A History of Lewiston, Maine

With Genealogical Register of Early Families
(Revised Edition)

THE OLD LEWISTON CITY BUILDING
The structure dominated Park Street for eighteen years before its destruction by fire, 1890.

By Janus G. Elder
Edited by David and Elizabeth (Keene) Young

HERITAGE BOOKS
2007

HERITAGE BOOKS
AN IMPRINT OF HERITAGE BOOKS, INC.

Books, CDs, and more—Worldwide

For our listing of thousands of titles see our website
at
www.HeritageBooks.com

Published 2007 by
HERITAGE BOOKS, INC.
Publishing Division
65 East Main Street
Westminster, Maryland 21157-5026

Copyright © 1989 1997 Androscoggin Historical Society

All rights reserved. No part of this book may be reproduced or transmitted in any form or by any means, electronic or mechanical, including photocopying, recording or by any information storage and retrieval system without written permission from the author, except for the inclusion of brief quotations in a review.

International Standard Book Number: 978-0-7884-0628-7

TABLE OF CONTENTS

Cover Illustration
  Taken from *The Peoples of Lewiston-Auburn, Maine, 1875-1975*
  By John A. Rand, The Bond Wheelwright Co., 1975

Map insert of Lewiston, Wales, Lisbon and Webster taken from
  A Topographical Map of Androscoggin County, Maine by
  J.O. Page; J. Chace, Jr., Publisher, 1858

Map of Lewiston lots, 1795	iv
Foreword	vii
Preface	viii
Prologue	ix
Abbreviations	x
Introduction	1
History of Lewiston, Maine	6
Biographical Sketches	85
Appendices	
Military Records	367
Heads of Families in Lewiston Village 1847	369
Early Lisbon Cemetery Records	373
Cemetery Inscriptions	375
List of Works	419
Index	425

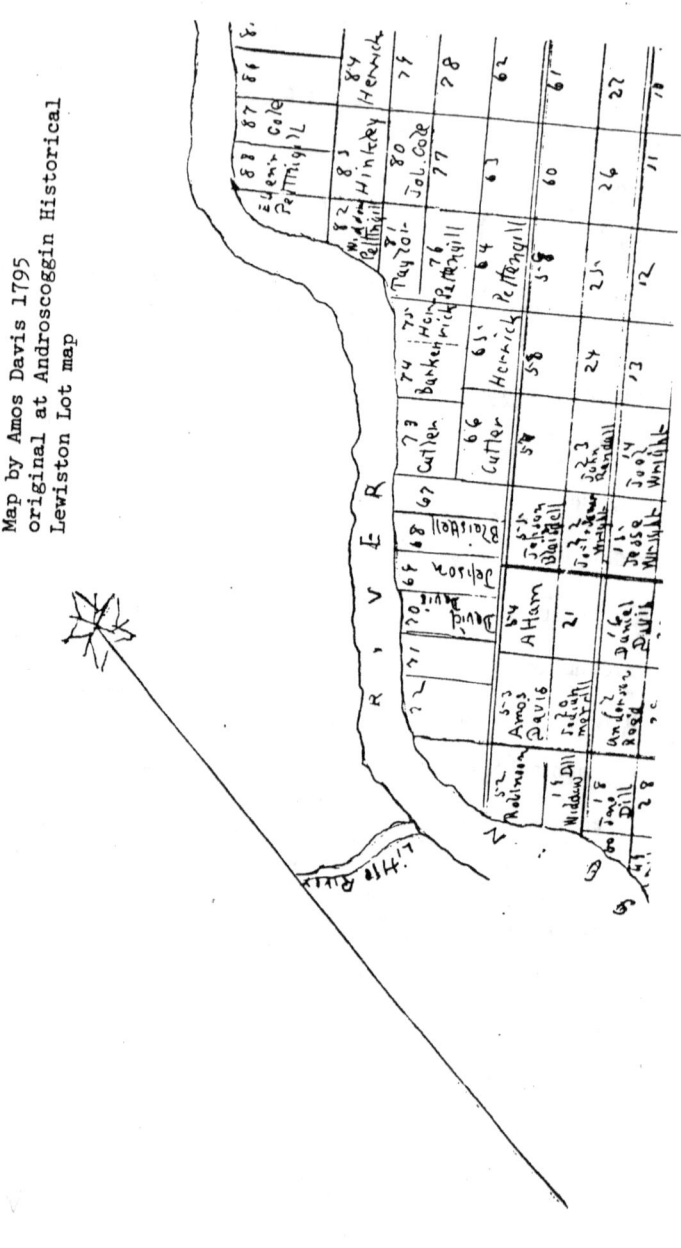

Map by Amos Davis 1795
original at Androscoggin Historical
Lewiston Lot map

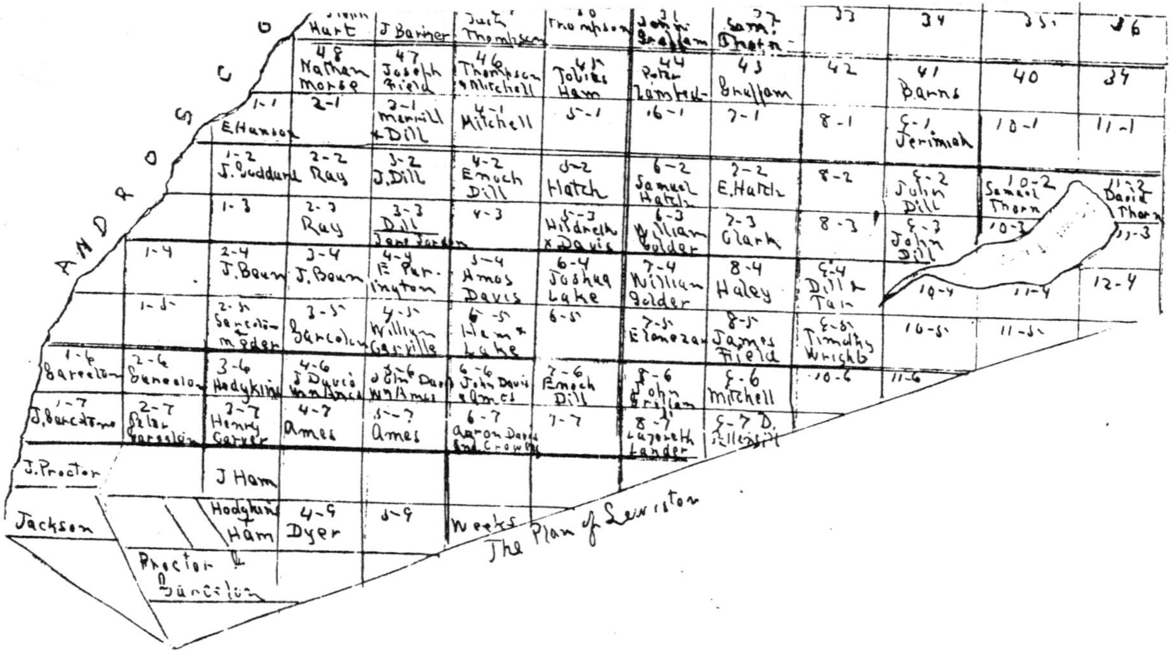
ANDROSCOG
The Plan of Lewiston
Hart
J Bariner
Thompson
Graffam
33
34
36
48 Nathan Morse
47 Joseph Field
46 Thompson & Mitchell
44 Peter
43 Graffam
42
41 Barns
40
1-1 E.Hanson
2-1
3-1 Merrill & Dill
4-1 Mitchell
5-1
6-1
7-1
8-1
9-1 Jerimiah
10-1
11-1
1-2 J.Goddard
2-2 Ray
3-2 J.Dill
4-2 Enoch Dill
5-2 Hatch
6-2 Samuel Hatch
7-2 E.Hatch
8-2
9-2 John Dill
10-2 Samuel Thorn
11-2 David Thorn
1-3
2-3 Ray
3-3 Dill
4-3
5-3 Hildreth & Davis
6-3 William Golder
7-3 Clark
8-3
9-3 John Dill
10-3
11-3
1-4
2-4 J.Baun
3-4 J.Baun
4-4 E Parington
5-4 Amos Davis
6-4 Joshua Lake
7-4 William Golder
8-4 Haley
9-4 Dill & Tan
10-4
11-4
12-4
1-5
2-5 Garcelon & Moder
3-5 Garcelon
4-5 William Garville
6-5 Ham & Lake
6-5
7-5 Elanezar
8-5 James Field
9-5 Timothy Wright
10-5
11-5
1-6 Garcelon
2-6 Garcelon
3-6 Hodgkins
4-6 J Davis
6-6 John Davis Ames
7-6 Enoch Dill
8-6 John Graffam
9-6 Mitchell
10-6
11-6
1-7 J.Garcelon
2-7 Peter Garcelon
3-7 Henry Garver
4-7 Ames
5-7 Ames
6-7 Aaron Davis
7-7
8-7 Lander
9-7 D.
J.Proctor
J Ham
Jackson
Hodgkins Ham
4-9 Dyer
5-9
Weeks
Proctor & Garcelon

FOREWORD

Having dabbled in the research of Lewiston's history, I have come to appreciate the significant contribution that Janus G. Elder made to the preservation of what we do know about the city's past. We all rely heavily upon Elder's research conducted when his sources and readers recalled persons and events involved in the founding and development of the town and city and of its commercial and business enterprises.

We who research our family histories must also express gratitude to David and Elizabeth Young for editing and making available in such convenient form the genealogical materials on Lewiston's early families. For the first printing of this work, they checked the accuracy of the typescript of Elder's material against his manuscript and against original sources, added many useful lists, and provided an index of names mentioned in the history. Now they have included a valuable index of subjects and places mentioned in the genealogy.

This work therefore includes priceless details on government, churches, business and industry, associations and the people of early Lewiston. A few researchers since then have added to our knowledge. Nevertheless, much more needs to be done. Most obvious is the need to cover our history since Elder's efforts of a hundred years ago. The details of our political, governmental, economic, and social development need to be recorded in accessible form with analysis of their meaning. How has Lewiston been typical and how has it been different from other cities? What does it tell us about life in the United States, New England, or Maine?

As we update our knowledge, we must consider topics that Elder neglected. Elder focused upon the Yankee families in Lewiston; as we know, there are Irish, French, Greek, German, Italian, Lithuanian, Jewish, and other stories to tell. We need to describe more of what we call social history. What was it like for people to live in Lewiston in such times as the 1890s, the 1930s, or the 1950s? What might we learn about the lives of women and children here throughout our history?

Even some of the topics that Elder covers need further attention. For example, he suggests that there was a major struggle over the establishment of The Lewiston & Auburn Railroad (pp. 60-61). An enterprising researcher might produce a splendid monograph on the political and legal battle, as well as the subsequent history of this joint enterprise between the cities.

As another example, Elder simply states that the Pejepscot Proprietors provided the name "Lewistown" (p. 12). In search of the origin of the name, I was able to discover that Job Lewis, a Boston merchant, was an influential Proprietor 1739 to 1752. His share passed to his son-in-law Samuel Waterhouse, who was the most active Proprietor when the grant was made in 1768; the name probably honored his father-in-law. (For documentation, please see the newsletter of the Androscoggin Historical Society, Androscoggin History, October 1995.)

We have a full agenda of research. I hope to be able to learn more about my home town, and invite others to join me. This book undoubtedly will continue to be our touchstone.

Douglas I. Hodgkin, Bates College, Lewiston, Maine
29 April 1996

PREFACE

The authorship of this book belongs to the late Janus G. Elder. He spent many long hours writing letters, interviewing the oldest citizens of Lewiston, visiting cemeteries, compiling vital records from old diaries, tax lists, etc. Elder started his history about 1860 and was still collecting information until his death in 1907. Building on the collections of William Garcelon, Thomas Hodgkins, and Amos Davis, he has made this priceless history of Lewiston's early settlers.

Because of a fire at City Hall in 1890, many of the records of Lewiston were lost; however, this record has survived the losses over time.

As many of the facts in this book are not cited we have listed the primary and secondary sources we used to double-check this work. Some errors were found in the typed copy when checked against Elder's manuscript and other primary sources. The late Everett Davis, a direct descendant of Amos Davis, had his secretary type Elder's work. We are in debt to Mr. Davis and his secretary for many hours of labor.

We would like to thank the Elder and Harris families for giving the Androscoggin Historical Society permission to publish and rights to this book. We would like to thank the following for their help and advice: *Lewiston Sun/Journal/Sunday,* Lois Wagner of Auburn Public Library, Gridley Barrows and Geneva Kirk of the Lewiston Historic Commission, Jeff Brown of the Maine State Archives, Willis Trafton Esq., Gordon Windle, historian, Alan Hawkins of Maine Genealogical Society, Prof. Douglas Hodgkin of Bates College, Mary Riley, Special Collections Librarian of Bates College, Lois Griffiths of Bates College and Robert Taylor of Androscoggin Historical Society, Herman Lord, computer advisor, of Danville, ME, and Timothy Herling of Durham, ME.

David C. and Elizabeth (Keene) Young
PO Box 152
Danville, Maine 04223

PROLOGUE

When this book was published in 1989, it was reviewed as a reprint. In fact, only the first 84 pages were taken from two publications by Janus G. Elder. One publication, *History of Lewiston, Maine* was printed in Boston, Massachusetts, for the Blue Store, the Androscoggin One-Price Clothing Co. of Lewiston, Maine, in 1882. The pamphlet was given to people when they made a purchase there. The other, Elder's *History of Lewiston*, was in the *History of Androscoggin County, Maine*, edited by Georgia Drew Merrill in 1891. Pages 85 thru 423 plus the everyname index was first published in 1989. In this edition a place and subject index is added to cover the history which is buried in the genealogical section. This new helping aid will greatly benefit the historian.

This history is a record of the early settlers of Lewiston, Maine. Those interested in a visual history of Lewiston will enjoy *Lewiston Memories, A Bicentennial Pictorial*, by Prof Douglas I. Hodgkin, 1994; *The Peoples Lewiston-Auburn, Maine, 1875-1975*, by John A. Rand, 1975. The Lewiston Historical Commission and Bicentennial Committees also produced pamphlets and videos on Lewiston subjects.

We hope you will enjoy this publication. We thank you for your interest. If you have additions, corrections, or questions about this publication you can direct them to: Androscoggin Historical Society, 2 Turner St., Auburn, Maine, 04223. A self-addressed, stamped envelope is necessary for a reply.

We regretfully report that Robert L. Taylor, Executive Secretary of the Androscoggin Historical Society since 1989 and our good friend, died 12 Mar 1996 at Danville, Maine. He will be greatly missed by all who knew him.

David C. Young
Elizabeth K. Young
PO Box 152
Danville, Maine
1 Apr. 1996

ABBREVIATIONS

AHS	Androscoggin Historical Society
bro/o	brother of
d/o	daughter of
int.	intention
L/A	Lewiston-Auburn, Maine
m	married
MSA	Maine State Archives
N. B.	New Brunswick
pub.	published
s/o	son of
sis/o	sister of
unm	unmarried
wid/o	widow of

State abbreviations are those currently in use by the United States Postal Service.

HISTORY OF LEWISTON

Written by J. G. Elder,
Expressly for

ANDROSCOGGIN ONE-PRICE CLOTHING COMPANY,

BLUE STORE

Corner Lisbon and Ash Streets,
Lewiston, ME.

1882

Lewiston, March, 1882

To the Public:

Having proved our first assertion, namely, that we have come to stay, we will now go further and say, we intend to be the leading Retail Clothing House in this State. For this reason we have built a store that is second to none, and where we can more fully merit the reward our established business principles have brought us.

Still we cannot work for glory alone. While we would fulfill our promises, we must sell our goods for a profit; for inasmuch as we would be honorable to you, we must be honorable to them from whom *we buy*.

But we shall at all times, as during the past *eight months* we have been among you, continue to sell at as small a profit as possible, continuing at all times the following principles, which have proved the secrets of our success:

STRICTLY ONE PRICE.

Marking the selling price ONLY on each and every article, on a tag, in plain English figures.

Warranting all goods to be as represented, holding ourselves personally responsible for any misrepresentations by anyone in our employ.

Treating all with *politeness*, whether *rich* or *poor*.

We are always willing to show our goods whether you wish to buy or not.

Always willing to exchange any article bought of us and returned to us unsoiled within thirty days.

A written guarantee accompanies every purchase made of us.

Very respectfully,

ANDROSCOGGIN O. P. CLOTHING CO.,
Blue Store, Lewiston, Maine.

What is One Price?

It seems wonderful that in such a growing community this question should be so often asked, yet such is the case.

"AND WHY?"

The clothing buyers have been humbugged to such an extent that it surprises them to think that anyone should dare to put a value on their goods and never take any less.

We have even met with people that have declared they would not buy of anyone unless they could beat them down in the price. To those we would say that in every instance after they have traded where they can beat the price down to their own satisfaction,

We will forfeit $10.00

for every instance where our price, marked in plain figures, is not as low for the same quality of goods.

Those who have friends in any of our sister States, viz.: Massachusetts, Rhode Island and Connecticut, ask them who are the reliable business houses of their respective towns or cities, and the answer will invariably be

"Those doing a Strictly One-Price Business."

The only responsible business men of the country are those who have adhered to this rule - selling goods for what they are, charging those who consider themselves sharpest at a trade the same as those who lack that quality of shrewdness.

Respectfully,

Androscoggin One-Price Clothing Co.,
Blue Store,
Lewiston, Maine.

Copyright, 1891

All Rights Reserved

From innumerable sources of information - many of them broken, fragmentary, and imperfect - from books, manuscripts, records, and private documents, we have gathered much of value respecting this valley of Androscoggin and its savage and civilized occupancy. In our labors we have endeavored to separate truth from error, fact from fiction, as they come down to us from the half-forgotten days in legend, tradition and the annals of the past.

We express our thanks to those who have willingly given of their time and labor to aid us; to those who have contributed the illustrations, thereby adding much to the value of this work; to those whose cheering words and earnest assistance have ever been at our service; and to those whose courtesy has been extended to us during our sojourn in this most progressive of counties.

AN HISTORICAL SKETCH OF LEWISTON, MAINE.

Pejepscot Claim.

Thomas Purchase settled on the Pejepscot, now the Androscoggin river, as early as 1630, perhaps before; the precise time as well as the exact location are not known. It was undoubtedly within the present limits of the town of Brunswick. Subsequently, it has been asserted, he lived at Lisbon Falls. Purchase was a farmer and trader, and carried on an extensive fur and peltry trade with the Indians. He is charged with taking advantage of the Indians in various ways, for which, at a later period, they fired his buildings and killed his cattle. Purchase was absent at the time. In 1632, the Council for New England granted to George Way and Thomas Purchase certain lands on "Bishopscotte" river, which unquestionably, included the territory occupied by Purchase. Way probably never occupied any of the land covered by the "Grant," and it is very doubtful if he ever visited this country. Purchase conveyed to Gov. Winthrop, in 1639, his land at Pejepscot, reserving the portion occupied and improved by himself. Within the limits of this "Patent" Purchase lived and continued actively in business until the first Indian war, 1675, when his buildings were destroyed and his family driven away. After the war he returned to his possessions on the Pejepscot, where he remained but a short time. He concluded to return to England to secure the provisions of his "Patent," and went to Boston, where he soon embarked for England, from which he never returned. He died before 1683. His widow married John Blaney, of Lynn. Purchase left three children - Thomas, Jane and Elizabeth.

Richard Wharton, a Boston merchant, an Englishman by birth and education, conceived the plan of establishing a manor, after the English style, and for that purpose bought, July 4, 1683, of the heirs of Purchase and Way, the land covered by their Patent of 1632, as well as lands bought by Purchase of the Indian sagamores. In this purchase of Wharton was included the claim of John Shapleigh. But this tract of land, extensive as it was, did not satisfy the Englishman's manorial ideas; for he sought and obtained from Worombus, and six other sagamores of the Androscoggin, a large tract of land on both sides of the river, and estending to the "uppermost falls on the Androscoggin river." Shortly after this transfer Wharton sailed for England for the purpose of securing from the crown a recognition of his claim, and the authority to establish a manor in the then "Province of Mayne." This magnificient enterprise failed, Wharton having died before the proper authority could be obtained.

In 1693 Ephraim Savage, of Boston, was appointed administrator of Wharton's estate, and four years later the Superior Court of Massachusetts Bay authorized and empowered him to sell the estate in order to liquidate the debts. Acting in accordance with the authority given him by the Court, Savage sold, on Nov. 5, 1714, the whole of Wharton's claim on the ancient Pejepscot to Thomas Hutchins, Adam Winthrop, John Watts, David Jeffries, Stephen Minot, Oliver Noyes, and John Buck, of Boston, and John Winthworth [Wentworth?], of Portsmouth, New Hampshire, for one hundred and forty pounds. These persons constituted the original Pejepscot Company, taking the name of the river below the "Twenty-mile Falls." In the early part of the next year the proprietors submitted to the General Court of Massachusetts Bay a series of propositions relating to their claim and its settlement, and on the tenth of June, 1715, the General Court passed resolutions in accordance therewith, giving validity to their title, and accepting the propositions submitted. By this act the Company became the undoubted legal owners of the land they had purchased.

Notwithstanding this recognition of their title by the General Court, controversies soon arose in regard to the limits of their claim. This question was forced upon them by the Plymouth Company, who had a Patent for lands on the Kennebec river. The question of boundaries is most important. The descriptions of the old patents are very obscure and often indefinite. Frequently they overlap each other, and occasionally the latter completely covers the former one. The bounds given to Purchase and Way are explicit in one direction, and Purchase, in his conveyance to Massachusetts, gives the limits in another; and there could be no doubt about Nicholas Shapleigh's claim being bounded by Purchase's claim and the "sea." But that which occasioned the greatest controversy was the description of the "Warumbee" deed, which included the above grants, but how much more? The contest became intense, and the rival corporations pushed their claims with tireless energy. If the Pejepscot company could not extend their bounds on the south and east beyond the limits of grants made to Purchase and Shapleigh, they were undoubtedly entitled to more on the north and west. The deed covered "all the aforesaid lands from the uppermost part of Androscoggin Falls" four miles westward, and so down to Maquoit, and on the other side of the river from the same falls to the Kennebec, on a line running southwest and northeast.

The Pejepscot proprietors as early as February, 1758, appointed a committee to carry into execution the "divisional line," who reported four years later "that they had exchanged proposals with the Plymouth Company" for the purpose of establishing the line between these conflicting claims; but the committee could not agree "Where to fix the mouth of said Cathance river." In 1766, a settlement was made which recognized the southern line of Bowdoinham and the Kennebec river as the "divisional line" between the Companies. The northern line was, however, unsettled. The Massachusetts Legislature, on the eighth of March, 1787, passed a resolution which declared; "That the Twenty Miles Falls, so called, in the *Androscoggin* river, being about twenty miles from *Brunswick* Great Falls, so called, be, and they are hereby considered, the uppermost falls, called the Uppermost Great Falls in *Androscoggin* river, referred to in the deed from Warumbee and six other Indian Sagamores, confirming the right of Richard Wharton, and Thomas Purchase, executed July the seventh, in the year of our Lord 1684, in the thirty-fifth year of the reign of King Charles the second."

At the same session of the General Court a resolution was passed, setting forth that the "Boundaries of the Pejepscot Company, so called, have not been ascertained, that the committee on the subject of unappropriated lands in the counties of *Lincoln* and *Cumberland*, be, and they are hereby directed not to locate or dispose of any lands claimed by the *Plymouth* Company to the southward of the south line of Bakerstown" – now Poland – bounded at the said Great Fall in *Androscoggin* river, aforesaid, on the west and south line of Port Royal" – now Livermore – on the east of said *Androscoggin* river. These boundaries were not satisfactory to the proprietors, and they refused to recognize them. In 1798, Col. Josiah Little, one of the Company, who had been elected agent of the proprietors, petitioned to the General Court, asking them to empower the Attorney General to enter into a rule of the Supreme Judicial Court all the controversies and disputes subsisting between the Commonwealth and the Pejepscot proprietors. The General Court readily acceded to this petition and authorized the Attorney General, Hon. James Sullivan, to enter into a rule of the Supreme Judicial Court, of the County of Lincoln, all the questions of dispute between the Commonwealth and the proprietors. By the terms of the resolve, Mr. Sullivan was to appoint the commissioners, subject to the approval of Col. Little, to whom "any or all" the controversies in dispute were to be submitted.

It was also stipulated that as there had been "disputes and controversies" between the proprietors and the persons who had settled and made improvements on lands claimed by them, that some equitable mode should be provided for adjusting the claims. The conditions imposed by the Court were, that these settlers should have one hundred acres of land so laid out as best to include the improvements made by them, and for such sums of money; and on such terms and conditions as three commissioners, appointed by the Governor, should judge reasonable. Mr. Sullivan informed the General Court, the next year, that he had agreed to submit to Levi Lincoln, Samuel Dexter, Jr. and Thomas Dwight, the dispute between the Commonwealth and the Pejepscot proprietors, and asked for an appropriation to defray the expenses of the commission, and the Legislature appropriated a thousand dollars for that purpose. The commissioners made their award February, 1800, which was substantially that affirmed by the General Court in 1787. This award was not satisfactory to the proprietors, who claimed that the "Uppermost Falls" mentioned in the "Warumbee" deed were not the "Twenty Mile Falls," but those now known as Rumford Falls. This claim was groundless, and the boundaries were finally established about 1814 by decisions in the Courts of Cumberland and Lincoln Counties, on the basis of the award of 1800.

The disputes between the Company and the settlers were settled according to the award made by the Commissioners, Nathaniel Dummer, Ichabod Goodwin, and John Lord, – who were appointed by the Governor, – who made the assignments and prescribed the terms and conditions of payment. About twenty thousand acres were conveyed to settlers in virtue of the conditions stipulated. Thus ended a controversy which had been waged for nearly a century, and been participated in by more than three generations. None of the parties were satisfied, but it gave substantial rest to those who, for a long time, held their homes by doubtful titles. As finally settled, the territory embraced Topsham, a part of Lisbon, all of Lewiston and Greene, three-fourths of Leeds, all of Brunswick, nearly all of Durham, most of Auburn, and a part of Poland.

HISTORY OF ANDROSCOGGIN COUNTY, MAINE.

"Out of monuments, names, words, proverbs, traditions, records, fragments of stone, passages of books, and the like, we doe save and recover somewhat from the deluge of time.

GEORGIA DREW MERRILL, Editor

LEWISTON

by J. G. Elder

CHAPTER II.

THE TOWN. Situation, Extent, Natural Features, Products, etc. - Conditions of Grant - Pioneer Settlers - Incorporation - Growth - Civil List - City Officers.

Lewiston is in north latitude 44 degrees 5' 45", and 70 degrees 10' west longitude. Its greatest length is 11 1/4 miles, and its greatest width is 6 1/3 miles, and it has an area of 35 square miles, or about 22,000 acres. The only body of water wholly in Lewiston is No Name Pond, one mile long and half a mile wide. It lies near Sabatis road, nearly four miles from the bridge. There is a small unimproved water-power at the outlet. There are some small streams. On several of these the early settlers erected lumber mills which long since disappeared. The surface is very uneven and considerably broken. This is especially true on the margin of the river, and in some places, extending a considerable distance from the river, the land is quite hilly, and the ledge occasionally crops out with more or less boldness. In some places the surface is quite level, but there are no plains and but little meadow land. While the surface is hilly and broken, it is not mountainous. Merrill Hill, formerly Randall Hill, is probably the highest elevation in the city, but its exact altitude has not been ascertained. David Mountain, which derives its name from Mr. David Davis, the owner for many years, is a dome-shaped ledge whose summit is 389 feet above tide water, and 123 feet above Main street at the corner of Riverside. It is a ledge of mica-schist; the base is skirted with small trees and shrubbery, and occasionally a dwarf pine; but near the summit there are a few plats of grass. Excavations to a considerable extent have been made on the northwesterly side of the mountain to obtain coarse stone for building purposes. Mr. Davis's heirs have given the summit of the mountain to Bates College with a right of way for an observatory, for which it is admirably fitted. Once upon the summit the eye catches a charming landscape which, when the atmosphere is clear, extends to the White Mountains, with a bird's-eye view of Lewiston and Auburn. The soil is a clayey loam, well adapted to agricultural purposes, and yields an average amount of produce. It is better adapted to the production of hay than to the growth of cereals, but corn, oats, and barley are grown in considerable quantities, and fruit is easily raised. Many of the farms whose soil is rugged produce excellent crops, and although husbandry may not be the most lucrative employment, yet the industrious farmer is sure to realize an average income. Clay banks especially adapted to the manufacture of bricks are numerous near the "Falls," and are also found in the rural portions of the city. These have been extensively worked, and large quantities of bricks are annually manufactured. The southern part abounds in sandy loam and is admirably fitted for agricultural purposes. The primeval forest was composed of hard and soft woods, with the stately pine in abundance. The early settlers did much in manufacturing pine lumber, and, in recent years, a large lumbering business was carried on by some enterprising citizens. The magnificent and romantic Lewiston Falls, with its water-power, one of the best in New England is not only the most striking natural feature of the city, but the great source of its wealth. The falls were first called the Uppermost Falls of the Pejepscot, but for years after the first settlement were known as Harris Falls. The lakes at the source of the Androscoggin are now used for the storage of water, dams having been built by the Union Water-Power Company to increase their capacity as reservoirs.

Grant to Little and Bagley. - The Pejepscot proprietors granted, January 28, 1768, to Moses Little and Jonathan Bagley, of Newbury, Mass., the tract of land commencing at Twenty-Mile Falls on the Androscoggin, from thence to extend five miles up said river, from thence to extend northeast five miles, from thence southeast four miles, from thence south to Androscoggin river, and so up the river to the falls. The conditions were that fifty families should be settled in as many houses before June 1, 1774, and a road be cleared to Royalsborough to meet the proprietors' road from Topsham. If less than fifty families were settled, only a proportion of the land was to be granted. The houses were to be "16 x 20 feet and 7 feet stud," and the town was named Lewistown. This grant was rescinded in June, 1771, notwithstanding the efforts made to comply with its conditions. The proprietors recognized what had been done by Bagley and Little, without offering any compensation for their services. We are unable to determine under what conditions the settlement was prosecuted. It is evident that Bagley and Little took measures to secure their title; but it was not until 1790 that the grant "was confirmed."

The First Settler. - Paul Hildreth moved into the plantation of "Lewistown" in the autumn of 1770. He built his log cabin on the bank of the river, just below the Continental Mill. Mr. Hildreth was a native of Dracut, Mass., and possessed a roving, as well as a resolute, spirit. He married Miss Hannah Merrill of Nottingham, N. H., where, it is said, he resided for nearly a year before he took up his residence here. In the autumn of 1770 his cabin was burned, and the family spent the winter in New Gloucester, but returned to Lewiston in the following spring, where he resided, with the exception of a short time in 1788, when he lived in Litchfield, until about 1802; he then removed to Gardiner, and died there about 1830. Tradition relates many adventures experienced during the early settlement of the place, of marvelous contests with venomous wild beasts which invaded the sanctity of the settlement; of women frightened; of children pursued by bears; of the destruction of cattle by huge and ferocious catamounts; of the dread experienced as the dusky forms of the aborigines were seen gliding through the forests in pursuit of game. With the pioneers life was a sad and checkered reality. A trackless forest, fifteen miles in extent, lay between them and the nearest white settlement. Provisions were frequently short, and once for four days they were without food or fire.

During these days of fasting and anxiety, Mrs. Hildreth and an infant were the only persons in the settlement. Tradition also informs us that the first grant of land made by Bagley and Little was a present of fifty acres to Mrs. Hildreth, as a testimonial of their respect for the first female settler of Lewiston. This tradition may be true, but so far no documents substantiate the claim. Mr. Hildreth occupied this lot (No. 52 on the plan of Lewiston) until 1795, when he sold to Samuel Robinson, and took up a new lot. Hildreth established the first ferry in town, about half a mile below the falls, which passed into Robinson's hands. Mr. Hildreth's family removed to Gardiner, where there are numerous descendants.

Shortly after Hildreth came, David Pettengill, of New Gloucester, moved into the place. Mr. Pettengill was a native of North Yarmouth, and born September 5, 1734. He married Mercy, daughter of Benjamin and Mercy (Eaton) Lake, November 23, 1758. Mr. Pettengill settled on the lot south of Hildreth, where he lived during the winter of 1770-71, the only settler in the plantation during that winter. He resided on this lot until after the commencement of the Revolution, when he entered the army, from which he never returned. His son, Benjamin, also entered the army, and after his return settled in Auburn. David, who married Thankful Graffam, settled on the lot now known as the Converse Farr place, and died October 1, 1848, aged 82 years. He had a family of eleven children, but only a small number of his descendants reside here.

Lawrence J. Harris was the third settler, and came from Dracut, Mass., in the spring of 1771. Mr. Harris had been here the previous autumn, and made arrangements towards a permanent settlement. It has been said that he was induced to settle by Bagley and Little, who made very liberal offers of land, not only for himself but for his children. In the fall of 1770 he got out the frame of a saw-mill, which was raised October 29, but not completed until the next season. Mr. Harris settled on what was known, after the survey of the plantation (1773), as the mill lot and comprised about 100 acres about the falls. Tradition informs us that this lot was one of those which he was to receive for settling here. Mr. Harris built a house on this lot, which was located just west of the Lower Maine Central depot, where he lived until his death in 1784. It does not now appear that Mr. Harris ever had a deed of a foot of this lot. The proprietors acknowledged their indebtedness to him at the time of his death, in the sum of 1.50, and in consideration of this conveyed to "Abner Harris, son and heir of Lawrence J. Harris, the whole of Mill lot, so-called," "excepting and reserving out of the same the mill privilege," also a piece of land 25 rods wide, extending from the "mill privilege" to the Hildreth lot. Abner Harris resided a short distance west of Lincoln street and a few rods north of the cross canal. The well connected with the house is now in constant use. In 1819 Mr. Harris sold this farm, the mill lot, and the one known as the Haley farm, to Dan and Lemuel Read, for $3,500, and removed to Ohio. The Reads sold to the Littles, who by this transfer came into possession of the most valuable portion of the Little and Bagley claim. Mr. Harris had a large family, and his son, Barron, was probably the first male child born in the plantation.

Several of these children settled in Greene, where descendants now live.

Asa Varnum, supposed to have been the fourth settler, came from Dracut about 1772, and built a log house nearly in front of the westerly end of Central block, and very near the center of Main street. He was probably employed by Mr. Harris in the saw-mill. His daughter, Abigail, born September 21, 1773, was the first child born in Lewiston. Mr. Varnum was drowned late in 1773, or the early part of 1774, nearly opposite the Catholic cemetery, while attempting to pass Dresser's Rips in a boat. His widow, Abigail, married Benjamin Winslow, of North Yarmouth, October 4, 1774, and died March 11, 1801. Mr. Varnum's daughter, Abigail, resided at North Yarmouth, in the Winslow family, until her death, December 17, 1846.

Israel Herrick, ancestor of the Herricks in this vicinity, was a native of Topsfield, Mass., born December 3, 1721, and died in Lewiston, September 14, 1782. He came February 1, 1774, and for a short time occupied a part of Amos Davis's house. Mr. Herrick's was the eighth family in the plantation. His son, John, settled at Barker's Mills and married Lydia Graffam, of Falmouth, March 14, 1780. For many years he kept the only public house in town. The Herrick house, built in 1800, is still standing, and is not [one?] of the oldest in town. Mr. Herrick was selectman for many years, chairman of the first board, a representative to the General Court of Massachusetts for seven years, and served as delegate in the convention which met October 11, 1819, at Portland, to frame the Constitution of Maine. In all these positions he performed his duties with singular fidelity and ability, and to the satisfaction of those who had confided these interests to his care. He died March 27, 1834. His sons, Oliver and Ebenezer, were prominent men in town. Oliver commanded a company in the War of 1812, and was captured in the disastrous battle of Lake Champlain. After his return he became colonel of his regiment. For several years he was selectman, represented his native town in the state legislature for a number of years, was postmaster under the Taylor administration, and died July 4, 1852. Ebenezer was a man of talent and culture; was delegate from Bowdoinham, where he then resided, to the convention which formed the constitution of Maine, in which he took an important part. Among the many able members of that convention, none were more clear in statement or more felicitous in expression. He was a representative to Congress from 1821-9, and a state senator in 1828 and 1829. His son, Anson, was founder, editor, and proprietor of the *New York Atlas*. He was naval store-keeper in New York under Buchanan, and in 1862-3 a member of Congress.

Jesse Wright, of Dracut, settled in 1774 on the lot now known as the Davis Nevens farm, which he bought of Bagley and Little, May 29, 1774, for "three pounds of lawful money." The deed, still in existence, was acknowledged before Stephen Longfellow, of Portland, and witnessed by Nathan and Jonas Coburn. Mr. Wright's first log house was just east of Meadow Brook. His brothers Joel and Timothy Wright came about 1777.

Amos Davis moved in from New Gloucester in 1774. He was born May 12, 1741, in Gloucester, Mass. Mr. Davis, it is supposed, first settled on what has been known as the Marston farm, where he built a log house. Subsequently he built a house where is now the corner of Sabatis and Wood streets. He occupied this lot until his death, March 20, 1815. Mr. Davis was a farmer, surveyor, and shoe-maker. In March, 1773, he was employed by the proprietors to make a survey of a part of the town. A plan of the town, made by him in 1795, showing the names and residences of the settlers at that time, is still in existence. He was a leading member of the Friends society, and a very exemplary man. His son, David, who kept the first store at Lowell's corner, was the second male child born in Lewiston. His children, four sons and a daughter, settled in Lewiston and have many descendants. His daughter, Mary, married Seth Tarr. Mr. Davis gave the land for the old burying-ground on Sabatis street, and erected, at his own expense, a small building within its present enclosure, which was occupied for some years as a meeting-house for the Friends society, and for a school-house.

Jacob Barker came about 1774 and settled at Barker's Mills, on the lot next below John Herrick's, where he built a grist and saw mill. His son Cyrus inherited the farm, and his grandson, Nelson P. Barker, resided at the "Mills" for many years, and rebuilt them about 1836.

James Garcelon with wife, Deliverance Annis, and six children, came in March, 1776, from Freeport. He was the son of Rev. Peter Garcelon, who graduated from a Roman Catholic college in Clermont, France, became a priest, and filled that position in London from 1721 to 1739, when he went to the island of Guernsey, renounced Romanism, and united with the Episcopalians; was ordained minister of a church called "St. Peters in the Wood," which position he held for 32 years. James Garcelon was great-grandfather of Dr. Alonzo Garcelon, H. G. Garcelon, and Capt. J. S. Garcelon. He soon took up land five miles down the river, that made him and his sons farms, erected buildings, established Garcelon's Ferry, and opened his house to entertain travelers. As this was when the settlement at the Falls was small and no bridge crossed the river, most of the travel was across his ferry. Here he died November 13, 1813, aged 74. His wife died November 16, 1828, aged 93 years. Mr. Garcelon had five sons and two daughters. His sons settled near the "Ferry." James was for many years a Baptist clergyman, doing much missionary work in destitute places, and died in 1838. William was one of the first merchants in town, and did an extensive business, was also engaged in lumbering and ship-building at Freeport. Lucy married Ezra Ames, and Sarah, the only child born in Lewiston, married Robert Moody. The Garcelon family have occupied a prominent place in the history of the town and city. Two of the family have been clergymen; four physicians (the most distinguished of whom is ex-Governor Garcelon, who, at the age of 78, is prosecuting with undiminished energy the duties of an exacting and laborious profession).

Josiah Mitchell came in the spring of 1776 and settled on the lot which had been taken up by Joel Thompson, who was then in the Revolutionary army. On his return the lot was divided and Mr. Mitchell took the southwest end. He died August 19, 1832, leaving his farm to his son James. Mr. Mitchell had a family of seven sons and five daughters.

Jonathan Hodgkin settled in Lewiston, April 1, 1777. His house was near the bank of the river a few rods above the Pingree mil stream. Subsequently he settled about four miles below the falls. He died February 2, 1814. Of his four children, one, Betsey, who married Lovell Lincoln, was a constant resident of Lewiston for more than 90 years. She was three years old when her father moved into the plantation. Mr. Hodgkin came from Cape Ann.

James Ames came from Oakham, Mass., in 1785, and settled on the farm now owned by Noah Litchfield, which he bought of William Garcelon. Mr. Ames was a blacksmith, and undoubtedly the first one in Lewiston. He carried on blacksmithing in connection with his farm, and did excellent service for the settlers. Previous to his arrival the settlers were compelled to go to New Gloucester for the services of a blacksmith. Mr. Ames kept a public house for many years. He died in 1815, and was buried in the old Garcelon burying-ground, on the bank of the river. His son Winslow cut his initials on a rude stone which marks his resting-place. This Winslow Ames was a man of considerable prominence in town affairs, and filled various offices. He was a member of the first board of selectmen, its chairman for two years, and captain of the Lewiston company of militia in 1804. Captain Ames was a man of fine presence and dignified bearing.

In November, 1788, Dan Read came from Attleborough, Mass., and settled in Lewiston. Mr. Read was a young man without any family. He married Susannah, daughter of Stephen Hart, of Lewiston. Soon after he came into the plantation he commenced teaching school, and was one of the earliest school teachers in the place. His education and ability soon brought him into prominence, and for more than 30 years, commencing with 1800, there was no more prominent man in town affairs. Mr. Read was selectman for 26 years, chairman of the board for 12 years, town clerk for 15 years, representative to the General Court of Massachusetts, and a representative to the Legistlature of Maine in 1820 and several subsequent years. He was the first postmaster in Lewiston, to which office he was appointed in 1799, a position which he held until 1837. In all these various and important trusts he brought unquestioned ability and integrity, an honest and noble purpose, and he was gathered to his fathers after having attained the unusual age of 87 years. He died February 15, 1854. Mr. Read had eight sons and five daughters.

Ebenezer Ham, grandfather of the late Colonel Ham, came from Shapleigh in March, 1789, and settled on a lot in the south part of Lewiston. He died [15] August, 1790 [1791]. His son, James, married Mary Brooks, and lived on the farm until his death, February 4, 1854, aged 79 years. The farm is now in possession of the family, owned and occupied by Nelson Ham. James Ham was the father of Colonel Ham, and the grandfather of the late ex-Mayor J. B. Ham, of this city.

John Marshall came here about 1780, and settled on the lot owned and occupied so long by Mr. David Davis. Mr. Marshall was a wheelwright. He removed from this place to Industry, about 1803. His son, Alfred, was a representative to Congress in 1841-2. Job Cole, the ancestor of the Coles in Lewiston, was a native of North Yarmouth. He first settled in Greene, but came here quite early and settled on what is now known as the Asa P. Taylor place. Mr. Cole had a large family of sons and daughters. His son, Rev. Benjamin Cole, was a Baptist clergyman for more than thirty years, preaching for the most of the time in Lewiston. Thomas Taylor came from Dracut, Mass., before 1788, and lived for many years on the place known as the Charles Taylor farm. This was one of the best farms in town and has remained in the Taylor family until recently. Mr. Taylor's family consisted of ten sons and two daughters. William Blaisdell came from North Yarmouth, and settled on the lot now occupied by Daniel Wood and others. He died in 1818, aged 70 years. His son, Colonel Walter R. Blaisdell, succeeded to the homestead, built the brick house near Mr. Wood's, and died in 1831, aged 55 years. There are no descendants in the city. William Golder came from New York when a young man, and purchased two lots of land in the Carville neighborhood. He married Dorcas, daughter of John Dill. His family consisted of five sons and three daughters. Mr. Golder died in 1846. One of his sons, Jacob, was for many years an honored and respected Baptist clergyman. Ezra Randall came from Bowdoinham about 1787, and settled on what has been known as the Randall place, near Thorne's Corner. His first house, probably built before 1790, is now standing, and is undoubtedly the oldest house in town. Mr. Randall was for many years deacon of the Old South (Baptist) church. He died in 1850, aged 84 years. His son, Foster Lee Randall, succeeded to the estate, and has occupied it until recently. Deacon Randall married first, Miss Mary Whitten; second, Miss Theoda Lee. Mr. Randall had a family of seven sons and nine daughters. John Graffam married Elizabeth Davis, sister of Amos Davis, Sr., and settled here in 1776-7. They lived on the Captain William Jepson place. Mr. Graffam had three sons and nine daughters. His son, John, married three wives, and had a family of ten sons and eight daughters.

Among the early settlers were Henry and William Carville, brothers, and the ancestors of the Carvilles in town. Henry was in the Revolutionary War, and for many years was a pensioner. He died in 1823 and William in 1829. Peter Lenfest came here about 1777, and married Lydia, daughter of Lawrence J. Harris. Mr. Lenfest was a native of the Isle of Guernsey, in the English Channel. The house which he occupied for nearly 30 years is still standing. He had eight sons and four daughters. He died in 1820. His daughter, Lydia, married Israel Glidden, who owned the Lenfest estate for many years. Joel Thompson, a Revolutionary soldier, came quite early into the plantation and settled on what is even now known as the Thompson place, on the Webster road. He came from Topsham. Mr. Thompson had six sons and five daughters. T. B. Thompson was one of his sons. Mr. Thompson was one of the prominent men in the early history of the town, and filled many official positions, was a representative to the General Court of Massachusetts, for several years a member of the board of selectmen, town clerk, and colonel of his regiment of militia, in all of which positions he showed ability. Colonel Thompson died in 1841, aged 87 years. Caleb Barker came here very early and settled on the Colonel Ham place. His son, Jacob, came into possession of the place and became quite a wealthy farmer. He died in 1824, aged 57 years. After his death the farm became the property of his son-in-law, the late Colonel Ebenezer Ham, who remained in possession until his death. Joseph Field was a native of Northampton, Mass., and came from Freeport to Lewiston. He settled on the place now occupied by the venerable Deacon Stephen Davis, and died there in 1815, aged 66 years. Deacon Field "fought at Bunker Hill." Only a few of his descendants now remain in Lewiston. Tobias Ham was one of the early settlers. He was a native of Brunswick, and married Elizabeth Herrick, sister of John Herrick, Esq. His farm was on the Webster road, some two miles from the city. He died in 1812, aged 60 years.

The growth of the southern part of the plantation was slow, the settlement incorporated as Greene, in 1788, attracting more. In 1790 Lewiston had 532 inhabitants, and February 18, 1795, it was incorporated the ninety-fifth town, with these boundaries: Beginning at the bank of Androscoggin river at the most westerly corner of the town of Greene, thence running southeast on the southerly line of Greene about 6 miles to the Plymouth Company's claim, 6 miles and 230 rods, thence southwest about 260 rods to Androscoggin river, thence northerly by said river to the bounds first mentioned. Daniel Davis was empowered by Benjamin Merrill, Esq., of Greene, to call the first town meeting, which was held at the house of Jedediah Morrell, April 6, 1795. John Herrick was chosen moderator; Noah Litchfield, clerk; John Herrick, Joel Thompson, Winslow Ames, James Garcelon, Daniel Davis, selectmen; Abner Harris, treasurer; Nathan Cutler, collector; James Ames, Nathan Cutler, constables; Nathan Cutler, Abner Harris, David Pettengill, Robert Anderson, Ezra Purrinton, James Garcelon, James Turner, Joel Wright, Amos Davis, Jr., highway surveyors; John Marshall, Oliver Barron, Benjamin Moors, Mark Garcelon, surveyors of lumber; Samuel Robinson, Ezra Purrinton, field drivers; Joseph Fields, William Blaisdell, Joel Wright, William Garcelon, "tidingmen" [sic]; Michael Little, Samuel Stephens, Ezra Purrinton, Thomas Rann, William Golder, Jacob Barker, hog-reeves. In 1807 Lewiston cast 40 votes for, 46 against separation from Massachusetts; in 1816 73 votes for, 83 against separation; in 1819 on the same question 92 voted for, 36 against. The vote to adopt the state constitution stood 66 in favor, 1 opposed. In the War of 1812 Captain Oliver Herrick raised a company which served in 1813 on Lake Champlain. Samuel R. Read, John P. Read, and Jonathan Ray were prisoners at Montreal and Quebec for one year from July, 1813. In September, 1814, Colonel Walter R. Blaisdell's regiment of militia was ordered into service. Two companies were from Lewiston, the North company, under Captain Nathaniel Sleeper, and the South company, under Captain George Williams. They were in service less than a month, but a small number drafted from them served some months.

It was not until the water-power was developed that Lewiston was anything more than a prosperous farming town, and its rapid growth is due to the application of that power by sagacious capitalists. In 1800 the population was 948; 1810, 1,038; 1820, 1,312; 1830, 1,549; 1840, 1,810. From 1840 there has been a wondrous growth, keeping pace with the increase in manufacturing. In March, 1849, the Androscoggin and Kennebec Railroad was completed as far as Lewiston, and the first engine crossed the bridge March 24th. Among the corporators were William R. Frye, James Lowell, Nathan Reynolds, N. B. Reynolds, John M. Frye, and Calvin Gorham, of Lewiston. In 1861 the Androscoggin railroad was opened for travel to Lewiston. These facilities brought large numbers of residents, and the town two years later became a city, which now bids fair to be the metropolis of Maine.

CIVIL LIST. - *Town Clerks* - Noah Litchfield, 1795 to 1800; Dan Read, 1801 to 1807, 1811, 1812, 1816 to 1823; Winslow Ames, 1802; Joel Thompson, 1808 to 1810, 1813 to 1815; Nathan Reynolds, 1821; William Garcelon, 1824 to 1830; Stephen H. Read, 1831 to 1834; John M. Frye, 1835; Samuel G. Phillips, 1836 to 1838; Edward P. Tobie, 1839 to 1862 except 1850 when John Smith was elected.

Selectmen - 1795, John Herrick, Joel Thompson, Winslow Ames, James Garcelon, Daniel Davis; 1796, William Garcelon, Daniel Davis, John Herrick; 1797, 1798, John Herrick, Joel Thompson, Winslow Ames; 1799, Oliver Barron, Ezra Randall, Winslow Ames; 1800, Winslow Ames, Dan Read, Oliver Barron; 1801, Dan Read, Oliver Barron, Joel Thompson; 1802, Winslow Ames, Noah Litchfield, Ezra Randall; 1803, Winslow Ames, Dan Read, Ezra Randall; 1804, 1805, 1806, Dan Read, Daniel Davis, Winslow Ames, 1807, Dan Read, Joel Thompson, Oliver Herrick; 1808, 1809, Joel Thompson, Winslow Ames, Ezra Randall; 1810, Joel Thompson, William Garcelon, Winslow Ames; 1814, 1815, Joel Thompson, Dan Read, William Garcelon; 1816, 1817, Dan Read, William Garcelon, Walter R. Blaisdell; 1818, 1819, 1820, Dan Read, William Garcelon, Calvin Gorham; 1821, Oliver Herrick, Nathan Reynolds, William Dingley; 1822, Oliver Herrick, Dan Read, William Dingley; 1823, Dan Read, William Garcelon, William Dingley; 1824, 1825, 1826, 1827, William Garcelon, Dan Read, William Dingley; 1828, 1829, William Garcelon, Dan Read, Walter R. Blaisdell; 1830, William Garcelon, William Dingley, Walter R. Blaisdell; 1831, William Garcelon, Stephen H. Read, John M. Frye; 1832, 1833, Stephen H. Read, John M. Frye, Samuel D. Garcelon; 1834, Stephen H. Read, Samuel D. Garcelon, Reuben Rand; 1835, Samuel D. Garcelon, Reuben Rand, Jeremiah Stanford; 1836, Samuel D. Garcelon, Ebenezer Ham, Daniel Garcelon; 1837, 1838, Ebenezer Ham, Stephen H. Read, Phineas Wright; 1839, Samuel D. Garcelon, William Garcelon, Samuel Litchfield; 1840, Stephen H. Read, Ebenezer Ham, Reuben Rand; 1841, Ebenezer Ham, Reuben Rand, Mark Lowell; 1842, Reuben Rand, Arthur Jameson, Ebenezer Ham; 1843, Ebenezer Ham, Arthur Jameson, James Carville; 1844, Ebenezer Ham, James Carville, Aaron D. Thorne; 1845, Stephen H. Read, Samuel D. Garcelon, Samuel Litchfield; 1846, Stephen H. Read, Stephen Davis, Samuel D. Garcelon; 1847, Stephen H. Read, Ebenezer Ham, Daniel Garcelon; 1848, William R. Frye, Samuel D. Garcelon, Mark Lowell; 1849, William R. Frye, Mark Lowell, Reuben Rand; 1850, Ebenezer Ham, Samuel D. Garcelon, Ham Brooks; 1851, William R. Frye, Ham Brooks, Reuben Rand; 1852, Stephen H. Read, Ham Brooks, John B. Jones; 1853, 1854, William R. Frye, Ebenezer Ham, Joseph S. Garcelon; 1855, John Read, Joseph S. Garcelon, Mark Lowell; 1856, Joseph S. Garcelon, Ebenezer Ham, Isaac N. Parker; 1857, William R. Frye, Howe Weeks, Archibald Wakefield; 1858, Isaac N. Parker, Timothy Walker, Joshua Merrill; 1859, William R. Frye, Jacob B. Ham, Archibald Wakefield; 1860, Jacob B. Ham, Mark Lowell, Abial M. Jones; 1861, Jacob B. Ham, Mark Lowell, Thomas Crowley; 1862, Jacob B. Ham, Mark Lowell, Isaac N. Parker.

CITY OF LEWISTON - The act to incorporate the city of Lewiston was approved March 15, 1861, and adopted by the town November 22, 1862. The first city election was in March, 1863, and the first Mayor was inaugurated March 16.

City Governments - 1863 - *Mayor*, Jacob B. Ham; *Aldermen*, Stephen I. Abbott, David M. Ayer, Edward Clark, Marshall French, Abial M. Jones, Samuel W. Kilvert, Thomas D. Thorne; *Councilmen*, Rhodes A. Budlong, George A. Clark, Jeremiah Crowley, Jr., Ezekiel S. Davis, Hersey Day, Joseph S. Garcelon, William F. Garcelon, Cyrus Greely, Converse J. Pettengill, George H. Pilsbury, Jordan K. Piper, John Y. Scruton, William N. Stevens, James Wood, Josiah G. Coburn; *Clerk*, Edward P. Tobie; *Marshal*, Isaac N. Parker.

1864 - *Mayor*, Jacob B. Ham; *Aldermen*, Abial M. Jones, Samuel W. Kilvert, Alonzo Garcelon, Linneus Cheetham, Josiah G. Coburn, Stephen I. Abbott, Edward Clark; *Councilmen*, Seth Chandler, Daniel Holland, Converse J. Pettengill, Josiah Day, Cyrus Greely, Alpheus C. Locke, Timothy E. Fogg, John Y. Scruton, George Webb, George H. Chandler, Samuel E. May, A. Byron Reed, Joseph P. Fessenden, Henry C. Goodenow, George H. Pilsbury, Jodan K. Piper, William S. Rogers, Chester C. Think, Joseph Blethen, John B. Garcelon, William H. Stevens; *Clerk*, Edward P. Tobie; *Marshal*, Isaac N. Parker.

1865 - *Mayor*, William P. Frye; *Aldermen*, Abial M. Jones, Josiah Day, Timothy E. Fogg, Henry C. Goodenow, Marshall French, Lorenzo L. Shaw (resigned), Allen P. Winslow (elected to fill the vacancy), George H. Pilsbury; *Councilmen*, Daniel Holland, Converse J. Pettengill, Lewis C. Peck, Lothrop L. Blake, Cyrus Greely, John W. Wood, George Webb, Theophilus B. Thompson, Plummer C. Tarbox, George H. Chandler, Benjamin R. Cotton, Albert O. Morgan, Joseph P. Fessenden, Wells W. Ayer, George A. Clark, William S. Rogers, Benjamin A. Bailey, R. E. Patterson, Joseph Blethen, John B. Garcelon, William H. Stevens; *Clerk*, Edward P. Tobie; *Marshal*, R. Jordan.

1866 - *Mayor*, William P. Frye; *Aldermen*, Daniel Holland, Samuel W. Kilvert, Timothy E. Fogg, Henry C. Goodenow, Marshall French, Benjamin A. Bailey, George H. Pilsbury, Seth Chandler (resigned), Albert O. Morgan (elected to fill the vacancy); *Councilmen*, Lewis C. Peck, Thomas D. Thorne, Sylvanus D. Thomas, Ransom C. Pingree, John Goss, John H. Randall, Theophilus B. Thompson, George Webb, Plummer C. Tarbox, Albert O. Morgan, Emery O. Bicknell, Ira W. Coburn, George A. Clark, Wells W. Ayer, John W. Danielson, Samuel W. Parmenter, John W. Farwell, Edward M. Dearborn, D. B. Sanderson, Noah Litchfield, Horace B. Bartlett, Joshua D. Rollins; *Clerk*, Edward P. Tobie; *Marshal*, William H. Waldron.

1867 - *Mayor*, George H. Pilsbury; *Aldermen*, Thomas D. Thorne, Ransom C. Pingree, Mark Lowell, Albert O. Morgan, George A. Clark, Jordan K. Piper, Ebenezer Ham; *Councilmen*, Abial M. Jones, David T. French, A. K. P. Knowlton, John Goss, Albert B. Nealey, Levi W. Gilman, Isaac G. Curtis, Isaac R. Hall, James B. Tracy, Ira W. Coburn, John D. Stetson, James Wrigley, Josiah G. Coburn, John W. Danielson, Samuel B. Harmon, Samuel B. Parmenter, John W. Farwell, George W. Bean, Horace B. Bartlett, Noah Litchfield, Natt E.

Davis, Lyman Prescott (resigned, and Pardon N. Dexter elected); *Clerk*, Edward P. Tobie; *Marshal*, Warren P. Laughton.

1868 - *Mayor*, Isaac N. Parker; *Aldermen*, Abial M. Jones (resigned), Ransom C. Pingree, Patrick McGillicuddy, Jesse S. Lyford, James Sands (resigned), Stephen I. Abbott, Horace B. Bartlett, Joseph P. Fessenden (to fill vacancy), William J. Burnham (to fill vacancy); *Councilmen*, A. K. P. Knowlton, James Wood, Dan Whittum, Albert B. Nealey, Joel Nevens, Seth Chandler, George Webb, Theophilus B. Thompson, Harmon Dixon, James Wrigley, William H. Monroe, John A. Rodick, Josiah G. Coburn, David Cowan, Benjamin T. Emery, John W. Farwell, Pardon N. Dexter, John B. Cotton, Joseph Blethen, Daniel B. Jones, John B. Garcelon; *Clerk*, Edward P. Tobie; *Marshal*, Isaac S. Faunce.

1869 - *Mayor*, Isaac N. Parker; *Aldermen*, Joseph P. Fessenden, Jacob B. Ham, Milton C. Wedgwood, James Wrigley, William J. Burnham, Stephen I. Abbott, Noah Litchfield; *Councilmen*, John F. Putnam, John N. Wood, Daniel Wood, William Robinson, Martin A. Jones, William F. Garcelon, Joseph H. Day, C. I. Barker, H. H. Richardson, John A. Rodick, George Hanson, Horace W. Barber, Josiah G. Coburn, David Cowan, Richard R. Ricker, John W. Farwell, Elijah M. Shaw, Joseph A. Pierce, John B. Garcelon, Jason Rand, Daniel B. Jones; *Clerk*, Edward P. Tobie; *Marshal*, Isaac S. Faunce.

1870 - *Mayor*, William H. Stevens; *Aldermen*, A. K. P. Knowlton, Mandeville T. Ludden, Alonzo Garcelon, Isaac C. Downes, William S. Rogers, Horace B. Bartlett, David Cowan; *Councilmen*, John F. Putnam, Alonzo D. Morton, Albert B. Furbush, Edward H. Cummings, Albert E. Frost, J. L. H. Cobb, Cyrus I. Barker, Roscoe C. Reynolds, H. H. Richardson, Aaron D. Thorne, Buel W. Dean, Rufus Carr, Richard R. Ricker, Cyrus Greely, Josiah G. Coburn, Benjamin P. Lowell, Joseph A. Pierce, Robert D. Sutherland, Jr., Jesse T. Stevens, William R. Wright, James Garcelon, 3d; *Clerk*, Edward P. Tobie; *Marshal*, Oscar G. Douglass.

1871 - *Mayor*, Alonzo Garcelon; *Aldermen*, John F. Putnam, Mandeville T. Ludden, David F. Noyes, George A. Drew, David Cowan, Stephen I. Abbott (resigned), Joseph P. Gill, William S. Rogers (to fill vacancy); *Councilmen*, Alonzo B. Morton, Albert B. Furbush, Abial M. Jones, Albert E. Frost, George A. Callahan, Benjamin Litchfield, Roscoe C. Reynolds, Thomas Ward, Eli B. Clark, Rufus Carr, John Riley, T. B. Rowell, Josiah G. Coburn, Cyrus Greely, Charles P. Wellman, Richard Skelton, David Pheteplace, Eaton Patterson (resigned), William J. Rodick, William R. Wright, George W. Crockett, Benjamin A. Bailey (to fill vacancy); *Clerk*, Edward P. Tobie; *Marshal*, Roscoe C. Reynolds (resigned); Ham Brooks (elected to fill vacancy).

1872 - *Mayor*, David Cowan; *Aldermen*, John F. Putnam, William F. Garcelon, Cyrus I. Barker, Ezekiel S. Davis, Cyrus Greely, William S. Rogers, Horace B. Bartlett; *Councilmen*, Abial M. Jones, Joseph H. Day, Alonzo E. Jackson, George A. Callahan, Benjamin Litchfield, Ai Brooks, Abial Daley, Nathaniel E. Skelton, Phil P. Getchell, Herbert C. Bradford, O. M. Maxwell, Linneus Cheetham, Josiah G. Coburn, N. R. Lougee, Horace C. Little, Richard Skelton, Benjamin A. Bailey,

21

David Pheteplace, John Goss, William F. Morrell, John S. P. Ham; *Clerk*, Edward P. Tobie; *Marshal*, H. H. Richardson.

1873 - *Mayor*, Nathan W. Farwell; *Aldermen*, Ransom C. Pingree, William F. Garcelon, Alonzo Garcelon, George A. Drew, Cyrus Greely, A. J. Morse, Horace B. Bartlett; *Councilmen*, Joseph H. Day, Daniel Holland, J. L. H. Cobb, Ai Brooks, Samuel W. Libby, Plummer C. Tarbox, James M. Small, Patrick McGillicuddy, A. L. Goss, Frank A. Conant, John Brophy, John H. Gooch, Edmund Russell, Z. H. Spinney, Charles H. Perkins, Joseph W. Quimby, Hiram Snow, Byron W. Getchell, Abel Goddard, Joseph Miller, William J. Rodick; *Clerk*, Edward P. Tobie; *Marshal*, H. H. Richardson.

1874 - *Mayor*, H. H. Dickey; *Aldermen*, Ransom C. Pingree, A. Wakefield, David F. Noyes, Michael A. Ward, Thomas Fillebrown, James Dempsey, Horace B. Bartlett; *Councilmen*, Abial M. Jones, John Y. Scruton, Benjamin F. Clough, Samuel W. Libby, Plummer C. Tarbox, Frederick B. Sprague, Jabez W. Murray, Moses D. Golder, William Collins, George Pottle, John Brophy, Clinton B. Heath, Edmund Russell, A. B. Watson, William D. Pennell, Edwin D. Wiggin, John Scott, Wilson Moody, Nathan W. Dutton, Joseph Miller, Gideon Perkins; *Clerk*, Edward P. Tobie; *Marshal*, David F. Noyes.

1875 - *Mayor*, Edmund Russell; *Aldermen*, Abial M. Jones, Warren E. Pressey, Alonzo Garcelon, Isaac C. Downes, William D. Pennell, David Pheteplace, Charles C. Cobb; *Councilmen*, John Y. Scruton, Benjamin F. Clough, Sylvanus D. Thomas, George S. Follansbee, George A. Chandler, Nelson Howard, William Collins, Patrick McGillicuddy, Selden A. Cummings, Thomas W. Murch, Thomas D. Thorne, Charles H. Hobbs, A. B. Watson, John H. Stetson, Milton C. Wedgwood, B. W. Getchell, Joseph J. Davis, Albert Cook, Nathan W. Dutton, D. Horace Holman, Gideon Perkins; *Clerk*, Edward P. Tobie (dec.), Everett A. Nash (to fill vacancy); *Marshal*, Oscar G. Douglass.

1876 - *Mayor*, Edmund Russell; *Aldermen*, Abial M. Jones, Warren E. Pressey, Alonzo Garcelon, Thomas Ward, William D. Pennell, Albert Cook, Charles C. Cobb; *Councilmen*, John Y. Scruton, Sylvanus D. Thomas, Frank E. SLeeper, Nelson Howard, Joseph W. Perkins, Albert E. Frost, William Collins, Patrick McGillicuddy, Moses D. Golder, George A. Drew, William Leader, Ervin V. Daly, John H. Stetson, John Garner, George A. Chandler, Menander Dennett; Hillman Smith, Frank E. Severance, D. Horace Holman, Joseph Blethen, Daniel B. Jones; *Clerk*, Everett A. Nash; *Marshal*, Oscar G. Douglass.

1877 - *Mayor*, Edmund Russell; *Aldermen*, J. L. H. Cobb, Nelson Howard, Alonzo Garcelon, Jesse S. Lyford, William D. Pennell, Dennis J. Callahan, John B. Garcelon; *Councilmen*, John Y. Scruton, Frank E. Sleeper, David B. Strout, Albert E. Frost, Joseph W. Perkins, Jacob L. Hayes, Alfred M. Hitchcock, William C. Bailey, Selden A. Cummings, Timothy J. Murphy, Ervin V. Daly (resigned), Richard Burke, George A. Chandler, John Garner, Fred B. Sands, Cyrus Haskell, Wilson Moody, G. G. Berry, Joseph S. Garcelon, Liberty H. Hutchinson, Frank W. Parker, W. W. Sanborn (to fill vacancy); *Clerk*, Everett A. Nash; *Marshal*, Warren P. Laughton.

1878 - *Mayor*, Jesse S. Lyford; *Adermen*, Joseph H. Day, Oliver Newman, Patrick McGillicuddy, Michael Eagan, John Garner, Dennis J. Callahan, William J. Rodick; *Councilmen*, David B. Strout, Joseph

K. Blanchard, Silas W. Cook, Roscoe C. Reynolds, Timothy O. Callahan, George G. Hartwell, Alfred M. Hitchcock, Calvin W. Clark, Thomas Sugrue, Timothy J. Murphy, Richard Burke, William W. Sanborn, Fred B. Sands, Richard R. Ricker, Isaac Goddard, Jr., Giles G. Berry, Wilson Moody, Cyrus Haskell, John W. West, Isaac A. Hayes, Ezra C. Kilgore; *Clerk*, Fred D. Lyford; *Marshal*, John C. Quinby.

1879 - *Mayor*, Joseph H. Day; *Aldermen*, David B. Strout, William F. Garcelon, George F. French, Dennis J. Callahan, John Garner, James Chandley, Mandeville T. Ludden; *Councilmen*, Joseph K. Blanchard, Silas W. Cook, Seth Chandler, John Given, Plummer C. Tarbox, Rendall Dresser, Calvin W. Clark, Thomas Sugre, William Collins, John Brophy, Thomas Kelley, William W. Sanborn, Fred B. Sands, Richard R. Ricker, William Lydston, Wilson Moody, Cyrus Haskell, Thomas Murphy, Daniel Allen, Elbridge G. Woodside, Andrew J. Hinckley; *Clerk*, Charles F. Goss; *Marshal*, Hillman Smith.

1880 - *Mayor*, Joseph H. Day; *Aldermen*, David B. Strout, Liberty H. Hutchinson, Alonzo M. Garcelon, Dennis J. Callahan, Fred B. Sands, James Chandley, Nathan W. Dutton; *Councilmen*, Joseph K. Blanchard, Addison Small, Seth Chandler, Rendall Dresser, Henry A. Torsey, Fred H. White, William Collins, Frank W. Martin, Thomas Sugrue, Royal Quimby, John Brophy, Eben Murch, William Lydston, Charles Horbury, Cyrus Greely, Palmer C. Thompson, John B. Smith, L. LeFebvre, Elbridge G. Woodside, Melvin J. Googin, Daniel Allen; *Clerk*, Everett A. Nash; *Marshal*, Hillman Smith.

1881 - *Mayor*, Mandeville T. Ludden; *Aldermen*, Seth Chandler, Liberty H. Hutchinson, Alonzo M. Garcelon, Daniel S. Fitzgerald, William Lydston, John B. Smith, Nathan W. Dutton; *Councilmen*, Addison Small, Isaac C. Merrill, Sylvanus B. Hayes, Henry A. Torsey, Fred H. White, Adelbert D. Cornish, Selden A. Cummings, Charles W. Waldron, Fred H. Thornton, Eben Murch, George W. Furbush, Joseph D. Montmarquet, Charles Horbury, Cyrus Greely, Fred F. Garcelon, Cyrus Haskell, George F. Drew, Leon LeFebre, Melvin J. Googin, Leonard P. Woodbury, William W. Clough; *Clerk*, Everett A. Nash; *Marshal*, Hillman Smith.

1882 - *Mayor*, David Farrar; *Aldermen*, Seth Chandler, Jacob L. Hayes, Howard N. Wagg, Daniel S. Fitzgerald, Cyrus Greely, John B. Smith, Horace B. Bartlett; *Councilmen*, Adelbert D. Cornish, Charles D. Lemont, Horace Libby, Sylvanus B. Hayes, Thomas B. Longley, Isaac C. Merrill, William Collins, Benjamin F. Peterson, Thomas Mansfield, George W. Furbush, Joseph D. Montmarquet, Everett O. Hilton, Fred F. Garcelon, Simeon H. Murray, Magloire Phaneuf, George F. Drew, Joseph E. Cloutier, Daniel Finn, Frank W. Parker, Albert L. Templeton, William W. CLough; *Clerk*, Everett A. Nash; *Marshal*, Hillman Smith.

1883 - *Mayor*, Alonzo M. Garcelon; *Aldermen*, Fessenden I. Day, Charles C. Wilson, Howard N. Wagg, Moses D. Golder, Samuel Booth, Cornelius O'Connell, Archie L. Talbot; *Councilmen*, Thomas H. Longley, Charles H. Miller, Albion K. Ordway, Roscoe C. Reynolds, John A. Tracy, Oren A. Norton, William Collins, Benjamin F. Peterson, George W. Ham, O. Everett Hilton, Timothy F. Callahan, Frank Peltier, Stanislas Marcous, Josiah G. Coburn, James Vaughn, Joseph E. Cloutier, John J. Burke, Jonathan F. Herrick, George G. Wagg, Albert

L. Templeton, Frank W. Parker; *Clerk,* William J. Rodick; *Marshal,* George W. Metcalf.

1884 - *Mayor,* Nelson Howard; *Aldermen,* Fessenden I. Day, Albert E. Frost, Howard N. Wagg, Timothy F. Callahan, Samuel Booth, Cornelius O'Connell, Archie L. Talbot; *Councilmen,* Charles H. Miller, Albion K. Ordway, Edwin H. Woodside, Isaac C. Downes, Charles S. Crowell, Charles D. Lemont, Cornelius J. Callahan, S. A. Baker, John E. Gagne, William Leader, Cleophas Thibault, Fred E. Leavitt, Stanislas Marcous, James Vaughn, Nathaniel W. Tarbox, John Scott, Charles Marchand, Anthony E. McDonough, George G. Wagg, Frank L. Hoyt, Ivory W. Emerson; *Clerk,* William J. Rodick; *Marshal,* James A. O'Brien (acting).

1885 - *Mayor,* Charles Walker; *Aldermen,* A. K. P. Knowlton, Roscoe C. Reynolds, Alonzo M. Garcelon, Timothy F. Callahan, Charles H. Osgood, Anthony E. McDonough, Frank W. Parker; *Councilmen,* Edwin H. Woodside, James T. Small, Everett A. Nash, Orin A. Norton, Alva D. Barker, Isaac M. Blake, Cornelius J. Callahan, Michael A. Ward, Fred E. Leavitt, William Leader, Louis Joncas, Charles E. Morgan, Magloire Phaneuf, Mathew McGawley, Wells H. Bates, Charles O. Godwin, Jeremiah F. Sullivan, Eli Roi, Frank L. Hoyt, Ivory W. Emerson, Frank L. Noble; *Clerk,* Wm. J. Rodick; *Marshal,* John French.

1886 - *Mayor,* David Cowan; *Aldermen,* A. K. P. Knowlton, Rendall Dresser, Charles G. English, Timothy Callahan, Pierre X. Angers, Michael A. Murphy, Frank W. Parker; *Councilmen,* Everett A. Nash, Isaac S. Faunce, James T. Tarbox, Isaac M. Blake, Charles D. Lemont, Edward Webb, Cornelius J. Callahan, Michael A. Ward, Benjamin F. Getchell, William Leader, Louis Joncas, Charles E. Morgan, Edwin C. Douglas, Israel B. Merrill, George W. Goss, James McManus, Charles O. Paradis, John O'Rourke, Frank L. Noble, Alonzo W. Sturges, Byron S. Adams; *Clerk,* John Sabin; *Marshal,* Daniel Guptill.

1887 - *Mayor,* Daniel J. McGillicuddy; *Aldermen,* Everett A. Nash, Alva D. Barker, Michael A. Coyne, Frank A. Conant, Pierre X. Angers, Michael A. Murphy, Frank L. Hoyt; *Councilmen,* Isaac S. Faunce, James T. Tarbox, Albert S. Plummer, Isaac M. Blake, Cyrus M. Lunt, George F. Reynolds, Benjamin F. Getchell, Newton J. Wedgwood, Thomas Robinson, William Leader, Charles E. Morgan, John E. Gagne, Edwin C. Douglas, Israel B. Merrill, George W. Goss, James McManus, Alfred W. Maillet, Menander Dennett, Alonzo W. Sturges, Byron S. Adams, Charles O. Morrell; *Clerk,* John Sabin; *Marshal,* Daniel Guptill.

1888 - *Mayor,* Horace C. Little; *Aldermen,* Wallace H. White, Alva D. Barker, Michael A. Coyne, Fred L. Tarr, Pierre X. Angers, Michael A. Murphy, Frank L. Hoyt; *Councilmen,* Albert S. Plummer, J. Frank Boothby, William F. Wood, Cyrus M. Lunt, Charles S. Crowell, Eben W. Dresser, Newton J. Wedgwood, Thomas Robinson, Alexander McWilliams, Augustus Marcous, Frank H. Johnson, Charles C. Benson, William Scott, James M. Sherman, Henri Lezotte, Menander Dennett, Alfred W. Maillet, Patrick J. Flaherty, Abram W. Garcelon, Charles O. Morrell, William A. Libby; *Clerk,* John F. Putnam; *Marshal,* Selden A. Cummings.

1889 - *Mayor*, Horace C. Little; *Aldermen*, Wallace H. White, Cyrus M. Lunt, Napoleon B. Stockbridge, Charles C. Benson, Daniel S. Fitzgerald, James L. Kenney, Charles O. Morrell; *Councilmen*, William F. Wood, J. Frank Boothby, William T. Smart, Eben W. Dresser, Benjamin Litchfield, Michael P. McGillicuddy, James J. Mottram, Edwin K. Smith, Frank Wright, Martin A. Ward, George W. Cappers, Ossian N. Briggs, James M. Sherman, Henry Lezotte, Daniel E. Murphy, John O'Rourke, Patrick J. Flaherty, Cornelius W. Murphy, William A. Libby, Abram W. Garcelon, George M. Coombs; *Clerk*, John F. Putnam; *Marshal*, Selden A. Cummings.

1890 - *Mayor*, Daniel J. McGillicuddy; *Aldermen*, Sylvanus B. Hayes, Cyrus M. Lunt, Henry Hines, Patrick J. Cronin, Louis J. Martel, John L. Kenney, William A. Libby; *Councilmen*, Samuel C. Leslie, Jr., George D. Armstrong, George W. Goss, Michael C. McGillicuddy, George C. Judkins, Jacob L. Hayes, George E. Harrison, Josiah B. Longley, Louis Langelier, Ossian N. Briggs, Oliver A. Frasier, Mathew McGawley, W. D. Crafts, John E. Gagne, Cornelius Russell, Frank Peltier, Cornelius W. Murphy, George W. Coombs, Andrew L. Marble, David A. Scannell; *Clerk*, Francois X. Belleau; *Marshal*, Mathew McGawley.

1891 - *Mayor*, William H. Newell; *Aldermen*, Sylvanus B. Hayes, Cyrus M. Lunt, Henry Hines, Alonzo M. Garcelon, Louis J. Martel, C. W. Murphy, William A. Libby; *Councilmen*, Samuel C. Leslie, Jr., George W. Goss, George M. Kavanaugh, Michael P. McGillicuddy, George C. Judkins, Jacob L. Hayes, Josiah B. Longley, Cornelius O'Connell, P. M. Doyle, Cleophas Thibeault, William Leader, George Welpley, John J. Sheehan, Regis Provost, A. K. P. Harvey, Cornelius Russell, Frank Peltier, William Scott, David A. Scannell, A. Llewellyn Marble, Arion C. Peirce; *Clerk*, Francois X. Belleau; *Marshal*, Mathew McGawley. *Treasurers*, David Farrar, from 1862 to 1871; John S. Adams, 1872; David Farrar, 1873 to 1877; A. Wakefield, 1878; David Farrar, 1879 to 1881; A. M. Jones, 1882; Charles Walker, 1883 to 1885; David Farrar, 1886 to 1889; Seth D. Wakefield, 1890, 1891.

CHAPTER III.

Ecclesiastical History - Church Organizations - Schools.

The Baptists. *The Old South Church*. -- In 1783 Rev. James Potter, of Bowdoinham, ME, a Baptist preacher, made his first missionary tour to the then plantation of Lewiston, undoubtedly the first minister who visited the place. Mr. Potter relates in his autobiography the circumstances and incidents connected with his first visit. His success was complete, but no effort was made to organize a church or society until 1789, and then a conference only was instituted, and the ordinances administered once in four months. The conference was composed of members residing in Lewiston, Greene, Bowdoin (now Webster), Freeport, Wales, New Gloucester, and Pejepscot (Danville), now the southern part of the city of Auburn. Scattered as they were, they maintained religious worship, receiving the ministrations of Rev. Messrs. Potter, Case, and Macomber. Gathering strength with every year, they were enabled to organize a church March 3, 1792, consisting of 55 members, Potter, Case, and Macomber taking part in the recognition. The organization was probably effected in the barn of Abner Harris, who was without doubt one of the first deacons and at whose residence, for the most part, until 1795, the church worshiped. From 1795 until the completion of the "Old South Church" in 1818, the church worshiped in the school-house on what is now known as Rose Hill.

It is utterly impossible at this time, and in the absence of the church records, to state definitely when the church engaged its first pastor, Rev. Levi Chadbourn, who was received by them with more than ordinary interest. Prepossessing in appearance, with a fine address and apparent piety, he soon won the confidence of the church and the esteem of the community. The society immediately commenced the erection of a parsonage on land owned by Abner Harris, now owned and occupied by William M. Chamberlin, Esq., but it was not completed. Mr. Chadbourn's stay was short. Slander assailed his character, and his usefulness in the community was destroyed. Notwithstanding these unfavorable circumstances the prosperity of the church was such that it was deemed expedient for the members who resided in other towns to organize conferences and churches in their respective communities; but this was not effected at once. The members who resided in Greene were constituted a church in 1793, and the same year those in Webster organized a conference, and in 1794 a conference was instituted in Pejepscot. The next year those living in New Gloucester were dismissed to form a new church, and those in

Freeport were dismissed in 1797 to join the church at North Yarmouth. The depletions made by these dismissals were more than filled by the accessions during 1794 and 1796, the fruits of interesting revivals which took place during those years. From the time of the organization of the church until 1802 the society received the occasional ministrations of Mr. Potter; but now one of their own members, Rev. Benjamin Cole, was called to the pastorate of the church. Mr. Cole remained the successful and honored pastor, with the exception of short intervals, when he supplied other places until near the time of his death, September 10, 1839. Rev. James Garcelon was pastor in 1815.

The continued prosperity of the church, the large accessions to its members, the necessity of a more commodious and convenient place of worship, induced the members of the church and some others, early in 1818, to take measures to supply this great want. The first public meeting for the purpose was held February 19, 1818, when Winslow Ames was chosen moderator and Noah Litchfield, clerk. At a subsequent meeting, William Garcelon, Jr., was chosen clerk and treasurer, and David Pettengill, Thomas Hodgkin, and Joseph Dill were chosen a committee "to look out a place to set a meeting house," who reported at a meeting held March 7, that the "southerly corner of James Mitchell's land" would be a desirable location. The society bought one-half acre of land at this place, it being valued at $8. The building committee, William Garcelon, Jr., Jacob Golder, and Thomas Hodgkin, carried forward the work with energy and success, for we find that the proprietors "met at the meeting-house frame, Monday, June 22, 1818." The meeting-house was finished in November, 1818, and the pews, 86 in number - 56 in the body of the house, and 30 in the gallery - were prized at $2,200, and sold at auction for choice, by Winslow Ames, November 28, 1818. The house was 41 x 45 feet and cost $2,260, and was dedicated December 1, 1818, Rev. Henry Kendall, of Topsham, preaching the sermon.

Among the proprietors of the "Old South Church" were a number of Universalists, who, in 1821, under the direction of Mr. Ezra Randall, formerly a deacon of the church, demanded their proportionate part of the time. To this end they petitioned the prudential committee, saying they "believed in an impartial Allmity," whom they desired to worship. Their request was promptly granted. In 1826 Rev. Mr. Frost, of Lisbon, was engaged to preach for the society, and finally a contract was made to settle him as pastor, after which he informed the society that he was a Universalist. He had secured a majority of the proprietors as a Baptist, but in his new role he was less successful. He was immediately dismissed. Rev. James Garcelon, Jr., was ordained in 1841, and soon after became pastor of the church, a relation which he sustained until the church became extinct, about 1847.

The "Old South Meeting-house" besides its use as a church was occupied for various public purposes, and for a number of years, until Jones's Hall was completed (1850) as a town-house. But after the organization of the First Baptist church in 1847, which included some of the members of the "Old South," which for more than fifty years had been vigorous and had enjoyed so large a share of prosperity, it became extinct and its members were mostly absorbed by the First Baptist. The church, not being occupied for religious purposes, and nearly all of the original proprietors having died or become interested in other places of worship, was sold in 1852, by order of the Supreme Court, for $250, to Samuel Litchfield and J. L. Cutter. It was taken down and removed to the "Falls," where it was rebuilt. It is situated nearly opposite the lower Maine Central depot. Five members of the Old South Church became ministers, viz., James Garcelon, Benjamin Cole, Joseph Roberts, Jacob Golder, and James Garcelon, Jr.

The Free Baptist Church. -- During his missionary tour in the autumn of 1783, Rev. Benjamin Randall, of New Durham, NH, the founder of the Free Baptist denomination, visited Lewiston, where he preached and baptized for the first time, but did not organize a church. It was his custom to receive all who desired to become members into his church at New Durham. But a membership so widely scattered was not easily controlled, and he soon found some of his Lewiston members expressing dissatisfaction with some of the doctrines he had so zealously advocated. Notwithstanding, however, the defection of some of the members, the number of adherents steadily increased, and it was deemed expedient to organize a church in Lewiston, which was done September 10, 1803, the usual services being conducted by Rev. Ephraim Stinchfield, of New Gloucester, who had preached in Lewiston as early as 1796. But little can be gleaned of the history of this church, which maintained its existence, however, with more or less prosperity until 1817. It is not probable that the church ever had a settled pastor, but was supplied with preaching by clergymen who visited the place, and undoubtedly, for much of the time by Rev. Benjamin Thorne, who was a member of the church. In 1817 there was an extensive revival under the labors of Rev. Josiah Farwell, and a church organized December 3, 1817, at the Herrick school-house, which embraced quite a number of the members of the First Church, and which finally supplanted it. The church as originally formed comprised twenty members, viz.: Rev. Benjamin Thorne, John Mooar, Oliver Herrick, Luther Litchfield, Wade Litchfield, Hannah Thorne, Elizabeth Graffam, Alice Thorne, Abigail Thorne, Mary Thorne, Hannah Thorne, 2d, Hannah Cutler, Martha Mooar, Sally Wright, Ruth Cole, Rhoda Litchfield, Lucy Lander, Susan Paul, Charlotte Pettengill, and Cyntha Cutler. At the organization of the church Oliver Herrick was chosen clerk, a position he held for many years. Jonathan Nash and Luther Litchfield were chosen deacons, August 6, 1818, and on the 19th of November of the same year "Elder Benjamin Thorne was received as the pastor and teacher agreeable to the New Testament Order," a relation which he long held. Soon after the church was organized and in connection with the labors of Rev. Mr. Farwell, measures were taken to construct a house of worship. Active operations were commenced in 1818, but the house was not completed and dedicated until December, 1820. It was located on Main street on the north side of Mountain avenue, on the lot now occupied by the residence of Mr. Fred H. White, where it remained until October 2, 1838, when it was removed to the corner of Main and Chapel streets - Haymarket Square - and occupied by the Main Street Free Baptists until February, 1856. The church had a nominal existence until about 1840, when only some eight persons retained their connection with it.

The Friends Society. -- The history of the denomination called the Friends is involved in much obscurity. Amos Davis was, undoubtedly, the first person of that persuasion in Lewiston. He was a very worthy and exemplary man, and took a great interest in the prosperity and usefulness of the society. Davis was the first *elder* and continued until his death, March 20, 1815. This office was then filled by his son, David, who died January 5, 1851. Levi Meader succeeded Mr. Davis. Mr. Meader died April 2, 1872. Mr. Amos Davis fitted up a small building in the old burying-ground on Sabatis street for a meeting and school, which was occupied for several years. The Friends built the first meeting-house in town, completed in 1811. It was situated on the Vining farm on the old Lisbon Road, where it remained until 1856, when it was taken down and removed to what is known as the Isaac Goddard farm, on the river road. For many years the town held its meetings in this house. There are now but few representatives in the society of the families who were once its chief supporters. It became small and feeble, and its place of worship was transferred to the city proper, where several families of Friends had settled. The old meeting-house was sold in 1875, taken down and removed to the city. They then held meetings in the Y.M.C.A. room until the completion of their house of worship on College street. This is a wooden structure 34x52 feet, and has a seating capacity of about 250, and cost about $3,500. The first service was held August 1, 1875. The ministers of the society at this meeting were Rev. Charles Varney, Freeman Andrews, David Douglass, William Jacob, Cyrus Cartland, George Douglass, Caleb Nichols. Mr. David Douglass made remarks and offered prayer, after which Mr. Jacob gave a brief account of the rise of the society. In the afternoon Mr. David Douglass delivered a sermon. Its pastors have been Charles Varney, Stephen Cartland, Freeman Andrews, George S. Williams, and the present pastor, George H. Farr.

The South Lewiston Church (Clough) Free Baptists. -- This church, consisting of 26 members, was organized July 26, 1826, Rev. Messrs. Ward, Lock, and Abiezer Bridges taking part in the services. The sermon was by Rev. Mr. Lock. The original members were: Noah Litchfield, Martha Litchfield, Amos Davis, Jr., Mariah Davis, Barzilla Rand, Thankful Rand, John Pettengill, Mary Pettengill, Aaron Davis, Jr., Samuel Mooer, Elizabeth Mooer, Joseph Webber, Joseph Jordan, Samuel Litchfield, Ames Litchfield, Mabel Williams, Mehitable Crowley, Jerusha Davis, Deborah Davis, Anna Davis, Sarah Bennett, Nabby R. Sleeper, Mary Lake, Sarah Hamilton, Lucy Gillpatrick, Anna Mitchell. The church held its meetings in Aaron Davis's barn, at the Clough school-house, and at various private residences in the vicinity, until 1846, when the present meeting-house was completed. The church had had no settled minister for many years, but has maintained worship for the greater part of the time, having its pulpit supplied by students from Cobb Divinity School.

Free Baptists (Main Street). -- April, 1838, a series of meetings were held at the North Meeting-house and conducted by Rev. Messrs. Isaac Libby, Gideon Perkins, Benjamin Thorne, and E. Phinney. An interesting revival ensued, and nearly 100 conversions were reported. As an immediate result of these meetings 36 were baptized May 20, 1838; 21 by Rev. Isaac Libby and 15 by Rev. Silas Curtis, and on May

28, 1838, a church was organized with these members; Ai Brooks, Isaac Barton, Josiah Blaisdell, James B. Cotton, John Curtis, William R. Frye, Stephen Field, Joseph Chamberlain, Amos Hersey, John B. Jones, John C. Jepson, Norris Litchfield, Harrison G. Otis, Eben H. Sleeper, Orin Sprague, Temple Tebbets, David Tracy, Thomas Thorne, Jeremiah Skinner, Joseph Winslow, Jane Brooks, Bathsheba Curtis, Christiana Caswell, Olive Chamberlain, Ann Dill, Joan Garcelon, Ann Hersy, Mary Jane Hersy, Lucinda Litchfield, Susan Merrill, Sarah Ann Nash, Joan Nash, Ann Pettengill, Julia Roberts, Sally Staten, Lucretia W. Tracy, Mary Ann Thompson, Laura C. Thorne, Sarah H. Tebbets, May Ann Webber, Mary Winslow, and Lydia Waterhouse. Rev. Messrs. Benjamin Thorne, Isaac Libby, and Silas Curtis took part in the organization. Additions were continually made to the church, and during May and June 52 were baptized and became members. The interest of the new church induced (October 2, 1838,) the change of the meeting-house from its original location to the corner of Main and Chapel streets where it now stands, the old building occupied by O. S. Ham. Here the church worshiped until February, 1856. Several years before this the church and society began to agitate the question of the erection of a new house of worship. The plan finally adopted was somewhat novel for this place. A stock company was incorporated with a capital of $10,000, consisting of 100 shares, and the work was commenced in 1854. The house, corner of Main and Bates streets, was completed in the winter of 1855-6, and dedicated February 14, 1856. Rev. Martin J. Steere, one of the most brilliant speakers of the denomination, preached the dedicatory sermon. In the evening Rev. James Drummond, of Auburn, delivered a very able sermon to a large audience. The house is a substantial brick structure and cost about $20,000.

Rev. Isaac Libby, the first pastor, was born in Buxton, February 22, 1809. He was licensed to preach in the fall of 1836. In April, 1837, he came to Lewiston and preached the greater part of the year to the First Free Baptist church. Mr. Libby was ordained by a council from the Gorham Quarterly Meeting in April, 1838, and became pastor of this church June 14, 1838, and resigned February 25, 1841. Mr. Libby was pastor at Brunswick, and subsequently at Cape Elizabeth. In July, 1843, he returned to Lewiston and assumed this pastorate for two years. In 1846 he became pastor of the Free Baptist church at Farmington Hill. He subsequently returned to Lewiston and resided for several years. He died in Auburn, October 18, 1866. He was a sound and effective preacher, and under his ministration prosperity was experienced. In manner he was dignified and grave, having but few of those qualities which captivate and charm the average audience. Rev. Daniel Jackson, a native of Madison, NH, became pastor in November, 1841, and resigned in December, 1842. He was ordained at East Ossipee, NH, September 14, 1826, where he was pastor for five years; at Wheelock, VT, for two years, he preached also in other states. He has recently deceased. He is remembered as a very genial man, prepossessing in manner, and an interesting and instructive preacher. Rev. George W. Bean became pastor in 1845, and resigned in 1848. He came from Farmington and after the close of his ministry here became pastor of the Free Baptist church at West Waterville, now Oakland.

Rev. Joseph S. Burgess, the fourth pastor, was born in Williamsburg, MA, August 15, 1814. He was a teacher eight years, then commenced the study of law, but becoming interested in religion he entered Whitestown Seminary, then under the direction of Rev. John Fullonton, D.D., and commenced study for the ministry. He accomplished the two years' course in one. In June, 1846, he became pastor of the Free Baptist church at West Waterville, and remained for two years. Mr. Burgess became pastor of the Main Street Free Baptist church September 18, 1848, and continued 12 years. The church was small - only 60 came to greet him the first Sabbath - and had little financial ability. At the close of his pastorate it had become one of the largest and strongest of the denomination in Maine. It was during his ministry that the church edifice, corner of Main and Bates streets, was built. Mr. Burgess's next pastorates were at Haverhill, MA, for two years; Bangor, three years; and at Harrisburg, PA, three years. In 1868, at the unanimous request of the friends of the new Pine Street Free Baptist church, he severed his connection at Harrisburg, and accepted its pastorate. Mr. Burgess labored here with zeal and success until December 31, 1868. Nineteen years of pastoral work in these two churches had so identified him with the interests of the place and people that his removal caused many expressions of regret. Mr. Burgess was corresponding secretary of the Home Mission Society, and passed nearly three years in assisting needy churches in Maine, Vermont, and Massachusetts, and for five years supplied churches of different denominations in Connecticut. He was a man of the people, and had a strong hold upon their affection and esteem. He was unassuming and without ostentation, ever hopeful and kindhearted. He died at Waterbury, CT, February 28, 1888, and was buried in Lewiston. Mr. John A. Lowell, a teacher in the Maine State Seminary, supplied the pulpit as early as October, 1860, and in March, 1861, the church applied for his ordination, which occurred in June. He closed his labors in 1869. Rev. W. H. Bowen, of Providence, RI, commenced his pastoral work June 6, 1869, and resigned in 1882. Rev. O. D. Patch was pastor from 1882 until 1884. Rev. Carter E. Cate was here as pastor from 1884 to 1888, when he was succeeded, October 11, by Rev. Martyn Summerbell, D.D.

Park Street Methodist Church. - There were but few Methodists in this community previous to the year 1845, and no attempt to organize a church. For nearly fifty years an occasional minister of the conference would visit the place, preach a sermon, and then go on his missionary tour, never, perhaps, to return. But in July, 1845, Rev. John Allen (Camp-meeting John) was appointed to the Little Androscoggin Mission, which embraced what was then called Lewiston Falls. In the two villages, Lewiston and Auburn, he spent nearly one-fourth of his time preaching in the school-houses on both sides of the river. In 1846 Mr. Allen was re-appointed and continued his labors in the same manner as the previous year. In July, 1847, Rev. William Summersides was appointed to the East Poland circuit, Lewiston being included within its limits. He preached here one-quarter of the time for a part of the year. Mr. Summersides was returned to this circuit by the conference in 1848, but spent only one or two Sabbaths at the "Falls." At the session of the conference in July, 1849, Rev. Charles Andrews was appointed to the Lewiston Falls Mission, which was limited to Lewiston and Auburn. Mr. Andrews commenced his labors immediately, and the Methodists here had for the first time a settled pastor. At this time it is very difficult to ascertain just how many Methodists there were in the two villages, but the following list is believed to be nearly complete: W. L. Davis, John Oakes, Ruth Oakes, Stephen Blethen, Charles Oliver, Mary Herrick, Sarah M. Cobb, L. J. R. Crocker, Hannah Crocker, Samuel Springer, Sarah N. Springer, Ami Read, Margaret Read, Lurania Jordan, Mrs. Daniel Wood, Charles D. Thomas, Jacob P. Smith, Ruby B. Additon, Winslow Kyle, Amos Bailey, Rachel Davis, Jemima Nevins, ---- Strout, Isaac Yetten, Anna Davis, Thomas J. Foss, Eliza Mitchell, Harriet D. Strout, William Staples, Harriet L. Yetten, Charles W. Kyle, Nathaniel French, Elizabeth French, Mrs. Charles W. Kyle.

It is possible that some others might have been connected with these two "classes," one on each side of the river, at the time Mr. Andrews came here. In the summer and autumn of 1849, Mr. Andrews preached in the school-houses in Lewiston and Auburn, but usually in the school-house in Lewiston. It was an old, dilapidated, brick building, located near the Main Street Free Baptist church, which they were compelled to abandon as cold weather approached. In the winter of 1849-50 they occupied Village Hall in Auburn; and subsequently the church worshiped in Union Hall, Auburn. Salaries in those days were not large, and Mr. Andrew's salary, as fixed by the board, was $175. He was re-appointed in 1850. In 1851 Rev. Ezekiel Robinson was appointed to the charge, with a salary of $350. It was during his pastorate that the place of worship was changed from Auburn to Jones's Hall in Lewiston. This hall, the first in Lewiston, had just been completed and occupied the upper story of what is now the lower Maine Central station. Here the church worshiped for several years. Mr. Robinson was re-appointed in 1852. In 1853 the conference sent Rev. Benjamin Foster to Lewiston. Mr. Foster was earnest and zealous in advocating the erection of a house of worship. Through his influence, and largely under his direction, a lot was procured on Park street and their present church edifice, a substantial wooden building, containing a basement, which is used for a vestry, was erected and dedicated September 9, 1854. Mr. Foster was pastor for two years. Rev. H. M. Blake was appointed by the conference as pastor in 1855, and served two years. The church became self-supporting under his pastorate. Rev. H. B. Abbott was pastor of the church for two years, commencing in the spring of 1857. In May, Rev. Charles Munger became pastor for two years. It was during this time, April 1, 1861, that the church was divided and the Methodist church in Auburn organized, the river being recognized as the "dividing line." This depletion did not seriously embarrass the Park street church. Rev. J. McMillan was pastor during the years 1861-62. In 1863 Rev. D. B. Randall became pastor. He was re-appointed in 1864. The conference appointed Rev. H. B. Abbott pastor in 1865. Mr. Abbott remained for three years. In 1868 Rev. Ezekiel Martin was then pastor for two years. Rev. Cyrus King became pastor in 1870; remained one year. He left the conference and removed to the West. Rev. Charles J. Clark was appointed in 1871, and occupied the pulpit for three years. He was followed by Rev. Horace W.

Bolton for three years; Rev. Roscoe L. Greene, three years; Rev. Israel Luce, three years; Rev. Fred C. Rogers, three years; Rev. Wilber F. Berry, two years; Rev. W. S. McIntire, three years. The present pastor, Rev. E. O. Thayer, was appointed in May, 1891.

The following is the necrology of the pastors of this church: Rev. James McMillan, born in Bartlett, N.H., August 3, 1806, and died in Gorham, September 15, 1874. Rev. Howard B. Abbott, born in Sidney, September 14, 1810; graduated at Bowdoin College in the class of 1836, and died February 2, 1876. Rev. Ezekiel Robinson, born in Norway in 1799. He entered the New England Conference in 1823, and for 50 years was an active minister. He died September 2, 1878. Rev. Charles Andrews was born in Berwick, October 23, 1811; died at Old Orchard in the eighties. Rev. Charles J. Clark was born in Portland, April 4, 1839, and died in New York, May 6, 1889. Rev. H. M. Blake died on his way to church, Sunday morning, January 15, 1865, aged 57 years. At the time he was pastor of the Pine Street Church at Portland. Rev. Ezekiel Martin was born in Hebron, March 19, 1820, and died at Lewiston, February 3, 1889.

The first Baptist (Bates Street). - Early in the spring of 1847, Mr. Daniel H. Wiggin, an earnest Baptist, who came from Greene the year before, took measures to ascertain the number of Baptists in Lewiston and Auburn who were desirous of organizing a church at the "Falls." The immediate result of this effort was a preliminary meeting which was held April 1, 1847, at the house of Mr. Edward Cobb, now Dr. Small's, on Park Street. Mr. Cobb was chosen moderator and clerk. Six persons were present at this meeting who "resolved themselves into a committee of vigilance to ascertain the names and number of Baptists in the community, and report at the next meeting." The report of the "vigilance committee," made on the 8th of April, showed 41 persons who were desirous of being organized into a church. Nineteen were present at this meeting and a committee of three was appointed to "ascertain where a place of worship can be obtained." At their next meeting, April 22, measures were taken to organize a church. The clerk was authorized to notify the "churches most convenient" to send delegates for the purpose of recognition, and Auburn, Danville, Durham, Greene, New Gloucester, and Topsham, responded to the call. The council met at the Free Baptist church (the building now occupied as a grain store on Haymarket Square) June 3, 1847, and organized by choosing Deacon O. C. Grose, of New Gloucester, moderator, and Deacon E. Barrell, of Greene, scribe. The proceedings of the council were as follows: Reading the records of the preliminary meetings, by Rev. George Knox; invocation, by Rev. J. Hutchinson, of Auburn; reading of the scriptures, by Rev. George Knox, of Cornish; introductory prayer, by Rev. James Drummond, Congregationalist, Auburn; sermon, by Rev. Joseph Kilpatrick, of Topsham; reading articles of faith, by Rev. Moses Hanscom, of Durham; right-hand of fellowship, by Rev. Samuel Owen, of Durham; address, by Rev. C. W. Reading, of Massachusetts; prayer, by Rev. P. Pillsbury, of Greene; concluding prayer and benediction, by Rev. George W. Bean, Free Baptist, Lewiston.

The church consisted of 25 members, viz.: Daniel H. Wiggin, Joel Morse, Calvin S. Titcomb, Stephen Davis, Simon Marston, Timothy Wright, William R. Wright, Israel Glidden, Jacob Golder, Charles

Wiggin, Levi Wiggin, Betsey Wiggin, Sarah Morse, Hannah McKenney, Mary Marston, Jane W. Miller, Ann M. Wiggin, Emeline Wiggin, Mary Titcomb, Abigail Kimball, Mary Mitchell, Eliza Field, Betsey Jepson, Betsey Wright, and Lucy Chamberlain. Of these the venerable Deacon Stephen Davis, now in his ninetieth year, is the only one living.

On the 5th of June William R. Wright was chosen clerk, and on the 12th of August Daniel H. Wiggin was chosen deacon, both for one year. Soon after Deacon Wiggin canvassed the three towns, Lewiston, Danville, and Auburn, Rev. George Knox, of Cornish, ME, visited the "Falls" and preached in the school-houses of Lewiston and Auburn. Mr. Knox spent May 16th, 23d, and 30th preaching in these places but did not become pastor of the church until the first Sabbath in August and then under the auspices of the Maine Baptist Missionary Society. He remained the pastor until January, 1860, nearly 13 years. Immediately after the organization, meetings were commenced in the old brick school-house near Lowell's Corner, but owing to its dilapidated condition they were obliged, on the approach of cold weather, to move to the Auburn side of the river into the Rechabite Hall. This was a very small hall, only about 22 x 40 feet and occupied the second story of the building. The lower story was occupied as a confectionery and "grog shop." The hall was found to be too close for warm weather and the society moved into the school-house on Turner street, where they continued to worship, with the exception of a few Sabbaths when Mr. Knox occupied Mr. Drummond's pulpit, until the completion of their chapel. This was built during the summer and autumn of 1848, under contract, by Captain Daniel Holland, and cost about $1,000, which, with the exception of $140, was raised by the society. The chapel was occupied for the first time November 9, 1848, when an interesting sermon was delivered by Rev. Mr. Beecher, of Portland. In the spring of 1849, owing to the extensive operations of the Water-Power Company, they were obliged to change the location of the chapel. During the summer it was moved several times.

The chapel was occupied until May, 1853, when it was exchanged with the Water-Power Company in part payment for the lot of land on which they subsequently built their brick church, corner of Main and Lisbon streets. From the chapel they moved to Union Hall in Auburn, where the church remained until December, 1853. In the spring of this year the society commenced the erection of the church at the head of Lisbon Street. This house cost about $10,000, and was dedicated December 9, 1853. Rev. L. B. Allen, of Yarmouth, preached the sermon and Rev. Arthur Drinkwater, of Greene, made the dedicatory prayer. The society occupied this house until May, 1870, the last meeting being held Tuesday evening, May 17. They removed from here to their new church edifice on Bates street, which was dedicated May 18, 1870. The sermon was by the pastor, Rev. E. M. Haynes, and the dedicatory prayer by Rev. N. M. Wood, D.D., of Illinois, a former pastor. The church was built in 1869-70, is of brick with granite trimmings and pressed brick beltings laid in black cement, and will seat about 800. It cost, including lot, $54,000. It is situated on Bates street at the southern extremity of the park, which it commands, being a very pleasing structure and a fine, though not gorgeous, specimen of

English Gothic architecture. The "structural idea" is carried out in every part, embracing the interior as well as the exterior of the building, and including also the furniture as well as the organ. The entire wood-work of the interior is black walnut, highly polished, with ceilings frescoed and tinted in a manner which admirably relieves the dark effect of the wood.

Rev. George Knox, son of Ebenezer and Sarah L. (Dorset) Knox was born in Saco, October 24, 1816. He fitted for collect at North Yarmouth Academy; was graduated from Waterville College in 1840; studied at Newton Theological Seminary in 1840-41; was ordained pastor of the Baptist church in Topsham in December, 1841, and remained until 1845, then was partor in Cornish about two years. But his chief pastorate was with the First Baptist church in Lewiston, which he was instrumental in gathering, and which under his wise and judicious care, became one of the most prosperous in the community. His labors here were abundant and frequently discouraging, but with tireless energy he prosecuted his work, winning in an especial degree the love and respect not only of his church and society but that of the whole community. Mr. Knox was a Christian gentleman; kind, courteous, and dignified in all his ways, his presence was a gentle but a positive rebuke to everything unmanly and ignoble. Mr. Knox resigned this pastorate to take effect January 1, 1860, and afterwards became pastor of the Baptist church at Brunswick. When, in April, 1861, the President issued his call for 75,000 volunteers, Mr. Knox offered his services to the governor, and was appointed chaplain of the First Regiment, and when its term of service expired he was commissioned chaplain of the Tenth, shared the hardships of his comrades and endeared himself to all. At the close of this service he became pastor of the Baptist church of Lawrence, Mass. When the Twenty-ninth Regiment was organized Mr. Knox was again commissioned chaplain. He resigned his pastorate, and October 18, 1864, joined the regiment in Virginia, and October 31 met with an accident, and survived only a few hours. His sudden death was deeply lamented by the officers and members of the regiment and the people of this community, where he had been so long and favorably known. His remains were brought to Lewiston for interment.

Rev. Nathaniel Milton Wood, second pastor, son of Ephraim and Prudence (Myrick) Wood, was born in Camden, May 24, 1822. He was fitted for college in Camden, and was graduated from Waterville College in 1844, one of the best scholars of a very able class. He subsequently entered the Western Theological Institute, at Covington, KY, where he remained till 1847, when he returned to Maine. In May, 1848, he was ordained pastor of the Baptist church in Bloomfield, now Skowhegan. Here he labored with marked success until January, 1852, when, at the earnest solicitation of the college faculty at Waterville, he commenced his pastorate at that place, which he resigned January, 1860. From January, 1860, to March, 1866, he was pastor of the First Baptist church in Lewiston, and from August, 1866, to May, 1868, at Thomaston. He then accepted the charge of the Baptist church at Upper Alton, IL, which he held until March, 1872, when he was elected professor of Systematic Theology in Shurtleff College, a chair he had provisionally filled for two years, and for which he was especially qualified. In June, 1874, he came East and located at South Boston, hoping by this change to regain his health, a hope never realized. While here he preached in several places in Massachusetts, until April, 1876, when waning strength compelled him to relinquish further effort. He died in Camden, August 2, 1876. Mr. Wood's labors met with marked success; he was a close and accurate thinker, a keen and logical writer; his style was terse and epigrammatic, and his preaching was effective.

Rev. George W. Holman, of Fort Edward, NY, was the third pastor, commencing his labors in July, 1866, and continuing until November, 1868. He was an earnest and successful preacher. Rev. E. M. Haynes succeeded Mr. Holman; came from Palmer, Mass., and assumed the pastorate in April, 1869. His resignation took effect May 4, 1873. Rev. W. T. Chase became pastor in 1873, and closed his pastorate August 3, 1879, to accept that of the Baptist church in Cambridgeport, Mass. He was a very successful pastor, and was regarded with much affection by his people. Rev. George B. Ilsley, of Yarmouth, was the next pastor, commencing work November 2, 1879. Rev. William C. Barrows, the seventh pastor, came from Rockland. His pastorate closed September 1, 1885. Rev. C. C. Tilley came from Dover, and assumed the pastorate in March, 1886. His resignation took effect in March, 1891. The present pastor, Rev. D. F. Wyman, began his services in June, 1891.

Episcopal Church. - The parish of Trinity church was organized in June, 1854, by the efforts of Rev. George P. Giddings, of Illinois (a native of Danville), then on a visit to Auburn. He held his first service in Union Hall, Auburn, June 11, 1854, and July 15 the parish was legally constituted and these parish officers elected: Byron W. Watson, senior warden; S. W. Keeler, junior warden; George L. Drinkwater, Nathaniel I. Jackson, and George H. Merrill, vestrymen. W. B. Watson was chosen treasurer and collector. Mr. Giddings ministered to the church until November 5, 1854, when he returned to Illinois. July 11, 1856, Rev. Frederic Gardiner became rector, but resigned November 10, 1856. The public worship of the parish was removed to the Lewiston side of the river during Mr. Gardiner's ministry, and was held for some time in Lisbon Small Hall. In August, 1857, Rev. John B. Southgate entered upon his duties as pastor, and resigned on account of ill health in June, 1858. He was followed by Rev. D. C. Ingraham. In 1859 the parish built their first house of worship, on the corner of Ash and Park streets. This was consecrated to the worship of God by Bishop Burgess, September 21, 1858. In April, 1860, Rev. Nicholas Ludlam was elected rector; he resigned in June, 1862. Rev. W. H. Collins was employed for some time, and in February, 1864, was elected rector. Mr. Collins resigned in April, 1866. Rev. W. M. Willian became pastor in April, 1867, and resigned in September, 1868. Mr. Willian had officiated from some time before he became rector for the church. Rev. E. Folsom Baker was elected rector in May, 1869, and resigned in 1870. Rev. Harry L. Yewens was the next pastor of the parish, and remained rector until November, 1875, when he resigned. Rev. Robert Wyllie commenced his labors as pastor soon after Mr. Yewens's resignation, and having been ordained priest, entered upon his duties as rector in May, 1877, and continued as rector until April, 1890, when he resigned. In 1869 the Franklin Company gave a bond for a lot, on the corner of Bates and Spruce streets, to Trinity parish, agreeing to give the lot on condition that the parish erected thereon a church edifice within 10 years. In September, 1877, work was commenced on the church under the supervision of a committee, consisting of Rev. W. H. Washburn, John Garner, John Straw, Samuel Booth, T. W. Kanada, and H. H. Dickey. The cornerstone was laid with appropriate ceremonies by Bishop Neely, June 21, 1879, and the church was consecrated by him October 6, 1882. The sermon was delivered by Rev. Samuel Upjohn, pastor of St. Mark's church, Augusta. The church is built of granite, the entrance to the audience room being from Bates street. The interior is finished in oak, and the whole building has the appearance of a substantial structure. The vestry is in the basement of the church, with the entrance from Spruce street. The building cost about $21,000. The parish also have a rectory on Horton street which was commenced in 1883. Rev. D. V. Gwilym, the present rector, came from Houlton, and assumed the pastorate of the parish in June, 1890. The church wardens for 1891 are John Garner and Edward Byron.

The Pine Street Congregational Church. - It was early in 1854 that the members of the Lewiston Falls Congregational church who resided in Lewiston began to agitate the question of the organization of a Congregational church in Lewiston. The importance as well as the necessity of a church on the "east side of the river" became more apparent and measures were instituted by the friends of the new society to perfect its organizaiton. Accordingly a petition was directed to the church in Aburun, in which the petitioners express the opinion "that the time has arrived when we feel it our duty to ask a dismission from your church, that we may be formed into a church in Lewiston." The petition was signed by R. A. Budlong and 30 others and dated July 15, 1854. It was presented to the church at a "regular meeting," held July 18, and the petitioners were accordingly dismissed to form a new church on the "east side of the river." At this meeting the church voted to unite with the petitioners in calling an ecclesiastical council, to be held August 8, 1854, for the purpose of organizing a second Congregational church. The pastor, Rev. James Drummond, Deacon R. Bradford, Samuel Pickard, Esq., Jordan K. Piper, and Davis E. Verrill, two of the petitioners, were appointed a committee to make the necessary arrangements. The church was organized August 8, 1854, with 42 members, 34 of whom were members of the Lewiston Falls church, and eight by letter from churches in Maine and Massachusetts. Their names were: Rhodes A. Budlong, Jordan K. Piper, Davis E. Verrill, Simeon H. Murray, Charles C. Burgess, George R. Smith, William F. Fitch, William Hayes, William L. Fitch, Benjamin Murray, Josiah G. Coburn, Horatio G. Cilley, John W. Marston, Joseph R. Greenwood, Charles C. Niebuhr, Hannah Hayes, Lydia W. Prescott, Mrs. John M. Frye, Sarah E. Frye, Mrs. N. B. Nevens, Alura E. Lowell, Betsey Riggs, Sarah P. Verrill, Clarinda Murray, Mrs. Charles C. Burgess, Charlotte Fitch, Ann M. Fitch, Mary H. Hayes, Harriet A. Hayes, Lucy S. Davis, Octavia D. Garcelon, Susan Marston, Sarah W. Greenwood, Mrs. Charles C. Niebuhr, Mrs. David M. Ayer, Eliza D. Lowell, Mrs.

L. Cushing, Miss E. Cushing, Maria Herrick, Mrs. Edward P. Tobie, and Alice L. Field.

The services at the organization were: Reading the scriptures and prayer by Rev. Thomas W. Lord, of West Auburn; sermon by Rev. George E. Adams, D.D., of Brunswick; reading Articles of Faith and Covenant by Rev. John W. Chickering, D.D., Portland; prayer by Rev. Elijah Jones, of Minot; right-hand of fellowship, Rev. James Drummond, Auburn; charge to the church, Rev. Asa Cummings, D.D., of Portland; prayer and benediction,, Rev. Charles Pickard. From the organization of the church until the completion of the chapel (in 1855), at the corner of Pine and Bates streets, the society worshiped in Jones's Hall. It was a plain and neat building and was occupied by the church and society until April, 1866, when it was removed to the rear of the present church edifice on Bates street, and was subsequently converted into a tenement block. While the new church was being built the society held their meetings in Central Hall, with the exception of a short time when they united with the Main Street Free Baptists. Their present church edifice is built after the Romanesque style of architecture, and is one of the finest in the state. It was erected in 1866-7, and dedicated May 22, 1867. The dedicatory services were: Prayer by Rev. Aaron C. Adams, of Auburn; reading the scriptures by Rev. John A. Lowell, pastor of the Main Street Free Baptist church; sermon by Rev. Uriah Balkam, the pastor; and the prayer by Rev. John O. Fiske, D.D., of Bath. The church is a substantial brick structure with granite beltings and trimmings, and the interior is finished in oiled black walnut and chestnut, with softly-tinted walls and frescoed ceilings, which produce a very fine effect. The basement is fitted up as a lecture-room with parlors and a library-room. It is located on the corner of Pine, which it fronts, and Bates streets, at the northeast corner of the Park, which it commands, and from which it presents a substantial and imposing appearance. It cost $70,000 exclusive of the lot.

The church did not settle a pastor until January, 1856, but sustained public worship more or less regularly, the desk being supplied the most of the time by Rev. Isaac Weston, of Cumberland. Rev. Uriah Balkam, the first pastor, was born in Robbinston, March 27, 1812. He was graduated from Amherst College in 1837, and from the Bangor Theological Seminary in 1840. Soon after he supplied the Congregational church at Union, and was ordained its pastor June 15, 1841. Mr. Balkam remained in Union until September 20, 1844, when he was dismissed. His next pastorate was at Wiscasset, where he was installed January 22, 1845; dismissed October 26, 1854. He then commenced his labors as "stated supply" at Lewiston, and was installed as pastor, January 30, 1856. The sermon on this occasion was by Rev. H. S. Carpenter, of Portland; prayer by Rev. Elijah Jones, of Minot; right-hand of fellowship by Rev. James Drummond of Auburn, and charge to the church by Rev. George E. Adams, D.D., of Brunswick. Mr. Balkam continued here for more than 14 years. His pastorate covered the more important events in the history of the church, having commenced his ministry during its infancy, and closing after it had received mature strength. Dr. Balkam was appointed chaplain of the Sixteenth Maine, December 18, 1863. He performed his duties with care and fidelity. He resigned October 8, 1864. In August, 1873, he was elected to the chair of Logic and Christian Evidences in Cobb Divinity School, Bates College, and while on his way to the college he was thrown from his horse and instantly killed, March 4, 1874. In 1867 Bates College conferred upon him the honorary degree of S.T.D. Dr. Balkam was a person of commanding presence; as a preacher, scholarly, thoughtful, and singularly zealous; as a pastor, faithful and instructive.

Rev. Francis F. Ford, the second pastor, was born in East Haddam, Conn., November 25, 1828. He was a graduate of Hamilton College in the class of 1851, was at Union Seminary in 1853-4, and Princeton in 1856; and ordained by the Presbytery of Genessee in 1857. Mr. Ford had filled several pastorates before he came to Lewiston. He was installed pastor June 22, 1871, and dismissed November 25, 1872. He died at Kansas City, Mo., January 26, 1886. Rev. George S. Dickerman, who had been pastor at West Haven, Conn., was installed pastor March 12, 1874, and resigned June 17, 1883. He was dismissed by a council convened July 20, 1883. Mr. Dickerman accepted a call to the First church in Amherst, Mass., where he was installed pastor September 19, 1883. Rev. George Milton Howe, the present pastor, was born in Westminster, Mass., July 23, 1844. His parents were Daniel M. and Harriot [Harriet?] Woodbury Howe. His father died when 37, and Mrs. Howe subsequently married Mr. Z. M. Larned, of Oxford, where the family resided a few years and moved to Charlton. Mr. Howe's early education was acquired by utilizing his time after his farm work was accomplished. In the fall of 1863 he entered Nichols Academy, Dudley, Mass., and was graduated in 1867. He then became a student at Amherst College, graduating in the class of 1871, and was a graduate of Andover Theological Seminary in July, 1874. July 8, 1874, Mr. Howe was ordained and installed pastor of the Congregational church in Princeton, Mass. Ten years prior, May, 1864, he united with the Congregational church of Oxford. Rev. Mr. Howe remained in Princeton over nine years, where he was an able and esteemed minister and pastor. He was scribe of the Worcester Central Conference for five years, several years one of the prudential committee of the Worcester County Sabbath School Association, and for seven years one of the directors of the Worcester Musical Association. He resigned at Princeton to accept the call to Lewiston, where he was installed pastor, February 13, 1884, and during the seven years of his pastorate here the results of his work have been exceedingly satisfactory. The congregations have largely added to their number, and the financial prosperity of the church rests on a firm foundation, as at the close of each year it is free from debt; the benevolent offerings have increased tenfold; the church membership has been greatly augmented, additions on confession of faith being made every communion Sunday for nearly five years. The energy and earnestness of Rev. Mr. Howe, his forceful sermons on practical Christianity inspire one and all to help forward the good works of righteousness of which he is such a spirited leader and teacher. His wife, Mrs. Sarah M. (Kendall) Howe, and estimable Christian lady, takes an active interest in progress and reform.

The Sabbath school of this church, established 34 years ago, is the second largest of the denomination in the state, and has progressed wonderfully in the past seven years, its membership having increased from 125 to 550. Mr. F. B. Sands has been its efficient superintendent for the past ten years, also church clerk for twenty years.

Universalist Society. - In February, 1858, 15 persons, residents of Lewiston, petitioned John Smith, Esq., to issue a warrant to one of their number directing him to notify a meeting of the subscribers for the purpose of organizing a religious society, to be known as the First Universalist Society of Lewiston. Judge Smith issued a warrant dated February 16, 1858, and the first legal meeting was held at the house of Mr. O. H. Littlefield on Bates street, February 23, 1858. At this meeting, John Smith, Esq., was chosen clerk, and a committee consisting of Timothy Walker, John Smith, and George W. Farr were chosen to draft a constitution and by-laws. The by-laws were reported and accepted March 12. Subsequently, May 28, the society chose a committee, consisting of Samuel Haley, George W. Farr, and Timothy Walker, to "present the society to the Maine Convention of Universalists for admission into the fellowship of that body." The society voted July 6, 1858, to instruct the assessors to engage the services of Rev. C. H. Webster for nine months. Mr. Webster had been for some time pastor of the High Street Universalist church in Auburn, but at this time was not engaged in pastoral labors. He immediately assumed the pastorate of the new society, which he retained for about two years. Soon after Mr. Webster's resignation the society became extinct. The society first held their meetings in Jones's Hall, but subsequently worshiped in Lisbon Hall.

Bates Street Universalist Society. - This society was organized August 17, 1863, the meeting being held in the Municipal Court Room. Mr. B. F. Furber was chosen moderator, and John Smith, clerk. On the 23d of August, a constitution and by-laws were adopted. At this meeting the clerk was instructed to correspond with Rev. Martin J. Steere for the purpose of securing his services as pastor. Mr. Steere accepted the invitation to become pastor of the society and commenced his labors in April, 1864. The society held its services in Lisbon Hall, in what is now College Block, Lisbon street, until the completion of their house of worship. In December, 1863, the question of the erection of a house of worship was presented to the society, and measures instituted to secure the speedy erection of a commodious and convenient church edifice. A lot of sufficient size on the easterly side of Bates street, between Ash and Pine, was procured in September, 1864, of the Franklin Company, and ground was broken in December of that year. Subsequently the lot was abandoned, and the lot on which their house of worship now stands was presented to the society by N. W. Farwell, Esq. The house was commenced in 1865 and finished in March, 1866. It is 55 x 75 feet, and the front is elaborately finished, the Tuscan order of architecture. The audience room is 55 x 61 feet, and contains 106 pews, with a seating capacity sufficent to accommodate 500 persons. The church was dedicated March 15, 1866. The sermon was preached by the pastor, Rev. Martin J. Steere, and prayer was made by Rev. George Bates, of Auburn. In the evening Mr. Steere was formally installed pastor and an appropriate sermon was delivered by Rev. Mr. Bolles, of Portland. The church is a wooden structure, substantially constructed and finely finished and furnished, and was built at a cost of $22,000.

During the ministry of Mr. Steere, July 2, 1865, a church was organized, consisting of 15 members, viz.: John Smith, Ezekiel Martin, Daniel B. Jones, Roana D. Jones, I. W. Coburn, Abby Coburn, Moses H. Harris, Martin J. Steere, Harriet M. Steere, Hattie A. Steere, Henry Hamilton, Almira W. Hamilton, Jesse H. Field, and Mrs. B. F. Furber. Mr. Steere remained pastor of the church and society until October, 1869, when he closed his pastorate, greatly to the regret of his people, who had under his ministry enjoyed unusual prosperity. Mr. Steere was succeeded in April, 1870, by Rev. J. H. Armies, of Ridgeway, NH, who remained until May, 1871. He removed to Long Island. Rev. J. W. Hines became pastor of the church in August, 1872. Rev. Almon Gage assumed the pastorate of the church in 1874. In 1876 Rev. C. P. Nash was called to the pastoral care of the society. Rev. W. G. Haskell became pastor in 1878. Rev. W. S. Perkins commenced his pastoral work in 1884. The present pastor, Rev. R. F. Johonnot, was called in 1889.

Rev. Martin J. Steere, the first pastor of the church, was born at Smithfield, RI, October 15, 1814. He commenced preaching in 1834, and subsequently was a student at Parsonsfield Seminary. So strongly was he imbued with the missionary spirit that he offered himself as a missionary to Orissa, India, but ill health compelled him to relinquish the design. He was prepared for college at Fruit Hill, RI, but was compelled to abandon study on account of sickness. He was ordained and became pastor of the Free Baptist church in Georgiaville in 1837, and resigned in 1839. Mr. Steere was pastor of the church at Apponaug for three years, at North Scituate three years, and at Greenville one year. He then became pastor of the Free Baptist church at Waterford, Mass. In 1851 Mr. Steere refused the pastorate of a church in Boston, preferring to remain at Waterford. He delivered the oration at the laying of the corner-stone of the Maine State Seminary, now Bates College, June 26, 1856. A few years later Mr. Steere announced a change in his religious views, and embraced the doctrines of the Universalists. He was a man of marked ability, a graceful and brilliant speaker, and was held in high esteem. His pastorate in Lewiston was very successful and he endeared himself to his people, and his resignation was accepted with many regrets. Mr. Steere became pastor of the Universalist church at Poland, November 30, 1873, and resigned May 19, 1876. He died in Connecticut in January, 1877.

Pine Street Free Baptist Church. - The constituent members of this church, consisting of 52 persons, were dismissed from the Main Street Free Baptist church, and organized, January 3, 1869, by a council consisting of Rev. O. B. Cheney, D.D., Prof. B. F. Hayes, of Bates College, and Rev. John A. Lowell, pastor of the Main Street Free Baptist church. These persons constituted the church at its organization: Rev. J. S. Burgess, Mrs. Laura A. Burgess, Rev. Gideon Perkins, Mrs. Gideon Perkins, Roland E. Patterson, Mrs. R. E. Patterson, D. B. Sanderson, Mrs. D. B. Sanderson, S. E. Buker, Mrs. S. E. Buker, Noah Litchfield, Benjamin P. Lowell, Mrs. Benjamin P. Lowell, James R. Blaisdell, Mrs. James R. Blaisdell, Caleb Gilbert, Mrs. Caleb Gilbert, Henry N. Eastman, Mrs. Henry N. Eastman, Ezekiel Wakefield, Mrs. Ezekiel Wakefield, Thomas D. Thorne, James Wood, Edward Clark, Mrs. Edward Clark, Lewis W. Pitman, Mrs. Lewis W. Pitman, William Hersey, Henry A. Chanell, Mrs. Henry A. Chanell, Mrs. Drusilla Swift, Mrs. Orinda Squirs [Squires?], Miss Emma J. Caston, Mrs. Carolina Phillips, Mrs. Mary Whittemore, Mrs. Araxsenie Rowell, Miss Lizzie Brackett, Mrs. Laura Thorne, Mrs. Julia French, Mrs. Olive Turner, Mrs. Laura J. Webster, Mrs. Sarah C. Litchfield, Mrs. Lucinda E. Lane, Mrs. Mary L. Mitchell, Mrs. Hulda Cole, Miss Eliza Bickford, Miss Lydia Small, Miss Sarah E. Sawyer, Miss Arvesta Towle, Miss Sarah Pettengill. They worshiped in Lisbon Hall until the completion of their house of worship in December, 1869. This neat church edifice is located on Pine street, corner of Blake, and was dedicated December 9, 1869, by the pastor Rev. J. S. Burgess, assisted by Rev. Gideon Perkins, a member of the church; Rev. W. H. Bowen, of the Main Street Free Baptist church; Rev. U. Balkam, of the Pine Street Congregational church; and Rev. E. M. Haynes, of the First Baptist church. The house is a plain and substantial wooden structure, with a basement which is occupied as a vestry and lecture-room, and cost the society $14,000.

The church was fortunate in securing the services of Rev. J. S. Burgess, so long the pastor of Main Street Free Baptist church. Mr. Burgess commenced his labors October 1, 1869, and remained as pastor until December 31, 1875. Mr. Burgess's pastorate was marked with his usual success, and his resignation caused deep regret. Rev. Richard L. Howard, the second pastor, was a native of New York, and had been pastor in Fairfort for three years. His pastorate commenced here in May, 1876, and closed in January, 1879. He was succeeded by Rev. A. C. Hogben, in February, 1879, who resigned in February, 1880. Rev. John B. Jordan, the fourth pastor, was born in Auburn, and was licensed to preach June 11, 1878. He commenced to supply this pulpit in February, 1880, and was ordained as pastor of the church May 22, 1882. His pastorate, which was a very successful one, closed September 1, 1883. Mr. O. L. Gile, a student at the Cobb Divinity School, supplied the pulpit from September, 1883, to September, 1885. Rev. William J. Twort, the fifth pastor, came from Canton, and commenced his work as pastor in March, 1886, and closed his labors in September, 1889, to accept the pastorate of the Free Baptist church in Lynn, Mass. The present pastor, Rev. S. A. Blaisdell, came from Bath, and was publicly installed January 31, 1890. The services were by the clergymen of Lewiston and Auburn, viz.: Prayer, by Rev. C. C. Tilley, of the First Baptist church; sermon, by Rev. Martyn Summerbell, D.D., of the Main Street Free Baptist church; installing prayer, by Rev. A. S. Ladd, of the High Street Methodist church, Auburn; right-hand of fellowship, by Prof. B. F. Hayes, D.D., of Bates College; charge to the pastor, by Rev. T. H. Stacy, Free Baptist church, Auburn; charge to church, by Rev. F. S. Root, of the High Street Congregational church, Auburn; welcome to the city, by Rev. G. M. Howe, of Pine Street Congregational church; welcome in behalf of church, by Prof. J. A. Howe, D.D., of Cobb Divinity School.

The Hammond Street Methodist Church. - This church was organized in June, 1870, with these members: Samuel R. Bearce, Betsey Bearce, William Robinson, Abbie P. Robinson, Joel Nevens, Julia Nevens, Warren S. Butler, Elize M. Butler, Joshua G. Richardson, Maria S. Richardson, William G. Richardson, A. J. Aiken, Sarah C.

Aiken, Lizzie S. Abbott, and Etta J. Robinshon. It now has a membership of about 140. Rev. H. B. Abbott, who for five years had been pastor of the Park Street Methodist church, was appointed pastor of the church and commenced his labors the first Sabbath in June, 1870. He closed his pastorate in May, 1873. The society worshiped in the old Baptist church on Main street, corner of Lisbon, until the early part of 1876, when their church edifice was completed. It was commenced in the spring of 1875, and is situated on the easterly side of Hammond street. The erection of a suitable house of worship for the convenience of the society had been a subject of discussion for some time, but no definite arrangements had been perfected until this year. Mr. Samuel R. Bearce, who had been one of the original promoters in the organization of the church, and its principal patron, gave the lot on which the house is built, and also gave towards its construction the sum of $10,000. This munificent gift encouraged the society, though small, to commence their present house of worship. The church has a basement which is used as a vestry, over which is the audience room, neatly and tastily finished, capable of seating about 500. The exterior is of wood, with pleasing design and finish. The whole cost was not far from $18,000, and it was dedicated January 24, 1876, by Bishop Foster. Rev. Messrs. E. Martin, the presiding elder of the district, S. F. Wetherbee, the pastor, A. S. Ladd, N. C. Clifford, and other members of the ministry of the denomination were present.

Rev. D. W. LeLacheur was appointed as a supply in 1873, and in 1874 was appointed as pastor. Rev. S. F. Wetherbee was appointed to the pastorate of the church in 1875, and remained three years. Rev. J. Benson Hamilton was appointed to the charge in 1878 and was continued for three years. In 1881 Rev. A. S. Ladd was pastor. He was followed in 1882 by Rev. W. S. McIntire. Rev. Roscoe Sanderson was pastor for three years commencing with 1883; Rev. C. L. Libby in 1886, and re-appointed in 1887. Mr. Libby left the conference quite early in the year, removed to Utah, and is serving the denomination as a missionary. His place was supplied for the remainder of the year by Mr. William B. Dukeshire, a student at Kent's Hill. Rev. Perry Chandler came here in 1888 and remained as pastor for three years. Rev. J. A. Corey, the present pastor, was appointed to the pastorate of the church in May, 1891. Only two of the pastors of the church have died; Rev. H. B. Abbott, whose death is mentioned in the sketch of Park Street church, and Rev. S. F. Wetherbee, who died April 24, 1890. Mr. Wetherbee was born in Harvard, Mass., January 23, 1815. He entered the Maine Conference in 1845, and served in quite a number of the most important charges in the Maine and East Maine Conferences.

St. Joseph's Catholic (Irish) Church. - The first Catholic service in Lewiston was held at the house of P. McGillicuddy, Esq., in June, 1850, by Rev. Charles McCollion, of Portsmouth, NH. Mr. McGillicuddy's house was on the old street leading from Main street down the river, and near where the Continental Mills are situated. The building had been a school-house, but was purchased May 1, 1850, by Mr. McGillicuddy, and converted into a dwelling-house. Subsequently meetings were held by Father McCollion in the Bates dye-house, the Cowan Mill, as well as in several other places. Father McCollion continued to visit Lewiston at regular intervals, once in four weeks, until worship was established in the chapel formerly occupied by the First Baptist church, on Lincoln street. The Catholics bought the chapel of the Franklin Company. The chapel was provided with settees, but these were removed and the Catholics purchased the pews, 52 in number, in the Old South Baptist meeting-house, and had them set up in the chapel.

It was during Father McCollion's ministry that Miss Augusta A. Davis, daughter of Deacon Stephen Davis, of this city, and a teacher in the high school, became interested in the moral and religious welfare of the Irish children, and established a Sabbath school for their instruction, which was held for the most of the time in the high school building. Miss Davis received the co-operation of Father McCollion and the leading Catholics, as well as many of the Protestants of the place. Miss Davis married Rev. Joseph K. Greene, and for more than thirty years has been a missionary in Turkey, being located at Constantinople.

Subsequently Rev. Peter McLaughlin, of Bath, held services here one-half of the time. He was succeeded by Rev. Thomas Kenney, whose time was equally divided between Lewiston and Biddeford. Rev. John Cullin was the first Catholic clergyman permanently located here, and remained about two years. He was succeeded by Rev. Daniel Wheelon, whose ministry occupied nearly six years. Rev. J. A. T. Durnin was the immediate successor of Father Wheelon, and remained 16 months. Rev. Michael Lucy came here in October, 1862. The church, St. Joseph's, located on Main street, was built under the immediate direction of Father Lucy. The corner-stone was laid with appropriate ceremonies, June 13, 1864, Bishop Bacon, of Portland, officiating. The foundation was completed in the autumn of that year, and the building finished in 1867. The church cost $55,000. Rev. Clement Mutsaers succeeded Father Lucy as pastor of the church.

Rev. T. H. Wallace assumed charge of the church in August, 1876. During his ministry of 15 years he has done a marked work for St. Joseph's church. It is now one of the strongest churches of the denomination in the state. Besides his ordinary church work he has superintended the building of the new church, St. Patrick's, on Bates street, facing the park. It was commenced in the spring of 1887, and the outside completed that year, and is now ready for occupancy. It is one of the finest church edifices in the state, all of its appointments being in the best and most approved style. It has magnificent windows of stained glass, and the altars are of superior design and workmanship. Connected with the church is the chapel, having an entrance from Walnut street, capable of seating 500 persons. The main building is about 180 x 65 feet, with a seating capacity for 1,000 persons. The whole cost of the church is not far from $78,000. The lot, which is one of the most desirable in the city, cost $25,000.

St. Peter's Catholic (French) Church. - The first service held by the French Catholics was at the chapel (Irish) on Lincoln street, on July 2, 1870, by Rev. Edward Leternearn, who remained until October, 1871. He was succeeded by Rev. Peter Hevey, who held his first service October 11, 1871. October 22, Father Hevey addressed his congregation on the importance of the erection of a house of worship, to which the society responded with marked enthusiasm. A lot was first purchased on Bates, corner of Ash street, but was soon abandoned, and the lot on Bartlett street secured instead. The corner-stone of the new church edifice was laid July 7, 1872, in the presence of Bishop Bacon. The church was dedicated May 14, 1873, Bishop Bacon conducting the services. The building is of the Gothic style of architecture, and is built of brick with granite trimmings. It will seat 1,500 persons and cost $75,000. Father Hevey was succeeded by Rev. A. Mothon, the preent pastor. The assistant pastors are Reverends B. Charmont, T. H. Morard, A. Maricourt, P. Duchaussoy, and R. Grolleau.

Schools. - Previous to 1795 the schools were undoubtedly conducted by private contributions. Tradition furnishes all the information we have of the schools. Daniel Davis, who came in 1777, taught for several winters in his house, and his brother Amos, who came earlier, was probably employed in teaching. Amos Davis built, it is said, a small house for Mrs. Poor, his relative, near the residence of Daniel B. Jones on Sabatis street, probably as early as 1780, in which she taught school for a number of years. Dan Read, Esq., who came in 1788, was a school-teacher for several years. Noah Litchfield, who came in 1792, was employed in teaching. In the north part of the town John Chandler also taught, a part of the time, for nearly 10 years. In 1791 Mr. David Gross taught in James Garcelon's house at "Garcelon's Ferry," and Mrs. Thomas Mitchell taught in the west end of the Mitchell log house about 1793. Mr. Mitchell lived on the farm formerly owned and occupied by Colonel William Garcelon, and now owned by Captain Silas B. Osgood. Benning Wentworth taught in Mr. Mitchell's house in 1799 and 1800; and Dr. Barrett also taught in a small room in one end of James Ames's blacksmith shop. Nearly all were private schools, supported by voluntary contributions, and were maintained for a long time after 1795. At the first town meeting, held April, 1795, it was voted to raise L-60 for schools. May 6th, "voted to accept the districts as the Select men have Laid them out for schooling." It was also "voted the Maj'r Part of Each District Should have power to Lay their money out as they See proper Either in Schools or building a house for that Purpose." The town was divided into six "Classes" or "Districts," and a "Collector" or "head" chosen for each. First Class. - Nathan Cutler was elected collector, comprising the northern part of the town. Second Class. - Abner Harris was collector, embracing what is now the city proper. Third Class. - Joel Thompson was collector, now known as Rose Hill district. Fourth Class. - Ezra Randall was elected collector, the Thorne district. Fifth Class. - Isaac Cotton, now the Clough district. Sixth Class. - William Garcelon was elected collector, at Garcelon's Ferry.

By authority granted by the town, district No. 3 built a school-house in 1795, on the farm of Deacon Josiah Mitchell, opposite the house of Deacon Stephen Davis, the first in town. It served not only for a school-house but for a town-house, and meeting-house for the Baptist church for nearly a quarter of a century. After several changes in the boundaries of the district, it was removed to Rose Hill, where it remained until the present school-house was erected in 1856. Subsequently it was sold to Horace B. Bartlett and removed to Orange street. It was torn down a few years since. The annual town meeting for 1796 was held in this house, and these appropriations made for building new school-houses: First class, Nathan Cutler, head, $166.67; second class, Noah Litchfield, head, $100; third class, Robert Anderson, head, $183.33; fourth class, Samuel Thorne, head $50; fifth class, Isaac Cotton, head $40; sixth class, Ezra Purinton, head $100; seventh class, Ezra Randall, head, $66.66. The town also raised $100 for the support of schools. In 1797 $100 was raised for schools, and the usual school officers - "Heads" - elected. District No. 7 was probably discontinued. The first district was authorized to expend their school money in completing the school-house which they commenced the previous year. District No. 2 commenced a school-house in 1797, but the town, April 1, 1797, refused to raise money towards its completion; but in 1801 the district voted to build, selected a site, and chose a building committee. In March, 1802, the building committee decided to build "brick and mortar," but for some cause the enterprise failed, and the school-house was not built until 1804, and then of wood. This was the fifth in town, school-houses having been built in No. 4 in 1802, and in No. 8 in 1803.

About 1802 Richard D. Harris came and commenced teaching. Mr. Harris was a very energetic as well as a very enthusiastic teacher, and infused new life and vigor into our schools, but it did not assume a permanent form, for they lapsed into their former methods. Year after year the town voted money for schools, gradually increasing the sum, but not in proportion to the increase of population, until 1831, when $700 was voted. Previously the interest in education had somewhat advanced and private schools were opened in several parts of the town, under the direction of competent instructors. Rev. Benjamin Thorne, William Bond, and Aaron D. Thorne taught with unusual success and acquired more than an ordinary reputation as instructors of youth. During the decade previous to 1850 little progress was made in our schools. No one was especially interested in placing before the people the importance of appropriating more money for their support, or furnishing better accommodations. The school-houses, as a rule, were poor, and constructed by persons having meagre knowledge of proper school buildings, and who knew as little how they ought to be furnished. In 1847 Rev. George Knox located here, and soon after commenced teaching private schools. He had progressive views of school work and soon won the confidence of the community, as well as the town, as a prudent and wise educator. He was soon placed on the school committee and afterwards elected supervisor, and could usually carry any appropriation he asked for. Under his supervision there was an advance not only in the village, but throughout the rural portions of the town. In 1841 district No. 2, the village district, was divided, and that portion lying next the river was constituted a district by itself, and called No. 16; but in 1850 this district was united with No. 2.

During the summer of 1850 a two-story school-house was built in the village district, and a high school established under the direction of George W. Jewett, a teacher of much experience and rare ability. Mr. Jewett remained about two years. From this date the schools in the village assumed new life, and their progress has been constant. They are now justly recognized as among the best in the state. In 1860 this district was authorized by act of the legislature, approved March

6, to choose three directors, who were invested with all the authority of school agents, and school committee, or supervisor. They were to determine the number of grades of schools and the number of schools in each grade, to classify the scholars, and to expend the money apportioned by the town to the district for the support of schools. The inhabitants were authorized to adopt by-laws and regulations, not contrary to the constitution and laws of the state for the regulation of the schools. This was the first substantial movement for a system of graded schools. The two small schools in 1850 have become 21 primaries, 8 intermediates, with a two years' course, a grammar school of ten classes with a four years' course, a high school having a four years' course with three courses of study, viz., an English, English classical, and college preparatory. Many of the school-houses are models in design, in architectural beauty and finish, as well as the character and style of the furniture. By a special act of the legislature in 1864, the district system was abolished and the town system adopted. For more than a quarter of a century this method has been tried with marked success. The great advantage which has grown out of this system is especially recognized in the rural schools of the city. These schools, whether large or small, have the same number of terms and generally the same number of weeks, are provided with better teachers, have an improved course of study, and many of the scholars have been prepared for and have entered the high school and have graduated with credit to themselves as well as the school. All scholars of the city are admitted free who have the necessary qualfications.

In 1872 the school board were authorized to supply each pupil with textbooks and school appliances free. Since that time our schools have been free indeed. Everything needed in the school-room, from the sub-primary to the high school, is furnished by the city and paid for with the money appropriated for this purpose. Besides the schools already mentioned, there has been in successful operation the most of the time for 20 years a Normal Training school, where young ladies, mostly graduates of the high school, have had the advantages, under the direction of a skillful and experienced teacher, of training in the best methods of instruction and in school economy. Unquestionably, this school has had much to do with the present high standard of the Lewiston schools. Every teacher enters the school-room with a commendable knowledge of the best methods of instruction recognized by the best educators in the country. Nor are they novices in teaching, for they have had a year's experience, and some of them more, under the instruction of a competent teacher, for this school unites the theory as well as the practice of teaching. The school board consists of 14 members, two from each ward in the city, one of whom is elected at the annual meeting in March for the term of two years. By this method at least one-half of the board has had an experience of one year in the management of the schools. In 1871 the school board elected a superintendent of schools, and since that time the office has been maintained. Mr. G. A. Stuart is the present superintendent.

CHAPTER IV.

Saw and Grist Mills - Lewiston Falls Water-Power Co. - R. C. Pingree & Co. - Read, Small & Co. - Barker's Mills - Other Mills - Lewiston Falls Manufacturing Co. - The First Cotton Mill - Lewiston Water-Power Co. - Franklin Co. - Lincoln Mill - Bates Manufacturing Co. - Hill Manufacturing Co. - Androscoggin Mill - Continental Mills - The Lewiston Mill - Avon Mill - Lewiston Bleachery - Cowan Woolen Co. - Cumberland Mill - Union Water-Power Co. - Lewiston Machine Co. - Gay-Woodman Co. - Jordan, Frost & Co. - Lewiston Bobbin Shop - H. H. Dickey & Son - Lewiston Monumental Works - Other Manufactures.

Saw and Grist Mills. - The saw-mill erected by Lawrence J. Harris in 1770-71, on the river nearly where the Cowan Mill stands, was burned about 1785, soon after the death of Mr. Harris. It is supposed the mills - saw and grist-mill - remained under his control during his life-time; but they soon passed into the hands of Little and the heirs of Bagley. The mill was simple. There was no dam across the river, or canal, but the water was conveyed into a small pond by a small flume which extended into the river and rested on the ledge near the summit of the falls. A dam was built across the valley, just above the mill, which reached the hill on the eastern side, touching a spur of ledge on the river bank that formed part of the western portion of the dam. Several years after the erection of the saw-mill, Mr. Harris built a grist-mill, taking the power from the same pond, but it was so near the river that after standing a few years it was undermined, and became a total loss. Soon after the destruction of the mill in 1785, it was rebuilt by the proprietors, but like its predecessor, it was burned. In 1808-9 the first dam across the river here was built, and a canal made. The dam was built of timber, rudely constructed, and did not occupy the same position of those built later. On this canal, and on ground now covered by the northerly wing of the Lincoln Mill, Mr. Little built, in 1809, a large wooden building, and had, under one roof, saw, grist, and fulling mills. There was also a carding machine. In the spring of 1814 this mill was consumed by fire, a total loss to Mr. Little and a great misfortune to the people. These mills were undoubtedly burned by the torch of the incendiary. Mr. Little was much grieved by these manifestations of enmity. There was unquestionably much feeling in the community against Mr. Little, but the sentiment was almost universal and pronounced against this wanton destruction of property. In a letter to Mr. Amos Davis, written in March, 1815, Mr. Little writes:

My son, Michael, writes that the people of Lewiston and Minot are desirous to have a grist-mill and saw-mill built this season on the falls, and that the people would get in the timber that will be suitable for them, provided I would consent to put them up this season. If the people think the mills will be safe from the base incendiary, who has no more regard for one man than another, I will, with the assistance of the people, make one more trial to rebuild them. But I should like to have the timber cut on the old of the moon, that if it should be preserved from fire it might be more durable.

A new mill much better than the one destroyed was built that season, which remained until about 1850, when it gave place to valuable improvements.

The Lewiston Falls Water-Power Company, in 1851, built a large saw-mill on the site now occupied by the pumping station of the Lewiston water works. It was a commodious building, furnished with the best of machinery for manufacturing lumber, cost $7,000, and was leased to Captain Daniel Holland for five years. This mill was also destroyed by fire, on the evening of August 28, 1852. Besides that part of the building occupied by Captain Holland, the basement was used by Charles Dean for planing lumber, having two planing machines; the chamber by Cyrus Parsons, who had one planing machine, and the attic by Wedgewood & Prescott, carpenters. There were 28 persons employed in the building. The Water-Power Company immediately rebuilt the mill, which, in March, 1856, was leased to Samuel R. Bearce & Co., and used by them until the property was sold to the city.

R. C. Pingree & Co. - In 1865 S. R. Bearce & Co. built a large steam mill, 60 x 114 feet, costing nearly $60,000, on the river about a fourth of a mile about the Maine Central station, where they commenced the manufacture of lumber in 1866. It is one of the best mills in the state, has gang, circular, shingle, clapboard, and lath saws, and planing machines. The power is a 250 horse-power engine. The annual production is about 13,250,000 feet of long lumber, 6,000,000 shingles, 850,000 laths, and 600,000 clapboards, valued at $250,000, and employs 100 men. Since the death of Mr. Bearce the business has been carried on by R. C. Pingree & Co. Mr. Pingree has been identified with the management of the mill ever since it was put in operation.

Read, Small & Co. - A steam-mill, which cost $7,500, was built at Barker's Mills, in 1847, by Read, Small & Co. It had one shingle saw, one shingle and one lath machine. The mill was burned September 10, 1852, and rebuilt the same year. In October, 1859, it was purchased by James Wood & Co., and removed to the "Falls," about one-half mile above the Maine Central station. The company purchased about 14 acres of land on the river for a mill-yard and other purposes. In 1860 the company was incorporated as the Lewiston Steam-Mill Company, with a capital of $50,000, which, in 1867, was increased to $100,000. The corporators were Stephen H. Read, James Wood, John N. Wood, and John N. Small. The company bought 35,000 acres of timber land, mostly spruce, on the Androscoggin and its tributaries, employed 60 men, disbursed about $3,500 per month, and manufactured annually 4,700,000 long lumber, 2,400,000 laths, 1,900,000 shingles, and 195,000 clapboards, valued at $100,000. The company suspended operations in September, 1887, and in October, 1888, the mill and adjoining land was sold to R. C. Pingree & Co. for $18,000. July 5, 1889, the mill was destroyed by fire. James Wood, Esq., was agent of the company from the commencement.

Barker's Mills. - About 1775, Jacob Barker built a grist-mill on the stream which takes its rise in the Mine Meadow, Greene, and flows into the Androscoggin two miles above the falls. For some years after the destruction of the Harris grist-mill this was the only one in the plantation. A few years later Mr. Barker built a saw-mill on the same stream, where he did considerable business in manufacturing lumber. These mills were rebuilt once or twice by his son, Cyrus Barker, and once in 1834 by his grandson, Nelson P. Barker. About 1870 they passed into the hands of Dwelley & Moore, who did an extensive business in the manufacture of meal and lumber. The mills have passed through several hands since 1865, and are now owned by Messrs. Libby & Dingley. For more than a year they have not been in operation.

Not far from 1800 a saw-mill was built on the rips opposite Boxer's Island, by William Blaisdell and Thomas Jepson, which was burned about 1812. A saw-mill was early built on Stetson brook, by James Randall, which was removed to Auburn. A shingle mill, erected by Jamison and Given, below the saw-mill was standing in 1847. About 1800 Colonel Joel Thompson, Captain Isaac Cotton, and Captain Joseph Dill built a saw-mill at the outlet, of No Name pond, where they manufactured considerable ship timber. Edward Estes had a saw-mill on the brook below the Stephen Hart place. It was built about 1820. The remains of a stone dam are now visible.

MANUFACTURES. - *Lewiston Falls Manufacturing Company.* - Some years previous to 1819 there was on the site of the new mill recently owned and operated by the Home Manufacturing Company, a small carding and fulling mill, owned, it is probable, by Mr. Michael Little. The discovery of two or more leases given by Michael Little to different parties to operate these mills seems conclusive. Hitherto Colonel Josiah Little, father of Michael, has been regarded as the owner. Michael Little came here quite early, and resided in Lewiston and Minot for many years. He died in Minot, April 2, 1830. Mr. Little graduated from Dartmouth College in the class of 1792. We are unable to fix the date when this mill was built, and it does not appear to have been very successful. It was in 1819 that the services of Mr. Dean Frye, father of Colonel John M. Frye, were obtained. Mr. Frye came from Brunswick. He had had large experience in carding wool and finishing cloth. Under his management the business readily assumed an importance which it had never experienced. The mill was burned in 1829, but in 1830 a new mill, 38 x 60 feet, and three stories high, was completed. The basement was occupied as a clothier's fulling mill, and the second story for carding rolls and finishing cloth. It was under the management of Mr. Dean Frye and his son, John M. Frye, whose previous experience and skill in business soon gave character and influence to the enterprise. Successful in these operations to an extent unusual for those days, the Messrs. Frye were induced to make the experiment of manufacturing satinet. This new effort required more capital, as well as a broader basis of action, and to secure these a legislative charter for the Lewiston Falls Manufacturing Company ($100,000 capital) was obtained February 26, 1834. This was the first charter granted for manufacturing purposes in Lewiston. The corporators were John M. Frye and William R. Frye. The organization was completed at once, the directors being Edward Little, Samuel Pickard, John A. Briggs, William R. Frye, and John M. Frye. The first meeting of the directors was held June 12, 1834, when Edward Little was elected president, Samuel Pickard, treasurer, and William R. Frye, clerk. June 30, 1834, John M. Frye was elected agent, with a salary of $300 per annum, with the promise that if the business was successful $50 should be added. The company immediately bought the fulling mill and water privilege, with sufficent land for the new enterprise, of the Littles. The fulling mill was converted into a satinet mill, with two sets of machinery. These were the first looms "started up" in Lewiston. The success which attended this mill induced the company to enlarge their business, and, in 1836, the brick mill called the cassimere mill was built, taking the name from the goods manufactured. Hardly was the mill completed before the spring freshet of 1837 undermined the mill on the river side, causing the whole wall to fall into the river. This misfortune, followed by the financial embarrassments of that year, were peculiarly disheartening. But, although young, without experience, and comparatively unknown in the market, yet the quality and texture of their goods secured the favorable notice of purchasers, commanded good prices, and brought early sales. For more than forty years these mills enjoyed unexampled prosperity. They were very prudently and wisely managed and their goods were readily sold. Much of the prosperity was due to the judgment and sound business ability of the agent, Colonel John M. Frye, and Samuel Pickard, Esq., who for many years was the treasurer. Colonel Frye remained agent until age and infirmities compelled him to retire. There were manufactured repellents, meltons, and cassimeres to the amount of 230,000 years per annum. There were six sets of machinery, which required 90 operatives, about one-half females. The monthly disbursements were $2,000, and the annual consumption of wool 250,000 pounds, about one-half purchased in Maine. For several years after the retirement of Colonel Frye the mills were in operation but a part of the time, but in November, 1881, they were sold to D. Cowan & Co., and in January, 1882, passed into the control of the Home Manufacturing Company, a local corporation having a capital of $100,000. The company ran six sets of cards, 20 looms, manufactured 2,000 yards of flannels daily, and employed 50 operatives. The daily consumption of wool was 1,000 pounds, and the monthly pay-roll $1,800. Recently the company closed operations and the plant has been sold to the Gay-Woodman Company.

The First Cotton Mill. - About 1836 Mr. John A. Briggs put up a wooden building on the site of the Cowan woolen mill. The rear of the building was three stories high, and the basement was occupied by a Mr. Johnson, a machinist who did a small business. The second story was occupied by Colonel Temple Tebbets, a cabinet maker who did wood-turning, confining his business mostly to cabinet work. Mr. Tebbets was a native of Lisbon and came here about 1831-2. The upper story was occupied by Ephraim Wood for manufacturing cotton warps and batting. He was the pioneer in this place in the manufacture of cotton. He finally removed to Winthrop. Jospeh B. Harding, of Gorham, became proprietor after Mr. Wood. This was in 1840-41. He continued the manufacture of batting and cotton warps, and about 1844 made additions to the mill, putting in three looms for weaving cotton cloths. Mr. Harding made the first cotton goods in Lewiston, and continued their manufacture for several years with considerable success. After Mr. Harding sold out he removed to Yarmouth. The "old mill" was partially destroyed by fire March 17, 1850, and the remainder was removed by the Water-Power Company in April, to make room for the flour and grist-mill. For several years it had been owned by the Water-Power Company and operated to some extent by them.

Lewiston Water-Power Company. - The predecessor of this company, the Great Androscoggin Falls, Dam, Locks, and Canal Company, was incorporated February 23, 1836, with a capital of $100,000, the charter being granted to Edward Little, Josiah Little, of Newbury, Thomas B. Little, Josiah Little, of Minot, Samuel Pickard, and Edward T. Little, their associates, etc., "for the purpose of erecting and constructing dams, locks, canals, mills, works, machines, and buildings on their own lands, and also manufacturing cotton, wool, iron, steel, and paper in the towns of Lewiston, Minot, and Danville." The corporators owned the water-power and a large amount of land on both sides of the river in the immediate vicinity of the falls. In 1837 the company procured the services of Mr. B. F. Perham, of Boston, a civil engineer, who made a survey and a plan, showing the survey and levels as well as profiles of different sections of the territory. This plan the company published. Desiring, a few years later, to establish cotton and woolen manufacturing to an extent hitherto unknown at the "Falls," the corporation, in 1845, secured a change of name to the Lewiston Water-Power Company, which was formally inserted in the charter by a vote of the company, November 19, 1845. Certificates of stock under the new name were issued to the share-holders, who soon sold them to parties in Boston. The Water-Power Company, from 1846 to 1850, purchased several valuable lots of land on both sides of the river. In the spring of 1850 work was commenced on the canal. The first section, as far as the Bates Mills, was completed in May, 1851. The canal is 62 feet wide, 14 feet deep, and the extensions made since 1851 have made it about three-fourths of a mile in length. There are several short, or cross canals, connecting the main canal with the river. The locks at the head of the canal are a fine piece of masonry, built of granite laid in cement, and contain 18 large gates, and two fly-gates whose capacity is equal to six of the other gates. The capital of the company was increased, June 18, 1849, "$1,500,000, to be divided into shares of $100 each." From the commencement of operations in 1850, and for several years afterwards, the company continued to improve and utilize the great water-power, and did much to develop the growth and prosperity of the town. Much of its land was put into the market, new streets were laid out and graded, and Lewiston assumed an air of activity and genuine thrift.

Franklin Company. - This company was incorporated April 3, 1854, with a capital of $1,000,000, but was not organized until November 25, 1856. It purchased the property of the Water-Power Company, assumed control in April following, and still controls a large portion of the original purchase. The spring freshet of 1862 carried away a section of the dam adjoining the eastern shore, which was replaced by a substantial granite dam during that year. In 1863 and 1864 the remaining portions of the dam were built, the whole costing about $100,000. This is one of the most substantial granite dams in the country. The company owns the land near the falls on both sides of the river, and several hundred acres in and around the thickly settled portions of Lewiston and Auburn. It owns the Lincoln Mill, the Cowan Mill building, the DeWitt House, about one-fourth of the Bleachery, and many shops and buildings. The agents of the Lewiston Water-Power Company and the Franklin Company have been Mr. Luke Bemis, Mr. George L. Ward (who came about 1850), Benjamin I. Leeds, who remained until 1860, when Amos D. Lockwood, Esq., assumed the agency, which he retained about 11 years. Mr. N. W. Farwell became agent in 1871, and resigned in February, 1873. From Mr. Farwell's resignation the company had no local agent (the business being done generally by the clerk) until the appointment of the present agent, Mr. Stephen Lee.

Lincoln Mill. - The success which attended the manufacture of cotton cloths in the "Old Cotton Mill," induced a number of the most enterprising citizens of Lewiston to apply to the legislature for a charter to enable them to enter upon the business of making cotton cloths to an extent not before attempted. The charter to the Lewiston Falls Cotton Mill Company, with a capital of $100,000, was granted March 1, 1845, the corporators being Calvin Gorham, James Lowell, Elisha Stetson, Daniel Cary, Daniel Briggs, John M. Frye, Nelson B. Reynolds, Howe Weeks, Stephen Davis, Edward Little, and Alonzo Garcelon. The proprietors soon commenced the construction of the mill, Captain Daniel Holland, contractor. There was a large excavation to be made in the ledge where the eastern extremity of the mill was to rest, that consumed considerable time. The foundation was completed and the brick work commenced September 1, 1845. Before the mill was completed it was bought (March 5, 1846) by the Water-Power Company. It was finished during the summer, and the first loom "started up" October 5, 1846. Mr. Zeba Bliss was superintendent of the mill for several years. The building was 46 x 102 feet in size, and five stories high. This enterprise was very successful. The goods made were plain sheetings of a standard quality, and found a ready market. In 1867 and 1868 additions were made, increasing its capacity several fold. The Franklin Company concluded to make an addition to the Hill machine shop, connect it with the Lincoln Mill, and convert it into a cotton factory. Besides this the mill received an addition of 53 feet on the eastern end. These extensions and additions increased its capacity from 5,472 to 21,747 spindles. The Lincoln Mill, as it now stands, is 56 x 182 feet, and five stories high. With its present machinery it is capable of annually producing 3,000,000 yards of forty-inch sheetings, and consuming 1,040,000 pounds of cotton. It requires 124 males and 280 females when in full operation. The mill has not run since July, 1884.

Bates Manufacturing Company. - Bates, No. 1, was the first cotton factory erected after the Water-Power Company commenced the development of the manufacturing interests. This company was incorporated in 1850. The corporators were Alexander DeWitt, Thomas B. Little, Jacob W. Pierce, Thomas I. Hill, Silas Titcomb, and George L. Ward. Immediately after incorporation the company commenced the construction of this mill, which was completed and put in operation in 1852. As originally built it was 60 x 280 feet, and four stories high. It is situated on the west side of the main canal, less than one-fourth of a mile south of Main street. Soon after it was in operation the company commenced a second mill situated only a few rods south of No. 1. No. 2 "was started" in 1854, and was the same size of No. 1 (60 x 280), and four stories high. In 1863 the company began its third (woolen) mill, which commenced manufacturing in 1865. No. 3 is 50 x 170 feet in size and three stories high. When operated as a woolen mill it manufactured Moscow beavers, repellents, fancy cassimeres and slasher cloths, making 118,925 yards per annum. It had 8 sets of machinery, 30 broad looms, and required 125 operatives, 50 of whom were females. More than 350,000 pounds of wool were consumed yearly. July 16, 1878, the woolen mill was damaged by fire, and in October it was changed to a cotton mill. In 1882 there were large additions made to No. 1 and two other mills by putting on another story to each, extending No. 1 to the cross canal, and adding about 30 feet to the southerly end of No. 2. These mills have been run with more than ordinary success, under the direction of Messrs. D. M. Ayer, C. I. Barker, and H. L. Pratt, who have successively been agents. The number of spindles is 58,392. There are 1,333 narrow and 262 broad looms. There are 1,865 operatives employed; 1,039 are females. There are annually consumed 5,230,132 pounds of cotton, and the value of dyes used is more than $63,000. The Bates manufactures fancy goods, Marseilles, crochet, and common quilts, dress goods, ginghams, etc., etc., amounting to 15,032,077 yards per annum. The pay-roll for two weeks is $23,125. Besides the mills there is a large dye-house, cloth-hall, two pickers, two cotton houses, and a repair shop. Its capital is $1,000,000.

Hill Manufacturing Company. - Among our manufacturing enterprises none, with a single exception, has been so long under the management of one agent as the Hill Corporation. This company was incorporated August 16, 1850. Benjamin E. Bates, Thomas B. Little, Albert H. Kelsey, Seth W. Fowle, and George L. Ward were the corporators. The capital was $350,000, which has been increased to $1,000,000. The company operates two mills and manufactures cotton goods exclusively. The first mill, No. 1, was completed in 1854 and put in operation immediately. Its second mill, No. 2, was not finished until 1864, when manufacturing commenced. These mills are 69 x 216 feet, and six stories high. Connected with the mills are two pickers, four stories high. There are 53,976 spindles, and 1,238 looms; 700 persons are employed, 500 of whom are females. There are 8,700,000 yards of fine sheetings, shirtings, sateens, contils, and twills manufactured, annually, which require 2,400,000 pounds of cotton. The monthly pay-roll amounts to $20,000. Mr. J. G. Coburn has been agent since it commenced operations until recently. Mr. William D. Pennell is now agent.

Androscoggin Mill. - This is one of the mammoth cotton mills of the country. It was incorporated in 1854 as the Arkwright Company, with a capital of $500,000, Benjamin E. Bates, A. H. Kelsey, and George L. Ward being the corporators. It does not appear that any business was done by this corporation, but in 1860 the name was changed to the Androscoggin Company, and the capital increased to $1,000,000. Immediately the company began the mill, and commenced manufacturing in 1861. The mill is 74 x 542 feet, five stories high, with two wings each 48 x 100 feet, with four stories. The second mill is 74 x 180 feet, and three stories high. This mill commenced operations in 1867. The third mill is 74 x 166 feet and three stories in height, and was started up in 1872. The Androscoggin Mill has 61,912 spindles, and 1,455 looms. It employs 960 operatives; 610 are females. The annual production is 10,400,000 yards of sheetings, seersuckers, shirtings, and satteen jeans, and 3,000,000 seamless bags. They consume 60 tons of starch. A. D. Lockwood was agent from 1861 until 1870, when J. W. Danielson became agent. W. F. Goulding succeeded Mr. Danielson, and retained the position until his death, April 16, 1885, when David Phetplace became agent. Mr. Phetplace was succeeded by George W. Bean, the present agent.

Continental Mills. - This company was incorporated February 4, 1865, with a capital of $1,500,000. The corporators were A. H. Fiske, Benjamin E. Bates, and Josiah Bardwell. In 1866 the company purchased the Porter Mill, which commenced manufacturing as early as 1858, and changed the name to Continental Mills. In 1872 the company enlarged the original mill by an addition of 230 feet in length by 75 feet in width, five stories high, making the building 554 feet long. There was also added a wing, 346 feet in length and 75 feet in width. The building is covered with a Mansard roof. It has 75,000 spindles and 1,650 looms. The whole number of employees is 1,200; 900 females. There are used annually 6,000,000 pounds of cotton. The annual production is 18,500,000 yards of brown sheetings and drills, and 150,000 pounds of batting. The monthly pay-roll is $40,000. There have been four agents, viz.: R. A. Budlong, Stephen I. Abbott, E. S. Davis, and the present agent, H. L. Adrich, Jr.

Lewiston Mill. - This company was incorporated February 8, 1853, as the Lewiston Bagging Company, with a capital of $50,000; A. H. Kelsey, George L. Ward, Edward A. Raymond, and Marshall French, corporators. For several years the company leased rooms in the Cowan Woolen Mill, and subsequently occupied rooms in the Continental Mill. In 1860 it commenced the erection of its first mill, which was completed and put in operation in 1861. This mill is 72 x 164 feet and four stories high, with a wing 50 x 121 feet, also four stories in height. The second mill was completed in 1866, and is 72 x 108 feet, having a wing 43 x 95 feet, four stories in height. In 1863 the corporation was authorized to change its name to Lewiston Mill and increase its capital $300,000. The mill had 18,792 spindles, and manufactured tickings, cottonades, osnaburgs, fancy, plaid, stripe, and plain, - colored ducks, and cotton bags. It also manufactured 800,000 pounds of yarn per annum. It employed 800 operatives, 520 of whom were females. The annual consumption of cotton was 4,200,000 pounds. In July, 1886, the company suspended operations and the mill was idle until May 1, 1889, when a new company was formed, and the plant purchased. The new company was incorporated in 1889 with a captial of $300,000. The stock is largely owned in this community. The company runs 23,140 spindles and 593 looms, and employs 300 males and 400 females, and manufactures tickings, cottonades, osnaburgs, fancy, plaid, stripe, plain, and colored ducks, turkey-red damasks, domett-flannels, horse-netting, and fly-cloths, and up to January, 1891, cotton bags. The company consumes 4,200,000 pounds of cotton per annum. It dyes 800,000 pounds of goods annually, and expends for dyes about $30,000. The monthly pay-roll and disbursements in Lewiston is $16,000. C. I. Barker, agent.

Avon Mill. - This company was incorporated in 1882, commenced the erection of the mill June 1, 1882, and began manufacturing in March, 1883. The mill is 50 x 100 feet in size, with bleachery, 24 x 50 feet; dye house, 50 x 67 feet; 75 persons are employed, 50 of whom are females. The whole number of looms is 56, 24 of which are broad. At the Avon are manufactured fancy, colored, and crochet quilts and Turkish towels. The number of quilts produced annually is 204,000, and 840,000 towels. Monthly disbursements, $2,000. January 1, 1891, the captial was $100,000; A. D. Barker, agent; F. H. Packard, treasurer.

Lewiston Bleachery and Dye Works. - The bleachery commenced operations in 1860, having been leased by the Franklin Company to Mr. N. W. Farwell, who did an extensive business until 1870. On the expiration of Mr. Farwell's lease extensive repairs were made, and, in January, 1872, the Lewiston Bleachery and Dye Works was incorporated, with a chartered right to hold property to the amount of $1,000,000. The corporators were Lyman Nichols, Benjamin E. Bates, and William B. Wood. The bleachery is now owned by the Franklin, Androscoggin, and Bates companies, and the Pepperell and Laconia companies, of Biddeford. It is now able to turn out 30 tons of bleached goods a day, and employs 438 operatives, 35 of whom are females. The monthly pay-roll is $45,000. The dye works consume $100,000 worth of drugs and dye per annum; and the value of finished goods amounts to $5,400,000. A box-shop connected with the bleachery manufactures 180 cases daily, and used yearly 2,100,000 feet of spruce lumber. The annual consumption of coal is 6,000 tons; lime, 1,800 barrels; soda-ash, 360,000 pounds; bleaching powders, 260,000 pounds; sulphuric acid, 6,000 carboys; potato starch, 80 tons; wheat and corn starch, 200 tons; sago flour, 50 tons; flour, 24 tons.

Cowan Woolen Company. - Early in 1864, D. M. Ayer & Co. leased rooms in the grist-mill building, now the Cowan Mill, for manufacturing cotton and woolen goods. In the autumn the machinery was completed and manufacturing commenced. Subsequently Mr. Ayer sold to D. Cowan & Co., who continued the business. For a number of years the company was known as the Aurora Mills, but was finally changed to the Cowan Mill. The mill was started with 3 sets of machinery and 12 broad looms. Mr. Cowan continued his connection until his death, and under his supervision the goods produced here were justly recognized as among the best in the market. The Cowan Woolen Company was organized in 1888, purchased the property, and have made additions, and put in much new machinery. They now have 8 sets of machinery, run 40 broad looms, have 180 employees (60 females), manufacture 300,000 yards of fancy cassimeres, suitings, and overcoatings. The monthly pay-roll is $3,700. Frederick Olfene, agent.

Cumberland Mill. - This mill commenced manufacturing in 1868, and was owned by J. L. H. Cobb & Co. Subsequently it came into the possession of Mr. P. M. Thurlow, one of the original proprietors. It is now owned by Messrs. W. S. Libby and H. M. Dingley. It is 50 x 72 feet, and three stories in height. It commenced operations with three sets of machinery which has been increased to six sets. There are 50 employees, 25 females. The monthly pay-roll amounts to $2,000. They manufacture Cumberland repellents (blacks, browns, blues, and grays), the annual production being 300,000 yards. The annual consumption of wool is 325,000 pounds.

Union Water-Power Company. - This company was organized September 18, 1878. The organization was the result of the purchase by the city of the water-works rights. It has a capital stock of $400,000, owned by the Franklin, Bates, Androscoggin, Continental, Hill, and Bleachery corporations. This company purchased of the Franklin Company the canals and water privileges in Lewiston, and are the owners of all the lands, dams, and water privileges (purchased of Coe & Co.), controlling the head waters of the Androscoggin. It rents to the several corporations their water-power.

Lewiston Machine Company. - This was incorporated February 4, 1865, with a capital of $200,000, the corporators being Samuel W. Kilvert, Josiah G. Coburn, Nathaniel W. Farwell, David M. Ayer, and Rhodes A. Budlong. Soon after organization it purchased the machinery and tools of the old Hill machine shop, which was subsequently removed to the foundry building near the Maine Central depot. This was built about 1852, enlarged in 1865 and again in 1866. In 1868 the interior was remodeled, and is now one of the best-appointed establishments in the state. The company employs 200 persons, and has a monthly pay-roll of $10,000. It manufactures iron and brass castings, and cotton machinery.

Gay-Woodman Company. - This is the only shoe manufacturing company in the city, and is incorporated with a capital of $150,000. It occupies a wooden building, 125 x 75 feet, and six stories high, on lower Main street, opposite Maine Central station, and commenced to manufacture here in July, 1883. It employs 400 males and 150 females, and manufactures 40,000 cases of men's boots and shoes annually. They run 150 stitching machines, six McKay sewing machines, two standard sewing machines, one Goodyear welt, one Goodyear stitcher, and two Hautin sewing machines. Weekly pay-roll, $3,000. Charles Gay is president, and T. E. Eustis, treasurer. This firm had its commencement in 1875, when Charles Gay & J. O. Foss employed 75 hands and produced 200 cases of shoes weekly, at No. 2 Roak Block, Auburn. This firm became Gay, Foss & Co., in 1878, by W. H. Foss joining it. In 1879 200 hands were employed. In 1883 the firm became Foss, Packard & Co., by the advent of H. M. Packard and R.

M. Mason; Mr. Gay retiring to form, with J. C. Woodman, Willard Linscott, and H. A. Packard, the firm of Gay, Woodman & Co.

Jordan, Frost & Co., manufacture mouldings and all kinds of finishing material. They employ 25 men. Their weekly pay-roll is $250. They handle about 7,000,000 feet of lumber yearly.

R. C. Pingree & Co. - In connection with their large lumber mill before mentioned, this firm manufactures all kinds of moulding and house finish, doors, sash and blinds; also stair rails, posts, and wooden mantels in their mill near lower Maine Central station, where they employ 38 men.

H. H. Dickey & Son (William Dickey) manufacture belts, rolls, etc., on the canal, near Main street, and employ 10 men. (See page ---).

Lewiston Monumental Works, 12 Bates street, John P. Murphy, manager, employs over 100 men, and does an extensive business in manufacturing monuments, mural tablets, etc. J. J. McKenna employs six men in marble and granite working at 182 Main street. J. J. O'Connell, in same business, employs six hands at 137 Main street.

Carman & Thompson, 48 Main street, employ nearly 50 men in making and fitting steam-heating apparatus, engines, etc.

FURNITURE, ETC. - *Bradford, Conant & Co.*, 199-201 Lisbon street, manufacturers and wholesale and retail dealers, continue the business established by Pinkham & Bradford in 1835. This firm later became Bradford & Conant, and in 1863 Bradford, Conant & Co. (J. C. Bradford, Granville Blake, Mrs. L. W. Conant). The factory is at East Auburn. *L. L. Blake & Co.*, 155 Lisbon street, manufacturers and dealers in furniture, etc., began business in 1856, the firm then being A. K. P. & L. L. Blake. Since 1864 the latter has conducted trade alone. *Daniel Allen & Co.*, 225 Lisbon street, manufacturers and dealers in furniture, have been in trade for 20 years, first as Carter, Allen & Maxwell, and since 1878 with present name.

CONTRACTORS AND BRICK MAKERS. - The skill of the contractors and builders of Lewiston has been often commented upon, and the elegant houses springing up under their hands in every part of the two cities bear witness to this and to their business capacity. Among those in stone work prominently stands the *Bearce & Clifford Construction Co.*, 242 Main street, who at times employ 100 men, and in their trucking department from 20 to 30 men and 60 to 70 horses. Others in this line are: George W. Lane & Co., 90 Pierce street; B. M. Dixon, 35 Sabatis street; S. D. Thomas, Sabatis street; W. A. Libby, 26 Pine street. Among those in wood-work are: Hodgkins, Foss & Co. (also sash, doors, and blinds), 7 Main street; J. E. Cloutier, 217 Blake street; G. E. Lown & Sons 268 Main street; Wood & Crockett, 266 Main street. Several are extensively engaged in brick-making. J. H. Pettengill & Son have a yard on Upper Main street near Jepson brook. The Burnt Woods District has furnished many bricks, and the Franklin Company have extensive operations there.

OTHER INDUSTRIES. - *Adams & Johnson* employ 10 men in manujfacturing doors, sash, etc.; *D. B. Stevens* has 10 men in the same business. Both are on the cross canal. *Gibbs & Dain*, in Grand Trunk yard, manufacture sash; employ 14 men; use over 250,000 feet of lumber annually and are increasing their business. *E. M. Leavitt* employs six men in making lasts; makes 15,000 pairs yearly. *J. B. Ham & Co.* (established 1872), and *O. S. Ham* have grist-mills. The first firm, near Grand Trunk station, grinds 200,000 bushels of meal yearly; employs four hands. *Edward Joyce* employs 10 hands in mking loom harnesses, on Lincoln street and cross canal. *P. P. Getchell* manufactures furs to the amount of $10,000 yearly, employing eight hands. *Bates Street Shirt Company* employ a large number in making shirts, doing a business of $75,000 yearly. *E. C. Andrews & Co.*, 72 Lisbon street, employ from 8 to 10 men in making felt hats, and do a fine business. *Charles W. Covell* employs 7 men in making harnesses. *W. H. Hackett* and *Wade & Dunton* make carriages; the later employ 18 men at 29 to 35 Park street. There are numerous others, employing from 2 to 10 hands.

CHAPTER V.

Railroads - County and State Agricultural Societies - Fire Department - Lewiston Gas Light Company - Manufacturers and Mechanics Library Association - Lewiston City Buildings - City Park - Soldiers' Monument - Lewiston Water Works - Lewiston & Auburn Horse Railroad - First National Bank - Manufacturers National Bank - Androscoggin County Savings Bank - People's Savings Bank - Board of Trade - Central Maine General Hospital - French Hospital - Y.M.C.C. - Nealy Rifles - Frye Light Guards - Associations.

RAILROADS. - In 1849 railroad facilities came to Lewiston. On March 24 the Androscoggin & Kennebec Railroad was opened to Lewiston. The legislature, February 15, 1860, authorized the Androscoggin Railroad Company to extend its railroad from Leeds to the Kennebec river, or to form a junction with the Portland & Kennebec at Topsham or Brunswick. The company decided to locate the road from Lewiston to Brunswick, and to extend the road from Leeds Junction to Crowley's. It was opened for travel in October, 1861. In July, 1871, it was consolidated with the Maine Central. The company has completed this season an elegant station house at the Upper station. Charles C. Benson has been station agent for many years. The Lower (Main street) station is handsomely arranged. Henry H. Hanson, station agent.

The Lewiston & Auburn Railroad. - The high tariff and unjust discrimination of the Maine Central Railroad against Lewiston and Auburn was sufficient, in the estimation of the citizens of these two cities, as well as the management of the several corporations, whose directors resided out of the place, to justify them in securing a charter for the construction of a competing line to connect with the Grand Trunk Railway. The legislature was petitioned in 1872 for a charter. The Maine Central vigorously opposed the measure, but February 10, 1872, the legislature granted a charter to N. W. Farwell, J. G. Cogurn, George H. Pilsbury, C. I. Barker, E. S. Davis, J. W. Danielson, and 39 other citizens of Lewiston and Auburn, for a railroad "from some point in the city of Lewiston to some point on the Atlantic & St. Lawrence Railroad, within the limits of the city of Auburn." After the charter was obtained, satisfactory terms were made by the manufacturing corporations with the Maine Central Railroad for transportation; but this arrangement did not include any reduction in passenger or freight tariff for the citizens. The public mind was somewhat stirred by this movement on the part of the Maine Central. Having secured all they desired (the reduction in freights), the corporations exhibited strong opposition to the construction of the new railroad. The people soon showed that they were determined that the railroad should be built, and, April 9, 1872, by an almost unanimous vote, they requested the mayor to subscribe for 2,245 shares of the stock at $100 per share. This action was opposed by a few in the interests of the corporations, who presented a petition at the January term of the Supreme Judicial Court in 1873, for an injunction to restrain the treasurer of Lewiston from paying the installments as they mature. Able counsel was employed by both sides, and, after a hearing of nearly three days, the court, Judge Kent presiding, dismissed the petition for want of jurisdiction. An appeal was taken, and the case went to the law court. In April another petition for an injunction was presented, which also went to the law court. These cases were kept in court several years and dismissed. After the railroad was completed it was leased to the Grand Trunk for 99 years. The stock held by the two cities would sell for more than its face value. The Lewiston station is on Lincoln street; Thomas N. Brown, general agent.

Androscoggin County Agricultural Society. - September 13, 1851, many of the farmers of this vicinity met at Lewiston to consider the formation of an agricultural society, embracing towns in this locality, and it was voted to petition the legislature for a charter. The legislature of 1852 granted a charter to Samuel Moody, Alonzo Garcelon, Ebenezer Ham, William R. Wright, John M. Frye, Archibald Wakefield, Samuel Pickard, Sewall Moody, James Lowell, John Lombard, Jesse Davis, Elisha Stetson, Elijah Barrell, and Asa Garcelon, for the purpose of organizing a society to be called the *West Lincoln Agricultural and Horticultural Society*, which was to embrace the towns in the county of Lincoln west of the Kennebec river, also Durham, Danville, Poland, Auburn, Minot, Greene, and Wales. The society organized in 1852, and elected Elijah Barrell, of Greene, president; William R. Wright, of Lewiston, recording secretary; Mark Lowell, treasurer; Ebenezer Ham, agent. The society held its first show and fair at Lewiston, October 18 and 19, 1852, when the Rev. D. T. Stevens, of Auburn, delivered an able and interesting address. The society then numbered 284 members, and the proceds of the fair amounted to about $300. In 1854 the name was changed to the *Androscoggin County Agricultural and Horticultural Society*, and embraced in its territory all the towns of this county. In 1856 land was purchased on the west of the Maine Central Railroad, now crossed by Holland and other streets, where the society held annual shows and fairs for several years; but the grounds were finally abandoned, and the stock was exhibited elsewhere. For several years the society united with the state society, but recently have held their annual exhibits at Livermore Falls.

The Maine State Agricultural Society. - In the latter part of 1881, the Maine State Agricultural Society bought the track and land which had been occupied by the Androscoggin Driving Park Association, and fitted them up for the use of the society. These grounds are less than two miles from the city and adjoin the line of the Maine Central Railroad. While the society did not vote to locate permanently at Lewiston, it did decide to secure these grounds, and has since enlarged them by purchase. They now have grounds not only large enough for a half-mile track, but sufficient for their accommodations. The society has built several buildings for the accommodation of those who exhibit at the fair, among which is a large hall for the exhibition of dairy products, agricultural implements, and machinery. Access to the fair grounds from the city is secured by means of the steam and horse cars.

Fire Department. - Androscoggin, No. 1, Fire Company was organized October 26, 1849, with Luke Bemis, foreman; Jacob B. Ham, first assistant foreman; Benjamin Dunn, second assistant foreman; and Zeba F. Bliss, clerk. The engine, the first owned by the Village Corporation, was built for the town by Hunneman & Co., of Boston, in 1849, and was in active service for more than 25 years. After a few years a second engine was purchased, and these two engines were the only ones belonging to the department until 1866, when the city ordered of J. B. Johnson, of Portland, one of his steam fire engines, which cost $4,500, but it was constantly out of repair and was finally condemned. In 1868 the city ordered of the Amoskeag Manufacturing Company a steam fire engine. Although rated a second class it has done excellent service and is now a very valuable machine. In 1878 the steamer L. C. Peck, No. 4, was built by the Amoskeag Company at a cost of $4,250. This engine is a first-class machine, is larger than the previous one and more effective. Connected with the department are three hose companies and one hook and ladder company. The force of the department consists of a chief engineer, four assistant engineers, superintendent of fire-alarm, engineer of steamers, and 55 men. The fire-alarm telegraph was put in in 1880, and has 27 signal boxes connected with it and about 21 miles of telegraph wire. The legislature of 1891 passed a bill which places the first department under the control of a commission consisting of five members. It was the design of the framer of the bill to place the department under the control of a non-partisan commission, hoping thereby to make it more effective and permanent.

Lewiston Gas Light Company. - This company was incorporated in 1853, John M. Frye, Samuel Pickard, William R. Frye, George L. Ward, Alonzo Garcelon, Edward T. Little, Daniel Holland, and Mark Lowell being the corporators. The company has a capital of $75,000, and commenced the manufacture of gas in 1854. These works are situated near the bank of the river, in the rear of the Androscoggin Mill. There are three brick buildings connected with the works. The gasometer is 60 feet in diameter, and 40 feet in depth, with a capacity of 120,000 feet. In 1886 the works were changed from coal to water-gas, the company operating under the Granger patents. They manufacture 17,000,000 cubic feet of gas annually.

Manufacturers and Mechanics Library Association. - This association was started by the munificence of the several corporations of Lewiston, over 30 years ago, and donations were made by them, books purchased, rooms fitted up, and a library opened in 1860. It was the intention to make it self-supporting. To secure this, two grades of membership were established, one, a life membership, costing $5, and an annual membership, costing $1. The founders purposed to continue annual subscriptions to purchase new books, hoping thus to secure, in a few years, a valuable library. But these expectations were only partially realized. The income only paid a part of the expenses, and the growth was slow. The library was opened in College Block, and was removed to the City Hall on its completion, and a new era in the life of the library association then began. The city gave the rent, the subscriptions paid the expenses, and the donations of the corporations were applied to the purchase of books. Care was exercised in the selection of books, so that in a few years Lewiston possessed one of the most valuable libraries, of its size, in New England. When it was burned with the City Hall, it contained 11,000 volumes, some of them rare works on local history.

City Buildings. - In 1866 the city purchased a lot on the corner of Park and Pine streets, for the purpose of erecting at some time a city building. Rooms had been obtained for the accommodation of the city government first in the Journal Block, and subsequently in Central Block, where they remained until June 12, 1870, when Central Block was partially destroyed by fire, and the rooms occupied by the city government and Central Hall, the largest in the city, was destroyed. The city found other rooms in the Savings Bank Block, just completed. In the reconstruction of Central Block the proprietors decided not to rebuild the hall, and Lewiston had no place for public meetings. This want of a suitable hall, the inconvenience of the rooms occupied by the city government, and other considerations, caused the erection of a city building to be earnestly advocated. Land was purchased on Pine and Lisbon streets, extending the lot to Lisbon street. Discussions were long and earnest in the city government, in which the people participated. Finally it was determined to submit the subject to the citizens for settlement. A meeting was called February 18, 1871, at which the people, by a vote (768 to 85), decided in favor of a city building, and William H. Stevens, John M. Frye, Archibald Wakefield, Cyrus I. Barker, David Cowan, William S. Rogers, Horace B. Bartlett, and Isaac C. Downes were appointed to superintend the construction. The plans and specifications presented by Mr. Meacham, of Boston, were accepted. The mason work was awarded to Mr. J. P. Norton, of this city, and the carpenter work was done by the day under the direction of ex-Mayor William H. Stevens. The corner-stone was laid by the mayor, Alonzo Garcelon, July 4, 1871, who delivered a very interesting historical sketch of Lewiston. The building was completed in December, 1872, and dedicated with imposing ceremonies, December 5, Dr. Alonzo Garcelon reading a very interesting sketch of the town and city.

It was built of brick with granite trimmings and decorations, and was generally of Gothic architecture, with an immense mansard roof, 32 feet high, which was broken into almost every variety of shape by gables and Gothic devices. The windows of the mansard were luthern, faced with turned columns with beautiful capitals that blended harmoniously with the surrounding decorations. The building extended 165 feet on Park street, with a frontage of 180 feet on Pine street, covering the whole distance between Park and Lisbon streets, and 40 feet on Lisbon street. From the sidewalk the walls rose 106 feet to the cornice. The mansard roof crowned the whole, with the exception of about 50 feet which fronted on Lisbon street. The corner of Pine and Park streets possessed one of the chief architectural ornaments of the building. A tower projecting eight feet from the main wall on the Pine street side contained one of the main entrances and the great staircase which extended from the ground floor to the roof. This tower was surmounted by a turret belfry. The spire rose 206 feet from the sidewalk, ending in a finial, bearing an immense vane. The interior, in point of design and beauty, was on a scale commensurate with the exterior. It contained 80 rooms. The basement contained the police quarters, city prison, boiler-rooms, etc., and the first story the municipal court room, aldermen's and councilmen's rooms, library rooms, and rooms for the city officers; in the second story, whose plane was 31 feet above the sidewalk, was the city hall, anterooms, cloak rooms, etc. The hall was of beauty and magnificence, then unequaled by any in New England. It was 80 x 165 feet, surrounded by over 400 feet of corridors, with galleries on all sides. The ceiling was 37 feet in the clear, and was beautifully frescoed. The hall would seat 2,272 people. The size of the building, which cost over $200,000, is shown by these statistics: There were two acres of flooring and 80 rooms in it. 20,000 yards of plastering, 1,400,000 feet of lumber, 3,000,000 bricks, 60 tons of slate, and 150,000 pounds of iron, were used in its construction, and it was lighted by 741 gas jets. This magnificent structure, for nearly 20 years the pride of our people, was destroyed by fire on the evening of January 7, 1890, and nothing of value was left. Competent judges pronounced the standing walls dangerous, and they were removed. In 1890 work was commenced on the new city building. This is 160 x 90 feet in size, fronts Pine and Park streets, and is a graceful and elegant building; its estimated cost is $130,000.

Park. - Early in 1861 the municipal authorities were informed that the Franklin Company purposed to donate the square in front of the DeWitt House to Lewiston, on certain conditions, for a park. At the annual meeting of 1861 A. D. Lockwood; Esq., made this proposition for the Franklin Company: "The Franklin Company proposes to donate to the town the grounds laid out or reserved for a park, containing about eight acres, on condition it shall always be kept open for a park and that the town shall expend in grading, fencing, and planting trees, etc., the sum of $5,000 upon it by July 1, 1863." The gift was accepted, and A. D. Lockwood, J. G. Coburn, D. M. Ayer, Marshall French, B. I. Leeds, J. M. Frye, and Daniel Holland were appointed to execute the wishes of the company. The grounds were immediately graded and fenced, walks laid out and ornamented with shade trees. It is now one of the most delightful places in the city, an ornament to the place, and a favorite resort of the people.

Soldiers' Monument. - Lewiston sent 1,153 soldiers to the Civil War (of whom 16 were drafted), paid $100,275 for bounties, and furnished aid to soldiers' families amounting to $31,970.26. The monument is located near the northeasterly corner of the park, and occupies a commanding position. It was designed and executed by the eminent sculptor, Frankin Simmons, a native of Webster. The monument has a square granite base, 10 feet in height, to which are secured four bronze tablets, with arch tops, and on which are the names of 112 officers and soldiers who were killed or mortally wounded in battle, died from disease contracted in camp, or wasted their lives in southern prisons by the slow process of starvation and neglect. The granite base is surmounted with a statue of a common soldier, cast in bronze and fully equipped, which is seven feet high and weighs 1,000 pounds. The statue was unveiled by the artist, assisted by Mayor Pilsbury, February 28, 1868, with appropriate military and civic ceremonies. Prayer was offered by Rev. Geo. W. Holman, and Hon. Wm. P. Frye delivered an appropriate address.

Lewiston Water Works. - Previous to 1873 attention had been frequently called to the necessity of the introduction of water into the city. In many localities great inconvenience was experienced in obtaining a sufficient supply, and the water obtained from many wells was so impure as to make it unsafe for use. The discussion of this subject frequently became animated, and the most conservative were convinced that the demand for a new source of supply was imperative. February 27, 1873, the governor approved "An act to supply the cities of Lewiston and Auburn with pure water." A committee was appointed in December, 1873, to consider the practicality, the best plan, and cost of procuring water, and to see if Auburn would join, and if it did not, it was authorized to secure an amendment to the act for Lewiston to proceed alone. They did this, and in March, 1875, reported in favor of the Holly system. In April, 1875, the city council elected a board of water commissioners of six members, which appointed a committee to investigate the merits of different systems in New England and New York cities. This committee reported unanimously in favor of the reservoir system, which was adopted. The plan of taking water from the saw-mill site was favored by the water commissioners, and, after much discussion, the city council submitted to the votes of the city (April 22, 1876,) a series of questions which included the purchase of the saw-mill site and the issue of city bonds for construction of water works. The vote was 995 yeas and 139 nays. This action was sufficiently decisive to warrant the city council to proceed with the work; but it was not until November 5, 1877, that the Franklin Company conveyed to the city the saw-mill site, with the special rights necessary to the proper construction of the works. The city paid $200,000 in water works bonds, running 40 years. The discussion was animated and prolonged on the method of supply, but January 15, 1878, the city council voted that the reservoir system was best adapted to meet the requirements and interests of the city. In the spring of 1878 work was commenced and pushed with commendable energy. The reservoir was located on Mitchell Hill, about a mile and three-fourths from the pumping station. It has a capacity of over 10,000,000 gallons, cost $39,000, and was completed in October, 1878. The water works were fully completed in December, and on Christmas eve the mayor, Hon. Jesse S. Lyford, raised the gates,and within one hour the water was entering the reservoir, and the most important public work of Lewiston was completed. The entire cost of the water works was $255,509.11. There are now 28 miles of pipe (mains) and 100 hydrants for fire service. I. C. Downes is superintendent of the water works.

Lewiston & Auburn Horse Railroad. - July 22, 1881, the city of Lewiston granted to George F. Mellen and Edward D. Chaffee, of Fall River, Mass., William P. Craig and Henry Masters, of New York, the right to construct a horse railroad, in the usual form. This grant was made without compensation, but the managers of the railroad agreed to lay regular street rails; to furnish plans of the manner of laying the rails to the city council and accept their direction as to their location in the several streets; to complete and operate the road in one year; and to operate the railroad to the reasonable convenience of the people. If these conditions were not fulfilled, the company was to forfeit its license. No other conditions were imposed. Articles of association of the Lewiston & Auburn Horse Railroad were signed July 28, by George F. Mellen and his associates, to organize a railroad corporation under the statutes of the state, with a capital of $100,000. August 15, 1881, the articles were approved by the railroad commissioners, and the company was declared a corporation. Work was at once begun, and Main and Lisbon streets were soon ready for the cars. The track was also extended to the fair grounds; but it soon became evident that the company would not occupy all the streets mentioned in the license, and in May, 1882, the company petitioned the city government to be released from further extension of their road. This petition was referred to a joint committee, who reported in favor of granting the petition on certain conditions. These terms, which the company regarded as unfavorable to its interests, were not accepted. After considerable discussion, the city council passed this order:

Ordered, That the Lewiston & Auburn Horse Railroad Company be and they are hereby released from further extending their tracks beyond the terminal points to which they are already built, except Pine street, upon the condition that at such time as the public convenience may demand its further extension, it shall be done upon such terms and conditions as the city council and the said railroad company may agree upon.

The action was satisfactory to the company, and is the condition on which its subsequent plans have been perfected. It was thought by many that the action of the city council in granting the license was not legal, and the city government was notified by the company that it should apply to the legislature to confirm not only the acts of the company, but to ratify the proceedings of the city. Accordingly acts were passed by the legislature of 1883 to make valid the doings of the cities of Lewiston and Auburn in granting the license, and to confirm and make valid the organization of the company. In the spring of 1882 the track up Pine street was laid, and in the fall the one to Perryville, Auburn. In July, 1883, the road was opened to Lake Grove. In December, 1889, the New Auburn belt line was completed. In June, 1891, the College and Pine streets circuit and the Denison street circuit were opened to the public. The company employs 30 men, has 14 miles of road in operation, and the service requires 20 cars and 90 horses. Colonel F. W. Dana has been president since 1885.

BANKS. – *The First National Bank* is the successor of the Lewiston Falls Bank, which was incorporated in February, 1852, the corporators being Daniel Holland, James Lowell, Samuel Haley, George L. Ward, and Albert H. Kelsey. The capital was fixed at $50,000, the shares being $100 each. The first meeting of the corporators was held June 29, 1852, and the organization was completed by the choice of these directors: James Lowell, Daniel Holland, Paul C. Tebbetts, Jacob H.

Roak, Howe Weeks, Albert H. Kelsey, and George L. Ward; and, at a meeting of the directors, James Lowell was chosen president, and Silas Titcomb, cashier. The bank continued to do business under the charter until February, 1864, when it was changed to a national bank. The stockholders, February 15, 1864, completed the organization by the election of these directors: Amos D. Lockwood, Samuel W. Kilvert, Josiah G. Coburn, Samuel R. Bearce, Timothy Walker, David M. Ayer, Archibald Wakefield, Nathan W. Farwell, Oren B. Cheney; the directors chose A. D. Lockwood, president, and Albert H. Small, cashier. The capital was limited to $50,000. It has since been increased to $400,000. The present officers are: President, John Y. Scruton; vice-president, F. H. Packard; cashier, A. L. Templeton; teller, George W. Goss; directors, John Y. Scruton, John N. Wood, David Farrar, R. C. Pingree, S. D. Wakefield, Charles H. Osgood, F. H. Packard, Wallace H. White, and Charles Walker.

Manufacturers National Bank. - This bank was organized under the act of Congress, January 26, 1875, with a capital of $200,000. The officers were: J. M. Robbins, president; George H. Pilsbury, vice-president; William Libby, cashier. The directors were J. M. Robbins, George H. Pilsbury, C. I. Barker, James Wood, E. S. Davis, James Dempsey, Jesse Davis. The present officers are: J. M. Robbins, president; C. I. Barker, vice-president; Addison Small, cashier; directors, J. M. Robbins, C. I. Barker, James Munroe, Oliver Newman, L. L. Blake, T. E. Eustis, William H. Newell.

The Androscoggin County Savings Bank was incorporated in March, 1870. The corporators were Samuel R. Bearce, C. I. Barker, F. O. Sands, E. F. Packard, R. C. Pingree, J. A. Pierce, Thomas Fillebrown, John G. Cook, S. H. Murray, George H. Pilsbury, R. C. Pennell, and E. H. Cummings. The organization was effected April 2, 1870, and the following persons were elected trustees: Samuel R. Bearce, E. F. Packard, George H. Pilsbury, C. I. Barker, and Ai Brooks, Jr. E. F. Packard was chosen president and A. L. Templeton, treasurer. The amount of deposits are $1,150,000. The present officers are: Cyrus Greely, president; J. Frank Boothby, treasurer; trustees, Cyrus Greely, John Y. Scruton, Charles Greenwood, H. L. Pratt, E. S. Paul, Charles Walker, Joseph H. Stetson, Seth M. Carter, and Frank W. Parker.

The People's Savings Bank. - February 12, 1875, the governor approved a bill to incorporate the People's Savings Bank of the city. Corporators: C. I. Barker, William H. Stevens, J. M. Robbins, N. W. Dutton, George H. Pilsbury, John G. Cook, Luther P. Martin, George A. Chandler, Mark Lowell, James Wood, Edmund Russell, J. L. H. Cobb, and A. M. Jones. The organization was immediately completed and the bank commenced business in the rooms of the Manufacturers National Bank. The resources November, 1890, were $1,033,418.60. The present officers are: C. I. Barker, president; C. F. Wellman, treasurer; C. I. Barker, H. W. Maxwell, A. D. Barker, A. B. Nealey, S. A. Cummings, John Garner, W. M. Chamberlin, A. R. Savage, and D. B. Sawyer, trustees.

The private banking house of Samuel E. May & Co., 17 Lisbon street, was established in 1863. Since January, 1887, it has been conducted by F. B. Wheelock.

Board of Trade. - The Lewiston Board of Trade was organized March 29, 1887. The officers were: C. I. Barker, president; B. Peck, secretary; and L. Linn Small, treasurer. As originally constituted its membership embraced business men in both cities. It is composed of business men of all classes, and has for its special object the promotion of the business interests of Lewiston. All questions affecting the interests of the city are discussed at its rooms, the general welfare of the place is carefully protected, and important business enterprises owe their origin to this very useful organization. Its present officers are: C. I. Barker, president; Noel B. Potter, secretary; and T. F. Callahan, treasurer.

Asylum and Hospital of Notre Dame de Lourdes. - Three sisters of charity of the congregation of Notre Dame de Lourdes came to Lewiston, in November, 1878, and founded a school, the asylum of Notre Dame de Lourdes, at 29 Walnut street, corner of Pierce. This sisterhood purchased the former residence and lands of Isaac Golder, and removed the asylum to its present location in November, 1888. It is now an orphan asylum, and connected with it a hospital was established. Sister Bernard is the superior. This hospital is located about one mile from the head of Lisbon street, on Sabatis street, and is owned and managed by the Sisters. It is a fine wooden building, having two wards, one for males and one for females, each containing eight beds. There are also 10 private rooms. There is also a ward for those who are not sick, but who wish to occupy a bed, for which a fee is charged. The building contains a drug store and an operating room. The asylum has now about 30 inmates. There are extensive grounds connected with the hospital, and all the surroundings are neat and attractive. It was opened in 1888.

Central Maine General Hospital. - This institution, which was opened to the public July 4, 1891, is finely located on the corner of Main and Hammond streets. This is largely the work of public subscription, and all classes contributed freely to bring it to being. The state offered to give $5,000 for every $10,000 raised by the people for a specified length of time, and in the very short time $12,000 were subscribed in the two cities. During the early part of the year the property was purchased at a cost of $21,000, and one of the buildings has been converted into a hospital. There are two wards, one for males, containing seven beds, and one for females, containing six beds. There is also a ward for children, containing four beds. Besides these there is a dormitory for nurses, superintendent of nurses, janitor, and a ward for contagious diseases, a large operating room, as well as other rooms for the general purposes of a hospital. It is under the care of the physicians of Lewiston and Auburn, and is open to all persons who desire to avail themselves of its advantages. The hospital staff is: Alonzo Garcelon, M.D., consulting surgeon; George P. Emmons, M.D., superintendent and resident physician; O. A. Horr, M.D., A. M. Peables, M.D., M. C. Wedgwood, M.D., J. W. Beede, M.D., attending physicians; E. H. Hill, M.D., W. K. Oakes, M.D., J. A. Donovan, M.D., B. F. Sturgis, M.D., attending surgeons; D. N. Skinner, M.D., C. E. Norton, M.D., ophthalmic surgeons; S. G. Bonney, M.D., pathologist; W. B. Small, M.D., E. W. Russell, M.D., adjunct physicians; F. L. Dixon, M.D., C. E. Williams, M.D., adjunct surgeons. The officers are J. L. H. Cobb, president; J. R. Learned, treasurer; D. J. Callahan, secretary; Ara Cushman, Prof. L. G. Jordan, John F. Cobb, R. C. Reynolds, George W. Wagg, D. J. Callahan, B. F. Wood, John Garner, Charles W. Hill, directors.

The Lewiston Y.M.C.A. was organized in 1867, and has continued active work since that time. Soon after its organization the association employed a city missionary, Rev. M. H. Tarbox, who did very efficient work for several years. He was succeeded by Rev. Samuel Boothby, of this city, who labored for a year or more. Rev. N. C. Clifford was also employed by the association as a city missionary. The employment of a general secretary since 1884 resulted in very excellent and systematic work. The Y.M.C.A. numbers among its nearly 200 members some of the best men of the city. A Woman's Auxiliary, with a large membership, and a Boys' Union are rendering much assistance, and are productive of great good. Thomas M. Singer, the general secretary, is a graduate of Bates College.

Nealey Rifles, Co. D, M.V.M. - About six years ago, the militia company formerly known as Lewiston Light Infantry, and later as Lewiston Zouaves, was disbanded. Col. A. B. Nealey, then a member of Governor Robie's staff, made strenuous efforts for a reorganization and was successful, and in compliment to his earnest labors the company named it Nealey Rifles. It is considered one of the finest companies of the state. Captain Walter A. Goss has been in command from organization. James A. Scott is first lieutenant, and Abram W. Garcelon, second lieutenant.

Frye Light Guards, Co. B, M.V.M. - This company was mustered into the state service February 28, 1888, and was named in honor of Senator Frye. The officers were: F. L. Hoyt, captain; C. F. Nealey, first lieutenant; E. M. Smith, second lieutenant. At the regimental competitive drill, July 4, 1889, at Bangor, the company won the prize. The only change in officers is that C. E. Hanscom is now second lieutenant. The company number 50 men.

Clan Campbell is the only society of its order in Maine, and was named from John Campbell, overseer of the Bates dye-house, its first "chief." It was founded here in 1888, is a fraternal and insurance society, admits only Scotchmen, or sons and grandsons of Scotchmen, and has 41 members.

ASSOCIATIONS. - *F. & A. M.* - Ashlar, Monday, on or before full moon; Rabboni, first Wednesday after full moon; King Hiram R. A. Chapter, second Friday; Dunlap Council, R. & S. M., second Tuesday; Lewiston Commandery, K. T., first Thursday; Lewiston Lodge of Perfection, first Friday; Androscoggin Masonic Relief Association, M. E. D. Bailey, secretary. *I.O.O.F.* - Manufacturers and Mechanics, No. 62, Wednesday; Golden Rule, No. 73, Thursday; Fidelity, No. 4, D. of R., second and fourth Tuesdays; Worombus Encampment, first and third Tuesdays; Grand Canton Worombus, P. M., No. 1, fourth Friday. *K. of H.* - Maine, No. 278, second Monday; Paul Hildreth, No. 1695, first and third Mondays. *K. of P.* - Industry, No. 2, Tuesday; Mt. David, No. 23, Thursday; Uniform Rank, Damon Divison, No. 1, first Monday; Pythian Sisterhood, Good Will, No. 3, second and fourth Mondays. *A. O. of Shepherds* - Excelsior, No. 1, second and fourth Tuesdays; Good Samaritan, No. 2, first and third Tuesdays.

Caledonian Club - first and third Thursdays. *I.O.G.T.* - United, No. 13, Wednesday; Mystic, No. 312, Monday; Dirigo, Tuesday. *R. T. of T.* - Banner, No. 3, Monday.. *A.O.U.W.* - Lewburn, No. 50, second and fourth Mondays. *G.A.R.* - Custer, No. 7, Monday; Custer Relief Corps, alternate Friday; Knox Relief Corps, No. 37, Wednesday. *S. of V.* - Custer Camp, Thursday. *I.O.R.M.* - Pokumkeswawaumokesis, No. 9, first and third Fridays. *Royal Conclave of Knights and Ladies* - No. 29, second and fourth Thursdays. *Y.M.C.A.* - Thomas M. Singer, general secretary. *Royal Arcanum* - first and third Mondays. *U.O.G.C.* - Androscoggin, No. 79, first and third Fridays; Eureka, No. 195, second and fourth Fridays. *W.C.T.U.* - Monday. *Ladies' Christian Union* - Monday. *Catholic Union* - Sunday. *U.O.P.F.* - Oriental, No. 32, second and fourth Mondays; Pine Tree, No. 33, first and third Fridays. *Lewiston Benevolent Society* - second Thursday. *P. of H.* - Lewiston, No. 2, Thursday; Androscoggin, No. 8, first and third Thursday. *A. O. of H.* - No. 1, Thursday; No. 2, Tuesday. *N. E. O. of P.* - Crescent, No. 70. *Bands* - Lewiston Brigade, F. G. Payne, Director; Union, Albert H. Beliveau, Manager; Wilson's Orchestra, George T. Wilson, leader; Given's Orchestra, F. A. Given, agent; Payne's Orchestra, F. G. Payne, manager. *French Societies* - Club Cremazie, Union, St. Joseph, Institut Jacques Cartier, Club National, Club St. Dominique. *Lewiston and Auburn Grocers' Association* - first Wednesday. South Lewiston: *I.O.G.T.* - Advance, Saturday. *Androscoggin Gun Club.* - E. F. Field, president; George W. Gifford, secretary.

CHAPTER VI.

Physicians - Merchants - Business Interests - Personal Sketches - Resume.

PHYSICIANS. - *Dr. Joel Wright* was undoubtedly the first person who practiced medicine in Lewiston. He came here, probably about 1776-7, and settled on what is now Eastern Avenue, on the lot above Davis Nevens's. Dr. Wright was a botanical physician. He died July 26, 1821.

Dr. Barrett was here for a short time about 1799 or 1800.

Dr. Alexander Dwelley was a native of Boylston, Mass. He studied medicine in Providence, RI, and came to Lewiston in 1803, and settled on a farm in the eastern part of Lewiston, where he lived until his death.

Dr. Calvin Gorham came here from Turner in 1816. He settled on Sabatis street, where, about 1825, he built a house, which is now standing. He was an allopathic physician, but in later life, about 1845, he became attached to the homoeopathic system. He died February 28, 1850.

Dr. Alonzo Garcelon was the next physician, and commenced the practice of medicine here in 1839. (See biography.)

Dr. Charles Millet was born in Norway, April 5, 1803. He was graduated from the medical school, Bowdoin College, in 1829, practiced medicine in Minot, and came to Lewiston about 1847. Dr. Millett died August 13, 1854.

Dr. Alcander Burbank was born in Shelburne, NH, June 26, 1822. He studied medicine with Dr. Barrows, of Fryeburg, and graduated at Dartmouth Medical College, April, 1847. He settled immediately in Lewiston, where he died, January 8, 1884.

Dr. H. C. Bradford is a native of Turner. He studied medicine with his father, Dr. Richmond Bradford, and graduated at the Homoeopathic Medical College of Philadelphia, in 1856. He immediately commenced the practice of his profession in Lewiston, and is the second oldest physician in the city.

Dr. M. C. Wedgwood was born in Bowdoin. He graduated from Bowdoin Medical School in 1859. Dr. Wedgwood was an assistant surgeon in the army and came to Lewiston in 1863, where he has practiced medicine with success. He has held the position of president of the Maine Medical and Androscoggin Medical associations, and also served in both branches of the Lewiston city government, and is now a member of the executive council, and secretary of the Board of U. S. Examining Surgeons.

Dr. John A. Donovan was born in Houlton, August 4, 1841, received his medical education in New York, London (England), and Paris (France), received his degree of M.D. from New York University Medical College, in March, 1866, located for practice at Lewiston, May 1, 1866, and has acquired an extensive practice. He is a member of the Maine Medical Association, was one of the founders of and has been president of the Androscoggin County Medical Association, and is treasurer of the Board of U. S. Examining Surgeons.

Dr. Edward H. Hill is a native of Harrison. He studied medicine with E. M. Wight, of Gorham, NH, and G. L. Kilgore, of Windham, and graduated from Harvard Medical College in March, 1867. He first settled in Durham, but in 1869 came to Lewiston and formed a copartnership with Dr. A. Garcelon, which continued about four years, and has since been in practice in Lewiston. He is an attending surgeon of the Central Maine General Hospital, of which he was one of the active promoters.

Dr. O. A. Horr was born in Waterford. He studied medicine with S. L. Weston, of Otisfield, and Dr. Charles Hutchinson, and graduated from Bowdoin Medical School in 1861. Practiced medicine in Minot, was assistant surgeon in the army, and came to Lewiston in 1870, where he has since been in practice.

Dr. J. M. Small is a native of New Gloucester. He studied medicine with Dr. Moses E. Swett, of Limington, and graduated at Bowdoin Medical School in 1847. Dr. Small settled in Exeter, and moved to this city in 1864.

Dr. R. R. Ricker was born in Acton. He studied medicine with Dr. Richard Russell, of Great Falls, NH, and graduated from Bowdoin Medical School in 1847. Dr. Ricker practiced medicine in Kittery, Ossipee, NH, and Minot, was an assistant surgeon in the army, and settled in Lewiston in 1865.

Dr. Edmund Russell was born in Temple, November 23, 1824. He pursued his medical studies with Dr. William Kilbourne, and graduated from Bowdoin Medical School in 1874, and the same year settled in Strong. He removed to Farmington in 1855, and came to Lewiston in 1869, forming a copartnership with the late Dr. S. Oakes, which was continued for a short time. Dr. Russell died December 20, 1880.

Dr. F. L. Dixon is a native of Jay. He studied medicine with Dr. Wright, of Readfield, and graduated from Dartmouth Medical College in 1880, and settled in Wayne. Dr. Dixon removed to Lewiston in 1884.

Dr. E. W. Russell was born in Temple, and prosecuted his professional studies with Dr. Edmund Russell, and graduated from the Medical University at Burlington, VT, in 1879. Dr. Russell practiced medicine six years in Minot, and removed to this city in 1885.

Dr. Elizabeth S. Horr studied medicine with Dr. O. A. Horr and graduated at the Woman's Medical College of New York, in 1872, and has since practiced her profession in this city.

Dr. L. J. Martel was born at St. Hyacinthe, P.Q., and was graduated from the college of St. Hyacinthe in 1869, from Victoria College in 1873, and soon after came to Lewiston, where he has been devoted to his profession and to the welfare of the French people. In 1874 he established the Institut Jacques Cartier, which has now a membership of over 200. In 1880 he was a delegate to the International Congress in Quebec. In 1881 he represented the French people of Lewiston in the Waterville conference, the first state convention held in Maine. In 1882 he was organizing president of the Maine and New Hampshire French Congress, held in Lewiston. He represented Lewiston in the legislature of 1884, and was city physician from 1883 to 1886. He has been vice-president and president of General French Convention of the United States, president of the French National Alliance, and was delegate to the Catholic Congress at Baltimore.

Dr. L. E. N. Matte is the city physician.

Dr. A. M. Garcelon is a native of Lewiston. He pursued his professional studies with his father, Dr. A. Garcelon, attended lectures at Montreal, and graduated at the College of Physicians and Surgeons in New York, 1876. Dr. Garcelon commenced practice in Lewiston in 1878. He was mayor in 1883.

Dr. W. S. Howe was born in St. John, NB, February 9, 1834, was educated at Acadia College, entered the Baptist ministry, and was in active work when he enlisted in the First Maine, and was a commissioned officer. He was nine months in Libby prison, and severly wounded at the battle of Five Forks. "He was a brave man, a good fighter, a magnificent soldier, and the boys all liked him." After the war he studied medicine, was graduated from Bowdoin Medical School in 1869; in 1870 from the College of Physicians and Surgeons in New York; in 1883 from the Hahnemann School of Homoeopathy in Philadelphia, and practiced in Pittsfield from 1870 to 1885, when he located in Lewiston, and has since been in practice. Dr. Howe was a chapter Mason and a Republican. He died August 24, 1891.

Dr. Charles E. Norton is a native of Gardiner. Graduated from Bowdoin Medical School in 1876. Dr. Norton practiced medicine for a time at Augusta, and then came to Lewiston.

Dr. Aurelia Springer is a native of Dresden. She studied with her father, Dr. W. W. Springer, graduated at the Woman's Medical College, Boston. Dr. Springer studied four years at the University at Zurich, Switzerland, and came to Lewiston in 1877.

Dr. A. K. P. Harvey studied with Drs. A. J. Marston and H. C. Bradford, and graduated at the Homoeopathic Medical College of Chicago in 1880.

Dr. W. B. Small, 147 Lisbon street, son of Addison Small, is the recording secretary of the Androscoggin County Medical Association. (For other physicians, see page ---.)

DRUGGISTS. - The drug store of *Charles A. Abbott*, corner of Lisbon and Main streets, is an outgrowth of the business established by Dr. Aaron Young in 1850, on the site of the gun shop near Main street bridge. This was removed to a building that stood where Hotel Atwood stands, and was there succeeded by George Garcelon, who removed it to the present location and sold it to William F. Garcelon. After his death, in 1884, Mr. Abbott became proprietor. John Cook, about 1851, commenced as a druggist on lower Main street, and about 1860 removed it to 145 Liston street. In or about 1880 *E. H. Gerrish* became proprietor. *Wakefield Brothers* (S. D. and E.), 114 Lisbon street, engaged in trade about 20 years since. Both of the proprietors are natives of Lewiston, and the senior member has held official positions of trust and is now city treasurer. *D. W. Wiggin*, 213 Lisbon street, a native of Leeds, established this extensive store in March, 1872. In January, 1863, he opened a drug store in Phoenix Block, Auburn, where he traded until 1871, when he purchased the bookstore then occupying the stand where his brother, W. H. Wiggin, is in trade, and carried it on until he came to Lewiston. *Warren E. Riker* and *B. F. Bradford* opened the drug store, corner of Lisbon and Pine streets, about 1879, and about six years ago Mr. Riker became sole proprietor. *R. W. Clark* has been in the drug business at the corner of Main and Bates streets for nearly 20 years.

There is one patent medicine manufactory in the city. *M. J. Rogers & Co.* manufacture Rogers' Inhalant and Cough Lozenges at 21 Lisbon street. These have been made for 18 years. Edgar J. Fogg, proprietor.

DENTISTS. - *N. Woodbury*, Pilsbury Block. *Ezra H. White* (White & Leavitt), Lyceum Hall Block, attends to the dental business in all its branches, and does excellent work. *Emery Bailey*, 20 Lisbon street, who has been established in Lewiston nearly 15 years, has availed himself of all the modern appliances pertaining to his profession, and has been successful.

MERCHANTS. - There is much obscurity about the early traders. It is not known who kept the first goods for the accommodation of the early settles. It is supposed that Amos Davis had a small amount of goods on sale at his house on Sabatis street. The wants of the pioneers were small and it required only a meagre quantity of merchandise to supply them.

William Garcelon, grandfather of Dr. Alonzo Garcelon, in 1797 opened a store in the southerly part of the town, on a scale then unknown in Lewiston, which he continued for several years. Mr. Garcelon did an extensive business, not only in his store, but also in lumbering, until about 1807. He was also engaged in ship-building in Freeport, but suffered from the effects of the embargo in 1807, and his business was ruined. Mr. Garcelon was one of the most active business men of his day.

David and Jackson Davis in 1799 built a house at the corner on the lot now owned and occupied by J. Y. Scruton, Esq., in the basement of which they commenced a small business. It is probable that they remained there only a few years. At that time only a few people had settled near the corner. Chase Wedgwood lived nearly opposite Mr. Davis. Noah Litchfield lived on the Nash farm, where J. M. Robbins now lives; Thomas Trafton, where A. D. Barker resides; John Marshall, where Mrs. A. Wakefield now lives; Stephen Chase, on the corner of Main and Mill streets, now occupied by Hotel Atwood; and Amos Davis, on what is now the corner of Sabatis and Wood streets. About 1800, a man by the name of Thomas Treadwell had a small stock of goods in one of the rooms of the old Harris house, situated on Main street, now occupied by the Lower Maine Central depot. He remained there only a short time, and was followed by *Michael Little* and *William Haskell*. *Richard D. Harris* had a small stock of goods, probably in his house near the corner of Main and Hammond streets. *Ebenezer Herrick* and *Dan Read* were in trade for a short time.

James Lowell came into the place in 1812 or 1813, and commenced trade at what for many years was known as Lowell's Corner. His store was on Main street, near the junction of Hammond. Mr. Lowell had the genius of a country trader, and in middle life did an extensive business. About 1822 he built a large two-story building, which he occupied for a store while he remained in business. Three years afterwards he built the two-story house on Main street, now owned by the Central Maine General Hospital. Mr. Lowell had an extensive tannery on the southerly side of Main street, and did an extensive business in the manufacture of boots and harnesses. His bark mill was burned in 1847 and was never rebuilt. He continued in business until near the close of his life. In 1855 he sold his store and residence at the "Corner," and removed to his farm on Webster street, where he died July 27, 1858.

Nathan Reynolds opened a store in the building occupied by David and Jackson Davis at Lowell's Corner in 1815 or 1816. A rivalry soon sprang up between him and Mr. Lowell, both of whom were keen discriminating business men. Soon after Mr. Lowell built his store, Mr. Reynolds built a two-story brick store, on the corner of Main and Sabatis streets, and within two years after Mr. Lowell built his house, Mr. Reynolds built the two-story brick house - which has since Mr. Reynold's death been remodeled and enlarged - now owned and occupied by J. Y. Scruton, Esq. Mr. Reynolds did an extensive business for those days, but about 1840 sold his goods, and, for a short time, retired from business. Subsequently he and his son, N. B. Reynolds, opened a store on lower Main street, where they continued in business until about 1852.

Gorham & Philips commenced to trade at Lowell's Corner, just below Lowell's store on Main street, about 1833, and continued in business for several years, and about the same time *Pickard & Little* opened a store on lower Main street. *Gideon D. Dickinson* commenced business on lower Main street about 1837. *John B. Jones* was also in business for a few years on lower Main street from 1839. *Herrick & Little* commenced trade in the Pickard store about 1847. Earlier than this *John W. Perkins* opened the first dry goods store of Lewiston, near the bridge.

Daniel Wood opened a store on lower Main street in 1848. Subsequently he took Howe Weeks as partner, and they built a store near the bridge which they occupied for several years, when the firm was dissolved, and Mr. Wood built the brick store on Lisbon street, which he now occupies with the most extensive stock of crockery and glass ware in the city. This is one of the oldest business houses in the city.

J. P. Longley, a native of Greene, commenced business here in 1847. Subsequently the firm name was Longley & Covell, and afterward changed to Longley & Jordan. They occupied a store near Lowell's Corner. In 1861 Mr. Longley became the sole owner (179 Main street) and has continued the business since. His son, J. B., is with him. This is the oldest business house in the city, and manufactures and sells furs, fine harnesses, trunks, traveling bags, etc., and makes a specialty of trotting and racing boots.

Messrs. E. S. Paul & Co. is the oldest dry goods house in the city. Business was commenced in 1867 as Goddard & Paul, which was continued for about a decade, when Mr. Paul assumed the entire control. It is now one of the largest dry goods establishments in the city. Mr. Paul, some years since, built the large brick block which he has since occupied. The firm manufactures cloaks and dresses, and employs about 30 persons.

Messrs. Oswald & Armstrong, dry and fancy goods dealers, were the successors of Arthur Sands, whose store and stock of goods they purchased in 1883. Besides their extensive stock of dry and fancy goods, they have departments of dress and cloak making which they carry on extensively. Oswald & Armstrong occupy five stores on Lisbon street, employ some 44 persons in their several departments, and their annual business amounts to about $140,000. Since March, 1890, Mr. Armstrong has been the sole owner of the establishement, but retains the firm name. Mr. Armstrong is a war veteran, a member of the Ancient and Honorable Artillery, Boston, has served on Governor Mitchell's staff, and is a member of the board of fire commissioners.

Mr. B. Peck, of the firm of the B. Peck Company, commenced business in Lewiston as a member of the firm of E. A. Plummer & Co. Subsequently Mr. Peck became sole manager of the business, remaining in Frye Block until 1885, when B. Peck & Co. transferred their stock to Sands Block, where they have since remained. The business embraces dry and fancy goods, including milinery, cloaks, and garments. The store has a frontage of 50 feet - equal to two stores - with a depth of 95 feet, and occupies two floors and one-half of the basement, about 12,000 square feet. The business is classified into 15 departments, and more than 60 persons are employed. The annual business amounts to $250,000. In April, 1890, the firm was reorganized and is now a stock company, with a capital of $100,000, one-half of which is paid in. The officers are: B. Peck, president; J. H. Crowley, manager; H. A. Free, treasurer; B. Peck, Lewis Lombard, J. H. Crowley, H. A. Free, William Nicoll, William Youland, L. T. Chabot, directors.

There are several other dry goods houses: *Lowell & Lowell, C. D. Farrar & Co., Bates Remnant Store, Greenberg Brothers, N. Greenberg*, etc.

CLOTHING. - *John Yeaton Scruton*, born in Farmington, NH, December 23, 1821, started in trade as member of the firm of Burleigh & Scruton in 1853. The firm was later Cobb & Scruton; then Mr. Scruton was alone. In 1884 his son, Edwin F., became a partner of the firm of *J. Y. Scruton & Son*, which conducts trade at 23 Lisbon street, and does a business of $40,000 a year. *Richards & Merrill* (D. O. Richards and J. L. Merrill) began trade on lower Main street in 1853, and later were in Jones's Block; from there they moved to Journal Block, and built their present store in Lyceum Hall Block in 1872. This house has not been changed in name or members since its foundation. The largest stock in ready-made clothing is carried by *Babbitt Brothers*, who in 1891 succeeded A. T. Neal, who conducted business as Bicknell & Neal. They occupy two stores on Lisbon street, corner of Ash. An old established house is that now in business as *S. A. Isaacson & Co.*, at the Blue Store, 152 Lisbon street, which was opened in 1881 and passed into the control of S. A. & I. B. Isaacson in 1886. Its connection as a branch of a large Boston house gives it many advantages. *W. H. C. Allen* (Allen & Co.), 85 Lisbon street, is another of the fair-dealing representative houses in this line, carrying a fine stock.

GROCERS, PROVISION DEALERS, ETC. - The oldest and leading grocery house is that of *Nealey & Miller*, 239 Main street. This business was started in 1850, by Hircy Day, in a cellar on Middle street. In August, 1860, Mr. Day, his son, Joseph H., and A. B. Nealey formed the firm of H. Day & Co., which continued until 1865, when H. Day retired, and the firm became Day, Nealey & Co. The store was removed in 1863 to Blanchard Block on Main street, and in 1867 to Bonnallie Block, when a hardware store was started in their old rooms in Blanchard Block by Joseph H. Day, A. B. Nealey, and Charles H. Miller, as J. H. Day & Co. Mr. Miller was later admitted a partner in the grocery business, and is treasurer of the Lewiston and Auburn Grocers' Association. The present establishment was purchased by them and fitted up into one of the most convenient stores in Maine, and about 1880 Day, Nealey & Co. dissolved partnership, Mr. Day taking the hardware store, and Nealey & Miller continuing as grocers. The business has had a healthy growth from the first, employs 13 males and two females, and its annual business reaches into the hundreds of thousands of dollars. Colonel Nealey is now the oldest grocer of Lewiston, and a director of the Grocers' Association.

Benjamin Litchfield established himself as a grocer in 1865 with George A. Chandler, on the corner of Main and Park streets, and in 1868 formed with Albert Tracy the firm of B. Litchfield & Co., on the opposite corner. In three years Mr. Tracy retired, and Mr. Litchfield, a year later, took as parner Marshall Emery, who 16 years later sold to S. C. Leslie, Jr., who retired in April, 1891. Mr. Litchfield is now alone, but retains the firm name. In 1871 he moved from his former location to the store adjoining his present store in the Dominican School (formerly Bonnallie) Block, and in 1886 occupied his present stand. Mr. Litchfield is a native of Lewiston, and was a soldier in the Thirteenth Massachusetts in the Civil War for 20 months, receiving his discharge November 29, 1862, in consequence of severe bullet wounds.

John Garner, 213 Park street, established his grocery business over a quarter of a century ago. He was born in England, and during his residence in Lewiston has been prominent in many ways. He has built up a large wholesale and retail trade, and among numerous official positions held by him is president of Lewiston and Auburn Grocers' Association. He conducts a foreign passenger and exchange agency.

J. C. White commenced business as a grocer, on Main street, about thirty years ago, and was in trade until 1890, when he retired from the firm of White & Ames, now Ames & Merrill, 187 Main street. *Maxwell & Nevens*, 10 Park street, are wholesale dealers in teas, spices, etc. *D. E. Parlin* conducts the Boston Tea Store, at 3 Journal Block, established in 1875, and is a wholesale and retail dealer. *Selden A. Cummings*, 223 Main street, manufactures confectionery,, which he sells at wholesale and retail. *Frank L. Hoyt & Co.* are wholesale and retail dealers in groceries, meats, etc., at 230 Lisbon street. *Merrifield & Brewer* (William E. Merrifield, Horace W. Brewer) conduct grocery business at 371 Lisbon street. *George A. Wiseman*, grocer and baker, does business at 146 Lincoln street. *Abram Atwood*, 159 Lisbon street, is a wholesale and retail dealer in groceries, meats, etc., established for nearly 25 years. He does an extensive business, and Hotel Atwood carries his name. *Edward W. Gross* and *Julius K. Briggs* have conducted a large business in wholesaling beef in Grand Trunk yard as Gross & Briggs.

SHOE DEALERS. - *Fessenden I. Day*, 5 Journal Block; *C. O. Morrell*, corner of Lisbon and Main streets; *A. S. Melcher*, 4 Frye Block.

WATCHES, JEWELRY, ETC. - *H. A. Osgood & Son* (wholesale) and *H. A. Osgood & Co.* (retail), 127 Lisbon street; *George A. Drew*, 2 Frye Block; *A. W. Anthoine*, 79 Lisbon street, established 1880, has a large stock of finely selected goods; *J. W. Perry & Son*, 90 Lisbon street; *E. E. Pomeroy*, 84 Lisbon street; *A. S. Wright*, 229 Lisbon street.

HARDWARE, CUTLERY, STOVES, ETC. - *Thomas R. Catland* makes a specialty of electrical appliances, cutlery, and sporting goods, does light machine work, is a locksmith, and has but one competitor in the city. *J. H. Stetson & Co.* (Joseph H. and George B. Stetson), 65 Lisbon street, successors to Bean & Stetson, deal in kitchen furnishings, stoves, furnaces, ranges, etc. *Charles Greenwood* was in extensive business from 1879 to 1890. J. H. Chase now occupies his former stand, 191 Lisbon street. Among other prominent houses are *Hall & Knight Hardward Co.*, 53 Lisbon street, successors to Owen & Hall, dealers in manufacturers' supplies, etc., and *A. L. & E. F. Goss*, Main street, corner Lincoln street, stoves, furnaces, etc.

COAL, WOOD, ETC. - *Bearce, Wilson & Co.*, 138 Main street, deal in coal and wood. This number is also headquarters of the extensive lumbering firm of *Bearce & Wilson* (George B. Bearce, Charles C. Wilson), large operators in the Upper Androscoggin valley. Other dealers in coal and wood are *John N. Wood*, 64 Middle street; *H. B. Skinner & Co.*, cross canal; *L. C. Robbins*, 270 Main street; *Harper & Googin* (John Harper, Melvin J. Googin), 138 Bates street; *O. A. Norton*, 51 Ash street.

FLOUR, GRAIN, MEAL, ETC. - *J. L. Hayes & Co.* (Jacob L. and Sylvanus B.) do a large business in the sale of these important articles and lime and cement, at 282 Main street (Lowell's Corner); *J. B. Ham & Co.*, Grand Trunk yard; *O. S. Ham*, Haymarket Square; *M. J. Davis*, 86 Park street.

PAINTERS AND DECORATORS. - *I. S. Faunce*, painter and decorator, of over 30 years' experience, 57 Bates street; *George W. Boardman*, plain and decorative paper-hanger, and house, wall, and ceiling painter, etc., 266 Main street; *James M. Sherman*, painter, grainer, glazier, paper-hanger, and fancy decorator, 96 Chestnut street.

INSURANCE. - *Chamberlin & Little*, 79 Lisbon street, is one of the oldest insurance agencies, succeeding a firm established 30 years or more ago. *F. A. Conant* represents good companies, with office in Sands Building. *Archie L. Talbot*, 19 Lisbon street, is general agent of that strong conservative, Quaker company, the Provident Life and Trust Company of Philadelphia. *Nazaire Payette*, 8 College Block, is manager of the Metropolitan Insurance Company. *Callahan & Durocher*, 226 Lisbon street, conduct insurance.

CIVIL ENGINEERS. - *John A. Jones*, Pilsbury Block. *Charles Bowers*, Franklin Company's office.

BOOKS AND STATIONERY. - The firm of *Douglass & Cook*, 188 Lisbon street, is an old established one, and keeps the name it had when S. W. Cook was a partner. It does a large business.

BOOK AND JOB PRINTERS. - *Nelson Dingley, Jr., & Co.*, Journal Block; *George A. Callahan*, 212 Lisbon street (established 1862); *W. H. Weeks*, 32 Main street.

BOOKBINDER. - *Mrs. C. A. Neal*, Journal Block.

Hon. James Lowell was born in Buckfield, January 5, 1791. (See merchants.) He was confident, even in early life, that Lewiston would ultimately become a large manufacturing city. Governed by this impulse he invested all his surplus funds in real estate, on which he realized large returns. For 20 consecutive years, commencing with 1829, Mr. Lowell was treasurer of the town of Lewiston, representative to the legislature in 1839, 1851, and 1852, and was a member of the state senate in 1841. In all of these places of responsibility he exhibited sound judgment, a conservative spirit, and devotion to the trusts confided to him. Mr. Lowell was quiet and unassuming in manner, and was highly esteemed in business circles. He married, in 1814, Hannah Paul, of New Gloucester. They had three sons, Mark, Daniel, and James, Jr., and one daughter, Vesta, who married Dr. A. Burbank. Mark Lowell was one of the selectmen for several years, and also a representative to the legislature. Mr. Lowell died July 27, 1858.

Colonel John M. Frye, a descendant of General Joseph Frye, of Fryeburg, was born in Westbrook, November 28, 1802. Mr. Frye, from early manhood, was intimately connected with the manufacturing industries of Lewiston, retaining his relation to the Lewiston Falls Manufacturing Company until he retired from business. In the municipal affairs of the town and city he took a deep interest. He served on the board of selectmen, was eleven years town treasurer, was a member of the Maine senate in 1841, and was elected a member of the governor's council in 1861. In these various positions he served with honor to himself and to the gratification of the people. In middle life he was elected colonel of his regiment of militia, a position in which he took much interest, making a model officer. Colonel Frye married Miss Alice Davis, daughter of Mr. David Davis, in 1828. They had two sons, Hon. William P. Frye, the distinguished senator, now in the U. S. senate, Dr. Albert S. Frye, who died in early life, and several daughters. Colonel Frye died January 1, 1885.

Major William R. Frye, a brother of Colonel John M. Frye, was born in Westbrook in 1808. He married Melicant Mower, of Greene. Major Frye in early life was one of the most successful of our school teachers, having taught a number of years at Lowell's Corner and at the Herrick school-house. He was interested in manufacturing, having for years an interest in the woolen mill here and at Sabatis. But it was in political life he was best known. Unquestionably he had the power of leadership, and had he been physically strong would have made it felt. For seven years he was chairman of the board of selectmen, was postmaster under Van Buren, Pierce, and Buchanan; and was a member of the state senate in 1841 and 1842. He was instrumental in securing the location of the Maine State Seminary here and was one of the trustees of Bates College. Mr. Frye had abilities of no ordinary character. As a speaker he was forcible, incisive, with a marked command of language. He drew around him many friends, and was not wanting in enthusiastic admirers, and in his intercourse with the public was kind and affable. His second wife was Miss Susan E. Caverly, of Lowell, Mass. Major Frye died March 5, 1865.

Edward P. Tobie, a native of Chesterville, married Miss Caroline Frye, daughter of Mr. Dean Frye, in 1829, and removed to Lewiston about 1836. Mr. Tobie was elected town clerk in 1839, and held the office of town and city clerk, with the exception of one year, until his death in 1875. His life was one of singular purity and commanded universal respect. His family consisted of two sons and two daughters. One of his sons, Edward P. Tobie, Jr., is one of the editors of the *Providence Journal*, and a brilliant writer.

Captain Daniel Holland, son of John and Rebecca Holland, who settled in the southern part of Lewiston early in this century, was born September 23, 1811, and died in March, 1891. He learned the tanning business of Asa Garcelon, and lived for a while in Durham. He married, October 22, 1835, Mary A., daughter of Deacon Joseph Field, and settled in Lewiston and became an active, vigorous, hard-working, honest-hearted business man of foresight and public spirit. Their children are Mrs. F. I. Day, of Lewiston, Mrs. H. S. Garcelon, of Dayville, Conn., and Alphonso B. Holland, of Lewiston. In 1836 Captain Holland and Stephen Field, his brother-in-law, put up a building on Sabatis street. It was a large building for those days, and they did a large business buying wool skins and pulling wool. The first residence of Captain Holland was in the Manning House, near Sabatis-street junction with Main street. About 1837 Captain Holland built a two-story brick house where Central Block is. He lived here many years, making famous thick boots, and selling them at retail at Portland and Bangor. He was an ardent militia-man, and captain of the Light Infantry Company. He did most of the lumbering in this city until the advent of Mr. Bearce, and was an extensive dealer in real estate. He was especially potent at the time the corporations (in 1847) were desirous of buying land. They found it difficult to purchase, and in connection with Colonel Reed and Mark Lowell, Captain Holland acted as a self-constituted committee, and bonded many farms and much land on both sides of the river. He built his fine brick residence on College street about 1872. He was president of the Lewiston Falls Bank, town treasurer in 1856 and 1857, and representative in 1866 and 1867. In 1868 he was a member of the governor's council, and in 1870 and 1871 was in the Maine State Senate. He was prominent in the establishment of Riverside Cemetery, and with John M. Frye, Wm. R. Frye, Alonzo Garcelon, A. H. Kelsey, Amos Nevens, D. H. Hamilton, Ammi R. Nash, and S. R. Bearce bought the property for $11,000, and established the corporation. Every one respected Captain Holland for his native integrity, his candid common sense, his wide acquaintance with business, his rare judgment on all matters of social and industrial welfare, his kind heart, and his honest soul.

John Read, Esq., son of Colonel Stephen and Abigail (Brown) Read, was born in Lewiston, December 21, 1820. Mr. Read's educational advantages were obtained in the public schools of the town and at the Lewiston Falls Academy, where he took a course in higher mathematics in order to prepare himself for the profession of civil engineer, which he subsequently pursued, having been engaged on several railroads in this state and in this west. In 1855 Mr. Read was elected chairman of the board of selectmen; was one of the county commissioners from 1869 to 1881; street commissioner of the city of Lewiston for three years; superintendent of the water works for two years; clerk of the water works for two years; and has been secretary of the Odd Fellows' Mutual Relief Association since 1885. He married Miss Mary A. Bonney, of Turner, May 18, 1848, and has two sons, Charles B. Reade, who graduated at Bates College in the class of 1873, and is now Deputy Sergeant-at-Arms of the U. S. Senate, and J. Leslie Reade, a graduate of Bates College, class of 1883, who is now connected with the *Auburn Daily Gazette.*

Hon. Jacob B. Ham, son of Colonel Ebenezer and Judith (Barker) Ham, was born in Lewiston, March 24, 1824. He was educated in the town schools and the Lewiston Falls Academy. He early engaged in trade and was always interested in mercantile pursuits. Mr. Ham's rugged character and evident ability soon brought him before the public, and he became one of the leading men in the county. He was representative to the legislature in 1854-6, and selectman of Lewiston in 1859, and in 1860-62 was chairman of the board. In 1863 Mr. Ham was elected with great unanimity, as the first mayor of Lewiston, and was re-elected in 1864. Mr. Ham was at the head of the municipal govenment of Lewiston during the entire period of the Civil War. During these years of anxiety and great responsibility he managed the affairs of the town and city with rare judgment and ability. Lewiston's quota was always ready at the time designated by the government, and in all of the affairs of the place which came under his control he showed executive ability and tact. He was appointed by the governor as Maine's commissioner to the New Orleans Exposition, and ably represented the state. His mind was so cast that he not only took great interest in the city, state, and county, but he also took much delight in intellectual pursuits, and traveled in almost every state in the Union, in Mexico, Cuba, and Europe. He had a fine appreciation of the rare and beautiful, and the instincts of the antiquary. His was an active, vigorous, and robust life, maintained with wonderful poise, until the end came, September 3, 1888.

Prof. Thomas Hill Rich, A.M., son of Hosea Rich, an eminent physician and surgeon, was born in Bangor, is a graduate of Bowdoin College and of the Theological Seminary in Bangor. For three years he taught Latin and Greek in East Maine Conference Seminary at Bucksport, for two years was in the Portland High School, and for six years was assistant teacher of Hebrew at Bangor. Since 1872 he has been professor of Hebrew in Cobb Divinity School. He has published metrical versions of portions of the Old Testament. Of his versions of Nahum *The Christian Mirror* said: "His purpose has been well accomplished. The paraphrase is in iambic measure, unrhymed, but easy and flowing; the diction pure, and the effect of the whole pleasing. It is remarkable how much of grace and power is added to these inspired productions by presenting them in a dress worthy of their originals." Other creditable critics have said that this version was comparable with and similar to Matthew Arnold's metrical versions of portions of Isaiah. Journals like the *New York Independent* have given high words of praise to his work. *Mrs. Caroline W. D. Rich* (wife of Prof. Thomas Hill Rich) is a lineal descendant on the paternal side from John Stockbridge, who came from Kent, England, in 1627, and on the maternal side from John Leavitt, who came from England in 1628. Mrs. Rich has written several books, some of which have been passed into second and third editions. A poem of considerable length was written for the centennial of Turner, is embodied in the "History of Turner," and also is in book form. Poems of the imagination, legends, and ballads have appeared in the leading publications of the day. Translations also have been added to her literary work as well as hymns, some of which may be found in hymn collections.

The early center of business was at Lowell's Corner, but, about 1845, business houses began to cluster around and on lower Main street, leaving but the store of James Lowell at the Corner when the railroad came in 1849. Lower Main street did not retain its commercial supremacy after Central Block was built and Lisbon street was laid out and partially opened. John W. Perkins (the first dry goods merchant, established early near the bridge,) moved to Central Block, others followed, the post-office was removed to a building standing where J. T. Small's office does, at the head of Lisbon street, and the tide of business enterprise flowed that way. As new stores were demanded, Lisbon street was by degrees opened and has developed into the great commercial thoroughfare of to-day. The old arcades near Cedar street were built by the corporations soon after their extensive surveys and laying out of streets, to draw trade that way, but it refused to come. With the opening of Sabatis road and the new road to Lisbon down Lisbon street, easy transportation for their produce was given to the farmers to the east, and that developed trade. The mills brought workmen who must have houses, food, and necessaries of life and business steadily increased. By 1860 the population was 7,424, and the valuation had increased fourfold in ten years and was $2,426,374. The growth has been very rapid, Bates College has made the city an educational center, and Lewiston is among the most prosperous cities of New England, and increasing in size, and wealth, and improvements with each year. It now has a valuation of $12,144,494. The French comprise from one-fourth to one-third of the population. The original seven wards of the city are unchanged in limits and have this population: Ward 1, 2,796; ward 2, 2,243; ward 3, 2,482; ward 4, 2,761; ward 5, 5,049; ward 6, 4,103; ward 7, 2,267; a total of 21,701. Jones's Block, now lower Maine Central station, was built about 1851, Central Block in the last of the 'fifties, Journal Block in 1862, Savings Bank Block in 1868, Lyceum Block in 1872, Centennial Block in 1876, Frye Block in 1877, Scruton Block in 1883, Sands Block in 1885.

The address of Mayor Newell, on assuming office, gave the financial condition of the city, March 1, 1891, thus: Liabilities, $1,099,000; resources, $182,752.11. He further says:

At the beginning of the last municipal year, the city report shows that the floating debt was $65,800. It is now $109,000, but of this sum $44,000 has been expended toward the construction of the new city building; and the floating debt then existing has not been increased by the ordinary expenditures, but has, as the figures show, been somewhat decreased. The amount of $44,000 this year added, is now invested in the city building.

The net debt of the city is $916,247.89, but of this sum $500,000 is represented by the water loan, which is more than self-sustaining, so that this is not a burden upon the city, nor in reality, a debt. The same may also be said of the 2,250 shares of the Lewiston & Auburn Railroad, whose face value is $225,000, and which is to-day worth $337,000. These two items of our indebtedness, aggregating, in money values, $837,000, do not constitute a burden upon the tax payers of our city, because they are a paying investment, not only from a money point of view, but they are important factors in the material progress and development of its business interests, and contribute in no small degree to the value of our taxable property. This leaves the debt, not self-sustaining, $79,247.89, with a valuation of $11,250,000 worth of taxable property, and makes a financial showing which compares favorably with that of any city in New England, and is in fact, equaled by that of very few. None of the outstanding bonds mature during the year. $100,000 of them become due on the first day of January, 1893; but it is thought that it will not be advisable to pay the same at maturity, owing to the heavy expenditures incident to the loss and reconstruction of our city building. For this reason, an act has passed the present legislature enabling the city to fund the same when due. This can be done at a low rate of interest, because the financial standing of our city is such that the bonds are looked upon as a safe investment.

Bates College

From the Blue Store 1882
History of Lewiston
By Elder

Maine State Seminary was chartered March 16, 1855*, by the Legislature of Maine, with an endowment, by the State, of $15,000. In June following the trustees met at Vienna, and after much deliberation decided by onevote to locate the seminary at Lewiston. Rev. O. B. Cheney*, of Augusta, was chosen president. The corner stone was laid with appropriate ceremonies June 26, 1856*. Rev. George Knox, of Lewiston, offered prayer, and Rev. Martin J. Steere (Portland, ME*), of

New Hampshire, delivered the address. It was open for students September 1st, 1857. The trustees instituted a collegiate course of study in 1863, and changed the name to Bates College, in honor of Benjamin E. Bates, of Boston, who had given the college $100,000. Subsequently Mr. Bates promised to give the college $100,000 more, on condition that the friends of the college would give an additional $100,000. The college accepted the offer of Mr. Bates, and received pledges for more than that amount from the friends of the institution. The action of the trustees was legalized by the Legislature, June 19, 1864, and Bates College graduated its first class, consisting of eight members, July 31st, 1867. Connected with the college is the Nicholas Latin School, being the preparatory department of the Maine State Seminary. The department for ladies was abolished, the last class graduating in June, 1870. There are a number of free scholarships, ten of which were founded by the State, the others are by donations of individuals, consisting of one thousand dollars each.

The theolgical department was established by a vote of the corporation July 21, 1870. It occupies Nicholas Hall. There are two courses of study, comprising the regular and English.

Faculty of the College - Rev. Oren* B. Cheney, D.D., President; J. Y. Stanton, A.M., Prof. of Latin and Greek; R. C. Stanley*, A.M., Prof. of Chemistry and Geology; Thomas L. Angell, A.M., Prof. of Modern Languages; Geo. C. Chase, Prof. of Rhetoric and English Literature; B. F. Hayes, Prof. Mental and Moral Philosophy; J. H.* Rand, Prof. Mathematics.

Faculty of the Theological School - Rev. Oren* B. Cheney, D.D., President; Rev. John Fullonton, D.D., Prof. of Ecclesiastical History and Pastoral Theology; Rev. B. F. Hayes, D.D., Prof. of the Evidences of Christianity, and Moral Science; Prof. J. A. Howe, D.D., Prof. of Homiletics; T. H. Rich, A.M., Prof. of Hebrew.

* Indicates corrections made by the Bates College Library Special Collection Dept.

BIOGRAPHICAL SKETCHES

AMES, ABNER CRAFT - Born 31 May 1773 [vital records of Lewiston, Maine, p. 4], d 13 Apr. 1814 in Industry, Maine, age 41 years, s/o James and Elizabeth (Craft) Ames. Abner Craft Ames resided in Lewiston and Industry, Maine. He m Betsy Bean, published 15 Apr. 1798. Children: **Jacob** b 24 Aug. 1799, d 10 May 1826; **David** b 11 May 1801, d 22 Aug. 1829; **Lydia Bean** b 4 Jul. 1808, m Aretus Hardy of Strong, Maine, pub. 12 Apr. 1830; and **Margaret** b 22 Jul. 1811, d 16 Jul. 1815.

AMES, ANNIS - Born 7 Aug. 1810, d ??, s/o Ezra and Lucy (Garcelon) Ames. Annis Ames m Priscilla Luce. Children: **Maria L.** b 3 Jun. 1840; **Franklin I.** b 22 Mar. 1842, enlisted 7 Oct. 1861, d 23 Sep. 1863; **Nancy S.** b 14 May 1844, m Charles Welch; **Charlotte T.** b 16 Jun. 1848, m Ebeneser I. Russell; and **Timothy H.** b 14 Oct. 1850.

AMES, DANIEL - Born 20 Feb. 1799, d 18 Jul. 1860 [Garcelon Cemetery, Lewiston, Maine], s/o Ezra and Lucy (Garcelon) Ames. Daniel Ames m 12 Jul. 1821 by Winslow Ames, Justice of the Peace, pub. 23 Jun. 1821, Polly Dingley/Dingly. Children: **Mary Jane** b 24 Nov. 1822, d 9 Jan. 1851; **Polly** b 2 Jul. 1824, d 8 Jul. 1824; **Sarah** b 2 Jul. 1825, m Moses Beal; **Lucy** b 18 Oct. 1827, m Clement King; **William D.** b 8 Nov. 1830, m ---- Greenwood; **Daniel** b 27 Jan. 1833 - went to Wisconsin; **Levi** b 14 Feb. 1837; and **Caroline D.** b 14 Jan. 1840, m Thos. Merriam.

AMES, EBENESER - Born 30 Sept. 1794, d Dec. 1865 [vital records of Freeman, Maine, p. 443], s/o Ezra and Lucy (Garcelon) Ames. Ebeneser Ames m Eleanor Weymouth [*Weymouth Family History* by Ruth Ella Weymouth, published by J. Grant Stevenson, Provo, UT, 1978]. Moved to Wisconsin. Children: **Rebecca L.** b 23 Oct. 1816; **Ivory W.** b 23 May 1818; **Lucy A.** b 1820, d 1824; **Alura H.** b 1822, d 1844; **Lucy A.** b Mar. 1824; **Eleanor**; **Isaac**; **Ebeneser**; **Alonzo G.**; **Fidelia**; **May E.** twin to Alma; and **Alma** twin to May E..

AMES, EZRA - Born 22 Apr. 1769, d 3 Jan. 1814 in Burlington, Vermont, s/o James and Elizabeth (Craft/Hall) Ames. Ezra Ames lived on a farm in Lewiston, Maine, until 1807 or 1808 when he sold it to Capt. George Williams and moved to Freeman, Maine, [Col. Wm. Garcelon's notes, 1825-1860+]. He m Lucy Garcelon. Children: **Isaac** q.v.; **Ezra Jr.** q.v.; **Ebeneser** q.v.; **Aaron** b 29 Jan. 1797, d 8 Dec. 1822, unm; **Daniel** q.v.; **James** b 7 Aug. 1801, d 20 Jan. 1803;

Diademia b 14 Jul. 1804, d 4 Apr. 1887, m Converse Moody; **James G.** q.v.; **Annis** q.v.; and **Betsy** [Vital Records of Lewiston, Maine, p. 4 and Vital Records of Freeman, Maine, p. 365] b 31 May 1813, m Rev. John Russell.

AMES, EZRA JR. - Born 15 Dec. 1792 [Vital Records of Lewiston, Maine, p. 4; this record was recorded circa 1801] twin to Issac Ames (see below), d 9 Mar. 1861, s/o Ezra and Lucy (Garcelon) Ames. Ezra Ames, Jr. m 20 Apr. 1817 Clarissa Luce [vital records of Freeman, Maine, p. 365]. Children: **Ezra**; **Prudence**; **Aaron**; **Sarah**; **Winslow** m? Marg. ----; **Cordelia**; and **Owen**. [*Freeman Records* by Leland Edwin Peary of Strong, Maine. The book (typescript) was presented, by his family, to the Colonial D. A. R. for use at Farmington Public Library, no date. Peary lived from the last part of the 1800s to the first part of the 1900s.]

AMES, ISAAC - Born 15 Dec. 1792, d 3 Nov. 1828 aged 36 years [Vital Records of Lewiston, Maine, p. 4; this record was recorded circa 1801] twin to Ezra Ames, Jr. (see above), s/o Ezra and Lucy (Garcelon) Ames. Isaac Ames m Polly Weymouth b 8 Dec. 1796 at Freeman, Maine [vital records of Freeman, Maine, p. 365]. Child: **Mary Ann** b 18 May 1817, m Robert T. Judkins, 26 Aug. 1836. [*Freeman Records* by Leland Edwin Peary of Strong, Maine. The book (typescript) was presented, by his family, to the Colonial D. A. R. for use at Farmington Public Library, no date. Peary lived from the last part of the 1800s to the first part of the 1900s.]

AMES, JAMES SR. - Born 27 Mar. 1739 in Groton, Massachusetts [*History of Oakham* by Henry B. Wright, published by Ernest Hayward, 1947, p. 386-7], d 3 Jun. 1815, s/o Jacob and Ruth (Shattuck) Ames. James Ames was a blacksmith by trade and kept an inn at Oakham, Massachusetts, 1776-1783. From 1780-1781, he was a member of the Committee of Correspondence, Inspection and Safety in 1775. [*History of Oakham* by Henry B. Wright and Edwin Harvey, published by Ernest Hayward, 1947, p. 386-7]. He m (1) 8 Dec. 1761 Elizabeth Hall, and m (2) Elizabeth Craft [*History of Industry, Maine*, by William C. Hatch, published by the author, 1893, p. 500-501 and *Ames Genealogy* by Wilmot Spofford Ames, published by the author, 1941]. Children: **Winslow** q.v.; **Ezra** q.v.; **Hannah** b 16 Feb. 1771, d 17 May 1819, m Mark Garcelon, 11 Oct. 1792; **Abner Craft** q.v.; **James** q.v.; **Lucy** b 3 Dec. 1776, d 4 Nov. 1814, m John Cummings, 19 Nov. 1795; **Elisabeth** b 1 Jun. 1780, m Samuel Mooer, published 30 Nov. 1799; **Martha** b 29 Mar. 1781, d 18 Mar. 1854, m Noah Litchfield, 28 Aug. 1803; **Aseneth** b 13 Oct. 1783, d 11 Feb. 1837, m Joseph Mooer, 15 Apr. 1802. [*History of Oakham, Massachusetts* by Henry B. Wright and Edwin D. Harvey, published by Ernest L. Hayward, 1947].

AMES, JAMES JR. - Born 22 Feb. 1774, d 3 Oct. 1837, s/o James, Sr. and ?? Ames. "James Ames started for Ohio on foot on 6 May 1817" [p. 20 of Thomas Hodgkin's diary, a typed script at the Androscoggin History Society.] James Ames, Jr. m Rebecca Crockett, published 15 Jul. 1797. Children: **Martha** b 25 Jul. 1798; **Rebecca** b 26

May 1800; **Susannah** b 2 Aug. 1802; **Mary** b 7 Jul. 1805; **Sally** b 23 Nov. 1807; **James** b 19 Aug. 1810; **Margaret** b 10 Feb. 1813; and **William G.** b 30 Nov. 1815.

AMES, JAMES G. - Born 9 Jul. 1807, d ??, s/o Ezra and Lucy (Garcelon) Ames. James G. Ames m 30 Oct. 1834 Nancy C. Decker. Children: **L a u r a F.** b 14 Jul. 1836, m Thomas B. Plummer, 22 May 1862; **Mary C.** b 3 Nov. 1839, d Aug. 1840; **Mary C.** b 15 Aug. 1841, d 2 Jun. 1844; and **George G.** b 15 Dec. 1846.

AMES, WINSLOW - Born 21 Oct. 1762, [Rutland, Massachusetts], d 8 Oct. 1851, aged 89 years, buried in the Garcelon Cemetery in Lewiston, s/o James & Elizabeth (Hall) Ames. Winslow Ames m (1) 10 Jul. 1788 Margaret Nichols, and m (2) 13 Aug. 1805 Betsey Litchfield. *Children by 1st wife:* **S a m u e l** b 11 May 1789, d 5 Apr. 1862, m Mary Benjamin; **J a m e s** b 4 May 1790, d 25 Jun. 1844, m Margaret (Peggy) Randall, 6 Mar. 1814; **Francis** b 2 Aug. 1791, d 3 Dec. 1866/1867, unm; **H a n n a h** b 29 Apr 1793, d 14 Mar. 1876, m Jesse Burbank Freeman, published 25 Dec. 1814; **Ruth** b 1 Feb. 1796, m Levi Gould, 11 Sep. 1817; **B e t s e y** b 18 Jun. 1797, m Robert Powers of Topsham, Maine, 7 Feb. 1822; **Jane N.** b 26 Feb. 1799, d 22 Mar. 1847, m Mark Garcelon; **J e a n** b 26 Feb. 1799, d 27 May 1805; **W i l l i a m** b 23 Nov. 1800, d -- Jul. 1872, m J. Hannah Cooper of Pittston, Maine; and **John** b -- May 1805, d in infancy, 30 May 1805. *Children by 2nd wife:* **Winslow N.** q.v.; and **Margaret** b 16 Aug. 1813, m Ham Brooks. [See *New England Historic Genealogical Register*, Vol. 9, July p. 216].

AMES, WINSLOW N. - Born 23 Sep. 1811, d 6 Sept 1892, s/o Winslow and Betsy (Litchfield) Ames. Winslow N. Ames was a captain in Lewiston's C Company, 3rd Infantry on 18 Apr. 1835. He resided in Lewiston in 1850 and was a blacksmith [census 1850]. He m 28 Aug. 1834 by Wm. Garcelon, J. P., to Sarah/Sarah J. Totman [Vital Records of Lewiston, Maine, p. 456]. Children: **A n g e l e n a** b 6 Jul. 1836, d 1902, m Isaac G. Curtis, 4 Mar. ----; **Margaret Ellen** b 23 Oct. 1838, m (1) Jeremiah Stimpson of Biddeford, ME, 10 Jun. 1876 and (2) George Kinne, 28 Jul. 1886; **Caroline Ann,** b 20 Aug. 1842, m Fred A. Howard; and **Albert Nichols** b 18 Jan. 1844.

ANDERSON, ROBERT - Born ??, d ??, s/o ?? Robert Anderson m Betsey ----. Children: **William** q.v.; **Jacob** b 13 Jul. 1782, m Rachael ----; **S a l l y** b 7 Sep. 1784, d 7 Apr. 1815, m James Field, 10 May 1811; **Martha** b 12 Aug. 1787, d 28 May 1831; **Barton** b 21 Feb. 1790, d 19 May 1845, m widow Hulda Anderson, 1 Jan. 1828; **Agnes** b 8 Nov. 1792, d 12 Sep. 1868, m Peter Nutley, 20 Feb. 1848; **Robert** b 24 Aug. 1795, d 19 Aug. 1843, m Abigail Smith, Mar. 1820; **J o h n** b 27 Dec. 1798, d 30 Jan. 1826; and **Hulda.**

ANDERSON, WILLIAM - Born 24 Aug. 1780, d 23 Mar. 1839, s/o Robert and Betsey Anderson. William Anderson m pub. 10 Nov. 1804 Mary Morrill, d 18 Jan. 1844. Children: **Elijah M.** b 25 Jul. 1805, m Sarah Vaughn of Strong, Maine, pub. 7 Feb. 1826; **Margaret** b 27 Oct. 1806, m Leander Daggett, 16 Mar. 1826 in New Vineyard, Maine; **William b 29 Mar. 1809, m Emeline Stewart, pub. 8 Aug. 1831, m 6 Sep. 1831; **Mary** b 23 Jun. 1810, m Ephraim Hackett, 26 Mar. 1829; **Robert** b 13 Sep. 1811, m Harriet Wallis, 25 Mar. 1832; **Barton** b 23 Jul. 1813, m Abigail H. Battle of Farmington, Maine, pub. 15 Jun. 1839; **Hiram** b 27 Dec. 1817; **Sarah** b 7 Apr. 1822, m John H. Ramsdell, pub. 8 Apr. 1844; and **John** b 7 Aug. 1826.

ATKINS - later changed to ATKINSON - note, Editor

ATKINSON, BENJAMIN FRANKLIN - Born in Lewiston, 13 Aug. 1825 [Topsham, Maine, records] or 28 Aug. 1827 [Pittsfield, Maine, town records], d ??, s/o William Jr. and Mary (Parker) Atkinson. Benjamin Franklin Atkinson m Martha ---- [Pittsfield town records]. Children: **William Franklin** b 10 Apr. 1854; and **Frederick Warren** b 21 Jul. 1856.

ATKINSON, CHARLES F. - Born 2 Jul. 1833 in Pittsfield, Maine, d ??, s/o William Jr. and Mary (Parker) Atkinson. Charles F. Atkinson m Emma A. Sanborn. Children: **Charles E.** b 17 Jun. 1858, d 3 Nov. 1858.

ATKINSON, GEORGE WASHINGTON - Born 14 Mar. 1817, d ??, s/o William Sr. and Anna (----) Atkinson. George Washington Atkinson m 14 Mar. 1839 Rhoda Proctor of Lisbon, Maine. Children: **H. Emma** b 9 Aug. 1840; **Ann Augusta** b 28 May 1842; **Mary Elura** b 22 May 1844; **Julia** b 17 Oct. 1846; **George William** b 3 Sep. 1849, d 1 Mar. 1862.

ATKINSON, JOHN - Born 4 Apr. 1805, d ??, s/o William Sr. and Anna Atkinson. John Atkinson m 26 Oct. 1828 Hannah Moore [Vital Records of Lewiston, Maine, p. 416]. Went to Minneapolis, MN. Children: **Warren** b 11 Mar. 1829; **Charles Henry** b 27 Oct. 1830; **Cynthia Ann** b 30 Mar. 1834; and **Martin Van Buren** b 17 Dec. 1837.

ATKINSON, RUFUS PARKER - Born 24 May 1831 in Pittsfield, Maine, d ??, s/o William Jr. and Mary (Parker) Atkinson. Rufus Parker Atkinson m Harriet Rogers, d/o Enoch Rogers. Children: **Grace** b Apr. 1858, d 1 Sep. 1865, age 7 years, 5 mos.; **Bessie**; and **Alma**.

ATKINSON, WILLIAM SR. - Born ??, d 5 Jun. 1849 in Lisbon, Maine, s/o ?? William Atkinson, Sr. m Anna ----. Children: **Anna** b 11 Jun. 1792, d 15 Dec. 1832, m Ezekiel Merrill, pub. 17 Apr. 1814, he d 26 Jul. 1855; **Sally** b 15 Mar. 1796, m Samuel Smith, 23 Sep. 1819; **Polly/Mary** [Vital Records of Lewiston, Maine, p. 401] b 9 Mar. 1799, m Edmund Thompson of Bangor, Maine, 15 Aug. 1824; **William Jr.** q.v.; **Ann** b 21 Nov. 1822, d 16 Jul. 1830; **John** q.v.; **Elvira** b 15 Jan. 1807, m James Vickery, Jr. of Danville, Maine; **Moses** b 25 Jun. 1809, m Emily Gerrish 29 Nov. 1837; **George Washington** b 2 Oct. 1811, d 12 Jan. 1815; **George Washington** q.v.

ATKINSON, WILLIAM JR. - Born 19 Mar. 1801, d 23 Mar. 1873 at Pittsfield, Maine, s/o William Sr. and Anna Atkinson. William Atkinson, Jr. m certificate granted 14 Nov. 1821 Mary Parker of Danville, Maine, b 25 Jul. 1800, d 17 Mar. 1856 age 56 years, 8 months. Children: **Mary** b 20 May 1822, m Sullivan R. Taylor; **William Davis** q.v.; **Frank (Fanny)** b 20 Aug. 1826; **James** b 28 Aug. 1827; **Benjamin Franklin** q.v.; **Rosanne/Roseanne**; **Rufus Parker** q.v.; **Charles F.** q.v.; **Levi** b 6 Jun. 1835, d 6 Jun. 1854; **Hannah** b 1 Jan. 1837, d 20 Jul. 1857; and **Amos**. [James Vickery of Bath, Maine, who is the source for the above information; he is likely the son of James Vickery, Jr., above, who married Elvira Atkinson, d/o William Atkinson, Sr. and see Charles Starbird's collections on Danville, Maine, families at Androscoggin Historical Society, a typescript.]

ATKINSON, WILLIAM DAVIS - Born 18 May 1824, d 9 Jun. 1894, s/o William Jr. and Mary (Parker) Atkinson. William Davis Atkinson m (1) Ada Avery, d 20 Feb. 1868, age 35-1-16, and m (2) 6 Feb. 1871 Margaret (Runnells) Rogers. Child: **Ada** b 3 Jan. 1874, d 5 Jan. 1876.

BACKMAN, GABRIEL - Born 1827 in Bavaria, Germany, d ??, s/o ?? Gabriel Backman occ' Dry and Fancy Goods. He m Emma ----, b 1834 in Rusia, Germany. Children: **Edwin** b 1854 in ME; **Henry** b 1854 in ME. Also listed in the family **Moses** b 1844 in Bavaria, Germany, occ' clerk; and **H. S. Friedman** b 1840 in Bavaria, Germany, perhaps brother and brother-in-law to Gabriel Backamn. [Lewiston 1860 Lewiston.]

BANGS, JOSHUA - Born ??, d ??, s/o ?? Joshua Bangs settled in Lewiston, Maine, 1788 [schedules of settlers or townships in Pegypscot (sic) patent, original at Maine Historical Society in Portland, Maine]. He m Anna ----. Children: **Edward** b 16 May 1785; **Almira** b 24 Aug. 1787; **Joshua** b 9 Dec. 1790. [Vital Records of Lewiston, Maine, p. 8.]

BARKER, RICHARD was probably the ancestor of the Barkers of Lewiston, **Jacob** and **Caleb**. He was a resident of Andover, Massachusetts, as early as 1643. He married Joanna ---- at or near the time he settled in Andover. He was a lumberman and died in Andover 18 Mar. 1692 or 1693. His wife died 11 Apr. 1787. Richard and Joanna had nine children of whom **S t e p h e n** was the eighth. Stephen was born 6 Jul. 1659, died 21 May 1741 (aged 71 years) in Methuen, Massachusetts, and married Mary Abott on 13 May 1687. Mary (Abott) Barker was living in 1709. Stephen and Mary had nine children of whom **Z e b e d i a h** was the second. Zebediah was born 2 Feb. 1689 or 1690 and married Elizabeth Lovejoy on 30 Dec. 1717, in Andover; he was a yeoman and lived in Haverhill, Massachusetts, until 1720 when he removed to Methuen, Massachusetts. Zebediah and Elizabeth had ten children, **Jacob** (q.v.) being the seventh and **Caleb** (q.v.) the ninth.

BARKER, ADDISON P. - Born 4 Dec. 1824, d 15 Feb. 1857 at Island Falls, Aroostook Co., Maine, killed by a falling tree [Maine State Archives], s/o Cyrus Jr. and Mary Jane (Berry) Barker. [A letter from

R. B. Sleeper of Sherman Mills, Maine, dated 1896, to J. G. Elder.] Addison P. Barker m (1) 27 Sep. 1846 Mary E. Joslin, d 9 May 1848, and (2) Susan A. Brown. Children: **Mary E.** b 24 Jun. 1856, m Luther B. Rogers, 7 Dec. 1869; **Clarissa**; and **Addison P.**

BARKER, ALPHONSO - Born 1847, d ??, s/o Jeddiah and ?? Barker. Alphonso Barker m Elisa Ramsdell, b 1850, d 1935, buried at the Notch Cemetery in New Vineyard, Maine [vital records of Franklin Co., vol. 1, typescript by Dorothy Wirth at Cutler Library of Farmington, Maine, p. 111.] Children: **Agnes** m Washburn Luce; **Margie** m True Luce; and **Ruphill.**

BARKER, AMOS - Born ??, d ??, s/o ?? Amos Barker m Elsie Keene. Children: **Hannah**; and **Waterman** q.v.

BARKER, ASA - Born ??, d ??, s/o ?? Asa Barker was one of the "embattled farmers" of the Revolution, and for his services as a soldier was granted lands in Bridgton, Maine, where he developed a fine home. [*History of Androscoggin County, Maine* edited by Georgia Drew Merrill, published by W. A. Ferguss & Co., 1891, p. 432.] Children: had at least one son, **Jonathan** q.v.

BARKER, AUGUSTUS L. - Born ??, d 6 May 1914 age 70 years and 7 months [Notch Cemetery, New Vineyard, Maine], s/o ?? Augustus L. Barker m (1) Emma Hackett, d 17 Mar. 1893 age 45 years and 2 months, and (2) Mrs. Elisabeth K. Hardy.

BARKER, CALEB - Born ??, d ??, s/o Zebediah and Elizabeth (Lovejoy) Barker. Children: **Caleb** b 24 Oct. 1758; **William** q.v.; **Jacob** b 21 Aug. 1761; **Jacob** q.v.; **Keziah** b Dec. ----, m Rev. Benjamin Cole, pub. in Topsham, Maine, 19 Feb. 1785; **Rhoda** b Apr. ----.

BARKER, CHARLES - Born 2 May 1816, d 1 Aug. 1896 in New Vineyard, Maine, s/o William and Dorcas Barker. Charles Barker m (1) Fanny ----, d 7 Feb. 1841 age 28 years [Hardy Cemetery, New Vineyard, Maine], and m (2) 8 May 1842 Sarah Robinson Barker, b 9 May 1821 in New Vineyard, Maine, d/o Jacob and Priscilla (----) Barker. Children: **Augustus** b 27 Dec. 1843, m (1) Emma Hackett and (2) Mrs. Elisabeth Keith Hardy; **Marcellous C.** q.v.; **Adalade F.** b 24 Jan. 1848, m Charles Hovey of Farmington, Maine; **Bertha E.** b 5 Sep. 1850, d 25 Nov. 1860; **Alma R.** b 20 Jul. 1854, d 23 Aug. 1855.

BARKER, CHARLES EDWARD - Born 23 Dec. 1850, d ??, s/o Jacob, Jr. and Annie (Ham) Barker. Charles E. Barker m Carrie Virginia Dyer, b 28 May 1859 in Phillips, Maine, [Maine State Archives], d/o Michael and Susan (Hanniford) Dyer of Farmington. Children: **Addie May** b 21 Aug. 1874, m Edward K. Fernald 13 Mar. 189-; **Edith Louise** b 23 Dec. 1875, m Winfield S. Welsh 3 Jun. 189-; **Lillian Alice** b 4 Jan. 1877; and **Edward Jacob** b 6 Dec. 1886.

BARKER, CYRUS - Born 9 Jan. 1765, d 25 Feb. 1838 age 72 years [Herrick Cemetery, Lewiston, Maine], s/o Jacob and May H. (Gove) Barker. Cyrus Barker m Rachel ----, who d 6 Dec. 1843 age 73 [Herrick Cemetery]. Children: **Sally** b 25 Jul. 1792, d 31 May 1850, m H.B. Ludden; **Deacon David** b 1 Sep. 1793, d 21 Oct. 1871 in North Turner, Maine; **Molly** b 8 Apr. 1796, d 27 May 1874; **Levi** b 13 Feb. 1798, d 27 Jul. 1803; **Cyrus, Jr.** q.v.; **Rachel** b 27 Mar. 1802, d 3 Apr. 1876, m Wlm. E. Adkins, 4 Jul. ----; **Lydia** b 14 Jan. 1804, d 19 Sep. 1835; **Jacob** b 15 Sep. 1805, d 8 Nov. 1883, m Mary Jane Berry of Patten, Maine; **Nelson P.** b 28 May 1819; **Cassandara** b 26 Oct. 1810.

BARKER, CYRUS JR. - Born 10 Oct. 1800, d 18 Apr. 1867, s/o Cyrus and Rachel (----) Barker. Cyrus Barker, Jr. m int. 16 May 1825, m 1 Jul. 1824 Mary Jane Berry of Minot, Maine, she residing in Island Falls, Maine, in 1860 [census]. [Vital Records of Minot, Maine, state, "John Barker, Jr., [sic] m. 14 Jul. 1825 Mary Jane, d/o Josiah and Molly (Bradbury) Berry" and Mrs. Sleeper of Sherman, Maine, writes in 1896 to Mr. Elder, stating that Mary Jane (Berry) d 15 Sep. 1872.] Children: **Addison P.** q.v. **Elisa M.** b 13 Jul. 1827, d 9 Aug. 1827; **May E.** b 9 Oct. 1828, m Winchell Woodard of Sherman, Maine, 16 Jan. 1849; **Silas Carlton** b 19 May 1832, m Flora Griffin of Jacksonville, Florida, -- Sep. 1854; **Stephen C.** b 13 Jul. 1837, d 14 Aug. 1865 in Monmouth, Maine, [*Morning Star*, issue 11 Oct. 1865]; and **Rodney C.** q.v.

BARKER, CYRUS I. - Born 27 Nov. 1827 in Bridgton, Maine, d 22 Jan. 1913 in Lewiston [probate court record], s/o Jonathan and Catherine (Mitchell) Barker. Cyrus I. Barker later moved to Lewiston, Maine. He m (1) 11 Aug. 1848, Almira B. Jewett, d 24 Aug. 1886, d/o Daniel Jewett of Denmark, Maine, and m (2) Mrs. Mary B. (Kilgore) Sprague. *Children by 1st wife*: **Alvarado D.** m Georgia Sanderson, a native of Oxford County, Maine, and they had one child, Grace W. Barker; and **Sarah Ida** m F. H. Packard, and they had one child, Cyrus F. Packard. [*History of Androscoggin County, Maine*, by Georgia Drew Merrill, editor, published by W. A. Ferguss, 1891, p. 432-432b.]

BARKER, DANIEL - Born 26 Feb. 1812, d -- Oct. 1864, s/o William and Dorcas (----) Barker. Daniel Barker resided in Farmington, Maine, in 1850 and was a blacksmith. He m (1) Mary J. Gilman and (2) Mary C. McIntire. *Child of 1st wife*: **Charles** killed in the Army. *Children of 2nd wife*: **Frances** b -- Jun. 1842, m (1) Geo. Dillingham and (2) Joseph Stores; **Elonora**; **Orland** q.v.

BARKER, DEACON DAVID - Born 1793, d ??, s/o Cyrus and Rachel (----) Barker. Deacon David Barker m Priscilla ----, b 1795. Children: **Marilla** b -- Oct. 1818; **Louisa** b 5 June 1821; **Harriet** b 7 Mar. 1823; **Albert** b 20 Feb. 1826; **Origen** q.v.; **Albert** b 29 Apr. 1830, m Susan M. Trask, d 13 Apr. 1906, d/o David and Sally (Barker) Trask [probate record]; **David** b 17 July 1832; **Betsey Ann** b 20 Jan. 1837. [Vital Records of Lewiston, Maine, p. 97.]

BARKER, DIAH - Born ??, d ??, s/o ?? Children: **Sophronia; Mary; Lydia; William; Zebadiah**, m Mary Merrill of Strong, ME; **Amos**; and **Orrin**.

BARKER, DIAH - Born 9 Sep. 1832, d 7 Apr. 1899 [Daggett Cemetery, New Vineyard, Maine], d ??, s/o Jacob and Priscilla (Robinson) Barker. Diah Barker m (1) -- Oct. 1857 Cordelia Cutler, and m (2) 30 Mar. 1860 Cynthia Matilda Mitchell. *Children of 1st wife*: **George N.** m 1885 Louisa Ramsdell. *Children of 2nd wife*: **Rose** m Allis Laskey of Union, New Hampshire; **Ernest; Elmer; Delia** m Fred Wentworth of Milton Mills, New Hampshire; and **Inez** m John Gray of New Vineyard, Maine. [Letter dated 1897 from Mrs. George W. Dobbin of Farmington to Marcellous Barker of Farmington, Maine.]

BARKER, GEORGE - Born 23 Oct. 1824 in New Vineyard, Maine, d 22 Mar. 1886, s/o Jacob and Priscilla (Robinson) Barker. George Barker m (1) 21 Apr. 1860 Phidelia Luce, and (2) -- May 1884 Lucinda Norton. Children: **Laura Ella** b 26 Oct. 1862, m Charles Williams, 1 Jan. 1890; **Alice Evelyn** b 17 Nov. 1865, m Geo. W. Dobbins, 1 Jan. 1885; and **Herbert Ernest** b 22 Jul. 1869, d 6 Jul. 1893 [letter from Mrs. G. W. Dobbins, 1896, of Farmington, Maine].

BARKER, HENRY M. - Born 13 Feb. 1841, d 9 Jun. 1873, s/o James R. and Nancy (Meryman) Barker. Henry M. Barker resided in Brunswick, Maine. He m 1 Jan. 1866/1867 in Augusta, Maine, Frances Gale, b 24 Jan. 1842, d/o John and Frances (Paul) Gale. Children: **Henry G.** b 8 Mar. 1868, m Lillian A. Turner of Bangor 8 Mar. 1893, was b 24 Oct. 1871; **George S.** b 2 Jan. 1870, m Blanch B. Jackson, b 21 May 1870, of Windsor, Maine; **Walter H.** b 8 Dec. 1872, unm.

BARKER, ISAAC - Born ??, d ??, s/o William and Annis (Austin) Barker. Isaac Barker resided in Strong and Vineyard, Maine. He was a twin to John Barker (see below). He m pub. 18 Feb. 1814 Mary W. Young [Hannah according to a letter from Mrs. Dobbins in 1896]. Children: **Isaac; Mary; William; Arabel; Helen; Hattie; George** of Norridgewock, Maine; **Charles; Greenleaf;** and **John**.

BARKER, JACOB - Born ??, d 17 Aug. 1803, s/o Zebediah and Elizabeth (Lovejoy) Barker. Jacob Barker m May H. Gove of Monmouth, Maine. Children: **Cyrus** b 9 Jan. 1765, d 25 Feb. 1838; **Asariah** b 26 Mar. 1762, m Henry A. Williams, 7 Jun. 1781; **Mary; Hannah** b 23 Nov. 1760; **Dinah** b 10 Mar. 1759; **Phebe** b 1777, d 25 Aug. 1848; **Esther** b 19 Sep. 1763; **Annis** b 12 Jan. 1767, d 18 Jan. 1831, m Priscilla Litchfield, 6 Nov. 1817; and **Anna** b 12 Jan. 1767, m Forest Seabury, 18 Jun. 1843.

BARKER, JACOB - Born 23 Apr. 1799 in New Vineyard, Maine, [letter from Alice Evelyn (Barker) Dobbins], d 1 Mar. 1869, s/o William and Annis (Austin) Barker. Jacob Barker m Priscilla Robinson, b 2 Jul. 1801, d 5 Jun. 1879. Children: **Sarah R.** b 9 May 1821; **George** q.v.;

Margaret b 10 Sep. 1827, d 15 Apr. 1867, m Ichabod Norton, pub. 18 Sep. 1861; **Diah** q.v.; and **Mary Ann** b 6 Sep. 1839.

BARKER, JACOB - Born 17 Jun. 1803, d 12 Dec. 1861 age 55 years [vital records of Lewiston, Maine, p. 81, 210], s/o Jacob and Martha Rose. Jacob Barker m 15 Oct. 1826, Anna/Annie Ham, b ??, d 29 Sep. 1866, s/o James and Nancy (Brooks) Ham. Children: **Vesta Ann** b 24 Aug. 1827, d 11 Feb. 1863, m Dean Weymouth of Abbott; **Mary Jane** b 12 Jul. 1829, d 18 Aug. 1833; **Nancy H.** b 16 Aug. 1831, d 8 Dec. 1862, m Sewall Works of Abbott, Maine; **Rodney F.** b 1 Mar. 1833; **Martha** b 29 Apr. 1837, d 4 Apr 1897, m Nathaniel Davis 1 Sep. 1856; **Jacob G.** b 30 Nov. 1840, d 29 Sep. 1882, unm; **Sarah J.** b 7 Apr. 1842, unm; **James** b 18 Sep. 1845, d 2 Oct. 1861, unm; **Mary A.** b 3 Jun. 1847, d -- May 1885, m Willard Carver; and **Charles E.** q.v.

BARKER, JACOB - Born 13 Mar. 1766, d 3 Jan. 1824 age 58 years, buried in the Davis Cemetery in Lewiston, Maine, s/o Caleb and ?? Barker. Jacob Barker m Martha Ross of Brunswick, Maine, b 17 Mar. 1777, d 8 Nov. 1835, aged 57 years [Davis Cemetery, Lewiston, Maine]. Children: two unnamed daughters b 1 Jul. 1799; **Judith** b 21 Sep. 1800, m Ebenezer Ham, pub. 15 Jun. 1822; **Jacob Jr.** b 17 Jun. 1803, d 13 Dec. 1861, m Anna Ham 15 Oct. 1826; **Polina** b 12 Apr. 1806, m Phillip Garcelon 1 Feb. 182-; **Rebecca** b 24 Jul. 1809, m Sumner Marston in 1834; **Jane G.** b 9 Apr. 1812, m James Lowell Jr., pub. 27 Mar. 1837, m Ebenezer Ham 27 Feb. 1855. He died 11 Oct. 1883; **James R.** b 2 Mar. 1815, d 14 Feb. 1897, m 24 Dec. 1838 Nancy Meryman of Brunswick, Maine, b 10 Jul. 1819 in Brunswick, d 24 Mar. 1888, d/o Nathaniel and Nancy (Woodside) Meryman; and **Martha A.** b 22 Jan. 1818, m Thomas Atwood, Lisbon, Maine, pub. 4 Apr. 1840.

BARKER, JAMES R. - Born 2 Mar. 1815, d ??, s/o Jacob and Martha (Ross) Barker of Lewiston, Maine. James R. Barker m 24 Dec. 1838, Nancy Meryman, b 10 Jul. 1819 in Brunswick, Maine, d 24 Mar. 1888, d/o Nathaniel and Nancy (Woodside) Meryman. Children: **Maria Ellen** b 18 Oct. 1839, d 13 Oct. 1840; **Henry M.** q.v.; **Ellen** b 7 Feb. 1845, d 28 Aug. 1846; **Harriet E.** b 8 Oct. 1847, m Rev. J.S. Richards 8 Jul. 1874; **James R. Jr.** b 20 Apr. 1851, d 21 Nov. 1880; **Willie H.** b 2 Jul. 1855, resided in Boston, Massachusetts [letter dated 1895 from James R. Barker while in Deer Isle, Maine].

BARKER, JEDDIAH - Born 14 Feb. 1821, d -- Feb. 1895, s/o William and Dorcas (Morrell) Barker. Jedediah Barker resided in New Vineyard, Maine, at the time of his death. He m May B. Norton, 17 Apr. 1843. Children: **Alonso** m Annie Ridgeway; **Lena** d age 5 years; **Jane** m Hiram Bangs of Farmington, Maine; **Alphonso** m Lisa J. Ramsdell; **Augusta**; **Edward** m Olive Ramsdell; **Lena** m Hiram Ramsdell; **Mary** m Daniel Wilcox.

BARKER, JOHN - Born ??, d ??, s/o William and ?? Barker. He was a twin to Isaac Barker (see above). He m Ruth Loller. Children: **Susan**; **John**; **Arad**; **Lorenso**; and **Mary Ann**. [Letter from Mrs. G. W. Dobbins, 1896.]

BARKER, JONATHAN - Born ??, d ??, s/o Asa and ?? Barker. Jonathan Barker m Catherine Mitchell. Children: had at least one son, **Cyrus I.** q.v. [*History of Androscoggin County, Maine*, by Georgie Drew Merrill, editor, published by W. A. Ferguss, 1891, pg. 432.]

BARKER, MARCELLUS C. - Born 23 Mar. 1845, d 1921, buried in Notch Cemetery in New Vineyard, Maine, s/o Charles and Sarah R. (Barker) Barker. Marcellus C. Barker m (1) Mary Morton, b 1846, d 1877, d/o George and Katherine (Storer) Morton, and m (2) 23 Dec. 1878 Mrs. Annie Rebecca (Rogers) Nottage, b 16 May 1846 in Moscow, Maine, d/o Francis and Rhoda (Rowe) Rogers, wid/o of Josiah T. Nottage. Children of 2nd wife: **Dana Hanson** b 3 Apr. 1872, m Minnie B. Smith, 30 Apr. 1896; **Grace Greenwood** b 11 Mar. 1882; **Goldie May** b 5 Sep. 1886. [Letter from Marcellus C. Barker, 1897, to Elder.]

BARKER, ORIGEN - Born 2 Nov. 1827 [vital records of Lewiston, Maine, p. 97], d ??, s/o David and Priscilla (Littlefield) Barker. Origen Barker m 5 Jul. 1857 Hannah Ludden, d/o Daniel and Catherine (----) Ludden of Canton, Maine. Children: **Preston C.** b 17 Apr. 1858, m Lucy Sampson 30 Mar. 1882; **Louisa C.** b 29 Apr. 1860, m Preston Knowlton 26 May 1881; **Estella C.** b 2 Jan. 1862, m John Briggs 14 Oct. 1881; **Emma F.** b 2 Nov. 1873, m Geo. Brown, 17 Oct. 1896; **Daniel L.** b 23 Sep. 1876/1877, resided in Canton, Maine, d 14 Sep. 1959 in Norway, Maine, buried in Pine Grove Cemetery in Canton, Maine [vital records of Turner, Maine, file cards at town office].

BARKER, ORLAND - Born -- Mar. 1846, d ??, s/o Daniel & Mary C. McIntire. Orland Barker m Fannie Whitcomb. Children: **Chester; Edward; Levi; Charles; Gertrude.**

BARKER, RODNEY C. - Born 14 Aug. 1840, d 5 Jan. 1886, s/o Cyrus Jr. and Mary Jane (Berry) Barker. Rodney C. Barker m 9 Jul. 1865 Mary E. Gove, d 24 Feb. 1889. Children: **Ella G.** b 20 Mar. 1867, m Sylvanus P. Hussey, 24 Nov. 1887; **Sara R.** b 23 Nov. 1869, m 27 Nov. 1890 Jacob Hersey, b 16 Jul. 1869; **Mattie** b 28 Aug. 1871, m 9 Jan. 1895 Edwin S. Rogers, b 29 Aug. 1871; **Ines C.** b 23 Nov. 1873, m 16 Apr. 1894 H. Beecher Sleeper, b 1 Aug. 1868 in Sherman Mills, Maine. [Letter dated 1896 from Mrs. Sleeper.]

BARKER, STEPHEN - Born 12 Oct. 1832, d 4 Jun. 1892, s/o William and Dorcas (Morrell) Barker. Stephen Barker m 4 Dec. 1859 Ellen Keith, who m (2) ---- Welch. Children: **William G.** b 3 Nov. 1860, m (1) Emma Wilcox, d 16 Mar. 1893, and (2) Mrs. Allie D. Walton, 27 Jul. 1895; **Ada** b 23 Oct. 1862, m F. A. Leavitt; and **Ida** b 23 Oct. 1862, m E. C. Winslow.

BARKER, WATERMAN - Born ??, d ??, s/o Amos and Elsie (Keene) Barker. Waterman Barker m (1) Elisa Leadbetter, and m (2) Carrie Norton (Baker) (Parsons) (Dayen) (Luce), her fifth husband. Children: **Wesley;** and **Ernest.**

BARKER, WILLIAM - Born 8 Mar. 1760, d ??, s/o Caleb and ?? Barker. William m Annis Austin. Children: **C a l e b** b -- Aug. 1782; Diah m Mary Merrill; **William** b 1784 q.v.; **John** q.v.; **Isaac** q.v.; **Jacob** q.v.

BARKER, WILLIAM - Born 1784, d 14 Apr. 1866 age 82 years and 11 months and 3 days, s/o William and Annis (Austin) Barker. William Barker resided in Farmington, Maine, in 1850. He m -- Nov. 1806 [Vital Records of Lewiston, Maine, p. 422] Dorcas Morrell, d 26 May 1858. Children: **Cynthia** b 31 Jul. 1808, d -- Aug. 1844, unm; **Annis** b 26 Feb. 1810, d in Baltimore, Maryland [see letter at AHS - Auburn], m Joseph Dyer, pub. 4 Jan. 1830; **Daniel** q.v.; **Joanna** b 2 Nov. 1814, d 2 Jan. 1852, m (1) Esekiel Gilman and (2) Wm. Corbett, -- Nov. 1851; **Charles** q.v.; **Jeddiah** q.v.; **Lucinda** b 7 Apr. 1822, d 13 Sep. 1862, m Nathan Cutler, Jr., 9 Sep. 1855; **Martha** b 17 Oct. 1825, d -- Sep. 1893, m Lemuel Childs; **William** b 20 Mar. 1828, d -- Feb. 1894; **Dorcas** b 22 Jul. 1830, d -- Apr. 1864, m Peter Corbett, 4 Nov. 1852; **Stephen** b 12 Oct. 1832, q.v.

BARKER, WILLIAM T. - Married (1) Flora E. Wheeler, Akron, Cal., m (2) Elizabeth Pongart.

BARKER, WM. C. - Child: **Almon C.** b 9 Aug. 1885.

BARRON, BENJAMIN - Born 10 Nov. 1804, d ??, s/o Jotham and Mehitable (Wood) Barron. Benjamin Barron m Olive Drinkwater of Cumberland, Maine. Children: **Margaret** b 3 Aug. 1842; **Benjamin Francis** b 15 Jun. 1846, d 23 Sep. 1847; **Olive Maria** b 23 Dec. 1847; **Frances G.** b 10 Oct. 1849; **Frederick W.** b 27 Mar. 1852; **Gilbert E.** b 18 Apr. 1856, m Mary Thompson.

BARRON, GEORGE - Born 4 Jul. 1824, d ??, s/o John and Martha (Crockett) Barron. Children: **John** b 14 Oct. 1858; **Frank** b 6 Jul. 1861.

BARRON, JAMES - Born 19 Jul. 1829, d 26 Aug. 1896, s/o John and Martha (Crockett) Barron. James Barron m (1) Martha Stinson and (2) 9 Aug. 1860, Irene Curts. Children: **F r e d** b 26 Mar. 1865, d 29 Jan. 1866; **Lillian** b 20 Nov. 1866, m Orrin Cash, 17 Oct. 1894; **Edgar** b 20 Feb. 1868; **Walter** b 5 Dec. 1870.

BARRON, JOHN - Born 17 Oct. 1792 in Everett, Mass., d 10 Apr. 1860 in Topsham, Maine, s/o Jothan and Mehitable (Wood) Barron. John Barron m Martha Crockett. Children: **L u c y** b 1 Jan. 1818, d 8 May 1885, unm; **Charles** b 5 Sep. 1821, d 9 Mar. 1871, m Nancy Crockett; **George** q.v.; **James** q.v.

BARRON, JOSEPH - Born 23 Feb. 1802, d ??, s/o Jothan and Mehitable (Wood) Barron. Joseph Barron m (1) Angeline Rollins, and (2) May Thompson, and (3) Mrs. Hannah Jordan (nee White), 9 Nov. 1867. Children: **Joseph Gerrish** b 12 Feb. 1834, m Mary Thu---; **Angeline Rollins** b 28 Jan. 1836, m James Robinson; **Martha Hale** b 10

Mar. 1839, d 11 Mar. 1846; **James B.** b 24 Apr. 1841, m Emma B. Read of Freeport, 10 Dec. 1884; **Mary** b 3 Sep. 1844, d 20 Jul. 1860.

BARRON, JOTHAN - Born 2 Dec. 1758, d 2 Mar. 1815 in Minot, Maine, m Mehitable Wood. Children: **Hitty** b 7 Jul. 1790; **John** q.v; **Charles** b 5 Feb. 1795; **William** b Jun. 1797 q.v.; **Harriet** b 19 Apr. 1799, m Rev. Wm. Johnson of Brunswick, ME; **Joseph** q.v.; **Benjamin** b 23 Feb. 1802, d 6 Apr. 18--; **Benjamin** q.v.; **Lucianna** b 25 Dec. 1806, d 10 Dec. 1880, unm; **Hosea** b 11 Feb. 1811, went west, unm.

BARRON, OLIVER - Born 3 Aug. 1769, d ??, s/o ?? Oliver Barron m Mrs. Molly Green, pub. 11 Oct. 1795. Children: **Nathan G.** b 27 Nov. 1799, d 6 Mar. 1815; **Mittie** b 7 Jan. 1802, d 3 Sep. 1804; **Asa** b 11 May 1803, d 13 Sep. 1804; **Justus** b 7 Oct. 1804; **Almira** b 31 Oct. 1806; **Aurealia** b 9 Oct. 1809; **Lydia** b 5 Oct. 1811. [Vital Records of Lewiston, Maine, p. 10.]

BARRON, WILLIAM - Born 4 Jun. 1797, d 18 Jan. 1866, likely s/o Jothan and Methilda/Methida (Wood) Barron. William Barron m Betsy Knights, 23 Nov. 1828. Children: **Hattie S./Harriet Sophia** b 4 Mar. 1825, d 13 Jul. 1847, m Lyman Jordan 7 Jul. 1845; **Sarah M.** b 10 Mar. 1827, m Rev. George Knox, 21 Feb. 1847; **William** q.v.; **Ann/Anne** b 5 Jul. 1834/1884, m D.C. Linscott, 29 Jul. 1855; **Jane** b 29 May 1836, m William Pierce.

BARRON, WILLIAM - Born 4 Sep. 1832, d ??, s/o William and Betsy (Knights) Barron. William Barron m 4 Aug. 1857 May/Mary N. Hall. Children: **Hattie S.** b 18 Jan. 1862; and **Bessie M.** b 6 Apr. 1874.

BATES, BENJAMIN EDWARD - Born 12 Jul. 1808 in Mansfield, d 14 Jan. 1878, s/o Maj. Elkanah and ?? Bates.

BATTEN, ABRAHAM - Born ??, d ??, s/o ?? Abraham Batten m (1) Naomi ----, d 25 Apr. 1798 [vital records of Lewiston, Maine, p. 203], and m (2) Dolla Dorothy ----, d 23 July 1826 [vital records of Lewiston, Maine, p. 203], and m (3) Mary ----. *Child by 1st wife*: **John** b 6 Oct. 1794. *Children by 2nd wife*: **Abraham** b 27 Sep. 1800; and **William Francis**. *Child by 3rd wife*: **Henry** b 16 Apr. 1831 [vital records of Lewiston, Maine, p. 8.]

BEAL, EPHRAIM - Born 11 Sep. 1801, d 10 Apr. 1861 in Lewiston, s/o Jonathan and Lucy (Doughty) [*History of Durham, Maine* by Stackpole, 1899, p. 151]. Ephraim Beal resided in Dover, New Hampshire, and Lewiston, Maine [vital records of Lewiston, Maine, p. 414]. He m (1) Mary Hatch, 27 Mar. 1828, d 21 Apr. 1850 [vital records of Lewiston, Maine, p. 204], and (2) Mrs. May Lowell, 19 Dec. 1853. Children: **Badford W.** b 12 Sep. 1829, d 28 May 1864, m Catherine O'Neal of Abington, Massachusetts, 3 Jul. 1852; **Leonard H.** b 3 Feb. 1831, m L. Randall, 2 Apr. 1859; **Benjamin R.** b 25 Sep. 1832, d 25 Jul. 1855, m Lucy Ann Cushing, 10 Jul. 1854; **Hannah M.** b 27 Apr. 1834, m Ira Goddor, 31 De. 1857; **Harriet M.** b 27 Apr. 1834, d 31 Aug. 1854; **Mary Jane** b 8 Apr. 1836, d 12 Jun. 1841; **Jonathon Knight** b 20 Sep.

1838, d 12 Jun. 1841; **Benson** b 28 May 1840, d 25 Aug. 1861; **George D.** b 10 May 1842, d 6 Sep. 1843; **James P.** b 22 Feb. 1844, m Mrs. Catherine Beal, -- Jul. 1865; **L u c y** b 29 Mar. 1846, d 13 Nov. 1860; **Lewis C.** b 27 Feb. 1848, d 2 Oct. 1872, m Miss Shaw, 1872.

BEAN, JOHN - Born 1 Sept. 1756, d ??, s/o John and Lydia (----) Bean. John Bean m Betsey Mody/Moody, b 25 Aug. 1758, d/o Sam and Hannah Mody/Moody. Children: **Betsey** b 10 Dec. 1780; **Samuel** b 7 Nov. 1782; **Nancy** b 5 Aug. 1784; **Lydia** b 15 Feb. 1787; **John** b 7 Apr. 1789; **Ivory** q.v.; **Hannah** b 7 Apr. 1794. [Vital Records of Lewiston, Maine, p. 9.]

BEAN, IVORY - Born 15 May 1791, d 26 Apr. 1842, s/o John and Betsey (Mody/Moody) Bean. Ivory Bean m Phileas Savage, 22 Dec. 1814. Children: **Orison** b 2 Jul. 1816; **Ivory** b 2 Jun. 1818; **Rosamond W.** b 20 Oct. 1820; **Loren** b 20 Oct. 1822, d 13 Apr. 1832; **Hiram P.** b 24 Feb. 1836; **Philena** b 10 Aug. 1839; **Thaxter W.** b 18 Sep. 1831.

BENNETT, NATHANIEL - Born 18 Nov. 1768, d 2 Oct. 1852, s/o ?? Nathaniel Bennett m (1) Betsy Whitney, b 10 Sep. 1774, d 17 Aug. 1819, and m (2) Hannah (Hildreth) (Douglas/Douglass) d 7 Aug. 1852, d/o Paul Hildreth, wid/o James Douglas/Douglass, Jr. Hannah (Hildreth) Douglas/Douglass and James Douglas/Douglass, Jr. had the following children: David Douglas/Douglass b 22 Aug. 1801 in Gardiner, ME; Paul Douglas/Douglass b 22 Jul. 1803; Thomas Douglas/Douglass b 31 Oct. 1804; George H. Douglas/Douglass b 26 Aug. 1806 in Litchfield, ME. Nathaniel Bennett had the following children from either one or both of his wives: **Thaddeus** b 7 Nov. 1811; **Sally** b 22 Feb. 1813; **Stedman** b 2 Feb. 1815; **Aseneth** b 2 Feb. 1817; **William** b 6 Apr. 1819; and **Robinson** b 26 Apr. 1822.

BENNETT, STEPHEN - Born -- Jan. 1791, d 30 Oct. 1855, s/o ?? Stephen Bennett m 21 Jul. 1811 Sarah Lake. Children: **S i l v i a** m Solomon Thompson; **Nathaniel** b 22 Mar. 1822, d 11 Oct. 1896, m Elisa J. Witham, 8 Oct. 1874; **Sarah C.** b 23 Aug. 1818, m Moses P. Manley of Auburn; and **James**.

BICKFORD, AARON - Born ??, d 6 Apr. 1863, s/o ??, came to Lewiston about 1810. Aaron Bickford m -- Jul. 1812 Sarah Higgins, b 12 May ----, d 12/27 Sep. 1861. Children: **M a r y** b 25 Mar. 1813, d 30 May 1886, m Isiah Dingley 29 Jul. 1832; **Ann** b 13 Apr. 1815, d 18 Sep. 1889, m Albert Meservy of Wiscasset; **J a m e s** q.v.; **J e s s e H.** **Nathaniel** b 13 Jun. 1824, d 2 Apr. 1865, m Rebecca Foss, d/o Salvan of Lewiston; **Rufus** d age 3 years; **Seth** b 6 May 1829, d 11 Jul. 1888, m (1) Lucy Crowell of Brunswick, and (2) Sophia Longey of Lewiston; **Sanie E.** b 9 Jan. 1832, m William Pattee of Bath, ME; **Elmira W.** b 17 Dec. 1835, m (1) Emery D. Sawyer of Lisbon, and (2) Robert Anis; **Jane C.** b 7 Jan. 1838, m Loyd Arnold 29 May 1858 of Damariscotta.

BICKFORD, GEORGE P. - Born ??, d ??, s/o Jesse H. and Mercy Ai (Talcott) Bickford. Children: **Jessie**; and **Earl**.

BICKFORD, JAMES - Born ??, d ??, s/o ??, bro/o Aaron Bickford. Children: **Martha Ann** b 13 Jul. 1821; **Mehitable** b 4 Jul. 1824; **Eliza Jane** b 24 Feb. 1827; **John**; **Silas**; and **James**.

BICKFORD, JAMES - Born 7 Jul. 1818, d 27 Aug. 1843, s/o Aaron and Sarah (Higgins) Bickford. James Bickford m Sarah Richardson of Greene, Maine, pub. 14 Aug. 1841. Children: **L u c y** b 1843, d California.

BICKFORD, JESSE H. - Born 27 Apr. 1822 [vital records of Lewiston, Maine, p. 81], d 5 Mar. 1892 in Auburn, Maine, s/o Aaron and Sarah (Higgins) Bickford. Jesse H. Bickford m (1) Sarah J. Spauford, d 27 Sep. 1882, 59-4-9 [gravestone, Crowley Cemetery, South Lewiston, Maine], m (2) Levina Hubbard 29 May 1886, and (3) Rolvin J. Hubbard of Oakland, Maine. Children: **George P.** m (1) Mary Mower of Greene, ME, and m (2) Mercy Ai Talcott; **Estella M.** m George Parker; **Hortense C.** m Frank Hunt of Auburn; and **Melissa** d 25 Aug. 1845, age 2 years.

BICKFORD, NATHANIEL - Born ??, d ??, s/o ?? Children: **Viola** b -- Dec. ----, m Samuel Goody of Lisbon.

BICKFORD, SETH - Born ??, d ??, s/o ?? Children: **Winfield S.** unm; **Wilber** m Fannie Ricker; **Willis** d young; **Ella** m William Gowell of Gardiner, ME; **Edward** unm.

BLAISDELL, JOHN T. - Born 18 Feb. 1808, d 24 May 1880 at Yellow Springs, Ohio, s/o Walter Robie and Sally (Tyler) Blaisdell. John T. Blaisdell m Mary G. Herrick 8 Jan. 1833, d 20 May 1870. Children: **Walter R.** b 5 Nov. 1833, d 23 Apr. 1834, age 5 months, 19 days; **Hannah H.** b 1 Oct. 1835, m Samuel McCullock 16 Oct. 1855; **Mary Elizabeth** b 28 May 1837, m Archibald McNair 21 Aug. 1862, who d in service 11 Mar. 1865; **Marinda Huntington** b 3 Oct. 1837/8, m Rev. Charles K. Marshall 2 Apr. 1861; **Elvira Priscilla** b 3 Jul. 1834, d 16 Feb. 1842, age 2 years, 7 months, 13 days; **Walter Scott** b 20 Sep. 1847, m -- Mar. 1873 to Mary Elizabeth Edwards of Paris, Bourbon Co., Ky., d.s.p. (died sine prole or died without issue) 30 Sep. 1878; **Elvina Susanna** b 24 July 1850, m Dr. James Madison Harris 6 Apr. 1884.

BLAISDELL, JOSIAH - Born ??, d ??, s/o ?? Children: **Sarah Jane** b 22 Sep. 1833, m Gilman Alden of Danville 24 Sep. 1848; and **Olive Caroline** b 21 Apr. 1840, m Joseph P. Gill.

BLAISDELL, MOSES PLUMMER - Born 3 Jun. 1855, d 1934, s/o Nathaniel and Rebecca (Plummer) Blaisdell. Moses Plummer Blaisdell m Mary Elizabeth Ware of Bangor 14 Sep. 1876, d/o Martha Ann Libby, b 21 Feb. 1853. Children: **Grace Greenwood** b 9 Oct. 1878; **Martha Ann** b 3 Jan. 1880; and **Olive Smith** b 16 Apr. 1891.

BLAISDELL, NATHANIEL - Born 25 Jul. 1814, d 15 Mar. 1888, s/o William Jr. and Rebecca (Tyler) Blaisdell. Nathaniel Blaisdell m 24

Apr. 1839 Rebecca Plummer of Bowdoinham, Maine, b 25 Jan. 1816. Children: **Jane Rebecca** b 15 Nov. 1840, d 1917, m Frank Phillips of Northport, Maine; **George Plummer** b 12 Apr. 1842; **William Plummer** q.v.; **Charlott** b 3 Jul. 1851, m William Glass of Bangor, ME; **Moses Plummer** q.v.; **Emma Estelle** b 1 Jul. 1861, d 1957, m 1878 Horatio Lewis. [See Blaisdell papers. Genealogical Outline Vol. II, #2, supplement, 1986, 185 Main St., Somersworth, NH 03878.]

BLAISDELL, ORIN W. - Born -- Dec. 1817, d 20 Jun. 1874, s/o Peter M. and Hannah (Morse) Blaisdell. Orin W. Blaisdell m Mary J. Kincaid of Whitefield, Maine, b -- Apr. 1820, d 3 Jan. 1899, d/o Gilman. Children: **Eldredge C.** b 1843, d 7 Aug. 1878, m Alice Chapman of New York City, New York, d 9 Aug. 1879, no children; **Martha** b 1845, m 1 Mar. 1874 Silas D. Cochran of Washington, D. C., d -- Nov. 1880.

BLAISDELL, PETER M. - Born 7 Jun. 1783, d 13 Sep. 1854 in Monmouth, Maine, s/o William and Rebecca (Pettingill) Blaisdell. Peter M. Blaisdell m 3 Nov. 1805 Hannah Morse, d 16 Feb. 1861, d/o Nathan. Children: **Submit** b 31 Jan. 1806, d 7 Apr. 1872, m Truxton Wood of Winthrop 1 May 1823, who d 23 Nov. 1869; **Orin** b -- May 1810, d 8 Aug. 1816; **Orin W.** q.v.; and **Lewis M.** b 26 Apr. 1819, removed west.

BLAISDELL, WALTER ROBIE - Born 14 Sep. 1775, d 19 Jan. 1831, s/o William and Rebecca (Pettingill) Blaisdell. Walter Robie Blaisdell m (1) Sally Mitchell, d 16 Nov. 1801, d/o Josiah, pub. 25 Dec. 1798, and m (2) 20 Sep. 1802 Sally Tyler of N. Gloucester, Maine, d 15 Apr. 1811, and m (3) Elizabeth Rogers of Harpswell, Maine, d 2 Jun. 1818 age 38 years in E. Argus, and m (4) 30 Jan. 1822 Ruby Adderton of Leeds, Maine. *Children of 1st wife*: **William** b 27 May 1800, unm; and **Sally** b 26 Oct. 1801, d 22 May 1831. *Children of 2nd wife*: **Dellia** b 5 Jun. 1803, d 30 Jul. 1849, unm; **Clarisa** b 24 Mar. 1805, d 19 Mar. 1807, scalded; **Josiah** b 2 Feb. 1807, d 30 Nov. 1856, m Olive H. Bradbury, Minot, 28 Apr. 1831, who d 23 Nov. 1869; and **John T.** q.v.; **Aphia** b 23 Feb. 1810, m Luther Kimball of Waterford, pub. 11 Sep. 1831. *Children of 3rd wife*: **Elizabeth** b 22 Sep. 1813, d 16 Dec. 1834; and **Polly** b 26 Feb. 1816, d 10 May 1836.

BLAISDELL, WILLIAM - Born 22 May 1748, d 23 Apr. 1816 age 68 years (Herrick Cemetery grave stone], s/o ?? William Blaisdell m 21 Mar. 1773 Rebecca Pettingill, b 22 Apr. 1750, d 9 Oct. 1831, d/o Abraham and Hannah (----) Pettingill. "He moved to N. Yarmouth, Maine, as a young man and owned a farm there. In 1774, moved to Lewiston, Maine." [Blaisdell papers, Vol. 3 #8, Jan. 1950.] Children: **Alijah** b 25 Nov. 1774, d 4 May 1787; **Walter Robie** q.v.; **Lydia** b 7 Sep. 1778, d 1 Jul. 1838, m Pettiah Barnes of Greene, pub. 13 Sep. 1795; **Mary** b 6 Aug. 1780, m David Baily of Poland, pub. 27 May 1898; **William Jr.** q.v.; **Peter M.** q.v.; **Dellia** b 30 Apr. 1785, d 2 May 1787; **Hannah** b 27 Jun. 1787, d 1 Sep. 1791; **Dellia** b 1 Apr. 1789; **Sarah** b 24 Jul. 1790, d 11 Sep. 1824, m William Jepson 12 Feb. 1815; **Nathaniel** b 6 Sep. 1792, d in the Army.

BLAISDELL, WILLIAM JR. - Born 15 Mar. 1781, d 11 Aug. 1860, s/o William and Rebecca (Pettingill) Blaisdell. William Blaisdell, Jr. m 21 Apr. 1805 Rebecca Tyler of N. Gloucester, b 4 Feb. 1774, d in Bangor 2 May 1862, age 88 years, 2 months, 29 days. Children: **Walter R.** b 27 Jan. 1806, d 1 Nov. 1888, m (1) Charlotte Legro, m (2) Maria ----, and m (3) Sarah Clement, no children; **Lucy Ham** b 30 Sep. 1807, m William Young of Woodstock, N. B.; **William** b 28 Jun. 1812, d 24 Feb. 1881, m Susan E. Dresser of Fryeburg, Me., no children; **Sullivan** b 25 Jul. 1810, d in infancy; **John J.** b 19 Jul. 1817; **Nathaniel** q.v.; and **Thomas Herrick**.

BLAISDELL, WILLIAM PLUMMER - Born 8 Mar. 1847, d 1931, s/o Nathaniel and Rebecca (Plummer). William Plummer Blaisdell m Sarah Lennon. Children: **Frank R.**; **Nellie P.**; **Sadie R.**; and **Harry G.**.

BLAKE, JOHN - Born ??, d ??, s/o ?? John Blake listed as 1-2-4 in Lewiston, Maine, 1790 census.

BLAKE, JOHN - Born ??, d ??, s/o ?? John Blake m 23 Jul. 1780 Mercy Dain [*Durham History* by Everett S. Stackpole, published by the Town of Durham, Maine, 1899, p. 152, 166.] Children: **Mary** b 17 Dec. 1787, she was the second wife of John Blethen of Lisbon, ME.

BLANCHARD, JOSEPH SR. - Born ??, d ??, s/o ?? Joseph Blanchard, Sr. m Hannah Mooer. He was elected Capt. of the First Military Co. in 1795, lived on the place occupied in 1892 by Sumner Sleeper, and left his family about ---- and never returned. Children: **Hannah B.** b 8 Mar. 1787, m Henry Cutter; **Polly** b 16 Apr. 1789, m Joseph Sawyer, 28 Jan. 1816; **Joseph** b 15 Jul. 1791; **Isaac** b 9 Sep. 1793, d 17 Apr. 1859; **Harmon** b 11 Mar. 1796, d 13 Jan. 1845.

BLETHEN, DEXTER - Born 4 Nov. 1817, d 28 Feb. 1902 age 81 years and 1 month [Crowley Cemetery], s/o ?? Dexter Blethen m 15 Nov. 1848 Charlotte H. Davis, d 1 Oct. 1880 age 57 years and 2 months [Crowley Cemetery]. Children: **Frederic** b 6 Feb. 1850; **Flora Augusta** b 28 Apr. 1852, m Holman Jordan, 9 Oct. 1883; and **Florence H.** b 9 Jun. 1864.

BLETHEN, JAMES - Born ??, d ??, s/o ??, bro/o John, who married three times. James Blethen m 1757 Miriam Day of Georgetown, Maine. Two James Blethens listed in 1790 census; one in Durham 1-1-1 and one in Lewiston and Gore adjoining 1-1-1 [age groups count of the first census, 1790]. (See *History of Durham* by Everett S. Stackpole, published by the Town of Durham, Maine, 1899, p. 151-152.)

BLETHEN, JOHN - Born ??, d ??, s/o ?? "Is belived (at age four) to have been in the garrison house at Small Point in 1722 when the Indians made an attack. Married (1) ---- and m (2) Dorcas Getchell in 1765?, b 25 Feb. 1743 at Brunswick, d/o Capt. John and Mary Getchell, and m (3) Hannah Hubbard, 27 Aug. 1789, of Durham, Maine. John d at Lisbon at the home of his daughter Hannah." (Starbird's records of Danville). Children: **Reuben** m (28 Nov.) 1799, Ruth Curtis of Little River; **Jonathan**; **William**; **Leas Polly**; **True**; **Ira**; **Chandler**; **Simeon** of Lisbon b 25 Dec. 1781 [vital records of Danville, Maine, p. 57], d 1846, m 25 Dec. 1803 [vital records of Danville, Maine, p. 57] (Polly Strout of Durham), d/o Josphua and Betsey (----) ---- [vital records of Danville, Maine, p. 57]; **Increase** (1777-1860) m widow Betsey Parker of Lisbon, ME; **Job** m Mary Jackson of Lisbon; **John** q.v.; **Jonathan**; **David**; **James** m ---- Longley lived in Durham on a farm Lot 62 SE of South West Bend; **Stephen** m Sally Black of Durham; **Esther** m Josiah Day; **Dorcas** m Edsel Webber; **Hannah** m William Green; **Rhoda** m Simeon Kimball; **Sarah** m ---- Sawyer; **Arie** m ---- Rideout of Freeport; **Judith**?; **Polly**? m (1795) Josiah True of Webster. John Blethen was reported to have been living in Lewiston 1790; however, was likely just over the line in what was later called Lisbon.

BLETHEN, JOHN - Born ??, d 11 Aug. 1844 at (76 years), s/o John who married three times. John Blethen m (14 Sept. 1794) in Durham, Maine, Sally Pomery/Pomroy, d 24 Mar. 1855. Children: **Rebecca** b 11 Feb. 1795 m John Blethen; **Polly** b 13 Apr. 1797 m Annis Garcelon; **Betsey** b 16 Aug. 1799 m Ira Green; **Judith** b 17 Jan. 1802 m William White; **Ebenezer** b 14 June 1804 m Peggy Coombs; **Sarah** b 29 June 1806 m Obedey Wonda? of Freeport; **William** b 9 Mar. 1809; **Nancy** b 29 Mar. 1812; **Phebe** b 24 Mar. 1815, d 22 Sept. 1877, 62 years, 6 months (obit), m (1) Lot Moulton and m (2) Feb. 1867 Rev. A. W. Purington; **Joseph** q.v. (This is a Bible record of a Lisbon, Maine, family plus addition from notes of Janus G. Elder). The 1790 census states that he was living on Lewiston Plt. and Gore.

BLETHEN, JOSEPH - Born in Lisbon 27 Nov. 1817, d 21 Jun. 1903 [Crowley Cemetery, South Lewiston, Maine], s/o John and Sally (Pomroy/Pomery) Blethen. Joseph Blethen m 20 Apr. 1843 Eleanor Jones. Joseph Blethen came to Lewiston in 1834 and served as apprentice with Stephen Myrick of Sabatus, who, at that time, was carrying on the furniture business. After leaving Myrick, he worked for Haly and Capt. Smith of Bath, Maine. He was also employed by Jonathan Raynes [a cabitnet-maker who resided in Danville, Maine, 1850 census group #37] of [now] Auburn, Maine, and George B. Smith of Lewiston. Soon after his marriage, he settled on the Jones place, near Crowley's Jct., South Lewiston, Maine, where he now (1903) resides. Child: **Geraldine** b 16 May 1846.

BOND, ELERY - Born 10 Dec. 1818, d -- Nov. 1888, s/o William and Mary (Wright) Bond. Elery Bond m Hannah Hatch, 9 Mar. 1842. Children: **Lizzie A.** b 23 Sep. 1844, m Alfred Richardson of Greene, pub. 7 Sep. 1867; **Stillman D.** b 10 Mar. 1846, m Ellen Frye of Portland; **Hortense** b 25 Feb. 1853, m Fred Donnell, 24 Feb. 1879; **Hilda** b -- Oct. ----, m Chas. Cappers, 1 Jan. 1875; and **Elson** b 1 Jul. 1857, unm.

BOND, GEORGE G. - Born 9 Mar. 1854, d ??, s/o Paris and ?? Bond. George C. Bond m 18 Jun. 1877 F. Webster. Children: **Harold W.** b 13 Jan. 1879.

BOND, PARIS - Born ??, d ??, s/o ?? Children: **Paris Newton** m Emma Carle; **George G.** q.v.; **Omar K.** m (1) ----, and (2) Annie M. Beals of Auburn, 25 Aug. 1880; and **Merinda** m Chas. W. Ray.

BOND, WILLIAM - Born 16 Apr. 1786, d ??, s/o ?? William Bond m 13 Jun. 1816 Mary Wright. Children: **William Pitt** q.v.; **Elery** q.v.; **Marinda** b 1 Jan. 1821, d 19 May 1876, m John Rodgers of Phippsburg, 14 Jun. 1849; **Phronissa** b 12 Apr. 1823, d 18 Mar. ----, m George Wing; **A. K. P.** b 6 Apr. 1825, m Delia Morey from Nantucket; **Newton** b 10 Aug. 1827, unm.; **Omar** b 17 Sep. 1829, d 16 Apr. 1861, m (1) Hattie A. Merrill, and (2) Helen Crowell of Lincoln, 10 Sep. 1882; **Houghton** b 10 Aug. 1834; **Benton** b 1 May 1836; **General Gaines** b 14 Feb. 1839, m S. Ellis of Searsport.

BOND, WILLIAM PITT - Born 29 Jan. 1817, d 17 Nov. ----, s/o William and Mary (Wright) Bond. William Pitt Bond m 15 Oct. 1843 Rebecca Barnes. Children: **Adrianna**; **Scott C.**; **Telotes**; and **Mary**.

BRACKETT, CHARLES - Born ??, d ??, s/o ?? Children: **Frank** b 30 May 1850, m Julia A. Braley; **William** b 17 Apr. 1853, m Prescott; **Mary** b 10 Apr. 1860; **George** b 27 Apr. 1861; **Edwin F.** b -- Sep. 1865; and **Fred** b -- Mar 1872.

BRACKETT, SAMUEL - Born in Gorham, Maine, 8 Jun. ----, d 14 Sep. 1883, s/o ?? Samuel Brackett m Louise Ingraham, -- Apr. 1821. Children: **Charles** b 18 Aug. 1823, d 20 Feb. 1894, m (1) Jennie Brailey, -- Apr. 1859, and (2) Mary Cook -- Jun. 185-, d 9 Jul. 1858 age 31 years [obit *Morning Star* issue 4 May 1858, see also issue 1 Jun. 1853 obit of Eva F. Cook, sister to Mary (Cook) Brackett], d/o Hanson and Nancy Cook; **Sarah A.** b 15 Aug. ----, m Charles H. Whitney, -- Oct. ----; **Julia A.** d 9 Jun. 1859, m Henry C. Simons, 25 Dec. 1854; **Caroline L.** b 17 Jul. 1831, m Washington Phillips, 5 Jun. 1855; **Mary J.** b 9 Jun. ----, m Chas. Whittemore, 29 Jul. 1855; **Arexine I.** b 8 Apr. ----, m Edwin Rowell, 26 Jul. 1864; **Elisa** b 31 Jul. ----, unm; **Edwin J.** b 30 Sep. ----, m Rosie Laughton Jewell, pub. 6 Nov. 1867; **Lissie I.** b 31 Jul. ----, unm.

BRIGGS, CHARLES C. - Born 24 Sep. 1840, d ??, s/o John A. and ?? Briggs. Charles C. Briggs m (1) 13 Jul. 1868 Margaret Haskell, and (2) Mary Geney. Children: **Betty**; **John H.**; **Carl**; **Helen**; **Margaret**; and **Mary**.

BRIGGS, EDWIN F. - Born 29 Aug. 1866, d ??, s/o George A. and ?? Briggs. Child: **Ethel M.** b 1888.

BRIGGS, GEORGE A. - Born 17 Jul. 1835, d ??, s/o Reubin and Mrs. Mary (Thompson) Briggs. George A. Briggs m Permelia Austin. Children: **Lissie E.** b 30 Apr. 1857, m 26 Jan. 1878; **Nellie F.** b 23 Apr. 1859, m Joseph Woodbury, 8 Sep. 1877; **Edwin F.** q.v.

BRIGGS, JOHN A. - Born in Minot, Maine, 6 Jan. 1810, d 14 Oct. 1885, s/o ?? John A. Briggs resided in 1850 Danville, Maine. His occ' - millwright [1850 census family #28]. He m (1) 20 Mar. 1837 Annett Swan of Waterford, Maine, and (2) m 15 Mar. 1842 Harriet Farrar of Waterford, and m 14 Jun. 1860 (3) Louisa Stinson of Woolwich, Maine. Children: **Emily E.** b 19 Feb. 1838, m George Aldrich, 23 Jun. 1856; **Charles C.** q.v.; **Annette Maria** b 11 Mar. 1843, d 16 Nov. 1847; **Fred Farrar** [named Frederick in 1850 census of Danville, Maine, census #28] b 8 Oct. 1845, d 18 Dec. 1866; **Harriet Farrar** b 11 Mar. 1847, d 1 Jan. 1853; **John Henry** b 6 Mar. 1851, d 2 Jan. 1853; **Herbert** b 8 Feb. 1853, m Ernestine Sampson of Chelsea; and **Anne Whitman** b 14 Mar. 1855, m Edwin Taylor of Sandwich.

BRIGGS, REUBIN - Born ??, d ??, s/o ?? Reubin Briggs m 7 Nov. 1830 [VR] widow Mrs. Mary Thompson. Children: **M a r i a h** b 27 Jan. 1831, d 1893, m Hewitt Bailey; **M o s e s** b 26 Mar. 1833, d 1878, m (1) Sarah Libby, and m (2) 14 Mar. 1857 Amanda Hill; **G e o r g e A.** q.v.; **M a r y A n n** b 18 Feb. 1838, m ---- Wheelock of Lowell, Massachusetts.

BROOKS, AI - Born 31 Jan. 1804, d 30 Sep. 1871 [*Morning Star*, issue 22 Nov. 1871], s/o ??. Ai Brooks m (1) 18 Jun. 1826 Martha Litchfield, d 25 Nov. 1828 age 25 years, and m (2) 3 Dec. 1829, pub. 8 Nov. 1829, Jane Field, and m (3) Eliza ----, d 5 Jan. ---- age 61 years [*Morning Star*, issue 23 Mar. 1870]. *Children of first wife*: **Martha Ann** b 12 Apr. 1827, d 16 Aug. 1828; and **Mary L.** b 16 Nov. 1828, m John Goss 11 Jul. 1847. *Children of second wife*: **M a r k G.** b 28 Dec. 1830, m Abbie Leaver of Industry; **Martha Jane** b 31 Dec. 1832, d 1 Nov. 1859, m Amos Crowley; **Albert S.** b 22 Nov. 1835, m Lovinia B. Chandler 25 Nov. 1858, d/o Seth of Lewiston; **Ai J r.** q.v.; **H a z o Field** b 2 Sep. 1841, d 13 Dec. 1862.

BROOKS, AI JR. - Born 28 Apr. 1837, d ??, s/o Ai and Jane (Field) Brooks. Ai Brooks, Jr. m 18 Jun. 1847 Threse Melcher of Danville, Maine. Children: **Nellie**; **Isaac**; and **Nettie**.

BROOKS, ALBERT - Born ??, d ??, s/o ?? Children: **Seth**; **Martha J.**; **George**; and **Warren**.

BROOKS, HAM - Born 21 Jun. 1809, d ??, s/o William Sr. and Anna (Ham) Brooks. Ham Brooks m (1) -- Aug. 1832, pub. 5 Aug. 1832, Margaret Ames, d 21 Jan. 1872 age 58 years and 5 months, d/o Winslow, and m (2) -- Jun. 1873 Maria Bickford. Children: **Cordelia Adaline** b 25 Dec. 1833, m Rev. George W. Quimby, pub. 9 Mar. 1861; **Elizabeth A.** b 23 Oct. 1835, d in Lowell 13 May 1867, m Charles D. Starbird, pub. 21 Feb. 1857; **Priscilla Jane** b 1 Oct. 1837, m Dr. B.F. Surgess of Auburn, 4 Feb. 1870; **Henrietta M.** b 10 Mar. 1841, m Alvory C. Pullen of Livermore, pub. 17 May 1866; **Georgiana W.** b 24 Mar. 1843, d 13 Aug. 1867, aged 24 years 4 months; **Sylvia E. M.** b 21 Oct. 1848, m Oscar S. Williams of Dunham who was b 2 Jul. 1844, d 14 Oct. 1893, m 20 Oct. 1870; **C h a r l e s E.** b 8 Aug. 1847, d 28 May 1881, age 33 years 9 months 20 days; **A r t h u r C.** b 28 Dec. 1851, m

Elizabeth Hilton of Augusta; **Walter M.** b 8 Feb. 1854, m Ada Bearce, d/o Pitt Bearce of Auburn; **Winslow H.** b n25 Jun. 1839, d 13 Apr. 1840, at 9 months; **Frank S.** b 30 Sep. 1852, d 22 Sep. 1853.

BROOKS, HAM JR. - Born -- Jan. 1875, d ??, s/o ??.

BROOKS, JOHN - Born 17 Nov. 1811, d ??, s/o William Sr. and Anna (Ham) Brooks. John Brooks m (1) 16 Sep. 1832, pub. 19 Aug. 1832, Susan Merrill, d/o Ezekiel, and m (2) 16 Aug. 1842 Mary Stinchfield. Children: **Anna** m ---- Larrabee, went to N. Carolina; **Sally** m ---- Haskell.

BROOKS, JOHN JR. - Born 12 Jul. 1775, d 1819, s/o John, Sr. and ?? Brooks. John Brooks, 2nd was chosen a highway surveyor 1802-1804. He was a private in Capt. Pelatiah Smith's company in 1813, and an ensign in Thomas Goss's company in 1815. It is thought that John, Jr. moved to Lewiston with his son, John III, about 1817 where John, Jr. d 21 May 1819. John Brooks, 2nd m 10 July 1796 at Cape Elizabeth, Maine, Ann Wheeler, b 11 Aug. 1772 at Cape Elizabeth. Children: **William** b 24 Dec. 1796; **Betsey** b 8 Oct. 1798 at Pejepscot, ME; **John III** q.v.; **Daniel** b 27 Nov. 1802; **Eunice** b 15 Feb. 1805; **Joseph Wheeler** b 11 Aug. 1807; **Joshua** b 26 Jan. 1810. [Vital Records of Danville, Maine, p. 77; vital records of Lewiston, Maine, p. 98; Starbird's records of Danville.]

BROOKS, JOHN III - Born 19 Nov. 1799 in Danville, Maine [Lewiston vital records, p. 98], d 9 Sep. 1831 age 32 years and 10 months [Garcelon Cemetery], s/o John Jr. and Anna (Wheeler) Brooks. John Brooks, III m 22 Dec. 1822 Martha Ham, d 14 Jan. 1879 [Garcelon Cemetery]. Children: **Josiah Robinson** b in Greene 18 Oct. 1823, d 19 Apr. 1848; **James Warren** b in Danville, 20 Aug. 1825, d 30 Nov. 1854 at Boston, MA, age 29 years 3 months 12 days, formerly of Lewiston, Maine [*Morning Star* obit issue 24 Jan. 1855]; **Joseph** b in Lewiston 5 May 1828; **Ann Wheeler** b 5 May 1828; and **Lydia Jane** b 2 Jul. 1830 [vital records of Lewiston, p. 98].

BROOKS, JOHN SR. - Born 5 Dec. 1739 [Old Style] in Portsmouth, New Hampshire, d 1807 age 67 years at Pejepscot [now Auburn], Maine, s/o Joshua and Ann (Staples) Brooks. John Brooks, Sr. was "an honest and industrious man" [*E. Argus and Portland Gazette*, 16 and 20 July 1807]. He settled first in Falmouth [now Portland] and later in 1797 moved to Pejepscot Claim with his son, John, Jr., settling in the southwestern part of Pejepscot. He was a farmer for over twenty years. He served as a tythingman in 1804. Children: **Abigail** b 3 Mar. 1774, d 25 Oct. 1846; **John, Jr.** q.v.; **Catherine; Martha; Lydia;** and **William.** [Starbird's records of Danville, Maine.]

BROOKS, JOSHUA - Born ??, d ??, s/o William and Mary (Fogg) Brooks. Joshua Brooks m 3 Aug. 1733 Ann, d/o John and Mary (Dixon) Staples of Portsmouth, New Hampshire. Child: **John, Sr.** q.v. [Starbird's records of Danville, Maine.]

BROOKS, MARK - Born ??, d ??, s/o ?? Child: **Annie**.

BROOKS, WILLIAM SR. - Born 24 Feb. 1777, d 18 Nov. 1867, aged 90 years 8 months, s/o ?? William Brooks, Sr. m Anna Ham, pub. 20 May 1798, b 17 Nov. 1781, d 19 Jun. 1867, aged 86 years 7 months [Garcelon Cemetery]. He walked to Ohio and back [Thomas Hodgkin diary]. Children: **Sally** b 13 Feb. 1799, d 29 Jan. 1836, aged 36 years 11 months 14 days, m Jonathan Hodgkins; **Anna** b 8 Jul. 1801, d 4 Feb. 1802; **Daniel** b 3 Dec. 1802, d 7 Dec. 1802; **Ai** q.v.; **Orpha** b 22 Sep. 1806, m (1) Jonathan Hodgkins, m (2) Benjamin Merrill 22 Mar. 1829; **Ham** q.v.; **John** q.v.; **William** b 26 May 1814, drowned -- Jun. ----, age 8 years; **Anna** b 6 Jul. 1818, d 27 Aug. 1828; **Henry C.** b 13 Oct. 1820, m Laura Dow of Mt. Vernon; **Octavia** b 16 Feb. 1824, d 1 Dec. 1865 in Virginia, was in the Army, m James P. Sutherland of Lisbon 16 Jul. 185-; **Israel** b 9 Jul. 1816, d age 10 months.

BUBIER, ANDREW - Born 10 Jun. 1768, d 12 May 1847 [Crowley Cemetery], s/o ?? Andrew Bubier m Miriam Grover. Children: **Lucy** b 8 May 1789, m Edward Lowell; **Mark** q.v.; **Miriam** b 2 Feb. 1795, m Lewis Ware; **Andrew** b 8 Jun. 1797, m Eunice Bickford, 25 Apr. 1819; **Stephen** b 15 Jul. 1799, d 1 Sep. 1799; **Stephen** q.v.; **Eunice** b 10 Sep. 1802, d 10 Oct. 1804; **Benjamin** q.v.

BUBIER, BENJAMIN - Born 18 May 1805, d ??, s/o Andrew and Miriam (Grover) Bubier. Benjamin Bubier m 1 Aug. 1826 Polly Howland of Bowdoin, Maine. Children: **Lorenso** b 10 Oct. 1826; **Eunice** b 12 Jan. 1828; **Miriam** b 21 Nov. 1829; **Benjamin** b 23 Jan. 1832; and **Mahitable** b 9 Dec. 1833. [*Bubier Family* by M. M. Bubier, published by John Greene Co., Inc., circa 1959, p. ?? - unknown due to loss of book.]

BUBIER, CHRISTOPHER - Born ??, d a pauper 1 Feb. 1841 age 78 years (VR 204 Lewiston), s/o ?? Christopher Bubier m Hannah Todd, d 1 Apr. 1841 age 78 years (VR 204) of Bath. Children: **Samuel** q.v.; **John** b 25 Apr. 1790; **Nancy** b 2 Apr. 1792; **Joseph** b 25 Mar. 1794; **Hannah** b 7 Jul. 1796; **Thomas** b 8 Sep. 1799; **Christopher Jr.** q.v.; **Filice** b 3 Jul. 1803; **Betsey** b 18 Sep. 1805; **Martha** b 18 Sep. 1810; **Gilbert** b 4 Jul. 1811, and **Julia Ann** b 29 Jun. 1813.

BUBIER, CHRISTOPHER JR. - Born 1 Jan. 1801, d ??, s/o Christopher and Hannah (Todd) Bubier. Christopher Bubier, Jr. m -- Oct. 1824, pub. 21 Sep. 1824, Mary Ann Chadbourn/Chadbourne. Children: **Darius King** b 7 Apr. 1825; **Abieser Bridges** b 19 Sep. 1826, d 28 May 1866, m Lydia A. Brown, -- Jan. 1847; **Nancy Watts** b 25 May 1828; **Dianna** b 10 Jun. 1830; **Mary Ann** b 19 Sep. 1831, d -- Dec. 1857; **Dorothy Malinda** b 31 Jul. 1835; **Thomas Locke** b 18 Jun. 1837; **Clarinda** b 22 May 183-; **James Henry** b 18 Jul. 1841; and **Amanda Jane** b 15 Jan. 1845.

BUBIER, GEORGE - Born 28 Apr. 1814, d 17 Sep. 1887 age 72 years and 5 months [Herrick Cemetery], s/o Samuel and Amy (Grover?) Bubier. George Bubier m (1) Rebecca Jepson, pub. 31 Mar. 1836, (2)

Callem Haskell, pub. 27 Mar. 1852, (3) Alilia Potter, pub. 17 Dec. 1859, and (4) Adelia Reonee of Gorham, pub. 2 Apr. 1865. Children: **Mary Abigail** b 6 Dec. 1836, m Edward Chadbourne, pub. 16 Dec. 1856; **George** q.v.; **Elisabeth** m David Davis, 18 Mar. 1866; **William D.** m Hattie Wait 13 May 1877; **Rebecca A.** b 17 Oct. 1855, m Samuel Chadbourne, 1873; **Fred G.** b 27 Jan. 1870.

BUBIER, GEORGE - Born 21 Dec. 18--, d ??, s/o George and ?? Bubier. George Bubier m Sarah A. Chadbourne, pub. 21 Sep. 1861. Children: **Edwin** b 15 Sep. 1863, m Jennie Estes; **Flora** b 11 Jun. 1865, d 16 May 1891, m Benjamin Morrison, 2 Jan. 1886; **Albert** b 1 Sep. 1872, d 29 Sep. 1875; **Alta May** b 21 Aug. 1879; **Alfred C.** b 21 Feb. 1884.

BUBIER, EDWARD/EDWIN T. - Born 15 Sep. 1863, d ??, s/o ?? Edward/Edwin T. Bubier m Jennie Estes of Troy. Child: **Frank Edson** b 15 Apr. 1889.

BUBIER, DEACON JOHN - Born 16 Feb. 1812, d 26 Sep. 1881 age 69-7-11 [Riverside Cemetery], s/o Samuel and ?? Bubier. Deacon John Bubier m 4 Feb. 1830 Mrs. Abigail Hanson/Vickery of Lewiston, d 8 Oct. 1868 [Riverside Cemetery]. *Child of Mrs. Abigail Hanson/Vickery and her previous husband*: **Mathias Hanson** b 8 Mar. 1826 in Turner, Maine. *Children of Mrs. Abigail Hanson/Vickery and Deacon John Bubier*: **Amy** b 23 May 1830; **William**; **Charles**; **Wheeler**; and **Dexter**.

BUBIER, JOSEPH - Born ??, d ??, s/o ?? Joseph Bubier m Phebe Cornish of Bowdoin, 17 Dec. 1815. Children: **Martha** b in Bowdoin, 14 May 1816, m Lewis Ware; **Stockbridge** q.v.; **Joseph** b 6 Mar. 1820, unm; **Otis** b 6 Apr. 1822; **Caroline S.** b in Dexter, 2 Mar. 1824, m Darius Bubur; **Elisha C.** b 22 May 1826; **Chas. Cornish** b 12 Oct. 1828.

BUBIER, MARK - Born 2 Jan. 1793, d ??, s/o Andrew and Miriam (Grover). Mark Bubier m (1) 17 mar. 1816 Betsey Shepard/Shephard, and m (2) Abigail Grover. Children: **Alfred** b 9 Dec. 1817, m Nancy Withee Bubier; **Daniel** b 9 Oct. 1819, m Happy Steward; **Nancy** b 6 Sep. 1821, m ---- Brackett; **Caroline** b 14 Nov. 1823, d 1 Mar. 1824; **Caroline** b 8 Jan. 1825, unm; **Horace** b 17 May 1827; **Sewall M.** b 28 Oct. 1830; and **Cyrus**.

BUBIER, SAMUEL - Born 18 Jan. 1788, d ??, s/o Christopher and Hannah (Todd) Bubier. Samuel Bubier m (1) Amy (Grover?), and m (2) Mary Vickery, pub. 19 May 1825 [VR 403.] Children: **Christopher the 3rd** b 1 Mar. 1810, m int. 7 Dec. 1830 Happy Steward d/o Edward and Abigail (Grover) Steward; **Deacon John** q.v.; **George** q.v.; **Asaneth** b 21 Mar. 1816, m David Purington; **Benjamin** b 5 Sep. 1818, unm.

BUBIER, STEPHEN - Born 11 Oct. 1800, d Clinton, Maine, s/o Andrew and Miriam (Grover) Bubier. Stephen Bubier m Sally Jenkins of Bowdoin, pub. 27 Oct. 1821. Children: **Mary Jane** b 30 Sep. 1822; **Alonso** b 19 Feb. 1824; **Stephen** b 23 Feb. 1827.

BUBIER, STOCKBRIDGE - Born 25 Mar. 1818, d 1892, s/o Joseph and Phebe (Cornish) Bubier. Stockbridge Bubier m Phebe Colby of Wales, Maine. Children: **Maria M.** b 21 Nov. 1832; **Allison Stockbridge** b 28 Jun. 1844; **Merritt Caldwell** b 20 Jun. 1849.

BURBANK, A. - Born ??, d ??, s/o ?? A. Burbank m 7 Apr. 1847 Alacin Burbank from Shelbun, New Hampshire, b 18 Jun. 1822, d 8 Jan. 1884. Children: **James L.** b 13 Aug. 1844, d 17 Aug. 1849; **James B.** b 5 Feb. 1852, d 13 Aug. 1852; **Guy H.** b 10 Aug. 1861, d 28 May 1861; and adopted child, **Willie T.** b 23 May 1867.

CALLAHAN, AUGUSTUS - Born 12 Apr. 1815 in Andover, Massachusetts, d 16 Feb. 1881, s/o Robert and Dorcas (Pettingill) Callahan. Augustus Callahan m 28 Jun. 1838 Mary Messer of Methuen, Massachusetts, d 28 Sep. 1899. Children: **George A.** q.v.; **Mary Agnes** b 10 Jun. 1843, m Geo. L. Dustin, -- May 1865; **Ellen Gardiner** b 26 Aug. 1845, m Fred Norcross of Augusta, ME, 1878; **Robert Newton** b 27 Feb. 1848; **May Adeline** b 4 May 1851, d 14 Mar. 1852. [Geo. A. Callahan, printer - 21 Lisbon St., Lewiston, ME, 189- - letter to Elder.]

CALLAHAN, GEORGE A. - Born 26 Apr. 1830/1839, d ??, s/o ??. George A. Callahan m 1859 Charlotte/Charlotte B. Turner. Children: **Alice Maud** b 20 Apr. 1862, m Chas. A Rounds of Portland, ME, -- Aug. 1882; **Lotta May** b 2 Oct. 1869, m Alphonso M. Sampson of Portland, ME, 14 Dec. 1892; **Agnes Estelle** b 1860, d 1866; **George** b 4 Sep. 1867, d 7 Feb. 1868; **Herbert Augustus** b 19 Aug. 1865, d 5 Aug. 1866; **Jennette Blake** b 16 Jul. 1868, d 28 Oct. 1869; **Augustus** b 3 Sep. 1873, d 21 Aug. 1875; and **Florence Mabel** b 26 Apr. 1877.

CARIGNAN, GEORGE - Born in Wotton, Wolfe Co., Quebec, Canada, d 19 Jan. 1890 age 73 years [was living on Broad St. in New Auburn, Maine, at the time of his death, probate #2895], buried at St. Peter and Paul's Cemetery [the necrology of St. Peter and Paul's Cemetery, 1870-1976 vol. 1 by Rev. Youville Labonte, p. 229, typed 1977?]. George Carignan moved to Lewiston, Maine, via Peabody, Vermont, in 1860 [liekly settled in Lewiston/Aubrun after 1860]. He is not listed in the 1860 or 1870 U. S. censuses of Lewiston, Maine; no vital records can be found, tax list, or dded can be found with his name on it. He has been published many times to have been the first French-Canadian to settle in Lewiston; however, Garcelon family, who are French first settled in Lewiston in 1776. Part of the Garcelon family moved to New Brunswick, Canada, only to return later and were the first French-Canadians to settle in Lewiston before 1860. George Carignan m Emilie Perreault [record in French: "et leur fille Clarissa est nee a Peabody, VT. C'est vers 1848-9. Que la famille se fixa a Wotton, et un fild Noe' est ne' la. La famille etait a Lewiston (Me) quand un autre fils, Henri, est ne'. Ce dernier fit au service avec l'arme'e americaine lors de la Guerre Espagnole en 1898, et est de'ce'de 'a Washington, D. C." See *Paroisse Saint-Pierre et Saint-Paul (CHURCH)*, a centennial history published 1971 by the parish under Rev. Father Anotonin Plourde O. P. on page no number.]

Children: **Clarissa** bc 1848-9 in Peabody, Vermont; **Noe'** b Wotton, Wolfe Co., Quebec, Canada; **Henri** b in Lewiston, served in the Army of USA during the Spanish War in 1898, d in Washington, D. C.

CARVILLE, ALMON A. - Born 20 Nov. 1843, d ??, s/o Amos H. and Eliza (Vaughan) Carville of Freeman, Maine. Almon A. Carville m Celeslia M. Hayford 22 Feb. 1874, d/o Zebedee and Nancy (Strinchfield) Hayford, b 11 Jun. 1851, in Salem, Maine. Children: **Effie E.** b 25 Apr. 1876 in Salem, ME; **Mystic L.** b 12 Dec. 1877 in Salem, ME, d 12 Apr. 1890; **Ella V.** b 21 Nov. 1879 in Salem, ME, d 20 Aug. 1880; **Alicia C.** b 10 Jun. 1881 in Salem; **Celinda T.** b 21 Aug. 1882 in Salem; and **Goldie M.** b 9 Jan. 1890 in Farmington, ME.

CARVILLE, ALONSO G. - Born 30 Nov. 1840, d ??, s/o Sewell and Tamar (Higgins) Carville. Alonso G. Carville m 3 Dec. 1865 (1) Frances A. Thompson, d 3 Dec. 1865, d/o ----, and m (2) 30 Apr. 1874 Frances J. Tracy, and m (3) 1 Jan. 1893 Edith Jones. Children: **Frank Alonzo** b 23 Dec. 1872, d 27 Jan. 1873; **Alonzo Harper** b 30 Aug. 1877; **Glenborn Alphonso** b 7 May 1898.

CARVILLE, AMOS H. - Born 20 Jun. 1820, d 10 Jun. 1890, s/o Henry and Nancy (Dyer) Carville of Freeman, Maine. Amos H. Carville m 7 Nov. 1841 Eliza Vaughn/Vaughan, b 17 Jan. 1821, d 10 Mar. 1898, d/o Zenus and Eunice (Knapp) Vaughn/Vaughan. Children: **Almon A.** q.v.; **Betsy Ann** b 10 Dec. 1848; and **Zenus Vaughan** q.v.

CARVILLE, BENJAMIN - Born 27 Feb. 1801, d 3 Apr. 1881, s/o Henry and Mary (Dyer) Carville. Benjamin Carville m 14 Apr. 1822 Abigail Hatch. Children: **Otis** q.v.; **Mary** b 16 Nov. 1823, d 20 Sep. 1873, m (1) Benson Merrill 16 Mar. 1845, and m (2) Jonathon Wright 20 Nov. 1859; **Harriet** b 15 Nov. 1825, d 19 Feb. 1851, m Elisha Hanson 5 Oct. 1845, who d 1 Jan. 1881; **Alonso** b 30 Apr. 1827, d 5 Nov. 1827; **Emery J.** b 3 Aug. 1831, d 30 Apr. 1843.

CARVILLE, BENJAMIN - Born -- Nov. 1824, d ??, s/o Joseph and Eunice Woodman (Watson) Carville of New Portland, Maine. Benjamin Carville m 25 Apr. 1852 Mary Murphy of Augusta, Maine.

CARVILLE, CHARLES - Born -- Feb. 1837, d 2 Apr. 1889, aged 52 years and 2 months, s/o of James and Harriet (Randall) Carville. Charles Carville m Maria Doyle, d 16 Dec. 1879, aged 42 years and 8 months. Children: **Annie**; **Minnie** d 7 Dec. 1889, m Loretus A. Strout of Wales, ME; **William L.** b 12 Aug. 1868; **Edith G.** b 22 Aug. 1870, m David Estes 23 Nov. 1892; and **Emmie J.** b 25 Oct. 1872.

CARVILLE, CLARENCE - Born in Lewiston 12 Aug. 1853, d ??, s/o Daniel W. and Drusilla (Dyer) Carville. Clarence Carville m 16 Dec. 1880 Harriet Ann Bagster, b 12 Apr. 1856, d/o Thomas and Sophia (Holcombe) Bagster. Children: **Helen Barber** b in Clinton, MA, 18 Nov. 1881. [Letter from Helen B. Carville, 1904.]

CARVILLE, DANIEL WATSON - Born in New Portland, Maine, d 17 Jan. 1903 in Clinton, Massachusetts, s/o Joseph and Eunice Woodman (Watson) Carville of Kinfield, Maine. Daniel W. Carville m 4 Aug. 1850 Drusilla Dyer of Lewiston, d/o Barsilla. Children: **Clarence** q.v.; **Drusilla** m Asa Smith; and **Charles**. [Obit. of Daniel Carville.]

CARVILLE, EZEKIEL - Born 13 Dec. 1798, d 11 Jun. 1829, s/o Henry Sr. and Mary (Dyer) Carville. Ezekiel Carville m pub. 18 May 1823 Lois H. Cotton of Bowdoin, Maine. Children: **Henry** b 25 Nov. 1823, d 3 Mar. 1893 in Brunswick, Maine, m Carolin A. Hale, who was b 24 Sep. 1832; **Elizabeth/Mary E./Mary Elizabeth** b 13 Nov. 1827, m 28 Mar. 1850 Samuel A. Merrill of Lawrence, Massachusetts; and **Ruth** b 13 Jun. 1826, d 30 Oct. 1826.

CARVILLE, EZRA - Born 1827, d 22 Aug. 1908, s/o James and ?? Carville. Ezra Carville m Dorcas A. Jordan, b 20 Dec. 1829, d 11 Jun. 1912, d/o Joshua and Abigail R[oberts] (Dennett) Jordan of Webster, Maine. [See *Jordan Memorial*, by Tristram Frost Jordan, published by New England History Press, 1882, reprinted 1982, pg. 277-278.] Children: **Georgia A.** b 10 Mar. 1852, m Leonard Dingley, of Lewiston, 4 years 7 months and 17 days; **Herbert J.** q.v.; **Helen R.** b 27 Oct. 1857, m Thomas ---- of Daluth, MN; **Henrietta/Etta H.** b 21 Jan. 1861, ---- Anderson; **Edwin L.** b 15 Mar. 1862; **Dora** b 6 Jun. 1866, m Clifton N. White of Belfast, ME, 4 Jul. 1889; **Walter E.** b 27 Apr 1869, d 16 Jan. 1880; and **Blanch M.** b 17 Aug. 1871, m William H. Shailon of N. Gloucester, ME, in -- Oct. 1892. [Will of Ezra Carville and will of James Carville, #2177 probate court, Androscoggin Co. and probate #7151 Androscoggin Co.]

CARVILLE, FRANK - Born ??, d 6 Feb. 1969, s/o Isaac T. and Julia Ann (----) Carville. Frank m Luella H. ---- (Carville) Carville. Children: **Rhea Maria** m ---- Horner; **Virginia Emily** m ---- Martin. [Will of Frank Carville #35859 and will of Julia Carville dated 1920.]

CARVILLE, FRANK E. - Born 4 Apr. 1869, d ??, s/o Henry Jr. and Elmira (Kilkenney) Carville. Frank E. Carville m Minnie Chandler 1 Sep. 1891, d/o Timothy T. Chandler, who was b 28 Jun. 1871. Children: **Myra F.** b 22 Apr. 1892.

CARVILLE, HARRY - Born 3 Dec. 1859 in Freeman, Maine, d ??, s/o John B. and Augusta C. (Presson) Carville of Freeman. Harry Carville m Georgia E. Woodbury of Temple, Maine, d 21 Mar. 1896. Children: **Shirley W.** b 7 Apr. 1883, d 19 Feb. 1900; **Alice Nora** b 17 Sep. 1885, d 26 Oct. 1894; and **Erlon P.** b 5 Feb. 1887, d 16 Nov. 1894.

CARVILLE, HENRY - Born ??, d 12 Jul. 1823 aged 68 [E. Argus 5 Aug. 1823], s/o ??. Henry Carville was a Revolutionary soldier and pensioner [Garcelon Cemetery, Lewiston, Maine]. He m Mary Dyer 1 Sep. 1782, who was b 17 Sep. 1759, d 11 Oct. 1845. Children: **Betsy** b 18 Mar. 1783, m Thomas Henderson of Webster, ME; **Henry** q.v.; **Sally** b 15 Jul. 1787, d 19 Nov. 1882, m (1) Amos S. Glover 1 Oct.

1815, and m (2) John Wright 12 Jun. 1834; **John** q.v.; **Luce** b 7 Sep. 1791, m Reuben Farrar of Lisbon, ME, 8 Apr. 1810; **Joseph** q.v.; **Mercy** b 22 Aug. 1796, d 19 Mar. 1799; **Ezekiel** q.v.; **Benjamin** b 27 Feb. 1801, d 3 Apr. 1881, m Abigail Hatch, who d 5 Feb. 1883, d/o John, 14 Apr. 1822; **James** q.v.; **Mercy** b 5 Jan. 1805, d in Bismark, ND, m Isaac C. Thompson, pub. 8 Oct. 1825, who d 14 Jul. 1861. [Vital Records of Lewiston, Maine, p. 11.]

CARVILLE, HENRY - Born ??, d ??, s/o Ezekiel and ?? Carville. Children: **Ada Lois** b 7 Dec. 1867, m D. Merrill.

CARVILLE, HENRY - Born 1 Jun. 1818, d 22 Apr. 1894, aged 75 years 10 months 22 days, s/o Henry and Nancy (Dyer) Carville of Freeman, Maine. Children: **Alonzo**; **Irving**; and **Almire** m Orin Brackley.

CARVILLE, HENRY - Born 4 Apr. 1785, d 17 Oct. 1864 aged 79 years and 6 months, s/o Henry and Mary (Dyer) Carville. Henry Carville m 2 Jul. 1809 Nancy Dyer, b 15 Feb. 1791, d 5 Jul. 1872, d/o Elkanah Dyer of Lewiston. Children: **Betsy** b 11 May 1810, d 4 Jun. 1835, aged 25 years; **Nancy** b 3 May 1812, d 19 May 1812; **Henry** b 2 May 1813; **Mary** b in 1814, d 8 Nov. 1839, aged 25 years; **Henry Jr.** q.v.; **Amos H.** q.v.; **Hiram** b 1824/1825, d 8 Sep 1839, aged 14 years and 10 months; **Jane** b 25 Jul. 1837, d 28 Jun. 1896, aged 69 years, m Samuel Luce, who d in Freeman, ME, 13 Dec. 1889?; **John B.** q.v.; **Elmira** b 5 Mar. 1830 in Freeman, Maine, d 25 Aug. 1899, m 7 Aug. 1853 Sewell Goss, d 28 May 1870, s/o Thomas and Sally (Jordan) Goss [see late Charles Starbird's notes on Auburn families at Androscoggin Historical Society]; and **Elvira** d in 1867, m John Luce of Freeman. [See Leland Edwin Peary's records of Freeman, Maine, families at Cutler Library, Farmington, Maine; placed in the library by Colonial Daughter Chapter N. S. D. A. R., vol. 9 of a set of typescripts.]

CARVILLE, HENRY JR. - Born 1 Jun. 1818, d 22 Apr 1894 aged 75 years and 10 months and 22 days, s/o Henry and Nancy (Dyer) Carville of Freeman, Maine. Henry Carville, Jr. m (1) 1840 Harriet Luce, d -- Feb. 1863, d/o Irvin Luce of New Portland, Maine, and m (2) 10 Aug. 1865 Elmira Kilkenny/Kilkenney, b 17 Mar. 1832, d 5 May 1898, and m (3) ----. *Children of 1st wife*: **Hiram** b 23 May 1840, d -- Apr. 1861; **Henry E.** q.v.; **Alonzo P.** b 14 Jun. 1844/1845, m Lydia A. Harvey 22 Aug. 1872, d/o Joseph Harvey, who was b 25 Jan. 1848; **Ellen/Mary Ellen** b 12 Dec. 1846/1847, d 2 Feb. 1891, m William L. Pratt, 4 Sep. 1864; **Elmira** b 1 Jan. 1849, m Orren/Orrin Brackley 1 Jan. 1867, who was b 2 Dec. 1846; **Frank** b -- Dec. 1850, d -- Apr. 1861; **Emma** b 1852, d 1861; **Walter**; and **John**. *Children of 2nd wife*: **Frank E.** q.v. *Children of 3rd wife*: **Myra F.** b 22 Apr. 1892.

CARVILLE, HENRY E. - Born 18 Apr. 1842, d ??, s/o Henry Jr. and Harriet/Harriet M. (Luce) Carville. Henry E. Carville m Mrs. Louisa/Luisa (Knapp) Thompson 1 Oct. 1865, d/o Levi Knapp, who was b 19 Mar. 1840, d 4 Mar. 1897. Children: **Harriet M.** b 25 Sep. 1866, d 11 Nov. 1891, m Alfred A. Newell 29 Sep. 1883; **Mary L.** b 16

May 1869, d 10 Nov. 1889; **Charlotte P.** b 23 Dec. 1870, m Clifford E. Wing -- Aug. 1897; **Nellie X.** 25 Nov. 1872, d 13 May 1891; and **Alonzo P.**

CARVILLE, HENRY W. - Born 1 Jan. 1837, d ??, s/o Joseph and Eunice Woodman (Watson) Carville of New Portland, Maine. Henry W. Carville m (1) 18 Mar. 1863 Sarah E. York in Carolina, Louisiana, and m (2) 28 Dec. 1886 Huldah Henderson, d/o James and Abigail (Church) Henderson. Children: **Cora E.** b 17 Oct. 1863; **George W.** b 14 May 1864; **Flora H.** b 27 Jul. 1869; and **John A.** b 4 Sep. 1872.

CARVILLE, HERBERT J. - Born 15 Feb. 1855, d 16 Oct. 1933, s/o Ezra and Dorcas A. (Jordan). Herbert J. Carville resided in Webster, Maine. He m -- Aug. 1879 Addie A. Campbell of Litchfield, Maine. Children: **E. Guy** of Rockland, ME, b 15 Jul. 1880; and **Addie Maud** of Portland, ME, b 24 May 1883. [Probate Androscoggin #18803.]

CARVILLE, ISAAC T. - Born 11 Aug. 1906, d 10 Oct. 1891, s/o ??. Isaac T. Carville m (1) Jane Ricker, and (2) m Julia Ann Carville, d 23 Jun. 1923, d/o Simon Carville. Children: **G e o r g e B .***+ b 23 Jan. 1874; **Ada L.***+ b 15 Mar. 1877; **Lena Etta** b 14 Feb. 1880, d 23 Mar. 1883; **Frank E.***+ of Lewiston, ME, b 6 Oct. 1882; and **Wallace L.***+ of Lewiston, ME, b 23 Oct. 1885. [#14375 Julia Carville probate d 23 Jun. 1923 and will and file #5472 probate will of Isaac Carville Androscoggin court d 11 Aug. 1906. * Indicates listed in Isaac T. Carville's will - file #5472 probate. + Indicates listed in Julia Ann Carville's will - file #14375 probate.]

CARVILLE, JAMES - Born 21 May 1803, d 6 Nov. 1879 [Androscoggin probate #2177], s/o Henry and Mary (Dyer) Carville. James Carville m (1) 8 Aug. 1824 Harriet Randall, d 9 Nov. 1837, d/o Ezra, and m (2) Anna Dennet, pub. 4 Dec. 1838. *Children of 1st wife*: **J a m e s F .** b 8 Jan. 1825; James q.v.; **Ezra** b 8 Jun. 1827, m Dorcas Ann Jordan, Webster; **Harriet** b 8 May 1829, m 15 Apr. 1849 William Lydston of Bowdoin, Maine; and **Helen M.** b 7 Sep. 1831, d 18 Jan. 1888, m Lysander Fuller of Stoneham, MA; **Willard** d 9 Mar. 1852 aged 18 years; and **Charles** q.v. *Child of 2nd wife*: **Robert D.** m Jane A. Powell 9 Jul. 1872, d/o John Powell.

CARVILLE, JAMES - Born ??, d ??, s/o James and Harriet (Randall) Carville. James Carville resided in Litchfield, Maine. He m Mervina/Minerva Purington, b 1 Mar. 1829, d/o Ira and Dorcas (Golder) Purington. Children: **James**; and **Willard** of Lawrence, MA. [Probate Court Androscoggin #2177 and will of James Carville, Sr.]

CARVILLE, JEFFERSON - Born 26 Feb. 1832, d ??, s/o Sewell and Tamar (Higgins) Carville. Children: **Alphonso**; and **Rebecca**.

CARVILLE, JOHN - Born 22 May 1789, d 6 Sep. 1862 [#261 probate court Androscoggin], s/o Henry and Mary (Dyer) Carville. John Carville m 2 Mar. 1815 Priscilla Higgins, b -- Mar. 1792, d 25 Jul. 1854, d/o Jesse. Children: **Samuel** q.v.; **Mary Ann** m Valentine G. Colby of

Webster, ME, pub. 26 Jun. 1840, moved to Brunswick, ME, and d; **Henry** b 3 Jul. 1820, m Rebecca Sanborn 6 Jun. 1842; **Elizabeth** m Eben Swett of Wales, ME, 31 Jan. 1841; **Sarah** b 20 May 1825, m William F. Marston 13 Feb. 1848; **Orrin Sprague** q.v.; **Priscilla** m Jeremiah Crowley 18 Dec. 1851; **Hannah F**. b 7 Sep. 1832, d 6 Nov. 1859, age 27 years, m Chas. E. Garcelon 28 Oct. 18--. [Vital Records of Lewiston, Maine, p. 13.]

CARVILLE, JOHN B. - Born 25 Jul. 1837, d ??, s/o Henry and Nancy (Dyer) Carville. John B. Carville m 13 Mar. 1859 Augusta C. Presson of Freeman, Maine, d/o Hiram and Celia (Savage) Presson. Children: **Harry** q.v.; **Edwin E**. b in Freeman, ME, 24 Dec. 1864, m Harriet Butts of Kinfield, ME, 27 Jun. 1901.

CARVILLE, JORDAN - Born ??, d ??, s/o ?? Jordan Carville m Harriet M. Elms, d/o Robert. Children: **Estele Viora** b 6 Apr. 1863, d 14 Feb. 1882; **Elzader L**. b 16 Dec. 1865; **Athea O**. b 7 Sep. 1867; **Albertie** b 6 Oct. 1868, d 11 Jan. 1890; **Willie S**. b 12 Jan. 1871; **Lillian I**. b 19 Oct. 1876; and **Luvertie E**. b 19 Oct. 1876, d 21 May 1893.

CARVILLE, JOSEPH - Born in Lewiston 12 May 1794, d 20 Feb. 1859 in New Portland, Maine, s/o Henry and Mary (Dyer) Carville. Joseph Carville was in the War of 1812. He m 4 Dec. 1818 Eunice Woodman Watson of Litchfield, Maine, b 22 Mar. 1798, d 30 May 1886, d/o Daniel, Jr. and Elizabeth (Webber) Watson. [Vital Records of Litchfield, Maine, p. 99 and see *Litchfield, Maine, History, 1795-1895* by ??, published by the author, 1897, p. 383, 384.] Children: **William Webber** q.v.; **Priscilla Higgins** b 12 Sep. 1821, d 21 May 1849; **Joseph Jr**. q.v.; **Benjamin** q.v.; **Daniel W**.; **Cynthia A**. b 12 Jul. 1828, d 4 Mar. 1894 in Clinton, Mass., m George Littlefield 25 Jan. 1840; **Eunice** b 12 Jun. 1831 in New Portland, ME, m Benjamin C. Webster 22 Mar. 1879 in Lewiston; **Melvina A**. b 12 May 1833, d 20 Feb. 1876 in Lexington, MA, m (1) George Perkins of Carthage, ME, and m (2) Carlo Luce in 1867; **John Wright** b 15 Apr. 1835, d 16 Jan. 1891 in New Portland, m Bell Tuesdale 29 Nov. 1865; **Henry W**. q.v.; and **Emily J**. b 16 Nov. ----, m Samuel Farrington. [Letter 1902 from Mrs. Benj. Webster.]

CARVILLE, JOSEPH JR. - Born 23 Jan. 1823, d ??, s/o Joseph and Eunice Woodman (Watson) Carville. Joseph Carville, Jr. m 1 Jan. 1850 Caroline A. Butts, d/o John and Abigail Butts. Children: **Flora** b 7 Oct. 1850, d 7 Oct. 1850; **Willard** b 18 Jan. 1852; **Joseph Lendal** b 22 Mar. 1854; **Abby B**. b 10 Mar. 1856, d 22 Jun. 1858; **Priscilla** b 16 May 1858; **Delphina/Delphina A**. b 28 Apr. 1860; **Charles P**. b 7 Jun. 1862; **Almond L**. b 14 Apr. 1864, d 30 Oct. 1866; **Emery B**. b 27 Mar. 1866, d 28 Jun. 1870; **John B**. b 31 Oct. 1867; **Abram B**. b 28 Jan. 1870, d 28 Jan. 1870, **Lucy J**. b 28 Jan. 1870; and **Amandia/Amanda M**. b 4 Apr 1871, d 25 Jan. 1876. [Letter from North New Portland, Maine, 1904 Mrs. Carville.]

CARVILLE, MILTON - Born 24 Oct. 1818, d in Greene, Maine, s/o Sewell and Tamar (Higgins) Carville. Milton Carville m 16 Mar. 1848

Lucy L. McKenney of Greene. Children: **Henry L.** b 11 Feb. 1849; **Edith M.** b 26 May 1855, d 19 May 1859; **Ida A.** b 18 Jan. 1861; and **Clarence Edwin** b 1 Dec. 1862.

CARVILLE, ORRIN SPRAGUE - Born 20 June 1827, d ??, s/o John and Priscilla (Higgins) Carville. Orrin Sprague Carville m 27 Jun. 1847 Nancy Dennett, d 13 May 1873, d/o Peter. Children: **Almon**; **Andristur** m James Steedman 22 Mar. 1873; **Abbie J.** m Edwin H. Judkins 24 May 1874; and **Alice**.

CARVILLE, OTIS - Born 1 Nov. 1827, d 16 Jun. 1872 [probate #1095 Androscoggin Co.], s/o Benjamin and Abigail (Hatch) Carville. Otis Carville m (1) 31 Jan. 1849 Harriet Dwelley, and m (2) 6 Jun. 1863 Christana Evelett/Eveleth of Auburn, Maine. Children: **Arvaletta Jane** [named in father's will]; and **Susan**.

CARVILLE, SAMUEL - Born ??, d 18 Nov. 1894, s/o John and Priscilla (Higgins) Carville. Samuel Carville was a sleigh and carriage manufacturer [letter 1904]. He m 4 Oct. 1836 Sophronia Wright d/o John. Children: **John Henry** b 23 Apr. 1837; **Charles Ellery** b 8 Feb. 1839; **Emma S.** b 8 Oct. 1844, m Chauncy Bangs of Farmington, ME.

CARVILLE, SEWELL - Born 16 Mar. 1794, d 8 Jun. 1879, s/o William and Rebecca (Bearth) Carville. Sewell Carville m 2 Mar. 1815 Tamah/Tamar Higgins, d 18 Nov. 1884, d/o Jesse Higgins. Children: **Milton** q.v.; **William** b 5 Sep. 1822, d 13 Sep. 1851 [d 28 Sept. 1851 at San Francisco, California, age 28 years, according to Sewall Merrill's record of Lewiston/Auburn AHS. Mr. Sewall Merrill was b 12 Apr. 1808 in New Gloucester, Maine; compiled records 1864-1890; manuscript at Androscoggin Historical Society Library, Auburn, Maine], m Mary Ann Edgecomb, d/o Bath, 14 Apr. 1850; **Mary** b 4 Jun. 1820, d 24 Sep. 1821; **Elijah** b 16 May 1824, d by drowning on 10 May 1836; **Submit** b 6 Apr. 1826, m Steven Smith, lived in Cambridge, Mass.; **Rebecca** b 23 Sep. 1827, m Orrin Whitney, lived in Minn.; **Mary** b 15 Feb. 1830, m George Coleman of Boston, MA, lived on Dight Street; **Jefferson** q.v.; **Jarusha** b 12 Jan. 1838, d 26 Nov. 1859, m Mary J. Brown; **Alonzo G.** q.v.; and **Alphonso H.** b 5 Feb. 1843, m Memima Gray.

CARVILLE, SIMON - Born 18 Nov. 1804, d 26/27 Dec. 1890 age 86 [Garcelon Cemetery, Lewiston], s/o William and Rebecca (Bearth) Carville. Simon Carville resided in Lisbon, Maine. He m (1) 30 Aug. 1831 Charlotte Dingley, d 18 Jul. 1841 age 37 years and 7 months [Garcelon Cemetery], and m (2) 28 Dec. 1845 Ednah/Ada Ricker of Webster, Maine, d 13 May 1888 age 69 years, d/o Levi of Webster, Maine. *Children of 1st wife*: **Sally** b 16 Jan. 1832, d 14 Feb. 1879; **Sarah D.** m Charles Haley of Limerick, ME; **Lucy D./T.** b 11 Mar. 1834, m (1) George Taylor from CT, and m (2) William D. Coombs of Lisbon, ME; and **Will/William D.** b 8 Feb. 1837, d 14 Jan. 1895 [probate record #3530 Androscoggin Co.], unm. *Children of 2nd wife*: **Julia Ann** b 6 Mar. 1849, m Isaac Carville; and **Juliett/Juliette** d 16

Jun. 1892, m -- Nov. 1882 Frebrick Hall of Portland, ME. [See probate #2107 Androscoggin Co. court.]

CARVILLE, WESLEY - Born ??, d in Lewiston, s/o ?? Wesley Carville m May Jane ----. Children: **Maria** b 17 Mar. 1857; **Marietta** b 20 Nov. 1858, d 28 Sep. 1884, m Benjamin Turner, Jr., 17 Jan. 1877; **Ellen** b 11 Aug. 1860, d 29 Jun. 1880; **Dency** b 1 Jun. 1862, d 15 Mar. 1879; **Addie** b 20 Aug. 1866, drowned 16 Aug. 1887; and **Grace Lee** b 21 Sep. 1874, unm, lived in Buxton, ME.

CARVILLE, WILLIAM - Born 10 Nov. 1762, d 20 Nov. 1829, s/o ?? William Carville m 24 Jan. 1791 Rebecca Bearth, b 23 Jul. 1767, d 14 Jul. 1861. Children: **Rachel** b 24 Oct. 1791, d 7 Jul. 1868, m James Tuck, Pan. No. 6 [means No. 6AP which is Berlin or Phillips, now located in Franklin Co., Maine], (he was later of Farmington, Franklin Co., Maine), this statement is an editor's statement backed up with census records, Rev. Greely's records of N. Yarmouth families and the *History of Farmington*; **Sewall** q.v.; **William Jr.** q.v.; **Mary** b 22 Mar. 1799, d 14 Apr. 1879, unm; **Simon** q.v.; **Elijah** b 30 Mar. 1802, d 19 Oct. 1824, unm; **Nathan** b 8 Jun. 1807, d 16 Oct. 1826, unm; **Rebecca** b 11 Jun. 1812, d 31 Dec. 1822; and **Anna** b 23 Sep. 1760. [Vital Records of Lewiston, Maine, p. 12.]

CARVILLE, WILLIAM JR. - Born 30 Sep. 1796, d 26 Oct. 1864, s/o William and Rebecca (Bearth) Carville. William Carville, Jr. m 9 Sep. 1827 Sally Golder, d 11 Dec. 1848. Children: **Nathan** b 5 Mar. 1828, d 29 Oct. 1851; **David William** b 17 Dec. 1829, m Sarah Jepson 8 Oct. 185-; **Elhanan** b 28 Feb. 1832, d 15 Jan. 1857; **Lewis** b 9 Dec. 1833, m Philenah Polden 24 Nov. 1854; **Rachel Ann** b 31 Dec. 1835, d -- Mar. 1899, m (1) on 11 Feb. 1854 to Sullivan Lane of New Sharon, ME, who d 1 Mar. 1882, and m (2) John Rankin of Monmouth, ME; **Jordan G.** b 9 Sep. 1837, d 25 Dec. 1901, m Hattie M. Elms 27 Jan. 1863; **Caroline** b 19 Apr. 1840, m Alfred A. Keene; **John** b 6 Apr. 1842, d 18 Jul. 1880 (killed at Leardville), m Nellie L. Worth of China, ME, 2 Sep. 1875; **Calvin Gorham** b 9 Oct. 1844, d 17 Jul. 1901, m Emma Susan Holey of Farmington, ME, b 13 Aug. 1850, d/o Merchange Holey and Susan; and **Melvina** b 10 Nov. 1846, m ---- Gledhill.

CARVILLE, WILLIAM WEBBER - Born 1 Nov. 1819, d 11 Dec. 1898, s/o Joseph and Eunice Woodman (Watson) Carville of New Portland, Maine. William Webber Carville m 19 Mar. 18-- Lucy J. Butts, d/o John and Abigail (----) Butts. Children: **Alton P.** b 17 Dec. 1847; and **Amanda** b 1852 in North New Protland, ME. [Letter 1904.]

CARVILLE, ZENUS VAUGHAN - Born 16 Feb. 1859, d 12 Apr. 1901, s/o Amos H. and ?? Carville. Zenus Vaughan Carville m 2 Mar. 1882 H. Hortie Teague, d 6 Jan. 1895, d/o Alvarus Teague. Children: **Celia M.** b 14 May 1883; **Earl A.** b 7 Nov. 1885; and **Ernest H.** b 16 Aug. 1888. Zenus Vaughan Carville was graduated from the Farmington Normal School. He taught school and then studied dentistry and settled in Phillips, Maine, where he remained for a few years, and then settled in Fall River, Massachusetts, and practiced his profession, being a very successful dentist.

CHADBOURNE, AUGUSTUS - Born 13 Oct. 1865, d ??, s/o ?? Augustus Chadbourne m May Davis, b 13 Mar. 1866, d/o William. Children: **Ada** b 21 Feb. 1886; and **Gracie** b 9 Sep. 1890.

CHADBOURNE, EDWARD - Born ??, d ??, s/o ?? Children: **Etta** b 17 Apr. 1860, m Albert Edgecomb of Lewiston; **Joseph Leroy** q.v.; **Edgar** b 26 Aug. 1866, m Mabel Gertrude Bemis 1 Sep. 1888; **Everett** b 26 May 1867, unm; **Bertie** d age 10 months; **Willie** d 25 Jul. 1877, age 1 year 6 months; and **Edith** b 9 Mar. 1879.

CHADBOURNE, EMERY - Born ??, d ??, s/o ?? Child: **Annie** b 6 May 1886.

CHADBOURNE, JAMES - Born ??, d ??, s/o ?? James Chadbourne m 26 Aug. 1837 May L. Bradly of Haverhill, Massachusetts. Children: **Mary Elizabeth** b 27 Jul. 1838; and **Enoch Bradley** b 5 Feb. 1840.

CHADBOURNE, JOSEPH - Born 27 Nov. 1797, d 18 Aug. 1887, s/o Thomas and Dolly (Tibbetts) Chadbourne. Joseph Chadbourne m 14 May 1820 Matilda/Mehitable Stewart/Steward, b 25 Oct. 1797, d 16 May 1857. Children: **Dorothy** b 18 Oct. 1820, m Nathan E. Stewart of Bowdoinham, ME, 7 Jul. 1844; **Patty** b 5 Jun. 1822, m (1) Joseph Whitten, pub. 23 Oct. 1842, and m (2) Nathan Stewart; **Rufus** b 27 Jun. 1824, m Charity Stewart, d/o Simeon of Bowdoinham, ME; **Joseph** b 25 Aug. 1826, unm, d 12 May 1863; **Eliza** b 29 Sep. 1829, d 24 Apr. 1864, m Joel G. W. Mitchell 17 Jun. 1860; **E m e r y** b 7 Jan ----, unm, d 1 Feb. 1891 in Calif.; **Catherine** b -- Sep. 1836, d 18 Nov. 1859; **Edward** b 20 Apr. 1835, m Abbie Bubier, d/o George, pub. 16 Dec. 1856; **Sarah A.** b 10 Nov. 1840, m George Bubier, Jr., s/o George, pub. 21 Sep. 1861; **Addine** b 17 Jul. 1845.

CHADBOURNE, JOPHAT/JAPHET - Born 13 Aug. 1799, d in Bowdoinham, Maine, s/o Thomas and Dolly (Tibbetts) Chadbourne. Jophat/Japhet Chadbourne m Ruth Stockman of Bowdoinham, Maine, pub. 3 Feb. 1822. Children: **Thomas** b 17 Aug. 1825, d 28 Sep. 1826; **John Stockman** b 30 Apr. 1829; **Caroline** m Samuel Sparks; **Margaret**; **Isaac**; **Lucy Ann**; and **Lucinda**.

CHADBOURNE, JOSEPH LEROY - Born 3 Aug. 1862, d ??, s/o Edward and ?? Chadbourne. Joseph Leroy Chadbourne m 16 Oct. 1886 Lula Earle of Webster, Maine. Children: **Bertha** b 30 Oct. 1888; and **Eva** b 12 Mar. 1892.

CHADBOURNE, RUFUS - Born ??, d ??, s/o ?? Children: **Mehitable J.** b -- May 1848, m Henry A. Jackson of Minot, ME; **Rachel Johnson** b 17 Mar. 18--, m John W. Johnson of Webster, ME; **Samuel B.** b 7 Jan. 1853, m Rebecca Bubier, d/o George M., 12 Oct. 1873; **J a m e s Emery** b 9 Feb. 1856, m Nellie Ellis; and **Carrie Emma** b 16 Jun. 1866, m William L. Littlefield 3 Apr. 1886.

CHADBOURNE, SAMUEL B. - Born ??, d ??, s/o ?? Children: **Millie Rose** b 7 Jan. 1887; and **Burtie.**

CHADBOURNE, THOMAS - Born ??, d ??, s/o ?? Thomas Chadbourne m Elizabeth Stewart of Bowdoin, ME, pub. 17 Oct. 1830.

CHADBOURNE, THOMAS - Came from Hollis, d 25 Mar. 1826 in Bowdoinham, Maine, s/o ?? Thomas Chadbourne m Dolly Tibbets. Children: **Patty** b 27 Dec. 1795; **Joseph** q.v.; **Jophat/Japhet** q.v.; **Polly** b 14 Jun. 1801, m Christopher Bubier, pub. 21 Sep. 1824, d 1 Feb. 1841; **Sally** b 17 Sep. 1803, m Stephen Stewart, pub. 4 Nov. 1827; **Olive** b 1 Feb. 1806; **Thomas** b 2 May 18-8, d 18 Aug. 1884, aged 75 years 3 months 17 days, m Eliza Stewart, pub. 17 Oct. 1830; **Elizabeth** b 6 Aug. 1810; **Belinda** b 18 Mar. 1812, d 19 Nov. 1891 in Lisbon, ME, m Hiram B. Higgins of Bowdoin, ME, pub. 7 Dec. 1834, and **Eliza** m Thomas Brimijohn of Bowdoin, pub. 29 Sep. 1833. [Vital Records of Lewiston, Maine, p. 99.]

CHAMBERLAIN, WILLIAM - Born ??, d ??, s/o ?? William Chamberlain m Mary ----, b 16 Mar. 1776. Children: **Isaac** b 22 Jan. 1799 at Livermore, ME; **Loranah** b 7 Feb. 1801; **Mary** b 20 Oct. 1802; **Julia** b 9 Sep. 1804. [Vital Records of Lewiston, Maine, p. 13.]

CHANDLER, CHARLES B. - Born ??, d ??, s/o ?? Children: **Loantha** b 28 Jul. 1865, m Irving L. Field; **Howard B.** b 28 Sep. 1863, m Elvira Andrews; and **Haste Bell** b 3 Feb. 1895.

CHANDLER, HOWARD B. - Born ??, d ??, s/o ?? Child: **Irene May** b -- Jun. 1888.

CHANDLER, SETH - Born 17 Jun. 1805, d 25 Sep. 1872, s/o ?? Seth Chandler m Lydia Banks of Hartford, Maine. Children: **Lovinia B.** b 18 Mar. 1830, m Albert S. Brooks, 25 Nov. 1858; **Charles B.** b 9 Jun. 1832, m Mary E. Penney, -- Mar. 1861; **Augusta J.** b 22 Jul. 1834, m Lyman Prescott, 16 Sep. 1853; **Howard** b 1 Mar. 1836, m Emily Prevo; **Horace Gould** b 1 Apr. 1836; **Seth** q.v.; **George A.** b 1 Nov. 1860, m Cornelius B. Pennell, 14 Jun. 1869; **Daniel Jones** b 30 Nov. 1840; **Loantha J.** b 16 Feb. 1842, d 6 Nov. 1889, m Warren C. Dorrah, 16 Sep 1861; and **Lydia Ann** b 3 Sep 1832, m Horace Richardson, 8 Dec. 1854.

CHANDLER, SETH - Born 3 May 1838 in Showhegan, Maine, d 13 Jan. 1903, s/o Seth and Lydia (Banks) Chandler. Seth Chandler moved to Lewiston, with his family, when he was twelve years old. He m 3 Mar. 1869 Ella A. Cutler. Child: **Louis.**

CHASE, STEPHEN - Born 19 Jan. 1772, d ??, s/o ?? Stephen Chase m 4 Dec. 1798 Ruth Tyler, b 12 Mar. 1778, d/o John and Ruth (----) Tylor. Children: **Clarence** b 22 Sep. 1799, m Daniel Curtis; **Ruhamah** b 28 Jun. 1801, m Benjamin Davis; **Ruth** b 6 Jul. 1803, m Simon Fickett; **Betsey** b 28 Dec. 1804, m Solon Gates; **Thomas H.** b 22 Dec.

1806, m Mary Gates; **Peter M.** b 28 Dec. 1808, m Mary Cole; **Cyrus H.** b 30 Nov. 1810, m Harriet Bailey; **Stephen S.** b 29 May 1813, d -- Jul. 1872; **Noah C.** b 29 Oct. 1815; **Dudley P.** b 14 Feb. 1817, m Olivia Carpenter; and **Abner B.** b 12 Dec. 1819, m Hannah B. Norton. [Vital Records of Lewiston, Maine, p. 12.]

CHENEY, OREN BURBANK - Born 10 Dec. 1816 in Holderness (Ashland), New Hampshire, d ??, s/o Deacon Moses and Abigail (Morrison) Cheney. Oren Burbank Cheney moved to Lewiston in 1857. He m (1) 1839 Caroline A. Rundlett, d 13 Jun. 1846 in Stratham, New Hampshire, and m (2) Nancy S. Perkins of West Lebanon, Maine, d 21 Feb. 1886, d/o Rev. Thomas Perkins. *Child of 1st wife*: **Horace R.** d 13 Dec. 1876. *Children of 2nd wife*: **Caroline A.** m ---- Swan; and **Emeline R.** m ---- Boothby.

CLARK, DANIEL - Born ??, d ??, s/o ?? Daniel Clark m int. (1) 13 Aug. ----, m 1 Nov. 1808 [vital records of Lewiston, Maine, p. 423] Eunice Tarr of Greene, Maine, and m (2) Nancy Harris. *Children of 1st wife*: **Phebe** b 18 Nov. 1812, m James Tarr, 14 Dec. 1828; **Nancy** b 16 Mar. 1814; **A a r o n** b 28 Aug. 1818; **S a r a h** b 28 Apr. 1821, m Samuel Whitney, 6 Jan. 1846; and **Eunice** b 1 Nov. 1823. *Children of 2nd wife*: **Daniel F.** b 11 Apr. 1827; and **Mary Mehitable** b 4 Sep. 1830, m Hiram Aino.

CLOUGH, AUGUSTUS - Born ??, d ??, s/o Josiah and ?? Clough. Augustus Clough m 27 Apr. 1872 Flora D. James/Jones. Children: **Edith M.** b 30 Mar. 1876; **Bessie M.** b 23 Jan. 1878; **Delia A.** b 23 Oct. 1884; and **Fred A.** b 14 Oct. 1889.

CLOUGH, BENJAMIN F. - Born 25 Oct. 1831, d ??, s/o Josiah S. and Mary (Crowley) Clough. Benjamin F. Clough m 13 Apr. 1857 Vesta Bowie. Children: **F r a n k** b 4 Jan. 1858, m Ena Warren, -- Sep. 1881; and **Minnie** b 21 Apr. 1860, m Samuel Woodrow, -- Nov. 1888.

CLOUGH, JEREMIAH - Born 12 Feb. 1768 at Epping, New Hampshire, d 26 Apr. 1848 age 81 years, s/o ?? Jeremiah Clough moved to Monmouth, Maine, 1797 and removed to Lewiston, Maine, 1816. He was a reader of the *Morning Star* for more than twenty years [obit was written by David Libby]. He m Mehitable Straw, d 16 Jun. 1848 age 76 years [*Morning Star* issue 7 Jun. 1848 and 19 Jul. 1848]. She was a member of the 2nd Freewill Baptist Church of Lewiston [obit written by David Libby]. Children: **B e t s e y** b 23 Nov. 1795, d 17 Dec. 1873, m William Woodward, 19 Oct. 1845; **Aseneth** b 1 Jan. 1803, d 22 Jun. 1878, unm; **Jeremiah** b 20 Jan. 1805, d 18 Jun. 1867, m Sarah Wright; and **Josiah S.** q.v.

CLOUGH, JOSIAH S. - Born 10 May 1810, d ??, s/o Jeremiah and Mehitable (Straw) Clough. Josiah S. Clough m 15 Dec. 1831 Mary Crowley. Children: **Benjamin F.** q.v.; **William W.** q.v.; **Mary M.** b 12 Aug. 1838, m Isaac G. Tarr, 28 Oct. 1865; and **Augustus** b 18 Sep. 1845, m Flora D. James/Janes, 27 Apr. 1872.

CLOUGH, WILLIAM W. - Born 10 May 1835, d ??, s/o Josiah S. and Mary (Crowley) Clough. William W. Clough m 21 Nov. 1885 Hattie/Hattie A. Robinson. Child: **Alice May** b 25 Mar. 1890.

COBB, CHIPMAN - Born ??, d ??, s/o ?? Chipman Cobb m Abigail ----. Children: **James** b 27 Dec. 1800; and **Hannah** b 11 Feb. 1803. [Vital Records of Lewiston, Maine, p. 13.]

COBB, JONATHAN LOVETT HASKELL - Born 5 Aug. 1824 in Poland, Maine, d ??, s/o Zenas and Charlotte (Haskell) Cobb. Jonathan Lovett Haskell Cobb was in Lewiston by 1857. He m 10 Dec. 1848 Abigail L. P. Morrell, d/o Nathaniel and Mary (Hall) Morrell of Poland, Maine.

COBURN, ALBERT - Born 12 Mar. 1816 in Greene, Maine, d 15 Mar. 1856 in Clarendon, New York, s/o ?? Albert Coburn m Elizabeth Harris Pettingill Coburn. Children: **Charles W.** b 18 Sep. 1844, d 15 Feb. 1893, m Jennett E. Spurr -- Jan. 1875, d 1895; **John P.** b 16 May 1847, m Bell Barr -- Sep. 1884; **Marcia E.** b 25 Aug. 1854, m Charles Cocker 11 Mar. 1887; and **Mary A.** b 13 Jan. 1856, m Geo. Coburn 7 Nov. 1879. [Loran and Jean Coburn - Fremont, CA.]

COBURN, CHARLES - Born ??, d ??, s/o ?? Children: **Mary** b 24 May 1814, m John Lowell, Jr.; **Albert** b 12 Mar. 1816, m Elizabeth Pettingill, 16 Dec. 1843; **Alanson** b 16 Nov. 1820, m Mary Ann Wright, 25 Apr. 1844; **Levi** b 22 Feb. 1823, d 16 Mar. 1825; **Marcia** b 3 Oct. 1825, d 15 May 1832; **Rachel** b 5 Aug. 1827, d 9 Apr. 1842; and **Benjamin** b 26 Aug. 1831, d 15 Nov. 1834.

COBURN, CHARLES - Born ??, d ??, s/o ?? Children: **Bertha F.** b 2 Aug. 1878; **Albert J.** b 8 Nov. 1881; **Mona B.** b 9 Nov. 1883; **Charles C.** b 24 Aug. 1885; **Avis E.** b 28 Oct. 1888; and **Ella Jenett** b 19 Jan. 1893.

COBURN, ELEAZER - Born 4 Mar. 1735 in Dracut, Massachusetts, d 7 May 1810 in Canan, District of Maine, s/o Aaron and Mercy (Varnum) Coburn. In 1791, Eleazer Coburn removed to Lewiston, Maine, with his family from Dracut, and two years later to Bloomfield (Maine) [obit of Bridget, his wife]. Family tradition states that he owned slaves. He m Bridget ----, b 6 May 1737, d 18 Aug. 1836 in Bloomfield, (now Skowhegan, Maine) [obit], d/o Robert and Sarah (Abbott) Hildreth. Children: **Bridget** b 12 Mar. 1762, d 18 Apr. 1824, m Dr. Shattuck; **Deborah** b 23 Dec. 1763, d 12 June 1857, m John Emery, removed to Canaan, ME; **Esther** b 1 Nov. 1765, d 9 Jan. 1846, m Ephraim Bigelow; **Sarah** b 7 Oct. 1768, m John Pierce, removed to Vermont; **Aaron** b 10 Sep. 1769, d 13 Jan. 1790 killed by the falling of a tree in Dracut, MA; **Prudence** b 16 Jan. 1772, d 20 Sep. 1851, m Robinson Landers; **Rachel** b 18 Nov. 1774, m 1796 Samson Parker; **Eleazer** b 24 Feb. 1777, d 9 Jan. 1845, m Mary Weston; **Robert** b 29 Jul. 1780, d 8 Mar. 1862, m Mary Parker; **Betsey** b 15 May 1785, d 5 Nov. 1855, m John Whitter of Cornville. [*(History of) Skowhegan on the Kennebec* by Louise Helen Coburn, published by the author, 1941,

p. 991, 671-673 and see *Early Settlers of Canaan* by Eben Weston, formerly of Skowhegan, a brother of Eleazer Coburn, Esq.'s wife, p. 146-147.]

COBURN, ELEAZER - Born ??, d 9 Jan. 1845 age 68 years, s/o ?? Eleazer Coburn m Mary Weston, d 21 Dec. 1860. Children: **Nahum** b 28 Oct. 1801, d 28 Oct. 1822; **Abner** b 22 Mar. 1803, d 4 Jan. 1885; **Fidelia** b 2 Feb. 1805, d -- Jan. 1850, m Rev. John Brooks; **Philander** b 19 Feb. 1807, d 8 Mar. 1867; **Eliza** b 6 Feb. 1809, d 1874, m Isaiah Marston; **Elivira** b 5 Feb. 1811, d 17 Aug. 1867; **Alonzo** b 6 Dec. 1812, d 19 Nov. 1882, m Vine Osgood; **Samuel** b 14 Jul. 1815, d 1873, m Sarah Bigelow; **Stephen** b 11 Nov. 1817, d 4 Jul. 1882, m Helen Miller; **Eleazer, Jr.** b 9 Feb. 1820, d 10 Mar. 1850, m Eleanor Emery; **Charles** b 5 Mar. 1822, d 30 Oct. 1844; **Mary Weston** b 30 Sep. 1824, d 21 Apr. 1874; **Sylvanus Pitts** b 5 Mar. 1827, d 18 Jan. 1874; **Sarah Pitts** b 5 Mar. 1827, d 28 Aug. 1827.

COBURN, LEVI - Born ??, d ??, s/o ?? Levi Coburn m -- Mar. 1856 Mrs. Susan Leighton. Child: **Eunice** b 5 Jan. 1857 in Cambridge, Maine, m 14 Sep. 1879 Greenwood B. Moody.

COBURN, REUBEN - Born 16 Aug. 1761, d 6 May 1813, s/o Reuben and Mary (----) Coburn. Reuben Coburn m Jane Austin. Children: **Betsey** b 16 Nov. 1792; **Ellis** b 5 Jul. 1794; **Hannah** b 12 Apr. 1796; **Polly** b 3 Apr. 1798; **Jane** b 7 Mar. 1800; **Justus** b 11 Aug. 1804; **Enoch** b 3 Aug. 1806; **Mary** b 20 Feb. 1810; and **Bartholomew** b 10 Jan. 1813. [Loran and Jean Coburn - Fremont, CA.]

COBURN, REUBEN JR. - Born 19 Oct. 1780 at Dracut, Massachusetts, d 1 Feb. 1857 at Cambridge, Maine [vital records of Cambridge, Maine, p. 35], s/o ?? Reuben Coburn, Jr. m (1) -- Feb. 1806 Eunice Lander, b 25 Apr. 1777, d 1 Apr. 1834 in N. Cambridge, Maine, and m (2) likely Abigail ----, d 20 Oct. 1861 age 80 years, widow of Reuben Jr. [vital records of Lewiston, Maine, p. 241]. Children: **Charity** b 5 Jan. 1810, d -- Jan. 1829 in Cambridge; **Clarisa** b 31 May 1812, d -- Jan. 1856; **Levi** b 25 Apr. 1815; and **Aaron** b 17 Jul. 1822 d 28 Sep. 1822 in infancy, age about 2 months old. [Letter - Levi Coburn - 1902 of Cambridge, ME, and Mrs. Eunice C. Moody of Cambridge, ME, 1894. Vital Records of Cambridge, Maine, p. 35.]

COLE, REV. BENJAMIN - Born 1761, d 10 Sep. 1839, s/o Job and Sarah (Reaves) Cole. Rev. Benjamin Cole m (1) Keziah Barker, d 6 May 1808, d/o Caleb, pub. 19 Feb. 1785 in Topsham, Maine, m (2) 27 Jan. 1809 Mrs. Ruth/Ruth Smith of Litchfield, Maine, b 19 Sep. 1778 in Chatham, Massachusetts, d 6 Dec. 1843, d/o Herman Smith of Litchfield, Maine. Children: **Benjamin Jr./2d** q.v.; **Keziah** b 7 Mar. 1789, d 12 Aug. 1869, m Philip Jenkins 27 Nov. 1807, who d 21 Sep. 1862; **Sarah** b 17 Apr. 1794, d 6 Jan. 1874, m Zaccheus Arno; **John** b in 1800, d 19 Jul. 1882, m Margaret Marston, who d 1 Jun. 1874, d/o Simon 31 Jan. 1828; **Otis** b 2 Feb. 1812, d 13 Apr. 1882, m Mrs. Hulda J. Dill, who d 28 May 1873, d/o William Stevens, wid/o Joseph Dill,

Jr., 30 Aug. 1846; and **Harriet** b 13 Nov. 1817, d 27 Jul. 1846, m 5 Jan. 1895 George D. Stetson, d 23 Jul. 1846.

COLE, BENJAMIN JR./2d - Born 9 Jan./19 Jul. 1787, d -- Nov. 1872, s/o Rev. Benjamin and ?? Cole. Benjamin Cole m (1) Sally Gookins of Monmouth, Maine, pub. 22 Apr. 1810 [vital records of Lewiston, Maine, p. 178] or 10 May 1810 Sarah Jenkins, d 28 May 1842, d/o Phillip, and m (2) Hannah Frances, pub. 31 Jul. 1830 [vital records of Lewiston, Maine, p. 178] or 11 Mar. 1846 Hannah Foster. Children: **Benjamin** q.v.; and **Abner** b 5 Apr. 1821, d -- Jan. 1883.

COLE, BENJAMIN - Born 5 May 1811, d 20 Jun. 1891, s/o Benjamin Jr./2d and ?? Cole. Benjamin Cole m (1) Julia A. Jenks of Wales, Maine, and m (2) Mehitable (Colby) Sto--. Child: **Benjamin F.** b 31 Dec. 1850 in Litchfield, ME, d -- Sep. 1863. "Here lies old Ben Cole as tall as a haypole, Who used to steal cabbage and hay, Here under the ground he may be found, If the devil hasn't carried him away." [Grave stone.]

COLE, CHARLES EDWARD TAYLOR - Born 14 Oct. 1861, d ??, s/o Isaac and Josephine Marie (Sleeper) Cole. Charles Edward Taylor Cole m 30 Aug. 1883 Ella Estelle Philips, d 6 Mar. 1861. Children: **Charles Irvin** b 18 Aug. 1888 in Bath; and **Maria Amelia** b 4 Feb. 1892 in Lynn, Mass.

COLE, EPHRAIM - Born 14 Jun. 1688, d before Nov. 1756, s/o Nathaniel and Sarah (----) Cole. Ephraim Cole m 2 Mar. 1724 Hannah/Susanna Waste/Waite. He moved to N. Yarmouth, Maine, in 1753. Children: **Job** b 20 Mar. 1725; **Noah** b 26 mar. 1727; **Rebecca** b 28 Nov. 1729; **Ebenezer** b 28 Oct. 1732; **Ruth** b 8 May 1735; and **Eunice** b 12 Feb. 1740. [*Cole Genealogy*, by Frank T. Cole, published by the author, p. 62.]

COLE, HARRISON L. - Born 8 Sep. 1815, d ??, s/o Samuel Jr. and Charlotte (Litchfield) Cole. Harrison L. Cole m Elvira S. Cole, d/o Jeremiah, pub. 7 Mar. 1838, d 14 Aug. 1853 age 34 years. Children: **Augusta Arvilda** b -- Oct. 1843; **Marcellus H.** b 2 Sep. 1858; and **Charlotte E.** b 1850, d 23 Mar. 1851.

COLE, ISAAC - Born ??, d ??, s/o ?? Children: **Llewellyn, Charles, John, Dorothy, Matilda,** and **Jennie**.

COLE, ISAAC - Born 26 Aug. 1800, d -- Jun. 1848 by drowning at Sabattas Point, Maine, s/o Samuel and Anna (Pettingill) Cole. Isaac Cole m 25 Aug. 1825 Dorothy Moulton of Lisbon, Maine, d/o John, pub. 30 Jul. 1825. Children: **Lorenzo/Lorenzo N.** q.v.; **Isaac** q.v.; **Eleanor B.** b 8 Nov. 1829, d 31 Oct. 1900, m Cyrus Hayford 10 Jan. 1850, d 12 Jan. 1879; **Roxie M.** b 23 Mar. 1837, m (1) Darius Sawyer, and m (2) Leander Robinson of Lawrence; **Andrew J.** b 20 Apr. 1832, d 6 Mar. 1893, m Clara Baker 15 Sep. 1855; **Jeremiah** b 30 Nov. 1839, unm; and **Anna** d 26 Dec. 1845. [Vital Records of Lewiston, Maine, p. 92.]

COLE, ISAAC - Born 28 Jul. 1828 [vital records of Lewiston, Maine, p. 92], d ??, s/o Isaac and Dorothy (Moulton) Cole. Isaac Cole m (1) 16 Sep. 1851 [family record] or 9 Aug. 1853 Josephine/Josephine Marie Sleeper, b 1 Nov. 1829, d 16 Sep. 1876, pub. 31 Aug. 1851, and m (2) 14 Feb. 1878 Addie Hunt. *Children of 1st wife*: **Frances Ann Marie** b 4 Jan. 1853, d 17 Dec. 1833, m Frederick M. Furbush 1 Jan. 1873, who was b 7 Aug. 1856, s/o Henry; **Llewellyn Henry** b 1 May 1859, d 1 Oct. 1881, m Myra Ellen Jones of Farmington, ME, -- Mar. 1881; Charles Edward Taylor q.v.; **Matilda Alice Jane** b 13 May 1864; **Florence Minerva Estell** b 14 Oct. 1867, d 3 Dec. 1874; **Flora Dorothea Jesie** b 15 Apr. 1870; and John Alcender q.v.

COLE, JENNIE - Died 4 Dec. 1874, aged 7 years, d/o Isaac.

COLE, JEREMIAH - Born 10 Jun. 1789/1790 in Greene, Maine, d 11 Aug. 1882 age 92 or 93 years and 2 months [Herrick Cemetery, Lewiston], s/o Samuel and Anna (Pettingill) Cole. Jeremiah Cole m 25 Feb. 1816 Lucinda Snell of Minot, Maine. Children: **Hulda H.** b 31 Jan. 1818, d 3 Jan. 1895, m George Fogg of Greene, Maine, d 27 May 1892, pub. 12 Jun. 1842; **Elvira Snell** b 18 Aug. 1819, d 14 Aug. 1853, m Harrison Cole; **Orrin/Orin P.** b 4 Apr. 1822, m (1) Hasadiah Jackson, d/o Solomon, pub. 12 Mar. 1843, m (2) ---- Wright, d/o Timothy; and **Sumner H.** b 7 Jan. 1824, m Osca Gilbert 9 Jan. 1855, who d 30 Nov. 1889. "A little sketch of the history of Lewiston as far forth as my memory serves me: My father, I believe was born in Yarmouth, Maine, then the Commonwealth of Mass. He came to Lewiston after the Revolutionary War and married Ann Pettingill, a sister to Capt. Nathaniel Pettingill, and I am the fourth child of their family. I was born in the Town of Greene, Maine, in the year 1789, June 10th and we moved to Lewiston when I was one year and a half old, onto the farm that Asa Taylor now lives on. We lived there five years and then moved down to where Mr. Marrow now lives, and I have lived here ever since. The first teacher that taught school here was John Chandler, a transient man. He kept school here as much as ten years, I should think, and then he got drowned in the river, and I think that Noah Litchfield was the first teacher at the Falls. [Lewiston Falls, the area located both sides of the Androscoggin River near the present - 1989 - Gov. Langley Bridge.] He was the first Town Clerk, and Dan Read was the next. My father was in his 88th year when he died, and my mother was 83, I think. The fruit of my father's marriage was seven children, five boys and two girls. They lost a boy and a girl when they were about two years old with the cancor rash." (Signed) Jeremiah Cole.

COLE, JOB - Born ??, d ??, s/o ?? Job Cole removed from Duxbury, Massachusetts, to Eastham, Massachusetts, in 1639. He m 15 May 1634 Rebecca Collier. Children: **John** b 1667; **Job**; **Rebecca**; **Daniel**; and perhaps others. [Justin Windsor's *History of Duxbury*, published by Crosby & Nichols, 1849, p. 247.)

COLE, JOB - Born 10 Mar. 1725, d ??, s/o Ephraim and ?? Cole. Job Cole moved to Lewiston previous to 1788 and lived on lot 87. He m 4 Dec. 1748 Sarah Reaves of N. Yarmouth, Maine, d 10 Feb. 1826, aged 99 years and 6 months. Children: **Susannah** b 9 Feb. 1750; **Mary** b 6 Oct. 1751, m John York of N. Yarmouth 5 Jul. 1770; **Elizabeth** b 8 Jan. 1754, m Kenelm Winslow of Royalstown, now Durham, ME, 9 Sep. 1775; **John**; **Samuel** q.v.; **Sarah**; **Rev. Benjamin** q.v.; **Hannah** b 11 Jul. 1764; **Lydia** b 7 Jun. 1767; **William** b 15 Apr. 1770; **Rebecca**; and **Rhoda** b 28 Mar. 1775.

COLE, JOHN ALCENDER - Born 3 Jan. 1872, d ??, s/o Isaac and Josephine Marie (Sleeper) Cole. John Alcender Cole m 5 Sep. 1891 Inetta Packer. Children: **Harold B.** b -- Jun. 1892; and **Ernest K.** b 10 Jun. 1893.

COLE, LORENZO/LORENZO O. - Born 1 Jul. 1827, d ??, s/o Isaac and Dorothy (Moulton) Cole. Lorenzo/Lorenzo O. Cole m 20 Oct. 1850 Mary R. Littlefield. Children: **Charles**, **Eddie**, **John**, **Clara**, and **Nellie**.

COLE, NATHANIEL - Born probably in Maine, d ??, s/o James Jr. and Mary (Tilson) Cole. Nathaniel Cole was of Duxbury, Massachusetts. He was originally guessed by Elder to be a descendant of Job of Eastham and Duxbury, (because) he had land granted him in 1679, and was alive in 1710. [However], he was descendant of James Cole of Plymouth [*Cole Families* compiled by Frank Theodore Cole, published by the author, 1887, p. 60). He m Sarah ----. Children: **Rebecca** b 21 Sep. 1680; **Mary** b 13 Nov. 1782; **Nathaniel** b 11 Oct. 1685, m 4 Aug. 1714 Abigail West; **Ephraim** q.v. [See *Old Times in North Yarmouth*, by Augustus Corliss, published by New Hampshire Publishing Co., 1977 (reprint of 1877-1884), , p. 966.]

COLE, ORRIN/ORIN P. - Born 4 Apr. 1822, d ??, s/o Jeremiah & Lucinda (Snell) Cole. Orrin/Orin P. Cole m (1) Hasadiah Jackson, b 20 Sep. 1819, d 5 Oct. 1865, d/o Solomon, pub. 12 Mar. 1843, and m (2) ----Wright, d/o Timothy. Children: **Florilla J.** b 3 Apr. 1845, d 3 Feb ----, m Dance Eaton of Greene; **Fidelia A.** b 24 Jan. ----; **Frances A.** b 7 Apr. 1850, m ---- Libby; and **Solomon J.** b 1 May 1852, m Lora J. Dill, d/o Eben of Greene, ME, 1 May 1876.

COLE, REEVES - Born 9 Jun. 1783, d in Andover, Maine, s/o Samuel and Anna (Pettingill) Cole. Reeves Cole m 2 Mar. 1808 Ruth Remmick. Children: **Benjamin** b 7 Nov. 1808, m Hannah Francis 19 Aug. 1830; **Samuel** q.v.; **Ira** b 2 Jun. 1817; **Anna** b 25 Mar. 1821, m ---- Ireland; and **Mary T.** b 27 May 1824. [Vital Records of Lewiston, Maine, p. 13.]

COLE, SAMUEL - Born 13 Jul. 1756 or 21 Jan. 1759, d 29 Mar. 1844 age 88 years and 8 months [Herrick Cemetery, Lewiston], s/o Job and Sarah (Reaves) Cole of N. Yarmouth, Maine. Samuel Cole was a "revol. soldier in actual battles yet received no wound nor injury..." [*Death Notices from Freewill Baptist Publications* by Young and Taylor, published by Heritage Books, Inc., 1985, p. 76]. He m Anna Pettingill, d 26 Dec. 1845, d/o Mark. Children: **Reeves** q.v.; **Benjamin** b 8 Feb. 1785, d 8 Mar. 1787; **Samuel Jr.** q.v.; **Jeremiah** q.v.; **Rhoda** b 19 Apr. 1793, d 24 Nov. 1856, m Luther Litchfield -- Aug. 1812, who d 11 May 1852; **Hannah** b 16 Jan. 1796, d 10 Apr. 1798; and **Isaac** b q.v. [Vital Records of Lewiston, Maine, p. 11.]

COLE, SAMUEL - Born 16 Feb. 1811, d ??, s/o Reeves and Ruth (Remmick) Cole. Samuel Cole m 29 Jan. 1833 Mary Haskell/Hackett. Children: **Holman** b 20 Nov. 1833; **Oliver**; and Lydia m David Tarr.

COLE, SAMUEL JR. - Born 3 Nov. 1786, d 11 Aug. 1828, s/o Samuel and Anna (Pettingill) Cole. Samuel Cole, Jr. m 5 Nov. 1810 Charlotte Litchfield. Children: **Allen P.** b 22 Mar. 1811; **Charlotte** b 28 Feb. 1813, d in Lisbon, ME, m Jesse Greene of Lisbon 25 Dec. 1882; **Harrison L.** q.v.; **Hester Ann** b 5 Nov. 1817, d 23 Mar. 1869 in Portland, ME, m Walter Cory of Portland 7 Jul. 1846, who d 31 Jul. 1889; **Mabel Wade** b 15 Oct. 1819, m (1) ---- Proctor of Lisbon, and m (2) Actor Ross of Lisbon 27 Nov. 1842; **King Samuel** b 20 Jun. 1823; and **Jackson** b 30 Apr. 1825. [Vital Records of Lewiston, Maine, p. 160.]

COLE, SUMNER H. - Born ??, d ??, s/o Jeremiah and Lucinda (Snell) Cole. Sumner H. Cole m 9 Jan. 1855 Osca Gilbert, b 18 Aug. 1828, d 30 Nov. 1889. Children: **Ella F.** b 7 Jan. 1858; and **Margery E.** b 15 Jan. 1859.

COLE, WILLIAM - Born 7 Jan. 1824, d ??, s/o ?? William Cole m Rhoda Barker. Children: **Prudence** b 27 Mar. 1803; **Susanna** b 16 Jun. 1804; **Rebecca** b 18 May 1806; **Hiram Barker** b 24 Jul. 1808; and twins **Mary** and **Martha** b 7 Apr. 1811.

CONANT, DANIEL - Born in Lewiston, 16 Oct. 1805, d ??, s/o ?? Daniel Conant m Abigail B. ----. Children: **William Thomas** b 7 May 1834; **Alfred P.** b 3 Feb. 1836; **Elisabeth** b 7 Jan. 1838; **Clement P.** b 29 Nov. 1839, d 1 Oct. 1841; **Jane W.** b 17 Jul. 1842; and **Daniel J.** b 12 Sep. 1844.

COOMBS, JOSEPH D. - Born ??, d ??, s/o ?? Joseph D. Coombs m Jane ----. Children: **Nancy Jane** b 27 Aug. 1815; **Abigail** b 20 May 1815; **William** b 9 Aug. 1820; **Joseph** b 15 Apr. 1822; **Clark McKenney** b 17 Jul. 1824; **Samuel Cole** b 16 Feb. 1827; and **John Quincy** b 10 Feb. 1829. [Vital Records of Lewiston, Maine, p. 93.]

CORLISS, SAMUEL - Born 1 Sep. 1800, d 7 Nov. 1872, s/o ?? Samuel Corliss m 9 Apr. 1892 Ann Davis. Children: **Mary Ann Tarr** b 9 Jan. 1843, m Phineas Skinner, 2 Jul. 1864; **Aaron Tarr** b 26 Sep. 1844, d 20 Jul. 1881, m Maria E. Marrinal, 14 Oct. 1865; **Lucy** b 12 Feb. 1847, m Charles N. Ware, 14 Oct. 1865; **Samuel** b 12 Sep. 1840, d 12 Oct. 1849; **Stephen** b 12 Mar. 1851, m Hannah Worcester, 1 Jan. 1874; and **William W.** b 12 Apr. 1854, d 30 Jun. 1857.

COTTON, ISAAC H. JR. - Born 21 Jul. 1811, d 23 Mar. 1888, s/o Isaac Hinckley and Elisabeth (Sylvester) Cotton. Isaac H. Cotton, Jr. m Rhoda Potter. Children: **Joseph Potter** b 8 May 1837, m Isabella Cole of Philadelphia, PA; **Henry C.** b 17 Oct. 1840, m Emily Edgecomb of Lisbon, Me.; **Clara A.** b 9 Feb. 1845, d 6 Dec. 1865; and **Emma Elisabeth** b 10 Jun. 1854, m James W. Coombs of Waltham, Mass.

COTTON, ISAAC HINKLEY - Born 5 Sep. 1766, d 3 Sep. 1843 [VR Bowdoin], s/o Thomas and Agnes (Smith) Cotton. Isaac Hinckley Cotton m Elisabeth Sylvester of Freeport, Maine, pub. 8 Nov. 1794. Children: **Sarah** b 18 Jul. 1796, m Cornelius Thompson, pub. 4 Oct. 1817; **Ruth** b 26 Aug. 1798, d -- Feb. 1823; **Lois** b 1 Aug. 1803, m (1) Esekiel Carville, pub. 13 May 1823, and m (2) John Merrill, pub. 15 Apr. 183-; **Alicia** b 21 Jul. 1806, m Ephraim Hall; **Isaac H. Jr.** q.v.; **William Sylvester** q.v.; **Mary Elisabeth** b 8 Jun. 1819, m Amasa Field; and **Thomas** q.v. [Vital Records of Lewiston, Maine, p. 14.]

COTTON, THOMAS - Born 10 Jul. 1820, d 29 Dec. 1881, s/o Isaac Hinckly and Elisabeth (Sylvester) Cotton. Thomas Cotton m Susan Merrill of Vineland, New Jersey. Child: **Thomas Edwin.**

COTTON, WILLIAM SYLVESTER - Born 5 Jul. 1815, d 13 Apr. 1888, s/o Isaac Hinckley and Elisabeth (Sylvester) Cotton. William Sylvester Cotton m Mary Dunham of Bowdoin, Maine. Children: **Lovisa D.** b 4 Feb. 1846, d 14 Feb. 1859; **Minerva J.** b 2 Apr. 1848, d 29 Mar. 1860; **William S.** b 2 Jun. 1851, m Hattie M. Abell, 28 Feb. 1878; and **Ella M.** b 2 Jul. 1857, d 8 Aug. 1874.

COURSON, IVORY - Born ??, d ??, s/o ?? Ivory Courson m Mercey ----. Children: **Emily Augusta** b 18 Jul. 1838; and **David Henry** b 13 Dec. 1842. [Vital Records of Lewiston, Maine, p. 155.]

COURSON, JOHN - Born ??, d ??, s/o ?? John Courson m 2 Oct. 1824 Mary Chase. Both were of Lewiston. [Vital Records of Lewiston, Maine, p. 424.]

COURSON, WILLIAM - Born ??, d ??, s/o ?? William Courson m Abigail ----. Children: **James** b 27 Mar. 1823; **Rufus** b 15 Mar. 1830; and **Mary Elisabeth**. [Vital Records of Lewiston, Maine, p. 92.]

COWAN, DAVID - Born 1 Jan. 1825 in Belgium, d 6 Apr. 1887, s/o ?? David Cowan went to Lewiston in 1856. He was Mayor Lewiston 1872 and 1886. He married twice and had two children neither of which survived him.

CROWLEY, FREDERICK T. - Born 20 Nov. 1850, d ??, s/o James and Jane (Mitchell) Crowley. Frederick T. Crowley m (1) 28 Nov. 1875 Alice Litchfield, and m (2) 27 Nov. 1890 Elisabeth Greenleaf. Children: **Bessey**; **Herbert**; and **Ernest.**

CROWLEY, JAMES - Born 23 May 1814, d ??, s/o Jeremiah and Mehitable (Davis) Crowley. James Crowley m 6 Jan. 1839 Jane Mitchell. Children: **Sarah A.** b 22 Dec. 1840, m (1) James Thompson of Webster, ME, pub. 16 Dec. 1885, and m (2) Albert Foss, pub. 27 Mar. 1865; **Lissie J.** b 22 Apr. 1843, d 31 Dec. 1860; **Jerusha E.** b 18 Sep. 1846, d 4 Oct. 1868; and **Frederick T.** q.v.

CROWLEY, JEREMIAH - Born 1786, d 16 May 1868, s/o ?? Jeremiah Crowley m 18 Jun. 1809 Mehitable Davis. He was of Lisbon, Maine, and she was of Lewiston, Maine, when married [vital records of Lewiston, Maine, p. 423]. Children: **Aaron** b 17 Jul. 1809 [vital records of Lewiston, Maine, p. 91], d 17 Apr. 1877, m Martha Annis of Lisbon, 31 Nov. 1833; **Mary** b 12 Apr. 1811, d 26 Oct. 1886, m 15 Dec. 1831 Josiah Clough, s/o Jeremiah; **James** q.v.; **William** q.v.; **John** q.v.; **Jerusha** b 8 Nov. 1821, d 27 Mar. 1892, m (1) Hiram Tibbetts, 7 Sep. 1845, and m (2) George Crowley of Addison, ME, pub. 16 Sep. 1852, and m (3) Asa Taylor, 31 Oct. 18--; **Jeremiah** q.v.; **Thomas** q.v.; **Amos** b 25 Nov. 1829, m (1) Martha J. Bank, 23 Feb. 1852, and m (2) Lissie Hatch.

CROWLEY, JEREMIAH - Born 10 Sep 1825, d 25 Dec. 1866, s/o Jeremiah and Mehitable (Davis) Crowley. Jeremiah Crowley m 18 Dec. 1851 Priscilla H. Carville/Carolls. Children: **Henry C.** b 20 Apr. 1856, d 12 Apr. 1857; **Ella P.** b 8 Jan. 1854, m Charles C. Jordan, 23 Nov. 1876; **Hannah G.** b 11 Sep. 1858, m George W. Cobb, 13 Jun. 1883; **Ida M.** b 6 Nov. 1860, m John M. Wallace, 28 Dec. 1880; and **Rose L.** b 27 Jan. 1863, m Edwin F. Goss of Auburn, ME, 29 Nov. 1887.

CROWLEY, JOHN - Born 16/17 Jan. 1819, d ??, s/o Jeremiah and Mehitable (Davis) Crowley. John Crowley m Sarah A. Annis. Children: **Elisabeth P.** b in 1841 in Lewiston, m J. Frank Mallett; **George A.** b in Topsham, ME, 1 Oct. 1843, m Hunter; **William H.** b in Topsham, 3 Dec. 1845, d 15 Oct. 1846; **Martha A.** b 26 Apr. 1848, m (1) Sanford Johnson and (2) Lemont Stimpson; **Sarah Alice** b 7 Nov. 1851, m Warren W. Gould, 16 Jan. 1879; **Rosetta E.** b 6 Mar. 1854, m Charles Goud; **Adela** b 22 May 1856, m Cyrus Key of Brunswick, ME; and **Hattie B.** b 13 Sep. 1858, m Charles Alexander.

CROWLEY, THOMAS - Born 24 Jul. 1827, d -- Apr. 1899, s/o Jeremiah and Mehitable (Davis) Crowley. Thomas Crowley m (1) 17 Jun. 1854 May/Mary Jane Whitney, and m (2) 6 May 1876 May/May A. Gould. Children: **Frank E.** b 30 Aug. 1857, m Carrie Sargent; and **Jennie Gertrude** b 17 Aug. 1862.

CROWLEY, WILLIAM - Born 20 Sep. 1816, d ??, s/o Jeremiah and Mehitable (Davis) Crowley. William Crowley m (1) Sophia Garcelon, d before 1864 age 41 years 6 months 14 days in So. Lewiston, Maine, d/o Annis and Mary (----) Garcelon [*Morning Star* issue 1 Jun. 1864, p. 40, Vo. 39 #10, whole #1986], and m (2) M./Mahala B. Moulton of Lisbon, Maine, pub. 1 May 1865. Children: **Mary P.** b 2 Oct. 1852, m

Gilman N. Holmes, 15 Apr. 1874; and **William, Jr.** b 28 Dec. 1864, m Carrie F. Jordan, 23 Dec. 1890.

CUMMINGS, AMMI C. - Born 6 Jun. 1796, d ??, s/o ?? Ammi C. Cummings m 4 Jan. 1818 Brittania Smart of Greene, Maine. Child: **Eliphalet N.** b 20 Sep. 1818.

CUMMINGS, JACOB - Born 19 Apr. 1790, d ??, s/o Solomon and Susannah (Ames) Cummings. Jacob Cummings went to N.B. He m Thankful Norcross. Children: **Jacob, Alonzo, Lydia,** and **Nancy.**

CUMMINGS, JAMES - Born on 3 Oct. 1791, d 15 Nov. 1853 or 14 Mar. 1854 age 62 years [d age 63 years on 14 Mar. 1854 at Greene, Maine, according to *Morning Star* 3 May 1854], s/o Solomon and Susannah (Ames) Cummings. James Cummings m (1) Betsey Jack, d 11 Oct. 1841, certificate granted 31 Oct. 1818, and m (2) Eunice Starbird, d 26/27 Mar. 1853/1854 age 42 years. *Children of 1st wife*: **Jesse Avander** b 13 Nov. 1818, and **Mary Jane** b 4 Feb. 1826, d 26 Nov. 1829.

CUMMINGS, JOHN - Born ??, d 11 Dec. 1819, s/o ?? John Cummings m (1) 19 Nov. 1795 Lucy Ames of Lewiston, d 8 Nov. 1815, d/o James, and m (2) Betsey Berry of Portland, Maine. Children: **Sally** b 30 Sep. 1796, d 28 Apr. 1812; **Aseneth** b 1 Sep. 1798, d 10 Aug. 1828; **Lucy** b 31 Jan. 1801, d 22 May 1810; **Joseph** b 2 Apr. 1803, d 17 Oct. 1825; **John** b 16 Aug. 1805, d 15 May 1828, m Polly Drake; **Margaret** b 30 Sep. 1807, d 11 Dec. 1886, m Edward Sylvester of Turner, ME; **Sylvanus Boardman** b 22 Apr. 1811, d 21 Aug. 1881, m Lovica Cummings, d/o Peter; **Silas Stearns** q.v.; **May;** and **Peter.**

CUMMINGS, JOHN - Born 1 Jan. 1800, d 23 May 1828, s/o Lemuel Jr. and ?? Cummings. John Cummings m Mary Cutter Merrill. Child: **Mary Ann** b 14 Sep. 1828, d -- May ----, m Timothy Wells -- Sep. 1856.

CUMMINGS, JOHN FRANKLIN - Born 18 Nov. 1854 in Berwick, Maine, d ??, s/o Rev. Silas S. and ?? Cummings. John Franklin Cummings m 7 Nov. 1877 Carrie Sniffen of San Francisco, California. Child: **Herbert** b 27 Aug. 1870.

CUMMINGS, JOHN H. - Born 3 Jul. 1834, d ??, s/o Lemuel and ?? Cummings. John H. Cummings m 1 May 1860 Mary Ann Hatch, d/o ---- of Jefferson, Maine, pub. 23 Apr. 1860. Children: **Edward Payson** b 26 Dec. 1862, d 7 Jan. 1864; **Hattie May** b 10 Dec. 1864, d 2 Mar. 1875; and **Minnie** b 12 Nov. 1872, d 13 Nov. 1872.

CUMMINGS, LEMUEL SR. - Born 21 Feb. 1745, d -- Aug. 1827, s/o ?? Lemuel Cummings, Sr. settled on Lot #49 in Lewiston, 1775 [#3 of William Garcelon's "History of Lewiston" published in the *Lewiston Journal*, Feb. 1-8, 1935, was written in 1863]. He m Rachel Stevens. Children: **Solomon** q.v.; **Lemuel Jr.; John** d 11 Dec. 1819, m Lucy Ames, pub. 27 Sep. 1795; **Peter A.** q.v.; **Mary** m Joshua Coburn;

Martha m Elisha Record; **Rachel** d 16 Nov. 1805, aged 34 years, unm; **Elizabeth** unm; and **William** m Deborah Harris, d/o Silas, pub. 14 Sep. 1814.

CUMMINGS, LEMUEL JR. - Born 10 Oct. 1769, d 11 Mar. 1852, s/o Lemuel Sr. and Rachel (Stevens) Cummings. Lemuel Cummings, Jr. m (1) 11 May 1796 Anna True, d 26 Mar. 1826, and m (2) 29 Nov. 1826 Polly Pitts, d/o Ebenezer and May (Ellis) Pitts. Children: **Laura** b 4 Dec. 1796, d 13 Dec. 1796; **Olive** b 1 Dec. 1797, d 8 Jan. 1845, m Aaron Stevens; **John** q.v.; **Sarah** b 18 Jan. 1802, d 23 Sep. 1840, unm; **Benjamin True** b 31 Dec. 1803, d 5 Mar. 1806; **Rachel** b 17 Nov. 1805, d 31 Mar. 1866, m Josiah Robinson; **Nathaniel True** b 14 Jul. 1808, d 25 Oct. 1809; **Lemuel III** q.v.; **Anna** b 10 Jun. 1812, d 1 Dec. 1820; **Jane** m David Parker, who d in Tyler, TX, 9 Jun. 1864; **Lucinda** m 18 Mar. 1817 Benjamin C. Robinson; **Jemima** b 18 Jul. 1819, m (1) William Hanneford, and (2) m An---- Harris, and m (3) M---- Thompson; **Polly Ann** b 21 Feb. 1830, m William E. Sawyer 9 Dec. 1850, who d 1 Oct. 1882, **Anna** b 9 Jan. 1828, d 25 Jul. 1829; and **Harriet** b 26 Apr. 1832, d 28 Jul. 1840.

CUMMINGS, LEMUEL III - Born 24 Jul. 1810, d 5/6 Dec. 1846, s/o Lemuel Jr. and ?? Cummings. Lemuel Cummings, III m Pameala/Pamelia Wing, d/o Asa. Children: **John H.** q.v.; **Benjamin Perley** b 28 Jul. 1836, d 9 Jan. 1877, m Lovina P. Hilton, pub. 11 Aug. 1862; **Joseph and Josiah** b -- Aug. 1835, d age 2 days; **Asa Wing** b 10 Oct. 1839, d -- Dec. 1862; **Silas Stearns** b 27 Sep. 1841, d 22 Feb. 1870, m Abbie A. Kent, 28 Jul. 1863; and **Sarah A.** b 7 Jun. 1843, d 29 Mar. 1879, age 36 years, m William Taylor, pub. 10 Nov. 1860.

CUMMINGS, OLIN/OLEN M. - Born 30 Dec. 1856 in Providence, Rhode Island, d ??, s/o Rev. Silas Stearns and ?? Cummings. Olin/Olen M. Cummings m 25 Dec. 1882 Hattie Dodge of Somerville, Massachusetts, d/o A. T. Children: **Eleanor** b at Baltimore 10 Mar. 1886; **Leslie Olin** b 19 Jun. 1888; and **Alice E.** b in El Paso, TX, 25 Dec. 1892.

CUMMINGS, PETER A. - Born ??, d ??, s/o Lemuel, Sr. and Rachel (Stevens) Cummings. Peter A. Cummings m 5 Nov. 1806 Sally Andrews, b 27 Dec. 1784, d/o Benjamin and Kasiah Andrews. Children: **Sally** m ---- French; **Caroline** m Asa Rice of Guilford; and **Levina** m Sylvan Cummings, s/o John.

CUMMINGS, SILAS STEARNS - Born 22 May 1814 [family record], d ??, s/o John and Lucy (Ames) Cummings. Silas Stearns Cummings m (1) 17 Jul. 1842 Mary A. Cram, d 22 Apr. 1855 age 34 years, d/o Smith Cram of Montville, Maine, and m (2) 19 Aug. 1855 Elizabeth Hodsdon of Ossippee, New Hampshire, d/o J. A. Children: **John Franklin** q.v.; **Olin/Olen M.** q.v.; **Arthur Irving** b 10 Nov. 1859, d 6 Aug. 1861; and **Charles S.** b at Thompson, CT, 15 Jun. 1865, unm.

CUMMINGS, SOLOMON - Born ??, d 6 Sep. 1827, s/o Lemuel Sr. and Rachel (Stevens) Cummings. Solomon Cummings m Susannah Ames, d 16 Mar. 1838, d/o James (1735-1815). Children: **Jacob** q.v.; **James** q.v.; **Ebenezer** b 28 Jul. 1794, m Tamy Lander; **Ammi Cutter** b 6 Jun. 1796, m Brittania Smart 4 Jan. 1818 of Greene, ME; **Susanna** b 25 Jun. 1799, d 8 Nov. 1809; **Cynthia** b 2 Apr. 1802, m (1) Lemuel Allen, and m (2) David Dolloff of Mt. Vernon, ME; and **Betsey** b 8 May 1807, d 22 Feb. 1854, unm.

CURTIS, JOHN - Born in Boston, Massachusetts, 29 Jun. 1793, d 10 Jun. 1875, s/o ?? John Curtis m (1) 23 Mar 1814 Phebe Jipson, d 27 Jun. 1826, d/o Thomas Jipson, and m (2) int. 16 Dec. 1826 Sarah Dresser [vital records of Lewiston, Maine, p. 411. *Children of 1st wife*: **Betsey** b 13 Jan. 1815, m David Perry of Minot, ME, 14 Jul. 1833; **Stephen** b 18 Feb. 1817, m Percis Davis of Minot, ME, 17 Nov. 1839; **John** b 18 Feb. 1819, d 16 May 1819 [vital records of Lewiston, Maine, p. 205]; **M a r y** b 9 Apr. 1820, m Welcome Hersey of Minot, ME, 17 Mar. 1841; **James** b 27 May 1822, d 1822; and **Abigail** m John Q. A. Atwood, 7 Dec. 1845, who was b 2 Jun. 1823. *Children of 2nd wife*: **John, Jr.** b 26 Sep. 1827, d 24 Nov. 1881 [Mt. Auburn Cemetery, Auburn, Maine], m his step 1st cousin, Lizzie Jepson, d/o William Jepson; **Phebe** b 16 Nov. 1828, d 13 Feb. 1830; **Lendall** b 18 Nov. 1830, m Angelia ----, 3 Oct. 1850; **S a r a h A n n** b 4 Sep. 1832, d 22 Feb. 1867, m 29 Nov. 1849; **W m. P.** b 20 Jun. 1834, m 2 Aug. 1857; **Olive T.** b 26 Jun. 1831, d 25 Aug. 1838; **Alanson T.** b 7 Mar. 1838, m 4 Apr. 1863; and **Chas. H.** b 22 Oct. 1840, m (1) Anna Pullen, 10 Mar. 1865, and m (2) Edith Rewon, 22 Nov. 1888. [Letter from the late Helen McPhee, Bath, Maine, 1980.]

CURTIS, JOHN JR. - Born ??, d ??, s/o ?? John Curtis, Jr. m Elizabeth G. Jepson. Children: **Herbert F.** b 1855; and **Flora E.** b 19 Aug. 1858, m Charles L. Wright.

CUSHING, JOHN SR. - Born 22 Aug. 1755, d ??, s/o ?? John Cushing, Sr. m (1) Meletiah ----, and m (2) 22 Jul. 1807 Eunice Parsons, and m (3) 18 Jun. 1809 Experience Weeks, and m (4) 2 Mar. 1815 Priscilla Higgins [vital records of Lewiston, Maine, p. 423]. Children: **Isaac** b 15 May 1778; **Experience** b 20 Feb. 1784; **John** q.v.; **Ruth** b 14 Feb. 1792, m Experience Weeks, 18 Jun. 1809; and **Rachel** b 12 May 1796.

CUSHING, JOHN - Born in Freeport, 18 Apr. 1802, d 3 Feb. 1894, s/o ?? John Cushing m Lucretia Shaw. Children: **Emaline** b 9 May 1833, m Jacob M. Shaw, 28 Oct. 1858; **Laura** b 30 Mar. 1835; **Olive A.** b 2 Nov. 1837, d 17 Apr. 1859; **Joseph C.** b 21 Dec. 1839, d 1 Sep. 1861; **L i s s i e** b 18 Jul. 1842, d 27 Nov. 1879, m Nathaniel S. Fogg of Monmouth, ME, 21 Jul. 1867; **John M.** b -- Feb. 1845, d 6 Oct. 1868; **Cornelia A.** b 24 Feb. 1848, d 31 May 1864; and **Prentice M.** b 1851, d 3 Aug. 1854.

CUSHING, DR. JOHN - Born 30 Apr. 1789, d 22 Dec. 1870, s/o John Sr. and ?? Cushing. Dr. John Cushing m (1) Experience Weeks, 18 Jun. 1809, and m (2) Rebecca Small, 9 Jun. 1853. Children: **S e t h** b 2 Jul. 1811, d 8 May 1887; **R u t h** b 30 Nov. 1816, d 7 Mar. 1842; **P r i s-**

cilla b 9 Aug. 1819; **Rachael** b 7 Sep. 1821, d 19 Nov. 1843; **Tamer** b 16 Nov. 1826; and **Mary** b 5 Jun. 1830.

CUTLER, DAVID - Born 14 Jul. 1793, d ??, s/o Nathan Sr. and Ruth (Nelson) Cutler. David Cutler m Lucy Lander/Landers, pub. 18 Mar. 1820 or 8 Dec. 1820. Children: **Jason** b 28 May 1821, d 1864; **Elvira** b 14 Feb. 1822, d 2 Dec. 1838; **Rosetta** b 2 Oct. 1827, d 8 Jan. 1845; **Matilda** b 29 Jul. 1832, m Augustus Prescott, 29 Feb. 18-2; and **Mahalia** b 1 Jul. 1838, m Robert Sargent.

CUTLER, HARVEY - Born in Minot, Maine, 26 Sep. 1803, d 27 Sep. 1880 in Warren, s/o Nathan and Polly (Moor) Cutler. Harvey Cutler m 11 Nov. 1830 Lucy Mathews of Warren, Maine. Children: **Mary E.** b in Warren, 30 May 1832, m Alden M. Watts; **Silvia J.** b 28 Jul. 1834, d 12 Mar. 1873 in New Sharon, ME, m James B. Gilmore, pub. 7 Feb. 1858; and **Lucy M.** b 4 Apr. 1837.

CUTLER, JASON - Born ??, d ??, likely s/o David and Lucy (Lander/Landers) Cutler. Jason Cutler m 16 Dec. 1840 Susan Piper of Lewiston, might have been the d/o Thomas and Hannah Piper. Children: **Fanny** b 17 Apr. 1842, m (1) Thomas Merrill and m (2) Wm. French; **Rosetta** b 9 May 1845, d -- Nov. 1854; **Emma** b 3 Oct. 1854, d -- Nov. 1854; **Olive** b 3 Jun. 1856, d -- Apr. 1872; and **Charles F.** b 5 Jul. 1858, m Mary Belle Bessie Weyes, 4 Dec. 1884.

CUTLER, NATHAN SR. - Born ??, d 8 Dec. 1827, s/o ?? Nathan Cutler, Sr. m Ruth Nelson. Children: **Nathan Jr.** q.v.; **Henry** b 26 Aug. 1781, d 26 Mar. 1815, m Hannah Blanchard, pub. 14 Mar. 1806; **Ruth** b 13 Oct. 1783, d 28 Jun. 1798; **Betsey** b 10 Aug. 1785, d -- Jan. 1811; **Olive** b 10 Mar. 1788, m Green Farmington; **Josiah** b 25 Feb. 1791, m Sally B. Hanscom, pub. 18 Mar. 1820; **David** q.v.; **Esther** b 12 Aug. 1795, d 17 Jul. 1812; **Stephen** q.v.; and **Cynthia** b 7 Jul. 1801. [Vital Records of Lewiston, Maine, p. 11.]

CUTLER, NATHAN JR. - Born 14 Sep. 1779, d 1 Nov. 1859, s/o Nathan and Ruth (----) Cutler. Nathan Cutler, Jr. m (1) Polly Mooar, pub. 15 Mar. 1800, and m (2) Lydia Baker of Wilton, Maine, pub. 16 Jan. 1823. *Children of 1st wife:* **Henry** b in Lewiston 9 Jun. 1800, d in Indiana, m Esther Hall of Strong, ME, pub. 29 Oct. 1825; **Hopestill** b in Minot, ME, 8 Jan. 1802, m James Hardy of Strong, 18 Apr. 1822; **Harvey** q.v.; **Nelson** b 25 Apr. 1805, d in Union, ME, 27 Dec. 1852, m Love Thompson, 8 Mar. 1827; **Levi** b 27 Feb. 1807, d 3 Jan. 1880, m (1) Margaret Moore Norton 3 Nov. 1831, and m (2) Lydia C. Norton, 21 Oct. 1861;**Seth** b 4 Feb. 1809, m Abigail S. Norton, 12 Jun. 1834; **Betsey** b 29 Dec. 1810 m Barsilla D. Dyer, pub. 24 Mar. 1834; **Esther** b in New Vineyard, ME, m William Heald; **Nathan** b 11 Feb. 1815, m (1) Lucinda Barker, 9 Sep. 1855, and m (2) Mrs. May Brown, 1 Mar. 1866; **Josiah** b 26 Mar. 1817, m Nancy Stanley, pub. 20 Aug. 1840, and m (2) May M. Craig, 28 Nov. 1848; **Ruth** b in Industry, ME, m James B. Wood 10 Sep. 1845; and **Hiram** b in Industry. *Children by 2nd wife*: **Mary Mooar** b 17 Oct. 1825, m Ephraim Hartwell of Strong, 2 Sep. 1847; **Sarah A.** b in Industry, m Joshua Williams 11 Jan. 1846;

Charles b in Industry, unm; **Ira Vaughan** b in Industry, m Deborah Norton, pub. 6 Oct. 1849; **Lydia Ann** b 17 Sep. 1833, m James Norton, 13 Oct. 1852; and **Cordelia J.** d 7 Nov. 1859, m Zebadiah Barker, pub. 10 Oct. 1857.

CUTLER, CAPT. STEPHEN - Born 3 Jan. 1799, d 1 Nov. 1837 age 39 years at Lewiston leaving wife and four children, youngest s/o Nathan Sr. and Ruth (Nelson) Cutler. Stephen Cutler was formerly of Milford, Massachusetts [*Morning Star*, issue 20 Dec. 1837, p. 135, vol. xii]. He m 15 Feb. 1821 Roxcyllanis Berry. Children: **Otis Nelson** b 19 Feb. 1824, d 5 Oct. 1885, m (1) Rachel Mills, 1845, and m (2) May Tibbetts, 1867; **Stephen Coroden** b 8 Jul. 1826, d 3 Sep. 1861, m Emily Taintor from Orford, NH, in -- Jul. ----; **Vesta Augusta** b 16 Oct. 1828, d 5 Mar. 1895, m (1) Lewis C. Peck, 14 Feb. 1846, and m (2) Charles Jellison, 13 Apr. 1892; and **Olive Armanda** b 27 Jun. 1835, m (1) Ambrose Turner, and m (2) O. S. Carville.

DAIN, JAMES - Born ??, d ??, s/o ?? James Dain was of Lisbon, Maine. He m 15 Feb. 1821 Hannah Jordan of Lewiston. Children: **Mary Loisa** b 18 Jan. 1822 in New Portland, ME; **Minerva** b 7 Apr. 1823 in N. Portland; **Isaac** b 26 Feb. 1825 in Lewiston, d 29 Mar. 1825 [vital records of Lewiston, Maine, p. 207]; and **Dianna** b 27 Jan. 1826. [Vital Records of Lewiston, Maine, p. 102.]

DAVIS, AARON - Born 14 Dec. 1767, d 11 Aug. 1841 [Crowley Cemetery, Lewiston, Maine] or 15 Aug. 1841 [vital records of Lewiston, Maine, p. 207] age 73 years and 8 months, s/o Amos and Ellis/Alice/Elice (Meserve/Merserve) Davis. Aaron Davis m Mary Wilkins. Children: **Mehitable** b 30 Jul. 1791, d 15 Jan. 1877 age 85 years 5 months 15 days, m Jeremiah Crowly 18 Jun. 1809; **William** q.v.; **Jerusha** b 3 Apr. 1794, d 30 Jan. 1884, m Sewall Merrill, 17 Jul. 1831; **Aaron** q.v.; **Amos** q.v.; and **Stephen** q.v.

DAVIS, AARON - Born 6 Jul. 1796, d 18 Jan. 1864, s/o Aaron and Mary/mehitable (Wilkins) Davis. Aaron Davis m Mehitable Graffam, pub. 16 Sep. 1827. Children: **Elisa Elen** b 26 Oct. 1828, d 14 Jun. 1874; **Olive G.** b 3 Jun. 1830, m (1) Samuel Dingley, and m (2) Albert Foss 30 Dec. 1854; **Marrietta W.** b 21 Jan. 1832, d 19 Mar. 1841; **Sophronia** b 10 Jul. 1834, d -- Sep. 1847; **Harriett W.** b 17 Feb. 1837, m Increase Gould 1 Jan. 1859; **Marietta** b 25 Aug. 1841, d 2 May 1871; **Anna** b 26 Oct. 1846, d 25 Dec. 1846; **Joseph W.** b 11 Mar. 1848, d 20 Jul. 1848; and **Ann M.** b 13 Jan. 1849, d 20 Apr. 1858.

DAVIS, ABEL - Born 10 Jul. 1712, d ??, s/o Aaron and Hannah (Haskell) Davis. Abel Davis unintentionally was the first settler of what is now Auburn, Maine. He settled near the Royal River in 1762. [Amos Davis diary]. Abel Davis m Sarah Millett. Children: **Sarah** b 11 Aug. 1734, m David Purington; **Abel** b 16 Aug. 1736; **Mary** b 17 Jul. 1739; **Amos** q.v.; **Hannah** b 16 Jul. 1743; **Anna** b 13 Jun. 1745, m Hubbard Haskell; **Elisabeth** b 30 Dec. 1747, m John Graffam; and **Daniel** b 7 Feb. 1750, m Mary Collins, 10 Sep. 1776.

DAVIS, ABEL - Born 4 Jun. 1797, d 18 Nov. 1846, s/o Daniel and ??
Davis. Children: **Pembrook** b 31 Mar. 1831, d 25 Jul. 1850; **Somerset** b 24 Mar. 1833, d 20 Dec. 1860, m ----; **Daniel** b 19 Feb. 1837, m Elisha J. Abbott, 2 May 1859; and **Mary** b 6 Feb. 1840, m Charles E. Chase of Lynne, MA.

DAVIS, AMOS - Born 1 May 1741, d 20 Mar. 1815, s/o Abel and Sarah (Millett) Davis. Amos Davis m (1) 22 Aug. 1765 Alice or Elice [vital records of Lewiston, Maine, p. 207] or Ellis [vital records of Lewiston, Maine, p. 16] Meserve/Merserve, b 22 Oct. 1735, d 30 Sep. 1803, and m (2) Susannah ----, d 24 Mar. 1815. *Children of 1st wife*: **Mary** b 18 Jul. 1766, d 9 Dec. 1822, m Seth Tarr, d 1838; **Aaron** q.v.; **Amos Jr.** q.v.; **John** b 17 Aug. 1772, d 3 Mar. 1849, m Jenny McKenny, pub. 9 Aug. 1796; and **David** q.v.

DAVIS, AMOS - Born 14 Jun. 1798, d 21 Feb. 1870/1871, s/o Aaron and Mary/Mehitable (Wilkins) Davis. Amos Davis m (1) 11 Jul. 1819 Maria/Mariah Graffam, d 11 Jun. 1841 [Crowley Cemetery, Lewiston, Maine] age 41 years and 9 months, and m (2) Mrs. Annah Jones, 27 Feb. 1844. *Children of 1st wife*: **Mary** b 23 Dec. 1819; **Rufus** b 18 Jul. 1821, m Clarissa Mitchell; **Joseph F.** b 28 Sep. 1825, m Elmira Seavey; and **Amos** q.v.

DAVIS, AMOS - Born 18 May 1833, d ??, s/o Amos and Maria/Mariah (Graffam) Davis. Amos Davis m 2/5 Feb. 1861 Mary E. Judkins. Children: **Everett A.** b 16 Nov. 1863; and **Gertrude A.** b 20 May 1868, m Wilber Sawyer, 26 Nov. 1889 of Gray, Maine.

DAVIS, AMOS JR. - Born 3 Dec. 1769, d 27 Jul. 1848, s/o Amos and Ellis/Elice/Alice Meserve/Merserve. Amos Davis, Jr. m Mary/Mehitable Wilkins. Children: **Mary** b 21 Jul. 1793, d 4 Dec. 1868, m Aaron Tarr, pub. 13 Mar. 1825; **Alice** b 25 Oct. 1795, d 19 Mar. 1889, m Daniel Garcelon, 5 Mar. 1825; **Eunice** b 10 Oct. 1797, d 1 Jul. 1874; **Anne** b 12 Apr. 1799, m Daniel W. Graffam, 2 Nov. 1859; **Deborah** b 6 Feb. 1801, d 6 Oct. 1804; **Henry** b 5 May 1805, d 16 Nov. 1874, m Olive Woodard of Lisbon, ME, pub. 23 Oct. 1831; **Deborah** b 24 Aug. 1808, d 22 Sep. 1884, m George D. Frost, 8 Apr. 1827; **James** b 3 Jun. 1810, d 16 Aug. 1810; **Levi** b 13 May 1811, d 20 Jun. 1816; **Amos** b 25 Mar. 1813, d 12 Dec. 1815; and **Ruth** b 17 Jan. 1816, d 19 Aug. 1833.

DAVIS, BENJAMIN FRANK - Born 13 Dec. 1834, d ??, s/o Daniel and Lucy (Jordan) Davis. Benjamin Frank Davis m Abbie/Abbit T. Stevens, 27 Feb. 1855. Children: **Frank A.** b 27 Apr. 1847, m Emma L. Bailey, 7 Oct. 1881; **James L.** b 18 May 1859; **Cora B.** b 23 May 1862, m George E. Stone, 31 Aug. 1891; **George W.** b 7 Jul. 1866, m Cora A. Smith, 21 Oct. 1889; **Charles C.** b 22 Jul. 1868; **Tena R.** b 13 Feb. 1871; and **John L.** b 18 Jan. 1874.

DAVIS, DANIEL - Born in Salisbury, Massachusetts, 7 Feb. 1750, d 12 Oct. 1827 age 78-8-29 [vital records of Lewiston, Maine, p. 207], s/o Abel and Sarah (Millett) Davis. Daniel Davis m 10 Sep. 1776

Mary Collins. Children: **Jackson** q.v.; **Mary** b 23 Mar. 1780, d 7 Apr. 1864, m Col. William Green Garcelon, 12 Jul. 1810; **Sarah** b 24 Sep. 1781, m Simeon Estes, 9 Mar. 1797; **Rebecca** b 14 Mar. 1784, d in Canada 26 Mar. 1812, m M. Austin; **Dorris** b 28 Dec. 1785, d in Hampden, ME, 1 Mar. 1856, m Abel Pettingill, 3 Feb. 1805; **Tace** b 19 Jun. 1788, d 15 Jul. 1874, m Benjamin Hackett, 21 Jul. 1811; **Daniel** q.v.; **John P.** b 10 Mar. 1793; **Lydia** b 28 Mar. 1795, d 7 Jan. 1859, m David Graffam; **Abel** b 4 Jun. 1797, d 18 Nov. 1846, m Fanny Hubbard, -- Nov. ----; **Mehitable** b 3 Oct. 1801, d 10 Aug. 1803; and **Mehitable** b 3 Oct. 1805, d 1814.

DAVIS, DANIEL - Born 24 Feb. 1797, d ??, s/o Nathaniel and Hannah (Vickery) Davis. Daniel Davis m Lucy Jordan 4 Apr. 1825. Children: **Joseph** b 9 Nov. 1826; **Dorcas** b 10 Jun. 1828, d 1831; **Jane** b 29 Jul. 1830; **James** b 23 Dec. 1832; **Benjamin Frank** q.v.; **John** b 3 Jan. 1838; **Colomore** b 1842; and **Charles N.** b 8 Jun. 1844.

DAVIS, DANIEL - Born 9 Nov. 1790, d 5 Nov. 1846, s/o Daniel and Mary (Collins) Davis. Daniel Davis m Jeanna Hook. Children: **Gilman** b 15 Mar. 1821; **Daniel** b 30 Dec. 1822; **Harriet N.** b 23 Jan. 1825; **Charles S.** b 3 Dec. 1826; **Abby Frances** b 1 Dec. 1828; **Clara Ann** b 29 Jan. 1831; **George H.** b 22 Jul. 1833, d 23 Oct. 1834; **George S.** b 2 Sep. 1834, d 11 Oct. 1836; **Mary C.** b 22 Jul. 1837, d 19 Feb. 1839; **Levi Y.** b 18 May 1840; and **Albert H.** b 31 May 1843.

DAVIS, DANIEL - Born ??, d ??, s/o ?? Daniel Davis m Louisa Ray. Children: **William Garcelon** b 8 Mar. 1829; and **Asa** b 6 Apr. 1830 [vital records of Lewiston, Maine, p. 20].

DAVIS, DAVID - Born 1 Sep. 1775, d 5 Jan. 1851, s/o Amos and Ellis/Elice/Alice (Meserve/Merserve) Davis. David Davis m Mary Pierce, d Nov. 1821 age 51 years [vital records of Lewiston, Maine, p. 207, E. Argus 27 Nov. 1821], pub. 9 Mar. 1800. Children: **Dan R.** b 4 May 1801, d 12 Apr. 1802, **Alice** b 10 May 1804, d 9 Nov. 1873, m John M. Frye, 28 Jan. 1828; **Seth** b 10 Jan. 1807, d 31 Jul. 1827; **Mary** b 7 May 1810, d 3 Mar. 1813; and **Sarah** b 18 Dec. 1812, d 17 Nov. 1892, m Archibald Wakefield 27 Nov. 1834.

DAVIS, DAVID - Born 9 Apr. 1803, d 20 Mar. 1839, s/o ??. David Davis m (1) Sally Eames of Greene, Maine, pub. 4 Jul. 1829, and m (2) 26 Feb. 1835 Betsy Reed. Children: **Seth** b 30 May 1830; and **Oliver R.** b 8 Jun. 1832, m Katie Clay, -- May 1866.

DAVIS, FREDERICK L. - Born 8 Sep. 1846, d ??, s/o Stephen and ?? Davis. Frederick L. Davis m 25 Nov. 1879 Clara Elisabeth Chough of Littleton, New Hampshire, or Clara Clough. Children: **Mabel Catherine** b 22 Aug. 1880; **George Melvin** b 23 Dec. 1882; and **Willard Henry** b 29 Jul. 1888.

DAVIS, GEORGE K. - Born 8 Sep. 1848, d ??, likely s/o Stephen and Katherine/Catherine (Field) Davis. George F. Davis m 31 Oct. 1876 Clara Anna Merrill. Children: **Fred Merrill** b 8 Oct. 1877; **Emma**

May b 1 Feb. 1879; **Rodney Clinton** b 11 Nov. 1880; and **Arthur Milton** b 2 Oct. 1882.

DAVIS, JACKSON - Born 24 Feb. 1778 [vital records of Lewiston, Maine, p. 19], d in Oldtown, Maine, 4 Sep. 1826, s/o Daniel and Mary (Collins) Davis. Jackson Davis m 5 Jul. 1804 in Portland, Maine, [vital records of Lewiston, Maine, p. 19] Mrs. Lydia (Taber) Merrill/Morrill, b 9 Sep. 1780 in Vassalboro, Maine, d/o John and Elizabeth (----) Taber. Mrs. Lydia (Taber) Merrill/Morrill was previously married on 26 Nov. 1801 to Levi Merrill/Morrill, d 4 Jun. 1802, and they had one child, Levi Merrill/Morrill, Jr., b 2 July 1802. Children: **John Taber** q.v.; **Daniel** b 22 Dec. 1807 in Orono, ME; **Mary** b 9 Nov. 1809 in Orono, d 10 Nov. 1853; **Elisa Taber** b 16 Aug. 1811 in Orono, m 31 May 1829 Harris Garcelon; **A s a** b 30 Oct. 1813 in Orono; and **Rebecca** b 3 May 1815 in Orono, d 8 Jul. 1815 in Orono. [Also, in vital records of Lewiston, Maine, p. 19: **Lydia Ann Spencer**, b 5 Mar. 1823, a twin child which Jackson and Lydia took when she was 4 days old. Col. William Garcelon was the town clerk who recorded the family in the town records of Lewiston, Maine; Jackson Davis was his brother-in-law.]

DAVIS, JOHN - Born 17 Aug. 1772, d 3 May 1849, s/o ?? John Davis m Jennie H. Kenney of Georgetown, Maine, pub. 9 Oct. 1796. Children: **S a r a h** b 28 Oct. 1797, d 7 Nov. 1890, m William Dudley of China, ME, 22 Nov. 1814; **John** b 3 Dec. 1799, d 27 Aug. 1846; and **D a v i d** b 9 Apr. 1803, d 20 Mar. 1839, m (1) Sally Eames of Greene, ME, pub. 4 Jul. 1829, and m (2) Betsy Reed, 26 Feb. 1835.

DAVIS, JOHN C. - Born ??, d ??, s/o ?? John C. Davis m Betsey ----. Children: **Katharine** b 17 Dec. 1820 in Lisbon, ME; **Betsey** b 3 May 1824 in Durham, ME; and **William James** b 5 Mar. 1827 in Lewiston, ME. [Vital Records of Lewiston, Maine, p. 64.]

DAVIS, JOHN TABOR - Born 5 Apr. 1805 in Portland, Maine, d 22 Apr. 1878 age 74 in Oldtown, Maine, [Sewall Merrill records of L/A deaths AHS], s/o Jackson and Lydia (Taber) (Merrill/Morrill) Davis. John Taber Davis m -- Jan. 1834 Harriet Jane Moore of Brunswick, Maine. Children: **Joanna Roberts** m James A. Purington -- Sep. 1859; **Ira Wadleigh**; **James Henry**; **Frances Ellen**; **Frances Ellen** m Charles A. Bailey 1872, d 1889; and **Emela Alice**.

DAVIS, JOHN V. - Born 10 Nov. 1794, d 14 Aug. 1881, s/o Nathaniel and Hannah (Vickery) Davis. John V. Davis m Prudence Estes, 13 Aug. 1818. Children: **S u s e y** b 28 Jan. 1819, d 4 Jan. 1891, m Alvin Whitney; **Ruth** b 11 Apr. 1820, d 23 Feb. 1822, unm; **Mary** b 27 Jan. 1822, d 27 Oct. 1889, m Simeon Hunt; **W e a l t h y** b 18 Jul. 1823, d 8 Feb. 1850, m Joshua Kenney; **Nathaniel D.** b 28 Mar. 1825, m Ruth Estes; **Rosannah** b 24 Sep. 1827, m Leonard Jepson, 4 Feb. 1849; **Jackson** b 1 May 1829, m Roxanna Conant; **Henry** b 2 Apr. 1831, m Deannah Bubier, 13 Jan. 1852; **Charlotte** b 15 May 1833, m David Farr; **Coolage Graves** [vital records of Lewiston, Maine, p. 63] b 13 Jul. 1835, d 10 Sep. 1863, m Dorcas Wright Jordan; **S a r a h** b 1 Oct.

1838, m Isaac Golder 18 Dec. 1854; **Elisa** b 1 Oct. 1838, m Hiram Holmes; and **Orevill** b 10 Feb. 1841, d 24 Jan. 1883, m Augustus Lane.

DAVIS, JOSEPH F. - Born ??, d ??, s/o ?? Joseph F. Davis m Elmira Seavey of Troy, Maine. Children: **Elmer E.** b 3 Sep. 1859, m Susie Ruggles; **George C.** b 13 Jun. 1864, m Nellie Mitchell; **Ernest L.** b 18 Apr. 1870; and **Lottie** b 11 Jan. 1873.

DAVIS, NATHANIEL - Born ??, d ??, s/o ?? Nathaniel Davis m Hannah Vickery [Danville, Maine, records compiled by Starbird], d 23 Oct. 1828, d Mathias & Hannah (Parker) Vickery. Children: **Hannah** b 24 Oct. 1792 [William b 22 Nov. 1812 is listed as s/o Hannah Davis in Lewiston VR 17]; **John V.** q.v.; **Daniel** q.v.; **Ruth** b 26 Jul. 1799, d -- Feb. 1822; **Nathaniel Jr.** q.v.; **Nancy** b 22 Feb. 1806; **James** b 1 Oct. 1811, d 25 Dec. 1811; and **Charlotte** b 30 Mar. 1809.

DAVIS, NATHANIEL - Born ??, d ??, s/o ?? Children: **Annie May** b 3 Feb. 1858, m Dennis D. Merrill, -- Nov. 1878; **Merl L.** b 10 Mar. 1862; **Grace Mabel** b 29 Apr. 1868, d 23 Feb. 1870; **Dana Ross** b 16 Jul. 1876, d 6 Jan. 1880; and **Bertha M.** b 10 Apr. 1870.

DAVIS, NATHANIEL JR. - Born 15 May 1802, d 27 Oct. 1847 a pauper [vital records of Lewiston, Maine, p. 63], s/o Nathaniel and Hannah (Vickery) Davis. Nathaniel Davis, Jr. m Abigail Smith. Children: **Jason** b 25 Mar. 1833; **William** q.v.; and **Nathaniel** b 25 Mar. 1833, m Martha Barker, 1 Sep 1856.

DAVIS, OTIS F. - Born 9 Aug. 1827, d ??, s/o Stephen and Katherine/Catherine (----) Davis. Otis F. Davis m (1) 13 Dec. 1857 Sophia A./S. Garcelon, and m (2) 27 Nov. 1876 Hannah C. Merrill. Children: **Stephen G.** b 7 May 1859; **Addie F.** b 21 Oct. 1860, m Rodney A. Swift, 6 Apr. 1882; **Alice M.** b 12 Oct. 1862; **Lillian S.** b 18 Sep. 1864; **Susie A.** b 14 Jul. 1866; and **Harry O.** b 2 Aug. 1870.

DAVIS, RUFUS - Born ??, d ??, s/o ?? Rufus Davis m Clarissa Mitchell of Wales, Maine, pub. 31 Oct. 1847.

DAVIS, STEPHEN - Born 21 Jun. 1801, d 18 Jan. 1892, s/o Aaron and Mary (Wilkins) Davis. Stephen Davis m (1) 27 Jan. 1827 Katherine/Catherine Field, and m (2) 7 Dec. 1856 Susan B. Jackson. Children: **Otis F.** q.v.; **Asa M.** b 23 Sep. 1829, m Sarah Willard, 22 Dec. 1857; **Augusta E.** b 12 Aug. 1831, m Rev. Joseph K. Greene, 24 Aug. 1857; **Angeline S.** b 16 Apr. 1833, m A. H. Hardy, 16 Nov. 1856; **Albert F.** b 7 Sep. 1836, d 16 Feb. 1894; **Rodney** b 19 Jun 1838, d 5 Mar. 1862; **Emma** b 16 Apr. 1840, m Marcellus S. Merrill, 9 Apr. 1862; **Melvin** b 16 Feb. 1842, m Etta Olmstead; **Cornelia W.** b 9 Apr. 1844, m Frank Baker, 18 Oct. 1870; **Frederick L.** q.v.; **George K.** q.v.; and **Everett C.** b 16 Apr. 18--, d 20 May 1868.

DAVIS, WILLIAM - Born 21 Dec. 1792, d 7 Nov. 1869/1870, s/o Aaron and Mary (Wilkins) Davis. William Davis m (1) Hannah

Thompson, pub. 2/22 Oct. 1820, and m (2) Jane M. Jordan, pub. 18 Nov. 1843. Children: **William** b 23 Oct. 1821, d 28 Apr. 1870; **Charlotte H.** b 23 Jul. 1823, d 1 Oct. 1880; **Matt E.** b 25 Jan. 1826, d 18 May 1876, m (1) Mrs. Mary Clark, 9 May 1847, and m (2) Abbie B. Charles, 17 Nov. 1866; **M a r t h a C.** b 29 Mar. 1828, d 24 Feb. 1861; **Augusta** b 29 Jul. 1831, d 1 Jun. 1864, m Charles O. Libby of Lisbon, ME, 18 Oct. 1862; and **Joel T.** b 29 Jul. 1836, d 1 Jun. 1864.

DAVIS, WILLIAM - Born 2 Jul. 1834?, d ??, s/o Nathaniel and Abigail (Smith) Davis. William Davis m Eunice/Eunice J. Smith. Children: **Abbie Elisabeth** b 22 Feb. ----, m Charles Moses; **Martha E.** b 19 Dec. ----, m William Merrill; **G e o r g e W.** b 28 Oct. ----; **Effie J.** b 8 Jan. ----, m Elmer Arnold; and **Ida E.** b 13 Nov. 1874.

DAVIS, WILLIAM - Born ??, d ??, s/o ?? William Davis m 3 Jan. 1857 Emma J. Smith of Topsham, Maine. Children: **Abbie Elizabeth** b 22 Feb. 1859, m Charles M. Morse, 25 Oct. 1879; **Emma M.** b 19 Dec. 1863, d 11 Oct. 1882, m William Morrett, -- Oct. 1879; **M a r y** b 13 Mar. 1866, m Augustus Chadbourne, 4 Jan. 1886; **George** b 28 Oct. 1868, unm; **E f f i e J.** b 8 Jan. 1872, m Elmer Arno of Bath, ME; and **Elizabeth J.** b 13 Mar. 1874, unm.

DAY, ABIAH - Born ??, d ??, s/o John and Eliza (Gray) Day. Abiah Day m (1) Elvira Haywood, and m (2) Mrs. Mary M. Coomb. Children: **Anna** m Leslie Haywood, had two children; **Ella** m Devereaus Faulson, had two children, d in Mass.; **Alice**; **Elsie**; **Willie**, unm, lived in Lawrence, Mass.; **Veranus** m Meada Frost of Cooper, ME; **Bert**; and **Alphonso** m Hattie Lydick of Upper Falls, N.B., had five children, was a member of the Maine Signal Corps and an active participant in the San Juan engagement of the Spanish War.

DAY, ABRAHAM - Born ??, d ??, s/o ??. Abraham Day m Mary ----. Children: **Miriam** b 2 Aug. 1790; **Rachel** b 5 Aug. 1790, m Alexander; **Stephen** b 1 May 1792; **Elisabeth** b 13 Mar. 1795, m Wallace ----; **Rhoda** b 23 Jul. 1798, m Robert Rogers; **Sylvina** b 23 Jul. 1798, m McIntire; **Ruth** b 30 Sep. 1803, m Chas. Toddbury; and **Nelson** b 30 Apr. 1807, m Mary Johnson.

DAY, DELISS - Born ??, d ??, s/o Joel and Catherine (Richardson) Day. Deliss Day m Katherine Brun, was a trader and resident of Princeton, Maine. Children: **Fred A.** m Mert Hoar, Princeton, lived in Port Ludlow, Wash., had three children; **Lillie E.** m Clarence Bates, Princeton, had four children; **Hattie A.** m Darius Feulason, Princeton, had two children; **Lowell L.** unm, lived in OH; **Morey G.**; **John F.**; **Floyd**; **Dora M.**; and **Nellie M.**

DAY, JACOB - Born in Georgetown, Maine, 12 Apr. 1777, d ??, s/o Jacob and Bathany (Bliffith) Day. Jacob Day m 28 Nov. 1799 Rebecca Gilbert, d 25 Feb. 1857. Children: **Stephen** b 20 Aug. 1800, d 20 Mar. 1845, m Rebecca Richardson; **Josiah** b 16 Jul. 1802, d 10 Apr. 1879, m Amy Ricker; **H e r s e y** b 18 Jun. 1804, d 27 Jun. 1884, m (1) Eunice Bailey, and m (2) Mrs. Judith Dwinal; **R a n d a l l** b 31 Mar. 1806, d 8

Apr. 1879, m Phebe Shaw; **Mary (Polly)** b 8 Apr. 1808, d 16 Aug. 1828; **Henry O.** b 1 Mar. 1810, m (1) Hester A. Cobb, and m (2) Olive M. Gove; **Christina B.** b 28 Sep. 1812, d 9 Nov. 1844, m Capt. John Hooper; **Judith** b 30 Mar. 1816, d 10 Sep. 1900, m Henry A. Torsey, 5 Feb. 1838; **Betsy E.** b 22 Nov. 1818, d 9 Nov. 1844, m Washington Hanscom; **Clarisa M.** b 5 Mar. 1821, m Samuel M. Parcher (she was his 2nd wife) [BRYANT, Samuel 1868-1955 *Notes on Leeds' Families* at MHS]; and **Ann B.** b 2 Mar. 1823, d 9 Dec. 1848, m Samuel M. Parcher.

DAY, JOEL - Born ??, d ??, s/o ?? Joel Day m (1) Elizabeth Jones, and m (2) Catherine Richardson. *Children by 1st wife*: **Randall** q.v.; **Josiah** q.v.; and **Elizabeth** m Mark Dudley. *Children by 2nd wife*: **Euphunia** *; **Deliss**, q.v.; **Emily**; **Doranda** *; **Alfred**; **Harris** *; **Lity** *; **Linnie** *; **Flora** *; **Harris**; and **Perry**. Those marked with an asterisk (*) died in less than three weeks after contracting Diptheria.

DAY, JOHN/JACOB - Born in Leeds, Maine, 17 Mar. 1799, d??, s/o Samuel and Mehitable (Grover) Day. John Day came to Wesley, Maine, about 1826. He m Eliza Gray of Wesley. Children: **John Alvin** d in youth; **Abiah** q.v.; **Samuel** q.v.; **Hannah** m Jordan Hall (a noted musician), had five children; and **John Wilber** d in Civil War.

DAY, JOSEPH HENRY - Born 1841 in Lewiston, d 8 Aug. 1898 in Lewiston, s/o Hersey and ?? Day. Joseph Henry Day at one time owned a beautiful and valuable farm in New Gloucester, Maine. He m (1) 1863 Lovonia Gilbert, and m (2) Rebecca R. Hatch whose daughter was Isabella (Mrs. George Whitney). [*Historic Lewiston: its government*, by The Lewiston Historic Commission, 1981/82, p. 22.]

DAY, JOSIAH - Born ??, d ??, s/o Joel and Elizabeth (Jones) Day. Josiah Day m Maria Bird, had 14 children but names of only six following are known. Children: **George A.** unm; **Alberto L.** unm; **Flora E.** m (1) Frank Seavey, Crawford, Maine, had one child, Herman, and m (2) Heman Dodge, Wesley, had one child, Bessie; **Lucy E.** unm; **Ida B.** m Melville Hawkins of Wesley, ME, had four children, Mina, Clarence, Thatcher, and Edna; and **John B.** unm.

DAY, RANDALL - Born ??, d ??, s/o Joel and Elizabeth (Jones) Day. Randall Day m Nancy Dudley, lived in Princeton, Maine, had 10 children, but names of only four following are known. Children: **Edward F.** unm; **Beatrice** m W. E. Choate of Waterville, ME, had two children; **Alonzo** unm; and **Cleaveland** unm.

DAY, SAMUEL - Born ??, d ??, s/o John and Eliza (Gray) Day. Samuel Day m Addia Elsemore, moved to Lawrence, Massachusetts, when she died. Children: **Arlington J.** m Sirena Gray, was a trader in Wesley, ME; **J. Wilber**; **Emma**; **Ann Ella** m (1) William Ohambis, and m (2) Wm. Roberts; **Justine** m Nettie Guptill, who m (2) Mr. Woodcock of Lawrence, MA, and had two children, one of whom d young; **Roy** m Alice Roberts; **Ralph** m Ida Roberts; **Julia** unm, lived w/bro Ralph in Yarmouth, ME; **Nellie; Lorenzo** unm; **Charlie** unm; **Louny** d in infancy; **Jennie;** and ---- dau d in infancy.

DEAN, JOHN - 1-0-1 Lewiston 1790 census. (See Stackpole's *History of Durham,* pp. 165-166, "Dain Family".)

DEAN, JOHN - 2-3-3 Lewiston 1790 census. (See Stackpole's *History of Durham,* p. 165.]

DEAN, WILLIAM - 1-2-1 Lewiston 1790 census. (See Plummer's *History of Lisbon, Maine.*)

DENNETT, EBENESER - Born 1757, d 9 Apr. 1834, s/o ?? Ebeneser Dennett m (1) Anna Roberts, and m (2) Sarah Thomas, pub. 17 Mar. 1817. Children: **Moses** q.v.; **Nathan** b 9 Jan. 1804, m Louisa Orcutt, 17 Sep. 1828; **Peter** q.v.; **Dorothy** b 22 Sep. 1787, d 3 May 1833, m Jacob Golder, 29 Dec. 1808; **Anna** b -- Mar. 1786, d 19 Aug. 1882, m William Dill, 29 Dec. 1808; **Abby Roberts** b 15 Jun. 1797, m Joshua Jordan, 28 Apr. 1826; **Sally** b 1796, m Fairfield Golder, 24 Feb. 1822; **Levi** b 1807, m 30 Jun. 1833 Sarah H. Frost, moved to Orono, ME; and **Mary** b 16 May 1810, d 28 Mar. 1871.

DENNETT, MOSES - Born -- Sep. 1792, d ??, s/o Ebeneser and ?? Dennett. Moses Dennet m Dorcas Aldrich of Freeport, Maine, pub. 7 Dec. 1816, d/o Nath and Mary (Googins) Dennett. Children: **Richard G.** b in Lisbon, ME, -- Jul. 1817, d 1873 in Sheboygan, Wisconsin, m Julia Conner of Greenville, moved to Wisconsin in 1848; **Mary Ann** b -- Apr. 1819, d 1875 in Sheboygan, Wisconsin, m Orin Rogers of Cambridge, moved to Wisconsin in 1845; **Nancy Aldrich** [letter to Mr. Elder from Nancy Aldrich Randall, Owatonna, Minnesota, postmarked 17 Jul. 1900] b in Turner, ME, -- Jan. 1822, m John H. Randall, pub. 18 Jan. 1846, moved to Wisconsin in 1871; and **Albert** b -- Oct. 1829, m Hattie Sage, moved to Wisconsin in 1849.

DENNETT, PETER - Born 6 Jun. 1800, d 3 Mar. 1884, s/o Ebeneser and ?? Dennett. Peter Dennett m (1) 4 May 1826 Mrs. Rebecca Holland, and m (2) Abby Johnson pub. 29 Oct. 1826. Children: **Nancy** b 20 Nov. 1826, d 11 May 1873, m O. S. Carville, 27 Jun. 1847; **Clarinda R.** m Samuel Jay, Jr., of Winthrop, ME, 4 Nov. 1852; **Rebecca** b 30 Dec. 1828, m Rushworth Jordan; **Eveline H.** b 28 Jun. 1842; **Julia A.** b -- Sep. 1836, d 2 Apr. 1853; and **Frank E.** b 10 Apr. 1846, d 27 Apr. 1853.

DICKEY, HENRY H. - Born 14 May 1816 in Amherst, New Hampshire, d 20 May 1884 in Lewiston, s/o ?? Henry H. Dickey started in business in Nashua, New Hampshire, moved to Lowell, Massachusetts, and then to Lewiston in 1854. He m (1) Frances Huse, and m (2) Eliza Gurney. Children: **William**, and three daughters. [*Historic Lewiston: its government*, by The Lewiston Historic Com., 1981/82, p. 20.]

DILL, BENJAMIN - Born ??, d ??, s/o ?? Benjamin Dill m 23 Apr. 1848 Mary E. Osborn. Children: **Ellen R.** b 6 Sep. 1849, d 12 Mar.

1875; **Charles F.** b 24 Sep. 1850, d 3 Feb. 1891; **Mary E.** b 1 Dec. 1851; **Ernest M.** b 17 Aug. 1857; **Edwin P.** b 22 Aug. 1861; **Ulysses G.** b 10 Jun. 1865, d 3 Aug. 1877; and **Minnie M.** b 7 Jul. 1871.

DILL, CHARLES H. - Born 6 Jul. 1830, d 8 Oct. 1878, s/o John and Rebecca W. (Hinckley) Dill. Charles H. Dill m 21 Nov. 1860 Sylance H. Dudley of Mattawamkeag, Maine. Child: **Ira B.** b 12 Apr. 1862.

DILL, CHARLES O. - Born 7 Nov. 1848, d ??, s/o Orrison and Mary J. (Hammond) Dill. Charles O. Dill m Mary N. Badger, 28 Aug. 1870. Children: **Daniel W.** b 26 Dec. 1871; **John O.** b 4 Sep. 1873; **Llewellyn H.** b 2 May 1879; **Rosa L.** b 3 Mar. 1882; and **Seward** b 28 Dec. 1890.

DILL, DANIEL - Born ??, d ??, s/o ?? Children: **Daniel** b 13 Jan. 1731; **Hannah** b 16 May 1735; **Joseph** b 2 Oct. 1738; and **Mary** b 2 Oct. 1738.

DILL, DANIEL - Born 4 Oct. 1790/1799, d 10 Feb. 1830, s/o Enoch Jr. and Joanna (Bishop) Dill. Daniel Dill m Polly Sawyer, 4 Dec. ----. Children: **Charles Henry**; and **Adaline** m William Colby of Wales, ME.

DILL, DANIEL JR. - Born ??, d ??, s/o ?? Daniel Dill, Jr. m 8 Nov. 1698 Elisabeth Frost. Children: **Mary** b 25 Nov. 1699; **Dorothy** b 9 Sep. 1700; **John** b 8 Nov. 1703; **Daniel** b 28 Feb. 1705; **Dorcas** b 16 Jul. 1708; and **Joseph** b 14 Jan. 1710.

DILL, EBEN M. - Born ??, d ??, perhaps s/o Enoch, Jr. and Daraca (----) Dill. Children: **Lora J.** b 9 Aug. 1850, m Solomon J. Cole of Lewiston, 1 May 1876; and **Walter E.** b 16 Mar. 185-, m Jennie Whittier, 2- Dec. 1887.

DILL, EDWARD C. - Born ??, d ??, s/o ?? Edward C. Dill m 15 Jun. 1887 Sophia Longil. Child: **Everline C.** b 9 Feb. 1892.

DILL, ELBRIDGE - Born 4 Oct. 1834, d ??, s/o ?? Elbridge Dill m 10 Mar. 1859 Octavia H. Banges. Children: **Myra B.** b 24 May 1861; **George B.** b 22 Apr. 1863; **Seward E.** b -- Aug. 1868; **Charles E.** b 4 Nov. 1870; **Lissie M.** b 27 Oct. 1874; **Robert O.** b 1 Oct. 1876; **William A.** b -- May 1881; and **Joseph H.** b 8 Jul. 1883.

DILL, ELIAS - Born 9 Nov. 1801, d 7 Sep. 1886/1896, s/o Enoch Jr. and Joanna (Bishop) Dill. Elias Dill m 20 Mar. 1835 Ether/Esther Mountford. Children: **Daniel**; **Lucy** m Elbridge Stiles of Deering, ME; **William**; and **Harrison** m Sarah Skillings of Gray, ME.

DILL, ENOCH - Born 1799, d -- Oct. 1846, s/o ?? Enoch Dill m 20 Jan. 1822 Elisabeth Edgecomb. Children: **Orrison** b -- Mar. 1823; **Sarah** b -- Jan. 1825; **Frank W.** b -- Mar. 1831; **William R.** b -- Oct. 1834; and **Enoch** b -- Jan. 1837.

DILL, ENOCH - Born 12 Feb. 1770, d 23 Oct. 1835 or 14 Jul. 1855, s/o John and Sarah (Coffin) Dill. Enoch Dill m (1) 19 Apr. 1791 Annie Ross, b 12 Feb. 1763 [vital records of Lewiston, Maine, p. 15], and m (2) 1828 [see scrapbook on Gardiner MHS] Sarah Robinson. Children: **William** q.v.; **Catherine** b 3 Apr. 1795; **Enoch, Jr.** b 19 Aug. 1799, d 15 Oct. 1846, m Elisabeth Edgecomb, 17 Jan. 1822; and **Martha** b 17 Sep. 1812.

DILL, ENOCH - Born ??, d ??, s/o ?? Enoch Dill m Joanna Bishop, pub. 29 Jan. 1774. Children: **M e r c y** b 14 Nov. 1774 in Lewiston, m Eleasor/Elwin Lake; **R u t h** b 13 Jun. 1776 in Lewiston, m Alpheus/Alphesus Field; **E n o c h** b 23 Sep. 1778 in N. Yarmouth, ME, m Miss D. Field.

DILL, ENOCH JR. - Born ??, d ??, s/o ?? Enoch Dill, Jr. was of Webster, Maine, in 1849 [deed book 13-168-Androscoggin Co.] Children: **Daniel** q.v.; **Elias** q.v.; **Lucy** b 30 Jun. 1803, d 1 Sep. 1804; **Mercy** b 14 Jun. 1805, d 26 Jan. 1874; **Salome M.** b 18 Jul. 1808, d 22 Sep. 1893, m Benjamin Skillings, 4 Aug. ----; **Eben M.** b 1 Jan. 1812, m Susan B. Grough, 18 Oct. 1847; and **Abigail** b 2 Jul. 1815, d 12 Dec. 1893, m David Thompson, 27 Dec. 1849.

DILL, FRANK W. - Born ??, d ??, perhaps s/o Enoch and Elizabeth (Edgecomb) Dill. Frank W. Dill m 11 Sep. 1855 Susan Neal. Children: **Frank E.** b in Gardiner, ME, 22 Apr. 1857; and **Emily W.** b 30 May 1871.

DILL, HARRY E. - Born ??, d ??, s/o ?? Children: **Elliot C.** b 30 Dec. 1874; and **Daisy M.**

DILL, HENRY F. - Born ??, d ??, s/o ?? Henry F. Dill m 11 Feb. 1846 Laura R. Wakefield. Children: **Henry W.** b 12 Sep. 1874; **Arthur H.** b 12 Jul. 1876; **Homer B.** b 30 Oct. 1877; **Fred W.** b 28 Nov. 1880; and **John H.** b 11 Sep. 1887.

DILL, JAMES - Born 16 Jul. 1781 [vital records of Lewiston, Maine, p. 15] in Lewiston, d 21 May 1867, s/o John and Sarah (Coffin) Dill. James Dill m (1) 4 Dec. 1806 Elisabeth Eliot, d 30 Jan. 1815 in No. 6, d/o Wm. Eliot of Brunswick, Maine, they moved to No. 6 (Oxford Co.) [later part of Phillips, Maine,] in Mar. 1808 and built the first frame house in town which was later lost in a fire 1814, and James m (2) 20 Aug. 1815 Mary Goff of Minot (now Auburn), Maine, and James m (3) 1 Aug. 1847 Nancy Nisbett, wid/o Charles Nisbett. [Charles Nisbett was b in Boston, Massachusetts, and d in what is now part of Madrid, Maine, in 1844]. *Children of 1st wife*: **S e w a r d** ** b 22 Jan. 1808 in Lewiston; **Orrison** q.v.; **Harrison** b 7 Jul. 1812 in No. 6, d 26 Aug. 1841 of yellow fever in Apalainda?, West Florida. *Children of 2nd wife*: **Elisabeth E.** b 30 Jan. 1816, m Jonathan Lowell, 16 Apr. 1840; **Delana G.** b 28 Nov. 1817, m Wm. Lake, 22 Jun. 1845; **James** b 22 Aug. 1819, d 14 Mar. 1863; **H a n s o n** b 29 Aug. 1821, d 3 May 1824; **Siras G.** b 4 Oct. 1822, d 13 Apr. 1825; **Sarah Ann** b 4 Feb. 1824, d 20 Sep. 1825; **Hannah C.** b 7 May 1825 in Berlin, m Fairfield Golder, Jr.,

9 Nov. 1854; **Mercy Ann** b 16 Mar. 1827, m Joseph Lamb, 5 Oct. 1854; **Ansel** ** b 6 Jul. 1828, m (1) Lucy D. French, 23 Jan. 1853, and m (2) Louisa F. Pray, 15 Sep. 1861; **John C.** q.v.; **Moses G.** b 19 Jan. 1833, d 27 Jul. 1863 in Greene, ME; and **Dorcas M.** b 10 Mar. 1837, d 4 Jun. 1841. [** Information from letters written by Seward Dill and Ansel to J. G. Elder in the 1880s.]

DILL, JOHN - Born 13 Nov. 1823, d 29 Apr. 1854, s/o ?? John Dill m twice. *Children of 1st wife*: **Albert F.** b 15 May 1846. *Children of 2nd wife*: **John F.** b 24 Jan. 1852, went to Pennsylvania, not heard from again; and **Cyrus H.** d -- Oct. 1854, age a few months.

DILL, JOHN - Born ??, d ??, s/o ?? John Dill m Sarah Coffin, d 27 Apr. 1850 [vital records of Lewiston, Maine, p. 208], pub. 11 Jul. 1761. Children: **Josiah** q.v.; **Dorcas** b 9 Apr. 1764, d 14 Oct. 1845, m William Golder; **Sarah** b 10 Apr. 1766, m Joshua Lake, pub. 8 Jan. 1785; **Polly** b 29 Mar. 1768; **Enoch** q.v.; **Hannah** b 12 Feb. 1773, m Joshua Haley; **Catey** b 12 Feb. 1773, d 15 Mar. 1795; **John Jr.** q.v.; **Joseph** q.v.; and **James** q.v.

DILL, JOHN III - Born 11 Oct. 1799, d ??, s/p John Jr. and Seviah/Survinah (Miller) Dill. John Dill III m 22 Dec. 1820 Rebecca W. Hinkley of Madrid, Maine. Children: **John** b 13 Nov. 1823, m Mrs. Nancy Kneeland 1844; **Belinda A.** b 24 Nov. 1825, m William Thornton of Providence, R.I., 8 Nov. 1853; **Warren N.** b 20 Nov. 1827, m Clarissa J. Ireland of Chester, Maine, 18 May 1848; **Charles H.** q.v.; **Hiram H.** b 13 Jun. 1832, d 16 Sep. 1862, m Chistana Davis 1852; **Rebecca W.** b 14 Apr. 1835 in Lincoln, Me., d 5 Aug. 1850; **Andrew J.** b 13 Jun. 1839, d 21 Jul. 1868; **Rachel S.** b 14 Apr. 1841; and **James P.** b 21 Nov. 1845, d 28 Jan. 1869, m Mathi Roundy 1867.

DILL, JOHN JR. - Born in Freeport, Maine, 18 Sep. 1775, d 28 Feb. 1853, s/o John and Sarah (Coffin) Dill. John Dill, Jr. m int. 21 Jul. 1798, m 2 Sep. 1798 Sevinah/Suvinah Miller of Freeport, Maine. Children: **John, III** q.v.; **Suvinah** b 11 Feb. 1802 in Lewiston, d 29 Oct. 1889, m Merrill Tenney of Raymond, ME; **Sally** b 25 Mar. 1804 in N. Yarmouth, ME, m (1) James Grover, and m (2) Daniel Tenney, and m (3) John Brown; **Betsey** b 15 Jul. 1806 in Lewiston, d 16 Apr. 1891, m Nathan Pillsbury; **Asa** b 27 Oct. 1808 in Berlin, ME, m Maria Pillsbury; **Hannah** b 23 Aug. 1811 in Berlin, m Grant Glidden of Freedom, ME; **Mercy A.** b 19 Mar. 1814 in Berlin, m Dummer Toward; **George W.** b 4 Mar. 1817 in Berlin, m Betsey Patterson; **Florinda** b 16 Aug. 1819 in Berlin, d 5 Aug. 1820; and **Deborah** b 11 Oct. 1821, m Rufus Patterson.

DILL, JOHN A. - Born ??, d ??, s/o ?? John A. Dill m Sarah Graffam. Children: **Harmon J.** b 9 Mar. 1840, m Hattie A. Blaney, -- May 1868; **Rufus**; **Emma** m John Walker; and **George**.

DILL, JOHN C. - Born 6 Dec. 1830, d ??, s/o James and Mary (Gott) Dill. John C. Dill m 2 Dec. 1860 Sarah C. M./M. C. Parker.

Children: **Charles H.** b 16 Sep. 1861 in Durham, ME; and **Marcia E.** b 21 Jun. 1870 in Lisbon, ME.

DILL, JOHN W. - Born 3 Jun. 1874, d ??, s/o ?? John W. Dill m 6 Jun. 1892 Ida Estelle Hunnewell. Children: **Mary Emma** b 28 Sep. 1893; and **George Rufus** b 8 Sep. 1895.

DILL, JOSEPH - Born 12 Feb. 1783, d 14 Oct. 1861, s/o Josiah and Abigail (Ray) Dill. Joseph Dill m 2 Dec. 1804 Polly Read. Children: **Abigail** b 6 Nov. 1805, m Aaron Hodgkins of Minot, ME, 27 Oct. 1825; **Anna H.** b 1 Mar. 1807, m John W. Hussey of Minot, 27 May 1830; **Owen/Orrin** q.v.; **Sally** b 21 Jan. 1811, d 31 Aug. 1858, m Jonathan Wright, Jr., 1 Jan. 1834; **Joseph** b 21 Jun. 1813, d 22 Jan. 1845, m Hulda Stevens, 25 Sep. 1842; **Mary** b 15 May 1815, m Wm. Dingley, 3 Jul. 1853; **George** b 5 Oct. 1817, m Lenore Cooledge, 7 Jun. 1859; **Washington** q.v.; **Harriet** b 11 Feb. 1821, d 27 Jul. 1843; **Ansel** b 11 Nov. 1822, m ---- Severance; **William G.** q.v.; **Alonzo G.*** b 19 May 1827, d 13 Jan. 1860; and **Charlotte** b 27 Dec. 1829, d 22 Apr. 1893, m Samuel Libbey, 30 Jun. 1860. [Vital Records of Lewiston, Maine, p. 101, and will of Alonzo Dill, Vol. 2 p. 450 of Androscoggin probate file *#433 at Androscoggin probate.]

DILL, JOSEPH - Born 6 Mar. 1777, d 6 Aug. 1819 or 14 Oct. 1861, s/o John and Sarah (Coffin) Dill. Joseph Dill m (1) Mary Goff, and m (2) Annie Buker. *Children of 1st wife*: **Josiah** b 4 Jun. 1799; **Elisabeth** b 28 May 1801, d 26 Apr. 1848, m John Jaquik; **Jonathan** b 1802, m Sally Doughty, 10 Mar. 1822. *Children of 2nd wife*: **John Abraham** d 16 Jul. 1863, m Sarah Graffam; **Enoch** d 1862 in Gardiner, ME, m Mary J. Marson; **Ann** b 14 Nov. 1810, d in Gardiner 26 Sep. 1895, m Caleb Taylor; and **Mary B.** b -- Oct. 1819, d 24 May 1888 in Gardiner, ME, m Wm. C. Dill.

DILL, JOSIAH - Born 31 Aug. 1762, d 20 Dec. 1827 at N. Yarville, Ohio [Lew VR 207], s/o John and Sarah (Coffin) Dill. Josiah Dill m 12/13 Sep. 1781 Abigail Ray of N. Yarmouth, Maine, d 1 Aug. 1839 [vital records of Lewiston, Maine, p. 207]. Children: **Joseph** q.v.; **Polly** b 20 Mar. 1785; **Sally** b 19 Mar. 1787, m Jonathon Wight, pub. 2 Oct. 1808; **William** q.v.; **Hannah** b 12 Feb. 1792, m Edwin Goff; **Dorcas** b 24 Jun. 1794, m Phineas Wright, 6 Jun. 1813; **Josiah** q.v.; **Samuel** q.v.; **Elias** d young; **Abigail** d young; and **Eliza** m Geo. W. Tibbetts, Litchfield, 6 Sep. 1827. [Vital Records of Lewiston, Maine, p. 15.]

DILL, JOSIAH - Born 3 May 1796, d 15 Nov. 1843 age 47 years and 6 months at Greene, Maine [vital records of Lewiston, Maine, p. 251], s/o Josiah and Abigail (Ray) Dill. Josiah Dill m 19 Sep. 1817 in Gardiner, Maine, [vital records of Lewiston, Maine, p. 143], Abigail M. Libby, b Scarboro, Maine, or Abigail Dyer of Scarboro. Children: **Rosilla G.** b 18 Jun. 1819 at Gardiner; **Dorothy B.** b 16 Feb. 1822 at Litchfield, m Joseph Davis; **Olive A.** b 21 Sep. 1824 at Litchfield, ME; **Sarah D.** b 17 Aug. 1826, m ---- Eaton; **Cyprus L.** b 23 Jul. 1828; **Mary Jane W.** b 8 Mar. 1830 at Gardiner, m ---- Eaton; **Dorcas**

W. b 8 Dec. 1833, m Elijah Guilford; **Arvista R.** b 15 Oct. 1836 at Lewiston; and **Hannah G.** b 10 Mar. 1839. [Vital Records of Lewiston, Maine, p. 143, recorded 3 Aug. 1857 by E. Tobie, town clerk.]

DILL, ORIN/OWEN - Born 7 Feb. 1809, d ??, s/o Joseph and Polly (Read) Dill [vital records of Lewiston, Maine, p. 101]. Orin/Owen Dill moved to Phillips, Maine. He m 7 May 1840 Abigail Miller Jordan or Abigail Jordan, d/o Apollos and Sarah (Miller) Jordan. Children: **Henry H.**; **Sarah E.**; **Harriet Ella**; **Alonso**; **Mary Asora**; and **Rovillah**. [*The Jordan Memorial* by Rev. Jordan, published by the New England History Press, reprint 1982, p. 389.]

DILL, ORISON - Born ??, d ??, s/o ?? Children: **Henry R.** b 29 Jan. 1849, m Laura R. Wakefield, 11 Feb. 1846.

DILL, ORRISON - Born 5/6 Aug. 1810 in No. 6, d 3 Apr. 1887, s/o James and Elisabeth (Eliot) Dill. Orrison Dill m 1833 Mary J. Hammond. Children: **Elbridge** b 4 Oct. 1834; **Lettice B.** b 1 Mar. 1837, m Joseph N. Fairbanks, 21 Sep. 1854; **Elisa J.** b 30 Jan. 1842, m John S. Harnden, 30 Apr. 1863; and **Charles O.** q.v.

DILL, PHINEAS/PHINEAS W. - Born -- Nov. 1820, d 12 May 1896 [vital records of Auburn, Maine, vol. 4 p. 16], s/o William and Anny/Amy (Dennett) Dill. Phineas/Phineas W. Dill m 23 Mar. 1843 Mary Randall. Children: **William R.** q.v.; **Dorcas W.** b 14 Nov. 1846, m David P. Field, 3 Jul. 1866; **Flavilla Jane** b 30 Sep. 1849, m Seth Burgess/Briggs of East Auburn, ME, d 17 Oct. 1907 [probate #6079]; **Wallace P.** q.v.; and **Samuel H.** b 24 Feb. 1858, m Nettie Tinkham, 16 Apr. 1890. [Will dated 23 June 1891 of Auburn, Maine, probate #3975 Androscoggin Co.]

DILL, SAMUEL - Born 8 Feb. 1799, d ??, s/o Josiah and Abigail (Ray) Dill. Samuel Dill m (1) 25 Dec. 1821 Sally Barnes, and m (2) Charlotte ----. *Child of 1st wife*: **Dexter** b 16 Jul. 1822. *Children of 2nd wife*: **Rufus McKenney** b 30 May 1827; **Rachel W.** b 19 Apr. 1832, d 30 Dec. 1857, m Joseph B. Lewis, 25 Apr. 1853; and **Samuel** b 20 Jan. 1835. [Vital Records of Lewiston, Maine, p. 64.]

DILL, SEWARD - Born in Lewiston 22 Jan. 1808, d ??, s/o James and Elisabeth (Eliot) Dill. Seward Dill m 14 Apr. 1833 Sarah W. Hammond. Children: **Florida** b in Phillips 26 Dec. 1835, d 14 Jan. 1860, m Jarvis Estey; and **Harry P.** b 11 Jul. 1895, m Colby of Lynn, Mass.

DILL, WALLACE P. - Born 22 Oct. 1855, d ??, s/o Phineas and Mary (Randall) Dill. Wallace P. Dill m (1) Sarah Blackwell of Auburn, Maine, and m (2) Katie Briggs or Kate Bryes. Children: **Mertie O.**; **Edward W.** b -- Aug. 1883; **Estella**; and **Carroll**.

DILL, WARREN A. - Born ??, d 29 Apr. 1864, s/o ??. Children: **Abby Frances** b 22 Dec. 1849, m Hestor Campbell; **Aura E.** b 13 Apr. 1852, m Jasper Reed; **M. Etter** b 8 Aug. 1857, m Thorndike A. Bonney; and **Cora** b 7 May 1859, d -- Oct. 1865.

DILL, WASHINGTON - Born 5 Oct. 1817 [vital records of Lewiston, Maine, p. 101], a twin, d 29 July 1878 age 60-9-23 [Crowley Cemetery, Lewiston, Maine], s/o Joseph and Polly (Read) Dill. Washington Dill m 16 Oct. 1845 Mrs. Caroline Purington/Punnton, nee Caroline Dingley, wid/o Joseph Purington/Punnton. Children: **Amanda** b -- Aug. 1848, d 3 Aug. 1852; and **Joseph F.** b -- Feb. 1851, d 3 Aug. 1852.

DILL, WILLIAM - Born 12 Sep. 1789, d 1823, s/o Josiah and Abigail (Ray) Dill. William Dill m 29 Dec. 1808 Anny/Amy Dennett. Children: **Adaline** d 13 Feb. 1848, m 3 Jun. 1828 William Jordan, 2nd, of Lisbon, ME, pub. 18 May 1828; **L o u i s a** b 15 Aug. 1812, d 8 Apr. 1872, m James A. Field, 29 Mar. 1833; **A n n** d -- May 1890, m Edwin Dzole/Dzido [a family by that name living in Lisbon, Maine, 1940], 25 Feb. 1843; **Ebeneser** d 25 Mar. 1846, m Ruth Covil of Bath, ME; **Almira** m Collins Edwards; **Phineas/Phineas W.** q.v.; and **Jane** d -- Jun. 1896 in Boston, MA, m David Huntington of Boston, MA.

DILL, WILLIAM - Born 30 Jan. 1793 [vital records of Lewiston, Maine, p. 15], d 2 Jul. 1825, s/o Enoch and Anne (----) Dill [vital records of Lewiston, Maine, p. 15]. William Dill m Elisa Church, 9 Feb. 1810. Children: **W i l l i a m C.** b 14 Aug. 1812, d 4 Jan. 1878, m Mary B. Dill; **Elisa** b 2 Sep. 1815; **James R.** b 9 Apr. 1817, d 12 May 1837; **Catherine** b 4 Dec. 1818; **Harriet N.** b 29 Mar. 1820, d 15 Jul. 1823; **Joseph C.** b 20 Jan. 1822; and **Charles H.** b 8 Dec. 1824, d 14 Nov. 1887.

DILL, WILLIAM G. - Born ??, d 14 Mar. 1904 in Lewiston, Maine, s/o Joseph and Polly (----) Dill. William G. Dill m Hulda Field. Children: **Alonzo G**; **William O.**; ---- (daughter) m ---- Babb. [Probate #5236 of Wm. G. Dill.]

DILL, WILLIAM R. - Born 20 Sep. 1844, d ??, s/o Phineas/Phineas W. and Mary (Randall) Dill. William R. Dill m 19 Mar. 1868 Olivia Conant. Children: **Bernice E.** b 8 Apr. 1873; **Celia May** b 16 Apr. 1875, m Ernest Leavitt, 5 Jan. 1898; and **Geo. W.** b 21 Nov. 1878.

DINGLEY, IRA - Born 14 Oct. 1805, d 15 Jun. 1860, s/o William, Jr. and Sally (Atkinson Dingley. Ira Dingley m Louisa Griffin of Freeport, Maine. Children: **William** b 30 Jan. 1830, m Cordelia Eastman, pub. 12 Dec. 1853; **Samuel** m Olive Davis; **Martha** m David Graffam, lived in Greene; **I r a** d 1 Apr. 1874, m Fannie Douglass, pub. 2 Sep. 1867; **Levi** b 14 Feb. 1840 in Lewiston, m Martha Mountfort; **Leonard G.** b 29 Dec. 1842, m Georgia A. Carvelli, 7 Apr. 1875; **Laura**; **Cordelia**; and **Emily** b 28 Mar. 1849, m John Hodgdon, 1 Jan. 1872.

DINGLEY, ISAIAH - Born ??, d ??, s/o ?? Isaiah Dingley m 29 Jul. 1832 Mary Bickford. Children: **William T.** b in Lisbon 20 May 1833, lived in Wales, ME, m Mrs. Marinda Ames, 4 Mar. 1862; **Nelson L.** d

9 Aug. 1870, m Sarah E. Cotton; **Mary** m William Stone; **Jane** m Charles Fish; and **Isaiah, Jr.** d 10 Apr. 1847.

DINGLEY, LEONARD G. - Born ??, d ??, s/o ?? Children: **Ernest L.** b 12 Jun. 1877; **Flora B.** b 2 Aug. 1879; **Helen M.** b 7 Oct. 1883; **Erlon J.** b 25 Jul 1886; and **Ethel B.** b 12 Sep. 1890.

DINGLEY, LEVI - Born 1 Oct. 1807, d 28 Feb. 1834, s/o William and Sally (Atkinson) Dingley. Levi Dingley m 9 Apr. 1829 Mary Davis. Children: **John Tabor** b 1 Oct. 1829, d 16 Nov. 1892, m Mary Ann Estes, 29 May 1856; **William J.** b 31 Aug. 1831, m Rachael Elisa Estes, 30 Nov. 1861; and **Harriet Augusta** b 7 Sep. 1834, m (1) Nelson Locke, and m (2) George W. Ryan. [Vital Records of Lewiston, Maine, p. 63.]

DINGLEY, LEVI L. - Born 2 Mar. 1842, d ??, s/o ?? Levi L. Dingley m 29 Nov. 1867 Delphina Edwards. Children: **Herbert Alton** b 18 Jul. 1871; and **George** b 15 Apr. 1873.

DINGLEY, NELSON JR. - Born 15 Feb. 1832 in Durham, Maine, d ??, s/o Nelson and Jane L. (----) Dingley. Nelson Dingley, Jr. m 1857 Salome McKenney, d/o a merchant of Auburn, Maine. Children: five sons and one daughter (the youngest). Four of the sons and the daughter were living in 1891. [*History of Androscoggin County*, edited by Georgia Merrill, published by W. A. Ferguson & Co., 1891, p. 422-426.]

DINGLEY, NELSON L. - Born 1832, d 8 Aug. 1870, s/o Isaiah and Mary (Bickford) Dingley. Nelson L. Dingley m Sarah E. Cotton. Children: **Julia A.** b 30 Dec. 1866, d 22 Aug. 1872; and **Albert** b 22 Apr. 1867.

DINGLEY, WILLIAM JR. - Born 25 Mar. 1774, d 10 Sep. 1852, s/o ?? William Dingley m 20 Aug. 1796 [vital records of Durham, Maine, p. ??] Sally Atkinson, pub. 21 Aug. 1796. Children: **Sally** b 3 Sep. 1798, d 7 Feb. 1865, m Esekiel Merrill, pub. 24 Feb. 1833; **Polly** b 15 Mar. 1799, d 21 Feb. 1858, m Daniel Annes, 12 Jul. 1821; **William** b 25 Nov. 1800, d 17 May 1814; **Lucy** b 28 Jun. 1802; **Charlotte** b 16 Oct. 1803, m Simon Carville, 30 Aug. 1831; **Ira** b 14 Oct. 1805, d 15 Jun. 1860, m Louisa Griffin of Freeport, ME, pub. 22 Feb. 1829; **Levi** q.v.; **Isaiah** b 2 Aug. 1809, d 18 Mar. 1897, m Mary Bickford, 29 Jul. 1832; **Caroline** b 15 May 1811, d 13 Sep. 1881, m (1) Joseph Purington, pub. 22 Jun. 1833, and m (2) Washington Dill, 16 Oct. 1845; **General** b 27 Mar. 1813, d 11 Feb. 1834; and **William Jr.**

DINGLEY, W. J. - Born ??, d ??, s/o ?? Children: **Fred E.** b 16 Oct. 1862; **Royal S.** b 7 Sep. 1866; **Nellie A.** b 22 Jun. 1871; **Grace M.** b 2 Nov. 1873; and **Chas. Frank** b 22 May 1888.

DINGLEY, WILLIAM JR. - Born 29 Nov. 1816, d 3 Jun. 1882, s/o William and Sally (Atkinson) Dingley. William Dingley, Jr. m (1) Mrs. May Dingley, pub. 17 Dec. 1836 and m (2) 3 Jul. 1863 Mary Dill.

Children: **Mary Elisabeth** b 18 Dec. 1837; **Lydia Ann** b 16 Jan. 1840, d 15 Sep. 1847; **Levie L.** b 2 Mar. 1842, m Delphia Edwards; **Elisa G.**; **Alice S.**; **Emily J.** d 24 Oct. 1850; and **Sarah E.** d 23 Aug. 1852.

DOANE, EDWARD - Born circa 1741?, d ??, might of been the s/o Ebenezer and Elizabeth (Skillings) Doane. Edward Doane was a soldier in the French and Revolutionary Wars. He m (1) pub. int. 3 Apr or 21 Oct. 1762 Anna Westcott, and m (2) 21 Nov. 1766 Sarah McDougle. Children (at least four): **William** moved to OH and had issue; **Charles** m Eunice ----, res. Cape Elizabeth, ME, in 1813; **R i c h a r d** m Mary Randall, had issue [see Stackpole's *History of Durham, Maine*, p. 171 & 172, 1899 reprint 1979 by New England History Press]; and **Joanna** m Joshua Elder, q.v. (see ELDER). "The old town of Cape Elizabeth, (Maine), is divided and the present (1894) town of South Portland retains the old records, which date back as to 1762. A few of the marriages only of the Doanes were recorded of which the town clerk sent me (Alfred Alder Doane) a certified copy last year (1893) and this copy with a few baptismal dates from the 2nd Parish records make the substance of my information...." [Letter to J. G. Elder from Alfred Alder Doane, 136 1st St., South Boston, MA, 26 May 1894. Mr. Doane published a genealogy on his family in 1902, see p. 149-150 of that book.]

DODD, STEPHEN - Born ??, d ??, s/o ?? Stephen Dodd m Eleanor ----. Child: **Mary** b -- Oct. 1794 [Vital Records of Lewiston, Maine, p. 17.]

DOUGLAS, JAMES JR. - Born ??, d ??, s/o ?? James Douglas m Hannah Hildreth, d 7 Aug. 1852, d/o Paul. She m (2) Nathaniel Bennett, b 18 Nov. 1768, d 2 Oct. 1852. Children: **D a v i d** b 28 Aug. 1801; **Paul Hildreth** b 22 Jan. 1803; **Annas** b 31 Oct. 1804; **George H.** b 26 Aug. 1806.

DOUGLASS, FRANCIS - Born ??, d 20 Jan. 1865, s/o ?? Francis Douglass m Susannah Hildreth. Children: **Mercy** b 18 Mar. 1805, d 8 Jun. 1879, m Robert Rhoades; **Jerusha** b 29 Dec. 1806, d 6 Mar. 1807; **Z e b u l o n W.** b 14 Apr. 1808, d 28 May 1882, m Hannah C. Johnson; **Robert H.** b 19 Feb. 1810, d 2 Jun. 1881; **William H.** b 17 Aug. 1813, d 18 Apr. 1856; **Hannah** b 15 Oct. 1814; **Joshua N.** b 4 Apr. 1819; and **Eleaser C.** b 20 Jun. 1824, d 20 Jun. 1880.

DUNN, BENJAMIN - Born 1 Jan 1813 in Cornish, Maine, d 6 Aug. 1861 [Androscoggin Co. Court probate #218], s/o Benjamin and Sally (Trafton) Dunn. Benjamin Dunn lived in Lewiston, Danville, and moved to Auburn, Maine, and d in 1861. He m Ruby N. Waterman of Poland Maine, b 21 Mar. 1813, d/o Daniel and Abigail (True) Waterman. Children: **Charles O.** b 6 May 1838, d 23 May 1839; **Martha A.** b 3 Nov. 1839, d 30 Aug. 1860, m Charles Kilord; **Sarah A.** b 30 Jun. 1844; and **Charles W.** b 19 Jul. 1846. [*Early Families of Cornish, Maine*, compiled by Robert Taylor, published by Robert Taylor, 1987, p. 37.]

DUNN, CHARLES - Born ??, d ??, s/o Benjamin and ?? Dunn. Child: **Ruby** b -- Jul. 1888.

DWELLEY, ALEXANDER - Born 22 May 1776 [vital records of Lewiston, Maine, p. 18], d ??, s/o ?? Alexadner Dwelley m 1799 Katherine/Catherine Lee of Barry, Mississippi, b -- Mar. 1775 [vital records of Lewiston, Maine, p. 18]. Children: **Darwin/Darloin** b 22 Nov. 1799, m Rowena Newton, 4 Feb. 1827; **H e n r y** b 5 Sep. 1802, m (1) 19 May 1839 Mary Ann Wellman, d 22 Dec. 1839, and m (2) May ---- 8 Apr. 1840; **Horace** b 27 Aug. 1805, m (1) Marinda ----, 16 Aug. 1832, and m (2) Lydia ----, 1 Aug. 1836; **K a t h e r i n e** b 23 Aug. 1807, d 2 Oct. 1837 age 30 years 1 month 9 days, m Alexander Hatch 14 Jul. 1835; and **Alexander** b 30 Apr. 1810, m (1) 17 Nov. 1836 Margaret R. ----, d 25 Dec. 1841 age 27 years 1 month, and m (2) Nancy Ashly, 6 Feb. 1842.

DWELLEY, DARWIN/DARLOIN - Born 23 Nov. 1799, d 18 Nov. 1884, s/o Alexander and Katherine/Catherine (Lee) Dwelley. Darwin/Darloin Dwelley m 4 Feb. 1827 Rowena Newton, b 14 Feb. 1808. Children: **Harriet N.** b 9 Mar. 1829, m Otis Carville, 31 Jan. 1849; **Horace D.** b 14 Feb. 1881; **Melsor (Melsar) S.** b 3 May 1833; **Catherine J.** b 9 Jul. 183?, m Leroy Kenniston, 27 Aug. 1861; **Samuel L.** b 29 Oct. 1838, killed 8 Jul. 1863; **Calvin** b 21 Jan. 1843; **Angeline A.** b 26 May 1847; and **Rowena M.** b 1 Aug. 1850.

DWELLEY, JOSEPH - Born 17 Oct. 1737 in Worcester, Massachusetts, d 9 Dec. 1807 age 70 years 1 month 22 days, s/o ?? Joseph Dwelley m Mary Dwelley, b 1 May 1737, d 23 Dec. 1834, age 97 years 7 months 23 days. Children: **Joseph** b 17 Mar. 1764; **Rachel** b 17 Dec. 1765; **Mary** b -- Jan. 1768; **Melzar** b 5 Feb. 1771; **Hannah** b 21 Mar. 1773; and **Lemuel** b -- Dec. 1774.

DWINAL, AARON - Born Sutton, Massachusetts, 10 Aug. 1762, d 5 Aug. 1844, s/o ?? Aaron Dwinal m (1) Susanna ----, and m (2) 18 Oct. 1799 Abigail Forks, and m (3) Hulda Watson of Poland, Maine, pub. 3 Feb. 1798, and m (4) 19 Nov. 1833 Judith Spifford. *Children of 1st wife*: **Susannah** b 2 Feb. 1787, m Nathaniel Herrick of Greene, ME, -- Oct. 1804; **Ruth** b 18 Mar. 1788, d 30 Sep. 1810, m Joel Thompson, Jr., pub. 11 Mar. 1809; **Sarah** b 30 Apr. 1890, unm; **Aaron** b 11 Dec. 1791, m Celia Cushman of New Gloucester, ME, 7 Mar. 1815; **Simeon** q.v. *Child of 2nd wife*: **Huldah** b 14 Jun. 1798, d 24 Apr. 1825, m Edmund Hinckley 1 Jan. 1818. *Children of 3rd wife*: **A b i g a i l** b 25 Oct. 1800, m Stephen Davis 14 Feb. 1822; **A m o s** b 26 Jan. 1802, m Sarah Small of Rumford, ME, pub. 18 Sep. 1832; **R u f u s** b 1 Nov. 1804, d in Bangor, ME, unm; **Oren** b 23 Aug. 1806, m Elisa; **Luther** b 9 Jan. 1809, m Priscilla R. Tebbets of Lisbon, ME, pub 1 Jan. 1835; **Calvin** b 30 Oct. 1810, m Elisa Bucknam, d/o Wm. and Sarah (Blackstone) of Lisbon, pub. 13 Oct. 1833; **Albert** b 29 Mar. 1813, unm; **Mary Ann** b 22 May 1815, m W.H.S. Cleveland; **Charles** b 24 Dec. 1817, unm; and **Celia** b 12 Dec. 1820, m Wm. C. Bruce of Bangor, 14 Oct. 1847.

DWINAL, AMOS - Born ??, d ??, s/o ?? Children: Warren; Henry; Lester; and Ellen.

DWINAL, CALVIN - Born ??, d ??, s/o ?? Children: Celia Frances b 11 Sep. 1835; Julia Adalade b 21 Sep. 1840, m Henry M. Prentiss of Bangor, ME; Frank b 7 May 1842, m Emma Crosby of Bangor; and Charles b 4 Feb. 1844, m Louisa Snow of Bucksport, ME.

DWINAL, SIMEON - Born 30 Dec. 1795, d ??, s/o Aaron and Susanna (----) Dwinal. Simeon Dwinal m Elisa Herrick of Greene, Maine, d 23 Oct. 1869. Children: Lydia b 3 Sep. 1820, m Joseph Kilgore; Sally b 24 Sep. 1822, m Daniel Smith; Rufus b 6 Apr. 1826, unm; and Elisa b 19 Aug. 1832, d 23 Oct. 1861.

DYER, BARZILLA J./BARSILLA - Born 12 Apr. 1793, d 26 Sep. 1870, s/o Elkanah and Catherine (Brooks) Dyer. Barzilla J./Barsilla Dyer m 30 Sep. 1818 Rebecca Jordan of Cape Elizabeth, Maine, d 31 Oct. 1846/1848, d/o Ephraim, pub. 24 Jun. 1818. Children: Susan J. b 22 Sep. 1821, d 19 Aug. 1842, unm; Reubin R. b 17 Mar. 1823, m Hannah Dyer, who d 6 May 1901, d/o Daniel 15 Jun. 1851; Rebecca b 7 Jan. 1825, d 30 Mar. 1847, unm; Drusilla b 19 Jan. 1827, d 31 Oct. 1857, m Daniel W. Carville, 4 Aug. 1850; Ann Jordan b 24 May 1829, d 4 Sep. 1831, age 2 years; Mary C. b -- Mar. 1831, d 30 Apr. 1899 at 68, m Antonio Fernandes Ceballos, who d in Spain 8 Jun. 1897 at age 66 years; Narcissa Ann b 29 Nov. 1839, m Oliver Welch 3 Dec. 1861, who d 24 Nov. 1902, age 72 years; Jane b -- Apr. ----, m Edwin M. Barnard 19 Mar. 1859; Ruth T. b 4 Apr. ----, d -- Jan. ---- age 49 years, m Seth Davis, pub. 1 Jun. 1855; Martha Ellen b 1 Feb. 1841, unm; and Maria D. b 18 Aug. ----, d 3 Nov. 1859, unm.

DYER, DANIEL - Born 26 Oct. 1806, d ??, s/o Elkanah and Catherine (Brooks) Dyer. Daniel Dyer m 23 Aug. 1827 Lois Curtis of Minot, Maine, b 19 May 1807, d/o William and Hannah (----) Curtis. Children: Daniel b 22 Nov. 1827, d 4 Dec. 1827; Hannah b 22 May 1829, d 6 May 1901, m Ruebin R. Dyer 15 Jun. 1851; James Libby b 18 Jul. 1831, m Abbie Brown of Auburn, ME, 9 Dec. 1851; William b 10 Aug. 1833, m Eleanor Philena Millary of New Portland, ME, pub. 24 Jun. 1863; John Stevens b 31 Aug. 1839, d age 7 months; Naomi R. b 5 Mar. 1837, m Joseph Chesley of New Portland, ME, 6 Aug. 1853; Sarah E. b 4 Aug. 1839, m Elkanah Dyer of New Portland, ME; Lydia b -- Nov. 1842, unm; Solomon b 28 Feb. 1845, m Julia Frufant; Martha b 9 Jul. 1846, unm; Rebecca unm; and Daniel b 13 Jun. 1852, m Lizzie Wood.

DYER, ELKANAH - [Original vital records of Lewiston, Maine, p. 17 spelling of Dyer was Diah.] Born 17 Sep. 1759, d 23 Jul. 1820 s/o Samuel and Thankful (----) Dyer. Elkanah Dyer m Catherine Brooks, d/o John and Martha (Staples) Brooks. Children: Elkanah Jr. q.v.; John Brooks b 8 Jan. 1787, m Sarah Dain of Lisbon, ME, pub. 31 Oct. 1812; Cate b 25 Feb. 1789, d 28 May 1882, age 93 years, m John Goss of Danville, ME, 28 Nov. 1816, who d 14 Mar. 1860; Nancy b 15 Feb. 1791, d 5 Jul. 1872, m Henry Carville of Lewiston 2 Jul. 1809, d 17

Oct. 1864; **Barzilla J.**/Barsilla q.v.; **Mattie** b 1 Mar. 1796, m Benjamin Tarr, s/o Seth, 5 Feb. 1817; **Polly** b 13 Aug. 1798, m Nathan Doleby; **Abigail** b 23 Jun. 1800, m Aaron Wetham of Danville 31 Jan. 1821; **Elmira** b 7 Oct. 1802, m Humphrey Whitney of Lisbon, ME, 17 Nov. 1822; **Ezekiel** b 1 Jul. 1804; **Daniel** q.v.; and **Cyrene** b 3 Feb. 1809, m Benjamin Goss of Danville 25 Dec. 1833. [Vital Records of Lewiston, Maine, p. 16.]

DYER, ELKANAH JR. - Born 7 May 1785, d age 78 years, s/o Elkanah and Catherine (Brooks) Dyer. Elkanah Dyer, Jr. m Sarah Hatch, d/o Samuel Hatch. Children: **Rufus** b 14 Apr. 1807, m Matilda Elder of New Portland, ME, 1 Oct. 1829, d/o Isaac; **Allen** b 3 Oct. 1808, m Amanda Starling of New Portland, ME; **Mary** b 19 Apr. 1810, m Samuel Jackson of Auburn, ME, 13 Mar. 1828; **Owen (Orren)** b 11 Oct. 1811, m Cynthia Bartlett, New Portland; **Katherine** b 15 Sep. 1813, m Daniel Metcalf of New Portland; **Rosannah** b 2 Jun. 1815, m Alvah Thompson of New Portland; **Martha** b 11 Jun. 1817, m William Dolbier of Kingfield, ME; **John** b 5 Jan. ----, m Matilda Clough; and **Warren** b -- Oct. ----, m Betsey Clough.

DYER, REUBIN R. - Born ??, d ??, s/o ?? Children: **Ella** b 9 Jul. 1852, m John E. Cole, pub. 6 Dec. 1871; **Minnetta** b 28 Feb. 1864, d 1 Aug. 1883, m V.A. Dunn, 21 Feb. 1882; and **Nellie P.** b 31 Dec. 1866, m Fred Durechey 9 Nov. 1887.

DYER, SAMUEL - Born ??, d 29 Dec. 1811, s/o ?? Samuel Dyer m Thankful ----. Children: **Luce** b 17 Sep. 1743; **Elizabeth** b 17 Nov. 1757, d 23 Nov. 1828, m Rev. James Garcelon, who d 28 Dec. 1838; **Elkanah** q.v.; **Mercy** b 27 Sep. 1759, d 11 Oct. 1845, m Henry Carville 1 Sep. 1782, who d 2 Jul. 1823; and **Abigail** b 13 Jul. 1761, d 19 Mar. 1850, m Thomas Rand 20 Mar. 1788, who d 6 Sep. 1837.

EASTMAN, JOHN - Born ??, d ??, s/o ?? John Eastman m Abigail ----. Children: **Mariah Elizabeth** b 1 June 1831; **Nancy** b 21 Sept. 1832; **Levi** b 22 July 1834; **Abigail R.** b 13 Nov. 1836. [Vital Records of Lewiston, Maine, p. 21.]

EDWARDS, COLLINS - Born ??, d ??, s/o ?? Collins Edwards m Almira ----. Child: **William Dill** b 6 Mar. 1838. [Vital Records of Lewiston, Maine, p. 21.]

EISEN, JOSHUA - Born 1831 in Hanover, Germany, d ??, s/o ?? Joshua Eisen occ' Dry Goods. He m Henrietta ----, b 1832 in Boden, Germany. Children: **Rebecca** b 1857 in Maine [1860 census Lewiston.]

ELDER, JANUS G. - Born 1835 in St, Albans, Maine, d 2 Feb. 1907 [obit *Journal* 4 Feb. 1907], s/o Joshua Jr. and Phebe B. (Day) Elder. Janus G. Elder started this history over one hundred years ago; it covers a little more than the first one hundred years of Lewiston's history. He m Pricilia G. Wing of Dover, Maine. Children: **George** b 1864, d 1949, no issue; and **Charles** d before 1949, no issue.

ELDER, JOSHUA - Born 28 Oct. 1763 in Cape Elizabeth, Maine, d 22 Jan. 1846 in Dexter, Maine, s/o John and Miriam (Purington) Elder. Joshua Elder was a revolutionary soldier. Application for pension 14 Apr. 1831 at Monmouth, Maine. He m 16 Dec. 1784 Joanna ---- [Maine Historical Records on Leeds, ME, manuscript] [letter from Bureau of Pensions, 1894] [Dexter, Maine, VR, card file at Maine State Archives], b 13 Sep. 1764, d 26 Jan. 1846, d/o Edward and Anna (Westcott) Doane [birth and parent information letter dated 1894 from Alfred Doane of South Boston, Massachusetts, to Elder]. Children: **William** b 28 Jun. 1785 in Littleboro Plt., Maine, (now Leeds, Maine), d 9 Jul. 1823 age 38 years [records on file at AHS], m pub. 21 Sep. 1805 [AHS] Sarah Bates, b 17 Aug. 1787, d 23 Jan. 1855 age 67 years; **Charles** b 19 Sep. 1788 d 1? May 1860 [AHS, Elder], m (1) 20 Mar. 1808 Sarah Labree, b 30 Jun. 1788, d 3 Feb. 1838, and m (2) 10 Feb. 1849 Phebe Miller, d 30 Sep. 1855; **Richard** q.v.; **Joshua Jr.** q.v. [*The Doane Family* by Alfred Doane, published by the author, 1902, p. 149.]

ELDER, JOSHUA JR. - Born 10 Apr. 1798 in Leeds, Maine, d 5 Jul. 1879 in Winthrop, Maine, s/o Joshua and Joanna (----) Elder. Joshua Elder, Jr. m (1) Phebe B. Day, d 25 Oct. 1849 in Lewiston, d/o Joseph and Ruth (Gilbert) Day. *Children of 1st wife*: **William Erastus** b 7 Feb. 1829, d 14 Feb. 1906, m (1) Annette Stafford, d 1 Oct. 1863 age 30 years, and m (2) Lydia Pellingill; **Joseph P.** b 22 Jul. 1842, d 29 Dec. 1905, no issue; **Rebecca** m and moved to Wakefield, Massachusetts; **Eben W.** b in Corinna, ME, d in Lewiston, see obituary in *Lewiston Journal* 24 Jan. 1898, m Ruby Ann Wing, b 17 May 1827 in Dover, ME, d/o Ezekiel Wing; **Lydia** m Emory Turner, had children; **Janus G.** q.v.; **Augusta** m R. W. Clark, no issue.

ELDER, RICHARD - Born 21 Sep. 1793, d 21 Mar. 1849, s/o Joshua and Joanna (----) Elder. Richard Elder resided in Greene and Dexter, Maine. He m twice; once on -- Jan. 1820 to Clarissa Dammon, b 8 Oct. 1799, d 25 Apr. 1866. Children: **Rosetta Cora** b 1 Feb 1821 in Monmouth, ME, m 24 Dec. 1843 Isaac M. Russ; **Richard Henry** b 3 Dec. 1823 in Monmouth, ME; **Emily** b 5 Feb. 1825 in Dexter, ME, m Mr. Buswell; **Camilla Snell**; **Lucy Ann** b 19 May 1833, d -- Dec. 1845; **Lizzie Weatherbeee** b 4 Jun. 1835 in Dexter, ME; **Gilman Burleigh** b 7 Apr. 1837 in Dexter, ME; **Olive Ellen** b 6 Aug. 1839; **William Frederick** b 14 Nov. 1841 in Dexter, ME; **Ann Delia** b 16 May 1846, d 21 Sep. 1848 in Dexter, ME. [Vital Records of Dexter, Maine, Maine State Archives' card file.]

ELDRIDGE, ISAAC - Born ??, d ??, s/o ?? Isaac Eldridge m Hannah ----. Child: **Isaac** b 8? Apr. 1788. [Vital Records of Lewiston, Maine, p. 19.]

EMINGER, FRANK - Born 1832 in Westemburg, Germany, d ??, s/o ?? Frank Eminger occ' Fcty Operative. He m Emma ----, b 1839 in Maine [1860 census Lewiston, Maine].

ESTES, DAVID - Born 22 Nov. 1803, d 1880, s/o ?? David Estes m Mary A. Grant. Children: **Daniel L.** b -- Dec. 1830, m Susan McCurdy of St. John, NB.; **Allen C.** b -- Mar. 1833 in Palmyra, Me., came to Lewiston with parents when a small boy, m Sarah Farr, pub. 14 Jun. 1860; **Simeon** b -- Feb. 1834; **Henry P.** b 10 Aug. 1835, m (1) Elisabeth Farr, 25 Dec. 1858, and m (2) Henrietta Farr on 11 Sep. 1862; **Mary Ann** b 13 May 1837, m John T. Dingley, 29 May 1856; **Alonzo G.** b -- Feb. 1839, d -- Aug. 1863, unm; **Jenette T.** b -- Sep. 1840, m Wm. G. Hackett, 23 Jul. 1865; **Rachel E.** b 17 Jul. 1842, m Wm. T. Dingley; **Reuben H.** b 1 Apr. 1844; and **Rebecca M.** b 10 Nov. 1846, d 17 Sep. 1875, m Notton Stewart. [See *Lewiston Journal*, 29 June 1906.]

ESTES, JOSIAH - Born 29 Feb. 1804, d 20 Feb. 1860, s/o Silas and Mary (----) Estes. Josiah Estes m Hannah Hoxie, b in Sidney, Maine. Children: **Olive Staten** b 29 Jan. 1828, m (2) Lemuel Jackson, 18 Sep. 1851, and m (1) Edwin E. Jasper, 30 Jul 1847; **Edward** b 25 Aug. 1829, d 13 Dec. 1854, unm; **Wealthy** b 24 Jul. 1831, d 20 Jul. 1862, m Wm. H. Frost of Litchfield, ME, 12 Mar. 1854; **Isaac H.** b 18 Apr. 1833, m Lizzie R. Lary, 20 Jun. 1863; **Josiah** b 2 Apr. 1835, d 9 Oct. 1840; **Joseph** b 10 Mar. 1837, m Elisa J. Farr, 3 Aug. 1862; **Siles** b 3 Mar. 1839, unm; **Stephen** b 4 Jun. 1843, m Theresa Thompson; **Calvin G.** b 3 May 1845, m Rhoda Ray, 26 Oct. 1867; **Sarah** b 11 Jun. 1841, unm; **Mary** d 22 Nov. 1856; and **Myrtle** b 13 May 1868. [*Durham, Maine, History* by Stackpole, published by Town, 1899, p. 179-181.]

FALES, HORACE - Born 3 Mar. 1820 in Freeman, Maine, d 26 Mar. 1892 in Lewiston, s/o ?? Horace Fales m 30 Oct. 1848 Elisabeth Graffam, d -- Apr. 1905, d/o David. Children: **Alphius B.** b 1 Dec. 1849; **Arianna** b 18 Jul. 1857, m (1) George Wilson, 28 Jun. 1879, and m (2) ----; and **Lorenzo D.** b 14 Nov. 1863, m Catherine Goodwin 13 Aug. 1891.

FARNHAM, JOHN W. - Born ??, d ??, s/o ?? John W. Farnham m Rachel Bangs of Wales, Maine, d/o Sylvanes and Ann (----) Bangs. Children: **Mary Susan** b 1 Oct. 1840, m Emery Skillings, Leeds, ME; **Ann Augusta** b 20 Jan. 1842; **John Henry** b 20 Feb. 1844, m (1) Anna Brown, and m (2) Sarah Farington; **Ann Augusta** b 12 Dec. 1845, m (1) Charles Clough 4 Jul. 1869, who d 12 Apr. 1873, and she m (2) Luther Lombard 18 Oct. 1882; **Ellen Maria** b 14 Feb. 1847, m Orin Sprague of St. Albans, Me.; and **Frederick Burgess** who lived in California.

FARNHAM, SAMUEL W. - Born ??, d ??, s/o ?? Samuel W. Farnham m Susan ----. Child: **John W.** b 19 Mar. 1819.

FARRAR, BENJAMIN - Born 25 Oct. 1824, d ??, s/o Nathan and ?? Farrar. Benjamin Farrar m (1) 9 Feb. 1847 Margaret/Margaret A. Riggs, d 4 Nov. 1862, age 38 years 8 months 23 days, sis/o Frank, and m (2) Polena Nutting, 19 Nov. 1863. *Children of 1st wife*: **Charles F.** b 22 Mar. 1848; **Eveline** b 5 Feb. 1852, d 5 Apr. 1852; **Walter Benjamin** b 31 May 1856, d 28 Sep. 1862; and **Ellen Frances** b 28 Dec. 1859. *Child of 2nd wife*: **Clorrie Estell** b 13 Sep. 1864.

FARRAR, DAVID - Born 5 Apr. 1825 in Lisbon, Maine, d 11 Dec. 1907 on the Farrar homestead on East Avenue, s/o James and Emily (Hamilton) Farrar. David Farrar m 1850 Lucy W. Purinton. Children: **Florence E.**; **Ella J.** (Ricker); **Clarence D.**; **Grace H.** (Whitmarsh); **Alice E.**; **Fred**; and **Ernest H.** [*Historic Lewiston: its government* by the Lewiston Historic Commission, 1981-2, p. 23.]

FARRAR, GEORGE W. - Born 25 Nov. 1804, d ??, s/o Nathan and ?? Farrar. George W. Farrar m (1) Lucy Dingley and m (2) Rachel ----, b 10 May 1806. *Child of 1st wife*: **Amanda** m ---- Richardson. *Children of 2nd wife*: **George H.** b 9 Apr. 1836, m Lucy J----, b 23 Oct. 1836; **William** b 23 Dec. 1838, m Lydia ----; **Frances Ann** b 6 Aug. 1840, d 17 Mar. 1854; **Harriet Maria** b 6 Mar. 1842, d 17 Nov. 1848; and **James Alonzo** b -- Mar. 1844.

FARRAR, JAMES - Born in Webster, Maine, d 26 June 1878 age 83 years 10 months 5 days in Lisbon, Maine, s/o ?? James Farrar m Emily ----, d 29 Nov. 1831 age 45 years in Lisbon, Maine. Children: **Mary Jane** m Daniel Farrar; **Olive Ann** m George Plummer; **James G.** m Rose Lancaster; **David** b 5 Apr. 1825 in Lisbon, m Lucy W. Purington; **John H.** m ---- Lancaster; **Emily** m George H. Boston of N. Yarmouth, ME; **Henry W.**; **Thomas L.**; **Desdemona**; **Frank** b 10 Sept. 1840; **Charles** b 22 May 1842; **Georgia Anne** b 15 Jan. 1845 in Lisbon, ME; and **Conbine** b 3 Dec. 1847.

FARRAR, JOHN - Came from Hingham, England, in 1635 with wife, Frances ----, and settled in Hingham, Massachusetts, d in 1678, had four daughters and two sons.

FARRAR, JOHN SR. - Born 1722/1724, d 25 May 1803 age 81 years, s/o Jonathan and Johannah (----) Farrar [see Greeley's notes on N. Yarmouth families]. John Farrar, Sr. settled in N. Yarmouth, Maine. He m 20 Jan. 1747 or 21 Jun. 1747 Jael/Jace Stubbs, d 7 Oct. 1809 age 83 years, d/o Richard Stubbs. Jael/Jace (Stubbs) Farrar joined the Church 23 May 1742 and John Farrar, Sr. joined the Church 31 Dec. 1749. Children: **Rachel** b 11 Sept. 1749 at Falmouth, ME, m David Drinkwater; **Hannah** b 17 Oct. 1751 at N. Yarmouth; **John** q.v.; **Nathan** bap. 25 Nov. 1759; **Rhoda** m Eliab Mitchell; **Hulda** bapt. 25 Nov. 1759; and **Sarah** bapt. 5 May 1765.

FARRAR, JOHN - Bapt. 17 Nov. 1754, d ??, s/o John Sr. and Jael/Jace (Stubbs) Farrar. John Farrar m (1) 9 Apr. 1776 Mary Vining of Durham, Maine, and m (2) 20 Sep. 1781 Hannah Shaw of Woolwich, Maine. Children: **Mary** b 20 Sep. 1782, m Joshua Haley; **Nathan** b 16 Dec. 1784, m Ester Garcelon of Lewiston; **Benjamin** b 5 Nov. 1786, lost at sea; **Reuben** b 8 Jan. 1789, m (1) Luce Carville, and m (2) Jane Small; **John** b 29 Dec. 1792, m Martha Ham; **James** b 21 Aug. 1794, m (1) Emily Hamilton 21 Apr. 1819, and m (2) Desdemona Wilson; **Josiah** b 6 Aug. 1796, m May Hanly; **Susanna** b 6 Aug. 1799, m ---- Clifford; **David** b 30 May 1802, m (1) Abbie Atwood, and m (2) Phebe Flint; **Hannah** b 6 Jan. 1806; and **Ira** b 29 Jun. 1809, m Lucy Hinley.

FARRAR, JONATHAN - Born 20 Jun. 1689, d ??, s/o Nathan and Mary (Garnett) Farrar. Jonathan Farrar m Johannah ----. Children: **Jonathan; David** settled in Buckfield, Maine, and **John** q.v.

FARRAR, NATHAN - Born 17 Sep. 1654, d ??, s/o ?? Nathan Farrar m 5 Dec. 1683 Mary Garnett. Children: five, including **Jonathan**, above.

FARRAR, NATHAN - Born ??, d ??, s/o ?? Children: **George W.** q.v.; **Jaila S.** b 21 Nov. 1806, m Elihu Anderson, pub. 5 Aug 1843, lived and d in Lisbon, ME; **Eliza G.** b 20 Nov. 1808 of Lisbon, m True G. Hatch of Lewiston 25 Oct. 1832; **Esther N.** b 25 Apr. 1811, m George Nutting, lived and d in Greene, ME; **Elvina** b 28 Jul. 1813, d 4 Apr. 1814; **Sewall** b 7 Nov. 1815, d 9 Aug. 1816; **William T.** q.v.; **Deborah G.** b 4 May 1821; and **Benjamin** q.v.

FARRAR, WILLIAM T. - Born 3 Jul. 1817, d ??, s/o Nathan and ?? Farrar. William T. Farrar m ----Thompson, d 8 Aug. 1851. Child: **William Henry.**

FARWELL, NATHANIEL W. - Born 9 Mar. 1818 in Plymouth, New York, d 7 Sep. 1886 in Lewiston but was buried in Boston, Massachusetts, s/o ?? Nathaniel W. Farwell m 1842 Eliza Fletcher. Children: two daughters and one son, **John W.** [*Historic Lewiston* by the Lewiston Historic Commission, 1981-2, p. 19.]

FIELD, BARTON A. - Born 6 Nov. 1833 in Lisbon, Maine, d 23 Dec. 1862, s/o James A. and Louisa/Louise (Dill) Field. Barton A. Field m 9 Jun. 1857 Esther A. Merrill, d/o Jacob of Greene, Maine. Children: **Willard Austin** q.v.; **Frederick Wallace** b 26 Sep. 1859; and **Charles Barton** q.v.

FIELD, BENJAMIN FRANKLIN - Born 31 Oct. 1828, d ??, s/o Benjamin H. and Nancy (Brown) Field. Benjamin Franklin Field m (1) 17 Apr. 1850 Frances J./Fannie Donnell, b 10 Jan. 1831, d 12 Sep. 1857, and m (2) 6 Sep. 1864 Alice Redman (Gordon) Leighton/Layton, d 15 Oct. 1880. Children: **James B.** b 18 Apr. 1851, m (1) Florence Poston, and m (2) Lydia Burgess; and **Charles Franklin** b 29 Nov. 1854, d 10 Apr. 1873.

FIELD, BENJAMIN H. - Born 29 Apr. 1788 in Lewiston, d 24 Jun. 1858 in Gardiner, Maine, s/o Joseph and Eunice (Hill) Field. Benjamin H. Field m 7 Feb. 1812 Nancy Brown of Litchfield, Maine, b 18 May 1796, d 21 Dec. 1891. Children: **Benjamin** b 24 Mar. 1813, d 26 Mar. 1813; **Pauline H.** b 30 Mar. 1814, m Constantine Dickman 5 Apr. 1832, who d 18 Dec. 1892; **Sewall Brown** b 5 Feb. 1816, d 4 Jan. 1820; **Ann Elizabeth** b 28 Dec. 1817, d 14 May 1890, m George Stone of Gardiner, ME, 1840; **Harriet Berry** b 23 Feb. 1820, d 30 Sep. 1875, m (1) John Winnett, 1860, and m (2) Reubin M. Smily; **Mary Purington** b 21 Jan. 1822, d 4 Apr. 1856, m Willard Byran; **Caroline** b 22 Feb. 1824, d 8 Aug. 1825; **Affia Jane** b 15 Jun. 1826, d 9 Mar. 1892, m Rufus B. Seaburg, Gardiner; **Benjamin Franklin** q.v.; **Nancy Louisa** b 31 Aug.

1830, m John S. Wilson; and **Emma Augusta** b 5 Oct. 1832, d 28 Jun. 1883, m Charles H. Marr, Gardiner. [Letter - 1890's from B. F. Field to Elder.]

FIELD, CHARLES BARTON - Born 5 Mar. 1862, d ??, s/o Barton A. and Esther A. (Merrill) Field. Charles Barton Field m pub. 2 Jan. 1885 Catherine O'Neal of Lewiston. Children: **Freddie** d young; **Walter** d young; and **Freddie**.

FIELD, DAVID P. - Born 13 Jul. 1838, d ??, s/o James A. and Louisa/Louise (Dill) Field. David P. Field m 3 Jul. 1865 Dorcas/Dorcas W. Dill, d/o Phineas/Phineas W. Children: **George A.** b 16 Sep. 1866, m Mary A. McCann 1 Mar. 1892; **James P.** b 3 Jul. 1869; **Ernest E.** b 20 May 1872; **Hattie May** b 30 Oct. 1874; and **David G.** b 23 Jun. 1883.

FIELD, HENRY - Born ??, d ??, s/o ?? Children: **Henry F.**; **Daniel**; **Phebe**; **Marchia**; **George W.** b 24 Aug. 1856, m Nellie Burleigh 18 Nov. 1879; **Mary Lizzie** m Henry Demerrett 12 Mar. 1874; **Nellie** m Daniel Chapman 19 Sep. 1881; **Daniel**; and **Mabel G.** m George W. Spenser 14 Jun. 1890.

FIELD, JACOB A. - Born 6 Oct. 1836, d ??, s/o James A. and Louisa/Louise (Dill) Field. Jacob A. Field m Dorothy J. Golder, d/o Rev. Jacob Golder. Children: **Elmer G.** b 9 Jan. 1861; **Edville J.** b 25 Dec. 1867; **Mamie** b 10 Feb. 1870, d 16 Jun. 1870; **Merton** b 2 Jun. 1871; **Willie** b 25 Mar. 1874; and ---- b 26 Nov. 1878, d 28 May 1879.

FIELD, JAMES - Born ??, d ??, s/o ?? Children: **James**; **Joseph**; **David** d of measles; **Sally** d of measles; **Mary** d in NY; **Elizabeth**; **John** d of measels; **Hannah** m Ado---- Flagg; **Silas**; **Thankful**; **George**; and **David**.

FIELD, JAMES - Born 26 Sep. 1786, d 6 May 1840, s/o Joseph and Eunice (Hill) Field. James Field moved to Lowell, Massachusetts. He m (1) 11 May 1810 Sarah Anderson, b 7 Sep. 1784, d 7 Apr. 1815 [vital records of Lewiston, Maine, p. 211] age 31 years, d/o Robert and m (2) 24 Sep. 1815 Sarah Pettingill, d/o David and Thankful (Graffam) Pettingill. *Children of 1st wife*: **James A.** q.v.; and **John B.** b 29 Mar. 1813, d -- May 1814. *Children of 2nd wife*: **Joseph** b 27 Jul. 1816; **David P.** b 12 Jan. 1818; **Sarah** b 3 Sep. 1819; **Mary P.** b 20 Nov. 1820; **John** b 28 Jun. 1822; **Elizabeth P.** b 19 Nov. 1824; **Hannah P.** b 4 Jan. 1827; **Silas Curtis** b 19 Dec. 1828; and **Thankful Ann** b 20 Jan. 1831.

FIELD, JAMES A. - Born 1 Feb. 1811, d 17 Sep. 1865, s/o James and Sarah (Anderson) Field. James A. Field m 24 Mar. 1833 Louise Dill, b 15 Aug. 1812, d 8 Apr. 1872. Children: **Barton A.** q.v.; **Robert A.** q.v.; **Jacob A.** q.v.; **David P.** q.v.; **Hulda A.** b 1 Aug. 1842, m William Dill 29 Nov. 1860, s/o Capt. Joseph; **James W.** q.v.; and **Frank E. D.** b 28 Nov. 1852, m Mary E. Austin.

FIELD, JAMES BENJAMIN - Children: Born ??, d ??, s/o ?? Frances Bergen b 31 Jan. ----; **Charles William** b 28 Nov. ----; **Lydia** b 23 Sep. ----; **Florence Poster**; and **Flo----** b 26 Nov. ----.

FIELD, JAMES W. - Born 1 Apr. 1849, d ?? s/o James A. and Louisa/Louise (Dill) Field. James W. Field m pub. 31 Dec. 1867 Abbie/Abigail Huff. Children: **Blance L.** b 16 Mar. 1872, and **Edmund R.** b 7 Jan. 1875.

FIELD, JOHN - Born 8 Jul. 1777, d in Durham, Maine, s/o Joseph and Eunice (Hill) Field. John Field m pub. 17 Mar. 1799 Betsey Ross of Brunswick, Maine. Children: **Jane** b 2 Dec. 1799, d 6 May 1867, m Ai Brooks 18 Jun. 1826; **Anna** b 2 Dec 1799, d 11 Sep. 1885, m Nowell Day of Gardiner, ME, removed to Chicago, IL [letter from Olive Field, 1893, to Elder]; **William** b 12 Dec. 1801, m Salome Merriman of Brunswick; **Eunice** b 16 Dec. 1803, m Joseph Wood, lived in Winslow, ME; **John** b 16 Oct. 1806; **Hazo** [sic] b 1 June. 1809; and **Sarah Maria** b 6 Apr. 1810, m Seward Ham 9 Jan. 1832.

FIELD, JOSEPH - Born 3 Jan. 1780, d 25 Dec. 1838, s/o Joseph and Eunice (Hill) Field. Joseph Field m pub. -- Nov. 1805 Elizabeth Stevens of Brunswick, Maine, d 3 Jun. 1865. Children: **Olive** b 13 Aug. 1806, m Isaac G. Field, Portland, 25 Oct. 1832; **Katherine** b 27 Aug. 1808, d 18 Jan. 1853, m Stephen Davis 31 Jan. 1827; **Stephen** q.v.; **Mary Ann** b 30 Mar. 1813, m Daniel Holland 25 Nov. 1835; **Eunice H.** b 5 Oct. 1815, m Henry McIntire of New Sharon, ME; **Benjamin** b 19 Mar. 1820, d 5 Jun. 1851, unm; **Joseph S.** b 2 Apr. 1822, unm, went to California, and probably died there; and **Elizabeth** b 4 Oct. 1824, m Freeman Irish of Turner, ME, 19 Oct. 1845. [Letter from Olive Field, 1891, to Elder.]

FIELD, JOSEPH - Born 1749 in Northhampton, Massachusetts, d 27 Mar. 1815, s/o ?? Joseph Field was a Revolutionary soldier. He m 21 Oct. 1773 Eunice Hill of Saco, Maine. Records in Yarmouth indicate Eunice Hill was from there, and she d 6 May 1830, age 79 years. Children: **John** q.v.; **Mary** b 14 Aug. 1774, d 7 Nov. 1857, m (1) Tobias Meader 28 Dec. 1794, and m (2) Ezra Purington, who d 28 Dec. 1838; **Joseph** q.v.; **Anne** b 29 Mar. 1782, d young; **James** q.v.; **Stephen** b 17 Apr. 1784, d 1787 "killed by dry beans fell onto himself" [letter 1893 from Olive Field of Melrose, MA, to Elder]; **Benjamin H.** q.v.; and **Eunice** b 10 Oct. 1790, d young.

FIELD, ROBERT A. - Born 30 Jan. 1835, d ??, s/o James A. and Louisa/Louise (Dill) Field. Robert A. Field m 1855 Elvira J. Randall of Litchfield. Children: **Ida F. Field** b 5 Jun. 1856, d 31 Jan. 1891, m Warren P. Douglas in Great Falls 11 Jun. 1881; **Mabel** b 2 Mar. 1860, d 4 Oct. 1869; **Irving** b 15 Jun. 1864, m Lonantha Chandler, d/o Charles, 12 Apr. 1883; **James A.** b 26 Feb. 1867, d 5 Jun. 1867; **Jennie L.** b 12 May 1868; and **Josie E.** b 29 Jun. 1878, d 13 Dec. 1894.

FIELD, SAMUEL - Born ??, d 22 Feb. 1854, s/o ?? Samuel Field came from Northampton, Massachusetts; occupation, tanning business. He "moved to Freeport, Maine, and later removed to Lewiston, Maine" [letter 1893 Olive Field of Melrose, MA]. He m Anna ----, d 21 Jan. 1845. Children: **M a r y** b 8 Jul. 1782, d 30 Nov. 1871, m Nicholas Varney, Jr., 7 Mar. 1805; **John** b 22 Nov. 1784; **Stephen** b 13 Apr. 1787; **Hannah** b 5 Feb. 1790, m John Crossman; **Sarah** b 13 Oct. 1792, m Ezra Sawyer; **James** b 24 Mar. 1795, d 21 Mar. 1798, **Absalom** b 18 Aug. 1799, d 4 Jan. 1802; **Abigail** b 23 Nov. 1801, d 1888, m Oliver Conant; and **Samuel** b 23 Jul. 1804. [See *Durham, Maine, History* by Stackpole, published by the Town of Durham, 1899, p. 185.]

FIELD, STEPHEN - Born 3 Apr. 1811 on the Stephen Davis farm, d 12 Mar./Nov. 1889, s/o Joseph and Elizabeth (Stevens) Field. Stephen Field was a Freewill Baptist; moved to Minot, Maine, about 1864 and later to Durham, Maine. He m 2 Nov. 1837 Mary Sleeper, b 13 Jul. 1817, d 26 Aug. 1899. Children: **Henretta** b 25 Jul. 1841, m George H. Blake of Harpswell, ME, 7 Jul. 1889; **Walter Franklin** b 9 Jun. 1843, d 20 Oct. 1850; **Elizabeth** b 22 Aug. 1845, m William A. Robinson 20 Aug. 1867; **Stephen Herbert** b 16 Jul. 1848, d 5 Sep. 1869 murdered in MI; **Henry** b 22 May 1851, d 26 Jul. 1851; **Arthur** b 22 May 1851, d 24 Jul. 1851; and **William Henry** q.v. [Letter from W. A. Robinson of Auburn, 1889.]

FIELD, WILLARD AUSTIN - Born 27 Apr. 1858, d ??, s/o Barton A. and Esther A. (Merrill) Field. William Austin Field m 7 Oct. 1878 May Conley of Lewiston. Children: **Essie Margaret** b 2 Jan. 1880; **Charles B.** b 10 Jun. 1883; and **May Belle** b 29 Dec. 1885.

FIELD, WILLIAM HENRY - Born 31 Mar. 1853, d ??, s/o Stephen and Mary (Sleeper) Field. William Henry Field served under Pope in U.S. Cavalry stationed Fort Wallace, Kansas, -- Aug. 1872, discharged 1873, also one year U.S. Bank stationed at Dover Island, New York. In 1864, while at Colis [sic] ---- enlisted in the Navy and served 9 months on *U.S. Lancaster*. He m 14 Aug. 18-- Cora I. Hackett, d/o James of Minot, ME. [Letter from W. A. Robinson of Auburn, 1889.]

FORD, BENJAMIN - Born ??, d ??, s/o ?? Child: **Henry Clay** b 12 Jul. 1829. [Vital Records of Lewiston, Maine, p. 25.]

FORD, MARCHAL - Born ??, d ??, s/o ?/ Marchal Ford m Susan ----. Children: **William Ripley** b 20 Nov. 1831, d 1852; **Algelone** b 28 Apr. 183-; **John** b 5 Mar. 1841; and **Susan** b 21 Aug. 1843/1848.

FORD, STEPHEN - Born ??, d in Portland, Maine, s/o ?? Children: **May Elizabeth**; **John** kept a store in Auburn, ME; and **James**.

FORD, WILLIAM - Born ??, d 27 Mar. 1854 age 100 years, s/o ?? William Ford m 2 Oct. 1790 Elizabeth Tarr at Georgetown, Maine. Children: **William Jr.** q.v.; **Salla** b 23 Sep. 1792, d at age 14 years; **Stephen** b 21 Feb. 1793; **Betsy** b 13 Oct. 1795, d 23 Aug. 1878, unm; **Benjamin** b 8 Sep. 1797, m Jane Farnham of Shepleight, ME, pub. 8 Sep. 1827; and **Joseph** b 19 Jul. 1799.

FORD, WILLIAM JR. - Born 25 Feb. 1791, d 27 Jan. 1852 age 61 years [vital records of Lewiston, Maine, p. 211 and Herrick Cemetery, Lewiston], s/o William and Elizabeth (Tarr) Ford. William Ford, Jr. was a soldier in 1812. He m pub. 29 Dec. 1817 Phebe Tarr of Georgetown, Maine, d 6 Apr. 1865 age 76 years 3 months [Herrick Cemetery]. Children: **Sally Mariah*** b 2 Feb. 1819, m Charles Arris, s/o Patrick, 11 Nov. 1851; **Elizabeth*** b 17 Dec. 1821, m Stephen Hill of Lisbon, ME; **Allen** b -- Dec. ----, m Ann Leighton; and **Nancy** b 24 Feb. ----, m David Smith of Newbergh, ME. [* Vital Records of Lewiston, Maine, lists only these two children for Wm., Jr. and Phebe Ford.]

FRANCIS, JOHN - Born 16 Aug. 1767 in Gloucester, Massachusetts, d 3 Apr. 1858 in Jay, Maine [g.s. cemetery off Crash Road], s/o George and Hepzibah (Varrel) Francis [vital records of Gloucester, Massachusetts, p. 263 births printed VR 1917 by Topshfield Hist. Soc.]. John Francis was in Lewiston 1791-1804 [census of Lewiston, Maine, 1800], in Weld 1810 census, in Lisbon 1820 and 1830 censuses, in Jay 1840 and 1850 censuses. He m (1) before 1791 Rebecca ----, probably d before 1812, and m (2) pub. 5 Jul. 1812 Mrs. Dorothy Perham [vital records of Greene, Maine, card file MSA], and m (3) 17 Jan. 1818 Miriam Cooper of Durham, Maine [vital records of Lisbon, Maine, p. 4 typescript by late Rachel E. Cox, typed by Marlene Graves of Rockland, ME, 1971, Maine State Archives]. *Children of 1st wife*: **A s a** b 6 Dec. 1791, 1868 [Brettuns Ce., Livermore], m Nancy ----; **Dolly/Dorothy** b 5 Jun. 1795, d 27 Feb. 1889 [vital records of Weld, Maine, card file MSA], m 29 Jun. 1815 Joel Ireland at Minot, ME; **Judith** b 31 Jul. 1797, m 1818 Abraham Whitney [vital records of Lisbon, Maine, p. 4, microfilm typescript by Cox]; **John** b 19 Feb. 1800, d 6 Jul. 1874 [vital records of Turner, Maine, MSA], m 1821 [vital records of Lisbon, Maine, p. 212; p. 7 by Cox] Mary Whitney of Minot 6 Jan. 1822 according to Lisbon Records, but it isn't certain that this John is the one on the Lisbon Records; **Rebecca** b 14 Jan. 1802, d 16 Oct. 1876 [g.s. North Chesterville Cemetery], m 27 Oct. 1824 Zadoc Ireland [vital records of Chesterville, Maine, MSA]; and **M o l l y** b 23 Jul. 1804. *Child of 1st marraige, from death certificate*: **William** bc 15 Jul. 1809, d 7 Feb. 1901, m (1) 1839 Susanna Whitney of Weld, and m (2) 1846 Serena Greene of Rumford, ME, and m (3) 1859 Achsa Holt of Weld [all vital records of Carthage, Maine, card file MSA]. *Children of 2nd wife*: no children known. *Children of 3rd wife*: **Sewall** b 12 Aug. 1819, d 24 Aug. 1895 in Carthage, m -- Dec. 1841 Anna Cole, both of Jay, ME, [bur. Crash Rd., Jay]; **David Neal** b 17 Jun. 1821, d 16 Jul. 1900 in Weld, m -- May 1841 Marindy Whitney of Carthage; **O r e n** b 23 Jun. 1823, living in Jay according to the 1850 census; **Hosea** b 15 Jan. 1826; **D i a n a** b 1 Dec. 1828, d 1899 [g.s. Newman Cemetery, Carthage], m 1 Oct. 1854 Sylvanus Holt, Carthage. [Letter from Lois Griffiths of Bates College, Lewiston, dated 5/1989 to David Young.]

FROST, GEORGE D. - Born 21 Jan. 1801 in Danville, Maine, d 30 July 1855, s/o late Henry Frost and ?? George D. Frost m 8 Apr. 1827 Deborah Davis, b 24 Aug. 1808, d 22 Sep. 1884, d/o Amos Davis.

Children (first three born in Lewiston): **Henry** b 1 Feb. 1828, d 7 Apr. 1881 age 53 years in Chicago, IL; **Charles Staples** b 28 Apr. 1829, living in Oakland, CA, 1896; **William A.** b 1 Aug. 1831, res. Chicago 1896; **V e s t a** b 24 Mar. 1833 in Lisbon, ME, d 5 Apr. 1833 in Lisbon, ME, age 12 days; **Ruth Ann** b 26 July 1834 in Lisbon, ME, res. Spring Valley, MN, 1896, m ---- St. Clair; **C e l e s t e** b 8 Aug. 1838, m ---- Pomeroy, lives in Chicago, IL, 1896; **Nancy E.** b 17 Mar. 1836, m ---- Blethen, res. Auburn, ME, 1896; **Alonzo** b 21 Dec. 1841, d in Virginia 17 Apr. 1863 age 21 years; **Elizabeth W.** b 21 Dec. 1841, res. Baltimore, MD, m Otis H. C. Junkins; **Cornelia C.** b 30 Nov. 1844 in Lisbon, ME, d 10 May 1866 age 21 years; **Geo. D.** [letter from Geo. D. Frost - Lisbon 29 Oct. 1896 ro Elder] q.v.; **Emery Frost** b 7 Apr. 1850 in Lisbon, ME, res. Maynard, IA, 1896. [Vital Records of Lewiston, Maine, p. 26; letter from Miss Alice G. Frost, 19 Oct. 1896, Lisbon Falls, ME, to Mr. Elder; see Starbird's records of Danville, ME, families AHS.]

FROST, GEORGE D. JR. [letter from Geo. D. Frost, 1896] - Born 10 Nov. 1847, d ??, s/o George D. and Deborah (Davis) Frost. George D. Frost, Jr. m M. Addie Golder, b 12 Jan. 1846 in Strong, Maine, d/o Fairfield and Cordelia (Rich) Golder. Children: **Alonzo G.** b 21 Aug. 1871; **Lizzie M.** b 13 Jul. 1873; **Alice G.** b 25 Oct. 1875; and **Nellie A.** b 11 Aug. 1878.

FRYE, DEAN - b 20 May 1775, d 18 Apr. 1834 in Lewiston, 6th s/o Capt. Joseph and Mary (----) Frye. Dean Frye was prominent in church matters and a fine singer. Before moving to Lewiston he was a woolen manufacture in Saccarappa, Maine. He m Joanna March, d 13 Jun. 1850 at Lewiston, d/o Pelletiah and Mary (Goodwin) March of Falmouth, Maine. Children: **John** q.v.; **Sophia** m Asa Garcelon; **Sarah** m Temple Tibbetts; **William** m (1) Millicent Moore, and m (2) Susan Caverly; **Caroline** m Edward P. Tobey; **Mary** d young; **Joseph** d young.

FRYE, COL. JOHN - Born 28 Nov. 1802 at Westbrook, Maine, d 1 Jan. 1885, s/o Dean and Joanna (----) Frye. Col. John Frye served as state senator, member of Governor's Council, and drummer boy to the rank of Colonel in the Maine Regiment of Militia. He was a Whig and then a staunch Republican. The Lewiston Falls Woolen Manufacturing Co. had his services for over forty years. He m Alice ----, b 10 May 1804, d -- Nov. 1871, d/o David Davis of Lewiston. Children, all born in Lewiston: **Mary** b 31 Dec. 1828, d 1917 in Medford, MA, m Dr. Pearl Martin; **William** q.v.; **Albert** b 6 Apr. 1834, d 1874, was a fine surgeon; **Sarah** b 4 Oct. 1837, unm; **John** b 1839, d young; **Addie** b 11 Nov. 1842, d 10 Jun. 1910, m Silas C. Dawes of Harrison, ME, Nov. 1863; and **Helen** b 9 Sep. 1845, d at 5 years.

FRYE, JOHN MARCH - Born 30 Dec. 1802 in Westbrook, Maine, d 1 Jan. 1885, s/o Dean and ?? Frye. John Frye m Alice M. Davis. Children: **Mary Davis** b 30 Dec. 1828; **William Pierce** b 2 Sep. 1830; and **A l b e r t** b 6 Apr. 1835. [Vital Records of Lewiston, Maine, p. 26 and Frye Genealogy, typescript at Bates College, Lewiston.]

FRYE, CAPT. JOSEPH - Born ??, d ??, s/o Joseph, Sr. and ?? Frye, gs/o John and ?? Frye, ggs/o Samuel and ?? Frye, gggs/o John Frye the progenitor [manuscript written by Joseph Frye, Sr. in 1783, original at Bates College, Lewiston, Maine]. Capt. Joseph Frye m 12 Feb. 1765 Mary Robinson, d/o Dean and Sarah (----) Robinson. Children: **Joseph** b 19 May 1765 in Andover, MA; **Mary** b 17 Oct. 1767 at Fryeburg, ME; **Mehitable** b 27 Dec. 1768; **John** b 27 Aug. 1771; **Nancy** b 25 Apr. 1773; **Dean** b 25 May 1775 "lived some years in Saccarappa, Maine, where some of his children were born"; **S a r a h** b 8 Oct. 1777; **William** b 30 Sep. 1780; **Sophia** b 6 Jun. 1784 [letter to Elder from Geo. B. Barrows of Fryeburg, Maine, dated 1894].

FRYE, WILLIAM PIERCE - Born 2 Sep. 1830 [vital records of Lewiston, Maine, p. 26], d 8 Aug. 1911, s/o John M. and Alice M. (----) Frye. Aftering graduating from Bowdoin College in 1850, William Pierce Frye studied law in Rockland and Portland, Maine, with William Pitt Fessenden, Vice President, U. S. Senate. He m 27 Feb. 1853 Caroline Frances Spear, d/o Archibald and Angelica (----) Spear of Rockland, Maine. Children: **Helen** b 11 Dec. 1853 in Rockland, ME, m ---- White; **A l i c e** b 1 Aug. 1859, m ---- Briggs; and **Emme/Emma** b 6 Dec. 1863, d at any early age. [*Historic Lewiston: its government* by the Lewiston Historic Commission, 1981-2, p. 15. and Frye genealogy typescript, Bates College, Lewiston.]

FRYE, WILLIAM ROBINSON - Born 1818 in Westbrook, Maine, d 1863, s/o Dean and ?? Frye. William Robinson Frye settled in Lewiston, 1819. He was Postmaster of Lewiston for many years. He m (1) ----, and m (2) Susan E. ----. *Children of 1st wife*: **Annie** m Dr. James Irish of Lowell, MA; **Caroline** m Henry W. Nieman of Schuyler, NE; and **Frank E.** m Flora Campbell. *Children of 2nd wife*: **Millicent** b 1859, m 21 Oct. 1891 Herbert R. C. Shaw who was the grandson of the late Randolph A. Codman, Esq. of Portland, ME; **Fred Mellen** b 2 Apr. 1861, d 1907, res. Omaha, NE; **Willie Robinson** b 21 Aug. 1862, d 30 Aug. 1863. [Frye genealogy, unpublished family records, given to Bates College by family member, John H. White, b 1878; letters from the Frye family to Elder, 1894; Frye genealogy compiled by Joseph Frye, written 1783, given to Bates College Library.]

FULLER, AMMI - Born ??, d ??, s/o ?? Ammi Fuller lived in Brunswick, Maine. Children: **J o s e p h** b 4 Nov. 1835, m Helen Brown; **Berry** b 12 Apr. 1837; **Alonso** b -- Jun. 1838; **Annie** b -- Aug. ----, m **William Ham**; **Alfred** b -- Dec. 1840, m Corson ----; **James**; **David**; **Everline**; **George**; and **William**.

FULLER, DAVID - Born -- Jan. 1777, d 6 Jun. 1850, s/o ?? David Fuller m 5 Jul. 1801 Sally Garcelon, d 7 Nov. 1871. Children: **John** q.v.; **J u l i a H**. b 20 Jan. 1804, m Edwin Blodgett, settled in Carmel, ME; **Otis** b 26 Nov. 1805, unm; **Sally Mariah** b 24 Sep. 1807, d 10 Jul. 1863, m Joseph Ham, pub. 7 Aug. 1831; **Hosea** q.v.; **David** q.v.; **Mary C.** b 4 Apr. 1815, m Charles Adams; **Jane** b 13 Dec. 1817, m Abraham

Woodard 15 May 1844, settled in Bangor, ME; **Charles** b 4 Jul. 1820, d 1847, unm; and **Frances Ann** b 13 Sep. 1826, d 20 Sep. 1889, m Lorenzo Garcelon.

FULLER, DAVID - Born 24 Jul. 1812, d ??, s/o David and Sally (Garcelon) Fuller. David Fuller m Elvira/Elisa Dennett and settled in Carmel, Maine. Children: **Ann Augusta** b 30 Dec. 1841, m Gordon Stanford 9 Apr. 1867; and **Mary E.** b 16 Mar. 1846, d 12 Oct. 1865.

FULLER, HOSEA - Born 14 Apr. 1810, d 19 Jul. 1880, s/o David and Sally (Garcelon) Fuller. Hosea Fuller m (1) 4 Jun. 1840 Harriet Woodward, d 23 Feb. 1843 age 24 years, and m (2) pub. 10 Sep. 1848 Rebecca Cowell/Gowell of Auburn, Maine. Children: **Harriet W.** b -- Oct. 1849, d 1 Nov. 1879; **Hellen**, b 13 Sep. 1851, d 18 Jul. 1888; and **Jennie W.** b 27 Sep. 1855, d 1 Nov. 1872.

FULLER, JOHN - Born 18 Dec. 1801, d 13 Nov. 1865, s/o David and Sally (Garcelon) Fuller. John Fuller m (1) Louisa Williams, settled in Carmel, Maine, and m (2) Josie Nevens. Children: **Frances Ann** b 5 Aug. 1829; **John M.** b 16 Oct. 1830, d 29 Feb. 1832; and **Georgia** b 1 Jan. 1838, m Millet Shaw, who d 4 Oct. 1865.

FULLER, JOSEPH - Born ??, d ??, s/o Seth and ?? Fuller [vital records of Lewiston, Maine, p. 25]. Joseph Fuller m pub. 3 Aug. 1803 Nancy Tarr, d 2 Apr. 1836. Children: **Joseph** b 26 Jul 1804; **Seth** b 26 Aug. 1806; and **Ammi Cutler** b 11 Sep. 1811, m Nancy Mitchell of Wales, ME, pub. 23 Nov. 1834.

FURBUSH, GEORGE WASHINGTON - Born 1 Dec. 1842 in Dresden, d 18 Apr. 1924, s/o Washington and Mehitabel (Colby) Furbush. George Washington Furbush m -- Aug. 1873 Josephine A. Leavitt. Children: **Edith**; **Mabel** m E. B. Call; and **Maude** m W. W. Bolster. [*Historic Lewiston* by the Lewiston Historic Commission, 1981-2, p. 31.]

See article on GARCELON genealogy in *Lewiston Journal*, 4 Jul. 1895.

GARCELON, A. M. - Born ??, d ??, s/o ?? A. M. Garcelon was a M. D. He m Jennie Skinner. Children: **Angelett**; and **William T.** m (1) Flora E. Wheeler of Akron, CA, and m (2) Elizabeth Pongart.

GARCELON, ABRAHAM GOLDER - Born 27 Dec. 1808, d 5 Sep. 1889, s/o Peter and Sarah (Golder) Garcelon. Abraham C. Garcelon m Nancy Day. [Vital Records of Lewiston, Maine, p. 30.]

GARCELON, ALBERT ALTON - Born ??, d ??, s/o ?? Children: **Donald Dean** b 16 May 1880; **Arthur Alton, Jr.** b 12 May 1884; and **Louisa Lizzie** b 21 Feb. 1887.

GARCELON, ALONZO - Born 6 May 1813 in Lewiston, d 8 Dec. 1906, an accidental death, in Medford, Massachusetts [obit in the *Lewiston Sat. Journal*, issue 8 Dec. 1906, p. 1 & 13 states d without illness in his sleep], s/o Col. William and Mary (Davis) Garcelon. Alonzo Garcelon m (1) Annie/Ann Augusta Waldron, d -- Dec. 1857, sis/o Col. William Waldron, d/o Job and Abigail (----) Waldron of Dover, New Hampshire [*Dictionary of American Biography*, Vol. VII, published by Charles Scribner's Sons, 1931, p. 131-132 and Col. William Garcelon's notes] or he m (1) Ann Augusta, d -- Dec. 1857, d/o Job Philpot [sic] of Somersworth, New Hampshire [obit. from *Lewiston Journal*, issue 8 Dec. 1906, p. 1, 13 and *Historic Lewiston: its government*, published by the Lewiston Historic Commission, 1981-2, and m (2) Olivia N. Speaker [sic], d 2 Jan. 1889 [obit. 8 Dec. 1906 from Journal and notes from Col. Garcelon], d/o Capt. Archibald and Angelica (Branton) Spear of Rockland, Maine. Children of 1st wife: **Charles Augustus** b 14 Nov. 1842; **Mary Ann** b 27 Jul. 1844; **William** b 15 Jun. 1846, d 28 Jan. 1848; **Ellen Elisabeth** b 17 Nov. 1848; **Edward L.**, and **Alonzo Marston** q.v.; and **Edward Little** b 15 Sep. 1855 [notes by William Garcelon]. Children of 2nd wife: **Edith** m ---- Dennis. [*Historic Lewiston*, published by the Lewiston Historic Commission, 1981-2, p. 18]

GARCELON, ALONZO MARSTON - Born 12 Nov. 1851 in Lewiston, d 14 Jan. 1935 in Lewiston, s/o Alonzo and Annie (Waldron) Garcelon. Alonzo Marston Garcelon m 1877 Jennie M. Skelton. Children: **Alonzo**, **William S.**, **Harold W.**, and **Louis**. [*Historic Lewiston Government*, published by the Lewiston Historic Commission, 1981-2, p. 24]

GARCELON, ANNIS - Born ??, d ??, s/o ?? Annis Garcelon m cert. 28 Jul. 1818 Polly Blethen of Lisbon, Maine [vital records of Lewiston, Maine, p. 371]. Children: **Horatio Gates** b 1 Feb. 1819; and **Sophia Frye** b 1 Nov. 1822 [vital records of Lewiston, Maine, p. 30.]

GARCELON, ANSEL GERRISH - Born 11 Jan. 1811, d 23 Jul. 1858, s/o Peter and Sarah (Golder) Garcelon. Ansel Gerrish Garcelon m 21 Jul. 1841 Almira P. Harville, both of Webster, Maine. [Topsham, Maine, records.] Children: **Mary Ann** b in Kingsfield, ME; and **William Henry** b 1 Jul. 1847, m 31 Mar. 1866 Harriet N. Small, d/o John M. of Lewiston.

GARCELON, CAPT. ASA - Born 24 Jul. 1799 in Lewiston [DAR Bible record; see also *Downeast Ancestry*, Dec. 1978, page 18], d (killed) 28 Mar. 1859 [probate record], s/o Mark and Hannah (Ames) Garcelon. Capt. Asa Garcelon m 8 May 1825 Sophie Frye, d 8 Mar. 1865 at age 65 years of pulmonary consumption [*Morning Star* obit notice, 24 May 1865], d/o Dean of Lewiston. Sophie (Frye) Garcelon was a member of the F. W. Baptist Church of Lewiston 35+ years. Children: **Dean Frye** b 15 Jun. 1826; **Charles E.*** q.v.; **William F.*** q.v.; **Asa Jr.*** q.v.; **Mary Caroline*** b 24 Feb. 1832, d 4 Mar. 1894, m Enoch Celman of Bath, ME; **Joanna F.** b 11 Jan. 1836, m George H. Gould of Bath, ME, 20 Jan. 1870; **Sophia Angelia*** b 25 Nov. 1837, m Otis F. Davis; and **Sarah Tibbetts*** b 23 May 1842, m Charles Haley. [Probate record #149, estate of Asa Garcelon, Androscoggin Co. *Listed in probate records, 7 Apr. 1859.]

GARCELON, ASA JR. - Born 14 Dec. 1833, d 6 Dec. 1890, s/o Capt. Asa and Sophie (Frye) Garcelon. Asa Garcelon, Jr. m 3 Dec. 1857 Louisa V. Penley, b 8 Oct. 1835, of Danville, Maine, d/o Capt. John of Auburn, Maine. Children: **Arthur Alton** b 12 Dec. 1858, m 11 Jul. 1880 Ada Florence Yelton, b 9 Jun. 1859 in S. Randolph, Massachusetts, d/o Seth and Elisabeth (Potter) Yelton; **John Penley** b 27 Nov. 1860; **Hattie Maria** b 24 Nov. 1865, d 27 Jan. 1866; **Albert Manchester** b 17 Jun. 1869, m 31 Jul. 1891 Ada Soper, d/o E. H. and Maria (Plummer) Soper; **Julia Winfield** b 30 Nov. 1873; and **Howard Asa** b 8 Nov. 1878. [Charles Starbird records of Danville, ME, families.]

GARCELON, CHARLES E. - Born 20/26 Mar. 1828, s/o Asa and Sophie (Frye) Garcelon. Charles E. Garcelon m (1) 28 Oct. 1852, Hannah F./Hannah/Hanah Carville/Corville, 7 Sep. 1832, d 6 Nov. 1858/1859, aged 27 years and 2 months, d/o John and Priscilla (Higgins) Carville, and m (2) Melissa/Melissa O. Jordan of Webster, Maine, 12 Jan. 1861. *Children of 1st wife*: **Fred M.** q.v.; **Rose/Rosa S.** b 31 Jan. 1856, d 20 Sep. 1872/1873. *Children by 2nd wife*: **Anna B.** b 25 Jul. 1863/1865; **Charles E. Jr.** b 17 Jan. 1865; **Clifton J.** b 20 Jul. 1866; **Iola/Iola M.** b 15 Aug. 1868, m L. Tuttle/Benjamin L. Tuttle of Auburn, ME, 24/25 Feb. 1891; and **Helen M.** b 5 Aug. 1872.

GARCELON, CONSTANE T./CONSTANT TRUE - Born 11 Feb. 1818, d 11 Feb. 1882, s/o Peter and Sarah (Golder) Garcelon.

GARCELON, DANIEL - Born 5 Feb. 1768, d 15 Nov. 1798 age 30 2/3 years, s/o James and Deliverance (----) Garcelon. Daniel Garcelon m Polly Parker of Yarmouth or Freeport, Maine, d 1849 at home of her grandson, Daniel Webber. Polly (Parker) Garcelon m (2) Elias Staten. Children: **Polly** b 11 May 1792, m (1) Jeremiah Walker of Danville, ME, d 10 Jan. 1812 [Starbird's records of Danville, Maine], and m (2) Joseph Webber; **Annis** b 12 Sep. 1794, d 30 Dec. 1853, m Mary Blethen. [Vital Records of Lewiston, p. 28; Rowley Cemetery, South Lewiston.]

GARCELON, DANIEL - Born 20 Feb. 1800, d 27 Nov. 1880, s/o Peter and Katherine (Millbanks) Garcelon. Daniel Garcelon m (1) 5 Oct. 1826 Mary A. Hinckley of Lisbon, Maine, d 13 May 1841 aged 36 years, 3 months, and m (2) 21 Apr. 1842 Ursula Ham, d 28 Sep. 1872 aged 49 years, 11 months. *Children by 1st wife*: **Peter** q.v.; **Samuel H.** q.v.; **Mary Ann** b 13 Aug. 1832, d 23 Nov. 1864 (?) m John C. Ring of West Bath, ME; **Daniel M.** q.v. *Children by 2nd wife*: **Nancy Jane** b 27 Sep. 1844 (?), m William S. Merrill 25 Dec. 1872, lived in Lisbon; and **Armine** b 31 Mar. 1847, m Alfonso B. Holland 27 Nov. 1867.

GARCELON, DANIEL M. - Born 6 Feb. 1836, s/o Daniel and Mary A./ A. L. (Hinckley) Garcelon. Daniel M. Garcelon m 1 Jan. 1866 Susan E. Woodward, d/o D. William. Children: **William Woodard** b 10 Aug. 1866, d 10 Nov. 1873; **Daniel Gardiner** b 31 Aug. 1869, d 1 Nov. 1873; and **Sarah** b 23 Sep. 1872, d 18 May 1882.

GARCELON, EBENEZER A. - Born 22 Nov. 1792, d 22 May 1869 in New Portland, Maine, s/o Peter and Katherine (Millbanks) Garcelon. Ebenezer A. Garcelon m Katherine Jordan of Lisbon, Maine, b 22 Sep. 1793 at Cape Elizabeth, Maine, d/o William of Lisbon, Maine. Children: **Peter** m Deborah Casley; **Ebenezer**; **Eunice**; **Almira** m John Moody; and **Jane**.

GARCELON, EDWARD A. - Born ??, d ??, likely s/o Fred M. and ?? Garcelon. Edward A. Garcelon occ. - mule skinner, boards at 15 Hill Corp, Lewiston, Maine. [Directory Androscoggin Co., Maine. Auburn-Lewiston 1904, 1905, 1906, 1907.] Child: **Raymond Dexter** b 25 Mar. 1897, m Margaret A. Hutton.

GARCELON, FRED ALMONT - Born 24 Nov. 1868, s/o William Golder and Miranda (Woodruff) Garcelon. Fred Almont Garcelon m 1 Jul. 1863 Georgia R. Grey, d/o William and Melinia (Bones) Grey. Children: **Ray M.** b -- Jun. 1893; **Elvia G.** b 4 May 1896; and **Helen Ruth** b 25 Nov. 1895, d 19 Feb. 1899.

GARCELON, FRED M. - Born 15 Apr. 1854/1855, d 6 Aug. 1905 [probate #5357], s/o Charles E. and Hannah F./Hannah/Hanah (Carville) Garcelon. Fred M. Garcelon m 25 Dec. 1873 Olive/Olive H. Channell, b -- Mar. 1853, d/o Henry A./H. H. and Sarah (Knowlton) Channel. Children: **Edward A.** b 14 Feb. 1875, m 1900 at 25 years, Margaret A. Hutton in 1905; **Herbert F.** b 7 May 1877, d 16 Sep. 1900, of Boston, MA; **George E.** b 15 Sep. 1884, of Lewiston, ME, in 1905; **Lucy Josephine** b 29 Apr. 1886, d 1999 at age 14 years; **E. May** b 10 Jan. ----; **Alice C.** b 22 Mar. 1879; and **Alice O.** b 3 Dec. 1881.

GARCELON, HOSEA - Born 9 Apr 1810, d 9 Jan. 1878, s/o Peter and Katherine (Millbanks) Garcelon, m Lucy/Lucy D. Rowe who lived in Durham, Maine. Children: **Henry H.**; and **Deliverance**.

GARCELON, ISAAC GOLDER - Born 24 Mar. 1825, d 9 Jun. 1849, s/o Peter and Sarah (Golder) Garcelon. Isaac Golder Garcelon m Jane Warner of Pennsylvania. No children.

GARCELON, JAMES - Born 4 Apr. 1739 in Guernsey, England, d 18 Nov. 1813 age 74 years in Lewiston, Maine, s/o Peter and ?? Garcelon. James Garcelon m 2 Mar. 1760 Deliverance Ames of Cape Ann, Massachusetts, d 16 Nov. 1828 age 93 years [biography of Col. William Garcelon with genealogy of early settlers of Lewiston, Maine, manuscript at Androscoggin Historical Society]. Children: **James Jr.** b 4 Sep. 1761; **William** q.v.; **Peter** q.v.; **Daniel** q.v.; **Mark** q.v.; **Lucy** b 27 Sep. 1773; and **Salley** b 27 Sep. 1776 in Lewiston, ME. [Garcelon cemetery records, Lewiston, Maine.]

GARCELON, ELDER JAMES - Born 4 Sep. 1761, d 28 Dec. 1838 age 77 years at Lewiston, Maine, s/o James and Deliverance (----) Garcelon. Elder James Garcelon m (1) Elisabeth Dyer and m (2) Jennet ----. *Children by 1st wife*: **Esther** b 9 Mar. 1784, m Nathan Farrow; **Lucy** b 13 Jul. 1785, m Jeremiah Dingley; **Abigail** b 21 Apr. 1787, m

Nathaniel Jordan; **Elisabeth** b 24 Mar. 1789, m Joshua Rowe; **James** b 3 Apr. 1791, m Sally Wentworth; **Samuel** b 22 Jun. 1793, m Hannah Robinson; **Sally** b 23 Aug. 1795, m (1) Jonathan Rowe, and m (2) John Barker; **Deborah** b 3 Jul. 1797, m James Jordan; and **Susan** b 25 Dec. 1804, m Joshua Lambert. *Child by 2nd wife*: **Justus** b -- Feb. 1833.

GARCELON, MARK - Born 15 Jan. 1771, d 28 Dec. 1830, s/o James and Deliverance (----) Garcelon. Mark Garcelon m (1) 1792 Hannah Ames, d 17 May 1819, d/o James Ames, and m (2) Elisabeth Field, d 17 Sep. 1863, at age 84 1/2 years. *Children by 1st wife*: **Mark** q.v.; **Daniel** b 5 Feb. 1795, d 7 Sep. 1863, m Alice Davis 5 May 1825, b 25 Oct. 1795; **Anna** b 17 Jul. 1797, d 29 Jul. 1867, m (1) Ephraim Jones 5 May 1824, and m (2) Nathaniel Merrill of Gray, ME; **Asa** q.v.; **William G.** b 16 Sep. 1801, d 2 Jun. 1822, unm; **Seward** b 28 Apr. 1806, d 5 Feb. 1877, moved to Oakland, Cal., in 1861, m Catherine Merritt; and **Washington** q.v. *Child by 2nd wife*: **Hannah E.** b 28 Dec. 1824, d 31 Aug. 1848, m A.M. Jones.

GARCELON, MARK - Born 31 Jul. 1793, d 29 Dec. 1850, s/o Mark and Hannah (Ames) Garcelon. Mark Garcelon removed to Lisbon, Maine. He m Jane Ames b 26 Feb. 1799, d 2 Mar. 1847. Children: **Hannah N.** b 15 Feb. 1821, d 27 Apr. 1840; **Winslow A.** b 1823, d 20 Nov. 1824; **Octoria D.** b 5 Sep. 1825; **Cressulla Jane** b -- Apr. 1827, d 20 Nov. 1851; **Nathaniel G./O.** q.v.; **Mark Jefferson** q.v.; **Rosan Curtis** b 6 Apr. 1833, d 13 Jun. 1856; **Paulina A.B.** b 14 Apr. 1835, d 5 Oct. 1853; and **Daniel Washington** b 27 Mar. 1837, d 25 Jul. 1847.

GARCELON, MARK JEFFERSON - Born 8 Jun. 1831, s/o Mark and Jane (Ames) Garcelon. Mark Jefferson Garcelon m 28 Dec. 1859 Maggie Pinto/Pinta of Chillroethe, Ohio, b 13 Jan. 1838, d 22 Oct. 1895, d/o H. M. and Elisa (Hutcheson) Pinto/Pinta. Child: **Rollin Lansing** b 14 Dec. 1860.

GARCELON, NATHANIEL G./O. - Born 20 Apr. 1829, d 13 Feb. 1892, s/o Mark and Jane (Ames) Garcelon. Nathaniel G./O. Garcelon m Lucy D. Jordan of Lewiston. Children: **Rose Jordan** b 24 Aug. 1859, m Robert Evenfight of Minneapolis, Minn., 1882; **Winfield Scott** b 26 Sep. 1863; **Octavia Lillian** b 15 Jun. 1865; and **Jennie L.** b 26 Mar. 1869.

GARCELON, PETER - Born 8 Jul. 1765, d 19 Jun. 1827, s/o James and Deliverance (Ames) Garcelon. Peter Garcelon m 2 Mar. 1787 Katherine Millbanks d 8 Apr. 1831. Children: **Peter** q.v.; **Thankful** b 23 Nov. 1790, d 7 Apr. 1873, res. in Abbott, ME, m Barsilla Rand, 6 Mar. 1814, d 13 Sep. 1861; **Ebenezer A.** q.v.; **Deliverance** b 17 Apr. 1797, d 1 Dec. 1832, unm; **Lucy** b 27 Jan. 1798, d 14 Jan. 1841, unm; **Daniel** q.v.; **Phillip M.** q.v.; and **Hosea** q.v. [Vital Records of Lewiston, Maine, p. 28.]

GARCELON, PETER - Born 26 Nov. 1788, d 20 Oct. 1867, s/o Peter and Katherine (Millbanks) Garcelon. Peter Garcelon m 10 Jul. 1808 Sarah Golder, b 27 Feb. 1787, d 20 Feb. 1876, d/o William. Children:

Abraham G. q.v.; Ansel Gerrish q.v.; Sarah Catherine b 27 Jun. 1813, d 5 Sep. 1898, m Foster Jordan 9 Feb. 1813, d 18 Apr. 1876; William Golder q.v.; Constant True q.v.; Dorcas Jane b 6 Aug. 1820, m ---- Rigby, lived in Wales, ME, went West when age 29 years; Peter James q.v.; Isaac Golder q.v.; Phillip Millbanks q.v.; Lucy Artimetia b 12 Aug. 1830 m B. Wilson of Wales, ME; Deliverance Cordelia b 12 Aug. 1830, d 26 Apr. 1853; and Elizabeth Frances b 2 Jul. 1832, d 25 Apr. 1833.

GARCELON, PETER - Born 5 Jul. 1827, d ??, s/o Daniel and Mary A/A. L. (Hinckley) Garcelon. Peter Garcelon m Rachel Cushing of Arlington, Massachusetts. They lived in S. Weymouth, Massachusetts. Children: Edith; Ira; Ammi; and Alice.

GARCELON, PETER JAMES - Born 6 Aug. 1820 or 18 Aug. 1822, d ??, s/o Peter and Sarah (Golder) Garcelon. Peter James Garcelon m 9 Mar. 1844 Elizabeth A. Thomas. Children: Erastus; and Winfield Scott.

GARCELON, PHILLIP M. - Born 7 Dec. 1805, d 4 Aug. 1880, s/o Peter and Katherine (Millbanks) Garcelon. Phillip M. Garcelon m 1 Feb. 1829 Pauline Barker, d 31 Jan. 1878, d/o Jacob. Children: Martha J.; Lucy M. m William F. Gay of Farmington, ME, 25 Oct. 1870; Frank A.; and Ellen.

GARCELON, PHILLIP MILLBANKS - Born 7 Aug. 1827, d 14 Jan. 1890, s/o Peter and Sarah (Golder) Garcelon. Phillip Millbanks Garcelon settled in Bath, Maine. He m (1) 20 Aug. 1851 Jane Warner, b 8 Aug. 1831, d 10 Apr. 1863, wid/o Isaac C. Garcelon, b/o Phillip, and m (2) 7 May 1881 Mrs. Marinda (Woodruff) Garcelon, who also m Wm. Golder Garcelon [letter Lila Garcelon, Spring Creek, Pennsylvania, 5 Mar. 1894]. Children: Lottie/Charlotte Delia b 10 Mar. 1856 in Bath, m 27 Sep. 1883 Robert C. Moore of Pittsburg, PA; and Lillian Leota b 19 Oct. 1857 in Bath.

GARCELON, SAMUEL HINKLEY [vital records of Lewiston, Maine, p. 57] - Born 6 Jun. 1830, d 15 Apr. 1867, s/o Daniel and Mary A./A. L. (Hinckley) Garcelon. Samuel H. Garcelon m (1) Emily Freeman, d 17 Aug. 1862, and m (2) Ellen March. Children: Fred F. b 1 Dec. 1854, lived in Watertown, MA, m Nellie A. Tucker; and Fannie Hinckley b 17 Oct. 1857, m J. Edwin Mosher of Farmington, ME, 25 Dec. 1883.

GARCELON, WASHINGTON - Born 17 Feb. 1809, d 11/12 Jun. 1849, s/o Mark and Hannah (Ames) Garcelon. Washington Garcelon m Rosann C. Curtis/Rose J. Curtiss, d 26 Jul. 1851/1857. Children: Rosann J. b 12 Apr. 1839, m Julius M. Swain 5 Feb. 1864; and Catherine C. b 27 Aug. 1841, m Henry Rogers, 18 Dec. 1864.

GARCELON, WILLIAM - Born 8 Jul. 1763, d 20 Jan. 1851 age 89 years 7 months, s/o James and Deliverance (Ames) Garcelon. William Garcelon m [vital records of Cumberland, Maine, p. 19 "William

Joslan (sic) to Maria Harris both of Lewiston m 8 May 1784"] Maria Harris, b 4 Mar. 1763. All the family except Col. William moved to St. David, N. B. about 1810. Children: Col. William q.v.; **Salley** b 8 Jan. 1785; **James** b 28 Jun. 1788; **Isaac** b 22 Jul. 1790; **Lydia** b 4 Feb. 1793; **Joseph** b 16 Feb. 1795; **Moses** b 23 Oct. 1797; **David** b 12 Apr. 1799; **Jane** b -- Jan. 1801 in Durham, ME; **Harvey** b 29 Jan. 1803 in Durham, ME; and **Harris** b 15 Sep. 1804 in Durham, ME. [Vital Records of Lewiston, Maine, p. 27 and Col. William Garcelon's notes.]

GARCELON, COL. WILLIAM - Born 21 Sep. 1786, d 13 Jan. 1872 age 85 years [see obit notice *Morning Star*, issue 21 Feb. 1872], s/o William and Maria (----) Garcelon. William Garcelon m 12 July 1810 Mary Davis, d/o Daniel and Mary (Collins) Davis. Children: **Alonzo** q.v.; **Charles** b 3 Nov. 1814, d 5 Jun. 1815; and **Mary Ann** b 9 Nov. 1818 [vital records of Lewiston, Maine, p. 27, 29], m 28 Dec. 1837 at Lewiston, ME, Charles Clark of Alfred, ME.

GARCELON, WILLIAM F. - Born 19 Dec. 1829, s/o Asa and Sophie (Frye) Garcelon. William F. Garcelon m Lucy/Lucy A. Taterson/Tatterson. Children: **Carroll C.** b 8 Dec. 1858, m Selina A. Harrison -- Nov. 1877; **Herbert Everett** b 2 Nov. 1861, d 17 Feb. 1866; and **William F.** b 24 Oct. 1868, m Grace F. Merrill 13 Sep. 1899.

GARCELON, WILLIAM GOLDER - Born 9 Oct. 1815, d 24 May 1876 in Pennsylvania age 60/66 years, s/o Peter and Sarah (Golder) Garcelon. William Golder Garcelon m Miranda Woodruff, d 25 May 1887, who was also the w/o Phillip Millbanks Garcelon. They had possibly: **Fred Almont** q.v.

GILBERT, AHIRAH - Born ??, d ??, s/o ?? Ahirah Gilbert m Olive Gilbert (his cousin), pub. 21 Mar. 1802. Children: **Deborah** b 16 Sep. 1802; **Leonard** b 14 Nov. 1805; and **Albion**.

GILBERT, ALANDA - Born ??, d ??, s/o ?? Alanda Gilbert m Deanna T. Children: **Rollin** b 11 Dec. 1844; **Abby Jane** b 21 Feb. 1848; **Lois Viola** b 21 Aug. 1852; and **Rosalin Victoria** b 6 Feb. 1855.

GILBERT, ALBERT HENRY - Born ??, d ??, s/o Orren and ?? Gilbert. Children: **Alice O.** b 27 Jan. 1872; **George C.** b 17 Feb. 1875; **Harry E.** b 17 Jul. 1878; **Frank O.** b -- Feb. 1877, d 27 May ----; **Iris Melvina** b 24 May 1889; and **Leslie Royal** b 17 Mar. 1892.

GILBERT, BAILEY - Born 29 Mar. 1793, d ??, s/o Samuel and ?? Gilbert. Bailey Gilbert m Salley/Sally Smart 13/30 Apr. 1815.

GILBERT, BENJAMIN - Born 25 Sep. 1805, d 6 Feb. 1856, s/o ?? Benjamin Gilbert m -- Sept. 1805 in Leeds, Maine, Lydia Jones, b 1 Mar. 1789, d 6 Apr. 1872, d/o Edward Jones. Children: **Nelson** q.v.; **Joanna Vaughan** b 11 Nov. 1808, unm; **Sanford** q.v.; **Wilson** q.v.; **Edward Jones** b 26 Oct. 1816, m Deborah Turner; **Judson** b 18 Apr. 1818;

Gustavus b 1 Aug. 1820; and **Benjamin** b 3 May 1822, d 6 Feb. 1856. [Bible rec Ralph Dakin of Auburn, Maine.]

GILBERT, BENJAMIN - Married Amanda T. Wagner, who d 2 Nov. 1875. Children: **Stella** b 13 Dec. 1873; **Eugenia**; and **Charles**.

GILBERT, CALEB - Born ??, d ??, s/o Elijah and Mrs. Hannah (Stetson (Randall) Gilbert. Caleb Gilbert m (1) Deanna/Diana/Deana Curtis 18 Nov. 1800, and m (2) Achsah Burgess of Wayne, Maine, who d 10 Sep. 1830 (they were published 24 Sep. 1815), and m (3) Miss Eliza Blaisdell of Phippsburg, Maine, 15 Oct. 1836. Children: **Lewis** q.v.; **Caleb** q.v.; **Deana** m Alden Rose 1 Jun. 1830; **Franklin** q.v.; **Melsar** q.v.; **Hiram** q.v.; **Eliza** b 5 Sep. 1820, d 4 Nov. 1833; **John**; **Frances** b 22 Sep. 1822, m Joseph Tuttle 9 Nov. 1845; **Achsah** b 4 Jul. 1818; **Elijah**; **Warbsell** b 10 Apr. 1825; **Mary** b 7 Jul. 1827; **Lovey** b 24 Dec. 1829; **Fairfield** b 16 Mar. 1840; and **Clinton**.

GILBERT, CALEB - Born ??, d ??, s/o Caleb and ?? Gilbert. Caleb Gilbert m Bathsheba Leavitt 23 Aug. 1827. Children: **Nancy** b 10 Jan. 1828; **Diana** b 17 Jul. 1830; **Alden** b 4 Dec. 1831; and **Orrin** b 2 May 1841.

GILBERT, CALEB S. - Born 26 May 1814, d 1893, s/o Hersey/Hursey, Jr. and ?? Gilbert. Caleb S. Gilbert m (1) Louisa Dorsey, who d 28 Jan. 1878, certificate granted in Nov. 1837, and m (2) Mrs. Rosetta Starbird 22 May 1879. Children: **Lucilla Alice** b 12 Sep. 1838, d 25 Sep. 1904, m Alonzo D. Morton 14 Nov. 1858, who d 8 May 1883; **Joseph Ransom** q.v.; **Livonia Josephine** b 1841, d 23 Jul. 1863, m Joseph H. Day 15 Nov. 1862, who d 9 Aug. 1898; and **Jetson Daniel** q.v.

GILBERT, CHARLES G. - Born 13 Feb. 1785, d 20 Aug. 1870, s/o ??. Charles G. Gilbert m Martha Day, 6 Dec. 1807. Children: **Rufus D.** b 10 Sep. 1810, d 13 Jul. 1828; **Everline** b 27 Dec. 1811, d 11 Jun. 1830; **Charles G. Jr.** q.v.; **Addison D.** b 3 Jan. 1816, d 26 Jul. 1843, m Elisabeth A. ----; **John Nelson** q.v.; **William Erastus** b 3 Jan. 1820, d 9 Jul. 1828; **James Cochran** b 11 Jan. 1822, m Martha Gile; **Joseph R. Harriet Amanda** b 2 May 1826, d 11 Sep. 1904, m Daniel Crossman of Greene, ME, 7 Mar. 1850; **Marinda J.** b 4 Apr. 1828, m John Hanscom, 22 Dec. 1850; **Everline R.** b 24 Sep. 1831, d -- Feb. 1870; and **Henrietta Anna** b 24 Nov. 1831, d 7 Oct. 1831. [Letter 1901 from L. Gilbert of Norway, Maine.]

GILBERT, CHARLES G., JR. - Born 7 Nov. 1813, d 5 Apr. 1894, s/o Charles G. and Martha (Day) Gilbert. Charles G. Gilbert, Jr. m Sarah Stover or Sarah Durgan, 24 May 1845. Children: **Hellen L.** b 29 Sep. 1846, m 1871 John A. Wheeler; **Lloyd A.** b 25 Sep. 1848, m Myra Brown 1883; **Alice M.** b 8 Sep. 1850; **Adrian L.** b 23 Jul. 1852, m Alice Gilson 1877; **Elwin B.** b 29 Jan. 1857; **William M.** b 24 Feb. 1861, d 17 Sep. 1884; **Helen L.** b 29 Sep. 1846, m John A. Wheeler -- Apr. 1871; **Alice M.** b 8 Sep. 1850, m Allelis W. Day 2 Jun. 1872; **Angelia M.** b 20 Jan. 1855; and **Florence Sarah** b 22 Apr. 1859. [All born in Leeds, Maine, except Hellen L. who was born at Hallowell Cross Roads, Maine, and Adriah L. who was born at Dover, New Hampshire according to a letter circa 1901 from Charles Gilbert.]

GILBERT, DANIEL - Married Isabella H. Annis, b in Hartland, Maine, d/o Solomon and Helen E. Annis.

GILBERT, DORA - Born 17 May 1839, d ??, d/o ?? Dora Gilbert m Josiah N. Eastman 1 Sep. 1860.

GILBERT, ELIJAH - Born ??, d ??, s/o ?? Elijah Gilbert settled in Turner, Maine.

GILBERT, ELIJAH - Born ??, d 19 Mar. 1825, s/o ??. Elijah Gilbert m Mrs. Hannah Randall nee Stetson. Children: **Josiah; Elijah Jr.; Nisa** or **Eunice** m Samuel Crockett 9 Mar. 1810; **Caleb Hannah;** and **James Drew** q.v.

GILBERT, ELIJAH, JR. - Born ??, d ??, s/o Elijah and Mrs. Hannah (Stetson) (Randall) Gilbert. Moved to Chesterville, Me., m 3 Jul. 1806 Huldah Gilbert.

GILBERT, FRANKLIN - Born ??, d ??, s/o Caleb and Deanna/Deana/Diana Curtis, m 8/25 Oct. 1831 Elivra Gilbert. Children: **Roscoe Lincoln** b 15 Oct. 1834; **Isabel** b 12 May 1835; and **Sophorina Curtis** b 12 May 1837.

GILBERT, GEORGE - Born ??, d ??, s/o ??. George Gilbert m Amanda. Children: **Mary Almeda** b 14 Mar. 1872.

GILBERT, HENRY - Born ??, d ??, s/o ??. Henry Gilbert settled in Leeds, Maine.

GILBERT, HENRY A. - Born 15 Feb. 1804, d in Turner, Maine, s/o Capt. William and ?? Gilbert. Henry Gilbert m Christina Alden. Children: **Ann** b 20 Jul. 1827, d 28 May 1851; **Betsy** b 29 Jan. 1830, m ---- Jewell; **Christina** b 21 Jul. 1831, d 16 Jul. 1850; **Julia** b 26 Dec. 1832, m (1) ---- Jones, and m (2) Hiram Phillips; **Alden** b 20 May 1834, unm; **Jercia** b 6 Mar. 1836; **Otis Hefford** b 11 Jun. 1838, d very young; and **James Henry** b 30 Apr. 1846, d 13 Mar. 1852.

GILBERT, HERSY/HURSEY, JR. - Born ??, d ??, s/o ??. Hersy/Hursey Gilbert Jr. was of Monmouth, Maine. He m Mehitable Morse 21 Jul. 1808. Children: **Dennis R.** b 10 Mar. 1811; **Arvillia B.** b 28 Mar. 1812, m Warren Foster; **Caleb S.** q.v.; **Levi J.** b 5 Sep. 1817; **Alfred L.** b 9 Aug. 1820; **Jerome B.** b 2 Jul. 1826; **Drusilla Jane** b 8 Aug. 1828, m Holman H. Dorsey; **L----** b 3 Aug. 1830, m Emily ----; **Joseph R.** b 7 Aug. 1833; and **Chandler** b 1832, d 12 Oct. 1893.

GILBERT, HIRAM - Born ??, d ??, s/o Caleb and Deanna/Deana/Diana Curtis. Hiram Gilbert m 19 Nov. 1835 Sarah Ann Bidwell. Child: **Harriet Whitney** b 22 Nov. 1836.

GILBERT, JAMES - Born ??, d ??, s/o ??. James Gilbert m 3 Jul. 1806 Hannah Jacobs of Waterville, Maine.

GILBERT, JAMES DREW - Born ??, d ??, s/o Elijah and Mrs. Hannah (Stetson) (Randall) Gilbert. James Drew Gilbert was of Turner, Maine. He m in Turner, Maine, Rebecca Day of Leeds, Maine, d 13 Nov. 1840, marriage certificate granted 4 Jul. 1813 [marriage notice in *Eastern Argus*, issue 2 Dec. 1813]. Children: **Hannah** m John S. Levitt 18 Nov. 1833; **Washington** m Jane Badger; **Carolus** b 22 Feb. 1818, m Olive R. Gilbert of Boston, ME, 1 Jan. 1849; **James Drew** b 20 Feb. 1820, m Adeline Curtis; **Roxanna** b 11 Jun. 1822, d 12 Aug. 1895 at Newton, Massachusetts, m (as his 2nd wife) George A. Hinkley [*Gilberts of New England* by Geoffrey Gilbert, 1959, Victoria, B.C., Canada, printed by Ward & Phillips Limited, p. 457]; **Octavie** b 30 Sep. 1824, m George A. Hinkley; **Ammi** b 19 Nov. 1827; and **Everline Rebecca** b 11 Sep. 1830, m Ralph Davenport of Newton, Mass.

GILBERT, JETSON DANIEL - Born 3 Jul. 1851, d ??, s/o Caleb S. and Louisa (Dorsey) Gilbert. Jetson Daniel Gilbert m (1) Inza D. Haville 5 Jun. 1875, who was b 11 Apr. 1857, d 12 Aug. 1891 in San Jose, d/o Joseph D. and Dorcas A. (Golder) Harville, and m (2) Addie ---- of Westbrook, Maine. Children: **Nina Komah**; and **Komah**.

GILBERT, JOHN NELSON - Born 21 Feb. 1818, d 12 May 1893 at age 76 years 2 months 21 days, s/o Charles G. and Martha (Day) Gilbert. John Nelson Gilbert m Silance/Silence H. Keene, d/o John, certificate granted 12 Dec. 1842.

GILBERT, JOSEPH R. - Born 4 May 1824, d 1 Mar. 1898, s/o ??. Joseph R. Gilbert m 30 Apr. 1843 Mary A. Crummett/Crommett. Children: **Martha Almeda** b 13 May 1843, d 27 Mar. 1864; **Erastus Everett** b 29 Oct. 1845; **George Elliot** b 5 Jul. 1848, d 5 Nov. 1880, m Amanda Chase of Turner, ME; **Elvetta Delilah** b 14 Oct. 1850, m George E. Wardwell of Turner; **Emma Aurelia** b 13 Nov. 1852, d 1 Jul. 1876; **Charles** d 14 Aug. 1870; and **Everline** d -- Feb. 1870.

GILBERT, JOSEPH RANSOM - Born 22 Sep. 1845, d ??, s/o Caleb S. and ?? Joseph Ransom Gilbert m 22 Jan. 1866 Anna L. Whitney. Child: **Josephine**.

GILBERT, JOSIAH - Born ??, d ??, s/o Elijah and Mrs. Hannah (Stetson) (Randall) Gilbert. Josiah Gilbert m 27 Feb. 1817 Bethany Day. Children: **Clarisa** b 24 May 1819; **Olive R.** b 20 Apr. 1821, m Carlous Gilbert of Turner, ME, 1 Jul. 1849; **Luther Bailey** b 23 Apr. 1823, m Penelope Gilbert; **Sarah Day** b 7 Nov. 1831, m Nathaniel Haskell; **Josiah Randall** b 22 Jun. 1827, m Lydia Durham; **Lois Am** b 14 Oct. 1833, m (1) Israel Durham, and m (1) ---- Webster; and **Lovicsa** unm.

GILBERT, LAFAYETTE - Born ??, d ??, s/o ??. Lafayette Gilbert m Elizabeth F. ----. Children: **Ida Eugenia** b 7 Jan. 1856; and **Minnie Vaughn** b 23 Sep. 1857.

GILBERT, LEVI - Born ??, d ??, s/o ??. Levi Gilbert settled in Buckfield, Maine.

GILBERT, LEVI - Born ??, d ??, s/o ?? Levi Gilbert m Ruth Robbins, certificate granted -- Aug. 1823. Children: **Levi Franklin** b 14 Apr. 1824; **Daniel** b 20 Dec. 1826; **Lucius Loring** b 16 May 1827; **Eliza Ann** b 19 Mar. 1829; and **Roxellea** b 16 May 1830.

GILBERT, LEWIS - Born 15 Apr. 1801, s/o Caleb and ?? Gilbert. Lewis Gilbert m 26 Feb. 1826 or 20 Apr. 1826 Eunice/Eunice J. Alden, b 13 Mar. 1801, d 25 Feb. 1867. Children: **Ellen** b 12 Mar. 1827, m Horace Bradford; **O s e a** b 18 Aug. 1828, d 30 Nov. 1889, m Sumner H. Cole 9 Jan. 1855; **Virginia** b 19 Dec. 1830, d 22 Feb. 1848; **Ziba Alden** b 4 Nov. 1832, m Clara Bradford; **Julius** b 7 Apr. 1836; and **Selden** b 9 Dec. 1837, m ---- Whitmore of Bowdoinham, ME.

GILBERT, MARKUS - Born ??, d ??, s/o ??. Markus Gilbert m (1) 22 Dec. 1816 Jane Samson, d 1 Feb. 1823, and m (2) Miriam Coburn, certificate granted -- Dec. 1823.

GILBERT, MELSER - Born ??, d ??, s/o Caleb and Deanna/Diana/Deana (Curtis) Gilbert. Melser Gilbert m 6 Oct. 1838 Alma P. Bradford. Children: **Horace Jones** b 10 Jan. 1840; **Celia Bradford** b 5 May 1841; and **Franklin Bailey** b 18 Aug. 184-.

GILBERT, NATHANIEL - Born ??, d ??, s/o ??. Nathaniel Gilbert m 1773 Hannah Hemps. Children: **Charles G.** b 13 Feb. 1785, d 20 Aug. 1870, m Martha Day, 6 Dec. 1809; **Spencer** q.v.; **Nathaniel** q.v.; **Rhoda**; **Judith A.** b 1 Jan. 1773, m Nathaniel Bishop of Winthrop, ME, ca. 1771; **Rebecca** b 3 Mar. 1774, m Zachariah Butterfield; **Huldah** m Elijah Gilbert 3 Jul. 1806; **Nancy** m Jonathon Danielson ca. 1799; **James**; and **Harriet** m George Pullen 11 Oct. 1798.

GILBERT, NATHANIEL - Born ??, d ??, s/o ?? Nathaniel Gilbert settled in Kingfield, ME.

GILBERT, NATHANIEL JR. - Born 8 Jan. 1781, d 6 Aug. 1872, s/o Nathaniel and Hannah (Hemps) Gilbert. Nathaniel Gilbert, Jr. m Sophia Stubbs, b 20 Apr. 1786, d 2 Oct. 1860, pub. 6 Oct. 1804, certificate granted 20 Oct. 1804. Children: **Agleon**; **Adeylon/Nathaniel Ajalon** b 1 May 1806, m Susannah Morley; **Nancy/Nancy Danielson** b 2 May 1808, m Benjamin Lane; **Alvin/Calvin** b 6 Feb. 1810, m Matilda Fillebrown; **Huldah/Hulda** m Patrick Mcloom/McCloom/McLoon; **William** b 17 Sep. 1818, m Hannah Chipman; **Henry** d young; **Charles**; **Chandler** b 4 Jul. 1820; **Joseph** b 1822, d 1822; **Sophia S.** b 28 May 1823, d 9 Sep. 1883, m Marcellus/Marcellus P. Lovejoy; and **Benjamin** b 2 Dec. 1828, d 1863, m Sophorina Longley. [Source: S. G. Lane of North New Portland, Maine, letter, 1902.]

GILBERT, NELSON - Born 16 May 1806, d 16 Sep. ----, s/o Benjamin and Lydia (Jones) Gilbert. Nelson Gilbert m Rebecca Sampson, who d 1 Oct. 1867, marriage certificate granted -- Apr. 1829. Children: **Oliver S.** q.v.; **Phils/Philo Clark** b 9 Feb. 1833, unm.; **Hannah Sampson** b 12 Oct. 1841; and **Emely/Emily Jane** b 17 Mar. 1850.

GILBERT, OLIVER S. - Born 18/19 Aug. 1830, d ??, s/o Nelson and Rebecca (Sampson) Gilbert. Oliver S. Gilbert m Lucie/Lucia/Lutia Turner. Children: **Ella Marr** b 4 Jun. 1859; and **Rosilla Augusta** b 31 Oct. 1864.

GILBERT, SAMUEL - Born ??, d ??, s/o ?? Samuel Gilbert m Martha ----, d 29 Mar. 1814. Children: **Aseneth Drew** b 13 Dec. 1787, m Stephen Hutchinson 29 Jul. 1810; **Chloe** b 22 Mar. 1791, m Edward Adams 30 Nov. 1809; **Bailey** q.v.; **Arad** b 27 Aug. 1796; **Alvah** b 10 May 1798; and **Rebecca** b 16 Jul. 1801.

GILBERT, SANFORD - Born 6 Jun. 1811, d ??, s/o Benjamin and Lydia (Jones) Gilbert. Sanford Gilbert m Adeline Day, certificate granted 3 Jan. 1836 [Bible record, Androscoggin Historical, Auburn, Maine]. Children: **Mahala Judson** b 11 Jun. 1837; **Roscoe Greene** b 28 Feb. 1839; **Josephine** b 29 Jul. 1840, m John Keene, was in 3d Me. Army, and killed therein.

GILBERT, SPENCER - Born 24 Jan. 1789, d 11 Jan. 1861, s/o ??. Spencer Gilbert m Nancy Dudley, b 5 Nov. 1790, d 10 Aug. 1858. Children: **Rebekah/Rebecca B.** b 8 May 1813, d 21 May 1877, m Tristram G. Norton 22 Sep. 1833; **William S.** b 26 Aug. 1814, d 3 Dec. 1815; **Harrison P.** b 10 Jun. 1816, d 21 Jun. 1898, m H. Jennie Sturgess, 22 Dec. 1869; **Mary A.** b 26 Jul. 1818, d 22 Mar. 1852, m Reubin B. Curtis in Jan.; **Hannah H.** b 13 Sep. 1820, m Irason P. Lander, 7 Dec. 1843; **Sarah P.** b 13 Aug. 1822, d 22 Nov. 1841; **William S.** b 18 Aug. 1824, d 26 Dec. 1897, m Ellen B. Church 30 Dec. 1859; **Joseph S. A.** b 1 Oct. 1826, d 15 Oct. 1853, m ----; **Elisa X.** b 1 Jan. 1829, d 4 Jan. 1900, m William Blanchard; **Cornelius W.** b 23 Oct. 1830, m Louise M. Trevylin; **Charles F.** b 5 Oct. 1832, d 8 Sep. 1896; m Aphia Vose. [Letter from Cornelius W. Gilbert of Kingfield, Maine, 1901.]

GILBERT, WILLIAM - Born ??, d ??, s/o ?? William Gilbert m Anna Samson 18 Oct. 1815. Children: **Aurelia J.** b 12 May 1816; **Guslina Bertram** b 11 Jan. 1821, d 3 Oct. 1823; and **William Earl** b 25 Mar. 1834.

GILBERT, CAPT. WILLIAM - Born in 1756, d 15/25 May 1816 at age 60 years, s/o ?? Capt. William Gilbert m Betsy Bailey of Hanover, Massachusetts, d 11 Aug. 1834, age 74 years. Children: **Betsy Bailey** b 22 Jul. 1785, d 8 Apr. ---- age 36 years, m George Turner, certificate granted 8 Sep. 1801; **Lucy** b 14 Jun. 1787, m Daniel Lothrop in Carroll -- Aug. 1808, pub. 18 Jun. 1808; **Jane** b 29 Jun. 1791, m Daniel Lindsey in Carroll 9 Nov. 1808; **Sally** b 8 Jul. 1794, m Codding

Drake 11 Nov. 1810, lived in Albion, ME; **William** b 18 Nov. 1798, unm; **Julia** b 25 Oct. 1800, m 30 Nov. 1820 James Warren Mitchell who d in Leeds, ME; and **Henry A.** q.v.

GILBERT, WILSON - Born 26 Jul. 1813, d 18 Feb. 1858, s/o Benjamin and Lydia (Jones) Gilbert. Wilson Gilbert m Catherine Day, who d 2 Mar. 1878, marriage certificate granted 1 Nov. 1841. Children: **Winfield Scott** b 26 Jul. 1843, d 22 Jul. 1847; **Herbert Melville** b 10 May 1846, d 13 Mar. 1885; **Llewellyn** b 13 May 1849, d 6 Apr. 1850; **Mallroy Wilson** b 19 Jul. 1851; and **Ada Manson** b 13 May 1854.

GILLPATRICK/GILPATRICK, JAMES - Born ??, d ??, s/o ?? James Gillpatrick m Elizabeth ----. Children: **Hannah** b 15 Feb. 1795, d young; **Samuel** b 5 July 1796; **Hannah** b 11 June 1798 in Lewiston (sic) [the statement that she was born in Lewiston is highly unlikely; however the record is most likely in error; it is more likely to have been in the Gore which became the town of Thompsonboro in 1799 (now part of Lisbon)]; **H a r r i e t** b 16 Aug. 1800, d 7 May 1804 [vital records of Lewiston, Maine, p. 213]; **Lucy** b 3 Jan. 1803; **Charles** b 30 Apr. 1805; **Harriet** b 28 Mar 1808 in Litchfield, ME; **Calvin** b 17 Feb. 1811 in Lewiston; **Simon** b 25 Feb. 1814 in Lewiston; **James** b 3 Dec. 1816 in Lisbon; **S a r a h** b 11 Nov. 1821 in Lisbon [vital records of Lewiston, Maine, p. 29]. The Gilpatrick family moved to Lewiston 1831-1849. The name of Gilpatrick can be found in Lisbon and Bowdoin, Maine. [Vital Records of Lewiston, Maine, p. 37.]

GILPATRICK, NATHANIEL - Born 1752, d 30 May 1834, age 85 years [vital records of Bowdoin, Maine, p. 67]. Nathaniel Gilpatrick was a revolutionary soldier and may have been a brother of James Gillpatrick (above) of Lewiston. Nathaniel Gilpatrick moved to Brunswick, Maine, after the war, then to Bowdoin by 1790. In 1799 the part of Bowdoin he lived in became Thompsonboro. He later lived in Lisbon and Webster (now called Sabattus) without moving. He m (1) Abigail Higgens, b 2 Jul. 1753 in Biddeford, Maine, d 28 Jul. 1805 [vital records of Bowdoin, Maine, p. 67], and m (2) Lydia ----. *Children by 1st wife*: **Timothy** b 19 Sept. 1787; **Christopher** b 6 Jan. 1790; **Joseph** b 12 May 1794; **Dyer** b 15 Oct. 1796; **Anna** b 22 May 1798; **John** b 10 Nov. 1802; **Nathan** b 6 Oct. 1800, d 3 Jul. 1804. *Children by 2nd wife*: **Nathan** b 13 Nov. 1807 [vital records of Bowdoin, Maine, p. 94-95, printed records, editor Rachel T. Cox, Maine Historical Society, 1944].

GILMAN, LYDIA EMMA - Born 4 Sep. 1852 in Farmington, Maine, d ??, d/o ?? Lydia Emma Gilman m 19 Mar. 1873 in Lewiston, Maine, ----.

GODDARD, ABEL - Born 23 Feb. 1773, d ??, s/o ?? Abel Goddard m Susannah ----, b 10 Sep. 1777. Children: **Hannah** b 22 May 1797; **John** b 9 Jun. 1799, had a house built for him on the River Road, Lewiston, ME, in 1838 by Samuel and Ira Nevens [*A Brief Journal of My Life* by Ira Nevens, manuscript at the Androscoggin Historical Society. Mr. Nevens built homes in Lewiston and Auburn, Maine, from 1834-1880.]; **Lydia** b 1 Jul. 1801; **Isaac** b 3 Feb. 1804; **Mary** b

26 Apr. 1806; **Sarah** b 10 Mar. 1809; **Robert** b 21 Feb. 1811; **Eunice** b 5 Feb. 1813; **Rebecca** b 17 Oct. 1815; **Levi** b 2 Apr. 1820. [Vital Records of Lewiston, Maine, p. 116.]

GODDARD, ISAAC - Born ??, d ??, likely s/o Abel and Susannah (----) Goddard. Isaac Goddard m int. 19 Feb. 1825, m 6 Mar. 1825 [vital records of Lewiston, Maine, p. 425] Betsey Staten [vital records of Lewiston, Maine, p. 372]. Children: **Caroline** b 10 Jun. 1825; **Matilda J. Fickett** (adopted) b 22 Dec. 1832; **Abel** b 25 Nov. 1838; **Levi** b 3 Dec. 1841; **Isaac** b 7 Jan. 1846. [Vital Records of Lewiston, Maine, p. 116.]

GODDARD, WILLIAM - Born 25 Jan. 1786 at Brunswick, Maine, d ??, s/o ?? William Goddard m Patience ----, b 12 Aug. 1783 at Durham, Maine. Children: **Lois** b 9 Apr. 1804; **Isiah** b 22 Feb. 1808; **Louisa** b 5 Feb. 1811; **Levi** b 27 May 1815; **Phebe** b 25 Nov. 1817; **Josiah** b 25 Mar. 1819; **Elizabeth** b 24 Nov. 1823; **Charles** b 1 May 1827. [Vital Records of Lewiston, Maine, p. 116.]

GOLDER, ALVAH A. - Son of Orren. Child: **Arthur Lewis** b 2 Jan. 1886.

GOLDER, DAVID TARR - Born 10/11 Oct. 1811, d 5 Nov. 1882, s/o William Jr. and Mrs. Rachel (Tarr) Golder. David Tarr Golder m 30 Oct. 1833 Elizabeth Stone, d 28 Feb. 1888, d/o Thomas Stone. Children: **Lydia Frances** b 18 Jun. or 8 Aug. 1835, d 1 Mar. 1880 in Portland, ME, m 10 Jul. 1861 Rev. Ammi G. Ladd; **Thomas S.** b 18 Jun. 1838; **Henry William** q.v.

GOLDER, FAIRFIELD - Born 1 Mar. 1800, d 8 Jan. 1880 and headstone states he was "79 years 10 months 8 days old", buried in Wales, Maine, on the Pond Rd., s/o William, Sr. and ?? Golder. Fairfield Golder m (1) 24 Feb. 1822 [vital records of Lewiston, Maine, p. 439] **Sally** ---- Peter or Sally Dennett, d 28 Sep. 1836, age 40 years, d/o Ebenezer and m (2) Polly Bar--- or Mary Sawyer (Dill), d 13 Feb. 1887, age 86 years 9 months, wid/o Daniel Dill. Children: **Fairfield, Jr.** b 28 Apr. 1823, d in Phillips, ME, 22 Feb. 1884, m Hannah/Hannah C. Dill, sis/o Seward and d/o James, 9 Nov. 1854; **Dorcas A./Ann** b 6 May 1829, d 20 Mar. 1895, m Joseph D. Harville 19 Apr. 1856, who was b 6 Jan. 1829 in Madison, ME, and d in 1875 in PA; **Sarah C./Caroline** b 19 Mar. 1831, m George H. Jones (Webster, ME) 7 Jan. 1858; **Nathan D.** q.v.; **Daniel D.** b 21 Sep. 1837, lived at Austin, Orange Co., Calif., m Isabel H. Annie 9 Sep. 1879, who was b at Hartland, Me., on 6 Jun. 1853, d/o Solomon and Hellen E. (Towle) Annie; and **Dora** b 17 May 1839, m Josiah N. Eastman 1 Sep. 1860.

GOLDER, FAIRFIELD - Born 18/19 Mar. 1807, d 19 Dec. 1885, s/o William Jr. and Mrs. Rachel (Tarr) Golder. Fairfield Golder m Cordelia/Cordalia Rich, who was b 2 Jul. 1817 and d 8 Apr. 1904, d/o Thophilus and Delia (Perry) Rich. Children: **Ellen Augusta** b 15 Mar. 1841, m William McKeene of Phillips 10 Aug. 1864; **Delia Ann** b 20 Nov. 1842, m S. Streeter Dunn 14 Sep. 1871; **Mary Adelaide** b 21 Jan.

1845, m George D. Frost of Lisbon, ME, 31 Dec. 1870; **Flora May** b 26 Apr. 1849, m Charles L. Roberts 16 Dec. 1882; **Clarence Fairfield** b 7 Jun. 1852, m Alice E. Huff -- Mar. 1878; **Eva Gertrude** b 12 Jan. 1859, d 17 Feb. 1903; and **Arthur Lee** b 13 Feb. 1863, m Mary Alice Grant 23 Sep. 1891.

GOLDER, GEORGE WASHINGTON - Born 9 Nov. 1873 in Webster, Maine, d ??, s/o John William and Lizzie Ann (Hubbard) Golder. George Washington Golder m 17 Sep. 1874 or 29 Aug. 1892 by J. W. Maxwell, Esq., in Webster, Maine, to Sarah H. Mellor, b 17 Sep. 1874 in Bridgeton, Maine. Child: **William Allne** b in Greene, ME, 3 Jan. 1893.

GOLDER, HARRY W. - Born 22 Apr. 1863 in Belgrade, Maine, d ??, s/o Thomas S. Golder. Harry W. Golder m 18 Sep. 1886 Minnie O. Tracy of Rome, Maine, d/o Ira and Martha (----) Tracy. Children: **Bernard Ryan** b 29 Jun. 1888; and **Elizabeth Tracy** b 2 May 1890.

GOLDER, HENRY WILLIAM - Born 14 Jan. 1844, d ??, s/o David Tarr and Elizabeth (Stone) Golder. Henry William Golder m 1 Nov. 1865 Elvira F. Chandler, b 6 Oct. 1846, d/o Joseph C. and Susan (Good----) Chandler of Belgrade, Maine. Child: **Maud E.** b 18 Sep. 1867.

GOLDER, ISAAC - Born 1 Dec. 1825, d 18 Aug. 1875, s/o Rev. Jacob and Dorothy (Dennett) Golder. Isaac Golder was having a house built for him on Sabattus St., Lewiston, but he d before it was finished [13 May 1875 to 8 Jan. 1876, Mr. Neven's (the builder) notes]. He m Sarah Jane Skinner 27 Dec. 1864. Children: **Leona May** b 3 May 1866; **Idella A.** b 28 Apr. 1868; and **Vergie E.** b 9 May 1871.

GOLDER, ISAAC S. - Born 7 Mar. 1835, d 29 Apr. 1898, age 63 years 1 month 23 days, s/o Capt. John and Susannah (Spofford) Golder. Isaac S. Golder m 28 Dec. 1854 Sarah J. Davis, d/o John V. Davis. Children: **Charles G.** b 27 Jan. 1847; **Eliza A.**; **Fred W.** m Jane Powell; and **Carrie**.

GOLDER, JACOB - Born 12 Mar. 1815, d -- Sep. 1893 or -- Jul. 1894 in Kansas, s/o Capt. John and Susannah (Spofford) Golder. Jacob Golder was of Auburn, Maine, in 1866 [father's will]. He m 6 Jun. 1839 Jane S. Wright, d 7 Jan. 1862, d/o Joel Wright of Lewiston, Maine. Children: **Mary Jane** b 17 Aug. 1840, m (1) Joseph Whitman, m (2) Harry W. Nye of Waterville; **Margaret Augusta** b 23 Dec. 1845, m Ellis L. Hunt of Auburn, ME, 25 Dec. 1873; **Dwight C.** b -- May 1849, m Cara Elden of Waterville, ME, in 1871; and **Charlotte S.** b in 1854, m Charles Edwin Jameson in 1876.

GOLDER, REV. JACOB - Born 13 Dec. 1785, d 12 Mar. 1872, s/o William, Sr. and Dorcas (Dill) Golder. Rev. Jacob Golder m (1) 29 Dec. 1808 Dorothy Dennett, d 5 May 1833, d/o Ebeneser and Susannah (Roberts) Dennett of Bowdoinham, Maine, married by Joel Thompson, J. P. [vital records of Lewiston, Maine, p. 427], and m (2) 30 Jul.

1834 to Mary Dennett who was b 16 May 1810, d 28 Mar. 1871, d/o Ebenezer and Anna (Roberts) Dennett. *Children of 1st wife*: **Dorcas*** b 30 Sep. 1809, d 27 Dec. 1830, age 21 years, m Ira Purington 27 Aug. 1828, who d 10 May 1888; **Affidele*** b 2 Jun. 1812, m James Maxwell of Webster, ME, 21 Mar. 1838; **Anna Dennett*** b 5 Oct. 1814, d 17 May 1886, m Sylvanus Ling of Lisbon, ME, 19 Mar. 1835; **Sally M.*** b 9 Jun. 1811, m Joel Dennett 11 Nov. 1841 of Bowdoin, ME; **Jacob Roberts** q.v.; **Lucinda*** b 6 May 1822, m Jacob B. Ham 20 Dec. 1846; **Isaac*** q.v.; and **Nathan** b -- Apr. 1829, d 31 Jan. 1830, age 9 months. *Children of 2nd wife*: **Dorothy J.*** b 26 Nov. 1837, m Jacob A. Field 24 Sep. 1859; **Flavilla E.*** b 23 Aug. 1841, m George S. Pettingill 6 Apr. 1867; **Melissa H.*** b 12 Feb. 1844, m A.P. Winslow 23 May 1877, who d 31 Dec. 1845, age 71 years 1 month 24 days; and **Moses D.*** q.v. [* Indicates probate #1076, will of Jacob Golder and Book 4 p. 345.]

GOLDER, JACOB ROBERTS - Born 31 Jun. 1818, d 20 Jan. 1865 of Lewiston [probate record #773], s/o Rev. Jacob and Dorothy (Dennett) Golder. Jacob Roberts Golder m Sarah Henderson 30/31 May 1846, who d 29 Aug. 1863, age 42 years. Child: **Everett H.** b 1852, d 19 Jul. 1865.

GOLDER, JAMES JOHNSON - Born 13 Nov. 1822, d 22 Feb. 1892, s/o Capt. John and Susannah (Spofford) Golder. James Johnson Golder m (1) Mary A. Jordan, who d 1 Apr. 1852, d/o John of Webster, Maine, and m (2) Arlitta B./Arletta Clark of N. Castle, Maine, d -- Oct. 1895. *Child of 1st wife*: **Eva Ann** b 4 Apr. 1850, d 23 Jan. 1878, m Charles Drinkwater of Webster, ME. *Children of 2nd wife*: **Nettie** b 22 Apr. 1859, m William H. Saymour of Portsmouth, NH, 16 Oct. 1884; and **Ella Florence** b 11 Dec. 1861.

GOLDER, CAPT. JOHN - Born 29 Aug. 1790, d 17 May 1867 [Androscoggin Co. probate record #627, will dated 1 Aug. 1866 names persons with asterisk (*)], s/o William, Sr. and ?? Golder. Capt. John Golder m Susannah Spofford/Sheppard of Lisbon, Maine, b 15 May 17--, d 25 Apr. 1865, pub. 26 Nov. 1812. Children: **General Washington*** q.v.; **Jacob*** q.v.; **Nathaniel Herrick** b 18 Jun. 1818, d 13 Nov. 1848, no family; **Orren S.*** q.v.; **James Johnson** b 15 Nov. 1822; **Dorcas*** b 27 Sep. 1824, m William S. Rogers* of Saco, ME, 13 Sep. 1849; **John William*** q.v.; **Peter Augustus** b 15 Jun. 1829, d 4 Apr. 1866, m Edna Williamson of Mercer, ME, -- Dec. 1865; and **Isaac S.*** q.v. [Vital Records of Lewiston, p. 56, 57.]

GOLDER, JOHN WILLIAM - Born 2 Apr. 1827, d 28 Jan. 1903 age 75 years, 9 months, 2 days, s/o Capt. John and Susannah (Spofford/Sheppard) Golder. John William Golder m (1) 9 Aug. 1851 (? 1857) in Montville, Maine, by Rev. Moses McFarland to Gertrude Leonard of Whitefield, Maine, b 31 Mar. 1838, d 16 Jan. 1860 (or 1 Mar. 1862 in Somerville, Maine), d/o Joseph of Whitefield, Maine, and m (2) 28 Jun. 1863 in Waterville, Me., by Rev. A. H. Morrell to Lizzie Ann Hubbard of Waterville, Maine, b 7 Feb. 1841, d 5 Dec. 1881 in Lewiston, Maine, d/o John of Waterville, Maine. *Children of 1st wife*: **Fred Clarence** b 18 Oct. 1858 in Waterville (? or Montville,

174

Me.); and **Nettie Gertrude** b in Somerville, Me., 10 Jan. 1861, d 19 Feb. 1862. *Children of 2nd wife*: **Lulu Frances** b in Somerville, Me., 7 May 1864, m John Henry Whitney 30 Apr. 1890 in Lewiston by Rev. Howe; **Lillie May** b in Lewiston 7 Apr. 1866; **Ulysses Grant** q.v; **George Washington** q.v.; and **Maud Ellen** b 9 Mar. 1878 in Lewiston, Maine.

GOLDER, JORDAN - Born 15 Dec. 1805, d 11/15 Dec. 1870/1880 at Parker's Head, Maine, s/o William, Jr., and ?? Golder. Jordan Golder m (1) 15 Mar. 1829 Eleanor (Maria?) Stone of Bridgeton, Maine, b 21 Jul. 1802, d 8 Jul. 1861 at Parkins Head, and m (2) 30 Nov. 1862 Mrs. Martha A. Farnham Wyman, b 21 Oct. 1834, and m (3) 15 Nov. 1867 Josephine Morse, b 19 May 1844, d/o Scott and Pauline (Weeks) Morse. Children: **Eliza Maria** or **Maria Elizabeth** b 29 (28?) Jun. 1830, m Oris/Oren S./G. or Orren S. Golder, who d 1 May 1882; **Eleanor Melvina** b 18 (19?) May 1832, m (1) 30 Sep. 1852 Samuel R. Penly (Percy?), who d 9 Jul. 1856, and m (2) George A. (W.?) Adams; **Harriet N.** or **Harriet Ann** b 19 Mar. 1834, d -- Mar. 1841 (or 18 Jan. 1843?); **Mary Frances ("Fanie")** b 19 Jan. 1836, m 3 Mar. 1858 David T. (J.?) Percy; **Lillian P.** or **Lectina Phillips** b 23 Dec. 1838 (1837?), m 6 Jan. 1863 Merrill T. Wyman; **Jordan** q.v.; **Ada Ann** b 25 May 1843, d -- Feb. 1868 (1869?), m Henry Wyman; **Augusta Jane** b 11 Apr. 1845, d 11 Mar. 1846; and **Mattie M.** b 25 Aug. 1863, m 28 Aug. 1883 Willard Duey.

GOLDER, JORDAN - Born 26 Jun. 1840, d ??, s/o Jordan and ?? Golder. Jordan Golder m 5 Nov. 1867 Josephine Morse. Children: **Scott**; and **Pauline**.

GOLDER, JOSEPH TARR - Born 11 Dec. 1816, d 10 Mar. 1859, s/o ?? Joseph Tarr Golder m Mary Jane Pinkham, Vassalboro, Maine. No children.

GOLDER, MOSES D. - Born 30 Dec. 1847, d 12 Oct. 1884, s/o Rev. Jacob and ?? Golder. Moses D. Golder m 27 Oct. 1868 Esther A. Gilmore, d 30 Mar. 1902.

GOLDER, NATHAN D. - Born 28 Sep. 1836, d 7 Apr. 1900, s/o Fairfield and Sally (----) Golder. Nathan D. Golder m 5 Nov. 1861 Desire Dingley Hackett of Auburn, b 19 Aug. 1834, d 16 Feb. 1899, d/o Jacob. Children: **Sherman C.** b -- May 1867; and **Lucy M.** b 25 Apr. 1869, m Fred R. Helms 21 Jun. 1894.

GOLDER, OREN/ORREN S. - Born 7 Jun. 1820, d 1 May 1882, s/o Capt. John and Susannah (----) Golder. Oren/Orren S. Golder m 25 Feb. 1848 Maria Elizabeth/Eliza Maria Golder, b 28/29 Jun. 1830, d/o Jordan Golder. Children: **Alfred H.** b 2 Jul. 1849, m Maggie E. Farr 15 Aug. 1870; **Alvah A.** b 15 Aug. 1852, m Nellie Hinckley of Penobscot, Me.; **Frances C.** b 20 Aug. 1854, d 31 Mar. 1900, age 45 years 7 months 10 days, m Louville Symonds 1 Jan. 1878; **Edgar J.** b 21 Nov. 1856, d 15 May 1899, m Carrie E. Bickford, d/o Charles B. of Lisbon, ME, 21 Aug. 1886; **Lizzie M.** b 22 Apr. 1859, m Frederick

Mitchell of Freeport, ME, pub. 25 Nov. 1881; **Frank L.** b 6 Oct. 1861, d 20 Nov. 1887, m May Dudley, Cambridge; **Ada A.** b 29 Oct. 1865, unm; **Loville O.** b 8 Dec. 1871, unm; and **Minnie** b 25 Mar. 1874, d 28 Mar. 1874.

GOLDER, RACHEL A. - Born 20 Jan. 1815, d ??, d/o ??. Rachel A. Golder m 28 Nov. 1844 John D. Lake, d 15 Nov. 1884 in Richmond, Maine.

GOLDER, THOMAS S. - Born 18 Jun. 1838, d ??, s/o David Tarr and Elizabeth (Stone) Golder. Thomas S. Golder m (1) 1/6 Jul. 1862 Jane C. Pray of Rome, Maine, d 10 Sep. 1865, d/o Samuel W. Pray and Clarinda Lord of Pownal, Maine, and m (2) Clara U. Peverlyn 29 Apr. 1866, who was b 30 May 1842 in Bethel, Maine. Children: **Harry W.** q.v.; **Edith J./Kimball** b in Belgrade, ME, 6 Sep. 1865, m Harry E. Burbank of Augusta, ME, 6 Jun. 1888, who d 19 Dec. 1894; and **Fred O.** b in Belgrade 6 Oct. 1870, m Stella M. Thompson 8 Jul. 1894, who was b in 1873.

GOLDER, ULYSSES GRANT - Born in Lewiston 3 Dec. 1868, d ??, s/o John William and Lizzie Ann (Hubbard) Golder. Ulysses Grant Golder m 17 May 1891 in Auburn, Maine, Rosa Ellen Carville, b 25 Jul. 1862 in Lewiston, Maine, by J. W. Mitchell, Esq. Child: **Ella Gertrude** b in Auburn 5 Mar. 1892.

GOLDER, GENERAL WASHINGTON - Born 29 Aug. 1813, d -- Feb. ----, s/o John and Susannah (Spofford) Golder. General Washington Golder res. California in 1866 [father's will; left $300 to him if he would return to Maine within nine years of this date]. He m Sarah Mary Jones (Pownal, Maine). Children: **Nathaniel** d age 6 months; **Willie** m Sarah Jones of Pownal, pub. 27 Jan. 1838; and **Frank** d ca. age 8 years.

GOLDER, WILLIAM SR. - Born ??, d 18 Mar. 1846, s/o ??. William Golder, Sr. m Dorcas Dill, pub. 4 Jul. 1783 at Topsham, Maine. Children: **William Jr.** q.v.; **Rev. Jacob** q.v.; **Sarah** b 27 Feb. 1788, d 27 Feb. 1876, m 10 Jul. 1808 Peter Garcelon, who d 20 Oct. 1867; **Capt. John** q.v.; **Dorcas** b 23 Jul. 1792, m Greenleaf Spofford of Lisbon, ME, pub. 19 Jun. 1812, who d 13 Sep. 1877, age 93 years 10 months; **Polly** b 20 Nov. 1796, m Benjamin Jordan of Lisbon, pub. 15 Aug. 1818, certificate granted 8 Nov. 1818; **Fairfield** q.v.; and **Isaac** b 3 Feb. 1807, d 8 Jan. 1824.

GOLDER, WILLIAM JR. - Born 21 Jan. 1784, d 24 Mar. 1837, s/o William and Dorcas (Dill) Golder. William Golder, Jr. m Mrs. Rachel Tarr, pub. 21 Nov. 1803 [vital records of Lewiston, Maine, p. 363], b 8 Feb. 1780, d 3 Apr. 1862. Children: **William** q.v.; **Jordan** q.v.; **Fairfield** q.v.; **Sally** b 18 Oct. 1809, d 11 Dec. 1848, m 19 Aug. 1827 William Carville, Jr., who d 26 Oct. 1864; **David Tarr** q.v.; **Rachel** b 20 Jan. 1815; and **Joseph Tarr** b 11 Dec. 1819. [Vital Records of Lewiston, Miane, p. 56.]

GOLDER, WILLIAM H. - Born ??, d ??, s/o David T. and ?? Golder. William H. Golder m 1 Nov. 1865 Elvira F. Chandler of Belgrade, Maine, b 6 Oct. 1846, d/o Joseph and Susan Goodridge. Child: **Maude E.** b 18 Sep. 1869.

GOLDER, WILLIAM HENRY - Born ??, d ??, s/o David and ?? Golder. Children: **Albert**; and **Isabelle**.

GOODWIN, ANDREW - Born 1 Jun. 1838, d ??, s/o George and Elizabeth (Harvey) Goodwin. Andrew Goodwin m 1 Jan. 1861 Mary L. Rich of Portland, Maine, b 1 Jan. 1837 in Yarmouth, Maine. Children: **Lillia** b 26 Feb. 1862, m Henry Collins 1 Jan. ----; and **Lewis I.** q.v.

GOODWIN, BENJAMIN - Born 10 Sept. 1773, d ??, s/o ??. Benjamin Goodwin settled in Lewiston, 1785. He m Sukey ----, b 1778. Children: **Comfort** b 18 Dec. 1798; **Rufus** b 6 Oct. 1800; **Lucy** b 4 Jul. 1803; **Sukey** b 17 Apr. 1805; **Darus** b 15 May 1807. [Vital Records of Lewiston, Maine, p. 29.]

GOODWIN, CHARLES H. - Born 18 Jun. 1841, d ??, s/o George and Elizabeth (Harvey) Goodwin. Charles H. Goodwin m -- Jul. 1862 Almeda Alden of Turner, Maine, b 11 Feb. 1842. Children: **George Albert** b 11 Jun. 1863; **Herbert A.** b 29 Apr. 1865, d 19 Feb. ----; **Fred W.** b 15 Mar. 1868, d 15 Sep. 1890; and **Carroll I.** b 2 Jan. 1878, d -- Mar. 1880.

GOODWIN, GEORGE - Born in Pittston, Maine, d 26 Dec. 1895, s/o ?? George Goodwin m Elizabeth Harvey, d/o John. George Goodwin came from Weld 10 Sep. 1846. Children: **Andrew** q.v.; **Charles H.** q.v.; **George Lewis**; and **George Albert** b 15 Aug. 1846, d 1 Aug. 1854.

GOODWIN, LEWIS I. - Born ??, d ??, s/o Andrew and Mary L. (Rich) Goodwin. Lewis I. Goodwin m Julia Chapin 17 Aug. 1896. Children: **Dudley C.** b -- May 1897; and **Elizabeth**.

GOODY, JOHN - Born ??, d 25 Aug. 1878, age 79 years 4 months, s/o ??. John Goody m (1) -- Aug. 1822 Mary Anderson, who d 3 Jun. 1830, age 31 years 5 months, and m (2) 29 Jan. 1832 Alice J. Anderson, who d 21 Oct. 1892, age 84 years 2 months. Children: **Olive Jane** b 11 Sep. 1822; **N a n c y** b 9 Dec. 1823; **J o h n** b 8 Jun. 1825, d 18 Mar. 1849; **M a r y   A n n** b 4 Jun. 1827, d 25 Dec. 1893, m Stephen Raynes; **Martha A.** b 21 Aug. 1833; **Thomas H.** b 18 Dec. 1835; **Helen M.** b 4 Nov. 1838, m 1 Jan. 1866 Josiah Raynes of Auburn, ME, s/o Jonathon; **George A.** b 16 Sep. 1843, killed 14 May 1864 at Druries Bluffs; **William W.** b 18 Mar. 1845, m 31 Dec. 1874 Rebecca J. Wilson, d/o Henry; **Samuel Hart** b 30 Mar. 1847; and **Effie Gertrude** b 5 Dec. 1848, d 4 Jan. 1849.

GORDON, DANIEL - Born 5 Feb. 1795, d ??, s/o Mark and Hannah (Ames), Godron. Daniel Gordon was an M.D. and he m 5 mar. 1825 Alice Davis. Children: **Mehitable** b 12 Jan. 1826, d 1 Apr. 1850; **Cornelia Ann** b 26 Oct. 1827, d 24 Mar. 1846, unm; **Mary** b 24 May 1830, m Peter Dunbar 8 (?) Aug. 1852, d 3 Mar. 1861; **Alice Cushman** b 18 Oct. 1835; and **Hannah Ames** b 20 Jul. 1842, m Henry Farr, 1 Dec. 1869.

GORHAM, CALVIN - Born ??, d 28 Feb. 1850, age 60 years, s/o ??. Calvin Gorham m 20 Sep. 1813 Lurana Briggs of Minot, Maine, d 3 Oct. 1852 in Turner, Maine. Children: **Julia G.** b 16 Feb. 1815, d 6 Nov. 1836; and **Betsey Briggs** b 16 May 1823, m 20 Oct. 1842 William H. Blair of Waterville, ME. [Vital Records of Lewiston, Maine, p. 30.]

GOSS, ALMON L. - Born ??, d 5 Mar. 1897, s/o ?? Almon L. Goss m 7 Oct. 1870 Mary A. Pettengill, b 12 Jun. 1846 in Lewiston. Children: **Eugene W.** m Sarah Wilsen; and **Henry E.**

GOSS, CHARLES FRANCIS - Born 27 Sep. 1848, d 20 Jun. 1921, s/o John III and Mary L. (Brooks) Goss. Charles Francis Goss m 9 Feb. 1871 Abbie P./R. Madison, d 28 Mar. 1930. He was associated with the E. S. Paul Co. of Lewiston, dealers in dry goods. Children: **Ralph Warren** b 17 Jun. 1879; and **Arthur Madison** b 25 Oct. 1881.

GOSS, EDWIN L. - Born 22 Oct. 1862, d ??, s/o John III and Mary L. (Brooks) Goss. Edwin L. Goss m (1) 7 Jul. 1886 Marion/Marion H. Wing of Lewiston, and m (2) at Bangor, Maine, 15 Sept. 1921, Cecilia Christensen. He worked for Elery Foxcroft Goss and Almon Libby Goss Co.

GOSS, GEORGE WILLIAM - Born 10 Mar. 1851, d ??, s/o John III and Mary L. (Brooks). He was educated in Lewiston public schools and employed by the First National Bank of Lewiston for 50+ years. He m (1) 25 Sep. 1873 Lillian/Lillian L. Ricker and m (2) Emily Gertrude Packard. Children: **Richard R.**; **Mira Hanson** b 10 Feb. ----; and **John** b -- Sep. ----.

GOSS, JOHN III - Born 8 Oct. 1816/8 in Danville, Maine, d 8 Aug. 1894, s/o John II and Catherine (Dyer) Goss. John Goss III m (1) 6 May 1841 [Starbird's notes] Eleanor F. Hackett of Danville, d 15 Jun. 1846, age 37 years [obit notice from *Morning Star*, issue 11 Nov. 1846], d/o Jude and Thankful (Penly) Hackett [notes by Starbird]. John Goss III m (2) 11 Jul. 1847 Mary L. Brooks, b 16 Nov. 1828, d 1 Jun. 1900, d/o Ai and Martha Brooks. John Goss III's early life was spent on the farm in Danville. After his second marriage, he moved to South Lewiston and was a tinsmith by trade which he later sold to Almon L. and Ellery F. Goss. He was elected to the Common Council for Ward 7 in 1872 and served as a Councilman from Ward 2, 1866 and 1867 [Starbird's notes on Lewiston/Auburn]. *Children by 1st wife*: **Mary L.** b 18 Jul. 1844 in Danville. *Children by 2nd wife* (all were born in Lewiston): **Charles Francis** q.v.; **George William** q.v.; **Martha Ellen** b 1 Apr. 1854, d 15 Apr. 1854; **Eliza Ella** b 16 Oct. 1855, d 22 Mar. 1856; **Etta L.** b 4 Jul. 1857 m 6 May 1871 George W. s/o Seward Ham [Starbird states she m George W. Lane in 1877]; **Cecil E.** b 9 Jun. 1859, d 7 May 1860; **Edwin L.** q.v.; **Lizzie Cedelle** b 28

Feb. 1866 m 1 Jan. 1885, Rev. John L. Smith, moved to West Haven, Connecticut; **Winnie Florence** b 11 May 1869; and **John Burgess** q.v. [Some of Starbird's records were used.]

GOSS, JOHN BURGESS - Born 22 Mar. 1871, d 4 Jul. 1939, s/o John III and Mary L. (Brooks) Goss. John Burgess Goss m Alice/Alice M. Wyman. He was in grocery business being the junior member of Howard & Goss firm.

GRAFFAM, ALONZO - Born ??, d ??, s/o ?? Alonzo Graffam m Mary Brown 29 Oct. 1871 in Chicago, Illinois.

GRAFFAM, BENJAMIN - Born 2 Jul. 1787, d 20 Jun. 1859 [obit notice from *Morning Star*, issue 24 Aug. 1859], s/o John and Elizabeth (Davis) Graffam. Benjamin Graffam m 20 Dec. 1810 Mary Ann Hipper of Brunswick, Maine, d 25 Jul. 1852 age 76 years [*Morning Star*, obit issue 25 Aug. 1852]. Children: **Benjamin**; **Charles**; and **Edward**. [Vital Records of Lewiston, Maine, p. 427.]

GRAFFAM, CORDELIA - Born ??, d ??, d/o ?? Cordelia Graffam m 14 Jul. 1867 Cyrus S. Cook.

GRAFFAM, DANIEL W. - Born 7 Sep. 1793/1794 [vital records of Lewiston, Maine, p. 107], d 8 Feb. 1884 in Salem, Maine, s/o John and Deborah (Wilkins) Graffam. Daniel W. Graffam m (1) by Dan Read 14 May 1820 Lydia Davis, pub. 16 Apr. 1820, certificate granted 14 May 1820, she d 7 Jan. 1859, and m (2) Anna Davis. Children: **Rufus** q.v.; **Daniel** b 2 Jan. 1822, d 6 Oct. 1823, age about 6 months; **Emily** b 10 Aug. 1824, d 20 Aug. 1852 unm; **Mary D.** b 15 Dec. 1825, m (1) Gardiner Woodard, and m (2) ---- Evans; **Daniel D.** b 23 Aug. 1828, m Sarah Witham -- Jan. 1862; **Lydia A.** b 11 Sep. 1831, m John Greeley, Readfield, ME; **Amelia** b 18 Aug. 1833, m Abner W. Mayo of Freeman, ME; and **Ruhamah** b 9 Aug. 1835, d 12 Jun. 1862, m John Wyman of Sidney, ME, d 17 May 1862.

GRAFFAM, DAVID - Born 22 Jun. 1785 [vital records of Lewiston, Maine, p. 27], s/o John and Elizabeth (Davis) Graffam. David Graffam m Betsy Pettingill 24 Nov. 1808 [vital records of Lewiston, Maine, p. 427], d 25 Dec. 1873. Children: **Mollie** b 21 Jul. 1809, d 5 Jun. 1814; **Sallie** b 8 Jan. 1811; **David** q.v.; **Mary** b 20 Mar. 1815; **Isaaiah** b 12 Mar. 1817; **Charlotte** b 25 Jan. 1819, d 22 Oct. 1853, m ---- Jackson [*Morning Star*, issue 15 Mar. 1854, obit notice]; **Almira** b 5 Aug. 1821, d 26 Feb. 1843; **Harriet** b 5 Aug. 1821, d 15 Feb. 1843; **Elizabeth** b 13 Jun. 1824, m Horace Fales; and **Davis N.** q.v. [In vital records of Lewiston also listed with this family is Enoch Graffam b 22 Mar. 1809, s/o Anna Graffam. Anna may have been a sister to David Graffam above.]

GRAFFAM, DAVID JR. - Born 1 Jan. 1813, d 18 May 1894, s/o David and Betsy (Pettingill). David Graffam m (1) 23 Oct. 1840 Phebe W. Goddard, d 20 Nov. 1855, d/o William, and m (2) 8 Apr. 1856 Happy/Happy A. Stanford, b 12 Jan. 1812 in Cape Elizabeth, Maine, d/o Jeremiah/Jeremial. [Sewall Merrill's records of Lewiston families AHS, manuscript from the years 1865-1872], d 15 Mar. 1879. Children: **Lovina J.** b 8 Nov. 1841 in Lewiston, d 10 Mar. 1883, m Nathan Locke 1 May 1859; **William H.** q.v.; **Alonzo** b 24 May 1845, m Mary Brown 29 Oct. 1871 in Chicago; **Elmira** b 9 Nov. 1849 in Lewiston, d 25 Feb. 1879; **Cordelia** b 20 Sep. 1847, m Cyrus S. Cook 14 Jul. 1867; and **Laura B.** b 12 Feb. 1853 in Lewiston, d 22 Jun. 1854.

GRAFFAM, DAVID - Born 1785, d 29 Aug. 1844, s/o John and Elizabeth (Davis) Graffam. David Graffam m Betsey Pettingill.

GRAFFAM, DAVID T. - Born ??, d ??, s/o ?? David T. Graffam res. Lisbon, Maine, 1868. He m Mary B. ---- [deed book 58, p. 7, Androscoggin]. Children: **George M.** b 24 Jul. 1849, d 30 Jul. 1851; **Joseph** b 7 Apr. 1851, m Georgia Daniels of Rumford 3 Jul. 1877, no children; **Elizabeth** b 25 Nov. 1852, m Alvin W. Talcott of Anson, ME, 26 May 1874; **Maria** b 25 Nov. 1852, m Franklin H. Newell of Durham 30 Jan. 1871; **M a r y S.** b 7 Apr. 1855, m Alfred Atwood 19 Jul. 1874; **G e o r g i a** b 25 Oct. 1857, m Nathan Coombs of Lisbon Falls, ME, 23 Jul. 1875; **Nellie M.** b 8 Aug. 1859, m George Pulsifer of Poland, pub. 14 Sep. 1876; and **Iva A.** b 28 Jun. 1861, m William Ridley in Lisbon, ME, -- Jun. ----.

G R A F F A M , D A V I D W . - Born 15 Jan. 1795, d 10 Jan. 1857 [Androscoggin Co. probate #92], s/o John Jr. and ?? David W. Graffam m Mary J. Trafant (Bath, Maine), b 3 Jan. 1802, d 17 Nov. 1881. Children: **David T.*** b 29 Feb. 1828, m 25 Feb. 1849 Mary Jackson*, b 15 Jan. 1831, d/o Lemuel; **Stephen H.*** q.v.; **William*** m Hannah; **A l m o n *;** and **M a r y** d young. [Deed Book #18, p. 339, Androscoggin Co., names those with asterick (*), 26 Apr. 1858; also an Eliza A. Graffam signed after Stephen was likely Stephen's wife.]

GRAFFAM, DAVIS N. - Born 14 Mar. 1847, m (1) 2 May 1853 Mary J. Paine, d 21 Nov. 1857, and m (2) 9 Dec. 1861 Emilie L. Adams. Children: **Bradley M.** b 17 Dec. 1855; **Davis N., Jr.** b 10 Feb. 1857; **Emma F.** b 21 Jul. 1865; and **Gertrude L.** b 7 Jun. 1872.

GRAFFAM, EDWARD - Born ??, d ??, s/o Benjamin and ?? Graffam. Child: **Louisa**.

GRAFFAM, FRANK G. - Born 6 Dec. 1851, d 21 Jun. 1882, s/o Rufus and Almira/Amanda (Atwood) Graffam. Frank G. Graffam m 4 May 1878 Ella M./Ellee E. Briggs, d 4 Oct. 1881. Child: **L e l i l a F .** b 12 Jan. 1881.

GRAFFAM, JOHN - Born c 1743, d -- Dec. 1801, s/o Abel and Sarah (Davis) Graffam. John Graffam moved likely to Plymouth, Massachusetts, and Gloucester, Massachusetts, then to New Gloucester, Maine, and settled in Lewiston, 1774. He m Elizabeth Davis, b 30 Dec. 1747, d 1830. Children: **Thankful** b 19 Jan. 1768, d 26 Jul. 1845, m David Pettingill, who d 1 Oct. 1848; **L y d i a** b 14 Feb. 1770, d 14 Feb. 1773; **John Jr.** q.v.; **L y d i a** b 10 Oct. 1773, d 13 Jan. 1859, m

Lazarus Lander; **Molly** b 8 Apr. 1775, d 19 Sep. 1795; **Betsey, Sr.** b 31 Nov. 1776; **Betsey, Jr.** b 12 Mar. 1779, d in Wales 29 May 1879, m Daniel Mitchell; **Hannah** b 6 Feb. 1781, d 20 Sep. 1860, m Davis Nevens 12 Jan. 1806; **Ellis** b 9 Mar. 1783, m Joseph Taylor 24 Apr. 1808; **Daniel** b 22 Jun. 1785, d 24 Aug. 1844, m 24 Nov. 1808 Patsy Pettingill, who d 25 Dec. 1873; **Benjamin** q.v.; and **Anna** b 5 Aug. 1791, m James Taylor 16 Apr. 1813. [See David Graffam and vital records of Lewiston, Maine, p. 27 and letter from Andover, Maine, 1898, Mary Bodwell.]

GRAFFAM, JOHN JR. - Born 23 Dec. 1772, d 20 Jan. 1836, s/o John and Elizabeth (Davis) Graffam. John Graffam, Jr. m (1) Deborah Wilkins, who d 29 Aug. 1801, and m (2) 19 Jan. 1802 Mariah Wilkins who d -- Feb. 1815, and m (3) Mrs. Nancy Patfield. *Children of 1st wife*: **Daniel W.** q.v.; **David W.** q.v.; **John N.** b 7 Sep. 1797, d 1835, m Mary (Deborah) Haskell of Minot, ME, 24 Nov. 1825; **Mariah** or **Maria** b 5 Sep. 1799, d 10 Jun. 1841, m Amos Davis 11 Jul. 1879, who d 21 Feb. 1871; and **Deborah** b 2 Aug. 1801, d 9 Sep. 1883 in Duxbury, MA, m 22 May 1825 John Wadsworth Cushman in Portland, ME, b 5 Sep. 1799 in Duxbury, MA, d 13 Apr. 1866. *Children of 2nd wife*: **Stephen** b 1 Apr. 1803, d 1803; **Stephen W.** b 1 Jun. 1805, d 9 Jan. 1850 (?) in California, m Taby Frost in Lewiston; **Oliver** q.v.; **Mehitable** b 20 Dec. 1809, m Aaron Davis, who d 18 Jan. 1864, pub. 16 Sep. 1827; **Mary W.** b 4 Aug. 1811, d 29 Jun. 1890 in Salem, ME, m 27 Nov. 1830 Harrison Clark, who d 23 Aug. 1866; and **Sarah** b 14 Jan. 1813, d 11 Dec. 1868 in Auburn, ME, m John Dill, who d 16 Jul. 1853 in the Army, br/o Harmon Dill. *Children of 3rd wife*: **Joseph** q.v.; **Benjamin** b 21 Mar. 1818, d 20 Jun. 1859 in Portland, ME, m Charlotte Gammon of Naples, ME, who d 25 Jul. 1852; **Hannah** b 8 Mar. 1820, m Henry Wiswell of Portland; **Annie Cook** b 23 Mar. 1822 in Portland, m John Renick of Portland 10 Nov. 1841, d 8 Nov. 1885; **Betsy** b 30 Mar. 1824, m George Rolfe of Portland; **Samuel H.** b 12 Aug. 1826, d 26 May 1860, m Louisa James of N.B.; and **Isaac** b 7 May 1828, d 24 Dec. 1833/1835. [Vital Records of Lewiston, Maine, p. 58, 107.]

GRAFFAM, JOSEPH - Born 22 Oct. 1816, d 18 Mar. 1869, s/o John and Mrs. Nancy (Patfield) Graffam. Joseph Graffam m 2 Nov. 1864 Ann Fanard/Farrin of Waterville, Maine. Child: **George W.** d 11 Aug. 1882 in Washington, Maine, age 40 years.

GRAFFAM, LOVINA - Born ??, d ??, d/o ?? Lovina Graffam m Nathan Locke 1 May 1859.

GRAFFAM, OLIVER - Born 22/25 Feb. 1807, d 3/7 Feb. 1884, s/o John and Mariah (Wilkins) Graffam. Oliver Graffam m 1 Mar. 1829 Olive Thompson, b in Otisfield, Maine, 22 Feb. 1807, d 22 Sep. 1890 in Lewiston. Children: **Frances O.** b 21 Mar. 1831, d 18 Aug. 1857, m Elbridge G. Heath; **Oliver H.** b 5 Apr. 1833, d 5 Sep. 1865, killed by Indians in Idaho; **John** b 27 Jan. 1836, d 25 Dec. 1864; **Mary J.** b 17 Aug. 1842, m Abel Goddard 31 Dec. 1862; **Anna M.** b 7 Mar. 1844, m George W. Graffam of Portland, ME; **Alonzo P.** b 5 Sep. 1846, m Susie

Grover; **Otis** b 20 Aug. 1848, d 2 Oct. 1851; and **Asa D.** b 20 Jan. 1852, m Mrs. Augusta Frye.

GRAFFAM, RUFUS - Born 4 Feb. 1821, d 4 Dec. 1889, s/o ?? Rufus Graffam m 13 May 1842 Amanda/Almira Atwood. Children: **Elmira M.** b 7 Aug. 1844, m Warren B. French 23 Jul. 1862; **Charles H.** b 14 Jun. 1846, m Sarah J. Chick 4 Apr. 1868; **Melvina** b 4 Dec. 1848, m George W. Harris 16 Jun. 1866; and **Frank G.** q.v.

GRAFFAM, SAMUEL D. - Born ??, d 26 May 1860, s/o ?? Samuel D. Graffam m Louisa James.

GRAFFAM, STEPHEN H. - Born ??, d ??, s/o David W. and ?? Graffam. Children: **Eva** m George Lovejoy; and **Frankie.**

GRAFFAM, WILLIAM H. - Born 26 Nov. 1843, d ??, s/o David and ?? Graffam. William H. Graffam was of Camden and m 10 May 1868 Lydia D. Merrow. Children: **Grace B.** b 29 Jul. 1869; **Fred W.** b 3 Dec. 1870; and **Perley E.** b 22 Jun. 1876.

GREEN, DANIEL - 1-2-1 Lewiston 1790. "He took up and cleared the farm below Boswell, married Jane Dustin." [*Androscoggin Co. Atlas* 1873, published by the Sanford Everts Co., 1873, p. 108-109.]

GREEN, WILLIAM - 1-1-4 Lewiston 1790, married (1790 Hannah Blethen), d/o John and Hannah (Hibbard) Blethen [*History of Durham*, published by Vote of Town - Durham, Maine, 1899, p. 151-152] William Green was the s/o Daniel Green [*Androscoggin Atlas* 1872, published by Sanford Everts & Co., date 1873, p. 108-109]. [See Plummer's *History of Lisbon*, published by Francis and Charles W. Plummer, 1970, p. 16, 17.]

GROVERS, JOHN - Born ??, d??, m??. Children: **Nabby** b 20 Aug. 1814; **Edward** b 6 Oct. 1816; **Pepples Maxfield** b 3 Nov. 1818. [Vital Records of Lewiston, Maine, p. 30.]

HACKETT, AMOS - Born 2/20 Jun. 1816, d in California, s/o Ezekiel and Susannah (Graffen) Hackett. Amos Hackett m Elizabeth S. ---- or Betsy Thompson. Children: **Eliza Jane** b 26 Jul. 1838, d in CA; **Charlotte Thompson** b 2 Aug. 1842; **Delia Annett** b 3 May 1845; and **Flora.**

HACKETT, BENJAMIN - Born 27 Oct. 1789, d 20 Aug. 1856 in Lewiston, s/o Ezekiel and Tamson (Lund) Hackett. Benjamin Hackett m 21 Jul. 1811 Tace Davis, d/o Daniel of Lewiston. Children: **James** q.v.; **John** b 4 Jan. 1816, d 9 Jul. 1890 at Paola, KS, m (1) 22 Jun. 1847 Minerva A. Chapman of Utica, NY, and m (2) 23 Jul. 1865 Jenette T. Estes, b -- Sep. 1840, d/o David and Mary A. (Grant) Estes; **Henry** q.v.; **Hiram** b 5 Aug. 1820, d 11 Mar. 1821; **Tamson** b 14 Feb. 1822, d 20 Feb. 1822; **Dorris** b 27 Jun. 1823, d 26 May 1831; **Davis** b 26 Jun. 1824, drowned 21 Jun. 1837 in Mill Pond; and **Sarah E.** b 19 Jan. 1827, m Barton Nichols of Durham, moved to IA.

HACKETT, CYRUS - Born 20 Nov. 1822/1823, d ??, s/o Samuel and ?? Hackett. Cyrus Hackett m 29 Aug. 1848 Rosella Quimby, b 27 Sep. 1828, d/o Aaron and Ann (Conck---) Quimby. Child: **Wallace** b 18 Nov. 1849, d 29 Mar. 1870, headstone reads 25 Feb. 1868, aged 21 years 3 months 7 days.

HACKETT, DAVIS - Born 10 Mar. 1799, d ??, s/o Judah and Abigail (Gordon) Hackett. Davis Hackett m 3 Nov. 1825 Rebecca Fitz, b 17 Jun. 1797, d/o Moses of Danville, [now part of Auburn, Maine]. Children: **Moses** unm; **Mary** unm; and **Loring** unm.

HACKETT, EZEKIEL - Born ??, d ??, s/o ?? Children: unm; and Ezekiel unm.

HACKETT, EZEKIEL - Born 12 May 1762 in Gloucester, Massachusetts, d 29 Mar. 1840, s/o ?? Ezekiel Hackett m (1) Tamson Lund of Sudsbury, Massachusetts, and m (2) 18 Sep. 1798 Suannah Graffen, b 9 Jun. 1775 in Brunswick, Maine, d 15 Sep. 1846. *Children of 1st wife*: **Benjamin** q.v.; **Susanah** b 8 Jan. 1792, d 14 Oct. 1859, age 68 years, m 1 Dec. 1816 Francis Wright; and **John** b 1795, d 3 Jan. 1858, age 63 years, unm. *Children of 2nd wife*: **Samuel** q.v.; **Tamson** b 21 Sep. 1801, d 28 Mar. 1882, m 27 Dec. 1818 Daniel Paul, d 27 Aug. 1865; **Elizabeth** b 18 Nov. 1803, d 25 Dec. 1827, m 22 Nov. 1827 Aaron Hiram Niles of Lisbon, ME, cert. of m int. 24 Sep. 1827; **Hannah** b 13 Apr. 1805, m 18 Nov. 1824 Jeremiah Nason of Greene, ME; **Mary** b 22 Oct. 1807; **Ezekiel** b 22 Nov. 1811, m Charlotte Thompson; **Joseph** b 22 Apr. 1815 (headstone), d 19 Jul. 1865, m 26 Jul. 1810 Lovinia Lander, b 26 Jul. 1810, d 20 Jan. 1868, d/o Freeman of Greene; **Amos** q.v.; and **Lucy** b 4 Apr. 1819, m Andrew Powers.

HACKETT, GEORGE WASHINGTON - Born 15 Jun. 1832, d ??, s/o Jude and ?? Hackett. George Washington Hackett m 22/26 Jun. 1856 Jane L. Peables, d/o James and Margaret (Jordan) Peables of Danville, Maine. Children: **Annetta A.** b 8 Apr. 1857, d 1 Oct. 1871, age 14 years 5 months 23 days; **Ella B.** b 5 Oct. 1859, d 1 Mar. 1865, age 5 years 4 months 24 days; and **George P.** b 19 Jul. 1871, m 1 Nov. 1899 Gertrude G. Doyle of Auburn, ME, d/o Edward Doyle.

HACKETT, HENRY - Born 13 Feb. 1818, d 30 Dec. 1886 in Lisbon Falls, Maine, s/o Benjamin and Tace (Davis) Hackett. Henry Hackett m (1) 18 Apr. 1844 in Lisbon, Maine, Dorcas Arvilla Blethan/Blethen, d in Freeport, Pennsylvania, d/o Jonathan and Mary (Rideout) Blethan/Blethen, and m (2) 19 Dec. 1850 Charlotte Plummer, d/o Henry and Wealthy (Estes) Plummer. Children: **Augusta M.** b 7 Apr. 1845, m 1884 Irving Lewis of Lynn, MA; **Cynthia Arvilla** b 27 Apr. 1846 in Lewiston, m 20 Dec. 1879 Charles H. Palmer of Exeter, NH; **Facie Anna** b 14 Aug. 1854, m Hermon Amback of Great Barrington, MA; **Martha Davis** b 29 Sep. 1857 in Salem, ME, m Henry Redding; **Martha Plummer** b 25 Feb. 1856 in Lisbon, m -- Jun. 1899 Harry Redding; **Henry Davis** b 29 Sep. 1857 in Salem, ME, m 3 Aug. 1883 Ada Batchelder, d/o Eben; and **Charles Freemond** b 15 Jan. 1859 in Salem, ME, unm.

HACKETT, HIRAM N. - Born 29 Oct. 1837, d 15 Aug. ----, s/o Samuel and ?? Hackett of Greene, Maine, in 1861 [deed book 27, p. 405]. Hiram N. Hackett m (1) 26 Mar. 1862 Mary E. Barker of Boston, Massachusetts, d 22 Dec. 1882, d/o George A., and m (2) 27 Mar. 1884 Etta M. Noble of Pittsfield, Maine. Children: **Harry N.** b 27 Dec. 1884; **Cyrus A.** b 3 Sep. 1886; and **Carrol** b 27 Apr. 1889.

HACKETT, JACOB - Born 22 Mar. 1801, d 7 Apr. 1863, s/o Judah and Abigail (Gordon) Hackett. Jacob Hackett m (1) 24 Dec. 1829 Minerva Penly/Penley, b 21 Oct. 1809, d 10 Mar. 1850, d/o Capt. John Penly/Penley, and m (2) pub. 29 Sep. 1853 Elsy/Elsey J. Maxwell, d/o Robert and Polly (Neven) Maxwell. Children: **Abigail Goden** b 15 Apr. 1830, m 12 Sep. 1872 Daniel Gage Todd of Rowley, MA?, b 14 Jul. ----, d 5 Feb. 1883; **Rufus Penly** q.v.; **Desiah Dingly** b 19 Aug. 1834, d 1899, m 5 Nov. 1861 Nathan D. Golbier; **John Allen** b 2 Jun. 1836, d 8 Oct. 1893, age 58 years in Togus, ME, m -- Dec. 1855 Bertha Brackett of Saco, ME; **Lucy Jane** b 22 Mar. 1838, d -- Nov. 1866, age 56 years, m Edward Colby of Webster, ME; **Hannah Mariah** b 9 Apr. 1840, d 13 Dec. 1901, m 9 Oct. 1879 Isaac Lombard, who was b 29 Jul. 1828 in Turner, ME, d 24 Jan. 1889; **Olive Ann** b 26 Oct. 1842, d 25 Jun. 1869, unm; **Esther Elizabeth** b 3 Sep. 1844, m George Judkins of Auburn, ME; **Mary Ellen** b 9 Jun. 1846, m George Stevens of Harpswell, ME; **Frank Allen** b 22 Jul. 1856, m -- Aug. 1888 Iva Tobie; **Jacob** b 25 Dec. 1854, d 28 Aug. 1855; **Edward Everett** b 21 Nov. 1859, m Alice Packard, d/o Lucias; and **Orland Jacob** b 28 Nov. 1863.

HACKETT, JAMES - Born 13 Oct. 1811, d 26 Dec. 1875 in Bradford, Maine, s/o Benjamin and Tace (Davis) Hackett. James Hackett m 1835 Belinda Hanson of Ossipee, New Hampshire, b 8 Dec. 1814, d 9 Oct. 1886, d/o Turner and Sally (Brown) Hanson. Children: **William H.** b 14 Jan. 1839, m 18 Jun. 1867 Geneva Graham; **Mary Jane** b 2 Mar. 1840, d 4 Aug. 1865, m -- Nov. 1862 Walker Brackett; **Susan** [letter from Mrs. Susan Plummer of Bradford, ME, 24 Jun. 1899] b 6 May 1846, m (1) 13 Oct. 1872 David Young, who d 17 Jun. 1894, and m (2) 20 Oct. 1895 Willard R. Plummer of Bradford; and **Orland T.** q.v.

HACKETT, JOHN - Born ??, d ??, s/o ?? Children: **Lillian** b 26 Apr. 1868; and **Mertie** b -- Aug. 1870.

HACKETT, JUDAH - Born c 1768, d 13 Jul. 1848 in Danville, Maine, age 80 years [vital records of Danville, Maine, p. ??, by Sewall Merrill's notes on Lewiston-Auburn, Maine, families and J. G. Elder's cemetery records of Danville, Maine, no page number], buried in Old Salbells Cemetery [my guess: the old Salbelle Cem. is what we now call the Fitz Cem. located on the Old Danville Rd., Auburn, ME - ed.], s/o ?? Judah Hackett m Abigail Gordan at Cape Ann, Massachusetts. [Lewiston 1-0-0 1790 census. 1790 Lewiston tax list.] Children: **Nabby** b 10 Nov. 1794, d 3 Nov. 1865, age 71 years, unm; **Loring** b 13 Mar. 1797, m 30 Dec. 1819 Sally Fitz, d/o Moses, who was b 5 Feb. 1791, no children; **Davis** q.v.; **Jacob** q.v.; **Polly** b 14 Oct.

1803, d 30 Sep. 1876; **Jude** q.v.; **Eleanor P.** b 9 Apr. 1809, d 15 Jun. 1846 age 37 years [Morning Star], m John Goss.

HACKETT, JUDE - Born 29 Dec. 1805, d 6 Feb. 1871 age 65 years 1 month 8 days, near Richmond, Maine, s/o Judah and Abigail (Gordon) Hackett. Jude Hackett m 5 Jul. 1829 Thankful Penly, b 9 Aug. 1810, d 26 Jan. 1885, age 74 years 5 months 17 days, d/o Joseph and Esther Penly of Danville, Maine. [Res. Danville in 1850 U. S. census record.] Children: **Lafayette** b 15 Jan. 1830, m 27 Nov. 1854 Lucy J. Wentworth of Lisbon, ME, b 23 Jul. 1834; **George Washington** q.v.; **Sullivan H.** b 14 Dec. 1834, m 7 Apr. 1860 Emily A. Chandler; **Emily B.** b 29 Jan. 1837, d 18 Aug. 1847; **Harriet S.** b 27 Dec. 1839, m James Henry Perkins; **Margaret J.** b 27 Feb. 1842; **Franklin** b 13 Nov. 1845, d 22 Jul. 1902, m Edith S. ----; **Julia** b 7 Jul. 1848, d 27 Jul. 1861, age 13 years; and **Eben** b 6 Feb. 1852, d 12 Oct. 1888, age 36 years 8 months 6 days.

HACKETT, ORISON W. - Born 14 Jun. 1830, d 13 Sep. 1887, s/o Samuel and Cindrilla/Cindrella (Austin) Hackett. Orison W. Hackett m 7 Jul. 1855 Mary F. Lovejoy of Vassalboro, Maine, b -- Apr. 1838, d/o Nathaniel and Lois (Clark) Lovejoy of Vassalboro. Children: **Frank P.** b 22 Mar. 1854, Washington near Sidney, m 13 --- 1887 Annie E. Sharron, d/o William and Margaret; **Lois E.** b 2 Sep. ----, m 17 Jun. 1880 Fred Tarr of Lewiston; **William A.** b 14 Mar. ----, m Jenny Carold; **John T.** b 7 Aug. ----, d 7 Oct. 1888; **Ida May** b 22 Oct. 1879; and **Ada P.** b 3 Dec. 1880.

HACKETT, ORLAND T. - Born 17 Jun. 1851, d ??, s/o James and Belinda (Hanson) Hackett. Orland T. Hackett lived in Bradford, Maine. He m 5 Oct. 1873 Mary J. Strout of Bradford, Maine. Children: **Hebron** b 20 Mar. 1877; and **Vesta G.** b 24 Nov. 1880.

HACKETT, RANK - Born ??, d ??, s/o ?? Children: **Wade** b 28 Jan. 1879, d 4 Jan. 1881; **Orville W.** b 2 May 1885, d 6 Dec. 1897; and **Bulen F.** b 15 Jun. 1889.

HACKETT, RUFUS PENLY - Born 11 Mar. 1832, d ??, s/o Jacob and Minerva (Penly/Penley) Hackett. Rufus Penly Hackett m 10 Dec. 1877 Laura Pearce, b 25 Jan. 1843, d/o Luther. Children: **Mary Merror** b 31 Jul. 1882; and **Rufus Allen** b 22 Sep. 1884.

HACKETT, SAMUEL - Born 26 Jun. 1798/1799, d 18 Aug. 1875, s/o Ezekiel and Susannah (Graffen) Hackett. Samuel Hackett m (1) 14 Jul. 1822 [4 Jul. 1823 according to the *History of Greene, Maine*, compiled by Walter Lindley Mower, 1938, p. 539] Cindrella/Cindrilla Austin of Greene, Maine, d 7 Oct. 1845, age 44 years 9 months, d/o Shedrick Austin, and m (2) 16 Oct. 1847 Olive Knox, who was his widow. *Children of 1st wife*: **Cyrus** q.v.; **Susannah T.** b 5 Mar. 1826, d -- Apr. 1886, m Luther Starbird of Greene and lived at Berkes Mills; **Consider** b 20 Oct. 1829, d 15 Aug. 1830; **Orison W.** q.v.; **Joseph Henry** b 19 Aug. 1832, m Sarah Totman of Richmond; **Hiram N.** q.v.; **Seth L.** q.v.; **Adrianna** or **Mary Adnona** b 31 Jul. 1840, d 17 Nov. 1856, age 16 years; **Lucy E.** b 5 Dec. 1849, m 3 Jul. 1873 Winfield Scott Jordan; and **Cindrella** b 20 Sep. 1845, m (1) Henry R. Perkins of Fairfield, ME, and m (2) 24 Jul. 1875 Virgil York. *Child of 2nd wife*: **Lucy E.** b 5 Dec. 1849, m 3 Jul. 1873 Winfield Scott Jordan. [Probate court #1217, Auburn, ME, and deed book 75, p. 410, dated 21 Nov. 1875.]

HACKETT, SARAH - Town Records pub. 12 Jul. 1804 show marriage to Edmund Lang.

HACKETT, SETH L. - Born 12 Dec. 1837, d -- Nov. 1869 in S. Boston, Massachusetts, s/o Samuel and ?? Hackett. Seth L. Hackett m Minnie Atkinson. Child: **Sethina** b -- Dec. 1859, lived in S. Boston, MA.

HACKETT, WILLIAM GARCELON - Born 14 Jan. 1818 in Danville, Maine, d 9 Jul. 1890, s/o Benjamin and Tacy (Davis) Hackett. William Garcelon Hackett m (1) 22 Jun. 1847 Minerva Axa Chapin of Utica, New York, b 22 Nov. 1829, d 9 Aug. 1863 in New York City, d/o Dr. David Seymour Chapin, and m (2) 23 Jul. 1865 Jenette T. Estes, d/o David of Lewiston. *Children of 1st wife*: **Clara Electa** b 28 May 1848 in Burlington, IA, d 8 Jul. 1883 in Paola, KS; **Lillian Elisa** b 21 Aug. 1850 in Kossuth, IA, m 8 Oct. 1874 William G. Hanson of Brentwood, NH; **Emma Kate** b 28 Jun. 1852, d 1855; **James Seymore** b 2 Oct. 1854, d 1855; **Mary Helen** b 31 Dec. 1856, living in Haverhill, MA, m Simeon Estes York of Pownal, ME; **Henry Francis** b 4 Feb. 1859 in Nebraska City, unm; and **Willie** b 26 Jul. 1863, d 9 Aug. 1863. [Letter dated 1899 from Lillian Culver of Lakeview, Madison Co., Montana.]

HAILEY, JOSHUA - Married (1) pub. 1797 Hannah Dill, d/o John, and m (2) 1805 Polly Farrow of Lisbon, Maine. Children: **Caty** b 18 Jul. 1798; **Ziba** b 2 Jan. 1810; **Lydia** b 7 Apr. 1814; **Nelson** b 7 Mar. 1816; **Rubin** b 7 Nov. 1818; **Aphia** b 11 Nov. 1820; **Susan** b 12 Apr. 1823; and **Sarah** b 24 Apr. 1825.

HALEY, ANDREW - Born ??, d ??, s/o ?? Andrew Haley m Theresia ----, d/o Jonathan ----. Children: **Andrew J.**; **Sidney G.**; **Melissa**; **John**; **Cyrus**; **Emma**; and **George**.

HALEY, CHARLES H. - Born 7 Apr. 1843, d ??, s/o Samuel and Elizabeth J. (Libbey) Haley. Charles H. Haley m 30 Nov. 1865 Sarah F. Garcelon, d/o Asa. Children: **Winnifred M.** b 21 Nov. 1866, m 24 Jun. 1891 Everett E. Howard, lived in Boston, MA; **Mary J.** b 13 Oct. 1870; **Gracie E.** b 11 Nov. 1872, d 4 Apr. 1877; **Charles H.** b 20 Nov. 1873, d 4 Aug. 1874; and **Charles G.** b 21 Jun. 1876, d 7 Apr. 1877.

HALEY, FRANKLIN M. - Born 24 Dec. 1852, d ??, s/o Nelson and ?? Haley. Franklin M. Haley m 15 Sep. 1875 Mary A. Sanborn of Webster, Maine. Children: **Bertha M.** b 4 Dec. 1876; and **Eva M.** b 22 Oct. 1878.

HALEY, GEORGE A. - Born 15 Aug. 1803, d -- May 1886, s/o Samuel, Sr. and Mary (----) Haley. George A. Haley m Mary Ward or Mary Lee Ward of Sidney, Maine. Children: **Samuel W.** b 4 Jan. 1831, lived in Troy, m (1) Maria Ward of Troy, ME, and m (2) Mary Brown; **Jeremiah J.** b 24 Sep. 1833; **Bryen W.** b 1837, d Oldtown, ME, m Susan Small of Troy; **Thomas C.** d 1867, unm; and **Lois E.** d 1858 in Sidney, unm.

HALEY, JACOB - Born 4 Nov. 1799 in Lewiston, d 13 Oct. 1858 in Milltown, N. B., s/o Joshua and Hannah (Dill) Haley. Jacob Haley m (1) pub. 16 Jan. 1825 Ruth E. Merrill, b 4 Sep. 1803 in Saco, Maine, d 18 Nov. 1830, and m (2) 17 Nov. 1833 Priscilla C. Farrow, b 8 Oct. 1810, d 9 May 1878 in Milltown, NB. Children of 1st wife: **Jacob** b 13 Feb. 1826 in Lisbon, d 8 Oct. 1900 in Milltown, N.B.; **M a r y A.** b 17 May 1827 in Lisbon; **D o l l y** b 17 Jan. 1828 in Lisbon, d 7 Sep. 1830; and **I s a a c M.** b 29 Oct. 1830 in St. Stephens, NB, m Anna Coy. Children of 2nd wife: **John H.** q.v.; **Reuben F.** b 22 Aug. 1839 in Milltown, NB, d 27 May ----; **Hattie F.** b 22 Dec. 1841 in Milltown, NB, d 29 Dec. 1900 in NY City, m 17 Nov. 1868 Thomas J. Robinson; **Lafa S.** b 16 Mar. 1844 in Milltown, NB, lived in Boston, m 1869 Joseph Bradshaw; **Lucy E.** b 12 Nov. 1847 in Milltown, NB, d 11 Dec. 1853; **Fannie** b 9 Sep. 1850 in Milltown, NB, d 13 Dec. 1858; and **Laura** b 20 Sep. 1853 in Milltown, NB, d 20 Sep. 1858.

HALEY, JAMES - Born 21 Jan. 1839, d ??, s/o Ziba and ?? Haley. James Haley m Louisa Rideout. Children: **Benjamin Joshua** b 18 Jul. 1867; and **Edwin Parker** b 8 Dec. 1868.

HALEY, JEREMIAH - Married 28 Dec. 1862 Mary Brown Geulfond. Children: **Alonzo G.** b 18 Nov. 1863, m Bertha Swan; **Anna A.** b 14 Apr. 1865, m Wyman Stevens; **L o i s M a y** b 1867, m Leander Wentworth; **Margie** b 16 Apr. 1869, m Wyman Stevens; **Jeremiah J., Jr.** b 12 Jun. 1871; and **Vesta** m William Chadbourn.

HALEY, JOHN - Born 5 Dec. 1797 in Lewiston, d 27 Sep. 1856 in Rangely, s/o Joseph and Mary (----) Haley. John Haley m 21 Jul. 1822, pub. 4 May 1822 Polly/Mary Polly Lowell, b 27 Jun. 1804 in Lewiston, d 27 Sep. 1883 in Rangely, Maine, d/o William Lowell. He was a member of the Legislature of Maine, a farmer and blacksmith, and resided in Rangely, Maine. Children: **J o h n J r.** b 24 Mar. 1824; **William** b 21 Sep. 1825, m Eunice Hoar; **Elias** b 8 May 1829; **George** m ---- Smith; **M a r y** m 18 Dec. 1849 in Phillips, ME, John William Lowell b in St. John, N. S., d 15 Jun. 1857 at Rangely, ME, s/o Stephen Lowell; **Jacob** b 8 Oct. 1829; **Catherine** b 5 Mar. 1834; **Dorcas** b 12 Aug. 1836, m ---- Niles; **Isaac B** b 8 Jun. 1839; **Sarah Ellen** b 29 Jun. 1841, m ---- Hoar; **Dorcas** m ---- Niles; **Hannah**; **David** b 20 Jan. 1847, m (1) ---- Robbins, and m (2) Abbie F. Lowell; **George** b 3 Jun. 1849, m ---- Smith; and **Rosina** m Sidney Gay. [*Lowell Genalogy, 1639-1899* by Delmar R. Lowell, published by the author, 1899, p. 699, 700 and vital cards at Maine State Archives of Rangely, Maine.]

HALEY, JOHN H. - Born 18 Oct. 1836 in Milltown, N.B., d 6 Oct. 1893, s/o Jacob and Priscilla C. (Farrow) Haley. John H. Haley m 29 Feb. 1868 Mary H. Gates of Carroll, Maine. Children: **Harry R.** b 6 Mar. 1869 in Milltown, NB; and **Fannie E.** b 6 Sep. 1870 in Milltown, NB.

HALEY, JOSEPH - Born ??, d ??, s/o Joseph and ?? Haley. Joseph Haley m Mary ----. Children: **M a r y** b 26 Jan. 1793, m 24 Oct. 1813 John Lowell; **John** q.v.; **Joseph** b 12 Nov. 1800, m Eunice Bubier Bowdoin; **Sally** b 20 Dec. 1804; and **Noah** q.v. [Vital Records of Lewiston, Maine, p. 110.]

HALEY, JOSEPH - Born 1738 in Kittery, d -- May 1800 in Topsham, Maine, s/o ?? Joseph Haley m Mary Goodwin, sis/o Samuel of Wells, Maine. Children: **Susannah**; **Joseph**; **Mary**; **Joshua** q.v.; **John** b 1777; **Samuel** d 18 Aug. 1817; and **Moses**.

HALEY, JOSHUA - Born 27 Dec. 1835, d 7 Sep. 1864, s/o Ziba and ?? Haley. Joshua Haley m 25 Mar. 1862 Huldah Hill, b 4 Mar. 1841 in Codyville, Maine, d 6 Dec. 1887. Child: **Jennie M.** [Letter from J. S. Haley of Topsfield, Maine, 1902.]

HALEY, JOSHUA - Born 23 May 1775, d 3 Jan. 1849, s/o Joseph and Mary (Goodwin) Haley. Joshua Haley m (1) pub. 2 Sep. 1797 Hannah Dill, d/o John, and m (2) pub. -- Oct. 1805 Polly Farrow. *Children of 1st wife*: **Jacob** q.v.; **Catherine/Caty** b 18 Jul. 1798, d 17 Aug. 1871, m -- Oct. 1821 Sewell Libby of Gardiner, ME, d 11 Mar. 1874, age 78 years; **James**; and **Eunice** m George Hutchins. *Children of 2nd wife*: **H a n n a h** b 6 Aug. 1806, d 14 Feb. 1809; **J o s h u a** b 2 May 1808, d 14 Feb. 1809; **Ziba** q.v.; **Otis** b 13 Feb. 1812, d 14 May 1814; **Lydia** b 7 Apr. 1814, m 21 Nov. 1833 John Stevens of Minot, ME; **N e l s o n** q.v.; **Ruben/Rubin** b 7 Nov. 1818, d 17 Jul. 1870, m Maria Lord; **Alphlia/Aphia** b 11 Nov. 1820, m 6 Jun. 1847 Nathaniel Barnes of Lisbon, ME; **S u s a n** b 12 Apr. 1823, d 16 Sep. 1899, m 30 Nov. 1845 John Yeaton of Stafford, NH, who d 19 Apr. 1900; and **Sarah** b 24 Apr. 1825. [Letter dated 18 Apr. 1902 from Mary Gates Haley of Milltown, N. B.]

HALEY, JOSIAH - Born 9 Sep. 1805, d ??, s/o Samuel, Sr. and Mary (----) Haley. Josiah Haley m Mary Crawford of Bath, Maine. Children: **John**; **Catherine/Catherine A.** m Noah Mayo; and **May**.

HALEY, NELSON - Born 7 Mar. 1816 or 14 Jan. 1848, d 25 Feb. 1871 or 17 Oct. 1894, s/o Joshua and ?? Haley. Nelson Haley m 31 May 1846 Nancy Torrens/Forrins of Lisbon, Maine, b 20 Oct. 1810 in Lisbon, d 7 Feb. 1902, d/o Samuel and Rebecca (Mooar) Torrens/Forrins. Children: **Leonard N.** b 14 Jan. 1848 in Webster, ME, d 25 Feb. 1871; **M a r y A.** b 30 Aug. 1849 in Webster, m 18 Nov. 1874 James L. Atwood of Lisbon; and **Moses F.** b 24 Dec. 1852 in Webster.

HALEY, NOAH - Born ??, d ??, s/o ?? Noah Haley m Sally M. Brock. Children: **Olive** m Jesse Wright; and **Ruby** m A---- Tyler, who d -- Jul. 1900.

HALEY, NOAH - Born 21 May 1806, d 7 Feb. 1862 age 54 years and 9 months, s/o Joseph and Mary (----) Haley. Noah Haley m Sarah E. Whitten, b 5 Jul. 1824, d 1892, d/o Joseph and Sally (Walker) Whitten of Bowdoin, Maine. Children: **Sarah K.** b 18 Mar. 1854; and **Mary** b 10 Feb. 1856, d 24 Aug. 1880.

HALEY, SAMUEL - Born 10 Aug. 1839, d 16 Jun. 1884 [named deceased in father's will, 18 Jun. 1885], s/o Samuel and Elizabeth (Stinson) Haley. Samuel Haley m 27 Nov. 1859 Annie A. Furber or Anna E. Turber, d -- Aug. 1888. Children: **Augusta Ann** b 23 Jan. 1861, m (1) Herbert Apling of South Boston, MA, and m (2) Frank Boise; **Edwin F.** b 3 Feb. 1863, d 22 Nov. 1886; **Mary J.** b -- Sep. 1866, d 1867; and **Blanch M.** b 12 Sep. 1872, unm.

HALEY, SAMUEL SR. - Born ??, d 18 Aug. 1817, s/o ?? Samuel Haley, Sr. m (1) Mary ----, and she m (2) after her husband's death: Jeremiah Jordan. Children: **George A.** q.v.; **Josiah** q.v.; **Samuel** q.v.; **Abigail** b 5 Apr. 1813; **Dorcas** b 28 Apr. 1816, m David Skinner; and **Sarah** m Joseph Tobie.

HALEY, SAMUEL - Born 4 Aug. 1810, d 1 Jul. 1885 age 74 years [probate #2443, Auburn, Maine], s/o Samuel, Sr. and Mary (----) Haley. Samuel Haley m (1) 24 May 1835 Elizabeth Stinson, d 22 Mar. 1836, d/o James and Abigail, and m (2) 29 Oct. 1838 Elizabeth J. Libby*, b 2 Apr. 1816, d 24 Aug. 1865, d/o Rufus Webster. *Children of 1st wife*: **Elizabeth S.*** b 1 Mar. 1846, m 12 Jun. 1866 Henry Wood* of Lewiston, ME; **S a m u e l *** [named deceased in father's will dated 18 Jun. 1885] q.v.; and **J o s i a h D.** b 9 Jun. 1841, d 22 Feb. 1867, m 24 Dec. 1863 Annie M. Sanborn, who d 12 Jun. 1869, no children. *Children of 2nd wife*: **Charles H.*** q.v.; **Mary Jane** b 21 Sep. 1845, d 20 Aug. 1850; and **Frances Jane*** b 31 Mar. 1850, m 30 Dec. 1869 William Libby* of Wales, ME. [* indicates names found in deed book 117, p. 522]

HALEY, ZIBA - Born 2 Jan. 1810, d 17 Nov. 1894, s/o Joshua and ?? Haley. Ziba Haley res. Topsfield, Maine. He m 1833 Betsy/Elizabeth Pomeroy of Pomeroy Ridge, N. B., b 7 Aug. 1808, d 12/21 Mar. 1881. Children: **Benjamin Joshua** b 27 Dec. 1853, d 7 Sep. 1864, m 25 Mar. 1862 Huldah Hill of Codyville, ME; **Mary Elizabeth** b 6 May 1837, d 29 Jan. 1888, m 30 Jun. 1858 John McPhail of Perry, ME; **James Shepard** b 21 Jan. 1839, m 15 Oct. 1866 Louise Rideout of Nashwaak, NB; **Hannah** b 6 Sep. 1840, d 3 Nov. 1840; **Amanda** b 3 May 1843, d 22 May 1888, m 22 May 1878 James Craft of Topsfield, Maine; and **J a n e** b 3 Nov. 1844, m 13 Mar. 1867 Harris Malhoon of Topsfield, Maine. [Letter from J. S. Haley of Topsfield, Maine, dated 9 Apr. 1902.]

HALLIE, ROSS - Born ??, d ??, s/o ?? Child: **Berneice** b 27 Feb. 1891.

HAM, ALBERT BROOKS - Born 27 Dec. 18--, d ??, s/o Seward and ?? Ham. Albert Brooks Ham m 4 Aug. 1870 Ardella B. Brann of N. Vassalboro, ME, b 4 May 18--, d/o Francis and F. (House) Brann. Children: **Walter B.** q.v.; **Foster F.** b 23 Aug. 1878; and **Ruth P.** b 24 Jun. 1892, d 17 Jan. 1899.

HAM, ALVAH V. - Born 1843, d ??, s/o Seward and ?? Ham. Alvah V. Ham m 8 Aug. 1871 Martha Ellen Marston, d/o Sumner Marston. Children: **Alfred B.** b 2 Aug. 1873 in Washington, DC; **Gertrude L.** b 4 Sep. 1875, d 22 Jun. 18--; **Robert B.** b 25 Dec. 1878 in Washington, DC; and **Charles C.** b 18 Feb. 1880.

HAM, CHARLES M. - Born 10 Jul. 1831, d ??, s/o Edmund H. and Margaret (Dunham) (Coombs) Ham. Child: **Marguerite Flora** b 11 Oct. 1895.

HAM, CHARLES SEWARD - Born 2 Jun. 1840 in Abbott, Maine, d 15 Nov. 1897, s/o Seward and ?? Ham. Charles Seward Ham m 7 Dec. 1865 at Blanchard, Maine, Thersa Davce Blanchard, b 14 Oct. 1841, d/o David and Metilda Chandler Blanchard. Children: **Emma Blanchard** b 13 Feb. 1867 in Wilton, Maine, d 10 Jan. 1892 in Dover-Foxcroft, Maine, m 4 Sep. 1888 Arthur F. Abbott, M.D.; and **Seward Brooks** b 21 Sep. 1869 in Wilton, Maine. [Letter from Charles Seward Ham 11 Nov. 1893 of Dover-Foxcroft, Maine.]

HAM, EBENEZER - Born 1746, d 15 Aug. 1791, age 45 years, s/o Joseph and Mary (Ham) Ham [New England HHistorical Genealogical Register 26:392]. Ebenezer Ham m Sarah Field, d 11 May 1837, age 91 years [Nelson Ham]. Children: **Israel** b 1772, d 10 Feb. 1795, age 23 years, unm; **James** b 3 Jan. 1775 in Dover, NH, d 4 Feb. 1854, m 8 Nov. 1798 Nancy Brooks, who was b 12 Sep. 1782; and **Anna** b 7 Nov. 1780, d 19 Jun. 1867, age 86 years 7 months, m pub. 20 May 1798 William Brooks, who d 18 Nov. 1867.

HAM, COL. EBENEZER - Born 29 Sep. 1800, d 11 Oct. 1883, s/o James and Nancy (Brooks) Ham. Col. Ebenezer Ham m (1) Judith Parker, d 2/26 Apr. 1851, age 50 years, and m (2) 27 Feb. 1855 Jane G. (Barker) Lowell, d 24 Oct. 1887, wid/o James Lowell, Jr. *Children of 1st wife*: **Elizabeth F.** b 12 Dec. 1822, d 22 Dec. 1822; **Jacob B.** q.v.; **Caroline F.** b 7 Sep. 1826, d 29 Sep. 1899, m 7 Sep. 1856 Samuel Wilson, who d 20 Nov. 1893; **William R.** q.v.; **John S. P.** q.v.; **James B.** b 7 Mar. 1834, d 7 Mar. 1834; **Alonzo G.** b 7 Sep. 1835, d 25 Jul. 1895, m 1 Jan. 1857 Sarah M. Pilsbury, d/o Levi Pilsbury of Lewiston; **Ebeneser** b 1 Jul. 1839, d 7 Jul. 1839; **Judith** b 1 Jul. 1839, d 10 Jul. 1839; and **Melissa J.** b 6 Sep. 1840. *Children of either 1st or 2nd wife*: **Nellie G.**; and **Judith A.** m pub. 10 Nov. 1877 George Pottle.

HAM, EDMUND H. - Born -- May 1806 or 10 Dec. 1816, d 13/18 May 1882, s/o John and Priscilla (Hinckley/Hinckly) Ham. Edmund H. Ham m Margaret (Dunham) Coombs of Bowdoinham or Lisbon, Maine, d/o William and Sarah (Ross) Dunham, wid/o ---- Coombs.

Children: **Edmund, Jr.** b -- Feb. 1848, d 18 Nov. 1892, unm; and **Charles M.** q.v.

HAM, EVERETT - Born ??, d ??, s/o ?? Children: **Lucy** b 23 May 1872; **Minerva** b 12 May 1888; and **James W.** b 27 Jan. 1892.

HAM, GEORGE W. - Born 29 Sep. 1820, d 7 Nov. 1890, m Sarah J. Additon of Dexter, Maine. Children: **Eva May** b 27 Nov. 1849, d 27 Oct. 1861; **Eda Eliza** b 30 Aug. 1851, d 26 Sep. 1852, age 1 year 27 days; **Carrie Matilda** b 29 Dec. 1854, d 13 Jan. 1902; **Hattie R.** b 26 --- 1855, m 5 Dec. 1870 Frank Wright; **George W.** d 5 May 1858, age 7 months; **Percy P.** b 9 Feb. 1859, m 21 Jun. 1880 Celia Bechard; and **Sevard E.** b -- Jan. 1869.

HAM, GEORGE W. - Born ??, d ??, s/o Seward and ?? Ham. George W. Ham m 6 May 1871 Etta L. Goss, d/o John Goss of Lewiston. Children: **Alice** b 1 Dec. 1880; **Florence** b 7 Apr. 1885; and **Everett G.** b 13 Dec. 1891.

HAM, HERBERT - Born ??, d ??, s/o Nelson and ?? Ham. Children: **Ethel**; and **Austin**.

HAM, HERRICK - Born ??, d ??, s/o Israel and Clarissa (Smith) Ham. Children: **Harriet** b 15 Dec. 1844; **Charles W.** b 8 Aug. 1847; and **Amanda J.** b 13 Jan. 1859.

HAM, HERRICK - Born 25 Jun. 1819, d 10 Apr. 1869, s/o Thomas and ?? Ham. Herrick Ham m 5 Feb. 1843 Elizabeth/Elizabeth J. Goddard. Children: **Harriet E.** b 15 Dec. 1844, m (1) pub. 18 Nov. 1861 Maurice S. Hussey, and m (2) pub. 2 Mar. 1867 Rufus L. Jordan (or Rubus Stewart); **Charles W.** b 8 Aug. 1847, m Anna Larrabbee; and **Armanda J.** b 13 Jan. 1859, m Fred Gowell.

HAM, ISRAEL - Born 25 Apr. 1786, d 2/26 Jul. 1854, s/o Tobias and Elizabeth (Herrick) Ham. Israel Ham had settled in Lisbon, Maine. He m (1) pub. 6/16 Jan. 1811 Lucy Hinckley/Hinckly of Lisbon, d 18 Jan. 1827, d/o Isaac and Priscilla Pennell Hinckley/Hinckly, and m (2) 7 May 1833 Clarissa Smith/South, b 19 Aug. 1806, d 12 Mar. 1887, d/o Lemuel ---- of Lisbon. Children: **Sarah H./Sarah/Sally** b 3 Mar. 1812, m Jonathon/Jonathan Sleeper; **Charles** b 21 Jan. 1815, d 22 Jan. 1862 in Bangor or Kenduskeag, ME, m Mary Doe; **Isaac Curtis** b 22 Dec. 1818 (or 30 Sep. 1818?), d 31 May 1883 in Levant, ME, m Mary Freese; **Israel** b 21/22 Dec. 1821, d 5 Jun. 1872, m (1) ---- Nevers, and m (2) Clarissa Smith of Lisbon; **John** b 4 Feb. 1834, m 13 Aug. 1859 Eveline Pinkham, who d -- Sep. 1868; and **Albert G./S.** b 19 Dec. 1837, m 4 Mar. 1865 Harriet E. Packard, lived in Lynn, MA, had one child: **Nellie H.** b 25 Dec. 1866, m 8 Apr. 1886 to George M. Spalding.

HAM, ISRAEL - Son of Ebenezer, d 10 Feb. 1795, age 23 years.

HAM, JACOB BARKER - Born 24 Mar. 1824 in Lewiston, d 3 Sep. 1886/1888, s/o Col. Ebenezer and Judith (Barker) Ham. Jacob Barker Ham m 20 Dec. 1846 Lucinda Golder, d/o Rev. Jacob Golder. Jacob was oldest of 11 children, educated at Lewiston Falls Academy, engaged in trade, owned hay/grain store on Main Street, lived on Chapel and Lowell Streets, then moved to Farwell area. He was elected to State Legislature in 1854 and 1856 as a Republican, named Selectman in Lewiston from 1859 - 1862, became mayor in 1863, and was re-elected to that position in 1864. He was appointed Maine's Commissioner to the New Orleans Exposition and traveled extensively in the United States, Mexico, Cuba, and Europe. Children: **Annie W.** b 2 Apr. 1850, m 27 May 1876 William Hayes; **Orland S.** b 1 Jul. 1855, m 8 Apr. 1880 Lizzie H. Blake; **Edmund P.** b 3 May 1857, m 2 Nov. 1878 Annie L. Harriman; and **Eben J.** b 17 Jul. 1860, m Carrie Dexter.

HAM, JAMES - (Also listed as HODGKINS, JAMES) Son of Betsy Hodgkins, b 1 Apr. 1797, m 25 Jun. 1821 Rachel Ackley.

HAM, JAMES - Born 10 Aug. 1822, d ??, s/o John and ?? Ham. James Ham lived in Lisbon, Maine. He m 16 Dec. 1853 Mineva J. Dunham of Bowdoin, Maine, b 23 Jul. 1826, d 6 Apr. 1899, d/o James and Sarah (Rodgers) Dunham. Children: **John** b -- Aug. 1854, d 2 Jan. 1855; **Agnes D.** b 23 Sep. 1857, m -- Jun. ---- Alfred L. Gonald of Lisbon; and **Everett** b 11 Sep. 1859, m Hattie R. Davis of MA, d/o William Davis and Elizabeth Brown.

HAM, JAMES - Born 3/31 Jan. 1775 in Dover, New Hampshire, d 4 Feb. 1854 [5 Feb. 1855 according to Nelson Ham], age 79 years, s/o Ebenezer and Sarah (Field) Ham. James Ham m 8 Nov. 1798 Nancy Brooks, b 12 Sep. 1782 in Falmouth, Maine, d 12 May 1874 age 93 years [Nelson Ham], d/o John and Martha Brooks. Children: **Martha** b 6 Mar. 1799, d 14 Jan. 1879, age 79 years 10 months, m 22 Dec. 1822 John Brooks, 3rd, who d 9 Sep. 1831; **Ebenezer** q.v.; **Joseph** b 6 Apr. 1801, d 29 Dec. 1804 age 2 years [Nelson Ham]; **Ann** b 30 Nov. 1803, d 29 Sep. 1866, m 15 Oct. 1826 Jacob Barker, who d 13 Dec. 1861; **Eliza** b 4 Jul. 1805; **Joseph** b 21 Mar. 1807, d 22 Aug. 1865, age 58 years 5 months, m 20 Sep. 1831 Sally M. Fuller, who d 19 Jul. 1863, age 55 years 10 months; **Seward** b 21/31 May 1809, m 9 Jan. 1832 Sarah M. Field, who d 19 Oct. 1857, d/o John Field; **Warren** b 11 Jun. 1811, d 18 Feb. 1855, age 44 years 8 months 7 days, m 20 Jul. 1834 Sarah Gorham, who d 18 Feb. 1859, age 47 years 8 months 6 days; **Mary** b 21 Sep. 1813, m (1) 25 Nov. 1835 David Garcelon, who d 5 Aug. 1837, and m (2) 5 Jul. 1846 Libbins Allen of Hebron, ME; **Nelson** q.v.; **Jane** b 7 Apr. 1818, d 3 Dec. 1830; **George W.** b 29 Sep. 1820, d 7 Nov. 1890, of Lewiston, m Sarah J. Additon of Dexter, ME; **Ursula** b 16 Nov. 1822, d 28 Sep. 1872, m 21 Apr. 1842 Daniel Garcelon; **Sarah** b 12 Jan. 1825, m ---- Goff and living in Mexico, ME; and **Nancy B.** b 17 Jul. 1827.

HAM, JAMES L. - Born ??, d ??, s/o Nelson and ?? Ham. Child: **Roscoe, Jr.** b 3 Apr. 1875.

HAM, JOHN - Born 28 Apr. 1792, d 8 Jan. 1880, s/o Tobias and Elizabeth (Herrick) Ham. John Ham m (1) pub. 30 Sep. 1815, m 29 Oct. 1815 Priscilla Hinckley/Hinckly, b 9 Oct. 1774, d 13 Jul. 1831, and m (2) Mary Colby, b 9 Oct. 1794, d -- Feb. ---- at Bowdoinham, ME, wid/o John Colby. Children: **Edmund H.** q.v.; **Hannah H.** b 18 Oct. 1819, d 18 Mar. 1842; **James** q.v.; **Priscilla** b 19 Dec. 1824, d 13 Mar. 1875, m -- Nov. 1852 John P. Hatch; **William** q.v.; and **Lucy** b 12 Jan. 1828, d 19 Aug. 1855, m John T. Edgecomb.

HAM, JOHN - Born 4 Feb. 1834, d ??, s/o Israel and Clarissa (Smith) Ham. Children: **Clara Eva** b 9 Sep. 1860; **James A.** b 24 Mar. 1863, d 10 Mar. 1883; and **Flora** b 22 Sep. 1868, d infant.

HAM, JOHN L. - Born 19 Mar. 1844, d ??, s/o Nelson and ?? Ham. John L. Ham m Emily Ford. Child: **William R.**

HAM, JOHN S. P. - Born 7 Nov. 1831, d 15 Jan. 1882, s/o Ebenezer and ?? Ham. John S. P. Ham m 7 Nov. 1860 Abbie L. Stetson, d/o Elisha of Auburn, Maine. Children: **Henry R.** b 21 May 1865; and **William F.** b 15 Mar. 1870.

HAM, NELSON - Son of James, who d 5 Feb. 1855 (s/o Sarah Ham, who d 11 May 1837, age 91 years), and Nancy, who d 12 May 1874, age 93 years. Children: **Joseph** d age 2 years; **Mary Allen** of Hebron, ME; **Nelson**; **George W.** of Lewiston; and **Sarah Goff** of Mexico, ME.

HAM, NELSON - Born ??, d ??, s/o ?? Children: **John L.** q.v.; **Alice R.** b 1 Apr. 1846, d 20 Oct. 1880, m (1) 28 Nov. 1866 Adelbert Holland, and m (2) 2 Sep. 1876 Warren Osgood; **J a m e s N.** b 16 Aug. 1848, m pub. 20 Dec. 1871 Florence Angella Billings of Hallowell, ME, d 23 Apr. 1875; **Clara L.** b 25 Oct. 1850, m (1) 12 Oct. 1870 Charles Sanborn of Boston, MA, who d 8 Jun. 1875, and m (2) 31 Oct. 1883 Albert B. M. Russell of Salem, MA; **E v a J.** b 25 Nov. 1852, m 17 Jun. 1880 William G. Snow; **Herbert B.** b 9 May 1857, m Ada Azelia Collins of New Portland, ME; and **Howard E.** b 16 Oct. 1862, m Gertrude Moody of Pittston, ME.

HAM, THOMAS - Born 17 Mar. 1790, d 27 Apr. 1827, s/o Tobias and Elizabeth (Herrick) Ham. Thomas Ham m 30 Sep. 1815 [Lisbon record] Anna Rand? [m int. cert. granted 2 Feb. 1817 according to the vital records of Lewiston, Maine, p. 394]. Children: **H u l d a** b 7 Mar. 1818, m Amasiah Nevens; **Herrick** q.v.; **Jonathan S.** b 7 Nov. 1820; **Sally R.** b 3 Jul. 1823, d young; **Nabby R.** b 12 Aug. 1825, d 14 Jun. 1827; and **Thomas** b 16 May 1827.

H A M , T O B I A S - Born 2 Jul. 1751, d 22 May 1812, s/o ?? Tobias Ham m Elizabeth Herrick, b 29 Aug. 1754, d 20 Mar. 1834. Children: **Abigail** b 31 Aug. 1779, d 10 Dec. 1805, m 6 Jul. 1800 Nathaniel Pettingill, who d 27 Feb. 1860; **Betsy** b 18 Mar. 1781, d 16 Aug. 1858, m 31 Dec. 1804 Jonathan Sleeper, who d 29 May 1805; **P o l l y** b 4 Jun. 1782, d 4 Apr. 1868, m 1800 Nathan Sleeper, who d 18 Feb. 1860; **Lydia** b 13 May 1784, d 8 Mar. 1832 in Lisbon, ME, unm; **Lucy** b 13

May 1789; **Israel** q.v.; **Tobias** b 3 Mar. 1788, d 1801; **Thomas** q.v.; and **John** q.v. [Vital Records of Lewiston, Maine, p. 31.]

HAM, TOBIAS - Born ??, d ??, s/o ?? Tobias Ham was of Brunswich, Maine. He m Abigail Smith. Children: **Benjamin** b 2 Jun. 1742, settled in Bath, ME; **John** b 1 Sep. 1744, settled in Bath; **Joseph** b 30 Dec. 1746, res. Brunswick, ME; **Judith** b 18 Apr. 1749 m ---- Arno; **Tobias** and **Thomas** (twins) b 2 Jul. 1751, settled in Lisbon, ME; **Nathaniel** b 17 Feb. 1756; and **Reuben**, settled in Lisbon or Wales, ME. [*History of Brunswick* by George A. and Henry W. Wheeler, published by the authors, 1877, p. 827.]

HAM, WALTER B. - Born 24 Apr. 1873, d ??, s/o Albert Brooks and Ardella B. (Brann) Ham. Walter B. Ham m 15 Sep. 1896 Lena Thompson Se----. Child: **Bernice Iown** b 24 Jul. 1898.

HAM, WARREN - Born 11 Jun. 1811, d 28 Feb. 1855 age 44 years 8 months 7 days [vital records of Lewiston, Maine, p. 222 states that he was buried in Garcelon Cem. in Lewiston], s/o James and Nancy (----) Ham. Warren Ham m 20 Jul. 1834 Sarah Gorham, d 18 Feb. 1859, age 47 years 8 months 6 days. Children: **Julia Ann** b 22 Feb. 1836, m Andrew Gowell of Auburn, ME, d in Portland, ME; and **John G.** b 19 Dec. 1845, d 25 Aug. 1846, age 8 months 6 days.

HAM, WILLIAM - Born 12 Jan. 1828, d 17 Jan. 1877, s/o John and Priscilla (Hinckly/Hinckley) Ham. William Ham m (1) 22 May 1857 Lucy A. Smith, b 21 Feb. 1831, d 3 Oct. 1871, d/o Edward and Mercy M. ----, and m (2) 11 Jun. 1873 Sarah Minerva Smith, b 13 Oct. 1842, d/o John and Philena (Tuttle) of Durham, Maine. Children: **Walter** b 20 Sep. 1860; **Wilber** b 18 Jul. 1865; **Thomas William** b 7 Jul. 1858, d 25 Sep. 1858; **Lucy** b 7 Jul. 1858, d 16 Oct. 1858; and **Lizzie** b 15 Sep. 1868, m 24 Dec. 1889 William D. Barnes.

HAM, WILLIAM R. - Born 22 Sep. 1829, d (killed in battle at Cold Harbor) 4 Jun. 1864, s/o Ebenezer and ?? Ham. William R. Ham m 1 Jan. 1855 Augusta D. Pilsbury, d/o Levi Pilsbury of Lewiston. Children: **William Ross** b 19 Dec. 1864, d 1870; **Clara Augusta** b 1855, d 1866; and **Kate Ross** b 1855, d 1863.

HAMILTON, HANNAH - Born ??, d ??, d/o ?? Child: **Edward Woodbury** b 5 Dec. 1829. [Vital Records of Lewiston, Maine, p. 41.]

HARDY, ALBION P. - Born 30 Nov. 1843, d ??, s/o Benjamin and Eliza (----) Hardy. Albion P. Hardy m 5 Dec. 1872 Mary J. Scott of North Gower. Children: **Edna Maud** b 22 Nov. 1873, m 9 May 1892 Frank Taylor of Dumlox, IA; **Emily Mabel** b 2 Nov. 1875; **Clarion DeWitt** b 2 Oct. 1877; **Leslie Miller** b 14 Mar. 1882; **Herbert Albion** b 25 Apr. 1884; **Elsie Mary** b 15 Aug. 1886; and **Maynard Nevens** b 3 Jul. 1891.

HARDY, AMORY NELSON - Born 17 Jul. 1834, d ??, s/o Benjamin and Eliza (----) Hardy. Amory Nelson Hardy m 16 Nov. 1856 Angeline Sewall Davis, d/o Stephen of Lewiston. Children: **George Everett** b 30 Mar. 1866, d 7 Aug. 1866; **Angelina Bertha** b 19 May 1868; **Grace Maud** b 12 Aug. 1871; and **William Amory** b 15 Jun. 1873.

HARDY, ARETAS - Born 25 Jan. 1805 in Lewiston, d 4 Jun. 1882 in Napa, California, s/o James and Priscilla (Mooar) Hardy. Aretas Hardy m 1 May 1832 Lydia B. Ames, b 4 Jul. 1808, d/o Abner C. and Betsy (Bean) Ames; was living in San Francisco, California, in 1890. Children: **Priscilla Mooar** b 22 Jul. 1833 in Strong, ME, d 16 Jul. 1890, m 6 Dec. 1857 Cyrus Willard of Boston, MA; ---- unnamed daughter b&d 6 Mar. 1841 in New Sharon, ME; **Achea Elizabeth** b 13 Jan. 1844 in Stark, ME, m 27 Dec. 1864 Henry Monroe Allen of San Francisco; and **Edwin Hawes** b 17 Jun. 1846 in Strong, m 5 Apr. 1870 Ella Van Hasen of San Francisco, CA.

HARDY, ARTHUR E. - Born 5 Apr. 1864 in Carmel, Maine, d ??, s/o Martin A. and Clara M. (Sparrow) Hardy. Arthur E. Hardy m 15 Sep. 1889 Minnie E. Rowell, b 15 Apr. 1866 in Hamilton, Maine. Children: **Lulu A.** b 3 Jun. 1890 in Hampden, Maine; and **Evelyn W.** b 18 Mar. 1893 in Hampden, Maine.

HARDY, BENJAMIN - Born 20 Jan. 1805 in Lewiston, d 10 Sep. 1894, s/o ?? Benjamin Hardy m Eliza ----, d 26 Jul. 1845. Children: **Lauriana** b 2 May 1832, d 11 Sep. 1835; **Amory Nelson** q.v,; **Martin A.** q.v.; **Harriet E.** b 15 Mar. 1838 in New Gloucester, ME; **James W.** b 9 Feb. 1839 in New Gloucester, ME; **Lewis E.** q.v.; and **Albion P.** b 30 Nov. 1843. [Vital Records of New Gloucester, Maine, p. 63 and manuscript in Maine Historical Society.]

HARDY, CHARLES W. - Born 1 Jul. 1821/1829, d ??, s/o John and Mehitable (Mooar) Hardy. Charles W. Hardy m (1) 10 Jan. 1851 Sarah H. Presson, b 15 Feb. 1828, d 26 Jul. 1887, d/o Leonard, and m (2) 30 Jan. 1890 Mary A. Hardy. Children: **Edmund R.** b 18 Oct. 1852, m Mary E. Hammond; **William G.** b 22 Sep. 1858; and **Emma L.** b 13 Feb. 1861, m (1) George M. Allen of New Haven, Connecticut, and m (2) E. E. Knight of Providence, Rhode Island.

HARDY, EVERETTE S. - Born 27 Jul. 1868 in Carmel, Maine, ??, s/o Martin A. and Clara M. (Sparrow) Hardy. Everette S. Hardy m 18 Aug. 1892 Laura E. Stone, b 8 Jan. 1867 in Oldtown, Maine. Children: **Harold A.** b 17 Dec. 1893 in Bangor, ME; and **Carl E.** b 4 Apr. 1895 in Bangor.

HARDY, FRED E. - Born 16 Jun. 1866 in Carmel, Maine, d ??, s/o Martin A. and Clara M. (Sparrow) Hardy. Fred E. Hardy m 1 Mar. 1893 Sylvia J. Loring, b 17 Sep. 1874 in Hampden, Maine. Children: **Ester E.** b 7 Mar. 1896 in Carmel, ME.

HARDY, GEORGE E. - Born ??, d ??, s/o ?? Children: **Belice** b 12 Dec. 1885; and **Perley** b 15 Oct. 1889.

HARDY, GILBERT - Born 5 Apr. 1839, d ??, s/o Oliver H. and Abigail (Merrill) Hardy. Gilbert Hardy m Jane Badger of Canaan, Maine. Children: **Carrie** b 14 Jan. 1862 in Carmel, Maine; and **Enos** b 19 Jun. 1880.

HARDY, HENRY PHILIPS - Born 19 May 1812 in Strong, Maine [L. Peary's records of Strong, Maine, p. 20, manuscript Farmington Library], d ??, s/o Simeon and Lois (Mooar) Hardy. Henry P. Hardy m Sarah D. Nichols, d 9 Jun. 1891, d/o James and Sarah (Dearborn) Nichols. Children: **Asbury H.** b 14 Jan. 1842, d 10 May 1842; **Charles H.** b 11 Apr. 1843, m 25 Apr. 1870 H. D. Pierce; **Weston N.** b 30 Sep. 1847, m 9 Jun. 1886 Lula K. Tunney; **S a r a h A.** b 14 Aug. 1858, d 13 Feb. 1864; and **Coris A.** b -- Oct.1853.

HARDY, JAMES - Born ??, d ??, s/o ?? James Hardy m pub. 9 Sep. 1798 Priscilla Mooar, d 4 Apr. 1828, age 49 years. Children: **James** d 27 Nov. 1862, age 63 years 9 months, m 18 Apr. 1822 Hopestill Cutter, who d 9 Nov. 1874, d/o Nathon of Industry, ME; **Aretas** q.v.; and **N a t h a n** d 26 Dec. 1883, age 80 years 11 months, m (1) Mary Vaughn, who d 3 Feb. 1836, age 26 years, and m (2) Angeline Willard, who d 16 Aug. 1873, age 59 years 4 months.

HARDY, JOHN - Born ??, d 20 Feb. 1883, s/o Simeon and ?? Hardy. John Hardy was of Strong, Maine. He m int. 2 Aug. 1825 [vital records of Lewiston, Maine, p. 436] Mehitable Mooar, b 23 Aug. 1798 or 16 Oct. 1803, d 29 May 1870 in Farmington, Maine, or 20 Feb. 1893, age 79 years 4 months 4 days. Children: **Matilda T.** b 27 Jan. 1827, d -- Jun. 1890, m (1) James P. Winslow, and m (2) Gideon Lambart, and m (3) Nathaniel Smith; **Charles W.** q.v.; and **Sophronia N.** b 2 Apr. 1832, m 1893 ---- Haven.

HARDY, LEWIS E. - Born 4 Sep. 1841, d ??, s/o Benjamin and Eliza (----) Hardy. Lewis E. Hardy m (1) 12 Mar. 1866 Addie C. Folsom, who was b 13 Apr. 1841 in Norway, Maine, d 8 Jan. 1873, and m (2) Mary A. Morrill, b 3 Jun. 1847 in Starkboro, Vermont. *Children by 1st wife*: **Sarah Gaetta** b 12 Oct. 1870 in Dow City, Iowa, m William Craft; and **Mark Raymond** b 6 Feb. 1872 in Dow City, Iowa. *Children by 2nd wife*: **Rolland Lewis** b 26 Mar. 1876, d 18 Sep. 1876; **Helen Grace** b 16 Aug. 1880 in Dow City, Iowa; and **Ernest Edward** b 16 Jan. 1884 in Dow City, Iowa.

HARDY, MARTIN A. - Born 18 Mar. 1837 in Strong, Maine, s/o Benjamin and Eliza (----) Hardy. Martin A. Hardy m 29 Jun. 1863 Clara M. Sparrow, b 8 Jan. 1841 in Winterport, Maine. Children: **Arthur E.** q.v.; **Fred E.** q.v.; **Everette S.** q.v.; **Cyrenus F.** b 18 Apr. 1871; **Herbert L.** b 12 Apr. 1874 in Carmel, ME, m 30 Nov. 1895 Daisey E. Bickford, b 14 Nov. 1872 in Dixmont, ME; and **R a l p h W.** b 25 Feb. 1878 in Carmel.

HARDY, MARTIN V. B. - Born 23 May 1838, d ??, s/o ?? Martin V. B. Hardy m 26 Sep. 1859 Hannah Spaulding, b 4 Jun. 1839, d 25 Jul. 1891. Children: **Wilbur Fisk** q.v.; **Julia Mira** b 9 Apr. 1871, d 24

Feb. 1874; **Macella Achsa** b 11 May 1873; **Austin Leon** b 26 Sep. 1878; and **Mattie Bell** b 19 Apr. 1880.

HARDY, OLIVER - Born 27 Apr. 1837, d ??, s/o Oliver and Abigail (Merrill) Hardy. Oliver Hardy m 18 Aug. 1863 Frances Benjamin of Carmel, b 9 Dec. 1850, d/o Eben and Ester (Barden) Benjamin. Child: **George E.** b 18 Aug. 1853, m 25 Dec. 1872 Frances Crabtree, who was b 19 Oct. 1857, d/o Greene Crabtree of Etna, Maine.

HARDY, OSMEN/OLIVER H. - Born 16 Sep. 1800, d 7 Oct. 1860, s/o Simeon and Lois (Mooar) Hardy. Osmen/Oliver H. Hardy was of Strong, Maine. He m 5 Jul. 1825 Abigail Merrill, d/o Benjamin and Sarah (----) Merrill of Lewiston, Maine [vital records of Lewiston, Maine, p. 407]. Children: **Delia Hardy** b -- Nov. 1827; **James E.** b 25 Feb. 1828, m Floretta Hatch of Passadumkeag, ME; **Linda** b 10 Oct. 1831; **Sumner** q.v.; **Oliver** q.v.; **Gilbert** b 5 Apr. 1839, m Jane Badger of Canaan, ME; **Jennie** b 31 Dec. 1841; **Enos** b 1 Nov. 1843, d 14 Dec. 1861; and **Flora M.** b 21 Jul. 1845, d 27 Jun. 1865.

HARDY, REUBIN - Born 30 Jun. 1802, d 1 Nov. 1871, s/o Simeon and Lois (Mooar) Hardy. Reubin Hardy m Rebecca Pratt of Farmington, Maine, b 18 Dec. 1800, d 15 Aug. 1848. Children: **Elizabeth** b 26 May 1827 in Farmington, ME, d 26 Aug. 1847 in Phillips, ME; **Lucy A.** b 11 Oct. 1829 in Freeman, ME, m 1 Jan. 1852 Mermon Stinson Houghton, b 7 May 1830 in Weld, Maine; **Sarah** b 9 Jan. 1832 in Strong, ME, d 10 Apr. 1832 in Freeman; **Simeon** b 17 Jul. 1833, d 19 Sep. 1893 in Natick, MA, m Ellen M. Rice of Natick, MA; and **Lauretta** b 18 Mar. 1839 in Phillips, ME, d 21 Sep. 1841 in Phillips.

HARDY, SIMEON - Born 14 May 1770 in Andover, Massachusetts, d 16 Mar. 1863, s/o ?? Simeon Hardy m Lois Mooar of Lewiston, b 15 May 1773, d 10 Apr. 1854. Children: **Lois** b 15 Jun. 1793 in Andover, MA, d age 91/92 years, m Solomon Gray; **Nabby** b 22 Sep. 1794, d 30 Sep. 1856, m (1) -- Sep. 1816 Abijah Wright, who d 17 Apr. 1843, and m (2) 9 Oct. 1845 Nathaniel Parker of Durham, ME; **Rhoda** b 18 May 1796 at Lewiston, ME, m (1) William Gray, and m (2) James Presson; **John** q.v.; **Oliver** q.v.; **Reuben** q.v.; **Benjamin** b 20 Jan. 1805; **Stephen** q.v.; **Sally** b 4 May 1809, d 9 Jun. 1891 in Canada, m 15 Jan. 1833 Abener M. Powell, b 4 May 1809 in Strong, ME, d 31 Jan. 1882 in Clinton, ME; and **Henry Philips** q.v. [Leland Peary's records of Strong, Maine, p. 20, Farmington, Maine, Library manuscript, no date.]

HARDY, STEPHEN - Born 11 Dec. 1806, d 16 Mar. 1863 or 24 Jan. 1895, s/o Simeon and Lois (Mooar) Hardy. Stephen Hardy m (1) Julia Nevens, b 9 Apr. 1807, d 9 Oct. 1839 in Etna, Maine, d/o Samuel and Lucy (Curtis) Nevens, and m (2) Eliza Hinkley of Carmel, Maine, d 22 Nov. 1844, and m (3) Mrs. ---- Doane, and m (4) Mrs. Clarissa Bunker. *Children of 1st wife*: **Melville C.** b 22 Feb. 1836, m Jennie Stockbridge; and **Martin V. B.** b 23 May 1838, m Hannah Spaulding, who was b -- Feb. 1848. *Child of 3rd wife*: **Osman O.** b -- Feb. 1848. *Children of 4th wife*: **Mary**; and **Jennie S.**.

HARDY, SUMNER - Born 16 Oct. 1835, d 6 Sep. 1895, s/o Oliver H. and Abigail (Merrill) Hardy. Children: **Cora A.** b 26 Nov. 1865, m 30 Aug. 1890 Stillman E. Dyer; and **Bertha L.** b 28 Oct. 1872, m 29 May 1896 T. B. Friend.

HARDY, WILBUR FISK - Born 22 Feb. 1861, d ??, s/o Martin V. B. and Hannah (Spaulding) Hardy. Wilbur Fisk Hardy m 25 Nov. 1886 Georgia A. Spaulding. Children: **Achsa Frances** b 3 Oct. 1890, d 28 Mar. 1894; and **Leslie Hardy** b 3 Feb. 1893.

HARRIDON/HARRADON, GEORGE W. - Born ??, d ??, s/o Washington Franklin and ?? Harridon/Harradon. George W. Harridon/Harradon m (1) 4 Jul. 1867 Jennie E. Waterhouse, d/o Samuel of Poland, Maine, and m (2) 8 Aug. 1876 Emma R. Grom, b 31 May 1855, d/o John Grom. Children: **Abee G.** b 7 Jan. 1887; **George E.** b 14 May 1888; **Charles W.** b 15 Dec. 1889; **Hattie E.** b 21 May 1891; **Edwin A.** b 11 Jul. 1893; and **Bernice** b 5 Mar. 1895.

HARRIDON/HARRADON, GEORGE WASHINGTON - Born ??, d ??, s/o ?? Children: **George W.**; and **Charles**.

HARRIDON/HARRADON, HARVEY S. - Born ??, d ??, s/o ?? Married 11 May 1862 Mrs. Mary A. Harris.

HARRIDON/HARRADON, HARVEY S. - Born 12 Sep. 1804, d 16 Jul. 1870, s/o William and ?? Harridon/Harradon. Harvey S. Harridon/Harradon m Sally West, b 28 Aug. 1837, d 2 Jun. 1861, d/o William Harlow and Stella S. Jone of Minot, Maine. Children: **Harvey S.** b 1826, d 28 Apr. 1892, age 66 years, m Louisa Macumber in Fall River, MA; **Rebecca** m Samuel Coffin, who d in Turner; **Mary Ann** m Charles E. Parsons of Turner, ME; **Sheppard W.** b 13 Oct. 1832, m 13 Oct. 1868 Flora Harlow, m (1) 20 Jun. 1862 May Jane Macomber of RI, who d 9 Dec. 1867, age 29 years 6 months 3 days; **Washington Franklin** q.v.; **Justus B.** d 10 Nov. 1891, age 44 years; and **Levina** d young.

HARRIDON/HARRADON, SHEPPARD - Born ??, d ??, likely s/o Harvey S. and Sally (West) Harridon/Harradon. Children: **Edward W.** b 23 Mar. 1863, m Lizzie Higgins of Bath, ME; **John A.** b 1 Nov. 1864, m Angie Marrow of Auburn, ME, d/o Orris; **Mary F.** b 27 May 1869, m Emery L. Feroo; **Addie L.** b 17 Nov. 1870; and **Millie R.** b 5 Jun. 1875.

HARRIDON/HARRADON, WASHINGTON FRANKLIN - Born 19 Mar. 1839, d ??, s/o Harvey S. and Sally (West) Harridon/Harradon. Washington Franklin Harridon/Harradon m (1) 17 May 1863 Marcella Potter of Litchfield, Maine, and m (2) 18 Feb. 1877 Helen/Hellen S. Collins of Lewiston, b 12 Mar. 1852, d 19 Dec. 1875, d/o Sam. Children: **Willie F.** b 4 Mar. 1864; and **Nellie M.** b 12 Apr. 1873, m 6 Oct. 1894 William Watson of A----.

HARRIDON/HARRADON, WILLIAM - Born 1771, d 4 Sep. 1834, age 63 years, s/o ?? William Harridon/Harradon m (1) Mary York, and m (2) Elizabeth ----, d 29 Feb. 1852, age 86 years. Children: **Elizabeth** b 3 Jun. 1787, m (1) ---- Moore, and m (2) ---- Larrabee; **Susanna** b 3 Aug. 1789; **Patience** b 31 Aug. 1791; **Drusilla** b 26 Aug. 1803, m Foster Wentworth; **Harvey** S. q.v.; **Sally** d in Greene, ME, m 3 Apr. 1823 William French, who d in Auburn; and **Washington** T. d 28 Mar. 1864 in the Army, m Mary Jane Dilldoe of Portland, ME.

HARRIS, ABNER - Born ??, d ??, s/o ?? Children: **Polly** b 18 Feb. 1783; **Lydia** b 6 Feb. 1785; **William** b 7 Nov. 1786; **Betsy** b 23 Nov. 1788; **Bridget** b 14 Jan. 1791; **Martha** b 22 Feb. 1793; **Deborah** b 1 Apr. 1795; **Abner** b 23 Aug. 1799; **Nat G.** b 16 Apr. 1801; and **Hosea** b 4 Jan. 1803.

HARRIS, ANDREW JACKSON - Born 22 Jan. 1815, d ??, s/o s/o Moses Little and Rachel (Hooper) Harris. Andre Jackson Harris m 28 Dec. 1843 Lucy Ann Greenwood, d -- May 1893. Children: **Lucinela** R. b 17 Apr. 1842, m Evan Allen of Greene, ME; **Moses Henry** b 14 May 1844, m 1871 Zelia E. Wilson of Canton, New York; **Greenwood** b 14 Nov. 1845, m Ada Gorman of Greene; and **Andrew Jackson** b 9 Jul. 1848, m 1895 Alice Starbird.

HARRIS, ARATIS/ARATUS - Born 19 Oct. 1807, d 12 Oct. 1878, age 70 years 11 months, s/o Silas and Mercy (Haskell) Harris. Aratis/Aratus Harris m (1) Jane Sheppard, and m (2) Jemima Cummings, d/o Lemuel. Children: **Aulenal Jane** b 26 Sep. 1837, d 3 Jul. 1853, m Dr. William Daly; and **William** b 24 Sep. 1843, m Mary Frances Hewens of Walpole, MA, b 11 Mar. 1846, d 1878, d/o Elis W.

HARRIS, ARTHUR - Born 10 Sep. 1856, d ??, s/o Dewitt Clinton and ?? Harris. Arthur Harris m 1 Jan. 1882 Sussi M. Simpson of Waterville, Maine, d/o Ripley. Children: **Eddie** b 16 Jun. 1887, d 1 Sep. 1887; and **Edna** b 10 Feb. 1892.

HARRIS, BARRON - Born 7 Apr. 1774, d 29 Oct./Nov. 1850 age 76 years, s/o Lawrence Jackson and Lydia (Barron) Harris. Barron Harris m (1) pub. 14 Jul. 1799 Cynthia Record, d 29 Feb. 1832 in Cambridge, Maine, and m (2) Mrs. Sally Hurd of W----, b 1 Jul. 1783, d 5 Nov. 1846. Children: **Zelotes** q.v.; **Lawrence Jackson** q.v.; **Betsey** b 20 Jan. 1805, m (1) 18 Dec. 1824 Jesse Hamilton, and m (2) Frank Jones; **Orson** b 7 May 1807, d 17 Jul. 1876, m Jane Watson, b 15 Jan. 1811, d 6 Sep. 1874; **Thomas** q.v.; **Abner** b 24 May 1811, d 15 Dec. 1888, m Annie Wilkins, d 1878; **Lydia** b 1814, m James Packard, d 30 Jun. 1887; **John** b 1816, d 12 Mar. 1880, m ---- Willis; **Jairum/Jairus** b 28 Jul. 1818, m 22 Sep. 1839 Olive Heard, d 25 Apr. 1869; and **Cynthia** b 6 Mar. 1820, m 5 Feb. 1838 Jacob Packard, d 1884.

HARRIS, DANIEL WEBSTER - Born 16 Apr. 1845 in Parkman, Maine, d 4 Apr. 1897 in Oshkosh or Washburn, Wisconsin, s/o Jairum/Jairus and Olive (----) Harris. Daniel Webster Harris m 1874 Eliza A. Corning, b in Londonderry, New Hampshire, d/o Daniel and Judith

(Webster) Corning. Child: **Byron C.** b 15 Jan. 1875, lived in Washburn, Wisconsin, unm.

HARRIS, DAVID - Born 5 Oct. 1809 in Greene, Maine, d 14 Mar. 1891 in Bath, Maine, s/o John and Nancy (Simmons) Harris. David Harris m 12 Sep. 1833 Phebe/Phebe R. Grows of Brunswick, Maine, b 14 Apr. 1809 in Brunswick, d 13 Mar. 1891 in Bath, Maine. Children: **John** q.v.; **Thomas F. G.** b 29 Dec. 1835 in Wales, Maine, m 8 Feb. 1859 Mary Pettie/Mary A. Pettes of Bath, Maine, b 11 Aug. 1833 in Bath; and **Roswell C.** q.v.

HARRIS, DAVID - Born ??, d ??, s/o Moses and ?? Children: **Betsy** m John Pease; and **Rachel** m Judge Williams.

HARRIS, DAVID HOOPER - Born 8 Feb. 1796, d 20/22 Aug. 1824 in Industry, Maine, s/o Moses Little and Rachel (Hooper) Harris. David Hooper Harris m 20 Jul. 1818 Polly/Polly C. Davis of Martha's Vineyard, who m (2) James Dickinson and moved to Georgetown, Maine, d/o James and Betsy (Look) Davis. Children: **Betsy** b 10 Apr. 1819 in Industry, m Abisha Pease; and **Rachel** b 15 Jun. 1820, m Hartley Williams.

HARRIS, DEWITT CLINTON - Born 17 Sep. 1816, d in Buckfield, Maine, s/o Richard D. and Martha (Reace) Harris. Dewitt Clinton Harris m 3 Apr. 1842 Lucy Ann Whitney. Children: **Walter** b 28 Aug. 1854, d 2 Aug. 1855; and **Arthur** b 10 Sep. 1856, m 1 Jan. 1882 Sussi M. Simpson of Waterville, ME, d/o Ripley.

HARRIS, DENNIE - Born ??, d ??, s/o Silas and ?? Harris. Children: **Lillian M.** b 1 Aug. 1875; and **Chester** b 13 Sep. 1888.

HARRIS, DOWNER - Born ??, d ??, s/o ?? Children: **Anabelle** m Leonard Conley; **Ella** m Horace Bowden of Dear Isle, ME; **Frances H.** m Henry Rogers; and **Ella** m Cotton Bradbury.

HARRIS, FRANK E. - Born ??, d ??, s/o ?? Children: **Eva May** b 15 Jun. 1881; and **Ina E.** b 28 Sep. 1889.

HARRIS, GEORGE W. - Born 17 Dec. 1839, d ??, s/o Phillip and Elizabeth M. (Heath) Harris. George W. Harris m (1) 16 Jun. 1866 Augusta M. Graffam, d 2 Jan. 1882, and m (2) 27 Apr. 1884 Minnie M. Moody. Children: **Emma A.** b 25 Sep. 1876 in Salem, ME; **G. Harold** b 26 Jan. 1885 in Salem; **John B.** b 19/29 Apr. 1889 in Salem; and **Augusta M.** b 17 Sep. 1891 in Salem.

HARRIS, GEORGE WASHINGTON - Born 12 Dec. 1859 in Bradley, Maine, d ??, s/o Jairum/Jairus/Jaris and Olive (Hurd/Heard) Harris. George Washington Harris m 6 Jan 1880 Mrs. Marguerit A. (Chapman) Mace, b 6 Jul. 1853 in Colden, Sue Co., New York, d/o Joseph and Dorothy (Elemdone) Chapman. Child: **Seymore E. A.** b 24 Nov. 1884.

HARRIS, HENRY S. - Born ??, d ??, s/o Moses and ?? Harris. Children: **Matilda Jane/Metilda** b 12 Nov. 1830, m 19 May 1855 Josiah Owen of Wales, ME; **Thursey Emeline/Emerline** b 8 Sep. 1832, m Zebulon Shaw or Zebelor Sharon; and **Christana Rebecca** b 26 May 1838, d 17 May 1883.

HARRIS, JARIUM/JAIRUS/JARIS - Born 28 Jul. 1818, lived in Medford, Wisconsin, s/o Barron and ?? Harris. Jarium/Jairus/Jaris Harris m 22 Sep. 1839 Olive Hurd/Heard, b 1822, d 25 Apr. 1869. Children: **James B.** q.v.; **Samuel Franklin** q.v.; **Daniel Webster** q.v.; and **George Washington** q.v.

HARRIS, JAMES B. - Born 17 May 1840, d 23 Sep. 1880, s/o Jairum/Jairus/Jaris and Olive (Hurd/Heard) Harris. James B. Harris m 6 Feb. 1865 Etta H. Melvin, d/o Joseph P. and Nancy A. (Philbrook) Melvin. Children: **Nancy E.** b 26 Dec. 1866, d 30 Jan. 1882 in Wisconsin; **Gracie O.** b 4 Jan. 1869, d 1 Mar. 1884 in Wisconsin; **Nellie A.** b 1 Nov. 1870, d 28 Mar. 1875 in Stetson, Maine; **Stella M.** b 22 Jan. 1872, m 23 Aug. 1891 Fred B. Baker of Albion, Maine; **James A.** b 30 Mar. 1874, m -- Mar. 1898 Hattie Peasley; and **Jennie N.** b 31 Dec. 1879 in Wisconsin.

HARRIS, JEBEDIAH - Born 5 Jun. 1803, d ??, s/o John and Mary (Pettingill) Harris. Jebediah Harris m 1827 Mercy Pettingill. Children: **Emily** b 15 Aug. 1827; **Albion** b 29 Dec. 1828; and **Henry Wilder** b 5 Mar. 1833.

HARRIS, JOHN - Born 13 Aug. 1758, d 12 Sep. 1844, s/o ?? John Harris m Mary Pettingill, d 18 Jul. 1841, d/o David, Sr. Children: **Betsy** b 1 Dec. 1782, m David Millett; **John** b 16 Oct. 1784, d at sea; **David** b 12 Feb. 1787; **Mercy** b 24 May 1789, d 19 Jun. 1850, m Charles Cohen; **Polly** b 11 Mar. 1791, d 29 Jan. 1842, age 51 years, m John Pettingill; **Joseph** q.v.; and **Jebediah** q.v.

HARRIS, JOHN - Born 23 Jun. 1834, d 16 Nov. 1895 in Boston, Massachusetts, s/o David and Phebe/Phebe R. (Grows) Harris. John Harris m 11 Oct. 1859 Laura Jones/Jone of Turner, Maine, b 20 Oct. 1838, d 6 Jan. 1898 in Boston, d/o Tilden and Abigail Jones/Jone. Children: **Helen Gertrude** b 28 Jan. 1862 in Bath, ME, unm; **Walter L.** b 6 Aug. 1867 in Bath, ME, unm; **Mabel Marshall** b 4 Feb. 1871 in Bath, unm; and **Conie/Carrie Estelle** b 2 Sep. 1874 in Bath, d 21 Apr. 1886 in Boston.

HARRIS, JOHN - Born 16 Oct. 1784 in Greene, Maine, d 1814/1815 at sea, s/o ?? John Harris m Nancy Simmons of Waldoboro, Maine, b 3 May 1790, d 7 Feb. 1877 in Wales, Maine. Children: **David** q.v.; **John** d age 1 year; **John Llewellyn**; John Llewellyn m Hannah Key; **John** q.v.; and **Nancy** b 9 Jul. 1814 in Greene, d 1 Feb. 1864, m 27 Apr. 1834 Richard Skelton of Lewiston.

HARRIS, JOHN - Born 18 Feb. 1812 in Greene, Maine, d 10 Jan. 1887 in Greene, s/o John and Nancy (Simmons) Harris. John Harris m 4

Nov. 1837 Hannah L. Kelly of Greene, d 26 Sep. 1880 in Boston, Massachusetts. Children: **John Llewellyn** b 12 Aug. 1842, d 11 Dec. 1848; and **John Llewellyn** b 5 Jan. 1850 in Bath, Maine, m 6 Sep. 1871 Lizzie S. Higgins of Townsend, Vermont.

HARRIS, JOHN LLEWELLYN - Born ??, d ??, s/o John and Hannah L. (Kelly) Harris. Child: **Maud L.** b 22 Jan. 1874.

HARRIS, JOSEPH - Born 29 Mar. 1794, d ??, s/o John and Mary (Pettingill) Harris. Joseph Harris m Cynthia Record, d 14 Feb. 1863 age 64 years and 4 months. Children: **Sarah** b 10 Apr. 1821; **Joseph Record** q.v.; **Cynthia** b 15 Aug. 1825; **Mary** b 7 Mar. 1827; **David Stillman** b 12 Jan. 1835; **Lucinda Crompton** b 29 Oct. 1839; **John** b 23 Dec. 1832, d 23 Feb. 1836; and **Chloe B.** b -- Dec. 1844, d 2 Oct. 1844 (?).

HARRIS, JOSEPH RECORD - Born 8 Apr. 1823, d ??, s/o Joseph and Cynthia (Record) Harris. Joseph Record Harris m Mary B. ----, b 3 Feb. 1829. Child: **Lois Abba** b 30 Sep. 1848.

HARRIS, JOSIAH - Born 15 Sep. 1809 [Greene records] or 8 Dec. 1809, d 18 Jul. 1884, s/o Silas and Mercy (Haskell) Harris. Josiah Harris pub. 27 Jun. 1835, m 12 Jul. 1835 Julia Wright, d/o Zebula or Tebe. Children: **M a r c i a** b 9 Sep. 1835, d 1892, m Jefferson Elmes; **Dennis** b 12 Oct. 1838, m Sarah Reynolds, d/o Galen; **William Haskell** m 7 Jul. 1845 Susan Mower, d/o Calvin; **Josiah Waterman** b 23 Feb. 1848, m Susan Rogers; **Julia Marcia** b 14 Apr. 1850, m Samuel Jones of Canton, ME; and **Silas Haskell** b 9 Oct. 1852, unm.

HARRIS, LAWRENCE JACKSON - Born 3 Jun. 1703, d 1838, s/o Barron and ?? Harris. Lawrence Jackson Harris m (1) pub. -- Jan. 1739 Phebe Russell, and m (2) pub. 31 Oct. 1753 Lydia Barron, b 1 Jan. 1734, d 1 Jan. 1824, and m (3) 13 Nov. 1828 Lucy Washburn , b in Parkman, Maine, d/o James. *Children of 1st wife*: **Ruth** b 20 Jul. 1741, m ---- Sewett; **Molly** b 18 Mar. 1743, m pub. 14 Mar. 1767 David Wilkins; **Deborah** m 9 Feb. 1769 David Trull; **Betsy** b 11 Apr. 1746, m William Wilson; **M e r c y** b 23 Apr. 1752, m Abijah Fox; and **L a w r e n c e J.** b 31 Mar. 1749, d age 19 years. *Children of 2nd wife*: **L y d i a** b 4 Aug. 1754, d 30 Aug. 1830, m Peter Lenfest; **A b n e r** b 26 Apr. 1756, d 1811 in OH, m pub. 2 Mar. 1782 Mary Gerrish of Durham, ME; **J o h n** b 13 Aug. 1758, d 12 Sep. 1844 age 87 years, m Mary Pettingill, d/o David, Sr.; **Hannah** b 13 Sep. 1759, d 18 Mar. 1851, age 90 years, m (1) Thomas Piper, and m (2) Moses Town; **Maria** b 14 Mar. 1763, d 2 Jul. 1850, age 87 years 4 months, m William Garcelon; **Silas** b 15 Feb. 1768, d 13 Jul. 1844, m 17 Nov. 1791 Mercy Haskell of N. Gloucester, ME; **S a r a h** b 14 Feb. 1769, d 24 Oct. 1854, m (1) Thomas Mower of Greene, ME, and m (2) Jacob Eames, and m (3) Samuel Clark; **Rebecca**; **Moses Little** q.v.; and **Barron** q.v. *Children of 3rd wife*: **William**; **Wesley**; and **George**.

HARRIS, MOSES LITTLE - Born 4 Oct. 1802, d 30 Aug. 1839, s/o Moses Little and Rachel (Hooper) Harris. Moses Little Harris m

Joanna Coffin, b 22 Apr. 1806, d 28 Mar. 1882, d/o James of Greene, Maine. No children or possibly: **Rosine** b 4 Apr. 1836, m Amasa W. Seeler; and **Moses**.

HARRIS, CAPT. MOSES LITTLE - Born 25 Dec. 1770/1772, d 1 Dec. 1820 at Greene, Maine, [*American Advocate*, 16 Dec. 1820], age 48 years, "buried with Masonic honors" [*E. Argus* 12 Dec. 1820], s/o ?? Moses Little Harris was a Captain. He m 1793 Rachel Hooper, b 24 Jun. 1774, d 21 Nov. 1869. Children: **Rachel H.** b 24 Jun. 1794, d 16 Sep. 1867, m John R. Baker, who d 20 Aug. 1824; **David Hooper** q.v.; **Polly White** b 18 Jan. 1798, d 14 Oct. 1837, m Joseph Blake of N. Sharon, ME; **Rebecca** b 18 Feb. 1800, d 1 Nov. 1820, unm; **Moses Little** q.v.; **Sukey Hooper** b 20 May 1804, d 7 May 1889, m George Trumpton, who d 8 Aug. 1870; **Henry Story** b 16 Feb. 1807, d 16 Jul. 1884, m Jane Thompson, who d 25 Feb. 1878; **Anna Sprague** b 12 Apr. 1809, d 13 Apr. 1894, unm; **Lucinda** b 28 May 1811, d 11 Apr. 1833, m 15 May ---- Isaac Trumpton; **Andrew Jackson** q.v.; and **Bethial Jane** b 17 Sep. 1817, d 4 Aug. 1888, m David Cushing, who d 20 Aug. 1864.

HARRIS, NATHANIEL - Born 28 Dec. 1793, d 6 Nov. 1860, age 66 years, s/o Silas and Mercy (Haskell) Harris. Nathaniel Harris m pub. 29 Apr. 1838 Mrs. Jome (Curtis) Benson, b 31 Jan. 1801, d 8 Dec. 1850, or Electa ----, sis/o Curtis. Child: **Elvira Eclecta** b 10 Jul. 1839, m Josiah H. Mower of Greene, ME, d -- Oct. 1898 in Denver, CO, Civil War vet., having served in the 23d and 30th regiments.

HARRIS, NELSON P. - Born ??, d ??, s/o ?? Children: **Frank N.** b 13 Jul. 1870, m 15 Dec. 1894 Laura B. Hinkley; **Fred M.** b 22 Aug. 1877; **Charles B.** b 27 Oct. 1881; **Clinton D.** b 15 Nov. 1882; **Edith M.** b 5 Apr. 1885; and **Edna Bell** b 9 Jun. 1893.

HARRIS, ORISON - Born ??, d ??, s/o ?? Children: **Martha** b 12 Feb. 1831, m 11 May 1852 Jacob F. Hatch; **Mary Jane** b 13 May 1832, d 26 Jul. 1875, m 22 Apr. 1850 William Woods; **Rebecca P.** b 28 Oct. 1833, d 26 Apr. 1876, m 9 Apr. 1849 Joseph Knowles; **Phebe** b 28 Jan. 1842, m (1) 30 Aug. 1862 Charles W. Huff, who d 29 Jun. 1872, and m (2) 5 Jun. ---- John Burns; **Betsey F.** b 25 Nov. 1851, d 25 Apr. 1889, m Davis Ellis; **Orison James/James Orison** q.v.; and **Thomas R.** b 25 Feb. 1848, d 28 Mar. 1874.

HARRIS, ORISON JAMES/JAMES ORISON - Born 28 Mar. 1844 in Parkman, Maine, d ??, s/o Orison and ?? Harris. Orison James/James Orison Harris m 4 Sep. 1869 Armenda A. Clifford, b in Belgrade, Maine, d/o David A. and Hannah (Ginn) Clifford. Children: **Frank D.** b 4 Sep. 1870; **Addie A.** b 16 Jun. 1873, d 22 Jan. 1874; **Eddie O.** b 29 Jul. 1875; and **Robert R.** b 1 Oct. 1880.

HARRIS, PHILLIP - Born 12 Apr. 1810, d 3 Oct. 1882 in Salem, Maine, s/o Richard D. and Martha (Reace) Harris. Phillip Harris m 8 Aug. 1838 Elizabeth M. Heath of Salem, who was b 6 Mar. 1823. Children: **George W.** q.v.; **Eugene A.** b 25 Jan. 1842, m 22 Apr. 1871 Aphie S. Turner; **Nelson P.** b 10 May 1844, m 21 Apr. 1868 Rachael L.

Mayo, who was b 15 Mar. 1851 in Freeman, ME; **DeWitt C.** b 10 Feb. 1847, d 8 May 1847; **Emma S.** b 4 May 1848, d 25 Jan. 1862; **Martha B.** b 25 Dec. 1850, m 12 Apr. 1868 Walter S. Heath of Salem, ME, b 5 Sep. 1840; **Marshall E.** b 20 May 1853, d 1 Apr. 1855; **Frank E.** b 18 Oct. 1856, m 23 Nov. 1879 Olive M. Hinds, who was b 2 Nov. 1853 in Kingfield, ME; **Horace E.** b 10 Mar. 1859, unm; **Lizzie E.** b 1 Nov. 1861, m 22 Dec. 1880 Frank S. Smith of Salem, b 24 Jul. 1856 in Eustus, ME; **Addie E.** b 6 Jun. 1864, m William J. Marshall, who was b 27 Jul. 1856 in VT; and **Carrie E.** b 11 Oct. 1867, m 23 Dec. 1889 Harry Harrison, b 13 Apr. 1863 in Calcutta, India.

HARRIS, RICHARD D. - Born in Albany, New York, d ??, s/o ?? Richard D. Harris m 8 May 1808 Martha Reace, d 12 Sep. 1840. Children: **Phillip** q.v.; **Deborah** b 9 Nov. 1812 (family record 2 Nov.), d -- Feb. 1813; **Samuel R.** b 24 Apr. 1814, d 18 Jun. 1864 in New Orleans during war, m Jane P. Dodge, who d 17 Apr. 1871; **DeWitt Clinton** q.v.; **Louisa R.** b 7 Nov. 1819 in Weld, d 6 Aug. 1822; **Richard D.** b 29 Aug. 1822, m (1) Julia Greenleaf of VT, and m (2) Hannah Dolly of Gray, ME; and **Cynthia S.** b -- Feb. 1825, m Charles H. Berry.

HARRIS, ROSWELL C. - Born ??, d ??, s/o David and Phebe (Grows) harris. Roswell C. Harris m Emma Woodside, d/o Stinson and Eleanor (Conly) Woodside. Children: **Fred Clark** b 11 Aug. 1864, m 1892 Ella Minchin; **Sherman**; **Roswell G.** b 1 May 1868; and **Herbert P.** b 8 Apr. 1874, unm.

HARRIS, SAMUEL FRANKLIN - Born 28 Apr. 1843 in Parkman, Maine, d ??, s/o Jairum/Jairus/Jaris and Olive (Hurd/Heard) Harris. Children: **Frederic Linwood** b 9 May 1873 in Omro, WI; **Mary Olive** b 1 Aug. 1878 in Oshkosh, WI; **Lanora Mabel** b 1 Nov. 1880 in Oshkosh, WI; **Joseph Byron** b 19 Mar. 1883 in Medford, WI; **Clara Purl** b 25 Sep. 1884 in Medford, WI; **Lottie Ada** b 23 Mar. 1888 in Medford, WI; and **Irven Franklin** b 30 Dec. 1890 in Medford, WI.

HARRIS, SAMUEL R. - Born ??, d ??, s/o ?? Children: **Cynthia J.** b 24 Feb. 1843, m 8 Dec. 1866 John Milton Atkinson; **Charles**; and **Eda** b 16 Sep. 1858, m 15 Mar. 1880 George T. Sanborn.

HARRIS, SILAS - Born 15 Feb. 1766, d 13 Jul. 1844, s/o ?? Silas Harris m 17 Nov. 1791 Mercy Haskell of New Gloucester, Maine, b 15 Dec. 1771, d 21 Jun. 1847. Children: **Deborah** b 4 Sep. 1792, m pub. 14 Sep. 1814 William Cummings; **Nathaniel** q.v.; **Silas** b 28 Sep. 1795, d 21 Dec. 1819, unm; **Clarina** b 18 Jun. 1797, m Phinneas Cohen; **Anna** b 14 Mar. 1799, m Nathan Smith; **Paulina** b 2 Apr. 1801, m William Haskell of Falmouth, ME; **William** q.v.; **Aratis/Aratus** q.v.; **Josiah** q.v.; **Mercy** b 2 Mar. 1812, m Rufus Brown; and **Mehitable** b 10 Sep. ----, m Silas Niles of Jay, ME.

HARRIS, THOMAS - Born ??, d ??, s/o David and ?? Harris. Children: **Emma** b 1858; **Winfield**; **Anna**; and **Nellie**.

HARRIS, THOMAS - Born 6 Apr. 1809, d 15 Nov. 1880, s/o Barron and ?? Harris. Thomas Harris m pub. 24/29 May 1834 Polly Packard, b 9 Feb. 1806 in Minot, Maine. Children: **Hiram P.** b 16 Aug. 1838, d 6 Nov. 1860, unm; **Sarah J.** b 20 Feb. 1838, d 29 Aug. 1890, m Haris Hamilton; and **Thomas Jefferson** q.v.

HARRIS, THOMAS JEFFERSON - Born 6 Feb. 1842, d ??, s/o Thomas and Polly (Packard) Harris. Thomas Jefferson Harris m 19 Oct. 1868 Lizzie Allen, b 29 Aug. 1844 in Parkman, Maine, d/o S---- and Mary (Harlow) Allen. Children: **H a r r y** b 7 Dec. 1869, unm; and **Eugene L.** b 4 Oct. 1878.

HARRIS, WILLIAM - Born 24 Sep. 1843, d ??, s/o Aratis/Aratus and ?? Harris. William Harris m Mary Frances Hewens. Child: **L i l l i an** May b 25 Aug. 1868, m 14 Jun. 1899 John L. Reade.

HARRIS, WILLIAM - Born 23 Jul. 1805, d 10 Sep. 1843, age 38 years, s/o Silas and Mercy (Haskell) Harris. William Harris m Wealthy True of Poland, Maine, b 26 Jun. 1811, d 3 May 1878. Children: **William Henry** b 3 Jul. 1838; **Charles Edwin** b 6 Sep. 1840; and **Silas** b 3 Jun. 1843.

HARRIS, ZELOTES - Born 15 Jun. 1801, d ??, s/o Barron and ?? Harris. Zelotes Harris m (1) 17 Dec. 1820 Desdemonia/Desdemona Tyler, who d 25 Jan. 1835, d/o Joseph, and m (2) Angeline Lane. Children: **Esther** b 31 May 1821, unm; **Pauline** b 2 Apr. 1823, d 12 Aug. 1856, m James Baine; **Louisa Haskell** b 26 Jan. 1825, m ---- Robinson; **Deborah R.** b 26 Nov. 1827, m Levi Packard; **Mary** b 11 Feb. 1830, d 13 Feb. 1854, m Alexander Whittemore; **Sullivan** b 18 Mar. 1832; and **Desdemona** b 1 Jun. 1834, d 6 Dec. 1834.

HART, STEPHEN - Born ??, d ??, s/o ?? Stephen Hart m Polly ----. Children: **Josiah** b 6 Mar. 1804; **William** b 5 Nov. 1805; **Jacob** b 25 Apr. 1807; **T h o m a s** b 23 Jul. 1809, had home built by Nevens brothers in 1838, Lewiston, ME [Neven's diary]; **Betty** b 3 Aug. 1811; **Samuel** b 20 Jun. (?) 1813; and **Jacob** b 7 Jun. 1815.

HASKELL, SUSANNA - Born 1757 at Cape Ann, Massachusetts, d 1838 in New Gloucester, Maine.

HEART, STEPHEN - Born ??, d ??, s/o ?? Stephen Heart m Betsey ----. Children: **Jenne** b 29 Jan. 1768; **Susanna** b 18 Jan. 1770; **Stephen** b 18 Feb. 1772; **Mary** b 15 May 1776; and **Cate** b 11 Apr. 1780.

HATCH, ELIHU - Born 1783, d 1874 and buried in Mt. Auburn Cem., Auburn, Maine, s/o Samuel and Hannah (Landers) Hatch, bro/o Samuel Hatch. Elihu Hatch m (1) 19 May 1805 Hannah Chamberlain, and m (2) Nancy Chamberlain, d 26 Nov. 1821. Children: **William** b 12 May 1806, d 27 Mar. 1876 in Oxford, ME, m (1) Lydia Lake, and m (2) Martha Gallemy of Bowdoin, ME, d 5 Feb. 1873; **R u t h** b 7 Mar. 1809, unm; **Samuel** q.v.; **Rebecca** b 16 Sep. 1813, m Charles Granger; **Gil-**

bert b 7 Dec. 1815, m 16 Jun. 1844 Julia Elkins, d/o Chase Elkins of Fayette, Maine; **Hannah** b 21 Jul. 1818, m 3 Dec. 1846 Henry Proctor of Lisbon, ME; and **Thomas** b 2 Apr. 1821, d in the Army, m (1) Nancy B. Sinclair, and m (2) Deborah Clark Howe.

HATCH, ELIHU - Born 1753 in Falmouth, Maine [*Soldiers, Sailors, and Patriots of the Revolutionary War* by Carleton E. Fisher, published by N. Sons of American Revolution, 1982, p. 351], d 14 May 1837, s/o ??, bro/o Samuel Hatch. Elihu Hatch was a Revolutionary soldier. He m Sarah Landers, b 3 Aug. 1759, d 9 Jan. 1839, d/o Freeman and Thankful (Hinckley) Landers. [Letter from Miss R. J. Allen of Skowhegan, Maine, 1902.]

HATCH, FREEMAN - Born 19 May 1800, d 28 Feb./7 Mar. 1873 age 72 years and 9 months, s/o John and ?? Hatch. Freeman Hatch m Charity Jackson, d 1 May 1892, d/o Lemuel. Children: **Isaac G.** b 5 Mar. 1834, m 23 Dec. 1860 Martha D. Montford; **Elizabeth A.** b 14 Aug. 1836; **Freeman Allen** q.v.; **Sarah B.** b 8 Dec. 1839, d 23 Aug. 1853, age 12 years 8 months; and **John L.** b -- Apr. 1848, d 20 Aug. 1852, age 4 years 4 months.

HATCH, FREEMAN ALLEN - Born 7 Jun. 1834, d 22 Aug. 1888, s/o Freeman and Charity (Jackson) Hatch. Freeman Allen Hatch m 1 Jan. 1873 Clarella Bucknam, d/o William and Eleanor (----) Bucknam of Lisbon, Maine. Children: **Lester Allen** b 11 May 1874, no children; **Lizzie L.** b 31 Aug. 1878, m (1) Fred Wapp, and m (2) William Frederick.

HATCH, GILBERT C. - Born 23 Dec. 1816 in Lewiston, d 21 Sep. 1900 age 83 years 8 months 28 days, s/o Elihu and Hannah (----) Hatch. Gilbert C. Hatch m Julia Elkins, d 14 Apr. 1906 age 87 years. Children: **Aldna C.** b 20 Apr. 1848, m -- Jun. 1870 John G. Roberts; **Gilbert Eldon** b 5 Oct. 1853, d 1 Oct. 1875; and **Marcia M.** b 18 Nov. 1855, d 8 Jan. 1861. [Mt. Auburn Cem., Auburn, Maine.]

HATCH, JOHN - Born 6 Mar. 1772 in Scitaute, Massachusetts, d 5 Jul. 1862 in Lewiston, s/o ?? John Hatch m Abigail (Turner) [*History of Durham, Maine* by Everett Stackpole, published by the Town of Durham, ME, 1899, p. 199]. Children: **Deborah** b 15 Dec. 1794; **John** b 15 Dec. 1796, d 25 Dec. 1796; **John** q.v.; **Freeman** q.v.; **Elisha** b 3 Sep. 1802, d 2 May 1817; **Abigail** b 11 Nov. 1805, m 14 Apr. 1822 Benjamin Carville; **Mary** b 4 May 1807; **True Glidden** q.v.; **Rosilla** b 28 Jan. 1814, m (1) pub. 4 Mar. 1834 Stillman Morse of Bath, ME, d 22 Aug. 1854, and m (2) 28 Jun. 1857 Enoch Littlefield of Auburn, ME; and **Eliza** b 25 Aug. 1816, m Joseph Gould.

HATCH, JOHN - Born 31 Jul. 1798, d ??, s/o John and Abiagil (Turner) Hatch. John Hatch m 9 Sep. 1821 Sarah Pettingill, d/o Nathaniel. Children: **Charles**; **John**; **Warren**; **Mansfield**; **Elminee** m James Hodgkins; **Mary Hamm**; **Nathaniel**; **Melvin**; and **Sophronia**.

HATCH, SAMUEL - Born 21 Apr. 1811, d ??, s/o Elihu and Nancy (Chamberlain) Hatch. Samuel Hatch m Sally Littlefield of Minot, Maine. Children: **Ruth** b 21 Feb. 1837; and **Alfred** b 5 Feb. 1840.

HATCH, SAMUEL - Born ??, d 4 Mar. 1841, age 84 years, s/o ?? Samuel Hatch m Hannah Lander, d/o Freeman and Thankful (Hinckley) Lander. Children: **P r u d e n c e** b 11 Dec. 1777, d 15 Dec. 1777; **P r u d e n c e** b 9 Mar. 1779, d 7 Feb. 1855, age 75 years 10 months 18 days, m pub. 10 Mar. 1798 William Ray of Minot, ME, d 5 Feb. 1855; **Fear** b 29 Mar. 1781, m 25 Mar. 1802 Thomas Ray of Minot; **Elihu** b 22 Apr. 1783, d 15 Sep. 1874, m 19 May 1805 Hannah Chamberlan, who d -- Sep. 1816; **S a r a h** b 12 Nov. 1785, m 27 Nov. 1806 Elkanah Dyer; **Ruth** b 7 May 1788, m James Merrill of Minot; **Molly** b 3 Aug. 1791, d 1 Sep. 1871 in Brunswick, m 26 Mar. 1812 Phineas Taylor of Brunswick, ME, d 4 Nov. 1855; **Samuel** b 12 Jul. 1793, unm, drowned when young; **O b e d** b 15 Oct. 1795, d 30 Oct. 1795; **H a n n a h** b 9 May 1797, d 14 Aug. 1798; and **H a n n a h** m 30 Sep. 1824 Simon Haskell of Minot.

HATCH, THOMAS - Born ??, d ??, s/o ?? Children: **Charles**; **Henry**; and **Eliza**.

HATCH, TRUE GLIDDEN - Born 25 Jul. 1810, d ??, s/o John, Sr. and ?? Hatch. True Glidden Hatch m 25 Oct. 1832 Eliza Farrow. Child: **True** b 26 Jun. 1838.

HATCH, WILLIAM - Born ??, d ??, s/o ?? Children: **Susan** b 8 Apr. 1822, d 2 Jun. 1862, unm; **M a r y A.** b 15 Dec. 1831, m 1 Jan. 1855 Lewis E. Strout; **Samuel O.** b 5 Mar. 1834, killed at Gettysburg, m Elvira Walker; **Dorcas C.** b 21 Aug. 1836, m -- Feb. 1856 Leonard White; **Lydia E.** b 4 May 1838, m 31 Dec. 1855 Jonas W. Strout; and **Louisia J.** b 6 Dec. 1842, m -- May ---- Joseph Bonney.

HAYES/HAYS, DAVID - Born 18 Nov. 1755, d 30 Aug. 1793, s/o John, Sr. and Judith (Moulton) Hayes/Hays. David Hayes m (1) 9 Sep. 1779 Dorcas Allen of New Gloucester, Maine, b 13 Nov. 1755, d -- Dec. 1784, and m (2) Lydia Eales/Edes, who later m Isaac Skillins. *Children by 1st wife*: **Joseph** b 22 Jul. 1780; **John** b 22 Nov. 1781, m wid Rachael (Griffin) Loring; and **William Allen** b 20 Oct. 1783, m 2 Jun. 1811 Susan Lord of South Berwick, ME.

HAYES/HAYS, JACOB - Born 5 Aug. 1757, d 21 Dec. 1848, s/o John, Sr. and Jane (Loring) [Mitchell] Hayes/Hays. Jacob Hayes/Hays m Jane Gray. Children: **Andrew** m (1) Betsey Drinkwater, and m (2) Lucy Loring, and m (3) Eliza Kelley; **Jacob Jr.** q.v.; **Sarah** m Joseph Clark; **Dorcas** m Rev. John Dutton; **Jane** m Jacob Loring; **Reuben** m 3 Feb. 1820 Hannah Prince; **John** m -- Oct. 1825 Sarah Porter; **David** b -- Jul. 1795, m -- Sep. 1826 Nancy Webb, res. at Westbrook, ME; **Rachael** m John Marston; and **Levi** m Emma Herrick. [Rev. Greeley's records of North Yarmouth, Maine, families, manuscript at Androscoggin Historical, Auburn, Maine, no page number and *John Hayes of*

Dover, NH compiled and published by Katherine F. Richmond, 1936, p. 240, 241.]

HAYES/HAYS, JACOB JR. - Born 17 Apr. 1785, d 7 Dec. 1848, s/o Jacob and Jane (Gray) Hayes/Hays. Jacob Hayes/Hays, Jr. m 16 Oct. 1808 Eleanor Skillan, b 15 Aug. 1789 in North Yarmouth, Maine, d 8 Nov. 1861. Children: **Samuel Skillan** b 6 Aug. 1809, d 29 Jan. 1884, m 10 Oct. 1833 Mary Richmond; **Lydia Skillan** b 14 Feb. 1812, d 5 Jul. 1836; **E d w a r d E e l l s** b 5 Nov. 1814, d 25 Feb. 1867, m 3 Dec. 1846 Sylvina Turner; **Isaac Skillan** b 28 Apr. 1817, d 11 Nov. 1865, m -- Oct. 1843 Aseneth Batchedler; **Jane Gray** b 20 Dec. 1819, d 24 Nov. 1870, m 4 May 1848 David M. Loring; **W i l l i a m** b 9 Oct. 1822, d 13 Oct. 1822; **Eleanor** b 27 Apr. 1826, d 28 Jul. 1856, m 4 Jul. 1854 Charles Mitchell; **Jacob 3rd** b 27 Apr. 1826, d 27 Apr. 1826; and **Achsah Fields** b 29 Dec. 1828, m 21 Oct. 1847 Edward Batchelder.

HAYES/HAYS, JOHN - Came from Dover, New Hampshire, c1750, d 19 Mar. 1793, s/o ?? John Hayes/Hays m (1) Jane Moulton, d 24 Nov. 1755, and m (2) Judith/Jane Loring, d 24 Aug. 1812, wid/o Jacob Mitchell. *Child of 1st wife:* **David** b 13/18 Nov. 1755, d 30 Aug. 1793, m 9 Sep. 1779 Dorcas Allen. *Children of 2nd wife:* **J a c o b** b 5 Aug. 1757; **Reuben** b 1759; **Sarah** b 28 Mar. 1762; **Elisabeth** b 17 Mar. 1764; **Levi** b 14 Oct. 1765; **Jane** b 5 Jul. 1767; **John** b 1 Jul. 1770, m Jane ----, wid/o Wm. Myrick; and **H u l d a** b 17 Aug. 1772, d 12 Oct. 1794. [Greeley's records of North Yarmouth, ME, families, manuscript at Androscoggin Historical, Auburn, Maine, no page number.]

HAYES/HAYS, JOHN - Born 1 Jul. 1770, d 27 Dec. 1841, s/o John and Jane (Gray) Hayes/Hays. John Hayes/Hays m Jane Myrick. Children: **H u l d a** b 1794, d 1 Oct. 1815; **E l i s a** m Samuel Soule; **Penelope** m Rev. George R. Giddings; **William** q.v.; **Sarah** m David P. Loring; **Rachael** m Samuel Burrell; **Jane** m Elijah Hayes of S. Berwick, ME; and **Hannah** m Rev. Dudley P. Bailey.

HAYES/HAYS, WILLIAM* - Born 2 Apr. 1802, d 8 Aug. 1868, s/o John and Jane (Gray) Hayes/Hays. William Hayes/Hays m 1835 Hannah Patterson Boynton/Boyington of Wiscasset, Maine, b 19 Dec. 1808. Children: **Mary Hannah** b 3 Jan. 1836, m -- Jan. 1853 Luther Jones; **Harriet Adams*** b 24 Oct. 1837, m 16 Aug. 1859 Melville Sawyer; **John*** b 20 Feb. 1840, d 8 Oct. 1862; **Caroline Elisabeth*** b 22 Apr. 1843, m 8 Sep. 1880 William E. Worthen of Amesbury, MA; **Susan Boynton*** b 17 Dec. 1844, m 23 Aug. 1871 Amos Hadley; **William, Jr.*** b 11 Oct. 1846, m 28 May 1876 Anna Ham; **Richmond Bradford*** b 20 Jun. 1849, m 13 Jul. 1886 Nellie Fairbanks of Auburn, ME; and **Ellen Cornelia** b 24 Dec. 1851, m 11 Jul. 1879 Frank C. Skinner. [* indicates those names listed in the 1850 census #81, Danville, ME. Letter from Wm. Hayes of Barker Mill, Auburn, ME, 26 Jan. 1893.]

HERRICK, ANSON - Born 21 Jan. 1812 in Lewiston, d 6 Feb. 1868 in New York, s/o Ebenezer and Hannah (Molloy) Herrick. Anson Herrick moved to New York City in 1836; was editor of *New York Attus*. He m

Lydia Wood of Wiscassett, Maine. Children: **Mary Wood; Moses Carlton** b 1836; and **Anson** b 1838.

HERRICK, BENJAMIN - Born 12 Aug. 1799, d ??, s/o Howard and Elizabeth (Richardson) Herrick. Benjamin Herrick m Sarah Keizer. Children: **Francis H.** b 4 Apr. 1827, d 26 Jun. 1874, unm; **Mary** b 15 Sep. 1829, m Asa Works; **Catherine Maria** b 2 Aug. 1831, m George Dawson; **Cordelia Ann** b 5 Aug. 1833, m Myrick Louse; **Charles I.** b 12 Jun. 1835, m Mary Spaulding; **John** b 8 Apr. 1837, m Abbie Spaulding; **Armanda** b 4 Jul. 1839, m 3 Feb. 1867 Hiram T. Brooks; **Ira** b 4 Jul. 1839, d 4 Jul. 1839; and **Sarah Augusta** b 14 Apr. 1843, m Joseph ----.

HERRICK, EBENEZER - Born 21 Oct. 1785, d 7 May 1839 in Lewiston, s/o ?? Ebenezer Herrick was of New Jersey [letter from H. M. Herrick of the *Hackensack Republican*]. He m 20 May 1810 Hannah Molloy of Litchfield, Maine, d/o Hugh. Children: **John** b 5 Aug. 1819, d 6 Dec. 1830; **Anson** q.v.; **Mary Gone** b 25 Jan. 1814, d 24 May 1880, m 8 Jan. 1833 John T. Blaisdell at Yellow Springs, OH; **James Lawrence** b 14 Jun. 1815, d 1838 in NY, unm; **Elvira P.** b 25 Oct. 1816, d 1850 in OH, teacher, unm; **Laura** b 1 May 1819, m George Ogden of Jersey City, NJ; and **Hugh Molloy** b 3 Jul. 1829.

HERRICK, HOWARD - Born ??, d 5 May 1857 at Rumford Falls, Maine, age 33 years.

HERRICK, HOWARD - Born ??, d ??, s/o ?? Howard Herrick m Elizabeth Richardson. Children: **Benjamin** q.v.; **Moses** b 15 Mar. 1801, d 20 Jan. 1840, unm; **Israel** b 20 Jul. 1807, d 30 Nov. 1847, m Mary Ford; **Charles** b 15 Oct. 1813, unm; **Hannah** b -- Mar. 1803, m Otis Corbett; **Obediah** b 20 May 1811; **Jonas** b 10 Nov. 1815, m Nancy Ford; **Eliza**; **Rachel** b 10 Nov. 1817, d 26 Jul. 1860, m John Perly; and **Lydia** b 6 Aug. 1819, m James Snowdown.

HERRICK, HUGH - Born ??, d ??, s/o Ebenezer and ?? Herrick of Lewiston. Hugh Herrick m 9 Aug. 1853 Louise M. Tremper, d/o Johnson and Laura A. Tremper of New Rich, OH. Children: **Alna Elvira** b 15 Jul. 1854; **Mary** b 11 Sep. 1856; **Richard C.**; and **Carlton Tremper** b 6 Jul. 1867, m 7 Sep. 1882 Mattie Kenyon, d/o John.

HERRICK, ISRAEL - Born 3 Dec. 1721, d 14 Sep. 1782, s/o ?? Israel Herrick m (1) Mary Bragg, and m (2) 1749 Abigail Kilham of Boxford, Massachusetts, b 30 Nov. 1725, d 8 Feb. 1817. *Children of 1st wife*: **Joseph** b 21 Sep. 1746, d -- Sep. 1748; and **Israel** b 27 Dec. 1747, d in the Army. *Children of 2nd wife*: **Joseph** b 14 Sep. 1750, d 17 Sep. 1820, m -- Oct. 1775 Mercie Preston of Wilmington; **John** b 9 Jul. 1752, d 27 Mar. 1834, m 14 Mar. 1780 Lydia Graffem of Falmouth, ME, b 2 Mar. 1752; **Elizabeth** b 19 Aug. 1754, d 20 Mar. 1834, m Tobias Ham; **Mary** b 24 Feb. 1756, m Eliphalet Booker of Wales, ME; **Eli** b 5 Sep. 1759, d 1813, m Hannah Thompson; **Samuel** b 5 Sep. 1759, d 5 Sep. 1834, m Abigail House of Turner, ME; and **Abigail** b 12

Oct. 1761, m (1) Thomas Smith of Topsham, Maine, and m (2) ----
Child of Livermore, ME.

HERRICK, JOHN - Born 23 Jul. 1816, d 9 Jul. 1856, s/o Col. Oliver and Lydia (Thompson) Herrick. John Herrick m 21 Oct. 1840 Maria Little, d/o Thomas B. Little. Children: **Maria Augusta** b 1 Aug. 1841, d 7 Aug. 1870, m 25 Aug. 1864 John S. Adams, d 7 Aug. 1870, s/o Rev. Aaron C.; **Lydia Thompson** b 10 Feb. 1845, m 7 Dec. 1870 Lester Dwinal, s/o Amos of Bangor, ME; **Eunice Thrasher** b 21 Mar. 1849, d 9 Sep. 1865; and **John Little** b 3 Jan. 1854, d 23 Mar. 1855.

HERRICK, JOHN - Born 9 Jul. 1752, d 27 Mar. 1834, s/o ?? Children: **Molly** b 23 Dec. 1780, m 1804 Elijah Gove of Monmouth, Maine; **Oliver** q.v.; **Ebenezer** q.v.; and **Lydia** b 3 Oct. 1790, unm. [Vital Records of Lewiston, Maine, p. 31.]

HERRICK, JOSEPH - Born ??, d 17 Sep. 1820, s/o ?? Joseph Herrick m 1775 Mercie Preston of Wilmington, Massachusetts, d 15 Aug. 1822. Children: **Elizabeth** b 16 Jul. 1776 in New Gloucester, Maine, m 18 Mar. 1801 Caleb Bates of Greene; **Joseph** b 23 Dec. 1777 in Lewiston, m 12 Mar. 1799 Anna Larrabee of Greene, ME; **Jedediah** b 7 Jan. 1780 in Lewiston, m 8 Feb. 1802 Mehitable Thompson of Lewiston, who d 22 Mar. 1839, d/o Joel Thompson; **Nathaniel** b 26 Jul. 1781, m -- Oct. 1804 Susanna Dwinal of Lisbon, ME, d/o Aaron; **Seth** b 12 Mar. 1783, d 6 Jan. 1818 in Cincinatti, OH, m 7 Oct. 1804 Ruth Sprague of Greene, who d 30 Dec. 1835, d/o Col. William; **Samuel** b 11 Dec. 1784, d 4 Jul. 1822 of yellow fever, m -- Oct. 1807 Catherine Molly; and **Henry** b 11 Apr. 1789, d 23 Jul. 1816 (1826 according to Greene Records), m 2 Jan. 1812 Martha C. Thompson, d/o Col. Joel.

HERRICK, COL. OLIVER - Born 29 Jul. 1782, d 4 Jul. 1852, s/o John and ?? Herrick. Col. Oliver Herrick m 24 Dec. 1809 Lydia Thompson of Lisbon, Maine, d 16 Mar. 1830, age 47 years, d/o Ezekiel. Children: **Ezekiel T.** b 13 Jan. 1811, m Mary Anna; **Elvira** b 4 May 1813; **Hannah** b 25 May 1815, m Phillip A. Briggs of Auburn, ME; **John** b 23 Jul. 1816, d 9 Jul. 1856, m -- Oct. 1840 Maria Little, d/o Thomas B.; **Oliver** b 15 Sep. 1821, d 18 Nov. 1878 at Togus, ME, was member of 10th Maine A. H., m Sarah Piper, d/o Thomas; and **Martha** d 1819.

HEWEY, SAMUEL - Born ??, d ??, s/o ??, bro/o William Hewey who was killed in Grand Trunk Railroad 1850. Samuel Hewey went west in fall of 1855. He m Betsy Potter [vital records of Lewiston, Maine, p. 402 shows her name as Betsey Vottar] of Wales, Maine. Children: **Margaret** b 28 Feb. 1822, m James Pinkham of Lisbon and Bucksport, ME; **William F.** b 15 Jul. 1827; **Arvesta** b 7 Oct. 1830, d 11 Jun. 1884, m Israel Herrick; **Emily** b 5 Apr. 1835, m Edward McLean, res. Albany, NY; and **Louisa** res. Ottawa, KS, m Aaron Haskell. [Letter from Margaret (Hewey) Pinkham dated 14 Jun. 1895, of Newtonville, MA.]

HIGGINS, CHARLES J. - Born ??, d ??, s/o ?? Children: **Henry G.** b 20 Feb. 1869; **Charles H.** b 18 Nov. 1871; and **Dwight** b 24 Dec. 1876.

HIGGINS, JESSE - Born ??, d 20 Mar. 1825, s/o ?? Jesse Higgins m (1) Tamah ----, and m (2) pub. 25 Sep. 1796 Jerrisha Wilkins, d 15 Jan. 1824. *Children of 1st wife*: **Mercy** b 1 Dec. 1789, d 10 Mar. 1870, m 2 Feb. 1814 Isaac Sprague of Greene, ME, d 8 Dec. 1863; **Priscilla** b -- Mar. 1792, d 25 Jul. 1854, m 2 Mar. 1815 John Carville, d 6 Sep. ----; and **Sally** b 12 May 1794, m 5 Jul. 1812 Aaron Bickford, d 6 Apr. 1863. *Children of 2nd wife*: **Tamah** b 13 Oct. 1797, d 19 Nov. 1884, m pub. 28 Mar. 1818 Sewall Carville, d 8 Jun. 1879; **Capt. Jesse** q.v.; **Mary** b 25 Jan. 1802, d 14 Jul. 1840, m Eben Swett of Wales, ME; and **Mitty** b 5 Nov. 1803, d 5 Feb. 1847, m Charles Swett of Wales.

HIGGINS, CAPT. JESSE - Born 11/13 Oct. 1797/1799 in Lewiston, d 11 Sep. 1863 in Farmingdale, Maine, or 19 Nov. 1884, s/o Jesse and Jerrisha (Wilkins) Higgins. Capt. Jesse Higgins m 15 Sep. 1820 Mary M. Hinkley, d 24 Mar. 1861, d/o James and Joanna (Norcross) Hinkley of Hallowell, Maine. Children: **Louisa M.** b 23 Mar. 1824, m 7 Aug. 1840 George H. Adams; **Henry H.** b 23 Mar. 1824, d 26 Mar. 1860; **Ann J.** b 31 Mar. 1828, m 3 May 1853 Caleb C. Burgess, who d 16 Dec. 1895; **Mary Elizabeth** b 18 Mar. 1830, d 14 Sep. 1858, m -- Oct. 1855 George H. Adams; **George Boardman** b 1832 (?), d 1833 [at Monmouth, ME according to the obit in the *Morning Star* and the *Death Notices From Freewill Baptist* compiled by Young and Taylor, published by Heritage Books, Inc., 1985, p. 166]; **James William** b 26 Jan. 1832; **Kathaleen A.** b 4 Feb. 1844; **Charles Jesse** b 20 Jan. 184-, m 4 May 1864 Sarah Rice, d/o Alden and Susan Rice. [Letter from Mrs. Burgess of Indianapolis, IN, Sep. 1896.]

HILDRETH, BENJAMIN SEWELL - Born 16 Jun. 1825, d ??, s/o Michael and Patience (Knox) Hildreth. Benjamin Sewell Hildreth m 6 Dec. 1867 Mrs. Mary F. Peacock. Children: **Eugene** b 16 Apr. 1868; **Edna**; **Richard W.** b 6 Feb. 1873; and **Julia E.** b 28 Nov. 1877.

HILDRETH, CHARLES A. - Born 22 Nov. 1844, d 15 May 1874, s/o Thaddeus and Sarah (Knox) Hildreth. Charles A. Hildreth m Cascelia E. Stilphen. Children: **Arthur E.** b 3 Jan. 1869, d 1878; and **Lillian B.** b 23 Jan. 1871.

HILDRETH, CHARLES S. - Born 15 Sep. 1823, d 3 Dec. 1887, s/o Daniel and Elmira (Smith) Hildreth. Charles S. Hildreth m (1) 3 Dec. 1847 Jane Woodcock, and m (2) 16 Oct. 1865 Annie/Anna F. Lennan. Children: **Ella M.** b 6 Aug. 1848, d 8 Mar. 1853; **Edward E.** b 1 Jul. 1853, d 14 Mar. 1857; **Franklin A.** b 24 Oct. 1854, d 30 Sep. 1856; **William A.** b 17 Apr. 1857, d 21 Aug. 1857; and **John D.** b 19 Nov. 1861, d 21 Aug. 186-.

HILDRETH, DANIEL - Born 1 Apr. 1801, d 21 Feb. 1875?, s/o David and Esther (Moody) Hildreth. Daniel Hildreth m 1822 Elmira Smith, b 21 Dec. 1802, d 22 Feb. 1859. Children: **Charles S.** q.v.; **Mary E.** b 26 Mar. 1825, d 5 Aug. 1850, unm; **Esther A.** b 15 Aug. 1827, d 31

Aug. 1850, m pub. 24 Feb. 1849 David Fuller; **Amasa S.** b 7 Nov. 1829, unm; **Susan J.** b 15 Jul. 1832, d 9 Aug. 1851, unm; **Emerline J.** b 9 Nov. 1834, m 21 Aug. 1862 Llewllyn Lennan; **Horace W.** b 28 Mar. 1837; **Augustine** b 14 May 1839, d 24 Nov. 1850; and **Ellen L.** b 30 Nov. 1841.

HILDRETH, DAVID - Born 9 Nov. 1770, d 12 Jul. 1848, s/o Paul and Hannah (Merrill) Hildreth. David Hildreth m 22 Apr. 1792 Esther Moody, b 16 May 1770. Children: **William** b 12 Dec. 1792, m pub. 25 Jan. 1811 Margaret Thompson of Industry, ME; **David** q.v.; **Nancy** b 19 Jan. 1797, d 7 Jun. 1822, m -- Sep. 1817 Ebeneser Swift; **Michael** q.v.; **Daniel** q.v.; **Esther** b 22 Jan. 1803, d 19 Oct. 1853, m 20 Jun. 1822 Joseph C. Syphens, who d 5 Oct. 1885; **Thaddeus** q.v.; **Love**; **Hiram** q.v.; and **Henry** q.v.

HILDRETH, DAVID - Born 12 Sep. 1794, d ??, s/o David and Esther (Moody) Hildreth. David Hildreth m (1) -- Jan. 1814 Mary Hammond of Industry, Maine, and m (2) 3 Jul. 1836 Martha Grant, b 10 Apr. 1802, d 27 Oct. 1873. *Children of 1st wife*: **Harriet** b 10 Apr. 1805 in Bingham, d 15 Jul. 1865, m pub. -- Mar. 1832 Jabes Stevens; **L o v e** b 23 Jun. 1816, d 21 Feb. 1846, m 22 Feb. 1834 James Peacock; **Clementine** b 4 Apr. 1818, d 19 Sep. 1887, m 1 Sep. 1850 William Totman of S. Walpole; **E s t h e r** b 22 Sep. 1820, m 1 Jun. 1848 John Baker; **William H.** b 13 Mar. 1823, d 18 Feb. 1881; **Almira** b 12 Mar. 1825, m (1) 3 Nov. 1853 Samuel P. Hicks, who d 1 Apr. 1854, and m (2) 16 Sep. 1865 Harvey Jewel; **Patience** b 12 Apr. 1827, d 20 May 1874, m 24 Apr. 1865 ---- Winn; **D a v i d** b 20 Sep. 1829, d 26 Aug. 1846; **George W.** q.v.; and **Wesley** b 23 Aug. 1833, d 24 Nov. 1846. *Children of 2nd wife*: **Rufus** b 24 May 1836, d 8 Jul. 1863 in New Orleans; **M a r y E.** b 24 Sep. 1840, m 6 Dec. 1861 B. F. Jewett of Gardiner, ME; and **Ann** b 14 Apr. 1842, m 23 Dec. 1862 E. C. Dodge of New Castle, ME.

HILDRETH, EPHRAIM - Born 1654 in Westford, d ??, s/o Richard and ?? Hildreth. Ephraim Hildreth m (1) ----, and m (2) Ann Moore.

HILDRETH, EPHRAIM - Born 9 Jun. 1680 in Chelmsford, Massachusetts, d 26 Sep. 1740 in Dracut, Massachusetts, s/o James and Margaret (Ward) Hildreth. Ephraim Hildreth m 1707 Mercy Richardson, d 25 Dec. 1743. Children: **Ephraim, Jr.** q.v.; **Josiah** b 14 Feb. 1710 in Chelmsford, d 7 Aug. 1754 in Dracut; **Robert** q.v.; **Mercy** b 27 Jan. 1715/1716, d 10 Dec. 1729; **Zachariah** b 26 Sep. 1718, d 10 Jan. 1745 in Dracut; **Thomas** b 5 Apr. 1721 in Dracut, d 4 Dec. 1755 in Fort Cumberland, Maryland, in the French and Indian Wars [*The Ancestry of Sarah Hildreth* by W. G. Davis, published by the author, 1958, p. 13]; **William B.** b 30 Aug. 1723 in Dracut, d 5 Sep. 1813; **Levi** b 13 Oct. 1726; **E l i j a h** b 23 May 1728, d 13 May 1814 in Dracut; and **Mercy** b 27 Nov. 1732, m 25 Jul. 1754 Jonathan Coburn.

HILDRETH, EPHRIAM JR. - Born 18 Jan. 1708 in Chelmsford, Massachusetts, d 5 Aug. 1769 in Dracut, Massachusetts, s/o Ephraim and

Mercy (Richardson) Hildreth. Ephraim Hildreth m 11 Feb. 1735 Mary Clark of Chelmsford, Massachusetts.

HILDRETH, FREDERICK - Born ??, d ??, s/o Thaddeus and Sarah (Knox) Hildreth. Frederick Hildreth m Mary E. Lawrence. Children: **Wilbur E.** b 7 Feb. 1870; and **Emma S.** b -- May 1877.

HILDRETH, GEORGE W. - Born 1 Jan. 1831, d ??, s/o David and Mary (Hammond) Hildreth. George W. Hildreth m 1856 Jane Wood of Bluehill, Maine. Children: **Lillian Florence** b 2 Jul. 1858, m 6 Jul. 1889 Willard G. Brown, lived in Randolph, MA; and **Hattie Grace** b 13 Dec. 1859, m 30 Jun. 1870 Fred L. Lovell of Sandwich, MA, resided in Jackson, MI.

HILDRETH, HENRY - Born 3 Apr. 1814, d 19 Aug. 1883, s/o David and Esther (Moody) Hildreth. Henry Hildreth m 5/25 Jul. 1834 Eliza Lemont, d 12 Jan. 1877. Children: **Laura A.** b 20 Apr. 1836, m 20 Sep. 1862 Charles Gifford; **Isabell** b 20 May 1838, m 27 Nov. 1858 Daniel H. Dorr; **Abbie E.** b 4 Feb. 1840, m 14 Aug. 1862 John E. Brann; **Malissa** b 9 Nov. 1842, d 25 Apr. 1843; **Weston H.** b 9 Nov. 1844, m 24 Dec. 1868 Ann Searles; **Augusta E.** b 25 Sep. 1846, m 15 Apr. 1865 John Mayo; **Henrietta** b 30 Dec. 1848, m 28 Nov. 1868 John M. Teague; and **Ossian E.** b 24 Aug. 1850, d 30 Mar. 1862.

HILDRETH, HIRAM - Born 9 Jun. 1809 in Industry, Maine, d 5 Mar. 1852, s/o David and Esther (Moody) Hildreth. Hiram Hildreth m (1) 2 Oct. 1836 Olive Plummer of Richmond, Maine, and m (2) 10 Sep. 1839 Hannah E. Libby of Parsonfield, Maine, d 15 Jan. 1858. *Child of 1st wife*: **Sarah A.** b 17 Dec. 1837, m James H. Peckham. *Children of 2nd wife*: **Olive** b 16 Feb. 1841, d 16 Jul. 1841; **Martha E.** b 31 May 1842, m 1 Apr. 1862 William R. Dill; **Mary F.** b 31 May 1842, m 9 Jun. 1861 James H. Peacock; **Maria G.** b 3 Oct. 1846, m George E. Joy; **Elizabeth L.** b 14 Oct. 1848, m Hubbard Goldsmith of Gardiner, ME; and **Floresta** b 10 Feb. 1850, d 6 Sep. 1868.

HILDRETH, JAMES/LEVI JAMES - Born 1631 in England, d 14 Apr. 1695, s/o Richard and Sarah (----) Hildreth. James/Levi James Hildreth m 1 Jun. 1659 Margaret Ward. Children: **Richard** d 28 Apr. 1760, age 83 years; **Margared/Margaret** m Israel Proctor; **Abigail**; **Dorothy**; and **Ephraim** b 9 Jun. 1680 in Chelmsford, MA, d 26 Sep. 1740 in Dracut, MA, m 1707 Mercy Richardson, who d 25 Dec. 1743.

HILDRETH, MICHAEL - Born 8 May 1799, d 29 Oct. 1869, s/o David and Esther (Moody) Hildreth. Michael Hildreth m 1 Jun. 1820 Patience Knox of Gardiner, Maine, d 1 May 1873. Children: **William Henry** b 11 Aug. 1821, d 1 Apr. 1842; **Nancy Swift** b 25 Feb. 1823, m 23 Oct. 1842 Hiram Libby; **Benjamin Sewell** q.v.; **Thaddeus** q.v.; **George Albert** b 12 Apr. 1829, d -- Dec. 1879; **Michael Sylvester** b 31 Aug. 1831, m 10 Sep. 1866 Hattie Williams; **Patience** b 25 Jan. 1834, d 29 Jan. 1865, m -- Oct. 1859 Dennie Libby; **Hannah Knox** b 25 Dec. 1835, m 16 Jun. 1864 F. D. Harmon; **Frances E.** b 1 Apr. 1838, d 15

Jul. 1852; and **Osgood** b 4 Jul. 1840, d 27 Jun. 1862, killed near Richmond, VA.

HILDRETH, MICHAEL S. - Born ??, d ??, s/o ?? Children: **George** b 8 May 1867; **Harry Augustus** b 12 Feb. 1869; **Frances Ellen** b 21 Jan. 1871; **Ida May** b 22 Nov. 1874; and **Lephy Love** b 11 Nov. 1878.

HILDRETH, NAHUM - Born 1 Apr. 1809, d 12 Jul. 1872, s/o ?? Nahum Hildreth m 13 Jun. 1830 Cordelia Wharff, b 3 May 1813. Children: **George H.** b 7 Apr. 1831, d 8 Jul. 1833; **Isaac** b 21 Dec. 1832, d 1 May 1836; **Lorina G.** or **Lenora J.** b 4 May 1834, d 13 Nov. 1867; **Lydia A.** b 18 Sep. 1836, d 19 Apr. 1865, m 26 Oct. 1854 Alexander Fuller; **Ferdernance F.** or **Ferdinand F.** b 28 Mar. 1839, d 14 Nov. 1839; **Sarah E.** b 28 Sep. 1840, m 20 Nov. 1860 Edwin Morse; **Frances G. H.** b 11 Apr. 1844, m (1) Parker Lunt, and m (2) David Roberts; **Maranda A.** b 28 Nov. 1847, d 7 Mar. 1849; **Clara M.** b 28 Apr. 1849, m 14 Dec. 1867 J. P. Elwell; and **Willie A.** b 29 Jan. 1854, m Jennie B. McPherson.

HILDRETH, PAUL - Born 5 Oct. 1746, d 26 Nov. 1820 in W. Gardiner, Maine, s/o Robert and Sarah (----) Hildreth. Paul Hildreth m Hannah Merrill. Children: **David** q.v.; **Sarah** b 17 Apr. 1773, d 17 Mar. 1857, m pub. 21 May 1796 Annes Spear, who d 17 Apr. 1858, age 83 years; **Betsy** b 12 Sep. 1775, d 17 Aug. 1819, m (1) ----, and m (2) pub. 25 Apr. 1799 Aaron Whitney of Bowdoin, b 15 Sep. 1744; **Hannah** b 18 Jul. 1778, d 7 Aug. 1852, m pub. 30 Aug. 1800 James Douglas of Pittston, ME; **Taddeus** q.v.; **Asa** b 17 Jul. 1784; **Robert** q.v.; **Mercy** b 2 May 1791, d 29 Jan. 1879, m 8 Sep. 1808 Levi Moore, who d 9 Jun. 1877; and **Susan** b 1784, d 28 Jun. 1847, m 17 Feb. 1803 Francis Douglass, who d 30 Jan. 1865.

HILDRETH, RICHARD - One of the first settlers of Massachusetts, admitted as a freeman 10 May 1643, ancestor of the American Hildreths, first settled in Woburn, then called Charlestown Village, Massachusetts. He was b 1605 in England, d 23 Feb. 1693, s/o ?? Richard Hildreth m (1) 1643 Sarah ---- in England, d 15 Jun. 1644, and m (2) Elizabeth ----, d after 1686, according to Richard's will. *Child of 1st wife* (or may have been a brother to Richard): **James/Levi James** q.v. *Children of 2nd wife*: **Joseph** b 16 Apr. 1658; **Persis** b 8 Feb. 1659; **Thomas** b 1 Feb. 1661; and **Isaac** b 20 Jul. 1663.

HILDRETH, ROBERT - Married (1) before -- Aug. 1735 Sarah ----, and m (2) pub. 15 Nov. 1752 Sarah Abbott. Children: **Sarah** b 31 Aug. 1735, m 16 Nov. 1754 Simeon Wood of Dracut; **Bridget** b 26 May 1737, d -- Aug. 1836 in Skowhegan, ME [obit], m pub. 1 Nov. 1760 Eleazer Coburn; **Robert** b 1 Mar. 1739, d young; **Robert, Jr.** b 23 Feb. 1740, d -- Aug. 1741; **Paul** b 5 Oct. 1746, m Hannah Merrill; **Susanna** b 5 Dec. 1748; and **Benjamin** b 23 Jan. 1754.

HILDRETH, ROBERT - Born 17/20 Oct. 1788, d 20 Oct. 1833, s/o Paul and Hannah (Merrill) Hildreth. Robert Hildreth m 4 Jan. 1814 Phoebe/Phebe Marston, d 4 Feb. 1871, age 84 years 7 months.

Children: **Emma J.** b 22 Dec. 1814; **William** b 16 Nov. 1816, unm; **Daniel** b 1 Sep. 1818, unm; **Mehitable** b 12 Oct. 1823, d 27 May 1883; **Robert G.** q.v.; **Thaddeus** b 17 May 1826, d 16 Sep. 1828; **Esther** b 28 Sep. 1829; and **Hannah** b 4 May 1832.

HILDRETH, ROBERT G. - Born 1 Sep. 1824, d 29 Jul. 1863, s/o Robert and Phoebe/Phebe (Marston) Hildreth. Robert G. Hildreth m 17 Oct. 1838 Huldah J. Hodgdon. Children: **Charles A.** b 18 Nov. 1856, m 1876 Carrie E. Channell; **Andrew G.** b 20 Dec. 1858; **Walter T.** b 17 Feb. 1861; and **William C.** b 10 May 1863, m 28 Jul. 1883 Lenore J. Weymouth.

HILDRETH, THADDEUS - Born 5 Aug. 1781, d 3 Aug. 1832, s/o Paul and Hannah (Merrill) Hildreth. Thaddeus Hildreth m (1) pub. 31 Mar. 1805 Relief Spear, d 5 Jan. 1826, age 36 years, and m (2) pub. 24 Mar. 1827 Lydia Gove of Litchfield, Maine. *Children of 1st wife*: **Mehitable** b 12 Feb. 1806, d 11 Oct. 1811; **Susanna** b 17 Jul. 1807; **Naham** b 1 Apr. 1809, d 12 Jul. 1872, m 13 Jun. 1830 Cordelia Wharf; **A n n i s** b 7 Oct. 1810, d 21 Sep. 1847, m 12 Feb. 1835 Caroline Knowlton of Litchfield, who d 2 Jun. 1886, age 74 years; **R e b e c c a** b 7 Feb. 1813; **Mary** b 7 Nov. 1814, d 21 Mar. 1869; **Hannah** b 28 Jan. 1817; **Thaddeus B.** b 8 Jun. 1819, d 9 Sep. 1847, m Nancy ----, who d 23 Aug. 1850; **Sally** b 28 May 1821; **Elias** b 13 Nov. 1823; and **Elizabeth** b 7 Sep. 1825. *Children of 2nd wife*: **Gove** d 8 May 1828; **Leonard** b 28 May 1829; and **Lydia A.** b 8 Aug. 1830.

HILDRETH, THADDEUS - Born 2 Mar. 1805, d 4 Sep. 1878, s/o David and Esther (Moody) Hildreth. Thaddeus Hildreth m 2 May 1830 Sarah Knox, who was b 7 Sep. 1808, d 16 Jan. 1885. Children: **Frederick** q.v.; **Augustus** b 2 Aug. 1835, d 13 May 1851; **Sarah E.** b 6 Apr. 1840, m 30 Jun. 1864 Charles J. Smith; and **Charles A.** q.v.

HILDRETH, THADDEUS - Born 1 May 1827, d ??, s/o Michael and Patience (Knox) Hildreth. Thaddeus Hildreth m 15 Nov. 1855 Ann Seavey of Farmingdale, Maine. Child: **Willie Osgood** b 15 Nov. 1865.

HINCKLEY, GIDEON - Born 21 Oct. 1731 [b 1730 and d after 9-25-1779, according to the D.A.R. Patriot's Index, p. 331], d 18 Apr. 1796 [vital records Lewiston, Maine, p. 215], likely s/o Seth and ?? Hinckley of Biddeford, Maine, who was killed by Indians. [*Lewiston History in Local Directory 1860* published by Stanwood Co., 1860, p. 17]. Gideon Hinckley m (1) Mary Russel/Russell, lived in Georegtown, Maine, and m (2) 8 Aug. 1782 Sarah Cole of Lewiston Plt., b 25/26 Jan. 1758 [vital records of Topsham, Maine, p. 133, printed vr published by Maine Historical Society, 1930]. He lived in Lewiston 1785-1796. *Children of 1st wife*: **Thankful** b Nov. 1756 at Georgetown; **Seth** b 30 Jul. 1758 in Brunswick, ME; **Jane** b 5 Apr. 1760; **Joseph** b 27 Oct. 1761; **Mary** b 19 Jul. 1763; **Russell** b 27 Feb. 1765; **Jesse** b 16 May 1766; **Experience** b 2 May 1768; **Lucy** b 29 Jan. 1770; **Sarah** b 27 Oct. 1772; **Samuel William** b 21 Sep. 1774, m Elizabeth Land; **Gideon, J r .** b 8 Mar. 1778, d 1833, buried in Cousin Scotts Graveyard. *Children of 2nd wife*: **Susanna** b 27 Nov. 1784; **Moses Merrill** b 4

Aug. 1786; **Anne** b 17 Oct. 1788; **Rebeccah** b 26 Mar. 1791; **Mercy** b 6 Jul. 1793; and **Dorcas** b 9 Apr. 1795. [Vital Records of Lewiston, p. 215, 31.]

HINCKLEY, DEACON SAMUEL - Born 24 Sep. 1684 at Barnstable, Massachusetts, d 1762. Deacon Samuel Hinckley first settled in York, Maine, then to Brunswick, Maine, about 1739, [*Brunswick History* by George and Henry W. Wheeler, published by the authors, 1877, p. 839], via Saco/Biddeford, Maine. He m (1) Mary Freeman, b 13 May 1687, d 10 Dec. 1717, d/o Edmond Freeman of Eastham, Massachusetts. They were dismissed from Harwich Church in Truro in Apr. 1719. Deacon Samuel Hinckley m (2) Mary Demond. Children: **Reliance** b 21 Nov. 1714, d 22 May 1751, m 13 Apr. 1732 Capt. James Thompson; **Experience** b 16 Jan. 1720, d 15 Sep. 1798, m Timothy Tebbets; **Mehitable** b 25 Dec. 1718, d 6 Jun. 1811, m 27 Aug. 1736 Lt. Samuel Scammon, Jr. of Biddeford/Saco, Maine; **Seth** b 25 Dec. 1707 in Harwich, Massachusetts; **Shubael** b 15 Mar. 1708/9, d 1 Feb. 1798 in Hallowell, m Mary Smith [the *History of Brunswick* states he moved to Machias, Maine]; **Samuel** (twin) b 7 Feb. 1711 at Harwich, d 18 Jun. 1767, m Sarah Miller; **Mary** b 7 Feb. 1711, m Joseph Tompson; **Edmund** b 20 Nov. 1712, m Sarah Smith; **Aaron** b 13 Sep. 1715 at Troro; **Experience** b 16 Jan. 1720 at Troro, Massachusetts; and **Isaac** b 27 Mar. 1726, killed by Indians in 1751. [*History of Brunswick and Lewiston Directory 1860* published by Stanwood Co., 1860, p. 17] and [*Hinckley Heritage and History* by E. Charles Hinckley, 2nd ed., published by author, 1976, p. 37.]

HINCKLEY, SETH - Born 25 --- 1684, d 2 May 1747 killed by Indians on his way to Thompson's Garrison up to Tobais Ham's Garrison, where was Ham's tan yard, for a strap for a cow bell - it was on his return he was killed and his remains were not found until the next Spring. [*Directory of Lewiston* published by Stanwood Co., 1860, p. 17.] Children: **Edmund** was captured by Indians; **Isaac** m ---- Smith of York, Maine, and she m (2) Thomas Cotton; **Gideon** bc 1728, he was 19y? when captured by Indians. [*Lewiston Directory 1860 and Hinckley Genealogy* 2nd ed. by Emmet Charles Hinckley, published by the author, 1976, p. 45.]

HINKLEY, EDMUND - Born ??, d 24 Jul. 1867 age 77 years, s/o ?? Edmund Hinkley m (1) 1 Jan. 1818 Huldah Dwinal of Lisbon, Maine, d 24 Apr. 1825, d/o Aaron, and m (2) Eliza Sinclair. *Children of 1st wife*: **Emerline** b 11 Sep. 1818; and **Ruth** b 12 Nov. 1822. *Children of 2nd wife*: **Hulda Jane** b 27 Sep. 1826, d 27 Dec. 1880; **Sanford** b 29 Feb. 1830, d 25 Feb. 1860; **Eliza Ann** b 15 Mar. 1832, d -- Apr. ----; **Emerline** b 19 Sep. 1834, d 20 Jul. 1879 age 44 years and 9 months, m 1859 Ezra A. Kilgore; **Moses** b 24 Aug. 1837, d 1893; **Edmund** b 10 Sep. 1839, d 29 Mar. 1840; **Edmund** b 6 Jan. 1841, m -- Feb. 1869 Emily L. Hathon; and **Abigail T.** b 28 Sep. 1844, d 13 Apr. 1895, m 1 Jul. 1880 Edward S. Corliss.

HINKLEY, MOSES - Born ??, d ??, s/o ?? Children: **Florence** b 9 Feb. 1869, d 12 Aug. 1889; and **Edward**.

Hodgkin - [see Hodgkins - some of the family dropped the "s"]. The Hodgkin/Hodgkins families were corrected by Prof. Douglas Hodgkin of Bates College, Lewiston, Maine, from family records he has.

HODGKIN, AI BROOKS - Born 20 Aug. 1822, d 20 Apr. 1877 age 54 years and 8 months, s/o Jonathan and Sally (Brooks) Hodgkin. Ai Brooks Hodgkin m Harriet M./N. Merrow, d/o Reuben. Children: **Eugene H.** b 28 Jan. 1853, m 2 Aug. 1892 Sadie Knight; **Franklin J.** b 21 Jan. 1856, d 19 Aug. 1860; **Nellie F.** b 30 Jan. 1858, m 17 Jun. 1822 J. Edgar Young; **Reuben W.** b 14 Mar. 1861, m 9 May 1883 Ella E. Holmes; **Arthur E.** b 5 Jun. 1863, m 12 Sep. 1888 Ruth S. McKeown; **Annie M.** b 7 Jan. 1866, m 2 Sep. 1890 Charles L. McKenney; **George K.** b 5 Sep. 1869, m 2 May 1891 Emma E. Davis; and **William H.** b 13 May 1873, m 19 Jun. 1893 Mary Brackett of Portland, ME.

HODGKIN, BENJAMIN - Born 5 Feb. 1771, d 12 Mar. 1815, s/o Jonathan and Betty (Meserve) Hodgkin. Benjamin Hodgkin m Sally ----. Children: **Hannah L.** b 20 Feb. 1799; **Sally** b 4 Aug. 1802; **Betsy** b 18 Feb. 1805; **Mary** b 18 Feb. 1805; **Joel** b 25 Oct. 1808; and **Lane** b 8 Apr. 1811.

HODGKIN, CHARLES - Born 7 Oct. 1829, d 28 Mar. 1911, s/o Jonathan and Sally (Brooks) Hodgkin. Charles Hodgkin m 1 Jan. 1862 Sarah D. Purinton. Children: **Joseph Edgar** q.v.; **Bertha Viola** b 16 Aug. 1863, m 23 May 1892 Joseph A. Brackenbury; **Forest Winfred** b 3 Jul. 1865, m 5 Oct. 1885 Abbie Stubbs of Rockland, ME; **Walter Corey** b 23 Jul. 1867, m Rosina Rice of Auburn, ME; **J. Russell** b 9 Sep. 1872, m 9 Aug. 1893 Lillian Maud Weed; **Lester Pearl** b 9 Apr. 1874; and **Irving Dana** b 6 Dec. 1880.

HODGKIN, CHARLES H. - Born 28 Jan. 1841, d ??, s/o James Ham and Rachel (Ackley) Hodgkin of Litchfield, Maine. Children: **Rachel E.** b 28 Aug. 1875; and **C. Elmer** b 24 Jan. 1877.

HODGKIN, FOREST - Born 3 Jul. 1865, d 23 Feb. 1923, s/o Charles Edgar and Sarah (Purinton) Hodgkin. Children: **Seldon A.** b 14 Feb. 1888; and others.

HODGKIN, JAMES - (According to Lewiston Birth Records, James Ham was) s/o Betsey Hodgkin, b 1 Apr. 1797 in Lewiston, d 19 Mar. 1889. James Hodgkin m 25 Jun. 1821 Rachel Ackley, who was b 30 Aug. 1799, d 6 Mar. 1887. They moved in 1842 to Litchfield, Maine, to farm later occupied by son Charles H. (see further). Children: **Charlotte** 24 Feb. 1822, m 26 May 1844 Robert Edgecomb; **John** b 24 May 1824, m 1 May 1853 Cordelia Weymouth; **Sarah Jane** b 13 Jul. 1826, m 5 Jul. 1848 John C. Jones, lived in Gardiner, ME; **James Caleb** b 10 Jun. 1831, m 14 May 1854 Ellen Weymouth, lived in Gardiner; **Thomas H.** b 31 Mar. 1833, d 17 Feb. 1850 in VA; **Ansyl D.** b 20 May 1839, d 18 Jul. 1865 in Gardiner; **Charles H.** b 28 Jun. 1841, m 24 Dec. 1870 Hannah L. Burnham; and **Harriet A.** b 22 Nov. 1843, m Stephen T. Merrill, lived in Gardiner.

HODGKIN, JOHN P. - Born ??, d ??, s/o ?? Children: **Elmer** b 14 Jul. 1890; and **Ernest** b 8 May 1892.

HODGKIN, JONATHON - Born 9 Sep. 1794/1795, d 28 Jan. 1876, s/o Jonathan and Anna (Welch) [or her sister] Hodgkin. Jonathon Hodgkin m (1) ----, and m (2) Orpha Brooks. *Children of 1st wife*: **Belinda** b 18 Feb. 1819, m 22 Nov. 1844 David Crockett, Jr., of Danville, ME; **George** b 2 Oct. 1820, m Harriet H. Morrell, who d 31 May 1892, d/o Amasiah; **Ai Brooks** q.v.; **Julia** b 1 Jun. 1824, m Artemus Bartlett of Portland, ME; **Abiah** (by act of Legislature in 1838, changed her name to **Sally Byam**) b 29 Jun. 1826, m pub. 14 Nov. 1846 in Lisbon, ME, to Chaneller Blake of Sharon, Massachusetts; and **Charles** q.v. *Children of 2nd wife*: **Anna B./H.** b 1/2 Oct. 1837, d 25 Dec. 1883, m Caleb C. Sturtevant; **John D.** q.v.; **James F.** b 30 Oct. 1841, m Elmira Hatch, d/o John of Lisbon; **Rosamond/Roseman W.** b 24 Oct. 1843, m John Hatch of Lisbon, ME, s/o John; **Martha B.** b 4 Mar./Nov. 1846, m Orren D. Hinckley of Lisbon, ME; and **Harriet L./Hattie L.** b 28 Feb. 1848, m John M. Jackson.

HODGKIN, JONATHON - Born 22 Aug. 1765, d 9 Feb. 1795, s/o Jonathon and Betsy (Meservey) Hodgkin. Jonathon Hodgkin m 27 Dec. 1792 Anna Welch by Rev. John Strickland of Turner, Maine. Children: **Esther** b 26 Dec. 1793, d 25 Jul. 1854; and **Jonathon** b 9 Sep. 1795, d 28 Jan. 1876.

HODGKIN, JOSEPH EDGAR - Born 14 Jun. 1861, d 4 Apr. 1906, s/o Charles Edgar and Sarah (Purinton) Hodgkin. Joseph Edgar Hodgkin m Flora Colburn of Hollis, New Hampshire. Children: **Charles Edgar** b 4 Nov. 1889; **Vinton** b 2 Sep. 1892; **Ida Frances** b 8 Jun. 1897; **Edwin Omer** b 7 Sep. 1900; and **Velma Alberta** b 6 Apr. 1904.

HODGKIN, MOSES - Born 30 Mar. 1824, d 30 Oct. 1895, s/o Thomas and Esther (----) Hodgkin. Children: **Thomas** b 27 Mar. 1859, d 12 Feb. 1863; **Hattie J.** b 1 Apr. 1863, m 5 Apr. 1890 Levi Ross of Lisbon ; **John Penly** b 1 Jul. 1865, m 1 Jun. 1889 Nellie Hunt; and **Julia Lillian** b 17 Feb. 1867, m 4 Mar. 1888 William Dill, s/o Alonso G. Dill.

HODGKIN, THOMAS - Born 6 Apr. 1778, d 20 Jun. 1855, s/o Jonathan and Betsey (Meserve) Hodgkin. Thomas Hodgkin m 29 Dec. 1811 Esther Hodgkin, d 25 Jul. 1854, d/o Jonathon. Children: **Anna** 4 Apr. 1812, d 29 Dec. 1872, unm; **Rachel** b 10 Sep. 1813, d 1888, m 7 May 1835 Samuel Penley of Danville, ME; **Pamelia** b 19 Jun. 1816, d at Little River, Lisbon, m Stephen Littlefield of Auburn, ME; **Amos D.** b 27 May 1818, lived in Farmington, ME, m 26 Mar. 1843 Lydia Porter of Greene; **Betsy** b 13 Jun. 1820, m Joseph Hatch of Wilton, ME; **Esther** b 5 May 1822, m Rufus Thomas of Durham, ME; **Moses** q.v.; **Olive** b 10 Mar. 1826, m (1) Hiram Williams of S. Gardner, Mass., and m (2) ---- Dunn; **Ruth** b 17 Oct. 1828, m 17 Oct. 1848 Daniel P.

Nichols of Bowdoin, ME; **Lois** b 21 Nov. 1830; **Hiram** b 21 Jul. 1833, unm; and **Jane** b 22 Jul. 1835, d 10 Jul. 1858.

See also Hodgkin - some of the family dropped "s".

HODGKINS, JOHN D. - Born 11 Oct. 1839, d 20 Jul. 1899, s/o Jonathan and Orpha (Brooks) Hodgkins. John D. Hodgkins m 5 Apr. 1864 Arabella Bucknam, d/o William of Lisbon, Maine. Children: **Nellie Adelaide** b 26 Dec. 1865, m 5 Jul. 1888 Eugene McFarland of Harpswell; **Mattie B.** b 23 Nov. 1867, m 28 Dec. 1892 E. D. Harrington of Harpswell, ME; **George William** b 18 Feb. 1876; and **John Bucknam** b 10 Jan. 1878.

HODGKINS, JONATHON - Born 18 Feb. 1736/1737, d 2 Feb. 1814, s/o Jonathan and Mary (Stockbridge) Hodgkins. Jonathon Hodgkins m Betsy Meservey, d 19 Dec. 1817, age 84 years. Children: **Jonathon** b 22 Aug. 1765, d 9 Feb. 1795, m 27 Dec. 1792 ----, sis/o Anna Welch; **Benjamin** b 5 Feb. 1771, d 12 Mar. 1815; **Betsy** b 15 Nov. 1774, d 4 Feb. 1868, m Lovell Lincoln; and **T h o m a s** b 6 Apr. 1778, d 20 Jun. 1855, m Esther Hodgkin.

HOLLAND, CHARLES H. - Born 27 May 1844, d 4 Aug. 1870, s/o Henry I. and Jane M. (Thompson) Holland. Charles H. Holland m Viola A. Chipman of Mechanic Falls, Maine. Child: **C h a r l e s M.** b 1864.

HOLLAND, DANIEL - Born ??, d ??, s/o ?? Daniel Holland m 25 Nov. 1835 Mary Field, d/o Joseph of Lewiston. Children: **A s a G a r celon** b 18 Jan. 1838, d 6 Aug. 1838; **Alphonso B.** b 7 Oct. 1839, m (1) 27 Nov. 1867 Minnie H. Garcelon, and m (2) Alice E. Laurie; **M a ry Alma** b 1 Jun. 1843, m 20 Dec. 1861 Fessenden I. Day; and **Ann A m e l i a** b 29 Sep. 1845, m 21 Dec. 1871 Harry G. Garcelon, who d 15 Aug. 1904.

HOLLAND, GEORGE EDGAR - Born 18 Oct. 1835, d ??, s/o Richard and ?? Holland. Charles Edgar Holland m 1 Feb. 1860 Elizabeth Whetmore/Whitmore. Children: **Franke Adele** b 20 May 1863, m 14 Oct. 1903 James H. Cutter of Utica, New York; **Mary Wetmore** b 29 Sep. 1865, d 17 Jan. 1868; **Jennie Isabel** b 13 Dec. 1869, m 25 Dec. 1895 Daniel G. Abbott of N. Redding, Massachusetts; and **Daniel** b 26 Aug. 1873, m 1 Nov. 1905 Lillian Geyer.

HOLLAND, HENRY I. - Born 1 Nov. 1815 in Lewiston, d -- Jan. 1904 in Portland, Maine, s/o John, Sr. and Rebecca (Ilsley) Holland. Henry I. Holland m (1) 22 Dec. 1842 Jane M. Thompson of Newfield, b 21 Jan. 1816, d 9 May 1873 age 52 years, and m (2) 19 May 1876 Anna D. Ling, who d 18 May 1887, d/o Jacob Golder, and m (3) 1 Dec. 1888 Mrs. Jessie D. McIntosh, nee Davidson. *Children of 1st wife*: **Charles H.** q.v.; **Frank D.** b 20 Jan. 1846/1847, m Amelia Dunn of Poland, d/o George; **Sarah Jane** b 24 Dec. 1848 or 25 Dec. 1848/1850, unm; and **Edith Caroline** b 20 Jan. 1862, unm.

HOLLAND, JOHN - Born 9 Jun. 1824, d 22 Aug. 1864, s/o ?? John Holland m 3 Nov. 1850 Emerlin G. Welch, b 25 Jul. 1827, d/o James and Eleanor (Nordstrum) Welch of Wilton, Maine. Children: **Ella A.** b 6 Sep. 1852, d 6 May 1874, age 21 years, m 21 Nov. 1872 Timothy B. Rowell of Vassalboro, ME; **Carrie E.** b 10 Sep. 1854, d 30 Dec. 1894, m 18 Jan. 1879 Melvin J. Googin; and **Lelia J.** b 15 Jun. 1863, d 29 Dec. 1889, m 15 Apr. 1884 Henry S. Roberts of Farmington, d at Great Falls, New Hampshire.

HOLLAND, JOHN SR. - Born 15 May 1771 in Gloucester, Massachusetts, d 23/25 Aug. 1823 by drowning at Harpswell, Maine, and he was later reburied in Lewiston on 25 Sep. 1823, s/o ?? John Holland, Sr.'s cabin was at the foot of Hog's Back Hill [diary of Thomas Hodgkin, printed in *Lewiston Journal*, date unknown, clipping file at the Androscoggin Hist. Society]. He m -- Aug. 1792 Rebecca Ilsley, who was b 5 May 1773 in Newbury, Massachusetts, d 19 Jul. 1850, age 76 years 2 months. Children: **John, Jr.** q.v.; **Susan H.** b 25 Sep. 1795 at Cape Elizabeth, ME, d 1 Mar. 1865, m Joshua Merrill; **Michael** q.v.; **Rebecca** b 5 Aug. 1799 in Lewiston, d 15 Feb. 1825, m Jarvis Lambert; **David** b 10 May 1802, d 22 May 1803; **Hannah** b 17 Oct. 1804 in Lewiston, d -- Oct. 1852, m (1) Jarvis Lambert, and m (2) James Welch; **Richard** q.v.; **Caroline** b 10 Jul. 1808 in Lewiston, d 28 Feb. 1825; **Daniel** b 23 Sep. 1811 in Lewiston, d 8 May 1890, m Mary Field; and **Henry I.** q.v.

HOLLAND, JOHN JR. - Born 25 Jun. 1793 at Lewiston, d 22 Jan. 1879, age 85 years 6 months, s/o John, Sr. and Rebecca (Ilsley) Holland. John Holland, Jr. m 13 Mar. 1817 Pamelia Towne, d 17 Oct. 1865, age 73 years, d/o Moses and Almira. Children: **Pamelia** b 27 Aug. 1817, m Silas Morse; **Elmira** b 6 Jul. 1819, d 28 Aug. 1839, unm; **William Garcelon** b 9 Oct. 1822; **John** b 9 Jun. 1824, d 22 Aug. 1864, m 3 Nov. 1850 Emeline S. Welch, who was b 25 Jul. 1827 in Wilton, ME, d/o James and Eleanor Welch; **Caroline** b 29 Jun. 1826, m Dexter Goodereen; **Hannah Harris** b 10 Mar. 1828, d 16 Dec. 1903 in Washington, KS, m (1) 18 Jan. 1852 William Davis, and m (2) J. Dan Webb, who d 10 Nov. 1899; and **Rebecca T.** m (1) Jeremiah Webber, and m (2) ---- Bates.

HOLLAND, MICHAEL - Born 10/13 Aug. 1797 at Cape Elizabeth, Maine, d ??, s/o John, Sr. and Rebecca (Ilsley) Holland. Michael Holland m 12/14 Apr. 1817 Dorcas Dresser, b 16 Sep. 1799. Children: **Susan I.** b 18/28 Sep. 1818, m 1 Jan. 1845 Jesse Royal of Paris, ME, d 4 Aug. 1890; **Harriet** b 2/20 Jul. 1820, d 1 May 1880 in Greene, m 2 Jul. 1854 Thomas Starbird, who d 29 Apr. 1895 in Minot, ME; **Gustavus** b 8 Jul. 1822, d 25 Nov. 1846; **Aaron** b 7 Dec. 1824; **Alice R.** b 20 Mar. 1827, m (1) 23 Jul. 1854 George Abbott, and m (2) 1881 Thomas Stockard; **Rebecca** b 6 Aug. 1829, d 6 Nov. 1850, m 6 Jan. 1850 Ammi Roberts of Durham, ME, d -- Jul. 1853; **Michael, Jr.** b 4 Jul. 1831, d 1 Nov. 1873, m (1) 7 Oct. 1855 Sophronia T. Jordan, and m (2) ----; **Mary Ann** b 6 May 1838, d 3 Sep. 1869, m 6 May 1866 Joseph Watson; and **Sarah Jane** b 24 Dec. 1840, m 5 Jul. 1865 Julius A. Hewins. [1850 census of Danville, Maine.]

HOLLAND, RICHARD - Born 8 Dec. 1806 in Lewiston, d 1807, s/o John, Sr. and Rebecca (Ilsley) Holland. Richard Holland m (1) 2 Jan. 1833 Mary/Mercy Jane Swift, b 8 May 1811, d 4 Mar. 1845, and m (2) 29 Nov. 1854 ---- Lyon of Brunswick, Maine, at New York. Children: **Helen M.** b 18/19 Nov. 1833, m Gustavus Bassett; **George Edgar** q.v.; **Mary Frances** b 4 Jul. 1839, m Autustine Heart; **Charles F.** b 16 Feb. 1841; and **Augusta Ann** b 21 Dec. 1843, d 10 Oct. 1846.

HOOPER, ISAAC - Born ??, d ??, s/o ?? Isaac Hooper m Eunice ----. Children: **Nathaniel Lincoln** b 3 Dec. 18--; and **David Story** b 20 May 18--.

HOWARD, NELSON - Born 1839 in Phillips, Maine, d ??, s/o Seth and Rachel (----) Howard. Nelson Howard served in both the 13th Maine Regt. and the 30th Regt. during three years of the Civil War. He m 1866 Emma Wood in Lewiston, d 23 Apr. 1909. Operated lumber business, concrete/gravel roof business, retired 1907, served as state rep. in 1872 and 1884, then aide-de-camp to Gov. Dingley, and state liquor agent 4 years. First commander of Knox Post (G.A.R.) and State Dept. Cmdr. of Grand Army of the Republic and had title of Colonel.

HOWE, CYRUS B. - Born ??, d ??, s/o Ephraim S. and ?? Howe. Cyrus B. Howe m 21 Nov. 1850 Everline M. Fogg. Children: **Lydia E.** b 23 Aug. 1852, d 20 Feb. 1857; **Luella C.** b 4 Mar. 1855, m 22 Dec. 1871 James Campbell; **Eddie S.** b 15 Mar. 1860; and **Abbie V.** b 21 Aug. 1861, m 1 Jan. 1881 George Works.

HOWE, EPHRAIM S. - Born 19 Jan. 1811 in Livermore, d ??, s/o ?? Ephraim S. Howe m (1) 12 Jun. 1825 Lydice Barker, d 19 Sep. 1835, d/o Cyrus, and m (2) 31 Jan. 1838 Casandaria Barker, d/o Cyrus. *Children of 1st wife*: **Cyrus B.** b 25 Mar. 1826, m 21 Nov. 1850 Everline M. Fogg; **Nancy M.** b 29 Mar. 1828, m 18 Dec. 1846 Austin Brown; and **Mary S.** b 8 Aug. 1831.

HUNT, CHARLES P. - Born 29 Aug. 18-- in Auburn, Maine, d ??, s/o Nathan L. and Hannah P. (Mitchell) Hunt. Charles P. Hunt m 22 Jan. 1878 Lizzie A. Hartley, b 3 Aug. 1859, d/o Thomas and Eliza (----) Hartley. Children: **Ella N.** b 16 May 1878; **Walter E.** b 17 May 1881; **Lester L.** b 20 Aug. 1883, **Thomas H.** b 20 Feb. 1887, d 1 Jan. 1888; **James Stone** b 24 May 1888; and **May Alice** b 26 Dec. 1890.

HUNT, ENOCH, VI - Born 25 Jun. 1731 [*Vital Records of Rehoboth, Massachusetts* by Arnold published by Narragansett Historical Soc., 1897], d 1800, s/o Enoch, IV and Miriam (Bliss) Hunt of Rehoboth. Enoch Hunt, VI m circa 1756 Jael Sabin. Children: **Enoch VII** q.v.

HUNT, ENOCH, VII - Born 5 Jun. 1757 [vital records of Attleboro, Massachusetts, p. 152 1934, by Essex Institute], d 1831, s/o Enoch, VI and Jael (Sabin) Hunt. Enoch Hunt, VII m (1) pub. 9 Oct. 1778 Anna Stone, and m (2) circa 1780 Silvie/Sylva Briggs. *Child of 2nd* *wife*: **Zebina** q.v. [*Hunt Genealogy* by T. B. Wyman, Jr., published by W. L. G. Hunt, 1862-3, p. 271-272.]

HUNT, JOHN A. - Born ??, d ??, s/o ?? Children: ---- unnamed son b 2 Jun. 1851, d 19 Jul. 1851; **Ida M.** b 27 Dec. 1855, m Allen B. Voter; and **Jessie E.** b 24 Mar. 1870, d 4 Jul. 1891, m 20 Oct. 1886 Euge B. Trendenthal, M.D.

HUNT, NATHAN L. - Born 24 Jul. 1829, d 15 Jun. 1882 or 13 Jun. 1883, s/o ?? Nathan Hunt m 30 Jun. 1850 Hannah P. Mitchell of Auburn, Maine, d 22 Nov. 1878, d/o Christopher. Children: **Ella E.** b 24 Mar. 1851 in Auburn, m 24 Dec. 1871 James T. Stover of Harpswell, who d 2 Mar. 1902; **Charles P.** q.v.; and **Frank C.** b 24 Apr. 18-- in Auburn, m Hortense Bickford of Auburn.

HUNT, SIMEON - Born -- May 1820, d ??, s/o Zebina and Hannah (Tibbetts) Hunt. Simeon Hunt m pub. 16 Dec. 1843 May J./May Davis, d 27 Oct. 1889, age 68 years, d/o John V. of Lewiston. Children: **Lewis A.** b 21 Jun. 1844, m Mary ----; **Franklin** b 14 Sep. 1845; **Armanda M.** b 14 Jul. 1849, d 24 Sep. 18--, m Charles Batchelder; **Edward H.** b 11 Oct. 1854; **Anna C.** b 21 Nov. 1841, d 6 Aug. 1863, m 1 Sep. 1860 Nelson J. Laughton, lived in Old Orchard, ME; and **Charles P.** b 30 Jul. 1844, d 8 Jun. 1848.

HUNT, ZEBINA - Born 23 Jan. 1795 in Attleboro, Massachusetts, d 11 Jan. 1864 in Lewiston, s/o Enoch, VII and Silvie/Sylva (Briggs) Hunt of Attleboro. Zebina Hunt m (1) 1818 Hannah Tibbetts in Attleboro, b 1 Jun. 1799, d 27 May 1825, d/o Andrew and Polly Lord Tibbets of Litchfield, Maine, and m (2) 25 Dec. 1825 Mrs. Dolly Watson Libby (nee Owen) [she was the wido of Nathan Libby], b 17 Mar. 1799 in Litchfield, d 15 Dec. 1897, d/o John Owen and Dolly (Watson). (Zebina and Dolly moved to Lewiston about 1825.) *Children of 1st wife*: **Mary O.** b 23 Jan. 1819, d 5 Oct. 1873, m 20 May 1844 Isaac P. Davis of Hallowell, ME; **Simeon** q.v.; **Sarah Ann** b 1822, d about age 5 years; and **James** b 14 Oct. 1824, d 29 Oct. 1851, unm. *Children of 2nd wife*: **John O.** b 6 Oct. 1826, d 23 Sep. 1900, m 7 Jul. 1850 Hannah S. Blanchard, who was b 25 Jul. 1827, d/o Jonas and Joanna Small of Springfield, ME; **Nathan L.** q.v.; **Almond B.** b 21 Apr. 1831, lived in MN, m 6 Feb. 1853 Abby H. Rankin; **Eliza P.** b 22 Dec. 1832, d 14 Oct. 1881, m (1) 11 Feb. 1855 Charles Taylor, and m (2) 11 Feb. 1871 Warren Lovejoy of Auburn; **Lorenzo D.** b 26 Jun. 1835, d 19 Feb. 1855, unm; and **Emma Jane** b 22 May 1837, m 23 Sep. 1857 Clark Mitchell, lived at 131 Pleasant Street, Auburn, in 1895. [*Hunt Genealogy* by Hunt and Wyman, published by W. L. Hunt, 1862-3, p. 272 and letter from Hannah (Tebbetts) Hunt, wid/o Zebina Hunt, 1896 and see *Lewiston Journal* article 16 Mar. 1895 on Dolly (Owen) [Libby] Hunt.]

HUNTOON/HUNTON, CROMWELL PITTS - Born ??, d ??, s/o ?? Cromwell Pitts Huntoon/Hunton moved to Lewiston, Maine, from Readfield, Maine. He m 1 Oct. 1836 Luvia Ann Currier of Lowell, Massachusetts. Children: **Angeline E.** b 27 Apr. 1838, d 1 Apr. 1905, m Jedediah Whitney; **Caroline** b 1 Dec. 1841; **Herbert** b 8 Sep. 1842; **Loring M.** b 10 Mar. 1844; a dau b 19 Feb. 1846, d 19 Jan. 1848; **Mellen** b 19 Feb. 1847; **Laurena** White b 24 Oct. 1848; **Fred Wood** b 25 Aug. 1850; **Jerome B.** b 27 Jul. 1852; and **Lua** b 4 Sep. 1854. [Most of this family is buried in Riverside Cemetery in Lewiston.]

JACKSON, ABEL - Born 11 Jan. 1826, d in Lisbon, Maine, s/o Elias and Lydia (Goddard) Jackson. Abel Jackson m Caroline Lewis of Lewiston, d/o Edroin Lewis. Children: **E d w a r d** who lived in Lisbon Falls, ME, and Greenwood, ME; **Frank**; **Cora**; and **Lizzie**.

JACKSON, ALONSO - Born ??, d 8 Aug. 1907, s/o Joseph and ?? Jackson. Alonso Jackson m Rebecca J. Wilkin, d/o Enos. Children: **Millecent F.** b 26 May 1868, m -- Sep. 1868 Geo. L. Folsom, lived in Livermore Falls, ME; **A l i c e** b 30 May 1871, m 10 Jun. 1905 Leon L. Reed; **Charles** b 15 Sep. 1873; and **Lewella F.** b 15 Jun. 1878, m 7 Sep. 1904 Ludon Willard Boies of Auburn, Maine. [Probate court #5621 (Alonso Jackson's will) and #12787 (will and probate of Delinda Jackson, sis/o Alonso Jackson).]

JACKSON, ELI - Born c1759 in Cape Elizabeth, Maine, d 29 Nov. 1825 age 63 years in North Limington, Maine [*History of Limington, Maine, 1668-1900* by Robert L. Taylor, published by the author, 1975, p. 175 and 176, and *Early Families of Limington, Maine* by Robert L. Taylor, published by the author, 1984, p. 163, 164], s/o Solomon and Sarah (Jordan) Jackson. Eli Jackson after his marriage moved from Cape Elizabeth to Lewiston, then returned briefly before moving to Limington, Maine, in 1814. He settled on Jackson flats, next to his father-in-law on Davis Brook. He is buried in an unmarked grave on his place, a Revolutionary soldier. He was a cousin to Robert and Bartholomew Jackson. He m 17 Nov. 1785 in Scarboro, Maine, Hannah McKenney of Cape Elizabeth, Maine, d 28 Dec. 1825 age 62 years in Limington, Maine. Children: **Solomon** b 23 Aug. 1788 in Lewiston, went to sea and never returned; **Martha (Patty)** b 3 Jun. 1790 in Lewiston, d 2 Dec. 1873 age 84 years 5 months 12 days in East Baldwin, ME, m 20 Oct. 1814 John Wentworth of Limington, b 6 Apr. 1791 in Limington, d 10 Mar. 1856 in Baldwin, ME; **J a m e s** b 23 Jun. 1793; **S a l l y** b 3 Jul. 1795 in Lewiston [stone gives 9 Jun. 1796], d 9 Aug. 1883 age 87 years in Westbrook, ME, m 17 Sep. 1815 Alexander Bailey; **Abigail/Nabby** b 3 Dec. 1796 in Lewiston, living 1855 Clinton, MA, m 29 Oct. 1815 in Falmouth, ME, Mark Sawyer of Westbrook, ME, d 21 Apr. 1852 age 58 years in Leominster, MA; **Eli** q.v.; **Daniel W.** b 1802, living 1850 in Westbrook, ME, m 20 May 1827 in Westbrook, ME, Ann T. Ross; **Betsey** b -- Feb. 1805 in Cape Elizabeth, d 9 Nov. 1889 age 84 years 7 months 28 days in Limington, ME, m 29 Nov. 1821 William McKenney of Limington, b -- May 1797 in Limington, d 20 Feb. 1881 in Limington [vital records of Lewiston, Maine, p. 37]; **A b e l** b 1809, living 1835 in Limington, ME, m 23 Mar. 1843 Abiah Merrill of Parsonfield, he recently of Limington; and **Catherine** b 1811, m 12 May 1833 in Westbrook, ME, Joseph French of Westbrook, d 20 Dec. 1847 age 37 years 6 months.

JACKSON, ELI - Born -- Jul. 1799, d 3 May 1872 age 72 years 9 months 5 days in Baldwin, s/o Eli and Hannah (McKenney) Jackson. He m 20 Oct. 1837 in Baldwin, ME, Betsey Sanborn of Baldwin, d 7 Apr. 1884 age 83 years 10 months 2 days in Baldwin. Children: **Maryann** b 1837, d 17 Dec. 1914 age 78 years 4 months in Baldwin, m 25 Dec. 1854 Noah Milliken of Baldwin, ME; **Hannah** m 19 Mar. 1865 Daniel Whitten of Baldwin, ME; and **A n d r e w** b 1842, d 11 Jul. 1866 age 25 years 10 months 6 days in East Baldwin.

JACKSON, ELIAS - Born 2 Mar. 1796, d 26 May 1850, s/o Lemuel and Belsey (Staten) Jackson. Elias Jackson m 23 Sep. 1819 Lydia Goddard, d/o Abel. Children: **Susan** b 18 Jul. 1820, d in Lisbon, m Geden Harmon, lived in Lisbon, ME; **Matilda** b 25 Mar. 1822, m John H. Merrill of Andover; **A b e l** b 11 Jan. 1826, d in Lisbon, m Caroline Lewis, lived in Lewiston, d/o Edroin Lewis; **Lemuel** b 5 Aug. 1827, m Olive Estes, d/o Josiah Estes; **Betsey** b 17 Feb. 1829, d 17 Feb. 1891 at Lockes Mills, m 18 Dec. 1845 Kendall Pollard; and **Polly** b 16 Jan. 1831, m (1) Leander Marston, and m (2) Darrat Graffen, s/o Dave W., and m (3) Charles Corsen (?), lived in Andover. [1850 census, Lewiston, p. 83 and vital records of Lewiston, Maine, p. 111.]

JACKSON, ELIAS - Born 14 Apr. 1860, d ??, s/o Lemuel and Olive (Estes) Jackson. Children: **H a r r y D.** b 30 Jun. 1883, lived in Skowhegan, ME, in 1905; **Frede E.** b 25 May 1886, lived in Hartland, ME, in 1905; and **M a r y** m (1) 25 Feb. 1849 David Graffam, and m (2) Leander Martin (they lived in Andover, Maine). [Probate #5811 of Lemuel Jackson.]

JACKSON, JOHN A. - Born 21 Oct. 1840, d ??, s/o Joseph and Betsey (----) Jackson. Children: **Joseph, Jr.** b 7 Jan. 1871; **J. William** b 15 Jun. 1880; and **Ada May** b 30 Oct. 1884, m ---- Pettengill, res. Leeds, ME. [1870 census Lewiston, p. 180 and probate court #12787.]

JACKSON, JOSEPH - Born 20 Nov. 1805 in Monmouth, Maine, d 4 Jul. 1878 age 73 years and 4 months, s/o Solomen and Hasadiah (Smith) Jackson. Joseph Jackson m 18 Apr. 1830 Belsey Moore, d/o John & Mehitable (Andrew) Moore, or Betsey E. Morron*, d 12 Jun. 1894 age 92 years. Children: **Delinda A.*** b 16 Jan. 1837, d 15 Nov. 1919 [probate court #12787 - Androscoggin Co.]; **Alonso E.*** b -- Jul. ----, d 8 Aug. 1907 [probate court #5621 - Androscoggin Co.], m Rebecca J. Wilkin, d/o Enos; **Delora M.*** b -- Jul. ----; and **John M.*** b 21 Oct. 1840, m 14 Feb. 1866 Harriet L. Hodgkins, d/o Jonathan and Orpha Brooks Hodgkins. [* indicates those named in will of Joseph Jackson book 5 page 329 who d 4 Jul. 1878 file #1340 probate.]

JACKSON, LEMUEL - Born 1770, d 28 Oct. 1862 age 92 years, s/o Solomon and ?? Jackson. Lemuel Jackson was from Cape Elizabeth, Maine. He m 17 Jun. 1792 Betsey Staten from Cape Elizabeth. Children: **Betsey** b 9 Oct. 1793, d 1887, unm; **Sally** b 12 Mar. 1794, d 12 Nov. 1868, m 10 Apr. 1814 Jos. Blethen, who d 1866, s/o John Blethen of Lisbon, ME; **Elias** q.v.; **Polly** b 21 Jul. 1797, d 1825 (?), m (1) 17 Sep. 1818 Daniel Blethen of Lisbon, and m (2) 21 Apr. 1822

William Jones; **Matilda** b 23 Jun. 1799, d 1833, m Benjamin Fickett of Portland, ME [vital records of Lewiston, Maine, p. 40]; **Lemuel** b 14 Aug. 1801, d 4 Nov. 1803; **Charity** b 19 Jun. 1804, m Freeman Hatch [vital records of Lewiston, Maine, p. 37]; and **Nancy** b 23 Aug. 1809.

JACKSON, LEMUEL - Born 5 Aug. 1827, d 2 Jan. 1905, s/o Elias and Lydia (Goddard) Jackson. Lemuel Jackson m 18 Sep. 1851 Mrs. Olive (Estes) Jasper, d/o Josiah Estes, wid/o Edwin E. Jasper. Children: **William Allen** b 24 Aug. 1852, m 20 Nov. 1876 Henrietta F. Luce; **Nancy Hammond** [in probate court #5811, Androscoggin Co., she is named as Annie Jones of Hyde Park, MA] b 8 Jul. 1854, m 3 Jul. 1875 Royal M. Jones; **Isaac H.** b 5 Mar. 1858, unm; **Betsey** [named as Bessie Taylor of Lewiston, ME, in probate court #5811 - Lemuel Jackson's file] b 12 Jun. 1856, m (1) Arthur Jones, and m (2) 17 Nov. 1886 Wm. A. Danforth; and **Elias H.** b 14 Apr. 1860, m (1) 26 Nov. 1880 Debby A. Coston of Athens, ME, and m (2) Minnie Cotton (?).

JACKSON, SAMUEL - Born ??, d ??, s/o ?? Samuel Jackson m Katharine ----. Child: **Aaron** b 5 Sep. 1795 [vital records of Lewiston, Maine, p. 38.]

JACKSON, SOLOMON - Born ??, bapt. 23 Jun. 1728 in Dover, New Hampshire, d 16 Apr. 1811 in Lewiston, s/o James and Sarah (Jordan) Jackson. Solomon Jackson came to Lewiston from Cape Elizabeth, Maine [Thomas Hodgkin diaries at the Androscoggin Historical Society]. He m 25 Feb. 1749 in Cape Elizabeth, Maine, Sarah Jordan, his cousin, b 1736, d 16 Aug. 1812 [vital records of Lewiston, Maine, p. 219], d/o Robert and Rachel (Huckins) Jordan, gd/o Jedediah. A complete list of their children is not known but there were: **Eli**; **Solomon, Jr.** d 6 Aug. 1777 in Cape Elizabeth in Rev. War; **Lemuel** b 1770, d 28 Oct. 1862 age 92 years in Lewiston, m 17 Jun. 1792 in Durham, ME, Betty/Betsey Staten; **Solomon III** b after his brother's death in 1778, d 11 Aug. 1853 age 75 years and 6 months in Lewiston; and **Samuel** m 22 Sep. 1794 in Durham, ME, Catherine Moody.

JACKSON, SOLOMON III - Born -- Feb. 1778, d 11 Aug. 1853, s/o Solomon, Sr. and Sarah (Jordan) Jackson. Solomon Jackson, III m Hasadiah Smith of Wareham, Massachusetts, b -- Mar. 1778, d 9 Jul. 1852. Children: **Joseph** q.v.; **Charlotte** b -- Aug. 1808, d 7 Oct. 1865, m Converse Pettengill; and **Salle** d -- Jul. 1869 in Greene, m Absalon McKenny. [Census 1850 Lewiston, p. 56.]

JACKSON, WILLIAM - Born ??, d ??, likely s/o Lemuel and ?? Jackson. Child: **Lemuel Jr.** b 9 Jan. 1880. [Lemuel, Jr. is named in his grandfather's will #5811.]

JAMESON, ----- - Born -- Oct. 1775, d -- Jan. ----, s/o John and ?? Jameson. ---- Jameson m Mary Hewey, b -- Nov. 1774, d -- Aug. 1873.

JAMESON, ARTHUR - Born -- Aug. 1799 in Topsham, Maine, d 31 May 1863, s/o ?? Arthur Jameson m Jane Given, b -- Jul. 1799 in Wales, Maine, d 18 May 1864, d/o Wm. of Wales, Maine. Children: **Mary Jane** b 12 Aug. 1829, m John Given of Lewiston; **John M.** b 24 Aug. 1824, d 22 May 1862, age 27 years 9 months [probate #278, Androscoggin Co., ME], m Elthera H. ----; **Charles D.** b 12 Dec. 1826, d 13 Dec. 1866 (drowned); and **Elisa Ellen** b 11 Jul. 1836, d 23 Mar. 1866, unm.

JENNINGS, HENRY - Born ??, d 27 Dec. 1867 [#641 probate court record, Androscoggin Co., Maine], s/o ?? Henry Jennings was a merchant in Lewiston in 1865. He m (1) Hannah ----, d after 1857 [Androscoggin Co. deed book 31, p. 190 and book 39, p. 183, and m (2) Martha J. ----, d 22 Jul. 1899, sis/o Howard Stetson of Monmouth, Maine [probate #4751, Androscoggin Co., Maine]. *Children by 1st wife*: **Almira J.** m ---- Morton; **Ward H.** ; **David L.**; **Amanda** m ---- Blood; **Mary A.** m ---- Prince; and **Hannah** m ---- Moore. *Child by 2nd wife*: **Elmer E.** living in Portland, ME, in 1899.

JEPSON, ALEXANDER B. - Born 24 May 1846, d 8 Jul. 1891, s/o William, Jr. and Mary (Vickery) Jepson. Aleander/Alezander B. Jepson m 23 Aug. 1874/1875 Georgiana/Georgia Oliver, d/o Warren. Children: **William** b 25 Jul. 1875; **Abbie S.** b 8 May 1877, d 20 Sep. 1877; and **John K.** b 14 Sep. 1878.

JEPSON, BRADBURY TRUE - Born 28 Sep. 1785, d 22 Jun. 1872, s/o Thomas and ?? Jepson. Bradbury True Jepson was about 8 years old when family came to Lewiston. He m prob. on 30 Jan. 1814 Hannah/Hannah M. Osgood of Bath, Maine, d -- Feb. 1866, d/o Jonathen and Mary J. (Duhor) Osgood of Richmond, Maine. Children: **John Curtis** b 22 Jun. 1815, d 3 Aug. 1900, m (1) 24 Jan. 1841 Ruth Bean, d 28 Dec. 1865, and m (2) Sarah Loise Paine; **Sarah** b 20 Jan. 1817, d 30 May 1844; **Hannah M.** b 24 Sep. 1819, d 3 May 1846, m 11 Aug. 1840 William P. Vickery of Minot, ME; **Leonard** q.v.; **James Clarinton** b 2 Jul. 1824, d 21 Oct. 1904, m Elizabeth H. Durell of Mendew, NJ, who lived in Linden, d 26 Jan. 1896 [Mary Ann P. Jepson of Stoneham, MA, claims to be his widow in #5790 probate court Androscoggin Co., ME]; **David** b 7 Mar. 1827, d 1 May 1849, unm; **Thomas B.** b 25 Jul. 1832, d 18 Jun. 1862, m 24 Nov. 1859 Caroline Hatch; **Mary M.** b 29 Mar. 1830, d 27 May 1843; and **Julien A.** q.v. [Vital Records of Lewiston, Maine, p. 38 and census 1850 of Lewiston, p. 50.]

JEPSON, EBENESER - Born 13 Feb. 1793, d 5 Feb. 1863, s/o ?? Ebeneser Jepson m 16 Oct. 1814 in Fayette, Maine, Dorcas/Dorcas B. Lander, d 6 Feb. 1863 or 15 Apr. 1871, d/o Abisha. Children: **Lucinda F.** b 26 Sep. 1815, d 31 Dec. 1878; **Sylvanus B.** b 1 Aug. 1820, d 1861, unm; **Thomas I.** b 27 Jul. 1822, d 11 Jul. 1896; **Joel C.** b 20 Mar. 1826, d 17 Jul. 1853, m in Newton MA, Anna Elizabeth Wright; **Jane A.** b 21 Jun. 1828, d 6 Aug. 1848; **Clarion P.** b 13 Oct. 1830; **Christiana R.** b 26 Aug. 1833, d 10 Jun. 1835; **Celia A.** b 23 Feb. 1818, d 7

Jul. 1883, m Levi Linten of Skowhegan, ME; and **Clarion P.** m 8 Jan. 1850 Elias S. Webber.

JEPSON, JOHN C. - Born ??, d ??, s/o ?? Children: **John C.** b 4 Jul. 1843, d 1 Oct. 1843, m ---- Jeffres of Boston, ME; **Mary Elizabeth** b 4 Nov. 1844; **Julie** b 20 Feb. 1847, d 9 Apr. 1848; **Hattie R.** b 30 Oct. 1868, m 22 Jun. 1887 Wilbert Rollins of Auburn; and **Florence A.** b 7 Dec. 1871.

JEPSON, JULIEN A. - Born 18 Apr. 1841, d -- Dec. 1904, s/o Bradbury True and Hannah (Osgood) Jepson. Julien A. Jepson m 28 Nov. 1862 Edwina J. Buker. Children: **Lane C. Charles; Charles; Milten Fillmore;** and **Lucy A.** m Edmond ----.

JEPSON, LENDALL - Born ??, d ??, s/o ?? Children: **Mildred** b 7 Jul. 1881; and **George L. B.** b 8 Oct. 1882.

JEPSON, LEONARD - Born 4 Dec. 1821, d 17 Jan. 1902, s/o ?? [Census 1850 of Lewiston, p. 50.] Leonard Jepson was 22 years on the New York Police Force. He m (1) 4 Feb. 1849 Rosanna Davis, d 21 May 1859, and m (2) 6 Oct. 1872 Frances A. Pray, d/o Joseph. Children: **Julia A.** b 17 Nov. 1849, m Lemuel C. Parker of Green; **Sarah L.** b 11 Nov. 1853, d 21 Jan. 1856; **Fred L.** b 17 May 1873; and **Cora May** b 6 Jul. 1881.

JEPSON, LEVI D. - Born 18 Jan. 1820, d 2 Apr. 1900, s/o William and ?? Jepson. Levi D. Jepson m (1) Ann Curtis, and m (2) Mary A. Getchell of Brunswick, Maine. Children: **Lendall** b 18 Apr. 1852, d 11 Apr. 1885, m 6 Oct. 1875 Hattie M. Stackpole, lived in Lynn; **Orlando L.** b 30 Aug. 1855, m 8 Dec. 1877 Carrie L. Harsie, lived in Lynn, MA; **Rose A.** b 14 Apr. 1860, d 12 Aug. 1885; **Charles A.** b 22 Feb. 1867, d 2 Aug. 1867; **John E.** b 25 Nov. 1871, d 10 May 1876; and **Frank C.** b 17 Jan. 1878.

JEPSON, ORLANDO - Born ??, d ??, s/o ?? Children: **Rosie May;** and **Elmer H.**

JEPSON, THOMAS - Born ??, d 28 Mar. 1818, age 65 years 1 month 14 days, s/o ?? Thomas Jepson m (1) 25 Sep. 1778 Sarah (Pettengill) True, d 15 Mar. 1795, and m (2) 22 Nov. 1795 Naomi (?) Reed of Freeport, Maine, d 5 Jul. 1842, age 88 years. Children: **Bradbury True** q.v.; **Abigail** b 7 Jan. 1787, d 9 Mar. 1866 in Richmond, m 11 Oct. 1807 John D. Parks of Bath, ME; **Mary** b 7 Jul. 1788, m 11 Feb. 1810 ---- Mason, lived in Leeds, ME, d 5 Jan. 1818, he m (2) Liva Fish; **William** q.v.; **Ebeneser** q.v.; and **Phebe** b 5 Sep. 1794, d 30 Jun. 1825, m 23 Mar. 1814 John Curtis. [Vital Records of Lewiston, Maine, p. 38.]

JEPSON, WILLIAM - Born 3 Apr. 1790, d 31 Jul. 1868, s/o Thomas and ?? Jepson. [1850 census of Lewiston, p. 60.] William Jepson m (1) 12 Feb. 1815 Sarah Blaisdell, d 11 Sep. 1824, and m (2) 16 Apr. 1825 Elizabeth Pettengell/Pettengill, d 16 Jun. 1870. Children: **Wil-**

liam b 30 Dec. 1816, d 186-?, m 13 Dec. 1842 Mary Vickery; **Rebecca** b 7 Apr. 1818, d 28 Aug. 1850, m 21 Mar. 1836 George Bubier; **Rosalinda** b 15 Jun. 1823, d 15 Jul. 1853, m Charles Foster (Rosalinda was his 2nd wife); **Edward Pettengill** b 3 Jul. 1827, d 1881 in KS, m Margaret Wright, d/o Joel, living in Janesville, WI; **Levi Dingley** q.v.; **Elizabeth G.** b 1 Apr. 1832; **Mary** b 1 Apr. 1832, d -- Apr. 1832, m 28 Oct. 1849 John Curtis, who d 8 Oct. 1854; and **Sarah N.** m 8 Oct. 1854, David W. Carville, s/o Wm. [Vital Records of Lewiston, Maine, p. 38.]

JEPSON, WILLIAM JR. - Born ??, d ??, s/o ?? William Jepson, Jr. m 13 Dec. 1842 Mary Vickery. [1850 census of Lewiston, p. 61.] Children: **Alonso** b 2 Mar. 1844, unm; **Alezander B.** b 24 Jul. 1846, m 23 Aug. 1874 Georgiana Oliver; **Charles Henry** b 12 May 1846, d 20 Sep. 1851; **John H.** b 21 Oct. 1851, m Lorentha Ann Whitney; **Charles W.** b 22 Dec. 1853, lived in Foxcroft, ME; **Rebecca** b 11 Apr. 1855, m George Piper, who lived in Weld, ME; **Harrison**; and **Vest B.** b 22 Feb. 1860, m 4 Nov. 1877 Frank A. Stevens.

JILLPATRICK, JAMES - Born ??, d ??, s/o ?? James Jillpatrick m Betsey ----. Children: **Hannah** b 12 Feb. 1795; **Samuel** b 11 Jul. 1796; and **Hannah** b 11 Aug. 1798.

JONES, ABIAL M. - Born c1823 in Vermont, d ??, s/o ?? Abial M. Jones was a depot master. He m (1) Hannah E. Garcelon, d 30 Aug. 1848, d/o Mark, and m (2) Ellen E. ----, bc 1826. Children: **Mary Elizabeth** or **H. Lizzie** [1860 census] b 29 Aug. 1847; **John Ambrose** b 25 Feb. 1851, m 2 Apr. 1879 Addie E. Skinner; **Frederick Augustus** b 8 Oct. 1861; **Ella Heloise** b May 1859, m 25 Nov. 1886; and **Emma C.** b 26 Dec. 1864. [Sarah Norton b 1770 in New Hampshire is living with this family in Lewiston in 1860. 1860 census Lewiston, p. 33.]

JONES, ALEXANDER - Born ??, d ??, s/o ?? Child: **Bessie E.** m Simon Lovejoy in Paris.

JONES, ARTHUR - Born ??, d ??, s/o Martin A. and ?? Jones. Child: **Effie** b 18 Apr. 1876.

JONES, DANIEL ILLESLEY/INSLEY [vital records of Lewiston, Maine, p. 113] - Born 29 Mar. 1794 in Standish, Maine, d 10 Apr. 1873 [probate court #1123, Androscoggin Co.; left everything to Lizzie Crocker, his dau. in will], s/o Ephraim and Judith (Philbrick) Jones. Daniel I. Jones m 30 Jan. 1820 in Lewiston, Maine, Betsey Bubier, d 31 May 1869, d/o Samuel. Children: **Jonathan Philbrick** b 30 Oct. 1825, d 17 Jun. 1893, unm [vital records of Lewiston, Maine, p. 40]; **Alexander** b 22 May 1828, m Mary Bunker; **Daniel** b 15 Mar. 1831, d 1867, m Mary Leavitt of Damariscotta, ME; **William** b 15 Oct. 1838, m Mattie Barnett of Augusta, ME; **Eunice F.** b 27 Jun. 1833, m Benjamin Fogg, lived in NH; **Martha** b 13 Sep. 1836, m Charles Soule of Freeport, ME; **Henry** b 20 Jan. 1842, unm; and **Elizabeth/Lizzie H.** b 23 Jun. 1843, m 31 Dec. 1870 Crosby N. Crocker of Corinth, ME.

JONES, DANIEL - Born ??, d ??, s/o ?? Children: **Rosetta** m John Atwood; **Walter**, unm; and **Elmer** d 1872.

JONES, DAVID - Born c1824 in Vermont, d 27 Mar. 1882, s/o ?? David Jones was a business partner of John B. Jones [probate court #2017]; occ. stair builder. He m 13 Jul. 1851 Sarah B. Banks. [1860 census of Lewiston, p. 33.]

JONES, EPHRAIM - Born 27 May 1749 in Portland, Maine, d 31 Mar. 1833, s/o Ephraim and Mary (Pearson) Jones. Ephraim Jones m Judith Philbrick, b 27 Aug. 1762 in Standish, Maine, d -- Jul. 1833. Children: **S a r a h** b 1 Mar. 1781 in Standish, m Thomas Pennell, lived in Standish; **Mary** b 19 Feb. 1783, m Oliver Dyer; **Jonathan P.** b 26 Dec. 1784 in Portland, ME, d 16 Aug. 1805 at sea; **B e t s e y** b 16 Aug. 1787 in Portland, d 27 Oct. 1821, m 1808 Benjamin Quimby; **Harriet** b 9 Mar. 1790 in Standish, m Rev. Josiah Merrill; **A n n i e T .** b 26 Mar. 1792 in Standish, m Annie R. Mitchell of Bath; **Daniel I.** q.v.; **Sophia** b 25 Sep. 1796 in Standish, d in Auburn, ME, m (1) ---- Adams, and m (2) Aaron Stevens of Rumford, ME; **Ephraim** q.v.; **Eunice F.** b 1 Jan. 1801 in Standish, d 23 Jun. 1841, m 18 Feb. 1835 Rev. Allen Greely of Turner, ME; **William** q.v.; and **Abigail F.** b 20 May 1805 in Standish, m James Edwards of Gorham, Maine, who lived in Gardiner, ME. [See *Early Families of Standish, Maine* compiled by Albert J. Sears, published by Robert L. Taylor, 1987, p. 91, 92.]

JONES, EPHRAIM - Born 7 Sep. 1798 in Standish, Maine, d 11 Oct. 1840, s/o Ephraim and Judith (Philbrick) Jones. Ephraim Jones m Ann Garcelon, d 29 Jul. 1867, d/o David. Child: **Hannah G.** b 19 Jun. 1824, d 13 Oct. 1837. [Vital Records of Lewiston, p. 111.]

JONES, JOHN B. - Born 26 Jan. 1811 in Vermont, d 21 Jun. 1885, s/o ?? John B. Jones was a R & R [railroad] builder. He was 45 years old in 1860. He m Joanna M. Nash, d/o John of Lewiston. [1860 census of Lewiston, p. 36.] Children: **Ellen Elizabeth** b 11 Feb. 1840, m 17 Apr. 1861 Samuel E. May; **Augustus Benson** b 29 Jun. 1841, d 10 Jul. 1877, m Vesta C. Wing of Leeds, ME; **Eudora** b 16 Sep. 1846, m Rodney G. Sargent of Sedgwick, ME; and **Sarah A.** m Frank H. Morrell.

JONES, JOSIAH - Born -- Apr. 1765, d 26 Aug. 1838, s/o ?? Josiah Jones m Eleanor Mitchell, b 29 Nov. 1767, d 28 Jan. 1841. Children: **Elizabeth** b 1 May 1792, d 28 Jun. 1873, m 15 Jun. 1843 Rufus K. Libby of Webster, ME; **Lettice** b 4 Feb. 1794, d 7 Sep. 1871, m Dominus Weymouth of New Portland, ME; **William** b 4 Feb. 1796, d 10 Apr. 1858, m Mary Heath of Webster; **Ezekial** b 30 Sep. 1801, d 5 Feb. 1836, m 26 Mar. 1835 Annah Jordan of Lisbon, ME, d 4 Dec. 1887; **Eleanor** b 20 Jan. 1805, d 29 Mar. 1890, m 20 Apr. 1843 Joseph Blethen; **Becher** b 10 Apr. 1793, d -- May 1793, age 7 weeks; and **Josiah** b 1 Apr. 1799, d 20 Sep. ----, age 5 years. [Family register at Androscoggin Historical, Auburn, Maine, and vital records of Lewiston, Maine, p. 113.]

JONES, LEVI - Born 31 Oct. 1790, d 5 Oct. 1861? [*History of Durham, Maine* compiled by Stackpole, published by the Town, 1899, p. 206], s/o ?? Levi Jones m Hannah Meader. Children: **Mary** b 9 Jun. 1824, m 12 Feb. 1844 William Robinson; and **Levi Meader** b 1 Jul. 1826, d 26 Oct. 1868, m 1 Feb. 1863 Janet Maxwell. [Vital Records of Lewiston, Maine, p. 112 and 1850 census of Lewiston, p. 74.]

JONES, LUTHER - Born ??, d ??, s/o ?? Luther Jones m -- Jan. 1853 Mary H. Hayes, d/o William.

JONES, MARTIN A. - Born c1819 in Vermont, d ??, s/o ?? Martin A. Jones was a joiner/carpenter. He m Almira ----, b 1820 in Massachusetts. Children: **Cornelia** b 1847 in Vermont; **Royal M.** in Maine; **Marcia** b 1852; **Arthur** b 1857; **Flora A.** b 1859 (twin); and **Alton H.** b 1859 (twin). [1860 census of Lewiston, p. 46 and 1870 census of Lewiston, p. 142. All birth dates were figured by how old they were in 1860 and 1870.]

JONES, ORRIN - Born ??, d ??, s/o ?? Orrin Jones m (1) Clarimond Clifford, and m (2) Phebe Garcelon, d 1844, d/o Rev. James. Children: **Theresa A.** b -- Mar. ----, m (1) 2 Oct. 1858 Van Buren Rawsen, and m (2) Otis ----; **James Garcelon** b -- Jul. ----, m Lemandi Hanscomb; **Alice S.** m 6 Sep. 1865 Charles D. Tukesbury of Falmouth, ME, d -- Aug. 1884; **George** b 1 May 1844, m Augusta Chadburn of Oxford, ME; **Eliza T.** m George Houghton; **Lorenso B.** m Emma ----; and **Mary** m Alvah Bumpus of Mechanic Falls, ME.

JONES, ROYCE - Born ??, d ??, s/o Martin A. and ?? Jones. Children: **Flora M.** b 21 Sep. 1877; and **Ella M.** b 26 Jun. 1879.

JONES, WILLIAM - Born 4 Feb. 1796, d 1858, s/o Josiah and Mary (----) Jones. William Jones m Mary Heath of Webster, Maine. Children: **Mary** b 23/24 Oct. 1821; **Josiah** b 24 Jul. 1823; **Otis** b 23 Apr. 1827; **Lydia** b 23 Dec. 1832; and **Maria** b 18 Apr. 1834. [Vital Records of Lewiston, Maine, p. 40.]

JONES, WILLIAM - Born 20 Apr. 1803 in Standish, Maine, d 15 Jan. 1848 [*Morning Star* obit 16 Feb. 1848], s/o Ephraim and Judith (Philbrick) Jones. William Jones moved to Lewiston at age 12 years. He m (1) 21 Apr. 1822 Mrs. Mary (Jackson) Blethen, b 21 Jul. 1799, d 1 Nov. 1825, d/o Lemuel Jackson, and m (2) 5 Jul. 1827 Theodola Sawyer, b 27 Feb. 1800, d 19 Feb. 1876. Children: **David B.** b 6 May 1823, lived in Sunnipee, NH; **William Augustus** b 13 May 1830; **Mary E.** b 20 Apr. 1832, m Stephen Cheney; and **Martha Ann** b 21 Jan. 1835, m Geo. Garfield. [Letter from M. A. Garfield, 1893, of West Pittsfield.]

JONES, WILLIAM - Born ??, d ??, s/o ?? Children: **Effie**, unm; **Albert**, unm; **Berther**, unm; **Grace**, unm; and **Mabel**, unm.

JONES, WILLIAM A. - Born c1830, d ??, s/o ?? William A. Jones m 1 May 1859 Emily F. Garfield. Children: **Herbert G.** [named Wm.

H. age 2/12 years in 1860 census] b 17 Mar. 1860, unm; **Willie E.** b 8 Jan. 1862, m 22 Jun. 1887 Hannah Titcomb of NY; and **Mary F.** b 19 May 1864, d 4 Aug. 1865. [In household in 1860, one Daty (sic) Jones, age 59 years. See 1860 census of Lewiston, p. 172.]

JORDAN, ABRAHAM - Born 16 Jun. 1781, d ??, s/o Jeremiah and Hannah (----) Jordan. Jeremiah Jordan was the s/o Jeremiah, s/o Jedidiah, s/o Jedidiah, s/o Robert. Abraham Jordan res. Mill Creek, Indiana. He m Betsey Miller of Durham, Maine. [Vital Records of Lewiston states wife's name as Melinda.] Children: **Eleanor Dunlap** b 27 Jul. 1827; **George Frances** b 27 Sep. 1829; **James** b 20 Jul. 1831; and **Delia** b 18 Aug. 1834. [Vital Records of Lewiston, Maine, p. 174.]

JORDAN, ALFRED E./EMERY - Born 23 Feb. 1831, d 12 Jun. 1917 [probate court #11890, Androscoggin Co., ME] leaving his wife/widow Anna F. ---- [according to his will], s/o James and Deborah (Garcelon) Jordan. Alfred E./Emery Jordan was of Lisbon, Maine. He m 26 Nov. 1857 Susan J. Blake, b 7 Aug. 1828 and lived in Lisbon, Maine. Children: **Francis J.** b -- Feb. 1858; and **Nellie M.** b 7 May 1869 in Lisbon, ME.

JORDAN, ANDREW - Born 2/28 Jul. 1783, d ??, s/o Jeremiah and ?? Jordan. Andrew Jordan lived in Durham, Maine. He m 3 Apr. 1808 Thankful Rand of Lewiston, d 1838 in New Portland, Maine.

JORDAN, ANN MARIA - Born ??, d ??, s/o ?? Ann Maria Jordan m ---- Randall, who went to California, a soldier in Cavalry and d in service. Child: **George** lived in Lewiston, 1876.

JORDAN, BENJAMEN - Born 23 Dec. 1787, d 1867 at Searsmont, Maine, s/o Jeremiah and Hannah (Marr) Jordan. Benjamen Jordan m (1) Mrs. Betsey Libby at Guilford, New Hampshire, and m (2) Lucy Jordan. Children: **Kesiah** b 7 Apr. 1812, d 27 Mar. 1845; **Mary** b 9 Sep. 1813, d 2 Jul. 1842; **Benjamin** b 8 Nov. 1815, d 12 Jul. 1863 in the Army; **Abial** b 12 Jan. 1815, m 4 Apr. 1844 at Belmont, ME, Harriet Ardway, d 14 Mar. 1824; **George Sylvester** b 6 Apr. 1821, d (drowned) 9 Jun. 1852 at Bangor, ME; **Louisa** b 6 May 1826, d 11 Dec. 1845, unm [m Frank Sevus according to *Jordan Memorial* compiled by Tristram F. Jordan, published by the author, 1882, reprinted 1982, p. 366]; **Lydia Ann** b 6 Mar. 1823, d 19 Nov. 1865, m John Amos; **Susan** b 6 May 1826, d 11 Dec. 1845, unm; and **Lucy M.** b 5 Jul. 1839, m L. P. Ness, lived at Searsmont.

JORDAN, BENJAMIN - Born 11 Feb. 1853, d 23 Mar. 1890, s/o ?? Benjamin Jordan m 21 May 1836 Sally Lincoln, b 9 Jun. 1810, d 6 Apr. 1868. Children: **Rufus** b 7 Nov. 1836, d 13 Apr. 1890, m (1) Harriet Ellen Harris, and m (2) Morris Hussey, who d -- Apr. 1894; **Matilda** b 16 Aug. 1838, d 27 Jan. 1861, m 3 Jul. 1860 Gilbert Proctor of Lisbon, ME; **Mary** b 28 Sep. 1840, m 27 Aug. 1870 Alexander Weaver, who d 1 Sep. 1886; **Deanna** b 6 Aug. 1845, m 24 Jun. 1865 ---- Stuart; and **Emeline** b 13 --- 1850, m (1) 24 Nov. 1870 Samuel Hodgon, and m (2) 29 Nov. 1880 John F. Casson.

JORDAN, BENJAMIN - Born ??, d ??, s/o Wm. and ?? Jordan. Wm. Jordan was the s/o Joshua, s/o Nathen, s/o Dominius, s/o Robert. Benjamin Jordan m 8 Nov. 1818 Polly Golder, who lived in Webster, Maine. Children: **Dorcus** 22 Sep. 1819, m Joseph Pray; **Appiah Andersen** b 21 Apr. 1821, m Lucius Lothrop; **Isaac Golder** q.v.; **Sarah Jane** b 31 May 1825, d 14 Jul. 1828; **Margaret** b 20 Aug. 1827, d -- May 1880, m (1) ---- Crockett, and m (2) John J. Tilton of NH, lived in Webster, ME; **Rebecca J.** m (1) Charles Sawyer, and m (2) 13 Jun. 1867 Clement Parker, and m (3) Samuel M. Parker, and m (4) 21 Mar. 1891 John Wakefield, when she was living at Empire Station with son William Sawyer; **A r v e s t a** m (1) ---- Swett of NH, and m (2) Arthur Cowley, who was living in Lisbon; and **Dorius** m Cosilla Tuttle of Pownal, living in CO.

JORDAN, CHARLES BISBEE - Born 16 Jun. 1829, d 30 Jan. 1886 [probate court #2590, Androscoggin Co., ME], s/o James and Deborah (Garcelon) Jordan. Charles Bisbee Jordan was late of Lisbon, Maine. He m 10 May 1847 Melisa/Melissa P. Porter, b 23 May 1838 or 1878 in Freeport, Maine. Children: **Iva Etta** b 29 Oct. 1849, d 8 May 1861; **Elona P.** b 19 Jun. 1861; **Lissie M. B.** b 24 Oct. 1863; and **Charles Alton** b 7 May 1866.

JORDAN, CHARLES R. - Born 29 Sep. 1801, d 13 Dec. 1874 [probate #1190 court, Androscoggin], s/o Joseph and Deborah (----) Jordan. Charles R. Jordan m Deborah ----. Child: **Charles Alarie** [sic] b 14 Jun. 1856, lived in Auburn, ME.

JORDAN, EDITH THOMPSON - Born 30 Sep. 1867, d ??, d/o ?? Child: **Eugene**.

JORDAN, GEORGE H. - Born 8 Jul. 1844, d ??, s/o James and Deborah (----) Jordan. George H. Jordan m Ella M. ---- [will dated 15 Jan. 1903]. Child: **P e r c y D.** b 13 Apr. 1869. [Probate court #10485, Androscoggin Co., ME.]

JORDAN, GEORGE WASHINGTON/WASHINGTON - Born 10 May 1811, d 17 Sep. 1895, was possibly the s/o Jonathan and ?? Jordan. Jonathan Jordan was the s/o Richard, s/o Robert, s/o John, s/o Robert. George Washington/Washington Jordan was possibly the s/o James and Abigail (Dingley) Jordan. He m 22/23 Apr. 1841 Joanna Garcelon, d 5 Apr. 1897, d/o James. Children: **Augusta O.** b 14 Jun. 1842; and **Eddie E.** b 21 May 1861, d 22 Aug. 1863.

JORDAN, ISAAC GOLDER - Born 18 Sep. 1822, d 17 Jan. 1896, s/o Benjamin and Polly (Golder) Jordan. Isaac Golder Jordan m Eliza A./Elisa Ann Jordan, b 27 Feb. 1832, d 24 Mar. 1893, d/o William & Adeline (Dill) Jordan of Webster, Maine. Children: **William F.** b 28 Dec. 1847, d 24 Jun. 1892, m 10 Jun. 1878 Lissie E. Briggs at Hyde Park, d/o George Austemput; **Vesta** b Aug./Oct. 1849, m 24 May 1869 Hall Page of Belgrade, ME, d 1901; **Winfield Scott** q.v.; **Ida May** m Fred Walker; **Lissie L.** b 27 Nov. 1857, m (1) William Howard of

Providence, RI, d 12 Apr. 1883, and m (2) Robert Howard of Providence, RI; **Helen** b -- Feb. ----, d 18 Aug. 1893, m William Greene of Boston; **Cora R.** lived in Boston, MA, with Ida; and **Alice M.** b -- Aug. 1866, d 28 Mar. 1867.

JORDAN, JAMES - Born ??, d ??, s/o ?? Child: **Sarah** m 13 Feb. 1855 Alvin Read, b 1 Oct. 1830, and they had one child, Everett E.

JORDAN, JAMES - Born 6 Apr. 1790, d 12 Mar. 1859 in Minot, Maine, s/o Jeremiah and Hannah (Marr) Jordan. James Jordan m 30 Nov. 1809 Sophia Moody, b in Hebron, Maine, d 2 Oct. 1871. Children: **Pemelia** b 14 Apr. 1810 at Lewiston, d 2 Nov. 1840, m 1833 Woodbury Thomas, who was b 14 Apr. 1804 at Cape Elizabeth, ME, d 26 Feb. 1874 at Lewiston; **M a r y g N.** b 21 Jan. 1812, d 15 Sep. 1853, m 26 Aug. 1837 Rufus Lincoln; **James** b 1 Mar. 1815; **Abigail** b 24 Apr. 1816 in Lisbon, ME, m 1836 Rufus Merrill of Lisbon, resided in Bath, ME; **Rufus** b 20 Nov. 1818 at Lewiston, m 1853 Harriet Groves, d 23 Nov. 1874 at Brunswick; **Hesikiah Moody** b 20 Jan. 1821, d 29 Aug. 185-; **William Ames** q.v.; **Winslow Ames** b 1 Jun. 1825, d at sea 24 Mar. 1878, m 4 Jul. 1848 Margueritte E. Briggs of Lisbon, ME; **James** b 10 Sep. 1827, carpenter at Bath, unm; **Sarah** b 19 May 1830; **Sophia** b 7 Jul. 1833 at Lisbon, d 10 Oct. 1876, m 7 Mar. 1852 Alvin Judkins, who was b 10 Jun. 1825 at Roxbury; and **Ellen** b 1 Aug. 1836 in Lisbon, m 5 Sep. 1861 Geo. L. Roberts of Brunswick, ME. [Vital Records of Lewiston, Maine, p. 111.]

JORDAN, JAMES - Born -- Apr. 1771, d 23 Aug. 1831, age 60 years, s/o Jonathan and ?? Jordan. Jonathan Jordan was the s/o Richard, s/o Robert, s/o John, s/o Robert. James Jordan m 20 Nov. 1796 Abigail Dingley, b -- Dec. 1772, d 11 May 1860, age 88 years 4 months. Children: **S a l l y** b 22 Jan. 1797, d 10 Dec. 1887, m pub. 24 Apr. 1825 Hugh Miller of Durham, ME, d 9 Oct. 1885 in Durham; **James** q.v.; **Lucy** b 20 May 1801, d 1891, m 8 May 1839 Jonathan D. Jordan of Lisbon, ME; **Charlotte** b 19 Nov. 1804, m 23 Mar. 1854 Elisha Hanson, d 1 Jan. 1884, age 77 years; **Rhoda** b 24 Apr. 1807, m 1835 Joshua S. Strout, who lived in Durham, ME; **A b i g a i l** b 10 May 1809, m 10 Mar. 1847 John L. Davis of Webster, ME; **G e o r g e Washington/Washington** q.v.; and **Harris** b 21 Aug. 1815, d 20 Dec. 1892, unm. [Vital Records of Lewiston, Maine, p. 38.]

JORDAN, JAMES JR. - Born 26 Dec. 1799, d 16 Apr. 1866 [probate #603 Androscoggin Co., ME, and *Morning Star* obit 9 May 1866], s/o James and Abigail (Dingley) Jordan. James Jordan, Jr. was a Freewill Baptist at Lisbon, Maine. He m 10 Jun. 1824 Deborah Garcelon, b 30 Jun. 1797, d 20 Aug. 1883 age 86 years and 20 days. Children: **Elizabeth Abigail** b 10 Aug. 1825, d 20 Feb. 1861, m 1 Mar. 1854 John Morrell; **James Garcelon** q.v.; **Charles Bisbee** q.v.; **Alfred S./Emery** q.v.; **Lucy Dingley** b 20 Mar. 1833, m 22 Nov. 1857 Nathaniel G. Garcelon; **Sarah Wentworth** b 30 Jun. 1835, unm, lived in Durham; **Harriet Newell** b 17 Oct. 1837, m 17 Oct. 1872 Henry Harrington, lived in Durham, ME; and **George Henry** q.v. [Vital Records of Lewiston, Maine, p. 112.]

JORDAN, JAMES GARCELON - Born 11 Jan. 1827, d 3 Nov. 1871 at Lisbon, Maine, s/o James and Deborah (Garcelon) Jordan. James Garcelon Jordan m 30/31 Oct. 1849 Nancy B. Ham, b 17 Jul. 1827, d 3 Nov. 1871, d/o James Ham of Lewiston. Children: **Eda M.** b 24 Apr. 1851, m 10 Apr. 1871 Wm. H. H. Atwood of Lisbon; **Frederick** b 17 Feb. 1853, d 9 Aug. 1870; and **James** b 26 May 1864 in Lisbon.

JORDAN, JEREMIAH II - Born ??, d 30 Aug./Nov. 1823 age 78 years, s/o Jeremiah and Keziah (Handscomb) Jordan. Jeremiah (the elder) was the s/o Jedidiah, s/o Jedidiah, s/o Robert. Jeremiah (the younger) Jordan m 8 Mar. 1774 Hannah Marr. Children: **Abraham** q.v.; **Jeremiah** q.v.; **Andrew** q.v.; **Benjamin** q.v.; **James** q.v.; **Kessiah** b 21 Feb. 1792, m 13 Jul. 1820 Andrew Dain at Lisbon, ME; **David** b 19 Sep. 1796, m 1 Jan. 1818 Polly Landers; **Hannah** b 28 Nov. 1798, m 15 Feb. 1821 James Dain of Lisbon; and **Joseph** b 17 Apr. 1803, d 15 Apr. 1823, m 7 Oct. 1825 Mary J. Moody, d/o Josiah Moody of Lewiston. [Vital Records of Lewiston, Maine, p. 37.]

JORDAN, JEREMIAH III - Born 29 Jul. 1785, d ??, s/o Jeremiah II and Hannah (Marr) Jordan. Jeremiah Jordan m (1) pub. 2 Aug. 1807 Anna/Dianna Pencock/Peacock of Gardiner, Maine, d -- Aug. 1821 due to a blood vessel which burst in her head, and he m (2) Mary (Dill) Haley. *Children of 1st wife*: **Hannah M.** m Alexander McIntosh, dc1885 at Topsham, ME; **Lucy** m Wm. Lunt of Gardiner, ME; and **Betsey** m Elisha Thurlow (?), lived at Leeds, ME. *Children of 2nd wife*: **Mary Ann Lulf** sis m Ivory Lord; **Jeremiah** b 1809, unm; **Benjamin** m Salley Lincoln; **Alexander** m Maria Webb; **Jerusha** m Elbridge Webber; and **Sarah** m Joseph Tobey. [Letter from O. B. Clason, Esq. of Gardiner, ME, 7 Jul. 1902.]

JORDAN, JOSEPH - Born 28 Jan. 1851 in Turner, Maine, d ??, s/o ?? Joseph Jordan m Deborah Bonney, d/o Isaac Bonney. Child: **Charles R.** b 9 Jun. 1826 at Lisbon, d 29 Dec. 1875 at Auburn.

JORDAN, JOSEPH - Born 12 Dec. 1834, d ??, s/o ?? Joseph Jordan m Ellen Turner, d/o James Turner of Lewiston.

JORDAN, NATHANIEL - Born ??, d ??, s/o ?? Nathaniel Jordan m (1) 18 May 1812 Abigail Garcelon, who d 11 Nov. 1818, and m (2) Alice Rowe. Nathaniel lived in Durham when married. Children: **Mary** b 18 Aug. 1812 in Lewiston, d 13 Jul. 1848, m 2 Jun. 1848 Simeon P. Fitz of Danville, who d 29 May 1890; and **Dorothy** b 1816, d 21 Mar. 1864, m Soloman Jordan. [Vital Records of Lewiston, Maine, p. 37.]

JORDAN, PETER D. - Born 1 Jul. 1828, m Isabel Turner, d/o James Turner of Lewiston.

JORDAN, RUFUS - Son of James of Lewiston, s/o James, s/o Jere, s/o Jere, s/o Jed, s/o Jed, s/o Robert. Children: **Hattie**; and **Caroline**.

JORDAN, DEACON TIMOTHY - Born 29 Sep. 1801, d ??, s/o Abner and Hannah (----) Jordan. Deacon Timothy Jordan lived on the John W. Mitchell place on Eastern Avenue, Lewiston. He m 15 Jan. 1827 at Monmouth, Maine, Climena Augusta Welch, d 21 Mar. 1868, age 63 years *Morning Star* obit 29 Apr. 1868]. Children: **Julius Augustus** b 23 Aug. 1828, d 17 Sep. 1848; **Delphina Adelade** b 2 Jun. 1830, d 17 Feb. 1833 at Greene, ME; **Abner A. Dolphus** b 10 Mar. 1832, res. KS; **George Mandeville** b 10 Apr. 1834, res. CA; **Irene Adelade** b 31 Dec. 1835, d 27 Aug. 1853; **Nathan Bartlett** b 10 Jan. 1838, eres. KS; **Isaac Libby** b 11 Aug. 1839; and **Octavia E.** b 1845, d 1 Aug. 1848, age 3 years.

JORDAN, WILLIAM AMES - Born 25 Nov. 1823, ----, d ??, s/o James, and Sophia (Moody) Jordan. William Omes/Ames Jordan was the br/o James, cousin/o Rufus. He m 14 Nov. 1846 Emelia W., d/o Jere P. Cummings. Children: **William F.** b 22 Aug. 1847 at Brunswick, d 20 Sep. 1849; **Mary Emma** b 18 Apr. 1850 at Brunswick, m 2 Dec. 1867 Calvin Glenn at Yreber (?), CA; **Lissie Etta** b 6 Apr. 1853 at Brunswick, ME, m 4 Jul. 1871 Lloyd Benjamin Tutrell, Lt., at Jones, CA; **Charles Henry** b 4 Aug. 1855 at Brunswick; **Edward Wilsen** b 29 Aug. 1857 at Brunswick; **Frank Cummings** b 2 Mar. 1866 at Scott Valley, CO, m 24 Dec. 1875 Lettie Taylor, Lt., at Jones, CA.

JORDAN, WILLIAM S. - Born 3 Feb. 1804, d 22 Apr. 1873, m 3 Jun. 1876 Adeline Dill, who d 13 Feb. 1848.

JORDAN, WINFIELD SCOTT - Married Lucy E. Thompson (nee Hackett), who was b 5 Mar. 1849, d/o Saml. and Olive (Meadler?) Hackett. Children: **Alice May** b 12 May 1873, m (1) 21 Nov. 1897 Joseph W. Chamberlane of Calais, ME?, and m (2) 4 Nov. 1889 Charles W. Towne of Lewiston, d 5 Sep. 1900; and **G r a c e E l v a** b 7 Aug. 1881, m Drew E. Drake.

JUDKINS, WILBUR H. - Born 19 May 1858 in Monmouth, Maine, d 5 Apr. 1934, s/o John G. and Aurelia (----) Judkins. Wilbur H. Judkins m 1886 Nellie Jones. He served as mayor of Lewiston in 1897, had been city solicitor from 1886 to 1888, among other positions. Child: **Florence**.

KIMBALL, SIMEON - Born ??, d ??, s/o ?? Simeon Kimball is listed as 1-2-2 in Lewiston, Maine, 1790 census. He m 26 Dec. 1785 Rhoda Blethen. [*History of Durham, Maine* published by the Town of Durham, 1899, reprint 1979, p. 152 and see vital records typescript at the Maine State Archives on the Ref. Shelves.]

LAKE, JOSEPH - Born ??, d 17 Mar. 1873, s/o ?? Joseph Lake moved to Bath, Maine. He m Loisa Johnson. Children: **Thaxter** b 11 Oct. 1836; **J. H.** b 1843; **Georgia**; and **Fannie**. [Vital Records of Lewiston, Maine, p. 119 and letter, 1896, from George Knight of Lowell, MA.]

LAKE, JOSHUA - Born ??, d ??, s/o ?? Joshua Lake settled in Lewiston in 1786. He m Sarah ----. Children: **Ebenezer** b 18 Jun. 1786; **Stephen** b 9 Jul. 1788; **Sarah** b 18 Sep. 1790; **Josiah** b 18 Apr. 1793; **Mercy** b 24 Mar. 1795; **John** b 30 Jun. 1797. [Vital Records of Lewiston, Maine, p. 43.]

LAKE, STEPHEN - Born 16 Mar. 1784, d 28 Jul. 1880 age 96 years 4 months 12 days at Richmond, Maine, s/o ?? Stephen Lake m Mehitable ----. Children: **Joseph** b 16 Aug. 1812; **Martha** b 4 Dec. 1814; **Melinda** b 18 Dec. 1816; **John** b 1 Aug. 1819; **William** b 8 Oct. 1822; **Joshua** b 4 Jan. 1825; **Almira** b 24 Jan. 1827; **Stephen** b 5 May 1828; and **Mehitable** b 5 Apr. 1833. [Vital Records of Lewiston, Maine, p. 46 and letter from John Lake of Richmond, 1896.]

LAMB, JOHN SANDERS - Born 26 Jan. 1805 in New Brunswick, Canada, d ??, s/o ?? John Sanders Lamb's parents were natives of U. S. A. Marriage int. 14 Nov. 1828 Prudence Lowell. Child: **Joseph** b 16 Sep. 1829 at Lewiston. [Vital Records of Lewiston, Maine, p. 119, 416.]

LAMBS, PETER - Born ??, d ??, s/o ?? Peter Lambs was listed as 1-4-5 in the Lewiston 1790 census. [See Lenfest.]

LANDER/LANDERS, ABISHA - Born ??, d ??, s/o Freeman and Thankful (Hinckley) Lander/Landers. Abisha Lander/Landers m Mary Frances Fuller, b in Falmouth, Massachusetts. Children: **Sealed** b 27 Jan. 1776, resided in Greene, ME; **Ansel** b 20 Nov. 1777, d 18 Apr. 1796; **Ansel** q.v.; **Archibald** q.v.; **Abisha, Jr.** q.v.; **Freeman** q.v.; **Dorcas** m 16 Oct. 1814 Ebenezer Jepson; **Thankful** b 1781, m David Ireland at Bloomfield; **Anna** b 11 Feb. 1783 (moved to Lagrange, ME), m 15 Mar. 1804 Joel Coburn; **Hannah** m pub. 1 Dec. 1808 Thomas Piper; **Olive** m Joseph Coburn; **Jerey** d 30 Apr. 1793; **Lucy** b 15 Mar. 1793; **Misha**; **Seth**; and **Levina**. [Letter from R. Allen of Skowhegan, 1904.] [*History of Greene, Maine* by Walter Lindley Mower, published by Merrill & Webber Co., 1938, p. 381, names four additional children: **Lucy** b 15 Mar. 1793; **Misha**; **Seth**; and **Levina**.]

LANDER/LANDERS, ABISHA JR. - Born ??, d ??, s/o Abisha and Mary Frances (Fuller) Lander/Landers. Abisha Lander/Landers, Jr. m (1) Kesiah Mills of Jay, Maine, and m (2) Abigail (Eustus) Brooks. Children: **Nancy** m Cyrus Weymouth; **Irsine/Iresin P.** q.v.; **Moses Mills** d 1840 in Kingfield, ME, m (1) Emily Searls, and m (2) Mary Garland of New Portland, ME; **William** b 13 Jun. 1832, d 4 May 1863 in the army, m 4 Sep. 1855 Jane Knapp of Blanchard, ME; **Sarah** m Moses Weymouth; and **Rebecca** m Reubin Winslow of Farmington Falls, ME.

LANDER/LANDERS, ABNER SR. - Born ??, d ??, s/o Freeman and ?? Lander/Landers. Abner Lander/Landers m Hannah Barker, d/o Jacob. Children: **Abner, Jr.** m Rebecca Peabody of New Portland, ME; **Stephen** q.v.; **Mary** m Wade Litchfield of Lewiston, pub. 22 Mar. 1818; **Lucy** m pub. 18 Mar. 1820 Daniel Cutler of Lewiston; **Tumah** m

Eben Cummings of Greene, ME; **Annis** m 30 Nov. 1820 Oliver Cushman of Leeds, ME; and **Amos** m Isabel Chapin.

LANDER/LANDERS, ANSEL - Born 11 Jun. 1796, d 11 Nov. 1865, s/o Abisha and Mary Frances (Fuller) Lander/Landers. Ansel Lander/Landers m 19 Nov. 1818 Bathsheba Cushman of Leeds, Maine, d 8 Feb. 1883. Children: **Samuel**; **Mary** b 16 Mar. 1820, m Benjamin Fellows; **Violet** b 13 Apr. 1822, lived in Freeman, ME, m 4 Jul. 1858 William R. Dudley, who d 3 Oct. 1890; **Albion** b 1824, d 1840, age 16 years; **Leonard** d in CA, unm; **Elizabeth** b 5 Sep. 1829, m 1 Jan. 1853 William Hull, who d 25 Apr. 1873; **Jason** b 1831, killed 16 Jun. 1864 in action with 17th ME Reg; **Prudence** m Ward Dudley, d in Lowell, MA?; **Oscar F.** b 17 Jul. 1836, m 6 Jun. 1883 Cynthia Fisher; and **Oinsa** d young.

LANDER/LANDERS, ARCHIBALD - Born 1783/1785, d 11 Jun. 1869, s/o Abisha and Mary Frances (Fuller) Lander/Landers. Archibald Lander/Landers m (1) Hannah Moody, and m (2) Lucy Mills. Children: **Joseph** q.v.; **Hiram** b 1816/1817, m Lucy Ann McKenny of Kingfield, ME; **Lonna** b 1819, d 1843, unm, school teacher; **Thankful** b 20 Jan. 1825, m 28 Apr. 1864 Sylognus M. Ruggles of Providence, RI, who d 19 Nov. 1895; **Ira Mills** b 1822, d 1870, m Deana Warl; and **Charles/Charles P.** q.v.

LANDER/LANDERS, ARCHIBALD/ARCHIBALD WELLES - Born 17 Mar. 1845, d ??, s/o Charles/Charles P. and Martha (Berry) Lander/Landers. Archibald Lander/Landers m 25 Jun. 1878 or 9 Jun. 1879 Fanny/Fannie Bickford. Children: **Adaline Evelyn** b 15 Aug. 1880; **Hattie May** b 25 Sep. 1882; **Archibald Willis** b 24 Jul. 1885; **John Joseph** b 10 Feb. 1887; **Everett** b 4 Nov. 1889; **Sewall Dinsmore** b 2 Feb. 1891; and **Lawrence Tucker** b 11 Oct. 1895.

LANDER/LANDERS, CHARLES/CHARLES P. - Born 16 Jul. 1829, d 23 Jan. 1899/1900, s/o Archibald and ?? Lander/Landers. Charles/Charles P. Lander/Landers m 7/27 Apr. 1853 Martha Berry of New Portland, Maine, b 14 Jun. 1830, d/o Soloman and Margaret E. (Drummond) Berry of New Portland. Children: **Leonard E.** q.v.; **Archibald/Archibald Welles** q.v.; **John J.** q.v.; **Wentworth V.** q.v.; and **Cathers Drummond** b 23 Aug. 1873, m 9 Apr. 1898 Mary Bartlett.

LANDER/LANDERS, CHARLES M. - Born ??, d ??, s/o ?? Children: **Lester A.** b 15 Dec. 1870; **Nellie M.** b 27 Feb. 1875; **Charles E.** b 3 Nov. 1884; and **Frank E.**

LANDER/LANDERS, ELBRIDGE F./T. - Born 21 Jun. 1833, d ??, s/o True and Elvira (Dresser) Lander/Landers. Children: **Eva L.** b 16 Dec. 1857, d 2 Jun. 1899; **Augusta A.** b 8 Jun. 1859; and **Charles F.** b 4 Apr. 1862.

LANDER/LANDERS, FREEMAN - Born ??, d ??, s/o ?? Freeman Lander/Landers m 20 Nov. 1755 Thankful Hinckley of Falmouth, Massachusetts. Children: **Abisha** q.v.; **Sarah** b 3 Aug. 1759, d 9 Jun.

1839, m Elihu Hatch, a Revolutionary Soldier who d 14 May 1837; **Hannah** b 31 Dec. 1760, d 6 Sep. 1831, m Samuel Hatch, who d 4 Mar. 1841, age 84 years; **Lucy** b -- Apr. 1763, d 5 Jun. 1858, unm; **Robinson** q.v.; **Dorcus** b 1770, d 12 Aug. 1849, age 89 years, m Ephraim Pettengill, who was b 1770, d 6 Sep. 1819, age 40 years; **Lasarus** q.v.; **Eunice** b 25 Apr. 1777, d 1 Apr. 1834 in Cambridge, ME, m -- Feb. 1806 Reuben Coburn of Lewiston; **Rachel** b 17 Feb. 1780, d 22 Apr. 1863; **Joana** b -- Jan. 1775, d 5 Feb. 1855, m Eliphalet Coburn, who d 7 Nov. 1828, age 56 years; and **Lucy**, unm.

LANDER/LANDERS, FREEMAN - Born 4 May 1779, d 24 Feb. 1842, s/o Abisha and Mary Frances (Fuller) Lander/Landers. Freeman Lander/Landers m Rebecca Wheeler. Children: **Seth** b 4 May 1803, d 9 Dec. 1826; **Lavinia** b 26 Jul. 1805, m Joseph Hackett; and **Freeman** q.v.

LANDER/LANDERS, IRESIN P./IRSINE/IRASIN P. - Born 5 Jan. 1819, d 25 Jun. 1884, s/o Abisha, Jr. and ?? Lander/Landers. Iresin P./Irsine/Irasin P. Lander/Landers m 7 Dec. 1843 Hannah/Hannah H. Gilbert of Kingfield, Maine, d/o Spencer Gilbert. Children: **Amelia K.** b 27 Oct. 1844, d 24 Jun. 1898; **Ellen N.** b 18 Apr. 1846, m 10 Oct. 1875 William Wagg; **Emma F.** b 2 Feb. 1848, m 5 Sep. 1872 Samuel Leadham; **Arvilla F.** b 16 Oct. 1850, d 28 Aug. 1900; **Franklin W.** b 6 Dec. 1852, d 15 May 1874; **Olin C.** q.v.; **Omer S.** b 26 Mar. 1856, m 9 Jun. 1883 Sarah Henderson; **Evelin R.** b 27 Jan. 1859, m 14 Dec. 1882 William E. Abbott; **Odell I.** b 3 Jul. 1861; and **Herbert H.** b 16 Mar. 1865, m 14 Nov. 1885 Menerva Goodwin.

LANDER/LANDERS, JOHN J. - Born 26 Feb. 1861, d ??, s/o Charles/Charles P. and Martha (Berry) Lander/Landers. John J. Lander/Landers m 17 Feb. 1884 Florence M. Baker, b 22 Feb. 1866 at Moscow, Maine, d/o Ellery R. and Mehitable (Bucks?) Baker. Children: **Nora M.** b 22 Nov. 1885; **Allen W.** b 14 Jun. 1888; **Eugean P.** b 14 Aug. 1889; **Mabel** b 27 Jul. 1891; **Janet F.** b 30 Dec. 1892; **Ruth B.** b 1 Mar. 1894; **William D.** b 14 Nov. 1895; and **Alice M.** b 12 Mar. 1898.

LANDER/LANDERS, JOSEPH - Born ??, d ??, s/o ?? Joseph Lander/Landers m Charity Littlefield. Children: **Hannah** b 4 Dec. 1826, m John Furbush; **Elisa** b 30 Jan. 1828; and **Elbridge** b 1 May 1829.

LANDER/LANDERS, JOSEPH - Born 24 Jun. 1814, d 11 Jun. 1869, s/o Archibald and ?? Lander/Landers. Joseph Lander/Landers m 6 Jun. 1841 Eliza/Eliza Ann Weymouth. Children: **Harris Philbrick** d 20 Feb. 1902, m (1) Melora Dennes, and m (2) Ethel Henniger; **Rufus K.** b 29 Oct. 1845, lived in Dedham, m 1878 Abbie Brinn; **Loantha** b 20 Nov. 1843, d 19 Jun. 1900; **Charles Albert** b 7 May 1848, m Annie Resinger; **Frank** b 27 Aug. 1851; **Ida H.**; and **Ida** b 22 Oct. 1853, m 1881 William Francis.

LANDER/LANDERS, JOSEPH/JOSIAH - Born 16 Sep. 1797 [14 Sep. 1796 according to Danville Records], d 22 Feb. 1856, age 57 years 5 months, s/o Lazarus and Lydia (Graffam) Lander/Landers. Joseph/Josiah Lander/Landers m (1) 13 Sep. 1821 Kesiah Haskell, d 13 Sep. 1821 or 27 Dec. 1837, d/o Samuel and Lydia (----) Haskell, and m (2) 10 May 1843 Pamelia/Pamela Jones of Danville, Maine, b 22 Mar. 1807.

LANDER/LANDERS, LAZARUS - Born 2 Dec. 1772, d 14 Jan. 1845 or 19 Jan. 1846 age 75 years, s/o Freeman and Thankful (Hinckley) Lander/Landers. Lazarus Lander/Landers settled in Lewiston in 1783. He m 13 Feb. 1809 Lydia Graffam, d 13 Jan. 1858, age 85 years 3 months. Children: **Luce** b 5 Jun. 1795, d 10 Feb. 1884, m John Chadbourne of Greene, ME, b 6/26 May 1795, d 30 Sep. 1877; **Joseph/Josiah** q.v.; **Emma** b 11 Apr. 1798, d 29 Mar. 1887, m Nathaniel Sawtelle of Oldtown, ME; **Isaac** b 6 Sep. 1799, d 12 Oct. 1881; **Alice** b 4 Mar. 1801, d 13 Sep. 1803; **Benjamin** b 23 Mar. 1803, d 9 Nov. 1893, m Ann Small; **Alice** b 5 Oct. 1804, d 1864, m George Moulton, d in Lewiston; **David** b 6 Jun. 1806, d 13 Aug. 1893 in Gardiner, ME, m 1827 Margaret Millay of Bowdoinham, ME; **True** q.v.; **Olive** b 8 Apr. 1810, d 19 Nov. 1884, m 14 Dec. 1830 Samuel Littlefield, b 27 Jun 1806, and d 20 Jan. 1891; **Lydia** b 15 Sep. 1811, d 11 Sep. 1819, m pub. 15 Jan. 1818 in Danville, ME, Foster Smith; **Anna** b 24 Aug. 1810, d 14 Nov. 1819; **Leonard** b 30 Apr. 1818, m (1) 1845 Elvira Abbott of Freeman, ME, and m (2) Susan Hinckley of Warren, ME; and **Mary I.** b 13 Dec. 1812, d 12 Sep. 1819.

LANDER/LANDERS, LEONARD - Born ??, d ??, s/o ?? Children: **Ellen**; and **Sarah** m Alonzo Grafton.

LANDER/LANDERS, LEONARD - Born 18 Feb. 1854, d ??, s/o Charles/Charles P. and Martha (Berry) Lander/Landers. Leonard Lander/Landers m 5 Apr. 1877 or 1878 Bell Vose. Children: **Nettie** m in Kansus; and **Charles**, unm, lived in East Pepperell, Massachusetts.

LANDER/LANDERS, MARSHALL - Born 24 Sep. 1840, d ??, s/o Stephen and Lydia (Bloomer) Lander/Landers. Marshall Lander/Landers m 5 May 1867 Elvira Moody. Children: **Lydia Jane** b 17 Jul. 1868, m 1887 Charles Wyman; **Herbert Stephen** b 14 Dec. 1870, m 1899 Kate McCrutchin; **Bertha** b 14 Mar. 1872, m 1898 George Douglass; **Lillian** b 30 Oct. 1873, m Hermon Lisherness; **Grace** b 24 Jan. 1877, m 1899 Herman Luce, lived in Kingfield, ME; **Carroll Granville** b 3 Apr. 1876; **Selinda** b 20 Jul. 1879, d 8 Aug. 1883; **Benjamin Marshall** b 14 May 1881; and **Eulalah Adelaid** b 1 Mar. 1885.

LANDER/LANDERS, MOSES MILLS - Born ??, d 1840 in Kingfield, Maine, s/o Abisha, Jr. and ?? Lander/Landers. Moses Mills Lander/Landers m (1) Emely Searls, and m (2) Mary Garland of New Portland, Maine. Children: **Willis**; **Etta** m John Walker; **Mabel** m Chester Dolbier; and **Burtram** m Mary Ella Fletcher.

LANDER/LANDERS, NASHUM D. - Born ??, d ??, s/o ?? Children: **Mertie E.** b 28 Jan. 1873; **Ethel B.** b 3 Sep. 1874; **Laura B.** b 26 Sep. 1875; **Frank N.** b 10 May 1877; **Lucy A.** b 24 Apr. 1879, d 15 Nov. 1881; **Nettie F.** b 4 Apr. 1881, d 11 Nov. 1888; **Edith E.** b 18 Jun. 1885; **Smith A.** b 25 Jul. 1887; and **Freeman A.** b 1 Jul. 1891.

LANDER/LANDERS, OLIN C. - Born 11 Jun. 1854, d ??, s/o Iresin P./Irsine/Irasin P. and Hannah H. (Gilbert) Lander/Landers of Kingfield, Maine. Olin C. Lander/Landers m 1 Oct. 1880 Theresa Brian. Children: **Grace H.** b 15 Jun. 1881; **Edith G.** b 10 Feb. 1883; and **Albert H.** b 5 Jun. 1886.

LANDER/LANDERS, OMER H. - Born 22 Jul. 1866, d ??, s/o Stephen, Jr. and ?? Lander/Landers. Omer H. Lander/Landers m 24 Mar. 1894 Blanche Dunton. Children: **Ola M.** b 7 Sep. 1896; and **Kathleen Ada** b 9 Jan. 1901.

LANDER/LANDERS, ROBINSON - Born 16 Mar. 1768, d 6 Jan. 1857, s/o Freeman and Thankful (Hinckley) Lander/Landers. Robinson Lander/Landers settled in Lewiston in 1784. He m 14 Jan. 1794 Prudence Coburn of Canaan, Maine, d 20 Sep. 1851, age 80 years, d/o Eleaser and Bridget (Hildreth) (sis/o Paul Hildreth) Coburn of Dracut, MA. Children: **Aaron** b 3 Mar. 1795, d 1831 in Fredricton, NB; **Sarah** b 24 Feb. 1797, d 11 Jan. 1890, m 14 Feb. 1871 Ansel Allen, who d 5 May 1858 in Bloomfield, ME; **Betsey** b 1799, d 1819 in Lewiston; **Jane** b 29 Jun. 1801, d 4 May 1822, m 15 Oct. 1825 Harper Allen, who d 6 Jun. 1865, age 66 years; **R a c h e l** b 12 May 1804, d 21 Jan. 1895, m 5 Mar. 1825 John Bennett, who d 1895, age 96 years; and **B r i d g e t** b 10 Jul. 1806, d 20 Dec. 1880, m 14 Dec. 1828 Peter Judkins, who d 1841. [Letter from Miss R. J. Allen of Skowhegan, ME, 1900.]

LANDER/LANDERS, SELIA SR. - Born ??, d ??, s/o Freeman, Sr. and ?? Lander/Landers. Children: **Selia, Jr.**; **Sarah** m Deacon Thomas Pratt; **Mary** m David Jordan; **Annie** m Luther Brown; and **Jacob** m Fidelia Pratt, who d in New Portland, ME.

LANDER/LANDERS, STEPHEN - Born ??, d ??, s/o Abner, Sr. and Hannah (Barker) Lander/Landers. Stephen Lander/Landers m Lydia Bloomer, d/o Capt. Benj. and Eunice (Owen) Bloomer of Bowdoinham, Maine. Children: **J a n e C o b u r n** b 2 Jun. 1832, m 30 Nov. 1854 Americus V. Hinds of Kingfield, ME; **Oliver** b 1 Jun. 1834; **Lois** b 1 Jun. 1836, d 28 Jan. 1899, m Capt. Edwin H. Lorry of Surry, ME; **Stephen, Jr.** b 5 Jun. 1838, m Eliza Morrow; and **Marshall** q.v.

LANDER/LANDERS, STEPHEN, JR. - Born ??, d ??, s/o ?? Stephen Lander/Landers, Jr. m (1) Eliza Morrow, and m (2) 11 Mar. 1895 Nellie Dunton. Children: **Cora Myrtle**; **Jeremiah**; **Omer H.** q.v.; **Blanch Nora** b 1 Aug. 1875, m 1 May 1895 Ernest E. Dunton of Concord.

LANDER/LANDERS, TRUE - Born 5 Apr. 1808, d 11 Dec. 1883, s/o Lazarus and Lydia (Graffam) Lander/Landers. True Lander/Landers m Elvira Dresser. Children: **Elbridge F./T.** q.v.; **Lucy J.** b 1 Dec. 1835, d 10 Mar. 1892, m Charles E. Nevers; **Charles M.** b 7 Sep. 1837, m (1) Lucy A. Blake, who d 27 Nov. 1867, and m (2) 21 Jun. 1894 Mrs. Nancy Snell (nee Chaffin), whose son lived in Auburn, ME; **Hattie A.** b 1 Sep. 1839, m Eliphlet Wight; **David N.** b 1 Mar. 1841, d 12 Nov. 1843; **Nathan H.** b 20 Dec. 1842, m 19 Dec. 1867 Mrs. Cathalina Woodman (nee Randall), d/o Robert; **David N.** b 18 Jan. 1845, m (1) 16 Sep. 1863 Lucy M. Sheban, and m (2) Nettie Johnson; **Lydia L.** b 2 Nov. 1846, d 21 Mar. 1863, unm; **Mary E.** b 24 Sep. 1848, d 4 Nov. 1866; **Adelaide E.** b 26 Sep. 1850, d 2 Nov. 1872; **Nellie D.** b 2 Jul. 1852, unm; and **Jermie** [sic] **F.** b 30 Aug. 1854, m 25 Dec. 1876 John F. Knight, lived in Auburn, ME, had three children: **Ida Knight** m A. Newhegin; **Lura Knight** m A. Wilsen, and **Charles Knight** was a lighthouse keeper in Portland Harbor, ME.

LANDER/LANDERS, WENTWORTH V. - Born 9 Jun. 1867, d ??, s/o Charles/Charles P. and Martha (Berry) Lander/Landers. Wentworth V. Lander/Landers m 15 Jun. 1889 Abbie/Alfie Hackett, d/o Hiram Carville Hackett. Children: **Nellie E.** b 1900; and **Cathus D.** m Mary ----, no children.

LARABEE/LARRABEE, ABRAHUM/ABRAHAM - Born 1896, d ??, s/o Isaac and ?? Larabee/Larrabee. Children: **Wm. Henry; Emery; Viola; Augusta; Martha;** and **George.**

LARABEE/LARRABEE, CHARLES - Born ??, d ??, s/o ?? Child: **Cora** b 1856, d 1860.

LARABEE/LARRABEE, ISAAC - Born 1799 in Durham, Maine or Pejepscot, Maine, d 22 Sep. 1866, age 70 years and 5 days, s/o Joseph and Abigail (McKenney) Larabee/Larrabee [vital records of Danville, Maine, Maine State Archives, file cards]. Isaac Larabee/Larrabee m Rebecca Adams, b 21/29 Mar. 1799, d 19 Apr. 1874. Children: **Abraham** b 30 Dec. 1820, d 1864 in the Army, m (1) 3 Mar. 1888 Abbe Rebecca Livermore, and m (2) Lovina Furbush, d/o Abraham of Green; **Isaac** b 2 Oct. 1822, m 15 Aug. 1848 Louisa Snell, d 19 Jul. 1886; **Abigail** b 4 Nov. 1824, m Henry Furbush; **Moses** d 16 Jul. 1843, unm; **Philip** b while living on Webster St., m (1) Abigail McDonald, and m (2) Elsia Stewart of Lewiston; **Charles H.** b 30 Nov. 1832, m 1855 Martha A. Bean of Ossipee, NH, likely d/o James and Eunice (Murphy) Bean [*History of Greene* by Mower, published by the author, 1938, p. 215]; **Eunice** b 1836 m Horace McDonald; **Stephen** m Louisa Philbrick of St. Albans, ME; **Edward** m Angelina Farewell of Greene; and **Rebecca** m William Sawyer. [Vital records of Lewiston, Maine, p. 118; 1850 census of Ossipee, NH, #120-123; notes on Ossipee, NH, families compiled by David Young of Auburn, ME.]

LARABEE/LARRABEE, JEAN? - Born ??, d ??, s/o Isaac and ?? Larabee/Larrabee. Children: **Frances E.** b 27 Dec. 1848; **Charles Edward** b -- Oct. 1850, d -- Jul. 19--; **Herbert W.** b 1 Nov. 1857, d 15 Feb. 1881; **Sarah J.** b 5 Apr. 1862 m Geo. French of Lewiston;

James B. b 2 Jan. 1860, m Mary Rich; **Anne B.** b 5 Sep. 1866; **Emma B.** b 5 Jun. 1870 m Llewelen Gould; and **Annett** d 1855.

LARRABEE/LARABEE, JOSEPH - Born 1801 in Pejepscot, Maine, *Saco Valley Settlements and Families* by G. T. Ridlon, Sr., published by the author, 1895, p. 847], d 1900, s/o Joseph and Abigail (McKenney) Larrabee/Larabee. Joseph Larrabee/Larabee m Charity Littlefield [*Saco Valley Settlements and Families* by Ridlon]. Children: **Hannah** b 4 Dec. 1826 in Lewiston, ME; **Eliza** b 30 Jan. 1828; and **Elbridge** b 1 May 1829, d 1913. [Vital Records of Lewiston, Maine, p. 118.]

LARABEE/LARRABEE, STEPHEN - Born ??, d ??, s/o ?? Children: **Wilmont; Oscar;** and **Edwin.**

LENFEST, PETER - Born 14 Nov. 1739 in Guernsey, England, d ??, s/o ?? Peter Lenfest m 2 Dec. 1774 in New Gloucester, Massachusetts, District of Maine, Lydia Harris, b 14 Aug. 1755 in Dracut, Massachusetts. Lydia Harris was the first white woman to settle in Lewiston. Children: **Judith** b 14 Aug. 1776; **Peter** b 7 Oct. 1777; **John** b 26 Jan. 1778; **Thomas** b 7 Sep. 1779, m Abigail Coburn of Pembroke, Massachusetts; **Lydia** b 18 Apr. 1781, m Joshua Getchell of Pittsfield; **Rebecca** b 12 Feb. 1783, m Isaiah Glidden of Lewiston; **Peter** b 23 Dec. 1784, m Margaret Campbell at Bowdoinham, Maine; **James** b 8 Sep. 1786, m Eunice Gilpatrick; **Judith** b 31 Aug. 1789 m Samuel Getchell at Topsfield, Maine; **Abraham** b 9 Sep. 1790, m Elmira Robinson at Palmyra, Maine; **Nicholas** b 4 Sep. 1792 m Hannah G---- at Washington, Maine; **Solomon** b 16 Apr. 1795, m Mary Ann Hancock. [Town vital records of Lewiston, Maine, p. 43, plus notes and letters of J. G. Elder.]

LIBBY, REV. DAVID - Born 2 Jun. 1822 in Poland, Maine, d 5 Jun. 1902, s/o Deacon David and Dorcas (Nason) Libby of Gray, Maine, [*Free Baptist Cyclopaedia* by Burgess and Ward, published by Free Baptist Cyclopaedia Co., 1889, p. 336]. Rev. David Libby came to Lewiston. He m (1) 12 Apr. 1847 Mary C. Smith of Lisbon, Maine, d/o Isaac and Susan (----) Smith, and m (2) 7 May 1868 Maria C. (Vining) Perley, d/o David Vining, wid/o Luther Perley of Harrison, Maine. *Children of 1st wife*: **Mary E.** b 11 Apr. 1851, m M. H. White; and **Isaac S.** b 14 Jul. 1853, d 1873. *Child of 2nd wife*: **Willis A.** b -- Dec. 1870. [*Libby Family Genealogy* by Charles Libby, published by the author, 1882, p. 435.]

LIBBY, NATHAN - Born 16 Mar. 1796, d 20 Apr. 1822, s/o ?? Nathan Libby m 23 Dec. 1819 Dolly Owen and she m (2) Zebina Hunt. Child: **Elizabeth May** b 16 Oct. 1821, d 16 Jun. 1822 age 9 months.

LIBBY, SAMUEL - Born 2 Sep. 1828, d ??, s/o Rufus and ?? Libby. Samuel Libby m Charlotte Dill, d/o Joseph. Children: **Edith** b 13 Dec. 1865, m (1) Stanley ----, and m (2) Edward Field; and **Frank** b 9 Feb. 1869, m Winnie ----.

LINCOLN, LEVI - Born 23 Jul. 1813, d ??, s/o Lovell/Loved and Betsey (Hodgkin) Lincoln. Levi Lincoln m 26 Aug. 1837 or 6 Aug. 1849 Sarah Peterson of Lisbon, Maine, d 13 Jul. 1868. Children: **Alphonzo** b 14/15 Sep. 1843/1844, m (1) Myrtle Whitney of Bowdoin, ME, and m (2) Addie Keene; **Allen P./T.** b 29 Nov. 1853, m Belle Irving of Lisbon; **Abby E.** b 2 Oct. 1856; and **Albert P./April** b 4 Apr. 1859, d age 85 years, unm.

LINCOLN, LOVEL - Born ??, d ??, s/o ?? Lovel Lincoln m Loraney House. Children: **Cyrus**; and **Nathaniel**.

LINCOLN, LOVELL/LOVED - Born ??, d ??, s/o ?? Lovell/Loved Lincoln m Betsey Hodgkin, d/o Jonathan and Betsey (----) Hodgkin. (Betsey had a child before this marriage.) Children: **Luraney** b 5 Oct. 1808, m pub. 10 Apr. 1827 Hale M. Huskings; **Sally** b 9 Jun. 1810, m Benjamin J. Litchfield, s/o Jeremiah; **Levi** q.v. and **Rufus** q.v.

LINCOLN, RUFUS - Born 5 Oct. 1815 in Lewiston, d ??, s/o Lovell/Loved and Betsey (Hodgkin) Lincoln. Rufus Lincoln lived in Vineland, New Jersey. He m (1) Mary/Mary N. Jordan, d/o James Jordan of Lisbon, Maine, and m (2) 7 Oct. 1854 Rosetta Smith, b 7 Jul. 1826 in Topsham, Maine. *Children of 1st wife*: **Mary E.** b 30 May 1843; **Sophia** b 9 Jan. 1845; **Alfred** b 15 Mar. 1847; **Emma** b 16 Mar. 1850; and **Sarah Abby** b Jul. 1852. *Child by 2nd wife*: **Charles Herbert** b 23 Jun. 1858.

LITCHFIELD, ALDEN FRED - Born 6 May 1855, d ??, s/o ?? Child: **Eta Louise** b 20 Oct. 1864, m 16 Nov. 1889 Geo. F. Taylor.

LITCHFIELD, ALVIN S. - Born 19 Jan. 1839, d ??, s/o Samuel and ?? Litchfield. Alvin S. Litchfield m 11 Oct. 1865 Anna K. Little of Portland, Maine. Children: **Mary Sturgis** b 9 Nov. 1860, m Carroll Augustus Leavitt of Portland; **Ida Josephine** b 29 Sep. 1868; **Clara Jumper** b 8 Aug. 1873; and **Walter Sherman** b 1 Oct. 1875.

LITCHFIELD, ANSELM P. - Born 2 Dec. 1834 or 28 Jan. 1837 in Greene, Maine, s/o Jacob and Mary Ann (Webb) Litchfield. Anselm P. Litchfield m 25 Aug. 1860 Melissa/Melissa W. Roberts, d/o John and Betsy (Thing) Roberts of Alfred, Maine. Children: **Lissie** b 25 Mar. 1860, m 8 Jul. 1889 George Kingsbury of Alfred, ME; and **Sarah** b 8 Apr. 1869, m 8 Apr. 1896 Fred E. Russell of South Berwick, ME.

LITCHFIELD, BENJAMIN - Born 13 Nov. 1836, d ??, s/o Samuel and ?? Litchfield. Benjamin Litchfield m 1866 Ella A. Fogg, d 1 Jun. 1881. Children: **Anna Watson** b 22 Dec. 1866; and **Charles Ames** b 6 Feb. 1869.

LITCHFIELD, BENJAMIN JR. - Born 26 Aug. 1812, d 3/8 Apr. 1884, s/o Benjamin, Sr. and Nancy (McLellen) Litchfield. Benjamin Litchfield, Jr. m 28 May 1838 Ruth P. Williams of Orono, Maine, d/o Ebenezer B. and Sally (Whitney) Williams. Children: **Julian/Julias B., Sr.** b 19 Feb. 1839, d (lost at sea) 30 May 1866, m Helen A.

Coombs, d 27 Apr. 1859, was returned to Rockland, ME, for burial; **Henry A.** b 17 Aug. 1841, d 13 May 1892, unm; **Frederic P.** b 23 Jan. 1844, d 12 Sep. 1891; **Emma** b 16 Apr. 1846; and **Georgiana F.** b 26 May 1844, m 25 Jan. 1871 A. Judson Shaw.

LITCHFIELD, BENJAMIN SR. - Born 19 Feb. 1782, d ??, s/o Noah, Sr. and Mabel (Wade) Litchfield. Benjamin Litchfield, Sr. m 15 Sep. 1800 Nancy McLellen of Cushing, Maine, d/o Capt. Simon and Deborah (Weed). Children: **Elisa Jane** b 30 Sep. 1810, d 1865, m Asa Moise of Rockland, ME; **Benjamin** q.v.; **Simon M./M. C.** q.v.; **Nancy M.** b 28 Feb. 1817, d 18 Feb. 1890, m Winslow Ames Litchfield, who d 28 Sep. 1899; **Orrin** b 9 Oct. 1820, d 24 Sep. 1824; **Almeda** b 27 Aug. 1818, d 24 Sep. 1843, m 17 Aug. 1837 Capt. John M. Coombs, d 23 Sep. 1843; **Matilda P.** b 16 Dec. 1822, m (1) 29 Sep. 1845 Capt. John M. Coombs, d 1843, and m (2) Wm. Hopkins; **Electa A.** b 10 Mar. 1825, d 17 Mar. 1896, m Hermon Mero; **Albee K.** b 15 Aug. 1828 living in Athol, MA, m (1) Cerena Young, and m (2) Kate Ulmer, then removed to Boston, MA; **Alden Fred** b 13 Apr. 1831 m 6 May 1855 Mary. B. Allen of Hope, ME, lived in Rockland; and **Silas C.** b 30 Oct. 1833, d 1897 in Boston, m Sarah Ulmer.

LITCHFIELD, CHARLES JORDAN - Born 18 Mar. 1853 at Salmon Falls, New Hampshire, d ??, s/o Lewis Kendall Litchfield and Sarah B. (Page). Charles Jordan Litchfield m 11 Aug. 1888 Mary E. Barthold. Children: **Dana Berthold** b 16 Apr. 1881; **Frederick Kendall** b 10 Sep. 1883; **Anna May** b 24 Apr. 1885; **Edith Hazel** b 28 Apr. 1887; **Pauline Isadore** b 28 Dec. 1889; and **Mildred Dawn** b 4 May 1893.

LITCHFIELD, EPHRAIM S. - Born 14 Mar. 1822, d ??, s/o ?? Ephraim S. Litchfield m (1) Emily Belden, and m (2) 24 Sep. 1866 Mrs. Mary Gould (nee Butler), b 16 Sep. 1834 in Harmony, Maine. Children: **Rosalia** b 21 Aug. 1848; **Wallace Jerome** b 26 Oct. 1849, d 16 Feb. 1853; **Elmer E.** b -- Jan. 1862, d 21 Jun. 1863 age 1 year and 5 months; **Carrie I.** b 27 Jun. 1864, d 19 Nov. 1868; **Elmer Elsworth** b 21 Jun. 1870, d 22 Nov. 1884; **Nellie** b 4 Feb. 1873; **Alfred** b 27 Jan. 1874; **George** b 28 Oct. 1878, d 28 Jun. 1889; and **Gertrude** b 25 Oct. 1880.

LITCHFIELD, HENRY C. - Born 23 Aug. 1847, d ??, s/o Samuel and Mary (Stanford) Litchfield. Henry C. Litchfield m 13 Jan. 1870 Hanrietta L. Rollins, b 1849 in Lowell, Massachusetts, d/o Joshua D. and Harriet L. (Eaton) Rollins. Child: **Harry A.** b 12 Jul. 1874 in Quincy, MA.

LITCHFIELD, JACOB - Born 7 Jan. 1800, d 27 Feb. 1876 in Winthrop, Maine, s/o Noah, Sr. and Mabel (Wade) Litchfield. Jacob Litchfield m 28 Feb. 1827 Mary Ann Webb, b 15 Jan. 1805, d/o Deacon Wm. H. and Ann Sieles (?) Webb of Warren, Maine. Children: **William Noah** q.v.; **Lewis Kendall** q.v.; **Alsaclovia (?) Maria** b 24 Feb. 1834 in Lisbon, ME, d 26 Mar. 1890, m 22 Dec. 1855 Charles Wood of Auburn, ME, d -- Aug. 1893; **Anselm Parker** q.v.; and **Augustus Lorin** b 21 May 1841 in Carmel, ME, m (1) 22 Mar. 1859

Delia A. Shory of South Berwick, ME, and m (2) Ella McCorrison, and m (3) 3 Nov. 1897 Annie Bryant.

LITCHFIELD, JULIAN/JULIAS B. SR. - Born ??, d ??, s/o Benjamin, Jr. and Ruth P. (Williams) Litchfield. Child: **Julian M.** q.v.

LITCHFIELD, JULIAN M. - Born 21 Sep. 1858, d ??, s/o Julian/Julias B., Sr. and Helen A. (Coombs) Litchfield. Julian M. Litchfield m -- Nov. 1855 Maria F. Emerson. Child: **Helen Emerson** b 10 Jan. 1887.

LITCHFIELD, JOSEPH M. - Born 19 Feb. 1842, d ??, s/o Samuel and Mary (Stanford) Litchfield. Joseph M. Litchfield m 22 Jan./Jun. 1885 Sarah Elizabeth Fritsh/Fitch, b 21 Sep. 1856 in San Francisco, California, d/o George and Margaret M. Fritsh/Fitch. Children: **Joseph M.** b 28 Nov. 1885; **George F.** b 2 Sep. 1887; **Samuel S.** b 5 May 1889, d 12 Aug. 1889; and **Reuben L.** b 9 Apr. 1892.

LITCHFIELD, LEWIS KENDALL - Born 20 May 1831 in Lisbon, Maine, d ??, s/o Jacob and Mary Ann (Webb) Litchfield. Lewis Kendall Litchfield m (1) 21 Jul. 1851 Sarah B. Page, d 4 Dec. 1891, and m (2) 15 Aug. 1893 Mrs. Jennie (Cromwell) Stover of Litchfield, Maine. Children: **Charles Jordan** b 18 Mar. 1853 at Salmon Falls, NH, m 11 Aug. 1888 Mary E. Berthold; **Mary Isadore** b 27 Feb. 1855 in Salmon Falls, d 30 Apr. 1863; and **Ida May** b 11 May 1868 in Winthrop, ME, m 3 Sep. 1895 Charles Mower.

LITCHFIELD, LUTHER - Born 6 Sep. 1788, d 11 May 1852, s/o Noah, Sr. and Mabel (Webb) Litchfield. Luther Litchfield m -- Aug. 1812 Rhoda Cole, d 4 Nov. 1856/1858. Children: **Norris** q.v.; **Vassel Edmond** b 5 Jan. 1816, d 31 Mar. 1892, m pub. 30 Nov. 1845 Nancy W. Parshly of Roxbury, MA, d 2 Sep. 1842; **Lucienda** b 2 May 1818, d 17 Jan. 1868, m 11 Sep. 1838 Geo. B. Swift, who d 20 Jul. 1888; **Ephraim S.** b 14 Mar. 1822, m (1) Emily Belden, and m (2) Mary Gould; **Harriet Haskell** b 13 May 1827, m 11 Sep. 1852 Daria Bumpus; **Luther** b 24 Nov. 1835, m (1) 13 Nov. 1858 Francis Getchell, and m (2) 12 Jun. 1874 Mrs. Eliza Ham; and **Maria** b 22 Jul. 1842, m (1) Charles Hall of Lowell, MA, and m (2) ---- Willson. [Vital Records of Lewiston, Maine, p. 45.]

LITCHFIELD, NATHANIEL - Born 22 Mar. 1797, d 18 Nov. 1878, s/o Noah, Sr. and Mabel (Wade) Litchfield. Nathaniel Litchfield m 23/27 Jan. 1817/1819 Rachel Barker, d 3 Apr. 1876, d/o Cyrus Barker. Children: **Nelson Porter** b 14 Aug. 1819 at Lowell, MA, d 1 Mar. 1884, m 26 Sep. 1847 Maria Arieyad Rinee; **Nancy Melinda** b 27 Apr. 1823, d 27 Aug. 1847; **Almeda** b 14 Sep. 1828, d 31 Aug. 1846; **Anson** b 11 Mar. 1830, d 14 Jan. 1832; **Sarah Emeline** b 27 Nov. 1831, d 11 Jan. 1845; **Lydia M.** b 6 Nov. 1835, m 23 Nov. 1856 A. K. P. Blake in Gray, ME, d 5 Nov. 1863; **Emelina Augusta**; and **Anson Edward** b 2 May 1839, m 13 Jun. 1861 Ester A. Haynes Bupert (?), d/o Saul P. [Vital Records of Lewiston, Maine, p. 118.]

LITCHFIELD, NOAH SR. - Born 24 Jan. 1753 in Scituate, Massachusetts, d 17 Nov. 1827 in Lewiston [vital records of Lewiston, Maine, p. 223 and Herrick Cemetery, Lewiston], s/o ?? Noah Litchfield, Sr. settled in Lewiston in 1774. He m 9 Jul. 1778 Mabel Wade, b 9 Jun. 1758 in Scituate, Massachusetts, d 12 Jul. 1838, d/o Jacob Wade. Children: **Noah** q.v.; **Mabel** b 28 Feb. 1780, d 1 Nov. 1853 in Durham, ME, m 16 Apr. 1801 George Williams, d 8 Feb. 1867 in Durham; **Benjamin, Sr.** q.v.; **Betsey** b 7 Mar. 1784 in Freeport, ME, d 20 Jul. 1857, m 13 Aug. 1805 Winslow Ames, who d 8 Oct. 1851; **Zachens/Zacheus** q.v.; **Luther** q.v.; **Charlotte** b 9 Apr. 1791, d 9 Sep. 1853, m 8 Nov. 1810 Samuel Cole, Jr., who d 11 Aug. 1828; **Wade** q.v.; **Priscilla** b 26 Mar. 1795, d 2 Feb. 1886, m 6 Nov. 1817 David Barker; **Nathaniel** q.v.; and **Jacob** q.v.

LITCHFIELD, NOAH - Born 28 Nov. 1817, d 19 Mar. 1893, s/o Noah, Jr. and Martha (Ames) Litchfield. Noah Litchfield m 20 Jun. 1840 Olive E./S. P. Miller, b 30 Apr. 1820, d 31 Dec. 180-, d/o James and Deborah Miller of Kennebunkport, Maine. Children: **Susan H.** b 5 Oct. 1841, m 10 Oct. 1867 George Henry Jordan, s/o James, Jr.; **Noah Ames** b 14 Jul. 1843; **Ednah W.** b 15 Oct. 1845, d 25 Oct. 1847; **Weber F. S.** b 30 May 1852, m 27 Oct. 1877 Florence I. Bartlett of Rumford, ME, lived in Lisbon, ME; and **Martha Alice** b 10 Nov. 1860, m (1) 28 Nov. 1875 Fred L. Crowley of Lewiston, and m (2) 14 Nov. 1888 Frank P. Griffin.

LITCHFIELD, NOAH, JR. - Born 4 Dec. 1778, d 2 Jan. 1863, s/o Noah, Sr. and Mabel (Wade) Litchfield. Noah Litchfield, Jr. m 28 Aug. 1803 Martha Ames, d 18 Mar. 1854, d/o James Ames, Jr. Children: **Martha** b 13 Oct. 1803, d 25 Nov. 1828, m 18 Jun. 1828 A. Brooks; **Samuel** q.v.; **Ames** b 24 Apr. 1807, d 18 Aug. 1835, m pub. 27 Oct. 1838 Susan H. Bean of Montville, ME; **Eliza** b 9 May 1809, d 17 Jun. 1870, m 21 Sep. 1867 A. Brooks; **Benjamin** b 11 Jun. 1811, d 22 Aug. 1835, age 24 years at Parsonsfield Seminary [vital records of Lewiston, Maine, p. 223 and *Morning Star*]; **Sally C.** b 9 Sep. 1813, d 8 Mar. 1888, m pub. 26 Oct. 1834 Norris Litchfield, who d 8 Feb. 1872; **Betsey** b 5 Nov. 1815, m pub. 14 Jun. 1840 Isaac Williams, who d 4 Apr. 1885, age 65 years 5 months 14 days; **Noah** q.v.; **Winslow Ames** b 8 Nov. 1820, d 18 Aug. 1835; and **William G.** b 3 Feb. 1823, m Mary ----, who d 7 Mar. 1848. [Vital Records of Lewiston, Maine, p. 117.]

LITCHFIELD, NORRIS - Born 9 Aug. 1813, d 8 Feb. 1872, s/o Luther and Rhoda (Cole) Litchfield). Norris Litchfield m pub. 26 Oct. 1834 Sarah/Sarah C. Litchfield/Lidstone, b 9 Sep. 1813, d -- Mar. 1887, d/o Noah of Lewiston. Children: **Martha Ann** b 13 Dec. 1836, d 18 Mar. 1837; **Lucinda E.** b 20 Apr. 1838, d 23 Mar. 1895, m 2 Dec. 1861 Oliver P. Lane; **Eliza Ellen** b 27 Jul. 1841, d 7 Apr. 1885, m 10 Dec. 1860 Jesse F. Swett; **Edmond W.** b 11 Jul. 1844, m 2 Sep. 1871 Clara W. ---- of Waldoboro, ME, d/o Wm. Bearce; and **Olivia D.** b 18 May 1836, d 16 Sep. 1840.

LITCHFIELD, SAMUEL - Born 10 Jun. 1805, d ??, s/o Noah, Jr. and Martha (Ames) Litchfield. Samuel Litchfield m (1) 8 Sep. 1833 Mary

Stanford, d 5 Dec. 1869, d/o Jeremiah, and m (2) Cynthia Stanford, d 10/11 Apr. 1881. Children: **Watson D.** b 5 Mar. 1835, d 14 Nov. 1889 in San Francisco, CA, m -- Aug. 1865; **Benjamin** q.v.; **Alvin S.** q.v.; **Charles A.** b 14 Nov. 1840, d 6 Jul. 1864 in the Army; **Joseph M.** q.v.; **Isaac W.** b 24 Jul. 1843; and **Henry C.** q.v.

LITTLEFIELD, SAMUEL - Born ??, d ??, s/o ?? Samuel Littlefield lived near the Nathan Morrel home near bridge. He m Olive Lander, d/o Abisha [sic]. [Abish'a daughter m Joseph Coburn.] Child: **William True** b 23 Apr. 1848.

LITCHFIELD, SIMON M./M. C. - Born 25 Dec. 1814, d in California, s/o Benjamin, Sr. and Nancy (McLellen) Litchfield. Simon M./M. C. Litchfield m (1) 10 Feb. 1845 Rebecca Crockett, b 1829, d/o Capt. Edward & Harriet (Spear) Crockett, and m (2) 3 Jan. 1853 Harriett Clark. Children: **Rebecca C. H. A.** m Samuel Fickett; **Ella**; and **Edmond M.** b -- Apr. 1861, d 20 Jul. 1861.

LITCHFIELD, VASSEL E. - Born ??, d ??, s/o ?? Vassel E. Litchfield m Nancy Ward, d/o Richard. Children: **Edward**; **Frances E.** b -- Aug. 1849, m 15 Jun. 1875 Myra Agnes Hurd; and **Clarence M.** b 20 Mar. 1854, m 2 Aug. 1888 Minnie F. Jones, d/o Edward.

LITCHFIELD, VINSON - Born 16 Jan. 1819, d ??, s/o Wade and Mary (Lander/Landers) Litchfield. Vinson Litchfield lived in Hartland, Maine. He m (1) 3 Jun. 1839 Mary Wyman of Dead River, Maine, d 13 Jun. 1852, and m (2) Rosina Rodgers of Winthrop, Maine, d/o Thomas J. Children: **Amanda** m Haskell Lawrence of Newport, ME; **Mary Jane** b 24 Jul. 1844, m ---- Ricker; **Daniel W.** b 14 Apr. 18--, d at Cold Hawkes [sic]; **Charlotte** m ---- Applebie of Boston, MA; **Melvina** m William Frost; **Alphonso**; **Alonso**; **Frances H.** b 29 Jul. 1876; **Rosetta** b 25 Sep. 1877, m 13 Jan. 1891 Melvin Turner of Athens, ME; **Lillian** b 19 Feb. 1879, m 18 Sep. 1894 Fred E. Turner; **George** b 9 Mar. 1881; **Ella** b 30 Mar. 1887; **Etta** b 25 Feb. 1884; **Mirtie J.** b 27 Jan. 1885; **Thomas J.** b 27 Nov. 1886; **Effie E.** b 24 Sep. 1888; and **Isabel** b 15 Feb. 1889.

LITCHFIELD, WADE - Born 17 Apr. 1793 in Lewiston, d 20 Jan. 1875 in Newport, Maine, s/o Noah, Sr. and Mabel (Wade) Litchfield. Wade Litchfield m -- Apr. 1818, pub. 22 Mar. 1818, Mary Lander of Greene, Maine, d 15 Nov. 1881. Children: **Vinson** q.v.; **Almira** b 20 Dec. 1820, lived in Walphole, NH, m (1) 9 Sep. 1838 James Savage of Madison, ME, d 13 Jan. 1866, and m (2) 1 Jul. 1889 John P. Murray of Rockingham, VT; **Leonard Wade** b 8 Jan. 1823; and **Clarissa** b 11 Mar. 1826.

LITCHFIELD, WM. E. - Born ??, d ??, s/o ?? Children: **Jesse/Tesse M.** b 14 Jan. 1873; and **Willie A.** b 3 Sep. 1875.

LITCHFIELD, WILLIAM NOAH - Born 1 Jan. 1828 in Union, Main, d ??, s/o Jacob and Mary Ann (Webb) Litchfield. William Noah

Litchfield m 5 Jun. 1853 Charity Baker Roberts of Alfred, Maine, b 5 Jan. 1828, d/o John and Betsey (Thing) Roberts.

LITCHFIELD, ZACHENS/ZACHEUS - Born 22 Mar. 1786, d in Bath, Maine, s/o Noah, Sr. and Mabel (Wade) Litchfield. Zachens/Zacheus Litchfield m -- Jan. 1812 Sally Barker, d 31 May 1850 in Manchester, New Hampshire. Children: **Alvin B.** b 17 Sep. 1813, d in Bath, ME, m Rebecca E. Pratt, d/o Olive and Joanna G. (Litus) Pratt, who was b 3 May 1821, then removed to Manchester, NH, and Bath, ME; **Elvira Jane** b 14 Sep. 1815, d 25 Aug. 1842 in Warren, ME, m 21 Mar. 1838 Samuel Cummings of Union, ME; **Sally Ann** b 23 Oct. 1819, d 9 Jul. 1836; **Rachel Antoinette** b 29 Mar. 1822, m Robert Donnell of Bath, ME; **Lydia Amanda** b 16 Aug. 1824; **Aurelus Ann** b 12 Feb. 1828, d 15 Mar. 1828; and **Henrietta C.** b 26 Nov. 1831, d 23 Feb. 1844. [Vital Records of Lewiston, Maine, p. 45.]

LITTLE, HORACE C. - Born 14 Jan. 1840 in Auburn, Maine, d 14 Mar. 1896, s/o Joseph and ?? Little, great-grandson of Colonel Moses Little, the Revolutionary War leader of the Minute Men. Horace C. Little m 1860 Rosa J. Roak. He was a newspaper editor in Portland, Maine, with James G. Blaine before the Civil War, during it he was a capt. of a regt., but also owner of the *Bridgton Reporter*. He owned a hardware store in the firm Owen & Little, which became Hall & Knight, was one of the builders of Lyceum Hall Block, in insurance business with William Chamberlain and his son, Jacob. He was Postmaster and established a delivery system from 1878 to 1888. Served the Franklin Company, Lincoln Mills, and Continental Mills as auditor. Elected in 1880 as a Republican, and again in 1889, and declined further nominations. Retired in 1892; was a member of the Red Order of Lewiston, Commander K. T., and of the Consistory of the Ancient and Accepted Order of Scotish Rites. Children: **Nellie R.** m Charles Clarke; **Nancy B.** m S. G. Bonney; **Lottie B.** m E. W. Emery; **Lucie**; and **Jacob**.

LITTLE, JOSIAH - Born 9 Apr. 1801 in Newburyport, Massachusetts, d ??, s/o Edward and ?? Little. Josiah Little m Mary H. ----. Children: **Elizabeth Mary Todd** b 24 Sep. 1823; and **Edward** 25 Jun. 1825 [Vital Records of Lewiston, p. 117].

LITTLE, THOMAS BROWN - Born ??, d ??, s/o Edward and ?? Little, Esq. Thomas Brown Little m Eunice Thrasher, d/o Capt. Josiah and Eunice (Tucker) Thrasher [See *Little Genealogy*, by George T. Little, published by the author, 1882, p. 440]

LONGLEY, JOSIAH P. - Born 5 Oct. 1818 in Greene, Maine, d ??, s/o ?? Josiah P. Longley m (1) Rebecca Colby of Wales, Maine, b 15 Nov. 1818, d 27 Jan. 1865, d/o Joseph, and m (2) 7 Mar. 1866 Mrs. Emily M. Cutler. Children: **Etta L.** b 1 Dec. 1846, d 8 Sep. 1887, m 15 Mar. 1870 Josiah D. Mitchell; **Enna L.** b 5 Jul. 1853, m 6 Nov. 1873 Lester R. Miller of Auburn, ME, b 3 Jun. 1854; **Alexander B.** b 16 Nov. 1848, d 18 Oct. 1877, m 26 Nov. 1872 Laura S. Nealey, who was b 18 Nov. 1847; **Leander** b 16 Nov. 1848, d 15 Feb. 1852; and

Josiah B. b 4 Oct. 1856, m -- Jul. 1876 Orella S. Nealy, who was b 4 Oct. 1854, d/o Geo. B. Nealy of Winthrop, ME.

LOWELL, CHARLES GORHAM - Born 12/17 Sep. 1852/1855, d ??, s/o Daniel and Amanda M. (Gorham) Lowell. Charles Gorham Lowell m 22 Apr. 1884 Maud/Maude F. Randall. Child: **Blanche/Blance L.** b 25 Sep. 1885, m -- Apr. 1898 Calvin C. Young of Auburn, ME.

LOWELL, DANIEL - Born ??, d ??, s/o ?? Daniel Lowell m Amanda M. Gorham, b 8 Jul. 1822, d 1 Aug. 1891. Children: **Henry Clay** b 15 Jun. 1846; **Francis Gorham** b 1 Nov. 1848; **James L./James, Sr.** q.v.; and **Charles Gorham** q.v.

LOWELL, EDWARD - Born ??, d ??, s/o ?? Edward Lowell m 9 Apr. 1812 Lucy Bubier. Children: **George** b 28 Jul. 1812; **Mary** b 23 Jun. 1814; **Andrew** b 7 Apr. 1816, d 18 Mar. 1857; **Jeremiah** b 2 Aug. 1818; **Elvira** b 6 Oct. 1820; **Mirian** b 3 May 1822; **Rufus** b 19 Nov. 1824; and **Ann** b 9 Jun. 1829. [Vital Records of Lewiston, Maine, p. 117.]

LOWELL, EDWARD/EDMOND MARK - Born 20 Nov. 1855, d ??, s/o Mark and Ann (Davis) Lowell. Edward/Edmond Mark Lowell m 3 Jun. 1880 Cora Hartshorn of Lunenburg, Vermont, d/o John. Children: **Anna Florence** b 13 Jan. 1881; and **Marion** b 11 Feb. 1890.

LOWELL, ELMER - Born ??, d ??, s/o ?? Children: **George** m Sarah Howling of Bowdoin, Maine, d/o Joseph; **Mary**; **Andrew**, unm; **Jeremy** m ----, widow who lived near town farm; **Elvira** m Zeba Dunham of Lakes in Merdred [sic]; **Marian**, unm; **Rufus**, unm; and **Ann**, unm.

LOWELL, GIDEON - Born 1672, d ??, s/o Percival and Mary (Chandler) Lowell. Gideon Lowell settled in Amesbury, Massachusetts, about 1720. He m 7 Jul. 1692 Mary Swett. Children: **Mary** b 1 Mar. 1692; **John** b 1 Feb. 1696; **Samuel** bc 1698; **Gideon** bc 1700; **Stephen** b 19 Feb. 1703 in Newbury, d 27 Oct. 1776, m 22 Dec. 1727 Miriam Collins [*History of Farmington* by Butler, published by the author, 1885, reprinted 1983, p. 524]; **Moses** b 1705 (?); **Hannah** b 11 Apr. 1707; **Joseph** b 1709 (?); **Abner** b 29 Nov. 1711; and **Jonathan** b 24 Mar. 1714.

LOWELL, JAMES - Born ??, d ??, s/o Daniel and ?? Lowell. Children: **Mildred**; **Walter**; **Grace**; **Bellie/Bertie**; **John Haley** b at Rangley Lakes; and **Joseph Haley** b in Phillips, ME.

LOWELL, JAMES SR. - Born 27 Jul. 1791 in Buckfield, Maine, d 27 Jul. 1858, s/o ?? James Lowell m 1 May 1814 Hannah B. Paul, b 19 May 1793 in New Gloucester, Maine, d 20 Feb. 1869. Children: **Mark** q.v.; **James Jr.** b 14 Aug. 1817, d 6 Aug. 1850, m 25 Dec. 1836 Ann S. T. Davis; **Daniel** b 16 Jul. 1869, m 3 Mar. 1845 Lucy A. Gorham, b 8 Jul. 1824 in Marshfield, MA, d 1 Aug. 1891 in Auburn, ME; and **Vesta** b 30 Mar. 1825, m 7 Apr. 1847 Alexander Burbank, d 9 Jan. 1884.

LOWELL, JAMES JR. - Born 1817, d 6 Aug. 1850, s/o James and Hannah (----) Lowell. James Lowell, Jr. m 20 Apr. 1837 Jane G. Barker. Children: **Vesta Jane** b 4 Mar. 1839, d 21 Jul. 1894, m 17 Dec. 1859 James B. K. Drake of FL; **Elizabeth M.** b 8 Jul. 1840, m 5 Dec. 1867 Alvin Woodman; **Phillip G.** q.v.; **Amelia W.** d 8 Sep. 1844; and **Georgiana** d 5 Jul. 1850, age 11 weeks.

LOWELL, JAMES L. - Born 13 Oct. 1851, d ??, s/o Daniel and Amanda (Gorham) Lowell. James L./James Lowell, Sr. m 10 Jun. 1875 Etta A. Crockett of Morrell, Maine, b 18 Jul. 1855. Children: **Grace B.** b 8 Sep. 1876, m -- Apr. 1899 Calvin C. Young of Auburn, ME; **Mildred G.** b 22 Jan. 1878, m 9 Jun. 1898 William R. Ricker; **Arthur J.** b 15 Jan. 1880, m 14 Apr. 1899 Alice C. Coburn; and **Walter C.** b 13 Oct. 1881.

LOWELL, JOHN - Born ??, d ??, s/o ?? John Lowell m (1) 24 Oct. 1813 [vital records of Lewiston, Maine, p. 431] Mary Haley, d 1821, wid/o Samuel ----, and m (2) 24 Nov. 1823 Mary Ann Gross [vital records of Lewiston, Maine, p. 431], and m (3) int. cert. 3 Mar. 1828 [vital records of Lewiston, Maine, p. 415] m 4 Mar. 1828 [vital records of Lewiston, Maine, p. 446] Hannah Davis, d/o Nathaniel, and m (4) (4) Sally Libby of Pownal, Maine. *Children of 1st wife*: **Dessalania** b 30 Jul. 1814, d 27 May 1826; **Mary** b 9 Jul. 1816, m pub. 13 Dec. 1837 Phillip Connor; **John** b 25 Oct. 1818, d 3 Oct. 1849, m Mary Coburn, who d 27 Aug. 1870, d/o Charles; and **Samuel** b 8 Mar. 1820, m (1) -- Feb. 1832 Rebecca Backus of Narr, and m (2) 13 Aug. 18-3 Merion Kenney, and m (3) 24 Nov. 1823 Polly Ann Goss, and m (4) Mary Catherine ----. *Children of 2nd wife*: **Julia Ann** b 19 May 1825, d 17 Oct. 1825. *Child of 3rd wife*: **Hannah** b 5 Feb. 1829, d 1845. [Vital Records of Lewiston, Maine, p. 46.]

LOWELL, JOHN, JR. - Born ??, d ??, s/o ?? Child: **Rachel J.** b 19 Aug. 1843, m Septimus Greenwood of Wales, ME.

LOWELL, JOHN WILLIAM - Born 7 Nov. 1823 at St. John, NS, d 7 Jun. 1887 at Rangeley, Maine, age 63 years 7 months, s/o Stephen, Sr. and ?? Lowell. John William Lowell was an active member of First Baptist Church, a farmer, and blacksmith. He m 19 Dec. 1849 in Phillips, Maine, Mary Haley, b 8 Oct. 1829 in Rangeley. Children: **Benj. Franklin** b 27 Feb. 1850, d 15 Jun. 1857 at Rangeley; **John H.** b 28 Apr. 1858 at Rangeley; **Elias Haley** d 30 ---- 1864; **Wm. Edwin** d 23 Jun. 1857; **Stephen Wesley** b 3 Jul. 1858, d 3 Dec. 1864; **Charles Edgar** b 21 May 1860, d 27 Nov. 1864; **James Rangeley** b 23 Jun. 1865, d 23 Sep. 1867; **Mary Corrilla** b 23 Nov. 1867, m 1 Oct. 1886 Ernest Ross; and **Bertha Victorro** b 20 Sep. 1875, d 31 Jun. 1879.

LOWELL, JONATHAN - Born ??, d ??, s/o Wm., Jr. and ?? Lowell. Child: **Harrison D.**, Co. F, 13 ME Reg. from Greene, ME, resident of ME 21 years.

LOWELL, MARK - Born 17 Mar. 1815, d 15 Sep. 1888, s/o ?? Mark Lowell m (1) 12 Oct. 1817 Ann Davis of Poland, d 17 Feb. 1845, d/o

Capt. Isaac, and m (2) 13 Jan. 1847 Alma Esther Burbank of Bethel, Maine. Children: **Eliza D.** b 9 Jan. 1838, m 14 May 1856 John G. Cook of Auburn, ME, d 12 Aug. 1898 in Chicago, IL; **Amanda G.** b 10 Mar. 1842, m 5 Dec. 1866 John B. Cotton of Lewiston, s/o Benjamin; **Hannah** b 22 Apr. 1844, m 19 Oct. 1865 Sam'l. G. French of Lunenburg, VT, which was his 2nd m; **Ann Clark** b 21 Apr. 1847 (?), d 26 Aug. 1851; **Alma B.** b 4 Oct. 1851, m 1 Jan. 1874 Willard M. Dunn of Waterville, ME; and **Edmond Mark** q.v.

LOWELL, PERCIVAL - Born -- Aug. 1571, d 1664 in Newbury, Massachusetts, s/o ?? Percival Lowell m Rebecca ----, d 28 Dec. 1645 in Newbury, Massachusetts. He resided in Somersetshire, England, also Gloucestershire, England, came to Colonies on ship *Jonathan* in 1639. Children: **John** b 1595 in England, d 10 Jul. 1647 in Newbury, m (1) Margaret ----, d 1639, and m (2) 1639 Elizabeth Goodale; **Richard** b 1602 in England, d 5 Aug. 1682 in Newbury, MA; and **Joan** b 1609 in England, d 14 Jun. 1677 in Newbury, m John Oliver.

LOWELL, PERCIVAL - Born 1639 [*Farmington, Maine, History* by Francis Butler, published by the author, 1885, reprint 1983, p. 534], d ??, s/o ?? Percival Lowell m 7 Sep. 1664 Mary Chandler. Children: **Richard** b 25 Dec. 1668 in Newbury, d 29 May 1749, m 8 Apr. 1695 Sarah Brown; **Gideon** b 3 Sep. 1672, m 7 Jul. 1692 Marion Swett; **Samuel** b 13 Jan. 1675 in Newbury, MA; **Edmond** b 24 Sep. 1684, m 18 Apr. 1706 Abigail Hadbook; **Margaret**; and **Johannah** bc 1690.

LOWELL, PHILLIP G. - Born 1 Nov. 1846, d ??, s/o James, Jr. and Jane G. (Barber) Lowell. Phillip G. Lowell m 4 May 1880/1881 Carrie Frances Perkins, d/o Sewall of Ellsworth, Maine. Children: **Kate** b 4 Feb. 1888; and **Dollie** b 6 Oct. 1890.

LOWELL, RICHARD - Born ??, d ??, s/o Percival and Rebecca (----) Lowell. Richard Lowell m (1) Margaret ----, and m (2) Margaret ----, b 27 Nov. 1604. Children: **Percival** b 1639 in Newbury, m 7 Sep. 1664 in Newbury May Chandler; **Rebecca** b 27 Jan. 1642, d 1 Jun. 1662, m 5 Dec. 1669 John Hall; **Sam'l.** b 1644; and **Thomas** b 28 Sep. 1649.

LOWELL, SAM'L. - Children: **Andrew C.**; **Mary** d age 6 years; **Sam'l. Jr.**; and **Eliza Ann** d age 3 months.

LOWELL, STEPHEN - Born 1703, d 1776, s/o Gideon and ?? Lowell. Gideon Lowell was the s/o Percival, s/o Richard, s/o Percival. Children: **Stephen** b 6 Oct. 1728 in Amesbury, d 15 Jun. 1800 in Buckfield, ME, m 20 Dec. 1753 Agnes Bolton of Falmouth, ME, d 13 Jun. 1801 in Buckfield, Maine (they lived in Windham, Maine, moved to Buckfield, and was an ancestor of the Minot and Lewiston Lowells); **Lewis** b 17 Dec. 1727 in Amesbury, MA, d 13 Jun. 1777, m 4 Jul. 1751 Miriam (Molly) Blaisdell; **Abner** b 2 Jul. 1731 in Amesbury, d 4/13 Apr. 1815, was a Capt., m (1) 28 Dec. 1852 in Amesbury Elizabeth Eaton of Seabrook, NH, who d 12 Mar. 1810 in Amesbury, age 75 years, and m (2) 25 Oct. 1810 in Amesbury June Bartlett, who d 17

Aug. 1822 in Amesbury, age 67 years; **Sarah** b 31 Jan. 1735 in Amesbury, m 17 May 1753 Stephen Blaisdell; **Miriam** b 20 Jan. 1735 in Amesbury, d 6 Jun. 1790, m Eliphlet Swett; **Elizabeth** b 9 Apr. 1737, m 16 Mar. 1758 in Amesbury, MA, Capt. Benj. Survey; **Reuben** b 29 Jun. 1739, d 1 Jun. 1824 in Chesterville; **Mary** b 16 Jun. 1743 in Amesbury, d 7 Jul. 1810, m 27 Jul. 1762 Samuel Kendrick, who d 9 Dec. 1811; and **Simeon** b 6 Oct. 1745, d 26 Aug. 1830 in Salisbury, MA, m (1) 23 Apr. 1770 Annie Wadleigh, who d 29 Jan. 1780 in Amesbury, age 39 years, and m (2) 13 Sep. 1789 Anna Webster, who d 4 Nov. 1819, age 67 years, wid/o ----.

LOWELL, STEPHEN - Born ??, d ??, s/o Stephen and ?? Lowell. Stephen Lowell (the elder) was the s/o Gideon, s/o Percival, s/o Richard, s/o Percival. Children: **Miriam** b 1755 in Falmouth, ME, d 7 Feb. 1823 in Buckfield, ME, m c1780 Richard Thurlow, who d 18 Jan. 1835, age 84 years; **Molly** b 1758 in Falmouth, ME, m Nat. Gammon in Buckfield; **Thomas** b 14 Jan. 1761 in Portland, d 10 Sep. 1810 in Buckfield, m 4 Jul. 1790 in Buckfield Judith Farrow of Buckfield, who d 1863; **Anne** bap. 31 Jul. 1763; **Stephen** bap. 7 Apr. 1765; and **William** b 28 May 1768 in Windham, ME, d 10 Jul. 1840 in Minot, ME, m (1) 9 Aug. 1790 Margery Irish, who was b 12 Apr. 1771 in Gorham, ME, and d 12 Nov. 1812 [obit *Portland Gazette*, issue 14 Dec. 1812], and m (2) Mrs. Betsy Blake Turner, who was b in Turner and moved to West Minot in 1804/1817.

LOWELL, STEPHEN, JR. - Born ??, d ??, s/o ?? Children: **Vesta**; **Edwin** or **Edward** d -- Apr. 1867; **A. Maud**; and **Claude**.

LOWELL, STEPHEN SR. - Born 15 Aug. 1798 in Yarmouth, Maine, d 6 Dec. 1877 in Greene, Maine, s/o William, Sr. and Lucy (Ray) Lowell. Stephen Lowell, Sr. resided at Lewiston and Greene. He m -- Mar. 1820 in St. John, NB, Ann Lamb of St. John. Children: **Mary Elizabeth** b 27 Oct. 1821; **John William** q.v.; **Lucy Ann** b 18/28 Dec. 1825, m ---- Foster while living in Stoneham, MA; **Maria Prudence** b 25 Jan. 1827, unm, lived in Taunton, MA; **Stephen, Jr.** b 2 Jun. 1830, d 1895, m Abbie Tibbetts, and they and their children lived in Rangeley; **Rebecca** b 2 Mar. 1832, m ---- Wilson who was living in Walnut, IA; **James P.** b 9 Nov. 1835; **Gideon Perkins** b 15 Jun. 1838, d in Civil War as a corporal in Co. C, 13 ME Reg. from Greene; **Octavia H.** b 15 Apr. 1841 in Phillips, ME, m 20 Jun. 1865 Byron G. Hill of Greene, ME, resided in Greene; and **Charles H.** b 15 Apr. 1841 in Phillips. [Vital Records of Lewiston, Maine, p. 44, 119.]

LOWELL, WILLIAM - Born ??, d ??, s/o Stephen and ?? Lowell. Stephen Lowell was the s/o Stephen, s/o Gideon, s/o Percival, s/o Richard, s/o Percival. Children: **James B.** b 5 Jan. 1791 in Buckfield, ME, d 27 Jul. 1858 in Lewiston, m 1 May 1814 in Lewiston, ME, Hannah Paul of New Glouchester, ME. (James was first president of Lewiston Falls Bank in 1829, treasurer of Lewiston for 20 years, representative to Legislature 1838, 1839, 1841, 1851, and 1852, senator 1857? and 1854.); **Mark** b 22 Apr. 1793 in Buckfield, ME, m 25 Feb. 1821 in Minot, ME, Lydia Atkinson, d 23 Nov. 1800?, d/o John; **Polly**

B. b 5 Sep. 1796 in Buckfield, d 1877, m -- May 1817 Ichabod Bonney of Turner; **Dorcus B.** b 11 Sep. 1798, d -- Apr. 1878, m Phillip Chamberlain of Turner, ME, d 19 Feb. 1878; **Stephen** b 11 Feb. 1801, d 12 Aug. 1858 at Sangerville, ME, m (1) 1826 Delora Goff of Auburn, ME, d 2 Aug. 1840, and m (2) 25 Mar. 1845 Mrs. Hald B. (Leadbetter) Anderson, who d 31 Oct. 1876; **Will** b 30 Oct. 1803, d -- Sep. 1889 in Auburn, ME, m (1) 7 Mar. 1826 Almira Dunham of West Minot, ME, d 7 Nov. 1833, and m (2) 28 Dec. 1836 Abosa Greenwood, who was b 5 Mar. 1805, d 4 Aug. 1851, and m (3) Hannah Shaw Atwood; **Elizabeth** b 20 Mar. 1805 in West Minot, d in Lewiston, age 78 years; **Margery** b 25 May 1809 in West Minot, d 28 Aug. 1861 in West Minot, m 2 Jun. 1836 Wm. Howard, Jr., who was b 10 Jun. 1808 in West Minot, d 1 Apr. 1879, s/o Wm. and Mary (Lyon) Howard; and **Miriam** b 6 Jul. 1812 in West Minot, m Edmund H. Shaw.

LOWELL, WILLIAM JR. - Born 26 Aug. 1807 in Lewiston, d ??, s/o ?? William Lowell, Jr. m int. 11 Dec. 1832 [vital records of Lewiston, Maine, p. 184] Harriet "Tylie" Gammon. Children: **Mahitable** b 15 Sep. 1832, m (1) William Maybury, and m (2) ---- Wight (?), resided in Industry, ME; **Sarah** b 15 Nov. 1834, m Foster Randall, resided in Lewiston; **Harriet Angeline** b -- Jan. 1836, m 1882 ---- Cunningham, a resident of St. Paul, MN; **James Mark** b 21 May 1835, W. G. 33 ME. Inf.; **Frances** m Alfred Roberts, resident of Omaha, NE; **Elvira** b 9 Oct. 1845, d 12 Aug. 1856, unm; and **Clarentine** b 19 Oct. 1857.

LOWELL, WILLIAM SR. - Born 21 Apr. 1778 in Augusta, Maine, d 10 May 1846 at Rangeley, Maine, s/o Stephen and ?? Lowell of Topsham (?). William Lowell, Sr. m 1797 Lucy Ray, b 17 Sep. 1775, d -- Jul. 1854 at Rangeley, age 78 years, d/o Sam'l. Children: **Stephen** q.v.; **Mary** b 27 Jun. 1804 in Lewiston, d 27 Sep. 1883 at Rangeley, m John Haley, b 5 Dec. 1797 in Lewiston, d 27 Sep. 1856 in Rangely; **Prudence** b 17 Feb. 1806 in Lewiston, d 28 Mar. 1890 in Rangeley, m pub. 14 Nov. 1828, m 4 Dec. 1828 John S. Lamb of Rangeley, d 18 Mar. 1873, age 67 years 10 months 23 days; **Elias** b 10 Feb. 1808, d 30 May 1870 at Rangeley, unm; **Jonathan William** b 10 Apr. 1813, d and buried in Greene, m Harriet "Tylie" Gammon, b 15 May 1814, resided in Lewiston and Industry, ME, sis/o Harriet F.; and **Catherine** b 4 Nov. 1818 in Lewiston, d 22 Nov. 1892 (?), m Cornelius Ellis, b 25 Dec. 1815, d 4 May 1889, resided in Rangeley. [Vital Records of Lewiston, Maine, p. 44.]

LUDDEN, MANDERVILLE T. - Born 17 Feb. 1830 in Canton, Maine, d ??, s/o ?? Manderville T. Ludden m 1856 Mary E. Jewett, d 21 Sep. 1882 in Lewiston. He graduated from Harvard Law School in 1854, and was the first to be admitted to the bar in Androscoggin County in 1854 at its incorporation. He moved to Lewiston in 1869, served as county attorney from 1863-1864, state senator from 1867-1868, and became mayor of Lewiston in 1881.

MCGILLICUDY, DANIEL J. - Born 17 Aug. 1859 in Lewiston, d 31 Jul. 1936 in Lewiston, s/o John B. and Ellen Byrnes. Daniel J.

McGillicudy m Minnie M. Sprague. Served as member of the local school board in 1881 and as a state legislator (Democrat) in 1884 and 1885, and as mayor in 1887 and 1890. It was while serving in the 62nd Congress that he drafted the first Workmen's Compensation Act, and a law limiting working days to 10 hours.

MANNING, SAMUEL - Born 9 Sep. 1801 in Brunswick, Maine, d 22 Jul. 1863, s/o Charles Henry and ?? Manning. Samuel Manning m (1) 28 Nov. 1820 Mary Stanwood of Brunswick, who was b 23 Mar. 1799, and m (2) Susanna Hunt (?), who d 10 Jul. 1887, d/o Stephen. Children: **Mary Ann** b 17 Dec. 1820 in Lewiston, d 6 Dec. 1860, m 16 Jan. 1845 Charles Hartshorn of Gardiner, ME; **Loisa** b 23 Feb. 1822, d 30 Jul. 1864 in Groton, MA, m James Stuart Parker of Groton; **Emeline** b 24 May 1824 in Danville, ME, d 19 Feb. 1854 in Stockton, CA, m 14 Feb. 1847 John T. Beckett of Monmouth, ME, d 1888; **Marie M.** b 15 Mar. 1826, m 27 May 1845 Samuel Record of Buckfield, ME; **Jane M.** b 28 Nov. 1827, m 25 Feb. 1847 Charles H. Reynolds; **Samuel** b 7 Jan. 1830; **Charles H.** b 19 Dec. 1831; **Stephen H.** b 24 Jul. 1834 in Lewiston, m 20 Jan. 1864 Sarah Walker, d/o Timothy; **Lemont A.** b 23 Nov. 1836 in Lewiston, unm; **Ellen A.** b 11 Jan. 1840 in Lewiston, m James Baker; **Isabelle B.** b 11 Jan. 1840 in Lewiston, m 1 Oct. 1873 George Bonellie, who d 6 Feb. 1893; and **Cordelia** b 5 Dec. 1841 in Lewiston, m John C. Baker.

MARCH, JOHN - Born 18 Jul. 1806, d 26 Mar. 1853, s/o ?? John March m Thursey L. Pratt, b 1 May 1812, d 5 Jul. 1887 in North Yarmouth, Maine. Children: **Charles Henry** b 6 Aug. 1832, d 1 Apr. 1852; **James Edmund** b 9 Jun. 1834, d 14 Feb. 1873; **Mary Hannah** b 16 Aug. 1836, m (1) ---- Bennett, and m (2) ---- Tabor; **Jennie E.** b 13 Jul. 1848, d 13 May 1877; and **John Frye** b 7 Apr. 1839, d 1 Apr. 1840. [Vital Records, Lewiston, Maine, p. 124.]

MARR, WILLIAM - Born ??, d 16 May 1849, age 50 years 3 months, s/o ?? William Marr lived with Hogan. William Marr came from Georgetown, Maine. William Marr m Olive S. Rogers, d 22 Aug. 1879, age 76 years 20 days. Children: **Rachael Catherine** b 25 Oct. 1836, d 6 Jul. 1860; **John Fairfield** b 29 Sep. 1838, d 19 Sep. 1873 (was blind); **Sarah Albina** b 20 Jan. 1841; **Arminta Uphrasin** b 8 Jan. 1843, m George Jay; and **Muriel** m Joseph Smith Trask. [Vital Records of Lewiston, Maine, p. 124.]

MARSHALL, ALFRED - Born 18 Apr. 1797, d 2 Oct. 1868, m 21 Dec. 1824 Lydia Brackett, who was b 15 Mar. 1802, d 30 Apr. 1874 (he was merchant in China, ME, and Congressional representative 1841-1842). Children: **Isabella I.** b 7 Mar. 1826, d 9 Oct. 1863, m 18 Jun. 1850 Prof. William Mathews; **Jacob Smith** b 26 May 1828, d 21 Aug. 1860, 1848 graduate Colby College; and **John Brackett** b 3 Dec. 1831, d 11 Aug. 1841.

MARSHALL, JOHN - Born ??, d ??, s/o ?? John Marshall m Sarah ----. Children: **Hannah** b 16 Dec. 1781; **John** b 28 Feb. 1785; **Samuel** b 1 Jun. 1787; **Daniel** b 13 Nov. 1790; **Isaac** b 31 Mar. 1794; **Alpha** [vital records of Lewiston, Maine, p. 48] (sic) b 18 Apr. 1797 (record states was a daughter (sic)); and **Sally** b 23 Mar. 1799.

MARSTON, SIMON - Born 3 Apr. 1779 in Portland, Maine, d 14 Feb. 1856, s/o ?? Simon Marston m Mary Frost, b 22 Dec. 1782 in Freeport, Maine, d 6 Jul. 1853. Children: **Brackett** b 10 Jun. 1802 in Pejepscot, ME, d 4 Aug. 1851, m pub. 5 Sep. 1829, m 8 Oct. 1859 Mary A. Field of Falmouth, ME; **Margaret** b 22 Apr. 1804 in Pejepscot, ME, d 1 Jun. 1874, m 31 Jan. 1828 John Cole, who d 19 Jul. 1882; **Sumner** q.v.; **John** b 25 Aug. 1808 in Pejepscot, ME, d 4 Sep. 1882, m Mary J. Fisher, who d 24 Jan. 1837; **Phineas** b 10 Feb. 1813 in Pejepscot, ME, d 21 Mar. 1896, m (1) Susan E. Fisher; **Eunice** b 22 Jan. 1815 in Pejepscot, ME, d 30 Aug. 1822; **Sylvanus Boardman** b 1 Mar. 1818 in Pejepscot, ME, d 9 Oct. 1861, unm; and **William Frost** b 15 Apr. 1824 in Lewiston, ME, d 31 Jul. 1892, m 13 Feb. 1848 Sarah Carville. [Vital Records of Lewiston, Maine, p. 122.]

MARSTON, SUMNER - Born 25 Feb. 1806 in Danville, Maine, d 30 Apr. 1851/1857, s/o Simon and Mary (Frost) Marston. Sumner Marston m 25 Feb. 1834 Rebecca/Rebecca C. Barker, b 24 Jul. 1809, d 14 Jan. 1892 in Bangor, Maine, d/o Jacob of Lewiston. Children: **John J.** b 13 Nov. 1836 in Bangor, d 8 Mar. 1843; **Charles S.** b 3 Dec. 1839 in Bangor, d 7 Jan. 1840; **Martha Ellen** b 21 Jun. 1843 in Bangor, m Alvah V. Ham 18 Aug. 1871; **Sophia Giddings** b 31 Aug. 1844 in Bangor; **John J.** b 22 Oct. 1845 in Bangor, d 24 Feb. 1864 in Libby Prison; and **Margaret C.** b 3 Sep. 1850 in Bangor, d 14 Jul. 1851.

MATTE, LOUIS EUGENE NAPOLEON - Born 9 Sep. 1851 in Quebec, Canada, d ??, s/o Hubert and Rose (Moffatt) Matte. Louis Eugene Napoleon Matte did not have a biography listed in the *Androscoggin History* by Merrill, published by W. A. Fergusson & Co., 1889, p. 408.] Dr. Matte was Lewiston's physician where he first practiced medicine. He later moved to Nashua, New Hampshire, in 1894, and to Keene, New Hampshire, in 1898.He m 3 Apr. 1883 Alice Bourque of Montreal, Canada. Births of all the children, except the last child, are recorded in Lewiston. Children: **Rose Cecile** b 6 Mar. 1884, d before 1904; **Hubert** b 12 Nov. 1885; **Lawrence** b 13 Apr. 1887; **Bertha** b 29 Apr. 1888; **Irene** b 3 May 1889; **Real** b 8 Oct. 1891; **Hugh** b 6 Jan. 1893; **Paul** b 28 Mar. 1894; and **Gerard** b 31 Jan. 1896. [Letter from Dr. Matte of Keene, NH, about 1904.]

MAY, JOHN - Born ??, d ??, s/o ?? Children: **Stephen** b 29 May 1796; **Mary** b 11 Apr. 1798; **Elizabeth** b 8 Mar. 1801; **Samuel** b 3 May 1803; **Nathan** b -- Jan. 1806; and **Franklin** b -- Aug. 1807.

MAY, JOHN - Born ??, d ??, s/o ?? John May m Sarah ----. Children: **Sarah** b 31 Jan. 1798; **William** b 9 Feb.? 1800; **Joseph** b 20 Sep. 1801 [vital records of Lewiston, Maine, p. 47.]

MEADER, AMOS - Born ??, d ??, s/o Tobias and ?? Meader. Children: **Albert A.** b 3 Dec. 1881; and **Lethea C.** b 22 Nov. 1886.

MEADER, EDWIN - Born ??, d ??, s/o ?? Children: **Guy L.** b 14 (?) Oct. 1881; and **Flora B.** b 5 Jun. ----.

MEADER, LEVI - Born 26 Feb. 1792, d ??, s/o ?? Levi Meader m (1) 27 Oct. 1813 [Davis diaries] Rebecca Austin, who lived with the Amos Davis family from 1806-1813, and m (2) Rebecca Totman. *Children of 2nd wife*: **Hannah** b 28 Nov. 1822, m pub. 6 Nov. 1842 Henry M. Wilson; and **Tobias** b 16 May 1827.

MEADER, TOBIAS - Born ??, d 28 Dec. 1794 [vital records of Lewiston, Maine, p. 225], s/o ?? Tobias Meader came from Marlboro, New Hampshire. Children: **Levi** b 26 Feb. 1792; and **Hannah** b 12 Feb. 1794, m Levi Jones. [Vital Records of Lewiston, Maine, p. 48.]

MEADER, TOBIAS - Born ??, d ??, s/o ?? Tobias Meader m 4 Oct. 1852 Caroline F. Goddard. Children: **Edwin W.** b 14 Feb. 1852, m Vesta Crowley, d/o Amos; **Aneetia Josephine** b 26 Aug. 1859, m 22 Apr. 1885 Herbert A. Whitney; and **Amos S.** b 8 May 1856, m 11 Mar. 1880 Mary S. Cross.

MERRILL, AMOS S. - Born 14 Jul. 1844, d 10 Jun. 1880, s/o Nathan and ?? Merrill. Amos S. Merrill m 1 Oct. 1873 Nellie A. Cleveland, who m (2) Reuben Tarr. Child: **Nathan** b 1876.

MERRILL, ASA - Born ??, d ??, s/o ?? Children: **Alvan** b 31 Aug. 1821; **Sally Morse** b 3 Mar. 1830; **Rachael**; and **Esther A.** b 8 Jan. 1835.

MERRILL, AZOR - Born 27 Jan. 1806/1808, d 16 Jun. 1871, s/o Benjamin, Jr. and Judith (Winslow) Merrill of Greene, Maine. Azor Merrill was of Parkman, Maine [vital records of Lewiston, Maine, p. 451]. He m 10 Feb. 1831 Adaline G. Wright, b 27 Aug. 1809, d 1884, d/o Lonzo C. and Sarah (Royal) Wright. Children: **Sarah Ellen** b 4 Sep. 1833, d 28 Aug. 1871; **Ozni Harris** [is the oldest child - ed.] b 18 Jun. 1832, d 29 Sep. 1894, m pub. 3 Oct. 1857, m 21 Oct. 1857 Mary J. Grant, d/o Elijah and Louisa (Curtis) Grant; **George Henry** b 18 Sep. 1836, d -- Sep. 1862 at Boliver, TN in the Civil War; **Olive Ann** b 4 May 1838, m (1) Adnesum Pillsbury, who d in Civil War, and m (2) George Thurston; and **Vesta Jane** b 1 Feb. 1840, m 7 Jun. 1864 Harrisen Porter Hood in Portland, ME.

MERRILL, BENJ. - Born ??, d ??, s/o ?? Benj. Merrill m 22 Mar. 1829 Orpha Brooks, d/o William. Child: **Asa** b 7 Jul. 1829.

MERRILL, BENJAMIN SR. - Born 28 Feb. 1741, d 7 Apr. 1824, Likely s/o Samuel and Anna (----) Merrill. Benjamin Merrill moved to [Lewiston Plantation now] Greene, Maine, from North Yarmouth, Maine, 15 Nov. 1775. He m 5 May 1763 Margaret Harris, b 28 Mar. 1738, d -- Dec. 1821. Children: **Benjamin Jr.** b 28 Feb. 1764, d 13 Feb. 1826, m Judith Winslow; **John** b 29 Sep. 1767, d 30 Jul. 1817; **Jeremiah** b 15 Aug. 1770, d 13 Apr. 1776; **Anna** b 12 Sep. 1772, d 28 Oct. 1845, m John Pickett; and **Levi** b 16 Feb. 1775, d 13 Aug. 1838.

MERRILL, CURTIS OZNI - Born in Greene, Maine, on Switzerland Rd, d ??, s/o Ozni Harris and ?? Merrill. Curtis Merrill m 16 Sep. 1891 Mary H. Downs, b 28 Feb. 1869, d/o Ezekiel C. and Eunice (Newbegin) Downs. Children: **Evelyn Irene** b 5 Jun. 1892 in Lewiston; **Egbert Harris** b 6 Oct. 1894 in Greene, ME; and **Evilona Grant** b 26 Mar. 1896 in Greene, ME.

MERRILL, DAVID - Born 28 Sep. 1790, d 22 Nov. 1865, s/o Moses and ?? Merrill. Children: **Louisa; Abby; Hannah** m Sewall Lane; **Mary Ann; Lydia; Louise** m Barber Lane; **George** m Charlotte Paul of Somerset, NH; and **William**.

MERRILL, ELBRIDGE G. - b 13 Dec. 1817, d 9 Oct. 1844/1899, s/o Jacob and Rachel (Stevens) Merrill. Elbridge G. Merrill m 22/23 Dec. 1846 Margaret R. Wright or Margaret Wright Francis, d 27 Feb. 1894/1897, d/o Francis. Children: **Emily Jane** b 11 Feb. 1849, d 1868; **Ann Eliza** b 7 Sep. 1850, m Benj. B. Foster of E. Livermore, ME; **Mary Ellen** b 11 Apr. 1852, m 29 Jun. 1889 Charles B. Chandler, s/o Elbridge G.; and **Elmer E.** b 24 Apr. 1862, d 19 Mar. 1892, unm.

MERRILL, ELIAS J. - Born 26 Feb. 1841, d ??, s/o Nathan and Nancy R. (Jackson) Merrill. Elias J. Merrill m (1) pub. 6 Jun. 1864 Pauline R. Forbes of Brunswick, Maine, and m (2) 19 Mar. 1880 Nellie Conley (Hamilton). Children: **Walter E.** b -- Feb. 1867; and **Hattie E.** d 8 Dec. 1878.

MERRILL, ENOCH - Born ??, d ??, s/o ?? Enoch Merrill m 21 Mar. 1824 Amy Smith. Children: **John Moore** b 16 Jun. 1826; and **Orpha Brooks** b 24 Aug. 1828. [Vital Records of Lewiston, Maine, p. 122.]

MERRILL, EZEKIEL - Born 24 Jul. 1790 in Greene, Maine, d 26 Jul. 1855 vital records of Lewiston, Maine, p. 226], s/o Benjamin and ?? Merrill. Ezekiel Merrill m (1) Anna Atkins, and m (2) pub. 24 Feb. 1833 Sally Dingley, d/o Wm., Sr. and Sally (Atkinson) Dingley. Children: **Susan** b 14 Sep. 1814; **Rufus** b 14 Nov. 1816, d -- May 1893, lived in Brunswick, ME, m Abigail Jordan, d/o James; **Susanna** b 14 Sep. 1814, m 16 Sep. 1832 John Brooks; **Ammi** b 7 Dec. 1818; **Mary J.** b 8 Jul. 1826, unm; **Anna/Amy** b 1 Dec. 1829, m Wm. Dingley; **Vesta Ann** b 7 Dec. 1831, m Horace Atwood; **Sarah D.** b 20 Sep. 1834, m S. J. Weber, lived in Lisbon, ME; **Lucy J.** m 29 Oct. 1859 Sydney Watson of Harpswell, ME; and **William** m Sarah Crockett.

MERRILL, FREEMAN H. - Born 8 Jun. 1834, d ??, s/o Nathan and Nancy R. (Jackson) Merrill. Freeman H. Merrill m (1) Georgia W. Garcelon, d/o Capt. Asa, or Georgia Gordan, d/o Sam'l D., and m (2) Mrs. Jennie E. Hutchins (nee Brown), d/o John Brown. Children: **Carrie E.; Joel C.; Herbert E.; Clarence A.** b 8 May 1888.

MERRILL, ISIAH/ISAIAH - Born 9 Aug. 1830, d 14 Aug. 1895, s/o ?? Children: **John H.** b 3 Aug. 1862; **Fred M.** b -- Feb. 1871; and **Frank H.** b 25 Dec. 1873.

MERRILL, JACOB - Born circa 1789, d 11 Nov. 1864, age 75 years, s/o ?? Jacob Merrill m Rachael* Stevens. Children: **Elbridge G.*** q.v.; **Mary*** b 18 Feb. 1820, d -- Feb. 1891, m Lorense Withen; **Jeremiah G.*** b 18 Jul. 1823, m Ann Upton; **Rachel*** b 1 Jun. 1833, m Calvin Stevens; **Laura C.** b 1812, d 2 Aug. 1883 age 71 years, buried at Herrick Cemetery in Lewiston, m (1) 18 Nov. 1831 Benjamin Thorne, and m (2) 3 Jun. 1841 Benjamin Foss [could not find any records to support this statement - editor's note]; **Abner** m 18 Feb. 1844 Becener Waugh; **Jane** d 19 Jun. 1807, m 8 Jul. 1835 Thos. D. Thorne; **Jeremiah**; **Mercy**; and **Susan** m Benj. Witham. [* Indicates listed in vital records of Lewiston, Maine, p. 121.]

MERRILL, JOB - Born ??, d ??, s/o John and ?? Merrill. Children: **Hannah B.** b 4 Oct. 1814; **Jeremiah Bean** b 2 Feb. 1816, d 16 Oct. 1817; **May** b 27 Feb. 1818; **Betsy**; **Selden**; **Franklin**; **John**; **Emily**; **Addisen**; and **Martha Jane**.

MERRILL, JOHN - Born 29 Jan. 1759, d 8 Oct. 1843, s/o Moses and ?? Merrill. John Merrill came from Freeport, Maine, as a Revolutionary War pensioner. He was a brother of Joseph Simon Merrill. He was in the army of George Washington. He m (1) Mary ----, and m (2) Sarah Smith, who was b 22 Dec. 1767, d 22 Mar. 1843, d/o Daniel. *Children of 1st wife*: **Joseph** b 2 Dec. 1785, m Sarah Smith, who was b 3 Oct. 1792, d/o Daniel Smith of Monmouth, ME; **John** b 26 Aug. 1787; **Sarah** b 5 Oct. 1789, m 15 Jan. 1815 John Bean of New Sharon, ME; **Phebe** b 7 Mar. 1792, m Alamon (?) Read of Bryon, ME; **William** b 5 Nov. 1793, m ---- from Gardiner, ME; and **Amos** b 30 Jan. 1795, lived in Mercer. *Children of 2nd wife*: **Stephen** b 29 May 1796, lived in Gardiner, m Emily Allen of Monmouth, b 29 Jul. 1813, d/o Joseph and Lydia (Billington) Allen; **Mary** b 11 Apr. 1798, m Joseph White, lived in Winsor, ME; **Elizabeth** b 8 Mar. 1801, unm; **Samuel** b 3 May 1803, m Sophiah Allen of Monmouth, who was b 15 Aug. 1807, d/o Joseph and Lydia (Billington) Allen; **Nathaniel/Nathan** q.v.; and **Franklin** b -- Aug. 1807, lived in Gardiner, m Louisa Towne of Gardiner.

MERRILL, JOHN H. - Born 8 Jan. 1843, d ??, s/o Nathan and Nancy R. (Jackson) Merrill. John H. Merrill m 26 Oct. 1875 Agnes Varney. Children: **Annie** b -- May 1877; and **Grace**.

MERRILL, JOSEPH - Born 1792 in Brunswick, Maine, d ??, s/o ?? Joseph Merrill m Sally Smith, d/o Daniel. Children: **Uncala** (?); **Hiram**; **Joseph A.** q.v.; **Aleander F.** b 18 Aug. 1824, m (1) Olive V. Andrews of Wales, ME, d/o John Andrews, Jr., and m (2) pub. 16 Dec. 1873 Lucinda T. Blaisdell of Lewiston; **Frances A.** b 10 Jun. 1827, m Joseph A. Basford of Monmouth, ME; and **Elvira A.** b 6 Jun. 1830, m George W. Norris of Monmouth.

MERRILL, JOSEPH A. - Born 12 Jul. 1821, d ??, s/o Joseph and Sally (Smith) Merrill. Joseph A. Merrill m (1) Sarah Robinson of Gardiner, Maine, sis/o Rev. Ezekiel Robinson, and m (2) pub. 21 May

1857 Hannah L. Haskell, d/o Simeon. Children: **George A.** b in Lewiston; **Grace F.** b in Boston.

MERRILL, JOSHUA - Born 2 Sep. 1788 in N. Yarmouth, Maine, d 18 Oct. 1845, s/o Samuel and ?? Merrill. Joshua Merrill m 14 Apr. 1814 Susanna Holland, b 25 Sep. 1795 in Cape Elizabeth, Maine [family Bible record AHS], d -- Mar. 1866, d/o John Holland. Children: **Silvira** b 9 Nov. 1814, m 31 Oct. 1840 Samuel Nevens; **Roxselana** b 9 Oct. 1817, [Roxselana's will probate #3191, d 14 Jul. 1890], m 15 Nov. 1840 Ira Nevens, b 1814, d 1892 [will of Ira Nevens #15861]; **Benson F.** b 30 Nov. 1820, d 14 Jan. 1850, m 16 Mar. 1845 Mary Carville; **Joshua** b 12 Oct. 1822, m 15 Aug. 1850 Hannah M. Maloon of Phippsburg, ME; **Orin** b 24 Jul. 1824, d 15 Oct. 1857, unm; **Caroline** b 23 Mar. 1827, d 28 Nov. 1881; **Susan Rebecca** b 18 Dec. 1831, d 28 Apr. 1865; and **Hannah True** b 23 Jan. 1835, d 6 Dec. 1860, m Charles W. Morrill, b 9 Oct. 1829 in Winslow, Maine [family Bible record AHS].

MERRILL, MOSES - Born 5 Jul. 1756, d ??, s/o ?? Moses Merrill m (1) Abigail ----, b 14 Jan. 1759, d 23 Apr. 1795, and m (2) Sally ----, b 20 Jul. 1756. *Children by 1st wife*: **Lydia** b 9 Sep. 1782; **William** b 7 Mar. 1783, d 21 Nov. 1783; **Moses** b 27 May 1784; **John** b 30 Mar. 1786 [Merrill Genealogy by Ernest L. Merrill, printed in the *Lewiston Journal*, c1907(?), clipping file at Auburn Library]; **Abigail** b 1 Mar. 1789; **David** b 28 Sep. 1790; **Polly** b 7 Aug. 1792; and **Richard** b 23 Apr. 1795. *Child by 2nd wife*: **Nancy Chandler** b 5 Mar. 1783 at Cape Ann, Massachusetts, (his sep daughter) ["sep" means Sally, his second wife, had a child before this marriage, likely by a Mr. Chandler].

MERRILL, NATHANIEL/NATHAN - Born 10 Apr. 1806, d 1 Apr. 1878, s/o John and Sarah (Smith) Merrill. Nathan Merrill m 29 Apr. 1830 Nancy/Nancy R. Jackson, b 23 Aug. 1811, d/o Lemuel of Lewiston. Children: **Isiah** b 9 Aug. 1830, d 14 Aug. 1895, m (1) 7 Jul. 1860 Electa M. Luce, who d 18 May 1863, d/o Robert of New Portland, ME, and m (2) Jennie Brown; **Freeman H.** q.v.; **Israel B.** b 26 Apr. 1837, m 17 Oct. 1862 Lizzie D. Bean, d/o Jeptha of Ripley, ME; **Mary H.** b 8 Apr. 1839, d 30 May 1891, m Lewis W. Blodgett; **Elias J.** q.v.; **John H.** q.v.; and **Amos S.** q.v.

MERRILL, OZNI HARRIS - Born 18 Jun. 1832, d 29 Sep. 1894, s/o Asor and Adeline (----) Merrill. Ozni Harris Merrill m 21 Oct. 1857 Mary Jane Grant, d/o Elijah and Louisa (Curtis) Grant. Children: **George** b -- Apr. 1863 in Portland, ME, d 1863; **Marietta R.** b 22 Jan. 1865 in Greene, m 5 Aug. 1886 Ralph A. Parker of Greene, ME; and **Ozni Curtis** b 22 Feb. 1869 in Greene, ME, [family records c1898], m 16 Sep. 1891 Mary Hannah Downs and they res. at Rumford Falls, ME.

MILLBANKS, PHILIP - Born circa 1739, d ??, s/o ?? Philip Millbanks was in the Revolutionary War from Falmouth to North Yarmouth, Maine [Mass. Soldiers & Sailors p. 729]. He was likely the same person living in Lewiston in 1790, one male, four females in his family [1790 census record]. Listed as 1-0-4 in the Lewiston 1790 census. Likely children: **Thankful** b -- Jan. 1772, d 7 Aug. 1864 age 92 years 7 months, m 15 Jul. 1790 Bela Vining [*Durham, Maine, History* by Stackpole, 1899, p. 275]; **Lisa** m 19 Dec. 1799 in Durham, ME, James Douglass [vital records of Durham, ME, no page number; **Katherine** d 8 Apr. 1831, m 2 Mar. 1787 Peter Garcelon; and likely one more daughter [1790 census list four females].

MITCHELL, ALGERNON M. - Born 12 Sep. 1837, d ??, s/o Jonathan, Jr. and Mary (Wright) Mitchell. Algernon M. Mitchell m 27 Nov. 1862 Sarah M. Perley, d 24 Feb. 1891. Children: **Lillian E.** b 12 Feb. 1864, m 6 Sep. 1892 Ralph Myrick; **S. Sherman** b -- Jun. 1867, m 24 Dec. 1892; **Alena M.** b 16 Feb. 1868, m 6 Mar. 1889 William Webster; **Guy L.** b 22 Apr. 1870; **Burton L.** b 26 Aug. 1872; **Rose Estelle** b 16 Feb. 1875; **Grace E.** b 25 Nov. 1878; **Blanche V.** b 6 Jan. 1880; and **Sarah A.** b 26 Jan. 1882.

MITCHELL, AMASSAH - Born ??, d ??, s/o Jonathan, Jr. and ?? Mitchell. Children: **Eva Gertrude** b 30 Mar. 1874, d 5 Dec. 1879; and **Alvin W.** b 8 Aug. 1867.

MITCHELL, AMASSAH CURTIS - Born ??, d ??, s/o ?? Children: **Elizabeth**; **Ellen**; **Harriet**; **Allen**; **Artemas**; and others.

MITCHELL, CHARLES R. - Born 10 Jan. 1829, d 15 Aug. 1892, s/o Jonathan, Jr. and Mary (Wright) Mitchell. Charles R. Mitchell m pub. 9 Oct. 1855 Priscilla Allexander, b 15 Jan. 1840, d 15 Jan. 1890. Children: **John**; **Edward M.**, m 15 Dec. 1859 Clora H. Masen of Monmouth, ME; and **Elmer E.**

MITCHELL, DAVID - Born ??, d 20 May 1858, s/o ?? David Mitchell was from Yarmouth, Maine. He m 11 Apr. 1778 in Lewiston Betsy Graffam, d/o John. Children: **Polly** b 4 Apr. 1799; **Josiah** b 10 Oct. 1801; **Sally** b 25 Jun. 1803, d 29 Aug. 1887, m Joseph Torsey, b 6 Mar. 1803, d 28 Nov. 1878; **M a r y** b 16 Feb. 1804, d 16 Jul. 1875, m (1) Alfred Ames of Wales, ME, b 29 Aug. 1804, s/o John, and m (2) Wilks Richardson of Litchfield, ME; **E l i z a** b 7 Oct. 1805, d -- Apr. 1869, m John Smith, b 12 May 1800, d 21 Feb. 1834 (*History of Monmouth*); **L e v i** b 2 Sep. 1807, d 12 Sep. 1807; **L e v i P.** b 30 Aug. 1808, d 3 Apr. 1833; **Nancy** b 24 Aug. 1810, d -- Jan. 1869, m pub. 22 Nov. 1834 Annie Fuller of Lewiston; **Rachael** b 16 Jun. 1812, d 13 Nov. 1815; **J a n e** b 4 Jul. 1814, d 13 Jun. 1894, age 79 years 11 months, m pub. 8 Dec. 1838, m 6 Jan. 1839 James Crowley, who d 19 Aug. 1897, age 83 years 2 months 26 days; **D a v i d** b 9 Mar. 1816, m Mary Thompson, b 16 Feb. 1821, d/o Joel and Margaret (Jewell), who lived in Sangeville, ME; **Susan** b 11 Oct. 1818, d 12 May 1818 (?); **Clarissa** b 25 Apr. 1820, lived in Jay, ME, m 31 Oct. 1847 Rufus Davis (pub. Clarissa from Wales); **Adaline M.** b 11 Nov. 1822, unm; and **John D.** b 17 Aug. 1825, d 30 Aug. 1862 in Wales, m Nancy Hall of Monmouth, ME.

MITCHELL, DAVID - Born ??, d ??, s/o Joshua and ?? Mitchell. David Mitchell m Mary Foster of Chambersburg, Pennsylvania. Child: **William G.**

MITCHELL, DAVID - Born ??, d ??, s/o David and ?? Mitchell. Children: **Harriet** m John Spooner of Sangerville, ME; **Laura** m ---- Estes; **Mehitable** m Zeaky Taylor; **John**; **Nellie** m ---- Small; **Judith**; **Charles**; **Sarah Jane**; **John**; **Estella**; and **Alonso**.

MITCHELL, F. W. - Born ??, d ??, s/o ?? F. W. Mitchell m ---- Golder. Children: **Cal G.** b 6 Feb. 1888; **Forest C.** b 24 Jan. 1886; **Gladys A.** b 11 Feb. 1889; and **Victor M.** b 11 Aug. 1894.

MITCHELL, FRED E. - Born 19 Jan. 1861, d ??, s/o George B./E. and Servia (Jenkins) Mitchell. Fred E. Mitchell lived on the homeplace. He m 31 Dec. ---- Effie M. Spear. Children: **Arthur** b 12 Apr. 1896; and **Ellen** b 12 Apr. 1896.

MITCHELL, GEORGE B./E. - Born 31 Aug. 1832, d 23/27 Sep. 1881, s/o Joshua and Nancy (Tarr) Mitchell. George B./E. Mitchell m 18 Mar. 1860 Servia Jenkins of Wales, Maine. Children: **Fred E.** q.v.; **Mary E.** b 30 Apr. 1863, m Jesse Stackford, lived in Bath, ME; **Frank G.** b 24 Jun. 1866, m Lulu Ray; **William H.** b 2 May 1869; **Lillian** b 3 May 1872, d 7 Sep. 1873; **Jennie S.** b 7 Jul. 1874, m Thomas French, lived in Andover, ME; and **Walter E.** b 30 Nov. 1878. [Letter from Joshua Mitchell, 1906.]

MITCHELL, HIRAM - Born ??, d ??, s/o ?? Children: **Ellen M.** b 17 Nov. 1834, m John Doughty; **Almon** b 28 May 1837; and **Joseph F.** b 29 Nov. 1840.

MITCHELL, ISAAC NEWTON - Born 15 May 1829, d 19 Nov. 1901, s/o James and Martha (Witherill) Mitchell. Isaac Newton Mitchell m 1 Jan. 1862 May Lucinda Stevens, d/o Thos. K. Stevens of Lewiston.

MITCHELL, ISAAC S./ISSAC - Born 8 Nov. 1823, d ??, s/o Joshua and Nancy (Tarr) Mitchell. Isaac S./Isaac Mitchell was living in Gardiner, Maine, in 1906. He m (1) 18 Oct. 1846 Catherine Sullivan/Catherine Johnson of Industry, Maine, b 7 May 1827, d 15 Jan. 1852, d/o Henry and Catherine (Sullivan) Johnson, and m (2) 15 Oct. 1854 Mary E. Lane, d/o Samuel Lane of Greene, Maine. Children: **Abbie M.** b 19 Dec. 1847; **Everett** b 1 Jan. 1857, m 29 May 1870 Chores H. Oldham; **Nellie R.** b 31 Mar. 1862, d 13 Jun. 1863; and **Eleanor C.** b 6 Feb. 1867.

MITCHELL, JAMES - Born 4 Feb. 1793, d 11 Sep. 1839, age 46 years 6 months, s/o Josiah and ?? Mitchell. James Mitchell m pub. 15 Jan. 1815 Martha/Polly (Martha) Witherill of Litchfield, Maine, d 30 Jan. 1865, age 70 years 3 months. Children: **Reull Barrows/Reuel Barrows/Rural** b 21 Jun. 1817, d 2 Jan./Jun. 1885 in Wales, ME, age 67 years 6 months, m (1) Ann Penley, d/o James of Auburn, ME, and m (2) 7 Jan. 1857 Sarah F. Warren; **Fred C.** bc1818, buried in Sabattus, m Dora Maxwell of Wales, ME, niece/o Mrs. Isaac Golder; **John Witherill** b 3 Feb. 1819, d 20 May 1897, age 78 years 3 months, m 19 Apr. 1898 Mary D. Frost of Litchfield, who d 5 Jul. 1905, age 78 years 4 months, d/o Simon of Brunswick, ME; **James Gardiner** b 7 May 1821, d 5 Sep. 1839; **Alfred Emery** b 24 Jan. 1823, d 3/30 Apr. 1903, m (1) 1 Apr. 1851 Ann J. Libby of Limerick, ME, who d -- Nov. 1851, and m (2) Sarah Tuttle (Smithfield) or Ann J. Libby of Limerick, Maine, d -- Nov. 1851; **Isaac Newton** q.v.; **Otis Washington** q.v.; **Sophia J.** b 13 Nov. 1832, m pub. 5 Nov. 1873 Chas. N. Merrifield; **Josiah W.** q.v.; **Martha E.** b 24 Aug. 1835, d 19 Jun. 1886, m 13 Nov. 1868 T. R. Herbert; and **James D.** q.v.

MITCHELL, JAMES D. - Born 24 Mar. 1838/1839, d 25 Jan. 1876/1877, age 37 years and 11 months, s/o James and Martha (Witherill) Mitchell. James D. Mitchell m 15 May 1867 Annie D. Bowen of Boston, Massachusetts.

MITCHELL, JOEL W./W. G./G. W. - Born 8 Aug. 1831, d 24 Feb. 1875, s/o Jonathan, Jr. and Mary (Wright) Mitchell. Joel W./W. G./G. W. Mitchell m (1) 17 Jun. 1860 Eliza/Elisa Chadbourne, d -- May 1862, d/o Joseph, and m (2) pub. 25 Aug. 1863 Isabel Russell. Children: **Fred A.** b 6 Oct. 1860, d -- Mar. 1874; **Wallace D.** b 3 Jul. 1865; and **Mary E.** b 3 Jan. 1867.

MITCHELL, JOHN - Born ??, d ??, s/o David and ?? Mitchell. Children: **John**; and **Lizzie**.

MITCHELL, JOHN W. - Born ??, d ??, s/o James and ?? Mitchell. Children: **John Edward** b 6 Apr. 1849, m 28 Sep. 1870 Minta M. Blake, d/o Orlando; **William H.** b 28 Dec. 1850, m 15 Nov. 1874 Nellie A. McLaughlin LaGrange; and **Vesta M.** b 7 Apr. 1862, d 21 Jul. 1885, m 26 Jun. 1884 George J. Densmore.

MITCHELL, JONATHAN JR. - Born 19 May 1802, d 9 Oct. 1880, s/o ?? Jonathan Mitchell, Jr. m 30 Dec. 1824 Mary Wright, b 29 Oct. 1804, d 10 Mar. 1884. Children: **Charles R.** q.v.; **Joel W./W. G./G. W.** q.v.; **Sylvanus D.** b 25 Oct. 1834, d 10 Jul. 1865 in the army, unm; **Algeron M.** q.v.; **Elizabeth G.** b 15 Jul. 1842, m 15 Nov. 1859 Theophilus H. Rowe, who was b 3 Mar. 1834; **Amansel A.** b 27 Dec. 1844, m 3 Feb. 1872 Etta G. Phemia; and **Benoni W.** b 23 Aug. 1847, d 9 May 1873.

MITCHELL, JOSEPH - Born 9 Feb. 1784, d 21 Apr. 1853 in Webster, Maine, s/o Josiah and ?? Mitchell. Joseph Mitchell m Mary Robinson, b 1785, d 13 Oct. 1853, age 68 years. Children: **Joseph** b 30 Mar. 1808, d 9 Apr. 1808; **Veremus** b 10 Sep. 1809, d 4 Feb. 1836; and **Betsey** b 8 Jul. 1812, d -- Nov. 1842, age 30 years 4 months, m Daniel Small of Webster, ME.

MITCHELL, JOSHUA - Born 8 Apr. 1786, d 4/25 Oct. 1877, s/o Josiah, Sr. and ?? Mitchell. Joshua Mitchell m 31 Mar. 1810/1811 Nancy Tarr, d 24 Feb. 1866, d/o Seth of Lewiston. Children: **William**

Greenleaf b 9 Sep. 1811, d 3 Jan. 1899, m Mrs. Annie Foster; **Mary** b 9 Jan. 1813, d 12 Apr. 1895, m (1) Isreal/Isaiah Stanford, and m (2) Daniel Johnson; **Sarah/Sarah C.** b 19 Jan. 1815, d 11 Sep. 1898, m 31 Mar. 1840 Oliver Dickson, who was b 29 Aug. 1805, d 8 Feb. 1882 in Concord, MA; **Nancy** b 25 May 1816, d 10 Dec. 1899, m Cyrus H. Ware of Litchfield, Maine, lived in Oshkosh, Wisconsin; **Seth F.** b 19 May 1818, d 24 Feb. 1867, m Mrs. Bright of Indiana or Mary Wright, lived in Pennsylvania; **Joshua*** b 1 Feb. 1820, lived in Boston in Nov. 1906, m 6 May 1846 Sarrah/Sevia Jane Small of Wales, ME, b 28 Oct. 1822, d 26 Jul. 1908, d/o Joel and Jane (Swett) Small; **Amanda** b 13 Nov. 1821, d 18 Jan. 1892, m Ingraham Clark of Litchfield, ME; **Isaac/Isaac S.** q.v.; **Emerson/F. Emerson** b 21 Jul. 1825, drowned 31 May 1846; **Daniel C.** b 22 Jan. 1828, lived in Chelsea, MA, m Mary Elizabeth/Nancy Merrill of Litchfield and lived in Chelsea, MA; **George B.E.** q.v.; and **David** b 28 Jan. 1834, d 11 Sep. 1864, m 6 May 1862 Mary Foster, lived in the West. [* Letter from Joshua Mitchell, 1906.]

MITCHELL, JOSHUA - Born ??, d ??, s/o Joshua and ?? Mitchell. Joshua (the younger) Mitchell removed to Sangerville, ME, in 1833. He m Pamelia Stevens. Children: **Harriett** m Eden Damon of Harpswell, ME; **Leonard**; **Martha G.** m Robert Anderson of Sangerville; **William James**; **Elisa** m ---- Richardson of Newport; **Ruth**; and **Frances** m ---- Oakes of Dexter, ME.

MITCHELL, JOSIAH - Born 14 Jun. 1749, d 9 Aug. 1832, s/o Joseph and Mary (----) Mitchell. Josiah Mitchell m (1) Sarah ----, d 8 Feb. 1792, and m (2) Martha Witherill, d 9 Jul. 1841, age 81 years. Children: **Rachel** b 1 Apr. 1771, d 6 Dec. 1843, m Cyrus Barker; **Josiah** b 5 Mar. 1773, d 14 Jun. 1795; **David** b 11 Mar. 1775, d 20 May 1858, was 4 years old when he moved to Lewiston, m pub. 18 Mar. 1798 Betsey Graffam, who d 29 May 1870, d/o John; **Sally** b 12 May 1777, d 16 Nov. 1801, m Walter R. Blaisdell; **Patty** b 8 Aug. 1779, d 1870, m pub. 9 Sep. 1798 Chase Wedgewood; **Rhoda** b 10 Nov. 1781, m (1) Daniel Smith of Monmouth, ME, and m (2) 8 Nov. 1827 James Shurtleff, who lived in Litchfield, ME; **Joseph** q.v.; **Joshua** q.v.; **Amassah** b 14 May 1788, d 3 Sep. 1851, m Sally Getchell (nee Witherill), who d -- Jun. 1852; **Mary** b 8 Oct. 1791, d 8 Jun. 1792; **James** q.v.; **Josiah** b 10 May 1796, d in Bangor, m 10 May 1818 Pamelia Stevens, d in Sangerville, ME.

MITCHELL, JOSIAH W. - Born 14 May 1834, d ??, s/o James and Martha (Witherill) Mitchell. Josiah W. Mitchell m 15 Mar. 1870 Etta E. Longley, d 8 Sep. 1889 age 48 years and 11 months.

MITCHELL, OTIS WASHINGTON - Born 24 Jan./Jun. 1831, d 3 Apr. 1832.

MITCHELL, WILLIAM G. - Born ??, d ??, s/o Joshua and ?? Mitchell. Children: **Rebecca**; **Nancy**; **Katie**; and **Sadie**.

Mooar was later changed to Moore - ed.

MOOAR, BENJAMIN - Born 1748, d 26 Sep. 1828, s/o ?? Benjamin Mooar m Hannah ----. Children: **Hannah** b 16 Nov. 1768, m (1) Joseph Blanchard, and m (2) -- Jan. 1818 Nathan Cutler; **Lois** b 15 May 1773, d 10 Apr. 1854, m Simeon Haney of Strong, ME, d 16 Mar. 1863; **Benjamin** b 3 Sep. 1770; **Samuel** q.v.; **Joseph** b 7 Nov. 1777, m 15 Apr. 1802 Aseneth Ames; **P r i s s y** b 16 Nov. 1778, d 4 Apr. 1828, m pub. 9 Sep. 1798 James Hardy of Strong; **J o h n B.** b 14 Aug. 1780, d 22 Dec. 1845, m 3 Sep. 1809 Martha Merrill, who d 12 Apr. 1869; **M a r y** b 24 Nov. 1782, d 1822, m 12 Mar. 1812 Nathan Cutler; **N a t h a n** b 14 Apr. 1787, m pub. 23 Sep. 1810 Sarah Merrill; **Timothy** b 5 Feb. 1785, m 12 Mar. 1812 Olive Cutler; and **Nathan** b 14 Apr. 1787.

MOOAR, JOHN - Born 14 Aug. 1780, d 20 Dec. 1848, s/o ?? John Mooar m 3 Sep. 1809 Martha Merrill, who d 12 Apr. 1869 age 80 years. Children: **Elbridge G.** b 13 Apr. 1810, d 1 Dec. 1874 in Auburn, m 31 Mar. 1835 Sarah White of Bath, ME, b 26 Jul. 1814 in Canaan, ME, d 6 Nov. 1883 in Auburn, ME, d/o Benjamin White; **Timothy** b 13 Oct. 1811, d 3 Apr. 1886, m 16 Jan. 1834 Sarah Vickery of Auburn, b 1811, d 8 Dec. 1883; **William D.** b 11 Nov. 1813, m June Potter (Lee); **Sarah** b 8 Jun. 1816, d 24 Jun. 1883, m -- Jan. 1838 William Thomas; **A b i g a i l** b 25 Mar. 1820, m (1) 25 Apr. 1849 Daniel Maxwell of Windham, ME, and m (2) 30 Dec. 1854 O. H. Littlefield of Kennebunk, ME; **Joanna F.** b 2 Jul. 1822, m Wm. H. Smith of Winslow, ME; **Anna** b 5 Apr. 1824, d 2 Sep. 1868, m 26 Apr. 1849 C. F. Getchell of Lewiston; and **Olive J.** b 15 Oct. 1823, d 22 Aug. 1893, m 5 May 1860 Geo. W. Farr of Lewiston, who d 8 Jul. 1882, age 77 years 5 months.

MOOAR/MOORE, JOSEPH - Born 7 Mar. 1777 in Andover, Massachusetts, d 23 May 1860 in Strong, Maine, s/o ?? Joseph Mooar/Moore moved to Wilton, Maine, c1826. He m 15 Apr. 1802 Aseneth Ames, b 13 Oct. 1782 in Oakham, Massachusetts, d 13 Feb. 1837 in Wilton, Maine. Children (all born in Lewiston): **Mehitable** b 16 Oct. 1803, d 20 Feb. 1883, m John Hardy of Strong, who d 29 May 1870 in Farmington, s/o Simeon; **C l a r i s a** b 23 May 1809, m 4 Mar. 1834 Harrison Greene, b 1 Jul. 1813 in Farmington, ME, d 17 Dec. 1882; **Joseph Jr.** b 17 Apr. 1812, m (1) 1 Jan. 1838 Polly Dresser of Wilton, who was b 6 Aug. 1819, and m (2) 1 Feb. 1844 Elizabeth Lawrence of Wilton, who was b -- Dec. 1822, d 11 Dec. 1888, and m (3) ----; **Ezra/Ezra H.** b 1/6 Oct. 1814, m (1) Florentine Mooar, d 13 Aug. 1839, d/o Nathan Mooar, and m (2) Nancy Winship of Weld, ME, d 20 May 1860, age 44 years, and m (3) Mary Butterfield, d 6 May 1891; **Lucy Ann** b 28 Oct. 1817, m Calvin Keyes of East Wilton; **Jane** b 14 Jan. 1821, m Samuel Holt; and **Roxelania B. C.** b 14 Jul. 1825, m Henry A. Stone.

MOOAR, NATHAN - Born ??, d ??, s/o ?? Nathan Mooar m Sarah ----, b 19 Dec. 1793. Children: **H a n n a h** b 19 Dec. 1810; **M a r y** b 2 Sep. 1812; **Martha** b 9 Feb. 1815; **Florentina** b 13 Jan. 1817; **Priscilla** b 16 Feb. 1819; **Harriot** b 20 Apr. 1821; **Nathan** b 7 Dec. 1823; **Orpha** b -- Nov. 1827; and **Orpha** b 5 Mar. 1829. [Vital Records of Lewiston, Maine, p. 52.]

MOOAR, SAMUEL - Born 7 Mar. 1775, s/o Benjamin and Hannah (----) Mooar. Samuel Mooar m pub. 3 Mar. 1799/30 Nov. 1802 Betsy/Betsey Ames, d/o James and Elizabeth (----) Ames. Children: **Zenas/Zenas A.** q.v.; **Samuel** q.v.; **Elizabeth Sarah** b 24 Aug. 1809 in Topsham, ME, d 28 Jan. 1884 in Newport, ME, m (1) W. Powrgess (?), and m (2) Gavon Chapman, d 16 Dec. 1854 in Newport, ME; **Henry/Harvey** q.v.; **Polivia Jane** b 23 Mar. 1815, m Thomas F. Dexter, b 1 Mar. 1815, d 30 Apr. 1883; and **Marshia Ann** b 11 Jul. 1821 in Lewiston, d 30 Jun. 1866 in Newport, m Lester Perkins of Newport, d 18 May 1873.

MOODY, DAVID F. - Born 3 Apr. 1807, d ??, s/o Robert and ?? Moody. Children: **Daniel M.**; **Elvira**; and **Sallie Ellen** b 13 Jul. 1842, m James A. Everett.

MOODY, JOSIAH - Born 12 Mar. 1765 in Falmouth, Maine, d ??, s/o Houchin, Sr. and ?? Moody. Josiah Moody lived in Pejepscot, Bethel, and Lewiston, Maine. He m (1) 10 Apr. 1790 Humility Proctor, d 15 Oct. 1795, they moved to Lewiston after their marriage, and m (2) pub. 20 Dec. 1795 Mehitable Hoosting of Falmouth. *Children by 1st wife*: **Sophia** b 26 Sep. 1790, d 2 Oct. 1871 in Minot, ME, m James Jordan of Lewiston; **Jeremiah** b 5 Oct. 1792; and **Hesikiah** b 1 Dec. 1794, m Hannah Estes. *Children by 2nd wife*: **Beniah** b 28 Aug. 1796; **Betsey** b 1 Jul. 1798; **Rebecca** b 10 Mar. 1800; and **Mary J.** b 3 Jun. 1806, m Joseph L. Jordan of Lewiston.

MOODY, ROBERT - Born ??, d 10 Apr. 1761/1861 in New Portland, Maine, s/o ?? Robert Moody m (1) pub. 20 Oct. 1799 Sally Garcelon, b 27 Jul. 1776, d 4 Sep. 1811, and m (2) 1 Mar. 1812 Rebecca Chandler. Children: **Clarisa** b 28 Sep. 1800, m Nathaniel D. Richardson of New Portland, ME; **Mariah** b 27 Dec. 1801, d 7 Jun. 1882, m 29 Mar. 1828/1829 John A. Davis, d 22 Dec. 1876; **Daniel** b 23 May 1803, m Mrs. Hildreth Spencer of Orono, ME; **Sally** b 13 Jul. 1805, d 1862, unm; **David** b 3 Apr. 1807, m Eliza Judkins; **Jane** b 24 Nov. 1808, m William Doyle of Orono; and **Rosillia** b 28 Dec. 1810, m Donia B. Miles.

MOORE, ALBERT - Born ??, d ??, s/o ?? Child: **Wm. James** b 6 Aug. 1875.

MOORE, CHARLES - Born in Revere, Massachusetts, d ??, s/o ?? Children: **Lionell**; and **Rhodolph**.

MOORE, ELBRIDGE/ELBRIDGE G. - b 13 Apr. 1810, d 1/11 Dec. 1874 in Auburn, Maine, s/o John and Martha (Merrill) Moore. Elbridge/Elbridge G. m 31 Mar. 1835 Sarah White of Bath, Maine, b 26 Jul. 1814 at Canaan, Maine, d 6 Nov. 1883 in Auburn, Maine, d/o Benjamin. Children: **Levi Davis** b 10 Jun. 1836 at Oldtown, ME, m 22 Aug. 1860 Mary A. Knight; **Julia Ann Gorham** b 17 Apr. 1840, m 19 Jan. 1867 Nathan M. York; **John Alvah** b 12 Nov. 1838 at Lewiston; **Sarah Jane** b 31 Mar. 1842, m 28 Dec. 1870 Albert H. Ricker; **Mary**

Frances b 19 Jan. 1844, m 24 Dec. 1878 David Johnson, Jr.; **Olive Marie** b 16 May 1846, m 23 Apr. 1866 Hiram B. Drake; **Elbridge Gerry, Jr.** b 15 May 1848, d 27 Jun. 1850; **Martha Helen** b 25 Feb. 1850, d 20 May 1857; **Frank Edwin** b 6 Nov. 1852 at Lewiston, m 4 Sep. 1871 Ida Farrar; **Emeline Oakes** b 23 May 1853, m 17 Apr. 1872 George A. Allen; **Alonso Garcelon** b 1 Nov. 1851, d 4 Aug. 1855; **Oscar Coburn** b 8 Jan. 1857, m 18 Dec. 1882 Lovena Beal; and **Henry Howard** b 30 Apr. 1859 at Auburn, m 1884 Annie Gorden.

MOORE, EZRA H. - Born 1 Oct. 1814, d ??, s/o Joseph and Azeneth (Ames) Moore. Ezra H. Moore m (1) Florentine Mooar, d 13 Aug. 1839, age 23 years, and m (2) Nancy Winship, d 20 May 1860, age 44 years, and m (3) Mary Butterfield, d 6 May 1891. Children: **Adler F.**; **Albertus**; **Anna M.** m Fred L. Tarr; and **Aseneth**.

MOORE, HARVEY/HENRY - Born 22 Nov. 1812 in Brunswick, Maine, d 18 May 1873, s/o Samuel and Betsy/Betsey (Ames) Moore. Harvey/Henry m (1) Sabina R./Salvinia Howe of Ripley, Maine, d 16 Dec. 1854 in Newport, Maine, and m (2) Mary E. Smith. Children: **Charles A.** b 17 Dec. 1842 in Carmel, ME, d 17 Feb. 1890 at Amesbury, MA; **Josephine** b 11 Mar. 1844 in Ripley; **Sarah E.** b 21 Oct. 1846, d 24 Feb. 1849 in Bangor, ME; **Georgetta** b 14 Mar. 1849 in Bangor, d 13 May 1873 in Corinna; **Fernaldo H.** b 8 Mar. 1850 in Newport; **Albert F.** b 9 May 1856, d 6 Mar. 1857 in Newport; **Perley P.** b 10 Jan. 1858, d 22 Oct. 1860 in Newport; **Walter A.** b 4 Mar. 1860; **Frank O.** b 12 Jan. 1862; **Ellie L.** b 14 May 1865; **Effie L.** b 14 May 1865; and **Flora B.** b 1 Mar. 1873.

MOORE, JOSEPH JR. - Born 17 Apr. 1812, d ??, s/o Joseph and Aseneth (Ames) Moore. Joseph Moore, Jr. m (1) 1 Jan. 1838 Polly Dresser of Wilton, Maine, b 6 Jul. 1819, d 21 Jan. 1842, and m (2) 1 Feb. 1844 Elizabeth Lawrence of Wilton, b -- Dec. 1822, d 4 Dec. 1888. Children: **James Farington** b 30 Dec. 1841 in Wilton; **Ordella A.** b 22 Sep. 1848 in Wilton; and **Osmond C. B.** b 22 Dec. 1858 in Paris.

MOORE, SAMUEL - Born 30 Jun. 1807, d 5 Feb. 1884 in Newport, Maine, s/o Samuel and Betsy/Betsey (Ames) Moore. Samuel Moore m Cynthia Sanderson, d 22 Jul. 1867. Children: **Charles Edwin** b 28 Oct. 1832 in Newport, m (1) 10 Oct. 1863 Ann Stevens of Newport, and m (2) 7 Feb. 1872 Mrs. Addie Allen; **Amanda M.** b 22 Nov. 1834 in Newport, m 3 Jul. 1856 Joseph Knight of Etna, ME; **Julia A.** b 27 Aug. 1836 in Newport, m 2 Dec. 1856 George E. Norton of Palmyra, ME; **Arthur E.** b 22 Feb. 1839, m 16 Aug. 1881 ---- St. Clair of New York; **Mary M.** b 11 Mar. 1841 in Newport; and **Samuel N.** b 26 Jan. 1844 in Newport.

MOORE, TIMOTHY - Born 13 Oct. 1811, d 3 Apr. 1886, s/o ?? Timothy Moore m 16 Jul. 1834 in Havill/Haverhill, Massachusetts, Sarah Vickery, b 26 Nov. 1811, d 8 Dec. 1883. Children: **Charles H.** b 8 Apr. 1835, m 17 Oct. 1858 Sarah Snow of Danville, ME; and **Caroline** b 26 Feb. 1838, d 31 Nov. 1884, m John Keyes.

MOORE, WM./WM. D. - Born 11 Nov. 1813, d 26 May 1856 in Lewiston, s/o John and Martha (Merrill) Moore. Wm./Wm. D. m 14 Jun. 1836 in Brunswick, Maine, June/Jane Potter (Lee) of Litchfield, Maine. Children: **Emma J.** b 27 Mar. 1837, m 27 Sep. 1857 Joseph White of Bath, ME; **Ellen R.** b 16 Apr. 1879, m 12 Sep. 1858 Artsen (?) A. Dennison of Freeport, ME; **Laura A.** b 20 Feb. 1841, d 6 Mar. 1842; **Laura E.** b 27 Jul. 1845, d 22 Nov. 1885, unm; and **Albert W.** b 23 Oct. 1850, d 30 Dec. 1891 in New Bedford, MA?, m 23 Jul. 1874 Mary E. Rigby.

MOORE, ZENAS/ZENAS A. - Born 22 May 1805 in Lewiston, d 30 Jan. 1871 in Newport, Maine, s/o ?? Zenas/Zenas A. Moore m (1) pub. -- Sep. 1827 Cyrena Abbott of Etna, Maine, and m (2) Melinda/Meleneca Gray, d 7 Apr. 1879 in Newport, Maine. Children: **William H.** b 2 Jun. 1834 in Newburyport, MA; **Harvey Augustus** b 12 Jul. 1836 in Dedham, MA; and **Lydia Parker** b 27 Oct. 1840 in Lewiston, m 17 Jun. 1861 Richard Libby of Newport.

MORRELL/MORRILL, ALONSO F. - Born 9 Aug. 1841, d ??, s/o Daniel/Daniel B. and Esther (Nash) Morrell. Alonso F. Morrell m 1 Apr. 1863 Loisa M. Bradbury, b -- May 1838, d/o Royal J. Bradbury of Auburn, Maine. Children: **Ida Estelle** b 27 Jan. 1864, m 16 Jun. 1886 Charles F. Curtis of Auburn; **Frank E.** q.v.; and **Angie B.** b 2 Aug. 1869, m 1 May 1889 Pearl C. Records of Auburn.

MORRELL/MORRILL, AMASIAH - Born ??, d 9 Feb. 1864, s/o ?? Amasiah Morrell/Morrill m 28 Jan. 1821 Elizabeth Read, d 30 Apr. 1877, age 78 years 9 months. Children: **Jedidiah** b 10 Nov. 1821, d 11 Oct. 1841; **Harriet H.** b 5 Jan. 1823, m 31 Oct. 1847 George Hodgkin; **Lemuel Read** b 29 Mar. 1825, m Orvida Mason; **Joann** b 19 Jan. 1827, d 16 Nov. 1863 in OH, m Charles D. B. Webster; **Mary R.** b 14 Sep. 1830, d 16 Jul. 1847; **John R.** b 13 Jun. 1836, d 7 Apr. 1841; **Betsey J.** b 1 Aug. 1838, m 31 Jan. 1884 Thomas B. Norris; and **George B.** b 7 Jan. 1842, d 7 Aug. 1890, m (1) 20 Jul. 1867 Anna G. Jordan, and m (2) 1871 Frances L. Gould.

MORRELL/MORRILL, ANDREW J. - Born 15 Jan. 1831, d ??, s/o Stephen and Lucinda (----) Morrell/Morrill. Andrew J. Morrell/Morrill m 25 May 1854 Annie Maria Hill. Children: **George Stillman** b 2 Aug. 1855, m 2 Aug. 1884 Maria G. Doten; **Orland Hill** b 30 Nov. 1856, m 2 Jul. 1889 Carrie C. McCarlie; **Laura Eva** b 6 Feb. 1860, m 19 Sep. 1892 David Orr; **Stephen Herman** b 8 Jun. 1862, m 6 Jul. 1892 Minnie V. Blake; **Frank Edward** b 2 May 1865, m 21 Jul. 1891 Clara B. Brown; **Oscar Millard** b 4 Nov. 1866, m 12 Dec. 1889 Lillian Finch; **Annie Blanche** b 29 Aug. 1868, m 7 Feb. 1888 Orren B. Doten; **Lucy Stevens** b 6 Aug. 1870, d 23 Feb. 1871; **Lucinda Hitching** b 12 Jul. 1872; **Amos Chester** b 4 Dec. 1874; and **Mabel Vinetta** b 13 May 1877. [Letter from A. J. Morrill, 1893, of Charlotte, N. B.]

MORRELL/MORRILL, BENSON - Born 3 Jan. 1803, d 1 Feb. 1867 in Topsham, Maine, s/o ?? Benson Morrell/Morrill m (1) 29 Mar. 1824

Philena Berry, d 16 Aug. 1851, and m (2) 12 Mar. 1854 Susanna Wait, b 1 Dec. 1814 in Dixfield, ME, d 22 Sep. 1872. Children: **Olive Berry** b 12 Jul. 1824, d 11 Jan. 1843; **Deanna Patterson** b 15 Feb. 1827, d 19 Jan. 1847; and **John Smith** b 13 Jan. 1831, d 21 Sep. 1857.

MORRELL/MORRILL, DANIEL/DANIEL B. - Born ??, d ??, s/o ?? Daniel/Daniel B. Morrell/Morrill m Esther Nash, d/o James (?). Children: **Alonso F.** q.v.; **David Edwin** b 10 Aug. 1847, d 10 Sep. 1853; and **Sanford** b 2 Dec. 1849, d 10 Aug. 1853.

MORRELL, DAVID - Born ??, d ??, s/o ?? Children: **David; Tloviman** (?) m Mary Leavitt; **Ann** m William Hatch; **Naham** d young; **Harriett; Rosetta;** and **Dennis** m Nettie Dahee of Cambridge, ME?.

MORRELL/MORRILL, FRANCES JUDITH - Born ??, d ??, d/o ?? Frances Judith Morrell/Morrill m pub. 20 Jul. 1801 Isaac Childs of Poland, Maine. Children: **Frances Dolly** m Abram Butler; **Weeks Experence** m -- May 1809 John Cushing; **Sally Atkinson** m pub. 21 Aug. 1796 Wm. Dingley of Pejepscot.

MORRELL/MORRILL, FRANK E. - Born 23 Feb. 1866, d ??, s/o Alonso F. and Loisa M. (Bradbury) Morrell/Morrill. Frank E. Morrell/Morrill m 21 Dec. 1889 Linda Merrill of Auburn, Maine, d/o Daniel and Mary (Noyes) Merrill. Child: **Alma Gertrude** b 31 Dec. 1891.

MORRELL/MORRILL, JEDIDIAH - Born ??, d 8 Nov. 1821, s/o ?? Jedidiah Morrell/Morrill m Joanna Beal, d 1 Jun. 1832. Children: **Mary** b 18 Aug. 1784, m 1804 William Anderson of New Vineyard, ME; **Daniel** b 21 Oct. 1785; **Stephen** q.v.; **Dorcas** b 19 Aug. 1789, m -- Nov. 1806 William Barker; **Jedediah, Jr.** q.v.; **Joannah** b 22 May 1793, d 3 Jun. 1846, m (1) 11 Mar. 1813 William Nash, and m (2) 16 Mar. 1824 John Smith, d 5 Sep. 1887; **A n a s h i a h** b 13 May 1795, d -- Feb. 1864, m 28 Jan. 1821 Elizabeth Reed, d 30 Apr. 1877, d/o Lemuel; **Elijah** b 2 Mar. 1797, d 5 Sep. 1803; **Jacob** b 4 Jan. 1799, unm; **Ebeneser** b 3 Jul. 1802, d 24 Oct. 1829; and **Benson** b 3 Jan. 1803, d in Topsham, ME, m (1) 29 Mar. 1824 Phelene Berry of Minot, ME, d 16 Aug. 1851, and m (2) 12 Mar. 1854 Susanna Wait, b 1 Dec. 1814 in Dixfield, ME, d 22 Sep. 1872.

MORRELL/MORRILL, JEDIDIAH, JR. - b 7 Aug. 1791, d 27 Jul. 1850, s/o Jedidiah and Joanna (Beal) Morrell/Morrill. Jedidiah Morrell/Morrill, Jr. m 3 Sep. 1811, Lydia Briggs of Auburn, Maine, b 30 Aug. 1790, d 16 Nov. 1868. Children: **Daniel B.** b 24 Apr. 1812, d 12 May 1883, m 17 Nov. 1840 Esther Nash, who was b 1813, d 14 Feb. 1893, d/o James Nash of Auburn; **C a l v i n** b 9 Jul. 1816, d 24 Mar. 1820; **Joann B.** b 25 Jul. 1821, d 7 Nov. 1865, m (1) 14 Sep. 1857 Albert W. Silver of NH, and m (2) Joseph Turner; **John C.** b 31 Jul. 1823, d 22 Oct. 1892, m 4 Nov. 1847 Olive Caroline Berry, who was b 16 Sep. 1826, d/o Charles Berry; **Julia A.** b 2 Jan. 1829, m 20 Nov. 1845 Hiram E. Woodman, who was b 2 Apr. 1824, d 5 Oct. 1865; and **Eben** b

9 Feb. 1831, d 24 Oct. 1850, unm. [Letter from Julia A. Woodman, 1892.]

MORRELL/MORRILL, JOEL - Born ??, d 8 Nov. 1821, s/o ?? Joel Morrell/Morrill m Joanna ----, who d 1 Jun. 1832. Children: **Mary** b 18 Aug. 1784, m 1804 Wm. Anderson in New Vineyard, ME; **Daniel** b 21 Oct. 1785, unm; **Stephen** b 3 Sep. 1787 in Lewiston, ME; **Dorcas** b 19 Aug. 1789, m -- Nov. 1806 Wm. Barker; **Jedidiah** b 7 Aug. 1791, m Lydia Briggs of Auburn, ME; **Joannah** b 22 May 1793, m John Smith; **Amasiah** b 13 May 1795, d 9 Feb. 1864; **Elijah** b 2 Mar. 1797, d 15 Sep. 1803; **Jacob** b 4 Jan. 1799, unm; **Ebeneser** b 22 Apr. 1801, killed 24 Oct. 1829, unm; and **Benson** b 3 Jan. 1803, m Philena Berry of Minot, ME.

MORRELL/MORRILL, JOEL JR. - Born ??, d ??, s/o ?? Children: **Daniel** m Esther Nash, sis/o Sumner; **Joannah** m ---- Silver; **Calvin** m ---- Berry of Auburn, ME; and **Julia** m Hiram Woodman.

MORRELL/MORRILL, JOHN C. - b 31 Jul. 1823, d 22 Oct. 1892, s/o Jedediah, Jr. and ?? Morrell/Morrill. John C. Morrell/Morrill m 4 Nov. 1847 Olive Garcelon/Caroline Berry, b 16 Sep. 1826, d/o Charles Berry. Children: **Ann B.** b 17 Sep. 1848, d 13 May 1849; and **John C.** b 3 May 1850, d 21 Sep. 1850.

MORRELL/MORRILL, STEPHEN - Born 3 Sep. 1787 in Lewiston, d 12 May 1841, s/o Jedidiah and Joanna (Beal) Morrell/Morrill. Stephen Morrell/Morrill m 5 Nov. 1829 Lucinda Hitchings of the Parish of St. Andrew, NB, or St. Andrews, N.S., b 22 Feb. 1809. Children: **Andrew Jackson** b 15 Jan. 1831, m 25 May 1854 Annie Maria Hill; **Joanna** b 22 Feb. 1832, d 17 Oct. 1854, m 31 Mar. 1859 Joseph Garcelon; **Lucinda** b 28 Feb. 1834, d 11 Apr. 1883, m -- Apr. 1862 William Wiley; **Stephen Decatar** q.v.; **Amos H.** b 13 Mar. 1838, killed 5 Jul. 1863 at Gettysburg, PA; and **Sophronia Herrick** b 12 Apr. 1840, d 15 Nov. 1876.

MORRELL/MORRILL, STEPHEN DECATAR - [Letter from A. J. Morrill of Oak Bay, Charlotte, N. B., 1893.] Born 17 Dec. 1835 in St. Andrews, NB, d ??, s/o Stephen and Lucinda (Hitchings) Morrell/Morrill. Stephen Decatar m 13 Oct. 1854/1855 at Calais, Maine, Almaria /Almatia Ann Doten, b 25 Apr. 1835. Children: **Ernest Decatur** b 31 Jan. 1855, m (1) 7 Dec. 1881 Nellie Lord, d 24 Apr. 1884, and m (2) -- Jan. 1891 Emma M. Wright; **Adelbert Fremont** b 9 Aug. 1857, m 1881 Laura S. Griggs; **William Edward** b 25 Apr. 1859, m Helen F. Armstrong; **Eben Doten** b 18 Sep. 1860; **Stephen Hitching** b 25 Jul. 1862; **John Frederic** b 25 Jun. 1863, m Clara A. Smith; **Herbert Philbrook** b 9 Mar. 1869; and **Edward Lorenso** b 27 Jul. 1871.

MORRELL/MORRILL, WM. FRANCIS - Born 27 Sep. 1835 in Poland, Maine, d 1 Apr. 1900 in Cambridge, Massachusetts, s/o Daniel and ?? Morrell/Morrill. Daniel was the s/o Joseph, s/o John, s/o Peter, s/o John, s/o John. Wm. Francis Morrell/Morrill m -- Apr. 1859 in Durham, ME, Sarah N. Newell, who was b 3 Feb. 1835 in

Durham, ME. Children: **Henry H.** b -- Jan. 1860 in Durham, ME, m 16 Nov. 1884 by Rev. Wm. S. Abesey in Cambridge, MA, Carrie Emery, who was b 6 Jun. 1864, d/o Thomas and Elizabeth Barrington; and **Frank Perceval** b 16 Oct. 1870 in Lewiston.

MORSE, BENJ. FRANKLIN - Born ??, d ??, s/o ?? Benj. Franklin Morse m ---- Brackett. Children: **Herbert**; and **Winniefred**.

MORSE, EDWIN AURELIUS - Born 28 Mar. 1820, d in Norway, Maine, s/o Nathan, Jr. and Mary (Crockett) Morse. Edwin Aurelius Morse m (1) E. P. Miles, and m (2) Sarah E. Blake of Lincoln, Maine, b 12 Dec. 1834. Child: **Edwin C.** b 2 Oct. 1862.

MORSE, EPHRAIM CROCKETT - Born 7 Apr. 1822, d 23 Jul. 1885 in Auburn, Maine, s/o Joel and Sarah (Crockett) Morse. Ephraim Crockett Morse m 15 Aug. 1849 in Auburn, Maine, Ann Marie McKenny. Children: **Henrietta** b 7 Sep. 1848; **Carrie**; and **Henry**.

MORSE, JOEL - Born 16 Oct. 1779, d 1 Aug. 1858, s/o ?? Joel Morse m 1809 Sarah Crockett. Children: **William B.** q.v.; **Sarah B.** b 14 Oct. 1812, d 25 Sep. 1819 in Lewiston; **Lucy Baker** b 18 Nov. 1814, m 23 Apr. 1835 John R. Merrill, d in San Francisco, CA; **Joel** b 16 May 1817, d 19 Aug. 1841; **Orren Blaisdell** b 26 Oct. 1819, m -- Apr. 1843 Sarah H. Harwood of Dublin, NH; **Ephraim Crockett** q.v.; **Nathan** b 12 Dec. 1825, m Emily Cobb of Brunswick, ME; **Reuben Crockett** b 24 Apr. 1828, d 12 Dec. 1877, m 4 Nov. 1847 Roland F. Read, d -- Dec. 1892; **James C.** b 9 Nov. 1830, d 22 Nov. 1839 in Durham; and **Sarah Marie** b 7 Sep. 1833, m 22 Mar. 1869 Rev. John M. Wedgwood, b 4 Jul. 1819 in Effingham, NH, and d 9 Apr. 1891. [Vital Records of Lewiston, Maine, p. 50 - spelling is Moss, not Morse; the spelling was changed or corrected to Morse later.]

MORSE, JOSEPH - Born ??, d ??, s/o Nathan and ?? Morse. Children: **Lydell**; **Daniel** b in Marlboro, NH; and **Frank**.

MORSE, NATHAN - Born 23 Jun. 1741, d 30 Jun. 1822, s/o Capt. Joseph and Sarah (Lewis) Morse. Nathan Morse m 28 Dec. 1763 Sarah Bacon of Dedham, Massachusetts. (The Morses all came from Dedham, MA). Children: **Paul**; **Joel** b 16 Oct. 1779, d 1 Aug. 1858 in Auburn, m 1809 Sarah Crockett, who d 13 Aug. 1850; **Abigail** b 29 Mar. 1783, m 22 Apr. 1810 James Nash; **Hannah** b 15 Jul. 1784, m 3 Nov. 1805 Peter R. Blaisdell; **Nathan Jr.** q.v.; and **Catherin** m ---- Billing. [Vital Records of Lewiston, Maine, p. 49 - spelt Morse as Moss; *Maine Families of 1790* edited by Ruth Gray, published by Maine Genealogical Society, 1988, p. 209.]

MORSE, NATHAN JR. - Born 6 Aug. 1787, d ??, s/o Nathan and Sarah (Bacon) Morse. Nathan Morse, Jr. m 2 Feb. 1809 Mary Crockett of Pejepscot, Maine. Children: **Joseph Roberts** b 4 Jun. 1810 in Danville, d 1882 in Paris, ME, m (1) ----, and m (2) Elvira Low; **Sally Bacon** b 15 Aug. 1811, d 1840, m Josiah Smale (?) of Greenwood, ME; **Betsey C.** b 2 Apr. 1813, d 10 Dec. 1815; **Judith** b -- Nov. 1814, d --

Oct. 1816; **Judith Crockett** b 24 Dec. 1817, m 21 Oct. 1837 Ansel Dinsmore, moved to Norway, ME; **Edwin Aurelius** q.v.; **Mary** b 9 Aug. 1822, d 8 Sep. 1823; **M a r y   J a n e** b 12 Jul. 1824, m John Woodman, moved to Pan, MI; **Lucinda Shackley** b 30 Jan. 1828; **Benjamin F.** b 20 Mar. 1830, m Eliza (?) Stone, moved to Church Hill, MD; **Julia Ann** b 4 Feb. 1833, m Albert M. Hammond of Paris, moved to Baltimore, MD; and **Hannah Blaisdell** b 30 Jun. 1836, m John J. Morton of South Paris.

MORSE, STILLMAN - Born ??, d ??, s/o ?? Stillman Morse m Rosilla Hatch, d/o John, and she m (2) Enoch Littlefield of Auburn, Maine. Children: **John H.** b 25 Sep. 1835; and **Ira F.** b 18 Sep. 1840.

MORSE, WILLIAM B. - Born 9 Oct. 1810, d 3 Apr. 1889, s/o Joel and Sarah (Crockett) Morse. William B. Morse m 21 Sep. 1837 in Auburn, Maine, Rebecca H. Merrill. Children: **James**; and **Alonso**.

MURRAY, BENJAMIN - Born ??, d ??, s/o ?? Benjamin Murray m 15 Mar. 1817 Priscilla Harris of New Gloucester, Maine, d 30 Sep. 1848. Children: **Jabez Woodman** b 22 Dec. 1820, m Amanda Brown of Machias, ME; **Simeon H.** q.v.; **Clarissa Ann** b 17 Mar. 1828, m Adino (?) J. Burbank; **Elizabeth Mary** b 21 Feb. 1832, d 4 Jun. 1855; and **V e s t a** b 17 Feb. 1834, d 17 Nov. 1855. [Vital Records of Lewiston, Maine, p. 123.]

MURRAY, HARVEY - Born ??, d ??, s/o ?? Harvey Murray m -- Nov. 1886 Vella Welch. Children: **E l s i e S.** b 13 Sep. 1887; and **Eleanor** b -- Dec. 1890.

MURRAY, JABEZ - Born ??, d ??, s/o ?? Jabez Murray was an M.D. He was a graduate of Bowdoin College of Brunswick, Maine.

MURRAY, SIMEON H. - Born 19 Aug. 1825, d ??, s/o Benjamin and Priscilla (Harris) Murray. Simeon H. Murray m 24 Jan. 1850 Clarian S. Stetson. Children: **Frank H.** b 3 Apr. 1852, d 8 Aug. 1853; **Harvey S.** b 15 Sep. 1860, m -- Nov. 1886 Vella Welch of Vineland; and **Ralph B.** b 27 Sep. 1865.

NASH, AMMI READ - Born 21 Nov. 1823, d 7 Nov. 1889, s/o John and Sarah (----) Nash. Ammi R. Nash m 30 May 1847 Julia Ann Sleeper. Children: **Everett A.** q.v.; **John F.** q.v.; **Sarah Frances** b 13 Jan. 1850, d 17 Sep. 1850; **Charles J.** q.v.; **James** b 30 Nov. 1853, d 17 Oct. 1884, m Mary E. Talbert of Turner, ME; **Arthur S.** b 19 Jan. 1856, d 16 Nov. 1871; **Helen** b 12 Jan. 1860, m 10 Feb. 1888 Frank L. Sleeper, M.D.; and **Walter H.** b 14 Sep. 1861, d 15 Nov. 1872.

NASH, CHARLES J. - Born 25 Dec. 1851, d ??, s/o Ammi R. and Julia Ann (Sleeper) Nash. Charles J. Nash m -- Feb. 1878 Eunice L. Buck, d/o Ambrose. Children: **Nina S.** b 1879, d 2 May 1881; **Charles H.**; **Ambrose L.**; **Cava S.**; and **Stephen M.**

NASH, EVERETT A. - Born 16 May 1848, d ??, s/o Ammi R. and Julia Ann (Sleeper) Nash. Everett A. Nash m 21 Jan. 1875 Emma A. Goodwin. Child: **George** b 17 Dec. 1878.

NASH, COL. JOHN - Born 15 Feb. 1789, d 19 Sep. 1847 age 58 years [vital records of Lewiston, Maine, p. 51 and Riverside Cemetery, Lewiston, Maine], s/o ?? Col. John Nash was the first tavern keeper [*Lewiston Journal* files]. He m 5 Dec. 1811 Sarah Read, b 28 Sep. 1794, d 24 Sep. 1863 age 64 years [Riverside Cemetery]. Children: **Susanna** b 9 May 1812, d 27 Aug. 1890, **Sarah** b 9 May 1816, d 9 Dec. 1892, m 15 Feb. 1838 Ebenezer H. Sleeper; **John** b 5 Apr. 1820, d 3 Nov. 1872, m 7 Jan. 1845 Matilda Wheeler; **Ammi Read** q.v.; and **Eliza P.** b 31 Aug. 1830, d 17 Nov. 1882, m 30 Jan. 1855 Charles F. Jefferson.

NASH, JOHN - Born ??, d ??, s/o ?? Children: **Ella Frances** b 5 Aug. 1854, m -- Jun. 1875 Lorenzo W. Daly; **Eddie** b 22 Jun. 1856, d 24 Aug. 1857; and **Herbert** b 24 Jun. 1860, d 8 Sep. 1876.

NASH, JOHN B. - Born 8 Jul. 1794 in Minot, [sic] [vital records of Poland, Maine, states Worcester, Massachusetts, as place of birth], d 16 Apr. 1883, s/o Capt. Jonathan and Ann (----) Nash [vital records of Poland, Maine]. John B. Nash m pub. 26 Jan. 1816 Rachael C. Banks, b 16 Jan. 1797 in North Yarmouth, Maine, d 2 May 1877 in Rockford, IL. Children: **Sarah A.** b 19 Feb. 1817, d 1842 in Bath, ME., m Winslow Morse; **Joan** b 26 Jan. 1819, d 6 Jan. 1864, m John B. Jones, who d 21 Jan. 1885 age 70 years; **Jacob** b 14 Nov. 1821, d 6 Feb. 1849, m Esther Frost; **Anarath** b 18 Aug. 1823; **William** b 29 Jul. 1825, d in infancy; **John** b 28 Nov. 1827, d in infancy; **Nancy** b 2 May 1828, d in infancy; **John B., Jr.** b 14 Feb. 1831, d 2 Feb. 1893, m 1858 Mary Ann Williamson of Flora, IL; **Nancy M.** b 6 May 1833, d 24 Aug. 1855, m Horace Johnson; and **Bardecia T.** b 31 Aug. 1834, d -- Sep. 1892, m George W. Hathaway of Rockford, IL.

NASH, JOHN B. - Born ??, d ??, s/o ?? Children: **George H.** b -- Dec. 1889, m ---- Sargent; **Earl**; and **Jay**.

NASH, JOHN F. - Born 13 Jan. 1850, d ??, s/o Ammi R. and Julia Ann (Sleeper) Nash. John F. Nash m 1 May 1870 Watie A. Carville of Poland, Maine, b 20 Jan. 1852, d/o John W. Carville. Children: **Grace Gertrude** b 7 Feb. 1871, m 9 Jun. 1892 James Leslie Folsom of Augusta, ME; **Julia Ann** b 20 Jun. 1872, d 29 Apr. 1873; **Waitie May** b 3 Oct. 1873; **Lucy Viola** b 5 Feb. 1876, d 20 Jul. 1876; **John Ammie** b 20 Sep. 1878; **Helen Weston** b 28 Jun. 1881; and **Lydia Winnifred** b 5 Dec. 1884, d 1 May 1889.

NASON, JEREMIAH - Born 30 Apr. 1803, d ??, s/o ?? Jeremiah Nason m 18 Nov. 1824 Hannah Hackett. Child: **Elizabeth** b 25 Dec. 1825.

The **NEVENS** came from the North of Ireland during the Scotch - Irish imigration. During the autumn of 1731, the following (**NEVENS**) named persons came to this county: **Robert; Molly; Rose; Oley; Hue** d 1776, m 1738 Joanna Burnham; **Robert**; one sister went to New Hampshire; one sister d in Boston, Massachusetts. Others all settled at Cape Ann, Massachusetts.

NEVENS, A. WILSON - Born ??, d ??, s/o Zedikiah and ?? Nevens. Children: **Ella Augusta** b 9 Jul. 1852; **Mary Olive** b 26 Jun. 1854, m J. Frank Conkling; **Carrie Elmira** b 8 Jul. 1858, m Joseph H. Conkling; and **Wilson Condit** b 14 Jan. 1860.

NEVENS, ALFRED DRUMMOND - Born 29 Aug. 1846, d ??, s/o Amasiah and Huldah J. (Ham) Nevens. Alfred Drummond Nevens m 4 Jan. 1871 Emma M. Hill of New Gloucester, Maine, b 30 Oct. 1849 in Walpole, New Hampshire, d 15 Apr. 1884 in New Gloucester. Children: **Jennie** b 1 Dec. 1871; **Marilla** b 25 Jun. 1873; **Stella H.** b 28 Jun. 1875; **Amasiah E.** b 27 Jul. 1876; **Marten G.** b 31 Jan. 1878, **Celinda True** b 11 May 1881; and **Ethel W.** b 5 Apr. 1883, d 14 Nov. 1883.

NEVENS, ALFRED I. - Born 26 Apr. 1820, d ??, s/o Joel and Jemima (Haskell) Nevens. Alfred I. Nevens m 1 Jan. 1844 Sarah Webb. Children: **Georgiana T.** b 2 Oct. 1844, m [James?] Polk Jordan; **Kate** b 25 Sep. 1854, m Clarence Bickford; **Frank H.** q.v.; **Elisa W.** b 15 Mar. 1860; **Frederick S.** b 14 Jan. 1862; and **Harriet H.** b 5 Sep. 1864. [Vital Records of New Gloucester, Maine, p. 120, 121 and a manuscript from the Maine Historical Society.]

NEVENS, AMASSIAH - Born 26 Feb. 1815 in Strong, Maine, d 16 Jun. 1900 in Stow, Massachusetts, s/o Joel and Jemima (Haskell) Nevens. Amassiah Nevens m pub. 7 Nov. 1841, m 25 Nov. 1841 Huldah J. Ham, b 7 Mar. 1816, d/o Thomas and Anna (Rand) Ham of Lewiston. Children: **Hannah Little** b 8 Apr. 1843; **Edward Little.** b 9 Mar. 1845, d 20 Sep. 1847; **Alfred Drummond** q.v.; and **Annah S.** b 28 Oct. 1851, d 18 Jul. 1864.

NEVENS, AMASSIAH/ANNASIAH/AMASIAH - Born 5 Dec. 1793, d 20 Nov. 1873, s/o Sam'l. and Susannah (Haskell) Nevens. Amassiah/Annasiah/Amasiah Nevens m 8 Apr. 1818 Ann Pierce of N. Gloucester, Maine, d 1 Nov. 1877. Children: **Robert B.** q.v.; **Jabez Pierce** q.v.; **Abram Pierce** b 1 May 1826, d 9 Dec. 1853; **George Henry** b 30 Sep. 1829, d 10 Jan. 1884 New Portland, ME; and **Almira Harris** b 12 Nov. 1835, m 5 Nov. 1850 Elizabeth Dumphy.

NEVENS, AMOS - Born 17 Dec. 1798 or -- Feb. 1799, d 4 Jan. 1869, s/o Sam'l. and Susannah (Haskell) Nevens. Amos Nevens m -- May 1805 Hannah Pierce. Children: **Lucy A.** b 2 Nov. 1827, d 2 Jul.. 1872, m 10 Dec. 1848 George Rose; **Sidney** b 22 Jan. 1829, d 10 Dec. 1890; **Eliza P.** b 4 May 1831/2, d 18 Mar. 1833 age 10 months [vital records of New Gloucester, Maine]; **George** b 15 Apr. 1833; **Hiram** b 5 Apr. 1835, d 26 May 1894; **Nannah** b 1 Feb. 1837, d -- Sep. 1839; **Webster** q.v.; **Harriet E.** b 1 Jun. 1841; and **John P.** b 26 Jun. 1843, d 3 Feb.

1849. [Vital Records of New Gloucester, Maine, p. 121 and a manuscript at the Maine Historical Society.]

NEVENS, AMOS - Born 24 Oct. 1816, d ??, s/o Davis and Hannah (Graffam) Nevens. Amos Nevens m Nancy B. Hutchins of Phippsburg, Maine, b 15 Mar. 1822, d/o William and Hannah (Batchelder) Hutchins. Children: **William Davis** b 24 Sep. 1845, d 20 Mar. 1840; **Henry Carville** b 27 Mar. 1847, d 21 Sep. 1848; and **Emma R.** b 24 Aug. 1850.

NEVENS, AMOS H. - Born ??, d ??, s/o Zedekiah/Zedediah and ? Nevens. Amos H. Nevens m 15 Oct. 1848 Mary Sutherland of Lisbon, Maine, b 2 Mar. 1827 in Lisbon. Children: **Wilson** q.v.; **Winifred Scott** b 6 Dec. 1841, m 22 Jan. 1881 Mary B. Leavitt, who was b 22 Jun. 1859 in Salem, MA.; **Helen** b 3 Feb. 1862; **Eben** b 2 May 1863, m 30 Oct. 1889 Olive M. Noyes, who was b 19 Feb. 1866 in Pownal, ME.; **Amos Ham** b 19 Jan. 1865, d 25 Jul. 1872; and **John P.** b 28 May 1868 (or 29 Jun. 1867).

NEVENS, CHARLES - Born ??, d 23 Jul. 1862, s/o James and Betsy (Reed) Nevens. Charles Nevens m 4 Oct. 1842 Marah A. Pettingill, d/o Nathaniel. Children: **William H.** b 9 Mar. 1845; **Eva M.** b 29 May 1855, d 6 Apr. 1857; and **Rosanna D.** b 23 Feb. 1859, m Annie K. Read of Creta, IL.

NEVENS, CHARLES FREEMAN - Born 18 Apr. 1830, d 7 May 1895 in Concord, Massachusetts, s/o Joel and Jemima (Haskell) Nevens. Charles Freeman Nevens m (1) 9 Mar. 1858 at Saco, Maine, Annie/Anna M. Corliss of Saco, b 7 Dec. 1829 in N. Yarmouth, Maine, d 7 Jul. 1874, and m (2) 26 Jan. 1876, as her second husband, Frances Anna (Elder) Strange, d 22 Sep. 1898 in Concord, Massachusetts, d/o Frances J. Elder of Bangor, Maine. Frances Anna (Elder) Strange m (1) John Strange. Children: **Hewett Augustus** b 15 Oct. 1859, d 4 Dec. 1870; **Imogene** b 3 Nov. 1861; **Lizzie May** b 3 Aug. 1867, d 18 Dec. 1868; and **Charles Freeman** b 6 Sep. 1877.

NEVENS, DANS/DAVIS - Born 26 Sep. 1812, d 4 Sep. 1891 [Ira Nevens's diary, p. 9], s/o Davis and Hannah (Graffam) Nevens. Dans/Davis Nevens (1) 9 Mar. 1837 Eliza Nason, d 4 Jul. 1847 age 38 years, and m (2) Amanda F. Pettingill, d 13 Apr. 1884 age 61 years 4 months, and m (3) 6 Jul. 1887 Abbie Packard/Parkard. *Child by 1st wife*: **Dennis** b -- Feb. 1843, d 19 May 1844. *Children by 2nd wife*: **Charles Taylor** b 2 Oct. 1851, m 10 Mar. 1874 Cora E. Randall, d/o Wm. M.; **John P.** q.v.; **Ira/Ira L.** q.v.; **Augusta E.** b -- Apr. 1881, d 5 Jun. 1883; and **George Davis** q.v.

NEVINS, DAVIS - Born 14 Sep. 1783, d 22 Sep. 1854 in Lewiston, s/o Sam'l. and Susannah (Haskell) Nevens. Davis Nevens m 4 Jan. 1807 Hannah Graffam, b 6 Feb. 1781, d 20 Sep. 1860, d/o John. Children: **Sarah Randall** b 14 Jul. 1807, d 6 Sep. 1883, m 18 Jan. 1841, John Skinner, who d 15 May 1868; **Eliza** b 14 Jul. 1808, d 22 Dec. 1881, m 9 Jul. 1831 Jordan Skinner, who d 18 Mar. 1863; **John Randall** q.v.;

Dans/Davis q.v.; **Ira** q.v.; **Samuel** q.v.; **Amos** q.v.; **Dennis** b 16 Jan. 1820, d 18 Sep. 1822; **Eunice** b 30 Jun. 1821, d 13 Sep. 1822; and **Eunice** b 2 Jul. 1823, m (1) 3 Jan. 1848 Aaron Osgood, who d 25 Aug. 1853, and m (2) 23 Sep. 1858 Charles H. Dearing.

NEVENS, DAVIS - Born in Lewiston, d ??, s/o ?? Davis Nevens m 6 Jun. 1887 M. A. Mower.

NEVENS, DEXTER - Born 24 Jul. 1808, d ??, s/o Joel and Jemima (Haskell) Nevens. Dexter Nevens m Cordelia Hillman. Children: **Justin L.**; **Augustus C.** m 27 Nov. 1863 Helen V. Marquis of Boston, MA., who was b 18 Jun. 1844; **Oren J.** m Laura J. Merrill; **Jason K.** m -- May 1881 Sarah Shepard of Montaque, MA.; and **Ira D.** m 22 Nov. 1882 Abbie L. Rogers of Harwich, MA.

NEVENS, EBEN - Born 2 May 1863, d ??, s/o Amos Harris and ?? Nevens. Children: **Ethel**; and **William H.**

NEVENS, EBEN - Born ??, d ??, s/o Amos H. and ?? Nevens. Amos H. Nevens was the s/o Zedidiah, s/o Sam'l., s/o Hugh. Children **Ethel M.** b 18 Aug. 1890; and **William Harris** b 16 Aug. 1892, d 22 Jan. 1899.

NEVENS, EBEN R. - Born 17 May 1844, d 8 Jun. 1897, s/o Isaiah and Ann (Rowe) Nevens. Eben R. Nevens m (1) 16 Oct. 1869 Fanny Haskell, b 7 Jul. 1850 in Portland, Maine, d 22 Jul. 1870 New Gloucester, Maine, and m (2) 3 Sep. 1872 ---- Keith, b 7 Oct. 1847 in New York, d/o Isaac. Children: **Hugh Keith** b 8 Jun. 1877, d 23 Jun. 1877; and **Matilda Keith** b 7 Jan. 1880.

NEVENS, ELIAS W. - Born ??, d ??, s/o Robert and ?? Nevens. Robert Nevens was the s/o Samuel, s/o Hugh. Elias W. Nevens m Martha Wescott. Children: **Charles** b 1858, d 1864; and **Clara** m A. J. Jenness.

NEVENS, EUNICE - Born ??, d ??, d/o ?? Eunice Nevens m (1) 3 Jan. 1848 Aaron Osgood, and m (2) 23 Sep. 1858 Charles H. Dearing. *Children by 1st husband*: **E u n i c e** b 24 Jan. 1850, d 27 Dec. 1853; and **Bernard** b 23 Jan. 1853, d 9 Nov. 1882. *Children by 2nd husband*: **Selden** b 24 Nov. 1861; and **Eliza** b 1 Jul. 1864.

NEVENS, FRANK H. - Born 28 Jan. 1859, d ??, s/o Alfred I. and Sarah (Webb) Nevens. Children: **Flora May** b 20 Nov. 1886; and **Carlton Alfred** b 27 Apr. 1889.

NEVENS, FRED H. - Born ??, d ??, s/o Amasiah and ?? Nevens of Danville, Maine. Fred H. Nevens m 11 Feb. 1856 Harriet S. Mitchell of Aran.

NEVENS, FREDERICK S. - Born 14 Jan. 1862, d ??, s/o Alfred I. and Sarah (Webb) Nevens. Frederick S. Nevens m Alice Sparrow at Upper Gloucester, Maine.

NEVENS, FREEMAN R. - Born 16 Sep. 1849, d ??, s/o Isiah and Ann (Rowe) Nevens. Freeman R. Nevens lived in Milton, Massachusetts. Children: **Bertha May** b -- May 1880, d 5 Jun. 1889; **Charles H.** b 24 Mar. 1883, d -- Mar. 1888; **Blanch May** b 17 Jun. 1885; **Florence Louise** b 5 Jun. 1888; and **George Arthur** b 24 Apr. 1891.

NEVENS, GEORGE DAVIS - Born ??, d ??, s/o Dans/Davis and Eliza (Nason) Nevens. Child: **Helen B.** b 3 Jul. 1898.

NEVENS, GEORGE DAVIS - Born 21 Oct. 1860, d ??, s/o Dans/Davis and Eliza (Nason) Nevens. George Davis Nevens m 6 Oct. 1897 Ella M. Johnson, b 28 Oct. 1869 in Canton, Maine, d/o Geo. K. and Eliza (Niles) Johnson.

NEVENS, GEORGE S. - Born ??, d ??, s/o ?? Child: **George S.** b 23 Dec. 1894.

NEVENS, HUE/HUGH - Born ??, d 1776 [1778 at New Gloucester, Maine, according to the family Bible and a manuscript compiled by Wilson Nevens, 1892, located at the Maine Historical Society], s/o ?? Hue/Hugh Nevens m 1738 Joanna Burnham. In 1766 the entire family moved to New Gloucester, Maine, on what was known as Morgan Hill. Children: **John** b 1745 Falmouth, d 1805 Lewiston, m Molly Ring, b 1747 Cape Ann, d 1832 Lewiston, settled in Poland, ME; **Robert** lived with uncle Robert in NH.; **William** m Betsey Ray, settled in Danville, ME; **Letty** m Asa Coburn; **James** m Joanna Haskell, settled in Danville; **Betsey** m William Warner of Boston, settled in New Gloucester; **Susan** b 4 Apr. 1760, m Nathan Woodbury; and **Samuel** q.v.

NEVENS, IRA - "Worked in Rev. Mr. Adams' house in Auburn and Luther Littlefield, also the Packard House and John A. Briggs shop built a shop [where the "Cowings Mill" now stands]. In the winter of 1834, I worked for Temple Tibbetts in the Briggs shop. In 1836, I built house for my father [Davis Nevens?] and the house for Capt. Wm. Jepson. In 1837 built wood work for Edward Estes' Brick house. In 1838 built houses [with brother, Samuel?] for Josiah and Thomas Hart and John Goddard and in the fall on Capt. Hollands' Brick house. In 1838 and 1839 worked on the Universalist Church in Auburn [where the Methodist Church later stood]. In the spring of 1840 bought 14 acres of land on Ephraim Wood on the south side of Webster Street, a part of the Amos Davis place. In the fall of the same year, built a house for myself [Ira Nevens] on the lot at the corner of Ash and Webster Street. In the summer of 1841 built a house on Lowell Street for Capt. Holland, house next the Brick store. Worked on Mark Lowells' house the summer and in the fall built a house for Thomas D. Thorne on the old Thorne farm. During the summer of 1843 built a house for Chas. Nevens about 100 rods above the Taylor farm and stands in from the road. Sold the lot on Webster Street in the spring of 1846 to Stephen H. Read. 23 Aug. 1847 bought of J. S. Randall the John Randall farm of 100 acres for $2,000. In 1863 sold the buildings and a part of the farm to William and Doner? Webster. On 19 Jul. 1871 went to work for

Capt. (Daniel) Holland on his Brick house on College Street, and quit 18 Nov. 1871. On 20 Jul. 1874 went to work for Fesonton Day on his house on College Street, and quit on 17 Oct. 1874. On 13 May 1875 went to work for Isaac Golder on his house on Sabattus Street, and quit 8 Jan. 1876." [Now the main part of the French Hospital (St. Mary's).] "In 1878 worked on Mays and Millers' houses on Pine Street." [Written circa 1 Jan. 1890 by Ira Nevens, b 3 Jan. 1814, d 1892.] [Corrections made from original journal of Ira Nevens.]

NEVENS, IRA - Born 3 Jan. 1814, d 21 Mar. 1892, s/o Davis and Hannah (Graffam) Nevens. Ira Nevens m (1) 15 Nov. 1840 Roxie Merrill, d 14 Jul. 1890 [Ira Nevens' diary, p. 11], and m (2) 25 Feb. 1891 Mrs. Lydia Laughton. [Probate #3191.]

NEVENS, IRA/IRA L. - Born 15 Jul. 1858, d 9 Mar. 1927 [probate #15861], s/o Dans/Davis and Eliza (Nason) Nevens. Ira/Ira L. Nevens m Lois ----. Child: **Byron** b 18 Nov. 1883.

NEVENS, ISAIAH - Born 28 Apr. 1810, d 26 Jul. 1871, s/o Joel and ?? Nevens. Isiah Nevens m 20 Aug. 1835 Ann Rowe, b 25 Aug. 1812/1813 in New Gloucester, Maine, d 25 Apr. 1883. Children: **Charles H.** b 24 May 1830/1836, m Mrs. Mary (Much) White; **Lucy R.** b 20 Jan. 1838, m John H. Adams; **Eben R.** b 31 Mar. 1840, d young; **Lydia A.** b 1 May 1842, m Enos O. Blanchard; **Eben R.** q.v.; **Hannah** b 17 Aug. 1846, d young; **Freeman R.** b 16 Sep. 1849; **Thomas Harry** b 4 Dec. 1852, m Annie McMurphy; and **Mellen Augustus** b 16 Dec. 1855, m (1) Almeda Blake of Winthrop, ME, b 21 Nov. 1878, d 18 Dec. 1894. [Vital Records of New Gloucester, Maine, p. 121.]

NEVENS, JABEZ P. - Born ??, d ??, s/o Amassiah and ?? Nevens. Amassiah Nevens was the s/o Sam'l., s/o Hugh. Child: **Mildred** b 21 Nov. 1886.

NEVENS, JABEZ PIERCE - Born 5 Apr. 1823 in Strong, Maine, d ??, s/o Amassiah/Amasiah/Annasiah and Ann (Pierce) Nevens. Jabez Pierce m 5 Nov. 1850 Elizabeth Dumphy, b 27 Mar. 1831 in Anson, Maine, or m Salinda (Weymouth) Libby of New Vineyard, Maine. Children: **Meribah E.** b 12 Aug. 1857, d 5 Sep. 1869, m Sidney S. Chase; **Olive E.** b 4 Aug. 1853, m Samuel P. Tinkham; **Alice A.** b 18 Oct. 1855, m Myron T. Bailey; **Nellie F.** b 8 Dec. 1860; and **George Ulyses** b 18 Dec. 1865.

NEVENS, JAMES - Born 15 Jan. 1756 in Gloucester, Massachusetts, d 19 May 1832 or 31 Jan. 1848, s/o Hugh and ?? Nevens. James Nevens m 15 Nov. 1778 Joanna Haskell, b 3 Aug. 1758, d 3 Aug. 1818. Children: **James** b 23 Dec. 1779 at Bakerstown, now Poland, Minot, or Auburn, Maine; **William** b 29 May 1781; **Jonathan** b 8 Dec. 1783; **Hugh** b 28 Jun. 1786; **Joanna** b 17 Dec. 1789; **Artimesa** b 10 May 1791; **Sally** b 17 Oct. 1793; **John** b 15 Jul. 1795; **Sally** b 15 Jul. 1797; **Daniel H.** b 2 Apr. 1800; and **Mary Thompson** b 7 Jun. 1802. [Vital Records of Danville, Maine, book 1, p. 44.]

NEVENS, JOEL - Born 3 May 1786, d 18 Apr. 1862, s/o Sam'l. and Susannah (Haskell/Haskall) Nevens. Joel Nevens m Minah/Jemina Haskell, b 29 Apr. 1790 in New Gloucester, Maine, d 31 Jul. 1869, d/o Nathan and Judith (Witham) Haskell. Children: Isiah q.v.; **Dexter** q.v.; **Mariam** b 16 Jan. 1813, d -- Jan. 1892, m (1) 17 Nov. 1855 John Bumper, who d 4 Apr. 1862, and m (2) 20 Nov. 1871 Seba Stevens, who d -- Sep. 1881; **Sarah D.** b -- May 1817, d 8 Jun. 1876, m -- Jun. 1832 Charles Hutchins, who d 5 Dec. 1888; Joel q.v.; **Amasiah** q.v.; **Alfred I.** q.v.; **Rhoda Hillman** b 6 Dec. 1818, d 1893, m 7 Dec. 1842 Benjamin Leach; **Eliza H.** b -- Mar. 1825, d 21 Dec. 1859, m 10 Jul. 1842 Isaac Allen of Worcester; **Clara M.** b 21 Nov. 1827, m 29 May 1859 John Whitman, from N. Gloucester; and **Charles Freeman** q.v.;

NEVENS, JOEL - Born in Strong, Maine, d ??, s/o Joel and Minah/Jemima (Haskell) Nevens. Joel Nevens m (1) 25 Aug. 1833 Matilda Haskell, b 2 Dec. 1812, d 17 Jan. 1846, and m (2) Mrs. Julia (Woodward) Blodgett or ---- Fuller. Children: **Sarah** b 4 Jun. 1834, d 16 Feb. 1854; **Harriet** b 6 Jan. 1836; **Matilda Haskell** b 28 Aug. 1838, m John Ruggles; and **Hubbard Haskell** m 24 Dec. 1866.

NEVENS, JOHN P. - Born ??, d ??, s/o Amos H. and ?? Nevens. John P. Nevens m (1) 26 Apr. 1889 Ida May Holland, d 18 Jan. 1894, and m (2) -- Sep. 1894 Mary A. Johnson. Children: **Guy Francis** b 2 Feb. 1890; **John Irving** b 23 Aug. 1891; **Helen May** b 10 Jun. 1893; and **Winfield S.** b -- Apr. 1895.

NEVENS, JOHN P. - Born 28 May 1868, d ??, s/o Amos Harris and ?? Nevens. Children: **Guy**; **Irving**; **May**; and **Winfilla**.

NEVENS, JOHN P. - Born in Lewiston, d ??, s/o ?? John P. Nevens m 10 May 1884 Alice M. Briggs of Auburn, Maine.

NEVENS, JOHN P. - Born 6/16 Nov. 1853, d ??, s/o Dans/Davis and Eliza (Nason) Nevens. John P. Nevens m 12 Jul. 1884 Agnes M. Bearce, b 12 Sep. 1867 at Meddybumps, Maine, d/o Bryon. Children: **Grace Amanda** b 30 Dec. 1883; **Charles** b 30 Dec. 1889; and **Charlotte May** b 12 Apr. 1893.

NEVENS, JOHN RANDALL - Born 17 Jun. 1811, d 15 Jul. 1863, s/o Davis and Hannah (Graffam) Nevens. John Randall Nevens m (1) 3 Aug. 1834 Caroline Plummer, d 6 Jul. 1854, and m (2) 18 Oct. 1855 Tamson/Lamson Lunt Wright. Children: **John D.** b 14 Jan. 1842, d 26 Feb. 1854, m 31 Jul. 1875 Thedosia Decker, d/o Albert of LaGrange; **Plummer R.** q.v.; **Alma** b 14 Aug. 1856, d 3 Sep. 1856; and **Esra** b 2 Aug. 1859, m 22 Jul. 1896 Florence Gertrude Campbell, b 13 Nov. 1856 in Poland, d/o Otis and Lizzie Campbell.

NEVENS, MELLEN - Born ??, d ??, s/o Isiah and ?? Nevens. Mellen Nevens m 30 Jun. 1888 Mary Clough of Milford, Masschusetts.

NEVENS, PLUMMER R. - Born 26 Apr. 1847, d ??, s/o John Randall and ?? Nevens. Plummer R. Nevens m 31 Jul. 1875 Thodosia Decker, d/o Albert. Children: **Ethel C.** b 1 Jun. 1879; **Plummer R., Jr.** b 28 Nov. 1888; and **Viola B.** b 24 May 1891.

NEVENS, ROBERT - Born 27 Jun. 1788 in Lewiston, d ??, s/o ?? Robert Nevens m 3 Apr. 1814 Miriam Whitney of North Yarmouth, Maine. Children: **Adeline** d young; and **Eben W.** d 1863 in Gorham, ME.

NEVENS, ROBERT B. - Born 6 Feb. 1820, d New Gloucester, Maine, s/o Amasiah/Annasiah/Amassiah and Ann (Pierce) Nevens. Robert B. Nevens m 3 Jul. 1854 Meribah E. Dane of Farmington, New Hmpshire. Children: **Violet** b 11 Aug. 1856, d 21 Oct. 1858; **Lilla** b 26 Aug. 1863, d 10 Oct. 1865; and **Florence** b 10 Dec. 1866.

NEVENS, SAMUEL - Born ??, d ??, s/o ?? Children: **Arvilla; Analetta; Florilla;** and **Henry Ward Beecher.**

NEVENS, SAMUEL - Born 1758 in Cape Ann, Massachusetts, d 1 Mar. 1837 in Lewiston or New Gloucester, Maine, s/o of Hue/Hugh and ?? Nevens. Samuel Nevens came to Lewiston in spring of 1783. He m 3 Oct. 1779 Susannah Haskell/Haskall of New Gloucester, Maine, b 20 Sep. 1761, d 23 Sep. 1838, d/o Joel and Joanna (Burnham) Haskell/Haskall [vital records of New Gloucester, Maine, p. 119, 478, found at Maine Historical Society]. Children: **Samuel Jr.** q.v.; **Davis** b 14 Sep. 1783, d 22 Sep. 1854 in Lewiston, m 4 Jan. 1807 Hannah Graffam, who d 20 Sep. 1860; **Joel** b 3 May 1786, d 18 Apr. 1862, m Minah Haskell; **Robert** b 27 Jun. 1788, m 3 Apr. 1814 Miriam Whitney of North Yarmouth; **Lovinia** b 24 May 1790, d 7 Feb. 1860 age 68 years, unm; **Amasiah** b 5 Dec. 1793, d 20 Nov. 1873, m 8 Apr. 1818 Ana Pierce, who d 1 Nov. 1877; **Zedidiah** b 21 Apr. 1796, d 14 Jul. 1869, m 4 Jul. 1820 Lydia Harris of Minot, who was b 30 Sep. 1791, d 28 May 1871, d/o Amos and Isabel Parsons; **Amos** q.v.; **Eliza** b 21 May 1803; and **Susannah** b 28 Sep. 1805, unm.

NEVENS, SAMUEL - Born 14 May 1815, d ??, s/o Davis and Hannah (Graffam) Nevens. Samuel Nevens m 1 Nov. 1841 Selvira Merrill. Children: **Arvilla S.** b 25 Dec. 1842, d 16 May 1874; **Angeletta S.** b 8 Aug. 1847, d 17 Oct. 1847; **Alonso** b 9 Aug. 1848, d 13 Sep. 1848; and **Florella M. N.** b 16 Sep. 1850, m 11 Nov. 1876 John Fred Smith.

NEVENS, SAMUEL JR. - Born 17 Oct. 1780, d 17 Oct. 1859, s/o ?? Samuel Nevens, Jr. moved to Strong, Maine. He m 12 Jan. 1806 Lucy Curtis, b 25 Aug. 1778 in Scituate, Massachusetts, d 4 Nov. 1850. Children: **Julia** b 9 Apr. 1807, d 9 Oct. 1839, m Stephen Hardy; and **Susanna** b 28 Jun. 1810, d 13 May 1854. [Letter from W. Nevens of Cambridgeport, Massachusetts, circa 1890s.]

NEVENS, THOMAS - Born ??, d ??, s/o Isiah and Ann (Rowe) Nevens. Children: **Frank A.** b 16 Jun. 1880, d 1 Oct. 1880; **Arthur O.** b 16 Jun. 1881, d 1 Nov. 1882.

NEVENS, WEBSTER - Born 12 Nov. 1839, d ??, s/o Amos and Hannah (Pierce) Nevens. Webster Nevsns lived in Lisbon, Maine. He m 2 Jul. 1864 Susan Plummer, b 9 Sep. 1838 [*History of Durham* by Stackpole, published by the Town of Durham, 1899, p. 239], d/o Henry and Martha (----) Plummer. Children: **Frank W.** b 29 Apr. 1866, m 11 May 1887 Hannah Wilson of Parsonfield, ME; **George S.** b 1 Nov. 1868, m 4 Aug. 1889 Annie Coffin of Lisbon, b 4 Apr. 1868; and **Martha G.** b 31 Jan. 1873, m 28 Oct. 1896 Horace Wood, b 11 Jun. 1867 in England.

NEVENS, WILLIAM - Born -- Mar 1750 in Gloucester, Massachusetts, d 23 Jul. 1800 in Pejepscot Claime, Maine, s/o ?? William Nevens m 22 May 1777 at New Gloucester, Maine, Elizabeth Ray, b 19 Jul. 1740/1749 Cape Elizabeth, Maine, d 3 Oct. 1824. Children: **Elizabeth** b 3 Mar. 1778; **William** b 7 Sep. 1779, d 3 Jul. 1804/1850; **John** b 19 Jul. 1780, m 16 Nov. 1804 Polly Ray of Lewiston, they moved to Hartland, ME; **Polly** b 14 Jun. 1782, m 20 Sep. 1806 Robert Maxwell, who d 12 Jul. 1858; and **Sally** b 22 Apr. 1785, m Amos Tucker.

NEVENS, WILSON - Born 21 Dec. 1849, d ??, s/o Amos H. and Mary (Sutherland) Nevens. Wilson Nevens m 1 May 1880 Josephine S. Stone, b 28 Dec. 1854 in Falmouth, Maine.

NEVENS, ZEDEKIAH/ZEDEDIAH - Born 21 Apr. 1796 in New Gloucester, Maine, d 14 Jan. 1864, s/o Sam'l. and ?? Nevens. Zedekiah/Zedediah Nevens m pub. 15 Jun. 1820, m 4 Jul. 1820 (Minot records) Lydia Parsons Harris, b 30 Sep. 1791, d -- May 1871. Children: **Samuel** b 5 May 1822, d 22 Dec. 1872, unm; **Amos H.** q.v.; **Adam Wilson** b 21 Jul. 1826, d 25 Jan. 1860, m Almira Condit of Orange, NJ; and **Olive Chipman** b 28 Jan. 1832, m 27 Jan. 1876 George Rose of Falmouth.

NEWELL, WILLIAM H. - b 16 April 1864, d 1933 in Lewiston, s/o William and Susannah (Weeks) Newell. William H. Newell m 10 Sep. 1883 Ida Plummer. Children: **Gladys** m Daniel Drummond; **Dorothy** m Roscoe Halliday; and **Augusta**.

NOBLE, FRANK L. - Born 22 Jul. 1865 in Fairfield, Maine, d 28 Mar. 1897 "only four weeks after his fourth re-election. He was the first mayor to die in service" [*Historic Lewiston: its government* by Geneva Kirk and Gridley Barrows, published by Historic Commission, 1981-82, p. 29], s/o Eleazar R. and Harriet (Lamb) Noble. Frank L. Noble m 1882 Clara Spofford. No children.

OLFENE, FREDERICK - Born 1827 in Hanover, Germany, d ??, s/o ?? Frederick Olfene occ' Designer. He m Louisa ----, b 1827 in Maine. Children: **Willie** b 1855; **Charles M.** b 1858; and **Herman** b 1860. [Lewiston 1860 census.]

OLIVER, CHARLES L. - Born 27 Dec. 1819 in Bethel, Maine, d 19 Jun. 1872 in Lewiston, s/o William and ?? Oliver. Charles L. Oliver came to Lewiston in 1844. He m 30 Jun. 1847 Mary E. Allen, b 10 Aug. 1814 in Hebron (then known as Oxford), Maine, d 22 Nov. 1888 in Auburn, Maine. [*History of Bethel, Maine* by Lapham; notes on Oliver family and letters at Androscoggin Historical Society.]

OTIS, HARRISON G. - Born ??, d ??, s/o ?? Harrison G. Otis was a carriage maker with Amos Hersey. Harrison G. Otis m pub. 1 Sep. 1839 Harriet Lambert of Durham, Maine.

PARCHER, JOHN - Born ??, d ??, s/o ?? Children: **Sally B.** b 27 Jan. 1821; **Sam'l. M.** b 22 Nov. 1822; **Olive L.** b 9 Nov. 1825; **Persis** b 22 Apr. 1828; **Otheneal** b 6 Jul. 1838; **John B.** b 18 Aug. 1835, d 2 Jan. 1855; and **Asenath** b 18 Aug. 1840.

PARSCHLEY, FREDERIC CHARLES - Born 10 May 1847 in Sangerville, Maine, d ??, s/o Gilbert Deblois and Fayette Delia (Turner) Parschley. Frederic Charles Parschley m Anna Flynt of Dexter, Maine. Child: **Fay.**

PARSHLEY, GILBERT DEBLOIS - Born 25 Jul. 1803 [vital records Lewiston, Maine, p. 62], d 30 Jul. 1898 in Dexter, Maine, s/o Joseph and Lucy (Coombs) Parshley. He m Fayette Delia Turner of Bath, Maine, b 2 Dec. 1804, d 29 Nov. 1887, d/o Tobes Turner. Children: **Augusta** b 22 Dec. 1827 in Lewiston, m Nathan F. Roberts of Sangerville, ME; **Emily Jane** b 2 Jan. 1830 in Lewiston, m Albion K. P. Swanton of Santa Croize/Cruz; **Elizabeth** b 13 Jun. 1832 in Lewiston, d 15 Jun. 1832; **Mary Frances** b 11 Apr. 1834 in Sangerville, m Capt. Vincent Davis of Long Island, NY.; **Julia Ann** b 26 Jun. 1836 in Sangerville, m John R. Herring; **Elvira** b 18 Jun. 1840 in Sangerville, m William N. Lane; **Caroline** b 14 Jul. 1842 in Sangerville, m 18 Mar. 1865 Frederic W. Elder of Dexter, who d 6 Oct. 1889; **Henry G.** b 17 Apr. 1845 in Sangerville, d 1865 in Dexter; and **Frederic Charles** q.v.

PARSHLEY, JOSEPH - Born 19 Mar. 1777 in Brunswick, Maine, d ??, s/o ?? Joseph Parshley m Lucy Coombs, b 9 Mar. 1778 in Bath, Maine. Children: **Gilbert;** and perhaps others. [Vital Records of Lewiston, Maine, p. 62.]

PARSONS, WILLIAM W. - Born ??, d ??, s/o ?? William W. Parsons m 13 Sep. 1863 Melissa Webber, d 19 Jul. 1889 age 44 years.

PATTEN, LEANDER - Born 11 Dec. 1807, d ??, s/o ?? Leander Patten m Jerusha Chase. Children: **Zemira Ellen** b 2 Jan. 1836; **Leander** b 28 Jan. 1837; **Lora Stevens** b 26 Sep. 1840; **Martha Jane** b 19 Jul. 1843; and **Esther Ann** b 22 Nov. 1845, d 11 Nov. 1860.

PAUL, CHARLES - Born ??, d ??, s/o ?? Charles Paul was from Greene, Maine. He m pub. 25 Oct. 1812 Betsey Wright. Children: **Judith** b 2 Apr. 1814; **John Hatch** b 10 Aug. 1816; and **James** b 23 Dec. 1820.

PAUL, DANIEL - Born 1787, d 27 Aug. 1865, s/o Daniel and Lucy (----) Paul. Daniel Paul m 27 Dec. 1818 Lamsen [Tamson according to the vital records of Lewiston, Maine, p. 62, 434] Hackett, d/o Ezekiel. Children: **Simeon** b 17 Nov. 1819, d 19 Apr. 1840; **Nelson F.** b 18 Jun. 1822, m 13 Dec. 1850 Frances O. Clarke; and **Lewis D.** b 25 Apr. 1829.

PAUL, DAVID - Born 1761, d 24 Aug. 1850, s/o ?? David Paul m Lucy A. Swift, b 1765, d 28 Mar. 1848. Children: **Daniel** q.v; **Simeon**; **Hannah** b 19 May 1793, d 22 Feb. 1860, m 1 May 1814 James Lowell, who d 27 Jul. 1858; **Betsey** m ---- Brown (?), went into Army c1812 or 1815; **Susan** b 18 Jan. 1799, d 9 Feb. 1890, m 11 Sep. 1824 George Washington Eaton, b 22 Feb. 1800, d 20 Aug. 1876; **Mary** m 27 Dec. 1818 Joseph Dunnell of Bath, ME, d 27 Aug. 1865; **Marshia** b 2 Jul. 1805, d 12 Feb. 1875, m 13 Jun. 1824 Luther C. Taylor, d 15 Sep. 1851; and **Sophronia** b 1807, d 28 Sep. 1878, m 14 Mar. 1870 Levi Pillsbury, d 13 Mar. 1872.

PEARCE, CHARLES - Born ??, d ??, s/o ?? Charles Pearce m Betsey ----. Children: **Judith** b 2 Apr. 1814; **John Hatch** b 10 Aug. 1816; and **James** b 23 Dec. 1818. [Vital Records of Lewiston, Maine, p. 61.]

PEAVY, MIRRAL - Born 1821 in Posen, Germany, d ??, s/o ?? Mirral Peavy occ' Merchant Tailor. He m Adalaide ----, b 1830 in Posen, Germany. Likely children: **Mark** b 1848 in Posen, Germany; **Charles** b 1853 in NH; **Samuel** b 1855 in NH; **Rebecca** b 1857 in NH. [Listed in the same family in 1860, Lewiston, ME: David L. b1828, occ' Merchant Tailor, likely brother of Mirral]. [Lewiston, ME, 1860 census, birth dates based on ages in 1860.]

PETTENGILL, ABEL - Born 15 Oct. 1779, d 18 Oct. 1844, s/o Abraham and ?? Pettengill. Abel Pettengill m 3 Feb. 1805 Dorris Davis. Children: **Thankful** b 6 Apr. 1805, d 3 Apr. 1850, m pub. 17 Oct. 1824 Alexander Hillman of Farmington, ME; **Mary** b 14 Aug. 1806, d 9 Oct. 1895, m 1826 Gilbert R. Hillman of Farmington; **Daniel** b 3 May 1808, d 1 Oct. 1891, unm; **Fay** b 14 Feb. 1810, d 1 Oct. 1893; **Abel** b 3 Jul. 1812, d -- Jul. 1892, m Mary Wiggins; **Abraham** b 6 Apr. 1814, d 4 Dec. 1890 in Harmony, ME., m Mary Emerson of Harmony, ME; **Lydia** b 4 Jan. 1816, d 1877; **John** b 23 Oct. 1819, d 16 Jan. 1844 in South America; **Amos** b 18 Jul. 1820, d 6 Sep. 1851 in Hampden, ME.; **Aaron** b 7 Apr. 1823, d 1 Mar. 1844; **William** b 4 Apr. 1825, d 28 Dec. 1844 at sea; **Simeon** b 12 Sep. 1827, d in California, m Eliza West of Orono, ME; and **Charles** b 29 Dec. 1829, m May Head.

PETTENGILL, ABRAHAM - Born 4 Dec. 1704 in Newbury, Massachusetts, d ??, s/o Abraham and ?? Pettengill. Abraham Pettengill (the elder) was the s/o Mathew, s/o Mathew, s/o Richard. Abraham Pettengill (the younger) m Hannah French of Salisbury, Massachusetts. He was admitted to Church in Salisbury on 18 Sep. 1727, and bought land on 26 Dec. 1729 in N. Yarmouth, Maine. Children: **Mark** b 12 Dec. 1728 in Salisbury, MA., moved to Lewiston, drowned in Androscoggin River in 1787, m 13 Jan. 1754 Sarah Clough, d/o

Ebenezer; **Ephraim** b 28 Dec. 1730 in N. Yarmouth; **Edward** b 11 Sep. 1732, d at sea; **David** b 5 Sep. 1734, was second settler in Lewiston, d in Revolutionary War, m 23 Nov. 1758 Mercy Lake; **Mathew** b 18 Oct. 1736; **Eliphalet** b 18 Nov. 1738, m pub. 17 May 1760 Sarah Dill; **Hannah** b 3 Aug. 1740, m 9 Nov. 1767 Sheribal Greeley; **Elisha** b 26 Apr. 1742, m 29 Nov. 1767 Rebecca Prince, b 19 Jul. 1749, d/o Benj. Prince; **Miriam** F. b 11 Feb. 1743, m 5 Jan. 1763 Amos Pinkham; **Mary** b 8 Jul. 1746; **Sarah** b 29 Jan. 1748, m (1) 28 May 1768 Bradbury True, and m (2) Thomas Jepson, who d 28 Mar. 1818; and **Rebecca** b 22 Apr. 1751, m 21 Mar. 1773 William Blaisdell, who d 23 Apr. 1818.

PETTENGILL, ABRAHAM - Born 4 Oct. 1754, d by drowning, s/o Mark and Sarah (Clough) Pettengill. Abraham Pettengill m Thankful Davis, d in Strong, Maine. Children: **Abel** b 15 Oct. 1779, m 3 Feb. 1803 Dorris Davis, lived in Strong, ME; **Mary** b 19 Sep. 1781, d after 1838, m 4 Aug. 1801 John Tarr, lived in N. Salem, ME; **Betsey** b 23 Apr. 1783, d 25 Dec. 1873, m 24 Nov. 1808 David Graffam, who was b -- Jan. 1785, d 24 Aug. 1844; **Abraham** b 13 Oct. 1787, m pub. 27 Jun. 1817, m 14 May 1817 Harriet Witham; **Mark** b 23 Jul. 1789, m 3 Feb. 1813 Betsey Smith; and **Charlotte** b 1792, d 5 Jul. 1869 in Augusta, ME, with son Leonard, m Benj. Holbrook of Mercer, d 1852. [Vital Records of Lewiston, Maine, p. 59.]

PETTENGILL, ABRAM - Born ??, d ??, s/o ?? Abram Pettengill lived north of the Herrick farm.

PETTENGILL, ALFRED H. - Born ??, d ??, s/o Chas. H. and ?? Pettengill. Alfred H. Pettengill m Helen A. Banks, d/o Evans C. and Ellen (Brewer). Children: **Alice** C. b 12 May 1889; and **Stella A.** b -- Jan. 1891.

PETTENGILL, ALLEN - Born 21 Jun. 1783 in Lewiston, d ??, s/o ?? Allen Pettengill lived in Rockport, Massachusetts. He m 21 Aug. 1783 Mary Higgins, b in Bath, Maine, d 2 May 1867 in Rockport, Massachusetts, d/o Benjamin and Hannah Higgins. Children: **Benjamin W.**; **Jeremiah** b 19 Jun. 1811; **Allen, Jr.** b 1812; **Mary Ann** m ---- Collins; **Rachel**; **Sophia** b -- Feb. 1819, m pub. 21 Mar. 1839 Evesen Noore, who d in Gloucester, MA; **Joseph** b 11 Dec. 1824 in North Yarmouth, ME; and **Harriet** d c1896, m (1) David Moxey, and m (2) Edmund Fitzgerald.

PETTENGILL, ALLEN A. - Born ??, d ??, s/o Stephen and ?? Pettengill. Children: **Nettie** W. b 5 Sep. 1885; and **Ella F.** b 5 Aug. 1887.

PETTENGILL, AMASHIAH/AMASIAH - Born -- Dec. 1798 in Minot, Maine, d ??, s/o Benj. and Phebe (Barker) Pettengill. Amashiah/Amasiah Pettengill m 1823 Persis/Plecis Sayre of Clarendon, New York, d 30 Aug. ----. Children: **Benjamin**; **Sarah**; **Cyrus**; and **Hiram**.

PETTENGILL, ANDREW JR. - Born 6 May 1829, d ??, s/o ?? Andrew Pettengill, Jr. m (1) 12 Feb. 1881 Esther L. Keene of Portland, Maine, b 19 Oct. 1832, and m (2) 29 Jul. 1883 Mrs. Octavia Cheney. Children: **Anderson** (?) b 4 May 1842, m 29 Mar. 1855 Emma Haskell of New Gloucester, ME; **Ella Endora** b 19 Jun. 1840, m 14 Jul. 1885 Edward Cheney from Stockton Springs, ME; and **Edward H.** b 17 Nov. 1866, m 27 Mar. 1893 Minnie Sision (?) of Wisconsin.

PETTENGILL, ANDREW C. - Born 22 Feb. 1816, d ??, s/o Nath./Capt. Nathaniel and Nancy (How) Pettengill. Andrew C. Pettengill m 19 Jun. 1842 Olive White, b 2 Feb. 1821, d/o Darius White of Auburn, Maine. Children: **William W.** q.v.; **Mary A.** b 12 Jun. 1846 in Lewiston, m 7 Oct. 1870 Almon L. Goss, who d 5 Mar. 1897; **George A.** q.v.; **Frank H.** b 2 Mar. 1852, d 19 Jun. 1881, m pub. 17 Jun. 1870 Carrie E. Payson of Belfast, ME; and **Dora** b 21 Jul. 1855, d 2 Jan. 1900, m 14 Dec. 1875 Ira W. Fites of Auburn.

PETTENGILL, ARCADIUS - Born 19 Jul. 1793, d 30 Oct. 1883, s/o Obidiah and ?? Pettengill. Arcadius Pettengill m Polly Tribou. Children: **Ann Pratt** b 9 Dec. 1815; **Joel** b 20 Mar. 1817, d 3 Oct. 1883; **William Henry** b 21 Jun. 1819, d 11 Jun. 1882, m 27 Nov. 1845 Betsey Smart of Vassalboro, ME, d/o Levi and Betsey Crowell Smart; and **Arcadius, Jr.** b 11 Dec. 1822, d 23 Jun. 1898, m (1) Ann C. Addition of Dexter, ME, d 18 Aug. 1866 age 43 years 10 months 18 days, and m (2) Lois J., d 24 Jun. 1881 age 58 years 3 months 2 days.

PETTENGILL, ARCADIUS, JR. - Born 11 Dec. 1822, d 23 Jun. 1898, s/o Arcadius, Sr. and ?? Pettengill.

PETTENGILL, ARVIDA - Born ??, d ??, s/o ?? Arvida Pettengill m Alvira Ann Sumner, d 11 Oct. 1899, d/o Houghton and Mary (Rogers) Sumner of Leeds, Maine. Children: **Elvira Jane** b 16 Oct. 1843, m (1) 16 Feb. 1879 Otis Kibby Prescott, and m (2) 1899 Andrew B. Pinkham; **Mary Rogers** b 17 Aug. 1849, d 23 Jul. 1866; **Augusta Winsor** b 27 Oct. 1851, m Frank E. Niles; **Frank Ellsworth** b 5 Jul. 1861, m Edith May Coffin, who d 27 May 1885 age 27 years 4 months.

PETTENGILL, CAPT. AUGUSTUS - Born 1 Dec. 1834, d 15 Dec. 1887, s/o ?? Capt. Augustus Pettengill m 29 Oct. 1858 Lucy Lord, b 2 Oct. 1840, d/o Capt. Isaiah and Nancy (Harmon) Lord. Children: **Augustus C.** b 7 Mar. 1861, d 27 Aug. 1883, lost at sea; and **Polly Louisa** b 19 Jun. 1864, d 16 Mar. 1886, m 1 Sep. 1881 Elgin B. Sayles.

PETTENGILL, BENJAMIN - Born 25 Oct. 1801, d 11 Apr. 1893, s/o Benj. and Phebe (Barker) Pettengill. Benjamin Pettengill m 1832 Mary Marshall of Oyden/Ogden, New York, d 1857. Children: **Mary Jane**; and **Orville**.

PETTENGILL, BENJAMIN - Born 23 May 1762, d 5 Oct. 1844, s/o David and Mercy (Lake) Pettengill. Benjamin Pettengill m (1) 17 Jul. 1785 Mary Briggs, and m (2) 2 Nov. 1795 Phebe Barker. *Children by 1st wife*: **Polly** b 1790, m (1) 1816 William Rice of Ogden, Monroe

Co., NY, who d 1839, and m (2) 1841 A. M. Cook, moved to Oregon; **Mercy** b 1792, d -- Aug. 1876, m 1818 Seth Woodworth, who d -- May 1843. *Children by 2nd wife*: **Hannah B.** b 24 Feb. 1797, d 30 Aug. 1866, m 1819 Benjamin G. Pettengill, s/o David and Thankful, who d 14 Apr. 1870; **Amasiah/Amashiah** q.v.; **Benjamin** q.v.; **Edward** b 24 Feb. 1803, d 9 Sep. 1890, m -- Nov. 1837 Lydia Pettengill, who d -- Aug. 1877, d/o David of Lewiston; and **Lucinda** b 10 May 1804, d -- Jun. 1869, m 1849 Abraham W. Salsbury.

PETTENGILL, BENJAMIN G. - Born 24 Jul. 1795, d 14 Apr. 1870, s/o ?? Benjamin G. Pettengill m Hannah B. Pettengill, d/o Benj. Children: **David Newton** q.v.; **Phebe H.** b 7 Feb. 1823 in Clarenden, NY, m James C. Hallock of Clarenden, NY; **Amos Nelson** b 24 Nov. 1824, d 22 Apr. 1845; and **True Edward G.** q.v.

PETTENGILL, CARLTON - Born 28 Jan. 1832, d ??, s/o Justin and ?? Pettengill. Carlton Pettengill m Mrs. Maria Field, b 19 Dec. 1830. Children: **Victor C.** b 17 Apr. 1855, m 1 Jan. 1877 Amanda Frances; **Arthur D.** b 8 Dec. 1857, m 1 May 1880 Flora I. Rounds, d/o Leonard Rounds; and **Carroll Alvin** b 8 Dec. 1869, m 14 Jun. 1897 Lucy Libby, d/o David B. Libby.

PETTENGILL, CHARLES A. - Born ??, d ??, s/o Charles H. and ?? Pettengill. Child: **Kenneth E.** b 8 Aug. 1893.

PETTENGILL, CHARLES A. - Born 28 Aug. 1829, d ??, s/o Wm. and Mary (Small) Pettengill. Charles A. Pettengill m (1) 21 Mar. 1856/1857 Elizabeth/Elizabeth M. Dyer, and m (2) 11 Apr. 1870 Mary E. Harmon, b 20 Nov. 1835. *Children by 1st wife*: **Addie L.** b 31 Mar. 1858, lived in Pleasantdale, m (1) 2 Nov. 1876 Edward E. Ricker, and m (2) 28 Aug. 1881 James B. Hayes; **Ella M.** b 23 Sep. 1860, d 3 Sep. 1898, m 23 Sep. 1877 George H. Kane; and **Emma C.** b 12 Mar. 1863, m Leroy Jackson. *Child by 2nd wife*: **George A.** q.v.

PETTENGILL, CHAS. E. - Born ??, d ??, s/o Sam'l and ?? Pettengill. Children: **Edith P.**; and **Charles W.** b 18 Oct. 1895.

PETTENGILL, CHAS. E. - Born ??, d ??, s/o ?? Chas. E. Pettengill m Etta E. ----. Children: **Maud M.** b 28 Aug. 1880, d 5 Feb. 1881.

PETTENGILL, CHARLES H. - Born 9 Nov. 1823, s/o Jacob and ?? Pettengill. Charles H. Pettengill m 22 Sep. 1846 P. Augusta Staples, b 12 Nov. 1823, d/o Capt. David and Elisabeth (Bartol) Staples. Children: **Wallace M.** b 20 Nov. 1847, m 11 Jan. 1873 Addie R. Gerry of Poland, ME; **Clara C.** b 10 Dec. 1849, unm; **Roscoe J.** b 5 Apr. 1851, m 31 Dec. 1877 Lizzie A. True; **Daniel L.** b 25 Jan. 1853, m 31 Oct. 1883 Gertrude C. Soule; **George B.** b 25 Jun. 1855, unm; **Alfred H.** b 9 Aug. 1857, m 19 Jun. 1886 Helen A. Banks; **Charles** b 27 Dec. 1860, m Sarah A. Trigg; and **Shirley A.** b 13 Jul. 1869, unm.

PETTENGILL, CHARLES H. - Born ??, d ??, s/o Jason and ?? Pettengill. Charles H. Pettengill m 3 Oct. 1866 Florence A. Seabury of

Auburn, Maine, d 1 Jul. 1896. Children: **Jason Charles** b 4 Aug. 1867 in Kingston, SC; and **Harry Stimson** b 22 Oct. 1860 Cheran (?), SC.

PETTENGILL, CHARLES L. - Born 1807, d 11 Aug. 1848, s/o Samuel and ?? Pettengill. Charles L. Pettengill m pub. 8 Nov. 1828 Eunice M. Griffin, d 21 Sep. 1852. Children: **Anna** d age 18 years, unm; **Elizabeth J.** b -- Aug. 1832, d 12 Feb. 1868, m pub. 20 May 1851 George M. Cushing; **Mary L.** b 1836, d 24 Apr. 1854; **Emerline** b 1837, d 26 Feb. 1868, m pub. 14 Oct. 1856 William N. Mann; **David P.** q.v.; **Emma G.** d age 8 years; and **Eunice E.** b 1847, m (1) 9 Dec. 1864 Archibald Kenney, and m (2) 1869 Asbury Libbey, lived at Buxton Center, ME.

PETTENGILL, CONVERSE/CONVERSE J. - Born 18 Jun. 1814, d 10 Apr. 1884/1889 in Everett, Massachusetts, s/o Capt. Nathaniel and Nancy (How) Pettengill. Converse/Converse J. Pettengill m (1) Philene Jackson, d 10 Apr. 1851, and m (2) Marcia Sylvester (nee Martin); d/o Ezekiel Martin. Children: **Converse M.**; and **Albion Martin**.

PETTENGILL, CYRANIUS - Born 27 Mar. 1820 [*History of Leeds* by J. C. Stinchfield, 1901, reprinted 1978, p. 154], d ??, third s/o Reuel and Lydia (Briggs) Pettengill. Cyranius Pettengill m 15 Jul. 1845 Ann A. Bates, b 15 Jan. 1826, d/o Harvey and Nancy G. (Rowe) Bates. Children: **Henry Franklin** b 20 Mar. 1846, m Adelia M. Gordon; **Emily Ann** b 14 Sep. 1850, d 27 Nov. 1855; **Emily Ann** b 28 Aug. 1860, m Manley Coffin; **Ermina Ellen** b 23 Oct. 1862, m Orin Curtis; and **Mary Emma Hammon** (adopted), b 21 Aug. 1859, m 6 May 1883 J. C. Wing [*History of Leeds, Maine*].

PETTENGILL, DANIEL F. - Born ??, d ??, s/o Charles H. and ?? Pettengill. Daniel F. Pettengill m Gertrude C. Soule, b 8 Mar. 1862, d/o Pomroy C. and Martha (Osgood) Soule. Children: **Flora** b 1884; **Jason H.** b 4 Jan. 1889; and **Martha P.** b 4 Mar. 1896.

PETTENGILL, DAVID - Born 4 Nov. 1766, d 1 Oct. 1848, s/o David and Mercy (Lake) Pettengill. David Pettengill m Thankful Graffin, d 26 Jul. 1845. Children: **Sarah** b 24 Oct. 1789; m 24 Sep. 1815 as his second wife, James Field; **John** q.v.; **Elizabeth** b 20 Jul. 1793, d 16 Jun. 1870, m 10 Apr. 1825 William Jepson; **Benjamin G.** b 24 Jul. 1795, d 14 Apr. 1870, m 1819 Hannah B. Pettengill, who d 30 Aug. 1866; **Mary** b 14 Jan. 1797, m Stephen Varney of Brunswick; **Hannah** b 11 Nov. 1800, d 1862 in Clarendon, NY., m 1839 Samuel Wetherbee of Calrendon, NY., who d 1879; **Mercy** b 15 Feb. 1803, d 26 Feb. 1890, m 12 Mar. 1827 Jedidiah Harris, who d 26 Aug. 1885; **David** b 24 Nov. 1805, d 1881, m Amanda Wickwire (?); **Edward** b 3 Jan. 1808, d 28 May 1815; **Lydia** b 8 Nov. 1809, d 19 Aug. 1877, m 1834 Edward Pettengill, who d 9 Sep. 1890; and **Amos** b 14 Aug. 1813, 1853 went to Clarendon, NY, d 1887, m 1857 Mrs. Betsey Jenkins in Clarendon, NY, d -- Jul. 1893.

PETTENGILL, DAVID - Born ??, d ??, s/o ?? David Pettengill m 23 Nov. 1758 Mercy Lake, d/o Benj. and Mercy (Eaton) Lake. Children: **Mary** b 20 Sep. 1759, d 18 Jul. 1841, m John Harris of Greene, ME, b 13 Aug. 1758, d 12 Sep. 1844 in Greene; **Benjamin** q.v.; **Rachel** b 1764, d 9 Oct. 1841, m 16 Mar. 1786 Elijah Briggs; **David** b 4 Nov. 1766, d 1 Oct. 1848, m Thankful Graffam, b 14 Jan. 1768, d 26 Jul. 1842, d/o John; **Ephraim** b 1770, d 6 Sep. 1819, m Dorcas Landers, d 12 Aug. 1859 age 89 years, d/o Freeman; **Edward** umn; **Mercy** b -- Jan. 1774 in Lewiston, buried in Greene, m pub. 28 May 1796 William Coburn, d 17 May 1774 in Dracut, MA., d 4 May 1826; and **Joanna** m 15 Mar. 1790 Moses Safford, lived in Augusta, ME.

PETTENGILL, DAVID - Born 24 Nov. 1805, d 16 Mar. 1882, s/o David A. and ?? Pettengill. In 1829, David Pettengill went to Clarendon, New York. He m Amanda Wickwire, d 1859. Children: **Eunice** b 1832, d 1877 in Lockport, Illinois, m Dr. Gibbs; **Adoniram Judson** b 1834, m Alma Lawrence; **Mary** b 1837, d 13 Feb. 1874 in Oakland, CA, and **Seward H.** b 1839, killed 2 Jan. 1865 at Franklin, MS.

PETTENGILL, DAVID/DAVID P. - Born ??, d ??, s/o Charles/Charles L. and Eunice M. (Griffin) Pettengill. David/David P. Pettengill m (1) 4 Jul. 1865 Adeline Griffen/Griffin, d/o David H. Griffen/Griffin, and she m (2) Charles Hammond. Children: **Bethiah C.** b 16 Sep. 1866, m 13 Oct. 1886 Herbert E. Cushing in Long Island, NY; **Susie C.** b 15 Jul. 1871, m 4 Jun. 1891 George Hewey in Long Island, NY; and **Alice M.** b 6 Jun. 1873, d 1899.

PETTENGILL, DAVID NEWTON - Born 8 Jul. 1820 in Ogden, New York, d 10 Apr. 1886, s/o Benj. G. and ?? Pettengill. David Newton Pettengill m 27 May 1845 Eliza D. Robinsen/Robinson of Clarendon, New York. Children: **Walter True** b 6 Jul. 1849, m -- Feb. 1873 Jennie Miller of Clarendon, NY; and **Beatrice Sone** b -- Nov. 1850, m David N. Salisbury.

PETTENGILL, EBENEZER - Born 28 Dec. 1756, d 1836 North Yarmouth, Maine, s/o Mark and Sarah (Clough) Pettengill. Ebenezer Pettengill m pub. 25 Oct. 1782 Esther Barker, d 1 Feb. 1824. Children: **Jacob** b 15 May 1783, d 24 May 1851 in Moozes (?) Island, m Esther Fogg of Freeport, ME; **Sally** b 22 Aug. 1784, unm; **Asa** b 26 Apr. 1786, drowned; **Percy** b 4 May 1788, m 7 May 1809 Joseph Chamberlin, who d 25 Mar. 1876; **Phebe** b 31 Dec. 1789, m Benj. Brown, d North Yarmouth; **Esther** b 27 Apr. 1792, m Geo. Bibber, lived in Falmouth, ME; **Ebenezer** b 2 Apr. 1794; and **Lydia** b 22 Feb. 1796.

PETTENGILL, EDWARD - Born ??, d ?? s/o Benj. and Phebe (Barker) Pettengill. Edward Pettengill m Lydia Pettengill, d 21 Jan. 1890, d/o David. Child: **Lydia Ann** b 1838, m 1860 Michael Hites in Wintersel, Iowa.

PETTENGILL, EPHRAIM - Born 7 Jul. 1800, d 1876, s/o Ephraim and ?? Pettengill. Ephraim (the elder) Pettengill was the s/o David. Ephraim (the younger) Pettengill m -- Jun. 1846 (?) Betsey Tyler of

New Gloucester, Maine. Children: **Betsey Tyler** b 17 Feb. 1826 in Dexter, m -- Nov. 1849 David Ham; **Phebe** b 19 Jan. 1828 in Cambridge, d 1861, m 1851 John Taylor; **Ephraim** b 28 May 1830 Cambridge; **Manassah** b 3 Apr. 1832, d 3 May 1895, m 8 Oct. 1855 Almira D. Harrington of Durham, ME; **Clara** b 19 Jul. 1834, m -- Apr. 1868 H. E. Stanton of NY; **Almon** b 14 May 1837; and **Ansel Freeman** b 28 Jan. 1840, was druggist in Pitkin, Colorado.

PETTENGILL, EPHRAIM - Born ??, d ??, s/o David, Sr. and ?? Pettengill. Children: **Mercy** m Asa Withee, lived in Harmony, ME; **Lucy** b 27 Jan. 1798, d 21 Mar. 1861, m 6 Nov. 1820 Martin Bailey; **Ephraim** b 7 Jul. 1800, d 1876, m Betsey Tyler; **Abigail** m Peter Hersom; **Sarah** b 1808, d 15 Jun. 1887, m (1) 20 Nov. 1861 Martin Bailey, and m (2) ---- Dam; and **John** m ---- Tucker.

PETTENGILL, ETHAN - Born ??, d ??, s/o Hugh and ?? Pettengill. Children: **Jennett** b -- Nov. 1824, d 23 Jan. 1852, m 25 Dec. 1847 Charles Wilson; **George B.** b 7 Nov. 1827, unm; **Daniel** b 15 May 1830, d 6 Nov. 1866; **Olevin H.** b 1 Jul. 1833, d 12 Jan. 1835; **Angeline** b -- May 1835, d 19 Sep. 1854; **Holmes** b 16 Aug. 1837, m 3 Apr. 1860 Vesta C. Carr; and **John F.** b 7 Feb. 1842, m 15 Sep. 1865 Martha J. Thomas.

PETTENGILL, FRANK ALTON - Born 20 Sep. 1868, d ??, s/o Richmond and ?? Pettengill. Frank Alton Pettengill m 17 Jun. 1893 Millie G. Nichols, b 2 Aug. 1876, d/o Wm. W. and Mary J. (Doyle) Nichols. Children: **William R.** b 18 Oct. 1894; and **Herbert Dean** b 26 Jul. 1898.

PETTENGILL, GEORGE A. - Born 26 Feb. 1846 in Auburn, Maine, d ??, s/o Andrew C. and Olive (White) Pettengill. George A. Pettengill m 12 Apr. 1868 Emma Grosman of Lisbon Falls, Maine. Child: **Herbert**.

PETTENGILL, GEORGE A. - Born 8 Apr. 1871, d ??, s/o Charles A. and Elizabeth/Elizabeth M. (Dyer) Pettengill. George A. Pettengill m 30 Jun. 1896 Jennie Read/Reed of Boothbay, Maine, b 14 Jul. 1874, d/o Franklin and Falora Eunice (Broser ?). Children: **Albion C.** b 10 Dec. 1896, d 5 Oct. 1897; and **George E.** b 9 Jan. 1898.

PETTENGILL, GEO. S. - Born ??, d ??, s/o ?? Children: **Charles D.** b 6 Jun. 1868, d 19 Apr. 1886; **John Harris** b 2 Nov. 1869, d 26 Apr. 1871; and **Arthur N.** b 8 Apr. 1877.

PETTENGILL, HEMAN - Born 18 Feb. 1795, d 18 Nov. 1866, s/o ?? Heman Pettengill m (1) Betsey Webber of Durham, Maine, b 13 Feb. 1792, d 2 Jun. 1847, and m (2) Rebecca Hamilton of Chebeaque Island, Maine, d 14 Feb. 1854, and m (3) Mary A. Colby, d 19 Mar. 1866. *Children of 2nd wife*: **Heman J.** b 8 Apr. 1851 in Brunswick, m Mary J. Keene, and lived in Boston, MA; and **George B.** b 4 Nov. 1853, d 1 Jul. 1854. *Child of 3rd wife*: **Malleville C.** b 7 Jan. 1861, m 6 Nov. 1882 John C. Gerry of Fryeburg, ME.

PETTENGILL, HENRY F. - Born ??, d ??, s/o Cyranus. Children: **Winnifred** b 26 Feb. 1874; **Carl Sheres** (?) b 9 Apr. 1876; **Ethel Gordan** b 29 Aug. 1878; and **Irving Henry** b 3 Jul. 1880.

PETTENGILL, HOLMES - Born 11 Feb. 1789, s/o Hugh and ?? Pettengill. Holmes Pettengill m Susannah Drake, d 10 Jan. 1874. Children: **Hannah H.** m pub. 3 Oct. 1846 Guilford Stickney; **Betsey D.** b 7 Sep. 1824, d 25 Nov. 1886, m Benjamin Bradbury, d 1 Nov. 1869; **Isaac D.** b 20 May 1826, m 28 Nov. 1855 Deborah M. Gowell, b 30 Jun. 1836, d/o Geo.; **Sarah A.** b 19 Apr. ----, d 11 Mar. 1895, m 28 Jul. 1849 Joseph C. Shaw, who was buried at Oak Hill Cemetery, Riverside Dr., Auburn, ME; **Jane M.** b 11 Aug. 1831, m 22 Apr. 1861 Russell B. Morse; and **Vesta Ann** b 13 Dec. 1833, m Thomas F. Record.

PETTENGILL, HUGH - Born 31 Aug. 1766, d 25 Mar. 1830, s/o ?? Hugh Pettengill m pub. 15 Apr. 1780 Mrs. Hannah Snell, b 1 Aug. 1762, d 1 Jan. 1824. Children: **Ethan** b 3 Dec. 1786, d 18 Sep. 1882, m Deborah Drake, d 3 Feb. 1889, d/o Isaac; **Holmes** b 11 Feb. 1789, m Susannah Drake, d/o Isaac Drake; **Jennet** b 13 Mar. 1791, d 7 Feb. 1860, m pub. 7 Dec. 1831 Rev. James Garcelon of Lewiston; **Betsey** b 8 Feb. 1793, d 11 Apr. 1875, m Capt. John Prince; **Heman** b 18 Feb. 1795, d 18 Nov. 1866; **Oren** b 7 Apr. 1797, m Jane Kendall, d/o Rev. Henry Kendall of Brunswick, ME; **Hannah** b 13 Apr. 1799, d 21 Dec. 1863, m Samuel N. Bradbury of Auburn, ME, d 10 Sep. 1868, age 63 years 10 months 22 days; **Justus** b 11 Apr. 1801; **Hugh** b 17 Jul. 1863; and **Justin** b 11 Oct. 1805, d 2 Jul. 1877.

PETTENGILL, ICHABOD A. - Born ??, d ??, s/o Joseph and Alice (Allen) Pettengill. Ichabod A. Pettengill m Martha Morse of Winthrop, Maine. Children: **Newland M.** b 24 Mar. 1850; **Isaac R.** b 1 Aug. 1854; and **Walter** b 8 Apr. 1859, d 31 Dec. 1885.

PETTENGILL, ISAAC - Born ??, d ??, s/o ?? Children: **Hannah** b 14 Jan. 1820; and **Mary** b 21 Aug. 1822.

PETTENGILL, ISAAC D. - Born 20 May 1826, d ??, s/o Holmes and ?? Pettengill. Isaac D. Pettengill m 28 Nov. 1855 Deborah M. Gowell. Child: **Laurence C.** b 22 Dec. 1856, m 26 May 1888 Mary E. Sawyer of Greene, ME, b 29 Jan. 1868, d/o Wm. and Polly (Cummings) Sawyer.

PETTENGILL, J. MANSFIELD - Born 26 Sep. 1819, d 2 Apr. 1887, s/o Capt. Nathaniel and Nancy (How) Pettengill. J. Mansfield Pettengill m 1 Jan. 1845 Elizabeth C. Young, d/o Thos. and Rebecca (Keyes) Young of Augusta, Maine. Children: **Frances Estell** b 28 Mar. 1846, m 14 Nov. 1878 Amos Baker of Pittston, ME.; **Abbie Maria** b 4 May 1849; and **Marcia Antoinette** b 15 Jan. 1856, m 8 Jun. 1883 Fred O. Harris, moved to Duluth, MN.

PETTENGILL, JACOB - Born 15 May 1783, d 21 May 1851, s/o ?? Jacob Pettengill m 24 Feb. 1805 Esther Fogg of Freeport, Maine, d 28 Dec. 1850 age 64 years. Children: **Olive** b 18 May 1806, d 4 Nov.

1891, m 1824 Charles Waite of Freeport, ME; **Jason** b 28 Feb. 1812, m 27 Nov. 1837 Dorothy Blethen of Lisbon, ME, d 4 Mar. 1897; **Martin R.** b 6 Oct. 1817, drowned in Yarmouth Falls, ME, 20 Apr. 1832; **Charles W.** b 20 Apr. 1820, d 16 Sep. 1824; **Joseph W.** b 16 Sep. 1822, d 22 Dec. 1823; **Charles H.** b 9 Nov. 1823, m 22 Sep. 1846 P. Augusta Staples, b 12 Nov. 1823, d/o Capt. David and Elisabeth Bartol Staples; **Delia A.** b 31 Dec. 1824, d -- Nov. 1827; **Alfred** b 18 Dec. 1827, d 29 Nov. 1857 at sea; and **Francis** b 29 Apr. 1829, d 11 May 1832.

PETTENGILL, JAMES - Born -- Feb. 1803, d 3 Dec. 1850, s/o Samuel and ?? Pettengill. Samuel Pettengill was the s/o Mark. James Pettengill m Dolly Hamlin of York, Maine, b 12 Sep. 1801, d/o Joseph and Magret/Margaret (Roberts) Hamlin. James was Capt. of Brig. *Olive Thompson* and was lost at sea 3 Dec. 1850 with sons, James M. and William G. Children: **James M.** b 19 Dec. 1824, d 3 Dec. 1850, m pub. 19 Sep. 1846 Lissie Ford of Portland, ME; **George W.** b 15 Feb. 1827, d infancy; **Andrew J.** b 1 May 1829, m (1) 12 Sep. 1850 Esther Keene of West Poland, ME, b 17 Oct. 1822, d 12 Feb. 1881, and m (2) Octavia Cheney; **William G.** b 3 Sep. 1832, d 3 Dec. 1850; **Augustus C.** b 1 Dec. 1834, d 15 Dec. 1881, m 29 Oct. 1858 Lucy Lord, b 2 Oct. 1840, d/o Capt. Isariah and Nancy (Harris) Lord; **Margaret Elisabeth** b 15 Nov. 1837, m 29 Jul. 1856 Granville (?) Mitchell of Portland, ME, d 19 Apr. 1894; and **Jeremiah Y.** b 1 Dec. 1839, d 28 Nov. 1865 in Havana, Cuba, Capt. of Brig. *Cal. Merck* (?), m 8 Sep. 1858 Nancy Dow Chappin.

PETTENGILL, JASON - Born ??, d ??, s/o Jacob and ?? Pettengill. Jason Pettengill was a sea captain. Children: **Frances E.** b 4 Nov. 1838, d 28 Oct. 1843; **Sarah L.** b 8 May 1842, d 21 Mar. 1851; **Charles H.** b 1 May 1844; **Jason** b 29 May 1845, d 2 Oct. 1845; **Albert** b -- Apr. 1848, d 7 Jan. 1850; and **Jasen/Jason** b 15 Jan. 1857, d 15 Jun. 1859.

PETTENGILL, JASON - Born 23 Feb. 1808 [*History of Leeds* by J. C. Stinchfield, 1901, reprinted 1978, p. 156], d 4 Apr. 1862, s/o Abadiah/Obediah and Eleanor (Cobb) Pettengill. Jason Pettengill m Lorretta/Lucetta Gordon, d 28 Aug. 1869, d/o George/George W. Gordon. Children: **George Boardman** b 27 Jan. 1846, d 4 May 1860, m Amasiah Wheeler; **Melentha Gordon** b 28 Dec. 1847, m Asa Gordon, s/o Crosby; **Louis Augusta** b 3 Mar. 1849; **Matilda Frances** b 16 Aug. 1850, m ---- Cushman; and **Wilbert Hamlin** b 2 Sep. 1856.

PETTENGILL, JEREMIAH - Born 1 Dec. 1839, d before 21 Jun. 1899, s/o ?? Jeremiah Pettengill m 8 Sep. 1858 Nancy D. Chappin, b 13 Dec. 1842, d/o Adiman and Lydia J. (Bean) Chappin of Buckfield, Maine. Nancy D. (Chapman) Pettengill m (2) 21 Jun. 1899 Charles M. Landers. Children: **Margaret Elizabeth** b 16 Dec. 1849/1859, m 30 Nov. 1876 Chas. Merrill Goodwin of Turner, ME, d 19 Dec. 1937 [probate #20680, Androscoggin Co. court]; **Mary Augustus** b 11 Mar. 1862, m 29 May 1883 David B. Rounds of Minot, ME; **Jeremiah York** b 24 Jul. 1864, m 23 Jul. 1887 Augusta A. Prince, d/o Stephen Prince.

PETTENGILL, JOHN - Born 6 Feb. 1791, d 8 May 1866, s/o David and Thankful (Graffin) Pettengill. John Pettengill m 30 Nov. 1815 Mary Harris, d 29 Jan. 1842. Children: **John Harris** q.v.; **Mary Harris** b 7 Apr. 1820, m (1) 27 Apr. 1841 Auran Clark, who d 4 Jul. 1845, and m (2) 23 May 1847 Nat. E. Davis, who d 18 May 1876; **Elizabeth Harris** b 25 Mar. 1825, m (1) 16 Dec. 1843 Albert Coburn, who d 15 Nov. 1856, s/o Charles, and m (2) 31 Mar. 1863 Orin Oakes of Sangerville, ME., who d 2 Jul. 1897, having lived in Wyomette, IL; **David H.** b 20 Jul. 1829, d 8 Mar. 1855, unm; and **Sarah F.** b 13 Dec. 1835, d 21 Mar. 1885, unm.

PETTENGILL, JOHN - Born 1762, d 29 Oct. 1844, s/o ?? John Pettengill m (1) Betsey Robinson, d 11 Nov. 1802, and m (2) 16 May 1809 Lucy Pettengill [vital records of Lewiston, Maine, p. 434], d 11 Apr. 1863, d/o Mark of Lewiston. Children of 1st wife: **Hannah** b 1 Mar. 1790, m Josiah Turner of Leeds, ME; **Sally** b 29 Dec. 1791; **John** b 7 Oct. 1794; **Deborah** b 27 Feb. 1797; **Eliphlet** b 28 Jan. 1799; and **Nancy** b 26 Feb. 1801. Children of 2nd wife: **Betsey** b 11 Mar. 1811, d 22 Apr. 1881, m Charles Taylor; **Olive** b 11 Nov. 1812, d 28 Jun. 1884, m Amos Clark, b 20 Oct. 1812, d 20 Jun. 1876; **Anna** b 22 Nov. 1815, d 13 Jan. 1893, unm; **Sarah Augusta** b 22 Jun. 1818, m 14 Feb. 1855 Barnum L. Townsand/Townsend, d 10 Apr. 1880; **Alvin H.** b 20 Aug. 1820, d 29 Sep. 1882, m 10 May 1859 Elizabeth Taylor, d/o Joseph; and **Amanda** b 30 Nov. 1822, d 18 Apr. 1884, m Davis Nevens.

PETTENGILL, JOHN - Born ??, d 7 Oct. 1858, s/o ?? John Pettengill m Maria ----, d 14 Jun. 1845.

PETTENGILL, JOHN A. - Born 26 Dec. 1813, d 25 Oct. 1867, s/o Joseph and Alice (Allen) Pettengill. Children: **Ellen A.** b 16 Jan. 1838, d 16 Nov. 1860; **Leonidas** b 23 Jun. 1840 in Monmouth, ME, m Adeline Augusta Prescott, b 3 Sep. 1840, d/o Ebeneser and Fanny (Will) Prescott of Yarmouth, ME; **Lantha J.** b 10 Aug. 1842; **Infant** b 15 Feb. 1846, d 3 Mar. 1846; **Willard F.** b 23 Mar. 1848, m Lillian Rounds; and **Luman E.** b 13 Dec. 1852, d 10 Nov. 1853.

PETTENGILL, JOHN FREEMAN - Born ??, d ??, s/o Manassah and ?? Pettengill. Manassah Pettengill was the s/o Ephraim, s/o Ephraim, s/o David. John Freeman Pettengill lived in Staples, Maine. Children: **George Freeman** b 10 Apr. 1895; **unnamed son** b 8 Mar. 1897.

PETTENGILL, JOHN H. - Born ??, d ??, s/o Nathaniel, Jr. and ?? Pettengill. John H. Pettengill m 4 Jul. 1874 Rebecca J. Hoer/Hoar, b 22 Oct. 1855, d/o Joseph Hoer/Hoar.

PETTENGILL, JOHN HARRIS - Born 11 Dec. 1816, d 29 Apr. 1893, s/o John and Mary (Harris) Pettengill. John Harris Pettengill m 19 Apr. 1842 Martha H. Sleeper. Children: **George S.** b 13 Jan. 1843, m 6 Apr. 1867 Flavilla E. Golder; **Mary Ellen** b 6 Jan. 1845, d 12 Nov. 1865; and **Amanda** b 11 Sep. 1850, m 7 Dec. 1874 Horace Libby.

PETTENGILL, JOSEPH - Born 4 Aug. 1784, d ??, s/o William and Lydia (Cobb) Pettengill. Joseph Pettengill m Alice Allen of Greene, Maine. Children: **Greenwood** b 9 Mar. 1810; **John A.** b 26 Dec. 1813, d 25 Oct. 1867, m 25 Feb. 1837 Mary Billings of Chesterville, ME.; **William P.** b 4 Dec. 1815, d 20 Apr. 1899, m (1) Mary A. Blake, d/o John S. and Betsey (Morrell), and m (2) 27 Aug. 1863 Hannah Owen of Leeds; **Cynthia** b 31 Mar. 1818, m Samuel Horace King, d 29 Oct. 1892; and **Joseph Gancello** q.v.

PETTENGILL, JOSEPH GANCELLO - Born 17 Aug. 1828, d ??, s/o Joseph and Alice (Allen) Pettengill. Joseph Gancello Pettengill m (1) Martha Morse of Winthrop, Maine, and m (2) 13 Sep. 1859 Mary Dillingham, b 15 Dec. 1840 in Pittsfield, IL, d 16 Aug. 1883, d/o Almond and Helen (Young) Dillingham. Children: **Alice** b 14 Oct. 1861, d 14 Nov. 1885, m 10 Dec. 1884 Oscar G. Bjerke; **Fred** b 18 Jan. 1863, m -- Aug. 1894 Ella Jones; **Maud** b 7 Aug. 1866, m 5 Jun. 1898 Stephen A. D. Ogden; **Helena** b 23 Aug. 1869; **Bertha** b 14 Apr. 1874, d 10 Apr. 1875; and **Frank M.** b 15 Nov. 1877.

PETTENGILL, JUSTIN - Born 11 Oct. 1805, d 2 Jan. 1877, s/o Hugh and ?? Pettengill. Justin Pettengill m Relief Harlow, d/o James and Susannah Harlow. Children: **Carlton** b 28 Jan. 1832, m 17 Nov. 1853 Mrs. Maria Field; **Royal** b 25 Apr. 1854, m 7 Jun. 1857 Adaline Dillingham, b 10 Feb. 1842, d/o Quincy and Minerva (Leavitt) Dillingham; **Richmond** b 21 Dec. 1837, d 15 Jan. 1892; and **Solyman** b 4 Dec. 1845, d 8 Dec. 1870, unm.

PETTENGILL, LAURENCE C. - Born ??, d ??, s/o Isaac D. and ?? Pettengill. Child: **Walter L.** b 25 Aug. 1892.

PETTENGILL, LEONARD A. - Born 6 May 1841, d 7 Oct. 1861, s/o Wm. and Mary (Small) Pettengill. Child: **Lewis S.**

PETTENGILL, MANASSAH - Born ??, d ??, s/o ?? Child: **Ethel May** b 29 Jul. 1893.

PETTENGILL, MARK - Born 29 Dec. 1728, d 1787, s/o Abraham and Hannah (----) Pettengill. Mark Pettengill m 13 Jun. 1754 Sarah Clough, d/o Ebeneser and Anna (Weber) Clough. Children: **Abraham** b 4 Oct. 1754, m 15 Mar. 1774 Thankful Davis; **Ebeneser** b 22 Dec. 1756, m pub. 25 Oct. 1782 Esther Barker; **Samuel** b 25 Apr. 1759, m 18 Jan. 1783 Hannah Cole; **Anna** bapt. 13 Jun. 1762, d 26 Dec. 1845, m Samuel Cole, b 13 Jul. 1756, d 29 Mar. 1844; **Martha** bapt. 21 Oct. 1764, d 28 May 1853, m 5 Apr. 1786 Jacob Stevens of Greene, ME, d 19 Nov. 1884; **Meriam** bapt. 16 Aug. 1767, d -- Apr. 1855, m 7 Jul. 1802 Thomas Taylor, d 18 Feb. 1825; **Susanna** bapt. 8 Oct. 1769; **Mary** bapt. 12 Jul. 1772, d 22 Nov. 1865, m Bartholomew Coburn of Greene; **Nathaniel** b 14 Nov. 1775, d 27 Feb. 1860, m 6 Jul. 1800 Abigael/Abigail Ham, and m (2) pub. 2 May 1806 Mrs. Nancy How of Jay, ME., d 18 Mar. 1854 age 74 years; **Lucy** b 22 Jul. 1779, d 11 Apr. 1863 in Greene, m 2 May 1809 John Pettengill of Greene, d 29 Oct.

1814; and **Andrew** b 22 Mar. 1782, m pub. 5 Jun. 1812 Polly Briggs of Greene, who m (2) 1818 David Wright.

PETTENGILL, MENASSAH - Born 3 Apr. 1832, d ??, s/o Menassah and ?? Pettengill. Menassah Pettengill (the elder) was the s/o Ephraim, s/o Ephraim, s/o David. Menassah Pettengill (the younger) had the following children: **Mary Ellen** b 2 Nov. 1857 in Durham, ME, m 22 Jun. 1841 Harry W. Barrett of Staples, MN; **Menassah** b 15 Nov. 1860 in Lewiston, m -- Arp. [sic - Apr.] 1893 Lithian Coates of Winneconne, WI; **Clara Abbie** b 13 Feb. 1863 in Oniro (?), WI, m 6 Nov. 1894 Herbert E. Barrett; **John Freeman** b 12 Oct. 1864 in WI, m 4 Jul. 1844 Kate Hemexson of Verndale, MN; **Josephine Betsey** b 26 Oct. 1868 in Leroy, MN; and **Orion** b 5 Aug. 1871 in Leroy, MN.

PETTENGILL, MOSES G. - Born 16 Sep. 1832, d ??, s/o Nathaniel and ?? Pettengill. Moses G. Pettengill m 16 Oct. 1853 Hannah Flower, b 10 Oct. 1834, d/o Geo. W. and Almira (Newbegin) Flower of Pownal, Maine. Children: **Almira F.** b 4 Jun. 1854, d -- Jun. 1888 (?), m 24 Nov. 1870 Benj. F. Hammond of Long Island; **Royal E.** b 20 May 1861, d 12 Jul. 1863; and **Ellva** (?) b 11 May 1864, m Elsie How.

PETTENGILL, NATH/CAPT. NATHANIEL - Born 14 Nov. 1775, d 27 Feb. 1860, s/o Mark and Sarah (Clough) Pettengill. Nath/Capt. Nathaniel Pettengill m (1) pub. 5 Apr. 1800, m (1) 6 Jul. 1800 Abigail Ham, b 31 Aug. 1779, d 10 Dec. 1805, and m (2) pub. 2 May 1806 Mrs. Nancy How of Jay, Maine, d 8 Mar. 1854 age 74 years. *Child by 1st wife:* **Sarah** b 7 Sep. 1801, d 25 Sep. 1864, m 9 Sep. 1821 John Hatch of Leeds, ME, b 20 Jul. 1798 in Durham, ME, d 7 Jan. 1878 in Lisbon, ME. *Children by 2nd wife:* **Abigail H.** b 16 Dec. 1806, d 16 May 1872, m 7 Feb. 1830 Washington Sprague, d 30 Aug. 1871; **Sophonia/Sophronia** b 11 Feb. 1808, d 16 Dec. 1809; **James Madison** b 24 Aug. 1809, d 17 Mar. 1830; **Nathaniel** b 20 May 1810, d 5 Oct. 1836; **Sophronia E.** b 28 Jan. 1813, d 13 Nov. 1869, m pub. 11 Nov. 1833 Lincoln Keene, d 17 Nov. 1877; **Converse/Converse J.** q.v.; **Andrew C.** b 22 Feb. 1816, m 19 Jan. 1842 Olive White; **J. Mansfield** b 26 Sep. 1819, d 2 Apr. 1887; and **Marie Antoinette** b 24 Nov. 1817, m pub. 13 Sep. 1840 Charles Nevens.

PETTENGILL, NATHAN JR. - Born ??, d 13 Aug. 1871, s/o ?? Nathan Pettengill, Jr. m 25 Nov. 1852 Ellen M. Johnson, b 12 Apr. 1837 in Portland, Maine, d/o David Johnson and Abigail (Snell) Johnson. Children: **John H.** b 20 Feb. 1854; **Deborah E.** b 5 Jul. 1856, m 14 Jul. 1882 Sam'l. C. McKenny; **George F.** b 29 Aug. 1860, m 18 May 1891 Rosella T. Frost, d/o Jacob R. Frost; and **Emma C.** b 24 Aug. 1865, m Geo. H. Griffin.

PETTENGILL, NATHANIEL - Born 3 Nov. 1797, d 1 Feb. 1882, s/o ?? Nathaniel Pettengill m Deborah T. Griffin, b 27 May 1803, d/o John and Nav. (----) Griffin. Children: **Nathaniel** b 1 Jun. 1829, d 13 Aug. 1871, m 25 Nov. 1852 Ellen M. Johnson; **Moses G.** b 16 Sep. 1832, m 18 Oct. 1853 Harriet Fowler; **Charlotte A.** b 25 Jan. 1823, m Joseph How; **Hannah** b 14 Aug. 1826, m 5 Dec. 1845 Joseph Small;

Samuel b 22 Dec. 1835, m 28 Sep. 1855 Susan Griffen, b 2 Jan. 1839, d/o David H. and Susan C. Griffen; **Deborah T.** b 12 Apr. 1831, d 22 Jul. 1853, m 6 May 1850 M. Witham; and **Lydia A.** b 26 Sep. 1840, m 3 Oct. 1859 Samuel H. Marston, lived in Long Island, NY.

PETTENGILL, OBADIAH/ABADIAH - Born in N. Bridgwater, Massachusetts, 29 Mar. 1846, s/o ?? Obadiah/Abadiah Pettengill m Eleanor Cobb, d 7 Apr. 1858 age 87 years 4 months 16 days. Children: **Arcadus** b 19 Jan. 1793, d 30 Oct. 1883, m 1814 Polby H. Tribou, d 15 Nov. 1869 age 80 years; **Abadiah** b 26 Sep. 1795, d 12 Feb. 1880; **John** b 29 Oct. 1798, d 7 Dec. 1858; **Phebe** b 20 Aug. 1801, d 31 Oct. 1896; **Phillips** q.v.; **Ivena** b 9 Feb. 1806, m ---- Clark; **Jason** q.v.; and Sarah Cobb b 22 Jul. 1814, d 4 Apr. 1892.

PETTENGILL, ORIN - Born 7 Apr. 1797, d in Kansas, s/o Hugh and ?? Pettengill. Orin Pettengill m Jane Kendall, d/o Rev. Henry Kendall of Brunswick, Maine. Children: **Sarah Jane Kendall** b 12 Feb. 1824; **Hugh** b 19 Aug. 1825, m 7 Sep. 1850 Cynthia B. Topsham; **Mary Ann Byram** b 10 Oct. 1827, m 1853 Benj. Richardson; **Susan Allen** b 2 May 1832, m 1853 F. A. Ledoton; **Almira**; **Charles Berry** b 19 Dec. 1829, m 30 Sep. 1854 Lizzie Downing; **Elisa** m Jesse Verrill, d in Auburn, ME; **Laura**, unm; and **Frank**.

PETTENGILL, ORIN - Born ??, d ??, s/o ?? Orin Pettengill m Marcetta Beechman, b 14 Aug. 1841. Children: **Anni/Annie** b 20 Feb. 1860, d 15 Aug. 1889; **Charles Asstroph** b 13 Aug. 1865, d 15 Jan. 1884; **Nicholas M.** b 6 Feb. 1865, d 16 Sep. 1866; **Georgianna** b 12 Apr. 1867, d 13 Sep. 1867; **Nellie J.** b 29 Aug. 1869, m 6 Jan. 1895 Wm. D. McLaughlin; **William** b 25 Apr. 1871, d 4 Oct. 1871; **Marcetta** b 25 Apr. 1871, d 6 Jan. 1894, m 12 Jul. 1892 Joesph A. McCarthy; **Georgiana M.** b 4 Mar. 1873, d 22 Feb. 1896, m Joseph Lovejoy; **Horatio** b 22 Apr. 1875, d 30 Apr. 1895; and **Maud Frances** b 21 Apr. 1879.

PETTENGILL, ORIN - Born ??, d ??, s/o ?? Orin Pettengill m Mary Beechan. Children: **Marion F.** b 21 Apr. 1879; and **Nellie J.** b 29 Aug. 1869.

PETTENGILL, PHILLIPS - Born 21 Jun. 1804, d 14 May 1884, age 79 years 10 months 23 days, fourth s/o Obadiah and Eleanor (Cobb) Pettengill. Phillips Pettengill m 2 Jun. 1844 Joan (Coffin) Harris, d 28 Mar. 1882, age 74 years 11 months, wid/o Moses Little Harris. Children: **Rosine** b 4 Apr. 1836; **Moses Little** b 1 Apr. 1838; **Eleanor** b 16 May 1845, m George Howe; **Joan Elizabeth** b 22 Apr. 1847, m Wallace Mower of Greene, Maine; and **Phillips, Jr.** b 16 Sep. 1850, d 12 Sep. 1852. [*History of Leeds* by J. C. Stinchfield, 1901, reprinted 1978, p. 156.]

PETTENGILL, RENSELLIER F. - Born 23 Oct. 1838, d 2 Dec. 1865, s/o Samuel and ?? Pettengill. Rensellier F. Pettengill m Mary Joanna Wait. Children: **Edward Albert** b 1 Aug. 1871, d 17 Jul. 1882;

Ella Gertrude May b 5 Jan. 1874, d 18 Nov. 1897, m 27 Jul. 1893 Edward Franklin Knight; and ---- b 23 Feb. 1877.

PETTENGILL, RICHMOND - Born 21 Dec. 1837, d 15 Jan. 1892, s/o Justin and ?? Pettengill. Richmond Pettengill m 22 Dec. 1861 Elizabeth Merrill, b 17 Aug. 1849, d/o Cyrus and Elizabeth (Noyes) Merrill. Children: **Frank Alton** b 20 Sep. 1868; and **William Adelbert** b 27 Aug. 1872.

PETTENGILL, ROSCOE I. - Born ??, d ??, s/o Charles H. and ?? Pettengill. Roscoe I. Pettengill m Lissie A. True, d/o Nathan O. and Mary A. (Anderson) True. Children: **Irving I.** b 27 Mar. 1881; and **Anna A.** b 14 Oct. 1885.

PETTENGILL, ROYAL H. - Born ??, d ??, s/o Justin and ?? Pettengill. Royal H. Pettengill m 7 Jun. 1817 Adeline Dillingham, d/o Quincy and Leavitt Dillingham. Children: **Edgar R.** b 11 Jun. 1859, m Almira Chase; **Carrie S.** b 8 Mar. 1870; and **Ralph E.** b 20 Oct. 1879.

PETTENGILL, RUEL - Born 17 Sep. 1792, d 23 Oct. 1862, s/o William and ?? Pettengill. Ruel Pettengill m 24 Mar. 1813 Lydia Briggs, b 14 Feb. 1794, d 21 Dec. 1873. Children: **Lydia** b 14 Dec. 1813, m 4 Mar. 1834 Calvin Briggs, d 21 Dec. 1873; **Ruel** b 18 Feb. 1816, d 26 Jan. 1899, unm; **Arvida B.** b 27 Jun. 1818, m 14 Jan. 1843 Alvira Ann Sumner, d 11 Oct. 1894; and **Cyranus** q.v.

PETTENGILL, SAM'L. - Born ??, d ??, s/o Nathaniel and ?? Pettengill. Children: **M a r y T.** b 18 Jan. 1857, d 10 Oct. 1893, m 12 Mar. 1874 Joseph H. Lewis; **Charles E.** b 12 Jul. 1862, d 7 Jul. 1899, m Elizabeth T. Johnson; and **Edwin S.** b 6 Feb. 1877.

PETTENGILL, SAM'L. - Born ??, d c1836, s/o Mark and ?? Pettengill. Sam'l. Pettengill m Hannah Cole, b 11 Jul. 1764, d/o John and Sarah (Reeves) Cole. Children: **Allen** b 21 Jun. 1783 in Lewiston, d 1 Aug. 1873, m Mary Higgins of Bath, ME, d 2 May 1867, d/o Benj. and Hannah Higgins; **Nathaniel** b 3 Nov. 1797, d 1 Feb. 1882, m Deborah T. Griffin, d/o John and Nancy (Eaton) Griffin; **Samuel P.** b 1814, d 28 Jan. 1857, m pub. 22 Oct. 1836 Abigail Littlejohn, d 2 Feb. 1894; **Jeremiah William** b 5 Jun. 1792, d 29 Jul. 1863, m 5 Sep. 1824 Mary Small, b 18 Dec. 1803; **Dorcas Banks** b 13 Jan. 1784, d 9 May 1883, m 25 Nov. 1805 Thomas Bibber of N. Yarmouth, ME, d 31 Jul. 1866; **H a n n a h** b 1 Dec. 1801, d 24 Jul. 1877, m pub. 20 Apr. 1822 Smyton Crossman in Portland, ME; **L y d i a** b -- May 1788, d 21 Feb. 1878, m David Hill, d 20 Mar. 1824 age 39 years; **Rhoda** b 1791, d 26 Oct. 1873, m Samuel Pettie, lived in Portland; **Charles L.** q.v.; **James** b 27 Oct. 1802, d 3 Dec. 1850, m Dolly York, b -- May 1801, d 4 May 1873, and she m (2) Geo. Hamlin; **Stephen** b 1 Jan. 1800, d 22 Mar. 1890, m (1) Polly Candler/Chandler (nee Woodbury), and m (2) Thankful Woodbury, who was m (1) Ezekial Cushing; and **Sarah** b 26 Jun. 1792, d 18 Nov. 1843, m 1 Jan. 1815 John York, b 4 Jul. 1794, d 26 Jul. 1855.

PETTENGILL, SAMUEL P. - Born 1814, d 28 Jan. 1857, s/o Samuel and Hannah (Cole) Pettengill. Samuel P. Pettengill m pub. 22 Oct. 1836 Abigail Littlejohn. Children: **Susan Alberta** b -- May 1842, d 2 Dec. 1865, m Capt. William E. Thomas of Portland, ME; **Rensellier Foster** b 23 Oct. 1838, d 26 Aug. 1885, lost at sea, m 3 Jul. 1870 Mary Joanna Wait of Portland, b 5 Sep. 1852 in Portland, d/o Albert Henry and Lucinda Ann (Paine) Wait; **Edward Dexter** b 11 Aug. 1840, d 30 Mar. 1885, m 2 Mar. 1868 Sarah J. Standish of Bath, ME, b 22 Aug. 1845; and **Alden Mitchell** b 7 May 1855, m 23 Jul. 1881 Sarah L. Hitchcock of Yarmouth.

PETTENGILL, STEPHEN - Born ??, d ??, s/o Sam'l. and ?? Pettengill. Stephen Pettengill m (1) 28 Apr. 1867 Melinda H. Clanage (?), and m (2) 11 Apr. 1859 Mary Woodbury (nee Chandler), d -- Jan. 1866, and m (3) ---- Cushing. Children: **Allen A.** b 8 Mar. 1860, m 29 Feb. 1884 Mary F. Dyer (Wiggin), b 17 Sep. 1857, d/o Ephram and Betsey (Roberts) Dyer.

PETTENGILL, TRUE EDWARD G. - Born 27 Sep. 1827, d ??, s/o Benjamin G. and Hannah B. (Pettengill) Pettengill. True Edward G. Pettengill m 18 Jul. 1854 Emma L. Sturges of Clarenden, New York, b 1 May 1834, d/o David. Child: **Edward True** b 4 Apr. 1847 in Clarenden, NY.

PETTENGILL, VICTOR C. - Born 17 Apr. 1855, d ??, s/o Carlton and ?? Pettengill. Victor C. Pettengill m 1 Jan. 1877 Amanda Frances. Children: **Earnest Herbert** b 23 Nov. 1877, d 25 Feb. 1880; **Charles E.** b 22 Nov. 1879; **Hebert Alton** b 15 May 1882; and **Asa Elmer** b -- Apr. 1896.

PETTENGILL, WALLACE M. - Born ??, d ??, s/o Charles H. and ?? Pettengill. Charles H. Pettengill was the s/o Jacob and Sarah (----) Pettengill. Wallace M. Pettengill m Adelia R. Gerry, d/o Wm. and Julia (Keene) Gerry. Children: **Ethel** b 30 Sep. 1873, d 23 Feb. 1896; **Frank L.** b 1 Feb. 1879; and **Mildred G.** b 15 Dec. 1882.

PETTENGILL, WALTER TRUE - Born 6 Jul. 1849, d ??, s/o ?? Children: **Agnes E.** b 1875; and **Ben. Miller** b 1879.

PETTENGILL, WILLIAM - Born 31 Oct. 1759, d 16 Nov. 1846, s/o ?? William Pettengill m Lydia Cobb, d 3 Dec. 1853 age 93 years 1 month. Children: **Joseph** b 4 Aug. 1784, d 25 Jan. 1869, m -- Jul. 1809 Alice Allen of Greene, ME, d 1 Jan. 1867 age 79 years 9 months 25 days; **Hannah** b 14 Feb. 1786, d 19 Jun. 1871, m 29 Jun. 1802 James Stinchfield; **Lydia** b 3 Nov. 1787, d 27 Feb. 1819, m 21 Jul. 1811 George Gordon of Wayne, ME, d 29 Aug. 1864 age 21 years 8 months; **Sarah** b 8 May 1791, d 22 Dec. 1881, m 25 Nov. 1808 Jonathan Gordan of Chesterville, ME; **Ruel** b 17 Sep. 1792, d 23 Oct. 1862, m 24 Mar. 1813 Lydia Briggs of Greene, d 21 Dec. 1873 age 79 years 10 months; **Jennet** b 3 Jan. 1795, d 14 Jan. 1883, m 29 Dec. 1814 Ebenezer Hammond of Wayne, ME; **Isaac** b 10 Apr. 1797, d 13 Sep. 1872, m (1) 25 Sep. 1819 Hannah Norris of Wayne, d 22 Mar.

1847, and m (2) Lucy ----, d 27 Oct. 1854 age 49 years 8 months 22 days; **Ruthy** b 18 May 1799, d 2 Dec. 1862, m 8 Feb. 1820 George Gordan, d 29 Aug. 1869 age 81 years 8 months; **William** b 10 Dec. 1801, d 11 Apr. 1881, m 20 May 1827 Eunice Day, d 3 Sep. 1896, d/o Joseph and Ruth; **Mary** b 20 Jan. 1805, d 6 Jan. 1895, m Orlando F. Blake, b 15 Dec. 1816, d 6 Aug. 1873 age 51 years 6 months; and **Amanda** b 22 Nov. 1807, d 5 May 1888, m 24 Feb. 1850, as his second wife, Joshua Elder, Jr. of Lewiston, d 5 Jul. 1879 father of J. G. Elder.

PETTENGILL, WILLIAM - Born 10 Dec. 1801, d 11 Apr. 1881, s/o William and ?? Pettengill. William Pettengill m Eunice Day, d/o Joseph and Ruth (Gilbert) Day. Children: **Ruth** b 26 Feb. 1828, d 12 Apr. 1890, m 17 Feb. 1850 Lewis Churchill, d 5 Nov. 1904; **Elisa** b 26 Apr. 1832, d 26 Nov. 1832; **Eunice Alleva** b 29 Jul. 1835, d 26 Mar. 1842; **Lydia** b 9 Jan. 1839, d 9 Feb. 1841; **Samuel Wesley** b 1 Mar. 1842, d 11 Jun. 1868; **Lucretia** b 23 Oct. 1845, twin, d 15 Oct. 1884, m 3 Jun. 1865 Wm. Henry Erskine, d 30 Aug. 1897; **Lydia** b 23 Oct. 1845, twin, m Wm. Erastus Elder; **William Russell** b 19 Oct. 1847, m 22 Aug. 1868 Fannie P. Libby; and **Eunice Ann** b 29 May 1854, d 11 Aug. 1854.

PETTENGILL, WILLIAM - Born ??, d ??, s/o Sam'l. and Hannah (Cole), Pettengill. William Pettengill m (1) ----, and m (2) 5 Sep. 1824 Mary Small of Lisbon, Maine, d 15 May 1882. Children: **William** b 21 Apr. 1814, d 15 Jan. 1813, m -- Jul. 1828 Eliza Randall, b 9 Feb. 1817, d 24 Dec. 1872, d/o Kanasum (?) Randall of Portland, ME; **Annie** m Noah Jordan; **Mary J.** b 26 Jul. 1825, d 8 Nov. 1845, unm; **Horace J.** b 10 Nov. 1827, d 2 Sep. 1849; **Charles A.** q.v.; **Hannah** b 28 Jul. 1831, d 12 Jun. 1899, m (1) 24 Feb. 1850 Earl Melaken, and m (2) 30 Nov. 1889 Iresen Greene; **George A.** b 8 Oct. 1833, d 3 Jul. 1863 (killed at Gettysburg); **Alonso L.** b 23 Oct. 1835, d 15 Nov. 1850, unm; **Cornelia E.** b 23 Jun. 1839, d 17 Jun. 1857, m 7 Jan. 1856 John Wright; **Leonard A.** q.v.; and **Martha A.** b 27 Sep. 1843, d 23 Aug. 1844.

PETTENGILL, WILLIAM - Born 21 Apr. 1814 in Lisbon, Maine, d 15 Jan. 1865, s/o William and ?? Pettengill. William Pettengill (the elder) was the s/o Samuel. William Pettengill (the younger) m -- Jul. 1838 Eliza Randall, b 9 Feb. 1817, d 24 Dec. 1872, d/o Kenacum. Children: **Elizabeth M.** b 28 Apr. 1839 in Portland, d 30 Mar. 1865, m 27 Nov. 1857 John H. Barberick (?); **Olive J.** b 11 Sep. 1840, m George Holt; **William M.** b 21 Jun. 1842, m 19 Apr. 1866 Mary C. Brown, b 19 Oct. 1843, d/o Wm. F. and Jane (Sampson) Brown; **Orin F.** b 21 Feb. 1844, m 16 Oct. 1862 Mary Beechan, d/o Michael; **Georgianna** b 21 Apr. 1846, m Joseph Lovejoy; **Ethel J.** b 13 Nov. 1851, d 1 Jan. 1873, unm; **Charles L.** b 17 Nov. 1854; and **Joseph Henry** b 27 Nov. 1849, d 15 Jul. 1881, m 29 Aug. 1867 Jennie Walker.

PETTENGILL, WM. ADELBERT - Born ??, d ??, s/o Richmond and ?? Pettengill. Wm. Adelbert Pettengill m 24 Dec. 1892 Carrie E. Nichols, d/o Wm. M. and Mary J. (Doyle) Nichols. Children: **Ethel**

W. b 20 Sep. 1893; **Lester E.** b 6 Aug. 1896; and **Stella M.** b 28 Mar. 1898.

PETTENGILL, WM. B. - Born ??, d ??, s/o Joseph and Alice (Allen) Pettengill. Children: **Henry D.** b -- May 1850, d 12 Nov. 1851; **Marietta M.**; **Georgiana D.** d 21 Dec. 1852; and **Nettie A.** d 1888, m 27 Jun. 1878 Walter C. Leavitt, d 11 Mar. 1893 age 78 years, 1876 graduated Bates, 1877 B.S.

PETTENGILL, WM. M. - Born ??, d ??, s/o Wm. and ?? Pettengill. Child: **Carrie May** b -- Jul. 1870.

PETTENGILL, WM. RUSSELL - Born ??, d ??, s/o ?? Children: **Grace Vernon** b 30 Jun. 1860; **Samuel Henry** b 31 Aug. 1870; **Emma Gertrude** b 18 Apr. 1872, m Sanford Adams; **William Tillotson** b 6 Oct. 1873; **Clara Eunice** b 30 Jul. 1875, d 4 Dec. 1877; **Ruth Eugenia** b 23 Dec. 1876; **Clara May** b 24 Mar. 1870; **James Garfield** b 6 Dec. 1880; **Fannie Louise** b 3 Jul. 1882; **Sarah Ruby** b 23 Feb. 1884; and **Fred Russell** b 24 Sep. 1886.

PETTENGILL, WILLIAM W. - Born 7 Apr. 1843 in Lewiston, d ??, s/o Andrew C. and Olive (White) Pettengill. William W. Pettengill m -- Jun. 1815 Helen Given, d/o David Given. Children: **Viola Helen** b 13 Feb. 1872, m John E. Wilson; **Wm. Albert** m Edna Thomas, d/o John Thomas of Auburn; **Arthur A.**; and **Frank**.

PICKARD, SAMUEL - Born ??, d ??, s/o ?? Samuel Pickard m Hannah [Little?]. Children: **Josiah Little** b 17 Mar. 1824 in Rowley, MA; **Joseph Coffin** b 7 Sep. 1826 in Rowley, MA; **Samuel Thomas** b 1 Mar. 1828 in Rowley, MA; **Daniel Webster** b 7 Jun. 1830 in Rowley, MA; **Sarah Little** b 4 May 1833; **Edward Little** b 25 Dec. 1834; **Charles Weston** b 28 Oct. 1836; **George Henry** b 2 Apr. 1838; **John** b 21 Apr. 1840; **Horace Chapin** b 24 Dec. 1841. [Vital Records of Lewiston, Maine, p. 127.]

PINKHAM, EBENESER - Born ??, d ??, s/o ?? Ebeneser Pinkham m Elenor ----. Children: **Miriam B.** b 17 Sep. 1787; **Hannah** b 12 Mar. 1793; **Ebeneser** b 1 Apr. 1795; **William Trew** b 25 Dec. 1797; **Ezekiel** b 24 Sep. 1799; **Anna** b 20 Aug. 1801; and **Susannah** b 6 Oct. 1807. [Vital Records of Lewiston, Maine, p. 61.]

PIPER, THOMAS - Born 26 Mar. 1787, d 11 Aug. 1827, s/o ?? Thomas Pinkham m (1) pub. 1 Dec. 1808 Hannah Lander of Kingfield, Maine, and m (2) Hannah Harris of Greene, Maine, d 18 Mar. 1851, d/o Lawrence J. Harris. Hannah (Harris) Piper m (2) Moses Towne. Children: **Mary** b 5 Dec. 1809, d 1 Mar. 1840, m 12 Feb. 1832 Gilbert Bubier; **Martha** b 24 Jun. 1811, unm; **Anna** b 9 Mar. 1813, m Freeman Lander of Greene; **Henry** b 13 Apr. 1815, m Lucinda (Ware) Stewart, who d 3 Feb. 1890, d/o Lewis; **Susan** b 5 Aug. 1817, m Jason Cutter, s/o David; **Olive** b 30 Dec. 1820, m Naham Decker; **Sally** b 23 Jul. 1822, m Oliver Herrick; and **Thomas** b 4 Feb. 1825, m 3 May 1857

Syrena B. Bradford of Turner, Maine, d/o Benjamin. [Vital Records of Lewiston, Maine, p. 59.]

PIPER, THOMAS - Born ??, d ??, s/o ?? Children: **Cynthia** b 18 Nov. 1844, unm; **Hannah**; **Harvey** b 5 May 1842, d 1 Dec. 1903; **Maria** m Sewall Austen who lived in Norway, ME; **Hattie** m John Susam (?) who lived in Augusta, ME.

PROCTOR, JOHN - Born ??, d ??, s/o ?? John Proctor m Jane ---- or m 19 Jun. 1814 Jean Robinson [vital records of Lewiston, Maine, p. 434]. Child: **Samuel** b 29 Jan. 1815. {Vital Records of Lewiston, Maine, p. 61.]

PROCTOR, SAMUEL - Born 24 Nov. 1719 in Portland, Maine, d ??, s/o ?? Samuel Proctor m 1745 Eliza Johnson. Children: **Samuel** b -- Apr. (?) 1749, Rev. soldier killed in Lewiston by a falling tree 29 Nov. 1795, m 6 May 1784 Joanna Berry, who m (2) Wm. Thompson of Wayne, ME; **Thomas** q.v.; and **Joseph** who lived and d in Durham, ME.

PROCTOR, THOMAS - Born 21 Jan. 1766 in Falmouth, Maine, d 21 Sep. 1855 in Danville, Maine, s/o Samuel and Eliza (Johnson) Proctor. Thomas Proctor m 13 Nov. 1792 [Starbird records] Deborah Jordan, b 12 Sep. 1761, d 13 Nov. 1843 in Danville, d/o Stephen and Mary of Cape Elizabeth, Maine. They settled on the Pejepscot Claim in 1793, about 1796 moved to Little River Plt. (now Lisbon Falls). They later returned to South River Rd., Danville [Starbird records]. Children: **Elijah** b 6 Sep. 1792/3 in Pejepscot; **Labetha** b 24 Aug. 1795; **Abigail** b 13 Jun. 1797 in Little River Plt.; **William** b 1 Jan. 1799 in Little River Plt., m 1 Jan. 1844 Abigail Fickett of Durham; **Joseph** b 30 Sep. 1801 and m Elizabeth Otis of Harpswell, ME; and **Thomas** b 1 Jul. 1804 at Pejepscot, ME.

PURINGTON, CHARLES E. - Born ??, d ??, s/o ?? Child: **Alcie** (?) b 1 Mar. 1872.

PURINGTON, DAVID - Born 1 May 1734, d 16 Feb. 1816, s/o ?? David Purington m Sarah ----, d 17 Mar. 1830. Children: **Mary** b 9 Aug. 1759; **Ezra** q.v.; **Phebe** b 23 Jun. 1766; **Anna** b 29 Aug. 1764, d 7 May 1777; **Sarah** b 26 Sep. 1768; **Mishna** b 9 Aug. 1771; **Daniel** b 20 Nov. 1772; **Lorannah** b 7 Apr. 1775; and **David** b 6 Sep. 1778, d 30 Jul. 1798.

PURINGTON, DAVID - Born 19 Jun. 1796, d 26 May 1848, s/o Ezra and Mary (Field) Purington. David Purington m (1) Hannah Goddard, d 20 May 1875, d/o Abel, and m (2) 16 Feb. 1843 Aseneth Bubier. Children: **Mary** b 17 Aug. 1820, m 6 Mar. 1848 Admiray/Admiral Hasey; **Anna Varney** b 8 May 1822, m David Baraby (?); **Ezra** b 19 Sep. 1824, d 6 Aug. 1886 in Auburn, m 13 Jul. 1850 Jesemine Hoxie, b 5 Feb. 1872, d 2 Feb. 1884; **Louise Goddard** b 17 Aug. 1826, d age 7 years in N. Gloucester; **David** b 18 Nov. 1828, d age 22 years; **Dorcas Goddard** b 21 Feb. 1831; **Phebe G.** b 13 Feb. 1833, m George Ross of

Rockport, MA; and **Isaiah General** b 10 Jun. 1835. [Vital Records of Lewiston, Maine, p. 59.]

PURINGTON, EZRA - Born 28 Oct. 1761, d 28 Dec. 1838, s/o David and Sarah (----) Purington. Ezra Purington m Mary Field, b 1772, d 7 Nov. 1857, d/o Joseph and Eunice (Hill) Purington. Children: **David** q.v.; **Joseph** b 1 Dec. 1798, d 28 Sep. 1842, m pub. 22 Jun. 1833, m 28 Jul. 1833 Caroline Dingley; **Tobias** q.v.; and **Ezra** b 25 Mar. 1803, d 10 May 1888, m 27 Aug. 1828 Dorcas Golder, who d 27 Dec. 1830.

PURINGTON, EZRA - Born ??, d 6 Aug. 1886 in Auburn, s/o Dorea and ?? Purington. Ezra Purington m 13 Jan. 1850 Jesemine Hoxie in Sidney, Maine, d 12 Feb. 1884. Children: **Alfred J.** b 12 Mar. 1852 in Durham, m Ella Smith of Hartland, ME; **Mary Ellen** b 31 Dec. 1853 in Sidney, d 26 Apr. 1863; **Lewetta** b 22 Nov. 1856 in Durham, m 28 Mar. 1876 James M. Jordan; **Everett Russell** b 17 May 1860 in Detroit, ME; **Romando** (?) S. b 12 May 1867 in Detroit, m Edith Austin of West Peru, ME; and **Eva May** b 29 Oct. 1874 in Fairfield.

PURINGTON, IRA - Born 25 Mar. 1803, d 10 May 1888, s/o ?? Ira Purington m (1) 27 Aug. 1828 Dorcus Golder, d/o Rev. Jacob, and m (2) pub. 27 Jul. 1834 Almira Snell of Fall River, Massachusetts, b 2 Jan. 1805 in Fall River, d 4 Jan. 1891. Children: **Charles E.** b 11 Dec. 1837, lived in Danville, ME, m Mary Goodwin of MA; **Arvesta** b 2 Sep. 1841, d 11 Feb. 1889, m Elvin Locke of Poland, ME; **Tobias** b 31 May 1840, unm; **Victoria** b 18 Jun. 1843, d 14 Dec. 1843; and **Minerva** b 1 Mar. 1829, m James Carville.

PURINGTON, JOSEPH - Born ??, d ??, s/o ?? Joseph Purington m Caroline ----. Children: **Mary** b 18 Dec. 1834, m 19 Sep. 1854 Rufus Stevens; **Almira** b 6 Sep. 1836, d 1 Mar. 1859; **Sarah** b 13 Aug. 1838, m Chas. Hodgkins; and **William Dingley** b 3 May 1840, d 12 Apr. 1842. [Vital Records of Lewiston, Maine, p. 127.]

PURINGTON, TOBIAS - Born 19 Mar. 1800, d 2 May 1880, age 79 years 1 month 14 days, s/o Ezra and Mary (----) Purington.

RAINARD, GEORGE - Born 1829 in Hurtemburg, Germany, d ??, s/o ?? George Rainard occ' Dyer. He m ----, b 1828 in Maine. Children: **Henry** b 1858 in Maine; **Rufus W.** b 1859 in Maine. [Lewiston, Maine, 1860.]

RAND, BARSILLA - Born 14 Sep. 1792, d 13 Sep. 1861 in Abbott, Maine, s/o ?? Barsilla Rand m 6 Mar. 1814 [vital records of Lewiston, Maine, p. 435] Thankful Garcelon, d 26 Feb. 1851 age 71 years. Children: **Jane** b 3 Dec. 1814, d 17 Mar. 1816; **Catherine** b 22 Apr. 1816, m Deneteus Crediford; **Jane** b 7 Nov. 1818, d 2 Aug. 1821; **Joan** b 30 Aug. 1821, m Albert Pierce; **Daniel** b 28 Oct. 1823; **Lucy Millbanks** b 5 Apr. 1827; and **Rosemond** m ---- from Ireland. [Vital Records of Lewiston, Maine, p. 68.]

RAND, JAMES - Born ??, d 9 Mar. 1945 in Lisbon, Maine [probate record], s/o Jason and ?? Rand. James Rand m Bertie Brann. Children: **Fred** b 17 Jul. ----; and **Eugenia** b 5 Oct. 1885, m ---- Young, res: Lewiston, ME, in 1945.

RAND, JASON K. - Born 14 Nov. 1824, d 15 Sep. 1892, s/o Samuel and ?? Rand. Jason K. Rand was of Lisbon, Maine. He m 27 May 1849 Susan Smith, b 3 Jul. 1827, d 23 Sep. 1904 [#5781 Susan's will probate], d/o Isaac Smith. Children: **Audretta** b 24 Jun. 1850, d 31 Jul. 1887, m William Foss of Gardiner, ME; **James S.** b 30 Oct. 1853, m Ina Brann of E. Harpswell, ME; **Sarah Eva** b 20 Feb. 1856, m WIlliam Treefant [according to the probate record of Adalade and Jason Rand, Sarah Eva's last name was Flanders and she was of Auburn, ME, in 1904 and 1907]; **Mary E.** b 19 Dec. 1860, m 24 Dc. 1892 William Whitney; **Jordan A.** b 3 May 1858, m 24 Dec. 1891 Jennie E. Allen; **Adalade A.** b 26 Mar. 1863, d 22 Jul. 1907 in Auburn, ME [probate #6075 and her will; probate and will of Jason Rand]; and **Lillian B.** b 25 Nov. 1869, m 22 Dec. 1890 Benjamin Thorne [Lillian B.'s last name was Coombs and she was living in Lewiston in 1904].

RAND, JORDAN - Born ??, d ??, s/o Jason or Samuel and ?? Rand. Children: **Hattie May** m Willard Jones; **Everett** b 29 Apr. 1882; **Dora** b -- Aug. 1883; **Wallace** b -- Aug. 1884; and **Frank** b 1 Aug. 1887.

RAND, REUBIN/REUBEN - Born 28 Nov. 1800, d 25 Jan. 1871 in Lisbon, Maine, s/o Thomas and Abigail (Dyer) Rand. Reubin/Reuben Rand m Mary ----, b 10 May 1801, d 27 Dec. 1875 [letter from Augusta M. Taylor of Higgins, Class. Inst., Charleston, Maine, dated 7 Sep. 1897 to Elder]. Children: **William Augustus** b 27 Dec. 1826, d 26 Apr. 1856; **Josiah Clough** b 23 Nov. 1828, d 2 Mar. 1856, m Therida Dunham of Lisbon, d/o Duncan; **Reuben Daniel** b 10 Jan. 1831, m (1) Pauline Montfort, and m (2) Mary Montfort, and m (3) 27 Jan. 1872 Lena Fuller of Lewiston; **Charles Henry** b 23 Jan. 1833, d 19 Oct. 1853; **John Gilman** b 9 Jan. 1835, d 28 Sep. 1837; **James Benson** b 7 Dec. 1836, d 31 Jan. 1862; **Mary Elizabeth** b 15 Apr. 1839, d 25 Dec. 1863 [*Morning Star* 9 Mar. 1864]; **Ebenezer Eaton** b 27 Apr. 1841, m Georgian Harmon of Lisbon; **John Gilman** b 26 May 1844, d 3 Nov. 1847 [*Morning Star* 8 Dec. 1847]; and **Lavella Alviretta** b 23 Mar. 1848. [Vital Records of Lewiston, Maine, p. 132; will and probate #1041 of Reuben Rand of Lisbon, ME.]

RAND, SAMUEL D. - Born 1802, d 1886, s/o Thomas and ?? Rand. Samuel D. Rand m (1) 6 Jul. 1823 [vital records of Lewiston, Maine, p. 392] Mehitable Courson, b 4 Jul. 1804, d 6 Dec. 1864, d/o Zebulon and Thankful (----) Courson, and m (2) 15 Apr. 1866 Mary Cole (nee Coombs), wid/o Benjamin/Boynton Cole. Children: **Jordan** b 24 Oct. 1823, m 10 Jul. 1847 Margaret Cole, d/o Benjamin/Boynton of Topsham, ME; **Jason King** b 14 Nov. 1824, d 12 Sep. 1892 in Lisbon, ME, or New Portland, ME, m 27 May 1849 Susan Smith of Lisbon; **Thomas** b 19 Sep. 1827 in Lewiston, m 20 Oct. 1852 Clemenia W. Trask, no children; **Nancy Jordan** b 18 Mar. 1830, m (1) Jack P. Smith of New Gloucester, ME, and m (2) Moses Leavitt of Harpswell, ME; **Rebecca**

b 3 Feb. 1833, d 26 Jul. 1848; **James T.** b 11 Jan. 1837, m 19 Nov. 1857 Jno J. Lith of Gra---; **Almeda** (twin) b 11 Jan. 1837 [vital records of Lewiston, Maine, p. 132]; **Samuel** b 17 Apr. 1840, m (1) 5 May 1866 Eliza Brown of Greene, ME, d 25 Jun. 1872, and m (2) 4 Jun. 1875 Emily Lambert of Thorndike, ME, b 13 Dec. 1839 (Samuel had no children); and **Georgiana** b 17 Sep. 1845, d 16 Mar. 1883, m Ferdman H----. [Letter dated 20 Dec. 1893 from Samuel Rand of Brunswick.]

RAND, THOMAS - Born 30 Dec. 1760 in Rye, New Hampshire, d 6 Sep. 1837 age 77 years, s/o ?? Thomas Rand m 20 Mar. 1788 Abigail Dyer, b 1759 in Cape Elizabeth, Maine, d 19 Mar. 1850 age 91 years. Thomas was a soldier in the Revolutionary War. Children: **Thankful** b 27 Oct. 1788, d 1838 in New Portland, m Andrew Jordan; **Barsilla** b 14 Sep. 1792, d 13 Sep. 1861 in Abbott, ME, m Thankful Garcelon; **Elizabeth** b 8 Dec. 1794, d in Shapleigh, ME, m Thomas Mitchell; **Anne** b 1 Aug. 1797, d 16 Nov. 1870 in Lewiston, m (1) Thomas Ham, m (2) Thomas Stewart; **Reubin** b 28 Nov. 1800, d 19 Jan. 1871 in Lisbon, m 29 May 1825 Mary Rand, b 10 May 1801, d 27 Dec. 1875 [A. Taylor, Charleston, ME 1897 letter to Elder], d/o Daniel Rand; **Samuel D.** b 4 Jul. 1802, d 28 Mar. 1886, m pub. 15 Jun. 1823 Mehitable Courson, b 4 Jul. 1804, d 6 Dec. 1864, d/o Zebulon; **Mercy C.** b 27 Oct. 1810, d 1875, m Ivory Courson; and **Abigail** b 4 Jun. 1806, d 27 Feb. 1838, m Nat P. Sleeper. [Vital Records of Lewiston, Maine, p. 66; letter from Samuel Rand of Brunswick, ME, 1893.]

RANDALL, BENJAMIN - Born 3 Aug. 1795, d ??, s/o Ezra and ?? Randall. Benjamin Randall m pub. 17 Nov. 1821 Mary Randall, d/o Isaac. Children: **Humphry** b 21 Sep. 1822, d 23 Oct. 1845, unm; **Holman** b 28 Jan. 1825, d 26 Dec. 1893 in Bethel, ME, unm; **Foster** b 26 Feb. 1827, m Sarah J. Lowell, d/o William; **Arvesta** b 1 Aug. 1829, m Ezra Randall, s/o William; **Alva** b 17 Feb. 1831, d in New Orleans; **Franklin** b -- Jul. 1833, d in CA.; **Sylvanus** b -- Apr. 1835; and **Horace** b -- Sep. 1837, d in the army, 3rd of 7 days' battle. [Vital Records of Lewiston, Maine, p. 134.]

RANDALL, BENJAMIN 2ND - Born 26 Aug. 1823, d 6 Jan. 1878, s/o Levi C. and ?? Randall. Benjamin Randall, 2nd m 16 Nov. 1849 in Lisbon, Maine, Sallie M. Webster, d/o Joseph. Children: **Harriet Jane** b 15 Feb. 1850, d 9 Sep. 1852; **Levi E.** b 28 Aug. 1853, m Marsha E. Prescott, d/o George of Monmouth, ME, (their child: George Percy b 7 Aug. 1877).

RANDALL, CHARLES - Born 1 Sep. 1817, d ??, s/o William and ?? Randall of Litchfield, Maine. Charles Randall m (1) 13 Mar. 1844 Susan E. Johnson, b 21 Mar. 1822 in Dana, Massachusetts, and m (2) Mrs. ---- Lamb of Springfield, Maine. Children: **Theodosia J.** b 17 Aug. 1845 in Springfield, ME, d 8 Oct. 1884 in Winn, ME, m 26 Nov. 1863 S. B. Gates, lived in Winn, ME; **Susan E.** b 6 Sep. 1852, m 17 May 1875 James Stewart; **Adria L.** b 22 Apr. 1855, m 3 Jun. 1875 W. F. Lovejoy, lived in Bangor, ME; **Geo. H.** b 1856 in Winn, ME; and

James D. b 11 Aug. 1858, m 22 Aug. 1882 ---- Carl of MN, lived in Bangor. [Letter from Mrs. S. E. Randall, 1896, of Winn, ME.]

RANDALL, EZRA - Born 1808, d 1894, s/o Ezra and Theoda (Lee) Randall. Ezra Randall lived in St. Francis, Minnesota. He m in Ashburnham, Massachusetts, Ann E. Underwood/Unberhind. [See *Randall Family* by Frank A. Randall, 1943, p. 27-34.]

RANDALL, EZRA - Born 28 Aug. 1764 in Harpswell, Maine, d 10 Jun. 1850 age 86, s/o Ezra and Ann Margaret (Foster) Randall of Topsham, Maine. Ezra Randall m (1) 20/26 Oct. 1785 Mary/Molly Whitten/Whidden, b 18 Jul. 1766, d 1 Aug. 1807, and m (2) 26 Nov. 1807 Theoda Lee (left Ezra and lived with her son James in China, Maine, where she died). *Children by 1st wife*: **William** b 19 Feb. 1787, m Sarah Thompson, d 29 Mar. 1810, lived in Litchfield, ME; **John** b 18 Apr. 1789, d 29 Nov. 1863, m (1) 7 Jan. 1813 Rebecca Taylor, and m (2) Mrs. Lucy Taylor, wid/o Thomas Taylor of Brunswick, ME; **Polly** b 3 Jun. 1791, d in Topsham age 25 years, m 28 Aug. 1808 Robert Hunter of Litchfield; **Peggy** b 29 Mar. 1793, d in Lee age 20 years, m 6 Mar. 1814 James Ames; **Benjamin** b 3 Aug. 1795, d in MN, m pub. 17 Nov. 1821 Polly Randall, d/o Isaac, br/o Ezra of Bowdoin, ME; **Isaac** b 28 May 1797, d 17 Sep. 1872, m pub. 16 Apr. 1818 Susan Oliver; **Levi Chadbourne** b 14 Mar. 1800, d 10 Aug. 1863, m (1) 21 Jan. 1819 Lucy Jordan of Lisbon, ME, and m (2) 22 Jun. 1845 Mrs. Lydia Coombs; **Eleanor** b 4 Oct. 1802, m 9 Mar. 1826 Charles Williams of Lisbon; and **Harriet** b 26 Mar. 1805, d 9 Nov. 1837, m 8 Aug. 1824 James Carville. *Children by 2nd wife*: **Ezra** b 17 Sep. 1808, m 27 Oct. 1839 Eliza Umberhind of MA.; **Harvey** b 12 Apr. 1810, d -- Jun. 1812; **Clarissa** b 1812, d 25 Feb. 1815; **Laura** b 21 Feb. 1814, d 20 Oct. 1838, m 19 Oct. 1834 William Small of Wales, ME; **Jane** b 14 Nov. 1815, unm; **Malinda** b 10 Dec. 1817, m 27 Oct. 1839 William Small of Wales; **Orpha** b 8 Oct. 1819, d 20 Sep. 1826; **Isabella** b 8 Nov. 1821, m John McKenzie, lived in Crow, MN.; and **Foster Lee** b 6 Aug. 1823, m -- Nov. 1856 Elsie J. Lenfest, d/o Peter. [Vital Records of Lewiston, Maine, p. 133; letter from William Small of Fort Fairfield, ME, dated 18 Mar. 1894 to Elder; letter from Ella L. Staples of Bowdoinham, ME, 1890s.]

RANDALL, EZRA - Born 24 Mar. 1796, d ??, 2nd s/o John, Jr. and ?? Randall. Ezra Randall m Mary Given. Children: **Sarah/Sarah Ann** b 8 Nov. 1816, m (1) ----, and m (2) 14 Jan. 1841 Francis Wright; **William/William G.** b 17 Sep. 1818, m 10 Nov. 1844 Pemelia Stetson, d/o Stephen of Lewiston; **May/Mary G.** b 5 Feb. 1820, m 23 Mar. 1843 Phineas Dill of Auburn, ME; **John/John S.** b 6 Aug. 1821, m Ann White, d/o Darius; **Ezra** b 14 Oct. 1823, d 1842, unm; **Dorcas/Dorcas W.** b 8 Mar. 1825, m 22 Jun. 1845 David Given; **Margaret/Margaret Jane** b 18 Sep. 1826, m Charles Beade; **Vesta/Olive Vesta** b 27 Feb. 1828, m (1) Addison Whitman and lived in Auburn, and m (2) James Garland; **Teletus/Zelotes** b 4 Aug. 1830, m (1) Abbie Woodman, and m (2) Alice Skillen; and **Horace/Horace Hewey** b 24 Apr. 1832, m Louisa Bradbury, d -- Aug. 1861. [Vital Records of Lewiston, Maine, p. 133, 384.]

RANDALL, FOSTER - Born 1827, d 20 Jun. 1880, s/o Benjamin and ?? Randall. Foster Randall m 26 Oct. 1852 Sarah Jane Lowell, d -- Sep. 1889, d/o William. Children: **Fannie** b 1 Jan. 1853, m Edward Johnston; **Orpha** b 2 May 1855, m 23 Aug. 1873 Fred H. Storah, lived in Auburn, ME; **Ella** b -- Jun. ----, m 17 Mar. 1880; **Minnie** d 30 May 1880; **Gertie** twin; and **Gracie** twin.

RANDALL, FRED E. - Born ??, d ??, s/o ?? Child: **Freddie A.** b 2 Apr. 1890.

RANDALL, HENRY T. - Born 22 Mar. 1834, d ??, s/o William and Mehiatable Randall. William Randall was the s/o Ezra Randall. Henry T. Randall m 24 Nov. 1857 Ellen Lowell. Children: **Mabel** b 15 Nov. 1858; **Jessie L.** b 14 Mar. 1861; **Harry** b 31 Dec. 1863, d 18 Dec. 1888; and **Percy** b 18 Jan. 1867, d 27 Feb. 1870. [Letter dated 18 Jan. 1896 from Henry T. Randall of Lee, ME, to Elder.]

RANDALL, HERBERT L. - Born ??, d ??, s/o ?? Child: **Dora D.** b 16 Aug. 1891.

RANDALL, ISAAC - Born 28 May 1797, d 17 Sep. 1872, s/o ?? Isaac Randall m (1) Susannah Oliver, d 27 Aug. 1851, and m (2) 25 Feb. 1855 Mrs. Joanna Coffin of Auburn, Maine. Children: **Susannah** b 26 Jun. 1818 in Lewiston, m John Lamont; **Mary Ann** b 18 Apr. 1820 in Litchfield, ME, d 18 Jun. 1894 in N. Berwick, ME, m James McCorrison; **Elisabeth** b 9 Oct. 1822 in Litchfield, m (1) 31 Jul. 1842 Arthur Maxwell of Webster, ME, d 9 Sep. 1874, and m (2) 10 Apr. 1886 William Chase of Litchfield; **Isaac** b 14 Nov. 1824 in Litchfield, d 9 Nov. 1839; **William** b 9 Oct. 1827, d 11 Apr. 1893, m 1 Jan. 1851 Mary Spofford, b 15 Jul. 1823, d/o Greenleaf; **Harvey** b 5 Sep. 1829 in Litchfield, d 11 Nov. 1839; **Jane B.** b 1 Jan. 1832 in Litchfield, m 11 Jul. 1852 Albert Maxwell of Webster, ME, d 16 Apr. 1880 in Mendicino, CA, s/o William; **Oliver E.** b 8 Mar. 1835 in Litchfield, d 17 Oct. 1887, m 13 Feb. 1856 Margaret J. Read, d/o Ammi; and **Elvira** b 26 Mar. 1837 in Litchfield, m 8 Mar. 1855 Robert A. Field, b 30 Jan. 1835. [Letter dated 17 Oct. 1893 from Mary E. Maxwell of Lewiston, ME, to Elder.]

RANDALL, ISAAC - Born 29 Nov. 1813, d 24 Jun. 1883, s/o John and ?? Randall of Litchfield, Maine. Isaac Randall m 12 Apr. 1838 Eliza B. Libby of Litchfield, d 2 Jan. 1892. Children: **Sarah R.** b 27 Sep. 1840, d 30 Jun. 1886 in Bridgeport, CT, m 11 Jun. 1867 Charles F. Davis of Gardiner, ME; **John A.** b 8 May 1845, d 11 Oct. 1850; **Philiria E.** b 18 Apr. 1847, d 31 Mar. 1872 in Litchfield, unm; **Martha E.** b 13 Feb. 1850, m 15 Nov. 1882 Rufus C. Williams (Chick) of Boston, MA, d 3 Sep. 1887; **James J.** b 11 Oct. 1853, d 25 Feb. 1855; **George J.** b 27 Jan. 1856, d 2 Jan. 1863; and **Mary E.** b 8 Jan. 1860, d 8 Jul. 1892 in Litchfield Plains, ME.

RANDALL, ISAIAH - Born ??, d 12 Feb. 1905, s/o Levi C. and ?? Randall. Isaiah Randall m 27 Aug. 1853 Mary Dingley. Children: **Eldora A. d 25 Mar. 1878 age 25 years; and **Edwin** E. moved to Garland, ME, m Frank Orgon of Tampa, FL. [Will of Isaiah Randall #5323 probate.]

RANDALL, JAMES - Born 1794, d 1872, s/o John, Sr. and ?? Randall. James Randall m 8 Jan. 1815 [vital records of Lewiston, Maine, p. 383] Sally/Sarah Given, d -- Mar. 1852. Children: **Louisa Jane** b 24 Oct. 1816, lived in Dover, ME, m John Carlton of Wellington; **John Hewey** b 19 May 1818, d -- Jul. 1870, m 1846 Mary A. Bennett of Wellington; **Sally H.** b 29 Apr. 1820, d 20 Apr. 1855, m Dan Read; **Mary Given** b 29 Apr. 1820, d 18 Nov. 1890, m Jefferson Foss; **Theodosia Wadley** b 21 Sep. 1822, m Jacob True of Sangerville, ME; **Ann Maria** b 25 Dec. 1825, d 10 Jan. 1879, m James O. Foss; **James Stanwood Given** b 5 Sep. 1827, m -- Dec. 1851 Harriet K. Whaff of Auburn; **Martha E.** b 28 Jun. 1830, lived in Boston, MA, m Andrew Babb; **Samuel C.** b 1 Jun. 1833, d in the Army, unm; and **Ezra R.** b 29 Oct. 1835, d in the Army, unm. [Vital Records of Lewiston, Maine, p. 133.]

RANDALL, JAMES STANWOOD - Born 5 Sep. 1827, d 12 Aug. 1902 in Lewiston, s/o James and ?? Randall. James Randall m Harriet (Whaff) ---- [named in the will of James S. Randall probate #5058]. Children: **Henrietta** b 19 May 1858, d 15 Sep. 1858; **Corn** [sic] **Eva** b 2 Jun. 1861, d 25 Mar. 1862; **Fredda Abbit** b 14 Jan. 1865, d 20 Jul. 1865; and **Harriet Emma** b 14 Jun. 1867.

RANDALL, JOHN - Born ??, d ??, s/o ?? John Randall immigrated from Bristol, England, about 1660, and settled in Scituate, Massachusetts. He was the father of Joseph, who was the father of Benjamin, who was the father of Ezra. Ezra Randall settled in Topsham, Maine, then in Bowdoinham, Maine. John Randall m Margaret Foster. Children: **Margaret** b 6 Aug. 1762; **Ezra** b 23 Aug. 1764; **Heatherby** b 26 Aug. 1766; **John** b 24 Feb. 1769; **Nabby; Joseph; Isaiah** b 4 Nov. 1772; **Isaac** b 1 Jun. 1776; and **Elisabeth** b 28 Nov. 1779.

RANDALL, JOHN - Born 27 Feb. 1769, d ??, s/o Ezra and Margaret (Foster) Randall. John Randall m pub. 8 Feb. 1792 Sarah Howey (?). Children: **James** q.v.; **Ezra** b 24 Mar. 1796, m 3 Jun. 1816 Mary Given of Wales; **Sarah** b 9 Apr. 1799, m 16 Jun. 1818 John Given of Brunswick, ME; **Mary** b 2 May 1802, m 5 Apr. 1821 Benjamin Given; and **Margaret** b 19 May 1805, d 3 Nov. 1866, m 8 Feb. 1827 Ammi R. Read, d 9 Oct. 1878 age 77 years 5 months. [Vital Records of Lewiston, Maine, p. 65.]

RANDALL, JOHN - Born 18 Aug. 1789, d 29 Nov. 1868, s/o Ezra and ?? Randall. John Randall m 7 Jan. 1813 Rebecca Taylor, b 13 Apr. 1791, d 15 Sep. 1853, d/o Thomas of Lewiston. Children: **Isaac** b 29 Nov. 1813, d 24 Jun. 1885, m 12 Apr. 1838 Eliza P. Libby, b 14 Sep. 1817, d/o James; **Daniel** b 4 Oct. 1817, d 4 Sep. 1887 in Richmond, ME, m 7 Apr. 1844 Julia A. Williams; and **Sarah E.** b 12 Apr. 1825, lived in Pottertown, m 28 Apr. 1844 William G. Williams, s/o Joseph of Litchfield, ME. [Letter from Martha E. Williams dated Aug. 1895 of Litchfield, ME, to Elder.]

RANDALL, LEVI C. - Born 14 Mar. 1800, d 10 Aug. 1863 age 63 years, s/o Ezra and ?? Randall. Levi C. Randall m (1) 21 Jan. 1819 Lucy Jordan of Lisbon, Maine, and m (2) 22 Jun. 1845 Mrs. Lydia* Coombs, d/o Levi Hammond of Lisbon. Children: **Harriet*** b 22 Jun. 1822, m James Deane, lived in Lowell, ME, with James Dain; **Benjamin*** b 26 Aug. 1823, d 6 Jan. 1873, m Sally Webber, lived on Park Street near stable in Lewiston; **Isaiah*** b 30 Jul. 1827, m 27 Aug. 1853 Mary Dingley; **Ellen C.*** b 5 Sep. 1849, m 6 Sep. 1868 Abram A. Littlefield, lived in Auburn, ME, and Cambridge, ME; **Anna Lucy*** d 1865, buried at Lisbon Plains, ME, unm; **Emma A.*** d 1869 at Lisbon Plains, unm; **Lavinia C.***/**Vinnie B.** d 15 Nov. 1879, m 14 Nov. 1877 Edwin Nelson; and **Addie B.*** b 24 Sep. 1859, m 24 Sep. 1889 James C. Howard. [* Indicates persons named in Levi Randall's will & probate #520.]

RANDALL, OLIVER - Born 8 Mar. 1835, d 17 Oct. 1887 (?), s/o Isaac and ?? Randall. Isaac Randall was the s/o Ezra. Children: **Affie E.** b 21 Oct. 1857, m (1) 18 Feb. 1874 Willie Frank Claray, and m (2) T. R. Herbest, and m (3) 21 Aug. 1880 Garcelon Hopkins; **Susie M.** b 23 Aug. 1859, m 31 Dec. 1876 Hartwell S. Becker; **Grace Read** b 16 Feb. 1861, m 30 Aug. 1883 James A. Sampson; and **Jesse N.** b 19 Jun. 1869 in OH., m (1) 6 Jul. 1889 Lavona Becker, and m (2) -- Feb. 1893 Belle Randall, d/o Zelotes.

RANDALL, RUFUS D. - Born 11 Apr. 1831, d ??, s/o William and ?? Randall. Rufus D. Randall m (1) 9 Nov. 18-- Hattie A. Williams, d 12 Mar. 1865, and m (2) 15 Dec. 1867 Elizabeth D. Patrie, d 15 Jul. 1873, and m (3) 2 Sep. 1874 Catherine Ann Earl of Michigan City, Indiana, b 20 Apr. 1840 in Lake County, Ohio, d/o Henry and Catherine (Siphers) Earl of N. B. Canada. *Children by 1st wife*: **Ava E.** b 14 Aug. 1857 in Lisbon, ME; and **Charles F.** b 2 Nov. 1862 in Lisbon, m -- Oct. 1888 Hattie Fair. *Children by 2nd wife*: **Hattie A.** b 7 Oct. 1869; **William D.** b 4 Feb. 1871, d 29 Oct. 1872; and **Eddie E.** b 9 Jul. 1873, d 18 Sep. 1873. *Child by 3rd wife*: **Rilla** b 10 Jun. 1875, m 2 Dec. 1896 William W. Quigley. [Letter dated 22 Feb. 1897 from Rufus D. Randall of Kingsbury, La Port Co., IN.]

RANDALL, ZELOTES - b 4 Aug. 1830, d ??, s/o Ezra, 2nd and Mary (Given) Randall. Zelotes Randall m (1) 24 Apr. 1855 Abbie Woodman, and m (2) 30 Apr. 1873 Alice Skillen. *Children by 1st wife*: **Fred E.** b 28 Sep. 1856, d 17 Sep. 1887; and **Amelia** b 3 Sep. 1860, m 6 Jun. 1887 Charles Smith of New Auburn [formerly of Danville, ME]. *Children by 2nd wife*: **Eda M.** b 21 Jun. 1873, m Harry C. Patridge; **Salle C.** b 3 Feb. 1876, m Jesse N. Randall; and **Guy B.** b 18 Oct. 1879. [See *Lewiston Journal*, 13 Nov. 1915.]

RANDALL, WILLIAM - Born ??, 22 Sep. 1857, s/o Ezra and ?? Randall of Lewiston. William Randall lived in Lee, Maine. He m (1) Sally Thompson, d/o Col. Jack, and m (2) 28 Nov. 1816 Mehitable

Woodard, b 22 Sep. 1795, d -- Jun. 1883. Children: **Mary** b 11 Jun. 1811, d 21 Mar. 1815; **Martha** b 9 Apr. 1813, m William Cushman; **Charles** b 1 Sep. 1817, d 29 Mar. 1894, m 13 Mar. 1844 Susan Johnson; **Mary** b 28 Dec. 1818, m 6 Apr. 1846 Denman Bartlett; **William H.** b 26 Nov. 1826, d 2 Mar. 1884, m Margaret Kimball; **Ezra** b 12 Oct. 1823; **Harriet C.** b 24 Oct. 1828, m 25 Jan. 1856 Birks Comforth o' :, b 30 May 1825 in Oakland, lived in Sutton, MN; **Rufus D.** q.v.; y T. b 22 Mar. 1834; and **John W.** b 10 Dec. 1836, moved to Bradf PA. [Letter from John W. Randall, 1896, to Elder.]

RANDALL, WILLIAM M. - Born ??, d ??, s/o Isaac and William M. Randall. Children: **Herbert L.** b 21 Sep. 1851, m (1) 1886 Winne Compr, and m (2) 23 Apr. 1890 N. Duherst; **Cora B.** b 21 Sep. 1851, m 10 Mar. 1874 Charles T. Nevens; **Ella D.** b 24 Sep. 1855, m -- Nov. 1897 William N. Miller; **Edwin A.** b 1 Sep. 1858, m 20 Jun. 1885 Nellie Cross of Belfast, ME; **Fred E.** b 16 Feb. 1861; **Willie Berton** b 7 Oct. 1864; and **Mabel** b 21 Jun. 1867.

RAY, ALMON S. - Born ??, d ??, s/o ?? Almon S. Ray m 18 Aug. 1879 Sarah J. LaFrance.

RAY, ALONZO M. - Born 17 Jul. 1850 in Greene, Maine, d ??, s/o ?? Alonzo M. Ray m Clara E. Mottram, d/o David Mottram. Children: **Edwin Sprague** [vital records in the Maine State Archives] b 7 Jul. 1882; and **Nellie A.** b 26 Mar. 1886.

RAY, ARTHUR W. - Born ??, d ??, s/o Elbridge and ?? Ray. Arthur W. Ray m Minnie E. Fogg. Children: **Ernest Arthur** b 5 Jul. 1895; **Reuben Orland** b 22 Oct. 1901; and **Valmar L.** b 22 Jan. 1903.

RAY, BENJAMIN - Born ??, d ??, s/o ?? Benjamin Ray m pub. 5 Oct. 1800 Nancy Bean, d/o John of Lewiston. Children: **Betsey** b 9 Nov. 1801; and **Nancy** b 13 Sep. 180 [Vital Records of Lewiston, Maine, p. 67, 385.]

RAY, CHARLES H. - Born in Minot, Maine, d 8 Nov. 1900 age 73 years and 3 months at Auburn, Maine, s/o Jonathan and Phebe (Vickery) Ray. Charles H. Ray m (1) in Auburn, Maine, Sophia (Merrow) ----, d 3 Jul. 1874 age 51 years 2 months 25 days, buried in Fletcher Cemetery on Fletcher Rd. in Auburn, Maine, and m (2) Hannah Maria Shaw, living in Portland, Maine. Children: **Hiram M.** b 19 Mar. 1856, d 14 Apr. 1856; **Franklin** b 7 Sep. 1857, d -- Nov. 1857; **Lizzie Maira** b 20 Sep. 1861, d 14 Dec. 1861; **Lucretia Nellie** b 5 Apr. 1864, d 24 Mar. 1865; **Hiram F.** b 24 May 1867, d 1 Aug. 1867; and **Charles H.** b 19 Jul. 1853, d 1903.

RAY, CHARLES H. - Born 19 Jul. 1853, d 25 Mar. 1903, s/o Charles H. and ?? Ray. Charles H. Ray m 27 Dec. 1884 Rose M. Merrill, b 31 Aug. 1859, d/o John and Sophronia (Youland) Merrill of Lisbon, Maine. Child: **Amina E.** b 3 Jan. 1888.

RAY, CHARLES H. - Born 12 Aug. 1827, d 7 Dec. 1880, s/o Jonathan and ?? Ray. Charles H. Ray m (1) 13 Apr. 1852 Sophia Merrow, and m (2) H. Maria Shaw. Children: **Charles Henry** b 19 Jul. 1853, d 25 Mar. 1903; **Hiram M.** b 19 Mar. 1856, d 14 Apr. 1856; **Franklin** b 7 Sep. 1857, d 10 Nov. 1857; **Lizzie Maria** b 20 Sep. 1861, d 14 Dec. 1861; **Lucretia Nellie** b 5 Apr. 1864, d 24 Mar. 1865; and **Hiram F.** b 24 May 1867, d 1 Aug. 1867.

RAY, DANIEL HOYT - Born at Greene, Maine, d ??, s/o Reuben and Annie (Chesley) Ray. Daniel Ray m Laura Etta Harmon of Naples, Maine. Children: **Charles W.**; **Edgar**; **Etta**; **Ethelbert**; **Vernett**; and **Lilla E.** b 1 Oct. 1875 [birth record of Lilla MSA].

RAY, ELBRIDGE W. - Born 15 Jun. 1841, s/o Ruben and ?? Ray. Elbridge W. Ray m 10 May 1861 Jane L. Harmon. Children: **Mary A.** b 2 Mar. 1863, m Benjamin T. Howett; and **Arthur W.** b 15 Aug. 1873, m Minnie E. Fogg.

RAY, JAMES - Born 1826, d 18 Jul. 1870 age 44 years, s/o Samuel and ?? Ray. James Ray m Cordelia Fernald, d 28 Feb. 1900 age 69 years 5 months 15 days, d/o Samuel Fernald of Livermore, Maine. Children: **Ada Florence** b 12 Mar. 1856; **Anna S.** b 30 Mar. 1861, d -- Aug. 1867; and **Fred** b 1 Mar. 1870.

RAY, JONATHAN - Born 7 Dec. 1781, d 6 Dec. 1859 age 77 years, s/o Samuel, Sr. and ?? Ray. Jonathan Ray m (1) pub. 22 Nov. 1812 Susanna Chamberlain of Minot, Maine, and m (2) 1820 Phebe Vickery, d/o Matthias and Elizabeth (Wagg) Vickery. Jonathan Ray lived in Auburn, Maine, near Littlefield's Tavern and was buried in old cemetery near the house where he lived. Children: **Charles H.** b 12 Aug. 1827, d 13 Nov. 1900, m 13 Apr. 1852 Sophia Merrow of Auburn, d 3 Jul. 1874, and m (2) 3 Jan. 1877 Maria H. Shaw; **Isaiah** b 24 Aug. 1829, m 22 Apr. 1858 Olive W. Nason; **Julia Ann** b 17 Sep. 1833, m (1) ---- Merrill, and m (2) ---- Woodbury; **Caroline** b 2 Nov. 1835; **James** b 7 Jun. 1852 (?); **I. Jones** b 7 Jun. 1842 (?), d 1866; **Nathaniel** b 14 May 1825, d 21 Nov. 1900, unm; **George Washington** b 13 Jun. 1821, d 1871, m Rebecca ----; **Ammi R.** b 22 Oct. 1831, d 1859; and **Susan** b 15 Jun. 1823, m ---- Ayer. [See Starbird's Records. Starbird lists three older children: George b 1821; Susan b 1823; Nathaniel b 1825. Minot VR Book 1, p. 77; will of Jonathan Ray #255; vital records of Danville, Maine, p. ?; cemetery records of P. Lane, 1974.]

RAY, JONATHAN - Born ??, d 3 Mar. 1867 [probate #883 of Jonathan Ray], s/o ?? Jonathan Ray m Elsie P. Curtis. Children: **Frank L.** b 1 Mar. 1854, d 13 Jan. 1855 age 10 months; **Henrietta A.** b 1850, d 24 Dec. 1860 age 10 years 4 months; **Hattie E.** b 1858, d 27 Dec. 1860 age 2 years 6 months; **Fred A.** b 16 Oct. 1860, d 26 Mar. 1899; **Ella**; **Fannie E.** b 28 Feb. 1863, d 20 Mar. 1892; and **Ida**.

RAY, MARY C. - Born ??, d ??, d/o ?? Mary C. Ray m (1) Augustus Tobin, and m (2) Almon Brown, and m (3) John Bishop.

RAY, RACHEL - Born ??, d ??, d/o ?? Rachel Ray m 1 Jan. 1854 William W. Peakes.

RAY, REUBEN - Born 16 Oct. 1804, d 5 Mar. 1906 age 101 years 4 months 17 days, s/o Thomas and ?? Ray. Reuben Ray lived almost 102 years. He m 1834 Annie Chesley of Rome, Maine. Children: **Daniel H.**; **Mary Ann**; **Elbridge W.** b 15 Jun. 1841, d 1895 of Schattus, m 10 May 1861 Jane L. Harmon, b 2 Mar. 1846; **Sophronia**; and **Rhoda F.** m 1867 Calvin G. Estes of Lewiston. [See *Lewiston Journal*, 19 Oct. 1904, Reuben's 100th birthday.]

RAY, SAMUEL - Born ??, d ??, s/o William and Prudence (Hatch) Ray. Samuel Ray m Caroline P. Ridley. Children: **James R.** m Cordelia D. Fernald of Livermore, ME, b 13 Sep. 1830, d 28 Feb. 1900 in Lewiston age 69 years 5 months 15 days, d/o Sam Fernald; **Beulah Ann** m David Rounds; **Mary Caroline** d 11 Aug. 1876, m (1) Almon Brown, and m (2) John Bishop, and m (3) pub. 30 Jun. 1873 Augustus Tobin; **Samuel** b 26 May 1840 in Brunswick, ME, [his death record states "born in Auburn, Maine, d 7 Sep. 1906, Lewiston, Maine, occ' mill operative, MSA], m (1) 1862 Martha J. Orr of Bath, ME, d 4 Oct. 1877 age 49 years, and m (2) 1 Jun. 1878 Sarah Ann Chutham, d/o Joseph of Lewiston; and **William A.** b 17 Apr. 1844, d 4 Aug. 1903 age 59 years 3 months 17 days, m 22 Sep. 1868 Mary J. Perkins.

RAY, SAMUEL - Born ??, d ??, s/o ?? Samuel Ray m 1 Jun. 1878 Sarah A. Cheetham.

RAY, SAMUEL - Born ??, d ??, s/o ?? Samuel Ray m Hannah ----. Children: **Hannah** b 1 Oct. 1759, m Jeremiah Jordan of Minot, ME; **Abigail** b 3 Aug. 1763, m Josiah Dill; **Benjamin** b 12 Feb. 1769, m pub. 5 Oct. 1800 Nancy Bean, d/o John; **William** b 27 Jun. 1771, d 5 Feb. 1855 age 82 years 1 month 27 days, m Prudence Hatch, d 7 Feb. 1855 age 75 years 10 months 28 days, d/o Samuel; **Jonathan** b 7 Dec. 1780, m 24 Dec. 1812 Susanna Chamberlain of Minot; **Molly** b 3 Dec. 1783, m 16 Mar. 1805 John Nevens of Pejepscot, ME; and **Lucy** b 1786, d -- Jul. 1854 in Rangeley, ME, m William Lowell. [Vital Records of Lewiston, Maine, p. 66.]

RAY, SAMUEL - Born 26 May 1840, d ??, s/o Samuel and ?? Ray. Samuel Ray m (1) 1862 Martha J. Orr of Bath, d 4 Oct. 1877, and m (2) 1 Jun. 1878 Sarah Ann Cheetham, b 31 Dec. 1855 at Fall River, Massachusetts, d/o Joseph and Jane (Cooper) Cheetham. Children: **Carry Maud** b 21 Aug. 1879, m 24 Jun. 1903 Melvin G. Small; and **Frank S.** b 23 Jul. 1881, d 16 Jan. 1883.

RAY, THOMAS - Born ??, d 6 Jan. 1835 in Greene, Maine, age 55 years [Pearce Cemetery in Greene], s/o ?? Thomas Ray m pub. 1 Mar. 1802, m 25 Mar. 1802 [vital records of Lewiston, Maine, p. 435] Fear Hatch, d 14 Apr. 1871, d/o Samuel. Children: **Jonathan** b 5 Sep. 1802 in Livermore Falls, ME, m Esther Mason of Minot, ME, d in Livermore, ME; **Isaac** b 26 Dec. 1803, m Aurilla Morrill of Minot; **Ruth** b 31 Jan. 1807, m Benjamin Lane of Greene; **Reuben** b 16 Nov.

1807, m Ann Chesley, d 12 Mar. 1883 (1882?); **Lucy** b 24 Sep. 1812, d 10 Nov. 1889, unm.; **Sally** b 24 Apr. 1815, d 31 Jun. 1838 age 23 years 10 months; **May** b 19 Dec. 1810, d 6 Aug. 1829 age 18 years 8 months 17 days, unm.; **Susanna** b 11 Apr. 1818, d 26 Jul. 1882; **Thomas** b 4 Jul. 1820; **Wealthy** b 5 May 1822, d 15 Jun. 1872; **Albion** b 21 Jan. 1824, d 22 Sep. 1869 (?), unm; **William** b 18 Jan. 1816; and **William** d 1811. [Vital Records of Lewiston, Maine, p. 67.]

RAY, VERNETT L. - Born ??, d ??, s/o Daniel and ?? Ray. Vernett L. Ray m 10 Jul. 1893 Mary Locke, d/o Lynt and Elizabeth (Foss) Locke. Children: **Norman** b 1 Jun. 1897; **Florence Bertice** b 1 Nov. 1898, d 25 Oct. 1904; and **Virgil Vernette** b 8 May 1901, d 1965 [Pine Street Cemetery, Auburn, ME].

RAY, WILLIAM - Son of Samuel, Sr., b 27 Jun. 1771, d 5 Jul. 1855 age 82 at Auburn, Maine [MSA card file], m pub. 11 Mar. 1798 Prudence Hatch, d/o Samuel. Children: **S a m u e l** b 28 Apr. 1799, d 14 Mar. 1861 age 61 years 10 months 16 days, m Caroline P. Ridley, b 23 Jan. 1809, d 26 Sep. 1892; **Jonathan** m Elsie P. Curtis (their children: Ella, Fannie, and Ida), d/o John; **W i l l i a m** b -- Mar. 1819, d 30 Jul. 1839, m Alvary C. Pullen; **M a r t h a** m (1) William Warren Knowlton, and m (2) John Boutelle, and m ---- Pullen; **Abigail** m 1834 John Curtis, both of Minot, ME [*Morning Star* issue 1 May 1834]; **Sarah** d 4 Jun. 1867, m ---- Underhill; **A n n** m 8 May 1843 George Moore of Brunswick, ME; and **Hannah** m (1) Moses Allen of Brunswick, and m (2) Jeremiah Jordan.

RAY, WILLIAM A. - Born ??, d 4 Aug. 1903, s/o ?? William A. Ray m 22 Sep. 1868 Mary J. Perkins. Children: **Wm. Jr.**; **Lutalma** m ---- Mitchell [will of Wm. Ray #5156.]

RAY, WILLIAM A. JR. - Born 28 Jul. 1875, d ??, s/o William and ?? Ray. William A. Ray, Jr. m 12 Dec. 1900 Winifred White of Bowdoin, Maine, b 1 Aug. 1877, d/o Isaac and Phemah G. Bunker. Children: **Theda A.** b 21 Jun. 1904; and **Theo A.** b 21 Jun. 1904, d 22 Jun. 1904.

READ, ADOLPHUS S. - Born ??, d ??, s/o ?? Children: **Walter A.** b 17 Feb. 1873; and **Alice Gertrude** b 6 Apr. 1889.

READ, ALVAH J. - Born 29 Jan. 1828, d 27 May 1861, s/o Ammi and ?? Read. Alvah J. Read m Sarah Jordan [probate #297 and will of Alvah Read]. Child: **Everett E.**

READ, A M M I - Born ??, d ??, s/o ?? Ammi Read m 8 Feb. 1827 [vital records of Lewiston, Maine, p. 434] Margaret Randall. Children: **Alva J.** b 29 Jan. 1828, d 27 May 1861, m 13 Feb. 1855 Sarah J. Jordan of Webster, ME, b -- Oct. 1830, d/o Benjamin and Nancy (Pray); **Margaret J.** b 22 Sep. 1838, m Oliver Randall.

READ, AMMI C. - Born ??, d ??, s/o ?? Ammi C. Read m 8 Feb. 1827 Margaret Randall, b 19 May 1805, d 3 Nov. 1866.

READ, CHARLES T. - Born 8 Oct. 1795, d 19 Jan. 1877, s/o Lemuel and ?? Read. Charles T. Read m 13 Nov. 1828 Cynthia Swift [*Eastern Argus* 27 Jan. 1829], d 1 Mar. 1883 age 80 years. Children: **Mary Jane** b 24 Sep. 1829, unm, d 1845; **Amanda E.** b 24 Feb. 1829, d 1873; **Edwin** b 20 Sep. 1832; **Edgar** b 20 Sep. 1832; **Mark L.** b 29 Apr. 1835, m Mrs. Augusta Wentworth; **Charles A.** b 30 Nov. 1838, d 13 Oct. 1895 (their child: Mark L., and his child: Mark L.). [Vital Records of Lewiston, Maine, p. 131.]

READ, DAN - Born 27 Feb. 1766, d ??, s/o ?? Dan Read m Susannah Hart, b 18 Jan. 1770. Children: **Martha** b 7 Dec. 1789, m 8 May 1808 Richard D. Harris; **Samuel** b 6 May 1791, d -- Oct. 1881, m int. -- Apr. 1816 Hulda Nash; **John** b 25 Jan. 1793, d 28 Nov. 1829; **Sarah** b 28 Sep. 1794, m int. 5 Dec. 1811 John Nash; **Jacob** b 22 Jun. 1796, m -- Apr. 1817 Mercy Goff of Minot, ME; **Stephen** b 21 Nov. 1798; **Ammi C.** b 8 May 1801; **Louisa F.** b 8 Oct. 1803, d 11 Sep. 1821 age 18 years; **Debby** b 14 Sep. 1805, d 1 Nov. 1812 age 7 years; **Mary** b 2 Mar. 1808, m Stephen Raynes of Auburn, ME; **Joseph F.** b 14 Nov. 1810; **Dan** b 25 Aug. 1812; **Lemuel?** b 2 Sep. 1815, d 26 Mar. 1895. [Difficult to read last two names. Vital Records of Lewiston, Maine, p. 67.]

READ, FRANK H. - Born 3 May 1847, d 16 Oct. 1922 age 75 years 5 months 3 days, s/o ?? Frank H. Read m Mary Conant. Children: **Mabel M.** b 29 Sep. 1880; and **Frank A.** b 23 May 1885, d 19 Jul. 1968, buried in Oak Hill Cemetery, Auburn, ME.

READ, HART - Born ??, d ??, s/o ?? Children: **Eugene** b 5 Jun. 1856, m (1) 4 Nov. 1882 Ella Carville, and m (2) 1886 Ella Getchell; **Frank A.** b 7 Mar. 1861, m 28 Jul. 1888 Sarah H. Jordan; and **Isaac M.** b 9 Jul. 1865.

READ, ICHABOD - Born ??, d 10 Dec. 1797, s/o ?? Ichabod Read m Ann ----. Children: **Oliver** b 21 Feb. 1779, d 17 Jun. 1850, m 2 Sep. 1801 Catherine Hart, b 11 Apr. 1780, d 23 Jul.. 1854; **Betsy** b 29 Sep. 1782, d 22 Jan. 1855, m (1) 21 Apr. 1805 James Nevens of Bangor, ME, and m (2) 19 Jan. 1817 John P. Rand, d 23 Jul. 1839; **Miranda** b 12 Sep. 1784, d 8 Oct. 1846 age 62 years, m 12 Aug. 1804 Al Moses Sprague; **Polly** b 3 Jun. 1786, d 29 Nov. 1864, m 2 Dec. 1804 Joseph Dill, d 14 Oct. 1861; **Nancy** b 23 Jun. 1788, m 10 Mar. 1811 Daniel Austin; **Sophia** b 18 May 1790, m 10 Jun. 1810 Samuel Collins of Hallowell, ME; **Ichabod** b 12 Jul. 1792, m 1820 Ruth Hewey of Topsham, ME; and **Russell** b 24 Jun. 1795 and lived in Greene, ME, m 23 Nov. 1817 Sally Sprague of Greene, b 1794, d/o Col. William and Anna Marrow. [Vital Records of Lewiston, Maine, p. 65.]

READ, JACOB - Born ??, d ??, s/o ?? Children: **Grace** m George Bean, b 23 Mar. 1818 in Portland, ME, (their child: Ana Stone Bean b 2 Apr. 1855, m 10 Aug. 1880 Charles A. Gilmore); **Vilroy**; **Lois**; and **Mabel**.

READ, JACOB HAWES - Born 22 Jun. 1796 in Vassalboro, Maine, d 17 May 1879, s/o ?? Jacob H. Read "as a young man lived in Minot and Lewiston. In 1822 moved a small building from Lewiston to Danville, taking advantage of thick ice to provide a smooth highway." [see Starbird's *Annals of Danville*, compiled before 1960, unpublished typescript at the Androscoggin Historical Society in Auburn, Maine]. He m 13 May 1817 Mercy Goff of Minot, b 1798, d 2 Jan. 1858, d/o James and Ann (Stubbs) Goff. Children: **D a n** b 16 Jun. 1818, m 22 Aug. ---- Sarah Randall, d 20 Apr. 1855; **James Goff** b 18 Apr. 1820, m 1 Jan. 1846 Sarah Littlefield of Auburn; **L a u r a** b 6 Mar. 1822, m 9 Feb. 1843 Thomas Littlefield, b 15 Aug. 1818; **Rowland Freeman** b 1 Feb. 1824 in Danville, ME, d 27 Dec. 1929, m 4 Nov. 1847 Rebecca C. Morse; **William G.** b 22 May 1826, m (1) 31 Dec. 1857 Jennie Short, m (2) Lucy Runnels; **L o i s** b 22 Aug. 1828, d 1878 in Boston, m pub. 17 Oct. 1850 George Sykes; **Abigail** b 27 Jun. 1830, m 30 Sep. 1851 James R. Hoys; **J a c o b H.** b 26 Aug. 1834, m (1) Ellen Grendale of MN, and m (2) Mrs. Ellen N. Timcon of St. Anthony, MN.; **Rachel** b 22 Sep. 1832, m Soleman Gorham; **Frederick D.** b 14 Oct. 1836, was a baker in Togus, ME, 11 Jan. 1921 (Starbird's Records), m 28 Feb. 1863 Margery H. Strout; and **Helen** b 29 Apr. 1838, d 1877 in Portland, ME, m 20 Oct. 1858 George L. Swett of Portland.

READ, JOHN N. - Born 4 Sep. 1836, d ??, s/o Capt. Samuel and ?? Read. John N. Read m (1) Viola A. Heyford, d/o G. and Tilpia (Barrows), and m (2) Assenett Taylor of Canton, Maine. Children: **Arthur E.** b 30 Jun. 1833, d 19 Jul. 1871; **Telepha Bray** b 11 Jul. 1855, m 24 Dec. 1878 Edwin Thompson; **Harry R.** m Esther Brett (their children: **Fannie E.**; and **Esther**).

R E A D , J O H N P. - Born ??, d ??, s/o ?? John P. Read m 19 Jan. 1817 Mrs. Betsy Read Nevens, d 22 Jan. 1855 age 72 years. Child: **Amelia S.** b 16 Jun. 1820, d 17 Oct. 1853. [Vital Records of Lewiston, Maine, p. 129, 435.]

READ, JONATHAN - Born 8 Aug. 1752, d 2 Mar. 1838, s/o ?? Jonathan Read m Dorothy ---, b 3 Nov. 1764, d 18 Mar. 1834. Children: **Dorothy** b 5 Sep. 1787, d 3 Jan. 1851; **Abigail** b 24 Dec. 1789, d 31 Jan. 1847; **Rufus** b 29 Mar. 1793; **Samuel** b 11 Oct. 1794, d -- Nov. 1794; **Amos M.** b 18 Oct. 1795; **Samuel** b 15 Mar. 1798, d 18 Nov. 1848, m Betsy Read, d/o Lemuel and Mary Hart; **E l i z a M.** b 5 Dec. 1799; **John B.** b 2 Dec. 1801; **Daniel B.** b 9 Jan. 1804, d 28 Nov. 1872; **May Ann** b 7 Oct. 1807; **Louisa S.** b 9 Dec. 1809; and **Leonard F.** b 18 Feb. 1811, d 11 Mar. 1811.

READ, JOSEPH F. - Born in Lewiston, d ??, s/o ?? Joseph F. Read m Mary R. Sturgis, b 13 Aug. 1804, d 20 Apr. 1882, d/o David Sturgis of Norridgewock, Maine. Children: **Lucy Ann P.** b 10 Nov. 1834, d 22 Feb. 1836; **Lucy Ann P.** b 12 Dec. 1836, m 13 Jan. 1858 at Gorham, New Hampshire, James E. Young of Auburn, ME, b 28 Jul. 1832; **Charles W.** b 25 Mar. 1839, d 25 Nov. 1874, unm; **Joseph Corridon** m 28 Nov. 1880 Mrs. Jane Taylor (nee Cornwell); **Adolphus S.** b 28 May 1843, m 21 Jan. 1871 Ellen E. Merrill of Dexter, ME, b 17 Aug. 1874, d/o Allen and Lucy Hesilton; **George F.** m Ellen M. Bryant of Auburn; **Frank H.** b 3 May 1847 [letter 1897 from Mr. James Taylor of Chattaroy Washington to Elder], m 22 Mar. 1873 Mary E. Keith, b 20 Apr. 1848 Mary E. Keith, d/o Seth and Dora (Caswell) Keith of Auburn; and **Lee Clair** b 26 Feb. 1860, d 21 Mar. 1863. [Phillip, Maine, Auburn VR - card file.]

READ, LEMUEL - Born 2 Sep. 1815, d 26 Mar. 1895, s/o David, Sr. and ?? Read. Lemuel Read m 27 Jul. 1840 Eleanor Russell of Hallowell, Maine, d 1895. Children: **Lois A.** b 4 May 1840, m Milton Seargent; **Martha J.** b -- Jun. 1844, m Jerome York of Grafton, ME.; **Mary E.** b -- Apr. 1846, m Daniel Kelley; **Nellie A.** b 31 Mar. 1850, m 25 Nov. 1870 Alphonso Nichols of Somerset; **Ralph R.** b 21 Mar. 1854, m pub. 8 Mar. 1878 Hannah Osborn of St. Albans, ME; **Susie H.** b 19 Jan. 1861, m Herbert Willis; and **Willie A.** b 2 Sep. 1862.

READ, LEMUEL - Born 1 Feb. 1771, d 4 Apr. 1821 [*Eastern Argus* obit 17 Apr. 1821], s/o ?? Lemuel Read m int. 26 Apr. 1795 [vital records of Lewiston, Maine, p. 385] Mary Hart, b 15 May 1776, d 17 Jul. 1854. Children: **Charles** b 8 Oct. 1795, d 19 Jan. 1877, m 13 Nov. 1828 Cynthia Swift; **Elizabeth** b 29 Jul. 1797, d 30 Apr. 1877, m 28 Jul. 1821 Amasiah Morrell, d 9 Feb. 1864; **Lemuel** b 16 May 1799, d 30 May 1799; **Betsy** b 21 Nov. 1806, m 23 May 1824 Samuel Read; **Joel** b 18 Dec. 1802, d 3 Sep. 1804; **Patience** b 20 Nov. 1804, d 4 Dec. 1866, m 25 Dec. 1827 William Webster; **Nabby** b 13 Feb. 1807, d 10 Sep. 1891, m 28 Dec. 1828 Frederick Dana of Portland, ME; **Susanna** b 7 Feb. 1809, d 5 Apr. 1886, m Enos Dunham, lost between Portland and Boston; **Jane** b 10 Apr. 1811, d 28 May 1885, m Ammi Sonar of Yarmouth, ME, d 4 Jul. 1874; and **Cynthia** b 23 Dec. 1815, d 13 Jun. 1888, m 12 Oct. 1843 George Bean of Lewiston, b in Portland. [Vital Records of Lewiston, Maine, p. 67.]

READ, OLIVER - Born 21 Feb. 1779, d 17 Jun. 1850, s/o ?? Oliver Read m 2 Sep. 1801 Catherine Hart, d 23 Jul. 1854. Children: **Polly** b 4 Jul. 1802, d 27 Aug. 1803; **Chester** b -- Jun. 1805; **Betsey** b 1808, m David Davis; **Submit** b 4 Oct. 1810, d 13 Mar. 1875, m Daniel B. Read, s/o Jonathan; **Ichabod** b 1813, m Margaret Read, d/o Ichabod; **Hart** b 1 Oct. 1815, m 8 Sep. 1854 Abbie J. Maxwell; and **Katherine** b 30 Aug. 1824, m David Basworth. [Vital Records of Lewiston, Maine, p. 68, 385.]

READ, ROWLAND - Born ??, d ??, s/o ?? Rowland Read m Rebecca (Morsel) Crockett. Child: **Frank W.** b 4 Jun. 1848, lived in Almeda, CA, m 27 May 1850 Emma Kirby, b in Towanda, PA., d/o I. P. and Jemima Coolbaugh (their children: **Rachel Kirby** b 26 Dec. 1877; and **Frances** b 30 May 1890). [Letter from Frank W. Read dated 1894 to Elder.]

READ, RUSSELL H. - Born 24 Jun. 1795, d in Augusta, s/o Ichabod and ?? Read. Russell H. Read m 23 Nov. 1817 Sarah Sprague, b 19 Feb. 1794, d/o Col. William and Anna Merrow Sprague. Children:

Anna b 2 Oct. 1818; **William** b 13 Jan. 1820; **Cynthia** b 17 Dec. 1824; and **Emily Frances** b 13 Jun. 1833.

READ, STEPHEN H. - Born ??, d 15 Apr. 1860, s/o ?? Stephen H. Read m 7 Feb. 1820 Abigail Brown, b 17 Mar. 1803 in North Yarmouth, Maine [vital records of Lewiston, Maine, p. 384; will of Stephen H. Read #180], d/o Elezer. Children: **John** b 21 Dec. 1820, m 18 May 1848 Mary A. Bonney, b 1826, d/o Turner; **William N.** b 3 Dec. 1831, d -- Sep. 1881, m Mary Wilson of MO., d 1892; **Abby S.** b 9 Feb. 1844; **Adeline B.** b 21 Sep. 1846; and **Adelia** b 21 Sep. 1846, m Samuel B. Washburn of La----, d NY.

READ, WILL G. - Born ??, d ??, s/o ?? Children: **Helen**; and **William**.

REMUCK, RUTH - Born ??, d ??, d/o ?? Child: **Susanna** b 23 Mar. 1799. [Vital Records of Lewiston, Maine, p. 66.]

REYNOLDS, DANIEL BRIGGS - Born ??, d ??, s/o ?? Children: **Caroline**; **Estella** b 12 Sep. ----, d age 25 years; and **Josephine** b 3 Jan. ----, d age 1 1/2 years.

REYNOLDS, EDWARD CHARLES - Born 30 Oct. 1832, d 12 Sep. 1887, s/o ?? Edward Charles Reynolds m Lucy Hathaway of Medford, Massachusetts, d -- Dec. 1878. Child: **Frank A.** b 16 Feb. 1871.

REYNOLDS, GEORGE - Born ??, d ??, s/o ?? George Reynolds m 7 Nov. 1865. Children: **Mary L.** b 1 Sep. 1866, d 24 Jan. 1867; **Nelson B.** b 25 Dec. 1870; **Louise B.** b 5 Jun. 1872; **George K.** b 1 Oct. 1875; and **Frank W.** b 28 Jul. 1882.

REYNOLDS, NATHAN - Born 27 Jun. 1794, d 24 Oct. 1859 age 65 years 3 months 27 days, s/o ?? Nathan Reynolds m 30 Nov. 1815 Betsy Briggs, b 18 Jan. 1794 in Poland, Maine [vital records of Minot, Maine, book 1, p. 68], d -- Nov. 1856, d/o Daniel and Betsey (Bradford) Briggs of Minot, Maine. Children: **Nelson Briggs** b 16 May 1819, m 28 Nov. 1839 Hannah A. Chase, b 10 Aug. 1820, d/o Benjamin F. and Hannah (Andrew) of Bragdon; and **Charles Horace** b 6 Nov. 1827.

REYNOLDS, NELSON B. - Born ??, d 6 Feb. 1898, s/o ?? Nelson B. Reynolds m Harriet Chase. Children: **George Nelson** b 30 Oct. 1842; **Charles J.** b 20 Jun. 1845, d 7 May 1846; **Edward L.** b 11 Jul. 1848, d 14 Oct. 1849; **Nathan Howard** b 28 Jan. 1851, m 15 May 1877 Mary E. LaFrance; **Alice C.** b 28 Jan. 1854, d 7 Oct. 1856; **Nellie H.** b 15 Feb. 1857, d 27 Feb. 1877; **H e n r y S.** b 26 May 1860, d 20 Sep. 1861; and **Harriet C.** b 18 Feb. 1864. [Nelson B. Reynolds' probate #4609.]

RICHARDSON, CORNELIUS W. - Born ??, d ??, s/o ?? Children: **Emma A.** b 2 Jan. 1849, d 23 Jun. 1863; **Charles L.** b 14 Jan. 1851, d 19 Aug. 1857; **Frederick L.** b 14 Jan. 1851; **Anna A.** b 29 May 1854;

Hattie E. b 12 May 1856; **Minnie A.** b 10 May 1860; **Willie E.** b 21 Sep. 1863; and **Susan E.** b 27 Feb. 1868.

RICHARDSON, EPHRAIM - Born 11 Jun. 1793 in Baldwin, Maine, d ??, s/o ?? Ephraim Richardson lived in Lewiston from 1826 to before Jun. 1836. He m (1) 22 Oct. 1822 Charlotte Wellington, b 24 Apr. 1793, d 9 Jun. 1842, d/o Enoch and Sarah (Richardson) Wellington of Lexington, Massachusetts, and m (2) 12 Jan. 1843 Mary Sprague, b 10 May 1803, d/o John and Charity (----) Sprague. Children: **Cornelius** b 1 Jan. 1824 in Monmouth, ME, m 25 Nov. 1847 Amanda M. Farrow, d/o George and Lucy; **H a r r i e t W.** b 27 Jun. 1826, m 24 Nov. 1864 Joseph M. Davis of Durham, ME; **Elisabeth Ann** b 9 Jan. 1828, m -- Sep. 1847 Ira Hall; and **S a r a h A.** b 23 Nov. 1831. [Vital Records of Lewiston, Maine, p. 131.]

RIGGS, FRANCIS H. - Born 10 Feb. 1821 in Portland, Maine, d 1911, s/o Enoch and Nancy (----) Riggs. Francis H. Riggs m 29 Nov. 1849 Betsey Dinsmore of Auburn, Maine. Francis H. Riggs arrived in Lewiston 12 Mar. 1847. Children: **Frank H.** b -- Jan. 1851; **Charles M.**; **James Edward**; and **Carrie A.**. [For additional information see *Riggs Family* by Rev. C. Sinnett.]

ROBINS, LUTHER - Born 16 Jul. 1784, d 24 Nov. 1862, s/o ?? Luther Robins m Mary ----, b 5 Jul. 1789, d 12 Jan. 1850. Children: **Alvin** b 10 Mar. 1819; **Lousinna Daggett** b 13 Oct. 1821; **Servetus Wellington** b 7 Jan. 1824; **Clementine C.** b 19 Nov. 1826, d 7 Oct. 1847 age 21 years; and **Mary M.** b 21 Dec. 1828, d 5 Jan. 1856.

ROBINSON, JAMES - Born ??, d ??, s/o ?? James Robinson m Susan ---- [according to the vital records of Lewiston, Maine, p. 134], d/o Capt. Charles Barbour of Gray, Maine [see *Durham, Maine, History* by Stackpole, 1899, p. 246], or -- Dec. 1822 Mary Barbour of Gray, Maine. Children: **William Barbour** b 28 Jul. 1823, d 18 Mar. 1849; **Betsey Barbour** b -- Oct. 1825, d 29 Jun. 1826; **Charles Barbour** b 25 Apr. 1827, d 3 Mar. 1863, m Catherine Frances Robinson; **Mary Little** b 26 Jun. 1829, d 8 Mar. 1844; **Catherine C.** b 30 Mar. 1831, m 28 Oct. 1859 Alfred Walker of Portland, ME; **Clarissa Ann** b 7 Nov. 1833, m James Adams of Portland; **J a m e s E.** b 3 Jul. 1837, d 14 Jul. 1858; **Susan E.** b 3 Jul. 1837; **Lewis C.** b 8 Aug. 1839, d 22 Oct. 1840; **Lewis C.** b 2 Jun. 1844, m Rachael Bowie; and **Mary** b 2 Jul. 1844, d 1 Apr. 1845. [Vital Records of Lewiston, Maine, p. 134.]

ROBINSON, JOSHUA - Born ??, d ??, s/o Samuel and ?? Robinson. Joshua Robinson m Eleanor ----, b 1797. Children: **Katharine Francis** b 10 Nov. 1821; **Martha Ann** b 7 Sep. 1823; **Joshua** b 8 Aug. 1827; **William Andrews** b 24 Sep. 1827; **Samuel** b 19 Dec. 1829. [Vital Records of Lewiston, Maine, p. 134.]

ROBINSON, SAMUEL - Born ??, d ??, s/o ?? Samuel Robinson m Lydia ----. Children: **Rebecca** b 20 Jul. 1776; **Sarah** b 28 Dec. 1777; **David** b 15 Dec. 1779; **John** b 19 Dec. 1783; **William** b 25 Feb. 1786; **Lydia** b 3 May 1788; **Timothy** b 14 Jun. 1790; **Timothy** b 2 Feb. 1792;

Mary b 2 Mar. 1794; **Micajah** b 6 Feb. 1796; and **Anna** b 15 Nov. 1798.

ROFF, ISAAC - Born ??, d ??, s/o ?? Child: **John** b 6 May 1786. [Vital Records of Lewiston, Maine, p. 67.]

ROH, AUGUSTUS - Born 1834 in Poland, Europe, d ??, s/o ?? Augustus Roh occ' Fcty Operative. He m Ellen ----, b 1830 in Scotland, British Isles. Child: **Mary** b 1859 in Maine. [1860 census Lewiston.]

ROWE, JOSHUA - Born ??, d ??, s/o ?? Joshua Rowe was of Pejepscot, Maine. He m 15 Mar. 1813 Elizabeth Garcelon of Lewiston. Children: **Lucy** b 24 May 1813; **Belinda** b 15 Nov. 1815; **Abigail** b 31 Nov. 1818. [Vital Records of Lewiston, Maine, p. 134, 382, 435.]

RUBEL, JOHN - Born 1833 in Bavaria, Germany, d ??, s/o ?? John Rubel occ' Fancy Goods. He m Barbary ----, b 1831 in Barvaria, Germany. Child: **Albert** b 1859 in Maine. [Lewiston, Maine, 1860 census; birth dates based on age in 1860.]

RUSH, WILLIAM - Born ??, d ??, s/o ?? William Rush m Sarah ----. Child: **Christopher Sylvanus Robinson** b 2 Aug. 1826 in Bath, ME. [Vital Records of Lewiston, Maine, p. 131.]

SHEPHERD, JOHN - Born 17 Jun. 1802, d 29 Apr. 1839, s/o ?? John Shepherd m 15 Jul. 1824 Sally Stuart. Children: **Nathaniel** b 22 Oct. 1824, d 13 Oct. 1826; **Nathaniel** b 8 Jun. 1826, m Sally Crocker; **Emaline** b 25 Jul. 1828, m 1 Dec. 1849 Wm. Whitten; **Chester** b 3 May 1838; and **Nancy C.** b 25 Jul. 1842, m Charles Labree. [Vital Records of Lewiston, Maine, p. 72.]

SHEPHERD, JOSIAH - Born -- Oct. 1806, d ??, s/o ?? Josiah Shepherd m 9 Nov. 1824 [vital records of Lewiston, Maine, p. 436] Therzy Wright. Child: **Otis** b 29 Nov. 1825. [Vital Records of Lewiston, Maine, p. 72.]

SIMONS, ---- - Born ??, d ??, s/o ?? ---- Simons m ---- Golder. Children: **William G.** b 26 Mar. 1879; **Joseph** b 19 Jul. 1893; and **Ethelen E.** b 30 May 1890.

SKELTON, JOHN HENRY - Born ??, d ??, s/o Richard and ?? Skelton. John Henry Skelton m 1 Oct. 1854 Betsy Jacques of Bowdoin, Maine. Children: **N. Henry** b 27 Jul. 1855, m 22 Jun. 1885 Minnie Sullivan at Skowhegan, ME; **Richard F.** b 1 Jan. 1857, m 6 Dec. 1883 Nora Savage of Augusta; **Mary L.** b 10 Jul. 1859, d 15 Aug. 1882 in Richmond; and **Annie N.** b 26 Feb. 1862, m 9 Sep. 1885 W. G. Rogers of Topsham, ME.

SKELTON, N. HENRY - Born ??, d ??, s/o John Henry and ?? Skelton. Children: **William F.** b 24 Aug. 1886; and **Nathan Irving** b 9 Dec. 1890.

SKELTON, NATHANIEL - Born ??, d ??, s/o ?? Children: **Hattie M.**; and **Walter**.

SKELTON, RICHARD - Born 21 Apr. 1804, d ??, s/o Thomas and ?? Skelton. Richard Skelton m (1) Nancy Harris, b 9 Jul. 1814, d 1 Feb. 1864, d/o John and Nancy (Simmons) Harris, and m (2) 28 Dec. 1865 Frances E. Parker. *Children of 1st wife*: **John Henry** b 8 Dec. 1834, m 1 Oct. 1854 Betsy Jacques of Bowdoin, ME, d/o Nathaniel P. and Rose Ann (Raymond) Jacques; **Mary Jane** b 2 Apr. 1837, m Nathaniel S. Stevens of Brunswick, ME; and **Richard**.

SKELTON, RICHARD F. - Born ??, d ??, s/o John Henry and ?? Skelton. Children: **Leon G.** b 31 Aug. 1885; **Richard F.** b 8 Feb. 1888; **Bessie M.** b 23 Feb. 1892; and **Louise I.** b 15 De. 1895.

SKELTON, ROBERT T. - Born ??, d ??, s/o Robert and ?? Skelton. Robert T. Skelton m 1 Aug. 1868 Esther A. Johnson. Children: **Maud** b 12 Nov. 1860; **Carrie E.** b 18 May 1871; and **Horace W.** b 14 Oct. 1872.

SKELTON, SIDNEY D. - Born ??, d ??, s/o Thomas and ?? Skelton. Sidney D. Skelton m Mary A. Bell. Children: **James T.**; **Leonard B.**; **George J.**; **Mary E.**; **Sidney W.**; and **Lillian**.

SKELTON, THOMAS - Born in 1770, d 15 Dec. 1864, s/o ?? Thomas Skelton m Miriam ----. Children: **Mary** b 7 Apr. 1800, m 19 Mar. 1818 Joel Wright; **Jane** b 15 Oct. 1803, m pub. 18 Oct. 1829 Barnel Thorne; **Thomas** b 20 Mar. 1807, m Mehitable ----; **William** b 5 Jun. 1809, d 14 Apr. 1883, m Betsy Wright, d 9 Sep. 1888; **Sidney** b 12 Sep. 1812, m 30 Jul. 1835 Allura Wright; **Richard** b 21 Apr. 1814, d 13 Jan. 1891, m (1) 1834 Nancy Harris of Greene, ME, d/o John and Nancy (Simmons), and m (2) 28 Dec. 1865 Frances E. Parker; and **Robert** b 20 Nov. 1816, m (1) ---- Jacques, and m (2) Adeline Richards. [Vital Records of Lewiston, Maine, p. 71.]

SKELTON, THOMAS - Born 20 Mar. 1807, d ??, s/o Thomas and ?? Skelton. Thomas Skelton m 8 Jul. 1829 Mehitable Preble, b 10 Dec. 1807. Children: **Dorcas** b 4 Feb. 1831, m A. K. P. Merserve; **Sidney D.** b 10 Nov. 1832, m Mary A. Bell; **Miriam A.** b 9 Nov.1834, m Henry Wright; **Susan A.** b 5 Oct. 1836, m Washington Young; **Frances E.** b 21 Sep. 1838, m Albion Graves; **Rebecca E.** b 19 Jan. 1841, m Silas Adams of Waterville, ME; and **Thomas W.** b 3 Dec. 1845, m 7 Feb. 1870 Mary L. Holbrook, d/o John K. of Bowdoin.

SKELTON, THOMAS W. - Born ??, d ??, s/o Thomas W. and ?? Skelton. Children: **William B.** b 9 Aug. 1871, m 21 May 1894 Florence L. Larrabee of Bowdoin, ME; and **Linwood T.** b 25 Nov. 1872.

SKELTON, WILLIAM - Born ??, d ??, s/o ?? William Skelton m 28 Jan. 1836 Betsey Wright. Children: **Nathaniel E.** b 20 Dec. 1837, m

10 Jun. 1859 Harriet Thompson, d/o Isaac; **Elijah W.** b 1 Apr. 1839; **Elizabeth Ann** b 21 Nov. 1841, m (1) 18 Nov. 1861 William Alonzo Herrick, d 12 Apr. 1883, s/o Alexis of Greene, ME, and m (2) 12 May 1885 Edwin B. Webb of Brooklyn; and **Abby W.** m 29 Feb. 1876 Lamont O. Stevens in Akron, CA.

SKELTON, WILLIAM - Born ??, d ??, s/o William and ?? Skelton. Child: **Bessie**.

SKINNER, ANDREW - Born 10 Jan. 1781, d 26 Feb. 1857, s/o John and ?? Skinner. Andrew Skinner m 21 Aug. 1806 Wealthy Green of Lisbon, Maine, d 15 Dec. 1862 age 78 years, d/o Daniel (?). Children: **Jordan S.** b 18 May 1808 in Durham, ME, d 18 Mar. 1863, m 9 Jan. 1831 Eliza Nevens, d 22 Dec. 1861; **David Guston** b 27 Apr. 1810 in Lewiston, d 1 Feb. 1890, m 24 Sep. 1846 Dorcas W. Haley; **George Sawyer** b 27 Mar. 1812 in Danville, ME, m twice; **John S.** b 26 Jan. 1814 in Danville, d 15 May 1863, m 18 Jan. 1841 Sarah P. Nevens, d 6 Sep. 1883, d/o Davis, sis/o Eliza; **William Webster** b 24 Feb. 1816 in Danville, m and d in Raymond, ME; **Jeremiah Sawyer** b 16 May 1818 in Danville, d 30 Sep. 1830, unm; **Calvin Gorham** b 8 Apr. 1820 in Danville, d 2 Mar. 1897 age 76 years 10 months 9 days, m 11 Feb. 1844 Louisa Crockett, b in Danville, d 2 Mar. 1894 age 72 years 6 months, d/o David and Esther (Dingley); **Joseph Green** b 29 Sep. 1822 in Lewiston, d 11 Jan. 1878, m 10 Oct. 1880 Elizabeth Wright; and **Katherine Jane** b 13 Dec. 1828 in Lewiston, d 10 Sep. 1841.

SKINNER, CALVIN - Born 8 Apr. 1820, d 2 Mar. 1897 age 76 years 10 months 9 days, s/o Andrew and ?? Skinner. Children: **Alfred W.** b 29 Jan. 1845, d 21 Sep. 1861; **Adalade A.** b 24 Jun. 1847, m 11 Dec. 1870 Charles W. Campbell; **Frank S.** b 29 Aug. 1849, d 9 Nov. 1861; **Emma L.** b 3 Dec. 1852, unm; **Charles F.** b 17 Jan. 1856, m Georgia Dixon (their child: **Emma M.** b -- Oct. 1880); **Esther F.** b 29 Nov. 1858, m George Hayes; **Arthur W.** b 29 Feb. 1860, d 15 Mar. 1862; and **Lulla M.** b 17 Jun. 1865, m Wallis Manter.

SKINNER, DAVID G. - Born 27 Apr. 1819, d 1 Feb. 1890, s/o Andrew and ?? Skinner. David G. Skinner m 24 Sep. 1840 Dorcas W. Haley. Children: **Phineas W.** b 24 Apr. 1842, m 3 Jul. 1863 Mary A. Corliss; **Charles W.** b 1 Apr. 1844, d 16 Sep. 1849; **Dexter D.** b 15 May 1856, m 21 Oct. 1873 Maria Charles; **Wealthy** b 21 Nov. 1845, m 27 Nov. 1867 Charles H. Cobb; **Dorcas J.** b 7 May 1865, d 7 Feb. 1883, m 16 --- 1873 George H. Whittier; **Eva** b 21 Mar. 1856, m 23 Nov. 1873 George R. Bancroft; and **Josiah C.** b 31 Aug. 1857, d 29 Jul. 1864.

SKINNER, DAVID - Born ??, d ??, s/o John and Sally (Nevens) Skinner. Children: **Phineas** m Mary A. Corliss; **Wealthy** m Charles Cobe; **Dexter**; **Jane**; and **Eva** m ---- Riley.

SKINNER, DAVIS N. - Born 7 Nov. 1841, d 18 Jun. 1892, s/o Jordan and Eliza (Nevens) Skinner. Davis N. Skinner m 1868 Frances Ross of Wales, Maine, b 1844, d/o Joseph and Hannah (Owen). Children:

Carroll E. m 30 Mar. 1896 Maud M. Handy, d/o Morris C.; and Melicent Louisa d 6 Dec. 1896 age 17 years 2 months.

SKINNER, FREEMAN - Born 2 Oct. 1794, d 29 Dec. 1838 age 42 years 2 months 21 days, s/o John and ?? Skinner. Freeman Skinner m pub. 13 Dec. 1823 Joanna Robinson, b 6 May 1800, d 14 Nov. 1877, d/o Stephen of Cape Elizabeth, Maine. Children: **Stephen Robinson** b 20 Jan. 1825, d 18 May 1886 age 61 years, m Clara Garcelon, d/o Samuel D.; **Joanna** b 12 Jan. 1827, d 20 Dec. 1864, m 15 Feb. 1853 James Garcelon; and **Eleanor** b 15 Nov. 1829, m Thomas H. Longley of Greene, ME, d 25 Nov. 1857, s/o Samuel. [Vital Records of Lewiston, Maine, p. 135.]

SKINNER, JOHN - Born 27 Dec. 1749 at Cape Elizabeth, Maine, moved to Durham, Maine, about 1790, came to Lewiston in 1807/1808, d ??, s/o ?? John Skinner was a Revolutionary soldier. He m 1 Jun. 1775 Catherine Jordan, d 19 Jan. 1832. Children: **John, Jr.** b 26 Mar. 1777 at Cape Elizabeth, ME, d 16 Mar. 1844, m 21 Aug. 1806 Wealthy Greene, d 18 Dec. 1862 age 78 years; **Andrew** b 16 Jan. 1781, d 26 Feb. 1867; **Sarah** b 18 Aug. 1782; **Peter** b 17 Jan. 1784; **David** b 18 Nov. 1786; **Joseph** b 11 Oct. 1789; **Samuel** b 12 Dec. 1791; **Freeman** b 2 Oct. 1794, d 23 Dec. 1838, m pub. 13 Dec. 1823 Joanna Robinson of Durham, b 6 May 1800, d 14 Nov. 1877; and **Joanna** b 27 Dec. 1797, d 21 Feb. 1840. [See *History of Durham* by Everett S. Stackpole, published by the Town of Durham, 1899, p. 248.]

SKINNER, JORDAN S. - Born 18 May 1808, d 18 Mar. 1863, s/o Andrew and ?? Skinner. Jordan S. Skinner m likely 9 Jan. 1831 Eliza Nevens [vital records of Lewiston, Maine, p. 431]. Children: **David** b 16 Jun. 1832, d 7 Feb. 1840; **Sarah Jane** b 6 Jul. 1836, m 22 Dec. 1864 Isaac Golder; **Davis Nevens** b 7 Nov. 1841, d 18 Jun. 1892, m Fannie Foss, d 6 Feb. 1897, d/o Joseph of Wales, ME, and Hannah (Owen) of Lisbon, ME; and **John Albert** b 28 Apr. 1843, m 11 Sep. 1867 Lizzie Bonner. [Vital Records of Lewiston, Maine, p. 136.]

SKINNER, JOSEPH - Born ??, d ??, s/o ?? Joseph SKinner m 8 Oct. 1850 Elizabeth Wright, d 4 Mar. 1873, d/o John. Children: **Nanna B.** b 7 Sep. 1851, d 11 Dec. 1861; **Addie E.** b 27 Nov. 1852; **Robert** b 6 Apr. 1859, d 12 Nov. 1873 age 14 years 7 months; and **Walter J.** b 7 Sep. 1863, m Ella Philbrook.

SKINNER, STEPHEN R. - Born 20 Jan. 1825, d 29 Jul. 1888 age 66 years 4 months 2 days, s/o ?? Stephen R. Skinner m 7 Jul. 1849 Clarissa J. Garcelon, d 29 Jul. 1838 age 66 years 4 months 2 days, d/o Samuel D. Garcelon. Children: **Marcia J.** b 1 May 1850, m 1 Jan. 1873 J. Henry Farnham; and **Ellen M.** b 16 Apr. 1852, m 7 Jul. 1872 E. Turner Hatch.

SLEEPER, AARON - Born 20 Feb. 1661, d 9 May 1732 Kingston, Maine, s/o Thomas and Joanna (----) Sleeper. Aaron Sleeper m 23 May 1682 Elisabeth Shaw. Children: **Moses** b 22 Jan. 1695, d 13 Jan. 1754; **Thomas** b 3 Nov. 1686; **Aaron** b 23 Jul. 1688; **Joseph** b 14 Jun.

1690, twin; **John** b 14 Jun. 1690, twin; **Samuel** b 1 Dec. 1692; **Elish** b 9 May 1694; **Hezekiah** b 11 May 1696; **Ebeneser** b 18 May 1697; **Jonathan** b 17 Mar. 1699; and **Abigail** b 17 Apr. 1700, m 9 Nov. 1721 to Isaac Fellows.

SLEEPER, EBENESER H. - Born ??, d ??, s/o ?? Children: **Helen F.** b 27 Sep. 1838, m George S. Plummer; **Horace** b 30 Jan. 1841; and **Frank E.** b 12 Sep. 1846, m Helen Nash.

SLEEPER, GEORGE R. - Born 12 Jan. 1844, d ??, s/o ?? George R. Sleeper m 12 Apr. 1866 Betsy Goss. Children: **Benjamin W. G.** b 28 Jun. 1867, d 5 Jul 1892; **Serina F. D.** b 3 Sep. 1869, m 21 Sep. 1888 Walter Cooper; **George E.** b 15 Aug. 1871; **Melvin A.** b 4 Jul. 1874; and **Bertha M.** b 5 Mar. 1877.

SLEEPER, JONATHAN - Born 5 Sep. 1806, d 27 Sep. 1879, s/o ?? Jonathon Sleeper m 9 Dec. 1833 Sarah Ham, d/o Israel and Lucy (Hinkley) Ham of Lisbon, Maine [letter from Augusta M. Taylor, 1890s]. Children: **Henry Harrison** b 9 Oct. 1834, d 12 Apr. 1838 in Levant, ME; **Charles Ham** b 19 Aug. 1840, m H. T. Skillings of Garland, ME; and **Hiram Baxter** b 19 Aug. 1840 (twin), m Sarah Stackpole of Kenduskegg, ME.

SLEEPER, JONATHON - Born ??, d ??, s/o ?? Jonathon Sleeper m 31 Dec. 1804 Betsey Ham. Child: **Ruth** b 8 Jun. 1805, m Cyrus Weymouth.

SLEEPER, NATHAN - Born 13 Aug. 1777, d 18 Feb. 1860, s/o ?? Nathan Sleeper came from Chester, New Hampshire, to Lewiston in 1803. He m Polly Ham. Children: **Ira** b 11 Apr. 1801, d 13 Sep. 1804; **Tobias** b 27 Jan. 1803, d 10 Sep. 1804; **Nathaniel P.** b 25 Oct. 1804, d 1 Sep. 1881 in Lewiston, m (1) 25 Dec. 1827 Abigail Rand, and m (2) 28 Oct. 1838 Dorcas Wright, and m (3) pub. 24 Sep. 1879 Mrs. Marcia Brown; **Jonathon** b 5 Sep. 1806, d 27 Sep. 1879, moved to Kenduskeag, ME, m 9 Jan. 1834 Sarah Ham; **Ebeneser H.** b 23 Sep. 1808, d 14 Aug. 1881 in Lewiston, m 15 Feb. 1838 Sarah Nash; **Sophronia** b 31 Jan. 1811, d 15 Apr. 1876, m 17 Jan. 1833 Asa P. Taylor; **Nathan** b 10 Jan. 1813, d 28 Aug. 1841, m May E. White of Greenbush, ME; **Lydia** b 13 Mar. 1815, d 27 Jul. 1890, m 21 Feb. 1839 Bartholomew C. Taylor; **M a r y** b 13 Jul. 1817, d 28 Aug. 1899 in Durham, ME, m 2 Nov. 1837 Stephen Field; **Martha Herrick** b 13 Oct. 1819, d 13 Apr. 1900 in Lewiston, m 19 Apr. 1842 John Harris Pettengill; **Sumner** b 15 Mar. 1823, d 16 Feb. 1903 in Lewiston, m 11 Feb. 1860 Amelia Pratt of Clinton, ME; and **Julia Ann Davis** b 17 Aug. 1826, m 30 May 1847 Ami R. Nash.

SLEEPER, NATHANIEL - Born 26 Oct. 1804, d 1 Sep. 1881, s/o Nathan and Polly (Ham) Sleeper. Nathaniel Sleeper m (1) 25 Dec. 1827 Abigail Rand, d 27 Feb. 1838, and m (2) 28 Oct. 1838 Dorcas Wright, and m (3) pub. 24 Sep. 1879 Mrs. Marcia Brown. *Children by 1st wife*: **Josephine M.** b 1 Mar. 1829, d 16 Sep.. 1876, m Isaac Cole; **Mary Lois** b 3 Feb. 1832, m Thomas Bennett; **Sophronia** b 10 Sep.

1835, d 1874, m 1 Dec. 1859 Almond Collins of Durham; and **Nathaniel H.** b 20 Feb. 1838, m 1859 Kale Gass. *Children by 2nd wife*: **Charles M.** b 11 Jun. 1839, m 1866 Lydia Royal; **Laura Ann** b 11 Mar. 1841, d 28 May 1873, m Wm. Lovejoy; **Abbie Rand** b 5 May 1842, m Chas. Walker; **George R.** b 12 Jan. 1844, d 29 Jan. 1903 in Auburn, ME, m 12 Apr. 1866 Betsey Goss; **Fred H.** b 1 May 1846, m 1875 Sarah Robinson; **John P.** b 4 Jun. 1849, m 3 Sep. 1876 Hannah Colby; **Alexander B.** b 9 Feb. 1848, d 30 Aug. 1870; **Sarah Jennie** b 2 Jan. 1857, d 23 Mar. 1864; and **Ebeneser H.** b 13 Jun. 1860, m 29 Mar. 1874 Alice J. Richardson of Belfast, ME. *Child by 3rd wife*: **Herbert** b 15 Apr. 1865.

SLEEPER, NATHANIEL - Born 20 Feb. 1838 in Lewiston, d 1909 [obit 12 May 1909, *Lewiston Journal*], s/o Nathaniel and "Nabby" (Rand) Sleeper. Nathaniel Sleeper m 2 Jan. 1859 Catherine Dyer Goss, b 11 Dec. 1836 in Kingfield, Maine, d 1902. Children: **William H.** b 29 Jun. 1860, m 20 Apr. 1881 Nellie J. Lamb; **Sarah Jane** b 29 Jul. 1864, m 20 Sep. 1882 Joseph E. Sullivan; **Edith M.** b 27 Nov. 1866, m (1) 19 Jan. 1884 Edwin Caville, and m (2) David M. Smith; **Benjamin F.** b 19 Jul. 1869, m 21 Sep. 1892 Myrtle Eaton; **Albert** b 7 Dec. 1871; **Gertrude M.** b 15 May 1877; **Catherine A.** b 22 Oct. 1880; ----, daughter, b 7 Oct. 1862, d 10 Oct. 1862; ----, son, b 9 Feb. 1874, d 15 Mar. 1874; and ----, daughter, b&d 25 Jul. 1875. [Letter from Lisbon, Maine, Mrs. G. Goss, 5 Sep. 1892.]

SLEEPER, THOMAS - Born 1607 in England, 1640 came to Hampton, New Hampshire, d 30 Jul. 1696, s/o ?? Thomas Sleeper m Joanna ----, d 5 Feb. 1703 in Kingston. He lived several years near Jesse Lamphrey place; land granted 1646; later lived on Shaw's Hill; that part of town called Sleeper-town; corrupted into Sleepy-town. Children: **Elisabeth** m (1) Abraham Perkins, and m (2) Alexander Denham, and m (3) Richard Smith; **Mary M.** m Deacon Gersham Elkins; **Ruth** b 1 Jun. 1650, m Arelas Leavitt; **John** b 10 Sep. 1652; **Naomi** b 15 Apr. 1655, m Timothy Blake; **Moses** b 13 Mar. 1658 in Haverhill; **Aaron** b 20 Feb. 1661; and **Luther** b 14 Nov. 1668, d 19 May 1670. [*Genealogical Dictionary of ME and NH* by Libby, Noyes, & Davis, published by Davis, 1928-39, p. 638.]

SMALL, ADDISON - Born 16 Oct. 1841 in Lewiston, d ??, s/o John N. and Sarah (Hamilton) Small. Addison Small m 29 Nov. 1862 Florence S. Wilder of Manchester, ME. Children: **William Bryant** b 21 Sep. 1863 in Manchester, m 1 Sep. 1892 Maud H. Ingalls; and **Roscoe Addison** b 10 Jan. 1871 in Portland, d in Lewiston.

SMALL, JOHN NEVENS - Born 6 Jun. 1806 in Minot (Auburn), Maine, d 20 Apr. 1878 in Lewiston, s/o ?? John Nevens Small m -- Sep. 1838 in Bath, Maine, Sarah Hamilton, d 3 Aug. 1889 [probate #2801]. Children: **Elvira/Elvira M.** b 25 Dec. 1839 in Bath, d 27 May 1840; **Addison** b 16 Oct. 1841 in Herrick House at Barkerville [part of Lewiston], m 28 Nov. 1862 Florence S. Wilder; **Elvira** b 25 Nov. 1843 in Lewiston, m 31 Mar. 1866 Philander E. Noyes*, d 30 Jan. 1878 in Wilton, ME [three of her grandchildren named in Sarah (Hamilton)

Small's will were: John R. Noyes*, Alice L. Noyes*, and Florgence E. Noyes*]; **Celestia*** b 23 Jun. 1845 of 25 Nov. 1845 in Lewiston, m 18 Mar. 1865 Cyrenious P./Cyrenus Stevens, living in Beloit, KS, in 1889; **Aretus/Aratus*** b 11 Apr. 1847 in Lewiston, m 1 Jul. 1860 Emma L. Whitcher, d 6 Dec. 1886 in Charlestown, MA [Aretus/Aratas's children named who died before his mother: Herbert E. Small* of Medford, MA, and Walter A. Small* of Medford, MA]; **Harriet/Harriet N.*** b 10/11 Feb. 1844/1849 in Lewiston, m 31 Mar. 1866 William H. Garcelon; **Mary*** b 3 Oct. 1850 in Lewiston, m 30 Dec. 1871 J. S./Jeremiah S. Pain/Paine; **Sarah/Sarah H.*** b 14 Feb. 1852 or 7 Jul. 1852 in Lewiston, m (1) int. 22 Aug. 1868 Oliver F. Thompson, d 6 Apr. 1879 in Topsham [Sarah (Small) Thompson's children who died before her mother were: Frank*, Lizzie*, and Edla H.*, living in Topsham, ME, in 1889]; and **Edla/Ella H.** b 7 Jul. 1855 in Lewiston, m Oliver F. Thompson, d 18 May 1894 in Brunswick. [* Indicates named in will probate #2801 and will of Sarah (Hamilton) Small.]

SMITH, HENRY - Born ??, d ??, s/o ?? Henry Smith m 3 Jan. 1828 [vital records of Lewiston, Maine, p. 446] Jane Chase. Children: **William** b 29 Oct. 1828 in Lewiston; **Mary Jane** b 28 Sep. 1829 in Lewiston. [Vital Records of Lewiston, Maine, p. 135.]

SMITH, JAMES - Born 23 Mar. 1776, d ??, s/o ?? James Smith m Betsey ----, b 9 Apr. 1775. Children: **Stephen** b 28 Sep. 1797; and **Sally** b 13 Sep. 1799.

SMITH, JEREMIAH JR. - Born ??, d ??, s/o ?? Jeremiah Smith, Jr. Married (1) Dorothy ----, and m (2) Mary Chase of Brunswick, Maine. *Children of 1st wife*: **Persi** b 16 Apr. 1801 in Durham, ME; **Thomas** b 23 Dec. 1802 in Lewiston; **M. E.** b 3 Jan. 1804 in Durham; **Sarah** b 25 Jan. 1806 in Durham; **Henry** b 16 Mar. 1808 in Lisbon, ME; **Senah** b 3 May 1810 in Lisbon; **Abigail** b 3 May 1812 in Lisbon; **Libeus** b 26 Mar. 1817 in Lisbon; and **Rufus** b 8 May 1819 in Lewiston. *Children of 2nd wife*: **Dorothy** b 9 Sep. 1822 in Lewiston; **James C.** b 2 Mar. 1825 in Lewiston; **Jeremiah** b 26 Aug. 1827 in Lewiston; and **Nancy** b 21 Dec. 1830 in Lewiston. [Vital Records of Lewiston, Maine, p. 71.]

SMITH, JOHN - Born ??, d ??, s/o ?? John Smith m Joanna Nash. Children: **John** b in Gray, ME; and **Orland** b 2 May 1825. [Vital Records of Lewiston, Maine, p. 70.]

SMITH, ORLAND GENERAL - Born 2 May 1825, d in Chicago, Illinois, age 78 years and was buried in Columbus, Ohio, s/o John and Joanna (Nash) Smith. Orland General Smith lived for many years in Lewiston, Maine. He served in the War of the Rebellion and was vice-president of the Baltimore and Ohio Railroad. He m Miss Sargent of Gorham, Maine. Children: ----. [Obit Lewiston scrapbook Androscoggin Historical 1890-1920s.]

SMITH, SAMUEL - Born 11 Jun. 1799, d ??, s/o Jeremiah and ?? Smith. Samuel Smith m 23 Sep. 1819 [vital records of Lewiston,

Maine, p. 436] Sally Atkinson [the family name was spelt Atkins in early records and later changed to Atkinson]. Children: **Washington** b 17 Jan. 1820; **Loren** b 23 Jul. 1822; **Julia Ann** b 13 Aug. 1825; **Samuel** b 19 Jun. 1827; and **Rebecca** b 23 Jun. 1829. [Vital Records of Lewiston, Maine, p. 70.]

SOPER, HORATIO T. - Born ??, d ??, s/o ?? Horatio T. Soper was of Danville. He m pub. 24 Jun. 1863 Hattie E. Nevens of Danville, Maine.

SPOFFORD, GREENLEAF - Born 12 Nov. 1785, d 13 Sep. 1877, s/o ?? Greenleaf Spofford m pub. 19 Jun. 1812 Dorcas Golder. Children: **Isaac G.** b 27 Apr. 1813, d 17 Jun. 1891, m Sarah Harris; **Judith** b 22 Jul. 1815, d 1877, m (1) 19 Mar. 1838 Oren Record, and m (2) 3 Dec. 1844 Hiram Lane; **Sarah J.** b 18 May 1822, d 27 Sep. 1882, m Jesse N. Bickford; **Luther F.** b 22 Jan. 1825, d 1871, m Jane Hildreth; **Martha A.** b 15 Jul. 1828, m Wm. Randall; and **Dorothy M.** b 16 Apr. 1833, d 28 Aug. 1856, unm.

SPRAGUE, CORNELL S. H. - Born ??, d ??, s/o ?? Children: **Edgar F.**; and **Nina**.

SPRAGUE, VOLNEY - Born ??, d ??, s/o Washington and ?? Sprague. Children: **William Washington** b 20 Feb. 1856, m Elisabeth Titus of Monmouth, ME, d/o Cyrus; and **Carrie Elizabeth** b 11 Feb. 1860.

SPRAGUE, WASHINGTON - Born 2 Mar. 1807, d 30 Aug. 1871, s/o William and ?? Sprague. Washington Sprague m 7 Feb. 1830 Abigail Pettengill, b 16 Dec. 1806, d 16 May 1872, d/o Nathaniel and Nancy (----) Pettengill. Children: **Volney** b 9 Jun. 1832, d 11 Jan. 1862 age 29 years, lived in Cambridge, MA., m 22 Dec. 1854 Sophia C. Twombley of Lowell; **Cornelius H.** b 25 Sep. 1838, d 17 Apr. 1898 in Halifax, MA, m (1) 11 Oct. 1857 Elmira Foss of Athens, and m (2) Nellie Smith; **Weathey F.** b 25 Aug. 1844, m 20 Jul. 1868 Thomas W. Murch; **Mary Stone** b 23 Dec. 1856, m 2 Aug. 1870 Arthur W. Penley of Auburn, ME; **Sophonia K.** b 31 Aug. 1841, d 25 Oct. 1856 age 16 years; and **Nancy Ann** b 12 Feb. 1834, d 11 Jan. 1862, m 15 Jan. 1853 Andrew W. Marble.

SPRAGUE, WILLIAM W. - Born ??, d ??, s/o ?? Child: **Bradbury Faye**.

STACKPOLE, CORNELIUS - Born ??, d -- Oct. 1849, s/o ?? Cornelius Stackpole m Mary Richardson of Portland, Maine. Children: **Absalom** b 22 Feb. 1812, d 8 Feb. 1833; **Sarah Jane** b 7 Jan. 1814; **Abigail** b 26 Jun. 1816, d 10 Jul. 1894, m Ebeneser Campbell; **Rhoda** b 4 Oct. 1818; **James Henry** b 16 Apr. 1821, m (1) -- Oct. 1854 Mary Elisa Sprague, and m (2) 5 May 1863 Sarah E. Ellis; and **Cornelius** b 5 Jun. 1823, d 20 Jan. 1891, m Susan G. Dingley. [Vital Records of Lewiston, Maine, p. 135.]

STACKPOLE, CORNELIUS JR. - Born 5 Jun. 1823, d 20 Jan. 1891, s/o ?? Cornelius Stackpole, Jr. m Susan G. Dingley. Children: **Fred Elmore** b 16 Sep. 1852, d 23 Sep. 1872; **Jennie Dingley** b 9 Jun. 1863; and **Hattie Mathews** b 11 May 1867, d 11 Nov. 1874.

STACKPOLE, FRANK E. - Born ??, d ??, s/o ?? Frank E. Stackpole m 28 Aug. 1888 Ada C. Holt. Children: **Ethel L.** b 23 Aug. 1889; **Hattie E.** b 12 Jun. 1891; **Clara E.** b 4 Sep. 1892; and **Frank V.** b 20 Dec. 1895.

STACKPOLE, JAMES H. - Born 21 Apr. 1821, d ??, s/o ?? James H. Stackpole m (1) -- Oct. 1854 Mary Elisa Sprague of Calais, Maine, and m (2) 5 May 1863 Sarah E. Ellis. Children: **C. Freeman** b 5 Dec. 1856; **Mary B.** b 8 Nov. 1856, d 21 Aug. 1859; **Mary L.** b 19 Nov. 1860, d 9 May 1887; **Frank Elmer** b 22 Apr. 1864; **James Fred** b 28 Apr. 1866, d 5 Oct. 1875 in Calais; **Charles Abraham** b 18 Sep. 1868, d 21 Jun. 1869; **Wilmot Fish** b 1 Dec. 1870; and **Mabel N.** b 5 Apr. 1879, adopted.

STANFORD, ALVIN - Born ??, d ??, s/o ?? Children: **George H.** b 14 Jun. 1842; and **Joseph D.** b 13 May 1847.

STANFORD, BENJAMIN - Born ??, d ??, s/o ?? Benjamin Stanford m Adeline Southard. Child: **Frederick B.** b 10 Jul. 1850 in Gardiner, ME, m 25 Jul. 1873 Sarah F. Boothby of Lewiston.

STANFORD, FREDERICK B. - Born 10 Jul. 1850, d ??, s/o ?? Children: **Harold B.** b 17 Nov. 1875; and **Louise** b 17 Oct. 1883.

STANFORD, GEORGE H. - Born 14 Jun. 1842, d ??, s/o ?? George H. Stanford m 28 Jan. 1869 Augusta J. Burbank of East Boston, Massachusetts. Children: **Frederick** b 19 Apr. 1872, d 4 Jan. 1874; **Emma E.** b 6 Aug. 1876; **Forest G.** b 19 Jul. 1878; and **Beulah M.** b 22 Dec. 1884, d 26 Feb. 1855.

STANFORD, JEREMIAH - Born 3 Oct. 1775 in Cape Elizabeth, Maine, d 7 Oct. 1861 in Lewiston, s/o ?? Jeremiah Stanford m (1) Mary Richards, and m (2) Betsey Dyer. Children: **Jordan** b 22 Dec. 1803, d 1 Apr. 1886, m 19 Oct. 1829 Polly Miller; **Mary** b 26 Oct. 1805, d 5 Dec. 1869, m 8 Sep. 1833 Samuel Litchfield, ME; **Isabella** b 16 Dec. 1807, d 21 Oct. 1851, unm; **Isaiah** b 9 Feb. 1810, d 20 May 1843, m -- May 1829 Mary Mitchell of Litchfield; **Happy** b 12 Jan. 1812, m 8 Apr. 1856 David Graffam; **Cynthia** b 2 Oct. 1813, m 20 Feb. 1870 Samuel Litchfield; **Alvin** b 22 Dec. 1815, m 13 Jun. 1841 Dovina Miller of Union; **Benjamin** b 18 Sep. 1819, d 22 Apr. 1858, m Adeline Southard; **Joseph Dyer** b 19 Sep. 1822 in Lewiston, d 31 Jul. 1844, unm; and **Elvira** b 30 Oct. 1826, m 25 Dec. 1850 Charles H. Davis of Farmington, ME. [Vital Records of Lewiston, Maine, p. 136.]

STANFORD, JEREMIAH - Born ??, d ??, s/o ?? Jeremiah Stanford m Betsey ----. Children: **Joseph Dyer** b 19 Sep. 1822; and **Benjamin** b 18 Sep. 1819. [Vital Records of Lewiston, Maine, p. 72.]

STANFORD, JORDAN - Born 22 Dec. 1803, d 1 Apr. 1886, s/o ?? Jordan Stanford m 19 Oct. 1829 Polly Miller of Union, Maine. Children: **Sophronia** b 6 Oct. 1830, m 8 Jun. 1851 Charles G. Baxter; **Martha J.** b 13 Mar. 1832, d 6 Apr. 1837, m 26 Dec. 1854 Sherburn Lawrence; **Julia** b 9 Aug. 1834; **Joseph M.** b 21 Oct. 1836, m 1 Jan. 1864 Abbie J. Carville; **Martha Jane** b 17 May 1839, unm; **Emila Dyer** b 25 Jan. 1841, unm; and **Isaiah** b 15 Mar. 1843, d 4 Oct. 1871.

STANFORD, JOSEPH M. - Born 21 Oct. 1836, d ??, s/o Jordan and Polly (Miller) Stanford. Joseph M. Stanford m 1 Jan. 1864 Abbie J. Carville. Children: **Sherburn L.** b 28 Aug. 1866, d 19 Sep. 1874; **Lulu C.** b 14 Feb. 1878; and **Eva May** b 24 Dec. 1887. [Letter dated 13 Apr. 1890's - Gardiner, Maine, writer unknown.]

STATEN/STATON, AMOS - Born 27 Jul. 1806, d 18 Mar. 1852, s/o ?? Children: **Hannah B.** b 24 Jul. 1845, d 8 Aug. 1849; **Josephine B.** b 19 Nov. 1848, d 8 Aug. 1849; **Amosanna** b 13 Jan. 1852, d 21 Jan. 1863; **Deborah** b 31 Aug. 1843, m -- Aug. 1862 Abram Osgood; and **Carrie G.** b 10 Feb. 1850, m 2 Oct. 1870 Samuel Flewllin.

STATEN/STATON, ELIAS - Born ??, d ??, s/o ?? Elias Staten/Staton was of Pejepscot Gore, Maine. He m pub. 22 Jan. 1800 Mrs. Polly (Parker) Garcelon, d 29 Jul. 1849 age 82 years. Children: **Sally** b 11 Mar. 1802, m (1) 17 Jan. 1825 John Proctor, and m (2) 10 Jan. 1828 William Haines of Minot, ME; **Kesiah** b 11 Nov. 1800, m 28 Sep. 1826 Ruben Burrell; **Louisianna** b 12 May 180-, d 5 Aug. 1886, m 7 Sep. 1841 Alfred Davis; and **Samuel W.** b 3 Oct. 1806, d 17 Nov. 1846, m 11 Mar. 1824 Deborah Chandler of Minot, d/o Rubin.

STATEN/STATON, ELIAS - Born 2 Aug. 1827, d 24 Nov. 1862 age 35 years 3 months 22 days, s/o ?? Child: **Frank Henry** b 10 Jun. 1849, d 21 Sep. 1849.

STATEN/STATON, ELIAS - Born ??, d 24 Nov. 1862, s/o Samuel and ?? Staten/Staton. Child: **Frank Henry** b 10 Jun. 1849, d 21 Sep. 1849 (headstone).

STATEN/STATON, PESIA - Born ??, d ??, s/o ?? Children: **William**; **James**; and **John**.

STATEN/STATON, SAMUEL - Born 1775, d 2 Jun. 1867 age 92 years, s/o ?? Samuel Staten/Staton m pub. 31 Aug. 1799 Esther Robinson. Children: **Sally** b 8 Oct. 1799, d 2 Dec. 1869, m 29 Dec. 1842 Josiah Hart; **Betsey** b 26 May 1801, d 24 Nov. 1884, m 6 Mar. 1825 Isaac Goddard; **Olive** b 11 Sep. 1803, d 11 Sep. 1804; **Amos** b 27 Jul. 1805, d -- Mar. 1852, m Martha J. Bibber of Portland, ME; **Persia** b 21 Apr. 1807, d -- Mar. 1894; **Isaac** b 7 Sep. 1809 [vital records of Lewiston, Maine, p. 69], d in Florida War; **Moses** b 1 Nov. 1811 [vital records of Lewiston, Maine, p. 69], went to sea, never returned; and **Mary Ann** b 16 Feb. 1814, lived in Lisbon, m John H. Goddard.

STATEN/STATEN, SAMUEL W. - Born 3 Oct. 1806, d 17 Nov. 1875, s/o ?? Samuel W. Staten/Staton m Deborah Chandler, b 23 Sep. 1803, d 10 Jan. 1878, d/o Reubin and Hannah (----) Chandler. Children: **Vesta Ann** b 21 Oct. 1829 in Minot, m 29 Aug. 1852 Thomas Standwart of Bath, ME; **Elias H.** b 2 Aug. 1827, d 24 Nov. 1862, m 7 Nov. 1848 Jane Briggs, b 3 Oct. 1824, d/o Daniel and Rhoda (Donahue); **Andrew J.** b 16 Nov. 1835, lived in Auburn, m (1) -- May 1856 Rosian M. Frances, d 14 Dec. 1865, and m (2) 27 Jun. 1869 Mary E. Jordan, b 14 Apr. 1849; and **Sarah P.** b 15 Jul. 1842, m Seth Staples of Auburn, ME.

STETSON, STEPHEN - Born 28 May 1791 in Durham, Maine, d ??, s/o Elisha and Rebecca (Curtis) Stetson. Stephen Stetson m 1 Aug. 1813 Betsey Denison of Freeport, Maine. Children: **Jennett** b 23 Oct. 1815, m 19 Mar. 1838 Nelson West of Greene, ME; **Betsey** b 27 Mar. 1817, d 16 Feb. 1876, m 1 Jan. 1839 Capt. Dan Whitten; **George D.** b 13 May 1819, d 23 Jul. 1846, m 5 Jan. 1845 Harriet Cole; **Pamela H.** b 5 Dec. 1821, m 10 Nov. 1844 William G. Randall; **Elisha** b 30 Aug. 1824, m 23 Jan. 1848 Caroline M. Manson; and **Andrew J.** b 4 Nov. 1828. [See *Journal* 31 Oct. 1878 and 27 Dec. 1872.]

STEVENS, DAVID THURSTON - Born 17 Apr. 1809 in Strong, d ??, s/o ?? David Thurston Stevens m Julia French of Hartford, Maine?, b 7 Jun. 1810. Child: **Edwin Thurston** b 25 Aug. 1836.

STEWART, REUBIN - Born ??, d ??, s/o ?? Reubin Stewart m 24 Jun. 1865 Dianah Jordan. Children: **William H.** b 2 Feb. 1867, m 2 Jul. 1890 Nett Howard of N. Brunswick, ME; **Rose E.** b 25 May 1869, m -- Sep. 1891 Wm. Gulliver; **Adah C.** b 16 Jun. 1875, m 6 Oct. 1893 Elbert L. Brackett of Portland, ME; **Irving E.** b 13 Sep. 1877; and **Virgil C.** b 15 Dec. 1885.

STEWART, THOMAS - Born ??, d ??, s/o ?? Thomas Stewart m 23 Oct. 1831 Anna Ham. Children: **Hester Ann** b 5 Sep. 1831; **Adeline H.** b 15 Nov. 1832; **Mary Elisa** b 9 Jun. 1834; and **Lovina Rogers** b 2 Jan. 1836.

STODDARD, WILLIAM - Born ??, d ??, s/o ?? William Stoddard m 1 Dec. 1808 [vital records of Lewiston, Maine, p. 426] Lydia Bean. Child: **Lydia** b 25 Aug. 1809. [Vital Records of Lewiston, Maine, p. 70.]

STUART, EDWARD - Born ??, d 22 Aug. 1827 [vital records of Lewiston, Maine, p. 71, 237], s/o ?? Edward Stuart m Abigail Grover, d 1843. Children: **Elisabeth** b 17 Jun. 1793, m John Grover; **George** b 16 Apr. 1795; **Mehitable** b 23 Oct. 1798, m 14 May 1870 Joseph Chadbourne; **Isaac** b 17 Feb. 1800, d 18 Nov. 1846, m (1) 23 Jan. 1823 Dorcas Lake, and m (2) pub. 27 Dec. 1836 Sarah (?Hannah) Hamilton; **Sally** b 30 Jan. 1803, m pub. 26 Apr. 1829 John Shephard; **Happy** b 20 Jan. 1805, m 9 Dec. 1830 Christopher Bubier; and **Andrew** b 4 Aug. 1809, m 24 Nov. 1831 Louisa Cannon. [Vital Records of Lewiston, Maine, p. 71.]

STUART/STEWART, ISAAC - Born 17 Feb. 1800, d 18 Nov. 1846, s/o ?? Isaac Stuart m (1) 23 Jan. 1823 Dorcas Lake, and m (2) pub. 27 Dec. 1836 (?Sarah?) Hannah Hamilton. Children: **Orilla Lake** b 6 Aug. 1823, m Lewis Littlefield; **Warren Danville** b 27 Jul. 1825, m Pelenia Ross; **Sarah Dill** b 5 Jul. 1828, m John Lake; **Isaac** b 9 Dec. 1831, unm; **Josiah L.** b 8 Sep. 1837, m 22 Apr. 1872 Mary E. Donnell; **Mary E.** b 2 May 1839; and **Henry O.** [Vital Records of Lewiston, Maine, p. 135.]

TARR, AARON - Born 1792, d 13 Jul. 1870 age 77 years 10 months 17 days, s/o Joseph and ?? Tarr. Aaron Tarr was the br/o Seth Tarr. Aaron Tarr m 27 Mar. 1825 Mary Davis, d 3 Dec. 1868 age 75 years 4 months 12 days, d/o Amos, Jr. Children: **Amos Davis** q.v.; and **Jordan** b 26 Mar. 1828, d 11 Aug. 1854 age 26 years, m 13 Nov. 1852 Mary W. Smith.

TARR, ALVIN B. - Born 29 Jun. 1839, d 1904, s/o Seth, Jr. and Mary (Farnham) Tarr. Children: **Alvin**; **William N.** m 27 Dec. 1900 Evangeline Langley of Oakland, CA., d/o L. Langley; and **Emma**.

TARR, AMOS DAVIS - Born 12 Apr. 1826, d ??, s/o Aaron and Mary (Davis) Tarr. Amos Davis Tarr m 22 Apr. 1849 Dianna G. Smith, d/o John and Elsa (Mitchell) Smith of Monmouth, Maine. Children: **Eva M.** b 15 Dec. 1852, m 1874 James Carville, lived in Lisbon, ME; **Mary Eliza J.** b 14 Mar. 1859, buried So. Lewiston Davis Cemetery, unm; and **Carrie Amelia** b 7 Dec. 1874, m John O. Pierce of Monmouth, ME.

TARR, BENJAMIN - Born ??, d ??, s/o Seth and ?? Tarr. Benjamin Tarr m Martha ----. Children: **Benjamin** b 17 Aug. 1817; **Josiah M.** b 20 Dec. 1819; **George** b 17 Aug. 1822; **Martha Ann**; **Mary Jane**; and **Ellen**. [Vital Records of Lewiston, Maine, p. 76.]

TARR, DAVID H. - Born ??, d ??, s/o James and ?? Tarr. Children: **Ted L.** m 17 Jun. 1880 Lois A. Hackett, d/o Orin Hackett; **Rosie E.** m pub. 21 Nov. 1884 Shepard S. Shaw, Jr.; **M a r y A l i c e** m Clifton McKenny; **Elden H.** m Mamie Smith; **Flavilla** m Albert Barrows; **Mildred**; and **Nellie** m Walter Littlefield.

TARR, FANANCE C. - Born 15 Jun. 1841, d ??, s/o Seth, Jr. and Mary (Furnham) Tarr. Children: **William F.** b 14 May 1869, d 29 Oct. 1869; **Herbie C.** b 15 Apr. 1870, d 22 Jul. 1870; and **Milton C.** b 14 Apr. 1874, m 2 Jul. 1894 Bertha Hinckley, adopted d/o C. H. Hinckley.

TARR, HENRY L. - Born ??, d ??, s/o ?? Child: **LeRoy**.

T A R R , ISAAC - Born ??, d ??, s/o ?? Isaac Tarr m 30 Mar. 1834 ---- in Lisbon, Maine. Children: **Francis B.** b 28 Jan. 1835; **Alvina** b 17 Sep. 1836; **Charles H.** b 28 Mar. 1839; **Isaac G.** b 28 Apr. 1841, m 28 Oct. 1865 Mary M. Clough, d/o Josiah; **Georgia W.** b 13 May 1843; **Moses W.** b 1 Feb. 1845; **Olive D.** b 12 Jul. 1848, d 7 Apr. 1879, m 22

May 1878 Joseph H. Fisher; and **Carrie E.** b 10 Oct. 1850, m 17 Nov. 1872 Eben W. Blake. [Vital Records of Lewiston, Maine, p. 78.]

TARR, ISAAC G. - Born 28 Apr. 1841, d ??, s/o Isaac and ?? Tarr. Isaac G. Tarr m 28 Oct. 1865 Mary M. Clough, d/o Josiah. Children: **Bessie M.** b 1868, d 2 May 1877 age 9 years 5 months; **Willie A.** b 1873, d 13 Aug. 1874 age 9 months; and **Frankie** b 1881, d 23 Sep. 1881 age 3 weeks.

TARR, JAMES - Born 1803, d 17 Apr. 1858 age 55 years, s/o ?? James Tarr was from Georgetown, Maine. He m 14 Dec. 1828 Phebe Clark, b 18 Nov. 1812, d 16 Jun. 1888 age 76 years 7 months 16 days, d/o Daniel and Eunice (Tarr) Clark. Children: **Rebecca** b 15 Nov. 1831, d 23 Jan. 1893, m 6 Jun. 1883 Abe B. Batchelder; **David H.** b 13 Jan. 1833, m (1) 18 Nov. 1853 Charlotte Davis, d/o John, and m (2) 29 Aug. 1863 Lydia H. Cole; **James E.** b 24 Mar. 1835, d 5 Jul. 1863, unm; **Eliza J.** b 18 Feb. 1838, m 3 Aug. 1862 Joseph Eates; **Henry** b 11 Nov. 1841, m 3 Aug. 1866 Mary D. Towle; **LaRoy** b 25 Jan. 1844, m Nettie Wilson; **Mary A.** b 26 Apr. 1848, m 5 Aug. 1876 Charles H. Holbrook; **George W.** b 21 May 1858, unm. [Vital Records of Lewiston, Maine, p. 138.]

TARR, JOHN - Born 26 Sep. 1776, d 6 Aug. 1860 age 83 years in Salem, Maine, s/o ?? John Tarr m 4 Aug. 1801 Mary Pettingill, b 15 Oct. 1781. d 5 Feb. 1855 age 73 years. Children: **Thankful** b 21 Nov. 1801; **Abraham** b 17 Jan. 1804 in Lewiston; **John** b 24 Dec. 1805 in Lewiston; **Mary** b 21 Apr. 1808 in Strong, ME; **Mark** b 4 Aug. 1810 in Strong; **William** b 28 Sep. 1813, d 20 Jan. 1894; **Abigail** b 16 Apr. 1816; **Harriet** b 11 Jul. 1819; **Rufus** b 11 Mar. 1824. [Leland Peary's notes of Strong, Maine, families, p. 22, at Cutler Library, Farmington, Maine.]

TARR, JORDAN - Born 26 Mar. 1828, d 11 Aug. 1854, s/o Aaron and Mary (Davis) Tarr. Jordan Tarr m 13 Nov. 1852 Mary W. Smith, d/o James from Wales, Maine. Child: **Frank M.** b 1853, d 9 Jul. 1854 age 1 year 1 month.

TARR, MILTON C. - Born 14 Apr. 1874, d ??, s/o F. C. and ?? Tarr. Child: **Charles Hinckley** b 31 Mar. 1895.

TARR, SETH - Born ??, d ??, s/o ?? Seth Tarr practiced medicine in Livermore, Maine.

TARR, SETH - Born ??, d ??, s/o ?? Seth Tarr m (1) pub. 19 Jun. 1789 Mary Davis, d 9 Dec. 1822, and m (2) pub. 4 Jun. 1823 Mary Hamilton formerly of Lisbon, Maine, d 10 Apr. 1866 age 103 years 7 months. Children: **Nancy** b 5 Nov. 1789, d 24 Feb. 1866, m 31 Mar. 1810/1811 Joshua Mitchell, d 25 Oct. 1877; **Amos** b 4 Apr. 1791, d 12 Oct. 1797; **Seth** b 2 Aug. 1795 in Georgetown, ME., d 1875, m pub. 21 Aug. 1825 Mrs. Judith Dawes of Richmond, d 24 Apr. 1836 age 32 years, and m (2) Mrs. ---- Durgain, d 2 Dec. 1852; **Sarah** b 9 May 1797, m 6 Feb. 1817 Thomas Clark of Lyman, ME, moved to Oldtown,

ME; **Ellis** b 25 May 1799, d 20 Feb. 1875, m 29 Nov. 1818 James Turner; **Joseph** b 13 Mar. 1802, d 7 Oct. 1803; **Isaac** b 6 Dec. 1804, d 12 Mar. 1897; **Sargent** b 12 Sep. 1809, d 17 Jan. 1814; and **David** b 5 Nov. 1811, m (1) ---- Dolbier of Freeman, ME, and m (2) ---- Ricker of Anson, ME. [Vital Records of Lewiston, Maine, p. 74 and 76.]

TARR, SETH JR. - Born 2 Aug. 1795, d 1875 in Hiram, Maine, s/o Seth and ?? Tarr. Seth Tarr, Jr. m (1) pub. 21 Aug. 1825 Judith Dawes of Richmond, Maine, d 24 Apr. 1836 in Summerworth, New Hampshire, and m (2) Mary L. Farnham (Dergan) of Hiram, Maine, d 2 Dec. 1852, and m (3) Hannah Merrifield in Cornish, Maine. *Children of 1st wife*: **Francis Ellen** b 23 Jul. 1827, m Joseph Eastman; **Nathan Davis** b 15 May 1829; **Edwin**; and **Olive A.** m Edward Casson. *Children of 2nd wife*: **Alvin B.** q.v.; **Fanance C.** q.v.; **Thomas S.** b 21 Sep. 1843, d 2 Dec. 1876 in Lewiston, m Hannah M. White; **Sarah J.** b 4 Dec. 1846, m George Casson; **Alice** b 2 Dec. 1852; and **Emerline** b 29 Oct. 1848, m George Casson. *Children by 3rd wife*: **Scott** enlisted in regular army; and ----, daughter, d young.

TARR, WILLIAM N. - Born ??, d ??, s/o Alvin B. and ?? Tarr. Child: **Ruth**.

TAYLOR, ASA P. - Born 16 Feb. 1807, d ??, s/o Thomas and ?? Taylor of Dracut, Massachusetts - Thomas having arrived there in 1785. Asa P. Taylor m 30 Nov. 1845 Betsy Pettingill Green, d 22 Apr. 1886 age 75 years. Children: **Charles E.** b 13 Jul. 1834, d 24 Jul. 1862; **Alonso G.** b 23 Sep. 1836, d 11 Oct. 1836; **Madison P.** b 5 Nov. 1837, d 9 Nov. 1837; **May S.** b 12 Dec. 1838, d 23 Sep. 1891; **Nathan S.** b 11 Apr. 1841, m 17 Jan. 1833 Sophonia Sleeper, d 15 Apr. 1876; **Augusta Minerva** b 22 May 1843; and **Anne Julia** b 29 Jun. 1845.

TAYLOR, B. J. - Born ??, d ??, s/o ?? Child: **Julia Ann** b 17 Jul. 1847, m 3 Feb. 1891 E. S. Googins.

TAYLOR, CALVIN G. - Born 4 Nov. 1828, d ??, s/o Phineas and ?? Taylor. Child: **George Calvin**.

TAYLOR, CHARLES - Born ??, d ??, s/o ?? Charles Taylor m Elisa Hunt. Child: **Fred**.

TAYLOR, CHARLES - Born ??, d ??, s/o James and ?? Taylor of Wales, Maine. Charles Taylor m 20 Jul. 1879 ----, d/o Hezekiah and Hannah Smiley. Child: **Fred C.** m Lettie Wright, d/o Jonathan.

TAYLOR, EBEN - Born ??, d ??, s/o Joshua, Jr. and ?? Taylor. Eben Taylor m (1) Julia Greaton, d 16 Oct. 1846 age 21 years, and m (2) Margaret Juellaria. Children: **Winfield S.** d 25 Oct. 1851 age 2 years 1 month; **Almer O.** d 3 Apr. 1852 age 11 months; **Eben C.** d 12 Aug. 1855 age 1 year; and **Eugene W.** d 6 Jan. 1863 age 3 years 5 months.

TAYLOR, HORACE - Born 21 Mar. 1815, d ??, s/o Joseph and ?? Taylor of Plymouth, Maine. Horace Taylor m 29 Sep. 1883 Addie M.

Ward, d/o John C. of Troy, Maine. Children: **Lizzie M.** b 7 Apr. 1889; and **Dora B.** b 12 Sep. 1890.

TAYLOR, IRASON - Born ??, d ??, s/o Joshua, Jr. and ?? Taylor. Irason Taylor m Mercy Savage. Child: **Alfred.**

TAYLOR, JAMES - Born 20 Feb. 1799 at Cape Elizabeth, Maine, d 27 May 1880 in Lewiston, s/o ?? James Taylor m 24 Dec. 1823 in Durham, Maine, Eunice Robinson, b 28 Feb. 1796 in Durham, d 24 Sep. 1876 age 80 years 7 months 26 days. Children: **L i z z i e A.** b 24 Jan. 1824 in Durham, m 20 Mar. 1844 P. J. Garcelon; **James W.** b 28 Aug. 1826 in Lewiston, d 29 Mar. 1870 age 44 years 7 months; **Sylvanus D.** b 19 Jan. 1829 in Lewiston, m (1) 27 Jun. 1853 Mary M. Foss of Wales, ME, d 27 Jul. 1857, and m (2) 19 Dec. 1849 Julia M. Hammond; **Sarah J.** b 7 Oct. 1831 in Lewiston, d 20 Dec. 1850 age 19 years 2 months 1 day; **D e x t e r S.** b 21 Oct. 1833 in Lewiston, m 25 Oct. 1856 in Belvidere, IL; and **Elbridge G.** b 27 May 1837 in Lewiston, lived in Sabattus, ME.

TAYLOR, JAMES - Born ??, d ??, s/o James and ?? Taylor of Wales, Maine. James Taylor m 28 Nov. 1848 Alice Taylor, b 28 Dec. 1820, d 21 May 1892, d/o Joseph and Alice (Graffam) Taylor. Children: **Georgiana** b 9 Feb. 1851, d 16 Jan. 1853 age 2 year; **George** b 9 Feb. 1851, d 28 Jan. 1853 age 2 years; ---- unnamed son, d 6 Jan. 1855; **James Herbert** b 29 Apr. 1858, d 14 Aug. 1896, m 31 Dec. 1882 Helen Maria Roberts, b 16 Feb. 1863 in Chelsea, MA, d/o Nathan P. and Mary L.; and **A l i c e L.** b 21 Dec. 1862, d 29 Jul. 1886, m 1 Sep. 1883 Cyrus Seavey.

TAYLOR, JAMES - Born 11 May 1789 in Lewiston, Maine, d 18 Jan. 1842 in Wales, Maine, s/o Thomas, Sr. and ?? Taylor. James Taylor lived in Wales, Maine. He m 16 Apr. 1813 Ann Graffam. Children: **James** b 12 Oct. 1820, d 20 Jan. 1886 age 65 years 3 months 18 days, m (1) 28 Nov. 1848 Alice Taylor, d 21 May 1892, and m (2) 14 Mar. 1848 Emma Smiley, d age 64 years 3 months; **J o s e p h** b 12 Apr. 1825 in Wales, d 2 Feb. 1892 in Litchfield, ME, m 2 Jul. 1848 Mary Brown of Greene, d 26 Nov. 1878; **C h a r l e s** b 1827, d 15 Mar. 1864 age 37 years, m 11 Feb. 1855 Elisa Hunt; **William** b 17 Apr. 1833, d -- Dec. 1879, m 15 Nov. 1861 Sarah Ann Cummings, d 29 Mar. 1879 age 36 years; and **Mary** b 19 Dec. 1813, m Nason Dixon of Wales.

TAYLOR, JAMES C. - Born ??, d 2 Feb. 1864 of Co. G., 16th Maine Reg., s/o ?? James C. Taylor m (1) 2 Sep. 1844 Roxannah Blanchard, d 13 May 1848 age 23 years 5 months, and m (2) ----, and m (3) ----. *Children of 1st wife*: **J a m e s E d w i n** b 9 May 1826, d 18 Jan. 1866 of 31st Maine Reg., unm. *Children by 2nd wife*: **Ella A.** b 15 Oct. 1850, d 9 Jun. 1872 age 21 years 7 months, m Charles H. Blake of Hartland, ME.; **M a y H.** b 16 Jan. 1853, m Albert Warren of Detroit, ME.; **George T.** b 13 Feb. 1855, drowned, unm; and **Emily C.** b 6 Jul. 1857, d 18 Dec. 1891, m 11 May 1878 Albion S. Wright. *Children by 3rd wife*: **Nellie E.** b 23 Jan. 1861, m Roscoe L. Peterson of Kingfield,

ME; and **Ellsworth C.** b 18 Dec. 1863, d 24 Jul. 1887 in Manchester, NH., m Edith A. Moore of Manchester, NH.

TAYLOR, JAMES C. - Born ??, d ??, s/o Thomas or Thomas Jr. and ?? Taylor of Brunswick, Maine. James C. Taylor m (1) ----, and m (2) Mary Toole, and m (3) Cynthia ----. Children: **Edward**; **Mary/Mary Helen** m A./Albert Warren (see WRIGHT for children); **Ellen/Nellie** m Charles Balde/Blake; **Emily C.** b 6 Jul. 1856 or -- Jul. 1860, d 18 Dec. 1891, m 11 May 1878 Albion S. Wright; and **George** d 1877, unm.

TAYLOR, JOSEPH - Born ??, d ??, s/o ?? Joseph Taylor m ---- Brown.

TAYLOR, JOSEPH - Born 31 Jan. 1784, d 3 Apr. 1855 age 71 years 2 months, s/o ?? Joseph Taylor m 17 Apr. 1808 Alice Graffam, b 9 Mar. 1783, d 19 May 1869. Children: **May** b 25 Jun. 1809, d 7 Feb. 1884 age 74 years 7 months 12 days, m 1 Apr. 1834 Wilbert Damon, d 6 Apr. 1862 age 53 years; ---- two sons, b -- Dec. 1810; **Joseph, Jr.** b 2 Nov. 1812, m 3 Jan. 1852 Martha B. Moody; **William H.** b 25 Nov. 1813, m 18 Jul. 1840 Roxanna Cross; **Rebecca** b 8 Jan. 1816, d 17 Apr. 1887 age 71 years 3 months, m 18 Sep. 1837 William Conent, d 18 Sep. 1887 age 78 years 6 months; **Randall** b 13 Oct. 1817, d 6 Mar. 1867 age 49 years, m 9 Jul. 1846 Catherine F. Leach; **Elizabeth** b 2 Jun. 1819, m 10 May 1859 Alvin H. Pettingill, d 29 Sep. ---- age 62 years 1 month 9 days; **Alicia** b 28 Dec. 1820, d 21 May 1892, m 28 Nov. 1848 James Taylor, d 20 Jan. 1886 age 65 years 3 months; and ---- son, b&d 1829.

TAYLOR, JOSEPH - Born ??, d ??, s/o Thomas and ?? Taylor. Thomas Taylor was the s/o Luther C. Taylor. Joseph Taylor lived in Boston, Massachusetts. He m pub. 2 Mar. 1874 Annie Hughes of Lewiston. Children: **Hiram S.**; and **Lucy**.

TAYLOR, JOSEPH - Born ??, d 2 Feb. 1892 in Litchfield, s/o James and ?? Taylor of Wales, Maine. Joseph Taylor m 2 Jul. 1848 Mary Brown of Greene, Maine. Children: **Ann Augusta** b 25 Oct. 1849, d 14 Dec. 1862; and **Lewella May** b 17 May 1854, d 21 Dec. 1862.

TAYLOR, JOSEPH - Born 2 Mar. 1812 in Minot, d ??, s/o Joseph and ?? Taylor of Plymouth, Maine. Joseph Taylor m 3 Jan. 1852 Martha B. Moody, b in Parsonsfield, Maine, d/o Daniel. Children: **George H.** m 29 Sep. 1883 Addie M. Ward of Troy; **Horace R.** m Augusta A. Witham; **Lucy J.**; **Joseph, Jr.**; and **Elmer E.**

TAYLOR, JOSEPH - Born 27 Sep. 1852, d ??, s/o Thomas and ?? Taylor. Joseph Taylor m Elizabeth Pettingill Greene, d/o Joseph.

TAYLOR, JOSHUA - Born 2 Feb. 1772, d 24 Mar. 1837 age 63 years, s/o Thomas and ?? Taylor. Joshua Taylor m Mary Hackett, d 3 Oct. 1843 age 71 years. Children: **Mercy** b 1 ---- 1793; **Joshua** b 20 Dec.

1794; **Richard** b 26 Feb. 1800, m Mary Toothaker; **Sarah** b 9 Feb. 1804; **Relief** b 2 Aug. 1806; and **Thomas** b 8 Jan. 1809, d 15 Apr. 1855.

TAYLOR, JOSHUA JR. - Born ??, d ??, s/o Joshua, Sr. and ?? Taylor. Children: **E b e n** m (1) Julia Greaton, d 16 Oct. 1846 age 21 years, and m (2) Margaret Judkins; **Joshua, 3rd** m Mary Savage; **I r a s o n** m Susan Brooks; and **E n o s T.** b 1834, d 13 Apr. 1836 age 2 years.

TAYLOR, JOSHUA 3RD - Born ??, d ??, s/o Joshua, Jr. and ?? Taylor. Joshua Taylor, 3rd m Mary Savage. Children: **two sons.**

TAYLOR, LUTHER - Born 24 Sep. 1802, d ??, s/o Thomas and ?? Taylor. Luther Taylor m Marshia Paul, d/o David Paul. Children: **Thomas** b 19 Sep. 1824, d 29 Sep. 1826; **Thomas** b 23 Jun. 1827; **Mary C.** b 7 Apr. 1831, m ---- Hackett; **Lucy A.** b 10 Jun. 1833, m 7 Jan. 1802 Joseph Plummer of Durham, ME; **Hannah L.** b 9 Jan. 1835; **Miriam** b 9 Dec. 1835; **Marcha B.** b 9 Apr. 1840, m 7 Jan. 1813 John Randall of Litchfield, ME; and **Russell S.** b 9 Sep. 1842, m Lucy A. Cook, who m (2) John Randall.

TAYLOR, PHINEAS - Born 13 Sep. 1786, d 4 Nov. 1855, s/o Thomas, Sr. and ?? Taylor. Phineas Taylor m Mary M. (?May) Hatch of Minot, Maine, b 3 Aug. 1791, d 1 Sep. 1871, d/o Samuel. Children: **Sally P.** b 3/30 Nov. 1812, d 14 Feb. 1888 (?), m A. J. Murray of Greene, ME, d Bath, ME; **Jane** b 12 Jan. 1815, d 19 Dec. 1884, m George Williston (?Willister), b 23 ---- 1811, d 14 ---- 1864; **Angeline** b 21 Dec. 1816, d 18 Sep. 1879, m Ivory Swett of York, ME, d 18 Sep. 1884; **Cynthia** b 11 Nov. 1819 (or 21 Dec. 1816 - twin to Angeline?), d 16 May 1847, m David T. Given; **Mary M.** or **May R.** b 5 Sep. 1821, m 21 Oct. 1841 Jonathan B. Knights of Lisbon, ME.; **George C.** b 9 Mar. 1826, d 26 Jul. 1826, unm; and **C a l v i n G.** b 4 Nov. 1828, m 31 Mar. 1851 Mary Cole of Topsham, ME.

TAYLOR, RICHARD - Born ??, d ??, s/o Joshua, Sr. (?) and ?? Taylor. Richard Taylor m Mary Toothaker. Children: **Jacob** b 1825, d 15 Jun. 1855 age 29 years 10 months; **David** d in the army; **Abram** m Mary Brooks; and **Charles** unm.

TAYLOR, THOMAS - Born 25 May 1794, d 13 Feb. 1837, s/o Thomas and Jemima (Coburn) Taylor. Thomas Taylor m -- Apr. 1817 Lucy H. Cook, b 1 Oct. 1799, d 19 Jan. 1859 in Hartland, ME., d/o James of Topsham. Children: **M a r t h a A n n** b 2 Jul. 1826, d 20 Jul. 1844; **Caroline Augusta** d 24 Jan. 1847 age 11 years 7 months; **Mary Ellen** d 5 May 1852; **James C.** d 2 Feb. 1864; and **Thomas Smith** b -- Aug. 1824, d 5 Jan. 1825.

TAYLOR, THOMAS - Born 8 Jun. 1809, d 15 Apr. 1855, s/o Joshua, Sr. and ?? Taylor. Thomas Taylor m Harriet Libbey, d 31 Jul. 1849 age 39 years 4 months, d/o Samuel. Children: **Philena** d 1 Feb. 1862 age 25 years 5 months, Henry Presson; **Rosco T.** d 6 Jan. 1862 age 20 years 8 months; **C h a r l e s H.** d 15 May 1863 age 19 years 7 months;

Oriaan m Zachariah Norton; **True** b 24 Apr. 1854, m Jennie Dolloff; and **Washington L.** b 24 Jul. 1838, m 4 Jul. 1865 Mary E. Stevens.

TAYLOR, THOMAS - Born ??, d ??, s/o Luther C. and ?? Taylor. Thomas Taylor m (1) 19 Feb. 1859 Serena G. Lowden, d/o Josiah, and m (2) 1 Jan. 1849 Sarah A. Francis, d/o Thomas. Children: **Joseph M.** b 23 Sep. 1850; **Charles S.** b 22 Feb. 1865, d 30 Sep. 1863; and **May E.** b 21 Mar. 1865, d 5 Mar. 1876.

TAYLOR, THOMAS SR. - Born 22 Feb. 1748 in Reading, Massachusetts, d 1825, s/o ?? Thomas Taylor, Sr. m pub. (1) 30 Nov. 1776 Sarah Richardson, and m (2) pub. 15 Apr. 1780 Jemima Coburn, d 1 Jun. 1801 age 55 years, and m (3) -- Jul. 1802 Miriam Pettingill, d 6 Apr. 1855 age 88 years. Children by 1st wife: **Sally** b 18 June. 1781; **Joseph** b 31 Jan. 1784; **Phineas** b 13 Sep. 1786; **James** b 11 Jul. 1789; **Rebecca** b 13 Apr. 1791; **Thomas** b25 May 1794; **Charles** b 22 Mar. 1797. Children by 2nd wife: **Luther** b 24 Sep. 1802; **Asa** b 16 Feb. 1807; **Nathaniel** b 3 Mar. 1804; **Bertholmew** b 26 May 1810; **Nathaniel** b 6 Jul. 1808. [Vital Records of Lewiston, Maine, p. 73.]

TAYLOR, URIAH C. - Born ??, d 24 Nov. 1882 age 68 years, s/o Joshua, Sr. and ?? Taylor. Uriah C. Taylor m (1) Almira Patterson, d 20 Sep. 1847 age 24 years, and m (2) Lydia N. Hale, d -- May/June 1893 age 67 years. Child of 1st wife: **Albertus F.** b -- Apr. 1847, d 16 Nov. 1883 age 36 years 7 months. Children by 2nd wife: **Uriah C.** b -- May 1852, d 8 Aug. 1855 age 3 years 3 months; **Willie E.** b -- Oct. 1858, d 22 Aug. 1872 age 18 years 11 months; **John F.** b -- Nov. 1855, d 6 Jan. 1857 age 14 months; and **Warren** m Alice Morrow.

TAYLOR, WILLIAM - Born ??, d ??, s/o James and ?? Taylor of Wales, Maine. Child: **Ella M.** b 27 Jan. 1862, m 15 Jun. 1880 Charles A. Gassett of Millford, MA.

TAYLOR, WASHINGTON L. - Born ??, d ??, s/o Thomas and ?? Taylor. Thomas Taylor was the s/o of Joshua Taylor. Children: **Rosco T.** b 28 Apr. 1867, d 28 Jan. 1871; **Cora A.** b 23 Aug. 1872, m 23 Aug. 1890 Will J. Smith; **Fred W.** b 3 Jun. 1876; and **Ernest L.** b 18 Jan. 1885.

TEBBETS, TEMPLE - Born ??, d ??, s/o ?? Temple Tebbets m Sarah ----. Children: **Albien Walker** b 4 Aug. 1833; and **Alonzo Garcelon** b 7 Jun. 1837. [Vital Records of Lewiston, Maine, p. 138.]

THOMAS, ELBRIDGE G. - Born ??, d ??, s/o James and ?? Thomas. Elbridge G. Thomas m Lydia E. Lane of Greene. Children: **Fred L.** b 3 Oct. 1858, d 3 Aug. 1861; **Isora** b 10 Jun. 1860, d 6 Jul. 1861; **Sarah E.** b 24 Nov. 1862, m 20 Jul. 1889 William F. Tibbetts; **James T.** b 11 Sep. ----, d 27 Nov. 1885; **Eunice M.** b 26 Dec. 1874, m 17 Aug. 1895 William Ramsey; and **Blanch Stella** b 20 Sep. 1877.

THOMAS, JAMES - Born 21 Feb. 1799 in Cape Elizabeth, Maine, d 27 May 1880, s/o Theophilus and ?? Thomas. James Thomas m 24

Dec. 1823 Eunice Robinson of Durham, Maine, b 28 Feb. 1796, d 24 Sep. 1876, d/o Samuel and Catherine (Clark) Robinson. Children: **Elisabeth Ann** b 24 Jan. 1824, d 3 Oct. 1893 in Bellvidere, IL., m 20 Mar. 1844 Peter J. Garcelon of Webster; **James William** b 28 Aug. 1826 in Lewiston, d 29 Mar. 1870, unm; **Sylvanus B.** b 19 Jan. 1829 in Lewiston, m (1) 27 Jun. 1853 Marie M. Foss of Wales, ME, d 27 Jul. 1857, and m (2) 11 Dec. 1859 Julia M. Hammond; **Sarah J.** b 7 Oct. 1831, d 20 Dec. 1850; **Dexter S.** b 21 Oct. 1833; and **Elbridge G.** b 27 May 1837, m 1857 Lydia R. Lane of Greene, ME. [Vital Records of Lewiston, Maine, p. 137 and *History of Durham, Maine* by Stackpole, published by the Town, 1899, p. 263.]

THOMAS, SYLVANUS D. - Born 19 Jan. 1828, d ??, s/o ??

THOMPSON, ACTOR P. - Born ??, d ??, s/o ?? Children: **Lena A.** b 21 Jul. 1871 in Pittston, ME, m -- Oct. 1892 Frank W. Worthing of Hartland, ME; **Rachel W.** b 20 Jan. 1876 in Bath, ME, d 22 Apr. 1883, m ----; **Arthur P.** b 27 Mar. 1867 in China, ME, m -- Jul. 1890 Mary Estey of Waterville; and **Fenn** b 9 Aug. 1868 in Chelsea, MA, m Warren L. Whitney.

THOMPSON, CORNELIUS - Born 18 Apr. 1791, d 5 Nov. 1857, s/o ?? Cornelius Thompson m (1) Sarah Cotton, and m (2) 14 Mar. 1832 Abigail Sylvester. *Children by 1st wife*: **Caroline Mehetable** b 2 Jul. 1819, d 3 Oct. 1840; **Henry Herrick** b 1 Nov. 1821, d 20 Feb. 1874; **Elisabeth Sylvester** b 8 Nov. 1824, d 17 Sep. 1826; and **Sarah** b 3 Sep. 1829, d 11 May 1830. *Children by 2nd wife*: **Harriet** b 18 Dec. 1832, m Joseph Healey; **Martha** b 3 Jul. 1835, m Cyrus Cox; and **Sarah** b 26 Jun. 1837, m Abraham Healey. [Vital Records of Lewiston, Maine, p. 137.]

THOMPSON, DAVID - Born 14 Sep. 1786, d 29 Dec. 1874, s/o ?? David Thompson m pub. 20 Nov. 1807 Lydia Stackpole of Durham, Maine. Children: **Nehemiah** b 22 Aug. 1808, d 28 Apr. 1887, m Elisabeth ----; **Jane L.** b 27 Aug. 1810, d 25 Feb. 1878, m Henry S. Harris; **Hannah W.** b 10 ---- 1813, m ---- Furbush; **Mary W.** b 20 Jun. 1816; **Christina L.** b 18 Feb. 1818, m Reubin Stetson; **Rachael D.** b 29 Aug. 1820, d 4 Apr. 1849, m ---- Little; **James H.** b 12 Nov. 1822, m 11 Nov. 1858 Bethiah J. Buker; **Elisabeth L.** b 21 Jul. 1824, m ---- Fillmore; and **Phebe** b 15 Mar. 1826, m ---- Farrar.

THOMPSON, EUGENE CHAS. - Born ??, d ??, s/o ?? Child: **Edith A.** b 30 Sep. 1867, m 19 Oct. 1887 Rufus Menserean.

THOMPSON, HIRAM - Born ??, d ??, s/o ?? Hiram Thompson m Achsa Small. Children: **Augusta** m Edward Littlefield of Haverhill, MA; **Sarah** m John Paul; **Chas. Eugene** b 24 Aug. 1845, m Lucy E. Hackett; **Mary** m Horace Horan of Haverhill; **Walter** m Lissie Herinton of Durham, ME; **Albert**; **Andora**; **Caroline** m Perry Kuse of Newfield, NH; **Frank** m Ella Thompson; and **John**.

THOMPSON, ISAAC C. - Born 22 May 1801, d ??, s/o ?? Children: **Alfred H.** b 7 Dec. 1826, d 21 Jun. 1873; **Theophalus** b 15 Feb. 1831, d 31 May 1896 in Lewiston; **Harriett Augusta** b 6 Dec. 1833; and **Isaac Woodman** b 15 Apr. 1837. [Vital Records of Lewiston, Maine, p. 138.]

THOMPSON, JAMES H. - Born 12 Nov. 1822, d ??, s/o ?? James H. Thompson m 11 Nov. 1858 Bethiah J. Buker. Children: **Arabella M.** m Davis Sanborn; and **Nellie J.** m Milan Sanborn.

THOMPSON, COL. JOEL - Born 26 Oct. 1766, d 1 May 1841 at Lewiston [*Kennebec Journal*, issue 29 May 1841], s/o ?? Joel Thompson m 16 Jul. 1828 Martha Cotton. Children: **Mehitable** b 10 May 1782, d 22 Mar. 1839, m 8 Feb. 1802 Jedediah Herrick; **Joel** b 26 Jul. 1784, m (1) pub. 11 Nov. 1809 Ruth Dwinal, and m (2) Rachel Willson of Topsham, ME; **Phineas** b 23 May 1786, m 27 Feb. 1806 Mary Metcalf of Lisbon, ME; **Sally** b 12 Mar. 1789, d 29 Mar. 1815, m pub. 9 Mar. 1810 William Randall; **Cornelius** b 18 Apr. 1791, d 5 Nov. 1857, m (1) pub. 4 Oct. 1817 Sarah Cotton, and m (2) Abigail Sylvester; **Martha** b 17 Apr. 1793, d 13 Oct. 1880, m (1) 6 Jan. 1811 Henry Herrick, and m (2) 8 Sep. 1819 Nathaniel Eames, and m (3) 22 Feb. 1843 Jed Herrick; **Ruth** b 8 Feb. 1796, m pub. 12 Dec. 1818 Daniel Grant; **Hannah** b 3 Dec. 1798, d 1 Aug. 1837, m pub. 22 Oct. 1820 Wm. Davis of Lewiston; **Isaac** b 22 May 1801, d 14 Jul. 1861, m 5 Jan. 1826 Mercy Carvelle; **Theophilus B.** b 6 Jun. 1803, d 10 May 1890, m 1 Nov. 1841 Charlotte Corbett; and **Nelson** b 10 Dec. 1805, d 9 Sep. 1882, unm. [Vital Records of Lewiston, Maine, p. 73.]

THOMPSON, JOEL JR. - Born 26 Jul. 1784, d -- Sep. 1853 in Wayne, Maine, s/o ?? Joel Thompson Jr. m (1) -- Apr. (? 11 Nov.) 1809 Ruth Dwinal, and m (2) 12 Dec. 1813 Rachel Willson of Topsham, Maine. *Child of 1st wife*: **Joel Dwinal** b 24 Dec. 1810, d 21 Feb. 1853, m Hattie French. *Children of 2nd wife*: **Thomas Wilson** b 12 Nov. 1814 m Hannah Harmon; **Jedediah Herrick** b 1 Jan. 1817, d -- Jan. 1848; **William Owen** b 28 Apr. 1819, m Abbie Clark; **James Smullen** b 9 Apr. 1822, m (1) Lydia Bourne, and m (2) Margaret Alley; **Actor Patten** b 23 Apr. 1828, m (1) 7 Dec. 1869 Rose Ally, and m (2) 11 Jan. 1859 Martha R. Marston; **Josiah Sanford** b 4 Dec. 1832, m (1) Rose Hayford, and m (2) Lena Edson; **George Owen** b 11 Mar. 1826, m (1) Marietta Moulton, and m (2) Melissa Tyler; and **Rachel W.** b 21 Mar. 1835, d 21 Apr. 1889 in Bangor, m Warren L. Whitney.

THOMPSON, JOSEPH - Born 1755, d 26 May 1827, s/o ?? Joseph Thompson m Happy ----. Children: **Samuel** b 6 Apr. 1783, m (1) 31 Jul. 1814 Betsy Proctor, and m (2) 25 Jun. 1807 Charlotte Lincoln; **David** b 14 Sep. 1786, d 29 Dec. 1874, m Lydia Stackpole; **Sally** b 5 Apr. 1789, m 13 Jun. 1816 Elijah Briggs of Greene; **Charity** b 16 Sep. 1791, d 30 Apr. 1851, m 17 Aug. 1809 Zebulon Wright; **Jeremiah** b 1 Mar. 1794; **Nehemiah** b 8 Oct. 1796, d 6 Nov. 1802; and **Isaac Jones** b 23 Jun. 1800. [Vital Records of Lewiston, Maine, p. 75.]

THOMPSON, SAMUEL - Born 6 Apr. 1783, d ??, s/o ?? Samuel Thompson m (1) 25 Jun. 1807 Charlotte Lincoln, and m (2) 31 Jul. 1814 Betsey Proctor, b 26 May 1792. *Child of 1st wife*: **Caroline** b 5 Jan. 1808. *Children of 2nd wife*: **Mary Ann** b 26 Apr. 1813; **George** b 5 Feb. 1815, unm; **Charlotte** b 3 May 1817; **Hiram K.** b 11 Mar. 1819, m Achsa Small; **Charles** b 17 Aug. 1822; **John Proctor** b 14 Feb. 1826; and **Rachel Elisabeth** b 20 Mar. 1829. [Vital Records of Lewiston, Maine, p. 75.]

THOMPSON, SOLOMON - Born ??, d ??, s/o ?? Solomon Thompson m Silva ----. Child: **Hannah** b 29 Aug. 1829. [Vital Records of Lewiston, Maine, p. 78.]

THOMPSON, WARREN EDMOND - Born ??, d 1826 in Orono, Maine, s/o ?? Warren Edmond Thompson m 1826 Mary Atkinson. Children: **Julia Ann** b 6 Dec. 1824 in Lewiston; and **Edmond Warren** b 13 Dec. 1825? in Orono. [Vital Records of Lewiston, Maine, p. 74.]

THORNE, AARON D. - Born ??, d ??, s/o ?? Aaron D. Thorne m Mrs. Laura C. Thorne (nee Merrill), d 2 Aug. 1883. Children: **Ann Augusta** b 4 Feb. 1843, m 4 Feb. 1861 Albert Edwards; **Susan Ellen** b 16 Jun. 1844, d 24 Jan. 1869, m John A. Willard; **Laura Eva** b 30 Apr. 1848, m 27 Oct. 1866 Augustus Royall; **Byron Orestis** b 22 Mar. 1846, m Eliza White; **Josephine** b 10 Jan. 1850, m Wilson Schwartz; and **Rachel Adelade** b 25 Feb. 1850, m Willard Linscott.

THORNE, BARNET - Born 26 Feb. 1826, d 28 Aug. 1891, s/o Samuel and Abigail (Lufkin) Thorne. Barnet Thorne m (1) Emily Fogg, d 1 Mar. 1862, and m (2) 27 Jul. 1862 Julia P. Farrow. Children: **Edwin E.** b 1866; and **Effie R.** b 1868.

THORNE, BARNET - Born 12 Mar. 1770, d 23 Apr. 1815, s/o Samuel and Hannah (Hoyt) Thorne. Barnet Thorne m Jane Lane, d 31 Mar. 1815, d/o Edmond Lane. Children: **Mary** b 12 Sep. 1796, m pub. 29 Dec. 1831 Benjamin Wilbur of Minot, ME; **Rachel** b 5 Aug. 1797, m 13 Sep. 1821 Daniel Lufkin; **Hannah** b 5 Aug. 1797, m 20 Feb. 1823 William Campbell of Minot; **Samuel** b 9 Dec. 1799, d 22 Jan. 1886 in West Sumner, ME, m Abigail Lufkin of Augusta, ME; **Barnet, Jr.** d in Bowdoinham, ME, m pub. 18 Oct. 1829 Jane Sketton; **Martha** d in infancy; **John**; **Martha** d in Bowdoinham, unm; **Edmund Lane** m (1) ---- Baker, and m (2) Rachel Pratt; and **Jane** m Jeremiah Niles. [Vital Records of Lewiston, Maine, p. 76.]

THORNE, REV. BENJAMIN - Born 30 Mar. 1779 in New Gloucester, Maine, d 4 Dec. 1864, s/o ?? Rev. Benjamin Thorne m 9 Aug. 1804, pub. 6 Aug. 1804, Allice Dresser of Pejepscot. Children: **Alice** b 26 Mar. 1805, d 1 May 1866, m 7 Nov. 1830 Samuel Given; **Olive** b 26 Jun. 1806, m 3 Jan. 1830 Samuel Turner; **Lois** b 26 May 1808, m 4 Feb. 1857 Edward S. Woodbury of Webster, ME; **Benjamin Hoyt** b 14 Nov. 1809, d 16 Feb. 1836, m 18 Nov. 1830 Laura C. Merrill; **Samuel** b 25 Apr. 1811, d 23 Jun. 1832, unm; **Elias Smith** b 11 Mar. 1813, d 30 Oct. 1818; **Thomas D.** b 29 Aug. 1814, m (1) 8 Jul. 1838 Jane M. Merrill, and m (2) 30 Dec. 1871 Mary H. Bickford; **Aaron D.** q.v.; and **Aurilla** b 20 Jun. 1820, m 11 Oct. 1856 Alfred Tuttle of Athens. [Vital Records of Lewiston, Maine, p. 76 and see *Free Baptist Cyclopaedia* by Burgess and Ward, published by the Free Baptist Cyclopaedia Co., 1889, p. 644.]

THORNE, BENJAMIN - Born circa 1810, d 16 Feb. 1836 [vital records of Lewiston, Maine, p. 239], s/o Eld. Benjamin and ?? Thorne [*Morning Star* obit. issue 13 Apr. 1836]. Benjamin Thorne m 18 Nov. 1830 Laura Merrill, d/o Jacob of Lewiston. Children: **Eliza Jane** m Andrew J. Lufkin; **Benjamin W.** m Mary Ella Smith; and **Samuel T.** b 2 Sep. 1833, d 28 Aug. 1846 age 12 years.

THORNE, BENJAMIN - Born ??, d ??, s/o ?? Children: **Chester W.** m Dell Haskell; and **Eliza G.** m 22 Oct. 1887 James W. White of Auburn, ME.

THORNE, CHESTER W. - Born ??, d ??, s/o ?? Children: **Benjamin**; and **Chester B.**

THORNE, HARRY - Born ??, d ??, s/o Thomas D. and ?? Thorne. Child: **Asa Willett** b 3 Feb. 1901.

THORNE, SAMUEL - Born 7 Nov. 1772, d 15 Sep. 1798, s/o Samuel and Hannah (----) Thorne. Samuel Thorne m pub. 6 Mar. 1796 Rebecca Winslow, d/o Knelin. Child: **Rhoda** b 4 Mar. 1798, d 31 May 1891, m (1) John Barnes, s/o Peltish Barnes, and m (2) Benjamin Vinny.

THORNE, SAMUEL - Born 9 Dec. 1799, d 24 Jan. 1888, s/o ?? Samuel Thorne m (1) Abigail Lufkin of Augusta, Maine, d -- Sep. 1837, and m (2) Emma Dolloff, d 8 Mar. 18--. *Children by 1st wife*: **Barnet** b 26 Feb. 1826, d 28 Aug. 1891; **Louisa** b 1828, m Joseph N. Masterman; **Hannah** b 17 Jun. 1831, m Samuel Moore; and **Edmund** b 15 Sep. 1835, d 1864 in Libby Prison. *Children by 2nd wife*: **Samuel** b 26 Mar. 1841, d 4 Jul. 1864 on the Red River Expedition; **Abigail** b 16 Jan. 1843, m George Webster; **Sarah** b 29 Oct. 1844, m Charles Clark; **Rosannah** b 6 Dec. 1846, m Henry Caswell; **Emma Y.** b 14 Mar. 1849; and **William** b 11 Sep. 1851, m Viletta Wing.

THORNE, SAMUEL - Born 5 Nov. 1743, d 10 Feb. 1828, s/o ?? Samuel Thorne m Hannah Hoyt, d 27 Jul. 1821. Children: **Barnet** b 12 Mar. 1770, m Jane Lane; **Samuel** b 7 Nov. 1772, d 15 Sep. 1798, m pub. 6 Mar. 1796 Rebecca Winslow, d/o Knelin; **Abigail** b 13 Apr. 1775, d 10 Apr. 1848; and **Benjamin** b 30 Mar. 1779, m Alice Dresser.

THORNE, THOMAS D. - Born ??, d ??, s/o ?? Thomas D. Thorne m (1) 8 Jul. 1838 Jane M. Merrill, d 19 Jun. 1867, and m (2) 30 Dec. 1871 Mary H. Bickford, b 2 Apr. 1840. *Children by 1st wife*: **Lucinda H.** b 18 Nov. 1838, d in Kansas, m Frank P. Weymouth; **Thomas A.** b 18 Nov. 1840, m (1) Lizzie Linscott, d/o Harvey and Lizzie, and m (2) Augusta Gray; **Mary Frances** b 16 Sep. 1842, m Peter J. Dresser;

Weston E. b 10 Dec. 1844, d 13 Dec. 1856; **Samuel T.** b 26 Nov. 1847, d 1 Jan. 1865 in Saulsbury Prison; **Woodbury J.** b 6 May 1850, m Adelia Lathrop; and **Jennie Eliza** b 10 Jun. 1858, m Asa R. Millett. *Child by 2nd wife*: **Harry Weston** b 3 Dec. 1876.

THORNE, WILLIAM - Born ??, d ??, s/o ?? William Thorne m Viletta Wing. Children: **Abner** b 17 Oct. 1873; **Albert** b 1 Jun. 1876; **Isaac** b 24 Mar. 1877; **Daniel** b 17 Apr. 1880; and **Dexter** b 25 Jan. 1882.

THORPS, ELIHU E. - Born ??, d ??, s/o ?? Elihu E. Thorps m Mary ----. Children: **Peter** b 14 Feb. 1833; and **Mary Elizabeth** b 22 Jun. 1836. [Vital Records of Lewiston, Maine, p. 139.]

TOBIE, EDWARD P. - Born 13 Oct. 1800 in New Gloucester, d 1875, s/o Jonathan L. and Lydia (Parsons) Tobie. Edward P. Tobie m (1) Caroline Frye, d/o Dean, and m (2) 9 Feb. 1840 Elizabeth Jane Harmon. *Children by 1st wife*: **Sarah F.** b 16 Nov. 1829; **Mary March Frye** b 13 Feb. 1832 twin; **Edward Parsons** b 19 Mar. 1828; and **Joseph Frye** b 19 Mar. 1828 twin. *Child by 2nd wife*: **LeRoy** b 18 Jan. 1843. [Letter from family of Edward Tobie, Pawtucket, RI, 1891.]

TRACY, DANIEL - Born 6 Apr. 1796, d ??, s/o Christopher and ?? Tracy of Durham, Maine. Daniel Tracy m (1) Polly Bicknell of Buckfield, and m (2) Thesey Bickford, b 8 Aug. ----. Children: **Hannah** b 29 Aug. 1818, d 1 Jan. 1892, m John Cornish; **Belinda** b 2 Aug. 1820, m (1) 7 Feb. 1841 William Cornish, and m (2) 16 Sep. 1858 Samuel G. Hall; **James B.** b 11 Aug. 1822, d 27 Dec. 1872, m (1) Helena Sampson, and m (2) pub. 11 Jan. 1864 Martha Ellen Eldridge, and m (3) pub. 20 Dec. 1867 Mary E. Manter, b 31 Nov. 1835, d/o Goff and Abilene Coleman Manton; **Mary** b 5 Jan. 1825, m Boyington Hervey of Lisbon; **Anna** b 23 Nov. 1827, d 19 Feb. 1893, m Edward Edgecomb of Bath, ME; **Aveline B.** b 14 Jun. 1830, m Charles Allen of Woodfords; and **Margaret** b 27 Jun. 1832, d 4 Jan. 1893, m Emery Bicknell. [See *History of Durham* by Everett Stackpole, published by the Town of Durham, ME, 1899, reprinted by New England History Press, 1979, p. 265-268.]

TRACY, JAMES B. - Born ??, d ??, s/o ?? James B. Tracy m (1) Helena Sampson of Bowdoinham, Maine, and m (2) Martha Ellen Eldridge of Greenbush, Maine, d/o Samuel and Selina (Spencer) Eldridge, b 27 Jan. 1834. *Child by 1st wife*: **Helena May** b 7 Aug. 1850, d 4 Oct. 1870. *Child by 2nd wife*: **Daniel** b 7 Aug. 1865, d 28 Feb. 1892 age 26 years 6 months 21 days, m 18 Jun. 1887 Emma Page of Lewiston. *Children by 3rd wife*: **James Henry** b 25 Jun. 1869; and **Ellen E.** b 23 Sep. 1871. [Letter from Mary E. (Mantor) Tracy, James's third wife, dated 26 Feb. 1897 - North Anson, ME, to Elder.]

TRAFTON, JOHN - Born ??, d ??, s/o ?? John Trafton m Nancy ----. Children: **John Crosby** b 27 Dec. 1801; and **Mary** b 3 Sep. 1812. [Vital Records of Lewiston, p. 76.]

TRAFTON, THOMAS - Born ??, d ??, s/o ?? Thomas Trafton m Mary ----. Children: **John** b 9 Sep. 1781; **Mary** b 6 Jul. 1783; **Betsey** b 31 Jan. 1785; **Charles; Thomas** b 25 Jun. 1788; **Mary** b 13 Dec. 1789; and **William** b 2 Dec. 1792. [Vital Records of Lewiston, Maine, p. 74.]

TREADWELL, JOSEPH - Born ??, d ??, s/o ?? Joseph Treadwell m Polly ----. Children: **Sukey** b 18 Mar. 1793; **Ruth** b 11 Oct. 1794; **Polly** b 20 Aug. 1796; and **John** b 6 Mar. 1798. [Vital Records of Lewiston, Maine, p. 73.]

TURNER, JAMES - Born 19 Jun. 1791, d 12 Jan. 1875, s/o ?? James Turner m 29 Nov. 1818 Alice Tarr. Children: **Susan** b 1 Apr. 1821, d 16 Sep. 1881, m pub. 5 Oct. 1845 Jacob F. Drinkwater; **James** b 30 Nov. 1822, m Nancy Jordan; **Mary** b 17 Nov. 1824, m 18 Feb. 1874 Frank Fowles; **Alice** b 13 Aug. 1826, m 4 Jul. 1844 Wm. Vickery; **Mary Jane** b 25 Oct. 1828, m pub. 27 Aug. 1855 James Vickery; **Sarah Ann** b 13 Apr. 1831, m Charles S. Whitney; and **Isaac Tarr** b 23 Oct. 1833, m 31 Dec. 1864 Mrs. Elizabeth Sowell of Litchfield, ME. [Vital Records of Lewiston, Maine, p. 137.]

TURNER, JAMES - Born ??, d ??, s/o ?? James Turner was a Revolutionary soldier, and resident of Andover, Massachusetts, when he enlisted (in Zebulon K. Harmon's Pension Records at the Maine Historical Society). He m 3 Sep. 1784 in Cape Elizabeth, Maine, Isabell (Simonton) Ranes, d 16 Jan. 1843 in Lewiston - she m (1) 4 Jan. 1784 Edward Ranes who died immediately afterwards. James and Isabella Turner came to Lewiston and he died there in 1800. She married next 10 May 1804 David Wilkins of Lewiston. Children: **Polly** b 6 Jun. 1785; **Sally** b 14 Apr. 1878; **Priscilla** b 1 Jan. 1789, m Cyrus Marr of Lisbon, ME; **James** b 19 Jun. 1791, d 12 Jan. 1875, m 29 Nov. 1818 Alice Tarr; **Isaac** b 20 Jun. 1793; **Suca** b 20 Jun. 1793, m pub. 23 Oct. 1823 Dr. Alexander Hutch; **Betsey** b 19 Dec. 1795; and **Samuel** b 14 Dec. 1797, m Olive Thorne. [Vital Records of Lewiston, Maine, p. 75.]

TUCK, SAMUEL - Born 1760 at Gloucester, Massachusetts, [*History of Farmington* by Francis Gould Butler, published by ??, 1885, reprinted by New England History Press, 1983, p. 593], d 1841 age 81 at Farmington, Maine, [*Kennebec Journal* 29 May 1841 obit], s/o Andrew and ?? Tuck. Samuel Tuck m Mary Baird. Children: **John** b 13 Oct. 1783, m Elizabeth Todd; **Polly/Mary** b 10 Sep. 1785; **Samuel** b 11 Oct. 1787, m Mercy Lincoln; **Joseph** b 3 Sep. 1789, m Annie Richmond; **Enos** b 8 Feb. 1792; **Jeremiah** b 8 May 1794, m Charlotte Walker; **James** b 23 Jul. 1796, m Rachel Carville; **Josiah** b 19 Jun. 1799; **William** b 25 Jan. 1802, m Eliza Grant. [Vital Records of Lewiston, Maine, p. 74; *History of Farmington*; Rev. Allen Greeley's records of North Yarmouth; Bragg Cemetery, Farmington, ME.]

TURNER, SAMUEL - Born 14 Dec. 1797, d 25 Sep. 1868, s/o ?? Samuel Turner m 3 Jan. 1829 Olive Thorne. Children: **Olive Amanda** b 30 Apr. 1830, d 6 Aug. 1858; **Benjamin H.** b 30 Sep. 1831, d 21 May

----, m 13 Jan. 1864 Lissie A. Woodbury; **John S.** b 23 Apr. 1833, d 4 Feb. 1863, m pub. 31 Oct. 1857 Deborah J. Webster; **Laura Jane** b 21 Feb. 1835, d 17 Mar. 1878, m 5 Dec. 1854 Frederick Dana Webster; **Samuel G.** b 6 Nov. 1836, d 4 Apr. 1860, unm; **Nathan R.** b 29 Nov. 1838, m pub. 9 Feb. 1861 Cemantha Tuttle; **Elias T.** b 19 Mar. 1841, d 19 Jan. 1861; **Aurelia A.** b 14 Jun. 1843, d 31 May 1860; and **Lois Amelia** b 15 Nov. 1845, d 4 Apr. 1859. [Vital Records of Lewiston, Maine, p. 138.]

TURNER, WILLIAM - Born 26 Feb. 1825, d 13 May 1863, s/o ?? William Turner m 3 Sep. 1848 Celia C. Robinson. Children: **Fred Allen** b 30 Mar. 1850; **Ellen E.** b 2 Jul. 1853; **Benjamin F.** b 24 Dec. 1855; **William H.** b 19 Jun. 1858; and **Edwin F.** b 21 Mar. 1862, d 11 Apr. 1863.

VARNAM, ASA - Born 14 Dec. 1743, d 1773/1774, s/o Abraham and ?? Varnam of Dracut, Massachusetts. Asa Varnam m Abigail East, d/o Joseph East. Abigail (East) Varnam m (2) Benjamin Winslow. Children: ---- b 19 Sep. 1773 in Lewiston, d 17 Dec. 1846 in North Yarmouth, Maine. "First female white child born in Lewiston," according to the Lewiston vital records, p. 79. [Letter from Asenath Winslow House, date unknown.]

VICKERY, MATTHIAS - Born 19 Jul. 1743 in Boston, Massachusetts, d ??, s/o David and Hannah (Parker) Vickery. Matthias Vickery settled first in Portland, then Cape Elizabeth with his mother circa 1746, where he lived for about three years. In 1770, he moved to Bluehill, Maine, where he farmed and fished. The next year he moved his family to [Lewiston Plantation, Maine] Greene, Maine, took up a farm there. After three years residing in Lewiston Plantation (now part of Greene) sold his farm and purchased land on South River Road in [Pejepscot now] Auburn, Maine. He spent a great deal of his early life at sea. He m (1) 9 Nov. 1767 at Cape Elizabeth, Maine, Ruth Horton, b 1748 at Cape Elizabeth, d 26 Dec. 1779 at Bluehill, and m (2) 14 Apr. 1780 at New Gloucester, Maine, Elizabeth Wagg. *Children of 1st wife*: **David** b 1768; **Hannah** b 8 Jun. 1770, m Nathaniel Davis of Lewiston; **John** b 1 Feb. 1772, d 2 Feb. 1780; **David** b 2 Sep. 1773; **James** b 1 Aug. 1775, m Rebecca Penley; **Matthias, Jr.** b 6 Mar. 1777; and **Isaac** b 7 Apr. 1779. *Children of 2nd wife*: **Ruth** b 20 Jun. 1781 at Greene, m John Lane and moved to Dexter, Maine. [Vital Records of Danville, Maine, p. 55, 56 and Starbird records and family records.]

VIDETO, JOSEPH - Born ??, d 11 Jul. 1839, s/o ?? Joseph Videto was in the area as early as 1801. He was a Revolutionary soldier and at the time of his marriage with Rachel Hammond, he belonged to New Gloucester, Maine. He lived in No. Yarmouth, came to Lewiston. His fourth wife drowned herself in the little stream in Auburn, Maine, nearly opposite the Bearce Stream Mill. After learning she was not in the stream, they commenced to search the main river when Videto remarked: "Don't look downstream for her. She was too g-- d--- contrary to do downstream," and sure enough, she was found above the little stream where she was drowned. Videto was a basketmaker. He m (1) 14 May 1787 Rachel Hammond of No. Yarmouth, Maine, and m (2) ----, and m (3) int. 9 Jun. 1799 Mary Mugford, d 10 Mar. 1801, and m (4) pub. 3 May 1801 Lydia Mugford of Windham, Maine. Children by 4th wife: **Ebenezer** b 2 Jan. 1802 [vital records of Lewiston, Maine, p. 79]; and **Sophia** d -- Aug. 1823.

VINING, BENJAMIN - Born 3 Aug. 1764, d ??, s/o Benjamin, Sr. and ?? Vining. Benjamin Vining m Sally Ring, d/o Barchelder Ring. Children: **Bacheldier** b 17 Feb. 1798; **Benjamin Brooks** b 30 Mar. 1799; **Thomas** b 31 Mar. 1800; **David** b 15 Jan. 1802; **Page** b 29 Mar. 1803; **Seward** b 8 Feb. 1805; **Converse** b 27 Feb. 1807; **Edward** b 17 May 1809; **John** b 2 May 1811; **Nathaniel** b 16 May 1813; and **Salley** b 8 Sep. 1814. [Vital Records of Lewiston, Maine, p. 79 and see *History of Durham* by Everett S. Stackpole, published by the Town of Durham, 1899, p. 274.]

WAKEFIELD, ARCHIBALD - Born ??, d 2 Feb. 1882, s/o Elisha and ?? Wakefield. Archibald Wakefield came from Buxton, Maine. He m 27 Nov. 1834 Sarah Davis, d 17 Nov. 1892, d/o David. Children: **David D.** b 12 Jan. 1837, d 12 May 1837; **Seth D.** q.v.; **Edwin** b 15 Mar. 1840; **Harriet** b 5 Jul. 1843, m 1869 Rufus Carr; **Mary A.** b 9 Mar. 1846, d 13 Oct. 1848; **Hannah** b 21 Nov. 1849, m 23 Dec. 1873 Phinney Mellen; **Sarah Alice** b 30 Sep. 1853; and **Helen** b 13 Nov. 1855.

WAKEFIELD, SETH D. - Born 23 Feb. 1838, d ??, s/o Archibald and Sarah (Davis) Wakefield. Seth D. Wakefield m 25 Aug. 1859 Mary E. Coffin, a descendant of Tristam Coffin of Dorsetshire, England. Children: **Archie C.** lived in Worcester, MA; and **Fred S.**

WALDRON, CHARLES - Born in Auburn, Maine [then most likely Danville, Maine], d 13 Apr. 1908 age 54 years and 3 months and 5 days, s/o William and Jane A. (Hitchcock) Waldron. Children: **Mary C.** of Vassalboro, ME, class of 1911, Bates College, Lewiston; and **Gertrude** of Vassalboro. [Probate records of Androscoggin Co. and Vital Records at the Maine State Archives.]

WALDRON, WILLIAM H. - Born 1822 in Dover, New Hampshire, d 25 Feb. 1881 age 59 years, s/o Job and ?? Waldron. William H. Waldron was a lineal descendant of the Indian-fighting Col. Waldron who figured in King Philip's War and whose fighting qualities were valuable to the early New England colonists. He married Jane Hitchcock of Strong, Maine. Children: **Grace** m Thomas E. Calvert; and **Charles W.** [Obit 26 Feb. 1881, *Lewiston Journal*.]

WARE, BENJAMIN L. - Born ??, d ??, s/o Isaac and ?? Ware. Children: **Aramenta Lois** b 9 Jul. 1878; and **Ethel Ione** b 12 Dec. 1880.

WARE, ISAAC - Born ??, d 12 Sep. 1851/1852, s/o Lewis and ?? Ware. Isaac Ware m 1 Jan. 1836 Eleanor Arris, b 5 Dec. 1814, d 2 Jul. 1867, d/o Patrick and Sarah (Jordan) Arris [*The Jordan Memorial* by T. F. Jordan, reprinted by New England History Press, 1982, p.

103; Starbird's records of Danville, Maine]. Children: **Elizabeth Ellen** b 9 Jun. 1839, m 3 Aug. 1854 Daniel Trask; **Benjamin L.** b 24 Oct. 1851, m 3 Jul. 1873 Louise Leighton, Auburn, ME, b 3 Oct. 1857, d/o Elias H. Leighton and Linett; **George A.** b 27 May 1837, d -- May 1839; **Sarah M.** b 1 Oct. 1841, d 12 Oct. ----; **Levi Greely** d 12 Oct. ----; **Isaac Wentworth** b 16 Apr. 18--, d 12 Oct. ----; and **Isaac E.** b 8 Aug. 1847, d 6 May 1851.

WARE, LEVI S. - Born ??, d ??, s/o Lewis Sr. and ?? Ware. Levi S. Ware m Sally Ware, d/o James. Children: **Charles N.** b 6 Feb. 185-; **Franklin**; **Hiram**; **Levi S., Jr.** b 25 Sep. 1850; **Prudence**; **Lucy Ann** d young; **Ardella**; **Lenora**; **Sophronia** d 17 Apr. 1880 age 23 years; **Rosalina**; **Amelia** m 14 Jun. 1882 Rev. Charles A. Peakes; **Ida May**; **Alsada** d 11 Aug. 1886 age 21 years; and **Lillian B.**

WARE, LEVI S. JR. - Born ??, d ??, s/o ?? Children: **Lola B.** b 6 May 1868, m 23 Feb. 1889 Thomas Garohen; **Reginald S.** b 1 Jan. 1872; **Charles W.** b 23 Jan. 1876, d 17 Mar. 1876; and **Genoa M.** b 9 Apr. 1879.

WARE, LEWIS - Born 30 May 1789 in Sudbury, Massachusetts, d 13 Aug. 1882, s/o Isaac and Sally (Howard) Ware. Lewis Ware m 9 Apr. 1812 Miriam Bubier, d 12 May 1872. Children: **Isaac** q.v.; **Eunice** b 3 Jan. 1814, d 1 Mar. 1894 in Pittston, ME, m William Ware of Pittston; **Lucinda** b 27 Feb. 1816, d 3 Feb. 1889 in Greene, ME, m (1) 21 Jul. 1833 William Stewart, s/o Thomas, and m (2) Harry Piper; **Lewis** b 18 Apr. 1818, m (1) 17 Apr. 1839 Martha Bubier, and m (2) 20 Sep. 1850 Ellen Moody; **Levi S.** b 17 Mar. 1820, d 20 Feb. 1904 in Newton, MA., m Sally Ware; **Sally** b 6 Jan. 1823, d 17 Jun. 1862 in Pittston, ME, m George Washington James of Pittston; **Hannah** b 6 Jul. 1825, m -- Aug. 1850 Benjamin Turner of China, ME, d 6 Jul. 1893; **Lucy Ann** b 30 Sep. 1835, m 11 Oct. 1858 Moses King; **Margaret Jane** b 7 Oct. 1839, d 25 Jun. 1841 in Lisbon, ME; **Caleb** b 19 Jun. 1833, d 16 Apr. 1860 age 27 years at Lewiston [*Lewiston Journal*, 23 Apr. 1906, "Old Men of 1878 in Lewiston, Some Ancient Sires"]; and ---- three children who died in infancy.

WARE, LEWIS - Born 18 Apr. 1818 in Lisbon, d -- Jan. 1900, s/o ?? Lewis Ware m (1) 17 Apr. 1840 Martha Bubier, b 10 May 1816 in Bowdoin, Maine, d 13 Feb. 1800, and m (2) 20 Sep. 1846 Eleanor Moody, b 10 May 1827 in Pittston, Maine. Children: **Amanda J.** b 8 Oct. 1841 in Woolwich, ME, m (1) 16 Sep. 1860 Orrinton Chadbourne, and m (2) pub. 6 Nov. 1877 Edward Hayes; **Martha C.** b 22 Oct. 1843 in Leeds, ME, m pub. 18 Jul. 1863 Francis M. Stewart; **Scribner M.** b 1 Oct. 1847 Hallowell, d 19 Feb. 1868; **Miriam** b 20 Feb. 1849 in Lewiston, m John Remick; **Eleamenzo** b 9 Nov. 1850 in Lewiston, m 4 Jul. 1876 Eliza Golder; **Sarah E.** b 9 Mar. 1852 in Lewiston, m 16 Mar. 1873 Silas W. Patterson of Pittston; **Isaac** b 8 Jul. 1854 in Lewiston, d 29 May 1873; **Lewis A.** b 18 Apr. 1856 in Lewiston; **George F.** b 7 Apr. 1858 in Lewiston, m 27 May 1892 Bertha Kawfenans; **Horatio G.** b 20 Nov. 1860, d 31 Aug. 1863; **Eleanor** b 26 Nov. 1862, m 21 Nov. 1881 John W. Moody of Pittston; **John H.** b 11 Aug. 1863 in Lewiston;

Lucinda b 5 Aug. 1865 in Lewiston, m 15 Mar. 1886 Ransom Lane of Greene; **Lama A.** b 9 Sep. 1867 in Lewiston, m 9 Jun. 1888 Joseph F. Davis of Webster, ME; **Angenette** b 21 Dec. 1868 in Lewiston, d 21 Aug. 1882; and **Edith E.** b 6 Apr. 1872 in Lewiston.

WEBBER, ARZA B. - Born ??, d ??, s/o ?? Children: **Bertram**; and **Fannie**.

WEBBER, CHARLES M. - b 18 Jan. 1851, d ??, s/o Daniel G. and ?? Webber. Charles M. Webber m -- Oct. 1887 Hannah J. Sweeney. Children: **Charles** b 12 May 1890; and **Lottie** b 13 Jan. 1892.

WEBBER, CLARENCE VERNIER - Born 26 Oct. 1869, d ??, s/o Mark G. and ?? Webber. Clarence Vernier Webber m 2 May 1891 Roschester Walker. Child: **Mina Lucy** b 20 Apr. 1905.

WEBBER, DANIEL G. - Born 15 Jan. 1816, d 24 Jan. 1904, s/o ?? Daniel G. Webber m 10 Sep. 1843 Betsey Staten, d 18 Jan. 1904. Children: **Otis** b 27 Mar. 1846, d 13 May 1894; **Susan** b 12 May 1848; **Adda** b 28 Dec. 1849, m (1) pub. 11 Oct. 1871 Henry F. Brown, and m (2) Leon Parker of Lewiston; **Charles Millett** b 18 Jan. 1851, m -- Oct. 1887 Hannah J. Sweeney; **Ellen** b 15 Mar. 1856; **Henry** b 15 Mar. 1856, d 24 Sep. 1856; and **Frank** b 24 Mar. 1862.

WEBBER, DAVID - Born ??, d ??, s/o ?? David Webber m 1 Jun. 1845 Caroline Edmond.

WEBBER, EDSEL - Born ??, d ??, s/o ?? Edsel Webber m pub. 6 Dec. 1812 Dorcas Blethan. Children: **Hannah** b 7 Jun. 1813, m Stover Bibber; **Jesse** b 23 Jan. 1815, d 4 Feb. 1869 age 54 years, m pub. 24 Nov. 1839 Eliza D. Harmon; **Abigail** b 19 May 1819, m Isaac Douglass of Lisbon, ME; **Charlott** b 10 Oct. 1819, m 17 Sep. 1856 Sewall Chamberlain of Auburn, ME; **Edsel B.** b 11 Mar. 1822, m Clementine Brown; **Orpha** b 4 Aug. 1824, m ---- Thompson; **Lydia Jane** b 5 Feb. 1828, d 16 Dec. 1832; **Cordelia R.** b 18 Jun. 1832; and **David S.** b 6 Feb. 1839, d 13 Jun. 1843.

WEBBER, ELIAS S. - Born 23 Jun. 1827, d 29 Jun. 1898, s/o ?? Elias S. Webber m 8 Jan. 1850 Clarion P. Jepson, b 13 Oct. 1830, d/o Ebeneser. Children: **Medora** b 8 Aug. 1853, d 8 Aug. 1853; **Cora A.** b 14 Oct. 1855, d 14 Oct. 1855; **Eldora L.** b 10 Sep. 1856, d 18 Feb. 1879, m 25 May 1877 William I. Small; **Wallace W.** b 8 Apr. 1859; **Elmer E.** b 22 May 1864, m 12 Aug. 1886 Savina Walker, d/o Jonathon of Norway, ME; **Mary D.** b 12 May 1866, m 1 Jan. 1888 George E. Famedan of Farmington, ME; **Ellsworth** b 14 Oct. 1868, m (1) 12 Apr. 1890 Lilla J. Small, d/o Newry, d 12 May 1893, and m (2) 5 Oct. 1898 Mary Collen in Brunswick, ME; and **Archella M.** b 11 Aug. 1873, d 15 Jul. 1892.

WEBBER, ELLSWORTH G. - Born ??, d ??, s/o Elias and ?? Webber. Child: **William E.** b 1 May 1891.

WEBBER, ENOS S. - Born ??, d ??, s/o ?? Enos S. Webber m 2 Mar. 1862 Mahalie Sewall.

WEBBER, FRANK M. - Born ??, d ??, s/o ?? Frank M. Webber m 17 Dec. 1876 Florence P. Jack.

WEBBER, FORRIDON ANNIS - Born -- Oct. 1866, d ??, s/o Mark G. and ?? Webber. Forridon Annis Webber m 30 May 1891 Maud A. Verrill. Children: **Myrtle Elizabeth** b 17 Aug. 1892; **Marjory Vere**; and **Fred**.

WEBBER, JEREMIAH - Born 7 Aug. 1818, d 29 Dec. 1876 at Galesville, Wisconsin, s/o ?? Jeremiah Webber m 10 Jun. 1849 Rebecca Holland, d/o John. Children: **Frank A.** b 4 Mar. 1850, d 16 Oct. 1870 in Mankato, MN; **Alton E.** b 3 Jun. 1853, m 12 Feb. 1884 Eva Thorsander; **Arthur T.** b 26 May 1857, m 1 Jun. 1879 Bell Frueap; **Oscar B.** b 12 Sep. 1861, m 9 Aug. 1884 Maybell Mean; **Otho H.** b 12 Sep. 1861, d 22 Aug. 1864 at Green Castle, IN.; and **Elmer** b -- Oct. 1863, d 16 Nov. 1863 at Galesville, WI.

WEBBER, JESSE - Born 4 Sep. 1763, d 30 Jan. 1809, s/o ?? Jesse Webber m Charlott ----, b 29 Nov. 1760. Children: **Joseph** b 9 Sep. 1791, d 2 Feb. 1874 age 82 years, m (1) pub. 1 Jul. 1814 Mrs. Polly Walker (nee Garcelon), d 29 Nov. 1854, and m (2) 3 Feb. 1855 Nancy F. Heath, d 14 May 1856 age 62 years 6 months, and m (3) 7 Aug. 1856 Fanny Butler; **Edsel** b 11 Jan. 1793; **Benjamin** b 7 Apr. 1795; **Desire** b 16 Jul. 1797, d 30 Nov. 1800; **William** b 1 Oct. 1799; and **Mary** b 6 Sep. 1807.

WEBBER, JESSE - Born 23 Jan. 1815, d 4 Feb. 1869, s/o Edsel and ?? Webber. Jesse Webber m pub. 24 Nov. 1839 Eliza D. Harmon. Children: **Mary Mellisa** b 26 Sep. 1840, m 29 Jan. 1857 Addison B. Parsons of Hartford, ME; **William D.** b 30 Nov. 1842, m 15 Apr. 1865 Melissa N. Hilton; **Arza B.**; **Levi H.** b 22 Jan. 1847, m (1) 12 Mar. 1874 Abbie J. Cole, and m (2) 21 Apr. 1877 Abbie H. Auburn; **Alice** m Cyrus Rich of Standish, ME; **Edna** m William Perkins of Paris, ME; **Delia** m pub. 18 Dec. 1876 William Moore; **George W.** m 1 Jan. 1876 Mattie A. Larrabee; **Ella** m Sidney Smith; and **Josiah**.

WEBBER, JOHN - Children: **Frank M.** b 4 Aug. 1860, m Florence P. Jack of Lisbon; **Fred W.** b 12 Jan. 1863, m 28 Feb. 1885 Eleanor Cobbree of Etna; and **Herbert S.** b 15 Nov. 1866, m 30 Sep. 1893 Josephine Foss.

WEBBER, JOSEPH - Born 9 Sep. 1791, d 2 Feb. 1874, s/o Jesse and ?? Webber. Joseph Webber m pub. 1 Jul. 1814 Mrs. Polly Walker (nee Garcelon), d 29 Nov. 1854, and m (2) 3 Feb. 1855 Nancy F. Heath, d 14 May 1856 age 62 years 6 months, and m (3) 7 Aug. 1856 Fanny Butler of Greene, Maine. *Children by 1st wife*: **Daniel G.** b 15 Jan. 1816, d 24 Jan. 1904, m 10 Sep. 1843 Betsey Staten, d 18 Jan. 1904; **Jeremiah W.** b 7 Aug. 1818, d 29 Jan. 1876, m 10 Jun. 1849 Rebecca Holland, d Washington, KA.; **Mary Ann** b 10 Oct. 1821, m

Willilam Lyon; **William G.** b 22 Apr. 1825, d very young; **Elias Staton** b 23 Jun. 1827, d 28 Jan. 1898, m 8 Jan. 1850 Clarion P. Jepson; **Sally Maria** b 21 Apr. 1830, d 14 Feb. 1904 age 73 years 10 months 8 days, m pub. 28 Oct. 1849, m 16 Nov. 1849 Benjamin Randall; **Mark G.** b 24 Apr. 1833, m Mary Robinson; and **Olive Jane** b 8 Oct. 1837, m 13 Jan. 1854 John D. Lane of Greene.

WEBBER, LEVI H. - Born ??, d ??, s/o Jesse and ?? Webber. Levi H. Webber m (1) 12 Mar. 1874 Abbie J. Cole, and m (2) 21 Apr. 1877 Abbie H. Swan. Child: **Effie A.** b 6 Jan. 1905/1906, m 30 May 19-- Fred E. Whittle.

WEBBER, MARK G. - Born 24 Apr. 1833, d 19 Jun. 1890, s/o Joseph and ?? Webber. Mark G. Webber m 7 Jan. 1861 Sarah Robinson of Oxford, Maine, d 25 Jul. 1895, d/o Orin and Hannah (----) Robinson. Children: **Fred** m Maud A. Verrill, d 25 Jul. 1895; **Vern** m Rochester Walker; and **Rose** m Llewellyn Hoffses. [Letter from ---- Norway, Maine, 1905, was one of the children of Mark G. Webber.]

WEBBER, PERLEY W. - Born ??, d ??, s/o Elias and ?? Webber. Children: **Chester W.** b 19 Jun. 1889; **Elsie A.** b 23 Sep. 1892, d 30 Oct. 1893; and **Lensea A.** b 30 Jul. 1894.

WEBBER, SAMUEL J. - Born ??, d ??, s/o ?? Samuel J. Webber m 10 Nov. 1853 Sally D. Merrill of Lewiston.

WEBBER, WILLIAM - Born ??, d ??, s/o ?? William Webber m Abigail Jackson, d 22 Sep. 1879. Children: **Sally M.** b 15 Aug. 1828; **Samuel Jackson** b 28 Sep. 1829; **Lovina Smith** b 14 Apr. 1831; **Mary Catherine** b 20 Sep. 1835; **Owen Blake** b 27 Sep. 1836; **Alfred** b 31 Oct. 1829; and **John Henry** b 6 Sep. 1841.

WEBBER, WILLIAM - Born ??, d ??, s/o ?? Child: **Angeline** d 28 Mar. 1852.

WEBBER, WILLIAM D. - Born ??, d ??, s/o Jesse and ?? Webber. Children: **Edwin W.** m Alice Haskell, d/o Rev. Wm. G.; **Perley LaForest; Jessie;** and **Eben.**

WEBBER, WILLIAM H. - Born ??, d ??, s/o ?? William H. Webber m 14 Jun. 1864 Emerline Thompson.

WEBSTER, F. DANA - Born 20 Jan. ----, d 26 Jan. 1882, s/o ?? F. Dana Webster m (1) 5 Dec. 1854 Laura Turner, d 18 Feb. 1878, and m (2) 2 Nov. 1880 Martha J. Patton. Children: **Florence A.** b 2 Dec. 1856, m George D. Bond; **Jennie** b 25 Apr. 1859, d 7 Aug. 1860; **William E.** b 30 May 1861, m -- Oct. 1886 Jennie McKenney, d/o Charles D. of Auburn, ME; and **Gertrude** b 25 Feb. 1870.

WEBSTER, WILLIAM - Born ??, d 1 Dec. 1879, s/o ?? William Webster m 25 Dec. 1827 Patience Read, d 4 Dec. 1856. Children:

Deborah b 9 Jan. 1832, d 26 Apr. 1872, m John S. Turner; and **F. Dana** b 20 Jan. ----, d 26 Jan. 1882.

WEBSTER, WILLIAM E. - Born ??, d ??, s/o ?? Children: **Laura M.** b 1 Aug. 1887; **Ethel M.** b 25 Feb. 1890; and **Inez D.** b 10 Jul. 1893.

WEDGEWOOD, CHASE - Born 29 Mar. 1806, d -- Sep. 1893, s/o ?? Chase Wedgewood m pub. 9 Sep. 1798 Martha Mitchell of Lewiston, b 8 Aug. 1779, d age 91 years.

WEDGEWOOD, CHASE - Born 19 May 1773 in Chester, New Hampshire, d 7 Apr. 1861 in New Hampshire, s/o Samuel and Martha (Godfrey) Wedgewood. Chase Wedgewood m pub. 9 Sep. 1798, m 29 Nov. 1798 Martha C. Mitchell of L----, b 8 Aug. 1779, d 1870 age 91 years. Children: **Isaac** b 7 Sep. 1800 in Lewiston, d 1889 in Dover, ME, m 15 Jul. 1821 Judith Kelley of Durham, ME; **Chase** b 3 May 1802 in Lewiston, d 20 Apr. 1824 in Tamworth, NH, unm; **Anasiah** b 10 Mar. 1804 in Lewiston, d 1891 in Grand Rapids, MI, m Mary Kelley of Durham; **Curtis** b 29 Mar. 1806, d -- Sep. 1893, m 2 Sep. 1831 Hannah Springer, b 12 Feb. 1807, d 21 Nov. 1877, d/o David and Hannah (Smith); **Samuel** b 11 Jan. 1808 in Lewiston, d -- Aug. 1890 in Brownville, ME, m Clariss Kelly of Durham in Newportland, ME; **Dana** b 16 Feb. 1810 in Lewiston, d in Old Town, ME, m Mary House of Brooks, ME; **Martha G.** b 12 Jun. 1813 in Tamworth, NH, d 1 Mar. 1892 in Sandwich, NH, m David Atwood of Sandwich, NH; **John G.** b 22 Sep. 1817 in Tamworth, NH, d 1864 in Hannibal, MO; **Charles Alonso** b 21 Jun. 1815, d 10 Oct. 1839 in Somerville, NH, m Elizabeth Moulton of Sandwich, NH.; **Josiah** b 28 Jun. 1819, d 1864 in Tamworth, unm; and **Mary Melissa** b 11 Apr. 1821 in Tamworth, m 15 Dec. 1844 Samuel Door of Sandwich, NH, b 30 Sep. 1822 in Newfield, ME. [Letter from O. J. Dorr of Sandwich, New Hampshire, dated 1897, to Elder.]

WEDGEWOOD, CURTIS - Born ??, d ??, s/o ?? Children: **M. C.** b 23 Dec. 1832, m -- Dec. 1861 Lizzie Webster; **Thomas S.** b 9 Apr. 1834, m Addie Leavitt of Salem, ME; **John** b 25 Nov. 1836, d 21 Jul. 1842; **Martha** b 4 Apr. 1840, m 25 May 1861 James T. Purington of Topsham, ME; **George G.** b 7 May 1842, m Bessie Hutchings; **N. J.** b 19 Jun. 1846, m 18 Jun. 1870 Maria Ring of Richmond, ME; and **Luella P.** b 20 Mar. 1848, m 21 Dec. 1870 Arista Webber of Litchfield, ME.

WEDGEWOOD, DAVID - Born ??, d ??, s/o ?? David Wedgewood m 4 Jan. 1863 Hannah Hobbs, lived in Hampton, New Hampshire. Children: **John**; and **Mary**.

WEDGEWOOD, JOHN - Born ??, d ??, s/o ?? JOhn Wedgewood m 31 Jan. 1712 Hannah Shaw, lived in Hampton, New Hampshire. Children: **David**; and **Jonathan**.

WEDGEWOOD, JOHN - Born ??, d 1654, s/o ?? John Wedgewood lived in Hampton, New Hampshire, 1644 to 1654 (?). He m Mary ----. Children: **John; Jonathan; Mary; Abigail;** and **David.**

WEDGEWOOD, JONATHAN - Born ??, d ??, s/o ?? Jonathan Wedgewood m 25 Jan. 1737 Mary Marston, lived in Hampton, New Hampshire. Children: **Jonathan; Hannah; David; Samuel; Hephsibah; James; Mary; Jonathan; Catherine; John; Jonathan;** and **Josiah.**

WEDGEWOOD, SAMUEL - Born 8 Feb. 1742, d ??, s/o ?? Samuel Wedgewood m Deborah ----, lived in Hampton, New Hampshire. Children: **Lydia; Mary; Sarah;** and **Chase.**

WEEKS, JAMES - Born ??, d ??, s/o ?? James Weeks m Priscilla ----. Children: **Lydia** b 18 Nov. 1785; **Betsey** b 11 Feb. 1788; **Experience** b 25 Dec. 1791; **Anna/Anne** b 14 Jun. 1795; and **Hannah/Tamah** b 26 Apr. 1797. [Vital Records of Lewiston, Maine, p. 84.]

WHITE, EDWARD - Born ??, d ??, s/o ?? Edward White m Hannah ----. Children: **Charles** b 27 Sep. 1818; **Edward** b 16 Oct. 1819; **Nathan Chase** b 8 Jun. 1821; **Hipsibeth Joanna** b 21 Apr. 1823; **Calvin Gorham** b 3 Apr. 1825; **Mariah** b 6 Apr. 1827; and **John B.** b 15 Feb. 1829. [Vital Records of Lewiston, Maine, p. 88.]

WHITE, THOMAS - Born ??, d ??, s/o ?? Thomas White m 20 Jul. 1823 in Lisbon, Maine, Mercy Colson. Children: **Francis Dillin** b 11 Nov. 182?; **Alonzo Durgin** b 10 May 182?. [Vital Records of Lewiston, Maine, p. 89, 440.]

WHITTEMORE, BARSTONE - Born ??, d ??, s/o ?? Barstone Whittemore m Jane ----. Children: **Mary Ann** b 13 Nov. 1829; **Laura Jane** b 29 Jul. 1834; **James** b 27 Jul. 1836; and **Otis** b 21 Jul. 1838. [Vital Records of Lewiston, Maine, p. 90.]

WHITTUM, DAN - Born 13 Oct. 1808, d 23 Dec. 1874, s/o ?? Dan Whittum m Betsey Stetson, d 16 Feb. 1876 age 58 years 10 months 20 days. Children: **George Dennison; Walter S.** b 6 Jul. 1842, d 3 May 1862; **Rodney** b 20 Oct. 1843, m 27 Nov. 1867 Annie B. Ayer; **Harriet N.** b 13 Dec. 1846, d 8 Apr. 1899, m 16 Aug. 1873 Herbert L. Foss; **Eben; Stephen** unm; **Charles M.** b 5 Oct. 1854, d 11 Feb. 1858; **Etta A.** b 20 Jun. 1857, m 8 Nov. 1875 Levi M. Pettingill of Monmouth, ME; and **Charlie** b 7 Mar. 1859.

WHITTUM, EBEN - Born ??, d ??, s/o Dan and ?? Whittum. Eben Whittum m 1873 Mary M. Prescott of Pittsfield, Maine. Children: **Leslie D.; Lulia A.; Minnie M.;** and **Elmer E. P.**

WHITTUM, EBENESER - Born ??, d ??, s/o ?? Child: **George** b Arlington, MA.

WHITTUM, EBENEZER - Born 13 Feb. 1780 [vital records of Lewiston, Maine, p. 86], d 11 Jan. 1849 age 69 years, s/o ?? Ebenezer Whittum m 13 Apr. 1806 Clarissa Tyler, b 25 Jan. 1786, d 10 Mar. 1862. Children: **John** b 15 Feb. 1807, d 22 Feb. 1889, m pub. 20 Nov. 1840 Mrs. Roxcyllania Cutter, d 9 Sep. 1865; **Dan** b 4 Oct. 1808, d 23 Dec. 1874, m pub. 10 Dec. 1838 Betsy Stetson, d 16 Feb. 1876; **Clarissa** b 22 Jul. 1810, d 8 May 1888; **Ebeneser** b 10 Jan. 1812, d 1 Jan. 1890, m Sarah Smith of Lexington, MA; **Sargent** b 16 Jan. 1814, d 13 Sep. 1887, m pub. 3 Mar. 1838 Sarah D. Mitchell, b -- Jul. 1811, d 1 Jan. 1894 age 81 years 6 months 16 days, d/o Samuel and Betsy (Dingley) Mitchell; **Moses** b 9 May 1816, d 5 Jul. 1865, m Sarah Rice of Woburn, MA; Sarah b 10 Feb. 1819, d 16 Jan. 1899, unm; **James** b 25 Sep. 1820, d 8 Jul. 1894, m Abbie Welch Fowles, d -- Nov. 1896, d/o Willmot and Permilia Hodgdon of Woolwich, ME; **Harriet** b 11 Aug. 1822, d 8 Oct. 1891, m James Bowker, d WI.; **George** b 19 Aug. 1824, m Elizabeth Gowing; **Martha Ann** b 26 Nov. 1826, d 5 Feb. 1878; and **Stephen C.** b 13 Oct. 1830 in Woodland, CA, m Susie Stanley, widow. [Vital Records of Lewiston, Maine, p. 86.]

WHITTUM, GEORGE - Born ??, d ??, s/o Ebeneser and ?? Whittum. Children: **G. Edward**; **William**; and **Lizzie**.

WHITTUM, JAMES - Born ??, d ??, s/o ?? James Whittum lived in Woolwich, Maine. Children: **Lizzie**; and **Frank**.

WHITTUM, JAMES - Born ??, d ??, s/o Ebeneser and Clarissa (Tyler) Whittum of Woolwich, Maine. Children: **Clara Permelia** m Homer F. Corliss; **Sarah Lizzie**; **Jennie Wright**; **James Frank** b 16 Aug. 1859, m 2 May 1894 Hattie Florence Corliss, b 3 Nov. 1870, d/o Howard and Abigail H. Nason of Woolwich; and **Ella**.

WHITTUM, JAMES F. - Born ??, d ??, s/o ?? Children: **James Howard** b 3 Mar. 1895; and **Florence Edith** b 3 Apr. 1899.

WHITTUM, JOHN - Born ??, d ??, s/o Ebeneser and ?? Whittum. Children: **Albert** b Dorchester, MA; and **Mary M.** b Wardsworth.

WHITTUM, J. FRANK - Born ??, d ??, s/o ?? J. Frank Whittum was from West Woolwich, Maine. He m H. Florence Corliss of West Woolwich.

WHITTUM, MOSES - Born ??, d ??, s/o ?? Children: **Sarah Jane**; **Caroline** of Worcester, MA; **Charles** of Worcester, MA; **Joshua Wm.** of Mt. Vernon, NY; and **Eliza**.

WHITTUM, RODNEY - Born ??, d ??, s/o ?? Children: **Harry W.** b 11 Oct. 1870; **Albert R.** b 21 Dec. 1874, d 5 Dec. 1886; **Arthur N.** b 24 Mar. 1877, d 25 Jul. 1887; and **Bessey Gertrude** b 17 Oct. 1878.

WHITTUM, SARGENT - Born 1813, d 13 Sep. 1887 age 74 years [buried in Riverside Cemetery, Lewiston], s/o Ebeneser and ?? Whittum. Children: **Mary Elizabeth** b 29 May 1839, m Albion W. Jordan of Webster, ME; and **William Henry** b 25 Apr. 1843, d 11 Dec. 1888, m 4 Feb. 1869 Abbie C. Jordan, d/o Nathaniel, d 25 Apr. 1894 age 48 years 3 months.

WHITTUM, WILLIAM H. - Born ??, d ??, s/o Sargent and ?? Whittum.

WIGGIN, DANIEL H. - Born 22 Mar. 1786 in Newmarket, New Hampshire, d 7 Aug. 1852, s/o Henry and ?? Wiggin. Daniel H. Wiggin m 24 Feb. 1818 Betsy Key, d 25 Jul. 1875, d/o Love Key. Children: **Henry L. K.** b 30 Apr. 1820 in Wolfborough, NH, d 25 Aug. 1875, m 18 Jul. 1847 Harriet A. Parker of Greene, ME; **Ann Mary** b 12 Mar. 1823 in Leeds, ME, d 1891, m 21 Jan. 1849 John C. Davis of Poland, ME; **Emeline Augusta** b 21 Mar. 1825 in Leeds, d 1885, m 18 Nov. 1847 James W. Strout of Poland; **Charles S.** b 26 Oct. 1827 in Leeds, d 12 Nov. 1850; **Levi Augustin** b 7 Apr. 1830 in Leeds, d 1 Feb. 1848; **Amy Elizabeth** b 3 Jul. 1833, m J. Alden Smith; **Daniel W.** b 20 Mar. 1836 in Leeds, d 1893, m (1) 17 May 1857 Lucinda E. Libby of Auburn, ME, and m (2) 1 Jul. 1863 Adarina H. Smith of Lewiston, d/o George B. Smith; and **William Harrison** b 13 Oct. 1839 in Greene, ME, m Mary A. Packard of Hallowell, ME.

WIGGIN, DANIEL W. - Born ??, d ??, s/o ?? Child: **Ralph L.** b 24 Jan. 1867, m 19 Sep. 1888 Gertrude E. Yetten of Auburn, ME, b 18 Jun. 1868.

WIGGIN, H. L. K. - Born ??, d ??, s/o ?? H. L. K. Wiggin was a medical doctor. Children: **Harriet Blaine** m John W. May of Auburn, ME; and **Henry Dwight** m Mary Sturdefant.

WIGGIN, RALPH L. - Born ??, d ??, s/o D. W. and ?? Wiggin. Ralph L. Wiggin m Gertrude E. Yetten. Children: **Alice Margaret** b 9 Sep. 1889; and **Daniel Webster** b 4 Aug. 1894.

WIGGIN, WILLIAM H. - Born ??, d ??, s/o ?? Children: **Agnes Beals** b 26 Sep. 1862, d 8 Feb. 1886; **William H., Jr.** b 20 Aug. 1867, m Grace Town Pomroy; **Maud E.** b 5 Feb. 1869, d 7 Jun. 1889; **Mary P.** b 10 Aug. 1872; and **Blanch E.** b 11 Feb. 1875.

WILKINS, AUGUSTINE - Born 26 Aug. 1838, d ??, s/o ?? Augustine Wilkins m (1) Josephine Farwell, and m (2) ---- Moulton of Greene, Maine. Children: **Marcia A.** b 13 Nov. 1862, m Henry Ashton of Sabatis, ME; **Alice May** m Julius Ambach; **Addie E.** m Samuel Sewall; **Clara Emma**; **Walter L.**; **Bertha M.**; **Harry A.**; and **Lena Maud**.

WILKINS, DANIEL - Born 12 Dec. 1796, d 30 Jan. 1876, s/o David and ?? Wilkins. David Wilkins was the s/o David Wilkins, Sr. Children: **Seth H.** b 7 Apr. 1830, m Lydia A. Coburn of Monmouth, ME, b 17 Jun. 1835; **Minerva Jane** b 13 Nov. 1832, m 9 Jan. 1872 Israel W. Longly, b 7 Feb. ----; **Ruth** b 4 Aug. 1835, d 15 Jul. 1893, unm; and **Daniel** b 4 Feb. 1837, d 30 Jan. 1865 age 28 years, unm.

WILKINS, DANIEL - Born 12 Jan. 1768, d 6 Oct. 1853, s/o David, Sr. and Molly (----) Wilkins. Daniel Wilkins m Jane ----, d 10 Feb. 1817. Children: **David** b 15 May 1794, m Dorcas Hill; **Daniel** b 12 Dec. 1796, d 30 Jan. 1876, m 26 Apr. 1827 Lavine Herrick, d 14 Jan. 1882 age 74 years, d/o Seth Herrick; **Anna** d 20 Sep. 1803; **Polly** b 24 Mar. 1806, m 24 Dec. 1829 Eliphlet Coburn of Greene, ME; **Enos** b 22 Jun. 1809, m pub. 25 May 1833 Hannah Libby of Wales, ME; and **Cedora Jane** b 8 Feb. 1815.

WILKINS, DAVID SR. - Born ??, d 18 Nov. 1834, s/o ?? David Wilkins, Sr. m (1) pub. 14 Mar. 1767 Molly Mary Harris, d 6 Oct. 1802/1803, d/o Lawrence J., and m (2) 10 May 1804 Mrs. Isabell Turner, d 16 Jan. 1843, wid/o James. Children: **Daniel** b 12 Jan. 1768, d 6 Oct. 1853, m Jane ----, d 10 Feb. 1817; **Molly** b 31 Oct. 1769, d 5 Jul. 1801, m Aaron Davis, d 11 Aug. 1841; **Mehitable** b 22 Sep. 1771, d 28 Jul. 1847, m Amos Davis; **Jerusha** b -- Jan. 1773, d -- May 1773; **Jerusha** b 1 Jun. 1774, d 15 Jan. 1824, m Jesse Higgins; **Deborah** b 1 Oct. 1777, d 29 Aug. 1801, m 20 Jan. 1836 John Graffam; **Mariah** b 29 May 1780, d -- Feb. 1815; **Anne** b 21 Jan. 1783, d 12 Jan. 1796; **David Jr.** q.v.; and **Stephen** b 26 Jul. 1788, d 24 May 1854 in Moscow, ME, buried in Bingham, ME, m 14 Jun. 1812 Ruth Eames of Greene.

WILKINS, DAVID JR. - Born 26 Dec. 1784, d 1 Apr. 1867 in St. Albans, Maine, s/o David and Molly (Harris) Wilkins. David Wilkins, Jr. m (1) Annie Eames of Greene, Maine, b 15 Mar. 1787, d 17 Apr. 1840 in Parkman, Maine, and m (2) Sarah Wall. Children: **Stephen** b 22 Feb. 1809, d 6 May 1857 in Parkman, m 1 Jan. 1835 Sarah Pingree; **Sally** m Robert Cushman, b 7 Sep. 1803 in Hebron, ME., d 9 May 1888; **Jacob**; **Nathaniel Ames** b 10 Mar. 1813 in Greene, ME, m (1) Sarah Davis of Bangor, ME, b 1815, d -- Mar. 1843, and m (2) Achsia Knowles, b 26 Feb. 1825 in Winterport, ME, d 19 Sep. 1870; **Eliza G.** b 27 Nov. 1815 in Parkman, d 11 Jul. 1893 in Exeter, ME, m Daniel Nevens of Exeter, b in Litchfield, ME; **William Warren** b 1827 in Parkman, d 29 Apr. 1880 in St. Albans, ME, m Ann Patten of Hampden, ME, d 20 Oct. 1896 in St. Albans; **David, Jr. (3rd)** b 1822 in Harmony, ME, d 1869 in St. Charles, IL, m Almira Lane of Parkman, d in St. Charles, IL; **Rosemond** b 1826 in Parkman, d 16 Mar. 1863, m Lowell Knowles of Corinna, ME; **Charity S.** b 25 Dec. 18-- in Parkman, m 19 Nov. 1848 Joseph Richardson of Newport, ME, b 5 Dec. 1824 in Guilford, ME., d 31 Jul. 1895; and **Almeda** b 1832 in Parkman, d 16 Apr. 1878, m James Russell of Newport.

WILKINS, DAVID - Born 15 May 1794, d ??, s/o Daniel and ?? Wilkins. David Wilkins m pub. 16 Sep. 1820, m 23 Nov. 1820 Dorcas Hill, b 18 Jan. 1798, d/o Nathaniel and May (Litchfield) Hill of Wells, Maine. Children: **Almon** b 22 Jan. 1822, m 7 Jun. 1850 Mary Cory of Buxton, no children, they went west; **Ellen** b 3 Feb. 1826, d -- Nov. 1893, m 6 Jan. 1844/1849 Verres Greenwood; **Eveline** b 15 Feb. 1828, d 23 Oct. 1846, unm; **Anaxine** b 31 Jul. 1831, m 28 Feb. 1867 Marshall Sawyer, lived in Greene, b 22 Feb. 1818 in Gorham, ME; **Mellen** b 4

May 1836, m Martha Ellen Clay of Buxton, ME, d/o Samuel and May; and **Augustine** b 26 Aug. 1838, lived in Livermore, m (1) Josephine Farwell, b 23 Oct. 1842, and m (2) Matilda Moulton.

WILKINS, DAVID II - Born 26 Dec. 1784 in Lewiston, Maine, d ??, s/o ?? David Wilkins, II m (1) 1808 Anna Ames of Greene, Maine, (sic: Grune), b 15 Mar. 1787, d 17 Apr. 1840 in Parkman, Maine, they moved to Parkman soon after marriage, but moved back to Greene, since most of their children were born there, and m (2) (?) Sarah Wall. Children: **Stephen** b 22 Feb. 1809 in Greene, m 1 Jan. 1835 Sarah Pingree of Parkman, d 6 May 1857; **Sally** m Robert Cushman, descendant of Robert Cushman of Plymouth Rock fame, settled in Corinth, ME; **Jacob** d young; **Nathaniel Ames Wilkins** b 10 Mar. 1813 in Greene, m (1) 1838 Sarah Davis in Bangor, ME, b 1815 in Bangor, d 1843 in Bangor, and m (2) Achsia Knowles, b 26 Feb. 1825 in Winterport, ME, d 19 Sep. 1870 in Glenburn, ME; **Eliza G.** b 27 Nov. 1815 in Parkman, d 11 Jul. 1893 in Exeter, ME, m Daniel Nevens (shoemaker), b in Litchfield, ME, d 1870 age 70 years in Exeter; **William Warren W.** b in Parkman, d in St. Albans, ME, m Ann Patten of Hampden, ME, d 20 Oct. 1896 in St. Albans; **David, Jr.** (3rd) b in Harmony, m Almira Lane of Parkman, both d in St. Charles, IL; **Rosemond** b in Parkman, m Lowell Knowles of Corinna, ME; and **Charity S.** b 25 Dec. ---- in Parkman, m 19 Nov. 1848 in Cambridge, ME, Joseph Richardson of Newport, ME, b 5 Dec. 1824 in Clifford, ME.

WILKINS, FRANCIS MARION - Born ??, d ??, s/o Stephen and ?? Wilkins. Children: **Joy G. W.** b 13 Apr. 1869 in St. Albans, ME, d 7 Mar. 1876 in St. Albans; **Maurace M.** b (?) 2/20 Feb. 1871 in St. Albans, drowned 15 Jul. 1896 in Indian Lake, St. Albans; **Leola W.** b 28 Jan. 1873, d 12 May 1873; **Albertie W.** b 20 Jan. 1874 in St. Albans; **Florence E.** b 5 Oct. 1875 in St. Albans; **Wilbur M.** b 24 Jan. 1879 in St. Albans, d 24 Mar. 1879; and **Jessie M.** b 20 Sep. 1882 in St. Albans.

WILKINS, FRANCIS M. - Born ??, d ??, s/o Stephen and ?? Wilkins. Children: **Walter W.**; and **Lucretia A.** m A. B. Tyler.

WILKINS, I. N. - Born ??, d ??, s/o David, Jr. and ?? Wilkins. Children: **Jennie**; and **Annie Ames**.

WILKINS, JOSIAH F. - Born ??, d ??, s/o ?? Josiah F. Wilkins m 11 Apr. 1885 Leetta Rowe in Lewiston, b 4 Oct. 1859, d/o David and Elizabeth Peary Rowe of G----.

WILKINS, LEVI - Born 30 Mar. 1816, d ??, s/o ?? Levi Wilkins m 26 Sep. 1874 Sadie E. Spencer. Children: **Charles E.** b -- Apr. 1854, d 19 Aug. 1882 age 28 years 5 months; **Laura**; and **Martha**.

WILKINS, MELLEN - Born 4 May 1836, s/o David and Dorcas (Hill) Wilkins. : Children: **Angella G.** b 2 Jan. 1863; **Samuel C.**; and **A. Judson**.

WILKINS, NATHANIEL AMES - Born 10 Mar. 1813 in Parkman, Maine, d ??, s/o ?? Nathaniel Ames Wilkins m (1) 1838 Sarah Davis in Bangor, b 1815, d 11 Mar. 1843, and m (2) Achsia Knowles. *Children of 1st wife*: **Helen M.** b 6 Aug. 1839 in Bangor, d 19 Apr. 1870 in Glenburn, ME, m 27 Jun. 1859 Harland Frost of Lowell, MA; **Isabella B.** b 30 May 1841 in Bangor, ME, d 16 Dec. 1890/1895 in St. Albans, m 1869 H. W. Brackett in Palmyra, ME; and **Francis** b 20 Aug. 1843 in Bangor, d 1 Sep. 1844 in Bangor. *Children of 2nd wife*: **Jasper** b 27 Oct. 1850 in Winterport, unm; **Leslie** b 22 Oct. 1855 in Glenburn, d -- Aug. 1864; **Jennie** b 12 Dec. 1861 in Glenburn, d 23 Sep. 1889 in Glenburn; and **Annie Ames** b 3 Jul. 1864 in Glenburn.

WILKINS, NATHANIEL W. - Born ??, d ??, s/o David, Jr. and ?? Wilkins. Nathaniel W. Wilkins m (1) Sarah Davis of Bangor, Maine, and m (2) Achsa Knowles. Children: **Helen Marr** m Harland Frost of Haverhill, MA.; and **Isabella B.** m H. W. Brackett. [Letter dated 1896 from M. L. Brackett of Newport, Maine, to Elder.]

WILKINS, SETH H. - Born 7 Apr. 1830, d ??, s/o Daniel, Jr. and ?? Wilkins. Children: **George M.** b 15 Jul. 1857; **John H.** b 16 Sep. 1859; and **Arthur C.** b 24 Oct. 1872, m Jennie Ashton.

WILKINS, STEPHEN - Born ??, d ??, s/o ?? Stephen Wilkins m Ruth ----. Children: **Anna** b 30 Sep. 1825 in Greene, Maine; **Levi** b 30 Mar. 1816; and **Amos** b 20 Nov. 1823.

WILKINS, STEPHEN - Born 26 Jul. 1788, d 24 May 1854 in Moscow, Maine, buried in Bingham, Maine, s/o David and ?? Wilkins. Stephen Wilkins m Ruth Eames, d 9 May 1831 in Moscow age 41 years. Children: **Levi** b 30 Mar. 1816, d 15 Apr. 1882 in Litchfield, ME, m 31 Jul. 1873 Mrs. Villa F. Grover; **Amos** b 20 Nov. 1823, d 16 Oct. 1826; and **Anna** b 30 Sep. 1825. [Letter from M. L. Brackett, special agent for the Prudential Insurance of America, dated 19 Sep. 1905, to Elder.]

WILKINS, STEPHEN - Born ??, d ??, s/o David, Jr. and ?? Wilkins. Stephen Wilkins m Sarah Pingree. Children: **Levcretia F.** b 13 Aug. 1838 in Parkman, ME, m A. B. Tyler of Parkman, s/o John Tyler, lived in St. Albans, ME; **Francis Marion** b 2 Dec. 1841, m 31 May 1868 Emily Knights of Gray, ME., lived in St. Albans, enlisted in 1861 in 2nd ME. Regt. Vols., wounded severely in the second battle of Bull Run, and honorably discharged and sent home; and **Walter Balfour** b 1853 in Cambridge, ME, m 10 May 1874 Mary Ellen Wing of St. Albans, ME.

WILKINS, STEPHEN - Born 22 Feb. 1809, d ??, s/o David, Jr. and ?? Wilkins. Children: **Lucretia F.** b 13 Aug. 1838, m A. B. Tyler; **Francis Marion** b 2 Dec. 1841 in Parkman, ME, m 31 May 1868 Emily Knight; and **Walter Balfour** b 1853 in Cambridge, m 10 May 1874 Mary Ellen Wing of St. Albans, ME.

WILKINS, WALTER BALFOUR - Born ??, d ??, s/o Stephen and ?? Wilkins. Stephen Wilkins was the s/o David Wilkins, Jr. Walter Balfour Wilkins m 10 May 1874 Mary Ellen Wing of St. Albans, Maine. Children: **Vesta M.** b 31 Oct. 1879; **Walter H.** b (?) 16/19 Feb. 1886; **Eldin E.** b 27 May 1890; **Alma M.** b 28 Nov. 1891/1892; **Clifford H.** b 20 May 1893; and **Wilmar** (?**William**) **G.** b 28 Feb. 1895.

WILKINS, W. S. - Born ??, d ??, s/o ?? W. S. Wilkins m 29 Mar. 1873 Martha Weymouth of Litchfield, Maine, d 18 Aug. 1880 age 31 years. Children: **Walter Leroy** b 21 Jan. 1876; and **Hannah Mary** b 27 Nov. 1879.

WILLIAMS, BARNARD - Born 15 Feb. 1807 in Lewiston, d ??, s/o George and ?? Williams. Barnard Williams m Elisabeth Augusta Herrick, b 9 Feb. 1815, d/o Jacob, Jr., and Abigail (Scott) Williams. Children: **George J.** d 27 Dec. 1870 age 27 years; **Oscar Scott** b 2 Jul. 1844, d 14 Oct. 1893, m 20 Oct. 1870 Silva M. Brooks, d/o Ham; **Charles E.** b 6 Apr. 1848, m Emma J. Harlow; **Josiah H.** lived in Durham, ME, m Edith Norton; and **F r e d M.** d -- Nov. 1897, m Ida Scammon of Saco, ME.

WILLIAMS, CHARLES - Born ??, d ??, s/o ?? Charles Williams m Eleanor ----. Children: **Margaret Ann** b 11 Mar. 1827; **Eleanor Jane** b 19 May 1829, d 25 Oct. 1829; and **E l e a n o r** b 24 Dec. 1830. [Vital Records of Lewiston, Maine, p. 90.]

WILLIAMS, CHARLES E. - Born ??, d ??, s/o ?? Charles E. Williams was an Auburn, Maine, M.D. He m 31 Mar. 187- Emma J. Harlow, b 17 Sep. 1852, d/o Abram D. and Roseta (Bard) Williams. Children: **Ethel Elisabeth** b 25 Apr. 1873; **Charles Edward, Jr.** b 12 Jun. 1875; and **Annie** b 18 Jul. 1880, d 4 Oct. 1891.

WILLIAMS, GEORGE - Born 3 Aug. 1777, d 8 Feb. 1867 in Durham, Maine, s/o Samuel and ?? Williams from Harpswell, Maine. George Williams was a Revolutionary Soldier. He moved to Thomaston, Maine. He m pub. 15 Mar. 1801 Mabel Litchfield, d 1 Nov. 1853 in Durham. Children: **C h a r l e s** b 17 Aug. 1801, m 9 Mar. 1826 Eleanor Randall, d/o Ezra and Molly; **Samuel** b 18 Dec. 1802, m pub. 20 Dec. 1834 Elisa F. Thomas; **M a r y S.** b 2 Sep. 1804, m 7 Oct. 1828 Capt. John Filler of Carmel, ME; **Barnard** b 15 Feb. 1807, m 16 Dec. 1841 Elisabeth Augusta Herrick, b 9 Feb. 1815, d/o Jacob, Jr., and Abigail (Scott); **Lucinda** b 26 Nov. 1808, d 13 Mar. 1810; **Auvila C.** b 15 Aug. 1810, m 25 Feb. 1836 James Jack of Portland, ME; **Lucinda** b 30 Mar. 1812, d 28 Aug.1866, m 22 May 1834 Joseph Webster, b 26 Mar. 1806, d 24 Aug. 1877; **George Summer** b 12 Dec. 1813, m Ann ----; **Elvira** b 13 Nov. 1815, m 20 May 1836 Jesu Snow, Jr., of Brunswick, ME; **Mabel Jane** b 24 Nov. 1817, d 1867, m 4 Mar. 1841 Nelson Strout of Durham; **Otis** b 1 Oct. 1819, m Frances ----; **Minerva** b 14 Jul. 1822, d 4 Mar. 1862, m 29 May 1845 Jeremiah Dingley, Jr.; and **Vesta Ann** b 5 Nov. 1824, m 29 May 1845 Harrison Strout of Durham. [Vital Records of Lewiston, Maine, p. 86.]

WILLIAMS, JOSIAH H. - Born ??, d ??, s/o ?? Josiah H. Williams m Edith Norton of Metinicus Isle, Maine. Child: **Ralph E.**

WILLIAMS, OSCAR SCOTT - Born 2 Jul. 1844, d 14 Oct. 1893, s/o Barnard and ?? Williams. Oscar Scott Williams m 20 Oct. 1870 Sylvia E. Brooks, d/o Ham Brooks. Of his children "none of the family married" [in 1897. Letter from W. S. Williams of Webster, Massachusetts, 1897]. Children: **Walter Scott** b 12 Dec. 1872; **George Brooks** b 29 Jun. 1875; **Fannie Elisabeth** b 7 Oct. 1877; **Winslow Oscar** b 14 Oct. 1878; **Sylvia Louise** b 15 Dec. 1880; **Frank E.** b 9 Nov. 1885, d 14 May 1889; **Harrison Morton** b 14 May 1888; **Adaline Marguerite** b 19 Dec. 1891. All from letter dated 26 Jul. 1897.

WILLIAMS, SAMUEL - Born ??, d ??, s/o ?? Samuel Williams was from Harpswell on Mercy, Maine. He was a soldier of the Revolution, enlisted 10 Jun. 1775 in Capt. James Curtis' Co., served 2 months 4 days. Possibly this Samuel was Sergeant in Capt. Nathan Lourdie's Co., enlitry 9 Jul. 1775 and served 6 months and 7 days. He m int. 14 Sep. 1754 Mercy Coombs, d -- Sep. 1824 age 94 years. Children (had others most likely): **Benjamin** b 14 Jan. 1767, lived in S. Thomaston near St. George line, d there, was a tanner, m c1790 Jane Otis of Thomaston; **D. Daniel** b 14 May 1775, moved c1885 to Thomaston, ME, settled in S. Thomaston on lot next to his brother's, d 13 Jun. 1858, m Hannah Page; **Peter** went to Thomaston in 1806, settled there was a joiner (?), m Margaret Bucklin of Warren, ME; and **George** b 3 Aug. 1777 in Harpswell, ME, first three children are recorded as b in Durham, ME, where he was probably working as a joiner, the rest were b in Lewiston, he moved to Durham about 1825 and settled on the Stoddwell farm, River Road, d 8 Feb. 1867, m Mabel Litchfield, b 29 Feb. 1780 in Scituate, MA., d 1 Nov. 1853 in Durham, d/o Noah of Lewiston, ME. [*Durham, Maine, History* by Stackpole, published by the Town of Durham, 1899, p. 286-287.]

WILSON, HENRY M. - Born ??, d ??, s/o ?? Henry M. Wilson m pub. 6 Nov. 1842 Hannah S. Meader. Children: **Caroline** b 11 May 1843; **Ellen C.** b 24 Apr. 1845; **Rebecca M.** b 24 Sep. 1846, m 31 Dec. 1874 William W. Goody of Lisbon, ME; **Edwin** b 7 Sep. 1848; and **Henrietta**.

WILSON, ISAACE - Born ??, d ??, s/o ?? Children: **Samuel**; **Willard**; **Henry**; **Ruth** m Samuel Goss; **Sarah** m Jeremiah Lovell; and **Eunice** m Dexter Goss.

WILSON, SAMUEL H. - Born 26 Aug. 1812, d 20 Nov. 1893, s/o Isaac and ?? Wilson. Children: **Adolphos P.** b 15 Nov. 1842, m 5 Nov. 1837 Deborah G. Gould, d 26 Mar. 1846; **Edward Alton** b 13 Apr. 1859, d 5 Mar. 1860; **John S. P. H.** b 9 Aug. 1860; and **Margaret Lenora** b 15 Jan. 1862.

WILSON, WILLARD H. - Born ??, d ??, s/o ?? Willard H. Wilson m (1) (?) Ellen R. ----, and m (2) Eliza R. Eastman of Fairfield, Maine.

Children: **Charles Emery** b 25 Sep. 1846; **Dwight Bagdon** b 6 May 1848; **Annie** m Ora Miller of Wilton, ME; and **Willard** m Clara Miller of Wilton.

WINSLOW, HORATIO N. - Born ??, d ??, s/o Jeremiah and ?? Winslow. Jeremiah Winslow was the s/o Jeremiah Winslow. Child: **Fred** m Clara Brown.

WINSLOW, JEREMIAH - Born 15 Jan. 1782, d 18 May 1836 in Bath, Maine, s/o Jeremiah Kenelmn Winslow. Jeremiah moved 1807 to Litchfield, Maine. He m 7 Jan. 1808 Eunice Richardson of Litchfield, b 2 Nov. 1793, d 27 Jul. 1848, d/o Abigail and Emma Thompson Richardson. Children: **Cornelius T. R.** b 7 Feb. 1809, went to sea and never was heard from again; **Horatio N.** b 22 Aug. 1810, d 20 Mar. 1878 in Bath, m (1) Mary T. Brimijohn, and m (2) Mary Patten; **Phebe R.** b 8 Jun. 1812, d 1865 in Bath, m Levi Huntington; **Mary Ann** b 26 Mar. 1814, m 18 Jul. 1842 Rufus L. Gary; **Kenelon** b 14 Mar. 1816, d 1875 in Lowell; **Sarah R.** b 18 Jul. 1818, d 17 Aug. 1864 in Cornville, ME., m Samuel Longfellow; **Jesse** b 25 Jun. 1823, d -- Jun. 1842 at sea; **Eunice Caroline** b 21 Dec. 1825, d 7 Dec. 1885 in Bath, m Levi Oliver; and **Jeremiah** b 17 Sep. 1829, d 30 Dec. 1881, m Lydia Cook.

WINSLOW, JEREMIAH - Born 17 Sep. 1829, d ??, s/o ?? Jeremiah Winslow m Lydia Cook. Children: **Horatio N.** m Ella Fuller; **William** m (1) Carrie Hill, and m (2) Louise Puster; and **Albert**.

WINSLOW, JOHN - Born ??, d ??, s/o ?? John Winslow m pub. 13 Sep. 1800 Dorcas Andrews of Brunswick, Maine. Children: **Stephen** b 1 Oct. 1801; **Deborah** b 24 Nov. 1803; and **Jemima** b 4 Aug. 1805.

WINSLOW, KANELON/KENELEM - Born 14 Mar. 1816, d ??, s/o Jeremiah and ?? Winslow. Children: **Horatio**; **John**; and **Levi** m Jane Pease.

WINSLOW, KENELEM - Died 13 Feb. 1796, d at Lewiston, Maine, s/o ?? Kenelem Winslow m pub. 9 Sep. 1775 Elizabeth Cole, b 8 Jan. 1754, d 17 Mar. 1800, d/o John. Children: **Rebecca** b 15 Sep. 1776, m pub. 6 Mar. 1796 Samuel Thorne; **John** m Dorcas Andrews of Brunswick, ME; **Job** b 15 Jan. 1781, m pub. 5 Jun. 1803 Betsey Andrews; **Jeremiah** b 15 Jan. 1783, d 18 May 1836 in Bath, ME, m Eunice Richardson of Litchfield, ME, b 2 Nov. 1783, d 27 Jul. 1848; **Elizabeth** b 13 Jun. 1785; **Lydia** b 17 Dec. 1787, m 10 Aug. 1809 Nathaniel Lincoln; **Samuel** b 6 Mar. 1790; **Lucretia** b 8 May 1792; and **Rhoda** d 13 May 1797. [Vital Records of Lewiston, Maine, p. 245.]

WINSLOW, WILLIAM - Born ??, d ??, s/o Jeremiah and ?? Winslow. Jeremiah Winslow was the s/o Jeremiah Kanelon Winslow. Children: **Arthur**; and **William**.

WOOD, DANIEL - Born 11 Nov. 1819 in Shapleigh, Maine, d 26 May 1906 in Lewiston, s/o Samuel S. and ?? Wood. Samuel S. Wood was the s/o Job Wood of Acton, Maine. Daniel Wood 1 May 1848 came to

Lewiston and commenced trade in Aug. of the same year. He m 23 Jul. 1843 Betsy Ann Leonard of Wilton, Maine, b 19 Feb. 1821, d 14 Mar. 1904, d/o Berry and Betsy (Powers). Children: **Betsey Eveline** b 16 Aug. 1846 in Wilton, d 17 Nov. 1870 age 25 years 3 months; **Benjamin Franklin** b 27 Mar. 1849, (Frank) d 1922; **Herbert Milo** b 11 Aug. 1851, d 8 Oct. 1847; **Sarah Addie** b 14 Aug. 1854, m 11 Sep. 1879 Alvin W. Fowles; **Hattie Silva** b 31 Jan. 1858, (Harriett) d 1940, m 16 Oct. 1879 Charles A. Robinson; and **Mattie Jane** b 25 May 1861. [Family Bible record at AHS.]

WOODARD, ABRAM - Born ??, d ??, s/o D. Ivan Woodard. Children: **Sarah J.** b 17 Apr. 1858, m 30 May 1867 Frank A. Sargent; **Charles F.** b 19 Apr. 1848, m Carrie Varnet of Bangor, ME; **Marcia Ann** b 26 Jun. 1851, m ---- Atwater; and **William** b 9 Sep. 1858, d 5 Jan. 1861.

WOODARD, WILLIAM - Born 15 Aug. 1784, d 28 Jan. 1880, s/o John and May (Hodgkins) Woodard. William Woodard m 1 Jan. 1812 Sarah Whitney, d 20 Feb. 1845. Children: **Moses** b 22 Oct. 1812, d 18 Dec. 1852 in Portland, ME, m 15 Jun. 1837 Almira Myrick; **Nathan** b 17 Aug. 1814, d 17 Jan. 1868 in Washington, D.C., m 11 Dec. 1843 Ann M. Washburn; **A b r a m W .** b 4 Feb. 1817, d 24 May 1876 in Bangor, ME, m 15 Jun. 1844 Jane Fuller; **Harriet W.** b 1 Mar. 1819, d 24 Feb. 1843, m 4 Jun. 1840 Hosea Fuller; **J a n e S .** b 2 Dec. 1820, m 28 Jan. 1841 Joseph S. Gordon; **William** b 6 Oct. 1822, d 22 Oct. 1822; **Mercy G .** b 6 May 1824, d 11 Jan. 1852, m 8 Sep. 1849 Thomas G. Godfrey; **G a r d i n e r F .** b 24 Apr. 1830, d 18 Dec. 1868 in Portland, ME, m 26 Oct. 1858 May D. Graffam; **S u s a n E .** b 22 May 1837, m Daniel Garcelon; and ---- son, m 19 Oct. 1845 Betsy Clough, d 17 Dec. 1873.

WOODSOM, GIDEON - Born ??, d ??, s/o ?? Gideon Woodsom m Anna ----. Child: **J o h n** b 11 Nov. 1805. [Vital Records of Lewiston, Maine, p. 85.]

WRIGHT, ABEL - Born ??, d ??, s/o ?? Abel Wright m 29 Apr. 1804 Hannah Baker of Bowdoin, Maine. Children: **D e l a n a** b 14 Apr. 1810; **Lorenzo Dow** b 3 Aug. 1812; **Dimick Baker** b 10 Oct. 1814; **Hannah** b 10 May 1817; **Mary** b 27 May 1817; **Mary** b 27 Mar. 1819; **Abel** b 10 Jan. 1822; and **Benjamin R.** b 10 Jun. 1825.

WRIGHT, ABIJAH - Born 8 Dec. 1787 in Lewiston, d 17 Apr. 1843, s/o ?? Abijah Wright became an M.D. He m -- Sep. 1816 Abigail Hardy of Strong, Maine, d 30 Sep. 1886, d/o Simeon. Children: **Alluria** b 8 Nov. 1817, m 30 Jul. 1835 Sidney Sketton; and **H o r a c e** b 15 Apr. 1819, d -- Sep. 1864, m 14 May 1840 Mary Ann Lincoln, d/o Nat Lincoln of Durham, ME.

WRIGHT, ALBION - Born ??, d ??, s/o Isaac and Diantha (----) Wright. Child: **Inez E.** b 14 Nov. 1880.

WRIGHT, BEAUMONT - Born ??, d ??, s/o ?? Beaumont Wright m Sarah Ann ----. Child: **Edmund** b 29 Jun. 1829.

WRIGHT, BENJAMIN FRANKLIN - Born 22 Nov. 1828, d 10 Nov. 1850, s/o Joel, Jr. and ?? Wright. Joel Wright, Jr. was the s/o Joel Wright, Sr. Benjamin Franklin Wright m 29 Oct. 1848 Mary E. Beal. Child: **Frances Elizabeth.**

WRIGHT, BENJAMIN F. - Born ??, d ??, s/o Sidney S. and ?? Wright. Children: **Clay P.** b 24 Feb. 1889; **Dorrice G.** b 24 Mar. 1895; and **Marjorie** b 3 Jan. 1897.

WRIGHT, CEPHAS - Born 7 Mar. 1817, d 9 Aug. 1889, s/o ?? Cephas Wright m 29 Sep. 1838 Nancy P. Merrill, b 8 Dec. 1816, d 24 Feb. 1875, d/o Samuel and Mehitable (----) Merrill. Children: **Harriet A.** b 22 Jul. 1839, d 28 Jan. 1855; **Emma E.** b 29 Oct. 1840, m 18 Nov. 1876 Thomas W. Alexander of Orr's Island, ME; **Lois M.** b 22 Apr. 1842, d 20 Jan. 1855; **Olive C.** b 6 Nov. 1844, m 8 Sep. 1892 Waterman Trafton, b 14 Dec. 1821 in Georgetown, ME, d 4 Apr. 1894; and **Margaret F.** b 9 Aug. 1853, d 28 Apr. 1888.

WRIGHT, CHARLES L. - Born ??, d ??, s/o Horace and ?? Wright. Charles L. Wright m Flora E. Curtis, b 19 Aug. 1858, d/o John Jr. and Elizabeth G. (Jepson) Curtis. Child: **Ona/Onie May** b 10 Nov. 1856 or b 15 Nov. 1888, d 1966.

WRIGHT, DAVID - Born ??, d ??, s/o ?? David Wright m Mrs. Polly Pettengell. Children: **Abigail** b 8 Feb. 1819; and **Jesse** b 13 Feb. 1821.

WRIGHT, DAVID T. - Born ??, d ??, s/o Zebulon and ?? Wright. David T. Wright m Mary Jane Hodgdon of Troy, Maine. Child: **Arthur.**

WRIGHT, EZRA R. - Born 12 Jul. 1829 in Lewiston, d in Phillips, Maine, s/o Francis and Susanah (Hackett) Wright. Ezra R. Wright m (1) Polena Daggett of Phillips, d/o William Daggett, and m (2) Rachel Daggett. Child: **Fred A.** b 18 Nov. 1860 in Phillips.

WRIGHT, FRANCIS - Born --- Apr. 1789, d 5 Oct. 1861, s/o ?? Francis Wright m 1 Dec. 1816 Susanna Hackett, b 1791, d 14 Oct. 1859, d/o Ezekiel. Children: **Arixona Southgate** b 29 Aug. 1817, d 14 Mar. 1852, m 24 Jan. 1847 Peter Gledden; **Margaret Randall** b 3 Nov. 1819, d 27 Feb. 1894, m 3 Dec. 1846 Elbridge Morrell; **Rufus Rogers** b 25 Jun. 1821, d in Westport, ME, m (1) Emeslene Dunton, and m (2) Esther McFadden of Georgetown, ME; **Tamson Lunt** b 14 May 1823, d 12 Sep. 1900, m 18 Oct. 1855 John R. Nevens, d 15 Jul. 1863; **Sumner Downing** b 15 Nov. 1827, d 2 Feb. 1896 in Jay, ME, m (1) Dorothy Stover of Harpswell, ME, and m (2) Mehitabell Lovell; **Ezra Randall** b 12 Jul. 1829, m (1) Polenia Daggett of Phillips, and m (2) Rachel Ramsdell (nee Daggett); and **Emily Jane** b 3 Sep. 1833, d 21 Sep. 1865, m 6 Mar. 1855 Robert J. Arris.

WRIGHT, FRANCIS - Born 15 Apr. 1815, d ??, s/o John and ?? Wright. Francis Wright m 14 Jan. 1841 Sarah A. Randall, d/o Ezra

Randall. Children: **Horace A.** b 19 Jan. 1842, m (1) Drusilla Libby, and m (2) Helen Libby; **Mary E.** b 17 Dec. 1843, m 12 May 1863 Milford S. Cummings; **John C.** b 15 Mar. 1844, d 29 Nov. 1844, m 21 Jul. 1883 Fannie D. Robinson; **Melissa E.** b 28 Aug. 1845, d 4 Jul. 1851; **Ezra R.** b 13 Nov. 1846, m ---- Libby; **Francis** b 2 Apr. 1848, unm; **Melissa A.** b 4 Jul. 1851, m (1) James Albert Ray, and m (2) -- May 1902 Elmer R. Bailey of Auburn, ME; **Herbert W.** b 11 Jul. 1852, m ---- Libby; and **William B.** b 29 Aug. 1854, d -- Oct. 1895, m Jane Coburn, lived in Greene, ME.

WRIGHT, FRANK - Born ??, d ??, s/o George Washington Wright. Frank Wright m Hattie R. Ham, b 26 Mar. 1853, d/o George W. Ham. Children: **Arthur** b 15 Dec. 1872, d 21 Jun. 1875; **Carl** b 4 Sep. 1874, d 21 Jun. 1875; **Allie** b 21 Jul. 1871, d 21 Oct. 1879; and **Lester C.** b 31 Jul. 1880.

WRIGHT, FRED LAFOREST - Born 1 Mar. 1877 in Lewiston, d ??, s/o ??

WRIGHT, GEORGE W. - Born ??, d ??, s/o ?? George W. Wright m Aurelia H. ----. Children: **Sarah** b 6 Aug. 1839, m 18 Feb. 1861 Theodore M. Varney; **Margett** b 29 Jan. 1842, d 11 Nov. 1851; **Mercy Ellen** b 5 Dec. 1843, d 4 Nov. 1851; **Gardiner A.** b 19 Nov. 1846; **Willard T.** b 12 Oct. 1849; **Franklin** b 6 Jun. 1852; **Elhanan W.** b 25 Nov. 1857, d 25 Apr. 1875; and **Costello A.** b 14 Dec. 1854, d 19 Mar. 1874.

WRIGHT, HORACE - Born ??, d ??, s/o Abijah and ?? Wright. Children: **Harriet** b 14 Dec. 1840; **Arabine** b 11 Jun. 1845, m Albert Walker of Melville, NH; **Horace Lyman** b 3 Jun. 1847; **Leander Hussey** b -- Jul. 1849, drowned 18 Jul. 1847; **Mary** b -- Jul. 1852, m 14 Jul. 1872 Henry S. Colby of Portland, ME; **Charles L.** b 2 Apr. 1857, m Flora Curtis, d/o John of Auburn; and **Hattie** b 6 May 1860, m Jefferson Wheeler of Brunswick, ME.

WRIGHT, ISAAC T. - Born ??, d 24 Oct. 1892, s/o Zebulon and ?? Wright of Lewiston. Isaac T. Wright lived in Troy, Maine. He m 23 Jan. 1834 Diantha Oliver, b 18 Sep. 1814, d 3 Aug. 1874. Children: **Isaac J.** b 26 May 1837; **Elizabeth O.** b 1 Aug. 1840, m Eugene Hopkins; **Albion Scott** b 15 Mar. 1843, m 11 May 1878 Emily C. Taylor of Palmira, d/o James; **Henrietta** b 23 Oct. 1846, m Timothy Hawes; **Alfred B.** b 26 Dec. 1850, m Blanch Read; and **Helen L.** b 28 Feb. 1855, m Enoch Bagley of Troy.

WRIGHT, JAMES - Born ??, d ??, s/o Timothy and ?? Wright. Children: **Violia** b 1849; **Ellen** b 1851, m John McIntire of Lawrence; **Marshall G.** m Ida Furbush, d/o Henry; and **Mabel** m ---- Choate.

WRIGHT, JAMES F. - Born ??, d ??, s/o ?? Children: **Annie E.** b 19 Jan. 1873, d 1 Mar. 1874; **Ben F.** b 2 Mar. 1863, m 8 Nov. 1886 Margaret A. Parker, d/o Francis and Mary Parker; **Melville O.** b 24 Jul. 1864; **Harold B.** b -- Aug. 1870, m 7 May 1893 Winnifred Hunter, d/o

Winchel and Alma A. Hunter; and **Linwood P.** b 4 Dec. 1874, m 4 Feb. 1899 Martha M. Varney, d/o John.

WRIGHT, JAMES P. - Born 10 May 1790, d 17 Feb. 1877 age 86 years 9 months 7 days, s/o Timothy and ?? Wright. James P. Wright m 14 Mar. 1816 Fanny H., d 28 Feb. 1878 age 86 years 6 months, d/o John Hewey of Wales, Maine. Children: **Timothy** b 20 Dec. 1816, m 14 Jul. 1842 Catherine Oliver, d/o John and Catherine of Phippsburg, ME; **Mark Fernald** b 26 Jul. 1818, d 27 Dec. 1898 age 80 years 5 months in Bath, ME, unm; **Josiah F.** b 1 May 1820, d 7 Jan. 1843, unm; **Fanny Maria** b 8 Apr. 1822, d 15 Feb. 1840, m 16 Oct. 1837 George F. Austin; **James Chandler** b 1 Jun. 1824, d 3 Apr. 1825, **Elisa B.** b 23 Oct. 1826, m 7 Sep. 1845 James A. Crooker of Bath; **Benjamin Rowe** b 19 May 1828, d 11 Jul. 1853, unm; **Christania** b 23 Oct. 1831, d 3 Jan. 1832; **Isabel Jane** twin b 28 Dec. 1832, m 30 Apr. 1857 Melvin C. Williams of Bath; **Mary J.** twin b 28 Dec. 1832, m William F. Crooker; **James F.** b 2 Oct. 1835, m int. 14 Nov. 1861 Oleavia A. Hooker of Gardiner [vital records of Phippsburg, Maine], d 24 Jan. 1906 at Bath; and **Frances A.** b 23 May 1838, m Samuel H. McFadden.

WRIGHT, JESSE SR. - Born ??, d ??, s/o ?? Jesse Wright, Sr. m Abby Cook of New Gloucester, Maine. Children: **Jesse** b 23 Apr. 1776, m pub. 18 Nov. 1798 Sally Buker of Bowdoin, ME; **Josiah** b 11 Apr. 1778, m pub. 12 Oct. 1800 Polly Buker; **Hannah** b 12 Mar. 1780, m pub. 26 Apr. 1803 Abraham Young; **Molly** b 12 Feb. 1782, m pub. 24 Nov. 1803 Daniel Young; **Abel** b 23 Apr. 1784, m 29 Apr. 1804 Hannah Buker of Bowdoin; **Christian** b 2 Jul. 1786, m 3 Nov. 1808 Sarah Royal of New Gloucester, ME; **Sarah** b 11 Jan. 1790; **Deborah** b 13 Nov. 1792, m 4 Nov. 1824 Jotham Briggs; and **Mina** b 22 Aug. 1795, m 22 Mar. 1814 James Grover of Avon, ME.

WRIGHT, JESSE JR. - Born 23 Apr. 1776, d 1812/1815 in the army, s/o Jesse, Sr. and ?? Wright. Jesse Wright, Jr. m 18 Mar. 1798 Sally Buker of Bowdoin, Maine. Children: **Abby** b 25 May 1800; **Jesse** b 23 Sep. 1802; **Jonah** b 18 Aug. 1804; **David** b 21 May 1806, d 21 Aug. 1879; **Christian** b 21 Sep. 1808; **Abie H.** b 22 Sep. 1810; and **David Buker** b 9 Jan. 1813.

WRIGHT, JOEL - Born ??, d 26 Jul. 1821, s/o ?? Joel Wright m Mary Peacock. Children: **Joel** b 14 Nov. 1776, d 15 Dec. 1860, m pub. 18 Jun. 1797 Betsy Elery, d 15 Dec. 1864 age 87 years 6 months; **Thomas** b 15 Jul. 1778, m pub. 15 Nov. 1800 Priscilla A. Barns of Berwick, ME; **Jonathan** b 3 Nov. 1780, m 1 Dec. 1808 Sally Dill; **Phineas** b 21 Mar. 1783, d 22 Jun. 1852, m 6 Jun. 1813 Dorcas Dill, d 25 Apr. 1872; **John** b 21 Apr. 1785, d 20 Jul. 1858, m (1) 8 May 1808 Betsey Buker, and m (2) 12 Jun. 1834 Sally Glover; **Abijah** b 8 Dec. 1787, d 17 Apr. 1842, m -- Sep. 1816 Abigail Hardy; **Francis** b 27 Apr. 1790, d 5 Oct. 1861, m 1 Dec. 1816 Susannah Hackett, d 13 Oct. 1859; **Ebeneser** b 22 Jan. 1793, d 21 Jun. 1796; **Molly** b 9 Mar. 1795, d 15 Jan. 1873, m 13 Jun. 1816 William Bond, d 10 Mar. 1873; and **Jacob** b 17 Aug. 1798, d 10 Dec. 1798. [Vital Records of Lewiston, Maine, p. 83.]

WRIGHT, JOEL - Born 16 Oct. 1821 in Strong, Maine, d 4 Dec. 1892, s/o Jonathan and Sally (Dill) Wright. Joel Wright m Mary P. Stoyell, b 11 Apr. 1827 in Farmington, Maine, d/o Auron and Alfreda (Greenleaf) Stoyell. Children: **Abbie** b 16 Apr. 1848, m 13 Dec. 1874 Melvin P. Tufts of Farmington; **Mary** b -- Jan. 1852, d -- Feb. 1852; **John M.** b 5 Feb. 1855, m 25 Oct. 1890 Mittie Lambert of Farmington, d/o Matilda Harvey and Gideon Lambert; and **Augusta L.** b 29 Mar. 1859, d 27 Feb. 1896, m 5 Nov. 1890 Charles Butler of Farmington.

WRIGHT, JOEL - Born 14 Nov. 1776, d 15 Dec. 1860, s/o ?? Joel Wright m pub. 18 Jun. 1797 Betsey Elery, d 15 Dec. 1864. Children: **Ebeneser** b 10 Jan. 1798, d 18 Jan. 1799; **Joel** b 5 Apr. 1800, d 10 Jan. 1884, m 19 Mar. 1818 Mary Skelton, d 26 Apr. 1883; **Nathaniel** b 8 Jan. 1802, d 18 Mar. 1815; **Mary** b 29 Oct. 1804, d 10 Mar. 1884, m 30 Dec. 1824 Jonathan Mitchell, d 9 Oct. 1884; **Betsey** b 5 Sep. 1806, d 26 Oct. 1806; **Phineas** b 7 Dec. 1807, m 1 Jul. 1837 Ruth Libby, d 12 Jul. 1893; **Betsey** b 18 Nov. 1811, d 10 Sep. 1839, m 28 Jan. 1836 William Skelton; **Nathaniel** b 26 Jun. 1815, m Claunda Savage; and **Sylvanis**.

WRIGHT, JOEL JR. - Born 5 Apr. 1800, d 10 Jan. 1884, s/o ?? Joel Wright, Jr. m 19 Mar. 1818 Mary Skelton, b 7 Apr. 1800, d 20 Apr. 1883, d/o Thomas. Children: **George Washington** b 18 Aug. 1818, m (1) pub. 9 Mar. 1839 Aurelia H. Clover, d 25 Jan. 1864, and m (2) pub. 11 Feb. 1865 Hattie H. Patten; **Jane S.** b (?5) 11 Jul. 1820, d -- Sep. 1893, m 6 Jun. 1839 Jacob Golder of Lisbon, ME; **Precena G.** b 1/3 Oct. 1822, d 7 Jun. 1899, m 18 Feb. 1844 Abner Merrill; **Mary A.** b 11/23 Jun. 1824/1825, m 25 Apr. 1844 Alanson Coburn, d 27 Jul. 1889; **Margaret M.** b 3 Aug. (?11 Oct.) 1826, d 9 Mar. 1899, m Edward Jepson, s/o Capt. William; **Benjamin F.** b 18/22 Nov. 1828, d 10 Nov. 1850, m 29 Oct. 1848 Mary E. Beal; **Betsey Elizabeth** b 26 Oct. (?29 Nov.) 1830, m 2 Apr. 1846 Nathan Merrill, lived in Pittsfield, ME; **Henry C.** b 14 Oct. (?1 Nov.) 1832, m Miriam Skelton, b 9 Nov. 1834, d/o Thomas; **Bulah P.** b 26 Sep. 1834, d 13 Jul. 1894, m 27 Oct. 1863 Roscoe N. Phillips, s/o Autetus of Auburn; **Clara A.** b 1 Sep. 1836, m James M. Gulliver; **Sydna S.** b 1 Jul. 1838, d 12 Sep. 1863, m pub. 5 Sep. 1859 Nancy Perkins, who m (2) ---- Spear of Pittsfield); **Winfield S.** b 17 Sep. 1840, d 31 Dec. 1875, m Mary A. Fuller of Hartland, ME, d 6 Aug. 1892; and **Serapline C.** b 14 May 1843, m Frank E. Perkins of Biddeford, ME.

WRIGHT, JOHN - Born ??, d 20 Jul. 1858, s/o Dr. Joel and ?? Wright. John Wright m (1) 8 May 1808 Betsy Buker, d 20 Sep. 1833, and m (2) 12 Jun. 1834 Sally Carville, d 19 Nov. 1882, d/o Henry. Children: **Almira B.** b 21 Jul. 1811, m 25 Dec. 1834 Daniel Cobbett of Strong, ME; **Sophronia** b 15 Mar. 1813, d 16 Feb. 1889, m 4 Oct. 1836 Samuel Corvill, d 8 Nov. 1894; **Francis** b 17 Apr. 1815, d in Greene, m 14 Jan. 1841 Sarah A. Randall, d/o Ezra; **William B.** b 14 Feb. 1817, d 17 Apr. 1889 at the town farm, m 27 Feb. 1848 Esther Brown; **Matilda M.** b 13 Jan. 1821, m George Hersey; **Elizabeth Haskell** b 30

Mar. 1825, d 4 Mar. 1873, m 10 Oct. 1850 Joseph Skinner, d 11 Jan. 1878; and **John Gledden** b 11 Oct. 1827, d 18 Aug. 1833.

WRIGHT, JOHN - Born 15 Mar. 1844, d 29 Nov. 1884, s/o ?? John Wright m 21 Jul. 1883 Rannie D. Robinson, b 28 Apr. 1861, d/o Jacob and Mary E. (Hall) Robinson. Child: **Willie H.** b 15 Apr. 1884.

WRIGHT, JOHN - Born ??, d ??, s/o Joel and Mary P. (Stoyell) Wright. John Wright m ---- in Farmington, Maine. Children: **Dana L.** b 6 Dec. 1893, d 7 Dec. 1893; **Mildred A.** b 19 Feb. 1896; and **Helen I.** b 13 Aug. 1899.

WRIGHT, JONATHAN - Born 28 Feb. 1810, d 31 Jan. 1865, s/o ?? Jonathan Wright m 1 Jan. 1834 Sally Dill, d 31 Aug. 1858. Children: **Sarah** unm; **Mary D.** m 16 Jul. 1856 Stephen F. Woodard of Poland, ME; **Francilla H.** m 19 Oct. 1867 Silas Libby; **Lettie**; and **Elisa**.

WRIGHT, JONATHAN - Born 3 Nov. 1780, d 29 Mar. 1837 in Farmington, Maine, s/o ?? Jonathan Wright m 22 Oct. 1808 Sally Dill, b 19 Mar. 1787, d 5 Feb. 1870, d/o Jesieh Dill of Lewiston. Children: **Jonathan** b 28 Feb. 1810, d 31 Jan. 1865, m 1 Jan. 1834 Sally Dill; **Louisa** b 6 Jul. 1811, m Henry Kempton; **Mary P.** b 16 Oct. 1813, d 17 Dec. 1837; **William** b 15 Dec. 1816 in Strong, d 12 Jun. 1879, m 27 Nov. 1839 Mary H. Backus; **Sarah** b 7 Jan. 1819, d 23 May 1831; **Joel** b 16 Oct. 1821 in Strong, ME, d 4 Dec. 1892, m 11 Apr. 1867 Mary P. Stoyell; **Dorcas** b 18 Jan. 1824, m Henry Wormell; **Olive Ann**; and **Abigail** b 25 Dec. 1829, d 30 Nov. 1885.

WRIGHT, JOSEPH - Born 11 Oct. 1778, d 26 Dec. 1850, s/o Timothy and ?? Wright. Joseph Wright m 11 Mar. 1802 Mrs. Patience Harmon, d 9 Dec. 1818. Children: **Nabby** b 30 Nov. 1802, d 28 Jun. 1833, "Whispering Nabby"; **Ruth** b 9 Jan. 1805; **Jonathan** b 9 Apr. 1807; **Judith** b 15 Dec. 1809; **Dorcas** b 23 Dec. 1811, d 11 Jun. 1874, m 28 Oct. 1838 Nathaniel Sleeper; **Jacob H.** b 17 Jul. 1814; **Ruben C.** b 10 Feb. 1817, d 30 Jul. 1893, m 20 Jan. 1848 Hannah H. Wescott, d 2 Jul. 1893, d/o Josiah of Lewiston; and **Patience** b 20 Nov. 1818, d 25 Nov. 1818.

WRIGHT, LANG CHRISTIAN - Born 2 Jul. 1786, d ??, s/o ?? Lang Christian Wright m 3 Nov. 1808 Sally Royal of New Gloucester, Maine. Children: **Adeline** b 27 Aug. 1809, d 10 Feb. 1831, m 10 Feb. 1831 Azor Morrill of Parkman, d 16 Jun. 1871; **Octavius** b 27 May 1811, m pub. 27 May 1837 Mariah Rice of Hallowell, ME; **Ferdinand** b 11 Apr. 1813, m Mary J. Wood of Hartford, ME; **Jane M.** b 7 Jul. 1815, m 24 Sep. 1881 George West of Bowdoin, ME; **Cephas** b 7 Mar. 1817, d 9 Aug. 1889, m pub. 8 Sep. 1838 Nancy Morrill of Greene, ME; and **Olive** b 17 Jan. 1824, m John M. Clark of Solon, ME.

WRIGHT, LEROY ALLSTON - Born 19 Apr. 1853 in Lewiston, d ??, s/o ?? Leroy Allston Wright m 19 Nov. 1873 age 40 years.

WRIGHT, LINWOOD P. - Born ??, d ??, s/o James F. and ?? Wright. Linwood P. Wright m 4 Feb. ---- Martha M. Varney, d/o John. Child: **Carrold L.** b 4 Feb. 1899.

WRIGHT, NATHANIEL E. - Born 26 Jun. 1815, d ??, s/o Joel, Jr. and ? Wright. Nathaniel E. Wright lived in New Vineyard, Maine. He m Clarinda T. Savage, b 31 Dec. 1816 in Anson, Maine. Children: **Anjoulette E.** b 20 May 1839 in Farmington; and **Alonzo P.** b 24 Nov. 1840 in Farmington, ME.

WRIGHT, PHINEAS - Born ??, d ??, s/o ?? Phineas Wright m 16 Jul. 1837 to Ruth Libby of Lisbon, Maine. Children: **Lorenzo B.** b 24 Sep. 1837, d 19 Nov. 1851; **William Henry** b 16 Nov. 1839; **Raymond L.** 1 Feb. 1842, d 23 Feb. 1851; **Rufus L.** b 24 Mar. 1844, d 11 Apr. 1884; **Elizabeth H.** b 3 Jul. 1847, d 17 Feb. 1851; **Emma E.** b 14 Dec. 1848, d 20 Jan. 1851; and **Phineas B.** b 20 Jan. 1851, d 19 Mar. 1851.

WRIGHT, RUBEN C. - Born ??, d 30 Jul. 1893, s/o ?? Ruben C. Wright m 20 Jan. 1848 Hannah H. Wescot, d 2 Jul. 1893. Children: **Noel R.** b 19 Mar. 1898, m (1) 21 Feb. 1871 Lucy Haley of Webster, and m (2) 24 Jan. 1891 Ida M. Sampson of Auburn; **Leroy A.** b 19 Nov. 1853, m 19 Nov. 1873 Lydia E. Gilman, b 4 Sep. 1852 in Farmington; and **Charles Myrick** b 1854, d 13 Aug. 1855.

WRIGHT, SIDNEY S. - Born ??, d ??, s/o Joel and ?? Wright. Sidney S. Wright m 12 Sep. 1859 Nancy Perkins, b 20 Aug. 1839 in Litchfield, d/o Edward S. and Lucy A. (Farrar) Perkins. Children: **Benjamin F.** b 27 Aug. 1851, m 31 Jan. 1888 Laura M. Clay; and **Sidney** b 30 Apr. 1863, d 7 Jul. 1864.

WRIGHT, SUMNER D. - Born 15 Nov. 1827, d 2 Feb. 1896, s/o Francis and Susanna (Hackett) Wright. Sumner D. Wright m (1) Dorothy Stover of Harpswell, Maine, and m (2) 27 Mar. 1876 Mrs. Mehitable Maburry. Children: **Sylvester S.** b 20 Oct. 1857; and **Sumner Wesley** b 31 Dec. ----, d 4 Apr. 1901.

WRIGHT, SUMNER WESLEY - Born ??, d ??, s/o Sumner D. and ?? Wright. Sumner Wesley Wright m 3 Oct. 1886 Statina L. Leathers, d/o Thomas J. Leathers. Child: **Harold Sylvester** b -- Nov. 1890.

WRIGHT, TIMOTHY - Born ??, d ??, s/o James R. and ?? Wright. Children: **Olive V.** b 13 Apr. 1845, m 10 Feb. 1857 James H. Commens, d 18 Sep. 1879; **Katherine A.** b 29 Jul. 1848, m George C. Preble; **Josiah F.** b 18 Jan. 1850, m Mrs. Margaret Samson; **Eliza F.** b 5 Jul. 1852, m Roswell Pushard; **Mary I.** b 23 Sep. 1854, m Charles E. Furbish; **Elbridge F.** b 11 Oct. 1857, m Susan McIntire; **James A.** b 23 Jun. 1859, m Carrie E. Spinney; **John C.** b 3 Jun. 1859, m (1) Edith Wilson, and m (2) Eva Rollins; and **Cora L.** b 23 Apr. 1862, m Charles Robinson.

WRIGHT, TIMOTHY - Born ??, d 7 Apr. 1827, s/o ?? Timothy Wright m pub. 13 Dec. 1777 Judith Rowe. Children: **Joseph** b 11 Oct.

1778, d 26 Dec. 1859, m 11 Mar. 1802 Mrs. Patience Harmon, d 9 Dec. 1818; **Judith** b 18 Mar. 1780, m 16 Oct. 1806 Abraham Pierce; **Abigail** b 3 Aug. 1781, d 20 Oct. 1861, m 9 Aug. ---- Reuben Coburn; **Zebulon** b 15 Jun. 1783, d 24 Jun. 1879 age 96 years, m 17 Aug. 1809 Charity Thompson; **Jonathan** b -- Apr. 1785; **Ellis** b 11 Oct. 1787 in Greene, m 4 Nov. 1816 John Wade; **Timothy** b 15 Jun. 1789, d 2 Mar. 1861, m 11 Feb. 1813 Suzannah Rowe of New Gloucester, ME, d 16 Jun. 1869; **James P.** b 10 May 1790, d 23 Mar. 1826, m 14 Mar. 1816 Fanny Hewey of Wales; and **Betsy** b 7 Nov. 1794, m pub. 25 Oct. 1812 Charles Perie of Greene, ME.

WRIGHT, TIMOTHY JR. - Born ??, d ??, s/o ?? Timothy Wright, Jr. m 11 Feb. 1813 Susanna M. Rowe in New Gloucester, Maine. Children: **William Rowe** b 7 Feb. 1814, d 9 Aug. 1888, m 19 Sep. 1847 Olive Turner, d/o Amos; **James** b 21 Aug. 1815, d 31 Mar. 1897, m 11 Jun. 1848 Sarah Marden of Vienna; **Catherine** b 21 Jun. 1817, d 7 Aug. 1854, m 18 Mar. 1840 William Rowe of New Gloucester; **Susan Blaisdell** b 1 Mar. 1820, m 18 Oct. 1847 Eben Dill of Webster, ME, lived in Greene, ME; **Otis Allen** b 31 Dec. 1821, d 3 Apr. 1879, m (1) 29 Nov. 1849 Mary A. Graffam, d/o Benjamin, and m (2) 1 Feb. 1856 Susan R. Purington; **Garcelon Chandler** b 31 May 1826, m Sophia Hyron; **Elvira** b 28 Jun. 1828, d 16 Feb. 1891, m (1) Frances Taylor, and m (2) ----; **Alfred Stone** b 11 Feb. 1831, d -- Nov. 1895, m 12 Nov. 1859 Aravester V. Labree of Wales, ME, b 3 Apr. 1840; **Clarissa Ann** b 30 Sep. 1833, m 25 Dec. 1867 Orin Cole of Greene, ME; **Charles Henry** b 29 Mar. 1836, m (1) 6 Nov. 1855 Angie King, and m (2) Helen Blythen; and **Sarah Jane** b 17 Jan. 1824, d 1 Nov. 1850, m 12 Sep. 1847 James Hamilton.

WRIGHT, THOMAS - Born ??, d ??, s/o Joel and ?? Wright. Thomas Wright m pub. 15 Nov. 1800 Priscilla A. Barnes. Children: **Thomas** b 1806, d -- Dec. 1876, m 21 Apr. 1830 Helena True of Pownal in Durham, ME, b 11 Jun. 1808, d 27 Dec. 1897, d/o Ebenezer of Pownal, ME; **Jonathan** m Maria Lumber; **Naomi** m Richard Doyen (?Doine); **Mary** m Jesse Chandler; **Israel** m Sarah Young, d/o Daniel; **Ruth** m Charles Hamblet; **Jacob** m Judith Low; and **Hiram** m Lydia Heath.

WRIGHT, THOMAS JR. - Born ??, d ??, s/o Thomas and Priscilla (Barnes) Wright. Thomas Wright, Jr. m 21 Apr. 1830 Helena True of Pownal, Maine, in Durham, Maine, b 11 Jun. 1808, d 27 Dec. 1897. Children: **Christiana T.** b 13 Oct. 1833; **Silas L.**; **Julia M.** m -- Apr. 1862 J. Weston Swift of Farmington, ME; and **Statina E.**

WRIGHT, WILLIAM RILEY - Born 15 Dec. 1816 in Strong, Maine, d 12 Jun. 1879, s/o ?? William Riley Wright m 27 Nov. 1839 Mary H. Backus of Farmington, Maine. Children: **Bell J.** m Samuel K. Gilman of Boston; and **Josiah Lester** b 22 Dec. 1850 in Farmington.

WRIGHT, ZEBULON - Born ??, d ??, s/o ?? Zebulon Wright m (1) -- Jun. 1839 Charity Edgcomb of Bath, and m (2) 17 Aug. 1809 Charity Thompson, d 23 May 1838. Children: **Isaac Thompson** b 6 Feb. 1810, d 24 Oct. 1892, m 23 Jan. 1834 Diantha Oliver, b 18 Sep. 1814, d 3 Aug. 1874; **Julia Ann** b 31 Dec. 1811, d 11 Oct. 1905, m 13 Jul. 1835 Josiah Harris of Greene, d 4 Apr. 1894, member of Co. D, 17th ME. Regt.; **Happy Proctor** b 3 Apr. 1814, d 12 Feb. 1890, m Josiah Marr of Gardiner, ME, d 23 Jan. 1878; **Judith Rowe** b 22 Mar. 1816, d 30 Dec. 1872, m 31 Mar. 1842 Waterman Trafton of Gardiner; **Zebulon, Jr.** b 8 Nov. 1821, d -- May 1890, m 7 Apr. 1853 Martha D. Packard of Woodstock, ME, d/o Stephen and Eleanor Robinson Packard; **Joseph Thompson** b 16 Mar. 1819, d 9 Oct. 1841; **David T.** b 7 Dec. 1824, d 20 Nov. 1879, m Mary Jane Hodgdon of Troy, ME.; **Sally D.** b 27 Jan. 1827, d 11 Mar. 1917, m 30 Apr. 1854 A. K. P. Edwards, d 22 Sep. 1904; **Louisa J.** b 7 May 1829, m (1) William Trafton, and m (2) Alvin W. Brann of West Gardiner; **Dexter Crosby** b 17 Jun. 1831, d 27 Mar. 1902, soldier, unm; and **Tryphena** b 18 Jul. 1836, m 9 Jan. 1854 Edward Wakefield of Gardiner, d 23 Aug. 1865.

WRIGHT, ZEBULON R. - Born ??, d ??, s/o Zebulon and ?? Wright. Zebulon R. Wright m Martha D. Packard. Children: **Ida May** b 22 Dec. 1854; **Abby Packard** b 8 Jun. 1856; **Herbert Z.** b 2 Sepf. 1858; **Grace Darling** b 21 Sep. 1860; **Walter**; and **Mattie**.

YOUNG, ABRAHAM D. - Born 3 Oct. 1784 in Andover, Massachusetts, d ??, s/o ?? Abrahm D. Young was a J. P. in Avon, Maine, in 1816, and a house carpenter in Guilford, Maine, in 1850. He m Hannah Wright, b 11 Mar. 1781 in Lewiston. Children: **Anna J.** b 1 Dec. 1803 in Lewiston, ME; **Jonathan W.** b 12 Oct. 1805 in Lewiston, ME; **George W.** b 10 Dec. 1807 in Avon, ME; **Hannah Jr.** b 1 Dec. 1809 in Avon, ME; **Abraham D., Jr.** q.v.; **Elmira** b 12 Apr. 1814 in Avon, ME; **Elvira** b 29 May 1816 in Avon, ME; **Rolla** b 11 Jul. 1818 in Avon, ME; **Joseph** b 18 Apr. 1820 in Philips, ME; and **Julia** b 20 Oct. 1823 in Guilford, ME. [U. S. Census 1850 of Guilford, Maine; Lewiston, Maine, poll tax 1804 & 1806.]

YOUNG, ABRAHAM D. JR. - Born 23 Apr. 1812 in Avon, Maine, d ??, s/o Abraham D., Sr. and Hannah (Wright) Young. Abraham D. Young, Jr. m Eliza ----, b 3 Feb. 1816 in Pittston, Maine. Children: **Emily** b 21 Oct. 1833 in Dover, ME; **Bothwell** b 10 Feb. 1834 in Dover, ME; **Grimsley** b 29 Aug. 1835 in Dover, ME; **Augusta** b 13 Nov. 1836 in Dover, ME; **Edwin** b 13 Apr. 1838 in Dover, ME; and **Lucy Jane M.** b 30 Jan. 1840 in Guilford, ME.

YOUNG, GEORGE W. - Born ??, d ??, s/o Abraham D., Sr. and ?? Young. George W. Young m Richamah R. ----. Children: **Andrew W. P.** age 17 years in 1850; **Washington** age 15 years in 1850; **Rodolphus** age 13 years in 1850; **Sarah L. P.** age 9 years in 1850; **George E.** age 2 years in 1850; and **James R.** age 8 years in 1860.

YOUNG, RODOLPHUS - Born ??, d ??, s/o ?? Rodolphus Young was from Minot, Maine. He m 22 Nov. 1803 Nancy (Anna) Tarr of Pejepscot, Maine, d/o Solomon and Anna (Rowe) Tarr of Gloucester, Massachusetts, who lived also in Sanford, Maine, and Ossipee, New Hampshire. Children: **Annie** m Asa Holt; **Ruby** b 16 Oct. 1806 of

Lewiston, ME, d 22 Dec. 1884 of Keene, NH, m Allen Perry; **Lovisa** m ---- Philbrick; **Sally** m 4 Jan. 1827 at Gloucester Allen Smith; **Rhoda**; **Clarissa A.** of Ossipee, NH, m 6 Dec. 1836 William Colby in Gloucester; **Betsey Jane**; **Mary**; **Lydia Frances** b 13 Feb. 1819 in Ossipee, NH, m Jesse Johnson Morgan, moved from Bow, NH, to Sherman, ME; **Joseph Lorenzo** b 1824, moved to Aroostook Co., ME; **Moses Colby** b 1825 in Ossipee, NH, m (1) Mary Tibbetts, and m (2) Sarah (Sprague) Gallison, wid/o Dr. Sylvanus Gallison of Dover, ME [*Morning Star*, issue 27 Jul. 1853]; **Benjamin**; and **Solomon** m (1) Lyida A. Gowen, and m (2) Eliza B. Larrabee. (Some records place this family in Lewiston; however, it is most likely that they settled on the West side of the river - then Minot or Pejepscot, now Auburn.)

BATES MILLS.

MILITARY RECORDS

The following records are from the Col. William Garcelon papers at the Androscoggin Historical in Auburn, Maine.

MILITIA ROLL of the Lewiston/Danville/Minot/Lisbon area in May 1806

Ames, Winslow, CAPT.
HODSKIN, Thomas, Sergant
DILL, Joseph Jr. Sergant

GOLDER, Wm, corporal
MICHEL, Joseph, corporal

the remainder are enlisted:

ATKINSSON, Wm
Ames, Craft
Bean, Samuel
BUBIER, Andrew
CURRANT, Thomas
COBB, Chitman
CHADBURN, Thomas
COBURN, Reuben
DILL, John Jr
DYER, Eleony?
DAVIS, Nathaniel
DAVIS, Joseph
DWELLEY, Eles'r
DYER, John
Field, John
FARRAR, Nath
FORD, Wm
Field, Joseph
Field, James
Garcelon, Mark
GARCELON, Peter Jr
Garcelon, Wm
GARCELON, Peter
GOODWIN, Benjamin
Harris, Richard
HALEY, Joshua
Holland, John
HALEY, Joseph
HALEY, Samuel
HODSKINS, Benjamin
Jackson, Lemuel
JACKSON, Samuel
JORDAN, Jere y
Jordan, Benj
Thomas, David
Jordan, James
LAKE, Eben'r
Lincoln, Nathan'l
Lincoln, Synus
LITCHFIELD, Noah
LOWELL, Wm
Morse, Joel
Moody, Robert
MICHELL, Joshua
MOODY, Sam'l
MERRILL, Joseph
MICHAL, David
PIPER, Thomas
RAY, Thomas
RAY, Jonathan
RAND, Thomas
Ray, Benj.
STEVENS, Caleb
STATON, Samuel
WRIGHT, Joseph
WRIGHT, Zebulon
WAGG, John
WEEKS, James

LEWISTON COMPANY of Foot 1800 from the Garcelon files Androscoggin Historical follows:

OFFICERS

COTTON, Isaac Capt
BARKER, Jacob Jr
DILL, Josiah.

Sergeants & musicians

Blasidell, Walter R
Herrick, Howard
Merrill, Moses
Mooar, Joseph
Pettengill, Nathaniel

enlisted

Atkinson, William Jr
Ames, Craft
Ames, James Jr
BARRON, Shearman
Bubier, Andrew
Bubier, Christpher
Blaisdell, William
Brooks, William
BATTEN, Abraham
CHAMBERLAIN, William
COAL (now spelling is COLE), Lemuel
Cutler, Nathan Jr
Coburn, Reuben Jr
CHADBURN, Thomas
DILL, Enoch
DILL, Enoch Jr
DILL, John
DILL, Joseph
DAVIS, Joseph
DAVIS, Nathaniel
DIAH, Elkimah
DINGLEY, William
Ford, William
FIELD, Joseph Jr
Garcelon, William
GRAFFAM, John
Garcelon, Benjamin
Gilpatrick, James

HARTS, Stephen Jr
HAM, James
Hatch, Jesse
Hatch, Samuel
HACKETT, Richard
Handy, Simeon
Handy, James
Hodgkins, Thomas
HALEY, Joseph
Hodgkin, Joshua
HILDRITH, Shadeau?
JONES, Josiah
JACKSON, Lemuel
JACKSON, Samuel
Jordan, James
Jordan, Abraham
LAKE, Joshua
Larreus, ohn?
Landers, Roberson
Landers, Lazaras
LOWELL, William
LITCHFIELD, Noah
LENFEST, Thomas
MERRILL, John
MOODY, Josiah
MOODY, Charles
MERRILL, Jedediah
MORSE, Joel
MOOAR, Samuel
MITCHEL, Davis
Pettengill, David
Prasley, Phillip
RANDALL, Ezra
RAY, Benjamin
RAY, William
RAY, Jonathan
READ, Oliver
SMITH, James
TUCK, Samuel
THORNE, Barrel
TRAFTON, John
THORNE, Benjamin
WRIGHT, Joel Jr
WRIGHT, Joseph Jr
WRIGHT, Joseph

HEADS OF FAMILIES IN LEWISTON VILLAGE 1847
compiled by Janus G Elder

Name	occupation	# in family	settled	built
ADAMS, Hiram	Boarding House		1846	1846
BEAN, George W	Minister	2	1845	
BENNETT, D	Operative	6	1847	1845
BIKETT, John	Harnessmaker	10	1835	
BISBEE, A	Woolen Mill	8	1840	1845
BLAIR, William	Farmer	3	1847	
BLISS, Zeba	Machinist	4	1845	
BLISS, Zeba F	Machinist	2	1845	
BRACKETT, S	Boarding House	?	1847	1846
BRIGGS, H C	Baker	8	1846	
BRIGGS, John A	Millwright	9	1837	1835
BROOKS, Ai	Watchman	13	1834	1843
BROOKS, Barber	Blacksmith	6	1835	
BUCKMAN, E T	Tin Ware	4	1845	
BURBANK, A	Physician	2	1847	
CALLAHAM, Aug.	Machinist	7	1847	1835
CALLAHEN, A	Machinist		1845	
CLARK, E D	Cotton Mill	4	1847	1845
COBB, E	Masterbuilder	6	1847	1847
COBB, Samuel	Mason	2	1847	1846
COTTON, James B	Operative	5	1843	1843
DAGGETT, Horace	Painter	8	1846	
DAVIS, David	Farmer	1	native	1816
DONNELL, N	Mason	6	1867	
DOYLE, E	Teamster	4	1846	
DUNN, Benjamin	Dept Shff	7	1841	
FARNHAM, John W	Tailor			
FARNHAM, S W	Tailor			
FIELD, Stephen	Woolshop			
FITCH, William	Machinist	6	1846	1845
FORD, Marshal	Joiner	6	1846	
FRENCH, Marshal	scribe	5	1844	1842
FRENCH, W R	Minister	3	1842	1845
FRYE, John M	Agt Woolen Mill	9	1809	
FRYE, W R	Manufacturer	6	1819	1844
GARCELON, Alonzo	Physician	9	1839	
GARDINER, Charles	Jack of all trades	7	1846	1846
GODDARD, J H	Jack of all trades	6	1845	1845

Name	Occupation			
GOODWIN, George	House Carpenter	4	1847	1846
GORHAM, Dr	Physician	2	1815	1820
GOSS, John	Store	5	1846	
GOULD, L A	Tailor	3	1846	1846
GRIGGS?, R	Operative	3	1847	1845
GROVER, A	Jobber	4	1847	
HAM, George W	Joiner	2	1845	
HAM, J B	Provision	2	1846	
HARRIS, Downes	Woolen Mill	2	1847	1846
HAYES, William	Carragemaker	8	1837	1845
HERRICK, John	Trader	4	1840	
HERRICK, Oliver		2	1839	
HEWEY, S	Shoemaker	9	1834	
HIGGINS, Charles	Tin Ware	6	1845	
HINKLEY, Maj	Jobber	9	1846	
HOLLAND, Daniel	Boots, shoes etc	7	1835	1837
IRISH, Freeman	Shoemaker	2	1846	1837
JONES, Hiram	Shoemaker	5	1840	1846
JONES, J B	Carragemaker	7	1846	
JONES, John B	Builder	5	1847	
KEENE, E, Jr	Trader	4		
KNOW, George	Minister	4	1847	
LINSCOTT, Daniel	Boarding House	30	1846	1836
LITCHFIELD, Isaac	Shoemaker	12	1847	1843
LITCHFIELD, L	Hotel	4	1834	1834
LITCHFIELD, Nels.	Dyer in Mill	9	1835	1837
LITCHFIELD, Wm.	Store	3	1847	1847
LITTLE, Josiah	Agt Woolen Mill	10	1846	1840
LONGLEY, Isiah P	Harnessmaker	4	1847	
LOWELL, Daniel	Farmer	2	1841	
LOWELL, James	Trader	2	1812	1825
LOWELL, Mark	Trader	7	native	1844
MERRILL, Benson	Teamster	3	1846	
MERRILL, S	Overseer	4	1834	1837
MILLETT, Charles	Physician	4	1847	
MOORE, T	Shoemaker	13	1846	1847
MOWER, P B	Brickmaker	2	1846	
MUCHFORD, H F	Shoemaker	3	1847	
MURRAY, Benjamin	Farmer	7		
NASH, A____	Farmer	2	1847	
NASH, John		2	1844	
NASH, Mrs		2	1832	1817?
NASH, William	Livery Stable	4	1845	1847
OAKES, John	Operative	7	1847	
OLIVER, Charles	Operative	3	1847	
PETTINGILL, H	Farmer	13	1847	1846
PICARD, Samuel	Manufacturer	11	1832	1834
PICKARD, S H	Farmer	4	1837	1833
Potter, L	Worker	13	1847	1846
RANDALL, J H	Joiner	4	1845	1847
READ, Dan	Joiner	3	1842	
READ, Samuel	Farmer	8	1829	

REYNOLDS, Charles	Machinist	2	1846	
REYNOLDS, Nathan	Trader	2	1816	
RICKER, H	Mason	3	1847	
ROBINSON, W			1847	
SAMPSON, Mr	Wool Cleaner	4	1840	1845
SCRIBNER, Daniel	Boarding House	36	1837	1836
SHAW, James	Saddler	5	1835	1845
SLEEPER, E	Joiner	8	1837	1843
SMITH, George B	Cabinetmaker	4	1837	1845
STATEN, Elias	Farmer	2	1847	
STEWART, F	Machinist	3	1846	1843
STICKNEY, D	Shoemaker	3	1847	1846
SYLVESTER, L	Fuller in Mill	9	1841	1837
TEBBETTS, Temple	Overseer	7	1832	1844
TOBIE, E P	Barber	7	1837	1840
TRACY, D	Boarding House	13	1835	
TRACY, D	Jack of all trades	5	1846	1837
TRACY, J P	Dyer in Mill	6	1846	1837
TURNER, E	Joiner	10	1845	1847
VERRILL, D E	House Carpenter	9	1847	1847
WAKEFIELD, A	Farmer	8	1834	
WARE, Levi	Brickmaker	5	1842	
WEBBER, Daniel	Teamster		1842	
WEBBER, Jesse	Joiner	5	1825	
WHITE, William	Shoemaker	6	1846	
WHITNEY, Alvin	Painter	6	1847	
WHITTUM, Sargent	Operative	7	1838	1837
WIGGIN, D H	Boarding House		1846	1845
WOODBURY, L P	Miller	4	1844	

LEWISTON FALLS.

PARK WALK.

EARLY LISBON CEMETERY RECORDS
Published in *Lewiston Journal*

ANDREWS, Shirley - 1804-1844 Lisbon Yard
BARD, Samuel - 1845 ae 62y Lisbon Center Yard
BARTON, Samuel - d 1846 ae 63y Lisbon Center Yard
BLAKE, John - 1780-1858 Lisbon Yard
BLAKE, William - 1782-1858 Lisbon Yard
BLETHEN, Increase - 1868 ae 91y Lisbon Center Yard
BLETHEN, John - 1858 ae 90y Lisbon Center Yard
CHENEY, Asa - 1767-1830 Lisbon Yard
COBBETT, Horace - 1797-1875 Lisbon Yard
COOMBS, Robert - 1847 71y Lisbon Center Yard
COURSON, Thankful - 1777-1851 Lisbon Yard
CUSHMAN, Isaac - 1780 1828 Lisbon Yard
DUNHAM, Ammi - 1804-1861 Lisbon Yard
DURGAN, Benjamin - 1775-1864 Lisbon Yard
FARNSWORTH, Cephas - d 1881 ae 88y Lisbon Center Yard
FARRAR, James Capt - 1795-1878 Lisbon Yard
FOSS, Simeon - 1795-1868 Lisbon Yard
FROST, George - 1855 ae 58y Lisbon Center Yard
GOODY, John - 1799-1878 Lisbon Yard
GREEN, John - 1807-1889 Lisbon Yard
GREENE, David - 1833 58y Lisbon Center Yard
HAM, Isreal - 1766-1854 Lisbon Yard
HAMMOND, Levi - 1869 ae 77y Lisbon Center Yard
HARDING, Richard - 1802-1859 Lisbon Yard
HASSY, Jacob - 1795-1868 Lisbon Yard
HINCKLEY Joseph - 1843 ae 75y Lisbon Center Yard
HINKLEY, Samuel - 1802-1885 Lisbon Yard
HOTTON, Asaph - 1791-1870 Lisbon Yard
JACK, Robert - 1818-1834 Lisbon Yard
JACK, Robert Esq - 1795-1865 Lisbon Yard
JORDAN, Winslow Capt - 1826-1878 Lisbon Yard
JORDAN, Abijah - 1877 76y Lisbon Center Yard
JUDKINS, Stephen - 1779-1841 Lisbon Yard
LYNG, Sylvanus - 1844 70y Lisbon Center Yard
MCFARLAND, David - 1787-1849 Lisbon Yard
NILES, Joseph Lisbon Yard
NUTTING, Aaron - d 1847 Lisbon Yard
NUTTING, Abel - 1755-1829 Lisbon Yard
PURINGTON, John - d 1840 ae 88 Lisbon Center Yard

PURINGTON, Joshua - d 1872 74 Lisbon Center Yard
RAND, Rhuban - 1801-1871 Lisbon Yard
ROBERTS, Oliver - 1769-1815 Lisbon Yard
SMITH, Isaac - 1766-1838 Lisbon Yard
TIBBETTS, Enoch - 1781-1858 Lisbon Yard
TIBBETTS, Paul - 1792-1864 Lisbon Yard
VINING, David - 1801-1867 Lisbon Yard
WEBBER, William - d 1890 91y Lisbon Center Yard
WHITNEY, Samuel - 1842 ae 72 Lisbon Center Yard
WOODBURY, Edward - 1780-1849 Lisbon Yard

CEMETERY INSCRIPTIONS

Janus G. Elder compiled names of people buried in Lewiston's oldest cemeteries. The cemetery records cover the years 1777-1900+. We have merged the town vital records for the years 1785-1875. The source LewVR 202 means, Lewiston Vital Records page 202. The name of the cemetery is regular type face. "*" means we have added this information from the sexton's cemetery records. The names of some of the revolutionary soldiers who were buried in Lisbon, Greene, Leeds, Webster, & Lewiston are also included as the lines of Lewiston were once larger than it is today. The name of the towns are all in caps.

ADAMS, Charles P s/o Hiram & Betsey - 15 July 1852 1-5-17 Davis
    Samuel revol soldier - (d 1828) bur. GREENE
ALDEN, Benjamin revol soldier - b 1752 bur. GREENE
    John revol soldier - bur. MINOT
ALLEN, John - d 1834 bur. GREENE
AMES, Aaron - 8 Dec 1822 26y Garceleon
    Daniel - 18 July 1860 61-4-28 Garceleon
    Elizabeth w/o James - d 18 Jan 1817 Lew VR 201
    Elizabeth w/o Winslow - 20 July 1857 74y Garceleon
    Ezra s/o James & Elizabeth - died in Burington 3 Jan 1814 LewVR 201
    Fanny - 3 Dec 1876 76y Garceleon
    Isaac - 3 Nov 1828 36y Garceleon
    James s/o Ezra & Lucy - d 20 Jan 1803 LewVR 201
    James - d 3 June 1815 LewVR 201
    John s/o Winslow & Margaret - 27 May 1805 LewVR 202
    Margaret w/o Winslow - 1 June 1805 LewVR 202
    Mary w/o Daniel - 21 Feb 1858 59y Garceleon
    Polly d/o Daniel & Polly - d 8 July 1824 LewVR 201
    Winslow - 12 Oct 1851 89y Garceleon
ANDERSON, Albert s/o Joseph - d 25 Mar 1851 LewVR 201
    Barton Capt - 19 May 1845 53y Davis
    Elizabeth w/o Robert - 29 Oct 1824 70y 6 mos Davis
    John s/o Robert - d 30 Jan 1825 LewVR 201
    Martha d/o Robert - 28 May 1831 43y Davis LewVR 201
    Robert, revol soldier - 19 Aug 1843 87-5-4 Davis
ANER, Chars [German] - 1880 Riverside*
ARNOLD, Elmer E s/o L - 14 Jan 1865 3y 9m Crowley
    Lloyd - 2 June 1879 43y Crowley

Samuel revol soldier LEEDS
ATKINSON, Ame d/o Wm & Anne - 16 July 1830 ae 28y LewVR 201
   George Washington s/o Wm & Anna - d 12 Jan 1815 LewVR 201
BABCOCK, William M of Lowell, Ma - 22 Nov 1870 BleedingNose Riverside
BACKNELL, Charles s/ Edwin - 1 Jan 1857 LewVR 210
BAGERT, Cloud [German] - 1877 Riverside*
BAILEY, Edmund revol soldier MINOT
BAILEY, Lois Ann l/o St Albans - 31 Oct 1851 21y? LewVR 210
BAKER, Cynthia w/o Shubael - 7 Feb 1884 79y 6m Herrick
BALD, Mary [colored] - 1886 40y Riverside*
BALKHAM, John s/o I??iah - 12 Dec 1861 LewVR 210
BANGS, Almira - 3 Apr 1807 LewVR 203
   Edward - 12 May 1808 LewVR 203
BANKS, Joseph - 23 Oct 1857 84y LewVR 210
   Philip - d 23 Feb 1811 [Hodgkins Diary]
BARKER, Albert s/o David/Priscila - 15 Oct 1828 LewVR 203
   Cyrus - 25 Feb 1838 72y Herrick
   Eliza Mittet d/o Cyrus - 9 Aug 1827 4 weeks Herrick Cem LewVR 203
   Fred A s/o N P - 25 May 1865 10y Herrick
   Geo L s/o N P - 3 Mar 1847 14 mos Herrick
   Jacob - 13 Dec 1861 55y LewVR 210
   Jacob - 17 Aug 1803 LewVR 203
   Jacob s/o Caleb - 3 Jan 1824 58y Davis Cem LewVR 203
   John - 25 Oct 1865 67-3-22 Garcelon
   Levi s/o Cyrus/Rachel - 27 July 1803 LewVR 203
   Martha w/o Jacob 8 Nov 1835 57y Davis
   Mary E w/o A P - 9 May 1848 24y 1m Herrick
   Mary H w/o N P - 12 Aug 1888 75y Herrick
   Rachel w/o Cyrus 6 Dec 1843 73y Herrick
   Sally w/o John - 21 Apr 1868 72y 8m Garcelon
   two d/o Jacob/Martha - 7 July 1799 LewVR 203
BARLOW, c/o John B - 29 July 1855 LewVR 210
BARNES, John - 21 July 1821 LewVR 210
BARNS, Marinda d/o Rhoda - 27 May 1828 LewVR 203
BARRELL, Olive w/o Samue - 12 Jan 1837 54y Davis
BARRON, Asa - 13 Sept 1804 LewVR 203
   Green Nathan - 6 Mar 1815 LewVR 203
   Mittel - 3 Sept 1804 LewVR 203
   Molly w/o Oliver - 31 Mar 1815 LewVR 203
BATCHELDER, Frances w/ J C B - 3 Nov 185622y LewVR 210
BATCHELDOR, Joseph - 11 July 1861 38 LewVR 210
BATES, Jabez revol soldier - d 1849 GREENE
BATTIN, Dorothy w/ Abraham - 23 July 1826 LewVR 203
   Naomi w/o Abraham - 25 Apr 1798 LewVR 203
BAYLEY, Edmund revol soldier POLAND
BEACE, Charles O s/o Daniel A - 17 Dec 1862 4y 1m Herrick
BEACE, Clara E d/o Daniel M - 17 Nov 1862 Herrick
   Daniel A - 3 June 1870 43-7-18 Herrick
   Edwin C s/o Daniel - 23 Nov 1862 6-1-11 Herrick
BEAL, Mary - 27 Oct 1876 57y 7m NoNamePond

BEAN, Cynthia w/o George - 13 June 1888 73y 6m Riverside
George Riverside
BECKETT, Julia d/o John - 23 July 1852 18m LewVR 210
BEGEIT, Henry [German] - 1881? Riverside*
Lewis [german] - 1 Sept 1874 36y Riverside*
BEGERT, Mary [German] - 12 Aug 1872 5m Riverside*
BENJAMIN, Samuel Lt revol soldier LIVERMORE
BENNER, Katie [scotch] - 26 Nov 1869 consumption Riverside*
BENSON, Lucy A w/o E T - 21 Feb 1898 81y Quaker Cem
Lydia w/Asa St David NB - 4 July 1830 37y 5m LewVR 203
Samuel s/Saml - 18 Apr 1861 31y LewVR 210
BERRY, Eugene M - born 13 Jan 1854 26 Mar 1885 Garcelon
George revol soldier - d 1846 GREENE
w/Ira - 17 Nov 1866 LewVR 252
BICKFORD, Aaron - 6 Apr 1863 75y Crowley
d/o Aaron Crowley
James - 27 Aug 1843 29 or 25 Crowley
Mary E w/o Geo P - 27 July 1872 26y 5m Crowley
Melissa d/o Jesse - 25 Aug 1845 2y 6m Crowley
Nathaniel - 2 Apr 1865 41y Crowley
Rufus s/o Aaron 3y Crowley
Sarah J w/o Jesse - 27 Sept 1882 59-4-9 Crowley
Sarah w/o Aaron - 12 Sept 1861 68y? 4m? Crowley
d/o Jesse - 1 Oct 1856 9d Crowley
BIXBY, Grace L d/o Geo L - 4 June 1864 3m Herrick
BLACK, Agnes [Scotch] - 16 Oct 1872 36y Riverside*
BLACK, Lewis M [Scotch] - 1873 teething Riverside*
BLAISDELL, Abijah s/o Wm & Rebeca 7 May 1787 LewVR 203
Clarisa d/o W R - 19 Mar 1807 LewVR 203
Delia d/o W R - 30 July 1849 46 or 16 Herrick
Dille d/o WM & Rebeca - 2 May 1787 LewVR 203
Elizabeth 3d w/o W R - 2 June 1818 38y Herrick LewVR 203
Elizabeth d/o W R - 16 Dec 1834 21y Herrick
Elizabeth d/o W R - 16 Dec 1834 Lew VR 203
Elvira P d/o John - 16 Feb 1842 2-7-13 Herrick
Hannah d/o Wm & Rebeca - 1 Sept 1791 LewVR 203
Polly d/o W R - 10 May 1836 20y Herrick LewVR 203
Rebecca w/o William - 9 Oct 1831 Lew VR 203
Sally 2dw/ W R - 15 Apr 1811 LewVR 203
Sally w/o Walter - 16 Nov 1801 LewVR 203
Sarah d/o W R - 22 May 1831 29y LewVR 203 Herrick
W R s/o John - 24 Apr 1834 Herrick
Walter R Esq - 19 Jan 1831 55y Lew VR 203 Herrick
Walter R s/John/Mary - 23 Apr 1832 Lew VR 203
William - 23 Apr 1816 (sic) 68y Herrick
William - 23 Apr 1818 LewVR 203
BLAKE, John - 23 Jan 1855 68y LewVR 210
BLANCHARD, Elizabeth w/o J K - 6 Apr 1884 59-6-11 Riverside
Isaac, blind pauper - 17 Apr 1859 LewVR 210
J K - 16 Sept 1885 65y 3m Riverside
BLETHEN, Betsey w/o Increase - 13 Oct 1852 80-3 *Morn. Star*
Charlott H w/o Dexter - 1 Oct 1880 57y 2m Crowley

Dexter - 28 Feb 1902 81y 1m Crowley
Eleanor - born 20 Jan 1805 29 Mar 1890 Crowley
Ings s/o Joseph - 26 Nov 1844 Crowley
Joseph - born 27 Nov 1817 21 June 1903 Crowley
Stephen of Lewiston - 2 July 1855 38y *Morning Star* FWB
BLODGETT, d/o L W - 1839-1891 ?????? Goddard
BOND, Mary w/o William - 15 Jan 1873 77y 10m Riverside
   Omar s/o William - 16 Apr 1861 31y 7m Riverside
   William - 10 Mar 1873 86y 10m Riverside
BORTHEWICK, Kate [Irish] - 30 Apr 1879 Riverside*
BRADBURY, Sarah Hellen (formerly of Athens) - 2 Nov 1857 LewVR 210
BRALEY, Angeline E d/o Sumner - 21 Mar 1852 15y LewVR 210
BROOKS, Anna w/o William - 19 June 1867 86y 7m Garcelon
   Charles E s/o Ham - 28 May 1881 33-9-20 Garcelon
   Frank S s/o Ham - 22 Sept 1853 11y 22m Garcelon
   Georgianna d/o Ham - 13 Aug 1867 24y 4m Garcelon
   James s/ widow Martha - 30 Nov 1854 LewVR 210
   James W l/o Lewiston - 30 Nov 1854 at Boston *Morn. Star*
   John - 9 Sept 1831 32y 10m Garcelon
   Josiah R - 29 Apr 1849 25y Garcelon
   Margaret w/o Ham - 21 Jan 1872 58y 5m Garcelon
   Martha Ann d/o Ai/Martha - 16 Aug 1828 LewVR 203
   Martha w/o Ai - 25 Nov 1828 25y LewVR 203
   Martha w/o John - 14 Jan 1879 79y 10m Garcelon
   William - 18 Nov 1867 90y 8m Garcelon Cem, 19 Nov 1866 90y LewVR 252
   Winslow H s/o Ham - 13 Apr 1840 9m Garcelon
BROWN, Melissa w/ Joel - 6 Aug 1856 LewVR 210
BRYANT, James J s/ James - 15 Nov 1866 LewVR 252
BUBIER, Abigail old age - 8 Oct 1868 [American] Riverside*
   Abigail w/o Dea John - 8 Oct 1868 81y Riverside
   Adelia A w/o Geo - 3 Sept 1863 33y 3m Herrick
   Adelia C w/o Geo - 11 Sept 1882 42y 6m Herrick
   Andrew - 12 May 1847 79y Crowley
   4 Sept 1871 74y 3m Crowley
   Caroline d/o Mark & Betsy - 1 Mar 1824 LewVR 203
   Catherine A w/o Geo - 26 Nov 1858 34y Herrick
   Delia w/o George - 6 Sept 186? smallpox LewVR 210
   Eunice d/o Andrew & M - 10 Oct 1804 LewVR 203
   George - 17 Sept 1887 72y 5m Herrick
   John Deacon - 26 Sept 1881 69-7-11 Riverside
   Larry s/o Geo - 29 Sept 1856 3m Herrick
   Levi s/o Geo - 24 June 1851 8y Herrick
   Louisa w/o Dea John - 8 Apr 1871 58y 8m Riverside
   Martha dChristopher/Hanna - 3 Apr 1811 LewVR 203
   Miriam w/o Andrew - 22 Dec 1837 78y Crowley
   Rebecca w/o Geo - 28 Aug 1850 32y Herrick
   Sadie B d/o E F - 21 Aug 1887 15m 6d Herrick
   Samuel - 24 Apr 1863 75y 3m Crowley
   Samuel s/o Christopher/Happy - 1819? NoNamePond
   Stephen s/o Andrew/Miriam - 1 Sept 1799 LewVR 203

BUCKLEY, Timothy, an Irishman - 16 Apr 1852 27y LewVR 210
BUCKNELL, Sarah d/ Edwin - 12 Dec 1866 21y LewVR 252
BUDLONG, Laroy s/o Rhodes A - 21 Feb 1852 LewVR 210
   Leroy R s/o R A & Betsey - 21 Feb 1852 4-9-15 Davis
BULLEN, J Roscoe s/o John & Mary - 24 Jan 1853 10y 11 mos Davis
   LewVR 210
BUMPER, d/o David/Harriet - 13 Aug 1855 LewVR 210
BURBANK, James - 19 Aug 1852 Riverside*
   James L - 17 Aug 1849 Riverside*
BURNS, Bridget widow (Irish) - 18 Feb 1855 LewVR 210
   Katherine d/o Bridget - 7 Feb 1857 9y LewVR 210
BUTLER, Emma J w/ Warren - 12 Sept 1855 24y LewVR 210
   Roscoe s/ Warren/Emma - 15 Apr 1857? 3y 3m LewVR 210
BUZZELL, John s/ John - 6 Sept 1855 8y LewVR 210
CALLAHAN, Agnes d/o George - 28 Oct 1866 6y? 4m Lew VR 241
   Loisa Adaline d/Augustus - 14 Mar 1852 Lew VR 206
CANNEBLE, Mitchell (Irish) - 2 Aug 1854 Lew VR 206
CANNELLE, widow of Michael - 12 Aug 1854 Lew VR 206
CAREY, Susie A R [colored] - 1880 27-11-9 Riverside*
CARR, Jane [Scotch] - 1881 Riverside*
CARRILLE, Mary - 24 Sept 1821 1y? 8m Crowley
   Tamar w/o Sewell - 19 Nov 1884 87y Crowley
CARVER, Mary A - 2 May 1885 Garceleon
CARVILLE, Abijail w/o Benj - 5 Feb 1883 78-3-24 Garceleon
   Ada w/o Simon - 13 May 1888 69y Garceleon
   Alonzo s/o Benjamin - 7 Nov 1827 1y 7m Garceleon
   Anna Celestia d/ Lewis - 14 Dec 1857 27y Lew VR 241
   Benjamin - 3 Apr 1881 81-1-6 Garceleon
   c/o Simon - 6 May 1840 Lew VR 205
   Celestia d/o Lewis - 14 Dec 1857 2y 4m Garceleon
   Charlotte w/o Simon - 18 July 1841 37y 7m Garceleon
   Drusilla w/o D W - 31 Oct ?? 31y Garceleon
   Elhanus W s/o Wm - 15 Jan 1857 in Chicago? LewVR 206
   Elijah s/ Sewall - 10 May 1836 11-11-24 Crowley LewVR 205
   Elijah s/o Wm & Rebeca - 19 Oct 1824 22y 6m Garceleon Lew VR 205
   Elisa J d/o Benj - 30 Apr 1843 11-8-27 Garceleon
   Elisabeth - 9 June 1829 33y Garceleon
   Elkanan - 15 Jan 1857 26y Garceleon
   Emily Jane d/o Benj. - 30 Apr 1843 11-8-7 Garceleon LewVR 205
   Ezekiel - 9 June 1829 33y Garceleon
   Harriet w/o James - 9 Nov/Oct 1837 32y LewVR 205 Riverside
   Henry revol soldier - 12 July 1823 68y Garceleon LewVR 205
   Itis - 16 June 1872 44y 7m Garceleon
   James - 6 Nov 1879 Riverside
   Jane F w/o Isaac T - 22 Aug 1872 43-7-25 Garceleon
   Jarusha Ann d/ Sewall - 26 Nov 1859 21y Lew VR 241
   John - 18 July 1880 38y 3m Garceleon
   6 Sept 1862 73y Crowley
   Mary - 14 Apr 1879? 80y 24d Garceleon
   Mary d/o Sewell/Tarnah - 25 Jan 1822 Lew VR 205
   Mercy d/o Henry/ Mary - 19 Mar 1799 Lew VR 205

    Mercy w/o Henry - 11 Oct 1845 88y Garceleon LewVR 205
    Nancy D - 11 May 1873 46-4-23 Crowley
    Nathan s/o Mary - 17 Mar 1851 19y 7m Garceleon LewVR 206
    Nathan s/o Wm/Rebeca - 16 Oct 1826/1 19y 6m Garceleon LewVR 205
    Nathan s/o William/Sally - 29 Oct 1851 23y 7m Garceleon LewVR 206
    Otis - 16 June 1872 44y 7m Garceleon
    Priscilla w/o John - 25 July 1854, 62y 5m Crowley, Lew VR 206
    Rebecca d/o Wm/Rebecca - 31 Dec 1822 10y 6m LewVR 205 Garceleon
    Rebecca w/o William - 14 July 1861/7 94y Garceleon
    Ruth d/o Ezehiel/Lois - 30 Oct 1826 Lew VR 205
    Sally w/o William C - 11 Dec 1848 39y 2m Lew VR 206 Garceleon
    Sewell - 8 June 1879 85-2-21 Crowley
    Simon - 26 Dec 1890 86y Garceleon
    Willard s/o James C - 9 Mar 1852 Lew VR 206
    William - 14 June 1895 59y 4m Garceleon
    26 Oct 1864 68y 26d Garceleon
    William Sr - 20 Nov 1829 67-0-10 Garceleon Lew VR 205
CARY, Emma S [colored] - 1884 Riverside*
    Jennie M [colored] - 1879 Riverside*
    ___ I H S Davis
CASWELL, Horatio, hung himself - 21 Mar 1853 50y Lew VR 206
CATEN, John, bank fell & killed - 6 Nov 1852 an Irishman LewVR 206
CHADBOURN, Abbie w/o Edward - 1836-1918 Randall Rd
    Catharine - 18 Nov 1859 23y Lew VR 241
    Edward - 1834-1900 Randall Rd
    Everett - 1869-1902 Randall Rd
    Thomas - 25 Mar 1826 Lew VR 205
CHADBOURNE, Alverton s/o S B - 25 Aug 1875 3m 1d Herrick
    Augustus - 1865-1931 Randall Rd
    Mary - 1865-1933 Randall Rd
CHADBURN, Orrington L - 25 June 1876 37 7 11 Randall Rd
    Rosila G pd Webster - 22 Mar 1858 36y LewVR 251
    s/o Orrington - 18 Aug 1864 6 mos Randall Rd
    Thomas s/o Jophat/Ruth - 28 Sept 1826 Lew VR 205
CHAMBERLAIN, Philip s/o William - 12 July 1799 Lew VR 205
CHAMBERS, Cudgo [a black] revol soldier LEEDS
CHANBURN, s/o Orrington C - 1862-1862 4mos Randall Rd
CHASE, Jerusha d/Ekeziel/Jerusha - 1 July 1853 Davis
    Jerusha d/o Ezekiel - 1 July 1858 Lew VR 206
    Josephine d/Ezekiel & Mary - 15 Dec 1854 4 weeks 5d Davis
    Silas A at Alms house - 22 Dec 1865 33y Lew VR 241
CHICK, Henry died suddenly - 23 Mar 1863 Lew VR 241
CHILDS, Judith, widow pauper - 5 May 1848 76y Lew VR 206
CLANCY, Thomas , a Irish pauper - 11 Jan 1858 68y Lew VR 241
CLARK, Charles, lived with Daniel - 13 Mar 1826 Lew VR 205
    d/o Emery D - Oct 1856 Lew VR 241
    Daniel - 8 Jan 1858 77y Randall Rd LewVR 241
    Eunice w/o Daniel - 15 Mar 1826 Lew VR 205
    Horace M s/o Horace C - 30 Dec 1849 Lew VR 206

Joseph H of Greene - 20 May 1871 80y Riverside*
Mary Ann w/o Charles - 4 Dec 1840 22y Garceleon LewVR 205
Matilda d/o W W - 17 Jan 1887 30y 6m Herrick
widow mother of Daniel C - 18 Feb 1825 Lew VR 205
CLARY, Edward, [Irishman] - 8 May 1853 Lew VR 206
Margaret d/ Edward [Irish] - 15 July 1851 8y Lew VR 206
CLEEVER, James L - 21 Dec 1851 25y Lew VR 206
CLOUGH, Aseneth - 22 June 1878 75-5-22 Crowley
Benjamin F - b 25 Oct 1832 19 Nov 1888 Crowley
Flora w/o A J - 11 Apr 1901 56-1-11 Crowley
Jeremiah - 18 June 1867 62-4-28 Crowley
26 Apr 1848 81y Crowley
Jeremiah Deacon - 26 Apr 1848 81y Lew VR 206
Josiah - 22 July 1895 85-2-12 Crowley
Mary d w/o Josiah S - 26 Oct 1886 75-6-14 Crowley
Mehitable wid/o Jeremiah - 16 June 1848 76y Crowley LewVR 206
Sarah A w/o Jere - 20 May 1889 73y Crowley
COBB, Angie A w/o Llewellyn - 31 May 1872 25y 5d Riverside
Hannah w/o Samuel-N Yarmou - 24 Dec 1831 Lew VR 205
Joel S - 5 Feb 1873 39-6-3 Garceleon
COBURN, Abigail wid/o Reuben - 20 Oct 1861 80y Randall Rd LewVR 241
Freeman - 24 Sept 1875 72y 3m Herrick
Hannah w/o Freeman - 30 June 1866 58y 2m Herrick
Mrs m/o Freeman C - 8 Feb 1858 80y Lew VR 241
w/o Josiah C - 30 Apr 1867 Lew VR 241
COFFIN, Fear of old age - 6 Mar 1880 72y Riverside*
COLBY, Mary W at Lewiston Falls - 14 June 1853 39y *Morn. Star*
COLE Alvira w/o Harrison C - 14 Aug 1853 34y? Lew VR 206
Anna - 26 Dec 1845 85y Herrick
Benjamin Elder - 10 Sept 1839 78y Davis Lew VR 205
Benjamin s/o Samuel/Anna - 8 Mar 1787 Lew VR 205
Charlotte E d/o Harrison 23 Mar 1851 9mos Herrick
Charlotte w/o Samuel Jr - 9 Sept 1853 62y Herrick
Ella F d/o Sumner - 4 Mar 1870 13y 2m Riverside
Elmisa w/o Isaac C - 2 Mar 1852 Lew VR 206
Elvira w/o H L - 14 Aug 1853 34y Herrick
Elvirus w/o Sumner C - 15 Aug 1853 Lew VR 241
Hannah d/o Samuel/Anna - 10 Apr 1798 Lew VR 205
Huldah J - 28 May 1873 51y 2m Riverside
Jere'h - 11 Aug 1882 93y 2m Herrick
Job revol Soldier bur. LEWISTON
John - 19 Jul 1882 82y Riverside
Lizzie d/o James/Rozetta - 25 Oct 1856 2y Lew VR 241
Lucy S w/o Jere'h - 25 Jan 1846 64y Herrick
Margaret w/o John - 1 June 1874 Riverside
Osca G w/o Sumner - 30 Nov 1889 61y 3m Riverside
Otis s/o John - 13 Apr 1882 70-2-11 Riverside
Ruth relict of Elder Cole - 4 Dec 1843 - Lew VR 205
s/o Isaac/Elmira - 26 Feb 1852 Lew VR 206
Samuel revol soldier - 29 Mar 1844 88y LewVR 205 Herrick Cem
Samuel Jr - 11 Aug 1828 42/43y Herrick LewVR 205

Sarah m/o Eben C - 10 Feb 1826 99y 6m Lew VR 205
Sumner H - 19 Dec 1899 75y 5m Riverside
COLEMAN, Charles E 25y Garceleon
  Hattie H - 4 Jan 1863 22y Lew VR 241
  Ursula B - 4 Mar 1886 69y Garceleon
COLLINS, Charles Franklin s/Dan. - 12 Nov 1851 Lew VR 206
  Charles s/o Samuel/Mary - 11 Nov 1851 at Lewiston *Morn. Star*
CONANT, Clementine w/o Winslow - 7 Oct 1847 21y Herrick
  Daniel at Lewiston - 13 Jan 1854 48y *Morn. Star*
  Daniel late of Topsham - 13 Jan 1854 48y Lew VR 206
  Olevia C w/ Winslow - 7 Oct 1847 Lew VR 205
CONDON, John - 2 Aug 1854 Lew VR 206
COOK, Hanson - 28 Dec 1871 69y Riverside
  Mary at Alms house - 11 June 1865 54y Lew VR 241
  Nancy w/o Hanson - 29 Dec 1869 67y Riverside
  Silas - 22 June 1898 61y Riverside
COOMBS, Hezekiah revol Soldier - d 1839 LISBON
COOPER, Jemnie [Gipsey] - 1881? Riverside*
CORLISS, Lucy wid m/o Samuel - 29 Dec 1849 78y Lew VR 206
COTTON, Thomas s/o James - 12 July 1848 Lew VR 206
COURSON, Abigail w/o Wm - 5 Sept 1874 81y Crowley
  Edora F d/o Rufus - 13 Oct 1865 14-2-3 Crowley
  Hattie E d/o Rufus - 11 July 1864 9y 11d Crowley
  Thankful widow - 26 Feb 1851 71y Lew VR 206
  W H Crowley
  William B - 13 June 1874 74 Crowley
COWEN, Calvin revol Soldier LISBON
CRAWFORD, Beatrice dead in canal - 28 Sept 1858 60y Lew VR 206
CROCKETT, Austin s/o D M - 23 Oct 1872 17-4-16 Crowley
  Daniel M - 31 May 1872 45-11-2 Crowley
  Harriet N w/o Wm D - 10 Mar 1882 58-11-8 Garceleon
  Immogene R D d/o D M - 24 Sept 1872 5m 21d Crowley
  William D - 6 May 1876 58-4-11 Garceleon
CROVER, Jonas ????? - 7 Nov 1897 61y Goddard
CROWLEY, Henry C s/o Jere - 12 Apr 1857 11m 22d Crowley
  Henry s/o Jeremiah - 12 Apr 1857 11m 22d Crowley
  Jere. Jr s/o Jeremiah - 25 Dec 1866 41y Crowley
  Jeremiah - 15 May 1868 82y Crowley
  Jeremiah Jr s/o J C - 24 Dec 1866 42y Lew VR 241
  Jerusha E d/o James - 4 Oct 1868 22y 16d Crowley
  Lizzie J d/o James - 31 Dec 1860 16-8-7 Crowley
  Martha Jane w/ Amos - 1 Nov 1859 27y Crowley LewVR 241
  Mehitable w/o Jere - 14 Jan 1877 85y Crowley
  Sophia F w/o William - 15 May 1864 41-6-14 Crowley
CUMMINGS, Edward P s/o J H - 7 Jan 1864 1y 12d Riverside
  Hattie May d/ John - 2 Mar 1875 10-2-20 Riverside
  John H Riverside
  Minnie d/o J H __ - Nov 1872 Riverside
CURTIS, James revol soldier - d 1824 WEBSTER
  James s/o John/Phebe - 7 June 1822 Lew VR 205
  John s/o John & Phebe - 16 May 1819 Lew VR 205
  Mrs Paul - 30 Sept 1857 39y *Morn. Star*

Phebe d/o John / Sarah - 13 Feb 1830 Lew VR 205
Phebe w/o John - 27 June 1825 31y Davis
Phebe w/o John C - 30 June 1826 Lew VR 205
CUSHING, Cornelia A d/o John - 31 May 1864 16-3-7 Crowley
  Experience w/o Dr John - 4 Nov 1848 57y Crowley
  John revol soldier WEBSTER
  John Dr - 22 Dec 1870 81y 8m Crowley
  John M s/o John - 6 Oct 1868 23y 8m Crowley
  Jos G s/o John - 1 Sept 1861 21y 8m Crowley
  Olive A d/o John 17 Apr 1859 21y 5m Crowley
  Prentice M s/o John - 3 Aug 1854 3y 5m Crowley
  Rebecca w/o Dr John - 28 June 1869 79y 2m Crowley
  w/o John C - 5 Nov 1848 Lew VR 206
CUTLER, Betsey d/ Nathan/Ruth - __ Jan 1871 Lew VR 205
  Esther d/o Nathan/Ruth 17 July 1812 Lew VR 205
  N Henry s/o Nathan/Ruth - 26 __ 1815 Lew VR 205
  Nathan revol Soldier LEWISTON
  Nathan, ae nearly 73y - 8 Dec 1827 Lew VR 205
  Ruth d/o Nathan/Ruth - 28 June 1798 Lew VR 205
  Ruth w/o Nathan - 12 July 1819 Lew VR 205
  Stephen - 1 Nov 1837 Lew VR 205
  Stephen C - 8 July 1826 Riverside
DAGGETT, John revol soldier - d 1816 GREENE
DAIN, Isaac s/o James/Hannah - 29 Mar 1825 Lew VR 207
DANCAN E A [French] - 28 Apr 1874 Riverside*
DANCOAN, child of chol. - 4 Aug 1854 Lew VR 208
  Cornelius [Irish] - 3 Aug 1854 of Chol. Lew VR 208
  Joanna an Irish girl - 4 Aug 1804 of chol. Lew VR 208
DANNEL, Emily w/o Nathaniel - 5 Feb 1848 Lew VR 208
DAUCLAN?, w/o Barnelius - 31 July 1854 of Chol. Lew VR 208
DAVIS, Aaron - 11/15 Aug 1841 73y 8m Crowley Lew VR 207
  14/18 Jan 1864 67y Crowley LewVR 218
  revol soldier POLAND
  Abigail w/o David - 29 May 1837 51y Davis
  Alice Meservey w/o Amos D - 1740-1803 Davis
  Almira w/o Jos F - 24 Apr 1882 47y 7m Crowley
  Ammi d/o Aaron - 20 Apr 1858 8y 10m Crowley
  21 Feb 1871 72-8-7 Crowley
  27 Jul 1848 78y 8 m Davis
  revol Soldier LEWISTON
  Amos - 1741- 20 Mar 1815 Davis LewVR 207
  Amos s/o Amos/Mehitable - 27 Dec 1815 Lew VR 207
  Anah w/o Amos - 4 Dec 1878 84y 10m 23d Crowley
  Anna d/o Aaron - 25 Dec 1846 2m Crowley
  Betsey R w/o David - 20 Mar 1869 62-9-20 Crowley
  Coolage s/o John V - 10 Sept 1863 28y Lew VR 218
  Dan R s/o David/Mary - 12 Apr 1802 11 mos Davis LewVR 207
  Daniel - 12 Oct 1827 78-8-24 Lew VR 207
  David Davis
  David - 14 May 1894 45y Riverside
  5 Jan 1851 75y Davis LewVR 208
  David 2d - 20 Mar 1839 Lew VR 207

Deborah d/ Amos/Mehiable - 10 Oct 1804 Lew VR 207
Dorcas w/o Daniel - 4 Nov 1825 Lew VR 207
Elice w/o Amos - 30 Sept 1803 Lew VR 207
Elizabeth w/o John H Davis - 26 July 1854 Lew VR 208
Ellen E d/o Aaron - 14 June 1874 45y 8m Crowley
George B - _ Dec 1889 59y Garcelon
Hannah w/ William - 2 Aug 1837 Lew VR 207
Hannah w/o Amos - 4 Dec 1887 84-10-23 Crowley
Hannah w/o Nathaniel - 23 Oct 1828 Lew VR 207
Hannah w/o Wm - 1 Aug 1837 38y Crowley
Harriet d/o Aaron - 2 Sept 1847 Lew VR 208
Henry D - 13 Nov 1865 32y Garcelon
Jackson s/o Daniel/Mary - 2 Sept 1826 in Orono Lew VR 207
James L - 29 June 1855 19y 8m Garcelon
James s/ Nathaniel/Hannah - 25 Dec 1811 Lew VR 207
James s/o Amos/Mehitable - 16 Aug 1810 Lew VR 207
Jane M w/o Wm - 2 Feb 1882 75y 8m Crowley
Jane wid/o John - 3 Nov 1853 90y Lew VR 208
Jesse revol Soldier LISBON
Jesse revol Soldier WEBSTER
John - 3 Mar 1849 76y Lew VR 208
John A - 22 Dec 1876 75y Garcelon
John formerly of Standish - 2 Jan 1864 Lew VR 218
John s/o John - 27 Aug 1846 46y Lew VR 208
Joseph W s/o Aaron - _ July 1848 5m Crowley
Katharine w/o Stephen - 18 Jan 1855 Lew VR 218
Levi s/o Amos/Mehitable - 20 Jan 1816 Lew VR 207
Lucy S w/o Ezekiel - 30 Sept 1856 Lew VR 218
Lydia wid/o Jackson D Esq - 10 Apr 1855 75y Garcelon LewVR 208
Margette d/o Aaron - 2 ??y 1871 25y 9m Crowley
Maria G w/o John A - 7 June 1882 80y 5m Garcelon
Maria w/o Amos Jr - 11 June 1841 41y 9m Crowley LewVR 207
Marietta d/Aaron/Mehitable - 19 Mar 1841 Lew VR 207
Martha C d/o Wm - 24 Feb 1861 32-10-26 Crowley
Mary - 3 Mar 1815 Bates College Campus
Mary d/ D & M - 3 Mar 1816 3y ?m Davis
Mary d/o David/Mary - 3 Mar 1815 Lew VR 207
Mary Elizabeth w/o David - 5 Jan 1858 Lew VR 218
Mary H w/o Nat - 20 Jan 1866 45y 9m Riverside
Mary w/o Daniel - 5 Jan 1858 30-2-11 Herrick
Mary w/o David - 10/19 Nov 1821 Davis 51y Lew VR 207
Mehitable d/o Daniel/Mary - 10 Aug 1803 Lew VR 207
Mehitable d/o David/Mary - 17 Nov 1815 Lew VR 207
Mehitable w/o Aaron Jr Crowley
Mehitable w/o Amos - 28 Jan 1847 75y Davis
Molley w/o Aaron - 5 July 1807 Lew VR 207
Murietta d/o Aaron - 19 Mar 1841 9y Crowley
Nathaniel d/o Orleans - 5 Sept 1864 38y 5m Riverside
Nathaniel, pauper - 27 Oct 1847 Lew VR 208
Ruth d/o Amos - 15 Aug 1833 Lew VR 207
Ruth d/o Nathaniel - 1822 Lew VR 207
Sarah w/o David - 24 Apr 1834 Lew VR 207

Sarah w/o G B - 18 June 1884 54y 5m Garcelon
Seth s/o David/Mary - 31 July 1827 Davis 21y Lew VR 207
Sophronia W d/o Aaron - 5 Sept 1847 2-1 Crowley LewVR 208
Unice - 1 July 1871 76y Crowley
William - 7 Jan 1853 Lew VR 208
7 Nov 186976-10-16 Crowley
William G - 28 Aug 1862 23y 11m Garcelon
William Jr - 28 Apr 1870 48y 6m Crowley
DAY, Elija d/o Heirey - b 1835 d 13 Jan 1853 Riverside Lew VR 208
Eliza w/o Eliphas P - 5 Oct 1856 18y 1m Davis Lew VR 218
Ellen L - born 3 Mar 1834 8 Dec 1854 Riverside
Ellen L d/o Hersey - 8 Dec 1854 20y Lew VR 208
Eunice w/o Hierey - 1811-1885 Riverside
Hierey - 1804-1884 Riverside
Joseph H - 1841-1898 Riverside
Levinia w/o J H - 1841-1863 Riverside
Livonia w/o Joseph H - 23 July 1863 21y Lew VR 218
Lydia B of Greene - 25 Nov 1849 Lew VR 208
Lydia J - 16 July 1859 19y 5m Riverside
DEARNELY, Wm s/o David & Eunice - 17 Mar 1869 Goddard
DELANO, Adaline - 1 Dec 1866 Lew VR 218
DELANO, Adelia d/l John of Abbott - 1 Jan 186721y Lew VR 218
DENNET, Ebenezer - 2 Apr 1836 Lew VR 207
DENNETT, Abigail w/o Peter - b 1806 d 27 Sept 1886 Crowley
Ann w/o Ebenezer - 8 Sept 1852 Crowley
Ebenezer - 2 Apr 1834 77y Crowley
Frank E s/o Peter - 27 Apr 1853 ae ?? Crowley
Julia A d/o Peter - 2 Apr 1853 16y 7m Crowley
Norton - 16 Aug 1862 21y Lew VR 218
Peter - b 6 June 1800 3 Mar 1884 83y Crowley
Rebecca - 18 July 1850 Lew VR 208
Sarah w/o Eben'r - 25 Aug 1825 65y Crowley
DICKEY, Eliza G w/o H H - 10 Nov 1879 Riverside
Henry H - 21 May 1884 68y Riverside
DILKS, Anna [German] - 18 Apr 1877 25y Riverside*
DILL, Abigail Dill Cem
Abigail d/o Josiah/Abigail - before 1814 Lew VR 207
Abigail w/o Josiah of Ohio - 1 Aug 1839 Lew VR 207
Alonzo Dill Cem
Amanda C d/o Washington 4y Crowley
Ann Huney Dill Cem
Caroline d/o Washington - 8 Aug 1852 Lew VR 208
Caroline w/o Washington - 13 Sept 1881 71y 3m Crowley
Caty d/o John & Sarah - 15 Mar 1795 Lew VR 207
Elias s/o Josiah/Abigail - before 1814 Lew VR 207
Ella A - 18 Aug 1889 35-10-? Crowley
Franklin s/o Washington - 3 Aug 1853 Lew VR 208
Hannah G died at Webster - 25 Dec 1850 11y 9m LewVR 251
Harriet d/o Joseph - 27 July 1843 Dill Cem? Lew VR 207
Joseph Capt Dill Cem
Joseph F s/o Washington - 3 Aug 1852 1y 6m Crowley
Joseph s/o Joseph - 22 Jan 1845 Dill Cem? Lew VR 207

Joshiah Dill Cem
Josiah died at Greene - 15 Nov 1843 47y 6m LewVR 251
Josiah s/o John - 20 Dec 1827 NYarville OH Lew VR 207
Mary Dingley Dill Cem
Olive Ann died in Strong - 29 Sept 1825 1y 15d LewVR 251
Polly Dill Cem
Sally w/o John - 27 Apr 1850 Lew VR 208
Washington - 29 July 1878 60-9-23 Crowley
DINGLEY, C Frank s/o John - 27 June 1876 16y 3m Garcelon
    Effie E d/o Wm F - 29 Apr 1863 8m 27d Crowley
    Emily J C d/o Wm - 24 Oct 1850 5y 7m? Garcelon
    Emma G d/o Ira - 24 Sept 1850 18m Crowley
    Emma w/o Wm - 12 Sept 1858 28y 9m Garcelon
    General s/o Wm - 11 Feb 1834 21y Garcelon
    Ira - 15 June 1860 54y 8m Crowley
    Isaiah b - 25 Mar 1814 31 May 1885 Crowley
    Isaiah Jr - 10 Apr 1847 10y 5m Crowley
    John T - 16 Nov 1892 63y Garcelon
    Levi w/o William - 28 Feb 1834 27y Garcelon
    Lydia d/o William - 15 Sept 1847 7y 8 mos Garcelon
    Mary w/o William - 9 Dec 1852 26y Lew VR 208
    Mary w/o Wm - 11 Jan 1860 44y 8m Garcelon
    9 Nov 1852 43y Garcelon
    Nelson L - 9 Aug 1870 35y 8m Crowley
    Sally w/o Wm - 4 Oct 1854 81y 10m Garcelon
    Sarah E d/o William - 23 Aug 1852 1y 2m Garcelon
    William - 10 Sept 1852 78y 7m Garcelon
    3 June 1882 62-6-4 Garcelon
    William s/o Wm Jr - 17 May 1814 b 25 Nov 1800 Garcelon
    William s/o Wm/Polly - 17 May 1814 Lew VR 207
DIVINAL, Aaron revol Soldier LISBON
DIXON, Mary w/o Hermon D - 26 Oct 1866 Lew VR 218
DOLOFF, Frances - 26 Apr 1881 75y unknown
Donahough,?? James - 1 Sept 1852 26y Lew VR 208
DONNELL, Thomas O - 18 Dec 1849 45y Davis
D'Onset, Prince [a blackman] revol soldier LEEDS
DOULASS, Augustus s/o Abner - 24 July 1844 Lew VR 208
DOYLE, Sarah J - 24 Jan 1895 44-1-2 Riverside
DUCKWAITH, Jesse E s/o John - 29 Dec 1855 Lew VR 218
DUNCAN, Robert revol soldier WEBSTER
DUNHAM, David A drowned - 19 June 1854 Lew VR 208
DUNN, Charles A [scotch] - 1880 Riverside*
    James, Irishman of Boston - 8 Oct 1851 Lew VR 208
DWELLY, Samuel L - 8 July 1863 24y 8m Riverside
DWINAL, Amos revol soldier WEBSTER
    Sarah 2d w/o Ebenezer - 3 Aug 1825 Lew VR 207
DYER, Alkanah revol soldier - 23 July 1820 62y Garcelon
    Annda d/o Barsilla - 4 Sept 1831 2yr Garcelon
    Burrilla - 26 Sept 1870 77-5-14 Garcelon
    Catherine w/o Alkanah - 21 Mar 1854 94y Garcelon
    Daniel s/o Daniel/Lois - 4 Dec 1827 Lew VR 207
    Elkanah Sr - 23 July 1820 Lew VR 207

Hannah w/o R R - b 21 May 1829 6 May 1901 71y Garcelon
Maria D d/o Barsilla - 3 Nov 1859 15y Garcelon
Rebeca w/o Barsilla - 31 Dec 1848 49y 5m Garcelon LewVR 208
Rebecca d/o Barsilla - 30 Mar 1847 22y Garcelon
Susan J d/o Barsilla - 19 Aug 1842 21y Garcelon
EASTMAN, Ina - 7 Dec 1890 1y 10m unknown
EATON, Mary Jane pd Portland - 15 Oct 1858 27y 8m LewVR 251
EDGECOMB, Eli Dr - 24 Oct 1891 80y Riverside
   L w/o Dr Eli - 28 Sept 1881 62y Riverside
ELDER, Phebe at So Gardiner, Me - 30 Sept 1855 67y *Morn. Star*
   Phebe w/o Joshua - 25 Oct 1849 48y Lew VR 209
EMERY, Elisa O - 30 Nov 1858 72-2-18 unknown
   Harriet E d/o Alfred H - 10 Oct 1883 32-7-22 Riverside
ERSKINE, Adaline w/o Alexander - 3 Dec 1857 48y Lew VR 209
ESTES, Edward - 7 Jan 1863 66-3-18 Quaker Cem
   Josiah - 20 Feb 1860 Lew VR 209
   Josiah s/o Josiah/Hannah - 9 Sept 1840 5y 6m Lew VR 209
EVANS, Francis V s/o E. M. & E. - 24 Sep 1852 9m 3d Davis
FALES, Alpheus B s/ Horace/Elizabe - 18 Oct 1852 12-10-18 Davis
FANNING, Joshua Doct - 6 Dec 1866 69-9 Lew VR 211
FARL, David Jr, Irishman - 13 Dec 1857 17y Lew VR 211
FARNHAM, Anna Augusta - 6 Nov 1842 9-0-22 Davis
   John W - 7 Nov 1850 32y Davis
   Susan w/o Samuel W - 29 Oct 1849 Lew VR 211
FARR, Geo W Dr - 8 July 1882 77y Riverside
   Hannah w/o Dr G H F? - 31 Jan 1852 Lew VR 211
FARROW, Lucy w/o George - 8 June 1828 26y Garcelon
FAUNCE, Cybelia w/o A L - 20 Aug 1886 63y 3m Garcelon
FELLOWS, Joseph, telegraphman - 16 Jan 1860 80y 9m Lew VR 211
FERGUSON, Lillie [scotch] - 1880 Riverside*
FICKETT, Josiah revol Soldier LEWISTON
   Nasthaniel revol soldier AUBURN
field stone marker L.A.D. Davis
field stone marker R.D. Davis
FIELD, Barton A - 23 Dec 1862 29-1-17 Riverside
   Benjamin s/o Joseph - 5 June 1851 61y Lew VR 211
   Eunice H w/o Joseph - b 1753 d 1831 Davis
   Eunice wid/o Dea Joseph - 6 May 1830 79y Lew VR 211
   James A - 17 Sept 1865 54y 7m Riverside
   James pd Lowell, Ma - 1 May 1840? Lew VR 211
   Joel revol soldier LEWISTON
   John B s/o James F - May 1814 Lew VR 211
   Joseph - 25 Dec 1838 Lew VR 211
   - 27 Mar 1815 Lew VR 211
   Joseph Deacon - born 1749 d 1815 Davis
   Joseph revol soldier Davis
   Sarah w/o James - 7 Apr 1815 Lew VR 211
   31y Davis
FILLEBROWN, Lucy A - 23 May 1857 21y 3m Davis
FISH, Thomas Maj revol soldier LIVERMORE
FISHER, Elijah revol soldier LIVERMORE
   Isaiah revol soldier LEEDS

FLANDERS, Anna Jr - 5 July 1865 22y Herrick
FOGG, Abba S w/o Beniah - 16 Apr 1888 71y 4m Herrick
   Abbi R w/o Geo - 20 Dec 1882 40y Herrick
   Beniah - 7 Oct 1887 78y Herrick
   Lester s/o Nath - 18 Nov 1879 10y 5m Crowley
   Lizzie w/o Nathaniel - 27 Nov 1879 37-4-9 Crowley
   Moses s/o Rev Fogg - 21 Aug 1859 Lew VR 211
FORD, Pheba w/o William - 6 Apr 1865 76y 3mos 76y Herrick
   William - 27 Jan 1852 Lew VR 211
   61y Herrick
   William s/o Marshal - 1 Jan 1852 Lew VR 211
FORSITH w/o James - 11 Feb 1856 24y Lew VR 211
FORSYTHE, Jemima w/o Samuel - 10 Feb 1850 28y Davis
FOSS, Almon L s/o Nathaniel - 6 Sept 1862 23-10-25 Crowley
   Caroline d/o Nathaniel - 19 Feb 1842 1y 20d Crowley
   Deborah w/o Nath - 18 Sept 1843 35y Crowley
   Holman - 15 Oct 1836 23y Crowley
   Lessie J d/o Albert - 19 July 1880 4y 8m Crowley
   Mary w/o Stephen - 15 Oct 1818 45y 5m Crowley
   Nabby H w/o Silvanus - 9 Oct 1847 48-11-4 Crowley
   Nancy H w/o Varranas - 1 Jan 1852 52y Crowley
   Odretta - 31 July 1887 36-1-7 unknown
   Silvanus - 12 Dec 1872 73y 6m Crowley
   Stephen - 18 Aug 1849 77y Crowley
   - 19 Aug 1849 Lew VR 211
   Stephen 2d - 25 June 1843 18y Crowley
   Stephen s/o Sylvanus - 25 June 1843 drowned Lew VR 211
   Varranas - 5 May 1873 66y 5m Crowley
FOSTER, Rosalinda w/o Charles - 15 July 1853 30y 8 day Herrick
   Stephen revol soldier LEEDS
FRANCIS, Thomas D revol soldier LEEDS
FRASIER, Olive, from Elsworth - 15 Feb 1859 d No 4 Bates Lew VR 211
FREEMAN, Roland bp Cape Ann? - 13 Apr 1821 Lew VR 211
   Rowland - 13 Apr 1821 47y Davis
FRENCH, Clara w/o Marshall - 27 Apr 1846 Riverside
   Marshall - born 13 Nov 1794 30 Jan 1877 Riverside
FRYE, Alma S, at alms house - 17 July 1865 20y Lew VR 211
   Dean - 18 Apr 1834 59y Riverside
   - 25 Apr 1834 Lew VR 211
   Joanna - 13 June 1850 Lew VR 211
   Joanna w/o Dean - 13 June 1850 74y Riverside
   John M - 1 Jan 1885 Riverside
   Joseph D - 7 June 1838 23y Riverside
   Joseph s/o widow Joanna - 7 June 1838 Lew VR 211
   Mary - 5 Nov 1835 23y Riverside
   Mary M d/o widow Joanna - 5 Nov 1835 Lew VR 211
   Melicent w/o Wm R - 28 June 1854 Lew VR 211
   38y Riverside
   William R s/ Dean F - 5 Mar 1865 57y Lew VR 211
FULLER, David - 6 June 1850 Lew VR 211
   73y 6m Garcelon

Harriet w/o Hosea - 23 Feb 1843 24y Garcelon
Harriet w/o Hosea F - 23 Feb 1843 Lew VR 211
Helen Riverside
Nancy w/o Joseph - 2 Apr 1836 Lew VR 211
Sally w/o David - 7 Nov 1871 86y 10m Garcelon
Seth - 10 Feb 1825 89y Garcelon
Seth of Pembrook, Ma - 27 Feb 1821 Lew VR 211
FYRE, William R - 5 Mar 1865 57y Riverside
GAFFAM, George s/ David 2d - 30 July 1851 37y LewVR 214
GAMMON, Sarah Jane w/ Rev E H 28 Aug 1855? Batavia, ILL *Morn. Star*
GARCELON, Anis - 30 Dec 1853 b 12 Sept 1794 Crowley
Annis - 30 Dec 1853 59y *Morn. Star*
Annis s/ Daniel - 30 Dec 1853 LewVR 214
Arrabella w/o Horatio - 25 Oct 1851 LewVR 214
Asa - 28 Mar 1859 59y 8m Garcelon
Asa Capt s/Mark - 28 Mar 1850 59y LewVR 214
Benning Wentworth twin - 13 July 1830 Lew VR 213
Bennings s/o James - 12 Aug 1830 Garcelon
Charles s/o Wm - 6 June 1815 7m 2d Garcelon
Charles s/o Wm/ Mary - 5 June 1815 Lew VR 213
Crissilla d/o Mark - 10 Jan 1851 LewVR 214
Cussilla d/o Mark - 10 Jan 1851 23y 9m Garcelon
Daniel - 1 July 1847 21y 15d Garcelon
- 15 Nov 1795 30y Garcelon
Daniel s/o James & Del - 15 Nov 1798 Lew VR 213
David s/ Wm/ Maria - 5 Aug 1837 Lew VR 213
David s/o William - 5 Aug 1837 38y Garcelon
David W s/o Mark - 25 July 1847 10y 4m Garcelon
Delivence w/o James - 16 Nov 1828 98y Garcelon
Deliverance A - 1 Dec 1832 37-7-14 Garcelon
Deliverance d/ Peter - 30 Nov 1832 Lew VR 213
Deliverance w/o James - 16 Nov 1828 b 1735 Garcelon
Deliverane w/ James Sr - 16 Nov 1828 93y Lew VR 213
Eliza d/o James - 29 Aug 1827 3y Garcelon
Eliza T w/o Harris - 5 Nov 1897 86-2-19 Garcelon
Eliza Taber d/ James Jr - 29 Aug 1827 Lew VR 213
Elizabeth w/ Elder G - 18 Nov 1828 71y Lew VR 213
Elizabeth w/o Mark - 16 Sept 1863 84y Garcelon
Elizabeth w/o Rev James - 23 Nov 1828 71y Garcelon
Frances w/o Lorenzo - 12 Aug 1889 58y Garcelon
Fred s/o Jos - 23 June 1850 3y 9m Garcelon
Fredric s/ Joseph - 23 June 1850 LewVR 214
Hannah 3w/o Charles E - 6 Nov 1859 27y 2m Garcelon
Hannah N d/o Mark - 27 Apr 1841 18y Garcelon
Hannah w/ Charles - 6 Nov 1859 LewVR 214
Hannah w/o Mark - 17 May 1819 Lew VR 213
- b 16 Feb 1771 Garcelon
Hannah w/o S D - 9 Dec 1864 69-8-23 Crowley
Hannah w/o Samuel D - 9 Dec 1864 69-8-23 Garcelon
Harris - 25 Dec 1879 75-3-10 Garcelon
Henry M - b 27 Feb 1819 30 May 1884 Garcelon

James - 1 Apr 1804 76y 9m Garcelon
  - 3 Feb 1874 86y Crowley
  86y Garcelon
James - b 4 Apr 1739 13 Nov 1813 Garcelon
James Elder - 14 Oct 1850 LewVR 214
James F s/o James - 21 Nov 1858 2-6-27 Crowley
James Rev - 14 Oct 1850 59y 6m Garcelon
  - 28 Dec 1838 77y Garcelon
James s/ J. /Deliveran - 28 Dec 1838 Lew VR 213
James s/o James - 12 Aug 1830 Garcelon
James s/o Peter - 17 Nov 1813 74y Lew VR 213
James s/o Rev Peter - 13 Nov 1813 74y Garcelon
James T s/o James - 21 Nov 1858 2-6-27 Garcelon
James twin - 13 July 1830 Lew VR 213
Jane S w/o J S Garcelon
Jane w/o Mark - 2 Mar 1847 45y Garcelon
Joanna J w/o James - 20 Dec 1864 37y 11m Garcelon
Jos - b 26 Mar 1817 d 1897 Garcelon
Katherine w/o Peter - 8 Apr 1831 63-4-24 Garcelon
LIZZIE d/o Harris F - 18 Jan 1855 2y 6m Garcelon
Lucinda w/o James - 17 July 1872 83y Crowley
  83y Garcelon
Lucy d/ Peter & Cote? - 14 Jan 1841 Lew VR 213
Lucy M - 14 Jan 1841 42-11-17 Garcelon
Maria w/ Wm G - 2 July 1850 LewVR 214
Maria w/o William - 2 July 1850 88y Garcelon
Mark - 27 Dec 1830 60y Garcelon
  29 Dec 1850 LewVR 214
  57y 5m Garcelon
Mark s/ James/Delivera - 28 Dec 1830 Lew VR 213
MARY Ann d/o Alonzo - 14 Feb 1848 3y 5m Garcelon
Mary Ann w/o Daniel - 13 May 1844 36y 3m Garcelon
Mary d/o Anis - 25 Feb 1841 3y 1m Crowley
Mary w/ Col Wm - 7 Apl 1854 LewVR 230
Mary w/o Anis - 29 Jun 1874 76-2-16 Crowley
Mary w/o Col Wm - 7 Apr 1864 84y 15d Garcelon
May w/o Col William - 7 Apr 1864 84y 15d Crowley
Paulina A d/ Mark - 6 Oct 1853 LewVR 214
Paulina A d/o Mark - 5 Oct 1853 18y 5m Garcelon
Peter - 19 June 1827 61y Garcelon
Peter s/James/Delivanc - 19 June 1827 62y Lew VR 213
Rose d/o Mark - 13 June 1856 23y 2m Garcelon
s/o Jos - 23 Oct 1851 16d Garcelon
Sally B w/o Rev James - 7 Mar 1861 61y Garcelon
Samuel D - 9 July 1864 71y 17d Crowley
  71y 17d Garcelon
SOPHIA w/o Asa - 18 Mar 1865 65y GARCELON
Sophia widow of Asa - 8 Mar 1865 LewVR 230
Ursula w/o Daniel - 28 Sept 1872 49y 1m Garcelon
Wiliam H - b 31 July 1846 10 May 1902 Riverside
William - 20 Jan 1851 87y 5m LewVR 214
William 2d - 2 June 1827 28y Garcelon

William 2nd s/ Mark - 2 June 1829 28y Lew VR 213
William s/o Alonzo - 28 Jan 1848 1y 7m Garcelon
William Sr - 20 Jan 1851 88y Garcelon
Winslow A s/o Mark - 20 Nov 1824 11m Garcelon
GARNER, John - 1835-1898 Riverside
GELDER, Wm Dercas - 8 Jan 1824 17y Randall Rd
GEORGE, Francis revol soldier LEEDS
GERRISH, Charles revol soldier DURHAM
   Nathaniel revol soldier DURHAM
GETCHELL, Lulie M d/o J F - 20 Apr 1886 26y 10mos Herrick
GIBBONS, Mildred 17 May 18?5 33y 5m unknown
GIDDINGE, Robinson Andrew revol soldier AUBURN
GILBERT, Caleb S Riverside
   Dolly C - born 31 Jan 1855 6 July 1862 Riverside
   Louisa w/o Caleb - 28 Jan 1878 63-4-? Riverside
   William Lt revol soldier LEEDS
GILLISPIE, George [Irish] - 17 Nov 1871 Riverside*
GILLPATRICK, Harriet d/o James G - 7 May 1804 Lew VR 213
GILLSON, n - Oct 1854? LewVR 214
GILMAN, Mary C w/o Enoch - 26 Feb 1894 62y 2d Garcelon
GILPATRICK, Ann W w/o Nathaniel - 4 Aug 1873 45y 3m Garcelon
   Nathaniel - 13 Nov 1862 39y 1m Garcelon
   revol soldier WEBSTER
GIVEN, Louise d/ Samuel - 13 Sept 1863 LewVR 230
GLIDDEN, Hilton s/o Isreal - 18 June 1825 Lew VR 213
   Israel - 31 Mar 1868 80y LewVR 230
   Joseph Hilton s/ Israel - 18 June 1825 Lew VR 213
GLIDDIN, Arixena w/o Peter - 14 Mar 1852 34y LewVR 214
   Lydia d/Isreal/Rebecca - 28 Oct 1839 Lew VR 213
GODDARD, Betsey w/o Isaac - 24 Nov 1884 83-5-28 Goddard
   Carrie d/o ?? & Mary L - 25 May 1869 Goddard
   Charles W - 21 Feb 1889 61y 9m Quaker Cem
   Isaac - 9 June 1883 79-4-6 Goddard
   Isaac s/o John & Judith - 16 Feb 1833 Goddard
   Isaac s/o John/Judith - 16 Feb 1833 Lew VR 213
   Jane M w/o Robert - 29 June 1884 79y 1m Goddard
   John 68y Goddard
   Josiah s/o Wm/Priscila - 1 21 Mar 1863 11y Quaker Cem
   Judith w/o John G - 31 May 1889 87y Goddard
   Levi s/ Wm/Patience - 15 Dec 1815 Lew VR 213
   Lois d/o Wm/Patience - 19 Jan 1807 Lew VR 213
   Louisa d/o Wm/Patience - 19 Mar 1826 Lew VR 213
   Mary d/ John - 14 Apr 1843 Lew VR 213
   Mary d/o John & Judith - 14 Apr 1843 Goddard
   Mary w/o Charles W Quaker Cem
   Susanna w/o Abel G - 4 Feb 1854 Goddard
   Susanna widow - 4 Jan 1854 75y LewVR 214
   William 11 Mar 1865 - 79y Quaker Cem
GODFEY,? Marcia A w/o Thomas G - 11 Jan 1852 27y 8m Garcelon
GODFREY, Mercy w/o Thomas - 11 Jan 1852 28y LewVR 214
GOFF, James revol soldier AUBURN
GOLDER, D w/o William - Oct 1845 81y Randall Rd

Dorothy w/ Jacob - 5 May 1833 Lew VR 213
Dorothy w/o Rev Jacob - 5 May 1833 45y Riverside
Everett H s/o Jacob R - 19 July 1865 13y Riverside
Isaac s/ Wm/Dorcas - 8 Jan 1824 Lew VR 213
Jacob R - 20 Jan 1865 46 Riverside
   46y Riverside
   46y Riverside
Jacob Rev - 12 Mar 1872 86y Riverside
Mary - 28 Mar 1871 60y 10m Riverside*
Mary w/0 Oct 1870 78-7-7 Riverside
Julia d/o Calvin - 6 Nov 1855 Lew VR 213
Mary w/o David - 12 Feb 1879 86-8-26 Riverside
Samuel - 2 Oct 1861 16-8-16 Riverside
GOSS, Eleanor P w/o John - 15 June 1845 36y Riverside
   John - 8 Aug 1894 75y 11m Riverside
   Mary d/o John Jr - 3 Jan 1858 13y LewVR 214
   Mary L w/o John - 1 June 1900 71y 6m Riverside
   Wm s/o John of Danville - 28 Dec 1849 20 Oct 1870 78-7-7 Riverside
   Julia d/o Calvin - 6 Nov 1855 Lew VR 213
   Mary w/o David - 12 Feb 1879 86-8-26 Riverside
   Samuel - 2 Oct 1861 16-8-16 Riverside
GOSS, Eleanor P w/o John - 15 June 1845 36y Riverside
   John - 8 Aug 1894 75y 11m Riverside
   Mary d/o John Jr - 3 Jan 1858 13y LewVR 214
   Mary L w/o John - 1 June 1900 71y 6m Riverside
   Wm s/o John of Danville - 28 Dec 1849 22y LewVR 214
GOULDING, Martha w/o Wm F - 25 Oct 1876 b 24 Mar 1821 Riverside
   William F - 16 Apr 1885? b 22 May 1822 Riverside
   Wm F - 17 Apr 1885 63y unknown
GRAFFAM, Almon L s/ David W - 13 May 1860 23y LewVR 230
   Almon s/o David - 13 May 1860 23-9-6 Riverside
   Betsey d/o John/Eliza - 4 Dec 1778 Lew VR 213
   Daniel s/ Daniel/Lydia - 6 Oct 1823 Lew VR 213
   David - died in Mercer 24 Aug 1844 Lew VR 213
   David W - 10 Jan 1857 61y Riverside
   - 10 June 1857 62y LewVR 214
   Deborah w/o John - 29 Aug 1801 Lew VR 213
   Isaac s/ John/Nancy - 24 Dec 1835 Lew VR 213
   John - 20 Jan 1836 Lew VR 213
   John Oliver - 25 Dec 1863 28y LewVR 230
   John s/o John - 21 Jan 1836 63y Davis
   John s/o Oliver - 25 Dec 1863 27y 11m Riverside
   Lydia d/o John /Eliza. - 14 Feb 1773 Lew VR 213
   Mariah w/o John - __ Feb 1815 Lew VR 213
   Mary Ann d/o Benjamin - 25 July 1852 75y LewVR 214
   Molly d/o David/Betsey - 8 June 1814 Lew VR 213
   Molly d/o John/Eliza - 19 Sept 1795 Lew VR 213
   Otis s/o Oliver - 2 Oct 1851 3y 2m Riverside
   Phebe w/o David G - 21 Nov 1855 LewVR 214
   Stephen s/o John - _____ 1803 Lew VR 213
GRAY, Alexander revol soldier WEBSTER

GREEN, Daniel revol Soldier LISBON
   Dennis (Irish) - 20 Dec 1850 LewVR 214
GROSS, David revol soldier AUBURN
GUCE, Benj [colored] - 1886 40y Riverside*
GUCE, Frank [colored] - 1886 22y Riverside*
GUILD, William O s/ Harmon - 18 Nov 1852 4y LewVR 214
GUTHRON, Haman [German] - 1 July 1874 Riverside*
HACKETT, Dorice d/o Benjamin/Tace - 26 May 1831 LewVR 216
   David s/o Benjamin/Tace - 21 June 1837 drowned LewVR 216
   Eliphalth revol soldier GREENE
   Hiram s/o Benjamin/Tace - 11 Mar 1821 LewVR 215
   John - 3 Jan 1858 63y LewVR 222
   John s/ Benjamin/Tace - 24 June 1816 LewVR 215
   Tamson d/ Benjamin/Tace - 20 Feb 1822 LewVR 215
HADLEY, Clarissa widow - 23 Aug 1855 51y LewVR 222
HAGGARTY, Joanna w/ Michael - 2 Aug 1854 of chol LewVR 216
   Michael (Irish) - 4 Aug 1854 of chol. LewVR 222
HALEY, Caty d/ James H - 6 Aug 1855 27y LewVR 222
   Josiah D s/o Samuel - 22 Feb 1867 25y LewVR 222
   Samuel - 18 Aug 1817 LewVR 215
   Sarah D Mrs - 14 Feb 1879 47y 1m Crowley
HALL, Emma J w/o Freeman - 27 Mar 1864 33y Riverside
HALLAND, Ann A d/ Richard - 17 Nov 1846 LewVR 216
HAM, Ada E d/o Geo W - 26 Sept 1852 1y 27d Garcelon
   Alonzo G - born 8 Sept 1835 25 July 1895 Riverside
   Clara A d/o Capt Wm R - 1855-1866 Riverside
   Ebeneser - b 29 ___ 1800 11 Oct 1883 Riverside
   Ebenezer - 15 Aug 1791 45y Garcelon
   Eliza Garcelon
   Elizabeth F d/ Eben/Judith - 29 Dec 1822 LewVR 215
   Elizabeth w/ Tobias - 20 Mar 1834 LewVR 216
   Geo W - 1820-1890 70y Garcelon
   Geo W Jr - Apr 1857 7m Garcelon
   Herrick - 10 Apr 1869 49y CROWLEY
   Isael s/o Ebenezer - 10 Feb 1795 23y Garcelon
   J S P Capt - 15 Jan 1882 50-2-28 Riverside
   Jacob B Riverside
   James - 4 Feb 1854 79y Garcelon
      79y LewVR 216
   James - b 1776 4 Feb 1854 79 Garcelon
   Jane Garcelon
   Jane d/o James - 3 Dec 1837 12y Garcelon
      - 3 Dec 1839 12y 8 m Garcelon
   Jane d/o James/Nancy - 3 Dec 1830 27y LewVR 215
   Jane G w/o Ebeneser - 24 Oct 1887 b 9 Apr 1812 Riverside
   John G s/o Warren - 25 Aug 1846 8mos 6d GARCELON
   Joseph Garcelon
      22 Aug 1865 58y 5m Garcelon
   Joseph s/ James - 29 Dec 1804 LewVR 215
   Judith w/ Ebenezer - 26 Apl 1851 50y LewVR 222
   Judith w/o Ebeneser - 26 Apr 1851 b 21Sept1800 Riverside
   Kate R d/o Capt Wm - 1855-1863 Riverside

Nabby d/ Thomas/Anna - 14 June 1827 LewVR 215
Nancy Garcelon
Sally w/o Joseph - 14 Jul 1863 55y 10m Garcelon
Sarah w/o Ebenezer - 11 May 1837 91y Garcelon
Sarah w/o Warren - 18 Feb 1859 47-8-6 Garcelon
Sarah widow of Ebenezer - 11 May 1837 LewVR 216
Thomas 37y - 27 Apr 1827 LewVR 215
Tobias - 22 May 1812 LewVR 215
Warren - 28 Feb 1855 44-8-7 Garcelon
Warren s/ James - 28 Feb 1855 LewVR 222
William R Capt - 4 June 1864 killed Riverside
Willie R s/o Capt Wm R - 1864-1870 Riverside
HAMILTON, Rebecca w/o H - 10 June 1858 44y Herrick
  Sarah Jane w/o James Jr ? ? Randall Rd
  Sarah w/ James - 1 Nov 1850 LewVR 216
HAMMON, Jacob - 20 June 1816 LewVR 215
HANDY, Abbie S - 30 July 1889 3y unknown
HANSON, Charlotte w/o Elisha H - 17 Jan 1897 86y Goddard
  Elisha - 1 Jan 1881 77y Goddard
  Emily d/ Elisha & Harriet - 23 July 1843 2y 5m Goddard
  Harriet w/o Elisha - 19 Feb 1851 26y Goddard
  Hattie M d/Elisha/Harriet - 29 Sept 1911 60y Goddard
  Matilda w/o Fred E - 13 Feb 1921 52y Goddard
HARLOW, Harrlett w/o Silas - 11 Jan 1867 32y LewVR 222
HARMON, Sally w/o Thomas - 23 Jan 1854 56y LewVR 216
HARRIS, Deborah d/ Richard - Feb 1813 LewVR 215
  Walter s/ Clinton - 2 Aug 1855 LewVR 222
HARRISON?, Harriet w/ Elisha - 19 Feb 1851 LewVR 216
HART?, - 2 Dec 1869 69y Goddard
HART, Betsey w/ Capt Stephen - 25 Oct 1812 LewVR 215
  Jacob s/ Stephen Jr - 29? Dec 1813 LewVR 215
  Jacob s/o Stephen - 11 Apr 1811 LewVR 215
  Josiah - 28 Aug 1871 67y 5m Goddard
  Mary w/o Stephen - 15 Oct 1828 53y 2mos Goddard
  Polly w/ Stephen - 15 Oct 1828 LewVR 215
  Samuel - 25 Nov 1846 33y 5m Goddard
  Samuel s/ Stephen - 25 Nov 1846 LewVR 216
  Stephen - 27 Oct 1844 72y 9m Goddard
  - 30 June 1817 83y LewVR 215
  Stephen Jr - 27 Oct 1844 LewVR 216
  Thomas - 8 Apr 1880 70y 9mos Goddard
  William s/ Stephen Jr - 11 Feb 1806 LewVR 215
  Wm the 2d s/ Stephen Jr - 11 Jan 1814 LewVR 215
HARVEY, William s/ Samuel - 7 Sept 1850 LewVR 216
HATCH, Allen - 20 Aug 1888 50y 2m Garcelon
  Charity - b 19 June 1806 1 May 1892 Garcelon
  Elihu revol pentioner - 14 May 1837 LewVR 216
  Elisha s/ John - 2 May 1817 LewVR 215
  Freeman - 28 Feb 1873 72-9-9 Garcelon
  Hannah d/ Sam/Hannah - 14 Aug 1798 LewVR 215
  John L s/o Freeman - 20 Aug 1852 4y 4m Garcelon
  John s/ John in Durham - 25 Dec 1796 LewVR 215

Obed s/ Samuel/ Hannah - 30 Oct 1795 LewVR 215
Prudence d/ Samuel/Hannah - 15 Dec 1777 LewVR 215
Sarah d/o Freeman - 23 Aug 1852 12y 8m Garcelon
Sarah wid/o Ehihu - 9 Jan 1839 LewVR 216
HAWS, Sarah w/ John - 9 Oct 1854 58y LewVR 222
HAYES, Amanda J - 14 Mar 1901 60y Randall Rd
HAYHURST, Josiah [German] - 19 Sept 1871 3m Riverside*
HAYS, John DEacon 1/o N Yarmouth - 27 Dec 1841 LewVR 216
HEATH Ella - 16 Aug 1854 Riverside*
    Frances d/o Elbridge - 31 Aug 1857 LewVR 222
    Frances O w/o E G - 18 Aug 1856 25y 5m Riverside
    Mrs F O - 18 Aug 1856 25y Riverside*
HEBIRD?, Lucy Mrs - 3 July 1871 65y 7m Riverside
HEFFRAN, Carnelius (Irish) - 25 July 1854 of Chol LewVR 216
HELLMERICK, Marion w/o John - 29 July 1898 No Name Pond
HERRICK, Ebenezer Esq s/John & - 7 May 1839 LewVR 216
    Elvira d/ Oben/Lydia LewVR 215
    Elvira d/o Oliver - 16 Oct 1815 2-7-12 Herrick
    Israel - 14 Sep 1782 66y Herrick
    - 14 Sept 1782 66y Herrick
    Isreal revol Soldier LEWISTON
    J Lawrence s/i Ebeneser Herrick
    John - 27 Mar 1834 82y Herrick
        revol soldier MINOT
    John 2nd s/o Ebenezer - 6 Dec 183? 20y LewVR 215
    John Esq - 27 Mar 1834 LewVR 216
    John s/o Ebenezer - 6 Dec 1830 20y Herrick
    Lydia w/ John H Esq - 18 Feb 1830 67y LewVR 215 (E. Argus)
    Lydia w/ Oliver Esq - 16 Mar 1830 47y LewVR 215
    Lydia w/o John - 18 Feb 1830 78y Herrick
    Lydia w/o Oliver - 16 Mar 1830 47y Herrick
    Martha d/o Oliver - 26 Sept 1819 15days Herrick
    Nancy w/o - 26 Nov 1821 LewVR 215
    Oliver - 4 July 1852 70y Herrick
    Oliver Col - 4 July 1852? 70y LewVR 216
HILL, Fannie B - 13 Feb 1859 27y LewVR 222
    Martha P d/ George P - 22 Aug 1849 4y 5m LewVR 216
HILTON, William F - 25 Oct 1889 70-2-15 Herrick
HINKLEY, Gideon - 18 Apr 1796 LewVR 215
    Peggy - 4 Nov 1814 LewVR 215
    Sanford - 26 Feb 1860 LewVR 222
HODGE, Albert 1/o Bangor - 24 Dec 1861 27y LewVR 222
HODGKIN, Ai B - 20 Apr 1877 54y 8m GARCELON
    Benjamin - 12 Mar 1815 LewVR 215
    Frankie Garcelon
    Jane F d/o Thomas - 10 Jul 1858 22-11-18 Garcelon
    John D - b 11 Oct 1839 20 Jul 1899 Garcelon
    Jonathan - 28 Jan 1876 81-4-19 Garcelon
    Orpha w/o Jona - 29 Aug 1899 93y Garcelon
    Sally w/o Jona - 29 Jan 1836 36-11-14 Garcelon
    Thomas - 20 June 1855 77-2-14 Garcelon
    Thomas s/o Moses - 12 Feb 1863 3-10-15 Garcelon

HODGKINS, Betsey w/ Jonathan - 19 Dec 1817 LewVR 215
   Charles W s/o George - 7 Jul 1861 2y 5 m Herrick
      - 7 July 1861 2y 5m Herrick
   Esther w/ Thomas - 25 July 1854 LewVR 222
   Esther w/o Thomas - 25 July 1854 60y 7m Garcelon
   Harriet w/o Ai B - 11 Sept 1892 64y Garcelon
   Hattie of Washington - 23 Dec 1866 27y LewVR 222
   Jonathan - 2 Feb 1814 LewVR 215
   s/ Benjamin/Sally - 24 Feb 1810 LewVR 215
   Thomas - 20 June 1855 77y LewVR 222
HODSDON, James revol soldier WALES
HODSKIN, Jonathan s/ Jonathan - 9 Feb 1795 LewVR 215
HOGAN, Andrew D - 23 May 1859 62y 18d Herrick
   Ruth - 22 Sept 1853 38y LewVR 216
   Ruth w/o A D - 22 Sept 1853 49y 21d Herrick
HOLEY, Elizabeth w/o Sam - 22 Mar 1836 LewVR 216
HOLLAND, Abbie F w/o Michael - 23 Jan 1866 38-2-6 Riverside
   Caroline - 15 Feb 1825 16y Garcelon
   Caroline d/ John - 28 Feb 1825 LewVR 215
   David s/ John - 22 May 1803 LewVR 215
   Elmira - 28 Aug 1839 20y Garcelon
   John Garcelon
      - 23 Aug 1823 52y GARCELON
      - 25 June 1793 Garcelon
   John in Harpswell - 23 Aug 1823 LewVR 215
   Mary w/o Richard - 4 Mar 1845 34y Davis
   Michael - 1 Nov 1873 43y Riverside
   Pemela - 17 Oct 1865 73y Garcelon
   Rebecca w/o John - 19 Jul 1850 76y GARCELON
   Sarah Jane d/ Richard - 12 Mar 1845 LewVR 216
   Sophronia w/o Michael - 2 Feb 1861 28-11-18 Riverside
   Susie W w/o Michael - 29 Nov 1869 38-4-3 Riverside
   W M - 23 Apr 1863 40y Garcelon
   w/o Richard - 4 Mar 1845 LewVR 216
   Willie M s/o Michael - 11 Aug 1866 7m 7d Riverside
HOPKINS, Gancelo C - 7 May 1883 30y 10m Herrick
   Isaac W - 25 Apr 1878 33y 5m Herrick
HOUGHTON, Frank T s/o Francis - 11 Mar 1863 3m NoNamePond
HOW, Licha w/o Ephraim - 19 Sept 1835 LewVR 216
   Lydia M d/o E S - 8 Nov 1844 5y Herrick
HOWARD, Alvin - 4 Dec 1859 48y LewVR 222
   Charles [colored] - 1886 Riverside*
HOWE, Lydia Mary d/ Ephraim - 8 Nov 1844 LewVR 216
   Lydia w/o E S - 19 Sept 1835 31y Herrick
HULLY, John s/ John (Irish) - 14 Aug 1854 39y LewVR 222
HUNT, Elizabeth Ellen d/ George - 15 July 1854 19y LewVR 216
   Hannah w/o Zebina - 25 May 1825 25y Davis
   Lorenzo s/ Zebina - 19 Feb 1855 LewVR 222
   s/o John O & Hannah - 19 Jul 1857 1m 17d Davis
   Simeon - 1820-1887 Herrick
   w/o Zebina - 27 May 1825 LewVR 215
   Zebina - 11 Jan 1864 69y LewVR 222

HUNTON, Crowell Pitts - b 1812 Riverside
　　Frank H - 27 Oct 1870 of Auburn Riverside*
　　Luvia (Currier) w/o C P Riverside
HUSSEY, Susan w/ Charles H - 1 Aug 1849 LewVR 216
HUTCHINS, Joseph - 9 Dec 1827 LewVR 215
JACKSON, Betsey w/o Lemuel - 27 July 1842 66y Garcelon
　　Charles w/o Andrew J - 22 Oct 1853 LewVR 219
　　Charlotte - 14 Aug 1856 49y 7m Herrick
　　Elias - 26 May 1850 LewVR 217
　　　　54y Garcelon
　　Hasadiah w/o Sol - 9 July 1852 76y 4m Herrick
　　James [scotch] - 21 July 1872 41y Riverside*
　　Lemuel s/ Lemuel - 4 Nov 1803 LewVR 219
　　Sarah w/ Solomon - 16 Aug 1812 LewVR 219
　　Soloman - 12 Aug 1853 75y LewVR 217
　　Solomon - 11 Aug 1853 75y 6m Herrick
　　　- 16 Apr 1811 LewVR 219
JEPSON, Angeline d/ Eben - 6 Aug 1848 LewVR 219
　　Betsey w/o Willliam - 16 June 1870 76-10-26 Herrick
　　Bradbury T - 22 June 1872 86-8-25 Herrick
　　Charles H s/o Wm Jr - 20 Sept 1851 5y 4m Herrick
　　Eliena d/o Edward/Marian - 18 Mat 1852 1y 21d No Name Pond
　　Hannah w/ William Vickery - 3 May 1846 26y 8m Herrick
　　Jane A d/o Eben D - 6 Aug 1848 20y Herrick
　　Marry d/o Bradbury - 27 May 1843 LewVR 217
　　Mary d/ Bradbury - 27 May 1843 LewVR 219
　　Mary twin d/ Wm/Elizabet - Apr 1832 LewVR 219
　　May M d/o Bradbury - 27 May 1843 13y Herrick
　　Rosanna - 21 May 1859 81y LewVR 217
　　Sarah d/o Bradbury - 30 May 1844 LewVR 217
　　　　27y Herrick
　　Sarah d/o Leonard - 21 Jan 1856 2y 2m2y Herrick
　　Sarah w/ William - 11 Sept 1824 LewVR 219
　　Sarah wid/o Thomas - 5 July 1842 LewVR 217
　　Thomas - 28 Mar 1818 LewVR 219
　　　　revol Soldier LEWISTON
　　William - 31 Jul 1868 78-4-2 Herrick
JEWELL, Benjamin - 2 Apr 1851 LewVR 217
　　　- 2 Apr 1857 LewVR 219
　　Henry Martin s/ Benjamin - 27 Aug 1849 7y acc't LewVR 217
　　Priscilla - 23 Jan 1848 70y LewVR 217
JILLSON, Nat R - 7 Oct 1854 19y Crowley
JIPSON, Sarah w/ Thomas - 15 Mar 1795 LewVR 219
JOHNSON, Cad [colored] - 1879 6m Riverside*
JOHNSON, Nancy w/ Horace - 24 Aug 1855 LewVR 217
JONES, c/ James - 12 Sept 1855 LewVR 219
　　c/o Daniel/Sarah - 12 Sept 1855 LewVR 219
　　Clarissa w/ Olison - 9 Oct 1854 51y LewVR 219
　　Daniel revol soldier LEEDS
　　Eleanor - 28 Jan 1842 76y Crowley
　　Ephraim - 31 Mar 1833 83y 10m Davis
　　Ezekiel - 5 Feb 1836 35y Crowley

Ezekiel s/ Josiah - 5 Feb 1836 LewVR 219
Ezekiel s/o Josiah LewVR 217
Hannah D w/o Abial M - 31 Aug 1848 23y 8 mos Davis
Hannah d/ Ephraim/Anna - 13 Oct 1837 LewVR 217
Hannah G d/o Ephraim - 13 Oct 1837 13y Garcelon
Hollis s/ David - 13 Dec 1857 LewVR 219
Josiah - 26 Aug 1837 75y Crowley
   - 26 Aug 1837? LewVR 217
Judith - 1 July 1833 70y 10m Davis
Laura d/o Wm J - 22 July 1852 LewVR 217
Laura M d/o Wm H & Almira - 27 Jul 1852 1-9-23 Davis
Martha A d/o Levi - 11 June 1855 20y LewVR 219
Mary J w/o Wm - 1 Nov 1825 26y Garcelon
Polly w/ Wm - 1 Nov 1825 LewVR 219
William - 15 Jan 1848 LewVR 217
   4y 9m Davis
JORDAN, Abigail w/ Nathaniel - 11 Nov 1818 LewVR 217
   Abigail w/o James - 11 May 1860 88y Garcelon
   Benjamin Capt - 7 Sept 1810 28y Crowley
   Deborah w/o James - 20 Aug 1883 86y 20d Garcelon
   Eddie E s/o Geo W - 22 Aug 1863 2y 3m Crowley
   Eddie s/o Geo W - 22 Aug 1863 2y 3m Crowley
   Evelina d/ John - 11 Aug 1850 LewVR 217
   Flora w/o Holman - b 1852 27 Dec 1899 46-7-29 Crowley
   Geo W - 17 Sept 1895 84y 4m Crowley
   Horace C - 20 Dec 1892 77y Crowley
   Humphrey revol soldier AUBURN
   James - 12 Mar 1869 78-11-6 Garcelon
      - 16 Apr 1866 66-3-20 Garcelon
      - 18 Mar 1895 67y 6m Garcelon
      - 23 Aug 1831 60y Garcelon
      - 25 Aug 1831 LewVR 219
   James s/o James/Sophia - 17 Mar 1815 LewVR 217
   Jeremiah - 30 Nov 1823 77y LewVR 217
      78y LewVR 219
   Joanna w/o Geo W - 5 Apr 1897 77y 10m Crowley
   Joseph - 6 Sept 1847 30y Crowley
   Joseph D - 15 Apr 1829 25y Garcelon
   Joseph s/ Andrew - 6 Sept 1847 28y LewVR 217
   Laura d/o Hiram & Phebe - 29 Aug 1859 Davis
   Mary w/o Jeremiah - 11 Apr 1845 60y LewVR 217
   May w/o Jeremiah - 11 Apr 1845 61y Riverside
   Nathaniel w/o Benjamin - 20 Feb 1853 70y Crowley
   Samuel - 8 Aug 1871 52y Crowley
   Sarah Jane d/ Benja - 14 July 1828 LewVR 219
   Sarah W - b 39 June 1835 29 June 1895 Crowley
   Sophia w/o James - 2 Oct 1871 81y 5d Garcelon
JORDON, Rishworth - b 8 Jul 1826 24 Aug 1888 Crowley
JUBB, James A s/o Thomas - 10 Apr 1877 24y 2m Crowley
KALAHERN, Michael s/ Michael - 30 Aug 1855 LewVR 221
KEENE, Lincoln - 17 Nov 1877 70-9-6 Herrick
   Sophronia w/o Lincoln - 18 Nov 1869 58y 9m Herrick

KELLEY, James d/ Thomas - 30 Aug 1855 LewVR 221
KENNISTON, Sarah w/o ? - 16 Nov 1885 65y Riverside
KEYER, Albert [German] - 1875 Riverside*
KINCAID, Emnily w/ Geo K - 22 June 1859 LewVR 221
KINCALD, Roxania w/ John A K - 30 Mar 1864 LewVR 221
KLEUSENER, Albert C - 1875 Riverside*
KNOWLTON, William K Maj - 19 Sept 1864 killed 34y Riverside
   William Maj - 19 Sept 1864 34y 5m LewVR 221
KRAMER, Franz Robert [German] - 31 July 1873 7y Riverside*
LAKE, Elisha (pauper) - 27 Dec 1806 LewVR 223
   Joshua s/o Stephen - 4 Apr 1825 LewVR 223
   Mehitable w/ Stephen - 26 Mar 1840 LewVR 223
   Susannah w/o Elisha - 20 Oct 1828 77y LewVR 223
LAMB, Russell - 19 Nov 1886 75y 7m Herrick
LAMBERT, Isaac G s/o Joshua - 7 Oct 1838 2y 11m Garcelon
   Joshua - b 17 Apr 1807 20 Aug 1890 83y Garcelon
   Rebecca w/o Jarvis - 15 Feb 1825 26y Garcelon
   Rebecca w/o John - 28 Feb 1825 LewVR 223
   Susan w/o Joshua - b 1806 22 Feb 1890 b 25 Dec Garcelon
LANCASTER, Elijah M - 12 Apr 1891 91y Crowley
   Clarinda w/o Elijah - 22 Dec 1892 92y Crowley
LANDER, Elice d/o Lazanus/Lydia - 13 Sept 1803 LewVR 223
LANE, Albion s/ Elizabeth - 12 July 1852 LewVR 224
   Cornelius (Irishman) - 21 Sept 1849 24y LewVR 224
   Daniel revol soldier LEEDS
   Jothan S - was frozen on the 11 Mar 1856 LewVR 224
   Orison s/ Orison - 5 Aug 1854 of Chol. LewVR 224
   Vesta d/ Jane Thorn - 4 Nov 1842 12y LewVR 223
LANEGAN, Wm (Irish) - found in canal 16 Sept 1854 LewVR 224
LARRABEE, Ruamah w/o Isaac - 19 Jul 1886 60-10-22 Herrick
   Herbert W s/o Isaac - 15 Feb 1881 23-3-15 Herrick
LAUGHTON, Anna C w/o Nelson J - 6 Aug 1863 22-9-6 Herrick
LAVERTY, Archabold [Scotch] - 1877 Riverside*
LAWERTY, Robert [scotch] - 1876 Riverside*
LAWLESS, Ann at Alms House - 3 Feb 1866 1y LewVR 224
LEAVITT, Adaline d/ James - 30 Dec 1864 4y LewVR 224
LECHTENBERG, Susan [German] - 1881? Riverside*
LEEMAN, c/o Wm - 23 Oct 1855 LewVR 224
LENFEST, Judith d/ Peter/Lydia - 17 Dec 1779 LewVR 223
   Lydia wid/o Peter L - 20 Aug 1830 LewVR 223
   Peter - pb Guernsey, Eng. 17 Mar 1820 LewVR 223
   Peter s/ Peter/Lydia - 14 June 1783 LewVR 223
LENKERSDEORSFER, Ida [German] - 3 Sept 1877 Riverside*
LEWIS, Rachel w/ Benson - 29 Dec 1857 24y LewVR 224
LIBBEY, Harriet E d/ Phineas - 14 Oct 1853 LewVR 224
   Phineas - 10 Nov 1852 LewVR 224
LIBBY, Ann A w/o Charles O - 1 June 1864 30-1-26 Crowley
   Betsey w/o Rufus - 28 June 1873 82y Crowley
   Francilla H w/o Silas C - 3 Sept 1897 Riverside
   Georgianna C d/ Phineas - 22 Dec 1854 9-6-9 Davis
   Harriet d/ Phineas/Celinda - 15 Oct 1853 22 mos Davis
   Miram w/ Elder Isaac L - 16 Nov 1840 LewVR 223

Phineas J - 10 Nov 1852 31y 5m Davis
  Silas C - born 6 June 1841 17 May 1892 Riverside
LINCOLN, David - 9 Apr 1850 LewVR 224
  Loved revol Soldier LEWISTON
  Loved? - 9 Apr 1850 92y 7m Garcelon
LITCHFIELD, Almeda d/ Nath'l - 31 Aug 1848 LewVR 223
  Ames Rev s/o Noah - 18 Aug 1835 28y Garcelon
  Ames s/ Noah - 18 Aug 1835 LewVR 223
  Anson s/ Nathan/Rache - 14 Jan 1832 LewVR 223
  Benjamin s/o Noah - 22 Aug 1835 LewVR 223
  Benjamin w/o Noah - 22 Aug 1835 24y Garcelon
  Luther - 11 May 1832 63y 8m LewVR 224
  Mabel wid/o Noah - 12 July 1838 LewVR 223
  Martha w/ Noah - 18 Mar 1854 75y LewVR 224
  Martha w/o Noah - 18 Mar 1854 73y Garcelon
  Mary A w/o Wm - 6 Mar 1848 25y Garcelon
  Mary w/ Wm - 7 Mar 1848 LewVR 223
  Nancy M d/ Nath'l - 27 Aug 1847 24y LewVR 223
  Noah revol Soldier LEWISTON
  Noah - 17 Nov 1827 75y 22-9-6 Herrick
  Noah Deacon - 2 Jan 1863 84y 22d Garcelon
    - Jan 1863 84y LewVR 224
  Noah Sr - 17 Nov 1827 74y LewVR 223
  Rhoda wid/o Luther - 24 Nov 1856 LewVR 224
  Sarah E d/ Nath'l - 11 Jan 1845 LewVR 223
LOCK w/ A C L - 31 Apl 1855 LewVR 224
LOCKE, Mrs H A - 30 Apr 1855 33y Riverside*
LORING, Calvin (pauper) - 4 June 1845 54y LewVR 223
LOTHROP, Deliance d/ Eaton - 5 Nov 1853 LewVR 224
  Lemuel s/ Lemuel - 28 July 1852 LewVR 224
LOVEJOY, Abba d/ Asabel - 1 May 1847 LewVR 223
  Charles - 7 Nov 1856 LewVR 224
LOW, Oscar Edwin s/ John - 13 Aug 1851 LewVR 224
LOWELL, Alma E w/o Mark - 17 Oct 1900 75y Riverside
  Amelia W d/ James Jr - 8 Sept 1844 LewVR 223
  Amelia W d/o James Jr - 8 Sept 1844 13m Riverside
  Andrew s/ Edward - 18 Mar 1837 LewVR 223
  Ann S w/o Mark - 17 Feb 1845 27y Riverside
  Disalania d/ John/Mary - 27 May 1826 LewVR 223
  Georgianna d/ James Jr - 5 July 1850 LewVR 224
  Hannah w/o James - 20 Feb 1869 75y 9m Riverside
  Harriet T w/o William - 27 Feb 1774 61y 9m 5d Herrick
  James - 27 July 1858 67y 6m Riverside
  James Esq - 27 July 1858 LewVR 224
  James Jr - 16 Aug 1850 LewVR 224
  John - 3 Oct 1849 32y LewVR 224
  Julianna d/ John & Polly - 17 Oct 1825 LewVR 223
  Mark - 15 Sept 1888 73y Riverside
  Mercy w/ Stephen (pauper) - 29 May 1825 LewVR 223
  Stephen (pauper) - 15 Dec 1826 LewVR 223
LUDDEN, Timothy - 16 Mar 1859 LewVR 224
  wid/o Timothy - 27 Mar 1859 LewVR 224

LUFKIN, Eliza - 3 June 1861 29 Herrick
MANNING, Charles H - b 19 Dec 1831 10 Aug 1899 Riverside
MARDENCE, Nancy L w/ Benjamin - 28 Dec 1856 LewVR 226
MARR, John F - 19 Sept 1873 33-11-21 Herrick
   Olive S w/o Wm - 22 Aug 1879 76y 20d Herrick
   Rachael - 6 July 1860 23-8-11 Herrick
   William - 16 May 1849 50y 3m Herrick
MARROW, Emma J w/o Samuel - 26 Apr 1881 36y 8m Herrick
   Emma J w/o Samuel H - 26 Apr 1881 36y 8mos Herrick
   Geo M s/o Wm N - 14 Oct 1856 8 weeks Herrick
   M Jane d/ Wm - 14 Feb 1858 13y 8m LewVR 228
   M Jane d/o Wm N - 14 Feb 1858 13y 8m Herrick
   _____ s/o Samuel - 28 Oct 1872 11d Herrick
MARSHAL, John s/ Patrick - 26 July 1855 LewVR 226
MARSTON, Eunice d/ Simon/Mary - 30 Aug 1822 LewVR 225
   Freddie S s/o Wm F - 17 June 1855 1-3-23 Crowley
   Mary w/ Simion - 6 July 1853 70y LewVR 226
   Simon - 13 Feb 1855 75y LewVR 226
MAXWELL, Abby d/o Daniel - 24 Mar 1859 5 weeks Herrick
   Daniel W - 7 Aug 1852 39y 7m Herrick
   Isabel d/o Daniel - 28 Feb 1857 5y Herrick
   Isahell d/ Mrs Abigail - 28 Feb 1867? 5y LewVR 226
MAYNER, Charles [German] - 1879 Riverside*
McCALLUM, David [Scotch] - 1880 Riverside*
McCARMIE, Dauris (Irish) - 3 Oct 1856 LewVR 226
McCARTHY, w/o Patrick - 1857 Davis
McCRATE, John (Irish) of Chol - 9 Aug 1854 LewVR 226
McFARLON, Jane d/o James of WALES - 5 May 1848 LewVR 226
McGEATH, James (Irish) of Chol. - 29 July 1854 LewVR 226
McKEE, John of Ireland - 11 July 1827 LewVR 225
McKINNEY, Joseph revol soldier GREENE
McWILLIAMS, Richard [Irish] - 25 Feb 1872 stillborn Riverside*
MEARS, Cilla Augusta d/ Mose - 6 Nov 1849 LewVR 226
MEEDER, Tobias - 28 Dec 1794 LewVR 225
MEGUIRE, Lawrence (Irishman) - 27 July 1851 67y LewVR 226
MERRILL, Abigail w/ Moses - 23 Apr 1795 LewVR 225
   Amaziah - 9 Feb 1864 LewVR 228
   Ammi s/ Ezekiel/Anna - 15 July 1828 LewVR 225
   Amos S - 10 June 1880 30-10-27 Goddard
   Ann - 28 Jul 1867 70-0-11 Garcelon
   Ann w/o Ezekiel - 14 Dec 1832 41y Garcelon
   Anna w/ Ezekiel - 15 Dec 1832 LewVR 225
   Asa - 9 May 1857 62y LewVR 228
   Benson - 14 Jan 1855 LewVR 226
      34-1-14 Riverside
   Caroline d/o Joshua - 28 Nov 1881 55y 8m Riverside
   David at Alms House - 22 Nov 1865 74y LewVR 228
   Edmund - 13 Apr 1849 13y 10m Crowley
   Elizabeth w/o John - 20 Feb 1861 35-4-10 Garcelon
   Ezekiel - 27 July 1855 64y Garcelon
   Ezekiel d/ Benjamin - 26 July 1855 LewVR 226
   Georgia w/o F W - b 1840 29 Feb 1872 Garcelon

    Gilman Henry s/ Sewall - 23 Feb 1866 LewVR 225
       LewVR 225
       LewVR 225
    Gilman s/o Sewell - 23 Feb 1846 12y 6m Crowley
    Henritta d/Nathan/Betsey - 28 Nov 1856 6y 9m No Name Pond
    Imlak, a town pauper - 30 Jan 1823 drowned LewVR 225
    Jeddediah s/ Amariah - 11 Oct 1841 at Topsham LewVR 225
    Jerusha w/o Sewell - 30 Jan 1884 88-9-27 Crowley
    John - b 27 May 1811 16 Oct 1882 Garcelon
    John, a pentioner - 8 Oct 1843 84y LewVR 225
    Joshua - 18 Oct 1845 51 y LewVR 225
       57y Riverside
    Josie C s/o F H - 21 Mar 1863 7m 13d Garcelon
    Lois w/ John - 9 Mar 1853 49y LewVR 226
    Lois w/o John - 10 May 1853 48y 6m Garcelon
    Mary D d/o Sewell - 15 Nov 1848 16y 9m Crowley
    Mary H d/o N & N ????? Goddard
    Mary J - 7 Dec 1865 38y Garcelon
    Mary J w/o Onzie - 20 May 1888 58y Herrick
    Orren s/ Joshua - 15 Oct 1857 33y LewVR 228
    Precend? w/o ? - b 1828 7 June 1899 Riverside
    Rufus s/o Sewell - 7 Feb 1839 44 days Crowley
    Sally w/o Ezekiel - 9 Feb 1865 77y 5m Garcelon
    Sarah - 28 Apr 1837 Garcelon
    Sarah d/ Asa - 28 June 1861 21y LewVR 226
    Sarah d/ John SMITH Esq - 20 Feb 1859 LewVR 228
    Sarah w/ John - 22 Mar 1843 75y LewVR 225
    Sewell - 25 Dec 1888 80-8-13 Crowley
    Susan d/o Joshua - 28 Apr 1865 33y 6m Riverside
    Susannah w/o Joshua - 1 Mar 1866 70y Riverside
    William - 7 June 1870 32y 4m Garcelon
    Wm s/o Moses/Abigail - 21 Nov 1783 LewVR 225
MERSERVE, Albert - 15 Nov 1854 LewVR 226
MERSERVY, Aaron s/o Albert - 24 Aug 1847 3y 5m Crowley
    Almond s/o Albert - 28 Aug 1847 7y 7m Crowley
    Ann w/o ALbert - b 1815 18 Sep 1889 Crowley
    Charles B s/o Albert - 11 Dec 1864 16-1-24 Crowley
MESERVEY, Albert - 15 Nov 1854 40y Crowley
METCALF, Abbie E d/o W H - 8 Aug 1884 26-3-2 Crowley
    Abijah revol Soldier LISBON
    Frank A - 11 Oct 1892 28y 8m Crowley
    Milton D - 12 July 1854 21y 7m Garcelon
    William H - 30 Nov 1878 43y 8m Crowley
    Willie H s/o W H - 2 Dec 1878 12y Crowley
MILLER, Harriet A d/o Hugh - 31 Dec 1861 27-3-24 Garcelon
    Hugh - 1799-1895 Garcelon
    Martha A d/o Hugh - 31 Dec 1861 27-3-24 Garcelon
    Sally - 1797-1889 Garcelon
MILLET, Charles Dr of Cholera - 13 Aug 1854 LewVR 226
MITCHEL, Mary d/ Josiah/Sarah - 8 June 1792 LewVR 225
MITCHELL, Ann J w/ Alfred E - 14 Nov 1852 21y 4m LewVR 226
    Benoni W - 9 May 1873 25-7-16 No Name Pond

Clarinida S d/o John - 15 Aug 1837 3m No Name Pond
George [German] - 1873 Riverside*
 - 27 Aug 1871 Riverside*
J G W - 24 Feb 1874 42-6-21 No Name Pond
James - 11 Sept 1839 LewVR 225
James Gardner s/ James - 5 Sept 1839 LewVR 225
John Jr - b 19 May 1802 9 Oct 1881 78y 4m No Name Pond
Joseph [German] - 1873 Riverside*
Joseph H [German] - 22 Sept 1873 8y Riverside*
Joseph s/Joseph/Mary - 9 Apr 1808 LewVR 225
Josiah - 19 Aug 1832 LewVR 225
Josiah s/ Josiah/Sarah - 14 June 1795 LewVR 225
Martha widow of Josiah - 9 Jul 1841 81y? LewVR 225
Mary w/o John - 10 Mar 1884 79-4-10 No Name Pond
Otis W s/ James/Martha - 3 Apr 1832 LewVR 225
Priscilla L w/Charles - 15 Jan 1891 53y 6m No Name Pond
Rachel d/ David/Betsy - 12 Mar 1815 LewVR 225
s/o ___ & Mary P - 6 July 1831 No Name Pond
Sarah w/ Josiah - 8 Feb 1792 LewVR 225
Sylvanus D - 11 July 1864 29-8-16 No Name Pond
MONROE, Abby Ann d/ Abel - 14 Aug 1849 LewVR 226
MOOAR, Benjamin - 26 Sept 1828 84y LewVR 225
 John - 22 Dec 1848 68y Herrick
 Martha w/o John - 12 Apr 1869 79y 9m Herrick
 Orpha d/o Nathan/Sarah - 4 Aug 1828 LewVR 225
MOODY, Charles drowned - 27 Apr 1807 LewVR 225
 Diedamia w/o Converse - 4 Apr 1887 82y 9m Garcelon
 Humility w/o Josiah - 15 Oct 1795 LewVR 225
 Josiah in Rumford - May 1830 LewVR 225
 Sally w/o Robert - 4 Sept 1811 LewVR 225
 35y Garcelon
MOORE, Alonzo G s/o E G - 4 Aug 1855 9m Herrick
 Frank A s/o G G - 19 Sept 1887 23-7-10 Herrick
 John L s/o G G - 3 Nov 1867 5-9-19 Herrick
 Sarah w/o Timothy - b 1811 8 Dec 1883 Riverside
 Riverside
 Timothy - b 13 Oct 1811 3 Apr 1886 Riverside
 Riverside
 William - 26 May 1856 42y 7m Herrick
MORE, Thomas revol soldier GREENE
 William - 18 May 1849 LewVR 226
MORES?, John 22 Dec 1848 68y LewVR 226
MORGAN, Jabez - 19 Sept 1863 23y LewVR 228
MORGON, Samuel revol soldier POLAND
MORRELL, Amaziah - 9 Feb 1864 68y 9m Herrick
 Benjamin - 10 Dec 1886 64y Crowley
 Charles E - 9 Sept 1871 43y Riverside
 Charles E s/o Charles - 30 Dec 1878 18y 6m Riverside
 Ebenezer s/ Jedediah - 24 Oct 1829 28y LewVR 225
 Elisabeth w/o Amaziah - 30 Apr 1877 78y? 9m Herrick
 Jedediah - 8 Nov 1821 LewVR 225
 Joanna w/o Jedediah - 1 June 1832 LewVR 225

Onie d/o Benjamin H – 25 Dec 1887 25y 9m Crowley
MORRILL, Elijah – 15 Sept 1803 LewVR 225
   Hannah w/o Charles W – 6 Dec 1869 Riverside
   Losiza d/o David/Naomi – 4 Mar 1826 LewVR 225
   Mary d/ Amaziah – 16 July 1847 LewVR 225
MORRISON, Dorcas – 3 Jan 1841 93y Davis
MORSE, Betsey w/ Mason A – 14 Dec 1866 73y LewVR 228
   Nathan – 30 June 1822 a pauper LewVR 225
   Peela – 6 Jan 1853 36y Crowley
   Rufus W s/ Henry – 4 May 1848 24y 6m LewVR 226
   Sarah, pauper, w/ Nathan – 30 Apl 1823 LewVR 225
   Stillman – 22 Aug 1854 LewVR 226
MORTON, Alice Riverside
   Alonzo D – b 11 Sept 1833 8 May 1883 Riverside
MOTHES, George [German] – 1881? Riverside*
MOWER, Ida d/ widow Deborah – 26 Jan 1857 LewVR 226
   John revol soldier GREENE
   Samuel revol soldier GREENE
MURRAY, Mary d/ Benjamin – 4 June 1852 LewVR 226
   Vesta d/ Benjamin – 17 Mar 1855 LewVR 226
NASH, Arthur S s/o Ammi C – b 1857 16 Nov 1871 Riverside
   d/o John – 1883-1889 Riverside
   Eddie s/ John – 24 Aug 1857 14m LewVR 227
   Jacob s/ John – 6 Oct 1849 LewVR 227
   James s/o Ammi C – b 1853 17 Oct 1884 Riverside
   John revol soldier MINOT
   John Col – 19 Sept 1847 58y LewVR 227
   John Col – b 15 Feb 1789 19 Sept 1847 Riverside
   Julia d/o John – 1872-1876 Riverside
   Lucy d/o John – 1876-1876 Riverside
   Sarah F d/ Ammi Jr – 18 Sept 1850 LewVR 227
   Sarah w/o Col John – b 1794 24 Sept 1863 Riverside
   Sarah wid/ Col John – 24 Sept 1863 69y LewVR 227
   Walter H s/o Ammi C – b 1866 5 Mar 1872 Riverside
NASON, Elizabeth d/Jermiah/Hannah – 3 Feb 1826 LewVR 227
   Lane d/ Wm Nason of Avon – 11 Feb 1841 LewVR 227
   Sumner – 16 Dec 1863 LewVR 227
NELSON, Caroline w/ A J – 26 Feb 182 19y LewVR 214
   – 26 Feb 1852 19y LewVR 227
NEVENS, Amanda F w/o Davis – 13 Apr 1884 61y 4m Riverside
   Augusta E d/o Davis – 5 June ____ Riverside
   Caroline w/o Randall – 6 Jul 1854 47y 6m Riverside
   Charles H – 23 July 1872 64y 4m Herrick
   Davis – 23 Sept 1854 71y Riverside
   Dennis s/ David/Hannah – 18 Dec 1821 LewVR 227
   Dennis s/o Davis – 19 May 1844 15m Riverside
   Eliza w/ Davis Jr – 4 July 1847 LewVR 227
   Eliza w/o Davis – 4 July 1847 38y Riverside
   Eunice d/ Davis/Hannah – 13 Sept 1822 LewVR 227
   Eva M d/o Charles H – 6 Apr 1857 1y 10m Herrick
   Hannah w/o Davis – 20 Sept 1860 79y 5m Riverside
   J R – 15 July 1863 52y Riverside

John revol soldier POLAND
John D s/o Randall - 26 Feb 1854 12-2-12 Riverside
Olive A d/o J R - 25 Mar 1863 1y 10m Riverside
William D s/ Amos & Nancy - 20 Mar 1816 6 mos Davis
NEVINS, Davis - 22 Sept 1854 LewVR 227
   Louina of N Gloucester - 7 Feb 1860 68y LewVR 227
   Randall s/ Davis - 15 July 1863 52y LewVR 227
NEWBEGIN, Hannah C H d/o George - 5 Sept 1856 18-3-19 Herrick
   Louisa A d/o George - 27 June 1859 15? Herrick
NICHOLS, Frank [colored] - d 1886 6y Riverside*
NOWELL, Paul revol soldier WEBSTER
NUTTING, Abel revol Soldier LISBON
NYE, Georgianna d/ Geath - 18 Jan 1867 8y LewVR 227
OAKES, Hellen C - 25 Sept 1852 LewVR 229
   Jenny P - 3 Sept 1852 LewVR 229
   Lucinda of Oldtown - 28 Dec 1848 LewVR 229
O'BRIEN, Ellen w/ Michael - 29 July 1852 LewVR 229
   Hannah w/ John - 25 Feb 1867 LewVR 229
   John (Irish) of consump - 26 Aug 1854 LewVR 229
   Michael (Irsih) - 20 Mar 1853 LewVR 229
OFINE c/o from Poland [German] - 1874 Riverside*
OLFINE, Augusta [German] - 9 July 1873 14y Riverside*
   Eliza C [German] - 10 Nov 1874 Riverside*
   Henry [german] - 4 Apr 1874 54y Riverside*
O'NEAL, John (Irish) killed acc' - 18 June 1861 LewVR 229
OSGOOD, J E Herrick
   William B s/o S B - b 1865 22 Sept 1893 Garcelon
O'SHAY, Stephen (Irishman) - 2 Nov 1852 drowned LewVR 229
PALMER, Charles s/ Martha P _ Dec 1863 poor house LewVR 232
PARCHER, John B s/ John - 2 Jan 1855 LewVR 232
   Olive Elsada d/ Saml - 16 July 1853 LewVR 231
PARSHLEY, d/ Gilbert/F D - 15 June 1832 LewVR 231
PARSONS, William s/ Daniel - 9 Mar 1855 LewVR 232
PATTERSON, Catherine w/o John W - 8 May 1887 71y 27d Crowley
   John W of Freeman - 25 Sept 1848 20y LewVR 231
PAUL, David - 24 Aug 1850 revol soldier Herrick 89y LewVR 231
   David revol soldier LEEDS
   John revol soldier WEBSTER
   Lucy w/ David - 28 Mar 1846? 83y LewVR 231
   Lucy w/David - 20 Mar 1848 83y Herrick [MaimeFarmer 6Apl848]
   M T revol soldier LEEDS
   Simeon s/ Daniel/Tenson - 19 Apl 1840 LewVR 231
PEARSON, Joseph C [Irish] - 9 May 1872 16m Riverside*
PECKHAM, Betsey M w/o Rev F H P - 22 July 1892 45y Riverside
   Fred H Rev Riverside
PEKINS, Joseph W - 22 July 1898 67y Riverside
PERKINS, Eldora d/ Edward - 2 Jan 1862 16y LewVR 232
   Gideon Rev - 25 Jan 1884 82y Riverside
   John W - 25 Mar 1872 44-7-10 Riverside
   Josie F w/o L M Thompson - 1864-1894 Riverside
   Martha w/o John W - 13 Oct 1867 34y Riverside
   Mary (Murray) w/ Rev C S - 7 June 1985 44y 5m ?d Riverside

Mary w/o Rev Gideon - 20 Nov 1877 78y 18d Riverside
　　Sarah E - 11 Feb 1896 57y Riverside
PEROWOOD, Simon [a blackman] revol soldier LEEDS
PETENGILL, Nathaniel s/ Nathl/Na - 1856 LewVR 231
PETTENGILL, Abigail w/ Nathl - 10 Dec 1805 LewVR 231
　　David Dea - 1 Oct 1848 82y LewVR 231
　　Edward s/David/Thankful - 29 May 1815 LewVR 231
　　Mary w/ John - 29 Jan 1842 51y LewVR 231
　　Nancy w/ Capt Nathl - __ Mar 1854 LewVR 231
　　Nathaniel Capt - 27 Feb 1860 LewVR 232
　　Philena w/ Converse - 10 Apl 1851 LewVR 231
　　Sophronia d/ Nathl - 16 Dec 1809 LewVR 231
　　Thankful w/ David - 26 July 1845 LewVR 231
PETTERSON, Hannah w/o Samuel - 18 Feb 1878 73y 7m Crowley
PETTINGILL, Benjamin revol Soldier LEWISTON
　　David revol Soldier LEWISTON
　　David Deacon - 1 Oct 1848 82y Riverside
　　David H s/o Dea John - 8 Mar 1855 25y 7m Riverside
　　James Madison s/o Nath'l - 17 Mar 1830 20y 6m Herrick (E Argus)
　　John Deacon - 8 May 1866 75-3-2 Riverside
　　Madison s/Nathl/Nancy - 17 Mar 1830 LewVR 231
　　Mark revol Soldier LEWISTON
　　Mary w/o Dea John - 29 July 1842 50y 11m Riverside
　　Nat s/o Nat - 5 Oct 1836 25y 7m Herrick
　　Philena w/o Converse - 10 Apr 1851 37y Herrick
　　Sarah F d/o John - 21 Mar 1885 49y 3m Riverside
　　Sarah widow - 20 Dec 1827 LewVR 231
　　Thankful w/ Dea David - 26 July 1845 77y Riverside
PHILLIPS, Ichabod Capt revol soldier GREENE
　　Joseph revol soldier GREENE
PIERCE, Alfred revol soldier GREENE
PIKE, Sophia F d/ Dr of Lynn, Ma - 29 Aug 1855 LewVR 232
PINKHAM, Elijah - 1 Mar 1861 50y LewVR 232
PIPER, Thomas s/ Thos/Hannah - 16 Aug 1827 40y LewVR 231
　　Zebiah d/ J W - 5 Sep 1852 1y LewVR 231
　　Zibeah d/ J K - 2 Oct 1853 LewVR 231
POLLARD, Sally w/o Isaac - 16 Mar 1848 Davis
　　w/ Isaac - 18 Mar 1846 LewVR 231
POLLOCK, John [scotch] - 16 Aug 1867 13m Riverside*
POWERS, John (Irish) of consump - 8 Aug 1854 LewVR 232
　　wid/o John (Irish) - 12 Aug 1854 of Chol LewVR 232
PRATT, w/ John - 17 Dec 1857 30y LewVR 232
PRAY, Mary Jane d/ Joseph - 8 Oct 1857 12y LewVR 232
PRENTIS, Samuel of Athens - 22 Oct 1853 LewVR 231
PRESCOTT, Lucy Jane d/ Samuel - 16 Sept 1851 LewVR 231
　　Lydia W - 21 Jan 1857 45y LewVR 232
PRINGTON, Joseph - 28 Sept 1842 44y Crowley
PROCTOR, Samuel revol Soldier LEWISTON
PURINGTON, Almira d/o Joseph - 1 Mar 1859 22-6-23 Crowley
　　Aseneth w/o David - 12 Apr 1873 56y 23d Herrick
　　Dorcas w/o Ira - 27 Dec 1830 21y Riverside
　　Ezra - 28 Dec 1838 LewVR 231

Harriet d/o Joseph - 14 Mar 1866 24-4-17 Crowley
Joseph s/ Ezra - 22 Sept 1842 LewVR 231
William D s/o Joseph - 16 Apr 1842 2y Crowley
PURINTON, David at Wiscasset Fall - 26 May 1848 LewVR 231
PURKINSON, John (Englishman) - 24 Dec 1866 27y LewVR 232
PURRINTON, Mary wid/o Ezra - 7 Nov 1857 85y LewVR 232
PURTINGTON, Benjamin F s/o David - 20 Sept 1860 12y 8m Herrick
PUTMAN, Ward - 30 Dec 1855 drowned LewVR 232
QUIMBY, Benjamin revol soldier GREENE
   Mary M w/o Aaron - 4 Jan 1890 60-8-4 Herrick
   Mildred d/o Aaron - 1 Dec 1866 3-7-12 Herrick
RAND, Abigail w/ Thomas - 19 Mar 1860 LewVR 235
   c/o Jordan - 2 Oct 1850 Crowley
   - 25 Feb 1852 Crowley
   Jane d/ Baezilla - 2 Aug 1821 LewVR 235
   Jane d/ Barzilla/Thankful - 17 Mar 1816 LewVR 235
   Mehitable w/o Samuel D - 6 Dec 1864 60y 5m Crowley
   Nabby w/o Thomas - 18 Mar 1850 91y Crowley
   Rebecca d/ Saml - 26 Jul 1845 LewVR 235
   Rebecca d/o Samuel - 26 July 1848 15y 6m Crowley
   Samuel - 28 Mar 1886 83-9-23 Crowley
   Thomas - 6 Sept 1837 LewVR 235
     77y Crowley
   Thomas revol Soldier LEWISTON
RANDALL, Clarrisai d/ Ezra/Theoda - 5 Feb 1815 LewVR 235
   Ezra - 10 June 1850 LewVR 235
   Ezra s/o Ezra - 14 Nov 1845 22y Herrick
   Humphrey s/ Benjamin - 23 Oct 1845 LewVR 235
   James s/o Wellington - 29 Jul 1872 78y Riverside
   John - 23 Oct 1845 LewVR 235
   Levi C s/ Ezra - 10 Aug 1863 63y LewVR 236
   Mary d/ Wm/ Sally - 21 Mar 1815 LewVR 235
   Rhoda M sis/o Isaac - 4 Jan 1854 LewVR 236
   Sally w/ William - 29 Mar 1815 LewVR 235
RANDELL, Oryeah d/ Ezra/Theoda - 20 Sept 1826 LewVR 235
READ, Abby S d/o Stephen - 20 Feb 1844 4 days Herrick
   Abigail B w/o Col S - 17 Dec 1883 b 17 Nov1813 Riverside
   Albert s/ Rufus - 15 Sept 1849 LewVR 235
   Ammi - 27 May 1861 33y LewVR 236
   Aurelia d/ John - 7 Oct 1853 LewVR 236
   Aurelia S d/o John P - 7 Oct 1853 33y 4d Herrick
   Betsey w/o John P - 22 Jan 1855 72y Herrick
   Betsey wid/o John - 22 Jan 1855 72y LewVR 236
   Catharine wid/ Oliver - 23 July 1854 74y LewVR 236
   Charles B - 4 Aug 1894 Riverside
   Dan - 15 Feb 1853 87y Herrick
     87y LewVR 236
   Debby d/ Danl/Susana - 1 Nov 1812 LewVR 235
   Deborah d/ Leml/Mary - 1 Mar 1815 LewVR 235
   Elizabeth d/ Saml - 8 Feb 1867 42y LewVR 236
   Huldah w/ Samuel - 3 Dec 1859 66y LewVR 236
   Ichobod - 10 Dec 1797 LewVR 235

    Joel s/ Leml/Mary - 3 Sept 1804 LewVR 235
    John P - 28 Nov 1849 57y Herrick
    John s/ Dan - 28 Nov 1849 67y LewVR 235
    Jonathan - 2 Mar 1838 LewVR 235
    Lemuel - 4 Apr 1821 LewVR 235
    Lemuel s/ Lemuel/Mary - 30 May 1799 LewVR 235
    Lois d/ Dan/Susanna - 16 Sept 1821 LewVR 235
    Margaret w/ Ammi - 19 May 1850 LewVR 235
       - 3 Nov 1866 59y LewVR 236
    Mary wid/o Lemuel - 17 July 1854 78y LewVR 236
    Mercy w/ Jacob H - 2 Jan 1858 LewVR 236
    Oliver - 15 June 1850 72y LewVR 236
       - 17 June 1850 LewVR 236
    Polly d/ Oliver/Catey - 27 Aug 1803 LewVR 235
    Stephen Col - 14 Apr 1860 b 21 Nov 1798 Riverside
    Susanna w/ Dan - 12 May 1847 LewVR 235
    Susannah w/o Dan - 12 May 1847 77y Herrick
    Daniel revol Soldier LEWISTON
REYNOLDS, Betsey w/ Nathan - 4 Nov 1856 62y LewVR 236
    Nathan Esq - 24 Oct 1859 65y LewVR 236
RICE, Harriet from Waterford - 27 Sept 1848 20 LewVR 235
RICHARDSON, Wm W s/ Wm T/Machael - 3 Sept 1856 2y 6m Davis
RICHMOND, Abiathar revol soldier GREENE
RICKER, Frances Ann d/ Harris - 29 Apr 1847 4m LewVR 235
    Martha A w/o Harrison - 2 Dec 1863 36y LewVR 236
    Simeon revol soldier WEBSTER
RIGGS, Enoch - 15 June 1855 LewVR 236
RING, Timothy (Irishman) - 15 Aug 1848 LewVR 235
ROBBINS, Daniel revol soldier LEEDS
    Luther revol soldier GREENE
    Lydia w/ H - 31 Dec 1860 36y LewVR 236
    Mary w/ Luther - 18 Jan 1852 60y LewVR 236
ROBINS, Luthur Deacon - 24 Nov 1862 78-4-14 Herrick
    Mary M d/o Luther - 5 Jan 1856 26y 14days Herrick
    Mary w/o Luther - 18 Jan 1852 62-6-13 Herrick
ROBINSON, Anna of Cape Ann - 7 Feb 1831 63y LewVR 235
    Betsey d/ James/Susan - 29 June 1826 LewVR 235
ROSE, Morice [German] - 18 Oct 1870 1m Riverside*
    Orrin - 12 Aug 1898? 61y 7m Crowley
ROWE, John revol soldier LISBON
    Jonathan - May 1835 43y 10m Garcelon
    Samuel D - 8 May 1859 40y 2m Garcelon
ROYAL, Israel revol soldier LEEDS
    Widow l/o New Gloucester - 4 Apr 1813 LewVR 236
SANBORN, Charles H s/ Dudley - 24 July 1852 16m LewVR 238
SAWYER, George revol soldier LISBON
    Sannah G l/o Durham - 12 July 1861 86y LewVR 242
SCHEIPNER, Charley [German] - 1880 Riverside*
SCHULZE, Agnes [German] - 1880 Riverside*
SCRIBNER, Hannah widow formerly - 27 Jan 1857 LewVR 238
    Margaret d/ Samuel - 27 Dec 1847 3y 6m LewVR 238

SHAPLEIGH, Primusa (black) - 27 Feb 1830 76y LewVR 237 (Danville 1798-1815?)
SHATTUCK, Annette w/ J H - 3 Dec 1857 18y LewVR 238
SHAW, Alinonda s/ Alvin - 14 Oct 1844 LewVR 237
  Ebenezer - 16 Jan 1820 60y LewVR 237
  Sarah w/ Ebenezer - 28 May 1826 72y LewVR 237
SHEEHAM, Cornelius [Irish] - 22 Dec 1871 21y 9m Riverside*
  William D [Irish] - 8 July 1872 9m Riverside*
SHEHAN, John (Irish) - 26 Aug 1854 cholera LewVR 238
SHEPPARD, Sarah w/o John - 18 Apr 1851 48y NoNamePond
  Calista d/o John/Sarah - 4 Aug 1851 13y NoNamePond
  John - 29 Apr 1841 39y NoNamePond
  Nathaniel - 11 Jan 1861 34y 7m NoNamePond
  Sarah w/o Nathaniel - 29 May 1895 68y NoNamePond
SIMMONS, Samuel revol soldier WEBSTER
SIMONS, Harriet d/ Loring - 16 Mar 1847 LewVR 237
  Julia w/o Henry - 20 June 1859 LewVR 238
SINCLAIR, Charenec W s/ J D - 9 July 1853 1y LewVR 238
SKETLON, Flora E w/o Wm T - 2 June 1880 26-2-22 Riverside
  William - 16 Apr 1883 74y Riverside
SKILLING, William l/o Leeds - 12 Sept 1851 17y LewVR 238
SKILLON, James (Irish) - 7 Feb 1860 70y LewVR 238
SKINNER, Andrew - 26 Feb 1857 LewVR 238
  76y Riverside
  Catharine d/ Andrew & W - 10 Apr 184? Davis
  David s/ Jeremiah - 30 Sept 1839 21y 4m Davis
  David s/ Jordan/Eliza - 7 Feb 1840 LewVR 237
  Elbridge (l/o Jefferson - 26 Oct 1866 LewVR 242
  Elias N w/o Jordan - 22 Dec 1886 73y 5m Riverside
  Freeman - 23 Dec 1838 LewVR 237
  Jeremiah s/ Andrew/Weal - 30 Sept 1839 LewVR 237
  Joanna d/ John/Katherin - 21 Feb 1840 LewVR 237
  John - 15 May 1868 54y 4m Riverside
  John (revol. Pensioner) - 16 Mar 1844 LewVR 237
  Jordan - 18 Mar 1863 54y 10m Riverside
  Jordan acc't w/ pung - 18 Mar 1863 55y LewVR 242
  KAtharine w/ John - 19 Jan 1832 LewVR 237
  Katherine d/ Andrew - 11 Sept 1841 LewVR 237
  Neathy w/o Andrew D - 15 Dec 1862 78y 6m Riverside
  Sarah R w/o John - 6 Sept 1883 76y Riverside
  Wealthy wid/ Andrew - 15 Dec 1862 78y LewVR 242
SLEEPER, Abigail w/ N P - 27 Feb 1838 LewVR 237
  David revol soldier LEWISTON
  Elizabeth w/o Jonathan - 1781-1858 Riverside
  Ira s/ Nathan/Polly - 13 Sept 1804 LewVR 237
  Jonathan - 1769-1805 Riverside
  Nathan - 18 Feb 1860 82y LewVR 238
  Tobias s/ Nathaniel/Pol - 10 Sept 1804 LewVR 237
SMALL, David revol soldier WALES
  Ferarcis Celia d/ Nathl - 23 Aug 1857 LewVR 238
SMITH, Abraham R - 1 Apr 1857 33y LewVR 238
  Amy d/o Samuel 9y - 10 Jan 1857 poor farm LewVR 238

Dolly w/ Jeremiah Jr - 5 June 1821 LewVR 237
George B - 19 July 1888 72y 3m Riverside
Jeremiah Sr - 10 May 1829 LewVR 237
Joanna w/ John - 3 June 1846 LewVR 237
L s/o George B - 18 Oct 1857 LewVR 238
Lucinda w/o George B - 17 Jan 1868 49y 8m Riverside
Sally d/ Jeremiah Jr/Dorot - 23 Feb 1821 LewVR 237
Thomas (pauper) - 20 Dec 1809 LewVR 237
THomas s/ Jeremiah Jr - __ Oct 1825 a pauper LewVR 237
SNELL, Robert Capt revol soldier AUBURN
SOULE, Albert B Maj - 8 Feb 1864 38y LewVR 242
   w/ Samuel Capt - 5 Sept 1843 LewVR 237
SPENCER, Lydia Ann by burns - 7 Feb 1828 LewVR 237
SPOFFORD, Dorothy M - 28 Aug 1856 23y 4m Randall Rd
   Phineas revol soldier WEBSTER
SPRAGUE, d/o Washington S - 25 Oct 1850 LewVR 238
   Nolney c/ Washington - 11 Jan 1862 29y LewVR 238
   William revol soldier GREENE
STACKPOLE, Absalom s/ Cornelius - 8 Feb 1833 LewVR 237
STAFFORD, Margaret poor house - 4 Oct 1865 40y LewVR 242
STAMFORD, Benjamin - 22 Apr 1858 38y Crowley
STANFORD, Augusta J w/o George H - 26 Feb 1885 34y 4m Crowley
   Betsey w/o Jere. - 6 Nov 1855 70y Crowley
   Isabella - 21 Oct 1851 43y Crowley
   Isabella d/ Jeremiah - __ Oct 1851 40y LewVR 238
   Isaiah - 20 May 1843 33y 3m Crowley
   Jeremiah - 7 Oct 1861 86y 4d Crowley
   Joseph D - 31 July 1844 22y Crowley
   Mary w/o Benjamin - 3 Aug 1831 77y 6m 6d Crowley
   Mary w/o Jere - 3 Dec 1820 42y Crowley
STANLEY, Julia d/ Edward - 18 Oct 1847 18y LewVR 237
STANTON, Paul revol soldier POLAND
STANWOOD, Ebenezer of Brunswick - 9 Apr 1828 LewVR 237
STATEN, Amos - 18 Mar 1852 47y Goddard
   Amos s/ Samuel - 18 Mar 1852 45y LewVR 238
   Amosanna d/o Amos/Martha - 21 Jan 1863 11y Goddard
   Josephine R d/o Amos & M - 8 Aug 1849 9m Goddard
   Olive d/ Samuel - 11 Nov 1821 LewVR 237
   Polly w/ Elias - 29 July 1849 82y LewVR 238
STEEL, Joseph [scotch] - 1880 Riverside*
STETSON, Batchelder revol soldier GREENE
   George D s/ Stephen - 23 July 1846 LewVR 237
   Harriet N w/ George - 27 July 1846 LewVR 237
STEVENS, Adeleaide B d/o Wm H - 11 May 1899 53y 19d Riverside
   Henrietta P d/o Wm H - 10 Aug 1898 52-3-19 Riverside
   Isaac - 1 Nov 1852 80y LewVR 238
   Jane R w/? - 18 Dec 1862 19y LewVR 242
   Julia R w/? - 18 Dec 1862 19y LewVR 242
   William (l/o Gardiner) - 3 July 1855 LewVR 238
   William H Riverside
STEWART, Edward - 22 Aug 1827 LewVR 237
   Fred s/ William - 12 Mar 1865 13y P Farm LewVR 242

Isaac Dea - 18 Nov 1846 LewVR 237
Mary Ellen d/ Robert - 2 Sept 1855 LewVR 238
Rebecca M w/o Nathan - 18 Sept 1875 28y 10m Garcelon
  w/ Thomas LewVR 237
  w/ Thomas S LewVR 237
STIMPSON, Alphaus s/ Josiah - 2 Apr 1857 LewVR 238
STINSAN, Josiah - 14 Jan 1864 LewVR 242
  Sarah w/ Josiah - 12 Jan 1860 41y LewVR 238
STORER, Elias revol soldier WEBSTER
STOWELL, Joseph (worker in Facto) - 19 Oct 1844 LewVR 237
STRAW, Ebenezer - 16 Jan 1820 69y Crowley
  Josiah - 8 Apr 1858 82y Crowley
  Sarah w/o Ebenezer - 28 May 1826 72y Crowley
STRICKROTT, Albert [German] - 6 Sept 1871 13m Riverside*
  Frank H [German] - 5 Aug 1873 4m Riverside*
STROUT, Enos revol soldier WALES
STUART, Addie d/o Stacy - 1 May 1867 2-3-9 Crowley
  Flavilla A d/o Stacy - 6 Feb 1871 16y 4d Crowley
  Stacy R - 20 May 1880 54-1-15 Crowley
SULLIVAN, James (Irish) - 3 Aug 1854 cholera LewVR 238
  Patrick (Irish) - 1 Aug 1854 cholera LewVR 238
SWETLAND, Sarah? w/o ? - 4 Apl 1851 LewVR 238
TARR, Aaron - 13 Jan 1870 77-10-17 Crowley
  Amos s/ Seth/Mary - 12 Dec 1797 LewVR 239
  Benjamin - 4 Feb 1838 LewVR 239
  Bessie M d/o J G - 2 May 1877 9y 5m Crowley
  Frank M s/o Jordan - 9 July 1854 1y 1m Crowley
  Frankie s/o J G - 23 Sept 1881 3 weeks Crowley
  James - 17 Apr 1858 55y LewVR 240
  Jordan s/o Aaron - 11 Aug 1854 26y Crowley
  Joseph s/ Seth/Mary - 7 Oct 1803 LewVR 239
  Mary w/ Seth - 7 Dec 1822 LewVR 239
  May w/o Aaron - 3 Dec 1868 75-4-12 Crowley
  Sargent s/ Seth/Mary - 17 Jan 1814 LewVR 239
  Willie A s/o J G - 13 Aug 1874 9m Crowley
TAYLOR, Charles - 15 Mar 1864 37y Herrick
  - 23 Nov 1880 83y Herrick
  Charles E s/o A P - 24 July 1862 28y Herrick
  Charles s/o Charles - 18 May 1861 20d Herrick
  Edward s/ Thomas - 1 July 1809 LewVR 239
  George - 9 Nov 1869 45y 6m Garcelon
  George s/o James - 28 Jan 1853 2y Herrick
  Georgeanna d/o Janus - 16 Jan 1853 2y Herrick
  Jemina w/o Thomas - 1 June 1801 55y Herrick
  Jerusha w/o Asa P - 23 Mar 1892 70y 5m Crowley
  Lerella? M d/o Joseph - 21 Dec 1862 8y Herrick
  Luther C - 15 Sept 1851 48y 6m Herrick
  Marcia w/o Luther C - 17 Feb 1875 69y 6m Herrick
  Mariam widow - 6 Apl 1855 LewVR 239
  Mary E d/o Thomas - 5 Mar 1876 10-11-16 Herrick
  Miriam w/o Thomas - 6 Apr 1855 88y Herrick
  Nathaniel - 20 Oct 1804 LewVR 239

   - 24 Apr 1808 LewVR 239
s/o James - 6 Jan 1855 Herrick
Sophronia w/o A P - 5 Apr 1876 65y Herrick
Thomas - 18 Feb 1825 LewVR 239
   89y Herrick
   revol Soldier LEWISTON
Thomas s/ Luther/Marsha - 29 Apl 1826 LewVR 239
w/ Thomas - 18 June 1802 LewVR 239
TEAGUE, Pauline F w/ Greenleaf - 1 Feb 1864 26y LewVR 240
TEEL, Hannah M w/o Henry C - 16 Jan 1912 b 20May 1837 NoName Pond
Henry C - 11 Apr 1900 69y NoNamePond
THING, Frank Edwin s/ Chester - 16 Oct 1856 LewVR 240
THOMAS George E s/o William - 7 Aug 1835 2-6-20 Herrick
   Ebner - 1863-1896 Riverside
   Esther - 5 Oct 1896 73y 5m Garcelon
   Lottie M d/o William E - 1878-1889 Riverside
   May M w/o S D - 1830-1858 Riverside
   William E - 1853-1881 Riverside
THOMPSON, Charlotte w/ Samuel - 6 Aug 1812 LewVR 239
   Elbridge - 1850-1902 Randall Rd
   Hannah d/ Solomon - 15 Aug 1851 88y LewVR 239
   Isaac C - 14 July 1861 60-1-22 Riverside
   Isaac C Esq - 14 July 1861 68y LewVR 240
   Joel revol Soldier LEWISTON
   Joel Col - 1 May 1841 LewVR 239
      87y 5m Davis
   Joel Col revol soldier Davis
   Joseph - 26 May 1827 72y LewVR 239
   Josie F w/o L M Riverside
   Martha J - 1859-1940 Randall Rd
   Martha L (from Bingham) - 5 Nov 1857 21y LewVR 240
   Martha w/ Col Joel - 16 July 1828 LewVR 239
   Martha w/o Col Joel - 16 July 1828 68y Davis
   Nehemiah s/Joseph/Happy - 6 Nov 1802 LewVR 239
   Ralph - 1881-1914 Randall Rd
   Ruthg s/ Joel - 30 Sept 1810 LewVR 239
   Samuel revol soldier LISBON
   Solomon - 15 Jan 1893 97y Randall Rd
   Sylvia w/o Solomon - 9 Jan 1871 83y Randall Rd
THORN, Abigail sis/o Elder Benj. - 10 Apr 1848 73y LewVR 239
   Barnett - 23 Apr 1815 LewVR 239
   Benjamin H - 16 Feb 1836 LewVR 239
   Benjamin? - 17 Jan 1842 90y LewVR 239
   Elias s/ Benjamin - 26 Apr 1841 LewVR 239
      - 30 Oct 1817 LewVR 239
   Hannah w/ Samuel - 27 July 1821 LewVR 239
   Martha d/ Barnett LewVR 239
   Saml gs/o Elder T - 28 Aug 1846 12y LewVR 239
   Samuel - 10 Feb 1828 LewVR 239
   Samuel s/ Samuel/Hannah - 15 Sept 1798 LewVR 239
THORNE, Alice w/o Rev Benjamin - 1 May 1866 86y 1m Herrick

Benjamin H - 16 Feb 1836 26y Herrick
Benjamin Rev - 4 Dec 1864 86-9-? Herrick
Elias - 26 Apr 1841 23y Herrick
Elias S s/o Rev Benjamin - 30 Oct 1817 4y Herrick
Jane w/ Bernett - 31 Mar 1815 LewVR 239
Laura C w/o A D - 2 Aug 1883 71y Herrick
Samuel - 23 June 1832 21y Herrick
Samuel T s/o Benjamin H - 28 Aug 1846 13y Herrick
THORNTON, James (Irsihman) - 4 July 1854 drowned LewVR 240
TIBBETTS, Patience - 4 Sept 1860 49y LewVR 240
   Sarah w/o Col Temple - 30 Aug 1886 77-11-15 Riverside
TIBBITTS, Temple Col - 8 Mar 1882 74y 7m Riverside
TIBOR, John (from New York) - 3 Sept 1855 LewVR 240
TOBIE, Caroline Frye w/o E P - 24 Dec 1838 38y Riverside
   Edward P Riverside
   Jane E w/o E P - 5 Nov 1891 84y Riverside
   Joseph F s/o E P - 7 Feb 1838 6m 18d Riverside
   Sarah F d/o E P - 13 Oct 1877 48y Riverside
TOBY, Caroline w/ Parson - 24 Dec 1838 LewVR 239
TORSEY, Emma [Irish] - 20 Jan 1879 Riverside*
   Joseph - 28 Nov 1878 75-8-22 Crowley
   w/o Joseph - 29 Aug 1887 85y Crowley
TOWNS, Hannah - 18 Mar 1851 90y 4m Garcelon
   Hannah widow - 18 Mar 1851 90y LewVR 240
TRACY, Elizabeth of Farmington - 15 Nov 1845 LewVR 239
TRAFTON, F Lincoln s/o Waterman - 18 May 1862 1-2-18 Riverside
   Judith w/o Waterman - 30 Dec 1872 54-9-8 Riverside
   Waterman - 4 Apr 1894 72y Riverside
TRIMBACK, Elizabeth [German] - 25 Aug 1872 Riverside*
   Henry [German] - May 1879 8m Riverside*
TRUE, Charles H s/ Jacob - 6 Jan 1848 6y LewVR 239
   Charles H s/Jacob/Theodocia - 7 Jan 1849 6y Davis
   William revol soldier WEBSTER
   William Maj revol soldier LISBON
TRULL, David near bend in River Porter Mill Cemetery
   Jonathan - buried 1 Apr 1777 in Lewiston [Garcelon Records]
TUCKER, Harriet d/ Jonathan - 31 July 1851 LewVR 240
TULLIS, Ellen [scotch] - 9 Dec 1869 23y Riverside*
   Isabell [Scotch] - 19 July 1872 77y Riverside*
TURNER, Amelia d/ Saml - 4 Apl 1859 LewVR 240
   Caleb S s/o Benjamin - 11 Jan 1881 22y 6d Crowley
   Charles B - 5 July 1883 28y 6m Crowley
   Cybelia A w/o A L - 20 Aug 1886 63y 3m Garcelon
   Deborah w/o John S - 26 Apr 1872 40-5-17 Riverside
   Jason A s/o Benjamin - 16 Mar 1881 28y 5m Crowley
   John S - 4 Feb 1864 30y 10m Riverside
   Marilla S w/o Charles - 28 Sept 1884 25-10-8 Crowley
   Olive d/ Daniel - 6 Aug 1858 28y LewVR 240
   Rosell d/o Benj - 27 Oct 1872 15y 8m Crowley
   Velsora M d/o Benj - 19 Oct 1865 16y 9m Crowley
   William revol soldier LEEDS
VARNEY, Joel Mrs. (keft boarders) - 8 Dec 1859 63y LewVR 243

VERRILL, Davis d/ Davis S - 28 May 1857 17y LewVR 243
   Davis E - 14 Aug 1855 LewVR 243
   Fanny Isabel d/ Davis - 3 Oct 1853 LewVR 243
   Freddie s/ Davis - 31 Mar 1863 LewVR 243
   Harland P s/o Davis E - 24 Aug 1866 24y 10m Riverside
   Harriet L d/ Davis - 19 June 1855 9y LewVR 243
VICKERY, Hannah w/ William - 3 May 1846 LewVR 243
VIDETO, Ebenezer s/ Joseph/Lydia LewVR 243
   Joseph - 11 July 1839 LewVR 243
   Lydia 4th w/ Joseph LewVR 243
   Mary 3rd w/o Joseph - 10 Mar 1801 LewVR 243
   Sophia d/o J & L - __ Aug 1823 LewVR 243
WAGG, Elizabeth of Lisbon - 24 Nov 1870 palsy Riverside*
WAITE, Joanna - 20 Jan 1881 74y Clough
WAKEFIELD, David s/ Archibald - 12 May 1837 LewVR 245
WALSH, James s/ William - 8 Aug 1854 LewVR 246
   w/ William of chol. - 8 Aug 1854 LewVR 246
WARE, Isaac s/o Lewis & Eleanor - 29 May 1872 18-10-22 NoNamePond
   Lewis - 13 Aug 1882 93y Riverside
   Lewis A s/o L & E - 7 Nov 1896 40y NoNamePond
   Lewis b - 18 __ 1818 1 Dec 1899 NoNamePond
   Nettie A - 21 Aug 1862 13-8-0 NoNamePond
   Scribner s/o L & E - 19 Feb 1868 20-3-19 NoNamePond
WARREN, Mary d/ Rev Silvanus - 16 May 1857 9y 6m Clough
WARTE, Horatio s/o Lewis/Eleanor - 31 Aug 1867 6-9-11 NoNamePond
WASHBURN, Elizabeth A w/Wentworth - 1848-1897 Randall Rd
   Wentworth F - 1845-1906 Randall Rd
WATSON, John [scotch] - 1880 Riverside*
   Lucy w/o Sidney - 15 Jan 1874 37-1-10 Clough
WEAR w/ Lewis Jr - 13 Feb 1845 LewVR 245
WEBBER, Desire d/ Jesse/Charlott - 30 Nov 1800 LewVR 245
   Jesse - 30 Jan 1809 LewVR 245
   Mary d/ Jesse/Charet - 6 Sept 18?7 LewVR 245
   Nancy w/ Joseph - 14 May 1856 LewVR 246
   Polly w/ Joseph - 29 Nov 1854 62y LewVR 246
   Polly w/o Joseph - 29 May 1854 (age missing Davis
   Samuel - b 28 Sept 1829 19 Aug 1902 Garcelon
   Sarah w/o Samuel - 20 Sept 1835 Garcelon
WEBSTER, John l/o N Gloucester - 12 May 1847 of palsy LewVR 245
   Patience w/o William - 4 Dec 1866 62y 14d Riverside
   William Riverside
WEEKS, Sarah w/o How W - 5 Nov 1847 LewVR 246
WELCH, Daniel (pauper) - 11 Feb 1851 LewVR 246
   Oliver - 24 Nov 1902 72y Garcelon
WENTWORTH, Foster revol soldier WEBSTER
WEST, William revol soldier LISBON
WEYMOUTH, Cyrus - b 1811- Riverside
   Dominicus - 6 Jan 1852 64y LewVR 246
   Rebecca d/ James - 26 Jan 1861 LewVR 246
   Ruth w/o Cyrus - 1805-1890 Riverside

WHEELER, Rachel d/ Ezra of Phil - 29 Aug 1857 LewVR 246
WHITE, George L s/ Job of N Glou - 4 Sep 1853 LewVR 246
WHITHAM, John - 16 Jan 1852 44y LewVR 246
  Ann w/o David S - 19 Aug 1882 96y 5m Riverside
  David - 9 Nov 1843 LewVR 245
    69y Riverside
WHITNEY, Abram revol soldier LISBON
  Amos revol soldier LISBON
  Phincas from Jay - 10 Aug 1857 LewVR 246
WHITTIUM, Ebenezer - 11 Jan 1849 59y LewVR 246
WHITTUM, Abbie C w/o Henry - 25 Apr 1891 Riverside
  Alma - 14 Apr 1853 3y Riverside
  Betsey w/o Dan - 16 Feb 1876 58-10-20 Herrick
  Charles M s/o Dan - 11 Feb 1858 3-4-6 Herrick
  Clarissa w/o Ebenezer - 10 Mar 1862 76-1-13 Herrick
  Dan - 23 Dec 1874 66y 1m Herrick
  Ebenezer - 11 Jan 1849 69y Herrick
  Sarah w/o Sargeant - 1 Jan 1894 82y Riverside
  Sargeant - 13 Sept 1887 74y Riverside
  Walter s/o Dan - 3 May 1862 20-3-27 Herrick
  Wm Henry - 11 Dec 1888 Riverside
WIGGIN, Levi s/ Daniel W - 1 Feb 1849 LewVR 246
WIGGINS, Charles s/ Daniel - 12 Nov 1850 LewVR 246
  Daniel H - 7 Aug 1852 66y LewVR 246
WIGHT, Joseph - 15 July 1895 70y 4m Clough
  - 26 Dec 1850 74y LewVR 246
  Mary w/o Joseph - 9 Oct 1882 62y 2m Clough
WILKINS, Amos s/ Stephen/Ruth - 16 Oct 1826 LewVR 245
  Anna d/ David/Molly - 12 Jan 1796 LewVR 245
  David - 18 Nov 1834 LewVR 245
  Isabella wid/ David - 16 Jan 1843 LewVR 245
WILKINS, Jerusha d/ David/Molly - __ May 1773 LewVR 245
  Molly w/ David - 6 Oct 1809 LewVR 245
WILLARD, Ellen S w/o John A - 24 Jan 1869 24-7-5 Herrick
  George A s/o J A - b 1866 5 May 1885 Herrick
WILLIAMS, Betsey - 17 Oct 1892 77y Garcelon
  Eleanor Jane d/ Charles - 25 Oct 1829 LewVR 245
  Isaac H - 4 Apr 1885 65y 5m Garcelon
  Lucinda d/ George - 13 Mar 1810 LewVR 245
WILSON, Edwin s/ Henry/Hannah - 24 June 1853 4y 9m Goddard
  Ellen w/ ? - 12 Jan 1853 34y LewVR 246
  Kottie [colored] - 1883 26y Riverside*
WINSLOW, Elizabeth w/ Kenelem - 17 Mar 1800 LewVR 245
  Kenelem - 13 Feb 1796 LewVR 245
  Rhoda d/ Kenelem/Elizab - 13 May 1797 LewVR 245
WITHAM, Joshua at town farm - 26 Apr 1859 65y LewVR 246
WITHERETL, John revol soldier WALES
WOOD, Annetta A Riverside
  B Eva d/o Daniel - 17 Nov 1871 25y 3m Riverside
  Ephraim - b 14 Aug 1797 1 Aug 1880 Riverside
  Harriet L w/Wm - b 28 July 1840 Riverside
  Ira L d/ Wm F - 2 Dec 1868 Riverside

    Joseph M Riverside
    Lulu E d/o William F - 8 Feb 1869 Riverside
    Martietta Riverside
    Mary T w/ Ephraim - b 12 Feb 05 24 Oct 1848 Riverside
    Ralph E s/o Wm F - 17 Mar 1872 Riverside
    Wm F - b 29 Mar 1835 ? Riverside
WOODARD, Betsy w/ William - 17 Dec 1873 78y Clough
    Gardiner - 18 Dec 1868 38y 7m Clough
        38y 7m Garcelon
WOODBURY, d/o Leonard - 25 Aug 1848 LewVR 246
WOODROW, Henry [Scotch] - drowned 1874 Riverside*
WRIGHT, Abigail (Paupar) - 28 June 1833 LewVR 245
    Albion - 1842-1911 NoNamePond
    Albion A - 1843-1905 NoNamePond
    Alvah s/o S D - 14 Apr 1864 1-6-23 Herrick
    Angelia w/o Charles 25 May 1851 24y Randall Rd
    Angier L s/o Charles H - 9 Sept 1851 Randall Rd
    Aurelia w/ George W - 25 Jan 1864 43y LewVR 249
    Aurelia w/o G W - 25 Jul 1864 47-10-28 Riverside
    Betsey d/o Joel Jr - 26 Oct 1806 LewVR 245
    Betsey w/o Joel Jr - 15 Dec 1864 87y 6m NoNamePond
    C B NoNamePond
    Charity L w/o Zebulon - 30 Apr 1851 54y Randall Rd
    Charity w/o Zebulon - 23 May 1838 47y Randall Rd
    Charles N d/Reuben/Hannah - 13 Aug 1855 LewVR 246
    Christiania d/ James - 5 Jan 1832 LewVR 245
    Costello A s/o Geo W - 19 Mar 1874 19-3-5 Riverside
    Dorcas w/o Phineus - 25 Apr 1872 72y Riverside
    Ebenezer s/ Joel Jr - 20 Jan 1806 LewVR 245
    Ebenezer s/ Joel Jr/Bety - 18 Jan 1799 LewVR 245
    Ebenezer s/ Joel/Mary - 21 June 1796 LewVR 245
    Edna E - 1903 8y NoNamePond
    Elbert s/o S D - 13 Apr 1867 5m 4d Herrick
    Eliza d/o Jona - 16 June 1873 11y 5m Garcelon
    Eliza d/o Jonathan - 16 June 1973 11y 5m Clough
    Elizabeth H d/o Phineas - 17 Feb 1851 4y 1m NoNamePond
    Elizabeth w/o Albion NoNamePond
    Elizabeth wid/ LewVR 245
    Elmer M s/o Charles - 17 Aug 1859 9-6 Randall Rd
    Emily M w/o W H - 12 Sept 1891 53y 4m NoNamePond
    Emmaett d/o Phineas - 20 Jan 1851 2y 1m NoNamePond
    Flora d/o S D - 10 Mar 1869 3m Herrick
    Francis - 5 Oct 1861 71y 6m Herrick
    Harriet d/ Cephias - 28 Jan 1855 16y LewVR 246
    Jacob (pauper) on Farm - 8 June 1817 LewVR 246
    Jacob s/ Joel/Mary - 10 Dec 1798 LewVR 245
    James C s/ James/Fanny - 3 Apl 1825 LewVR 245
    Jesse revol Soldier LEWISTON
    Joel - 26 July 1821 LewVR 245
    Joel W Jr - 15 Dec 1861 84y 1m NoNamePond
    Jonathan Capt - 31 Jan 1865 54y 11m Clough
        54y 11m Garcelon

Joseph s/o Zebelon - 3 ___ 1810 21y Randall Rd
Judath w/ Timothy - 28 May 1830 LewVR 245
Judith w/o Timothy ? ? Randall Rd
Leander d/ Horace - 18 July 1857 10y LewVR 246
Louis d/ Cephias - 20 Jan 1855 13y LewVR 246
Mary A w/o Wm - 6 Aug 1892 49-6-6 Riverside
Mary w/o Jonathan - 20 Sept 1873 50y 6m Garcelon
  56y 6m Clough
Mary w/o Joseph - 9 Oct 1882 62y 10m Clough
Maryette d/o Geo W - 11 Nov 1851 9y 9m Riverside
Melinder Jane d/ Jonatha - 19 Jan 1851 LewVR 246
Melissa d/o Francis 2d - 4 July 1857 67y LewVR 246
Mercy E d/o Geo W - 4 Nov 1851 7y 11m Riverside
Nathaniel Es/Joel/ Betsey - 1815 NoNamePond
Nathaniel s/ Joel/Betsey - 18 Mar 1815 LewVR 245
Otis A - 3 Apr 1879 51y Randall Rd
Patience d/ Joseph/Patie - 25 Nov 1818 LewVR 245
Patience w/ Joseph - 9 Dec 1818 LewVR 245
Paurretta M d/ Jonathan - 14 Feb 1851 12y LewVR 246
Phicas Esq - 22 June 1852 69y LewVR 246
Phineas - 22 June 1852 69y 3m Riverside
  - 7 Dec 1898 90y NoNamePond
Phineas Jr - 8 APr 1908 54-2-19 NoNamePond
Phineas s/ Phineas/Ruth J - 19 Mar 1851 13y 6m NoNamePond
Phineus Esq - 22 June 1852 69y 3m Riverside
Roxanna L d/o Phineas - 23 Feb 1851 9y 23d NoNamePond
Ruth w/o Phineas - 12 July 1893 80y 5m NoNamePond
s/o S D - 20 May 1865 1m 19m Herrick
Sarah w/o Jona - 31 Aug 1858 47y 7m Garcelon
Sarah w/o Jonathan - 31 Aug 1858 47y 7m Clough
Sidney S - 12 Sept 1863 25-1-28 Riverside
Susan w/o Francis - 14 Oct 1859 67y 9m Herrick
Susannah w/o Timothy - 16 June 1869 Randall Rd
Timothy ? ? Randall Rd
  - 7 Apr 1827 LewVR 245
  83y Randall Rd
William - 22 Aug 1918 79y 4m NoNamePond
Winfield Scott - 31 Dec 1875 34-3-14 Riverside
Zebulon - 23 June 1879 96y Randall Rd
Zebulon Jr s/ Zeb'n/Char - 14 May 1818 LewVR 245
WRIGLEY, Mary A [scotch] - 27 Dec 1869 consumption Riverside*
WYMAN, Albie - 1824-1866 Clough
  Ellen - 1836-1888 Clough
  Susan G w/o Sylvanus - 13 Mar 1873 38y 6m Clough
YOUNG, Lydia W w/o Isaac - 21 Jul 1869 23y Davis
  Rebecca d/ Isaac & Lydia - 23 Aug 1859 Davis
  Warren W - 15 Mar 1864 LewVR 250

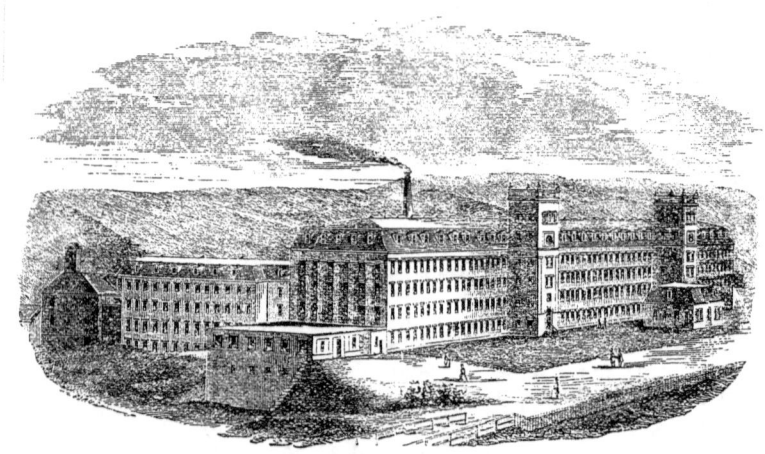

ANDROSCOGGIN MILLS.

LITTLE INSTITUTE, AUBURN.

LIST OF WORKS

AMES, Wilmot Spofford. Ames Genealogy. Gardiner, Me: typed by compiler, 1941

Andover, Mass. Vital Records. Topsfield, Mass, Historical Society. 1912

Androscoggin Probate Court Records 1854-1900+

APPLEBY, Miss Vital Records for Early Lisbon (Maine) Families. *Downeast Ancestry* Vol 1. No 5 Feb 1978 & Vol 2, no 1, June 1978

Attleboro, Mass Vital Records. Published by Essex Institute

Blasidell Papers Vol 11 # 2 Supplement. Somersworth, NH: Blasidell Family Assoc. May 1987

Bowdoin Vital Records to 1892. Portland, Me: Maine Historical Society. 1944

BRYANT, Mrs Harry. Garcelon & Haley Vital Records. *Downeast Ancestry* Vol 2, #4 Dec 1978

BUTLER. Francis G. History of Farmington, Maine 1776-1885. Farmington, Me: 1885

CARVER, Fred & his wife. Gravestone Inscriptions of Leeds. Maine. type by compilers. 1967

COLE, Frank. Cole Genealogy. Columbus, Ohio: by compiler. 1887

CORLISS, Au9usus. Old Times of North Yarmouth, Maine. printed 1877 1884

COX. Rachel. Lisbon. Maine. Vital Records. Rockland, Me: typed by M Groves. 1971

DAVIS, Amos. Diaries 1790-1810 at AHS

DANVILLE. Maine. Vital Records at Maine State Archives

DAVIS, Walter Goodwin. The Ancestry of Sarah Hildreth. Portland, Me: Anthoensen Press. 1958

DOANE. ALfred A. Doane Family Genealogy. Boston. MA: by Author. 1902

DURHAM, Maine. Vital Records at Maine State Archives

ELDER, Janus G. Early Lewiston Cemetery Records compiled before 1907.

ELDER, Janus G. *History of Lewiston*. Boston. Mass: Blue Store publisher. A. G. Daniels, printer. 1882

ELDER. Janus G. Early Lewiston Family Histories. at AHS

ELDER, Janus G. Letters written to him 1850's-1905 at AHS

ELDER, Janus G. Interviews with old settlers of Lewiston 1860-1880. at AHS

Frye Genealogy. typescript at Bates College Library

GARCELON, William. Notes on Early History of Lewiston at AHS

GARCELON, William. Records of Lewiston Miliitia 1800 & 1806

GRAY, Ruth. Maine Families in 1790 Vol 1. Camden, Me: Maine Genealogical Society. Picton Press 1988

GREELY, Rev Allen. Notes on North Yarmouth, Maine Families before 1860 at AHS

HATCH, William C. History of Industry, Maine. 1893

HILL, Mary P. Vital Records of Topsham, Maine to 1892. Portland, Maine: Maine Historical SocietY 1929

HILL, Mary P. Vital Records of Phippsburg, Maine to 1892. Maine Historical Published. 1935

HILL, Mary P. Vital Records of Georgetown, Maine to 1892. Maine Historical Published. 1939

HAWKINS, ALlen. Notes on Jipson/Jepson Families. 1988

HINCKLEY, E Charles. Hinckley Heritage & History. Fort Wort, TX: 1976

HODGKIN, Douglas. Notes on Ham/Hodskin/Hildreth Families

HODGKINS, Thomas. Diaries 1804-1826 at AHS

HOUGHTON, Vinal A. History of Lee, ME. Wilton, ME: Nelson Print 1926

HUNT, W. L. G. & T. B. Wyman. Genealogy of Hunt Family. Boston, MA: 1862-3

KIRK, Geneva & Gridley Barrows A.I.A. *Historic Lewiston: Its Government.* Auburn, Maine: published by the Historic Commission. printed by C.M.V.T.I. 1981-82

LANE, Patricia. Cemetery Records of Auburn, Maine. typed by compiler 1974 at AHS

LAPHAM, William B. History of Bethel, Me. 1891

LEAMON, James S. Historic Lewiston: a textile city in transition. Auburn, ME: Lewiston Historical Commission 1976

Lewiston/Auburn Directory 1860. Stanwood # Co. Publishers. Printed by Waldron. 1860

Lewiston, Maine - Schedules of Settlers of Townships in Pegypscot Patent [sic] cira 1805 - original at Maine Historical Society - photocopy at AHS

Lewiston Falls Journal. Lewiston, Maine 1847-1861

Lewiston Journal. Lewiston, Maine. 1861-1900+

Lewiston, Maine. US Censuses 1790-1860

Lewiston, Maine. Vital Records 1774-1851+

Lewiston, Maine: Maps 1795, 1805, 1858

LOUD. Eva Blake & Mabel E Blake. Early Cemetery Records of Ossipee, NH. 1976

LOWELL. Delmar. *Lowell Genealogy.* Tuttle Co 1899

MERRILL. Georgia Drew. editor. *History of Androscoggin Co.* [chapter on Lewiston is written by J G Elder] Boston, Mass: W. A. Ferguss & Co. 1891

MICHAUD, Charlotte. Historic Lewiston: Franco-American Origins. Auburn, ME: Central ME Vocational Technical Institute 1974

Minot, Maine, Vital Records at MSA

MOWER, Walter Lindley. History of Greene. 1938

NEVENS, Ira. Notes on Nevens family 1814-1892 at AHS

New Gloucester, Maine, Vital Records to 1850. manuscript at Maine Historical cira 1940

North Yarmouth, Maine - Vital Records to 1850. Warwick, RI: Society of Mayflower Descendants in RI 1980

OAKHAM, Mass., Vital Records to 1849. Worcester, MA: Franklin P Rice. 1905

PEARY, Leland Edwin. Notes on Freeman Families. D.A.R. typescript at Cutler Public Library. Farmington, Maine

PENLEY, Clarence. Historic Lewiston (Maine) - Its Fire Deptment. Auburn, Me: C.M.V.T.I. 1989

PLUMMER, Francis & Charles W. Lisbon (Maine) History. Lewiston, Maine: Twin City Printers. 197?

PRINCE, Marjorie. Gravestone Inscriptions: Rond Rd. Cemetery. Wales, Maine. *Downeast Ancestry* Vol 2 # 3 Oct 1978

RAND, John A. The Peoples Lewiston - Auburn, ME, 1875-1975. Published for Peoples Bank, 1975

RICHMOND, Katherine. *John Hayes of Dover, NH.* Tuttle Printing Co. 1936

SINNETT, Charles. The Riggs Family in Maine. Solon, Me: typed by Virginia Merrill no date

SKINNER, Ralph B Auburn (Maine) History 1869-1969. Lewiston. Me: Twin City Printery 1968

STACKPOLE, Everett. *Durham, Maine, History.* Lewiston. Maine: by the town. 1899

STARBIRD, Charles. Notes on Early Lewiston/Auburn (Maine) Families at AHS

STINCHFIELD, J C. History of Leeds (Maine). Lewiston, Me: by author. 1901

TAYLOR. Robert L. Early Families of Limington, Maine. Danville, Me: by the Author 1984

Tax Lists of Lewiston 1785, 1797, 1815 at AHS

WARREN, William & Samuel Warren. The History of Waterford (Maine). Portland, Me: Hoyt, Fogg, & Donham 1879 reprint 1977

WEYMOUTH, Ruth. Weymouth Family History. Provo, Utah: J Grant Stevenson. 1978

WHEELER, George Augusta & Henry Warren Wheeler. *History of Brunswick-Topsham-Harpswell.* Boston. Mass: Alfred Mudgers. 1878

WINDOR, Justin. History of Duxbury (Ma). Crosby & Nichols, P Samuel Drake. printer. 1849

WIRTH, Dorothy. Franklin County Vital Records. typescript at Cutler Public Library. Farmington, Maine

YOUNG, David C. Vital Records from *Maine Baptist Herald* 1826-1830+. Brunswick, Me:

YOUNG, David C. Vital Records from *Eastern Argus.* 1803-1824+ Portland, Me:

YOUNG. David C. Vital Records from *Morning Star* 1824-1871. Limerick, Me & Dover, NH:

YOUNG, David C. Vital Records from *Portland Gazette* 1798-1820. Portland, Me:

YOUNG. David C. Vital Records from Sherman Mills, Me. 1840-1900+. typed by compiler 1981

BATES COLLEGE.

BAPTIST CHURCH.

INDEX

Every name mentioned in the section covering the history of Lewiston is indexed. For the biographical sketches, we have cross-indexed names buried in the text. All names from pages 367-374 are indexed. The final section of the book, cemetery inscriptions, is not indexed since all names are in alphabetical order.

Abbott, Alice R 220 Arthur F 190 Cyrena 267 Daniel G 219 Elisha J 131 Elvira 239 Emma Blanchard 190 Evelin R 238 George 220 H B 32 43 Howard B 33 Jennie Isabel 219 Lizzie S 43 Sarah 118 214 Stephen I 20 21 55 William E 238
Abell, Hattie M 124
Abesey, Wm S 270
Abott, Mary 89
Ackley, Rachel 192 217
Adams, Aaron C 38 210 Byron S 24 Charles 158 Chloe 170 Clarissa Ann 315 Edward 170 Eleanor Melvina 175 Emilie L 180 George A W? 175 George E 38 George H 211 Geroge H 211 Gertrude 298 Hiram 369 James 315 John H 277 John S 25 210 Louisa M 211 Lucy R 277 Maria Augusta 210 Mary 158 Mary Elizabeth 211 Rebecca 241 Rebecca E 317 Sanford 298 Silas 317 Sophia 229
Adderton, Ruby 99
Addition, Ann C 284
Additon, Ruby B 32 Sarah J 191 192
Adkins, Rachel 91 Wlm E 91
Adrich, H L Jr 55
Aiken, A J 42 Sarah C 42 43
Aino, Hiram 117 Mary Mehitable 117
Alden, Almeda 177 Christina 167 Eunice 169 Eunice J 169 Gilman 98 Sarah Jane 98
Aldrich, Dorcas 137 Emily E 103 George 103
Alexander, Charles 125 Emma E 357 Thomas W 357

Alexander (continued) Hattie B 125
Allen, Achea Elizabeth 195 Addie 266 Alice 289 291 292 296 298 Ansel 240 Aveline B 338 Charles 338 Cynthia 128 Daniel 23 Dorcas 207 208 Eliza H 278 Emeline Oakes 266 Emily 258 Emma L 195 Evan 199 George A 266 George M 195 Hannah 310 Harper 240 Henry Monroe 195 Isaac 278 Jane 240 Jennie E 301 John 31 Joseph 258 L B 34 Lemuel 128 Libbins 192 Lizzie 205 Lucinela 199 Lydia 258 Mary 192 205 Mary B 244 Mary E 281 Moses 310 R 236 R J 206 240 S--- 205 Sarah 240 Sophiah 258 W H C 77
Allexander, Priscilla 260
Alley, Margaret 335
Ally, Rose 335
Ambach, Alice May 349 Julius 349
Amback, Facie Anna 183 Hermon 183
Ames, 77 Abner C 195 Alfred 260 Anna 350 Aseneth 264 266 Azeneth 266 Betsey 246-266 Betsy 195 265 266 Captain 16 Craft 367 368 Deliverance 162 164 Elizabeth 265 Ezra 15 Hannah 160 163 164 177 James 16 18 45 126 128 163 303 James Jr 246 368 Jane 163 John 260 Joseph 265 Lucy 15 126 127 Lydia B 195 Margaret 103 Marinda 143 Martha 246 Mary 260 Peggy 303 Susannah 126 127 Winslow 16 18 19 27 103 246 367

Amos, John 231 Lydia Ann 231
Anderson, Alice J 177 Elihu 152 Etta H 109 Hald B 253 Henrietta 109 Hulda 87 Jaila S 152 Martha G 263 Mary 177 268 269 Mary A 295 Robert 18 45 153 263 Sarah 153 William 268 Wm 269
Andrew, Hannah 314 Mehitable 224
Andrews, Benjamin 127 Betsey 355 Andrews Charles 31 33 Dorcas 355 Elvira 116 Freeman 29 John Jr 258 Kasiah 127 Mr 32 Olive V 258 Sally 127 Shirley 373
Angell, Thomas L 84
Angers, Pierre X 24
Anis, Elmira W 97 Robert 97
Anna, Mary 210
Annes, Daniel 144 Polly 144
Annie, Hellen E 172 Isabel H 172 Solomon 172
Annis, Deliverance 15 Helen E 167 Isabella H 167 Martha 125 Sarah A 125 Solomon 167
Anthoine, A W 78
Apling, Augusta Ann 189 Herbert 189
Ardway, Harriet 231
Armies, J H 41
Armstrong, George D 25 Helen F 269 Mr 76
Arno, Effie J 135 Elmer 135 Zaccheus 119
Arnold, Effie J 135 Elmer 135 Jane C 97 Loyd 97 Matthew 82
Arris, Charles 156 Eleanor 341 Emily Jane 357 Patrick 156 341 Robert J 357 Sarah 341 Sarah Mariah 156
Ashly, Nancy 145
Ashton, Henry 349 Jennie 352 Marcia A 349
Atkins, Anna 257 Sally 323
Atkinson, Cynthia J 204 John 252 John Milton 204 Lydia 252 Mary 336 Minnie 186 Sally 143 144 257 322 William Jr 368
Atkinsson, Wm 367
Atwater, Marcia Ann 356

Atwood, Abbie 151 Abigail 128 Abram 78 Alfred 180 Almira 180 182 Amanda 180 182 David 346 Eda M 234 Hannah Shaw 253 Horace 257 James L 188 John 229 John Q A 128 Martha A 93 Martha G 346 Mary A 188 Mary S 180 Rosetta 229 Thomas 93 Vesta Ann 257 Wm H H 234
Auburn, Abbie H 344
Austemput, George 232
Austen, Maria 299 Sewall 299
Austin, Annis 92 95 Cindrella 185 Cindrilla 185 Edith 300 Fanny Maria 359 George F 359 Jane 119 M 132 Mary E 153 Permelia 102 Rebecca 132 256 Shedrick 185
Avery, Ada 89
Ayer, Annie B 347 D M 54 64 David M 20 57 67 Mr 56 Mrs David M 37 Susan 308 Wells W 20
Babb, 143 Andrew 305 Martha E 305
Backus, Mary H 361 363 Rebecca 250
Bacon, Bishop 44 45 Sarah 270
Badger, Jane 168 196 197 Mary N 138
Bagley, 14 48 Enoch 358 Helen L 358 Jonathan 12
Bagster, Harriet Ann 108
Bailey, Alexander 223 Alice A 277 Benjamin A 20 21 Betsy 170 Charles A 133 Dudley P 208 Elmer R 358 Emery 74 Emma L 131 Eunice 135 Frances Ellen 133 Hannah 208 Harriet 117 Hewitt 103 Lucy 288 M E D 69 Martin 288 Melissa A 358 Myron T 277 Sally 223 Sarah 288 William C 22
Baily, David 99 Mary 99
Baine, James 205 Pauline 205
Baird, Mary 339
Baker, 336 Amos 289 Carrie 94 Clara 120 Cordelia 250 Cornelia W 134 E Folsom 36

Baker (continued)
Ellen A 254 Ellery R 238
Florence M 238 Frances
Estell 289 Frank 134 Fred B
201 Hannah 356 James 254
John C 254 John R 203 Lydia
129 Mehitable 238 S A 24
Stella M 201
Balde, Charles 331 Ellen 331
Nellie 331
Balkam, U 42 Uriah 38
Bancroft, Eva 318 George R 318
Banges, Octavia H 138
Bangs, Ann 150 Chauncy 113
Emma 113 Hiram 93 Jane 93
Rachel 150 Sylvanes 150
Bank, Martha J 125
Banks, Ellen 283 Evans C 283
Helen A 283 285 Lydia 116
Rachael C 272 Sarah B 229
Bar---, Polly 172
Baraby, Anna Varney 299 David 299
Barber, Jane G 251
Barberick, Elizabeth M 297 John M 297
Barbour, Charles 315 Mary 315 Susan 315
Bard, Roseta 353 Samuel 373
Barden, Ester 197
Bardwell, Josiah 55
Barker, A D 56 67 74 Alva D 24
Ann 192 C I 54 56 60 67 68
Caleb 17 119 Casandaria 221
Cordelia J 130 Cyrus 15 50
221 245 263 Cyrus I 21 63
David 246 Dorcas 268 269
Elizabeth 89 Esther 287 292
George A 184 Hannah 236 240
Jacob 15 18 50 164 192 236
254 Jacob Jr 368 Jane G 190
250 John 163 Judith 81 192
Keziah 119 Lucinda 129
Lydice 221 Martha 134 Mary E
184 Nelson P 15 50 Pauline
164 Phebe 283 284 287 Priscilla 246 Rachel 245 263
Rebecca 255 Rebecca C 255
Rhoda 123 Sally 163 248
William 268 Wm 269 Zebadiah 130

Barnard, Edwin M 147 Jane 147
Barnes, Alphlia 188 Aphia 188
John 337 Lizzie 194 Lydia 99
Nathaniel 188 Peltish 337
Pettiah 99 Priscilla 363 Priscilla A 363 Rebecca 102
Rhoda 337 Sally 142 William D 194
Barnett, Mattie 228
Barns, Priscilla A 359
Barr, Bell 118
Barrell, E 33 Elijah 61
Barrett, Clara Abbie 293 Dr 45 71
Harry W 293 Herbert E 293
Mary Ellen 293
Barrington, Elizabeth 270
Barron, Lydia 199 202 Oliver 18 19 Shearman 368
Barrows, Albert 327 Dr 71 Flavilla 327 Gridley 280 Tilpia 312
William C 36
Barthold, Mary E 244
Bartlett, Artemus 218 Cynthia
148 Denman 307 Florence I
246 Horace B 20 21 22 23 45
63 Julia 218 June 251 Mary
237 3077
Bartol, Elisabeth 285
Barton, Isaac 30 Samuel 373
Basford, Frances A 258 Joseph A 258
Bassett, Gustavus 221 Helen M 221
Basworth, David 313 Katherine 313
Batchedler, Aseneth 208 Abe B
328 Achsah Fields 208 Ada
183 Armanda M 222 Charles
222 Eben 183 Edward 208
Hannah 274 Rebecca 328
Bates, Ann A 286 Benjamin E 54
55 56 84 Caleb 210 Clarence
135 Elizabeth 210 George 40
Harvey 286 Lillie E 135 Nancy
G 286 Rebecca T 220 Sarah 149
Batten, Abraham 368
Battle, Abigail H 88
Baxter, Charles G 325 Sophronia 325
Beade, Charles 303 Margaret 303

Beade (continued)
  Margaret Jane 303
Beal, Catherine 97 Joanna 268
  269 Lovena 266 Mary E 357
  360 Moses 85 Sarah 85
Beals, Annie M 102
Bean, Ana Stone 311 Betsy 85
  195 Cynthia 313 Eunice 241
  George 311 313 George W 20
  30 33 55 369 Grace 311 James
  241 Jeptha 259 John 258 307
  309 Lizzie D 259 Lydia 326
  Lydia J 290 Martha A 241
  Nancy 307 309 Ruth 226
  Samuel 367 Sarah 258 Susan H
  246
Bearce, 78 Ada 104 Agnes M 278
  Betsey 42 Byron 278 Clara W
  246 George B 78 Mr 80 Pitt
  104 S R 49 80 Samuel R 42 43
  67 Wm 246
Bearth, Rebecca 113 114
Becker, Hartwell S 306 Lavona
  306 Susie M 306
Beckett, Emeline 254 John T 254
Beechan, Mary 294 297 Michael
  297
Beecher, Rev Mr 34
Beechman, Marcetta 294
Beede, J W 68
Behcard, Celia 191
Belden, Emily 244 245
Beliveau, Albert H 70
Bell, Mary A 317
Belleau, Francois X 25
Bemis, Luke 53 Mabel Gertrude
  115 Eben 197
Benjamin, Ester 197 Frances 197
  Mary 87
Bennett, D 369 Hannah 145 John
  240 Mary A 305 Mary Hannah
  254 Mary Lois 320 Nathaniel
  145 Rachel 240 Sarah 29
  Thomas 320
Benson, Charles C 24 25 60 Jome
  203
Bernard, Sister 68
Berry, 269 Betsey 126 Caroline
  269 Charles 268 269 Charles H
  204 Cynthia 204 G G 22 Giles
  G 23 Joanna 299 Josiah 91

Berry (continued)
  Margaret E 237 Martha 237-
  239 241 Mary Jane 89 91 94
  Molly 91 Olive Caroline 268
  Phelene 268 Philena 268 269
  Roxcyllanis 130 Soloman 237
  Wilber F 33
Berthold, Mary E 245
Bibber, Dorcas Banks 295 Esther
  287 Geo 287 Hannah 343
  Martha J 325 Stover 343
  Thomas 295
Bickford, Aaron 211 Carrie E 175
  Charles B 175 Clarence 273
  Daisey E 196 Eliza 42 Eunice
  105 Fannie 237 Fanny 237
  Hortense 222 Kate 273 Maria
  103 Mary 143 144 Mary H 337
  Mercy Ai 97 Sally 211 Thesey
  338
Bicknell, Emery 338 Emery O 20
  Margaret 338 Polly 338
Bidwell, Sarah Ann 167
Bigelow, Ephraim 118 Esther 118
  Sarah 119
Bikett, John 369
Billing, Catherin 270
Billings, Florence Angella 193
  Mary 292
Billington, Lydia 258
Bird, Maria 136
Bisbee, A 369
Bishop, Joanna 138 139 John 308
  309 Judith A 169 Mary C 308
  Mary Caroline 309 Nathaniel
  169
Bjerke, Alice 292 Oscar G 292
Black, Sally 101
Blackstone, Sarah 146
Blackwell, Sarah 142
Blaine, James G 248
Blair, Betsey Briggs 178 William
  369 William H 178
Blaisdell, Eliza 166 James R 41
  John T 209 Josiah 30 Lucinda
  T 258 Mary Gone 209 Miriam
  (Molly) 251 Mrs James R 41
  Peter R 270 Rebecca 283 S A
  42 Sally 263 Sarah 227 252
  Stephen 252 Walter R 17 18 19
  263 William 17 18 50 283 368

Blake, A K P 58 245 Abiah 218
Almeda 277 Betsey 292 Carrie
E 328 Chaneller 218 Charles
331 Charles H 330 Eben W
328 Ella A 330 Ellen 331
George H 155 Granville 58 H
M 32 33 Henretta 155 Isaac M
24 John 373 John S 292 Joseph
203 L L 58 67 Lizzie H 192
Lothrop L 20 Lucy A 241
Lydia M 245 Mary 297 Mary A
292 Minnie V 267 Minta M 262
Naomi 321 Nellie 331 Orlando
262 Orlando F 297 Polly
White 203 Sally 218 Susan J
231 Timothy 321 William 373
Blanchard, David 190 Enos O 277
Hannah 129 264 Hannah S 222
Joseph 264 Joseph K 22 23
Lydia A 277 Metilda Chandler
190 Roxannah 330 Thersa
Davce 190
Blaney, Hattie A 140 John 6
Blasidell, Walter R 368
Blethan, Dorcas Arvilla 183
Jonathan 183 Mary 183 Daniel
224 Dorcas Arvilla 183 Doroth
290 Eleanor 229 Hannah 182
Increase 373 John 100 182 224
373 Jonathan 183 Jos 224
Joseph 20 21 22 229 Mary 100
161 183 230 Nancy E 157
Polly 160 224 Rhoda 235 Sally
224 Stephen 32
Bliffith, Bathany 135
Bliss, Miriam 221 Zeba 53 369
Zeba F 62 369
Blodgett, Edwin 158 Julia 278
Julia H 158 Lewis W 259
Mary H 259
Bloomer, Benj 240 Eunice 240
Lydia 239 240
Blythen, Helen 363
Boardman, George W 78
Boies, Lewella F 223 Ludon
Willard 223 Augusta Ann 189
Frank 189
Bolles, Rev Mr 40
Bolster, Maude 159 W W 159
Bolton, Agnes 251 Horace W 32
33

Bond, Florence A 345 George D
345 Molly 359 William 46 359
Bonellie, George 254 Isabelle B
254
Bones, Melinia 162
Bonner, Lizzie 319
Bonney, Deborah 234 Ichabod 253
Isaac 234 Joseph 207 Louisia
J 207 M Etter 142 143 Mary A
81 313 Nancy B 248 Polly B
252 253 S G 68 248 Thorndike
A 142 143 Turner 314
Booker, Eliphalet 209 Mary 209
Booth, Samuel 23 24 37
Boothby, Emeline R 117 J Frank
24 25 67 Samuel 69 Sarah F
324
Boston, Emily 151 George H 151
Bourne, Lydia 335
Bourque, Alice 255
Boutelle, John 310 Martha 310
Bowden, Ella 200 Horace 200
Bowdoin, Eunice Bubier 188
Bowen, Annie D 262 W H 31 42
Bowers, Charles 79
Bowie, Rachael 315 Vesta 117
Bowker, Harriet 348 James 348
Boyington, Hannah Patterson 208
Boynton, Hannah Patterson 208
Brackenbury, Bertha Viola 217
Joseph A 217
Brackett, 106 270 Adah C 326
Bertha 184 Elbert L 326 H W
352 Isabella B 352 Lizzie 42
Lydia 254 M L 352 Mary 217
Mary Jane 184 Nancy 106 S
369 Walker 184
Brackley, Almire 110 Elmira 110
Orin 110 Orren 110 Orrin 110
Bradbury, Benjamin 289 Betsey D
289 Cotton 200 Ella 200
Hannah 289 Loisa M 267 268
Louisa 303 Molly 91 Olive H
99 Royal J 267 Samuel N 289
Bradford, Alma P 169 B F 74
Benjamin 299 Betsey 314
Clara 169 Deacon R 37 Ellen
169 H C 71 73 Herbert C 21
Horace 169 J C 58 Richard 71
Syrena B 299
Bradly, May L 115

Bradshaw, Joseph 187 Lafa S 187
Bragg, Mary 209
Brailey, Jennie 102
Braley, Julia A 102
Brann, Abbie E 213 Alvin W 364 Ardella B 190 194 Bertie 301 F 190 Francis 190 Ina 301 John E 213 Louisa J 364
Branton, Angelica 160
Brett, Esther 312
Brewer, Ellen 283 Horace W 77
Brian, Theresa 240
Bridges, Abiezer 29
Briggs, Alice M 278 Betsey 314 Betsy 314 Calvin 295 Daniel 53 314 325 Elijah 287 335 Ella M 180 Ellee E 180 Estella C 94 Flavilla Jane 142 H C 369 Helen 158 Jane 326 John 94 John A 51 276 369 Jotham 359 Julius K 78 Katie 142 Lissie E 232 Lurana 178 Lydia 269 286 295 296 Margueritte E 233 Mary 284 Ossian N 25 Phillip A 210 Polly 293 Rachel 287 Rhoda 326 Sally 335 Sarah 359 Seth 142 Silvie 221 222 Sylva 221 222
Bright, Mrs 263
Brimijohn, Eliza 116 Mary T 355 Thomas 116
Brinn, Abbie 238
Brock, Sally M 188
Brooks, A 246 Abigail 236 Ai 21 22 30 154 178 369 Ai Jr 67 Albert S 116 Anna 190 Armanda 209 Barber 369 Catherine 147 148 Eliza 246 Fidelia 119 Ham 19 21 87 353 354 Hiram T 209 Jane 30 154 John 119 147 192 John 3rd 192 Lovinia B 116 Margaret 87 Martha 147 178 192 246 Mary 16 332 Mary L 178 179 Nancy 93 190 192 Orpha 218 219 224 256 Sally 217 Silva M 353 Susan 332 Sylvia E 354 William 190 256 368
Brophy, John 22 23
Broser, Falora Eunice 288

Brown, 331 Abbie 147 Abigail 81 343 Almon 308 309 Amanda 271 Anna 150 Annie 240 Austin 221 Benj 287 Betsey 282 Clara 355 Clara B 267 Clementine 343 Eliza 302 Elizabeth 192 Emma F 94 Esther 360 Geo 94 Helen 158 Henry F 343 Jane 297 Jennie 257 259 John 140 257 Lillian Florence 213 Luther 240 Lydia A 105 Marcia 320 Mary 179 180 187 330 331 Mary C 297 308 Mary Caroline 309 Mary J 113 May 129 Mercy 204 Myra 166 Nancy 152 Nancy M 221 Phebe 287 Rufus 204 Sally 140 184 Samuel 302 Sarah 251 Susan A 90 Thomas N 61 Willard G 213 Wm F 297
Bruce, Celia 146 Wm C 146
Brun, Katherine 135
Bryant, Annie 245 Ellen M 313 Samuel 136
Bryes, Kate 142
Bubier, Abbie 115 Andrew 367 368 Aseneth 299 Betsey 228 Chistopher 326 Christopher 116 368 Deannah 133 George 115 228 George Jr 115 George M 115 Gilbert 298 Happy 326 Lucy 249 Martha 342 Mary 298 Miriam 342 Polly 116 Rebecca 115 228 Samuel 228 Sarah 115
Bubur, Caroline S 106 Darius 106
Buchanan, 80
Buck, Ambrose 271 Eunice L 271 John 7
Bucklin, Margaret 354
Buckman, E T 369
Bucknam, Arabella 219 Clarella 206 Eleanor 206 Elisa 146 Em 146 Sarah 146 William 206 219
Bucks, Mehitable 238
Budlong, R A 37 55 Rhodes A 20 57
Buker, Annie 141 Bethiah J 334 335 Betsey 359 Betsy 360 Edwina J 227 Hannah 359 Mrs

Buker (continued)
  S E 41 Polly 359 S E 41 Sally 359
Bumper, John 278 Mariam 278
Bumpus, Alvah 230 Daria 245 Harriet Haskell 245 Mary 230
Bunker, Clarissa 197 Isaac 310 Mary 228 Phemah G 310
Bupert, Ester A 245 Saul P 245
Burbank, A 79 369 Adino J 271 Alcander 71 Alexander 249 Alma Esther 251 Augusta J 324 Clarissa Ann 271 Edith J 176 Kimball 176 Vesta 79 249
Burgess, Achsah 166 Ann J 211 Bishop 36 Caleb C 211 Charles C 37 Flavilla Jane 142 J S 41 42 Joseph 31 Laura A 41 Lydia 152 Mrs Charles C 37 Seth 142
Burke, John J 23 Richard 22 23
Burleigh, Nellie 153
Burnham, Hannah L 218 Joanna 273 276 279 William J 21
Burns, John 203 Phebe 203
Burrell, Kesiah 325 Rachael 208 Ruben 325 Samuel 208
Buswell, Emily 149 Mr 149
Butler, Abram 268 Augusta 360 Charles 360 Fanny 344 Frances Dolly 268 Francis 251 Francis Gould 339 Mary 244 Warren S 42
Butterfield, Mary 264 266 Rebecca 169 Zachariah 169
Butts, Abigail 112 114 Caroline A 112 Harriet 112 John 112 114 Lucy J 114
Byam, Sally 218
Byran, Mary Purington 152 Willard 152
Byrnes, Ellen 253
Byron, Edward 37
Call, E B 159 Mabel 159
Callaham, Aug 369
Callahan, 78 Cornelius J 24 D J 69 Dennis J 22 23 George A 21 79 T F 68 Timothy F 23 24
Callahen, A 369
Callahn, Timothy O 23
Calvert, Grace 341 Thomas E 341

Campbell, Abby Frances 142 Abigail 323 Adalade A 318 Addie A 111 Charles W 318 Ebeneser 323 Flora 158 Florence Gertrude 278 Hannah 336 Hestor 142 James 221 John 69 Lizzie 278 Luella C 221 Margaret 242 Otis 278 William 336
Candler, Polly 295
Cannon, Louisa 326
Cappers, Chas 101 George W 25 Hilda 101
Carcelon, Sally 159
Carle, Emma 102
Carlton, John 305 Louisa Jane 305
Carold, Jenny 185
Carolls, Priscilla H 125
Carpenter, H S 38 Olivia 117
Carr, Harriet 341 Rufus 21 341 Vesta C 288
Carter, Seth M 67
Cartland, Cyrus 29 Stephen 29
Carvelle, Mercy 335
Carvelli, Georgia A 143
Carver, Mary A 93 Willard 93
Carville, Abbie J 325 Abigail 206 Benjamin 206 Charlotte 144 Daniel W 147 David W 228 Drusilla 147 Ella 311 Esekiel 124 Eva M 327 Hanah 161 162 Hannah 161 162 Hannah F 161 162 Harriet 303 Harriet N 145 Henry 17 147 148 360 James 19 300 303 327 John 161 211 John W 272 Joseph M 325 Julia Ann 111 Lois 124 Luce 151 Mary 259 Mercy 148 Minerva 300 Nancy 137 147 O S 130 137 Olive Armanda 130 Otis 145 Priscilla 161 211 Priscilla H 125 Rachel 339 Rosa Ellen 176 Sally 176 360 Sarah 255 Sarah N 228 Sewall 211 Simon 111 144 Tamah 211
Carville Watie A 272 William 17 William Jr 176 Wm 228
Cary, Daniel 53
Case, Rev Mr 26
Cash, Orrin 95

Casley, Deborah 162
Casson, Emeline 231 Emerline 329 George 329 John F 231 Olive A 329 Sarah J 329
Caston, Emma J 42
Caswell, Christiana 30 Dora 313 Henry 337 Rosannah 337
Cate, Carter E 31
Catland, Thomas R 78
Caverly, Susan 157 Susan E 80
Caville, Edith M 321 Edwin 321
Ceballos, Antonio Fernandes 147 Mary C 147
Celman, Enoch 160 Mary Caroline 160
Chabot, L T 76
Chadbourn, Levi 26 Mary Ann 105 Vesta 187 William 187
Chadbourne, Amanda J 342 Augustus 135 Edward 106 Elisa 262 Eliza 262 John 239 Joseph 262 326 Luce 239 Mary 135 Mary Abigail 106 Mary Ann 105 Mehitable 326 Orrington 342 Rebecca A 106 Samuel 106 Sarah A 106
Chadburn, Augusta 230 Thomas 367 368
Chaffee, Edward D 65
Chaffin, Nancy 241
Chamberlain, Charlott 343 Dorcus B 253 Hannah 205 Jacob 248 Joseph 30 287 Lucy 34 Nancy 205 207 Olive 30 Phillip 253 Sewall 343 Susanna 308 309 William 248 368
Chamberlane, Alice May 235 Joseph W 235
Chamberlin, 78 Percy 287 W M 67 William M 26
Chamerlan, Hannah 207
Chandler, Charles B 257 Deborah 325 326 Elbridge G 257 Elvira F 173 177 Emily A 185 George A 22 67 77 George C 20 George H 20 Hannah 326 Jesse 363 John 45 121 Joseph C 173 Lonantha 154 Lovinia B 103 Mary 249 251 296 363 Mary Ellen 257 May 251 Minnie 109 Mr 259 Perry 43 Polly 295

Chandler (continued)
Rebecca 265 Reubin 326 Seth 20 21 23 103 Susan 173 Timothy T 109
Chandley, James 23
Chanell, Henry A 42 Mrs Henry A 42
Chanlder, Charles 154
Channel, Henry A 162 Henry H 162 Sarah 162
Channell, Carrie E 215 Olive 162 Olive H 162
Chapin, David Seymour 186 Isabel 237 Julia 177 Minerva Axa 186
Chapman, Alice 99 Daniel 153 Dorothy 200 Gavon 265 Joseph 200 Marguerti A 200 Minerva A 182 Nellie 153 Sarah 265
Chappin, Adiman 290 Lydia J 290 Nancy D 290 Nancy Dow 290
Charles, Abbie B 135 Maria 318
Charmont, B 45
Chase, Almira 295 Amanda 168 Benjamin F 314 Charles E 131 Elisabeth 304 Geo C 84 Hannah 314 Hannah A 314 Harriet 314 J H 78 Jane 322 Jerusha 281 Mary 124 131 322 Meribah E 277 Sidney S 277 Stephen 74 W T 36 William 304
Cheetham, Jane 309 Joseph 309 Linneus 20 21 Sarah A 309 Sarah Ann 309
Cheney, Asa 373 Edward 284 Ella Endora 284 Mary E 230 O B 41 83 Octavia 284 290 Oren B 67 84 Stephen 230
Chesley, Ann 310 Annie 308 309 Joseph 147 Naomi R 147
Chick, Sarah J 182
Chickering, John W 38
Child, Hannah 209 210
Childs, Frances Judith 268 Isaac 268 Lemuel 95 Martha 95
Chipman, Hannah 169 Viola A 219
Choate, Beatrice 136 Mabel 358 W E 136
Chough, Clara Elisabeth 132

Christensen, Cecilia 178
Church, Abigail 111 Elisa 143
  Ellen B 170
Churchill, Lewis 297 Ruth 297
Chutham, Joseph 309 Sarah Ann
  309
Cilley, Horatio G 37
Clanage, Melinda H 296
Claray, Affie E 306 Willie Frank
  306
Clark, Abbie 335 Amanda 263
  Amos 291 Arletta 174 Arlitta
  B 174 Auran 291 Calvin W 23
  Catherine 334 Charles 165 337
  Charles J 32 33 Daniel 328 E
  D 369 Edward 20 41 Eunice
  328 George A 20 Harriett 247
  Harrison 181 Ingraham 263
  John M 361 Joseph 207 Lois
  185 Mary 135 213 Mary Ann
  165 Mary Harris 291 Mary W
  181 Mrs Edward 41 Olive 291
  361 Phebe 328 R W 74 Samuel
  202 Sarah 202 207 328 337
  Thomas 328
Clarke, Charles 248 Frances O
  282 Nellie R 248
Clason, O B 234
Clay, Katie 132 Laura M 362
  Martha Ellen 351 May 351
  Samuel 351
Clement, Sarah 100
Cleveland, Mary Ann 146 Nellie
  A 255 W H S 146
Clifford, Armenda A 203 Clarimond 230 David A 203 Hannah
  203 N C 43 69 Susanna 151
Clough, Anna 292 Ann Augusta
  150 Benjamin F 22 Betsey 148
  Charles 150 Clara 132 Ebeneser 292 Ebenezer 282 283
  Jeremiah 125 Josiah 125 327
  328 Mary 125 278 Mary M 327
  328 Matilda 148 Sarah 282 283
  287 292 293 William W 23
Cloutier, Joseph E 23
Clover, Aurelia H 360
Coal, Lemuel 368
Coates, Lithian 293
Cobb, Charles C 22 Charles H
  318 Chitman 367 E 369

Cobb (continued)
  Edward 33 Eleanor 290 294
  Emily 270 George W 125
  Hannah G 125 Hester A 136 J
  L H 21 22 57 67 69 John F 69
  Lydia 292 296 Samuel 369
  Sarah 32 Wealthy 318
Cobbett, Almira B 360 Daniel 360
  Horace 373
Cobbree, Eleanor 344
Cobe, Charles 318 Wealthy 318
Cobly, Valentine G 111
Coburn, Abby 41 Abigail 242 363
  Alanson 360 Albert 291 Alice
  C 250 Anna 236 Asa 276
  Bartholomew 292 Bridget 214
  240 Charles 250 291 Eleaser
  240 Eleazer 214 Eliphalet 238
  Eliphlet 350 Elizabeth Harris
  291 Eunice 238 Geo 118 I W
  41 Ira W 20 J G 55 64 Jane
  358 Jemima 332 333 Joana
  238 Joel 236 Jonas 14 Jonathan 212 Joseph 236 247
  Joshua 126 Josiah G 20 21 23
  37 57 67 Letty 276 Lydia A
  349 Mary 126 250 292 Mary A
  118 Mercy 212 287 Miriam 169
  Nathan 14 Olive 236 Polly 350
  Prudence 240 Reuben 238 363
  367 Reuben Jr 368 William
  287
Cochrain, Martha 99
Cochran, Silas D 99
Cocker, Charles 118 Marcia E
  118
Codman, Randolph A 158
Coffin, Annie 280 Edith May 284
  Emily Ann 286 James 203
  Joan 294 Joanna 203 304
  Manley 286 Mary E 341
  Rebecca 198 Samuel 198 Sarah
  139 140 141 Tristam 341
Cogurn, J G 60
Cohen, Charles 201 Clarina 204
  Mercy 201 Phinneas 204
Colburn, Flora 218
Colby, Adaline 138 Clarissa A
  365 Edward 184 Hannah 321
  Henry S 358 John 193 Joseph
  248 Lucy Jane 184 Mary 193

Colby (continued)
　358 Mary A 288 Mehitabel 159
　Mehitable 120 Phebe 107
　Rebecca 248 William 138 365
Cole, Abbie J 344 345 Anna 156
　292 Benjamin 17 27 28 90 301
　Boynton 301 Charlotte 246
　Elizabeth 355 Ella 148 Hannah
　292 295-297 Harriet 326 Hulda
　42 Isaac 320 Isabella 124 Job
　16 John 255 295 355 John E
　148 Josephine M 320 Keziah
　90 Lemuel 368 Lora J 138
　Lydia H 328 Margaret 255
　Mary 117 301 332 Orin 363
　Osea 169 Rhoda 245 246 Ruth
　28 Samuel 292 Samuel Jr 246
　Sarah 215 295 Solomon J 138
　Sumner H 169
Coleman, George 113 Mary 113
Collen, Mary 343
Collier, Rebecca 121
Collins, Almond 321 Azelia 193
　Helen 198 Hellen S 198 Henry
　177 Lillia 177 Mary 130 132
　133 165 Mary Ann 283 Miriam
　249 Sam 198 Sophronia 320
　321 W H 36 William 22 23
Colson, Mercy 347
Comforth, Birks 307 Harriet C
　307
Commens, James H 362 Olive V
　362
Compr, Winne 307
Conant, Abigail 155 F A 78 Frank
　A 22 Mary 311 Mrs L W 58
　Oliver 155 Olivia 143 Roxanna
　133
Conck---, Ann 183
Condit, Almira 280
Conent, Rebecca 331 William
　331
Conkling, Carrie Elmira 273 J
　Frank 273 Joseph H 273 Mary
　Olive 273
Conley, Anabelle 200 Leonard
　200 May 155 Nellie 257
Conly, Eleanor 204
Conner, Julia 137
Connor, Mary 250 Phillip 250

Cook, A M 285 Abby 359 Albert
　22 Cordelia 179 180 Cyrus S
　179 180 Eliza D 251 Eva F
　102 Hanson 102 James 332
　John G 67 251 Lucy A 332
　Lucy H 332 Lydia 355 Mary
　102 Nancy 102 Polly 284 285 S
　W 79 Silas W 23
Coolbaugh, Jemima 313
Cooledge, Lenore 141
Coomb, Mary M 135
Coombs, Almeda 244 Emma
　Elisabeth 124 George M 25
　George W 25 Georgia 180
　Helen A 243-245 James W
　124 John M 244 Lillian B 301
　Lucy 281 Lucy D 113 Lucy T
　113 Lydia 303 306 Margaret
　190 Mary 301 Matilda P 244
　Mercy 354 Nathan 180 Peggy
　101 William D 113
Cooper, J Hannah 87 Jane 309
　Miriam 156 Serina F D 320
　Walter 320
Corbett, Charlotte 335 Dorcas 95
　Hannah 209 Joanna 95 Otis
　209 Peter 95 Wm 95
Corey, J A 43
Corlis, Abigail H Nason 348 H
　Florence 348 Howard 348
Corliss, Abigail T 216 Anna M
　274 Annie 274 Clara Permelia
　348 Edward S 216 Hattie
　Florence 348 Homer F 348
　Mary A 318
Corning, Daniel 199 200 Eliza A
　199 Judith 199 200
Cornish, Adelbert D 23 Belinda
　338 Hannah 338 John 338
　Phebe 106 107 William 338
Cornwell, Jane 312
Corsen, Polly 224
Corvill, Samuel 360 Sophronia
　360
Corville, Hanah 161 Hannah 161
　Hannah F 161
Cory, Hester Ann 123 Mary 350
　Walter 123
Coston, Debby A 225
Cotton, Amanda G 251 Benjamin

Cotton (continued)
 251 Benjmain R 20 Isaac 45
 46 50 368 James B 30 369
 John B 21 251 Lois H 109
 Martha 335 Minnie 225 Sarah
 335 Sarah E 144 Thomas 216
Courson, Ivory 302 Mehitable 301
 302 Mercy C 302 Thankful 301
 373 Zebulon 301 302
Covil, Ruth 143
Cowan, D 51 David 21 63 Mr 56
Cowell, Rebecca 159
Cox, Cyrus 334 Martha 334
Coy, Anna 187
Coyne, Michael A 24
Crabtree, Frances 197 Greene 197
Craft, Amanda 189 Elizabeth 85
 86 James 189 Sarah Gaetta
 196 William 196
Crafts, W D 25
Craig, May M 129 William P 65
Cram, Mary A 127 Smith 127
Crawford, Mary 188
Crediford, Catherine 300 Deneteus 300
Crocker, Crosby N 228 Elizabeth
 228 Hannah 32 L J R 32
 Lizzie H 228 Sally 316
Crockett, Belinda 218 David 318
 David Jr 218 Edward 247
 Esther 318 Etta A 250 Eunice
 167 George W 21 Harriet 247
 Louisa 318 Margaret 232
 Martha 95 Mary 270 Nancy 95
 Rebecca 86 247 313 Samuel
 167 Sarah 257 270 271
Crommett, Mary A 168
Cromwell, Jennie 245
Cronin, Patrick J 25
Crooker, Elisa B 359 James A
 359 Mary J 359 William F 359
Crosby, Emma 147
Crosen, Charles 224
Cross, Mary S 255 Nellie 307
 Roxanna 331
Crossman, Daniel 166 Hannah
 155 295 John 155 R Harriet
 Amanda 166 Smyton 295
Crowell, Charles S 24 Helen 102
 Lucy 97

Crowley, Amos 103 255 Fred L
 246 J H 76 James 260 Jane 260
 Jeremiah 112 Jeremiah Jr 20
 Martha Alice 246 Martha Jane
 103 Mary 117 118 Mehitable
 29 Priscilla 112 Thomas 19
 Vesta 255
Crowly, Jeremiah 130 Mehitable
 130
Crummett, Mary A 168
Cuimmings, Mary E 358
Cullin, John 44
Culver, Lillian 186
Cummings, Asa 38 Deborah 204
 E H 67 Eben 237 Edward H 21
 Elvira Jane 248 Emelia W 235
 Jemima 199 Jere P 235 John
 86 127 Lemuel 199 Levina 127
 Lovica 126 Lucy 86 Milford S
 358 Peter 126 Polly 289 S A
 67 Samuel 248 Sarah Ann 330
 Selden A 22 23 24 25 77
 Sylvan 127 Tumah 236 237
 William 204
Cunningham, Harriet Angeline
 253
Currant, Thoms 367
Currier, Luvia Ann 222
Curtis, Abigail 310 Adeline 168
 Angelena 87 Ann 227 Bathsheba 30 Charles F 267 Daniel
 116 Deana 166 167 168 Deanna
 166 167 169 Diana 166 167 169
 Elizabeth G 357 Elsie P 308
 310 Ermina Ellen 286 Flora
 358 Flora E 357 Hannah 147
 Ida Estelle 267 Isaac G 20 87
 James 354 John 30 227 228
 310 John Jr 357 Jome 203
 Lois 147 Louisa 256 259 Lucy
 279 Mary 228 Mary A 170
 Nancy 197 Orin 286 Phebe 227
 Rebecca 326 Reubin B 170
 Rosann C 164 Ruth 100 Silas
 29 30 William 147
Curtiss, Rose J 164
Curts, Irene 95
Cushing, 296 Bethiah 287 Bethial
 Jane 203 David 203 Elizabeth
 J 286 Ezekial 295 George M

Cushing (continued)
  286 Herbert E 287 John 268
  Lucy Ann 96 Miss E 38 Mrs L
  38 Rachel 164 Thankful 295
  Weeks Experence 268
Cushman, Annis 237 Ara 69
  Bathsheba 236 237 Celia 146
  Isaac 373 Martha 307 Matilda
  Frances Oliver 237 Robert 350
  351 Sally 350 351 William 307
Cutler, Cordelia 92 Cyntha 28
  Daniel 236 Ella A 116 Emily
  M 248 Hannah 28 264 Lucinda
  95 Lucy 236 Mary 264 Nathan
  18 45 46 264 Nathan Jr 95 368
  Olive 264
Cutter, David 298 Franke Adele
  219 Hannah B 100 Henry 100
  Hopestill 196 J L 28 James H
  219 Jason 298 Nathon 196
  Roxcyllania 348 Susan 298
Dakin, Ralph 166
Davis, Alice 163 Amos Jr 29
  William 192
Day, Adeline 170
Daggett, Horace 369 Leander 87
  Margaret 87 Polena 357 Pole-
  nia 357 Rachel 357 William
  357
Dahee, Nettie 268
Dain, Andrew 234 Hannah 234
  James 234 306 Kessiah 234
  Sarah 147
Daley, Abial 21
Daly, Aulenal Jane 199 Ella
  Frances 272 Ervin V 22
  Lorenzo W 272 William 199
Dam, Sarah 288
Dammon, Clarissa 149
Damon, Eden 263 Harriett 263
  May 331 Wilbert 331
Dana, Frederick 313 Nabby 313
Dane, Meribah E 279
Danforth, Betsey 225 Wm A 225
Daniels, Georgia 180
Danielson, J W 55 60 John W 20
  Jonathon 169 Nancy 169
Davenport, Everline Rebecca 168
  Ralph 168
Davidson, Jessie D 219

Davis, Aaron 29 181 350 Aaron Jr
  29 Abigail 146 233 Alfred 325
  Alice 79 157 163 177 Alice M
  157 Amos 14 29 45 48 74 156
  181 256 276 Amos Jr 18 327
  Amos Sr 17 Angeline Sewall
  194 195 Ann 123 249 250 Ann
  Mary 349 Ann S T 249 Anna 29
  179 Augusta A 44 Benjamin
  116 Betsey 313 Betsy 200
  Charles F 304 Charles H 324
  Charlotte 328 Charlotte H 100
  Chistana 140 Clarissa 260
  Daniel 18 19 45 165 182 David
  11 15 16 29 74 75 79 106 157
  313 341 369 Deborah 29 156
  157 Dorothy B 141 Dorris 282
  283 E S 55 60 67 Elisabeth
  106 Elizabeth 17 179 180 181
  Elvira 324 Emma E 217
  Ezekiel S 20 21 Hannah 250
  335 340 Hannah Harris 220
  Harriet W 315 Hattie R 192
  Isaac 250 251 Isaac P 222
  Jackson 74 75 James 200
  Jerusha 29 Jesse 61 67 John
  328 John A 265 John C 349
  John L 233 John V 173 222
  Joseph 141 367 368 Joseph F
  343 Joseph J 22 Joseph M 315
  Katherine 154 Lama A 343
  Louisianna 325 Lucy S 37
  Lydia 179 M J 78 Maria 181
  Mariah 29 181 265 Martha 93
  Mary 15 144 159 165 165 327
  328 Mary Frances 281 Mary
  Harris 291 Mary O 222 May
  115 222 May J 222 Mehitable
  125 181 350 Mr 15 Nat E 291
  Nathaniel 93 250 340 367 368
  Natt E 20 21 Olive 143 Otis F
  160 Percis 128 Polly 200
  Polly C 200 Rosanna 227
  Rufus 260 Ruhamah 116 Ruth
  T 147 Sarah 180 341 350-352
  Sarah J 173 Sarah R 304 Seth
  147 Sophia Angelia 160 Ste-
  phen 18 33 34 44 45 53 146
  154 155 195 Tace 182-184
  Tacy 186 Thankful 283 292

Davis (continued)
 Vincent 281 W G 212 W L 32
 William 115 192 220 Wm 335
Dawes, Addie 157 Judith 328 329
 Silas C 157
Dawson, Catherine Maria 209
 George 209
Day, Alice M 166 Alielis W 166
 Anna 154 Bethany 168 Catherine 171 Esther 101 Eunice 297
 Fessenden I 23 24 78 219
 Hersey 20 Hircy 77 Joseph 149
 297 Joseph H 21 22 23 77 166
 Josiah 20 101 Livonia Josephine 166 Martha 166 168 169
 Mary Alma 219 Miriam 100
 Mrs F I 80 Nancy 159 Nowell
 154 Phebe B 148 149 Rebecca
 168 Ruth 149 297
Dayen, Carrie 94
DeWitt, Alexander 54
Dean, Buel W 21 Charles 49
Deane, Harriet 306 James 306
Dearborn, Edward M 20
Dearing, Charles H 275 Eunice
 275
Decker, Albert 278 279 Naham
 298 Nancy C 87 Olive 298
 Thedosia 278 Thodosia 278
Demerrett, Henry 153 Mary
 Lizzie 153
Demond, Mary 216
Dempsey, James 22 67
Denison, Betsey 326
Dennes, Melora 238
Dennet, Anna 111
Dennett, Abigail 109 Amy 142
 143 Anna 174 Anny 142 143
 Dorcas 137 Dorothy 173 174
 Ebeneser 173 Ebenezer 172
 174 Elisa 159 Elvira 159 Joel
 174 Mary 137 174 Menander 22
 24 Nancy 113 Nath 137 Peter
 113 Sally 172 Sally M 174
 Susannah 173
Dennis, Edith 160
Dennison, Ellen R 267 Joseph A
 267
Densmore, George J 262 Vesta M
 262
Dergan, Mary L 329

Dexter, Carrie 192 Pardon N 21
 Polivia Jane 265 Samuel Jr 8
 Thomas F 265
Diah, Elkimah 368 (see Dyer 147)
Dickerman, George S 39
Dickey, H H 22 37 William 58
Dickinson, Gideon D 75 James
 200 Polly 200 Polly C 200
Dickman, Constatine 152 Pauline
 H 152
Dickson, Oliver 263 Sarah 263
 Sarah C 263
Dill, Abigail 309 Adeline 232 235
 Alonso G 218 Ann 30 Anna 137
 Caroline 144 Charlotte 242
 Daniel 172 Dorcas 17 153 173
 176 359 Dorcas W 153 Eben
 122 363 Enoch 368 Enoch Jr
 368 Hannah 172 186-188
 Hannah C 172 Harmon 181
 Hulda A 153 Hulda J 119
 James 172 Jesieh 361 John 17
 181 186 188 368 John Jr 367
 Joseph 27 50 153 242 311 368
 Joseph Jr 119 367 Josiah 309
 368 Lillian 218 Lora J 122
 Louisa 152 153 154 Louise
 152 153 154 Martha E 213
 Mary 144 234 Mary B 143
 Mary G 303 Mary Sawyer 172
 May 303 Phineas 153 303
 Phineas W 153 Polly 311
 Sally 359-361 Sarah 181 282
 Seward 172 Susan Blaisdell
 363 Washington 144 William
 137 153 218 William R 213
Dilldoe, Mary Jane 199
Dillingham, Adaline 292 Adeline
 295 Almond 292 Frances 91
 Geo 91 Helen 292 Leavitt 295
 Mary 292 Minerva 292 Quincy
 292 295
Dingley, Abigail 232 233 Amy
 257 Anna 257 Betsy 348 Caroline 143 300 Charlotte 113
 Esther 318 Georgia A 109 Gov
 221 H M 57 Isiah 97 Jeremiah
 162 Jeremiah Jr 353 John T
 150 Leonard 109 Lucy 151 162
 Mary 141 304 306 Mary Ann
 150 Minerva 353 Mr 50 Nelson

Dingley (continued)
   Jr 79 Olive G 130 Polly 85
   Rachel E 150 Sally 257 Sally
   Atkinson 268 Samuel 130
   Sarah 97 Susan G 323 324
   William 19 368 Wm 141 257
   268 Wm Sr 257 Wm T 150
Dingly, Polly 85
Dinsmore, Ansel 271 Betsey 315
   Judith Crockett 271
Dixon, F L 68 72 Georgia 318
   Harmon 21 Mary 104 330
   Nason 330
Doane, Alfred 149 Anna 149
   Edward 149 Joanna 149 Mrs
   197
Dobbin, George W Mrs 92
Dobbins, Alice Evelyn 92 Geo W
   92 Mrs G W 92
Dodge, Ann 212 Bessie 136 E C
   212 Flora A 136 Hattie 127
   Heman 136 Jane P 204
Doe, Mary 191
Dolbier, 329 Chester 239 Mabel
   239 Martha 148 William 148
Doleby, Nathan 148 Polly 148
Dolloff, Cynthia 128 David 128
   Emma 337 Jennie 333
Dolly, Hannah 204
Donahue, Rhoda 326
Donnell, Fannie 152 Frances J
   152 Fred 101 Hortense 101
   Mary E 327 N 369 Rachel
   Antoinette 248 Robert 248
Donovan, J A 68 John A 72
Door, Mary Melissa 346 Samuel
   346
Dorr, Daniel H 213 Isabell 213 O
   J 346
Dorrah, Loantha J 116 Warren C
   116
Dorset, Sarah L 35
Dorsey, Drusilla Jane 167
   Holman H 167 Louisa 166 168
Doten, Almaria 269 Almatia Ann
   269 Annie Blanche 267 Maria
   G 267 Orren B 267
Doughty, Ellen M 261 John 261
   Lucy 96 Sally 141
Douglas, David 97 Edwin C 24
   George H 97 Hannah 97 214

Douglas (continued)
   Ida F Field 154 James 214
   James Jr 97 Paul 97 Thomas
   97 Warren P 154
Douglass, 79 Abigail 343 Bertha
   239 David 29 97 Fannie 143
   Francis 214 George 29 239
   George H 97 Hannah 97 Isaac
   343 James 260 James Jr 97
   Lisa 260 Oscar G 21 22 Paul
   97 Susan 214 Thomas 97
Dow, Laura 105
Downes, Isaac C 21 22 24 63
Downing, Lizzie 294
Downs, Eunice 257 Ezekiel C 257
   Mary H 257 Mary Hannah 259
Doyen, Naomi 363 Richard 363
Doyle, E 369 Edward 183 Gertrude G 183 Jane 265 Maria
   108 Mary J 297 P M 25 William 265
Drake, Codding 170 171 Deborah
   289 Drew E 235 Grace Elva
   235 Hiram B 266 Isaac 289
   James B K 250 Olive Marie
   266 Polly 126 Sally 170 171
   Susannah 289 Vesta Jane 250
Dresser, Alice 337 Allice 336
   Dorcas 220 Eben W 24 25
   Elvira 237 241 Mary Frances
   337 Peter J 337 Polly 264 266
   Rendall 23 Sarah 128 Susan E
   100
Drew, George A 21 22 78 George
   F 23
Drinkwater, Arthur 34 Betsey 207
   Charles 174 David 151 Eva
   Ann 174 George L 36 Jacob F
   339 Olive 95 Rachel 151 Susan
   339
Drummond, Daniel 280 Gladys
   280 James 30 33 37 38 Margaret E 237 Mr 34
Duchaussoy, P 45
Dudley, Elizabeth 136 Mark 136
   May 176 Nancy 136 170
   Prudence 237 Sarah 133 Sylance H 138 Violet 237 Ward
   237 William 133 William R
   237
Duey, Mattie M 175 Willard 175

Duherst, N 307
Duhor, Mary J 226
Dukeshire, William B 43
Dummer, Nathaniel 8
Dumphy, Elizabeth 273 277
Dunbar, Mary 177 178 Peter 178
Dunham, Almira 253 Ammi 373
  Duncan 301 Enos 313 James
  192 Margaret 190 Mary 124
  Mineva J 192 Sarah 190 192
  Susanna 313 Therida 301
  William 190
Dunn, Alma B 251 Amelia 219
  Benjamin 62 369 Delia Ann
  172 George 219 Minnetta 148
  Olive 218 S Streeter 172 V A
  148 William M 251
Dunnell, Joseph 282 Mary 282
Dunton, Blanch Nora 240 Blanche
  240 Emeslene 357 Ernest E
  240 Nellie 240
Durechey, Fred 148 Nellie P 148
Durell, Elizabeth H 226
Durgain, Mrs 328
Durgan, Benjamin 373 Sarah 166
Durham, Israel 168 Louis Am 168
Durnin, J A T 44
Durocher, 78
Dustin, Agnes 107 Geo L 107
  Jane 182
Dutton, Dorcas 207 John 207 N W
  67 Nathan W 22 23
Dwelley, Alexander 71 Eles'r 367
  Harriet 113
Dwight, Thomas 8
Dwinal, Aaron 216 Amos 210
  Huldah 216 Judith 135 Lester
  210 Lydia Thompson 210 Ruth
  335 Susanna 210
Dyer, Abigail 141 301 302 Annis
  95 Barsilla 109 Barsilla D 129
  Betsey 296 324 Carrie Virginia
  90 Catherine 178 Cora A 198
  Drusilla 108 109 Eleony 367
  Elisabeth 162 Elizabeth 285
  288 Elizabeth M 285 288
  Elkanah 110 207 Ephraim 296
  John 367 Joseph 95 Mary 108
  109 110 111 112 229 Mary F
  296 Michael 90 Nancy 108 110
  112 Oliver 229 Sarah 207

Dyer (continued)
  Stillman E 198 Susan 90
Dzido, Ann 143 Edwin 143
Dzole, Ann 143 Edwin 143
Eagan, Michael 22
Eales, Lydia 207
Eames, Annie 350 Jacob 202
  Martha 335 Nathaniel 335 Ruth
  350 352 Sally 132 133 Sarah
  202
Earl, Catherine 306 Catherine
  Ann 306 Henry 306
Earle, Lula 115
East, Abigail 340 Joseph 340
Eastman, Cordelia 143 Dora 167
  172 Eliza R 354 Francis Ellen
  329 Henry N 41 Joseph 329
  Josiah N 167 172 Mrs Henry N
  41
Eates, Eliza J 328 Joseph 328
Eaton, Dance 122 Elizabeth 251
  Florilla J 122 George Wash-
  ington 282 Harriet L 244 Mary
  Jane W 141 Mercy 13 287
  Myrtle 321 Nancy 295 Sarah D
  141
Edes, Lydia 207
Edgcomb, Charity 363
Edgecomb, Albert 115 Anna 338
  Bath 113 Charlotte 217 Edward
  338 Elisabeth 138 139 Emily
  124 Etta 115 John T 193 Lucy
  193 Mary Ann 113 Robert 217
Edmond, Caroline 343
Edson, Lena 335
Edwards, A K P 364 Abigail 229
  Albert 336 Almira 143 Ann
  Augusta 336 Collins 143
  Delphia 145 Delphina 144
  James 229 Mary Elizabeth 98
  Sally D 364
Elden, Cara 173 Dwight C 173
Elder, 83 Amanda 297 Caroline D
  281 Frances Anna 274 Frances
  J 274 Frederic W 281 Isaac
  148 J G 90 297 Janus G 101
  Joanna 145 Joshua 145 Joshua
  Jr 297 Lydia 297 Matilda 148
  Mr 91 Wm Erastus 297
Eldridge, Martha Ellen 338
  Samuel 338 Selina 338

Elemdone, Dorothy 200
Elery, Betsey 360 Betsy 359
Eliot, Elisabeth 139 142 Wm 139
Elkins, Alexander 321 Chas 206 Elisabeth 321 Julia 206
Ellis, Betsey F 203 Catherine 253 Cornelius 253 Davis 203 May 127 Nellie 115 S 102 Sarah E 323 324
Elmes, Jefferson 202 Marcia 202
Elms, Harriet M 112 Hattie M 114 Robert 112
Elsemore, Addia 136
Elwell, Clara M 214 J P 214
Emerson, Abraham 282 Ivory W 24 Maria F 245 Mary 282
Emery, Benjamin T 21 Carrie 270 Deborah 118 E W 248 Eleanor 119 Elizabeth 270 Elmira W 97 John 118 Lottie B 248 Marshall 77 Thomas 270
Emmons, George P 68
Erskine, Lucretia 297 Wm Henry 297
Estes, Calvin G 309 David 108 182 186 Edith 108 Edward 50 276 Hannah 265 Jenette T 182 186 Jennie 106 Josiah 224 225 Laura 261 Mary A 182 Mary Ann 144 Olive 224 225 Prudence 133 Rachael Elisa 144 Rhoda F 309 Ruth 133 Sarah 132 Wealthy 183
Estey, Florida 142 Jarvis 142 Mary 334
Eustis, T E 57 67
Eustus, Abigail 236
Evans, Mary D 179
Eveleth, Christana 113
Evelett, Christana 113
Evenfight, Robert 163 Rose Jordan 163
Everett, James A 265 Sallie Ellen 265
Fair, Hattie 306
Fairbanks, Joseph N 142 Lettice B 142 Nellie 208
Fales, Almira Elizabeth 179 Horace 179
Famedan, George E 343 Mary D 343

Fanard, Ann 181
Farewell, Angelina 241
Farington, Sarah 150
Farmington, Green 129 Olive 129
Farnham, J Henry 319 Jane 155 John W 369 Marcia J 319 Martha A 175 Mary 327 Mary L 329 S W 369
Farnsworth, Cephas 373
Farr, Charlotte 133 David 133 Elisa J 150 Elisabeth 150 Geo W 264 George H 29 George W 40 Hannah Ames 178 Henrietta 150 Henry 178 Maggie E 175 Olive J 264 Sarah 150
Farrar, David 23 25 67 Harriet 103 Ida 266 James 373 Luce 110 Lucy A 362 Nath 367 Phebe 334 Reuben 110
Farrin, Ann 181
Farrington, Emily J 112 Samuel 112
Farrow, Amanda M 315 Eliza 207 Esther 162 George 315 Judith 252 Julia P 336 Lucy 315 Nathan 162 Polly 186 188 Priscilla C 187 188
Farwell, John W 20 21 Josephine 349 351 Josiah 28 N W 40 53 56 60 Nathan W 22 67 Nathaniel W 57 Rev Mr 28
Faulson, Devereaus 135 Ella 135
Faunce, I S 78 Isaac S 21
Fellows, Abigail 320 Benjamin 237 Isaac 320 Mary 237
Ferguss, W A 90 91
Fernald, Addie May 90 Cordelia 308 Cordelia D 309 Edward K 90 Sam 309 Samuel 308
Feroo, Emery L 198 Mary F 198
Fessenden, Joseph P 20 21
Feulason, Darius 135 Hattie A 135
Fickett, Abigail 299 Benjamin 225 Matilda 225 Matilda J 172 Rebecca C H A 247 Ruth 116 Samuel 247 Simon 116
Field, Alice L 38 Alphesus 139 Alpheus 139 Amasa 124 Catherine 132 134 David P 142 Deacon 18 Dorcas W 142

Field (continued)
  Dorothy J 174 E F 70 Edith
    242 Edward 242 Elisabeth 163
    Eliza 34 Elvira 304 Hulda 143
    Irving L 116 Jacob A 174
    James 87 286 367 James A
    143 Jane 103 Jesse H 41 John
    192 367 Joseph 18 80 219 367
    Joseph Jr 368 Katherine 132
    134 Loantha 116 Louisa 143
    Maria 285 292 Mary 219 220
    299 300 320 Mary A 80 255
    Mary Elisabeth 124 Miss D
    139 Olive 154 Robert A 304
    Ruth 139 Sally 87 Sarah 190
    192 286 Sarah M 192 Stephen
    30 80 320 369
Fields, Joseph 18
Fillebrown, Matilda 169 Thomas
    22 67
Filler, John 353 Mary S 353
Fillmore, Elisabeth L 334
Finch, Lillian 267
Finn, Daniel 23 Charles 144
Fish, Jane 144 Liva 227
Fisher, Carleton E 206 Cynthia
    237 Joseph H 328 Mary J 255
    Olive D 327 328 Susan E 255
Fiske, A H 55 John O 38
Fitch, Ann M 37 Charlotte 37
    George 245 Margaret M 245
    Sarah Elizabeth 245 William
    369 William F 37 William L
    37
Fites, Dora 284 Ira W 284
Fitz, Mary 234 Moses 183 184
    Rebecca 183 Sally 184 Simeon
    P 234
Fitzgerald, Daniel S 23 25
    Edmund 283 Harriet 283
Fitzgerld, Daniel S 23
Flagg, Ado--- 153 Hannah 153
Flaherty, Patrick J 24 25
Flanders, Sarah Eva 301
Fletcher, Eliza 152 Mary Ella
    239
Flewllin, Carrie G 325 Samuel
    325
Flint, Phebe 151
Flower, Almira 293 Geo W 293
    Hannah 293

Flynt, Anna 281
Fogg, Benjamin 228 Edgar J 74
    Ella A 243 Emily 336 Esther
    287 289 Eunice F 228 Everline
    M 221 George 121 Hulda H 121
    Lissie 128 Mary 104 Minnie E
    307 308 Nathaniel S 128
    Timothy E 20
Follansbee, George S 22
Folsom, Addie C 196 Geo L 223
    Grace Gertrude 272 James
    Leslie 272 Millecent F 223
Forbes, Pauline R 257
Ford, Emily 193 Francis F 39
    Lissie 290 Marshal 369 Mary
    209 Nancy 209 William 368
    Wm 367
Forks, Abigail 146
Forrins, Nancy 188 Rebecca 188
    Samuel 188
Foss, Albert 125 130 Ann Maria
    305 Benjamin 258 Elizabeth
    310 Elmira 323 Fannie 319
    Harriet N 347 J O 57 James O
    305 Jefferson 305 Joseph 319
    Josephine 344 Laura C 258
    Marie M 334 Mary Given 305
    Mary M 330 Olive G 130
    Rebecca 97 Salvan 97 Sarah A
    125 Simeon 373 W H 57
Foster, Ann Eliza 257 Ann
    Margaret 303 Annie 263 Arvillia B 167 Benj B 257 Benjamin 32 Bishop 43 Charles 228
    Hannah 120 Lucy Ann 252
    Margaret 305 Mary 261 263
    Rosalinda 228 Warren 167
Fowle, Seth W 54
Fowler, Harriet 293
Fowles, Abbie Welch 348 Alvin
    W 356 Frank 339 Mary 339
    Sarah Addie 356
Fox, Abijah 202 Mercy 202
Frances, Amanda 285 296 Hannah
    120 Rosian M 326
Francis, Hannah 122 Ida 238
    Margaret Wright 257 Sarah A
    333 Thomas 333 William 238
Frasier, Oliver A 25
Frederick, Lizzie L 206 William
    206

Free, H A 76
Freeman, Edmond 216 Emily 164 Hannah 87 Jesse Burbank 87 Mary 216
Freese, Mary 191
Frence, George F 23
French, Catherine 223 David T 20 Elizabeth 32 Elmira 182 Fanny 129 Geo 241 Hannah 251 282 Hattie 335 Jennie S 261 Joseph 223 Julia 42 326 Lucy D 140 Marshal 369 Marshall 20 55 64 Nathaniel 32 Sally 127 199 Sam'l G 251 Sarah 241 Thomas 261 W R 369 Warren B 182 William 199 Wm 129
Friend, Bertha L 198 T B 198
Fritsh, George 245 Margaret M 245 Sarah Elizabeth 245
Frost, Albert E 21 22 24 Deborah 131 Elisabeth 138 George 373 George D 131 173 Harland 352 Helen M 352 Helen Marr 352 Jacob R 293 Mary 254 255 Mary Adelaide 172 173 Mary D 262 Meada 135 Melvina 247 Rev Mr 27 Rosella T 293 Sarah H 137 Simon 262 Taby 181 Wealthy 150 William 247 Wm H 150
Frueap, Bell 344
Frufant, Julia 147
Frye, Albert S 79 Alice 79 132 Augusta 182 Caroline 80 338 Dean 50 80 160 338 Ellen 101 J M 64 John M 18 19 50 51 53 61 62 63 79 80 132 369 Joseph 79 Melicant 79 Mr 51 80 Mrs John M 37 Sarah E 37 Senator 69 Sophie 160 161 165 Susan E 80 W R 369 William P 20 79 William R 18 19 30 51 62 79 Wm P 65 Wm R 80
Fuller, 278 Alexander 214 Annie 260 David 212 Ella 355 Esther A 211 212 Harriet W 356 Helen M 111 Hosea 356 Jane 356 Lena 301 Lydia A 214 Lysander 111 Mary A 360 Mary Frances 236-238 Nancy

Fuller (continued) 260 Sally M 192
Fullonton, John 31 84
Furber, Annie A 189 B F 40 Mrs B F 41
Furbish, Charles E 362 Mary I 362
Furbush, Abigail 241 Abraham 241 Albert B 21 Frances Ann Marie 121 Frederick M 121 George W 23 Hannah 238 Hannah W 334 Henry 121 241 358 Ida 358 John 238 Lovina 241
Furnham, Mary 327
Gage, Almon 41
Gagne, John E 24 25
Gale, Frances 92 John 92
Gallahan, George A 79
Gallemy, Martha 205
Gallison, Sarah 365 Sylvanus 365
Gammon, Charlotte 181 Harriet ""Tylie""" 253 Molly 252 Nat 252 Harriet F 253
Garcelon, 107 A 72 73 A M 73 Abigail 234 Abram W 24 25 69 Alice 131 Alonzo 15 20 21 22 53 61 62 68 71 74 80 369 Alonzo M 23 24 25 Ann 229 Ann Amelia 219 Annis 101 125 Asa 61 80 157 186 257 Benjamin 368 Char E 112 Clara 319 Clarissa J 319 Daniel 19 131 192 356 David 192 229 Deborah 231-234 Deliverance 15 Elisa Taber 133 Elisabeth Ann 334 Elizabeth 148 316 Ester 151 Franes Ann 159 Fred F 23 George 73 Georgia W 257 H G 15 Hannah 86 Hannah E 228 Hannah F 112 Harriet 322 Harriet N 322 Harris 133 Harry G 219 J S 15 James 15 18 19 21 27 28 45 148 230 232 289 319 James Jr 27 28 Jane 87 164 Jennet 289 Joan 30 Joanna 232 269 319 John B 20 22 Joseph 269 Joseph S 19 20 22 Katherine 260 Lizzie A 330 Lorenzo 159 Lucy 15 85 86 87 Lucy Dingley 233 Maria 202

Garcelon (continued)
  Mark 18 86 87 228 367 Mary 125 132 192 Minnie H 219 Mrs H S 80 Nathaniel G 233 Octavia D 37 Olive 269 P J 330 Peter 15 176 260 367 Peter J 334 Peter Jr 367 Phebe 230 Phillip 93 Polina 93 Polly 101 325 344 S 134 Sally 158 159 265 Samuel D 19 318 319 Sarah 15 176 Sarah F 186 Sophia 125 157 Sophia A 134 Susan E 356 Thankful 300 302 Ursula 192 William 15 16 18 19 45 74 126 133 202 368 William F 20 21 22 23 73 William Green 132 William H 322 William Jr 27 Wm 85 87 367 ex-Governor 15
Gardiner, Charles 369 Frederic 36
Garfield, Emily F 230 Geo 230 M A 230 Martha Ann 230
Garland, James 303 Mary 236 239 Olive Vesta 303 Vesta 303
Garner, John 22 23 37 67 69 77
Garnett, Mary 152
Garohen, Lola B 342 Thomas 342
Gary, MAry Ann 355 Rufus L 355
Gass, Kale 321
Gassett, Charles A 333 Ella M 333
Gates, Betsey 116 Mary 117 Mary H 188 S B 302 Solon 116 Theodosia J 302
Gay, Charles 57 Lucy M 164 Mr 58 Rosina 187 Sidney 187 William F 164
Geney, Mary 102
Gerrish, Emily 88 Mary 202
Gerry, Addie R 285 Adelia 296 John C 288 Julia 296 Malleville C 288 Wm 296
Gersham, Deacon 321 Mary M 321
Getchell, Anna 264 B W 22 Benjamin F 24 Byron W 22 C F 264 Dorcas 100 Ella 311 Francis 245 John 100 Joshua 242 Judith 242 Lydia 242 Mary 100 Mary A 227 Phil P 21 Sally 263 Samuel 242

Geulfond, Mary Brown 187
Geyer, Lillian 219
Gibbs, Dr 287 Eunice 287
Giddings, George P 36 George R 208
Giddins, Penelope 208
Gifford, Charles 213 George W 70 Laura A 213
Gilbert, Caleb 41 Carlous 168 Hannah 238 Hannah H 238 240 Lovonia 136 Mrs Caleb 41 Olive R 168 Osca 121 123 Rebecca 135 Ruth 149 297 Spencer 238
Gile, Martha 166 O L 42
Gill, Joseph P 21 98 Olive Caroline 98
Gillpatrick, Lucy 29
Gilman, Bell J 363 Esekiel 95 Joanna 95 Levi W 20 Lydia E 362 Mary J 91 Samuel K 363
Gilmore, Ana Stone 311 Charles A 311 Esther A 175 James B 129 Silvia J 129
Gilpatrick, Eunice 242 James 368
Gilson, Alice 166
Ginn, Hannah 203
Given, Alice 336 Benjamin 305 Cynthia 332 David 298 303 David T 332 Dorcas 303 Dorcas W 303 F A 70 Helen 298 Jane 226 John 23 226 305 Mary 303 305 306 Mary Jane 226 Sally 305 Samuel 336 Sarah 305 Wm 226
Glass, Charlott 99 William 99
Gledden, Peter 357
Gledhill, 114 Melvina 114
Glenn, Calvin 235 Mary Emma 235
Glidden, Grant 140 Isaiah 242 Israel 17 33 Lydia 17 Mercy A 140 Rebecca 242
Glover, Amos S 109 Sally 109 359
Goddard, Abel 22 181 224 299 Betsey 325 Caroline F 255 Elizabeth 191 Elizabeth J 191 Hannah 299 Isaac 29 325 Isaac Jr 23 J H 369 John 276 John H 325 Lydia 223-225 Mary Ann 325 Mary J 181 Phebe W 179

Goddard (continued)
　William 179
Goddor, Hannah M 96 Ira 96
Godfrey, Martha 346 Mercy G 356
　Thomas G 356
Godler, Anna D 219 Jacob 360
Goff, Ann 312 Delora 253 Edwin
　141 Hannah 141 James 312
　Mary 139 141 Mercy 311 312
　Sarah 192
Golbier, Desiah Dingly 184
　Nathan D 184
Golder, 261 316 Cordelia 157
　Dorcas 17 111 140 300 323
　Dorcas A 168 Dorcus 300
　Dorothy 137 Dorothy J 153
　Eliza 342 Fairfield 137 157
　Fairfield Jr 139 Flavilla 291
　Hannah C 139 Isaac 68 134
　262 277 319 Jacob 17 27 28 33
　137 153 192 219 300 360 Jane
　360 Lucinda 192 M Addie 157
　Moses D 22 23 Mrs 262 Polly
　232 Sally 114 137 Sarah 133
　134 159 160 161 162 163 164
　165 Sarah Jane 319 William
　17 18 140 163 Wm 367
Goldsmith, Elizabeth L 213
　Hubbard 213
Gonald, Agnes D 192 Alfred L
　192
Gooch, John H 22
Good---, Susan 173
Goodale, Elizabeth 251
Goodenow, Henry C 20
Goodereen, Caroline 220 Dexter
　220
Goodridge, Joseph 177 Susan 177
Goodwin, Benjamin 367 Catherine
　150 Emma A 272 George 370
　Ichabod 8 Mary 157 188 300
　Menerva 238 Samuel 188
Goody, John 373 Samuel 98 Viola
　98 William W 354
Googin, Carrie E 220 Melvin J 23
　78 220
Googins, E S 329 Julia Ann 329
　MAry 137
Gookins, Sally 120
Gordan, Abigail 184 George 297
　Georgia 257 Jonathan 296

Gordan (continued)
　Ruthy 297 Sam'l D 257 Sarah
　296
Gorden, Annie 266
Gordon, Abigail 183-185 Adelia
　M 286 Alice Redman 152 Asa
　290 Crosby 290 George 290
　296 George W 290 Lorretta
　290 Lucetta 290 Lydia 296
　Melentha Gordon 290
Gorham, Amanda 250 Amanda M
　249 Calvin 18 19 53 71 Dr 370
　Lucy A 249 Rachel 312 Sarah
　192 194 Soleman 312
Gorman, Ada 199
Gosell, Deborah M 289
Goss, A L 22 78 Almon L 284
　Benjamin 148 Betsey 321
　Betsy 320 Cate 147 Catherine
　Dyer 321 Charles F 23 Cyrene
　148 Dexter 354 E F 78 Edwin
　F 125 Elmira 110 Etta L 191
　Eunice 354 George W 24 25 67
　John 20 22 103 147 191 370
　Mary A 284 Mary L 103 Mrs G
　321 Polly Ann 250 Rose L 125
　Ruth 354 Sally 110 Samuel 354
　Sewell 110 Thomas 104 110
　Walter A 69
Gott, Mary 140
Goud, Charles 125 Rosetta E 125
Gould, Deborah G 354 Eliza 206
　Emma B 242 Frances L 267
　Harriett W 130 Increase 130
　Joseph 206 L A 370 Levi 87
　Llewelen 242 Mary 244 245
　May 125 May A 125 Ruth 87
Goulding, W F 55
Gove, Elijah 210 Lydia 215 Mary
　E 94 May H 91 92 Molly 210
　Olive M 136
Gowell, Andrew 194 Armanda J
　191 Deborah M 289 Ella 98
　Fred 191 Geo 289 Julia Ann
　194 Rebecca 159 William 98
Gowen, Lyida A 365
Gowing, Elizabeth 348
Graffam, Alice 330 331 Ann 330
　Anne 131 Augusta M 200
　Benjamin 363 Betsey 263 283
　Betsy 260 Daniel W 131 David

Graffam (continued)
132 143 224 283 324 Deborah 350 Elisabeth 130 150 Elizabeth 17 28 George W 181 Hannah 274 277-279 Happy 324 John 17 130 260 263 274 287 350 368 Lydia 14 132 239 240 Maria 131 Mariah 131 Martha 143 Mary 224 Mary A 363 May D 356 Mehitable 130 Sarah 140 141 Thankful 13 153 287
Graffem, Lydia 209
Graffen, Darrat 224 Dave W 224 Polly 224 Susannah 182 183 185
Graffin, Thankful 286 290
Grafton, Alonzo 239
Graham, Geneva 184
Granger, Charles 205 Rebecca 205
Grant, Daniel 335 Elijah 256 259 Eliza 339 Louisa 256 259 Martha 212 Mary A 149 182 Mary Alice 173 Mary J 256 Mary Jane 259 Ruth 335
Graves, Albion 317 Frances E 317
Gray, Augusta 337 Eliza 135 136 Inez 92 Jane 207 208 John 92 Lois 197 Meleneca 267 Melinda 267 Memima 113 Rhoda 197 Sirena 136 Solomon 197 William 197
Greaton, Julia 329 332
Greeley, Allen 339 Hannah 283 John 179 Lydia A 179 Rev 207 Sheribal 283
Greely, Allen 229 Cyrus 20 21 22 23 67 Eunice F 229 Rev 114
Green, Betsey 101 Betsy Pettingill 329 Daniel 318 Elizabeth Pettingill 331 Hannah 101 Ira 101 John 373 Molly 96 Wealthy 318 William 101
Greene, Augusta A 44 Augusta E 134 Charlotte 123 Clarisa 264 David 373 Hannah 297 Harrison 264 Helen 233 Iresen 297 Jesse 123 John 105 Joseph 331 Joseph K 44 134 Roscoe L

Greene (continued)
33 Serena 156 Wealthy 319 William 233
Greenleaf, Alfreda 360 Elisabeth 124 Julia 204
Greenwood, 85 Abosa 253 Charles 67 78 Ellen 350 Joseph R 37 Lucy Ann 199 Rachel J 250 Sarah W 37 Septimus 250 Verres 350
Grendale, Ellen 312
Grey, Georgia R 162 Melinia 162 William 162
Griffen, Adeline 287 David H 287 294 Susan 294 Susan C 294
Griffin, Adeline 287 David H 287 Deborah 295 Deborah T 293 Emma C 293 Eunice M 286 287 Flora 91 Frank P 246 Geo H 293 John 293 295 Louisa 143 144 Martha Alice 246 Nancy 295 Nav 293 Rachael 207
Griffiths, Lois 156
Griggs, Laura S 269 R 370
Grolleau, 45
Grom, Emma R 198 John 198
Grose, O C 33
Grosman, Emma 288
Gross, David 45 Edward W 78 Mary Ann 250
Grough, Susan B 139
Grover, A 370 Abigail 106 326 Amy 105 106 Elisabeth 326 James 140 359 John 326 Mehitable 136 Mina 359 Miriam 105 106 Sally 140 Susie 181 182 Villa F 352
Groves, Harriet 233
Grows, Phebe 200 201 204 Phebe R 200 201
Guilford, Dorcas W 142 Elijah 142
Gulliver, Rose E 326 Wm 326
Guptill, Daniel 24 Justine 136 Nettie 136
Gurney, Eliza 137
Gwilym, D V 37
Hackett, Abbie 241 Alfie 241 Benjamin 132 Cora I 155 Desire Dingley 175 Eleanor F

Hackett (continued)
 178 Emma 90 Ephraim 88
 Ezekiel 282 357 Hannah 272
 Hiram Carville 241 Jacob 175
 James 155 Jenette T 150
 Joseph 238 Jude 178 Lamsen
 282 Lavinia 238 Lois A 327
 Lucy E 235 334 Mary 88 123
 331 332 Olive 235 Orin 327
 Richard 368 Saml 235 Susanah
 357 Susanna 357 362 Susannah
 359 Tace 132 Tamson 282
 Thankful 178 Wm G 150
Hadbook, Abigail 251
Hadley, Amos 208 Susan Boynton 208
Haines, Sally 325 William 325
Hale, Carolin A 109 Lydia N 333
Haley, Charles 113 160 Dorcas W
 318 Hannah 140 John 253
 Joseph 367 368 Joshua 140
 151 367 Lucy 362 Mary 151
 234 250 253 Samuel 40 66 250
 367 Sarah D 113 Sarah Tibbetts 160
Hall, 78 Alicia 124 Belinda 338
 Charles 245 Elisabeth Ann 315
 Elizabeth 85 86 87 Ephraim
 124 Esther 129 Frebrick 114
 Hannah 136 Ira 315 Isaac R 20
 John 251 Jordan 136 Juliett
 113 114 Juliette 113 114 Maria
 245 Mary 118 Mary E 361
 Mary N 96 May 96 Nancy 260
 Rebecca 251 Samuel G 338
Halliday, Dorothy 280 Roscoe 280
Hallock, James C 285 Phebe H 285
Ham, Abigael 292 Abigail 292
 293 Alvah V 255 Anna 93 103-
 105 208 273 326 Anne 302
 Annie 90 93 158 Betsey 320
 Betsey Tyler 288 Colonel 16
 17 David 288 Ebenezer 16 17
 19 20 61 81 93 Eliza 245
 Elizabeth 18 209 Etta L 178
 George W 23 178 358 370
 Hattie R 358 Huldah J 273
 Israel 320 Isreal 373 J B 16 78
 370 Jacob 17 Jacob B 19 20 62
 81 174 James 16 90 93 234

Ham (continued)
 368 John S P 22 Joseph 158
 Judith 81 93 Lucinda 174 Lucy
 320 Martha 151 Martha Ellen
 255 Mary 16 Nancy 93 Nancy
 B 234 O S 30 78 Polly 320
 Sally Mariah 158 Sarah 320
 Sarah Maria 154 Seward 154
 178 Thomas 273 302 Tobais
 216 Tobias 18 209 Ursula 161
 William 158
Hamblet, Charles 363 Ruth 363
Hamilton, Almira W 41 Betsey
 199 D H 80 Emily 151 Hannah
 327 Haris 205 Henry 41 J
 Benson 43 James 363 Jesse
 199 Mary 328 Nellie 257
 Rebecca 288 Sarah 29 321 322
 326 327 Sarah J 205 Sarah
 Jane 363
Hamlin, Dolly 290 295 Geo 295
 Joseph 290 Margaret 290
 Margret 290
Hammond, Adeline 287 Albert M
 271 Almira F 293 Benj F 293
 Charles 287 Ebenezer 296
 Jennet 296 Julia Ann 271 Julia
 M 330 334 Levi 306 373 Lydia
 306 Mary 212 Mary E 195
 Mary J 138 142 Rachel 341
 Sarah W 142
Hancock, Mary Ann 242
Handscomb, Keziah 234
Handy, James 368 Maud M 319
 Morris C 319 Simeon 368
Haney, Lois 264 Simeon 264
Hanly, May 151
Hannah, Sarah 326
Hanneford, Jemima 127 William 127
Hanniford, Susan 90
Hanscom, Betsy E 136 C E 69
 John 166 Marinda J 166 Moses
 33 Sally B 129 Washington 136
Hanscomb, Lemandi 230
Hanson, Abigail 106 Belinda 184
 185 Charlotte 233 Elisha 108
 233 Harriet 108 Henry H 60
 Lillian ELisa 186 Sally 184
 Turner 184 William G 186

Harding, Joseph B 52 Mr 52 Richard 373
Hardy, A H 134 Abigail 356 359 Angeline S 134 Aretus 85 Elisabeth K 90 Elisabeth Keith 90 Hopestill 129 James 129 264 John 264 Julia 279 Lydia Bean 85 Mary A 195 Mehitable 264 Prissy 264 Simeon 264 356 Stephen 279
Harlow, Abram D 353 Emma J 353 Flora 198 James 292 Mary 205 Relief 292 Roseta 353 Susannah 292 William 198
Harmon, Eliza D 343 344 Elizabeth Jane 338 F D 213 Geden 224 Georgian 301 Hannah 335 Hannah Knox 213 Jane L 308 309 Laura Etta 308 Mary E 285 Nancy 284 Patience 361 363 Samuel B 20 Susan 224 Zebulon K 339
Harnden, Elisa J 142 John S 142
Harney, Lydia A 110
Harper, John 78
Harriman, Annie L 192
Harrington, Almira D 288 E D 219 Harriet Newell 233 Henry 233 Mattie B 219
Harris, Abner 13 18 26 45 An---- 127 Barron 13 Deborah 127 Downes 370 Elizabeth 118 Elvina Susanna 98 Fred O 289 George W 182 Hannah 298 Harriet Ellen 231 Henry S 334 James Madison 98 Jane L 334 Jedidiah 286 Jemima 127 Joan 294 John 287 317 Josiah 364 Julia Ann 364 Lawrence J 13 17 48 298 350 Lydia 17 242 279 Lydia Parsons 280 Marcia Antoinette 289 Margaret 256 Maria 165 Martha 311 Mary 287 291 Mary A 198 Melvina 182 Mercy 286 Molly 350 Molly Mary 350 Moses H 41 Moses Little 294 Mr 14 Nancy 117 290 317 Priscilla 271 Richard 367 Richard D 46 74 311 Sarah 323 Silas 127

Harrison, Carrie E 204 George G 25 Harry 204 Selina A 165
Harsie, Carrie L 227
Hart, Catherine 311 313 Josiah 276 325 Mary 312 313 Sally 325 Stephen 16 Susannah 16 311 Thomas 276
Hartley, Eliza 221 Lizzie A 221 Thomas 221
Harts, Stephen Jr 368
Hartshorn, Charles 254 Cora 249 John 249 Mary Ann 254
Hartwell, Ephraim 129 George G 23 Mary Mooar 129
Harvey, A K P 25 73 Edwin 86 Elizabeth 177 John 177 Joseph 110
Harville, Almira P 160 Ann 172 Dorcas A 168 172 Joseph D 168 172
Harwood, Sarah H 270
Hasey, Adimray 299 Admiral 299 Mary 299
Haskall, Joanna 279 Joel 279 Susannah 278 279
Haskell, 104 Aaron 210 Alice 345 Anna 130 Callem 106 Charlotte 118 Cyrus 22 23 Dell 337 Emma 284 Fanny 275 Hannah 130 207 Hannah L 259 Hubbard 130 Jemima 273-275 Jemina 278 Joanna 276 277 279 Joel 279 Judith 278 Kesiah 239 Louisa 210 Lydia 239 Margaret 102 Mary 123 Mary (Deborah) 181 Matilda 278 Mercy 199 202-205 Minah 278 Nathan 278 Nathaniel 168 Pauline 204 Sally 104 Samuel 239 Sarah Day 168 Simeon 259 Simon 207 Susannah 273 274 278 279 W G 41 William 74 204 Wm G 345
Hassy, Jacob 373
Hatch, Abigail 108 110 112 Alexander 145 Ann 268 Betsy 218 Caroline 226 Charity 225 E Turner 319 Elihu 238 Eliza G 152 Ellen M 319 Elmira 218 Fear 309 Floretta 197 Free

Hatch (continued)
 man 225 Hannah 101 238
 Jacob F 203 Jesse 368 John
 110 218 271 293 John P 193
 Joseph 218 Katherine 145
 Martha 203 Mary 96 Mary Ann
 126 Mary M 332 May 332
 Priscilla 193 Prudence 309
 310 Rebecca R 136 Rosamond
 218 Roseman W 218 Rosilla
 271 Samuel 148 238 309 310
 332 368 Sarah 148 237 238 293
 True G 152 William 268
 William C 86
Hathaway, Bardecia T 272 George
 W 272 Lucy 314
Hathon, Emily L 216
Haven, Sophronia N 196
Haville, Inza D 168
Hawes, Henrietta 358 Timothy
 358
Hawkins, Clarence 136 Edna 136
 Ida B 136 Melville 136 Mina
 136 Thatcher 136
Hayes, Addie L 285 Amanda J
 342 Annie W 192 B F 41 42 84
 Edward 342 Elijah 208 Esther
 F 318 George 318 Hannah 37
 Harriet A 37 Isaac A 23 Jacob
 L 22 23 25 78 James B 285
 Jane 208 Mary H 37 230
 Sylvanus B 23 25 78 William
 37 192 230 370
Hayford, Celeslia M 108 Cyrus
 120 Eleanor B 120 Nancy 108
 Rose 335 Zebedee 108
Haynes, E M 34 36 42
Hayward, Ernest 86
Haywood, Anna 135 Elvira 135
 Leslie 135
Head, May 282
Healey, Abraham 334 Harriet 334
 Joseph 334 Sarah 334
Heard, Olive 199-201 204
Heart, Autustine 221 Mary
 Frances 221
Heath, Clinton B 22 Elbridge G
 181 Elizabeth M 200 203
 Frances O 181 Lydia 363
 Martha B 204 Mary 229 230
 Nancy F 344 Walter S 204

Helms, Fred R 175 Lucy M 175
Hemexson, Kate 293
Hemps, Hannah 169
Henderson, Abigail 111 Betsy 109
 Huldah 111 James 111 Sarah
 174 238 Thomas 109
Henniger, Ethel 238
Herbert, Martha E 262 T R 262
Herbest, Affie E 306 T R 306
Herick, Lavine 350
Herinton, Lissie 334
Herrick, Abigail S Williams 353
 Alexis 318 Anson 14 Arvesta
 210 Ebenezer 14 74 Elisa 147
 Elisabeth Augusta 353 Eliza-
 beth 18 191 193 Elizabeth Ann
 318 Emma 207 Henry 335
 Howard 368 Israel 210 Jacob
 Jr 353 Jed 335 Jedediah 335
 John 14 15 18 19 370 Jonathan
 F 23 Lydia 14 Maria 38
 Martha 335 Mary 32 Mary G 98
 Mehitable 335 Nathaniel 146
 Oliver 14 18 19 28 298 370
 Sally 298 Seth 350 Susannah
 146 William Alonzo 318
Herring, John R 281 Julia Ann
 281
Hersey, Amos 30 281 George 360
 Jacob 94 Mary 128 Matilda M
 360 Sara R 94 Welcome 128
 William 41 42
Hersom, Abigail 288 Peter 288
Hersy, Ann 30 Mary Jane 30
Hervey, Boyington 338 Mary 338
Hesilton, Allen 313
Hesliton, Lucy 313
Hevey, Father 45 Peter 44
Hewens, Elis W 199 Mary
 Frances 199 205
Hewey, Fanny 363 Fanny H 359
 George 287 John 359 Margaret
 210 Mary 225 Ruth 311 S 370
 Susie C 287
Hewins, Julius A 220 Sarah Jane
 220
Heyford, G 312 Tilpia 312 Viola
 A 312
Hibbard, Hannah 182
Hickley, Andrew J 23
Hicks, Almira 212 Samuel P 212

Higgens, Abigail 171
Higgins, Belinda 116 Benj 295
  Benjamin 283 Charles 370
  Hannah 283 295 Hiram B 116
  Jerusha 350 Jesse 111 113 350
  Lizzie 198 Lizzie S 202 Mary
  283 295 Priscilla 111 113 128
  161 Sarah 97 98 Tamah 113
  Tamar 108 111 112 113
Hildreth, Bridget 118 240 Hannah
  12 97 145 Jane 323 Mr 13 Mrs
  13 Paul 12 69 97 145 240
  Robert 118 Sarah 118 Susannah
  145
Hildrith, Shadeau 368
Hill, Amanda 103 Annie Maria
  267 269 Byron G 252 Carrie
  355 Charles W 69 David 295
  Dorcas 350 351 E H 68 Edward
  H 72 Elizabeth 156 Emma M
  273 Eunice 152-154 300
  Huldah 188 189 Lydia 295 May
  350 Nathaniel 350 Octavia H
  252 Stephen 156 Thomas I 54
Hillman, Alexander 282 Cordelia
  275 Gilbert R 282 Mary 282
  Thankful 282
Hilton, Elizabeth 104 Everett O
  23 Lovina P 127 Melissa N
  344 O Everet 23
Hinckely, Mary A 161
Hinckley, A L 161 164 Bertha 327
  C H 327 Edmund 146 Eliza
  197 Huldah 146 Isaac 191
  Joseph 373 Lucy 191 320
  Martha B 218 Mary A 161 164
  Nellie 175 Orren D 218 Priscilla 190 193 194 Priscilla
  Pennell 191 Rebecca W 138
  Susan 239 Thankful 206 207
  236-238 240
Hinckly, Isaac 191 Lucy 191
  Priscilla 190 193 194 Priscilla
  Pennell 191
Hinds, Americus V 240 Jane
  Coburn 240 Olive M 204
Hines, Henry 25 J W 41
Hinkely, Rebecca W 140
Hinkley, George A 168 James 211
  Joanna 211 Laura B 203 Maj
  370 Mary M 211 Octavie 168

Hinkley (continued)
  Roxanna 168 Samuel 373
Hinley, Lucy 151
Hipper, Mary Ann 179
Hitchcock, Alfred M 22 23 Jane
  341 Jane A 341 Sarah L 296
Hitchings, Lucinda 269
Hites, Lydia Ann 287 Michael
  287
Hoar, Eunice 187 Joseph 291
  Mert 135 Rebecca J 291 Sarah
  Ellen 187
Hobbs, Charles H 22 Hannah 346
Hodgdon, Emily 143 Huldah J 215
  John 143 Mary Jane 357 364
Hodgkin, Betsey 16 243 Douglas
  217 Esther 219 George 267
  Harriet H 267 Jonathan 16 243
  Joshua 368 Thomas 27 86 105
  220 225
Hodgkins, Aaron 141 Abigail 141
  Betsy 192 Chas 300 Elminee
  206 Harriet L 224 James 192
  206 Jonathan 105 224 May 356
  Orpha 105 224 Sarah 300
  Thomas 368
Hodgon, Emeline 231 Samuel 231
Hodsdon, Elizabeth 127 J A 127
Hodskin, Thomas 367
Hodskins, Benjamin 367
Hoer, Joseph 291 Rebecca J 291
Hoffses, Llewellyn 345 Rose 345
Hogben, A C 42
Holbrook, Benj 283 Charles H 328
  Charlotte 283 John K 317
  Leonard 283 Mary L 317
Holcombe, Sophia 108
Hold, Ada C 324
Holey, Merchange 114 Susan 114
Holland, Adelbert 193 Alfonso B
  161 Alice R 193 Alphonso B
  80 Armine 161 Daniel 20 22 34
  49 53 62 64 66 80 154 277 370
  Ida May 278 John 80 259 344
  367 Mary A 80 Mary Ann 154
  Rebecca 80 137 344 Susanna
  259
Hollands, Capt 276
Holman, D Horace 22 Geo W 65
  George W 36
Holmes, Elisa 134 Ella E 217

Holmes (continued)
   Gilman N 126 Hiram 134 Mary
    P 125 126
Holt, Achsa 156 Annie 364 Asa
   364 Diana 156 George 297
   Jane 264 Olive J 297 Samuel
   264 Sylvanus 156
Hood, Harrisen Porter 256 Vesta
   Jane 256
Hook, Jeanna 132
Hooker, Oleavia A 359
Hooper, Christina B 136 John 136
   Rachel 199 200 202 203
Hoosting, Mehitable 265
Hopkins, Affie E 306 Elizabeth O
   358 Eugene 358 Garcelon 306
   Matilda P 244 Wm 244
Horan, Horace 334 Mary 334
Horbury, Charles 23
Horner, Rhea Maria 109
Horr, Elizabeth S 72 O A 68 72
Horton, Ruth 340
Hotton, Asaph 373
Houghton, Eliza T 230 George
   230 Lucy A 197 Mermon
   Stinson 197
House, Abigail 209 Asenath
   Winslow 340 F 190 Loraney
   243 Mary 346
Hovey, Adalade 90 Charles 90
How, Charlotte A 293 Ellva 293
   Elsie 293 Joseph 293 Nancy
   284 286 289 292 293
Howard, Addie B 306 Caroline
   Ann 87 Everett E 186 Fred A
   87 James C 306 Lissie L 232
   Margery 253 Mary 253 Nelson
   22 24 Nett 326 Richard L 42
   Robert 233 Sally 342 William
   232 Winnifred M 186 Wm 253
   Wm Jr 253
Howe, Daniel M 39 Deborah Clark
   206 Eleanor 294 G M 42
   George 294 George Milton 39
   Harriot 39 J A 42 84 Rev 175
   Sabina R 266 Salvinia 266
   Sarah M 39 W S 73
Howett, Benjamin T 308 Mary A
   308
Howey, Sarah 305
Howland, Polly 105

Howling, Joseph 249 Sarah 249
Hoxie, Hannah 150 Jesemine 299
   300
Hoys, Abigail 312 James R 312
Hoyt, F L 69 Frank L 24 77
   Hannah 336 337 Hannan 337
Hubbard, Fanny 132 Hannah 100
   John 174 Levina 98 Lizzie
   Ann 173 174 176 Rolvin J 98
Huckins, Rachel 225
Huff, Abigail 154 Abiie 154 Alice
   E 173 Charles W 203 Phebe
   203
Hughes, Annie 331
Hull, Elizabeth 237 William 237
Hunnewell, Ida Estelle 141
Hunt, Addie 121 Dolly 242 Elisa
   329 330 Ellis L 173 Frank 98
   Hortense C 98 Margaret
   Augusta 173 Mary 133 Nellie
   218 Simeon 133 Stephen 254
   Susanna 254 W L G 222
   Zebina 242
Hunter, 125 Alma A 359 Polly
   303 Robert 303 Winchel 359
   Winnifred 358
Huntington, David 143 Jane 143
   Levi 355 Phebe R 355
Hurd, Myra Agnes 247 Olive 200
   201 204 Sally 199
Huse, Frances 137
Huskings, Hale M 243 Luraney
   243
Hussey, Anna H 141 Harriet E
   191 John W 141 Maurice S 191
   Morris 231 Sylvanus P 94
Hussy, Ella G 94
Hutch, Alexander 339 Suca 339
Hutcheson, Elisa 163
Hutchings, Bessie 346
Hutchins, Charles 278 Eunice 188
   George 188 Hannah 274 Jennie
   E 257 Nancy B 274 Sarah D
   278 Thomas 7 William 274
Hutchinson, Aseneth Drew 170
   Charles 72 J 33 Liberty H 22
   23 Stephen 170
Hutton, Margaret A 162
Hyron, Sophia 363
Ilsley, George B 36 Rebecca 219-
   221

Ingalls, Maud H 321
Ingraham, D C 36 Louise 102
Ireland, Anna 122 Clarissa J 140
  David 236 Dolly 156 Dorothy
  156 Joel 156 Rebecca 156
  Thankful 236 Zadoc 156
Irish, Annie 158 Elizabeth 154
  Freeman 154 370 James 158
  Margery 252
Irving, Belle 243
Isaacson, I B 76 S A 76
Jack, Auvila C 353 Betsey 126
  Florence P 344 James 353
  Robert 373
Jackson, Abigail 345 Alonzo E 21
  Blanch B 92 Charity 206
  Charlotte 179 Daniel 30 Emma
  C 285 Harriet L 218 Hasadiah
  121 122 Hattie L 218 Henry A
  115 John M 218 Lemuel 150
  180 206 230 259 367 368 Leroy
  285 Mary 101 148 180 230
  Mehitable 115 Nancy 259
  Nancy R 258 Nathaniel I 36
  Olive Staten 150 Philene 286
  Samuel 148 367 368 Solomon
  121 122 Susan B 134
Jacob, William 29
Jacobs, Hannah 168
Jacques, 317 Betsy 317 Nathaniel
  P 317 Rose Ann 317
James, Flora D 117 George
  Washington 342 Louisa 181
  182 Sally 342
Jameson, Arthur 19 Charles
  Edwin 173 Charlotte S 173
Jaquik, Elisabeth 141 John 141
Jasper, Edwin E 150 225 Olive
  225 Olive Staten 150
Jay, Arminta Uphrasin 254 Clarinda R 137 George 254
  Samuel Jr 137
Jefferson, Charles F 272
Jeffres, 227
Jeffries, David 7
Jellison, Charles 130 Vesta
  Augusta 130
Jenkins, Betsey 286 Keziah 119
  Philip 119 Phillip 120 Sally
  106 Sarah 120 Servia 261
Jenks, Julia A 120

Jenness, A J 275 Clara 275
Jepson, Betsey 34 Clarion P 343
  345 Dorcas 236 Ebeneser 343
  Ebenezer 236 Edward 360
  Elizabeth 286 Elizabeth G 128
  357 John C 30 Leonard 133
  Lizzie 128 Margaret M 360
  Rebecca 105 Rosannah 133
  Sarah 114 283 Thomas 50 283
  William 17 99 128 286 360
  Wm 276
Jewel, Almira 212 Harvey 212
Jewell, Betsy 167 Rosie Laughton 102
Jewett, Almira B 91 B F 212
  Daniel 91 George W 46 Margaret 260 Mary E 212 253
Jipson, Phebe 128 Thomas 128
Johnson, Abby 137 Abigail 293
  Catherine 261 Daniel 263
  David 293 David Jr 266 Eliza
  276 299 Elizabeth T 295 Ella
  M 276 Ellen M 293 Esther A
  317 Frank H 24 Geo K 276
  Hannah C 145 Henry 261
  Horace 272 J B 62 John W 115
  Loisa 235 Martha A 125 Mary
  135 263 Mary A 278 Mary
  Frances 265 266 Mr 51 Nancy
  M 272 Nettie 241 Rachel
  Johnson 115 Sanford 125 Susan
  307 Susan E 302 Wm 96
Johnston, Edward 304 Fannie 304
Johonnot, R F 41
Joncas, Louis 24
Jone, Abigail 201 Laura 201
  Stella S 198 Tilden 201
Jones, A M 25 67 163 Abial M 19
  20 21 22 Abigail 201 Anna 163
  Annah 131 Annie 225 Arthur
  225 Betsey 199 225 Caroline
  172 Daniel B 21 22 41 45
  Edith 108 Edward 165 247
  Eleanor 101 Elijah 38 38
  Elizabeth 136 136 Ella 292
  Ephraim 163 Flora D 117
  Frank 199 George H 172
  Hannah 255 Hannah E 163
  Hattie May 301 Hiram 370 J B
  370 Joan 272 John A 79 John
  B 19 30 75 272 370 John C 217

Jones (continued)
　Josiah 368 Julia 167 Julia
　Marcia 202 Laura 201 Levi
　255 Luther 208 Lydia 165 170
　171 Mary Hannah 208 Minnie
　F 247 Myra Ellen 121 Nancy
　Hammond 225 Nellie 235
　Pamela 239 Pamelia 239
　Polly 224 225 Roana D 41
　Royal M 225 Samuel 202 Sarah
　176 Sarah C 172 Sarah Jane
　217 Sarah Mary 176 Tilden 201
　Willard 301 William 225
Jorda, Dorcas A 111
Jordan, Abbie C 349 Abby Roberts 137 Abigail 142 162 163
　257 Abigail Miller 142 Abijah
　373 Abraham 368 Adaline 143
　Albion W 348 Andrew 302
　Anna G 267 Annah 229 Annie
　297 Apollos 142 Benj 367
　Benjamin 176 310 Carrie F
　126 Catherine 319 Charles C
　125 David 240 Deborah 163
　299 Dianah 326 Dorcas A 109
　111 Dorcas Ann 111 Dorcas
　Wright 133 Ella P 125 Foster
　164 George Henry 246 Georgiana T 273 Hannah 95 130 309
　310 Harriet E 191 Holman 100
　James 163 243 257 265 367
　368 James Jr 246 James M
　300 James Polk 273 Jane M
　135 Jedediah 225 Jeremiah
　189 310 Jerey 367 Jermiah 309
　John 174 John B 42 Joseph 29
　Joseph L 265 Joshua 137
　Katherine 162 L G 69 Lewetta
　300 Lucy 131 132 303 306
　Lucy D 163 Lucy E 186 Lurania 32 Lyman 96 Margaret 183
　Mary 189 240 243 299 Mary A
　174 Mary E 326 Mary Elizabeth 348 Mary J 265 Mary N
　243 Melissa 161 Melissa O
　161 Nancy 310 339 Nathaniel
　163 349 Noah 297 Polly 176 R
　20 Rachel 225 Rebecca 137
　147 Robert 225 Rufus L 191
　Rushworth 137 Sally 110 Sarah
　142 223 225 310 341 Sarah

Jordan (continued)
　Catherine 164 Sarah H 311
　Sarah J 310 Sophia 265 Sophronia T 220 Stephen 299
　Susan H 246 T F 341 Thankful
　302 Tristram Frost 109 William 162 William 2nd 143
　Winfield Scott 186 Winslow
　373
Joslin, Mary E 90
Joy, George E 213 Maria G 213
Judkins, Abbie J 113 Alvin 233
　Bridget 240 Edwin H 113 Eliza
　265 Esther Elizabeth 184
　George 184 George C 25
　Margaret 332 Mary Ann 86
　Mary E 131 Peter 240 Robert
　T 86 Sophia 233 Stephen 373
Juellaria, Margaret 329
Junkins, Elizabeth W 157 Otis H
　C 157
Kanada, T W 37
Kane, Ella M 285 George H 285
Kavanaugh, George M 25
Kawfenans, Bertha 342
Keeler, S W 36
Keene, Addie 243 Alfred A 114 E
　Jr 370 Elsie 90 94 Esther 290
　Esther L 284 John 168 170
　Josephine 170 Julia 296
　Lincoln 293 Mary J 288 Silance 168 Silence H 168
　Sophronia E 293
Keith, 275 Dora 313 Elisabeth 90
　Ellen 94 Isaac 275 Mary E 313
　Seth 313
Keizer, Sarah 209
Kelley, Daniel 313 Eliza 207
　Judith 346 Mary 346 Mary E
　313 Thomas 23
Kelly, Clariss 346 Hannah L 202
Kelsey, A H 55 80 Albert H 54 66
　67
Kempton, Henry 361 Louisa 361
Kendall, Henry 27 289 294 Jane
　289 294 Sarah M 39
Kendrick, Mary 252 Samuel 252
Kenney, Archibald 286 Eunice E
　286 James L 25 Jennie H 133
　John L 25 Joshua 133 Merion
　250 Thomas 44 Wealthy 133

Kenniston, Catherine J 145 Leroy 145
Kent, Abbie A 127 Judge 61
Kenyon, John 209 Mattie 209
Key, Adela 125 Betsy 349 Cyrus 125 Hannah 201 Love 349
Keyes, Calvin 264 Caroline 266 John 266 Lucy Ann 264 Rebecca 289
Kilbourne, William 72
Kilgore, Emerline 216 Ezra A 216 Ezra C 23 G L 72 Joseph 147 Lydia 147 Mary B 91
Kilham, Abigail 209
Kilkenney, Elmira 109 110
Kilkenny, Elmira 110
Kilord, Charles 145 Martha A 145
Kilpatrick, Joseph 33
Kilvert, Samuel W 20 57 67
Kimball, Abigail 34 Aphia 99 Luther 99 Margaret 307 Rhoda 101 Simeon 101
Kincaid, Gilman 99 Mary J 99
King, Angie 363 Charles II 7 Clement 85 Cynthia 292 Cyrus 32 Lucy 85 Lucy Ann 342 Moses 342 Samuel Horace 292
Kingsbury, George 243 Lissie 243
Kinne, George 87 Margaret Ellen 87
Kirby, Emma 313 I P 313 Jemima 313
Kirk, Geneva 280
Knapp, Eunice 108 Jane 236 Levi 110 Louisa 110 Luisa 110
Kneeland, Nancy 140
Knight, 78 Amanda M 266 Charles 241 E E 195 Edward Franklin 295 Ella Gertrude May 295 Emily 352 Emma L 195 George 235 Ida 241 Jermie F 241 John F 241 Joseph 266 Lura 241 Mary A 265 Sadie 217
Knights, Betsy 96 Emily 352 Jonathan B 332 Mary M 332 May R 332
Know, George 370
Knowles, Achsa 352 Achsia 350-352 Joseph 203 Lowell 350 351 Rebecca P 203 Rosemond

Knowles (continued) 350 351
Knowlton, A K P 20 21 24 Caroline 215 Louisa C 94 Martha 310 Preston 94 Sarah 162 William Warren 310
Knox, Ebenezer 35 George 33 34 35 46 83 96 Olive 185 Patience 211 213 215 Sarah 211 213 215 Sarah L 35 Sarah M 96
Kuse, Caroline 334 Perry 334
Kyle, Mrs Charles 32 Winslow 32
LaFrance, Mary E 314 Sarah J 307
LaGrange, Nellie A 262
Labonte, Youville 107
Labree, Aravester V 363 Charles 316 Nancy 316 Sarah 149
Ladd, A S 42 43 Ammi G 172 Lydia Frances 172
Lake, Benj 287 Benjmain 13 Delana G 139 Dorcas 326 327 Eben'r 367 Eleasor 139 Elwin 139 John 327 John D 176 Joshua 140 368 Lydia 205 Mary 29 Mercy 13 139 283 284 286 287 Mercy Eaton 13 Rachel A 176 Sarah 97 140 Sarah Dill 327 Wm 139
Lamb, 302 Ann 252 Harriet 280 John S 253 Joseph 139 Mercy Ann 140 Nellie J 321 Prudence 253
Lambart, Gideon 196 Matilda T 196
Lambert, Emily 302 Gideon 360 Hannah 220 Harriet 281 Jarvis 220 Joshua 163 Matilda Harvey 360 Mittie 360 Rebecca 220 Susan 163
Lamont, John 304 Susannah 304
Lamphrey, Jesse 321
Lancaster, Rose 151
Land, Elizabeth 215
Lander, Abisha 226 247 Anna 298 Dorcas 226 Dorcas B 226 Eunice 119 Freeman 183 207 298 Hannah 207 298 Hannah H 170 Irason P 170 Lazarus 181 Lovinia 183 Lucy 28 129 Lydia 180 181 Mary 247 Olive

Lander (continued) 247 Tamy 128 Thankful 207
Landers, Charles M 290 Dorcas 287 Freeman 206 287 Hannah 205 Lazaras 368 Lucy 129 Mary 247 Nancy D 290 Polly 234 Prudence 118 Roberson 368 Robinson 118 Sarah 206 Thankful 206
Lane, Almira 350 351 Angeline 205 Augustus 134 Barber 257 Benjamin 169 309 Edmond 336 Elvira 281 Etta L 178 George W 178 Hannah 257 Hiram 323 Jane 336 337 John 340 John D 345 Judith 323 Louise 257 Lucinda 343 Lucinda E 42 246 Lydia E 333 Lydia R 334 Mary E 261 Nancy 169 Nancy Danielson 169 Olive Jane 345 Oliver P 246 Rachel Ann 114 Ransom 343 Ruth 309 340 Samuel 261 Sewall 257 Sullivan 114 William N 281
Lang, Edmund 186 Sarah 186
Langelier, Louis 25
Langley, Evangeline 327
Larned, Z M 39
Larrabbee, Anna 191 104 Anna 104 210 Eliza B 365 Elizabeth 199 Florence L 317 Mattie A 344
Larreus, ohn 368
Lary, Lizzie R 150
Laskey, Allis 92 Rose 92
Lathrop, Adelia 338
Laughton, Anna C 222 Lydia 277 Nelson J 222 Warren P 21 22
Laurie, Alice E 219
Lawrence, Alma 287 Amanda 247 Elizabeth 264 266 Haskell 247 Martha J 325 Mary E 213 Sherburn 325
Layton, Alice Redman 152
LeFebre, Leon 23
LeFebvre, L 23
LeLacheur, D W 43
Leach, Benjamin 278 Catherine F 331 Rhoda Hillman 278
Leadbetter, Elisa 94 Hald B 253
Leader, William 22 24 25
Leadham, Ellen N 238 Samuel 238
Learned, J R 69
Leathers, Statina L 362 Thomas J 362
Leaver, Abbie 103
Leavitt, Ada 94 Addie 346 Bathsheba 166 Carroll Augustus 243 Celia May 143 Ernest 143 F A 94 Fred E 24 John 82 Josephine A 159 Mary 228 268 Mary B 274 Mary Sturgis 243 Minerva 292 Moses 301 Nancy Jordan 301 Nettie A 298 Walter C 298
Ledoton, F A 294 Susan Allen 294
Lee, Catherine 145 Jane 267 June 264 267 Katherine 145 Theoda 17 303
Leeds, B I 64 Benjamin I 53
Legro, Charlotte 100
Leighton, Alice Redman 152 Ann 156 Elias H 342 Linnett 342 Louise 342 Susan 119
Lemont, Charles D 23 24 Eliza 213
Lenfest, Elsie J 303 Lydia 17 202 Peter 17 202 303 Thomas 368
Lennan, Anna F 211 Annie 211 Emerline J 212 Llewllyn 212
Lennon, Sarah 100
Leonard, Berry 356 Betsy Ann 356 Gertrude 174 Joseph 174
Leslie, S C Jr 77 Samuel C Jr 25
Leternearn, Edward 44
Levitt, Hannah 168 John S 168
Lewis, Augusta M 183 Caroline 223 224 Edroin 223 224 Emma Estelle 99 Horatio 99 Irving 183 Joseph 142 Joseph H 295 Mary T 295 Rachel W 142 Sarah 270
Lezotte, Henry 25
Libbey, Asbury 286 Charlotte 141 Elizabeth J 186 Eunice E 286 Harriet 332 Samuel 141 332
Libby, 122 358 Abigail M 141 Amanda 291 Ann J 262 Augusta 135 Betsey 231 C L 43

Libby (continued)
Catherine 188 Caty 188
Charles O 135 David 117
David B 285 Dennie 213 Dolly
Watson 222 Drusilla 358 Eliza
B 304 Eliza P 305 Elizabeth
229 Elizabeth J 189 Fannie P
297 Frances A 122 Francilla H
361 Hannah 350 Hannah E 213
Helen 358 Hiram 213 Horace
23 291 Isaac 29 30 James 305
Jane 189 Lucinda E 349 Lucy
285 Lydia Parker 267 Martha
Ann 98 Mr 50 Nancy Swift 213
Nathan 222 Patience 213
Richard 267 Rufus K 229 Ruth
360 362 Salinda 277 Sally 250
Samuel W 22 Sarah 103 Sewell
188 Silas 361 W S 57 William
67 189 William A 24 25
Lidstone, Noah 246 Sarah 246
Sarah C 246
Lincoln, Betsey 16 Betsy 219
Charlotte 335 336 Levi 8
Lovell 16 219 Lydia 355 Mary
Ann 356 Maryg N 233 Mercy
339 Nat 356 Nathan'l 367
Nathaniel 355 Rufus 233
Salley 234 Sally 231 Synus 367
Lindsey, Daniel 170 Lucy 170
Ling, Anna D 219 Anna Dennett
174 Sylvanus 174
Linscott, Ann 96 Anne 96 D C 96
Daniel 370 Harvey 337 Lizzie
337 Rachel Adelade 336
Willard 58 336
Linten, Celia A 226 227 Levi 227
Lisherness, Hermon 239 Lillian 239
Litchfield, Alice 124 Ames 29
Benjamin 21 25 77 Benjamin J
243 Betsey 87 Betsy 87 Charlotte 123 Cynthia 324 D B 41
Isaac 370 Jeremiah 243 L 370
Lucinda 30 Luther 28 123
Mabel 353 354 Martha 29 86
103 Mary 236 324 May 350
Nels 370 Noah 16 18 19 20 27
29 41 45 46 74 86 121 354 367
368 Norris 30 Priscilla 92
Rhoda 28 Sally 243 Samuel 19

Litchfield (continued)
28 29 324 Sarah C 42 Wade
28 236 Wm 370
Lith, Jno J 302
Little, 14 48 78 Anna K 243
Edward 51 52 53 Edward T 52
62 Hannah 298 Horace C 21 24
25 Josiah 8 50 52 370 Maria
210 Michael 18 49 50 74
Moses 12 Mr 48 Rachael D
334 Thomas B 210
Littlefield, Abigail 264 Abram A
306 Augusta 334 Carrie Emma
115 Charity 238 242 Cynthia A
112 Edward 334 Ellen C 306
Enoch 206 George 112 Laura
312 Lewis 327 Luther 276
Mary R 122 Nellie 327 O H 40
264 Olive 239 Orilla Lake 327
Pamelia 218 Priscilla 94
Rosilla 206 271 Sally 207
Samuel 239 Sarah 312 Stephen
218 Thomas 312 Walter 327
William L 115
Littlejohn, Abigail 295 296
Littlfield, Enoch 271
Litus, Joanna G 248
Livermore, Rebecca 241
Lock, Rev Mr 29
Locke, Alpheus C 20 Arvesta 300
Elizabeth 310 Elvin 300 Harriet Augusta 144 Lovina 181
Lovina J 180 Lynt 310 Mary
310 Nathan 180 181 Nelson 144
Lockwood, A D 55 64 67 Amos D 53 67
Loller, Ruth 93
Lombard, Ann Augusta 150
Hannah Mariah 184 Isaac 184
John 61 Lewis 76 Luther 150
Longey, Sophia 97
Longfellow, Samuel 355 Sarah R 355 Stephen 14
Longil, Sophia 138
Longley, 101 Eleanor 319 Etta
263 Isiah P 370 J B 75 J P 75
Josiah B 25 Samuel 319
Sophorina 169 Thomas B 23
Thomas H 23 319
Longly, Israel W 349 Minerva

Longly (continued)
 Jane 349
Look, Betsy 200
Lord, Clarinda 176 Isaiah 284 Isariah 290 Ivory 234 John 8 Lucy 284 290 Maria 188 Mary Ann Lulf 234 Nancy 284 290 Nellie 269 Polly 222 Susan 207 Thomas W 38
Loring, David M 208 David P 208 Jacob 207 Jane 207 208 Jane Gray 208 Judith 208 Lucy 207 Rachael 207 Sarah 208 Sylvia J 195
Lorry, Edwin H 240 Lois 240
Lothrop, Appiah Andersen 232 Daniel 170 Lucius 232 Lucy 170
Lougee, N R 21
Lourdies, Nathan 354
Louse, Cordelia Ann 209 Myrick 209
Lovejoy, Adria L 302 Bessie E 228 Eliza P 222 Elizabeth 89 90 92 Eva 182 George 182 Georgiana M 294 Georgianna 297 Joseph 294 297 Laura Ann 321 Lois 185 Marcellus 169 Marcellus P 169 Mary F 185 Nathaniel 185 Simon 228 Sophia 169 W F 302 Warren 222 Wm 321
Lovell, Fred L 213 Hattie Grace 213 Jeremiah 354 Mehitabell 357 Sarah 354
Low, Elvira 270 Judith 363
Lowden, Josiah 333 Serena G 333
Lowell, Abbie F 187 Alura E 37 Benjamin P 21 41 Daniel 79 311 370 Delmar R 187 Edward 105 Elisabeth E 139 Eliza D 37 Ellen 304 Ezra 302 Hannah 79 282 James 18 53 61 66 67 75 79 82 282 370 James Jr 79 93 190 Jane G 93 190 John 188 John A 31 41 John Jr 118 John William 187 Jonathan 139 Lucy 105 309 Mark 19 61 62 67 79 80 276 370 Mary 118 187 188 Mary Polly 187 May 96 Mrs Benjamin P 41 Polly 187

Lowell (continued)
 Prudence 236 Sarah J 302 Sarah Jane 304 Sophia 311 Stephen 187 Vesta 79 William 187 302 304 309 368 Wm 367
Lowsell, John A 38
Luce, Agnes 90 Carlo 112 Carrie 94 Clarissa 86 Electa M 259 Elvira 110 Grace 239 Harriet 110 110 Harriet M 110 Henrietta F 225 Herman 239 Irvin 110 Israel 33 Jane 110 John 110 Margie 90 Melvina A 112 Phidelia 92 Priscilla 85 Robert 259 Samuel 110 True 90 Washburn 90
Lucy, Michael 44
Ludden, Catherine 94 Daniel 94 H B 91 Hannah 94 Mandeville T 21 23 Sally 91
Ludlam, Nicholas 36
Lufkin, Abigail 336 337 Andrew J 337 Daniel 336 Eliza Jane 337 Rachel 336
Lumber, Maria 363
Lund, Tamson 182 183
Lunt, Cyrus M 24 25 G H 214 Lucy 234 Parker 214 Wm 234
Lydick, Hattie 135
Lydston, Harriet 111 William 23 111
Lyford, Fred D 23 Jesse S 21 22 65
Lyman, Harriet Sophia 96 Hattie S 96
Lyng, Sylvanus 373
Lyon, 221 Mary 253 Mary Ann 344 345 William 345
MCarthy, Joseph A 294
Maburry, Mehitable 362
Mace, Marguerit A 200
Macomber, May Jane 198 Rev Mr 26
Macumber, Louisa 198
Madison, Abbie P 178 R 178
Maillet, Alfred W 24
Malhoon, Harris 189 Jane 189
Mallett, Elisabeth P 125 J Frank 125
Maloon, Hannah M 259
Manley, Moses P 97 Sarah C 97

Mann, Emerline 286 William N 286
Mansfield, Thomas 23
Manson, Caroline M 326
Manter, Goff 338 Lulla M 318 Mary E 338 Wallis 318
Manton, Abilene Coleman 338
Mantor, Mary E 338
Marble, A Llewellyn 25 Andrew L 25 Andrew W 323 Nancy Ann 323
March, Ellen 164 Joanna 157 Mary 157 Pelletiah 157
Marchand, Charles 24
Marcous, Augustus 24 Stanislas 23 24
Marden, Sarah 363
Maricourt, A 45
Marquis, Helen V 275
Marr, Charles H 153 Cyrus 339 Hannah 231 233 234 Happy Proctor 364 Josiah 364 Priscilla 339
Marrinal, Maria E 123
Marrow, Angie 198 Anna 311 Mr 121 William 311
Marshall, Addie E 204 Alfred 16 Charles K 98 John 16 18 74 Marinda Huntington 98 Mary 284 William J 204
Marson, Mary J 141
Marston, A J 73 Eliza 119 Isaiah 119 John 207 John W 37 Leander 224 Lydia A 294 Margaret 119 Martha Ellen 190 Martha R 335 Mary 34 347 Phebe 214 215 Phoebe 214 215 Polly 224 Rachael 207 Rebecca 93 Samuel H 294 Sarah 112 Simon 33 119 Sumner 93 190 Susan 37 William F 112
Martel, L J 72 Louis J 25
Martin, E 43 Ezekiel 32 33 41 286 Frank W 23 Leander 224 Luther P 67 Marcia 286 Mary 157 224 Pearl 157 Virginia Emily 109
Masen, Clora H 260
Mason, Esther 309 Liva 227 Mary 227 Orvida 267 R M 57 58

Masterman, Joseph N 337 Louisa 337
Masters, Henry 65
Mathews, Isabella I 254 Lucy 129 William 254
Matte, L E N 73
Maxwell, 77 Abbie J 313 Abigail 264 Affidele 174 Albert 304 Arthur 304 Daniel 264 Dora 261 Elisabeth 304 Elsey J 184 Elsy 184 H W 67 J W 173 James 174 Jane B 304 Janet 230 Mary E 304 O M 21 Polly 184 280 Robert 184 280 William 304
May, 277 Ellen Elizabeth 229 Samuel E 20 67 229
Maybury, Mahitable 253 William 253
Mayo, Abner W 179 Amelia 179 Augusta E 213 Catherine 188 Catherine A 188 John 213 Noah 188 Rachael L 203 204
McCann, Mary A 153
McCarlie, Carrie C 267
McCarthy, Marcetta 294
McCloom, Hulda 169 Huldah 169 Patrick 169
McCollion, Charles 43 Father 44
McCorrison, Ella 245 James 304 Mary Ann 304
McCrutchin, Kate 239
McCullock, Hannah H 98 Samuel 98
McCurdy, Susan 149
McDonald, Abigail 241 Eunice 241 Horace 241
McDonough, Anthony E 24
McDougle, Sarah 145
McFadden, Esther 357 Frances A 359 Samuel H 359
McFarland, David 373 Eugene 219 Moses 174 Nellie Adelaide 219
McGawley, Mathew 25
McGillicubby, Michael P 25
McGillicuddy, Michael P 25 P 43 Patrick 21 22
McIntire, Ellen 358 Eunice H 154 Henry 154 John 358 Mary C 91

McIntire (continued)
94 Susan 362 Sylvina 135 W S 33 43
McIntosh, Alexander 234 Hannah M 234 Jessie D 219
McKeene, Ellen Augusta 172 William 172
McKenna, J J 58
McKenney, Abigail 241 242 Annie M 217 Betsey 223 Charles D 345 Charles L 217 Hannah 34 223 224 Jennie 345 Lucy L 113 Salome 144 William 223
McKenny, Absalon 225 Ann Marie 270 Clifton 327 Deborah E 293 Jenny 131 Lucy Ann 237 Mary Alice 327 Salle 225 Sam'l C 293
McKenzie, Isabella 303 John 303
McKeown, Ruth S 217
McLaughlin, Nellie A 262 Nellie J 294 Peter 44 Wm D 294
McLean, Edward 210 Emily 210
McLellen, Deborah 244 Nancy 243 244 247 Simon 244
McLoon, Hulda 169 Huldah 169 Patrick 169
McManus, James 24
McMillan, J 32 James 33
McMurphy, Annie 277
McNair, Archibald 98 Elizabeth 98
McPhail, John 189 Mary Elizabeth 189
McPhee, Helen 128
McPherson, Jennie B 214 Willie A 214
McWilliams, Alexander 24
Mcloom, Hulda 169 Huldah 169 Patrick 169
Meacham, Mr 63
Meader, Hannah 230 Hannah S 354 Levi 29 Mary 154 Tobias 154
Meadler, Olive 235
Mean, Maybell 344
Melaken, Earl 297 Hannah 297
Melcher, A S 78 Threse 103
Mellen, George F 65 66 Hannah 341 Phinney 341
Mellor, Sarah H 173

Melvin, Etta H 201 Joseph P 201 Nancy A 201
Menserean, Edith A 334 Rufus 334
Mercy, Pettengill 13
Mero, Electa A 244 Hermon 244
Merriam, Caroline D 85 Thos 85
Merrifield, Chas N 262 Hannah 329 Sophia J 262 William E 77
Merrill, 77 Abiah 223 Abigail 196-198 233 Abner 360 Anna 88 163 Annie May 134 Benjamin 18 105 197 Benson 108 370 Betsey Elizabeth 360 Chas 290 Clara Anna 132 Cyrus 295 Daniel 268 Dennis D 134 Elizabeth 295 Ellen E 312 Emma 134 Esekiel 144 Esther A 152 153 155 Ezekiel 88 104 Fanny 129 George H 36 Georgia Drew 10 90 91 Georgie Drew 94 Grace F 165 Hannah 12 212 214 215 Hannah C 134 Harriet 229 Harriet A 218 Hattie A 102 Isaac C 23 Israel B 24 J L 76 Jacob 152 337 James 207 Jane M 336 337 Jedediah 368 Jerusha 130 John 124 307 368 John H 224 John R 270 Joseph 367 Joshua 19 220 Josiah 229 Julia Ann 308 Laura 337 Laura C 336 Laura J 275 Levi 133 Levi Jr 133 Linda 268 Lois 124 Lucy Baker 270 Lydia 133 Marcellus S 134 Margaret Elizabeth 290 Martha 264 265 267 Mary 92 95 108 268 Mary Cutter 126 Mary Elizabeth 263 Matilda 224 Mehitable 357 Moses 368 Nancy 263 Nancy Jane 161 Nancy P 357 Nathan 360 Nathaniel 163 Orpha 105 Precena G 360 Rebecca H 271 Rose M 307 Roxie 277 Rufus 233 Ruth 207 Ruth E 187 S 370 Sally 144 Sally D 345 Samuel 357 Samuel A 109 Sarah 197 264 Selvira 279 Sewall 113 130 180 184 Sophronia 307 Stephen

Merrill (continued)
  T 218 Susan 30 104 124 Susan
  H 220 Thomas 129 William S
  161
Merriman, Salome 154
Merritt, Catherine 163
Merrow, Harriet M 217 Harriet N
  217 Lydia D 182 Reuben 217
  Sophia 307 308
Merserve, A K P 317 Alice 130
  131 132 Dorcas 317 Elice 130
  131 132 Ellis 130 131 132
Meryman, Nancy 92 93 Nathaniel
  93
Meserve, Alice 130 131 132
  Betsey 218 Betty 217 Elice
  130 131 132 Ellis 130 131 132
Meservey, Betsy 218 219
Meservy, Albert 97 Ann 97
Messer, Mary 107
Metcalf, Daniel 148 George W 24
  Katherine 148 Mary 335
Michal, David 367
Michel, Joseph 367
Michell, Joshua 367
Miles, Donia B 265 Rosillia 265
Millay, Margaret 239
Millbanks, Katherine 161 162 163
  164
Miller, 277 Annie 355 Betsey 231
  Charles H 23 24 77 Clara 355
  Deborah 246 Dovina 324 Ella
  D 307 Enna L 248 Helen 119
  Hugh 233 James 246 Jane W
  34 Jennie 287 Joseph 22
  Lester R 248 Olive E 246 Ora
  355 Phebe 149 Polly 324 325 S
  P 246 Sally 233 Sarah 142 216
  Seviah 140 Survinah 140
  William N 307
Millet, Charles 71
Millett, Asa R 338 Betsey 201
  Charles 370 David 201 Jennie
  Eliza 338 Sarah 130 131
Milliken, Maryann 224 Noah 224
Mills, Kesiah 236 Lucy 237
  Rachel 130
Minchin, Ella 204
Minot, Stephen 7
Mitchel, Davis 368

Mitchell, Anna 29 Annie R 229
  Annie T 229 Betsey Jr 181
  Betsy 348 Catherine 91 94
  Charles 208 Christopher 222
  Clarissa 131 134 Clark 222
  Cynthia Matilda 92 Daniel 181
  Eleanor 208 229 Eliab 151
  Eliza 115 Elizabeth 302 Elsa
  327 Emma Jane 222 Etta L
  248 Frederick 175 176 Governor 76 Granville 290 Hannah P
  221 222 Harriet S 275 J W 176
  Jacob 208 James 15 27 James
  Warren 171 Jane 124 125 207
  208 Joel G W 115 John W 235
  Jonathan 360 Joshua 328
  Josiah 15 45 99 Josiah D 248
  Judith 208 Julia 171 Lizzie M
  175 176 Lutalma 310 Margaret
  Elisabeth 290 Martha 346
  Martha C 346 Mary 34 324 360
  Mary L 42 Mrs Thomas 45
  Nancy 159 328 Nellie 134
  Rhoda 151 Sally 99 Samuel
  348 Sarah D 348 Thomas 302
Mody, Betsey 97 Hannah 97 Sam
  97
Moffatt, Rose 255
Moise, Asa 244 Elisa Jane 244
Molloy, Hannah 208 209 Hugh 209
Molly, Catherine 210
Monroe, William H 21
Montford, Esther 138 Martha D
  206
Montfort, Mary 301 Pauline 301
Montmaquet, Joseph D 23
Montmarquet, Joseph D 23
Mooar, Florentine 266 John 28
  Lois 196 197 Martha 28
  Mehitable 195 196 Polly 129
  Priscilla 195 196 Rebecca 188
  Samuel 368
Moody, Almira 162 Betsey 97
  Catherine 225 Charles 368
  Converse 86 Daniel 331
  Eleanor 342 Ellen 342 Elvira
  239 Esther 212 213 215 Eunice
  119 Eunice C 119 Gertrude 193
  Greenwood B 119 Hannah 97
  237 John 162 John W 342

Moody (continued)
   Josiah 234 368 Martha B 331
   Mary J 234 Minnie M 200
   Robert 15 367 Sam 97 Sam'l
   367 Samuel 61 Sarah 15 Sewall
   61 Sophia 233 235 Wilson 22
   23
Mooer, Aseneth 86 Elisabeth 86
   Elizabeth 29 Hannah 100
   Joseph 86 Samuel 29 86
Moor, Polly 129
Moore, Ann 212 310 Belsey 224
   Charlotte Delia 164 Delia 344
   Edith A 331 Elizabeth 199
   George 310 Hannah 88 226 337
   Harriet Jane 133 John 224
   Levi 214 Lottie 164 Mehitable
   224 Mercy 214 Millicent 157
   Robert C 164 Samuel 337 T
   370 William 344
Moors, Benjamin 18
Morard, T H 45
Morey, Delia 102
Morgan, Albert O 20 Charles E 24
   Jesse Johnson 365 Lydia
   Frances 365
Morley, Susannah 169
Morrel, Nathan 247
Morrell, A H 174 Abigail L P 118
   Amasiah 218 313 Betsey 292
   C O 78 Charles O 24 25
   Dorcas 93 94 95 Elbridge 357
   Elizabeth 313 Elizabeth
   Abigail 233 Frank H 229
   Harriet H 218 Jedediah 18
   John 233 Margaret Randall 357
   Mary 118 Nathaniel 118 William F 22
Morrett, Emma M 135 William 135
Morrill, Adeline 361 Aurilla 309
   Azor 361 Charles W 259
   Hannah True 259 Levi 133
   Levi Jr 133 Lydia 133 Mary 87
   Mary A 196 Nancy 361
Morrison, Abigail 117 Benjamin
   106 Flora 106
Morron, Betsey E 224
Morrow, Alice 333 Eliza 240
Morse, A J 22 Abbie Elizabeth
   135 Charles M 135 Edwin 214

Morse (continued)
   Hannah 99 Jane M 289 Joel 33
   367 368 Josephine 175 Martha
   289 292 Mehitable 167 Nathan
   99 Pamelia 220 Pauline 175
   Rebecca C 312 Rosilla 206
   Russell B 289 Sarah 34 Sarah
   A 272 Sarah E 214 Scott 175
   Silas 220 Stillman 206 Winslow 272
Morsel, Rebecca 313
Morton, Almira J 226 Alonzo B
   21 Alonzo D 21 166 George 94
   Hannah Blaisdell 271 John J
   271 Katherine 94 Lucilla Alice
   166 Mary 94
Moses, Abbie Elisabeth 135
   Charles 135
Mosher, Fannie Hinckley 164 J
   Edwin 164
Mothon, A 45
Mottram, Clara E 307 David 307
   James J 25
Moulton, 349 Alice 239 Dorothy
   120 121 122 Elizabeth 346
   George 239 Jane 208 John 120
   Judith 207 Lot 101 M 125
   Mahala B 125 Marietta 335
   Matilda 350 Phebe 101
Mountford, Ether 138
Mountfort, Martha 143
Mower, Calvin 202 Charles 245
   Elvira Eclecta 203 Ida May
   245 Joan Elizabeth 294 Josiah
   H 203 M A 275 Mary 98
   Melicant 79 P B 370 Sarah 202
   Susan 202 Thomas 202 Wallace 294 Walter Lindley 185
   236
Moxey, David 283 Harriet 283
Much, Mary 277
Muchford, H F 370
Mugford, Lydia 341 Mary 341
Munger, Charles 32
Munroe, James 67
Murch, Eben 23 Thomas W 22
   323 Weathey F 323
Murphy, C W 25 Cornelius W 25
   Daniel E 25 Eunice 241 John
   P 58 Mary 108 Michael A 24
   Thomas 23 Timothy J 22 23

Murray, A J 332 Almira 247 Benjamin 37 370 Clarinda 37 Jabez W 22 John P 247 S H 67 Sally P 332 Simeon H 23 37
Mutsaers, Clement 44
Myrick, Almira 356 Jane 208 Lillian E 260 Prudence 35 Ralph 260 Stephen 101 Wm 208
Nash, A 370 Abigail 270 Ami R 320 Ammi R 80 C P 41 Esther 267-269 Everett A 22 23 24 Helen 320 Hulda 311 James 268 270 Joan 30 Joanna 322 Joanna M 229 Joannah 268 John 229 311 370 Jonathan 28 Julia Ann Davis 320 Mrs 370 Sarah 311 320 Sarah Ann 30 Sumner 269 William 268 370
Nason, Abigail H 348 Dorcas 242 Eliza 274 276-278 Hannah 183 Jeremiah 183 Olive W 308
Neal, A T 76 Mrs C A 79 Susan 139
Nealey, A B 67 69 77 Albert B 20 21 C F 69 Laura S 248
Nealy, Geo B 249 Orella S 249
Neely, Bishop 37
Nelson, Edwin 306 Lavinia C 306 Ruth 129 130 Vinnie B 306
Ness, L P 231 Lucy 231
Neven, Mr 173 Polly 184
Nevens, 77 Amanda 291 Amasiah 193 Amos 80 Betsy 311 Betsy Read 312 Charles 293 Charles T 307 Cora B 307 Daniel 350 351 Davis 14 71 181 291 318 Eliza 318 319 Eliza G 350 351 Hannah 181 Hulda 193 Ira 171 259 James 311 Joel 21 42 John 309 John R 357 Josie 159 Julia 42 197 Lucy 197 Marie Antoinette 293 Molly 309 Mrs N B 37 Roxselana 259 Sally 318 Samuel 171 197 259 Sarah P 318 Silvira 259 Tamson Lunt 357
Nevers, 191 Charles E 241 Lucy J 241
Nevesn, Hattie E 323
Newbegin, Almira 293 Eunice 257

Newell, Alfred A 110 Franklin H 180 Harriet M 110 Maria 180 Mayor 83 Sarah N 269 William H 25 67
Newhegin, A 241 Ida Knight 241
Newman, Oliver 22 67
Newton, Rowena 145
Nicholl, William 76
Nichols, Alphonso 313 Barton 182 Caleb 29 Carrie E 297 Daniel P 218 219 Margaret 87 Mary J 297 Millie G 288 Nellie A 313 Ruth 218 219 Sarah 182 Sarah D 196 Wm M 297
Niebuhr, Charles C 37 Mrs Charles C 37
Nieman, Caroline 158 Henry W 158
Niles, Aaron Hiram 183 Augusta Winsor 284 Dorcas 187 Eliza 276 Elizabeth 183 Frank E 284 Jane 336 Jeremiah 336 Joseph 373 Mehitable 204 Silas 204
Nisbett, Charles 139 Nancy 139
Noble, Etta M 184
Noore, Evesen 283 Sophia 283
Norcross, Ellen Gardiner 107 Fred 107 Joanna 211 Thankful 126
Nordstrum, Eleanor 220
Norris, Betsey J 267 Elvira A 258 George W 258 Hannah 296 Thomas B 267
Norton, Abigail S 129 C E 68 Carrie 94 Charles E 73 Deborah 130 Edith 353 354 George E 266 Hannah B 117 Ichabod 93 J P 63 James 130 Julia A 266 Lucinda 92 Lydia Ann 130 Lydia C 129 Margaret 93 Margaret Moore 129 May B 93 O A 78 Oren A 23 Oriaan 333 Orin A 24 Rebecca B 170 Rebekah 170 Sarah 228 Tristram G 170 Zachariah 333
Nottage, Annie Rebecca 94 Josiah T 94
Noyes, Alice L 322 David F 21 22 Elizabeth 295 Elvira 321 Florgence E 322 John R 322 Mary 268 Olive M 274 Oliver 7

Noyes (continued)
    Philander E 321
Nutley, Agnes 87 Peter 87
Nutting, Aaron 373 Abel 373
    Esther 152 George 152 Polena 150
Nye, Harry W 173 Mary Jane 173
O'Brien, James A 24
O'Connell, Cornelius 23 24 25 J J 58
O'Neal, Catherine 96 153
O'Rourke, John 25
Oakes, Elizabeth Harris 291
    Frances 263 John 32 370 Orin 291 Ruth 32 S 72 W K 68
Odgen, Stephen A D 292
Ogden, George 209 Laura 209 Maud 292
Ohambis,, Ann Ella 136 William 136
Oldham, Abbie M 261 Chores H 261
Oliver, Catherine 359 Charles 32 370 Diantha 358 364 Eunice Caroline 355 Georgia 226 Georgiana 226 228 Joan 251 John 251 359 Levi 355 Susan 303 Susannah 304 Warren 226
Olmstead, Etta 134
Orcutt, Louisa 137
Ordway, Albion K 23 24
Orgon, Frank 305
Orin, Clarissa Ann 363
Orr, David 267 Laura Eva 267 Martha J 309
Orrin, Lillian 95
Osborn, Hannah 313 Mary E 137
Osgood, Aaron 275 Abram 325 Alice R 193 Charles H 24 67 Deborah 325 Eunice 275 H A 78 Hannah 226 227 Hannah M 226 Jonathen 226 Martha 286 Mary J 226 Silas B 45 Vine 119 Warren 193
Oswald, Mr 76
Otis, Elizabeth 299 Harrison G 30 Jane 354
Owen, 78 Dolly 222 242 Eunice 240 Hannah 292 318 319 John 222 Josiah 201 Matilda Jane 201 Metilda 201 Samuel 33

Packard, Abbie 274 Alice 184 Cynthia 199 Cyrus F 91 Deborah R 205 E F 67 Eleanor Robinson 364 Emily Gertrude 178 F H 56 67 91 H A 58 H M 57 Harriet E 191 Jacob 199 James 199 Levi 205 Lydia 199 Martha D 364 Polly 205 Sarah Ida 91 Stephen 364
Packer, Inetta 122
Page, Emma 338 Hall 232 Hannah 354 Sarah B 244 245 Vesta 232
Pain, J S 322 Jeremiah 322 Mary 322
Paine, J S 322 Jeremiah 322 Lucinda Ann 296 Mary 322 Mary J 180 Sarah Loise 226
Palmer, Charles H 183 Cynthia Arvilla 183
Parcher, Clarisa M 136 Samuel M 136
Parckard, Lucias 184 Mary A 349
Parkard, Abbie 274
Parker, Adda 343 Betsey 101 Clement 232 David 127 Frances E 317 Francis 358 Frank W 22 23 24 67 George 98 Hannah 134 340 Harriet A 349 Isaac N 19 20 21 James Stuart 254 Jane 127 Judith 190 Julia A 227 Lemuel C 227 Leon 343 M C 140 Margaret A 358 Marietta R 259 Mary 88 89 118 358 Mary Ann 254 Nabby 197 Nathaniel 197 Polly 161 325 Rachel 118 Ralph A 259 Rebecca J 232 Samson 118 Samuel M 232 Sarah C M 140
Parks, Abigail 227 John D 227
Parlin, D E 77
Parmenter, Samuel B 20 Samuel W 20
Parshly, Nancy W 245
Parson, Amos 279 Isabel 279
Parsons, Addison B 344 Carrie 94 Charles E 198 Cyrus 49 Eunice 128 Lydia 279 338 Mary Ann 198 Mary Mellisa 344
Patch, O D 31

Patette, Nazaire 78
Patfield, Nancy 181
Patridge, Eda M 306 Harry C 306
Patrie, Elizabeth D 306
Pattee, Sanie E 97 William 97
Patten, Ann 350 315 Hattie H 360 Mary 355
Patterson, Almira 333 Betsey 140 Deborah 140 Eaton 21 Hannah 208 Mrs R E 41 R E 20 Roland E 41 Rufus 140 Sarah E 342 Silas W 342
Patton, Martha J 345
Paul, Charlotte 257 Daniel 183 David 332 E S 67 75 178 Frances 92 Hannah 79 252 Hannah B 249 John 334 Marshia 332 Mr 76 Sarah 334 Susan 28 Tamson 183
Payne, F G 70
Payson, Carrie E 284
Peables, A M 68 James 183 Jane L 183 Margaret 183
Peaboy, Rebecca 236
Peacock, Anna 234 Dianna 234 James 212 James H 213 Love 212 Mary 359 Mary F 211 213
Peakes, Amelia 342 Charles A 342 Rachel 309 William W 309
Pearce, Laura 185 Luther 185
Pearson, Mary 229
Peary, Leland Edwin 86
Pease, Abisha 200 Betsy 200 Jane 355 John 200
Peasley, Hattie 201
Peck, B 68 76 L C 62 Lewis C 20 130 Vesta Augusta 130
Peckham, James H 213 Sarah A 213
Peirce, Arion C 25
Pellingill, Lydia 149
Peltier, Frank 23 25
Pencock, Anna 234 Dianna 234
Penley, Ann 261 Arthur W 323 James 261 John 161 184 Louisa V 161 Mary Stone 323 Minerva 184 185 Rebecca 340 Samuel 218
Penly, Eleanor Melvina 175 Esther 185 John 184 Joseph

Penly (continued)
185 Minerva 184 185 Samuel R 175 Thankful 178 185
Pennell, Cornelius B 116 R C 67 Sarah 229 Thomas 229 William D 22 55
Penney, Mary E 116
Percy, David T J? 175 Eleanor Melvina 175 Mary Frances 175 Samuel R 175
Perham, B F 52 Dorothy 156
Perie, Betsy 363 Charles 363
Perkins, Abraham 321 Carrie Frances 251 Charles H 22 Cindrella 186 Edna 344 Edward S 362 Elisabeth 321 Frank E 360 George 112 Gideon 22 29 41 42 Harriet 185 Henry R 186 James Henry John W 75 82 Joseph W 22 Lester 265 Lucy A 362 Marshia Ann 265 Mary J 309 310 Melvina A 112 Mrs Gideon 41 Nancy 360 362 Nancy S 117 Sewall 251 Thomas 117 W S 41 William 344
Perley, Luther 242 Maria C 242 Sarah M 260
Perly, John 209 Rachel 209
Perreault, Emilie 107
Perry, Allen 365 Betsey 128 David 128 Delia 172 J W 78 Ruby 365
Pescott, Otis Kibby 284
Peter, Sally 172
Peterson, Benjamin F 23 Nellie E 330 Roscoe L 330 Sarah 243
Pettengell, Polly 357
Pettengill, Abigail 323 Ada May 224 Ann 30 Benjamin G 285 Charlotte 28 Converse 225 Converse J 20 David 13 18 27 285 368 Dorcus 238 Elizabeth 227 Ephraim 238 Hannah B 285 John 29 John Harris 320 Lydia 285 Martha Herrick 320 Mary 29 Mary A 178 Nancy 323 Nathaniel 323 368 Sarah 42 227 Thankful 13 285
Pettes, Mary A 200
Pettie, Mary 200 Rhoda 295

Pettie (continued)
  Samuel 295
Pettingell, Elizabeth 227
Pettingill, Abel 132 Abigail 193
  Abraham 99 Alvin H 331
  Amanda F 274 Anna 120 121
  122 123 Betsey 180 Betsy 179
  Charlotte 225 David 153 180
  David Sr 202 Dorcas 107
  Dorris 132 Elizabeth 118 331
  Etta A 347 Flavilla E 174
  George S 174 H 370 Hannah 99
  John 201 Levi M 347 Marah A
  274 Mark 123 Mary 201 202
  328 Mercy 201 Miriam 333
  Nathaniel 121 193 206 274
  Patsy 181 Polly 201 Rebecca
  99 100 Sarah 153 206 Thankful
  153 180
Peverlyn, Clara U 176
Phaneuf, Magloire 23
Phemia, Etta G 262
Pheteplace, David 21 22
Phetplace, David 55
Philbrick, Judith 228-230 Louisa
  241 Lovisa 365
Philbrook, Ella 319 Nancy A 201
Philena, Eleanor 147
Philips, Ella Estelle 120
Phillips, Autetus 360 Bulah P
  360 Carolina 42 Caroline L
  102 Frank 99 Hiram 167 Jane
  Rebecca 99 Julia 167 Roscoe
  N 360 Samuel G 19 Washington 102
Philpot, Ann Augusta 160 Job 160
Phinney, E 29
Picard, Samuel 370
Pickard, Charles 38 S H 370
  Samuel 37 51 52 61 62
Pickett, Anna 256 John 256
Pierce, 80 Abraham 363 Albert
  300 Ana 279 Ann 273 279
  Carrie Amelia 327 H D 196
  Hannah 273 280 J A 67 Jacob
  W 54 Jane 96 Joan 300 John
  118 John O 327 Joseph A 21
  Judith 363 Mary 132 Sarah 118
  William 96
Pillsbury, Adnesum 256 Betsey
  140 Levi 282 Nathan 140 Olive

Pillsbury (continued)
  Ann 256 P 33 Sophronia 282
Pilsbury, Augusta D 194 George
  67 George H 20 60 67 Levi 190
  194 Mayor 65 Sarah M 190
Pingree, R C 49 50 67 Ransom C
  20 21 22 Sarah 350-352
Pinkham, Amos 283 Andrew B
  284 Elvira Jane 284 Eveline
  191 James 210 Margaret 210
  Mary Jane 175 Miriam F 283
Pinta, Elisa 163 H M 163 Maggie
  163
Pinto, Elisa 163 H M 163 Maggie
  163
Piper, George 228 Hannah 129
  202 236 Harry 342 Jodan K 20
  Jordan K 20 37 Lucinda 342
  Rebecca 228 Sarah 210 Susan
  129 Thomas 129 202 210 236
  367
Pitman, Lewis W 41 Mrs Lewis
  W 41
Pitts, Ebenezer 127 May 127
  Polly 127
Plourde, Anotonin 107
Plummer, Albert S 24 Caroline
  278 Charles W 182 Charlotte
  183 E A 76 Francis 182
  George 151 George S 320
  Helen F 320 Henry 183 280 Ida
  280 Joseph 332 Laura 87 Lucy
  A 332 Maria 161 Martha 280
  Olive 213 Olive Ann 151
  Rebecca 98 99 100 Susan 184
  280 Thomas B 87 Wealthy
  Estes 183 Willard R 184
Polden, Philenah 114
Pollard, Betsey 224 Kendall 224
Pomeroy, Betsy 189 Celeste 157
  E E 78 Elizabeth 189 Sally
  101
Pomroy, Grace Town 349 Sally
  101
Pongart, Elizabeth 95 159
Poor, Mrs 45
Porter, Lydia 218 Melisa 232
  Melissa P 232 Sarah 207
Poston, Florence 152
Potter, Alilia 106 Betsy 210
  Elisabeth 161 James 26 Jane

Potter (continued)
267 June 264 267 L 370
Marcella 198 Mr 27 Noel B 68
Rev Mr 26 Rhoda 124
Pottle, George 22 190 Judith A
190
Powell, Abener M 197 Jane 173
Jane A 111 John 111 Sally 197
Powers, Andrew 183 Betsey 87
Betsy 356 Lucy 183 Robert 87
Powrgess, Sarah 265 W 265
Prasley, Philip 368
Pratt, Amelia 320 Ellen 110
Fidelia 240 H L 54 67 Joanna
G 248 Mary Ellen 110 Olive
248 Rachel 336 Rebecca 197
Rebecca E 248 Sarah 240
Thomas 240 Thursey L 254
William L 110
Pray, Clarinda 176 Dorcus 232
Frances A 227 Jane C 176
Joseph 227 232 Louisa F 140
Nancy 310 Samuel W 176
Preble, George C 362 Katherine A
362 Mehitable 317
Prentiss, Henry M 147 Julia
Adalade 147
Prescott, Adeline Augusta 291
Augusta J 116 Augustus 129
Ebeneser 291 Elvira Jane 284
Fanny 291 George 302 George
Percy 302 Lydia W 37 Lyman
21 116 Marsha E 302 Mary M
347 Matilda 129
Pressey, Warren E 22
Presson, Augusta C 109 112
Celia 112 Henry 332 Hiram
112 James 197 Leonard 195
Philena 332 Rhoda 197 Sarah
H 195
Preston, Mercie 209 210
Prevo, Emily 116
Prince, Augusta A 290 Benj 283
Betsey 289 Hannah 207 John
289 Mary A 226 Rebecca 283
Stephen 290
Prison, Libby 337
Proctor, Betsey 336 Betsy 335
Gilbert 231 Hannah 205 Henry
206 Humility 265 Israel 213
John 325 Mabel Wade 123

Proctor (continued)
Margared 213 Margaret 213
Matilda 231 Rhoda 88 Sally
325
Provost, Regis 25
Pullen, 310 Alvary C 310 Alvory
C 103 Anna 128 George 169
Georgianna W 103 Harriet 169
Pulsifer, George 180 Nellie M
180
Punnton, Caroline 143 Joseph 143
Purchase, 7 Elizabeth 6 Jane 6
Thomas 6 7
Purington, A W 101 Asaneth 106
Caroline 143 144 David 106
130 Dorcas 111 174 Eunice
300 Ezra 154 Ira 111 174
James A 133 James T 346
Joanna Roberts 133 John 373
Joseph 143 144 300 Joshua
374 Lucy W 151 Martha 346
Mary 154 Mervina 111 Minerva
111 Miriam 149 Phebe 101
Sarah 130 Susan R 363
Purinton, Ezra 46 Lucy W 151
Sarah 217 218 Sarah D 217
Purrinton, Ezra 18
Pushard, Eliza F 362 Roswell
362
Puster, Louise 355
Putnam, John F 21 24 25
Quigley, Rilla 306 William W
306
Quimby, Aaron 183 Adaline 103
Ann 183 Benjamin 229 Betsey
229 George W 103 Joseph W
22 Rosella 183 Royal 23
Quinby, John C 23
Ramsdell, Elisa 90 Hiram 93
John H 88 Lena 93 Lisa J 93
Louisa 92 Olive 93 Rachel 357
Sarah 88
Ramsey, Eunice M 333 William
333
Rand, Abigail 148 320 Anna 193
273 Barsilla 163 Barzilla 29
Betsy 311 J H 84 John P 311
Mary 302 Nabby 321 Reuben
19 Rhuban 374 Thankful 29
163 231 Thomas 148 367
Randall, Ann Maria 231 Benjamin

Randall (continued)
  28 345 Cathalina 241 Cora E
  274 Deacon 17 Eleanor 353
  Elivra J 154 Eliza 297 Ezra 17
  19 27 45 46 353 357 358 360
  368 Foster 253 Foster Lee 17
  Hannah 166 167 168 Harriet
  108 111 Isaac 302 J H 370 J S
  276 James 50 John 276 332
  John H 20 137 Kanasum 297 L
  96 Lucy A 332 Marcha B 332
  Margaret 310 Margaret (Peggy)
  87 Maria 345 Martha A 323
  Mary 17 142 143 145 302 Maud
  249 Maude F 249 Molly 353
  Nancy Aldrich 137 Pamela H
  326 Robert 241 Sally 335 Sarah
  253 312 Sarah A 357 360
  Theoda 17 William 335 William G 326 Wm 274 323
Ranes, Edward 339 Isabell 339
Rankin, Abby H 222 John 114 Rachel Ann 114
Rann, Thomas 18
Rawsen, Theresa A 230 Van Buren 230
Ray, Abigail 141 142 143 Benj 367 Benjamin 368 Betsey 276 Chas W 102 Elizabeth 280 Fear 207 Frank G 261 James Albert 358 John 280 Jonathan 18 367 368 Louisa 132 Lucy 252 253 Lulu 261 Melissa A 358 Merinda 102 Polly 280 Prudence 207 Rhoda 150 Sam'l 253 Thomas 207 367 William 207 368
Raymond, Edward A 55 Rose Ann 317
Raynes, Helen M 177 Jonathan 101 Jonathon 177 Josiah 177 Mary 311 Mary Ann 177 Stephen 177 311
Reace, Martha 200 203 204
Read, Abigail 81 Alamon 258 Alvin 233 Ami 32 Ammi 304 Ammi R 305 Annie K 274 Betsy 313 Blanch 358 Dan 13 16 18 19 45 74 121 179 305 370 Daniel B 313 Elizabeth 267 Emma B 96 Falora Eunice

Read (continued)
  288 Franklin 288 Ichabod 313
  Jennie 288 John 81 John P 18
  Jonathan 313 Lemuel 13
  Margaret 32 305 313 Margaret J 304 Mary A 81 Oliver 368 Patience 345 Phebe 258 Polly 141 142 143 Roland F 270 Rosanna D 274 Sally H 305 Samuel 313 370 Samuel R 18 Sarah 233 272 Stephen 81 Stephen H 19 49 276 Submit 313 Susannah 16
Reade, Charles B 81 J Leslie 81 John L 205 Lillian May 205
Reading, C W 33
Reavers, Sarah 119
Reaves, Sarah 122
Record, Cynthia 199 202 Elisha 127 Judith 323 Maria M 254 Martha 127 Oren 323 Samuel 254 Thomas F 289 Vesta Ann 289
Records, Pearl C 267
Redding, Harry 183 Henry 183 Martha Davis 183 Martha Plummer 183
Reed, A Byron 20 Alice 223 Aura E 142 143 Betsy 132 133 274 Colonel 80 Elizabeth 268 Falora Eunice 288 Franklin 288 Jasper 143 Jennie 288 Lemuel 268 Leon L 223 Naomi 227
Reeves, Sarah 295
Remick, John 342 Miriam 342
Remmick, Ruth 122 123
Renick, Annie Cook 181 John 181
Reonee, Adelia 106
Resinger, Annie 238
Rewon, Edith 128
Reynolds, Charles 371 Charles H 254 Galen 202 Jane M 254 N B 18 75 Nathan 18 19 75 371 Nelson B 53 R C 69 Roscoe C 21 23 24 Sarah 202
Rhoades, Mercy 145 Robert 145
Rice, Alden 211 Asa 127 Caroline 127 Ellen M 197 Mariah 361 Polly 284 Rosina 217 Sarah 211 348 Susan 211

Rice (continued)
William 284
Rich, Alice 344 Carolin W D 82
  Cordalia 172 Cordelia 157 172
  Cyrus 344 Delia 172 Hosea 81
  Mary 242 Mary L 177 T H 84
  Thomas Hill 81 82 Thophilus
  172
Richards, Adeline 317 D O 76
  Harriet E 93 J S 93 Mary 324
Richardson, Abigail 355 Alfred
  101 Alice J 321 Amanda 151
  Benj 294 Catherine 135 136
  Charity 350 Charity S 351
  Clarisa 265 Elisa 263 Elizsabeth 209 Emma Thompson 355
  Eunice 355 H H 21 22 Horace
  116 Joseph 350 351 Joshua G
  42 Lizzie A 101 Lydia Ann
  116 Maria S 42 Mary 260 323
  Mary Ann Byram 294 Mercy
  212 213 Nathaniel D 265
  Rebecca 135 Sarah 98 315 333
  Wilks 260 William G 42
Richmond, Annie 339 Mary 208
Richmons, Katherine F 208
Ricker, 329 Ada 113 Addie L 285
  Albert H 265 Amy 135 Ednah
  113 Edward E 285 Ella J 151
  Fannie 98 H 371 Jane 111
  Levi 113 Lillian 178 Lillian L
  178 Mary Jane 247 Mildred G
  250 R R 72 Richard R 21 23
  Sarah Jane 265 William R 250
Rideout, 101 Arie 101 Louisa 187
  Louise 189 Mary 183
Ridgeway, Annie 93
Ridley, Caroline P 309 310 Iva A
  180 William 180
Ridlon, G T Sr 242
Rigby, Dorcas Jane 164 Mary E
  267
Riggs, Betsey 37 Frank 150
  Margaret 150 Margaret A 150
Riker, Warren E 74
Riley, Eva 318
Rinee, Maria Arieyad 245
Ring, Barchelder 341 John C 161
  Maria 346 Mary Ann 161 Molly
  276 Sally 341
Roak, Jacob H 66 67 Rosa J 248

Robbins, 187 J M 67 74 L C 78
  Ruth 169
Robers, William S 21
Robert, Betsey 296
Roberts, Abigail 109 Aldna C 206
  Alfred 253 Alice 136 Ammi
  220 Ann Ella 136 Anna 137
  174 Augusta 281 Betsey 248
  Betsy 243 Charity Baker 248
  Charles L 173 David 214 Ellen
  233 Flora May 173 Frances
  253 G H 214 Geo L 233 Helen
  Maria 330 Henry S 220 Ida 136
  John 243 248 John G 206
  Joseph 28 Julia 30 Lelia J 220
  Margaret 290 Margret 290
  Mary L 330 Melissa 243
  Melissa W 243 Nathan F 281
  Nathan P 330 Oliver 374
  Rebecca 220 Susannah 173
  Wm 136
Robie, Governor 69
Robinsen, Eliza D 287
Robinshon, Etta J 43
Robinson, Abbie P 42 Angeline
  Rollins 95 Benjamin 127
  Betsey 291 Catherine 334
  Catherine Frances 315 Celia C
  340 Charles 362 Charles A 356
  Dean 158 Eliza D 287 Elizabeth 155 Elmira 242 Esther
  325 Eunice 330 334 Ezekiel 32
  33 258 Fannie D 358 Hannah
  163 345 Hattie 118 Hattie A
  118 Hattie F 187 Hattie Silva
  356 Jacob 361 James 95 Jean
  299 Joanna 319 Josiah 127
  Leander 120 Louisa Haskell
  205 Lucinda 127 Mary 158 230
  262 345 Mary E 361 Orin 345
  Priscilla 92 Rachel 127
  Rannie D 361 Roxie M 120
  Samuel 13 18 334 Sarah 90 139
  158 258 321 345 Stephen 319
  Thomas 24 Thomas J 187 W
  371 W A 155 William 42 230
  William A 155
Rodgers, John 102 Marinda 102
  Rosina 247 Thomas J 247
Rodick, John A 21 William J 21
  22 24

Rogers, Abbie L 275 Annie 316
  Annie Rebecca 94 Catherine C
  164 Dorcas 174 Edwin S 94
  Elizabeth 99 Enoch 88
  Frances H 200 Francis 94
  Fred C 33 Harriet 88 Henry
  164 200 Luther B 90 M J 74
  Margaret 89 Mary 284 Mary
  Ann 137 Mary E 90 Mattie 94
  Olive S 254 Orin 137 Rhoda 94
  135 Robert 135 Sarah 192
  Susan 202 W G 316 William S
  20 21 63 174
Rolfe, Betsy 181 George 181
Rollins, Angeline 95 Eva 362
  Hanrietta L 244 Harriet L 244
  Hattie R 227 Joshua D 20 244
  Wilbert 227
Root, F S 42
Rose, Alden 166 Deana 166
  George 273 280 Lucy A 273
  Martha 93 Olive Chipman 280
Ross, Actor 123 Ann T 223 Annie
  139 Betsey 154 Frances 318
  George 299 Hannah 318 Hattie
  J 218 Herbert L 347 Joseph
  318 Levi 218 Mabel Wade 123
  Martha 93 Pelenia 327 Phebe
  G 299 Sarah 190
Rounds, Alice Maud 107 Beulah
  Ann 309 Chas A 107 David 309
  David B 290 Flora I 285
  Leonard 285 Lillian 291 Mary
  Augustus 290
Roundy, Mathi 140
Rowe, Alice 234 Ann 275-277 279
  Anna 364 Catherine 363 David
  351 Elizabeth G 262 Elizabeth
  Peary 351 Jonathan 163
  Joshua 163 Judith 362 Leetta
  351 Lucy 162 Lucy D 162
  Nancy G 286 Rhoda 94 Sally
  163 Susanna M 363 Suzannah
  363 Theophilus H 262 William
  363
Rowell, Araxsenie 42 Arexine I
  102 Edwin 102 Ella A 220
  Minnie E 195 Timothy B 220
Royal, Jesse 220 Lydia 321 Sally
  361 Sarah 256 359 Susan I 220

Royall, Augustus 336 Laura Eva
  336
Rubler, Elize M 42
Ruggles, John 278 Matilda
  Haskell 278 Susie 134 Sylog-
  nus M 237 Thankful 237
Rundlett, Caroline A 117
Runnells, Margaret 89
Runnels, Lucy 312
Russ, Isaac M 149 Rosetta Cora
  149
Russel, Mary 215
Russell, Albert B M 193 Almeda
  350 Betsy 86 Charlotte T 85
  Clara L 193 Cornelius 25 E W
  68 72 Ebeneser I 85 Edmund
  22 67 72 Eleanor 313 Fred E
  243 Isabel 262 James 350
  John 86 Mary 215 Phebe 202
  Richard 72 Sarah 243
Ryan, George W 144 Harriet
  Augusta 144
Sabin, Jael 221 John 24
Safford, Joanna 287 Moses 287
Sage, Hattie 137
Salisbury, Beatrice Sone 287
  David N 287
Salsbury, Abraham W 285 Lucin-
  da 285
Samll, L Linn 68
Sampson, Alphonso M 107 Ernes-
  tine 103 Grace Read 306
  Helena 338 Ida M 362 James
  A 306 Jane 297 Lotta May 107
  Lucy 94 Mr 371 Rebecca 170
Samson, Anna 170 Jane 169
  Margaret 362
Sanborn, Annie M 189 Arabella M
  335 Betsey 224 Charles 193
  Clara L 193 Davis 335 Eda
  204 Emma A 88 George T 204
  Mary A 186 Milan 335 Nellie J
  335 Rebecca 112 W W 22
  William W 23
Sanderson, Cynthia 266 D B 20 41
  Georgia 91 Mrs D B 41 Roscoe
  43
Sands, Arthur 76 F O 67 Fred B
  22 23 James 21
Sargent, 272 Carrie 125 Frank A

Sargent (continued)
356 Mahalia 129 Miss 322
Robert 129 Rodney G 229
Sarah J 356
Savage, A R 67 Almira 247 Celia 112 Clarinda T 362 Clauda 360 Ephraim 6 James 247 Mary 332 Mercy 330 Nora 316 Phileas 97
Sawtelle, Emma 239 Nathaniel 239
Sawyer, 101 Abigail 223 Anaxine 350 Charles 232 D B 67 Darius 120 Emery D 97 Ezra 155 Gertrude A 131 Harriet Adams 208 Joseph 100 Mark 223 Marshall 350 Mary 172 Mary E 289 Melville 208 Nabby 223 Polly 100 138 289 Polly Ann 127 Rebecca 241 Rebecca J 232 Roxie M 120 Sarah 101 155 Sarah E 42 Theodola 230 Wilber 131 William 232 241 William E 127 Wm 289
Sayles, Elgin B 284 Polly Louisa 284
Saymour, Nettie 174 William H 174
Sayre, Persis 283 Plecis 283
Scammon, Ida 353 Mehitable 216 Samuel Jr 216
Scannell, David A 25
Schwartz, Josephine 336 Wilson 336
Scott, Abigail 353 James A 69 John 22 24 Mary J 194 William 25
Scribner, Daniel 371
Scruton, Edwin F 76 J Y 74 75 John Y 20 22 67 John Yeaton 76
Se----, Lena Thompson 194
Seaburg, Affia Jane 152 Rufus B 152
Seabury, Florence A 285
Seargent, Lois A 313 Milton 313
Searles, Ann 213
Searls, Emely 239 Emily 236
Sears, Albert J 229
Seavey, Alice L 330 Ann 215 Cyrus 330 Elmira 131 134

Seavey (continued)
Flora E 136 Frank 136 Herman 136
Seeler, Amasa W 203 Rosine 203
Severance, 141 Frank E 22
Sevus, Frank 231 Louisa 231
Sewall, Addie E 349 Mahalie 344 Samuel 349
Sewett, Ruth 202
Shailon, Blanch M 109 William H 109
Shapleigh, 7 John 6
Sharon, Emerline 201 Thursey Emeline 201 Zebelor 201
Sharron, Annie E 185 Margaret 185 William 185
Shattuck, Bridget 118 Dr 118 Ruth 86
Shaw, Edmund H 253 Elisabeth 319 Emaline 128 Emerline 201 Georgia 159 Georgiana F 244 H Maria 308 Hannah 151 346 Hannah Maria 307 Herbert R C 158 Jacob M 128 James 371 Joseph C 289 Judson 244 Lorenzo L 20 Lucretia 128 Maria H 308 Millet 159 Millicent 158 Miriam 253 Miss 97 Phebe 136 Rosie E 327 Sarah A 289 Shepard S Jr 327 Thursey Emeline 201 Zebulon 201
Sheban, Lucy M 241
Sheehan, John J 25
Shepard, Betsey 106 Sarah 275
Shephard, Betsey 106 John 326 Sally 326
Sheppard, Jane 199 Sussannah 174
Sherman, James M 25 78
Short, Jennie 312
Shory, Delia A 245
Shurtleff, James 263 Rhoda 263
Silver, Albert W 268 Joann B 268 Joannah 269
Simmons, Frankin 64 Nancy 200 201 317
Simons, Henry C 102 Julia A 102
Simonton, Isabell 339
Simpson, Ripley 199 Sussi M 199 200
Sinclair, Eliza 216 Nancy B 206

Singer, Thomas M 70
Sinnett, Rev C 315
Siphers, Catherine 306
Sision, Minnie 284
Skelton, Betsey 360 Jennie M 160 Mary 360 Miriam 360 Nancy 201 Nathaniel E 21 Richard 21 201 Thomas 360 William 360
Sketton, Alluria 356 Jane 336 Sidney 356
Skillan, Eleanor 208
Skillen, Alice 303 306
Skilling, H T 320
Skillings, Benjamin 139 Elizabeth 145 Emery 150 Mary Susan 150 Sarah 138
Skillins, Isaac 207 Lydia 207 Salome M 139
Skinner, Addie E 228 D N 68 David 189 Dorcas 189 Eliza 274 Elizabeth Haskell 360 361 Ellen Cornelia 208 Frank C 208 H B 78 Jennie 159 Jeremiah 30 John 274 Jordan 274 Joseph 361 Mary Ann Tarr 123 Phineas 123 Sarah Jane 173 Sarah Randall 274
Sleeper, Abigail 302 Betsey 193 Dorcas 361 E 371 Eben H 30 Ebenezer H 272 Frank E 22 Frank L 271 H Beecher 94 Ines C 94 Jonathan 191 193 Jonathon 191 Josephine 121 Josephine Marie 121 122 Julia Ann 271 272 Martha H 291 Mary 155 Mrs 91 Nabby R 29 Nat P 302 Nathan 193 Nathaniel 18 361 Polly 193 R B 90 Sarah 272 Sophonia 329 Sumner 100
Smale, Josiah 270 Sally Bacon 270
Small, Achsa 334 336 Addison 23 67 73 Albert H 67 Ann 239 Betsey 262 Carry Maud 309 Daniel 262 Dr 33 Eldora L 343 Hannah 293 Harriet N 160 J M 72 J T 82 James M 22 James T 24 Jane 151 263 Joanna 222 Joel 263 John N 49 John M 160 Jonas 222 Joseph 293

Small (continued)
Laura 303 Lilla J 343 Lydia 42 Malinda 303 Mary 285 292 295 297 Melvin G 309 Nellie 261 Newry 343 Rebecca 128 Sarah 146 Sarrah 263 Sevia Jane 263 Susan 187 W B 68 73 William 303 William I 343
Smart, Betsey 284 Betsey Crowell 284 Brittania 126 128 Levi 284 Salley 165 Sally 165 William T 25
Smiley, Emma 330 Hannah 329 Hezekiah 329
Smily, Harriet Berry 152 Reubin M 152
Smith, 187 216 Abigail 87 134 135 194 209 210 Adarina H 349 Agnes 124 Amelia 306 Amy 257 Amy Elizabeth 349 Anna 204 Asa 109 Betsey 283 Capt 101 Charles 306 Charles J 215 Clara A 269 Clarissa 191 193 Cora A 131 333 Daniel 147 258 263 David 156 David M 321 Dianna G 327 Drusilla 109 E M 69 Edith M 321 Edward 194 Edwin K 25 Elisabeth 321 Eliza 260 Ella 300 344 Elmira 211 Elsa 327 Emma J 135 Eunice 135 Eunice J 135 Florella M N 279 Foster 239 Frank S 204 George B 101 349 371 George R 37 Gloucester Allen 365 Haly 101 Hannah 346 Hasadiah 224 225 Herman 119 Hillman 22 23 Isaac 242 301 374 J Alden 349 Jack P 301 Jacob P 32 James 328 368 Joanna 264 Joannah 268 269 John 19 40 41 260 268 269 327 John B 23 John Fred 279 John L 179 Lemuel 191 Lizzie Cedelle 178 179 Lizzie E 204 Lucy A 194 Lydia 239 Mamie 327 Mary 216 Mary C 242 Mary E 266 Mary Ella 337 Mary W 327 328 Matilda T 196 Mercy M 194 Minnie B 94 Nancy 156 Nancy Jordan 301 Nathan 204 Nathaniel 196

Smith (continued)
  Nellie 323 Pelatiah 104 Rhoda 263 Richard 321 Rosetta 243 Ruth 119 Sally 88 147 365 Samuel 88 Sarah 216 258 259 348 Sarah E 215 Sarah Minerva 194 Sidney 344 Steven 113 Submit 113 Susan 242 301 Thomas 210 Will J 333 Wm H 264
Smithfield, Sarah 262
Snell, Abigail 293 Almira 300 Hannah 289 Louisa 241 Lucinda 121 122 123 Nancy 241
Sniffen, Carrie 126
Snow, Elvia 353 Eva J 193 Hiram 22 Jesu Jr 353 Louisa 147 Sarah 266 William G 193
Snowdown, James 209 Lydia 209
Sonar, Ammi 313 Jane 313
Soper, Ada 161 E H 161 Maria 161
Soule, Charles 228 Elisa 208 Gertrude C 285 286 Martha 228 286 Pomroy C 286 Samuel 208
South, Clarissa 191 Lemuel 191
Southard, Adeline 324
Southgate, John B 36
Sowell, Elizabeth 339
Spalding, George M 191 Nellie H 191
Sparks, Caroline 115 Samuel 115
Sparrow, Alice 275 Clara M 195 196
Spauford, Sarah J 98
Spaulding, Abbie 209 Georgia A 198 Hannah 196-198 Mary 209
Speaker, Olivia N 160
Spear, Angelica 158 160 Annes 214 Archibald 158 160 Caroline Frances 158 Effie M 261 Harriet 247 Nancy 360 Relief 215 Sarah 214
Spencer, Hildreth Mrs 265 Sadie E 351 Selina 338
Spenser, George W 153 Mabel G 153
Spifford, Judith 146
Spinney, Carrie E 362 Z H 22
Spofford, Clara 280 Greenleaf 176 304 Mary 304 Susannah 173

Spofford (continued)
  174 176
Spooner, Harriet 261 John 261
Sprague, Abigail H 293 Al Moses 311 Anna Merrow 313 Charity 315 Elisa 323 Ellen Maria 150 Frederick B 22 Isaac 211 John 315 Mary 315 Mary B 91 Mary Elisa 324 Mercy 211 Minnie M 254 Miranda 311 Orin 30 150 Ruth 210 Sally 311 Sarah 313 365 Washington 293 William 210 313
Springer, Aurelia 73 David 346 Hannah 346 Samuel 32 Sarah N 32 W W 73
Spurr, Jennett E 118
Squires, Orinda 42
Squirs, Orinda 42
St Clair, 266 Ruth Ann 157
Stackford, Jesse 261 Mary E 261
Stackpole, Everett 338 Everett S 100 319 341 Hattie M 227 Lydia 334 335 Sarah 320
Stacy, T H 42
Stafford, Annette 149
Standish, Sarah J 296
Standwart, Thomas 326 Vesta Ann 326
Stanford, Ann Augusta 159 Cynthia 247 Gordon 159 Happy 179 Happy A 179 Isaiah 263 Isreal 263 Jeremiah 19 179 180 247 Jeremial 179 180 Mary 244-247 263
Stanley, Nancy 129 R C 84 Susie 348
Stanton, Clara 288 H E 288 J Y 84
Stanwood, Mary 254
Staples, Ann 104 David 285 290 Elisabeth 285 Elisabeth Bartol 290 Ella L 303 John 104 Martha 147 Mary 104 P Augusta 285 290 Sarah P 326 Seth 326
Starbird, Alice 199 Charles 89 110 161 Charles D 103 Elizabeth A 103 Eunice 126 Harriet 220 Luther 185 Rosetta 166 Susannah T 185 Thomas 220

Starling, Amanda 148
Staten, Belsey 224 Betsey 172 224 225 343 Betty 225 Elias 161 371 Polly 161 Sally 30 Samuel 367
Steedman, Andristur 113 James 113
Steere, Harriet M 41 Hattie A 41 Martin J 30 40 41 83
Stephens, Samuel 18
Steston, Pemelia 303
Stetson, Abbie L 193 Betsey 347 Betsy 348 Christina L 334 Clarian S 271 Elisha 53 61 193 George B 78 George D 120 Hannah 166 167 168 Harriet 120 Howard 226 J H 78 John D 20 John H 22 Joseph H 67 78 Martha J 226 Reubin 334 Stephen 303
Stevens, Aaron 127 229 Abbie 131 Abbit T 131 Abby W 318 Ann 266 Anna A 187 Caleb 367 Calvin 258 Celestia 322 Cyrenious P 322 Cyrenus 322 D T 61 Elizabeth 154 155 Frank A 228 George 184 Harriet 212 Hulda 141 Hulda J 119 Jabes 212 Jacob 292 Jesse T 21 John 188 Lamont O 318 Lydia 188 Margie 187 Mariam 278 Martha 292 Mary 300 Mary E 333 Mary Ellen 184 May Lucinda 261 Olive 127 Pamelia 263 Rachel 127 257 258 Rufus 300 Seba 278 Sophia 229 Thos K 261 William 119 William H 20 21 63 67 William N 20 Wyman 187
Stevenson, J Grant 85
Steward, Abigail 106 Edward 106 Happy 106 Mehitable 115 Metilda 115
Stewart, Anne 302 Charity 115 Dorothy 115 Eliza 116 Elizabeth 116 Elsia 241 Emeline 88 F 371 Francis M 342 Harriet E 191 James 302 Lucinda 298 342 Martha C 342 Matilda 115 Mehitable 115 Nathan 115 Nathan E 115 Notton 150 Patty

Stewart (continued)
115 Rebecca M 150 Rubus 191 Sally 116 Simeon 115 Stephen 116 Susan E 302 Thomas 302 342 William 342
Stickney, D 371 Guilford 289 Hannah H 289
Stiles, Elbridge 138 Lucy 138
Stilphen, Cascelia E 211
Stimpson, Jeremiah 87 Lemont 125 Margaret Ellen 87 Martha A 125
Stinchfield, Ephraim 28 Hannah 296 J C 286 290 James 296 Mary 104
Stinson, Abigail 189 Elizabeth 189 James 189 Louisa 103 Martha 95
Sto--, Mehitable 120
Stockard, Alice R 220 Thomas 220
Stockbridge, Jennie 197 John 82 Mary 219 Napoleon B 25
Stockman, Ruth 115
Stoen, Eleanor Maria 175
Stone, Ann Elizabeth 152 Anna 221 Cora B 131 Eliza 271 Elizabeth 172 173 176 George 152 George E 131 Henry A 264 Josephine S 280 Laura E 195 Mary 144 Roxelania B 264 Thomas 172 William 144
Storah, Fred H 304 Orpha 304
Storer, Katherine 94
Stores, Frances 91 Joseph 91
Stover, Dorothy 357 362 Ella E 222 James T 222 Jennie 245 Sarah 166
Stoyell, Alfreda 360 Auron 360 Mary P 360 361
Strange, Frances Anna 274 John 274
Straw, John 37 Mehitable 117
Strickland, John 218
Strinchfield, Nancy 108
Strout, David B 22 23 Emeline Augusta 349 Harrison 353 James W 349 Jonas W 207 Joshua S 233 Lewis E 207 Loretus A 108 Lydia E 207 Mabel Jane 353 Margery H 312

Strout (continued)
  Mary A 207 Mary J 185 Minnie 108 Nelson 353 Polly 101 Rhoda 233 Vesta Ann 353
Stuart, Deanna 231 G A 47
Stubbs, Abbie 217 Ann 312 Jace 151 Jael 151 Richard 151 Sophia 169
Sturdefant, Mary 349
Sturges, Alonzo W 24 David 296 Emma L 296
Sturgess, Jennie H 170
Sturgis, B F 68 David 312 Mary R 312
Sturtevant, Anna B 218 Anna H 218 Caleb C 218
Sugre, Thomas 23
Sugrue, Thomas 23
Sullivan, Catherine 261 James 8 Joseph E 321 Minnier 316 Sarah Jane 321
Summerbell, Martyn 31 42
Summersides, William 31
Sumner, Alvira Ann 284 295 Houghton 284 Mary 284
Surgess, B F 103 Priscilla Jane 103
Survey, Benj 252 Elizabeth 252
Susam, Hattie 299 John 299
Sutherland, James P 105 Mary 274 280 Octavia 105 Robert D Jr 21
Swain, Julius M 164 Rosann J 164
Swan, Abbie H 345 Annett 103 Caroline A 117 Bertha 187
Swanton, Albion K P 281 Emily Jane 281
Sweeney, Hannah J 343
Swett, Angeline 332 Charles 211 Eben 112 211 Eliphlet 252 Eliza Ellen 246 Elizabeth 112 George L 312 Helen 312 Ivory 332 Jane 263 Jesse F 246 Marion 251 Mary 211 249 Miriam 252 Mitty 211 Moses E 72
Swift, Addie F 134 Cynthia 311 313 Drusilla 42 Ebeneser 212 Geo B 245 J Weston 363 Julia M 363 Lucy A 282 Mary 221

Swift (continued)
  Mercy Jane 221 Nancy 212 Rodney A 134
Sykes, George 312 Lois 312
Sylvester, Abigail 334 335 Edward 126 Elisabeth 124 L 371 Marcia 286 Margaret 126
Symonds, Frances C 175 Louville 175
Syphens, Esther 212 Joseph C 212
Taber, Elizabeth 133 John 133 Lydia 133
Tabor, Mary Hannah 254
Taintor, Emily 130
Talbert, Mary E 271
Talbot, Archie L 23 24 78
Talcott, Alvin W 180 Elizabeth 180 Mercy Ai 97 98
Tarbox, M H 69 Nathaniel W 24 Plummer C 20 22 23
Tarr, Aaron 131 Alice 339 Anna 364 Anna M 266 Benjamin 148 David 123 Elizabeth 155 156 Eunice 117 Fred 185 Fred L 24 266 Isaac G 117 James 117 John 283 Lois E 185 Lydia 123 Mary 15 131 283 Mary M 117 Mattie 148 Nancy 159 261 262 Nancy Anna 364 Nellie A 255 Phebe 117 156 Rachel 172 176 Reuben 255 Seth 15 131 148 262 Solomon 364
Taterson, Lucy 165 Lucy A 165
Tatterson, Lucy 165 Lucy A 165
Taylor, Alice 330 Ann 141 Anna 181 Anne Whitman 103 Asa 121 125 Asa P 16 320 Assenett 312 Augusta M 301 320 Bartholomew C 320 Bessie 225 Betsey 291 Caleb 141 Charles 17 222 291 Edna Maud 194 Edwin 103 Eliza P 222 Elizabeth 291 Ellis 181 Elvira 363 Emily C 358 Eta Louise 243 Frances 363 Frank 194 Geo F 243 George 113 James 181 313 358 Jane 312 Jerusha 125 John 288 Joseph 181 291 330 Lettie 235 Lucy 303 Lucy D 113 Lucy T 113 Luther C

Taylor (continued)
282 Lydia 320 Marshia 282
Mary 89 Mehitable 261
Meriam 292 Molly 207 Phebe
288 Phineas 207 Rebecca 303
305 Robert 145 Robert L 223
Sarah A 127 Sophronia 320
Sullivan R 89 Thomas 17 292
303 305 William 127 Zeaky
261
Teague, Alvarus 114 H Hortie 114
Henrietta 213 John M 213
Tebbets, Experience 216 Priscilla R 146 Sarah H 30 Temple
30 52 Timothy 216
Tebbetts, Hannah 222 Paul C 66
Temple 371
Templeton, A L 67 Albert L 23
24
Tenney, Daniel 140 Merrill 140
Sally 140 Suvinah 140
Thayer, E O 33
Thibault, Cleophas 24
Thibeault, Cleophas 25
Thing, Betsey 248 Betsy 243
Think, Chester C 20
Thomas, Charles D 32 David 367
Edna 298 Elisa F 353 Elizabeth A 164 Esther 218 John
298 Martha J 288 Pemelia 233
Rufus 218 Sarah 137 264 Susan
Alberta 296 Sylvanus D 20 22
William 264 William E 296
Woodbury 233
Thompson, 152 Abigail 139 Alvah
148 Betsy 182 Charity 363
Charlotte 183 Colonel 17
Cornelius 124 David 139 Edla
322 Edmund 88 Edna H 322
Edwin 312 Ella H 322 Emerline 345 Emma 355 Ezekiel
210 Frances A 108 Frank 322
Hannah 134 135 209 Harriet
318 Isaac 318 Isaac C 110
Jack 306 James 125 216 Jane
203 Jane M 219 Jemima 127
Joanna 299 Joel 15 17-19 45
50 173 210 260 Joel Jr 146
Lena 194 Lizzie 322 Louisa
110 Love 129 Lucy E 235
Luisa 110 Lydia 210 M--- 127

Thompson (continued)
Mary Ann 30 Margaret 212 260
Martha C 210 Mary 88 95 102
103 260 Mehitable 210 Mercy
110 Olive 181 Oliver F 322
Orpha 343 Palmer C 23 Polly
88 Reliance 216 Rosannah 148
Ruth 146 Sally 306 Sarah 124
303 322 Sarah A 125 Sarah H
322 Silvia 97 Solomon 97
Stella M 176 T B 17 Telepha
Bray 312 Theophilus B 20 21
Theresa 150 Wm 299
Thonre, Benjamin 301 Thomas 30
Thorne, Aaron D 19 21 46 Abigail
28 Alice 28 Barnel 317 Barrel
368 Benjamin 28 29 30 46 258
301 368 Hannah 28 Hannah 2d
28 Jane 317 Laura 42 Laura C
30 258 Lillian B 301 Mary 28
Olive 339 Rebecca 355 Samuel
46 355 Thomas D 20 22 41 276
Thornton, Belinda A 140 Fred H
23 William 140
Thorsander, Eva 344
Thrasher, Eunice 248 Josiah 248
Thu--, Mary 95
Thurlow, Betsey 234 Elisha 234
Miriam 252 P M 57 Richard
252
Thurston, George 256 Olive Ann
256
Tibbets, Dolly 116
Tibbetts, Abbie 252 Andrew 222
Dolly 115 Eliza 141 Enoch 374
Geo W 141 Hannah 222 Hiram
125 Jerusha 125 Mary 365 May
130 Paul 374 Polly Lord 222
Sarah 157 Sarah E 333 Temple
157 276 William F 333
Tilley, C C 36 42
Tilson, Mary 122
Tilton, John J 232 Margaret 232
Timcon, Ellen N 312
Tinkham, Nettie 142 Olive E 277
Samuel P 277
Titcomb, Calvin S 33 Hannah 231
Mary 34 Silas 54 67
Titus, Cyrus 323 Elisabeth 323
Tobey, Caroline 157 Edward P
157 Joseph 234 Sarah 234

Tobie, Caroline 80 E P 371
Edward P 19 20 21 22 80
Edward P Jr 80 Joseph 189
Mrs Edward P 38 Sarah 189
Tobin, Augustus 308 309 Mary C 308 Mary Caroline 309
Todd, Abigial Goden 184 Daniel Gage 184 Elizabeth 339 Hannah 105 106
Toddbury, Chas 135 Ruth 135
Tompson, Joseph 216 Mary 216
Toole, Mary 331
Toothaker, Mary 332
Topsham, Cynthia B 294
Torrens, Nancy 188 Rebecca 188 Samuel 188
Torsey, Henry A 23 136 Joseph 260 Judith 136 Sally 260
Totman, Clementine 212 Peacock 212 Rebecca 255 Sarah 87 185 Sarah J 87
Toward, Dummer 140 Mercy A 140
Towle, Arvesta 42 Hellen E 172 Mary D 328
Town, Hannah 202 Moses 202
Towne, Alice May 235 Almira 220 Charles W 235 Hannah 298 Louisa 258 Moses 220 298 Pamelia 220
Townsand, Barnum L 291 Sarah Augusta 291
Townsend, Barnum L 291 Sarah Augusta 291
Track, Clemenia W 301
Tracy, Albert 77 D 371 David 30 Frances J 108 Ira 173 J P 371 James B 20 John A 23 Lucretia W 30 Martha 173 Minnie O 173
Trafant, Mary J 180
Trafton, John 368 Judith Rowe 364 Louisa J 364 Olive C 357 Sally 145 Thomas 74 Waterman 357 364 William 364
Trask, Daniel 342 David 91 Elizabeth Ellen 342 Joseph Smith 254 Muriel 254 Sally 91 Susan M 91
Treadwell, Thomas 74
Treefant, Sarah Eva 301 William 301
Tremper, Johnson 209 Laura A 209 Louise M 209
Trendenthal, Euge B 222 Jessie E 222
Trevylin, Louise M 170
Tribou, Polby H 294 Polly 284
Triggs, Sarah A 285
True, Abigail 145 Anna 127 Bradbury 283 Ebenezer 363 Helena 363 Jacob 305 Lissie A 295 Lizzie A 285 Mary A 295 Nathan O 295 Sarah 227 283 Theodosia Wadley 305 Wealthy 205
Trull, David 202 Deborah 202
Trumpton, George 203 Isaac 203 Lucinda 203 Sukey Hooper 203
Tuck, James 114 Rachel 114 Samuel 368
Tucker, 288 Amos 280 Eunice 248 Sally 280
Tuesdale, Bell 112
Tufts, Abbie 360 Melvin P 360
Tukesbury, Alice 230 Charles D 230
Tuner, Benjamin Jr 114
Tunney, Lula K 196
Turber, Anna E 189
Turner, Abigial 206 Ambrose 130 Amos 363 Aphie S 203 Benjamin 342 Betsy Bailey 170 Betsy Blake 252 Charlotte 107 Charlotte B 107 Deborah 165 346 E 371 Ellen 234 Ellis 329 Emory 149 Fayette Delia 281 George 170 Hannah 291 342 Isabel 234 Isabell 350 James 18 234 329 350 Joann B 268 John S 346 Joseph 268 Josiah 291 Laura 345 Lillian 247 Lillian A 92 Lucia 170 Lucie 170 Lutia 170 Lydia 149 Marietta 114 Melvin 247 Olive 42 336 363 Olive Armanda 130 Samuel 336 Sylvina 208 Tobes 281
Tutrell, Lissie Etta 235 Lloyd Benjamin 235

Tuttle, Alfred 337 Aurilla 337
  Benjamin L 161 Cemantha 340
  Cosilla 232 Dorius 232
  Frances 166 Iola 161 Iola M
  161 Joseph 166 L 161 Sarah
  262
Twombley, Sophia C 323
Twort, William J 42
Tyler, A B 352 Betsey 287 288
  Clarissa 348 Desdemona 205
  Desdemonia 205 John 352
  Levcretia F 352 Lucretia F
  352 Melissa 335 Rebecca 98
  100 Ruby 188 Ruth 116 Sally
  98 99
Tylor, John 116
Ulmer, Kate 244 Sarah 244
Umberhind, Eliza 303
Unberhind, Ann E 303
Underhill, Sarah 310
Underwood, Ann E 303
Upjohn, Samuel 37
Upton, Ann 258
Van Buren, 80
Van Hasen, Ella 195
Varnet, Carrie 356
Varney, Agnes 258 Charles 29
  John 359 362 Marth M 362
  Martha M 359 Mary 155 286
  Nicholas Jr 155 Sarah 358
  Stephen 286 Theodore M 358
Varnum, Abigail 14 Asa 14 Mercy
  118
Varrel, Hepzibah 156
Vaughan, Eliza 108 Eunice 108
  Zenus 108
Vaughn, Eliza 108 Eunice 108
  James 23 24 Mary 196 Sarah
  87 Zenus 108
Verrill, D E 371 Davis E 37 Elisa
  294 Jesse 294 Maud A 344 345
  Sarah P 37
Vicker, Hannah 133
Vickery, Abigail 106 Alice 339
  Elizabeth 308 Elvira 88
  Hannah 132 133 134 Hannah M
  226 James 89 339 James Jr 88
  Mary 106 226 228 Mary Jane
  339 Mathias 134 Matthias 308
  Phebe 307 308 Sarah 264 266
  William P 226 Wm 339

Vining, Bela 260 David 242 374
  Maria C 242 Mary 151 Thankful
  260
Vinny, Benjamin 337 Rhoda 337
Vose, Aphia 170 Bell 239
Voter, Allen B 222 Ida M 222
Vottar, Betsey 210
WAldron, William 160
Wade, Jacob 246 Mabel 244-248
Wadleigh, Annie 252
Wadsworth, Deborah 181 John
  181
Wagg, Elizabeth 308 340 Ellen
  238 George G 23 24 George W
  69 Howard N 23 24 John 367
  William 238
Wagner, Amanda T 166
Wait, Albert Henry 294 296
  Hattie 106 Lucinda Ann 296
  Susanna 268
Waite, Charles 290 Hannah 120
  Olive 289 290 Susanna 120
Wakefield, A 22 25 371 Archibald
  19 61 63 67 132 Edward 364
  Ezekiel 41 John 232 Laura R
  139 142 Mrs A 74 Mrs Ezekiel
  41 Rebecca J 232 S D 67 Sarah
  132 Seth D 25
Waldron, Abigail 160 Ann Augus-
  ta 160 Annie 160 Charles W
  23 Job 160 William H 20
Walker, Abbie Rand 321 Albert
  358 Alfred 315 Arabine 358
  Catherine C 315 Charles 24 25
  67 Charlotte 339 Chas 321
  Elvira 207 Emma 140 Etta 239
  Fred 232 Ida May 232 Jennie
  297 Jeremiah 161 John 140
  239 Jonathon 343 Polly 161
  344 Rochester 345 Roschester
  343 Sally 189 Sarah 254 Savina
  343 Timothy 19 40 67 254
Wall, Sarah 350 315
Wallace, Ida M 125 John M 125
  T H 44
Wallis, Harriet 88
Walton, Allie D 94
Wapp, Fred 206 Lizzie L 206
Ward, Addie M 329 330 331
  Edward 24 George L 53 54 55
  62 66 67 John C 329 330 Mary

Ward (continued)
187 Margaret 212 213 Maria
187 Martin A 25 Mary Lee 187
Michael A 22 24 Nancy 247
Rev Mr 29 Richard 247
Thomas 22
Wardwell, Elvetta Delilah 168
George E 168
Ware, Charles N 123 Cyrus H 263
Eunice 342 James 342 Levi
371 Lewis 105 106 298 Lucinda 298 Lucy 123 Martha 106
Mary Elizabeth 98 Miriam 105
Nancy 263 Sally 342 William
342
Warl, Deana 237
Warner, Betsey 276 Jane 162 164
Phillip 164 William 276
Warren, A 331 Albert 330 331
Ena 117 Mary 331 Mary Helen
331 May H 330 Sarah F 261
Washburn, Ann M 356 Lucy 202
W H 37
Waste, Hannah 120 Susanna 120
Waterhouse, Jennie E 198 Lydia
30 Samuel 198
Waterman, Abigail 145 Daniel
145 Ruby N 145
Watson, A B 22 Byron W 36
Daniel Jr 112 Dolly 222 Elizabeth 112 Eunice 108 109 111
112 114 Hulda 146 Jane 199
Joseph 220 Lucy J 257 Mary
Ann 220 Nellie M 198 Sydney
257 W B 36 William 198
Watts, Alden M 129 John 7 Mary
E 129
Waugh, Becener 258
Way, 7 George 6
Weaver, Alexander 231 Mary 231
Webb, Ann Sieles 244 Edward 24
Edwin B 318 Elizabeth Ann
318 George 20 21 Hannah
Harris 220 J Dan 220 Mabel
245 Maria 234 Mary Ann 243-
245 247 Nancy 207 Sarah 273
275 Wm H 244
Webber, Arista 346 Betsey 288
Daniel 161 371 Dorcas 101
Edsel 101 Elbridge 234 Elias
S 227 Elizabeth 112 Jeremiah

Webber (continued)
220 Jerusha 234 Jesse 371
Joseph 29 Luella P 346 May
Ann 30 Melissa 281 Rebecca
T 220 Sally 306 William 374
Weber, Anna 292 S J 257 Sarah D
257
Webster, Abigail 337 Alena M
260 Anna 252 Benjamin C 112
C H 40 Charles D B 267
Deborah J 340 Doner 276
Eunice 112 F 101 Frederick
Dana 340 George 337 Joann
267 Joseph 302 353 Judith 199
200 Laura J 42 Laura Jane 340
Lizzie 346 Lois Am 168
Lucinda 353 Patience 313
Rufus 189 Sallie M 302 William 260 276 313
Wedgewood, Chase 263 Patty 263
Wedgwood, Chase 74 John M 270
M C 68 71 Milton C 22 Newton
J 24 Sarah Marie 270
Weed, Deborah 244 Lillian Maud
217
Weeks, Ruth 128 Experience 128
Howe 19 53 67 75 James 367
Pauline 175 Susannah 280
Welch, 94 Anna 218 219 Charles
85 Climena Augusta 235
Eleanor 220 Emeline S 220
Emerlin G 220 Hannah 220
James 220 Nancy S 85 Narciss
Ann 147 Oliver 147 Permilia
Hodgdon 348 Vella 271
Willmot 348
Wellington, Charlotte 315 Enoch
315 Sarah 315
Wellman, C F 67 Charles P 21
Mary Ann 145
Wells, Mary Ann 126 Timothy
126
Welplely, Cornelius 25
Welsh, Edith Louise 90 Winfield
S 90
Wentworth, Augusta 311 Benning
45 Delia 92 Drusilla 199
Foster 199 Fred 92 John 7 223
Lucy J 185 Martha 223 Patty
223 Sally 163
Wescot, Hannah H 362

Wescott, Hannah H 361 Josiah 361 Martha 275
West, Abigail 122 Eliza 282 George 361 Jane M 361 Jennett 326 John W 23 Nelson 326 Sally 198
Westcott, Anna 145 149
Weston, Eben 119 Mary 119 Mary 118 S L 72
Wetham, Aaron 148 Abigail 148
Wetherbee, Hannah 286 S F 43 Samuel 286
Weyes, Mary Belle Bessie 129
Weymouth, Cordelia 217 Cyrus 236 320 Dean 93 Dominus 229 Eleanor 85 Eliza 238 Eliza Ann 238 Ellen 217 Frank P 337 Lenore J 215 Lettice 229 Lucinda H 337 Martha 353 Moses 236 Nancy 236 Polly 86 Ruth 320 Ruth Ella 85 Salinda 277 Sarah 236 Vesta Ann 93
Whaff, Harriet 305 Harriet K 305
Wharf, Cordelia 215
Wharff, Cordelia 214
Wharton, 7 Richard 6 7
Wheeler, Amasiah 290 Ann 104 Anna 104 Flora E 95 159 George 216 Hattie 358 Helen L 166 Hellen L 166 Henry W 216 Jefferson 358 John A 166 Matilda 272 Rebecca 238
Wheelock, F B 67
Wheelon, Daniel 44
Whetmore, Elizabeth 219
Whidden, Mary 303 Molly 303
Whitcher, Emma L 322
Whitcomb, Fannie 94
White, 77 Ann 303 Benjamin 264 265 Clifton N 109 Darius 284 303 Dora 109 Dorcas C 207 Eliza G 337 Emma J 267 Ezra H 74 Fred H 23 28 Hannah 95 Hannah M 329 Helen 158 J C 77 James W 337 John H 158 Joseph 258 267 Judith 101 Leonard 207 M H 242 Mary 258 277 Mary E 242 May E 320 Olive 284 288 293 298 Sarah 264 265 Wallace H 24 25 67 William 101 317

White (continued) Winifred 310
Whitman, Addison 303 Clara M 278 John 278 Joseph 173 Mary Jane 173 Olive Vesta 303 Vesta 303
Whitmarsh, Grace H 151
Whitmore, 169 Elizabeth 219
Whitney, Aaron 214 Abraham 156 Alvin 133 371 Aneetia Josephine 255 Angeline E 222 223 Ann 339 Anna L 168 Betsy 97 214 Charles H 102 Charles S 339 Elmira 148 George 136 Herbert A 255 Humphrey 148 Isabella 136 Jedediah 223 John Henry 175 Judith 156 Lorentha Ann 228 Lucy Ann 200 Lulu Frances 175 Mary 156 Mary E 301 Mary Jane 125 May 125 Miriam 279 Myrtle 243 Orrin 113 Rachel W 335 Rebecca 113 Sally 243 Samuel 117 374 Sarah 117 355 Sarah A 102 Susanna 156 Susey 133 Warren L 334 335 William 301
Whittemore, Alexander 205 Chas 102 Mary 42 205 Mary J 102
Whitten, Betsey 326 Dan 326 Daniel 224 Emaline 316 Hannah 224 Joseph 115 189 Mary 17 303 Molly 303 Patty 115 Sally 189 Sarah E 189 Wm 316
Whitter, Betsey 118 John 118
Whittier, Dorcas J 318 George H 318 Jennie 138
Whittle, Effie A 345 Fred E 345
Whittum, Dan 21 Sargent 371
Wickwire, Amanda 286 287
Wiggin, Ann M 34 Betsey 34 Charles 33 34 D H 371 D W 74 Daniel H 33 34 Edwin D 22 Emeline 34 Levi 34 Mary F 296 W H 74
Wiggins, Abel 282 Mary 282
Wight, E M 72 Eliphet 241 Hattie A 241 Jonathan 141 Sally 141
Wilbur, Benjamin 336 Mary 336
Wilcox, Daniel 93 Emma 94

Wilcox (continued)
Mary 93
Wilder, Florence S 321
Wiley, Lucinda 269 William 269
Wilins, David 339
Wilkin, Enos 223 224 Rebecca J 223 224
Wilkins, Annie 199 David 202 339 Deborah 179 181 Isabell 339 Jerrisha 211 Mariah 181 Mary 130 131 134 Mehitable 130 131 Molly 202
Will, Fanny 291
Willard, Angeline 196 Cyrus 195 John A 336 Priscilla Mooar 195 Sarah 134 Susan Ellen 336
Williams, Asariah 92 Betsey 246 C E 68 Charles 92 303 Ebenezer B 243 Eleanor 303 Elvin C 359 George 18 85 246 George S 29 Hartley 200 Hattie 213 Hattie A 306 Henry A 92 Hiram 218 Isaac 246 Isabel Jane 359 Joseph 305 Joshua 129 Judge 200 Julia A 305 Laura Ella 92 Louisa 159 Mabel 29 246 Martha E 304 306 Olive 218 Oscar S 103 Rachel 200 Rufus C 304 Ruth P 243 245 Sally 243 Sarah A 129 Sylvia E M 103 William G 305
Williamson, Edna 174 Mary Ann 272
Willian, W M 36
Willis, 199 Herbert 313 Susie H 313
Willister, George 332 Jane 332
Williston, George 332 Jane 332
Willson, 245 Maria 245 Rachel 335
Wilsen, A 241 Lura Knight 241 Sarah 178
Wilson, 78 Arianna 150 B 164 Betsy 202 Caroline F 190 Charles 288 Charles C 23 78 Desdemona 151 Edith 362 George 150 George T 70 Hannah 255 280 Henry 177 Henry M 255 Jennett 288 John E 298 John S 153

Wilson (continued)
Lucy Artimetia 164 Mary 314 Nancy Louisa 152 153 Nettie 328 Rebecca 252 Rebecca J 177 Samuel 190 Viola Helen 298 William 202 Zelia E 199
Windsor, Justin 121
Wing, Asa 127 Charlotte P 111 Clifford E 111 Emma Hammon 286 Ezekiel 149 George 102 J C 286 Marion 178 Marion H 178 Mary Ellen 352 353 Pameala 127 Pamelia 127 Phronissa 102 Pricilia G 148 Ruby Ann 149 Vest C 229 Viletta 337 338 William 337
Winlsow, Allen P 20
Winn, Patience 212
Winnett, Harriet Berry 152 John 152
Winship, Nancy 264 266
Winslow, A P 174 Abigail 14 340 Benjamin 14 340 E C 94 Elizabeth 122 Ida 94 James P 196 Joseph 30 Judith 255 256 Kenelm 122 Knelin 337 Mary 30 Matilda T 196 Melissa H 174 Rebecca 236 337 Reubin 236
Winthrop, Adam 7 Gov 6
Winthworth, John 7
Wirth, Dorothy 90
Wiseman, George A 77
Wiswell, Hannah 181 Henry 181
Witham, Augusta A 331 Benj 258 Elisa J 97 Harriet 283 Judith 278 M 294 Sarah 179 Susan 258
Withee, Nancy 106
Withen, Lorense 258 Mary 258
Witherill, Martha 261-263 Polly (Martha) 261
Wonda, Obedey 101 Sarah 101
Wood, Alsaclovia Marie 244 B F 69 Charles 244 Daniel 17 75 Elizabeth S 189 Emma 221 Ephraim 35 52 376 Eunice 154 Henry 189 Horace 280 James 20 21 41 49 50 67 James B 129 Jane 213 John N 49 67 78 John W 20 Joseph 154 Lizzie

Wood (continued)
 147 Lydia 209 Martha G 280 Mary J 361 Mehitable 95 96 Methida 96 Methilda 96 Mr 52 Mrs Daniel 32 N M 34 Nathaniel Milton 35 Prudence 35 Ruth 129 Sarah 214 Simeon 214 Submit 99 Truxton 99 William B 56 William F 24 25

Woodard, Abraham 158 159 Gardiner 179 Jane 158 159 Mary D 179 361 May E 91 Mehitable 306 307 Olive 131 Stephen F 361 Winchell 91

Woodbury, Edward 374 Edward S 336 Georgia E 109 Harriot 39 Joseph 102 Julia Ann 308 L P 371 Leonard P 23 Lissie A 340 Lois 336 Mary 296 N 74 Nathan 276 Nellie F 102 Polly 295 Susan 276 Thankful 295

Woodcock, Jane 211 Justine 136 Mr 136

Woodman, Abbie 303 306 Alvin 250 Calvin 269 Cathalina 241 Elizabeth M 250 Hiram E 268 J C 58 John 271 Julia 269 Julia A 268 269 Mary Jane 271

Woodrow, Minnie 117 Samuel 117

Woodruff, Marinda 164 Miranda 162 165

Woods, Mary Jane 203 William 203

Woodside, Edwin H 24 Elbridge G 23 Eleanor 204 Emma 204 Nancy 93 Stinson 204

Woodward, Betsey 117 Harriet 159 Julia 278 Susan E 161 William 117 161

Woodworth, Mercy 285 Seth 285

Worcester, Hannah 123

Works, Abbie V 221 Asa 209 George 221 Mary 209 Nancy H 93 Sewall 93

Wormell, Dorcas 361 Henry 361

Worth, Nellie L 114

Worthen, Caroline Elisabeth 208 William E 208

Worthing, Frank W 334 Lena A 334

Wright, 121 122 A S 78 Abijah 197 Adaline G 255 Albion S 330 331 Allura 317 Anna Elizabeth 226 Betsey 34 281 317 Betsy 317 Charity 335 Charles L 128 Cornelia E 297 David 293 Dorcas 141 320 Elizabeth 318 319 Emily C 330 331 Emma M 269 Flora E 128 Francis 183 257 303 Frank 25 191 Hannah 364 Hattie R 191 Henry 317 Henry B 86 Jane S 173 Jesse 14 188 Joel 14 18 71 173 228 317 368 John 110 113 297 319 Jonathan 329 Jonathan Jr 141 Jonathon 108 Joseph 367 368 Joseph Jr 368 Julia 202 Lamson Lunt 278 Lettie 329 Lonzo 255 Margaret 228 Margaret R 257 Mary 101 102 108 260 262 263 317 Mary Ann 118 Miriam A 317 Nabby 197 Olive 188 Phineas 19 141 Polly 293 Sally 28 110 141 Sarah 117 256 303 Sarah Ann 303 Sophronia 113 Susannah 183 Tamson 278 Tebe 202 Therzy 316 Timothy 14 33 121 122 William R 21 33 34 61 Zebula 202 Zebulon 335 367

Wrigley, James 20 21

Wyllie, Robert 36

Wyman, Ada Ann 175 Alice 179 Alice M 179 Charles 239 D F 36 Henry 175 John 179 Lectina Phillips 175 Lillian P 175 Lydia Jane 239 Mary 247 Merrill T 175 Ruhamah 179 T B Jr 222

Yeaton, John 188 Susan 188

Yelton, Ada Florence 161 Elisabeth 161 Seth 161

Yetten, Gertrude E 349

Yewens, Harry L 36

York, Cindrella 186 Dolly 295 Jerome 313 John 122 295 Julia Ann Gorham 265 Martha J 313 Mary 122 199 Mary Helen 186 Nathan M 265 Sarah 295 Sarah E 111 Simeon Estes 132 186 Virgil 186

Youland, Sophronia 307 William 76
Yound, Daniel 359
Young, Aaron 73 Abraham 359 Blance L 249 Blanche 249 Calvin C 249 250 Cerena 244 Daniel 363 David 241 Elizabeth C 289 Eugenia 301 Grace

Young (continued)
B 250 Hannah 92 359 Helen 292 J Edgar 217 James E 312 Lucy Ann P 312 Lucy Ham 100 Mary W 92 Molly 359 Nellie F 217 Rebecca 289 Sarah 363 Susan 184 Susan A 317 Thos 289 Washington 317 William 100

INDEX OF SUBJECTS AND PLACES
(Pages 11 - 418)

The location "Lewiston" has not been indexed as it is mentioned on almost every page, however, names of roads, streets, lakes and local names for Lewiston have been indexed.

ALMS HOUSE, 388 399 401
ANDROSCOGGIN COUNTY AGRICULTURAL SOCIETY, 61
ASSOCIATIONS, 69-70
AUBURN MAINE, Barker Mill 208 Bearce Stream Mill 340 Denison Street 66 Fletcher Cemetery 307 Fletcher Road 307 Littlefield's Tavern 308 Mount Auburn Cemetery 128 206 Oak Hill Cemetery 289 311 Old Salbells Cemetery 184 Phoenix Block 74 Pine Street Cemetery 310 Pleasant St 222 South River Rd 299 340 Turner St 34
BANK, Androscoggin County Savings 67 Lewiston Falls 252 Manufacturers National 67 People's Savings 67 Private Banking House of May 67 The First National 66
BELGIUM, 124
BLACKMAN, 386 393 405 406 409
BLACKWOMAN, 379
BOARD of Trade, 68
BRICK, Church 34 House 17 Makers 58 Mill 53 Town Hall 63 Two-story Store 75 Two-story House 75 80
BRISTISH Isles, Scotland 316
BUSINESS HOUSE, Oldest 75 One of the Oldest 75
CABBAGE STEALER, 120
CALIFORNIA, 150 154 176 231 237 282 Akron 95 159 318 Austin Orange Co 172 Fremont 118 119 Jones 235 Oakland 157 163 327 San Francisco 113 126 195 247 270 Woodland 348 Yreber 235
CANADA 197 Charlotte New Brunswick 267 Fredricton

CANADA (Cont.)
New Brunswick 240 Milltown New Brunswick 187 188 Montreal 255 Nashwaak New Brunswick 189 New Brunswick 107 126 306 Oak Bay Charlotte New Brunswick 269 Pomeroy Ridge New Brunswick 189 Quebec 255 St Andrews New Brunswick 269 St David New Brunswick 165 St David New Brunswick 377 St Hyacinthe, Quebec 72 St John New Brunswick 73 150 252 St Stephens New Brunswick 187 Upper Falls New Brunswick 135 Woodstook New Brunswick 100 Wotton Wolfe Co Quebec 107 108
CANTON MAINE, Pine Grove Cemetery 94
CENTENARIAN, 309
CHARLES II, King of England 7
CHURCH, FREE BAPTIST, 28 29 38 42 in Georgiaville 41
CHURCHES, St Mark's Church in Augusta 37 Universalist 27 Baptist 44 Bates Street Universalist Society 40 Catholics 44 Clough Meeting House 29 Congregationalist 33 Episcopal 36 First Baptist of Bates Street 33 Freewill Baptist 233 Friends Society 15 29 Hammond Street Methodist 42 High Street Congregational in Auburn 42 High Street Methodist in Auburn 42 Lewiston Falls Congregational 37 Lewiston Falls Mission 32 Lincoln Street 44 Little Androscoggin Mission 31 Main Street Free Baptist 29

483

CHURCHES (Cont.)
  32 41 42 North Meeting-house 29 Old South Baptist Meeting-house 44 Park Street Methodist 31 43 Pine Street Congregational 37 42 Pine Street Free Baptist 31 41 Rechabite Hall in Auburn 34 South Lewiston Church 29 St Joseph's Catholic (Irish) 43 44 St Patrick's 44 St Peter's Catholic (French) 44 Trinity Episcopal 36 Union Hall in Auburn 32 34 36 Univeralist Society 40 Village Hall in Auburn 32
CIVIL WAR, 91 105 136 247 248 256 262 287 302 305 322 Cavalry Soldier 231 Five Forks 73 Gettysburg 207 297 Libby Prison 73 337 Red River Expedition 337 Saulsbury Prison 338 Soldier's Monument 64 Surgeon 72 1st Maine Regiment 35 1st Maine 73 2nd Maine Reg Vols 352 2nd Battle of Bull Run 352 10th Maine A H 210 13th Maine 250 13th Maine Reg 221 252 13th Massachusetts 77 17th Maine Reg 237 23rd Maine Regiment 203 29th Maine Regiment 35 30th Maine Reg 203 221
CLOTHING STORES, 76
CLUBS & ORGANIZATIONS, Masonic Lodge 248 Red Order of Lewiston 248 Worcester County Sabbath School Association 39 Lewiston Y.M.C.A. 29 69 Baptist Missionary Society 34 Logic & Christian Evidences 39
COLORADO, 232 Pitkin 288 Scott Valley 235
COLORED, 379 393 405
COMPANY, Allen - Maxwell 58 Amoskeag Manufacturing 62 Androscoggin Mill 55-57 Aurora Mills 56 Avon Mill 56 Bates Manufacturing 52 54 56 57 Bleachery 57 Bradford - Conant 58 Carman & Thompson 58 Continental Mill 55 57 Cowan Woolen Mill 48 51 53 56

COMPANY (Cont.)
  Cumberland Mill 57 Dam 52 Daniel Allen & 58 Gay-Woodman 51 57 Great Androscoggin Falls 52 H H Dickey & Son 58 Hill Manufacturing 54 Hill Mill 57 Home Manufacturing 50 Hunneman & 62 J L H Cobb 57 James Wood & 49 Jordan, Frost & 58 Laconia 56 Lewiston Bagging 55 Lewiston Bleachery 53 Lewiston Bleachery & Dye Works 56 Lewiston Falls Manufacturing 50 51 Lewiston Falls Water-Power 49 Lewiston Falls Woolen Manufacturing 157 Lewiston Gas Light 62 Lewiston Machine 57 Lewiston Mills 55 Lewiston Monumental Works 58 Lewiston Steam-Mill 49 Lewiston Water Works 65 Lewiston Water-Power 34 52-54 Libbey & Dingley 50 57 Lincoln Mill 53 Locks & Canal 52 Pepperell 56 Pinkham - Bradford 58 R C Pingree & 58 R. C. Pingree & 49 Read - Small & 49 S. R. Bearce & 49 Union Water-Power 57
CONGRESSMEN, 14 16 254
CONNECTICUT, 31 41 113 Bridgeport 304 East Haddem 39 New Haven 195 Waterbury 31 West Haven 39 179
CONSTRUCTION COMPANY, Bearce - Clifford & 58
CUBA, 192 Havana 290
CUTLER, Olive (did not marry Green Farmington, see page 264, married Timothy MOORE/MOOAR) 129
DISTRICT of COLUMBIA, Washington 99 108 190 356
DENTIST, 74
DRUGGISTS, 73
EARLY HOUSES, 276 River Road 171 Sabattus Street 173
ENGLAND, 77 214 251 Bristol 305 Dorsetshire 341 Hingham 151 Kent 82 London 15 72

ENGLAND/FRANCE CHANNEL, Guernsey 15 17 162 242 399
ENGLISHMAN, 407
EUROPE, 192 Poland 316
FALLS, Androscoggin 7 Brunswick Great 7 Great 8 Harris 12 Lewiston 12 Rumford 8 Twenty-mile 7 8 12 Uppermost 8 12
FARMINGTON MAINE, Bragg Cemetery 339
FIRE DEPARTMENT, 62
FIRST THINGS, Blacksmith 16 Catholic Clergyman 44 Cotton Mill 51 Deacons 26 Doctor in Lewiston 71 Ferry 13 Female settler 13 Female White Child Born in Lewiston 340 French-Canadian 107 House Built 45 Log House 14 Male Child Born 13 Merchants 74 of the admitted freeman in MA 214 School District 46 Settlement 12 Settler 12 Tavern Keeper 272 Teacher in Lewiston 121 Teacher in Lewiston Falls 121
FLORDIA, 250 Tampa 305 Jacksonville 91 War 325 West Apalainda 139
FRANCE, Clermont 15
FRATERNAL INSURANCE SOCIETY, Clan Campbell 69
FREE MASON, 73
FRENCH, 383 Doctor 72 Congress 73
FRENCH & INDIAN WAR, 145 212
GERMAN, 377 393 395 399 401 403-405 408 411 413
GERMANY, Bavaria 89 316 Hanover 148 280 Posen 282 Rusia 89
GRAND ARMY OF THE REPUBLIC, 221
GREENE MAINE, Pearce Cemetery 309
GROCERS, 77
GROG SHOP, 34
HARDWARE, 78
HOSPITAL, Asylum of Notre Dame de Lourdes (Now St Mary's Hospital) 68 277 Central General (now CMMC) 68 72 75

HOSPITAL (Cont.)
French 277 St Mary's 277
HOTEL, Atwood 73 74 DeWitt House 53 64
IOWA, 182 Burlington 186 Kossuth 186 Maynard 157 Walnut 252
IDAHO, 181
ILLINOIS, 34 36 Batavia 389 389 Belvidere 330 Chicago 73 154 157 179 180 251 322 379 Lockport 287 Rockford 272 St Charles 350 351 Upper Alton 35 Wyomette 291
INDIA, Calcutta 204 Orissa 41
INDIANA, 263 Green Castle 344 Indianapolis 211 Kingsbury La Port County 306 Michigan City 306
INDIANS, captured by 216 Fighting 341 Sagamores 6 7 Warumbee deed 8
INSURANCE, 78
IOWA, Dow City 196 Wintersel 287
IRELAND, 300 North of 272
IRISH, 381 383 386 391 393 395 399 401 405 406 408 409 413 411 pauper 380 bank fell & killed 380
JAY MAINE, Crash Road Cemetery 156
JEWELRY, 78
KANSAS, 173 235 337 Beloit 322 Fort Wallace 155 Ottawa 210 Paola 186 Washington 344
KENTUCKY, Covington 35 Paris Bourbon Co 98
KING PHILIP'S WAR, 341
LANDHOLDER, 37 Franklin Company 40 53 56 57 64 65 248
LEWISTON MAINE, Ash Street 40 45 Baker's Mills 14 15 49 50 Barkerville 321 Bates St 30 37 38 45 58 74 Blanchard Block 77 Bonnallie Block 77 Boxer's Island 50 Burnt Woods District 58 Catholic Cemetery 14 Centennial Block 82 Central Block 14 63 82 Central Hall 63 Chapel Street 28 30 City Hall 63 City Buildings 63 Clough school-house 29 College St 29 66 277 College Block 40 63

LEWISTON MAINE (Cont.)
Continental Mills 12 43 Cowan Mill 43 Cowings Mill 276 Crowley Cemetery (typo "Rowley Cemetery") 161 Crowley Cemetery 98 100 101 105 131 143 David Mtn 11 Davis Cemetery 93 Dominican School (Formerly Bonnallie) Block 77 Dresser's Rips 14 Early Houses 205 276 Eastern Avenue 71 235 Farwell area 192 Garcelon Cemetery 104 105 109 113 Garcelon's Ferry 15 45 Hammond Street 74 75 68 Harris grist-mill 50 Haymarket Square 33 Herrick Cemetery 91 99 105 121 122 246 Herrick House 321 Herrick School-house 28 Hog's Back Hill 220 Jones Hall 40 Jones's Block 82 Journal Block 63 82 Land Grants 12 Lincoln Street 13 44 78 Lisbon St 34 40 43 63 68 73 74 Lisbon Hall 40 Lowell Corner 15 34 75 82 Lower Central Station 82 Lower Central depot 13 Lyceum Block 82 Main St 11 14 28 30 34 43 44 58 68 73-75 77 192 Maine Central depot 28 Manning House 80 Meadow Brook 14 Merrill Hill 11 Mill Street 74 Mill lot 13 Mountain Ave 28 No Name Pond 11 50 Old brick school-house 34 Old South Church 26 27 Old Garcelon burying-ground 16 Old Lisbon Road 29 Old South Baptist Church 17 Oldest houses 14 Orange Street 45 Park Street Stable 306 Park Street 33 63 77 Park (now called John F Kennedy Park) 64 Pierce St 68 Pine Street 38 40 63 66 74 277 Pingree Mill Stream 16 Poorfarm 409 Public House 14 Randall Hill 11 River Road 29 171 Riverside St 11 Riverside Cemetery 80 106 223 272 348 Sabatis Road 11 15 45 71 74 80 82 173 277 Sands Block 82 Savings Bank Block 63 82

LEWISTON MAINE (Cont.)
School-house 43 Scruton Block 82 Shaw's Hill 321 Sleeper-town 321 Sleepy-town 321 Spruce Street 37 St Peter & Paul's Cemetery 107 Stetson Brook 50 Switzerland Road 257 Thorne's Corner 17 Town farm 249 360 Walnut St 68 Webster St 18 75 241 276 Wood Street 15 74
LIBRARY, Manufacturers & Mechanics Assiciation 62
LIGHTHOUSE KEEPER, Portland Harbor 241
LISBON MAINE, Early Cemetery Records 373
LIVERMORE MAINE, Brettuns Cemetery 156
LOUISIANA, Carolina 111 New Orleans 302
MAINE, 31 Abbott 93 302 385 Acton 72 355 Addison 125 Albion 171 Alfred 165 243 Alfred 248 Andover 122 Andover 224 Anson 329 Anson 362 Aroostook Co 365 Athens 225 247 323 337 378 406 Auburn 9 13 26 31-34 36 38 40 42 50 53 58 61 65 66 98 101 103 104 110 113 125 130 139 142 144 145 147 148 155 157 159 161 166 173 175-177 181 183 184 186 189 193 194 198 199 206-208 210 217 221 222 227 229 232 234 241 244 248 249 251 253 261 265-271 276 278 284 286 289 301 304 307 310 311 313 315 321 326 340 341 343 345 349 353 358 360 362 365 367 387 391 393 Augusta 37 83 104 107 108 176 228 272 287 289 299 316 336 337 Avon 359 364 404 Bakerstown 8 277 Baldwin 223 224 315 Bangor 31 88 92 98 99 147 159 178 191 195 210 231 255 263 266 274 302 303 350-352 356 Bath 42 44 89 97 101 105 128 135 143 164 180 188 194 198 200-202 226 229 233 235 264 265 281-283 309 321 334 355 359 363 Belfast 284 307 307 321 Belgrade 173 176

MAINE (Cont.)
232 Belmont 231 Berkes Mills
185 Berlin 114 140 Berwick 359
Bethel 176 251 280 281 302
Biddeford 56 87 171 215 216
360 Bingham 350 352
Blanchard 190 Bloomfield 35
118 236 240 Bluehill 340
Boothbay 288 Boston 193 195
263 313 Bowdoin 26 71 105 106
109 111 116 124 171 174 192
205 214 219 243 249 316 317
342 359 361 Bowdoinham 7 14
17 26 99 115 169 173 190 193
239 240 303 305 336 338
Bradford 184 185 Bradley 200
Bridgeton 173 Bridgton 90
Brooks 346 Brunswick 9 18 30
35 38 50 92 93 96 97 100 109
112 125 133 139 154 158 171
183 194 200 215 216 221 227
233 235 257 262 267 270 286
288 289 294 302 303 305 309
317 322 331 343 353 355 358
410 Bryon 258 Buckfield 79 152
249 251 252 253 254 290
Buckport 81 147 210 Buxton 30
114 341 350 351 Buxton Center
286 Calais 235 324 Cambridge
199 238 268 351 352 Cambridge
Plains 306 Camden 35 36 182
Canaan 118 119 196 240 265
Canton 42 94 202 253 276 312
Cape Elizabeth 30 104 145 147
149 162 179 223-225 233 259
302 319 333 339 340 Carmel
159 195-197 244 266 353
Carroll 170 188 Carthage 112
156 Charleston 301 302
Charlton 39 Chebeaque Island
288 Chelsea 103 Chester 140
Chesterville 80 156 167 252 296
China 114 254 303 334 342
Clifford 351 Codyville 188 189
Concord 240 Cooper 135
Corinna 266 350 351 Corinth
228 Cornish 33-35 145 329
Cornith 351 Cornville 355
Cumberland 38 95 164
Cumberland County 8 Cushing
244 Damariscotta 97 228
Danville 26 33 34 36 61 88 89

MAINE (Cont.)
98 100 101 103 104 134 148
157 161 178 183-186 218 220
234 239 241 255 266 275-277
299 300 306 308 312 318 323
340-342 367 409 Davis Brook
223 Dead River 247 Deer Isle 93
200 Denmark 91 Detroit 300
Dexter 149 191 192 263 281
288 312 340 Dixfield 268
Dixmont 196 Dover 36 148 305
364 365 Dover-Foxcroft 190
Dresden 73 Durham (typo
"Dunham") 103 Durham 9 33 61
80 96 100 101 122 133 137 141
145 150 151 154-156 165 182
182 197 206 218 220 225 230
231 234 235 241 246 260 269
280 281 288 293 299 300 315
318-322 330 332 334 338 341
346 353 356 East Wilton 264
East Auburn 142 East Baldwin
224 East Harpswell 301 East
Livermore 257 East Poland 31
Ellsworth 251 388 Empire
Station 232 Etna 197 266 267
344 Exeter 72 351 Fairfield 186
280 300 354 Falmouth 14 104
151 192 204 206 209 223 251
252 255 259 265 276 280 287
299 Farmingdale 211 215
Farmington Falls 236
Farmington 72 86 88 90-93 95
108 110 113 114 121 164 171
196 197 218 220 249 251 264
279 282 324 339 343 360-363
413 Fayette 206 226 Foxcroft
228 Freeman 85 86 108 109 110
112 179 197 204 239 237 329
Freeport 15 18 26 27 74 96 101
124 128 137 140 143 144 155
161 176 255 258 267 287 290
326 Fryeburg 71 79 100 158
288 Gardiner 12 13 73 98 139
141 152-154 188 213 217 218
229 234 254 258 261 301 304
324 325 359 364 410 Garland
305 320 Georgetown 100 133
135 155 200 254 328 357
Glenburn 351 352 Gorham 102
106 229 279 312 322 350
Grafton 313 Gray 131 242 315

MAINE (Cont.)
Gray 352 Greenbush 320 338
Greene 9 14 16 18 26 33 34 61
98 99 101 112 113 117 121 122
126 132 133 140 141 147 149
152 156 173 183-185 199-203
210 220 225 235-237 239 241
248 250 252 256 257 259 261
289 292 294 296 298 302 307
309 317 318 326 331-335 340
342-345 349-352 358 361 363
364 375-377 383 406 407 410
Greenville 137 Greenwood 223
270 Guilford 364 Hallowell
Cross Roads 167 Hallowell 193
211 216 222 313 342 349 361
Hamilton 195 Hampden 195
Hampden 282 350 Harmony 244
282 288 350 Harpswell 99 220
257 299 301 303 353 354 362
Harrison 72 157 Hartford 116
326 344 361 Hartland 167 172
247 280 300 330 332 Hebron
192 281 233 Hiram 329 Hope
244 Houlton 37 72 Industry 16
85 103 129 196 200 212 213
253 261 Island Falls, Aroostook
Co 89 Jackson Falts 223 Jay 72
156 204 236 260 357 Jefferson
126 Kenduskeag 191
Kennebunk 264 Kennebunkport
246 Kingfield 109 148 160 169
170 236 237 Kingfield 239 240
321 330 Kingston 319 Kittery 72
188 Lagrange 236 Lawrence 358
Lee 304 306 Leeds 9 99 136 149
150 165 167 229 234 237 284
286 290 291 294 349 380 386
387 388 406 409 413 Levant
191 320 Lewiston Falls 31 381
Limerick 113 262 Limington 72
223 Lincoln 102 Lincoln County
8 Lisbon 27 52 88 93 97 98 100
101 110 113 123-125 131 135
137 141 143 146 147 151 152
156 157 160-163 171 173-175
180 182 183 185-188 190-193
206 210 216 218 219 223 224
229 231-234 242-244 246 257
274 280 290 297 301-303 306
307 318-322 327 328 332 335
339 342 354 360 362 367 382

MAINE (Cont.)
408 413 Lisbon Falls 6 223 288
299 Lisbon Plains 306 Litchfield
12 97 111 112 119 120 141 150
152 154 171 198 209 215 217
222 245 260-263 267 302-304
306 324 330 332 339 346 350
351 353 355 362 Litchfield
Plains 304 Little River 101 Little
River Plt 299 Littleboro' 149
Livermore 103 156 210 308 309
328 351 377 387 Livermore
Falls 309 Livermore 8 Lowell
306 Lyman 328 Machias 216
271 Madison 30 172 247 Madrid
139 140 Manchester 321
Marshfield 249 Mattawamkeag
138 Mechanic Falls (then part of
Poland & Minot) 219 230
Meddybumps 278 Mercer 174
258 283 Metinicus Isle 354
Mexico 193 Mexico 192 Mine
Meadow in Greene 50 Minot 38
49 50 61 71 72 91 99 103 115
121 128 129 139 147 155 178
181 188 198 205 207 220 226
233 251 265 269 272 279 283
290 307-311 314 321 325 326
336 364 365 367 375
Monmouth 91 92 99 114 120
128 149 167 224 235 254 258
260 263 302 315 323 327 347
349 Montville 174 Morrell 250
Moscow 94 352 Mount Vernon
105 128 N Cambridge 119
Naples 308 New Auburn 306 66
New Castle 174 New Castle 212
New Gloucester 13 14 16 26 28
33 72 79 99 100 109 113 136
146 195 202 204 205 207 210
242 249 252 271 273 275-279
288 299 301 336 340 359 361
363 405 408 415 New Portland
108-112 114 130 147 148 162
193 229 231 236 237 239 240
259 265 273 302 346 New
Sharon 114 129 154 195 203
258 New Vineyard 87 92-94 269
277 362 New Auburn 26 107
New Gloucester 12 26 New
Vineyard 90 Newburgh 156
Newfield 219 Newport 247 265

MAINE (Cont.)
263 266 Newport 350-352 Newry 343 Norridgewock 92 312 North Brunswick 326 North Chesterville Cemetery 156 North Limington 223 North New Portland 112 114 169 North Salem 283 North Yarmouth 13 14 16 17 27 99 114 120 122 139 151 207 208 254 259 272 279 282 283 295 339-341 381 395 North Anson 338 Northport 99 Norway 71 166 196 271 299 343 345 Number 6AP 114 Number 6 Oxford Co 139 Oakland 30 98 Old Orchard 222 Oldtown 133 187 195 239 265 328 346 Orono 133 137 265 282 336 Orr's Island 357 Otisfield 72 181 Oxford County 91 Oxford 39 205 281 Palmyra 242 266 352 Paris 220 228 270 271 Parker's Head 175 Parkman 199 205 256 350-352 Parsonsfield 213 223 280 331 Passadumkeag 197 Pejepscot Claim 6 104 280 299 Pejepscot Company 8 Pejepscot Gore 325 Pejepscot 7 26 104 241 242 255 265 268 270 309 336 340 Penobscot 175 Perryville 66 Phillips 90 114 139 142 172 187 197 221 249 252 313 357 364 Phippsburg 102 166 259 274 359 Pittsfield 73 88 184 242 347 360 Pittston Pittston 364 87 177 193 289 334 342 Plymouth 329 331 Poland 8 9 41 61 99 146 198 205 219 250 272 276 277 285 300 314 349 361 375 410 Port Royal 8 Portland Harbor 241 Portland 14 34 38 40 62 80 83 104 107 111 114 123 126 133 154 155 158 177 181 194 199 217 225 226 229 243 248 252 256 259 275 284 290 293 295-297 299 307 311-313 315 321 323 325 326 340 353 356 358 387 Pottertown 305 Pownal 176 186 232 250 274 293 363 Princeton 135 136 Province of Mayne 6 Rangeley 187 250 252

MAINE (Cont.)
253 309 Raymond 140 318 Readfield 72 179 222 Richmond 185 213 226 236 305 328 346 Ripley 266 Robbinston 38 Rockland 36 156 158 160 217 244 Rockland 111 Rome 173 176 309 Royalsborough 12 Royalstown 122 Rumford 146 156 180 229 Rumford Falls 209 259 Sabattas Point 120 Sabatus/Sabattus 101 171 261 330 349 Sacarappa 157 158 Saco 35 154 187 216 274 353 Saco Valley 242 Salem 108 179 183 200 204 328 346 Sanford 364 Sangerville 253 260 261 263 281 305 Scarborough 141 223 Searsmont 231 Searsport 102 Sedgwick 229 Shapleigh 302 355 Shepleigh 155 Sherman 91 Sherman Mills 90 94 Sidney 150 179 185 187 300 Skowhegan 35 118 119 206 214 224 227 236 316 Small Point 100 Solon 361 Somerset 313 Somerville 174 175 South Paris 271 South Gardiner 387 South Lewiston 101 245 327 South Berwick 207 243 South Thomaston 354 South West Bend 101 Springfield 302 St Albans 148 313 350-353 St George 354 Standish 228-230 344 384 Stetson 201 Stockton Springs 284 Strong, 72 86 87 92 129 157 195-197 264 273 278 279 283 328 341 361 Temple 72 Temple 109 Thomaston 353 Thompson 171 Thorndike 302 Togus 210 Topsfield 188 189 242 Topsham 9 12 33 35 87 88 90 95 119 125 135 210 215 226 243 265 268 303 305 311 322 332 335 402 Troy 106 134 187 330 331 357 358 364 Turner 71 81 94 137 156 167 168 177 178 184 198 201 209 218 234 252 253 271 290 Union 129 325 247 324 Upper Gloucester 275 Vassalboro 220 284 190 185 175 312 341 133 Vienna 83

MAINE (Cont.)
  Waldoboro 246 Waldoboro' 201
  Wales 26 61 108 112 120 134
  143 150 159 163 172 189 200
  201 209-211 226 248 250 260
  261 262 303 305 319 328 330
  331 334 350 359 363 396 409
  411 Warren 129 239 244 354
  Washington 185 Waterford 72
  99 103 408 Waterville 35 136
  168 173 174 178 181 199 200
  251 317 Wayne 72 299 296
  Webster 26 64 101 109 111-113
  115 125 139 151 160 Webster
  392 171 174 173 188 186 184
  229 230 232 233 262 386 383
  382 363 349 343 336 334 310
  304 410 411 413 409 Weld 264
  228 177 156 Wellington 305
  Wells 350 Wesley 136 West
  Auburn 38 West Gardiner 364
  West Lebanon 117 West Minot
  252 253 West Peru 300 West
  Poland 290 West Sumner 336
  West Waterville 30 31 Westbrook
  168 207 223 79 Whitefield 174
  99 Wilton 129 190 220 264 266
  321 355 356 Windham 251 252
  341 72 Windsor 92 258 Winn
  302 303 Winslow 259 264
  Winterport 196 350 352
  Winthrop 52 99 137 149 247
  249 277 292 Wiscasset 97 208
  38 209 Wiscasset Fall 407
  Woodstock 364 Woolwich 103
  151 348 Yarmouth 260 252 177
  161 137 121 290 291 296 313
  34 52 36 York 216 290 332
MAINE METHODIST
  CONFERENCE, 43 East 43
MAINE STATE AGRICULTURAL
  SOCIETY, 61
MARYLAND, Baltimore 127 271 73
  95 Church Hill 271 Fort
  Cumberland 212
MASONIC, honors 203
MASSACHUSETTS, 31 Abington 96
  Amesbury 251 208 252 249
  Amherst 39 Andover 89 181 197
  364 339 Arlington 164 347
  Attleboro 16 221 222 Boston 6
  41 52 73 93 113 128 139 143

MASSACHUSETTS (Cont.)
  186 187 233 244 247 262 273
  276 288 304 305 331 Boston
  (typo? "ME") 168 Boxford 209
  Boylston 71 Cambridge 113 119
  270 323 269 Cambridgeport 36
  279 Cape Ann 16 162 184 205
  259 273 279 388 408
  Charlestown 214 322 Chatham
  119 Chelmsford 212 213
  Chelsea 103 263 330 334
  Clinton 112 Clinton 108
  Concord 274 Dana 302 Dedham
  270 267 Dorchester 348 Dracut
  12 13 17 118 214 287 340 329
  212 Dudley 39 Duxbury 122
  121 East Boston 324 East
  Pepperell 239 Eastham 121 122
  Everett 95 286 Fall River 65 115
  300 Falmouth 236 237
  Gloucester 14 156 180 277 283
  339 364 365 Grafton 313 Great
  Barrington 183 Groton 86 254
  Halifax 323 Hanover 170
  Harvard 43 Harwich 216 275
  Haverhill 31 89 115 266 334
  Havill 266 Hyde Park 225 232
  Lawrence 35 109 111 120 136
  Lexington 315 348 Lowell 80
  103 137 153 222 235 237 244
  245 323 Lynn 6 183 191 227
  Lynn 120 Lynne 131 Mansfield
  96 Martha's Vineyard 200
  Medford 159 314 322 Melrose
  155 Methuen 89 107 Milford
  130 278 Millford 333 Milton 276
  Montague 275 Nantucket 102
  Natick 197 New Bedford 267
  New Gloucester 180 Newbury
  220 249 251 Newburyport 267
  Newton 168 226 Newtonville 210
  Northampton 18 154 North
  Redding 219 Oakham 16 86 264
  Palmer 36 Plymouth Company 8
  18 Plymouth 180 Princeton 39
  Randolph 161 213 Rehoboth
  221 Revere 265 Rockport 283
  300 Roxbury 233 245 Rutland
  87 Salem 193 274 Salisbury 131
  282 Sandwich 103 213 Scituate
  206 246 279 305 354 Sharon
  218 Somerville 127

MASSACHUSETTS (Cont.)
South Boston 36 145 149 186
189 South Gardner 218 South
Weymouth 164 Stoneham 226
252 Stoneham 111 Sudbury 342
Sudsbury 183 Taunton 252
Topsfield 14 Truro 216
Wakefield 149 Walpole 199
Wareham 225 Waterford 41
Watertown 164 Webster 354
Westford 212 Westminister 39
Williamsburg 31 Wilmington
209 210 Woburn 214 348
Worcester 272 341
MERCHANTS, 74
MEXICO, 192
MICHIGAN, 155 Grand Rapids 346
Jackson 213
MILITIA, 16-18 80 87 157 367 Frye
Light Guards 69 Lewiston Light
Infantry 69
MINISTER, Baptist 15 17 26
Episcopalian 15
MINNESOTA, 113 303 Owatonna
137 Crow 303 Duluth 289 Leroy
293 Mankato 344 Minneapolis
88 163 Oakland 306 Spring
Valley 157 St Anthony 312 St
Paul 253 Staples 293 Sutton
306 Verndale 293 St Francis
303
MISSISSIPPI, Franklin 287
MISSOURI, 314 Hannibal 346
Kansas City 39
MONTANA, Lakeview Madson Co
186
NEW HAMPSHIRE, 228 232 276
282 Ashland 117 Bow 365
Chester 346 320 Dover 160 190
208 341 Dublin 270 East
Ossipee 30 Effingham 270
Exeter 183 Gorham 72 Grafton
313 Great Falls 72 154 220
Guilford 231 Hampton 321 346
347 Holderness 117 Hollis 218
Keene 255 365 Littleton 132
Londonderry 199 Manchester
248 331 Marlboro 256 Marlboro
270 Melville 358 Milton Mills 92
Nashua 255 Nashua 137 New
Durham 28 Newfield 334
Newmarket 349 Nottingham 12

MASSACHUSETTS (Cont.)
Orford 130 Ossipee 72 127 184
241 365 Portsmouth 7 43 104
174 Ridgeway 41 Rye 302
Salmon Falls 245 Sandwich 103
346 Shelburne 71 Shelun 107
Somersworth 99 Somerville 346
Stratham 117 Summerworth
329 Sunnipee 230 Tamworth
346 Union 92 Walpole 247
White Mtns 11
NEW JERSEY, 209 Jersey City 209
Linden 226 Mendew 226
Vineland 243
NEW ORLEANS EXPOSITION, 192
NEW YORK, 14 42 72 73 231 275
288 314 413 Albany 204 210
Canton 199 Clarenden 285
Clarendon 286 287 Clarendon
283 Colden Sue Co 200 Dover
Island 155 Fairport (typo
"Fairfort") 42 Fort Edward 36
Genessee 39 Long Island 41 281
287 294 New York 99 186 187
208 227 Ogden 284 Ogden
Monroe Co 284 285 Oyden 284
St Clair 266 Utica 182 186 219
NEW VINEYARD MAINE, Daggett
Cemetery 92 Hardy Cemetery 90
Notch Cemetery 90 94
NEWSPAPER, Auburn Daily
Gazette 81 Bridgton Reporter
248 Christian Mirror 81 Eastern
Argus 104 Hackensack
Republican 209 New York Atlas
14 New York Attus 208 New
York Independent 82 Portland
Gazette 104 Providence Journal
80
NORTH CAROLINA, 104
OFFICERS, Aldermen 20-25 City
elections 20 Mayors 20-25
Selectmen 19 Town Clerk list 19
OHIO, 13 86 105 135 209 385
Chillroethe 163 Cincinatti 210
Columbus 322 Lake County 306
N Yarville 141 386 New Rich 209
Yellow Springs 98
OLDEST HOUSE IN LEWISTON, 12
(N.B. perhaps no longer
standing) 17
OREGON, 285

PATENT MEDICINE MANUFACTORY, Roger's Inhalant & Cough Lozenges 74
PAUPER, 377 399 400 404 416
PENNSYLVANIA, 140 162 Bradford 307 Chambersburg 261 Harrisburg 31 Philadelphia 71 73 124 Spring Creek, 164 Towanda 313
PHYSICIANS, 71
PLYMOUTH ROCK FAME, 351
POOR HOUSE, 410
RAILROAD, Androscoggin 19 Railroad Androscoggin & Kennebec 18 60 Baltimore & Ohio 322 Builder 229 Grand Truck 210 Grand Truck Station 58 Lewiston & Auburn 60 Lewiston & Auburn Horse 65 66 Lower Maine Central Depot 74 Maine Central 60 Maine Central Station 49 57
REVOLUTIONARY WAR, 13 15 17 86 90 109 121 122 145 149 154 171 206 215 223 238 248 258 259 302 319 339 340 353 354 Bunker Hill 18 Soldier Killed by Tree 299 Soldiers 375-377 381-384 386 387 391 392 397 405-408 410 411 413 416
RHODE ISLAND, Fruit Hill 41 Georgiaville 41 Greenville 41 North Scituate 41 Pawtucket 338 Providence 31 71 195 233 237
RIVER, Androscoggin 6 18 50 282 Bishopscotte 6 Kennebec 7 61 Pejescot 12 River Royal 130
SAW & GRIST MILLS, 48
SAW-MILL SITE, 65
SCHOOLS, 45 Acadia College 73 Amherst College 38 39 Andover Theological Seminary 39 Bangor Theological Seminary 81 Bates College 11 39 41 42 69 80- 83 156-158 298 384 Bowdoin Medical 71 72 Bowdoin College 71 73 81 158 271 City Proper District 45 Classical Inst of Charleston 301 Clough District 45 Cobb Divinity 29 39 42 81 Dartmouth College 50

SCHOOLS (Cont.) Dartmouth Medical College 71 72 District System Abolished 47 Early teacher 16 45 East Maine Methodist Conference Seminary 81 Farmington Normal 114 Free textbooks 47 Garcelon's Ferry District 45 Hahnemann of Homoeopathy 73 Hamilton College 39 Harvard Law 253 Harvard Medical 72 Homoeopathic Medical College 71 73 Kent's Hill 43 Lewiston Falls Academy 81 192 Maine State Seminary 31 41 80 83 Medical University at Burlington Vermont 72 New York University College 72 Newton Theological Seminary 35 Nichols Academy 39 Normal Training 47 North District 45 North Yarmouth Academy 35 Parsonsfield Seminary 41 246 Portland High 81 Princeton College 39 Private 46 Roman Catholic College in Clermont France 15 Rose Hill District 45 Systematic Theology in Shurtleff College 35 Thorne District 45 Union Seminary 39 University at Zurich Switzerland 73 Waterville College 35 Western Theological Institute 35Whitestown Seminary 31 Woman's Medical College of New York 72 73
SCOTCH-IRISH 272
SCOTCH, 377 386 387 399 401 406 413 414 416
SECOND, Male Child Born in Lewiston 15 Settler of Lewiston 283
SHIP, *U.S. Lancaster* 155
SHOE DEALERS, 78
SLEIGH & CARRIAGE MANUFACTURER, 113
SOUTH AMERICA, 282
SOUTH LEWISTON (perhaps Lisbon), Davis Cemetery 327
SPANISH WAR, 108 San Juan engagement 135
ST ALBANS, Indian Lake 351
SWITZERLAND, Zurich 73

TANNER, 75 354
TEXAS, El Paso 127
TENNESSEE, Boliver 256
TURKEY, 44
UTAH, 43
VERMONT, 31 118 204 228- 230
   Burlington 72 Lunenburg 249
   251 Peabody 107
   108Rockingham 247 Starkboro'
   196 Townsend 202 Wheelock 30
VICE PRESIDENT, (acting) 158
VILLAGE CORPORATION, 62
VIRGINIA, 105 217 Richmond 214
WAR OF 1812, 14 112 156 282 359
   Capt Pelatiah Smith's Company 104

WAR OF 1812 (Cont.)
   Lake Champlain 18 Montreal, Quebec 18
WASHINGTON, Chattoroy 313 Port Ludlow 135
WATER-POWER, 18
WEST LINCOLN AGRICULTURAL & HORTICLTURAL SOCIETY 61
WISCONSIN, 137 201 348
   Galesville 344 Janesville 228
   Medford 204 Oniro 293 Oshkosh
   199 263 Sheboygan 137
   Washburn 199
WORKMEN'S COMPENSATION ACT 254

ERRATA

Page 87, Robert ANDERSON Sr d 19 Aug 1843 not his son

Page 105, Orpha Brooks m(1) Benjamin Merrill, m(2) Jonathan Hodgkins

Page 105, under Benjamin BUBIER "circa 1959, p. ?? - unknown due .." should be circa 1959, p 117

Page 105, William Brooks Sr should read, died "18 Nov 1866 ae 89y 11m at his son's, Ham Brooks Esq at Lewiston" and not "18 Nov 1867 ae 90y 8m" [*Lewiston Falls Journal* 18 Oct 1866]

Page 111, Isaac Carville died 11 Aug 1906 (remove d 10 Oct 1891) s/o Mary Carville, who was the w/o Edward Estes Jr. He was a member of South Lewiston Grange and Old Fellows, served by wife and six children: Edward E of Bowdoin; William K of Leeds Center; George B; Mrs Ada L Williams; Frank E and Wallace of Lewiston. [*Lewiston Weekly Journal* 15 Aug 1906]

Page 121, under Jeremiah COLE 6 from the bottom should be "- 1989 - Gov Longley Bridge.]"

Page 129, under Nathan CUTLER Sr, Olive married Timothy MOOAR not Green Farmington, see page 264

Page 136, 7th line [BRYANT, Samuel 1868-1955 .... should be [BRYANT, Albert Scott 1868-1955...

Page 137, under Peter DENNETT, his dau, Clarinda R married Samuel JOY not Jay

Page 147, under Barzilla DYER his dau, Jane was born 17 Apr 1840

Page 150, Edward Estes b 25 Aug 1829, d 13 Dec 1854, s/o Josiah. [probate # 500 & will of Edward Estes]

Page 160, Mary Caroline d/o Capt Asa Garcelon, she m Enoch "Gilman", not "Celman"

Page 162, James Garcelon m 2 Mar 1760 Deliverance "Annis", not "Ames"

Page 163, Peter Garcelon "s/o James & Deliverance (Annis) Garcelon" not s/o James & Deliverance (Ames) Garcelon

Page 165 & 162, Fred Almont Garcelon was not the son of William Golder Garcelon as he had no issue.

Page 171, under James GILPATRICK his dau, Hannah was born in the part of Lewiston which was set off to Webster ME in 1895, now called Sabattus, Maine

Page 220, John HOLLAND Jr born in Newbury MA, not Lewiston ME, according to notes by Don Taylor of San Diego CA, letter dated 27 Apr 1995

Page 220, Children of John HOLLAND Jr
Pamela Holland Moses d 1851 at Plymouth MA
William Holland d 1861 at St Louis MO
John Holland d in Libby Prison in Richmond Virginia during Civil War
Rebecca's 2nd Husband was Sam Bates, she b 11 Aug 1831 Lewiston ME d 6 Nov 1923 at Hastings, Nebraska (from obit)

Page 229, Ephraim Jones m Ann Garcelon d/o Mark Garcelon, not David Garcelon

Page 258, John Merrill m(2) Sarah Henshaw and not Sarah Smith [source: Mrs Drisko of Boothbay Harbor ME]

Page 309, Elbridge W Ray ... was of Sabattus. MAINE & not of Schattus

Page 309, Thomas RAY's wife is Althea HATCH & not Fear Hatch

Page 318, Frances Ross wife of Davis N Skinner was "Francis FOSS" & not Ross

Page 337, Samuel THORNE his dau Rhoda m(2) Benjamin VINING & not Vinny

Page 339, Samuel TUCK family should be listed before James Turner family

Page 344, Jeremiah WEBBER & his children: (corrections & additions)
Jeremiah d 1886 not 1876 married Rebecca 10 May not June 10
Rebecca divorced Jeremiah 16 Apr 1872 at Galesville WI
Alton Webber d 29 Oct 1935 at Hastings Neb (obit)
Arthur's wife last name is TRUAX
Arthur died 6 Aug 1906 at Kentwood LA
Oscar's wife name was Mary Bell MEAD
Oscar d 3 Jan 1932 at Los Angeles CA

Page 343, Arza B WEBBER was b 17 Feb 1844 at Lewiston, d 3 Dec 1910 at Auburn ME

Page 356, Jane d/o William Woodard, She m Joseph S Garcelon not Gordan

Page 362, Phineas B Wright Jr b 20 Jan 1851, did not die 19 Mar 1851, died on 8 Apr 1905

Page 391, above the line GIVEN, Louise please insert "GILPATRICK Nathaniel 1752-1834" before the words "revol soldier WEBSTER"

Page 391, under GILPATRICK Nathaniel d 13 Nov 1862 ae 39y 1m at Garcelon Cem was a Civil War soldier, and the next line was Nathaniel Gilpatrick b 1752 d 1834 of the Revolutionary War.

Page 419, please correct CORLISS, Au9usus ..... to CORLISS, Augustus

Page 420, HAWKINS Allen should be HAWKINS Alan

Page 431, Index "Carcelon 159" should be Garcelon 159"

Page 433, Index "Cogurn J G 60" should read "Coburn J G 60"

www.ingramcontent.com/pod-product-compliance
Lightning Source LLC
Chambersburg PA
CBHW070836020526
44114CB00041B/1397